C0-ANH-572

Praise for Reformed Systematic Theology, *Volume 3*

"With the publication of this third volume of *Reformed Systematic Theology*, the monumental Beeke and Smalley journey of theological exploration now takes us into territory overseen by the Holy Spirit. Here we are given a reverent survey of the biblical witness to his ministry; a five-hundred-page exposition of the *ordo salutis*; and an extensive exploration of the Beatitudes, the fruit of the Spirit, and the Decalogue, leading us appropriately to the loving fear of the Lord and prayer. Here the comprehensive knowledge of the Reformed tradition characteristic of volumes one and two is now combined with the authors' specialist expertise in the experiential dimensions of biblical doctrine. Those who join them on the journey will find themselves traveling with reliable guides and agreeable companions. En route, students will find the information they require, pastors and teachers will discover the stimulus they need, and all Christian readers will receive a theological education that will help them to live *coram Deo*."

Sinclair B. Ferguson, Chancellor's Professor of Systematic Theology, Reformed Theological Seminary; Teaching Fellow, Ligonier Ministries

"I tell my students that I am not interested in theology that can't be preached. I sense the same when reading this third volume. What we have here is a systematic theology that covers all bases—scholarly and pastoral, Reformed and worshipful. No topic is left unaddressed. A monumental achievement."

Derek W. H. Thomas, Senior Minister, First Presbyterian Church, Columbia, South Carolina; Teaching Fellow, Ligonier Ministries; Chancellor's Professor, Reformed Theological Seminary

"One of Joel Beeke's most prized contributions to the field of systematic theology is his understanding that Christian theology is for living. A hallmark of Beeke's preaching and writing is that it follows Martin Bucer's dictum: 'True theology is not theoretical, but practical. The end of it is living, that is to live a godly life.' This present volume is no exception. Here is theology for the church of God and not just for the academy. It is a privilege to commend this latest volume, with the prayer that it will find its way into the bloodstream of the church."

Ian Hamilton, Professor, Westminster Presbyterian Theological Seminary, Newcastle, UK

"The third volume of Joel Beeke and Paul Smalley's *Reformed Systematic Theology* gives attention to the doctrines of the Holy Spirit (pneumatology) and salvation (soteriology). We are treated to, among many other significant features, a knowledgeable defense of the *ordo salutis*, which sincerely engages the main objections to this important formulation of classic Protestant soteriology. We meet a beautiful exposition of the Holy Spirit and the *historia salutis*, which nicely complements the treatment of the *ordo*. The volume concludes, as you might have expected in a book coauthored by Joel Beeke, with a rich summary of the Holy Spirit's work in the Christian experience of salvation (*experientia salutis*). I must confess that I turned immediately to peek at the section on preparatory grace and also that on assurance, knowing Beeke's interest and expertise in those areas. I will be utilizing this volume as I teach systematic theology, and will be commending it to others. I've already learned and benefited from it greatly. This is a welcome addition to the current flourishing of Reformed systematics."

Ligon Duncan, Chancellor and CEO, Reformed Theological Seminary

Praise for the Reformed Systematic Theology Series

"'Oh, the depth of the riches and wisdom and knowledge of God!' This expression of praise from Paul's great doxology is a fitting response to reading this wonderful work of doctrine and devotion. Though the Reformed faith is often caricatured as merely intellectual, this work demonstrates that Reformed theology is also profoundly experiential, as no chapter fails to move from theology to doxology."

John MacArthur, Pastor, Grace Community Church, Sun Valley, California; Chancellor, The Master's University and Seminary

"*Reformed Systematic Theology* not only takes readers into the depths of our triune God, but also shows what these great truths have to do with the Christian life. No contemporary systematic theology will bring the reader to a greater understanding of how theology blossoms into doxology than this one."

Matthew Barrett, Associate Professor of Christian Theology, Midwestern Baptist Theological Seminary; Executive Editor, *Credo Magazine*; editor, *Reformation Theology*

"Beeke and Smalley have written a work useful to the church at large that teaches Christians what they should believe and how they should love, but they have not sacrificed academic rigor to achieve these goals."

J. V. Fesko, Professor of Systematic and Historical Theology, Reformed Theological Seminary, Jackson, Mississippi

"Joel Beeke has continued his decades-long service to Christ and his church by presenting us with his mature reflections on the nature of systematic theology. This work is fully reliable, well written, easily understood, and thoroughly researched."

Richard C. Gamble, Professor of Systematic Theology, Reformed Presbyterian Theological Seminary

"Joel Beeke is a rare gift to the church, a noted Christian leader who combines the skills of a learned theologian, master teacher, noted historian, and yet also a caring pastor. *Reformed Systematic Theology* is a virtual gold mine of biblical doctrine that is systematically arranged, carefully analyzed, historically scrutinized, and pastorally applied."

Steven J. Lawson, President, OnePassion Ministries; Professor of Preaching, The Master's Seminary; Teaching Fellow, Ligonier Ministries

"Here is theology functioning as it ought to function—calling us to worship. You will not need to agree with the authors at every point to believe and to hope that this work will serve Christ's church well in our generation and for generations to come."

Jeremy Walker, Pastor, Maidenbower Baptist Church, Crawley, UK; author, *Life in Christ*; *Anchored in Grace*; and *A Face Like a Flint*

REFORMED SYSTEMATIC THEOLOGY

REFORMED SYSTEMATIC THEOLOGY

Volume 3:
Spirit and Salvation

Joel R. Beeke and Paul M. Smalley

WHEATON, ILLINOIS

Reformed Systematic Theology, Volume 3: Spirit and Salvation

Published by Crossway
1300 Crescent Street
Wheaton, Illinois 60187

Cover design: Jordan Singer

First printing 2021

Printed in the United States of America

Unless otherwise indicated, Scripture quotations are from the *King James Version* of the Bible.

All emphases in Scripture quotations have been added by the authors.

Hardcover ISBN: 978-1-4335-5991-4
ePub ISBN: 978-1-4335-5994-5
PDF ISBN: 978-1-4335-5992-1
Mobipocket ISBN: 978-1-4335-5993-8

Library of Congress Cataloging-in-Publication Data

Names: Beeke, Joel R., 1952– author. | Smalley, Paul M., author.
Title: Reformed systematic theology / Joel R. Beeke and Paul M. Smalley.
Description: Wheaton, Illinois: Crossway, [2021] | Includes bibliographical references and index.
Identifiers: LCCN 2018029011 (print) | LCCN 2018047407 (ebook) | ISBN 9781433559921 (pdf) | ISBN 9781433559938 (mobi) | ISBN 9781433559945 (epub) | ISBN 9781433559914 (hardcover) | ISBN 9781433559945 (ePub) | ISBN 9781433559938 (mobipocket)
Subjects: LCSH: Reformed Church—Doctrines.
Classification: LCC BX9422.3 (ebook) | LCC BX9422.3 .B445 2019 (print) | DDC 230/.42—dc23
LC record available at https://lccn.loc.gov/2018029011

Crossway is a publishing ministry of Good News Publishers.

SH 29 28 27 26 25 24 23 22 21
14 13 12 11 10 9 8 7 6 5 4 3 2 1

For

Mary Beeke,

my precious gift-of-God helpmeet, in whose
tongue is the law of kindness
and who beautifully models the doctrine of salvation for me,
for our children and grandchildren, and for our church and seminary.
Thank you for being easy to love and for your
unflagging loyalty and support.
I love you—your integrity, godliness, humility,
and joy—with all my heart.
—Your grateful husband, Joel

And for

Dawn Smalley,

my beloved Proverbs 31 wife and *ezer kenegdi*,
who has taught me much about the love of the Savior
by her daily kindness to me, our children, and many others.
You are one of the most diligent, generous, organized,
hopeful, and perceptive people I know.
I don't deserve you, but I am so thankful to have you as my bride.
—Love, Paul

Contents

Abbreviations

ACCS/NT	*Ancient Christian Commentary on Scripture, New Testament.* Edited by Thomas Oden. 12 vols. Downers Grove, IL: InterVarsity Press, 2005–2006.
ACCS/OT	*Ancient Christian Commentary on Scripture, Old Testament.* Edited by Thomas Oden. 15 vols. Downers Grove, IL: InterVarsity Press, 2001–2005.
ANF	*The Ante-Nicene Fathers.* Edited by Alexander Roberts and James Donaldson. Revised by A. Cleveland Coxe. 9 vols. New York: Charles Scribner's Sons, 1918.
CR	*Corpus Reformatorum.* Edited by Carolus Gottlieb Bretschneider et al. 101 vols. Halis Saxonum: Apud C. A. Schwetschke et Filium, 1834–1959.
LW	*Luther's Works.* Edited by Jaroslav Pelikan et al. 80 vols. St. Louis, MO: Concordia, 1958–2020.
NIDNTTE	*The New International Dictionary of New Testament Theology and Exegesis.* Edited by Moisés Silva. 5 vols. Grand Rapids, MI: Zondervan, 2014.

NIDOTTE	*The New International Dictionary of Old Testament Theology and Exegesis*. Edited by Willem A. VanGemeren. 5 vols. Grand Rapids, MI: Zondervan, 1997.
NIDPCM	*The New International Dictionary of Pentecostal and Charismatic Movements*. Edited by Stanley M. Burgess and Eduard M. Van der Maas. Revised and expanded edition. Grand Rapids, MI: Zondervan, 2002.
NPNF[1]	*A Select Library of Nicene and Post-Nicene Fathers of the Christian Church, First Series*. Edited by Philip Schaff. 14 vols. New York: Christian Literature Co., 1888.
NPNF[2]	*A Select Library of Nicene and Post-Nicene Fathers of the Christian Church, Second Series*. Edited by Philip Schaff and Henry Wace. 14 vols. New York: Christian Literature Co., 1894.
The Psalter	*The Psalter, with Doctrinal Standards, Liturgy, Church Order, and Added Chorale Section*. Preface by Joel R. Beeke and Ray B. Lanning. 1965; repr., Grand Rapids, MI: Eerdmans for Reformation Heritage Books, 2003.
Reformed Confessions	*Reformed Confessions of the 16th and 17th Centuries in English Translation: 1523–1693*. Compiled by James T. Dennison Jr. 4 vols. Grand Rapids, MI: Reformation Heritage Books, 2008–2014.
RST	Joel R. Beeke and Paul M. Smalley. *Reformed Systematic Theology*. 4 vols. Wheaton, IL: Crossway, 2019–.

TDNT	*Theological Dictionary of the New Testament*. Edited by Gerhard Kittel, Geoffrey W. Bromiley, and Gerhard Friedrich. 10 vols. Grand Rapids, MI: Eerdmans, 1964.
The Three Forms of Unity	*The Three Forms of Unity*. Edited and introduced by Joel R. Beeke. Birmingham, AL: Solid Ground, 2010.
Trinity Hymnal—Baptist Edition	*Trinity Hymnal—Baptist Edition*. Revised by David Merck. Suwanee, GA: Great Commission Publications, 1995.
WJE	*The Works of Jonathan Edwards*. 26 vols. New Haven, CT: Yale University Press, 1957–2008.

Tables

Preface to Volume 3

With much gratitude to God we present the third volume of *Reformed Systematic Theology*. In a sense, the project started here in 2016, when we began a significant revision of theological lectures, presented at Puritan Reformed Theological Seminary, on the doctrines of the Holy Spirit and his work in applying salvation. Those revised lectures became the seed from which this systematic theology grew.

The doctrine of the Holy Spirit is discussed in systematic theology under the locus of *pneumatology* (from Greek *pneuma*, "spirit," and *logos*, "word, speech").[1] However, here we encounter a complication, for the study of the Holy Spirit's work overlaps with another locus, *soteriology*, the doctrine of salvation (Greek *sōteria*). In God's plan of salvation, the Holy Spirit applies to the elect the salvation accomplished by the work of Christ as Mediator (Titus 3:5–6). Therefore, we have chosen to combine these two loci and consider them as one. Hence, this volume contains part 5 of our systematic theology, "Pneumatology and Soteriology: The Doctrine of Salvation Applied by the Holy Spirit."

However, in order to provide an orderly structure for our treatment of the various aspects of the Spirit's work, we consider it from three perspectives.

First, from the perspective of the history of salvation (Latin *historia salutis*), we trace the work of the Spirit through the history of God's mighty works: creation, God's covenantal and redemptive dealings with the patriarchs and Israel, the incarnation and work of Jesus Christ, the outpouring of the Spirit at Pentecost and its implications for the church today, and the Spirit's work in transforming God's creation into the new creation.

Second, from the perspective of the order of salvation (*ordo salutis*), we trace the Spirit's work in applying salvation to individual persons by

1. On the loci of systematic theology, see *RST*, 1:64–66.

union with Christ, including the general call of the gospel, conviction of sin, regeneration and conversion, justification, adoption, sanctification, and preservation and perseverance.

Third, from the perspective of the practical experience of salvation (*experientia salutis*), we explore the work of the Spirit with respect to the indwelling of the Spirit, assurance of salvation, the fruit of the Spirit in personal godliness, Spirit-worked obedience to God's commandments, the fear of God, various Christian virtues, and prayer.

We desire to make it clear from the outset that these are not three separate categories, but three perspectives on the work of God the Holy Spirit. God's mighty works in history (*historia salutis*) aim at the salvation of individuals (*ordo salutis*), and God's works in history and individual lives are profoundly experiential in producing piety (*experientia salutis*).

Before we proceed to these topics, we must review a doctrine introduced in volume 1 under the doctrine of the Trinity—the person of the Holy Spirit—for we must know who the Spirit is before we can adequately consider what he does. This we do in the introductory chapter, where we also answer objections to the study of the Spirit and offer reasons why this is such an important doctrine for us to know.

We thank Justin Taylor and the team at Crossway for their enthusiasm for this project and the Christian professionalism they constantly exhibit in their work. We particularly thank Greg Bailey, our editor, for the countless improvements he has made in our writing. We also gratefully acknowledge the labors of Ray Lanning, Keith Mathison, Wouter Pieters, and Liz Smith in reviewing our manuscript. And we thank God for our wives, Mary Beeke and Dawn Smalley, for their faithful love and prayers. They are both beautiful examples of the power of God's salvation and the reality of the Holy Spirit's indwelling his saints. Consequently, we gratefully dedicate this volume to them. *Soli Deo gloria*!

Joel R. Beeke and Paul M. Smalley

PART 5

PNEUMATOLOGY AND SOTERIOLOGY: THE DOCTRINE OF SALVATION APPLIED BY THE HOLY SPIRIT

Analytical Outline: Pneumatology and Soteriology

Section A: The Holy Spirit and the History of Salvation (*Historia Salutis*)

I. Introduction to the Doctrine of the Holy Spirit
   A. Objections to the Doctrine of the Holy Spirit
      1. We Should Not Study the Spirit but Be Filled with the Spirit
      2. Focusing on the Spirit Leads to Bizarre Behavior
      3. The Doctrine of the Spirit Divides Christians
      4. Studying the Spirit Distracts Us from Jesus Christ
   B. The Importance of Studying the Holy Spirit
      1. To Know the Spirit Is to Know Our God
      2. To Know the Spirit Is to Know Our Salvation
      3. To Know the Spirit Is to Understand Sanctification
      4. To Know the Spirit Is to Balance the Christian Life
      5. To Know the Spirit Is to Worship God Rightly
      6. To Know the Spirit Is to Appreciate Historic Christian Orthodoxy
      7. To Know the Spirit Is to Be Equipped to Speak to Our Culture
      8. To Know the Spirit Is to Be Prepared for Spiritual Warfare
      9. To Know the Spirit Is to Feel Our Dependence
      10. To Know the Spirit Is to Know Christ
   C. The Person of the Holy Spirit
      1. The Names of the Spirit
         a. The Spirit of God or the Spirit of the Lord
         b. The Holy Spirit

        2. The Deity of the Holy Spirit
            a. Names and Titles of Deity
            b. Attributes of Deity
            c. Relations of Deity
            d. Actions of Deity
            e. Presence of Deity
            f. Authority of Deity
            g. Honors of Deity
        3. The Personality of the Holy Spirit
            a. The Holy Spirit Is Someone, Not Something
            b. The Holy Spirit Is Someone with a Rational, Volitional Nature
            c. The Holy Spirit Is Someone Unique in Relationships with Other Persons
        4. Practical Implications of the Spirit's Divine Personality

II. The Work of the Holy Spirit in Creation and Common Grace
    A. The Holy Spirit and Creation
        1. The Spirit's Creation of the World
        2. The Spirit's Creation of Mankind
    B. The Holy Spirit and Providence
        1. The Spirit's Providence over All Things
        2. The Spirit's Providence over Human Life
    C. God's Common Grace to Mankind
        1. God's General Goodness
        2. God's Restraint of Sin
        3. The Reformed Controversy over God's Common Grace
        4. Common Grace in the Bible
        5. Common Grace in Reformed Theology
        6. Practical Applications of the Doctrine of Common Grace

III. The Spirit of God with Old Covenant Israel
    A. The Spirit of Prophecy
    B. The Spirit of Power
    C. The Spirit of Presence
    D. The Spirit of Piety
        1. Explicit Statements That the Spirit Sanctified Old Covenant Saints
        2. The Identity of the Spiritual Israel
        3. The Necessity of the New Birth to Enter the Kingdom
        4. The Necessity of the Indwelling of the Spirit for Obedience

Section B: The Holy Spirit and the Order of Salvation (*Ordo Salutis*)

2. The Implications of the Warning against Testing the Holy Spirit
   a. The Fear of the Lord
   b. The Warning to Unbelievers
   c. The Encouragement to Believers

C. Blaspheming the Holy Spirit
   1. The Meaning of Blasphemy against the Holy Spirit
   2. The Magnitude of Blasphemy against the Holy Spirit
   3. The Modern Implications of Blasphemy against the Holy Spirit

D. Concluding Applications regarding Sinful Responses to the Gospel Call
   1. We Should Humble Ourselves for Our Sin
   2. We Should Acknowledge Our Need for Inward, Transforming Grace
   3. We Should Thank God with Grateful Hearts If He Has Saved Us

XIV. Effectual Calling

A. A Basic Explanation of Effectual Calling

B. The Definition and Doctrine of Effectual Calling
   1. Sovereign Summons
   2. The Triune God
   3. Eternal Election
   4. Individuals
   5. Undeserved Grace
   6. Produces Gospel Faith and Repentance
   7. To Create a New People
   8. Spiritual Union with Christ
   9. Holiness
   10. God Infallibly Brings Them to Glory

C. Applications of the Doctrine of Effectual Calling
   1. The Church Must Preach the Gospel for the Salvation of Sinners
   2. A Person Must Be Effectually Called to Be Saved
   3. A Person's Election Makes Itself Known in His Calling
   4. Christians Should Glorify God Alone for Their Conversion
   5. The Called Must Pursue Practical Holiness
   6. The Called Must Cultivate the Unity of the Church
   7. The Called Should Joyfully Hope in a Happy Future

b. Heartfelt Confessing of Sins against the Righteous God
c. Praying for Saving Grace
d. Declaring God's Salvation to Others
e. Worshiping God with His Penitent Church

5. True Repentance Discerned by Its Character and Fruit
6. The Necessity of Repentance
   a. Necessary for Salvation
   b. Necessary for Growth and Perseverance
7. Motives for Unbelievers to Repent
   a. God's Command
   b. God's Mercies
   c. The Evil of Sin
   d. The Inevitability of Death
   e. The Justice of God's Judgment
   f. The Sufferings of Christ
   g. The Wrong of Your Sins against God
   h. The Consequences of Whether You Repent

C. Faith in Jesus Christ
   1. Biblical Terminology of Faith
   2. Kinds of Faith That Do Not Save
      a. Mere Mental Belief (Historical Faith)
      b. Transient Emotional Commitment (Temporary Faith)
      c. Confidence in Miracles (Faith of Miracles)
      d. Blind Submission to Church Leaders (Implicit Faith)
      e. Claiming Earthly Blessings with Confidence
      f. Saying a Prayer or Making a Physical Motion
   3. The Object of Saving Faith
   4. The Threefold Nature of Saving Faith
      a. Historical Background: Saving Faith Is More Than Assent
      b. Saving Faith as Experiential Knowledge of God
      c. Saving Faith as Submissive Assent to God's Word
      d. Saving Faith as Confident Trust in Christ
   5. Faith's Experiential Exercise
      a. Faith Empties Us of Self
      b. Faith Comes to Christ and Receives Him
      c. Faith Lives out of Christ
      d. Faith Strives against Obstacles
      e. Faith Produces Good Works

- 6. The Necessity of Faith in Christ
  - a. The Necessity for Salvation of the Lost
  - b. The Necessity for Growth in the Saved

XVII. Justification
- A. The Nature of Justification: Terminology and Definition
- B. The Basis of Justification: The Righteousness of God in Christ
  - 1. The Righteousness of God
  - 2. The Imputation of Christ's Righteousness
- C. The Execution of Justification: From Eternity to Glory
  - 1. God Decreed Justification in Eternity through Christ
  - 2. God Accomplished Justification by Christ's Obedience, Death, and Resurrection
  - 3. God Promises Justification in the Gospel of Christ
  - 4. God Grants Actual Justification by Faith in Christ
  - 5. God Imparts a Subjective Sense of Justification in the Conscience
  - 6. God Will Publicly Justify Believers on Judgment Day
- D. The Means of Justification: By Faith in Christ
- E. Justification by Faith Alone and the Place of Good Works
  - 1. The Opposite of Justification by Works of Obedience to the Law
  - 2. The Inseparable Companion of the Grace of Sanctification
- F. The Experiential and Practical Benefits of Justification by Faith Alone
  - 1. Peace of Conscience
  - 2. Joyful Communion with the Reconciled God
  - 3. Liberty to Confess Our Sins and Seek God's Fatherly Forgiveness
  - 4. The Gift of Eternal Life and Blessing
  - 5. Freedom of Conscience from Human Judgments
  - 6. Grounds for Assurance of Salvation
  - 7. Hope of Glory
- G. Historical and Polemical Theology of Justification (Ancient to Reformation)
  - 1. The Early Church Fathers on Justification
  - 2. The Medieval Catholic Theologians on Justification
  - 3. The Reformers on Justification
  - 4. The Council of Trent and Modern Roman Catholicism on Justification

XVIII. Adoption
- A. Biblical Theology of Adoption
  1. The Cultural Background of Adoption in the Ancient World
  2. God's Adoption of Sons in the Book of Moses
  3. God's Adoption of Sons in the Monarchy and Latter Prophets
  4. God's Adoption of Sons in the Gospels
  5. God's Adoption of Sons in Paul's Epistles
  6. God's Adoption of Sons in the Other Epistles
- B. Adoption as a Privilege Unique to Those in Christ
- C. Adoption as a Systematic Perspective on Salvation
  1. Election and Predestination Are the Planning of Adoption
  2. Incarnation Is Christ's Taking a Nature Suitable for Our Adoption
  3. Redemption by Christ's Blood Is the Objective Accomplishment of Adoption
  4. Resurrection and Ascension Are the Incarnate Son's Exaltation as the Mediator of Adoption
  5. Calling Is the Effectual Summons to Christ for Adoption
  6. Regeneration Is God's Giving Sinners a Nature Suitable to Live in the Relationships Granted by Adoption
  7. Repentance Is a Sinner's Turning to the Father for Adoption
  8. Faith Is the Human Instrument of Receiving Adoption
  9. Justification Is the Legal Prerequisite of Adoption
  10. Sanctification Is the Practical Outworking of Adoption
  11. Preservation and Perseverance Are the School of Adoption
  12. Glorification Is the Completion of the Aims of Adoption
- D. Adoption as the Transformation of Relationships
  1. A Transformed Relationship to the Triune God
     - a. God the Father
     - b. God the Son
     - c. God the Holy Spirit
  2. A Transformed Relationship to Oneself
     - a. God's Son or Daughter
     - b. One with the Son of God
     - c. An Identity That Transcends Earthly Categories
     - d. An Heir of God's Promises

3. A Transformed Relationship to the World
    a. The Formation of an Antithesis with the World
    b. A Call to Maintain Distinctiveness from the World
    c. A Peaceable and Kind Heart toward Enemies in the World
    d. Participation in the Son's Mission to the World
4. A Transformed Relationship to the Church
    a. True Membership in God's Family with His Brothers and Sisters
    b. Fundamental Spiritual Equality with His Brothers and Sisters
    c. Harmonious Relationships with His Brothers and Sisters
    d. Sacrificial Service to His Brothers and Sisters
    e. Giving and Receiving Exhortation among His Brothers and Sisters
    f. Ministry with Familial Affection to His Brothers and Sisters
    g. Communication with His Brothers and Sisters

XIX. Sanctification
- A. Biblical Teaching about Sanctification
    1. The Biblical Terminology of Sanctification
    2. The Theological Definition of Sanctification
    3. The Necessity of Sanctification
        a. God's People Must Be Sanctified Because He Is Holy
        b. God's People Must Be Sanctified Because They Are His Image Bearers
        c. God's People Must Be Sanctified Because They Are Born in the State of Sin
        d. God's People Must Be Sanctified Because Morality and Religiosity Are Not Holiness
        e. God's People Must Be Sanctified Because Regeneration Is Only the Beginning of Holiness
        f. God's People Must Be Sanctified Because Salvation Demands the Response of Holy Love
        g. God's People Must Be Sanctified Because Good Works Demonstrate the Reality of Their Salvation by Faith
    4. The Trinitarian Grace of Sanctification
        a. Election unto Holiness by the Father

        b. Union with Christ in His Death and Resurrection
        c. The Supernatural Agency of the Holy Spirit
    5. The Divine Implementation of Sanctification
        a. Definitive Sanctification
        b. Progressive Sanctification
B. Theological Controversies about Sanctification
    1. Celibacy, Poverty, and Asceticism (Roman Catholicism)
    2. Christian Perfectionism (Wesleyan Methodism)
    3. Modern Second-Blessing Theology
        a. The Holiness Movement
        b. The Higher Life Movement
        c. The Early Keswick Movement
        d. Classic Dispensationalism
        e. Broader Evangelicalism and Pentecostalism
    4. Exegetical Response to the Carnal Christian Doctrine (Romans 7–8)
        a. Paul's Present Experience as a Believer in Christ
        b. "Carnal" Not the Same as Lacking the Spirit
        c. Inward Conflict Characteristic of True Christians
        d. No Transition from Defeat to Victory
        e. Holy Ambition for Perfect Love, Not Total Failure to Obey
        f. The Law's Weakness and the Spirit's Power, Not Two States
    5. Theological Response to Second-Blessing Christianity
        a. The New Birth Produces a New Life
        b. All in Christ Are Justified and Sanctified
        c. No One in Christ Is a Slave of Sin
        d. Christians Do Not Need a "Second Blessing"
        e. Sanctification Comes by Our Faith and Work
        f. The Life of Sanctification Is Not Superhuman, but Truly Human
    6. Practical Conclusion
C. Practical Applications regarding Sanctification
    1. The Call to Cultivate Holiness
        a. A Holistic Task
        b. An Impossible Task apart from Christ
    2. The Life of Faith in Christ
        a. Depend on Christ in His Threefold Office
        b. Count Yourself Dead to Sin and Alive to God

3. The Pattern of Sanctification
    a. Covenantal Sanctification as the People of God
    b. Progressive Repentance in Its Positive and Negative Aspects
    c. The Imitation of God and Christ
    d. Warfare against Temptation and Indwelling Sin
    e. Obedience to the Law of God
    f. Submission to Providential Suffering
    g. Living unto God
4. Obstacles to Holiness
    a. Self-Centeredness
    b. Spiritual Lethargy
    c. Spiritual Pride
    d. Shirking Battle
5. Disciplines to Cultivate Holiness
    a. Meditate on God's Word
    b. Pray for More Sanctifying Grace
    c. Participate Fully in the Life of the Church
    d. Flee Worldliness as Pilgrims on Earth
    e. Fill Your Mind with the Glory of God
    f. Know Your Sinful Heart
    g. Look to the Blood of Christ

XX. Preservation and Perseverance
- A. Biblical Promises and Warnings
    1. Historical Background of the Debate over Perseverance
    2. Christ's Promises of Eternal Life
    3. The Necessity of Perseverance
    4. The Warnings against Apostasy
        a. Warnings in the Teachings of Our Lord
        b. Warnings in Acts and Paul's Epistles
        c. Warnings in the Epistle to the Hebrews
    5. The Divine Grace of Preservation
        a. Preserving Grace Promised in the New Covenant
        b. Preserving Grace Promised in the New Testament Epistles
- B. Resting and Running
    1. Resting in the Triune Preserver of Your Salvation
        a. Immutable Election and Comforting Support by the Father

b. Perfect Redemption and Effective Intercession by the Son
c. Powerful Sanctification and Incitement to Prayer by the Spirit
d. Summary: Resting on the Character of the Triune God

2. Running with Perseverance for the Heavenly Prize
a. Pay Careful Attention to God's Word
b. Establish in Your Mind the Supremacy of Christ
c. Lean on Christ's Intercession in Your Prayers
d. Stand upon the Promises of God
e. Share in the Worship, Love, and Accountability of the Church
f. Run the Race with Your Eyes on Christ the Victor

Section C: The Holy Spirit and the Experience of Salvation (*Experientia Salutis*)

XXI. The Indwelling, Leading, and Filling of the Holy Spirit
A. The Indwelling of the Holy Spirit
1. The Promise of the Spirit's Indwelling
2. The Spirit of Life, the Spirit of Christ
B. The Leading of the Holy Spirit
1. The Promise of the Spirit's Leading
2. The Warning against Grieving the Spirit
3. The Duty of Walking in the Spirit
C. The Filling of the Holy Spirit
1. The Promise of the Spirit's Filling
2. The Christian's Responsibility to Be Filled by the Spirit
3. Praying for Revival

XXII. Assurance of Salvation
A. Why Do Many Christians Lack Full Assurance?
B. Is Assurance of Faith Biblical and Normative?
C. Three Possibilities concerning Assurance
1. False Assurance
2. True Assurance
3. Saving Faith, Yet Little or No Conscious Assurance
D. The Foundations of Assurance
1. The Divine Promises in Christ
2. The Evidences of Saving Grace: The Syllogisms
3. The Testimony of the Holy Spirit

1. Christian Prayer Is Presenting Our Desires to God
2. Christian Prayer Is Offered Only to God
3. Christian Prayer Is Possible Only by the Power of the Holy Spirit
4. Christian Prayer Is Performed by Faith in Jesus Christ
5. Christian Prayer Is according to God's Preceptive Will
6. Christian Prayer Is Made with Confession of Sin
7. Christian Prayer Is Accompanied by Thanksgiving and Adoration

B. A Practical Exhortation to Prayerful Praying
   1. The Problem of Prayerless Praying
   2. Practical Steps toward Prayerful Praying
      a. Remember the Value of Prayer
      b. Maintain the Priority of Prayer
      c. Keep a Blood-Washed Conscience for Boldness in Prayer
      d. Speak with Sincerity in Prayer
      e. Cultivate a Spirit of Continual Prayer
      f. Exercise a Broad and Organized Ministry of Intercession
      g. Read the Bible for Prayer and Pray the Bible to God
      h. Use Biblical Variety and Balance in Prayer
      i. Believe That God Answers the Prayers of His Children
      j. Take Hold of the Triune God in Prayer

C. The Hope of Glorification
   1. The Grace of Christian Hope
   2. The Experiential Exercise of Christian Hope

Section A

The Holy Spirit and the History of Salvation (Historia Salutis)

1

Introduction to the Doctrine of the Holy Spirit

One of the most remarkable statements of the Bible appears in Christ's words to his disciples: "It is expedient for you that I go away: for if I go not away, the Comforter will not come unto you; but if I depart, I will send him unto you" (John 16:7). How could it possibly be "expedient"—that is, to our advantage—for the Lord Jesus Christ to leave us? Christ must highly value the ministry of "the Spirit of truth" (14:16–17). If we treasure Christ as the only Mediator between God and man (v. 6; 1 Tim. 2:5), then we will treasure the work of the Holy Spirit.

Jonathan Edwards (1703–1758) said, "The Holy Spirit, in his indwelling, his influences and fruits, is the sum of all grace, holiness, comfort and joy, or in one word, of all the spiritual good Christ purchased for men in this world: and is also the sum of all perfection, glory and eternal joy, that he purchased for them in another world."[1]

However, studying the doctrine of the Holy Spirit presents special challenges. Sinclair Ferguson says, "While his work has been recognized, the Spirit himself remains to many Christians an anonymous, faceless aspect of the divine being."[2] In part, this is because it is rare to find extended discussions of the Holy Spirit in the Bible; most references to him come

1. Jonathan Edwards, *An Humble Attempt*, in *WJE*, 5:341.
2. Sinclair B. Ferguson, *The Holy Spirit*, Contours in Christian Theology (Downers Grove, IL: InterVarsity Press, 1996), 12.

in connection with other doctrines.[3] This problem is further complicated when people stumble over the older usage of "Holy Ghost," which has nothing to do with ghosts but is another way of saying "Holy Spirit."[4]

However, these difficulties should not turn us aside from the great task of studying the Spirit's work and the application of redemption. The task is worthy of our highest effort. Instead, the difficulties should stir us up to take on this great work with determination, careful thinking, perseverance, submission to God's Word, and constant prayer for the Spirit to illuminate our minds (Ps. 119:18; Eph. 1:17–18). We need the work of the Holy Spirit if we are going to successfully study the Holy Spirit. Pause now, before you read further, and pray for the Holy Spirit to lead you into all truth by his Word.

Objections to the Doctrine of the Holy Spirit

A number of objections might be raised against doing a biblical and theological study of the Holy Spirit. Some of the more common ones are as follows.

Objection 1: We should not study the Spirit but be filled with the Spirit. In response, we agree that we must not rest in mere understanding, but must seek the Spirit's grace and serve the Lord with all our hearts. However, an individual may be filled with the influence of a "spirit" that is not the Holy Spirit (1 John 4:1–2). The apostle Paul was deeply concerned that churches not be deceived into receiving "another spirit" (2 Cor. 11:2–4). Therefore, we must cultivate discernment by knowing the true Spirit of God and his works. Knowing God's Spirit is knowing the person who gives life to the church. Geoff Thomas says, "The essential, vital, central element in the life of every congregation is the person and work of the Spirit of God as illuminated . . . by the Spirit-breathed Word."[5]

Objection 2: Focusing on the Spirit leads to bizarre behavior. In reply, we assert that we must not overreact against one error and fall into its opposite. Martyn Lloyd-Jones (1899–1981) said, "The doctrine of the Holy Spirit is neglected because people are so afraid of the spurious, the false, and the exaggerated that they avoid it altogether."[6] We must study

3. Millard J. Erickson, *Christian Theology*, 3rd ed. (Grand Rapids, MI: Baker Academic, 2013), 773.

4. "Ghost" is related to a German root (*Geist*) while "spirit" comes from Latin (*spiritus*), but both mean the same.

5. Geoffrey Thomas, *The Holy Spirit* (Grand Rapids, MI: Reformation Heritage Books, 2011), 2.

6. Martyn Lloyd-Jones, *Great Doctrines of the Bible*, vol. 2, *God the Holy Spirit* (Wheaton, IL: Crossway, 1997), 5.

this doctrine because the Spirit is a person in the Trinity, the Word of God teaches us of him, and, since "the Holy Spirit is the one who applied salvation, it is of the utmost practical importance that we should know the truth concerning Him."[7]

Objection 3: The doctrine of the Spirit divides Christians. In response, we acknowledge that aspects of this doctrine are flashpoints of debate among Reformed theologians, Lutherans, Arminian evangelicals, Roman Catholics, Pentecostals, and charismatics. The answer, however, is not to neglect Christian polemics—for they are necessary (Titus 1:9; Jude 3). The way to heal divisions among true Christians and distinguish them from false Christians is to learn the truth about the Holy Spirit from God's Word and to embrace that truth with humility, love, and the fear of God. The Holy Spirit is not a divisive force among God's children; there is "one Spirit," and he unites the church as one body (1 Cor. 12:13; Eph. 2:18; 4:4).

Objection 4: Studying the Spirit distracts us from Jesus Christ. In reply, we observe that it is possible to focus on the Spirit in an unhealthy manner that draws us away from Jesus Christ, but studying the biblical doctrine of the Spirit does not have this harmful effect. The Holy Spirit came to glorify the Son (John 16:14). To study the Spirit magnifies Christ, for the Spirit is the Spirit of Christ (Rom. 8:9). Richard Sibbes (1577–1635) wrote, "The Holy Ghost fetches all from Christ in his working and comfort, and he makes Christ the pattern of all; for whatsoever is in Christ, the Holy Ghost, which is the Spirit of Christ, works in us as it is in Christ."[8] Two Reformed theologians noted for their writings on the glory of Christ, John Owen (1616–1683) and Thomas Goodwin (1600–1679), also wrote lengthy treatises on the Holy Spirit.[9] If we neglect the doctrine of the Spirit, then we actually diminish the glory of Christ, for all the things of Christ are ours only by the Spirit.

The Importance of Studying the Holy Spirit

It is sufficient that God's Word speaks much of the Spirit, for the only warrant we need to study a truth is that God teaches it in his Word. However,

7. Lloyd-Jones, *Great Doctrines of the Bible*, 2:6.

8. Richard Sibbes, *A Description of Christ*, in *The Works of Richard Sibbes*, ed. Alexander B. Grosart, 7 vols. (1862–1864; repr., Edinburgh: Banner of Truth, 1973), 1:18.

9. John Owen, *Pneumatologia*, in *The Works of John Owen*, ed. William H. Goold, 16 vols. (1850–1853; repr., Edinburgh: Banner of Truth, 1965), vols. 3–4; and Thomas Goodwin, *The Work of the Holy Ghost in Our Salvation*, in *The Works of Thomas Goodwin*, 12 vols. (1861–1866; repr., Grand Rapids, MI: Reformation Heritage Books, 2006), vol. 6.

to strengthen our motivation to study this topic deeply, let us consider reasons why it is crucial that we study the Holy Spirit.

1. *To know the Spirit is to know our God.* The Holy Spirit is God. Therefore, to study the person and works of the Holy Spirit is a great opportunity to know God in a better way. Nothing is more valuable, transforming, or life-giving than the knowledge of God (Jer. 9:23–24; 31:33–34; John 17:3). In particular, the Holy Spirit is the third person of the Trinity, who especially brings us into communion with the Father and the Son (2 Cor. 13:14; Gal. 4:4–6). Millard Erickson writes, "The Holy Spirit is the point at which the Trinity becomes personal to the believer."[10] Christ promised that when he ascended to heaven he would not leave his disciples as orphans, but would come to them and dwell in them with the Father—all by the Holy Spirit (John 14:16–23). Wayne Grudem observes, "The work of the Holy Spirit is to manifest the active presence of God in the world, and especially in the church."[11]

2. *To know the Spirit is to know our salvation.* Man cannot discover the wisdom of God, but God reveals his salvation by the Holy Spirit (1 Cor. 2:9–16). Man by his own power cannot see or enter into the kingdom of God, but God brings sinners into the kingdom by causing them to be born again by the Spirit (John 3:3–5). No one can confess Jesus as Lord without the Holy Spirit (1 Cor. 12:3). Thus, in the Nicene Creed, the church confesses that the Spirit is "the Lord and Giver of life."[12] Just as the Father especially ordained salvation and the Son accomplished salvation, so the Spirit applies salvation to people's lives.[13] The Westminster Shorter Catechism (Q. 29) says, "We are made partakers of the redemption purchased by Christ, by the effectual application of it to us (John 1:11–12) by his Holy Spirit (Titus 3:5–6)."[14] The doctrine of the Spirit is crucial to knowing how God saves sinners and knowing whether or not *you* are saved.

3. *To know the Spirit is to understand sanctification*, the process of spiritual growth in holiness. Sanctification is "of the Spirit" (2 Thess. 2:13; 1 Pet. 1:2). William Perkins (1558–1602) said, "The Father sanctifies by the Son and by the Holy Ghost; the Son sanctifies from the Father and

10. Erickson, *Christian Theology*, 772–73.

11. Wayne Grudem, *Systematic Theology: An Introduction to Biblical Doctrine* (Grand Rapids, MI: Zondervan, 1994), 634.

12. *The Three Forms of Unity*, 7.

13. William Ames, *The Marrow of Theology*, trans. John D. Eusden (Grand Rapids, MI: Baker, 1968), 1.14.1–2 (149).

14. *Reformed Confessions*, 4:357.

by the Holy Ghost; the Holy Ghost sanctifies from the Father and from the Son by Himself immediately."[15] Owen said that sanctification is "the universal renovation of our natures by the Holy Spirit into the image of God, through Jesus Christ."[16] He noted, "All this increase of holiness is immediately the work of the Holy Ghost."[17] It is by the Holy Spirit that the people who belong to Christ are made holy (1 Cor. 3:16–17; 6:19–20), overcome sin (Gal. 5:16), pray (Rom. 8:15; Eph. 6:18), receive illumination (Eph. 1:17–20), are transformed into Christ's glory (2 Cor. 3:17–18), and magnify Christ in life and death (Phil. 1:19–20). If we listed every aspect of the Christian life, beside each item we could add, "by the Spirit."

4. *To know the Spirit is to balance the Christian life.* Christians and churches are prone to become imbalanced in their preaching and experience. We must maintain a proper balance between knowledge of doctrine and experience of spiritual life. This is the balance of the Word and the Spirit. To overemphasize the Word or the Spirit results in the coldness of intellectualism or the confusion of emotionalism, either of which can harden hearts so that people fall away into skepticism. J. van Genderen (1923–2004) and W. H. Velema (1929–2019) wrote, "The Word does not exist apart from the Spirit. It is the Word of the Spirit. The Spirit does not come without the Word. He is the Spirit of the Word. Whenever the Word is believed, it is entirely due to the work of the Spirit, who opens the heart to it."[18]

5. *To know the Spirit is to worship God rightly.* Our worship should be Trinitarian, just as we are baptized "in the name of the Father, and of the Son, and of the Holy Ghost" (Matt. 28:19). We worship one God in three persons and three persons in one God.[19] Thomas Watson (c. 1620–1686) wrote, "There is an order in the Godhead, but no degrees . . . therefore we must give equal worship to all the persons."[20] Furthermore, an appreciation for the Holy Spirit's work is essential to worship. Under the old covenant, God's people worshiped in a physical temple using a complex system of rituals through which the Spirit revealed Christ (Heb. 10:1). In the new covenant, the outward rituals have given way to simplicity as

15. William Perkins, *An Exposition of the Symbol*, in *The Works of William Perkins*, series eds. Joel R. Beeke and Derek W. H. Thomas, 10 vols. (Grand Rapids, MI: Reformation Heritage Books, 2014–2020), 5:305.

16. Owen, *Pneumatologia*, in *Works*, 3:386.

17. Owen, *Pneumatologia*, in *Works*, 3:393.

18. J. van Genderen and W. H. Velema, *Concise Reformed Dogmatics*, trans. Gerrit Bilkes and Ed M. van der Maas (Phillipsburg, NJ: P&R, 2008), 767.

19. Perkins, *An Exposition of the Symbol*, in *Works*, 5:322.

20. Thomas Watson, *A Body of Divinity* (Edinburgh: Banner of Truth, 1965), 112.

the church worships through Christ, with access to the Father, and in one Spirit (Eph. 2:18). It is the Spirit who binds us together in unity and peace despite our personal, ethnic, and social differences so that the church is one body of worshipers (1 Cor. 12:12–13; Eph. 4:3–4). The Spirit fills us with truth and joy so that we sing psalms, hymns, and spiritual songs to the Lord (Eph. 5:18–20). Therefore, the knowledge of the Spirit protects the simplicity, unity, and spirituality of worship.

6. *To know the Spirit is to appreciate historic Christian orthodoxy.* From the beginning of the church, Christians have treasured the fundamentals of right doctrine ("orthodoxy") and confessed it in their creeds. In the Apostles' Creed, the Christian confesses, "I believe in the Holy Ghost."[21] The doctrine of the Holy Spirit is rooted in the Scriptures, was developed in the early church, and was renewed and made all the more fruitful in the Reformation of the sixteenth century. B. B. Warfield (1851–1921) called John Calvin (1509–1564) "the Theologian of the Holy Spirit."[22] Warfield said, "The developed doctrine of the work of the Holy Spirit is an exclusively Reformation doctrine, and more particularly a Reformed doctrine, and more particularly still a Puritan doctrine."[23] Therefore, to neglect this doctrine is to neglect our Christian and Reformed heritage.

7. *To know the Spirit is to be equipped to speak to our culture.* Science has provided us with much technology but no answers to life's deepest questions. People desire to experience something transcendent and glorious, but our nations are adrift without direction from moral standards or divine wisdom. The doctrine of the Holy Spirit equips us to show people that Christianity offers true knowledge and genuine spiritual experience. As Erickson writes, "In a culture that stresses the experiential, it is primarily through the Holy Spirit's work that we feel God's presence within and the Christian life is given a special tangibility."[24] As long as people view Christianity as a mere social institution, system of beliefs, or set of behaviors, they will not recognize its uniqueness. George Smeaton (1814–1889) wrote,

21. *The Three Forms of Unity*, 5.

22. Benjamin B. Warfield, *Calvin and Calvinism*, in *The Works of Benjamin B. Warfield*, 10 vols. (Bellingham, WA: Logos Research Systems, 2008), 5:21.

23. Benjamin B. Warfield, introduction to Abraham Kuyper, *The Work of the Holy Spirit*, trans. Henri de Vries (Grand Rapids, MI: Eerdmans, 1946), xxxiii.

24. Erickson, *Christian Theology*, 773.

> Wherever Christianity has become a living power, the doctrine of the Holy Spirit has uniformly been regarded, equally with the atonement and justification by faith, as the article of a standing or falling Church. The distinctive feature of Christianity, as it addresses itself to man's experience, is the work of the Spirit, which not only elevates it far above all philosophical speculation, but also above every other form of religion.[25]

8. *To know the Spirit is to be prepared for spiritual warfare.* The Christian life consists of a battle against enemies that we can conquer only by means of the Spirit as our supernatural ally. When Christ engaged in direct combat with the Devil in the wilderness, Jesus did so as a man "full of the Holy Ghost" (Luke 4:1). Our great offensive weapon in the battle against the unseen powers of darkness is "the sword of the Spirit, which is the word of God" (Eph. 6:17), the same weapon Christ used. The only way for us to make effective use of the armor of God is by "praying always with all prayer and supplication in the Spirit" (v. 18). Though this world is full of evil spirits that would draw us away from Christ, John wrote, "Ye are of God, little children, and have overcome them: because greater is he that is in you, than he that is in the world" (1 John 4:4).

9. *To know the Spirit is to feel our dependence.* The doctrine of the Holy Spirit is full of man's inability and God's sovereignty. The Lord's word to Zerubbabel remains the banner that flies over all Christian endeavors: "Not by might, nor by power, but by my spirit, saith the Lord of hosts" (Zech. 4:6). While the doctrines of sovereign grace empower human activity (Phil. 2:12–13), they undermine the independence of man's proud spirit. A. W. Pink (1886–1952) warned, "In the great majority of cases, professing Christians are too puffed up by a sense of what they suppose they are doing for God, to earnestly study what God has promised to do for and in His people."[26] As Irenaeus (fl. 180) said, we are but "dry earth," and the Holy Spirit is the "water from heaven . . . [and] dew of God" that we must have in order to bear fruit pleasing to God.[27] John Dagg (1794–1884) said, "No believer, who has any just sense of his dependence on the Holy Spirit, for the divine life which he enjoys, and all its

---

25. George Smeaton, *The Doctrine of the Holy Spirit*, foreword by W. J. Grier (Edinburgh: Banner of Truth, 2016), 1.
26. Arthur W. Pink, *The Holy Spirit* (Grand Rapids, MI: Baker, 1970), 8.
27. Irenaeus, *Against Heresies*, 3.17, in *ANF*, 1:445.

included blessings, can be indifferent towards the Agent by whom all this good is bestowed. . . . And to him, therefore, the study of the Holy Spirit's character and office, will be a source of delight."[28]

10. *To know the Spirit is to know Christ.* This is so because of both the triune nature of God and the plan of salvation. In the Trinity, the Son and the Spirit are distinct in their personalities but inseparable in their being and activity. So closely united are they in all their works that Paul could write of Jesus Christ, "Now the Lord is that Spirit" (2 Cor. 3:17). Furthermore, God has so ordered salvation that the Spirit comes to apply what the Son has accomplished (John 16:13–14). The great work of the Spirit is union with Christ: "He that is joined unto the Lord is one spirit" (1 Cor. 6:17). Calvin wrote, "The Holy Spirit is the bond by which Christ effectually unites us to himself."[29] This union in the Spirit is the means of our personal communion with Christ. Wilhelmus à Brakel (1635–1711), echoing the Heidelberg Catechism, wrote, "The Holy Spirit makes believers partakers of Christ and His benefits. . . . This union results in the mutual use of possessive pronouns. 'My beloved is mine, and I am His' (Song of Sol. 2:16)."[30]

Do you know the Holy Spirit? Have you felt his convicting power, his converting power, his power to enable you to believe in the Lord Jesus Christ and be saved, his power to crucify the lusts of your flesh, his power to sanctify you, and his power to uphold you and cause you to persevere in grace? Have you come to see how much you need him in every aspect of your salvation and sanctification? Have you discovered the unity you have in the Spirit with other believers? Has the Spirit borne witness with your spirit that you have passed from death into life, that your sins are forgiven, and that you are an heir to everlasting life?

If so, then you will love the Holy Spirit and will want to have a right understanding of who he is and what he does. As the Spirit leads you into all truth, shedding the Father's love abroad in your heart and glorifying Christ in you as the hope of glory, you will say, "I do not know which of the divine persons I need the most, but one thing I know: I need each of

28. John Dagg, *Manual of Theology*, 2 parts (Charleston, SC: Southern Baptist Publication Society, 1859), 1:235.

29. John Calvin, *Institutes of the Christian Religion*, ed. John T. McNeill, trans. Ford Lewis Battles, The Library of Christian Classics, vols. 20–21 (Philadelphia: Westminster, 1960), 3.1.1.

30. Wilhelmus à Brakel, *The Christian's Reasonable Service*, trans. Bartel Elshout, ed. Joel R. Beeke, (Grand Rapids, MI: Reformation Heritage Books, 1992–1995), 1:184. See the Heidelberg Catechism (LD 1, Q. 1; LD 20, Q. 53), in *The Three Forms of Unity*, 68, 84.

them, and I love them all." If, however, you are a stranger to this Spirit, then you have an urgent need to know his saving work both in your understanding and, by faith, in your experience.

The Person of the Holy Spirit

Many people today are like the disciples in Ephesus who said, "We have not so much as heard whether there be any Holy Ghost" (Acts 19:2). He may be to them just a name in a creed that they recite in church, or even less. Some people have opinions of the Spirit that are in error, such as viewing him to be an angel or the impersonal energy of God. Other people may confess biblical truth about the Spirit but live in practical ignorance of him. If he were suddenly to withdraw his saving and sanctifying presence from the earth, it would make no difference at all in their lives.

There is a profound mystery to the Holy Spirit. Our Lord Jesus once compared being born of the Spirit to the blowing of wind: you cannot control it or see where it starts or ends, but you can observe the results (John 3:8). If it were not for the Word of God, we would not know God the Spirit. Yet he reveals himself in the Holy Scriptures. The Bible speaks of the Holy Spirit ninety-four times in the Old Testament and more than two hundred and fifty times in the New Testament.

The Names of the Spirit

At times the Bible gives to the Spirit names or titles related to works he does or graces he gives, such as the Spirit of wisdom, the Spirit of truth, the Spirit of holiness, the Spirit of life, the Spirit of adoption, the Spirit of faith, the Spirit of grace, and the Spirit of glory.[31] He is the Comforter or Advocate.[32] Although these titles teach us things about the Holy Spirit, they pertain more directly to his works than his nature. Some names speak of the Spirit's close relationship to God's Son. He is the Spirit of Christ, the Spirit of the Son, and the Spirit of Jesus Christ.[33] We will consider these functional and relational titles in other chapters.

31. Spirit of wisdom: Ex. 28:3; Deut. 34:9; Isa. 11:2; Eph. 1:17. Truth: John 14:17; 15:26; 16:13; 1 John 4:6. Holiness: Rom. 1:4. Life: Rom. 8:2. Adoption: Rom. 8:15. Faith: 2 Cor. 4:13. Grace: Heb. 10:29. Glory: 1 Pet. 4:14.

32. Comforter or Advocate (*paraklētos*): John 14:16, 26; 15:26; 16:7.

33. Spirit of Christ: Rom. 8:9; 1 Pet. 1:11. Spirit of the Son: Gal. 4:6. Spirit of Jesus Christ: Phil. 1:19. The unique expression "Spirit of Jesus" (Acts 16:7) appears in several early uncial manuscripts, but not in the Majority Text.

Here we want to give attention to three designations for this divine person, two used primarily in the Old Testament and the other almost entirely in the New Testament.

1. *The Spirit of God* or *the Spirit of the Lord*. These are his predominant names in the Old Testament, also occurring several times in the New, for a total of about sixty times. Of course, God is spirit in his divine nature (Isa. 31:3; John 4:24). Charles Hodge (1797–1878) wrote that *spirit* communicates "invisible power" and thus "immaterial, invisible agents."[34] All three persons of the Trinity share this same spiritual essence; they are invisible, intelligent, and alive without the limitations, needs, or complexities of a physical body.[35]

How then is the third person of the Trinity distinctly called "the Spirit of God" if God in the whole Trinity is spirit? The word *spirit* often refers to the wind that blows or the breath we breathe. This is mysterious, but the Bible implies that the Spirit is like the breath of God—the living, energetic, personal, intelligent, dynamic life of God. Herman Bavinck (1854–1921) wrote, "The Holy Spirit is the breath of the Almighty (Job 33:4), the breath of his mouth (Ps. 33:6). Jesus compares him to the wind (John 3:8) and 'breathes' him upon his disciples (John 20:22)."[36]

Owen connected the idea of breath to the abiding, living presence of a person, "as the vital breath of a man has a continual emanation from him, and yet is never separated utterly from his person."[37] The eternal procession of the Spirit of God from the Father and the Son is a matter properly discussed under the doctrine of the Trinity.[38] It suffices to say here that the name "Spirit of God" teaches us that the Spirit is the living and life-giving presence of God, invisible and yet personal and powerful in his being and operations. Calvin wrote, "Through him we come into communion with God, so that we in a way feel his life-giving power toward us."[39] If we desire God's life and nurturing presence, we should seek the Spirit of God from the Father.

2. *The Holy Spirit*. This name appears only three times in the Old Testament (Ps. 51:11; Isa. 63:10–11). However, it dominates the New

34. Charles Hodge, *Systematic Theology*, 3 vols. (repr., Peabody, MA: Hendrickson, 1999), 1:522.

35. On God's spirituality, see *RST*, 1:606–22 (chap. 32).

36. Herman Bavinck, *Reformed Dogmatics*, ed. John Bolt, trans. John Vriend, 4 vols. (Grand Rapids, MI: Baker Academic, 2003–2008), 2:277.

37. Owen, *Pneumatologia*, in *Works*, 3:55.

38. On the procession of the Spirit, see *RST*, 1:915–17, 940–44.

39. Calvin, *Institutes*, 1.13.14.

Testament descriptions of the Spirit, appearing ninety-four times. With the coming of Christ, the Spirit of God became known to us preeminently as the *Holy* Spirit.

As with spirituality, holiness is an attribute of God that pertains to the whole Trinity. The holiness of God is his majesty and moral excellence that sets him above all things and against all sin for the sake of his glory.[40] Ferguson writes that the word *holy* emphasizes "the 'otherness' of the Spirit's being."[41] Owen wrote about the Spirit, "This is the foundation of his being called 'Holy,' even the eternal glorious holiness of his nature."[42] Holiness sets the Holy Spirit apart from all that is not God, as Exodus 15:11 says: "Who is like unto thee, O Lord, among the gods? Who is like thee, glorious in holiness, fearful in praises, doing wonders?" Since the Spirit is holy, we should always relate to him with fear, awe, wonder, and reverence.

He is called the Holy Spirit because both his nature and his work are holy. Antonius Thysius (1565–1640) said, "He is called also Holy Spirit (Isaiah 63:10) and Holy Spirit of God (Ephesians 4:30) because of his nature, office, and effect."[43] Negatively, he is called the Holy Spirit because he implacably opposes the unclean spirits of this world. To slander the Spirit's work as being of the Devil is to blaspheme the Spirit, for it accuses the Holy Spirit of being an unholy spirit (Mark 3:29–30).[44] His very name, as Smeaton wrote, sets him in "antithesis to every unholy spirit, whether human or Satanic."[45] Consequently, those indwelt by the Holy Spirit must separate themselves from the sins and false worship promoted by the unclean spirits of this world (2 Cor. 6:14–17). As one in whom the Holy Spirit dwells, a Christian who gives himself to uncleanness and worldliness provokes God to jealousy (James 4:4–5).

The Spirit's greatest work of holiness is the sanctification of God's people. Martin Luther (1483–1546) summarized the Apostles' Creed when he said, "I believe in God the Father, who created me; I believe in God the Son, who redeemed me; I believe in the Holy Spirit, who makes me

40. On the holiness of God, see *RST*, 1:566–82 (chap. 30).
41. Ferguson, *The Holy Spirit*, 16.
42. Owen, *Pneumatologia*, in *Works*, 3:56.
43. Johannes Polyander, Antonius Walaeus, Antonius Thysius, and Andreas Rivetus, *Synopsis Purioris Theologiae, Synopsis of a Purer Theology: Latin Text and English Translation*, vol. 1, *Disputations 1–23*, trans. Riemer A. Faber, ed. Dolf te Velde, Rein Ferwerda, Willem J. van Asselt, William den Boer, and Riemer A. Faber, Studies in Medieval and Reformation Traditions: Texts and Sources (Leiden: Brill, 2014), 9.3 (230).
44. Owen, *Pneumatologia*, in *Works*, 3:56.
45. Smeaton, *The Doctrine of the Holy Spirit*, 101.

holy."[46] Francis Turretin (1623–1687) wrote that the Spirit is "called Holy by way of eminence" both "subjectively (because he is most holy)" and "efficiently (because he sanctifies us)."[47] Perhaps this is the reason why he is preeminently called the Holy Spirit in the New Testament. With the finished work of Christ, the old covenant emphasis on outward, ceremonial holiness has been replaced by the new covenant emphasis on inward, moral sanctification. Smeaton said that the frequent joining of the word *Holy* to the Spirit "gives us a nearer view of the Spirit's special work in connection with man's salvation."[48]

This is the great display of the Spirit's holiness throughout redemptive history: he makes God's people holy. Perkins said, "The third person [of the Trinity] is called holy, because besides the holiness of nature His office is to sanctify the church of God."[49] That is the thrust of Paul's argument in 1 Corinthians 6:19–20: "What? Know ye not that your body is the temple of the Holy Ghost which is in you, which ye have of God, and ye are not your own? For ye are bought with a price: therefore glorify God in your body, and in your spirit, which are God's." We dare not claim the Spirit as our own while living in unrepented sin. On the contrary, knowing the Holy Spirit should greatly increase our sorrow over sin, humility before God, meekness with men, and zeal to pursue practical holiness in every area of life. He is the *Holy* Spirit.

The Deity of the Holy Spirit

The Holy Spirit is God. Though the Spirit is not the Father or the Son, the Spirit shares the same divine nature with them and is rightly called God the Spirit. It is a serious mistake for us to view the Holy Spirit as a created spirit, such as an angel. When the Arians of the fourth century denied that Christ is God, they also denied that the Holy Spirit is God, and some

46. The Large Catechism (2.7), in *The Book of Concord: The Confessions of the Evangelical Lutheran Church*, ed. Robert Kolb and Timothy J. Wengert, trans. Charles Arand et al. (Minneapolis: Fortress, 2000), 432. See also the Heidelberg Catechism (LD 8, Q. 24), in *The Three Forms of Unity*, 75.

47. Francis Turretin, *Institutes of Elenctic Theology*, trans. George Musgrave Giger, ed. James T. Dennison Jr., 3 vols. (Phillipsburg, NJ: P&R, 1992–1997), 3.30 (1:303).

48. Smeaton, *The Doctrine of the Holy Spirit*, 101.

49. Perkins, *An Exposition of the Symbol*, in *Works*, 5:305. Thus also James Ussher: "Why is he called the Holy Spirit? Not only because of his essential holiness as God; for so the Father and the Son are also infinitely holy as he: but because he is the author and worker of all holiness in men, and the sanctifier of God's children. Why, does not the Father and the Son sanctify also? Yes verily: but they do it by him: and because he does immediately sanctify, therefore he hath the title of Holy." *A Body of Divinity*, ed. Michael Nevarr (Birmingham, AL: Solid Ground, 2007), 3rd head (75).

speculated that he is an angel—provoking a vigorous response from Athanasius (c. 297–373), the great champion of orthodox, biblical faith against Arianism.[50] Though the Qur'an is not explicit on this matter, it is commonly believed among Muslims that the Holy Spirit is the angel Gabriel.[51]

However, the Bible clearly reveals that the Holy Spirit is God and does so in a number of ways. The Holy Scriptures ascribe to the Holy Spirit:

1. The *names and titles of deity*, for the Holy Spirit is called "God" (Acts 5:3–4) and is identified in the New Testament as the source of statements in the Old Testament attributed to "the LORD" (*YHWH* or Jehovah).[52]

2. The *attributes of deity*, for the Bible reveals the Spirit's omniscience (Isa. 40:13; 1 Cor. 2:9–11), omnipotence (Luke 1:34–37), omnipresence (Ps. 139:7; 1 Cor. 6:19), eternity (Gen. 1:2), foreknowledge (Acts 1:16; 1 Pet. 1:11–12), goodness (Neh. 9:20; Ps. 143:10–11), love (Rom. 15:30), truth (John 14:17), holiness (Isa. 63:10–11; Rom. 1:4), infinity (John 3:34), vitality (2 Cor. 3:3, 6), and simplicity (Rom. 8:10; 1 John 5:6).[53]

3. The *relations of deity*, in which the Spirit is the Spirit of the Father (Matt. 10:20) who proceeds from the Father (John 15:26), and he is the Spirit of the Son (Gal. 4:6) and the Spirit of Christ (Rom. 8:9). The Father, the Son, and the Spirit appear together repeatedly in the New Testament as the three persons active in the works of the one God: the initiation of Christ's ministry (Mark 1:9–11); the salvation of sinners (Gal. 4:4–6; Titus 3:4–6); the exercise of spiritual gifts in the church (1 Cor. 12:4–6); and the spiritual strengthening and growth of believers (Eph. 1:17–20; 3:14–17). The Holy Spirit is one with the Father and the Son (Matt. 28:19; 2 Cor. 3:17), sharing with them the one divine knowledge, power, life, and will of the triune God.[54]

4. The *actions of deity*, for the Spirit created all things and people,[55] gives life to the creatures (Ps. 104:30), inspired God's Word,[56] worked

50. J. N. D. Kelly, *Early Christian Creeds*, 3rd ed. (London: Continuum, 1972), 339–40.

51. Norman L. Geisler and Abdul Saleeb, *Answering Islam: The Crescent in the Light of the Cross* (Grand Rapids, MI: Baker, 1993), 35. The Qur'an attributes its revelation both to Gabriel (Surah 2:97) and to the Holy Spirit (16:102).

52. Acts 28:25–27, citing Isa. 6:9–10; Heb. 10:16, citing Jer. 31:33.

53. See *RST*, 1:888. See the references to the Spirit's holiness (1:573–74, 579), vitality (1:619), simplicity (1:626), aseity (1:646), omnipresence (1:656), eternity (1:665–66), omniscience (1:726, 730–31), authority (1:769), power (1:363–68, 771–72), love (1:793), truth (1:809), and joy (1:845).

54. John 7:37–39; 1 Cor. 12:11; Rev. 5:6. See *RST*, 1:896–97.

55. Gen. 1:2; Job 26:13; 33:4; Ps. 33:6. See chap. 2.

56. 2 Sam. 23:2; Acts 1:16; Heb. 3:7; 9:8; 2 Pet. 1:21. On the inspiration of Scripture, see *RST*, 1:316–32 (chap. 17)

miracles through Christ and the apostles,[57] regenerates and gives spiritual life to sinners,[58] and raises the dead.[59] As we proceed in this volume, we will see that the Holy Spirit does works that can only be the works of God.

5. The *presence of deity*, by which we mean that the presence of the Holy Spirit is the presence of God, and the Spirit is the divine resident in the temple of God.[60] William Ames (1576–1633) said, "A temple is not legitimately consecrated to anyone except God. . . . But in this place, this temple is said to be set up [to be] especially holy for the Holy Spirit."[61] Since God's temple is a people scattered across the world among the nations, the Holy Spirit must be God to dwell simultaneously in them all.[62]

6. The *authority of deity*, for the Spirit exercises sovereignty over the church "as he wills" (1 Cor. 12:11 ESV; cf. Acts 13:2). The Spirit led Israel through the wilderness (Isa. 63:14), leads God's children in the ways of righteousness (Ps. 143:10; Rom. 8:14), and even led the incarnate Mediator (Matt. 4:1). Pink wrote, "Who but a Divine person had the right to direct the Mediator? And to whom but God would the Redeemer have submitted!"[63]

7. The *honors of deity*, as when the Spirit is equally honored with the Father and the Son in the ordinance of baptism (Matt. 28:19) and the invocation of God's blessing on his people (2 Cor. 13:14). Consequently, the church confesses in the Nicene Creed that the Holy Spirit "with the Father and the Son together is worshipped and glorified."[64]

The deity of the Holy Spirit is central to Christian orthodoxy. As Douglas Kelly writes, the theologians of the early church wrote of "the supreme and regal authority of the Holy Spirit."[65] Gregory of Nazianzus (330–389) said,

> The Holy Ghost, then, always existed, and exists, and always will exist. He neither had a beginning, nor will He have an end; but He was everlastingly ranged with and numbered with the Father and the

57. Matt. 12:28; Luke 4:14; Acts 10:38; Rom. 15:19; Heb. 2:4.
58. John 3:3–6; 6:63; 2 Cor. 3:6; Titus 3:5.
59. Rom. 1:4; 8:11; 1 Cor. 15:42–45.
60. Ps. 139:7; Hag. 2:1–5; 1 Cor. 3:16–17; Eph. 2:21–22.
61. William Ames, *A Sketch of the Christian's Catechism*, trans. Todd M. Rester, Classic Reformed Theology 1 (Grand Rapids, MI: Reformation Heritage Books, 2008), 104.
62. Ambrose, *Of the Holy Spirit*, 1.7, in *NPNF*², 10:104.
63. Pink, *The Holy Spirit*, 15.
64. *The Three Forms of Unity*, 7.
65. Douglas F. Kelly, *Systematic Theology: Grounded in Holy Scripture and Understood in the Light of the Church*, vol. 1, *The God Who Is: The Holy Trinity* (Fearn, Ross-shire, Scotland: Christian Focus, 2008), 341–42.

> Son. For it was not ever fitting that either the Son should be wanting to the Father, or the Spirit to the Son. . . . Himself ever the same with Himself, and with Those with Whom He is ranged; invisible, eternal, incomprehensible, unchangeable . . . self-moving, eternally moving, with free-will, self-powerful, All-powerful . . . Life and Lifegiver; Light and Lightgiver; absolute Good, and Spring of Goodness . . . ; the Right, the Princely Spirit; the Lord, the Sender, the Separator; Builder of His own Temple; leading, working as He wills.[66]

Since the Spirit is God, God's people should adore him. It is good and right to apply the great commandment to all the Trinity: "Thou shalt love the Lord thy God with all thy heart, and with all thy soul, and with all thy mind" (Matt. 22:37; cf. Deut. 6:5). Do you love the Holy Spirit? When you read the Bible and encounter one of the many references to the Spirit, does your soul respond in a sweet motion of worshipful love? When you hear the Bible preached faithfully in church, do you delight that you are hearing what the Spirit says to the churches? Do you desire the Spirit to fill you, not just to get power for service, but that you may know more of his glory and help others to do the same? Believers should pray and strive to grow in their love for the Holy Spirit.

The person who does not love God does not belong to Christ. However, even in this case the deity of the Holy Spirit can give you hope and motivate you to call on the name of the Lord Jesus to save you. The Holy Spirit is a miracle worker, the God who raises the dead. Though your soul may be as dead as a valley of dry bones, God the Holy Spirit can make you alive. Make this your prayer:

> Eternal Spirit, by whose breath
> The soul is saved from sin and death,
> Before Thy throne we sinners bend;
> To us Thy quickening power extend.[67]

The Personality of the Holy Spirit

Another major error concerning the Holy Spirit is to conclude that he is not a person, but only the energy or presence of God. The denial of the Spirit's personality is presently a more common heresy than the denial of

66. Gregory of Nazianzus, *On Pentecost*, chap. 9, in *NPNF*^{2}, 7:382.
67. Edward Cooper, "Father of heaven, whose love profound," cited in Kelly, *Systematic Theology*, 1:313.

his deity. We find it in Socinianism, historic Unitarianism,[68] and the teachings of the Watchtower Society or Jehovah's Witnesses.[69] The father of modern liberal theology, Friedrich Schleiermacher (1768–1834), spoke of the Holy Spirit as the presence of the divine essence active within human beings.[70] Such formulations reduce the Spirit to a mode of God's activity, "the old Sabellian error that the Holy Spirit is only an expression of God's power," as Geerhardus Vos (1862–1949) observed.[71]

The Bible reveals the Holy Spirit to be personal[72]—that is, someone with a rational, volitional nature; a unique "I" in relationships with other persons.[73]

1. *The Holy Spirit is someone, not something*. It may be argued that the Spirit's being poured out like water (Acts 2:17) or quenched like fire (1 Thess. 5:19) proves that the Spirit is impersonal. However, the Bible compares God himself to a "fountain of living waters" (Jer. 2:13) and "a consuming fire" (Deut. 4:24). These are figures of speech, "imagery, pure and simple."[74] They do not indicate that God or the Spirit is impersonal but refer to his operations. John Brown of Haddington (1722–1787) wrote, "In all these texts of Scripture, in which something not proper to an intelligent and eternal person is ascribed to the Spirit or Holy Ghost, his name must be understood as meaning not himself, but his gifts and influences."[75]

Close attention to the Greek New Testament reveals that the Scriptures speak of the Spirit grammatically as a person. In John 14:16, our Lord Jesus Christ did not say that the Father would give his disciples "comfort" but "another Comforter" (cf. 14:26; 15:26; 16:7).[76] The word translated

---

68. Robert Wallace, *A Plain Statement and Scriptural Defence of the Leading Doctrines of Unitarianism* (Chesterfield, England: for the author, by T. Woodhead et al., 1819), 34. Present-day Unitarian Universalism has morphed into vague humanism that encompasses those who are "agnostic, theist, atheist, and everything in between." "Existence of a Higher Power in Unitarian Universalism," Unitarian Universalist Association, December 21, 2015, http://www.uua.org/beliefs/what-we-believe/higher-power.

69. "In the Bible, God's holy spirit is identified as God's power in action. . . . God's active force." "Is the Holy Spirit a Person?" *Awake!* (2006), Watchtower Online Library, December 21, 2015, http://wol.jw.org/en/wol/d/r1/lp-e/102006245.

70. Friedrich Schleiermacher, *The Christian Faith*, ed. H. R. Mackintosh and J. S. Stewart, 2 vols. (New York: Harper and Row, 1963), 571–72, 738. Cf. Hodge, *Systematic Theology*, 1:534.

71. Geerhardus Vos, *Reformed Dogmatics*, trans. and ed. Richard B. Gaffin et al., 5 vols. (Bellingham, WA: Lexham Press, 2012–2016), 1:67. On Sabellianism, see *RST*, 1:904.

72. See *RST*, 1:889–90.

73. See *RST*, 1:931–33.

74. Gordon D. Fee, *God's Empowering Presence: The Holy Spirit in the Letters of Paul* (Peabody, MA: Hendrickson, 1994), 830.

75. John Brown of Haddington, *Systematic Theology: A Compendious View of Natural and Revealed Religion* (Grand Rapids, MI: Reformation Heritage Books, 2015), 143.

76. Louis Berkhof, *Systematic Theology* (Edinburgh: Banner of Truth, 1958), 96.

as "Comforter" (*paraklētos*) refers to an advocate, a person called upon to represent another person in court and speak on his behalf.[77] "Another" compares the Spirit to Christ, and the term *paraklētos* is used of Christ as the heavenly "Advocate" of his people (1 John 2:1). Though the Greek word translated as "Spirit" is neuter in gender,[78] the word translated as "Comforter" is masculine, and masculine pronouns are used of him: "He [*ekeinos*] shall teach you all things" (John 14:26); "he [*ekeinos*] shall testify of me" (15:26); and "when he [*ekeinos*], the Spirit of truth, is come . . . he [*ekeinos*] shall glorify me" (16:13–14).[79] By calling him "another Comforter," Jesus implied that the Spirit would be like Christ, standing in for him after he ascended to the Father (14:2–3, 12, 18; 16:7). In this way, our Lord taught us to view the Holy Spirit as a person who witnesses for God on earth just as Jesus did.

2. *The Holy Spirit is someone with a rational, volitional nature.* The Spirit knows glorious things: "No one comprehends the thoughts of God except the Spirit of God" (1 Cor. 2:11 ESV). Impersonal objects may contain information, but only a person knows truth. The Holy Spirit also makes moral judgments about actions: "It seemed good to the Holy Ghost, and to us, to lay upon you no greater burden than these necessary things" (Acts 15:28).

The Holy Spirit has a will that he exercises in making choices. Regarding the spiritual gifts, Paul writes, "All these are empowered by one and the same Spirit, who apportions to each one individually as he wills" (1 Cor. 12:11 ESV). Energy does not make choices. The will of the Spirit ardently opposes sin. When the people of Israel rebelled against the Lord in the wilderness, they "vexed" (grieved and provoked) the Holy Spirit (Isa. 63:9–10). Paul warned the saints in Ephesus, "Grieve not the holy Spirit

77. *TDNT*, 5:800–803.

78. The Greek language has three genders: masculine, feminine, and neuter, which are merely a matter of morphology (linguistic form). The neuter gender of the word translated as "Spirit" (*pneuma*) does not deny that the Holy Spirit is personal; the Greek word translated as "child" (*paidion*) is also neuter.

79. Bavinck, *Reformed Dogmatics*, 2:278. Many theologians argue that the use of the masculine demonstrative pronoun *ekeinos* for the Spirit in John 14:26, 15:26, and 16:13–14 contradicts the normal agreement of gender between a pronoun and its antecedent, and therefore indicates that the Spirit is a person. For example, see Brown, *Systematic Theology*, 140; and Erickson, *Christian Theology*, 784. However, others argue that in each context, the antecedent of the masculine pronoun is not the neuter Greek word translated as "Spirit," but the masculine word translated as "Comforter" (John 14:26; 15:26; 16:7). Thus, Daniel B. Wallace, "Greek Grammar and the Personality of the Holy Spirit," *Bulletin for Biblical Research* 13, no. 1 (2003): 97–125, especially 97–111. At the very least, we believe that the masculine word translated as "Comforter" is a manifestly personal term, which is confirmed by the masculine pronouns.

of God, whereby ye are sealed unto the day of redemption" (Eph. 4:30). While we should not attribute grief to God in a way that implies suffering or passion, the text teaches that the Spirit treats people in a personal and relational manner.[80] Hodge wrote, "He is represented, therefore, as a person . . . whom we may please or offend."[81]

3. *The Holy Spirit is someone unique in relationships with other persons.* As a person, he is distinct from the Father and the Son, relating to the other two persons according to the order of the Trinity.[82] He displays his personhood by relating to human beings in a personal manner. He teaches, testifies, reproves, and guides them (John 14:26; 15:26; 16:7, 13). He intercedes for them (Rom. 8:26). John Gill (1697–1771) wrote, "Now as the advocacy and intercession of Christ, prove him to be a Person, and a distinct one from the Father, with whom he intercedes; so the intercession of the Spirit, equally proves his personality, even his distinct personality also."[83]

The Holy Spirit speaks and acts as the personal Lord. The Spirit said to Peter, "Go with them, doubting nothing: for I have sent them" (Acts 10:19–20). When the church at Antioch gave itself to prayer and fasting, the Holy Spirit spoke, commanding the church to set apart for him Barnabas and Saul for the work to which "I have called them," and so they were "sent forth by the Holy Ghost" (13:1–4). The Holy Spirit is not an *it*, but an *I*, a person "who speaks of himself in the first person," as Bavinck said.[84]

Practical Implications of the Spirit's Divine Personality

Since the Holy Spirit is God and a living person, Perkins said that each Christian must "acknowledge the Holy Ghost as He has revealed Himself in the Word, . . . believe that He is my Sanctifier and Comforter, . . . [and] put all the confidence of my heart in Him for that cause."[85]

80. Owen wrote of grief and anger, "Such affections and perturbations of mind are not ascribed unto God or the Spirit but metaphorically." However, he also noted that our duty not to "grieve" the Spirit is an example of how we are to relate to him "as he is a holy, divine, intelligent person, working freely in and toward us for our good." Owen, *Pneumatologia*, in *Works*, 4:413–14. See also *Communion with God*, in *Works*, 2:265–66. On divine affections and impassibility, see *RST*, 1:829–73 (chaps. 43–44).

81. Hodge, *Systematic Theology*, 1:525.

82. Luke 4:1, 18; John 14:16, 26; 16:26. See *RST*, 1:890–91.

83. John Gill, *A Complete Body of Doctrinal and Practical Divinity* (1839; repr., Paris, AR: The Baptist Standard Bearer, 1995), 168. Henceforth cited as Gill, *Body of Divinity*.

84. Bavinck, *Reformed Dogmatics*, 2:278.

85. Perkins, *An Exposition of the Symbol*, in *Works*, 5:306.

This last point highlights how important it is to believe that the Spirit is God. Only God can bear the full weight of our total trust. No mere creature is worthy of such faith. The Spirit, however, is worthy. Do you honor him with your faith? Do you trust in the Spirit with all your heart and lean not on your own understanding? Does your faith in Christ lead you to trust in the Spirit of Christ, by whom the Lord Jesus works in your life?

The personality of the Spirit teaches us that true spirituality involves a personal relationship with the Holy Spirit. We must not treat him as a mere power to be used, much less manipulated for our selfish ends. We must not seek him in the pursuit of nothing more than a transcendent experience. He dwells in each believer as a divine person within a human person. He is grieved by sin and delighted by holiness. Marvel over his love, undeserved grace, and patience toward you. As Lloyd-Jones said, it is astonishing that the Holy One would lower himself so far as "to dwell in you and me."[86] He is the Author of the Scriptures, and there he will teach you how to please him. Hear what the Spirit says in the Word and obey him.

The deity of the Spirit calls us to worship him together with the Father and the Son. If we do not worship the Spirit, we undermine the doctrine of the Trinity.[87] Let us exalt the Spirit in our praises for his divine attributes. Let us celebrate the glory of the Spirit revealed in his mighty works. If you are a pastor, plan and lead the worship of your church to lift up the congregation's hearts to the triune God, to the glory of the Father, the Son, and the Holy Spirit. If you are the head of a household, make sure that your family worship does not neglect the Spirit. All Christians, take hold of every opportunity to give thanks to the Holy Spirit, for apart from him you would not exist, and without him you have no spiritual life.

Sing to the Lord

Praying for the Leading of the Spirit

When morning lights the eastern skies,
O Lord, Thy mercy show;
On Thee alone my hope relies,
Let me Thy kindness know.

86. Lloyd-Jones, *Great Doctrines of the Bible*, 2:21.

87. See Joel R. Beeke and Mark Jones, *A Puritan Theology: Doctrine for Life* (Grand Rapids, MI: Reformation Heritage Books, 2012), 422.

Teach me the way that I should go;
I lift my soul to Thee;
For refuge from my cruel foe
To Thee, O Lord, I flee.

Thou art my God, to Thee I pray,
Teach me Thy will to heed;
And in the right and perfect way
May Thy good Spirit lead.

For Thy Name's sake, O gracious Lord,
Revive my soul and bless,
And in Thy faithfulness and love
Redeem me from distress.

Psalm 143:8–11
Tune: Lynton
The Psalter, No. 391

Questions for Meditation or Discussion

1. What objections might be raised against the doctrine of the Holy Spirit? How can we answer such objections?
2. Why does knowing the Holy Spirit and his work help us to know God, Christ, and our salvation better?
3. How does the doctrine of the Holy Spirit contribute to the following?
   - a balanced Christian life
   - right worship
   - evangelism in our culture
   - spiritual warfare
4. What is "orthodoxy"? What do the authors mean when they say, "To neglect this doctrine [of the Holy Spirit] is to neglect our Christian . . . heritage"?
5. Why should studying the Holy Spirit increase our dependence on God and faith in Jesus Christ?
6. Why is the Spirit named "the Holy Spirit"?
7. List seven lines of argument to prove that the Holy Spirit is God, with a few Scripture references for each.
8. How do the Holy Scriptures show us that the Spirit of God is a person?

9. What is one practical application from this chapter that you needed to hear? How will you put it into practice?

Questions for Deeper Reflection

10. How can Christians from different traditions and churches talk with each other about the Holy Spirit and his work in a way that is faithful to the truth but not unnecessarily divisive?
11. The authors say, "This is mysterious, but the Bible implies that the Spirit is like the breath of God." What biblical truths does this comparison suggest? What might be possible dangers in comparing the Holy Spirit to "the breath of God"?
12. Someone from a heretical group says to you, "Everything that the Bible says about the Spirit of God can be explained simply by understanding 'spirit' to mean God's power." How do you answer this assertion?

2

The Work of the Holy Spirit in Creation and Common Grace

When modern Christians think of the Holy Spirit, they tend to think of the new birth or the spiritual gifts. They rarely connect the Holy Spirit with God's works of creation and providence. However, the Holy Spirit is the third person of the eternal Trinity. The Belgic Confession (Art. 8) says, "The Father hath never been without His Son, or without His Holy Ghost. . . . They are all three one, in truth, in power, in goodness, and in mercy."[1] God's people sing in the Psalter,

> Thy Spirit, O Lord, makes life to abound;
> The earth is renewed, and fruitful the ground.[2]

The Holy Spirit's work to save the lost was preceded by his work to create the world. A hymn dating back to the medieval period begins,

> Come, O Creator Spirit blest,
> And in our hearts take up Thy rest;
> Spirit of grace, with heavenly aid
> Come to the souls whom Thou hast made.[3]

These words remind us that when the Holy Spirit comes to renew lost sinners, he does not enter foreign territory, but returns to that which he

1. *The Three Forms of Unity*, 23.
2. *The Psalter*, No. 287 (Ps. 104:30).
3. "Veni Spiritus Creator," as translated and found in *Trinity Hymnal—Baptist Edition*, No. 251.

created. A full-orbed theology of the Spirit must begin not with redemption but with creation and God's providential mercies to all things, for as Ambrose of Milan (c. 339–397) said, the Holy Spirit "is above all things."[4]

The Holy Spirit and Creation

Here we focus on the particular work of the Spirit in creation and do not attempt to fully explore the doctrine of creation, which has its own place earlier in systematic theology.[5]

The Spirit's Creation of the World

Genesis 1:1–2 says, "In the beginning God created the heaven and the earth. And the earth was without form, and void; and darkness was upon the face of the deep. And the Spirit of God moved upon the face of the waters." God created the universe, but initially the earth was not inhabited by living creatures, nor could it be ("without form, and void").[6] At the very beginning of the process of creation, we meet the Holy Spirit working to craft a home for living creatures. R. C. Sproul (1939–2017) said, "The Spirit brings order out of disorder . . . the structure of wholeness, the integration of the parts of the cosmos with the whole. It is because of Him that we have cosmos instead of chaos."[7] The verb translated as "moved" (*rakhap*) is used elsewhere of the hovering of a mother bird over its young, a picture of God's care for Israel in the wilderness (Deut. 32:11). The same Hebrew word translated as "without form" (*tohu*) in Genesis 1:2 appears in that context ("the waste," Deut. 32:10), strengthening the link between the texts and confirming that Genesis is not describing a violent wind but depicting the Spirit as the agent of God's nurturing presence in the primeval, uncultivated wilderness.[8] This tender image communicates that the Spirit of God cared for creation in its infantile state and brought it to life and completion. John Owen wrote, "Without him all was a dead sea, a confused deep, with

4. Ambrose, *Of the Holy Spirit*, 1.1.19, in *NPNF*², 10:96.

5. See *RST*, 2:55–142 (chaps. 2–6).

6. See the use of *tohu* and *bohu* in Deut. 32:10; Job 12:24; Isa. 34:11; 45:18; Jer. 4:23.

7. R. C. Sproul, *The Mystery of the Holy Spirit* (Wheaton, IL: Tyndale House, 1990), 85.

8. Ferguson, *The Holy Spirit*, 19–20. See also Graham A. Cole, *He Who Gives Life: The Doctrine of the Holy Spirit*, Foundations of Evangelical Theology (Wheaton, IL: Crossway, 2007), 96–99. The Hebrew phrase translated as "Spirit of God" (*Ruakh Elohim*) is not used of "wind" in the Old Testament, but consistently refers to God's Spirit (Gen. 1:2; 41:38; Ex. 31:3; 35:31; Num. 24:2; 1 Sam. 10:10; 11:6; 19:20, 23; 2 Chron. 15:1; 2 Chron. 24:20; Ezek. 11:24), except for a few references to an evil spirit sent by God to trouble Saul (1 Sam. 16:15–16, 23; 18:10).

darkness upon it, able to bring forth nothing."[9] Sinclair Ferguson says that the activity of the Spirit here is "extending God's presence into creation in such a way as to order and complete what has been planned in the mind of God"—the same work the Spirit performs in salvation.[10]

As we read in the text that follows how God repeatedly spoke and sovereignly shaped the universe (Gen. 1:3–31), we are to understand that the Spirit accompanied the creative word at every stage of creation. Leon Wood (1918–1977) wrote, "Since the indication [of Gen. 1:2] comes immediately before the description of the six-day creative activity, the implication is that the work of the six days was performed by the Spirit."[11] Spirit and word go together in divine activity. Psalm 33:6 says, "By the word of the LORD were the heavens made; and all the host of them by the breath [Hebrew *ruakh*, "spirit"] of his mouth." Though the connections between "word," "mouth," and "spirit" imply that the latter is best translated as "breath," the allusion to Genesis 1 shows that "breath" pictures the activity of "the Spirit of God" (Gen. 1:2).[12] As Psalm 33 exhorts us, we should rejoice in the goodness of the Creator Spirit and stand in awe at his power. All the loveliness of the skies comes from the Holy Spirit: "By his spirit he hath garnished the heavens" (Job 26:13).[13] John Calvin said, "The beauty of the universe (which we now perceive) owes its strength and preservation to the power of the Spirit."[14]

Every work of God shines with the beautiful activity of the whole Trinity. Though theologians, following Scripture, emphasize the Father's work in creation, the Son's in redemption, and the Spirit's in applying salvation, all three persons act as one God in every divine work. Michael Horton says, "It is not different works but different roles in every work that the divine persons perform."[15] Gregory of Nyssa (c. 330–c. 395)

9. Owen, *Pneumatologia*, in *Works*, 3:98.

10. Ferguson, *The Holy Spirit*, 21.

11. Leon J. Wood, *The Holy Spirit in the Old Testament* (Grand Rapids, MI: Zondervan, 1976), 30.

12. E. W. Hengstenberg, *Commentary on the Psalms*, trans. P. Fairbairn and J. Thomson, 3 vols. (Edinburgh: Thomas Clark, 1845), 1:527–28.

13. The immediate context of Job 26:13 mingles descriptions of God's creative works and his judgments. There are other uses of "spirit" (*ruakh*) for God's creative activity in the broader context (27:3; 32:8; 33:4), though the word is also used for the "wind" (28:25; 30:15, 22). The word translated as "garnished" (*shiprah*) is apparently related to a verb meaning "be beautiful" (*shapar*, Ps. 16:6). The "crooked serpent" may refer to a constellation of stars. On this text, see John F. Walvoord, *The Holy Spirit: A Comprehensive Study of the Person and Work of the Holy Spirit* (Grand Rapids, MI: Zondervan, 1991), 38.

14. Calvin, *Institutes*, 1.13.14.

15. Michael Horton, *Rediscovering the Holy Spirit: God's Perfecting Presence in Creation, Redemption, and Everyday Life* (Grand Rapids, MI: Zondervan, 2017), 38.

noted that men cooperate in an endeavor as each does his own separate work,

> But in the case of the Divine nature we do not similarly learn that the Father does anything by Himself in which the Son does not work conjointly, or again that the Son has any special operation apart from the Holy Spirit; but every operation which extends from God to the creation, and is named according to our variable conceptions of it, has its origin from the Father, and proceeds through the Son, and is perfected in the Holy Spirit.[16]

Therefore, the Creator is the triune God, represented in the Old Testament as God, his Word, and his Spirit, and in the New Testament as Father, Son, and Holy Spirit. Irenaeus wrote of God the Father, "For with Him were always present the Word and Wisdom, the Son and the Spirit, by whom and in whom, freely and spontaneously, He made all things."[17] Athanasius said, "The Father creates all things through the Word in the Spirit; for where the Word is, there is the Spirit also, and the things which are created through the Word have their vital strength out of the Spirit from the Word."[18] We should worship our Creator as God the Father, the Son, and the Holy Spirit, and direct our thanksgiving with the knowledge that the Spirit of God is himself the God who gives all things.

The Spirit's Creation of Mankind

In the startling announcement "Let *us* make man in *our* image, after *our* likeness" (Gen. 1:26), the plural must include the divine person introduced in verse 2, the Spirit of God.[19] The Spirit is the Creator of mankind. This is confirmed when Genesis 2 gives us more details about man's creation: "The LORD God formed man of the dust of the ground, and breathed into his nostrils the breath of life; and man became a living soul" (v. 7). God gave life to the first man by an act of divine breathing, which, as we saw in the last chapter, is a metaphor closely connected to the Holy Spirit (John 20:22). Genesis elsewhere uses the word translated as "spirit" (*ruakh*) to speak of the "breath of life" (6:17; 7:15, 22). Job alluded to Genesis 2:7

16. Gregory of Nyssa, *On "Not Three Gods,"* in *NPNF*[2], 5:334.
17. Irenaeus, *Against Heresies*, 4.20.1, in *ANF*, 1:487–88.
18. Athanasius, *The Letters of Saint Athanasius concerning the Holy Spirit*, trans. and ed. C. R. B. Shapland (London: Epworth, 1951), 3.5 (174).
19. Ferguson, *The Holy Spirit*, 21. See *RST*, 2:65–67.

when he said, "The spirit of God is in my nostrils" (Job 27:3). Owen cited Job 33:4 and said, "The Spirit of God and the breath of God are the same, only, the one expression is proper, the other metaphorical; wherefore, this breathing is the especial acting of the Spirit of God."[20]

The words "Let us make man" indicate that God consulted within himself somewhat like a group of people consult to make a plan. The Spirit participated in the eternal divine counsel behind man's creation. He is not only the agent of creation, but also, together with the Father and the Son, is the author of the decree concerning mankind. Here again we see the personality and deity of the Spirit. The Spirit possesses the infinite wisdom of God, and by it he formed his perfect plan (Isa. 40:13).

Furthermore, together with the Father and the Son, the Holy Spirit is the God in whose image mankind was created. Therefore, when the Spirit works the sanctification of fallen sinners, he is renewing what he created in his image. We were made to be holy like the Holy Spirit, and though our sin has polluted us to the core, the Spirit comes again as the sovereign Creator to work holiness in us as he wills. He works "regeneration" (*palingenesia*, Titus 3:5), which could be rendered as "Genesis again"—a new creation. Since we know that the Spirit is our Creator, we should have great confidence in his ability to regenerate lost sinners. He who created the universe out of nothing has unlimited power and wisdom to save us.

The Holy Spirit and Providence

The Holy Spirit's activity in creation did not end in the first week, but continues in his constant preservation and governance of God's creatures.[21] The Holy Spirit is the divine person who manifests what Ferguson calls "God's power-presence"[22] in renewing and perpetuating life—even after man's sin brought death into the world.

The Spirit's Providence over All Things

All living things depend upon the Spirit for their sustenance and life: "Thou hidest thy face, they are troubled: thou takest away their breath, they die, and return to their dust. Thou sendest forth thy spirit, they are created: and thou renewest the face of the earth. The glory of the LORD

20. Owen, *Pneumatologia*, in *Works*, 3:101.
21. On the doctrine of providence, see *RST*, 1:1058–1105 (chaps. 52–53).
22. Ferguson, *The Holy Spirit*, 21.

shall endure for ever: the LORD shall rejoice in his works" (Ps. 104:29–31). Ambrose said, "The Holy Spirit gives life to all things; since both He, as the Father and the Son, is the Creator of all things. . . . And who can deny that the creation of the earth is the work of the Holy Spirit, whose work it is that it is renewed?"[23] Psalm 104 dwells on God's provision of water and food for the plants, animals, and people that he created (vv. 13, 27). The "face" of God is his gracious presence, manifest in his care for creation.[24] Owen said, "The Spirit of God, whose office and work it is to uphold and preserve all things continually, produceth by his power a new supply of creatures in the room of them that fall off like leaves from the trees, and return to their dust every day."[25] Smeaton wrote that this text proves "that the Spirit of God is the fountain of life; and that creation, amid all its necessary changes, receives from him its renovating or rejuvenating power."[26] The Spirit's sustaining work reveals the joy of God in his creation and makes known the glorious Giver of all good things (v. 31). In this work in his first creation, the Spirit gives us a picture of his work as the life giver of the new creation, restoring righteousness and peace to a world into which man's sin has brought only death (Isa. 32:15–17).

Therefore, the Holy Spirit manifests the blessed life of the triune God by giving vitality and joy to the created world. Augustine of Hippo (354–430) exalted "the Holy Spirit in the Trinity, not begotten, but the sweetness of the begetter [the Father] and of the begotten [the Son], filling all creatures according to their capacity with abundant bountifulness and copiousness, that they may keep their proper order and rest satisfied in their proper place."[27] Calvin said, "By his Spirit he keepeth us in life, and upholdeth us. For the power of the Spirit is spread abroad throughout all parts of the world, that it may preserve them in their state; that he may minister unto the heaven and earth that force and vigour which we see, and motion to all living creatures." This, Calvin said, refutes the idolatry of man that ascribes divinity to mere creatures; instead, the Scriptures reveal the continuing activity of the Creator.[28]

The Spirit's work to create and sustain shows us that he is truly God. He gives life, breath, and all things to all creatures; "in him we live, and

23. Ambrose, *Of the Holy Spirit*, 2.5.32, 34, in *NPNF*², 10:118–19.
24. On the Spirit as God's "face," see Ezek. 39:29.
25. Owen, *Pneumatologia*, in *Works*, 3:99.
26. Smeaton, *The Doctrine of the Holy Spirit*, 9.
27. Augustine, *On the Trinity*, 6.10.11, in *NPNF*¹, 3:103.
28. John Calvin, *Commentaries*, 22 vols. (Grand Rapids, MI: Baker, 2003), on Acts 17:28.

move, and have our being" (Acts 17:25, 28). Calvin wrote, "For it is the Spirit who, everywhere diffused, sustains all things, causes them to grow, and quickens them in heaven and in earth. Because he is circumscribed by no limits, he is excepted from the category of creatures; but in transfusing into all things his energy, and breathing into them essence, life, and movement, he is indeed plainly divine."[29]

Precisely at this point of the Spirit's immanence in creation, we must also affirm his transcendence as Lord of all. The omnipresence of the Spirit must not be distorted into a subtle denial that he is the *Holy* Spirit, infinitely exalted in glory above all. Much modern theology tends toward panentheism, the false teaching that God inseparably indwells and participates in the world like a soul in its body.[30] Horton warns, "The proliferation of panentheistic pneumatologies in recent decades has tended to depersonalize the Spirit, reducing the 'Lord and giver of life' to something divine in the world rather than someone divine who is at work in it."[31] As a consequence, the Spirit of God becomes the spirit of the cosmos, the life and energy of all things that needs us and suffers with us, as opposed to the biblical God who is "fully complete in himself, independent of the world, immutable, omniscient, and omnipotent."[32]

As the Lord, the Spirit preserves people and nations for God's glory. This may be the thought of Psalm 139:7, where David exults in the omnipresence of God's Spirit in the context of his providential care and protection. Earlier we noted the link between Genesis 1:2 and Deuteronomy 32:11, a link that joins the Spirit who creates with the God who cared for his people in the wilderness. Similarly, Isaiah wrote of God's leading of Israel through the wilderness, "As a beast goeth down into the valley, the Spirit of the Lord caused him to rest: so didst thou lead thy people, to make thyself a glorious name" (Isa. 63:14). The Spirit's ministry to Israel included the spiritual guidance that he gave through Moses (v. 11), but God also provided physical nourishment and protection in that harsh place. Whether it is manna in the wilderness or our ordinary bread and butter today, the Holy Spirit remains intimately involved in every detail of human existence. He feeds us, clothes us, preserves our health, and in all things providentially sustains and rules us as God's creatures.

29. Calvin, *Institutes*, 1.13.14.
30. On panentheism, see *RST*, 1:594–98.
31. Horton, *Rediscovering the Holy Spirit*, 69.
32. Horton, *Rediscovering the Holy Spirit*, 76.

Since the Spirit is the Holy One, he rules the world not only as its loving Sustainer but also as its righteous Judge. The Spirit judges the nations. The "breath" (*ruakh*) of the Lord was the overflowing river of fire that devoured the forces of Assyria (Isa. 30:28, 31, 33). The Spirit judges all of fallen mankind, rushing upon them like a scorching desert wind to wither all flesh like grass—even the princes are like stubble before the whirlwind (40:6–8, 22–24; cf. Ps. 103:15–16). The Spirit works inseparably with "the word of our God" (Isa. 40:8), by which the Spirit pronounces damnation upon the wicked and gives hope to his people.

Therefore, the Spirit works in every aspect of God's providence. When a nation gathers in the harvest and its tables are full of food, it owes thanks to the Spirit. When a nation falls under the calamity of war or natural disaster, we should tremble before the almighty Breath of the Lord. He is the sovereign Spirit, and we should fear him.

The Spirit's Providence over Human Life

The Holy Spirit personally makes and upholds every human being. Each individual should acknowledge, "The Spirit of God hath made me, and the breath of the Almighty hath given me life" (Job 33:4). Ferguson writes, "While the second half of the verse echoes Genesis 2:7, the first half appears to echo Genesis 1:2."[33] Thus, this is a statement about creation, applied to the individual person. Each human life depends on the Spirit. Geoff Thomas says, "How long will you live? You do not know. But you do know it will be as long as God's Spirit gives you life."[34]

The Holy Spirit not only sustains physical life, but also forms and sustains the inner life of the mind, giving understanding and wisdom: "It is the spirit in man, the breath of the Almighty, that makes him understand" (Job 32:8 ESV). This implies that we should give glory to the Spirit for every endowment of skill or ability that we possess. Calvin said of our ability to think, "We ought to ascribe what is left in us to God's kindness. For if he had not spared us, our fall would have entailed the destruction of our whole nature."[35]

The Spirit gives leadership ability, as we see in Joshua (Deut. 34:9) and Saul (1 Sam. 10:6, 10; 11:6). Calvin wrote, "God, in providing for

33. Ferguson, *The Holy Spirit*, 20.
34. Thomas, *The Holy Spirit*, 18.
35. Calvin, *Institutes*, 2.2.17.

the human race, often endows with a heroic nature those destined to command," though if they are unbelievers they are driven by "ambition" that makes all their works of "no value" before God.[36] Even the pagan kings of Egypt and Babylon acknowledged that the wisdom to lead well comes from the divine Spirit.[37]

Whenever God gives ability and skill for mankind to work in industry and the arts, or to teach others those skills, that ability is the gift of the triune God. Abraham Kuyper (1837–1920) said, "Gifts and talents come from the Father; are disposed for each personality by the Son; and kindled in each by the Holy Spirit as by a spark from above."[38] God filled people in Israel with the Spirit of wisdom so that they would have skill to work with wood, metal, and textiles, and the ability to teach others to do the same (Ex. 28:3; 31:1–11; 35:31–35).[39] These people were not preachers who needed the Spirit to teach the Word, but tradesmen who worked with their hands. The most practical, hands-on vocation on earth requires gifts of the Holy Spirit. Whenever a farmer understands how to plow, plant, and harvest, it is because "God doth instruct him" (Isa. 28:26; cf. vv. 23–28). Calvin said, "The excellent gifts of the Spirit are diffused through the whole human race."[40] This is not to confuse natural abilities with the spiritual gifts for ministry (1 Cor. 12:4), but it does teach us that we depend upon the Spirit for skill in every task. Charles Hodge said that the Spirit is "the source of all intellectual life," all the powers of the mind.[41]

The Spirit's involvement in all human wisdom and endeavor has several practical implications for the Christian life. First, we must depend

36. Calvin, *Institutes*, 2.3.4.

37. Gen. 41:38; Dan. 4:8–9; 5:11, 14.

38. Kuyper, *The Work of the Holy Spirit*, 39–40.

39. Cole objects that the Spirit's work in Exodus 28, 31, and 35 refers only to God's making sure that the tabernacle was constructed according to God's will and cannot be generalized to refer to all human knowledge and skill. Cole, *He Who Gives Life*, 111–12. However, these Scripture passages indicate that God filled people with the Spirit to equip them with "all craftsmanship, to devise artistic designs, to work in gold, silver, and bronze, in cutting stones for setting, and in carving wood, to work in every craft" (Ex. 31:3–5 ESV). He "filled them with skill to do every sort of work . . . by any sort of workman or skilled designer" (35:35 ESV). These are natural skills, for there is no indication that the construction of the tabernacle (an ornate but ordinary tent) required supernatural ability. Furthermore, that such natural skills are gifts from the Spirit implies that people lack these abilities without the Spirit's work. Finally, though the tabernacle was the place of God's special presence, its artistry represents it as a new Eden, implying a return to man's original state—with man vivified by the breath of God to rule the earth (Gen. 1:26; 2:7). God's dealings with Israel reflect his ways with all mankind, established in Adam and restored and glorified in Christ.

40. Calvin, *Commentaries*, on Gen. 4:22. He referred here to the "arts and sciences." See also *Commentaries*, on 1 Cor. 1:17.

41. Hodge, *Systematic Theology*, 1:530.

on the Holy Spirit daily for all skill and ability. Every day should begin with prayer for the tasks before us, throughout the day we should pepper heaven with petitions for divine assistance, and at the end of the day we should give thanks.

Second, we must value all human knowledge, including that of people outside of Christ. Calvin wrote that although the Holy Spirit does not dwell in unbelievers to make them holy (Rom. 8:9; 1 Cor. 3:16), nevertheless the Spirit distributes "excellent benefits . . . to whomever he wills, for the common good of mankind."[42] He added, "If we regard the Spirit of God as the sole fountain of truth, we shall neither reject the truth itself, nor despise it wherever it shall appear, unless we wish to dishonor the Spirit of God." Calvin included law and civics, scientific study of nature, rhetorical skill, medicine, and mathematics.[43] He said, "If the Lord has willed that we be helped in physics, dialectic, mathematics, and other like disciplines, by the work and ministry of the ungodly, let us use this assistance."[44]

Third, we must distinguish between the results of the Spirit's general activities to preserve human thinking and the Spirit's special revelation. Merely human teachings and writings contain a measure of truth as sustained by the Spirit, but are also distorted by much sin and foolishness (Rom. 3:11; Eph. 4:17–18). Only the Holy Scriptures have divine authority to command our total submission, inerrant veracity to evoke our absolute trust, and sufficiency to direct our faith and godliness (2 Tim. 3:15–17).[45] Calvin wrote, "The liberal arts, and all the sciences by which wisdom is acquired, are gifts of God. They are confined, however, within their own limits; for into God's heavenly kingdom they cannot penetrate. Hence they must occupy the place of handmaid, not of mistress: nay more, they must be looked upon as empty and worthless, until they have become entirely subject to the word and Spirit of God."[46]

Fourth, if all abilities come from the Spirit, then we must use them for God's glory. All skill, science, and art should serve for the glory of God. William Perkins said, "The skill of any handicraft is not in the power of man, but comes by the Holy Ghost. And by this we are taught

42. Calvin, *Institutes*, 2.2.16.
43. Calvin, *Institutes*, 2.2.15.
44. Calvin, *Institutes*, 2.2.16.
45. On the effects of sin upon the human mind, see *RST*, 2:403–4, 408. On the authority, inerrant veracity, and sufficiency of God's written Word, see *RST*, 1:334–43, 371–408.
46. Calvin, *Commentaries*, on 1 Cor. 3:19.

to use those gifts well whereby we are enabled to discharge our particular callings, that they may serve for the glory of God and the good of His church."[47] Let us, therefore, be grateful for our abilities, love our work as much as possible, and put our energy into it (Eccles. 9:10). The Scriptures say, "Whatsoever ye do, do it heartily, as to the Lord, and not unto men" (Col. 3:23).

God's Common Grace to Mankind

The Holy Spirit continues to give physical life and mental faculties to sinful men. However, these gifts are not saving graces that reconcile sinners to God through Christ and bring them to glory. Therefore, we must consider the topic of "common grace," which we define as the good gifts that God gives to both the righteous and the wicked, even to those who will never repent.

God's General Goodness

We have seen that the Holy Spirit, as the third person of the triune Creator, showers many gifts on mankind in general. The Lord's goodness extends to the whole world (Ps. 145:8–9). God is a model of unconditional, even counterconditional love. The Lord Jesus teaches God's children to love their enemies, "for he maketh his sun to rise on the evil and on the good, and sendeth rain on the just and on the unjust" (Matt. 5:44–45). God "is kind to the ungrateful and the evil" (Luke 6:36 ESV; cf. Acts 14:16–17).[48]

A prime manifestation of God's goodness to his fallen creation appeared after the flood, when God's righteous judgment had swept away all human beings and animals except those preserved in Noah's ark. Kuyper wrote that the "starting point for the doctrine of common grace lies in God's establishment of a covenant with Noah."[49] God renewed his creational blessings to Noah and his sons (Gen. 9:1, 7), instituted a new order regarding man's use of animals and punishment of crime (vv. 2–6), and established his covenant with all mankind and animals

47. Perkins, *An Exposition of the Symbol*, in *Works*, 5:309.

48. On God's universal goodness and general love, see *RST*, 1:797–98.

49. Abraham Kuyper, *Common Grace*, trans. Nelson D. Kloosterman and Ed M. van der Maas, ed. Jordan J. Ballor and Stephen J. Grabill, intro. Richard J. Mouw, 2 vols. to date, Abraham Kuyper Collected Works in Public Theology (Bellingham, WA: Lexham Press; Grand Rapids, MI: Acton Institute, 2015, 2019), 1:10.

that he would never again destroy the world in a flood (vv. 8–17). G. H. Kersten (1882–1948) pointed out, "We must distinguish the covenant of Noah from the Covenant of Grace."[50] The preservation of the world through Noah set the stage for God's promises of salvation (12:1–3). Kuyper wrote, "Apart from common grace, the elect would not have been born. . . . Particular grace presupposed common grace."[51] God's purposes center on Jesus Christ and his church, and therefore, "not common grace, but the ordained arrangement of particular grace dominates" God's plan for history.[52]

God's Restraint of Sin

Another manifestation of God's goodness to fallen man is the restraint of sin. Humanity has the capacity to be much more evil than it actually is. God restrains human sin by means of the conscience operating in every human soul and by civil government insofar as it seeks to maintain justice and order (Rom. 2:14–15; 13:1–7).[53] William Ames wrote that God inhibits the progress of spiritual death, working internally by the conscience so that "excess of sin is curbed in most people so that even sinners abhor the committing of many grosser sins."[54] When God withdraws his influence and gives sinners over to their sins, natural affections toward family members and friends die, and society degenerates into horrible lawlessness (Rom. 1:28–31; 2 Tim. 3:1–3).

A text often cited as evidence of God's restraint of sin is Genesis 6:3: "And the LORD said, My spirit shall not always strive with man, for that he also is flesh: yet his days shall be an hundred and twenty years." However, this Scripture passage is difficult to interpret, in part due to uncertainty regarding the verb translated as "strive" (*yadon*), the particular form of which appears only here. Some believe it is derived from a root meaning to judge, execute justice, or contend (*din*); others derive it from a root meaning to continue or abide, which is also the reading of the Septuagint and Vulgate translations. The reading "contend" could

50. G. H. Kersten, *Reformed Dogmatics: A Systematic Treatment of Reformed Doctrine Explained for the Congregations*, trans. Joel R. Beeke and J. C. Weststrate, 2 vols. (Grand Rapids, MI: Netherlands Reformed Book and Publishing Committee, 1980), 1:79. On the covenant with Noah and its relation to the covenant of grace, see *RST*, 2:614–16.

51. Kuyper, *Common Grace*, 1:265.

52. Kuyper, *Common Grace*, 1:266.

53. On conscience and civil government as human means to punish and restrain sin, see *RST*, 2:457–61.

54. Ames, *The Marrow of Theology*, 1.14.21, 27, 30 (123–24).

support the idea that the Spirit strove with people through the preaching of godly men such as Noah (2 Pet. 2:5). As to the second reading of "abide," John Currid writes, "The opening clause, 'My spirit will not remain', probably refers to the divine spirit of life (see [Gen.] 2:7). And so, God is promising to withdraw life from mankind, and thus end its terrible conduct."[55]

God often restrains the sins of the wicked in order to protect his people. After Abimelech took Sarah without knowing that she was married, the Lord said to him, "I know that you have done this in the integrity of your heart, and it was I who kept you from sinning against me. Therefore I did not let you touch her" (Gen. 20:6 ESV). Later, God somehow restrained the Canaanites from taking revenge on Jacob's family by "the terror of God" (35:5). When God commanded Israel to gather at the annual festivals, he promised that their pagan neighbors would not "desire" their land when they were absent, which implies that God was going to limit other nations' greed in order to protect his worshipers (Ex. 34:24). A significant part of the peace in this evil world arises from God's blessing on the godly who please him (Prov. 16:7).

Most people, though evil sinners, still give good things to their children (Matt. 7:11; 1 Tim. 5:8), avoid vices regarded as shameful in their culture (1 Cor. 5:1), and love those who love them (Matt. 5:46–47). Heinrich Bullinger (1504–1575) said, "The worthy deeds of the heathens are not to be despised nor utterly contemned; for as they were not altogether done without God, so did they much avail to the preserving and restoring of the tranquility of kingdoms and commonwealths."[56] However, as Christ's words in Matthew 5:46 show, such non-Christian virtues have no value in pleasing God. Calvin said, "God by his providence bridles perversity of nature, that it may not break forth into action; but he does not purge it within."[57]

55. John D. Currid, *A Study Commentary on Genesis: Genesis 1:1–25:18*, EP Study Commentary (Darlington, England: Evangelical Press, 2003), 175.

56. Heinrich Bullinger, *The Decades of Henry Bullinger*, trans. H. I., ed. Thomas Harding, 5 decades in 4 vols. (Cambridge: Cambridge University Press, 1850), 2:419. The original reads "commonweals." For this reference, we are indebted to J. Mark Beach, "The Idea of a 'General Grace of God' in Some Sixteenth-Century Reformed Theologians Other than Calvin," in *Church and School in Early Modern Protestantism: Studies in Honor of Richard A. Muller on the Maturation of a Theological Tradition*, ed. Jordan J. Ballor, David S. Sytsma, and Jason Zuidema, Studies in the History of Christian Traditions (Leiden: Brill, 2013), 102.

57. Calvin, *Institutes*, 2.3.3.

The Reformed Controversy over God's Common Grace

Kuyper distinguished between "a saving grace that ultimately cancels sin and completely neutralizes its consequences" and "a temporarily restraining grace that stems and arrests the continued effect of sin," the former of which is particular to the elect and the latter "common grace."[58] The doctrine of common grace has proven controversial. Ralph Janssen (1874–1942) wrongly appealed to the doctrine to support a higher critical approach to the Bible when he claimed that biblical miracles can be explained by natural causes and that the Old Testament borrowed from ancient mythology, "for truth is one." Some who opposed him affirmed common grace, but others opposed both his ideas and his appeal to common grace, particularly Herman Hoeksema (1886–1965).[59]

In 1924, the synod of the Christian Reformed Church affirmed,

1. "There is, besides the saving grace of God, shown only to those chosen unto eternal life, also a certain favor or grace of God which He shows to all His creatures." This is particularly evidenced in the free offer of the gospel to all who hear it.[60]
2. "God through the general operation of His Spirit, without renewing the heart, restrains sin in its unhindered breaking forth, as a result of which human society has remained possible."
3. "Concerning the performance of so-called civic righteousness . . . the unregenerate, though incapable of any saving good . . . can perform such civil good."[61]

Against this affirmation of common grace stood Hoeksema and others who subsequently formed the Protestant Reformed Churches in America.[62] Their objections to common grace included: (1) God hates the wicked, whom he has rejected eternally (Pss. 5:5; 11:5; Rom. 9:13); (2) the doctrine of common grace is used to deny the total depravity of unregenerate sinners,

58. Kuyper, *Common Grace*, 1:264.

59. John Bolt, "Common Grace and the Christian Reformed Synod of Kalamazoo (1924): A Seventy-Fifth Anniversary Retrospective," *Calvin Theological Journal* 35, no. 1 (April 2000): 9–12 (full article, 7–36).

60. On the free offer of the gospel, see chap. 12.

61. Cited in Bolt, "Common Grace and the Christian Reformed Synod of Kalamazoo (1924)," 7. Cf. Christian Reformed Church, *1924 Acts of Synod*, trans. Henry De Mots (Grand Rapids, MI: Archives of the Christian Reformed Church, 2000), 145–46. Proofs from Scripture, confessions, and Reformed divines appear on pp. 126–34.

62. Bolt, "Common Grace and the Christian Reformed Synod of Kalamazoo (1924)," 28–29, 33.

who cannot do any good (Rom. 3:9–18); (3) that doctrine undermines the church's antithesis against the wicked world in a misguided attempt to Christianize the world; and (4) that doctrine requires that two distinct purposes of God for creation and redemption be substituted for God's one decree.[63] The controversy continues today.[64]

The objections to common grace reflect legitimate concerns. The church must never allow the truth that "God is love" (1 John 4:8) to conceal or negate the reality of God's wrath against "all ungodliness and unrighteousness of men" (Rom. 1:18) or the ultimate damnation of the unrepentant (Matt. 25:41, 46). We must sharply distinguish common grace from saving grace. Saving grace is not an increased measure of common grace, a product of common grace, or the result of a right response to common grace, but a different work of the Holy Spirit given apart from the power, wisdom, or merit of fallen man. Christ alone is our wisdom, righteousness, sanctification, and redemption (1 Cor. 1:30). Apart from him we are dead in our sins and do nothing but hate God, even in our outward attempts to perform the duties of religion and do good to others (Rom. 8:6–8; Eph. 2:1). The church is not merely one human organization in society among many others, but God's peculiar, redeemed people (Titus 2:14), who are "not of the world" because the Lord chose them and called them out of the world (John 15:19).

Therefore, while we must thank God for common grace, we must never rest in it or think that common grace, if rightly used, will save a single soul. We need special, saving grace, the grace given in eternal election, purchased by Christ's redemption, and individually applied by the Holy Spirit to our souls by regeneration (John 3:1–8). Until one is born again into the fear of the Lord and hope in his mercy, no human endeavor pleases God (Ps. 147:10–11), and our religious acts are abominations in his sight (Prov. 15:8; 21:27; 28:9).

---

63. Herman Hoeksema, *A Triple Breach in the Foundation of the Reformed Truth* (Grand Rapids, MI: C. J. Doorn, 1925), 46–87, also available at Protestant Reformed Churches in America, http://www.prca.org/resources/publications/pamphlets/item/1598-a-triple-breach-in-the-foundation-of-the-reformed-truth; *Reformed Dogmatics*, 2nd ed. (Grandville, MI: Reformed Free Publishing, 2004–2005), 1:334–35, 378–81; 2:441–47; Barry Gritters, "Grace Uncommon: A Protestant Reformed Look at the Doctrine of Common Grace," Protestant Reformed Churches in America, http://www.prca.org/pamphlets/pamphlet_55.html; and Robert Harbach, "A Brief Answer to Common Grace," Protestant Reformed Churches in America, http://www.prca.org/resources/publications/articles/item/290-a-brief-answer-to-common-grace.

64. Other publications on this question include Cornelius Van Til, *Common Grace and the Gospel* (Phillipsburg, NJ: Presbyterian and Reformed, 1972); Richard J. Mouw, *He Shines in All That's Fair: Culture and Common Grace* (Grand Rapids, MI: Eerdmans, 2001); and David J. Engelsma, *Common Grace Revisited: A Response to Richard J. Mouw's* He Shines in All That's Fair (Grandville, MI: Reformed Free Publishing, 2003).

Common Grace in the Bible

Although we must guard the doctrine of common grace from abuse, it is a teaching of the Holy Scriptures. The history of Israel reveals that God judges unbelieving sinners in his wrath and yet may grant them temporal mercies in answer to their prayers because of his covenantal purposes (Ps. 106:7–45). God shows true kindness and goodness to many wicked men, though it will result in greater condemnation to those who refuse to repent (Rom. 2:4–5). There is a kind of grace or favor from God that does good to people but does not save them from sin.

There is biblical warrant for using the term common *grace*. The word translated as "grace" (*khen*) in the Old Testament does not mean friendship, but freely given favor, whether from God or man. The root "denotes the kind turning of one person to another as expressed in an act of assistance."[65] Sometimes this favor is shown in a lasting relationship,[66] but sometimes merely in the granting of a request.[67] Thus, temporal mercies from God are "grace," such as the deliverance of Lot out of Sodom before its destruction (Gen. 19:19), the provision of men to help Moses lead Israel (Num. 11:11, 15), the granting of a sign to Gideon to confirm God's calling (Judg. 6:17), and the return of David to Jerusalem after Absalom's insurrection (2 Sam. 15:25). Jacob's children were "graciously given" (*khanan*) to him by the Lord (Gen. 33:5). Isaiah 26:10 says, "Let favour be shewed [grace be given, *khanan*] to the wicked, yet will he not learn righteousness." The wicked kings of Israel did evil in God's sight and led their people into idolatry, and yet, "the LORD was gracious [*khanan*] unto them, and had compassion on them, and had respect unto them, because of his covenant with Abraham, Isaac, and Jacob, and would not destroy them, neither cast he them from his presence as yet" (2 Kings 13:23).

In the New Testament, with its emphasis on the salvation accomplished in Christ, "grace" (*charis*) most often refers to God's saving grace,[68] though it still appears occasionally as favor from men.[69] However, not all of God's gifts of grace pertain directly to salvation, for Mary's privilege of bearing the Messiah was "favour," literally "grace" (*charis*, Luke 1:30); the office of apostleship was grace (Rom. 1:5; Gal. 2:9; Eph. 3:2, 7–8); and all gifts for

65. *TDNT*, 9:377.
66. Gen. 6:8; Ex. 33:12–13, 16–17.
67. Gen. 47:25, 29; Num. 32:5; 1 Sam. 20:29; 2 Sam. 12:22; 14:22.
68. For example, Acts 15:11; Rom. 3:24; 5:21; 6:14; 11:5–6; Eph. 2:5, 7, 8.
69. Acts 2:47; 24:27; 25:3, 9.

service in the church are grace (Rom. 12:6; Eph. 4:7; 1 Pet. 4:10), though they may be possessed by hypocrites who will ultimately be damned.[70]

We may, therefore, speak of God's *common grace* when we refer to his goodness to all creation, including the reprobate. The word *common* indicates that these blessings do not belong only to the elect or to the regenerate but are shared broadly with many people. The word *grace* reminds us that no sinner deserves anything, not even a drop of water, but only the tormenting fires of hell (Luke 16:24–25). All of God's gifts are undeserved grace. If someone prefers to speak of this doctrine as *common goodness*, we have no interest in quarrelling about mere words. However, we do desire to preserve the important biblical teaching that God continues to shower undeserved kindness upon unrepentant sinners.

Common Grace in Reformed Theology

The language of common grace is rooted in the early Reformed writers. Calvin wrote of "the general grace of God" in preserving fallen man despite his total corruption by sin.[71] Calvin said that when we see non-Christians living with virtue, "amid this corruption of nature there is some place for God's grace; not such grace as to cleanse it, but to restrain it inwardly."[72] Wherever we encounter "moral integrity" in an unbeliever, we should not ascribe it to man's fallen nature but to the "grace the Lord has bestowed."[73]

Bullinger also wrote of the "general grace of God, which God has appointed for us all and which rains down upon the good and the evil," which Bullinger carefully distinguished from the saving grace that justifies and sanctifies.[74] Wolfgang Musculus (1497–1563) wrote that the covenant with Noah displays the "noble, manifest and general grace of our Creator, without which this world cannot endure," by which ungrateful men enjoy "earthly and temporal goods," even the air they breathe.[75] Perkins said that the "benefits" given by the Spirit of God to men "are of two sorts:

70. Matt. 7:22–23; John 6:70; Acts 20:28, 30.

71. Calvin, *Institutes*, 2.2.17. See Herman Kuiper, *Calvin on Common Grace* (Grand Rapids, MI: Smitter, 1928).

72. Calvin, *Institutes*, 2.3.3.

73. Calvin, *Institutes*, 2.3.4.

74. Heinrich Bullinger, *De gratia dei justificante* (Zurich, 1554), 4:7, cited in Beach, "General Grace," in *Church and School*, ed. Ballor, Sytsma, and Zuidema, 100.

75. Wolfgang Musculus, *Loci communes* (Basel, 1564), 179, translated in *Commonplaces of Christian Religion* (London, 1578), 285, cited in Beach, "General Grace," in *Church and School*, ed. Ballor, Sytsma, and Zuidema, 104.

some are common to all men both good and bad, and some proper to the elect and faithful."[76] The common gifts of the Spirit include skill to perform one's vocation in life, illumination to understand God's Word, the self-restraint to avoid "outrageous behavior," and the "grace and gift of the Holy Ghost" to listen to biblical preaching with temporary joy.[77]

Early Reformed theologians also distinguished between common grace and saving grace. Peter Martyr Vermigli (1499–1562) wrote that we may speak of "natural gifts" as "graces" because they are "freely granted by God"; however, we must use such language guardedly, never confusing such gifts with the "graces, which happen to the elect, through the redemption of Christ," for that is to fall into the heresy of Pelagianism and to reduce saving grace to human nature.[78] The Arminian Remonstrants appealed to common grace as the reason why natural free will can take steps toward salvation, but the Canons of Dort (Heads 3/4, Rej. 5) rightly reject the teaching "that the corrupt and natural man can so well use the common grace (by which they understand the light of nature), or the gifts still left him after the fall, that he can gradually gain by their good use a greater, namely, the evangelical or saving grace and salvation itself."[79] Common grace cannot save; people need the Word and Spirit to be converted.

The Westminster Assembly wrote of "common operations of the Spirit" that do not in themselves result in salvation by faith in Christ.[80] The Savoy Declaration (14.3) and the Second London Baptist Confession (14.3) contrast saving faith to "the faith and common grace of temporary believers."[81] Owen contrasted "gospel holiness" to "common grace or moral virtues."[82] He said,

> Concerning grace itself, it is either common or special. Common or general grace consisteth in the external revelation of the will of God

76. Perkins, *An Exposition of the Symbol*, in *Works*, 5:309.

77. Perkins, *An Exposition of the Symbol*, in *Works*, 5:309–11.

78. Peter Martyr Vermigli, *The Common Places*, trans. Anthonie Marten (1583), 3:50. See Beach, "General Grace," in *Church and School*, ed. Ballor, Sytsma, and Zuidema, 107.

79. *The Three Forms of Unity*, 150.

80. The Westminster Confession of Faith (10.4); the Westminster Larger Catechism (Q. 68), in *Reformed Confessions*, 4:247, 312. This topic is explored in more depth in chaps. 13 and 14 on preparatory grace and resisting the Spirit.

81. *Reformed Confessions*, 4:472, 549. The phrase was not original to the Westminster Confession (14.3), from which the Savoy Declaration and Second London Baptist Confession are derived.

82. Owen, *Pneumatologia*, in *Works*, 3:506; cf. 503–4. The quotes from Owen and Goodwin in this section reflect the use of "common grace" for the inward, moral, nonsaving effects of the Holy Spirit on the human soul, not the broader use of the term for God's general goodness to all creation, as employed by modern theologians.

> by his word, with some illumination of the mind to perceive it, and correction of the affections not too much to contemn it [view it with contempt]; and this, in some degree or other, to some more, to some less, is common to all that are called. Special grace is the grace of regeneration, comprehending the former, adding more spiritual acts, but especially presupposing the purpose of God, on which its efficacy doth chiefly depend.[83]

Common grace to mankind is a consequence of God's decree to grant saving grace to the elect in Jesus Christ. God did not punish mankind immediately after their fall as he did the angels that sinned (2 Pet. 2:4), but initiated an era of patience and mercy for sinners in Adam, during which God would give them "food and gladness, with all those fruits of kindness which the womb of his providence is still bringing forth for their benefit," as Owen said. The reprobate have no part in Christ's redemption as the Mediator of the covenant of grace, but they enjoy temporal blessings as "a necessary consequent" of Christ's office as Mediator.[84] God did not destroy the world upon the first entrance of sin, but instead, through Christ, he preserves it as "the great stage for the mighty works of God's grace, wisdom, and love."[85]

Thomas Goodwin said, "There is a different mercy or grace in God, out of which he bestows those gifts he vouchsafes unto men, whom in the issue he saveth not, different far from that mercy out of which he gives that grace and holiness which hath salvation accompanying it." Thus, Goodwin spoke of God's "common providential mercies," and called the working of the Holy Spirit in (as yet) unconverted people "common graces."[86] However, God makes no promise to grant saving graces to those who make good use of their "common graces."[87]

Therefore, we conclude that just as the Holy Scriptures give us warrant to speak of common grace, so we also find that this doctrine has long had a place in Reformed theology. However, both Scripture and the Reformed tradition caution us against an unbridled affirmation of common grace,

83. Owen, *A Display of Arminianism*, in *Works*, 10:134.

84. John Owen, *An Exposition of the Epistle to the Hebrews*, 7 vols. (repr., Edinburgh: Banner of Truth, 1991), 3:57–58.

85. Owen, *An Exposition of the Epistle to the Hebrews*, 3:107.

86. Goodwin, *The Work of the Holy Ghost in Our Salvation*, in *Works*, 6:327.

87. Goodwin, *The Work of the Holy Ghost in Our Salvation*, in *Works*, 6:353. On Goodwin's own experience, as summarized by his son, see the introduction to Goodwin, "Memoir," in *Works*, 2:lxvii.

but call us to make qualified and balanced statements lest we fail to guard the doctrine of salvation through faith alone in Christ alone.

Practical Applications of the Doctrine of Common Grace

One practical application of the doctrine of common grace is that we must seek the peace of the wider society or community we live in and pray for God's blessings on it. When the people of Judah were carried off by the Babylonians and forced to live in pagan cities, the Lord said that they must "seek the peace of the city whither I have caused you to be carried away captives, and pray unto the LORD for it: for in the peace thereof shall ye have peace" (Jer. 29:7). Likewise, Christians are pilgrims and exiles in this world (1 Pet. 2:11). We are citizens of the heavenly Jerusalem, and our hearts should be there (Phil. 3:20; Col. 3:1). However, while we live in exile on earth, we must seek the peace of our cities and nations, and pray for God's blessings on society around us. We do good works and pray for our world and its authorities in order to promote peace in our society so that we may live quiet lives of godliness and openly proclaim the gospel by which God is saving sinners through faith in Jesus Christ (1 Tim. 2:1–5).

Many an unbeliever, if honest, would have to admit to a Christian friend, family member, or coworker, "The LORD hath blessed me for thy sake" (Gen. 30:27; cf. 39:5). The prayers and presence of a few righteous people might preserve a wicked city from destruction, though God's patience does not endure forever.[88]

By loving, doing good to, and praying for the wicked in this world—even as they persecute us—God's children function as image bearers representing the goodness of their Father in heaven (Matt. 5:44–45). Kersten explained that God's common grace "serves to glorify God's goodness shown to Adam's posterity . . . perform God's good pleasure in the salvation of the elect [by sustaining the world into which they will be born and converted] . . . [and] exalt the righteousness of God even more in the judgment of the wicked," for it renders them "without excuse" (Rom. 1:20).[89] In the same way, godly Christians are the salt of the earth and the light of the world (Matt. 5:13–16) as they bear the fruit of saving grace.

In our application of the doctrine of common grace, we must guard the antithesis, the fixed opposition, between the church and the world.

88. Gen. 18:17–32; but note Jer. 7:16; 15:1; Ezek. 14:14–20.
89. Kersten, *Reformed Dogmatics*, 1:78.

J. van Genderen and W. H. Velema critique Kuyper for his "strong cultural optimism" and his statement that "God, with steady progress, protects human life more and more fully against suffering and brings it to richer and fuller inner development."[90] To be fair, Kuyper also said that human lawlessness always grasps the gifts of human progress as tools to deify proud man and dethrone God.[91] Kuyper sought to maintain the antithesis. Yet it is too easy for us, in our pride and love of human glory, to neglect the reality of depravity and admire the optimism of progress such that we become followers of the world. Scripture does not foresee moral and spiritual progress but degeneration in mankind's future until the return of the Lord—even as the gospel mission reaches all nations.[92] God's word to the church is still "Come out from among them."[93] "Friendship with the world is enmity with God" (James 4:4 ESV).

We must also take care that we do not rest in common grace for our own souls. Outward restraint of sin and morality in conduct are not evidence of salvation. The Spirit leads God's children to fight in mortal combat against their inner lusts (Gal. 5:16–24). Perkins explained,

> For it is not sufficient for a man to live in outward civility and to keep in some of his affections upon some occasion (for [that] a wicked man may do), but we must further labor to feel in ourselves the Spirit of God not only bridling sin in us but also mortifying and killing the same. Indeed, both of them are the good gifts of God's Spirit, but yet the mortification of sin is the chiefest, being an effectual sign of grace, and proper to the elect.[94]

Likewise, Perkins warned that the illumination of the mind to understand the Word is "a common gift and received both of good and bad," and therefore we must not "content ourselves with the bare knowledge of the Word, but therewithal we must join obedience."[95]

The irony of defending the doctrine of common grace is that common grace generally flourishes only when the church focuses its pursuit on saving grace. Let us, therefore, avoid both extremes of denying common grace or resting in it, and instead let us appreciate common grace with profound

90. Van Genderen and Velema, *Concise Reformed Dogmatics*, 294.
91. Kuyper, *Common Grace*, 1:531–32.
92. Matt. 24:1–14; 2 Thess. 2:1–12; 2 Tim. 3:1–5.
93. Isa. 52:11; 2 Cor. 6:17; Rev. 18:4.
94. Perkins, *An Exposition of the Symbol*, in *Works*, 5:311.
95. Perkins, *An Exposition of the Symbol*, in *Works*, 5:309–10.

gratitude to the triune God and set our hearts upon receiving, cherishing, and growing in saving grace through faith in Jesus Christ.

Sing to the Lord

The Spirit's Goodness to Creation

Thy Spirit, O Lord, makes life to abound;
The earth is renewed, and fruitful the ground;
To God ascribe glory and wisdom and might,
Let God in His creatures forever delight.

Before the Lord's might earth trembles and quakes,
The mountains are rent, and smoke from them breaks;
The Lord I will worship through all of my days,
Yea, while I have being my God I will praise.

Rejoicing in God, my thought shall be sweet,
While sinners depart in ruin complete;
My soul, bless Jehovah, His Name be adored,
Come praise Him, ye people, and worship the Lord.

Psalm 104:30–35
Tune: Aspinwall
The Psalter, No. 287
Or Tune: Houghton
Trinity Hymnal—Baptist Edition, No. 110, Stanzas 5–6 (one omitted)

Questions for Meditation or Discussion

1. What biblical evidence is there for the Holy Spirit's involvement in the creation of the world? Briefly explain the meaning of the text(s).
2. How do the Scriptures show us that the Holy Spirit created mankind?
3. What does the Bible reveal about the Holy Spirit's activity in preserving God's creation?
4. How is the Holy Spirit involved in general human thinking and culture?
5. How does God's Word make known that God exercises a general goodness to all creation?
6. How does God restrain sin in unbelievers?

7. What position did the Christian Reformed Church affirm about common grace in 1924?
8. What concerns did theologians such as Herman Hoeksema raise about the doctrine of common grace? Are these legitimate concerns? If so, how should we address them?
9. What are the biblical and theological bases of speaking about God's common grace?
10. How has reading this chapter expanded your view of the Holy Spirit's work? How should you respond with worship?

Questions for Deeper Reflection

11. A relatively new Christian says, "I have been reading a book lately that is making me wonder if the Holy Spirit is the life and energy of the cosmos." How would you explain the Holy Spirit's omnipresent activity in providence in a way that guards this new Christian against the error of panentheism?
12. You have been asked to teach a class of high school students on what it means to be in the world but not of the world. Outline your lesson plan, drawing upon the doctrine of common grace as well as other relevant doctrines.

3

The Spirit of God with Old Covenant Israel

The outpouring of the Holy Spirit at Pentecost marked such a signal event in redemptive history that one might assume that the Spirit was absent or idle prior to that day. Such an assumption could be encouraged by a misinterpretation of John 7:39: "The Holy Ghost was not yet given; because that Jesus was not yet glorified." Literally the text says that the Spirit "was not yet" (*oupō . . . ēn*), which might suggest he did not even exist or was inactive. That, of course, was not the case. The same Gospel tells us that the Spirit had already descended upon Jesus Christ (1:32) and that Christ proclaimed the new birth by the Spirit prior to his death (3:3–8).

In context, the statement that the Spirit "was not" (John 7:39) refers to the yet-awaited superabundant outpouring of the Spirit like "rivers of living water" (v. 38) from the ascended Christ, the promised baptism of the Holy Spirit granted first at Pentecost (Luke 3:16; Acts 1:5; 2:1–4). As Cyril of Jerusalem (c. 310–386) said, the Spirit was with godly men of ancient times, but since Pentecost he is "given lavishly."[1] John Owen said, "The Lord Christ was 'in all things to have the pre-eminence' (Col. 1:18); and, therefore, although God gave his Spirit in some measure before, yet he poured him not out until he was first anointed with his fulness."[2]

1. Cyril of Jerusalem, *Catechetical Lectures*, 16.26, in *NPNF*², 7:122.
2. Owen, *Pneumatologia*, in *Works*, 3:114.

It is certainly true that the Holy Spirit does not appear as prominently in the Old Testament as in the New.[3] He empowered relatively few people for ministry, not the whole people of God (Num. 11:29). However, the Spirit was not absent from Israel. God taught Israel through Moses that "the Spirit of God" was already present and active "in the beginning" (Gen. 1:1–2).[4] As we will see, the Spirit was constantly at work in God's ancient people.

The Old Testament does not present the Spirit as a mere force, but as a distinct divine person of infinite knowledge (Isa. 40:13–14) who spoke through the prophets (2 Sam. 23:2), was grieved by Israel's sin (Isa. 63:10), and was promised to be poured out by the Lord in great abundance (Joel 2:28–29). Neither do Christ and the apostles view the Spirit of God in the Old Testament as any other than the Holy Spirit. B. B. Warfield said, "There can be no doubt that the New Testament writers identify the Holy Spirit of the New Testament with the Spirit of God of the Old."[5]

Since the fall of man, the creative Spirit has been acting to restore the fallen world, beginning with the patriarchs and old covenant Israel.[6] As we survey the Old Testament in light of New Testament teaching, it is evident that the Holy Spirit worked among God's people as the Spirit of prophecy, power, presence, and piety.

The Spirit of Prophecy

The most prominent work of the Holy Spirit in the Old Testament was his inspiration of the words of the prophets: "For the prophecy came not in old time by the will of man: but holy men of God spake as they were moved by the Holy Ghost" (2 Pet. 1:21).[7] The prophets spoke of the

3. There are no explicit references to the Spirit of God in Leviticus, Joshua, Ruth, Ezra, Ecclesiastes, Song of Songs, Jeremiah, Lamentations, Obadiah, Jonah, Nahum, Habakkuk, and Zephaniah. Other books mention the Spirit only once (Deut. 34:9; 2 Sam. 23:2; Prov. 1:23; Hos. 9:7 [Hebrew]). Even the "evangelical prophet" Isaiah makes perhaps nineteen references to the Spirit, which may be compared to thirty references in Romans (twenty of which appear in chap. 8 alone), fourteen references in Galatians, nineteen in the Gospel of John, and perhaps seventy-two in Luke-Acts.

4. See Ambrose, *Of the Holy Spirit*, 2.1, in *NPNF*[2], 10:115.

5. Benjamin B. Warfield, *The Person and Work of the Holy Spirit*, intro. Sinclair B. Ferguson (Birmingham, AL: Solid Ground, 2010), 114. He cites Matt. 12:18; 22:43; Mark 12:36; Luke 4:18–19; Acts 1:16; 2:17; 7:51; 28:25; 2 Cor. 4:13; Heb. 3:7; 9:8; 10:15; 1 Pet. 1:11; 2 Pet. 1:21.

6. Cole, *He Who Gives Life*, 116.

7. The Old Testament speaks of the Spirit's work on prophets, judges, and kings, but there is no reference to his enablement of the ordinary work of priests. However, priests were anointed with holy oil, a type of Christ's priestly anointing by the Spirit (Ex. 28:41; 29:7, 21; 30:25–33).

grace to come through Christ's sufferings and glorification as "the Spirit of Christ" revealed it to them (1 Pet. 1:10–11). The great prophet of the old covenant, Moses, had the Spirit abiding "upon" him (Num. 11:17, 25). When Israel traveled in the wilderness, God gave the people his good Spirit "to instruct them," perhaps another reference to the prophetic ministry of Moses (Neh. 9:20).

The Spirit of God was the divine agent of the prophetic word, whether the occasional exercise of prophecy by men such as Balaam (Num. 24:2) and Saul (1 Sam. 10:6, 10; 19:20, 23), or the regular prophetic ministry exercised by men such as David, who said, "The Spirit of the Lord spake by me, and his word was in my tongue" (2 Sam 23:2). A "prophet" was a "spiritual man" (Hos. 9:7), literally "a man of the Spirit" (*ish haruakh*). Thus, the words of the prophets were the words of the Spirit, bearing divine authority by divine inspiration.[8]

Under the Spirit's direction, the prophets acted as God's covenantal prosecutors, declaring to Israel its transgressions and warning of divine judgment (2 Chron. 24:19–27; Mic. 3:8). After the exile, godly Israelites spoke of their forebears and confessed, "Many years didst thou forbear them, and testifiedst against them by thy spirit [or Spirit][9] in thy prophets: yet would they not give ear: therefore gavest thou them into the hand of the people of the lands" (Neh. 9:30; cf. 2 Kings 17:13; Zech. 7:12).

Whenever we read the words of the Old Testament, we should receive them as the words of the Holy Spirit. Behind "Moses said" and "Isaiah said" is what "the Holy Ghost saith" (Heb. 3:7). Therefore, we must believe all that the Hebrew Scriptures teach with fear and trembling, for the Holy One is speaking to us (Isa. 66:2), whose word is like a fire and a hammer (Jer. 23:29). However, the Spirit also is like a river of living water, and his words are full of life for all who trust in Christ (John 6:63; 7:37–39). Since God the Spirit put the words in the prophets' mouths, we should receive them as our spiritual food and our great joy, just as the prophets did (Jer. 1:5; 15:16). Only then may we sincerely confess

8. The doctrine of prophetic inspiration is treated extensively under the locus of prolegomena. See *RST*, 1:316–33 (chap. 17). Subsequent chapters in that volume explain the properties of the inspired Word.

9. The lowercase "spirit" in the translation of various biblical uses of *ruakh* and *pneuma* does not necessarily indicate that the reference is not to the personal Holy Spirit. Hebrew does not have distinct sets of capital and lowercase letters. Greek has both, but ancient manuscripts do not designate proper nouns by case. Even in English texts written in the sixteenth through eighteenth centuries, capitalization did not follow modern conventions.

with the church, "I believe in the Holy Ghost . . . who spake by the prophets."[10]

The prophets, already dependent on the Spirit for the revelation of their message, also received spiritual enablement for effective preaching. Micah said, "Truly I am full of power by the spirit of the LORD, and of judgment, and of might, to declare unto Jacob his transgression, and to Israel his sin. . . . Therefore shall Zion for your sake be plowed as a field, and Jerusalem shall become heaps, and the mountain of the house as the high places of the forest" (Mic. 3:8, 12). The "power" of the Spirit to which Micah referred included "holy courage" to speak hard truth, in contrast to false prophets, who preached what was pleasing to their hearers and financially profitable to themselves (v. 11).[11] However, it likely also included power to evoke repentance. We find this prophecy of Micah cited in the book of Jeremiah, where we learn that King Hezekiah and Judah received his hard message in the fear of God, turned from sin, and found mercy with God (Jer. 26:18–19). The Spirit of the Lord made Micah's preaching effective.

There may be another example of the Spirit's empowerment of preaching when Hezekiah sent messengers throughout Israel and Judah calling the people to repent and keep the Passover at the house of the Lord (2 Chron. 30:1–9). Most members of the northern tribes despised and mocked the king's heralds (v. 10), but some people "humbled themselves, and came to Jerusalem" (v. 11), and "in Judah the hand of God was to give them one heart to do the commandment of the king and of the princes, by the word of the LORD" (v. 12). God revived his people. The "hand of God" represents his supernatural influence (cf. Acts 11:20–24) and can function as an anthropomorphism for the activity of the Spirit.[12]

The church does well to remember that the ministry of the Word in the new covenant likewise depends entirely on the Spirit of God to give life to the hearer and to write the Word on the heart (2 Cor. 3:3–6). If our preaching is to be more than mere words, then the Spirit must accompany the Word with power for the conversion of sinners (1 Cor. 2:4; 1 Thess. 1:5). Preachers must pray for their preaching, and people must pray for their preachers, that the minister will receive the unction of the Holy Spirit.

---

10. The Nicene Creed, in *The Three Forms of Unity*, 7.

11. Kenneth L. Barker, *Micah, Nahum, Habakkuk, Zephaniah*, The New American Commentary 20 (Nashville: Broadman & Holman, 1999), 79.

12. Ezek. 3:14; 37:1. Compare "the Spirit of God" (Matt. 12:28) and "the finger of God" (Luke 11:20).

The Spirit of Power

The Holy Spirit not only reveals divine truth but also gives his servants effectual power to rule people for God's glory. After God enabled Joseph to interpret Pharaoh's dream, the king of Egypt said, "Can we find such a one as this is, a man in whom the Spirit of God is?. . . . Forasmuch as God hath shewed thee all this, there is none so discreet and wise as thou art: thou shalt be over my house, and according unto thy word shall all my people be ruled" (Gen. 41:38–40). The divine Spirit brought Joseph not only a supernatural ability to interpret divine revelation but also the skill to wisely rule a nation. We find the same in Daniel (Dan. 4:8–9, 18; 5:11–14).

The Lord commanded Moses to lay hands on Joshua, "a man in whom is the Spirit," to make him the leader of Israel (Num. 27:18 ESV). Evidently, Joshua was indwelt by the Spirit before his appointment to this office. Later Joshua was said to be "full of the spirit of wisdom" (Deut. 34:9), suggesting a greater gifting from the Spirit who already dwelled in him. Joshua's office was most comparable to that of a king, a political and military leader.[13] We have previously noted that God "filled" particular people in Israel with the Spirit to give them the wisdom and skill to craft the priestly garments and the tabernacle (Ex. 28:3; 31:3; 35:31).[14]

The Holy Spirit came upon the judges to enable them to deliver Israel from her foes. It is written of Othniel, "The Spirit of the Lord came upon him, and he judged Israel, and went out to war" (Judg. 3:10). Gideon was a fearful man by nature (6:11–24, 27), but when hostile nations invaded Israel, "the Spirit of the Lord came upon Gideon, and he blew a trumpet" and rallied nearby Hebrew tribes to go to war (vv. 34–35). When the Ammonites attacked Israel, "the Spirit of the Lord came upon Jephthah," and he led the people to advance against their enemies and win a great victory over them (11:29, 32).[15] The Spirit "rushed" upon Samson and gave him the supernatural strength to rip apart an attacking lion with his bare hands, kill thirty Philistine men, and then kill a thousand men with no weapon but the jawbone of a donkey (14:6, 19; 15:14–15 ESV).[16] It may be that David alludes to this gift of extraordinary strength from the Spirit when he sings of God giving him the power to bend a bow of bronze (Ps. 18:34).

13. Compare Num. 27:17 to the similar language used of kings (2 Sam. 5:2; 1 Kings 22:17).
14. See the section on the Spirit's providence over human life in chap. 2.
15. Owen, *Pneumatologia*, in *Works*, 3:149–50.
16. The verb translated as "rush" (*tsalakh*) can be used for the advance of a fire (Amos 5:6). For other examples of the Spirit "rushing" (*tsalakh*) on people, see 1 Sam. 10:6, 10; 11:6; 16:13; 2 Chron. 24:20.

Similarly, the Holy Spirit rushed upon Saul after he was anointed to be king (1 Sam. 10:6–10). When he heard that the Ammonites had besieged an Israelite city, "the Spirit of God came upon Saul . . . and his anger was kindled greatly" so that he mustered Israel for war, "and the fear of the LORD fell on the people, and they came out with one consent" (11:6–7). It appears that the Spirit stirred up natural courage in both Saul and the people to fight their enemies.

David's anointing with oil to designate him as the next king was accompanied by the gift of the Spirit: "The Spirit of the LORD came upon David from that day forward," even as "the Spirit of the LORD departed from Saul" (1 Sam. 16:13–14). After God judged the monarchy, sent the people into exile, and then restored them to the land, he empowered David's descendant Zerubbabel to rebuild the temple—"Not by might, nor by power, but by my spirit, saith the LORD of hosts" (Zech. 4:6). God's servants can accomplish his purposes by neither military force nor human resources in general; the Spirit alone makes their efforts effectual.[17]

The power to rule was promised in sevenfold fullness to the Christ: "The Spirit of the LORD shall rest upon him, the Spirit of wisdom and understanding, the Spirit of counsel and might, the Spirit of knowledge and the fear of the LORD" (Isa. 11:2 ESV). By the power of that Spirit, the Messiah administers the kingdom of justice, righteousness, peace, harmony, and the knowledge of God throughout the earth (vv. 3–9). Christ exercises spiritual power to enable his servants to practice biblical church discipline to guard and promote the righteousness of God's people (1 Cor. 5:3–5) and to exercise courage in the face of persecution (Acts 4:31). Therefore, the church should devote itself to prayer at all times, and the elders of the church should set aside significant portions of their meetings to pray for the power of the Spirit. The answer to the indifference or cowardice that our selfishness, unbelief, and guilt naturally engender is not to stir up our pride and bitter prejudice, but to call upon God for the boldness of the Spirit.

The Spirit of Presence

From the beginning of Israel's national history, the Holy Spirit was present with the people. When Isaiah reflected on the Lord's goodness to the

17. George L. Klein, *Zechariah*, The New American Commentary 21B (Nashville: Broadman & Holman, 2008), 159.

Israelites and redemption of them from Egypt, the prophet wrote, "But they rebelled and grieved his Holy Spirit; therefore he turned to be their enemy, and himself fought against them. . . . Where is he who brought them up out of the sea with the shepherds of his flock? Where is he who put in the midst of them his Holy Spirit" (Isa. 63:10–11 ESV).[18] Isaiah also said, "As a beast goeth down into the valley, the Spirit of the LORD caused him to rest: so didst thou lead thy people, to make thyself a glorious name" (v. 14). Sinclair Ferguson says, "The Spirit is the executive of the Exodus-redemption wrought by God the Saviour."[19] The text also mentions "the angel of his presence" with Israel (Isa. 63:9), who appears in the exodus narrative as another divine person sent by the Lord (Ex. 23:20–23). The Lord who sends the angel and the Spirit is especially characterized as the "father" of his people (Isa. 63:16). Thus, Isaiah gives us a dim revelation of the Trinity.

Isaiah's statements about the Spirit dwelling among the people of Israel and leading them to their rest in the land (Isa. 63:11, 14) allude to the manifest glory of the Lord in the cloud and fire that descended upon the tabernacle and led Israel through the wilderness (Ex. 13:21–22; 40:34–38). The Lord identified the Spirit as the agent of his presence in the temple: "I am with you, saith the LORD of hosts: according to the word that I covenanted with you when ye came out of Egypt, so my spirit remaineth among you: fear ye not" (Hag. 2:4–5). The Spirit of God dwelled with God's people, manifesting God's special presence with them in his holy temple in fulfillment of his covenant promise to be with them.[20] Michael Horton says, "The Holy Spirit is the one who turns a house into a home—created space into a covenantal space where God dwells with his people."[21] The presence of the Spirit anticipated the glorious dwelling of God with his people in the future, for he promised, "I will fill this house with glory" (v. 7). Yet the Spirit of God dwelled with them in the glory cloud as the Spirit of judgment and burning (cf. Isa. 4:4–5), who manifested the devouring fire

18. In contrast to the ESV's "in the midst of them" (Isa. 63:11), the KJV reads "within him." The Hebrew construction (*b-* plus *qereb* and a singular pronominal suffix) can be used either for "within an individual" (26:9) or "among a group considered collectively" (29:23). In Isa. 63:11, it is best to interpret it to refer to the Spirit's presence among Israel as a group (vv. 10, 14), not specifically his presence within Moses.

19. Ferguson, *The Holy Spirit*, 24.

20. Gen. 21:22; 26:24, 28; 28:13–15; 31:3; Ex. 29:45–46; 33:12–16; Lev. 26:11–12; Isa. 41:10; 43:2, 5; Jer. 30:11; 46:28. On God's special presence, see *RST*, 1:652–53. On God's promise to be "with" his people and its centrality to the covenant of grace, see *RST*, 2:658–61.

21. Horton, *Rediscovering the Holy Spirit*, 41.

of God's holiness in receiving sacrifices and purging all that offended him (Lev. 9:24; 10:1–3). He is the Spirit who judges fallen mankind as the desert wind withers the grass (Isa. 40:7). Horton writes, "He is the sovereign Lord who executes conviction, judgment, and justification."[22]

The Spirit was present with each Old Testament saint as his covenant Lord. The doctrine of God's omnipresence is rightly proven from David's words, "Where shall I go from your Spirit? Or where shall I flee from your presence? If I ascend to heaven, you are there! If I make my bed in Sheol, you are there!" (Ps. 139:7–8 ESV).[23] However, this psalm does not merely affirm God's omnipresence, but also his dynamic, special presence with his servant. David says, "Thou hast . . . laid thine hand upon me" (Ps. 139:5), and, "Even there [in the remotest part of the ocean] shall thy hand lead me, and thy right hand shall hold me" (v. 10). David celebrates God's formation of him in his mother's womb according to his decree, figuratively described as "thy book" (vv. 13–16). Therefore, God's Spirit manifests his divine presence by working to fulfill his purposes in the lives of individual believers (cf. Ps. 73:23–24). In the light of God's complete knowledge of him and presence with him, David takes the covenantal promise, "I am with thee" (Gen. 26:24; 28:15), and reverses it in a most personal manner: "When I awake, I am still with thee" (Ps. 139:18). God's covenantal presence by the Spirit is further revealed by his opposition to wicked men (vv. 19–22) and sanctifying work in his people to bring them to everlasting life (vv. 23–24). Therefore, the words "Where shall I go from your Spirit?" in this context communicate that the Spirit of God dwells continually with each believer as his covenant God. This psalm should comfort every child of God with a marvelous awareness of our divine companion.

In the old covenant, God's special presence by the Spirit was accessible to believers everywhere but was manifest with particular power where his glory dwelt in the tabernacle and later the temple in Jerusalem. The localized concentration of God's special presence required regular pilgrimages to the holy place and made it difficult for Gentiles to participate. Many Israelites participated in the ceremonies at Mount Zion, but they did not please God, for they lacked repentance and faith (Isa. 1:10–18). The godly in Israel worshiped as a living temple within the temple, so to speak, for the Lord inhabited their praises (Ps. 22:3).

22. Horton, *Rediscovering the Holy Spirit*, 110.
23. On God's attributes of immensity and omnipresence, see *RST*, 1:649–57.

In the new covenant, God's special presence is no longer limited to a holy place on one mountain (John 4:21–24) but is concentrated wherever God's people assemble in the name of Christ (Matt. 18:20). The church of Christ is now the temple where God dwells "through the Spirit" (Eph. 2:20–22; cf. 1 Cor. 3:16). Therefore, if the church seeks God's presence, then we are seeking the Holy Spirit. Furthermore, if churches grieve the Holy Spirit by rebellion and sin, then they may forfeit the manifestation of God's presence that the Spirit provides and experience his discipline (Acts 5:1–11; Eph. 4:30). Let us, therefore, walk in reverent obedience to the words of the Spirit—the Holy Scriptures—that we may live in the light of God's face.

The Spirit of Piety

The Holy Spirit is especially known to Christians in his works of regenerating lost sinners and indwelling the saints to produce practical holiness. Did the Holy Spirit perform these same works during the old covenant? The Westminster Confession of Faith (8.6) says, "Although the work of redemption was not actually wrought by Christ till after His incarnation, yet the virtue, efficacy, and benefits thereof were communicated unto the elect, in all ages successively from the beginning of the world."[24] Since "we are made partakers of the redemption purchased by Christ by the effectual application of it to us by his Holy Spirit," this implies that the Spirit has done essentially the same works of salvation throughout history.[25] We present seven arguments here that the Spirit of God performed essentially the same ministry of rebirth and indwelling for sanctification for the Old Testament saints as he does for Christians today.

Explicit Statements That the Spirit Sanctified Old Covenant Saints

The coming of God the Son incarnate to accomplish redemption brought a greater revelation of both the Trinity and the work of salvation. However, prior to Christ's incarnation there were explicit testimonies to the Spirit's work of producing godliness in his people.

In his penitential psalm after he committed adultery and murder, David prayed, "Cast me not away from thy presence; and take not thy holy spirit from me" (Ps. 51:11). Some theologians interpret this prayer as a

24. *Reformed Confessions*, 4:245.
25. The Westminster Shorter Catechism (Q. 29), in *Reformed Confessions*, 4:356.

request that the Holy Spirit will not cease to empower David for service.[26] However, it is unlikely that the Spirit's work in this text can be limited to empowerment. The words "cast me not away from thy presence" refer to God's banishment of sinners from his special presence, though not necessarily permanently.[27] In the context, David was not praying primarily about empowerment, but about cleansing, joy, forgiveness, and inward renewal (vv. 7–10).[28] Owen said, "It is the Spirit, and his presence as unto sanctification . . . that he is treating of with God." David had wounded God's graces in his soul, and so "he cries aloud that He whose they are, and who alone is able to revive and quicken them, may not be taken from him."[29] Warfield wrote, "All his hopes of continued power of new life rest on the continuance of God's holy Spirit, or of the Spirit of God's holiness, with him."[30]

It might be objected that David should never have prayed in this manner, because God cannot reject his children. However, praying for God not to forsake us is not inconsistent with the promises of divine preservation and perseverance of the saints.[31] Believers often turn God's promises into prayers by faith in their covenant God (cf. Ps. 71:1, 9, 12). Furthermore, David had committed grave sins that could (and should) shake the assurance of any believer; it is experientially appropriate for the backslider to ask God to forgive and not forsake him.[32] Therefore, we conclude that David's prayer "Take not thy holy spirit from me" is a poignant petition for the Spirit's continuing work, which involves both sanctification and empowerment.[33]

We find another testimony to the Spirit's sanctifying work in Psalm 143:10: "Teach me to do thy will; for thou art my God: thy spirit is good; lead me into the land of uprightness," or, "Let your good Spirit lead me"

---

26. Wood, *The Holy Spirit in the Old Testament*, 51; and Grudem, *Systematic Theology*, 636.

27. For examples of being "cast out" (*shalak*) from God's "presence" (*panim*), see 2 Kings 13:23; 17:20; 24:20; 2 Chron. 7:20; Jer. 7:15; 52:3. See also Jonah 2:4.

28. "On his lips the prayer has a personal-subjective-soteriological, and not merely an official-objective-theocratic, orientation." Ferguson, *The Holy Spirit*, 24. David links his prayer that God not take away his Spirit with the surrounding prayers for renewed spiritual graces by the three uses of the word translated as "spirit" (*ruakh*, Ps. 51:10–12).

29. Owen, *The Doctrine of the Saints' Perseverance*, in *Works*, 11:331.

30. Warfield, *The Holy Spirit*, 135. See Luther, *Selected Psalms*, on Ps. 51:11, in *LW*, 12:381; and Matthew Poole, *Annotations upon the Holy Bible*, 3 vols. (New York: Robert Carter and Brothers, 1853), 2:84, on Ps. 51:11.

31. On the doctrine of preservation and perseverance, see chaps. 30–31.

32. Calvin, *Commentaries*, on Ps. 51:11.

33. Matthew Henry, *Matthew Henry's Commentary on the Whole Bible: Complete and Unabridged in One Volume* (Peabody, MA: Hendrickson, 1994), 818.

(ESV).[34] In the midst of a prayer for deliverance from his enemies, David called upon his covenant Lord to "teach" him the way of obedience to his preceptive will (cf. Ps. 25:4–5). Psalm 119 often calls upon the Lord to "teach" the believer his commandments, which implies an inward work to reveal the meaning and glory of God's Word so that one obeys it.[35] Just as the Lord once led Israel by the pillar of cloud and fire,[36] so the Spirit still shepherds the flock of God in his good and righteous ways.[37]

In the last explicit testimony that we will adduce, Proverbs represents divine Wisdom as crying out to the public, "Turn you at my reproof: behold, I will pour out my spirit unto you, I will make known my words unto you" (Prov. 1:23). Here we have the gift of the Holy Spirit promised to individuals before Pentecost.[38] Wisdom promises to give the Spirit abundantly to those who repent of sin so that they will grow in their spiritual understanding of his Word. The verb translated as "pour out" (*naba'*) may suggest the gushing of water from a spring (18:4).[39] Wisdom offers this spiritual abundance to those who are already hearing the wisdom of the Word, but through repentance and the gift of the Spirit, "now there is joy, a power and sweetness, of which before we had no conception," as Charles Bridges (1794–1869) said.[40]

Therefore, although the Old Testament does not contain as much explicit teaching about the sanctifying work of the Spirit as the New Testament presents, it does teach us that the saints of Israel were renewed, taught, led, and abundantly blessed by the Holy Spirit.

The Identity of the Spiritual Israel

A second argument for the Spirit's sanctifying work in old covenant saints is that the Bible identifies people who truly are in covenant relationship

34. In Ps. 143:10, "Lead" could be a second person jussive, "may you lead," possibly accompanied by a noun clause, "your Spirit is good" (cf. KJV, following the punctuation of the Masoretic Text). Or the verb could be a third person jussive, "may your good Spirit lead" (cf. ESV), which is similar to Neh. 9:20 and makes good sense of the text. Leslie C. Allen, *Psalms 101–50, Revised*, Word Biblical Commentary (Nashville: Thomas Nelson, 2002), 352. In any case, the good Spirit of God is closely connected to God's leading his people to do his will.

35. Ps. 119:12, 26, 64, 66, 68, 108, 124, 135. See also vv. 18, 33–36, 102.

36. See "lead" (*nakhah*) in Ex. 13:21; 15:13; Deut. 32:12; Neh. 9:12, 19; Ps. 78:14, 53.

37. Cf. Pss. 23:3; 77:19; 78:70–72; 139:10.

38. All other instances of a divine figure speaking of "my spirit" in the Old Testament refer to the Holy Spirit (Gen. 6:3; Isa. 30:1; 42:1; 59:21; Ezek. 36:27; 37:14; Hag. 2:5; Zech. 4:6), including references to the "pouring" of "my spirit" on people (*yatsaq*, Isa. 44:3; *shapak*, Ezek. 39:29; Joel 2:28–29; cf. "the spirit be poured," *'arah . . . ruakh*, Isa. 32:15).

39. John A. Kitchen, *Proverbs*, A Mentor Commentary (Fearn, Ross-shire, Scotland: Christian Focus, 2006), 49.

40. Charles Bridges, *A Commentary on Proverbs* (Edinburgh: Banner of Truth, 1968), 9.

with the Lord as those who have received an inward circumcision. Beginning with the Abrahamic covenant, circumcision in the flesh was required of all males to be counted as part of the covenantal community or household (Gen. 17:9–14). However, God revealed through Moses that faithfulness to the covenant also required the circumcision of the heart: "And now, Israel, what doth the LORD thy God require of thee, but to fear the LORD thy God, to walk in all his ways, and to love him, and to serve the LORD thy God with all thy heart and with all thy soul. . . . Circumcise therefore the foreskin of your heart, and be no more stiffnecked" (Deut. 10:12, 16). The people of Israel needed the spiritual circumcision of their uncircumcised hearts in order to escape God's covenantal curses, repent of their rebellion, know him, love him, and receive his covenantal blessing.[41] By implication, those individuals who were delivered from the power and penalty of sin already enjoyed this inner circumcision.[42] Paul identifies the circumcision of the heart with the work of the Spirit to produce inner obedience and true worship toward God—the defining marks of the true "Jew" (Rom. 2:28–29; Phil. 3:3). Therefore, the true and spiritual Israel of all ages consists of those inwardly transformed by the Holy Spirit.

It might be objected that Paul is writing from the perspective of the new covenant, contrasting the "letter" to the "Spirit" and assuming that the requirement of physical circumcision has been abolished (Rom. 2:26, 29; cf. 2 Cor. 3:6–7; Gal. 6:15).

In response, we agree that Paul is writing from the perspective of the new covenant in Christ. However, he also affirms the doctrine of the old covenant, which, as we have seen, indicates that only those circumcised in the heart are true covenant keepers. Paul projects his distinction of a spiritual Israel within physical Israel back into old covenant history (Rom. 9:6–8). Therefore, Paul's definition of a true Jew as a man inwardly circumcised by the Spirit is illuminating not only for the present era but for all ages. Arthur Lewis said, "Within the total number of Jews there had always been a company of true Jews, all of those who were saved by faith and cleansed from within, having their hearts altered ('circumcised') to conform to the will of God."[43]

41. Lev. 26:40–42; Deut. 30:1–6; Jer. 4:4; 9:23–26.

42. On circumcision and the Abrahamic covenant, see *RST*, 2:618–23.

43. Arthur H. Lewis, "The New Birth under the Old Covenant," *Evangelical Quarterly* 56, no. 1 (January 1984): 37, cited in Erickson, *Christian Theology*, 911.

The Necessity of the New Birth to Enter the Kingdom

A third argument for the Spirit's renewing work in the Old Testament is that without regeneration it is impossible for anyone to be saved from sin and brought into God's kingdom. Our Lord Jesus Christ said, "Verily, verily, I say unto thee, Except a man be born again, he cannot see the kingdom of God. . . . Except a man be born of water and of the Spirit, he cannot enter into the kingdom of God" (John 3:3, 5). Christ also said that Abraham, Isaac, and Jacob—and the prophets who followed them—will be in the kingdom (Matt. 8:11; Luke 13:28). Therefore, the patriarchs were born of the Spirit.

It might be objected that regeneration is a new covenant grace. Dispensationalist theologian Lewis Sperry Chafer (1871–1952) said that the Old Testament saints were renewed to some level of moral obedience to the law, but we cannot affirm that this resulted "in the impartation of the divine nature, in an actual sonship, a joint heirship with Christ, or a placing in the household and family of God," or in being "justified on the ground of the imputed righteousness of Christ."[44] Bill Gillham (1927–2011) said that the old covenant saints will receive regeneration when God raises them from the dead, but during their lives they lacked both regeneration and spiritual participation in the kingdom of God, for those are new covenant realities that did not begin until Christ died on the cross.[45]

In reply, we acknowledge that there is no clear, explicit reference to God regenerating a sinner, causing a new birth, or giving a person a new heart under the old covenant.[46] However, this objection misses Christ's point to Nicodemus. The new birth is not an additional benefit, but is essential to salvation, for only the Holy Spirit can produce spiritual life:

44. Lewis Sperry Chafer, *Systematic Theology*, 8 vols. (Dallas, TX: Dallas Seminary Press, 1948), 6:73–74. On dispensational theology, see *RST*, 2:554–59.

45. Bill Gillham, *What God Wishes Christians Knew about Christianity* (Eugene, OR: Harvest House, 1998), 138.

46. One possible example of spiritual rebirth in the Old Testament might be when Samuel said to Saul, "The Spirit of the Lord will come upon thee, and thou shalt prophesy with them, and shalt be turned [*haphak*] into another man. . . . God is with thee," and the narrator says, "And it was so, that when he had turned his back to go from Samuel, God gave [*haphak*] him another heart: and all those signs came to pass that day. . . . And the Spirit of God came upon him, and he prophesied among them" (1 Sam. 10:6–10). Thus, Erickson, *Christian Theology*, 911. However, the context pertains entirely to Saul's empowerment to serve as king, and in subsequent narratives Saul does not demonstrate the godliness and perseverance associated with the new birth, making his spiritual state dubious at best. The verb *haphak*, which means to turn or overturn, is used with "heart" as its object to describe emotional disturbance (Lam. 1:20; figuratively of God in Hos. 11:8) or God's directing people's attitudes without saving them (Ex. 14:4–5; Ps. 105:25). Therefore, it is not clear that Saul was regenerated by the Spirit.

"That which is born of the flesh is flesh; and that which is born of the Spirit is spirit" (John 3:6; cf. 6:63). The new birth produces a life of righteousness, a radical break from sin, authentic Christian love, faith in Christ, and overcoming the world.[47] Unless we desire to argue that Abraham, Moses, David, and Isaiah had no repentance, faith, love, and obedience, we must conclude that they were born of the Spirit. Owen argued that men of all times must be saved "by the same kind of operation, and the same effect of the Holy Spirit on the faculties of their souls"; because all unregenerate men are in the same state of sin and spiritual death, salvation must rescue sinners from that state and bring them all into essentially the same state of grace and spiritual life.[48] To deny the new birth to those saved in ancient Israel is by implication to deny the corruption of man and the necessity of salvation by grace alone.

Christ said, "Ye must be born again" (John 3:7) to the teacher of Israel who was yet under the old covenant—and rebuked him for not knowing this doctrine from his studies of the Hebrew Bible (v. 10). Christ's reference to being "born of water and of the Spirit" (v. 5) alludes to the use of water as an image of renewal and cleansing, as in the promises of Ezekiel 36:25–27.[49] Furthermore, it makes no sense for Christ to say, "Ye must be born again," if regeneration were not possible before Jesus died and rose again.[50] Indeed, Ezekiel pressed upon his contemporaries their need for "a new heart"—which was a call for their immediate conversion (Ezek. 18:31).

The Necessity of the Indwelling of the Spirit for Obedience

Some theologians acknowledge that the Spirit regenerated those whom God saved under the old covenant but deny that the Spirit indwelt them, except as a temporary empowerment.[51] A key statement to support such a position is found in Christ's words in John 14:16–17: "I will pray the

47. 1 John 2:29; 3:9; 4:7; 5:1, 4, 18. On the new birth, see chap. 17.

48. Owen, *Pneumatologia*, in *Works*, 3:215.

49. Linda Belleville, "'Born of Water and Spirit': John 3:5," *Trinity Journal* 1NS (1980): 138–40 (full article, 125–41).

50. Wood, *The Holy Spirit in the Old Testament*, 67.

51. Walvoord, *The Holy Spirit*, 71–73, 131–32; John R. W. Stott, *Baptism and Fullness: The Work of the Holy Spirit Today* (Downers Grove, IL: InterVarsity Press, 1975), 27; Erickson, *Christian Theology*, 912; James M. Hamilton Jr., *God's Indwelling Presence: The Holy Spirit in the Old and New Testaments*, NAC Studies in Bible and Theology (Nashville: B&H Academic, 2006), 4; Cole, *He Who Gives Life*, 145; John MacArthur and Richard Mayhue, eds., *Biblical Doctrine: A Systematic Summary of Bible Truth* (Wheaton, IL: Crossway, 2017), 350–51, 368–69; and Horton, *Rediscovering the Holy Spirit*, 154. Hamilton gives the most extensive argument for this position.

Father, and he shall give you another Comforter, that he may abide with you for ever . . . ye know him; for he dwelleth with you, and shall be in you." It is argued that the Spirit was already "with" Christ's disciples, but would dwell "in" them only after Christ ascended.

In reply, we observe that there are good exegetical reasons to be cautious about drawing such a conclusion from John 14:16–17. First, the text does not explicitly say that the Spirit was *not* in the disciples at that time. It is possible that "he dwelleth with you, and shall be in you" does not describe two contrasting situations but instead indicates continuity in the Spirit's ministry by two parallel expressions,[52] a style of speaking found in this context.[53] A very similar statement appears in 2 John 2, which says the truth "dwelleth in us, and shall be with us for ever,"[54] but this clearly indicates continuity and not a contrast between two situations. Second, Christ describes a particular ministry of the Spirit, his work as *paraklētos* ("Comforter" or "Advocate"; cf. 1 John 2:1).[55] We should not conclude that this ministry exhausts the full meaning of his indwelling or that the indwelling could not exist apart from it. Third, Christ indicates that he will send the Spirit in this larger capacity to those who love him and keep his commandments, which implies that God already has given them saving grace by the Spirit.[56]

Answering this objection brings us to our fourth argument for the Spirit's sanctifying work in old covenant saints: both the Old and New Testaments teach that the indwelling of God's Spirit is necessary in order to keep God's commandments. After the Lord promised that he would wash Israel from its idolatry with "clean water" and give the people "a new heart," he also said, "I will put my Spirit within you, and cause you to walk in my statutes and be careful to obey my rules" (Ezek. 36:25–27 ESV). The gift of a new heart corresponds to regeneration; the gift of God's Spirit refers to his indwelling in the heart as a continual sanctifying influence.[57] The indwelling Spirit gives life to the dead (37:14). Similarly,

52. The expression translated as "dwell with" (*menō para* with dative) refers to staying together for a period of time (John 4:40; 14:25; Acts 18:20; 21:7), including staying with someone in his house (John 1:39; Acts 9:43; 18:3; 21:8). Cf. Wood, *The Holy Spirit in the Old Testament*, 87.

53. Similar parallelism appears in v. 17, when Christ says of the Spirit that the world "seeth him not, neither knoweth him," and in v. 18, when Christ says, "I will not leave you comfortless [orphans]: I will come to you."

54. Greek: *menousan en hēmin, kai meth' hēmōn estai eis ton aiōna* (2 John 2).

55. On the Spirit's coming as the other *paraklētos* after Christ's glorification, see chap. 5.

56. Augustine, *Tractates on the Gospel of John*, 74.2, in *NPNF*[1], 7:334.

57. Hamilton argues that Ezek. 36:27 does not refer to the Spirit's indwelling in an individual, but his dwelling "in your midst," that is, in his restored temple. *God's Indwelling Presence*, 49–51.

Paul contrasts life in the Spirit with death in the flesh, saying that "they that are in the flesh cannot please God," but "ye are not in the flesh, but in the Spirit, if so be that the Spirit of God dwell in you" (Rom. 8:8–9). Both Ezekiel and Paul indicate that the indwelling of the Spirit of grace is necessary for the spiritual life of obedience to God.

Therefore, we conclude that wherever we encounter spiritual life toward God, we meet a person indwelt by the Spirit. Just as the saints of old had to be regenerated to be saved, so too they had to be indwelt in order to walk in obedience. And they did walk in obedience to his laws (Gen. 26:5; Ps. 119:60, 63, 67). As the Reformation churches confess, "Good works are a testimony of his presence and indwelling,"[58] for "the Holy Ghost is our Sanctifier by His dwelling in our hearts."[59]

The Evidence of the Grace Promised in the New Covenant

It might be further objected that the indwelling of the Spirit revealed through Ezekiel is promised for the future spiritual restoration of Israel under what Jeremiah calls the "new covenant" (Jer. 31:31). Therefore, it is argued, it cannot pertain to people under the old covenant.

The answer to this objection leads us to consider a fifth line of argument for the Spirit's work of sanctification in the old covenant—namely, that godly individuals under that covenant already evidenced graces promised in the new covenant. Through Jeremiah, the Lord promised, "I will put my law in their inward parts, and write it in their hearts" (Jer. 31:33), and, "I will put my fear in their hearts, that they shall not depart from me" (32:40). The new covenant corresponds to promises of a new heart and the indwelling of God's Spirit (Ezek. 36:25–27). Yet God gave these graces to individuals saved under the old covenant. The Lord himself testified that Abraham feared him (Gen. 22:12). David prayed, "Unite my heart to fear thy name" (Ps. 86:11). David said of the righteous man, "The law of his God is in his heart" (37:31). The Lord said, "Hearken unto me, ye that know righteousness, the people in whose heart is my law" (Isa. 51:7).

However, v. 26 is clearly focused on an internal work of grace: "A new heart also will I give you." The promise of this heart work is paralleled by the clause "and a new spirit will I put within you" (*ve-ruakh khadashah eten beqirbekem*). The promise of the Spirit's dwelling in v. 27 is presented in almost identical words (*ve-et-rukhi eten beqirbekem*). This indicates that the giving of God's Spirit has the same internal locus as the giving of a new heart and new spirit. Furthermore, Ezekiel's prophecy links the promise of the indwelling Spirit to new obedience, which must proceed from the heart.

58. Formula of Concord (Epitome, 4.15), in *The Book of Concord*, 499. See the Scottish Confession (Art. 13), in *Reformed Confessions*, 2:194.

59. The Belgic Confession (Art. 9), in *The Three Forms of Unity*, 24.

Therefore, the promises of the new covenant reveal how the Spirit of God works in every person whom he saves.

In this regard, it is worth noting Paul's statement that we have "the same spirit of faith" as the author of Psalm 116:10, which Paul cites (2 Cor. 4:13). If "spirit" is taken for an attitude or disposition, then at least this text indicates continuity of faith in the Old and New Testaments (cf. Heb. 11:1–12:2). However, as Gordon Fee observes, "spirit" (*pneuma*) plays an important role in this part of Paul's epistle as a reference to the Holy Spirit, who gives life and inscribes the law on the heart.[60] Fee comments, "Paul's concern is twofold: that he and the Psalmist share the same faith, because they share the same Spirit who engendered such faith." Thus, even after strongly emphasizing the distinction between the old covenant and the new (2 Cor. 3:6), Paul reminds his readers of the essential continuity of salvation among believers through history.[61]

The Content of the Covenantal Blessing

Sixth, the gift of the Holy Spirit is an integral part of the covenantal blessing promised to Abraham (Gen. 12:1–3). Christ bore the law's curse to redeem us, "that the blessing of Abraham might come on the Gentiles through Jesus Christ; that we might receive the promise of the Spirit through faith" (Gal. 3:14).[62] Though Paul's treatment of the work of the Spirit in his epistle to the Galatians includes miraculous gifts (v. 5), he emphasizes the Spirit's work of salvation in connection to adoption as God's children (4:6) and the production of love and holiness (5:16–25)—graces belonging to believers in Christ as the "seed" of Abraham (3:29). Is it reasonable to think that Abraham himself had no part in the Spirit of salvation promised to his seed?

It might be objected that Paul is teaching the Galatians about the progress of redemptive history, in which the bondage of the law was replaced by the liberty of God's sons after Christ came (Gal. 3:22–4:7). Therefore, one might argue, Paul teaches that the Holy Spirit came only as the eschatological fulfillment of the Abrahamic promise—not to the patriarchs or Israel.

In reply, we acknowledge that "the promise of the Spirit" (Gal. 3:14) was fulfilled only after Christ accomplished redemption (v. 13), for only

60. 2 Cor. 3:3, 6, 8, 17, 18; cf. 5:5; 6:6.

61. Fee, *God's Empowering Presence*, 323–24. See also Smeaton, *The Doctrine of the Holy Spirit*, 253.

62. See the discussion of Gen. 12:1–3 in *RST*, 2:572–75.

then was the Spirit's work granted with extensive fullness to "the Gentiles through Jesus Christ" (v. 14) and intensive fullness as "the Spirit of his Son" (4:6).[63] It would be a mistake to read the fullness of the Spirit's operations in the new covenant back into the experience of the patriarchs and Israelites. John Calvin denied "that they were so endowed with the spirit of freedom and assurance as not in some degree to experience the fear and bondage arising from the law."[64] Even Moses experienced a terror at Mount Sinai that believers under the new covenant need never know (Heb. 12:18–24).

However, Paul aims to teach not only the progress of redemptive history, but also its continuity, for the apostle's gospel is the same gospel that God revealed to Abraham in the promise of "blessing" to him and his seed (Gal. 3:7–9). Abraham, too, was justified by faith (v. 6). That implies that long before Christ came and died, Abraham received the saving benefits of Christ's redemption, which include the Spirit (vv. 13–14). We also note that Paul grounds our reception of the Spirit by faith in Christ (vv. 1–5) on Abraham's justification by faith (v. 6). His point is that we who are counted righteous and given the Spirit through faith are following in Abraham's footsteps. We are not blessed with the Spirit apart from Abraham, but "blessed with faithful Abraham" (v. 9). In light of the Old Testament witness that the Lord was with the patriarchs as their God, we may conclude that they, too, had the Spirit of life.

The Westminster Confession of Faith (20.1) says that Christ purchased for believers liberty from sin's guilt, God's wrath and curse, and Satan's bondage so that they may enjoy free access to God and childlike love for him. These liberties "were common also to believers under the law." However, in the new covenant, "the liberty of Christians is further enlarged" with freedom from the ceremonial law, greater boldness in approaching God, and larger measures "of the free Spirit of God, than believers under the law did ordinarily partake of."[65]

Spiritual Communion with God

A seventh argument for the saving and sanctifying influence of the Holy Spirit upon the Old Testament saints is the fellowship with God that they

63. On the differences between the old and new covenants, see *RST*, 2:645–52.
64. Calvin, *Institutes*, 2.11.9.
65. *Reformed Confessions*, 4:257.

craved and enjoyed. The Psalms richly testify to their spiritual experience. They found abundant satisfaction in the spiritual pleasures, life, and light of God's "house" (Ps. 36:8–9). They thirsted for him and longed to worship in "the house of God," for he was their "exceeding joy" (42:1–4; 43:4). They declared that God was present in the holy place of his city, like a river whose streams make people glad (46:4–5). They thirsted to see his power, glory, and love as they had perceived it in the sanctuary, and earnestly meditated on him wherever they went (63:1–8). When at the sanctuary of God, they received spiritual illumination about the end of the wicked and the inheritance of the righteous, which is God himself (73:17–28). They longed to meet God in his courts and at his altars, and they counted one day in his house as better than a thousand spent with the wicked (84:1–12). Are we to imagine that they desired and experienced this powerful communion with the living God apart from the grace of the Holy Spirit?

However, these psalms also locate the nexus of the saints' communion with God at the physical house of the Lord. As we saw earlier regarding the Spirit of presence, during the old covenant God focused his special presence in the tabernacle and temple, though he was accessible to believers at any time and place (Pss. 63:5–6; 139:7). Today, he is the same Spirit performing the same saving works as in ancient times, but with Christ's exaltation the ministry of the Spirit has expanded dramatically in both place and power as Christ builds his temple not of stone, gold, and silver, but with people redeemed from all nations.

Practical Applications of the Spirit's Old Covenant Work

Although God's people are no longer under the old covenant (Heb. 8:13), the old covenant documents were written for our instruction and hope (Rom. 15:4). Some practical lessons we can take away from the Spirit's operations in the Old Testament are as follows.

First, *we must submit to the Spirit's ancient words*. Whenever we read the Old Testament Scriptures, we are hearing the Holy Spirit speaking to us. This is the voice of the same person who indwells us for our salvation and spiritual growth. Therefore, let us listen to what the Spirit says to the church through the Old Testament. We should love these ancient writings, receive them not as the mere words of men but as the words of God, cherish them as our very life, and obey them without rebellion or hesitation.

Second, *we must rely on the Spirit's empowering gifts*. Throughout history, no one has been able to serve the Lord without the assistance of the Holy Spirit. He has been the giver of wisdom to sages, strength to kings, power to warriors, and courage and effectiveness to preachers. Whatever ministry you may have for the Lord, you simply cannot succeed without the Spirit. Therefore, walk humbly, pray dependently, and serve confidently in the Spirit.

Third, *we must depend on the Spirit's saving work*. We are entirely dependent on the Spirit not just for his empowerment, but also, like the saints of ancient Israel, for all true faith and piety. Apart from the Spirit, all our spiritual experiences, spiritual fruit, and spiritual marks of grace (e.g., Matt. 5:3–12; Gal. 5:22–23; 2 Peter 1:3–7) are a sham. Without the Spirit's saving graces, we can go no further in our spiritual life than mere nominal Christianity or a false mystical imitation of Christianity. Genuine experiential Christianity is always inseparable from the work of the Holy Spirit in us (cf. 1 Cor. 2:10–16). This truth ought to make us realize our radical dependency on the Spirit on a daily basis for every aspect of our spiritual life.

Fourth, *we must pray for the church's worship of God*. The Spirit's special work is to manifest the active presence of God with his people. It was the Holy Spirit who made God's tabernacle and temple a place of spiritual worship and communion with God. It is the Spirit of the living God who dwells in the living temples of local churches today. Much has been said in recent decades about how to make the church's worship of God into a spiritually stimulating experience. Let us not neglect the great essential: the work of the Holy Spirit. Pray regularly and earnestly for the Spirit to unite his people in access to the Father through the Son.

Fifth, *we must be grateful for our new covenant privileges*. Though the Holy Spirit performed great acts of amazing grace for Israel, he has done much more since the ascension of our Lord Jesus Christ. We enjoy brighter revelation of Christ and his ways in the New Testament, broader empowerment for ministry given to every member of Christ's body, multiplied opportunities to enter God's special presence wherever churches gather in Jesus's name, and greater liberty and assurance as God's adopted sons and daughters by the finished work of Christ. As Geoff Thomas says, in the old covenant the Spirit sustained the life and fruitfulness of believers like a steady dripping of water into a sponge, but in the New Testament the Spirit comes through Christ like a jet of water that saturates us and overflows to the world.[66] Do not take these privileges for granted or God might remove them from your experience. Instead, thank God for them.

Sixth, *we must have faith in Christ alone*. The continuity of the Spirit's work among God's people of all eras reflects the fact that they are all saved by one Mediator, Jesus Christ. Athanasius said,

> Surely as, before His becoming man, He, the Word, dispensed to the saints the Spirit as His own, so also when made man, He sanctifies all by the Spirit and says to His disciples, "Receive ye the Holy Ghost." And He gave to Moses and the other seventy; and through Him David prayed to the Father, saying, "Take not Thy Holy Spirit from me." On the other hand, when made man, He said, "I will send to you the Paraclete, the Spirit of truth"; and He sent Him, He, the Word of God, as being faithful. Therefore "Jesus Christ is the same yesterday, to-day, and for ever."[67]

The ancient people of God served him in no other way than by the grace of Christ given in the Spirit of God. Surely we can and must trust in Christ alone for the same grace today.

Sing to the Lord

Calling upon the Holy Spirit

Spirit, strength of all the weak,
Giving courage to the meek,
Teaching faltering tongues to speak;
Hear us, Holy Spirit.

Spirit, aiding all who yearn
More of truth divine to learn,
And with deeper love to burn;
Hear us, Holy Spirit.

Spirit, Fount of faith and joy,
Giving peace without alloy,
Hope that nothing can destroy;
Hear us, Holy Spirit.

66. Thomas, *The Holy Spirit*, 24.
67. Athanasius, *Discourses against the Arians*, 1.12.48, in *NPNF*[2], 4:334.

Source of love and light Divine,
With that hallowing grace of thine,
More and more upon us shine;
Hear us, Holy Spirit.

Holy, loving, as thou art,
Come and live within our heart,
Never from us to depart;
Hear us, Holy Spirit.

May we soon, from sin set free,
Where thy work may perfect be,
Jesus' face with rapture see:
Hear us, Holy Spirit.

Thomas Benson Pollock
Tune: Gower's Litany
Trinity Hymnal—Baptist Edition, No. 244

Questions for Meditation or Discussion

1. A recently converted Christian comes to you and asks, "What does John 7:39 mean when it says that the Holy Spirit 'was not yet given'?" How do you answer?
2. What part did the Spirit of God play in the lives of the prophets?
3. Give examples of how the Holy Spirit empowered judges and kings.
4. How did the Spirit manifest God's presence in the exodus, the temple, and the lives of individual believers?
5. What Old Testament Scriptures explicitly speak of the Holy Spirit's work to make men holy prior to Christ's coming in the flesh?
6. What does Paul teach in Romans 2:28–29? What does that imply about the Holy Spirit's work during the old covenant?
7. Why might someone think that the new birth or regeneration was not given to anyone in the Old Testament? How can we show that it was given?
8. Someone says, "We know that the Holy Spirit did not indwell or sanctify people in the Old Testament because those works were promised in the new covenant." How do you respond?
9. What does Galatians 3:14 imply about the Holy Spirit's work in the Old Testament?

10. What do the Psalms reveal about the spiritual communion with God enjoyed by old covenant saints? What does this imply about the work of the Spirit?
11. Of the practical applications made throughout this chapter, including those listed at the end, which do you think is most important for your church? Why? What can you do about it?

Questions for Deeper Reflection

12. What arguments might be made for and against the doctrine that the Holy Spirit indwelt believers as a sanctifying influence during the old covenant? Which position is most biblical? Why?
13. If we deny that the Holy Spirit gave essentially the same saving graces to believers in ancient Israel as he does to Christians today, what would that imply about the following?
    - salvation by grace alone
    - how we interpret and apply the Old Testament
    - the mediation of Jesus Christ

4

The Spirit and God the Son Incarnate

Christ began his ministry in Nazareth by reading the prophecy "The Spirit of the Lord is upon me, because he hath anointed me" and announcing, "This day is this scripture fulfilled in your ears" (Luke 4:16–21, citing Isa. 61:1). Though all the saints share in his anointing (2 Cor. 1:21; 1 John 2:27), Christ is preeminently the Anointed.[1] The psalmist says, "God, thy God, hath anointed thee with the oil of gladness above thy fellows" (Ps. 45:7). John Flavel (1628–1691) paraphrased this text as follows: God "enriched and filled thee, in a singular and peculiar manner, with the fulness of the Spirit, whereby thou art consecrated to thy office: and by reason whereof thou out-shinest and excellest all the saints, who are thy fellows or copartners in these graces."[2]

John says that God "gives the Spirit without measure" to his Son (John 3:34 ESV). Christ is the reservoir containing all the living waters that overflow into the lives of his people. Isaac Ambrose (1604–1664) said, "In Christ there is a gracious mixture and compound of all the graces of the Spirit. . . . He received the Spirit out of measure; there was in him as much as possible could be in a creature, and more than in all other creatures whatsoever."[3]

1. On "Christ" or "Anointed One" as Jesus's official name, see *RST*, 2:742–44.
2. John Flavel, *The Method of Grace in the Gospel-Redemption*, in *The Works of John Flavel*, 6 vols. (1820; repr., Edinburgh: Banner of Truth, 1968), 2:141.
3. Isaac Ambrose, *Looking unto Jesus: A View of the Everlasting Gospel; or, The Soul's Eyeing of Jesus, as Carrying on the Great Work of Man's Salvation, from First to Last* (Philadelphia: J. B. Lippincott & Co., 1856), 280.

Francis Turretin noted that Christ's reception of the Spirit in his humanity is not "simply infinite," for his "humanity is finite in itself," but it is "a 'fulness of abundance,' which suffices not only for himself but for others also, so that we all can drink of his fulness (John 1:16)."[4]

When we consider Christ's anointing with the Holy Spirit, we must remember the doctrines of the Trinity and the incarnation.[5] The Son and the Spirit are each distinct persons, both fully God, sharing the one divine essence with the Father. The incarnate Son is both God and man in one person. As God the Son, the Mediator is anointed by the Father to give the Holy Spirit to sinful men. As the human Servant of the Lord, Christ needs and receives the graces of the Spirit to live and fulfill his office, for his deity does not replace a human mind and soul.[6]

The Holy Spirit and the Revelation of Christ

The Spirit of God is the divine agent of revelation.[7] He revealed the old covenant with its holy place and sacrifices, ordering its ceremonies in a manner that pointed ahead to a more perfect way into God's presence that Christ would accomplish (Heb. 9:8–12). The Holy Spirit also revealed the new covenant, in which he testified that Christ's one offering would accomplish both the justification and sanctification of his people (10:14–17).

When the prophets foretold "the sufferings of Christ, and the glory that should follow," they did so by the revelation of the Spirit (1 Pet. 1:10–12). In them was the "Spirit of Christ" (v. 11), evidently so named because God the Son was already making himself known to God's people by the work of the Spirit among them.[8] Edmund Clowney (1917–2005) said, "Not only does prophecy bear witness to Jesus, but Jesus bears witness through prophecy. . . . The eternal Logos is the source of the prophetic testimony."[9] The same Holy Spirit inspired the apostles and evangelists who proclaimed Christ after his coming (v. 12).

---

4. Turretin, *Institutes*, 13.12.3 (2:347).
5. On the Trinity, see *RST*, 1:876–953 (chaps. 45–47). On the incarnation, see *RST*, 2:783–865 (chaps. 39–42).
6. Smeaton, *The Doctrine of the Holy Spirit*, 112, 114–15.
7. See the discussion of the Spirit of prophecy in chap. 3. See also *RST*, 1:268.
8. The similarity among "Spirit of Christ," "Spirit of God," and "Spirit of the Lord" implies that the first title indicates that the Spirit was sent from Christ in his name (cf. John 14:26; 15:26; 16:7). See Poole, *Annotations upon the Holy Bible*, 3:901, on 1 Pet. 1:11.
9. Edmund P. Clowney, *The Message of 1 Peter: The Way of the Cross*, The Bible Speaks Today (Downers Grove, IL: InterVarsity Press, 1988), 58.

The Spirit's ministry is so tied to Jesus Christ that apostolic tests for the authentic Spirit of prophecy are, among other things, whether people are led to confess that "Jesus Christ is come in the flesh" (1 John 4:3) and "Jesus is the Lord" (1 Cor. 12:3). The aim of prophecy is to bear witness to Jesus for God's glory, "for the testimony of Jesus is the spirit of prophecy" (Rev. 19:10).

The Holy Spirit and Christ's Incarnation

The Holy Spirit formed Christ's human nature: Jesus was conceived in Mary "of the Holy Ghost" (Matt. 1:18, 20). This does not mean that the Holy Spirit is the father of Christ's human nature; the Spirit relates to the man Jesus simply as his Creator. Christ is one person in two natures, divine and human, and thus relates only to God the Father as his Father.[10]

The angel Gabriel told Mary, "The Holy Ghost shall come upon thee, and the power of the Highest shall overshadow thee: therefore also that holy thing which shall be born of thee shall be called the Son of God" (Luke 1:35). Christ's unique conception by a virgin mother was a sign that he is no mere man, but the vanguard of the new creation by the Holy Spirit, the divine glory dwelling among men.[11] The Holy Spirit who manifested God's glory with Israel in its earthly tabernacle and temple (Isa. 63:10–14; Hag. 2:5) prepared the human tabernacle of Immanuel, so that God the Son dwells among men in human flesh (John 1:14; 2:19–20).[12]

Christ would not be the God-man apart from the power of the Spirit forming his humanity from Mary's flesh. God's promises hinge upon this great work. All the Spirit's saving operations on men and women through Christ spring from his work in this one man, the last Adam. Therefore, let us glorify God the Holy Spirit forever for the virgin birth.

Christ's miraculous conception by the power of the Holy Spirit was not an isolated event, but rather set upon Christ's human nature a birthmark, as it were, of constant dependence on and filling by the Spirit. Herman Bavinck said, "This activity of the Holy Spirit with respect to Christ's human nature . . . began with the conception . . . [and] continued through-

---

10. Owen, *Pneumatologia*, in *Works*, 3:164–65.

11. See the section on the incarnate Lord's unique birth in *RST*, 2:790–94.

12. Edward Henry Bickersteth, *The Holy Spirit: His Person and Work* (repr., Grand Rapids, MI: Kregel, 1959), 75. Some draw a parallel between Christ's baptism and transfiguration, noting the Father's dual commendation of the Son and suggesting that the cloud of glory represents the Holy Spirit (Matt. 17:5; Mark 9:7; Luke 9:34–35)—but that is not explicit in the text. See Cole, *He Who Gives Life*, 163–64; and Horton, *Rediscovering the Holy Spirit*, 102.

out his entire life, even right into the state of exaltation, . . . [for] the true human who bears God's image is inconceivable even for a moment without the indwelling of the Holy Spirit."[13]

The Holy Spirit and Christ's Anointing at His Baptism

The power of the Spirit characterized Christ's ministry. God said, "Behold my servant, whom I uphold; mine elect, in whom my soul delighteth; I have put my spirit upon him: he shall bring forth judgment to the Gentiles" (Isa. 42:1). The Spirit of God imparted to the Servant of the Lord both assurance of God's approval and empowerment to do God's will. God fulfilled this promise in Christ by giving him the Spirit (Matt. 12:18). George Smeaton said that "all his official activity" sprang from "the personal life of Christ as the God-man full of the Spirit."[14]

Richard Sibbes anticipated an objection: "Christ was God himself; he had the Spirit, and gives the Spirit; therefore, how could the Spirit be put on him?" Sibbes answered, "Christ is both God and man. . . . Christ, as man, receives the Spirit. . . . Whatsoever Christ did as man, he did by the Spirit."[15] The Spirit, who proceeds from the Father and the Son, is their gift to his human nature. Antonius Thysius said, "To carry out such a great task, by the efficacy of its power, the Word truly shared with it the Spirit, and the spiritual and excellent gifts, without measure."[16]

The Father anointed his incarnate Son with the Spirit in a manner that fulfilled Isaiah 42:1 at Christ's baptism: "The Holy Ghost descended in a bodily shape like a dove upon him, and a voice came from heaven, which said, Thou art my beloved Son; in thee I am well pleased" (Luke 3:22). This was not Christ's adoption, but the warm acknowledgment that he was already God's delightful Son (1:35; 2:49; cf. Gal. 4:4). Afterward, "Jesus being full of the Holy Ghost returned from Jordan, and was led by the Spirit into the wilderness" (Luke 4:1). In that barren place, Christ exhibited the fruit of the Spirit in obedience to God's will. William Perkins commented that "Christ was always filled with the Spirit, . . . [but] at His baptism being inaugurated into His mediatorship, He received such

13. Bavinck, *Reformed Dogmatics*, 3:292.
14. Smeaton, *The Doctrine of the Holy Spirit*, 123.
15. Sibbes, *A Description of Christ*, in *Works*, 1:17.
16. Johannes Polyander, Antonius Walaeus, Antonius Thysius, and Andreas Rivetus, *Synopsis Purioris Theologiae, Synopsis of a Purer Theology: Latin Text and English Translation*, vol. 2, *Disputations 24–42*, trans. Riemer A. Faber, ed. Henk van den Belt, Studies in Medieval and Reformation Traditions 204, Texts and Studies 8 (Leiden: Brill, 2016), 25.30 (83).

fullness of the Spirit as was behooveful [necessary, suitable] for so high an office, which . . . was far greater than before He needed."[17]

There is a notable similarity between Luke's account of Christ's baptism and temptation and Paul's teaching that the adopted "sons of God" are "led by the Spirit of God," who also "beareth witness with our spirit, that we are the children of God" (Rom. 8:14, 16).[18] Paul intertwines our experience with that of Christ, for, having "the Spirit of Christ" dwell in us, "we suffer with him, that we may be also glorified together" (vv. 9, 17). Christ, the last Adam in the Spirit, was assured of the Father's love and led by the Spirit so that those adopted by his grace would be assured and led by the same Spirit. Sibbes said, "All things are first in Christ, and then in us. . . . We have the Spirit in us, but he is first in Christ; God hath put the Spirit in Christ, as the spring, as the second Adam. . . . Whatsoever the Holy Ghost doth in us, he doth the same in Christ first, and he doth it in us because in Christ."[19]

The Spirit descended upon Christ in visible form "like a dove" (Luke 3:22). The form of a bird alludes to the Spirit of God powerfully hovering over the unformed creation to bring order and nurture life (Gen. 1:2) and to the Lord caring for Israel in the wilderness as an eagle cares for its young (Deut. 32:11).[20] Thus, the Spirit of the Lord anointed Christ as the beginning of the new creation, the true Israel. Yet the Spirit did not appear as an eagle, but as a dove, an image of gentle beauty, purity, mourning, and sacrifice.[21] Thomas Goodwin said that a dove is "the most innocent and most meek creature . . . having no fierceness in it, expressing nothing but love and friendship to its mate."[22] This gentle image suits the Servant of the Lord, of whom it is said, "A bruised reed shall he not break, and the smoking flax shall he not quench" (Isa. 42:3). John Calvin said that here we find "the sweetest consolation, that we may not fear to approach Christ, who meets us, not in the formidable power of the Spirit, but clothed with gentle and lovely grace."[23] Smeaton said, "There was, in

17. Perkins, *The Combat between Christ and the Devil Displayed: or, a Commentary upon the Temptations of Christ*, in *Works*, 1:94.
18. Bickersteth, *The Holy Spirit*, 78; and Ferguson, *The Holy Spirit*, 47.
19. Sibbes, *A Description of Christ*, in *Works*, 1:18.
20. On the Spirit's work of creation, see chap. 2.
21. For examples, see the uses of the word translated as "dove" or "pigeon" (*peristera*) in Gen. 15:9; Lev. 1:14; 5:7, 11; 12:6, 8; 14:22, 30; 15:14, 29; Num. 6:10; Ps. 67:14 [68:13]; Song 1:15; 2:14; 4:1; 5:2, 12; 6:9; Isa. 38:14; 59:11; Nah. 2:8(9) LXX; and in Matt. 10:16; 21:12; Mark 11:15; Luke 2:24; John 2:14, 16.
22. Goodwin, *The Heart of Christ in Heaven unto Sinners on Earth*, in *Works*, 4:118.
23. Calvin, *Commentaries*, on Matt. 3:16.

the Lord's human life, a combination of all the graces that seem the most opposite—meekness and boldness, the assertion of truth and deep humility, greatness and gentleness."[24]

The Holy Spirit and Christ's Empowering in His Ministry

The Holy Spirit empowered Christ to preach the gospel (Luke 4:14–19). By the Spirit, Jesus spoke with supernatural grace and authority (vv. 22, 32). He received a limitless supply of the Spirit's grace to enable him to speak God's words. John says, "He whom God hath sent speaketh the words of God: for God giveth not the Spirit by measure unto him" (John 3:34). Christ's words are "spirit" and "life," for through them the Holy Spirit gives eternal life (6:63). After Christ's resurrection, he still taught his disciples "through the Holy Ghost" (Acts 1:2).

The Spirit directed and equipped Christ to wage spiritual warfare against Satan. The Spirit "led" Jesus "into the wilderness to be tempted of the devil" (Matt. 4:1). Satan did not start this fight; the Spirit of God sent Christ into holy conflict with the Tempter. Mark uses a more forceful verb: "The Spirit driveth him into the wilderness" (Mark 1:12).[25] Perkins said that this leading of the Spirit "was a motion of the Holy Ghost, wherewith Christ was filled above measure and made willing to encounter with Satan in that combat."[26] The same Spirit had led Israel through the wilderness, but the people grieved him with their rebellion (Isa. 63:10–14). Now the Spirit led the true Israel, God's Servant, who followed in perfect obedience to the prophetic Word (Matt. 4:3–10). Having overcome the Devil, Christ attacked his strongholds, casting demons out of many people (vv. 23–25). Christ said, "If I cast out devils by the Spirit of God, then the kingdom of God is come unto you" (12:28). Thus, by the power of God's Spirit, Christ did "bind the strong man" and rescued those whom he had taken captive (v. 29).

The Spirit of the Lord anointed Christ to heal the sick and crippled. Peter said, "God anointed Jesus of Nazareth with the Holy Ghost and with

24. Smeaton, *The Doctrine of the Holy Spirit*, 124.

25. The verb translated as "driveth" (*ekballō*) is used in Mark's Gospel for firmly telling people to leave (Mark 1:43; 5:40), pulling out an eye (9:47), throwing people out (11:15; 12:8) and often for casting out devils (1:34, 39; 3:15, 22, 23; 6:13; 7:26; 9:18, 28, 38; 16:9, 17). It does not appear to be used in Scripture for the driving force of the wind. Uses of *ekballō* similar to Mark 1:12 have to do with sending forth laborers to gather a large harvest (Matt. 9:38; Luke 10:2), which implies urgency, and God's servant sending out justice for victory (Matt. 12:20).

26. Perkins, *The Combat between Christ and the Devil Displayed*, in *Works*, 1:90.

power: who went about doing good, and healing all that were oppressed of the devil; for God was with him" (Acts 10:38). The phrase "healing all that were oppressed of the devil" does not limit this activity to exorcisms of the demonized. After Christ healed a woman who had been bent over for eighteen years, he said she had been "bound" by "Satan" (Luke 13:16). Though her disease itself was demonic in origin (cf. 4:39), nothing in the text suggests she was demon possessed.

It may be asked whether all of Christ's miracles were performed by the power of the Spirit. If so, then it could be argued that his miracles did not attest to his deity any more than the miracles of the prophets and apostles show that they were divine.

In reply to this question, we would clarify that the works of the Trinity toward creation are undivided: the Father always works through the Son by the Spirit.[27] Therefore, God the Son does nothing apart from the Holy Spirit, including the Son's acts toward his own human nature.[28] The question is not whether a miracle comes from the Son or the Spirit, but whether any of the miracles are distinct signs of the deity of Christ.

Some miracles of Christ resemble those that God worked by other men (2 Kings 4:18–44; Acts 9:36–43). Scripture ascribes Christ's healing of the sick and casting out of demons to the power of the Spirit (Acts 10:38). Christ is incarnate: "Jesus of Nazareth, a man approved of God among you by miracles and wonders and signs, which God did by him" (2:22). Luke prefaces Christ's ministry with the general comment that "Jesus returned in the power [*dynamis*] of the Spirit into Galilee" (Luke 4:14). Once when Jesus was teaching, "the power [*dynamis*] of the Lord was present to heal" (5:17). On other occasions, we read that "virtue" (*dynamis*) went out of him (6:19; 8:46). He gave "power" (*dynamis*) to others to work exorcisms and healings (9:1). These statements suggest that Christ healed by a divine source distinct from his own person—the person of the Spirit (cf. 24:49).[29]

However, in other respects Christ's miracles did not merely indicate that he was God's Servant but pointed to Christ's unique identity. Christ

27. On the one divine power and activity of the Trinity, see *RST*, 1:893–98.

28. See the discussion in Owen, *Pneumatologia*, in *Works*, 3:160–62.

29. Gerald F. Hawthorne, *The Presence and the Power: The Significance of the Holy Spirit in the Life and Ministry of Jesus* (Dallas, TX: Word, 1991), 155. However, Hawthorne made so much of the Spirit's activity in and through Christ that he embraced a form of the kenotic theory, the belief that "the Son of God willed to renounce the exercise of his divine powers, attributes, prerogatives, so that he might live fully within those limitations which inhere in being truly human" (208). For a rebuttal of kenotic theories, see *RST*, 2:855–58.

worked many miracles by a mere word (Matt. 8:8–9, 16, 26) and used his miracles to show that he is the King in whom the kingdom of God had arrived (12:28).[30] Some miracles revealed Christ's sovereignty over creation as its Lord and Creator, such as calming a violent storm, walking on water, causing a multitude of fish to fill the nets after the fishermen spent a night without a catch, and turning large quantities of water into excellent wine—which, the Scriptures say, revealed his glory and evoked wonder and worship toward Christ.[31] In these cases, Christ's miracles revealed that he is God the Son incarnate, essentially one with the Father in his divine power.

We see this mysterious interplay of the Trinity and the incarnation in Luke 10:21–22. Christ "rejoiced in spirit," or better, "in the Spirit" (*en tō pneumati*),[32] referring to the work of the Holy Spirit to produce godly joy in Christ's human nature (cf. Acts 13:52; 1 Thess. 1:6). He thanked the "Father" for concealing the truth from some and revealing it to others as "it seemed good in thy sight." Christ then said, "All things are delivered to me of my Father," referring to his mediatorial reign as the God-man. However, he also said no one knows the Son but the Father, implying the Son's infinite nature; and no one knows the Father "but the Son" and those to whom the Son chooses to reveal him, implying the Son's unique relation to the Father and divine will. Thus, in one text we have both the Son's deity and sovereignty on the one hand, and his human worship of the Father and dependence on the Spirit on the other. Christ's Spirit-formed, Spirit-filled humanity qualifies him to lead his brothers in the worship of God (Heb. 2:11). Consequently, Sibbes said, "all the communion that Christ as man had with God was by the Holy Ghost; all the communion that God hath with us, and we with God, is by the Holy Ghost: for the Spirit is the bond of union between Christ and us, and between God and us."[33]

The Holy Spirit and Christ's Passion, Death, Resurrection, and Ascension

If the Spirit led Christ in the path of obedience into the wilderness, then we would expect that the Spirit also led Christ in his obedience unto death on the cross. The Gospel narratives do not mention the Spirit when Christ

30. See the section on Christ's actions of deity in *RST*, 2:766–71.
31. Matt. 8:23–27; 14:25–33; Luke 5:4–11; John 2:1–11; 21:4–14.
32. Some manuscripts read *en tō pneumati tō hagiō*, "in the Holy Spirit" (Luke 10:21 ESV).
33. Sibbes, *A Description of Christ*, in *Works*, 1:17.

cried, "Abba, Father," in Gethsemane (Mark 14:36), but this is the very prayer that Paul says the Spirit moves God's adopted children to lift up to their "Abba, Father" (Rom. 8:15; Gal. 4:6). Again, we note that the experience of God's adopted children, as described in Romans 8:14–17, reflects the experience of God's only begotten Son. Christ is unique in both his person and his redemptive work, but just as Christ bore the punishment for the sins of his people, he also conquered the power of sin for their sake and forged a new humanity that he would impart to them by the Spirit.[34] Sibbes said, "He is a Spirit of union, to knit us to Christ, and make us one with him, and thereupon to quicken us [make us alive], to lead us, and guide us, and to dwell in us continually, to stir up prayers and supplications in us, to make us cry familiarly to God as to a Father, to comfort and support us in all our wants and miseries, as he did Christ."[35]

There is one explicit statement of the Spirit's empowerment of Christ as he died as a sacrifice to cleanse his people, though this is disputed. The writer to the Hebrews says that Christ "through the eternal Spirit offered himself without spot to God" (Heb. 9:14). Some people interpret the "eternal Spirit" as a reference to Christ's spiritual perspective on the eternal world, but "spirit" is not used in this abstract sense in Hebrews. Some theologians have taken it as Christ's divine nature (cf. "the power of an endless life," 7:16).[36] John Chrysostom (d. 407), Thomas Aquinas (1225–1274), and Calvin read it as a reference to the power of the Holy Spirit.[37] John Owen found it plausible to interpret the "eternal Spirit" as either Christ's divine nature or the Holy Spirit, both views being held by sound commentators.[38]

Several factors favor the interpretation of Hebrews 9:14 as a reference to the Holy Spirit. First, the word translated as "Spirit" (*pneuma*) often refers to the Holy Spirit in Hebrews, but never to the divine nature.[39] Sec-

34. On Christ's victory over sin, see *RST*, 2:1117–28.

35. Sibbes, *A Description of Christ*, in *Works*, 1:22.

36. There is a Reformed exegetical tradition that interprets "spirit" in several Christological texts as a reference to Christ's divine nature. See John (Giovanni) Diodati, *Pious and Learned Annotations upon the Holy Bible*, 3rd ed. (London: by James Flesher, for Nicholas Fussell, 1651), on Mark 2:8; Rom. 1:4; 1 Tim. 3:16; Heb. 9:14; 1 Pet. 3:18; and Polyander, Walaeus, Thysius, and Rivetus, *Synopsis Purioris Theologiae*, 26:19 (2:109–10).

37. John Chrysostom, *Homilies on Hebrews*, 15.5, in *NPNF*[1], 14:440; Thomas Aquinas, *Commentary on the Letter of Saint Paul to the Hebrews*, ed. John Mortensen and Enrique Alarcón, trans. Fabian R. Larcher (Lander, WY: The Aquinas Institute for the Study of Sacred Doctrine, 2012), sec. 444 (195); and Calvin, *Commentaries*, on Heb. 9:14.

38. Owen, *Pneumatologia*, in *Works*, 3:176, 180; and *An Exposition of the Epistle to the Hebrews*, 6:303–6. But see his earlier statement in *The Death of Death in the Death of Christ*, in *Works*, 10:178.

39. *Pneuma* as the Holy Spirit: Heb. 2:4; 3:7; 6:4; 9:8; 10:15, 29. Angels: 1:7, 14. Human spirit: 4:12; 12:9, 23.

ond, it seems a "superfluous repetition" to interpret the text as saying he offered himself through himself.[40] Third, the text does not say, "*his* eternal Spirit," as we would expect if it referred to Christ's divine nature. Fourth, the text emphasizes the moral perfection of Christ's sacrifice ("without spot," cf. 1 Pet. 1:19), which requires the Spirit's enablement. Fifth, Hebrews 9:28 alludes to Isaiah's prophecy of "my righteous servant" who "bare the sin of many" (Isa. 53:11–12), and Isaiah also foretold that the Lord would uphold his Servant with his Spirit (42:1).[41] Sixth, "eternal" in this context does not refer to a divine attribute or the divine nature, but pertains to the age to come, for the word also modifies "redemption" and "inheritance" (Heb. 9:12, 15). Hence, "the eternal Spirit" is the promised Spirit of the age to come (6:4–5). Seventh, the epistle emphasizes that God acted through Christ from beginning to end (1:2; 2:10; 5:4–6, 8–9; 13:20).[42] Therefore, Hebrews 9:14 almost certainly speaks of God's Spirit enabling Christ to offer the sacrifice.

How did the Spirit assist Christ at the cross? Aquinas commented that Hebrews 9:14 reveals "the reason why Christ shed His blood, because this was done by the Holy Spirit, through whose movement and instinct, namely, by the love of God and neighbor He did this."[43] Owen identified "those principal graces of the Spirit which he [Christ] acted in this offering of himself unto God" as follows: "love to mankind, and compassion towards sinners, . . . his unspeakable zeal for, and ardency of affection unto, the glory of God, . . . his holy submission and obedience unto the will of God, . . . [and] that faith and trust in God which, with fervent prayers, cries, and supplications, he now acted on God and his promises."[44] We may consider these graces in the dying Christ to be among the greatest works performed by the Holy Spirit, for in offering

40. Smeaton, *The Doctrine of the Holy Spirit*, 129.

41. Compare "having been offered to bear the sins of many" (*prosenechtheis eis to pollōn anenenkein hamartias*, Heb. 9:28) with "he bare the sin of many" (*autos hamartias pollōn anēnenken*, Isa. 53:12 LXX). Thus, F. F. Bruce, *The Epistle to the Hebrews*, The New International Commentary on the New Testament (Grand Rapids, MI: Eerdmans, 1964), 205, 223. The verb translated as "offer" (*prospherō*, aorist passive participle *prosenechteis*) ties together Heb. 9:14 and v. 28, indeed, this part of the epistle (9:7, 9, 14, 25, 28; 10:1, 2, 8, 11, 12).

42. Martin Emmrich, "'Amtscharisma': Through the Eternal Spirit (Hebrews 9:14)," *Bulletin for Biblical Research* 12, no. 1 (2002): 22 (full article, 17–32), available at https://www.ibr-bbr.org/files/bbr/BBR_2002a_02_Emmrich_Amtschrisma_Heb9.pdf. In the latter part of the article, Emmrich notes extracanonical Jewish writings that ascribe the empowerment of priests to the Holy Spirit (25–31).

43. Latin: *causam quare Christus sanguinem suum fudit, quia hoc fuit spiritus sanctus, cuius motu et instinctu, scilicet charitate Dei, et proximi, hoc fecit*. Aquinas, *Commentary on the Letter of Saint Paul to the Hebrews*, sec. 444 (195).

44. Owen, *Pneumatologia*, in *Works*, 3:177.

himself to God as a sacrifice for our sins, Jesus "acted all his graces to the utmost."[45]

Therefore, as Michael Horton says, "the Spirit not only applies redemption but was a principal agent of it."[46] Stating it more broadly, Owen wrote, "The agent in, and chief author of, this great work of our redemption is the whole blessed Trinity."[47]

When we contemplate the cross of our Lord, let us not neglect to marvel at the love of the Holy Spirit. Edward Bickersteth (1825–1906) said that Christ "died as he lived, full of the Holy Ghost. And as our souls glow with responsive love at the thought of the Father's love, who gave his only Son, and of the Son's love, who gave himself, let us not forget the coequal and coeternal love of the Holy Spirit, in whose efficient power the stupendous sacrifice was made."[48]

The redeeming death of Christ by the Spirit purchased the grace of the Holy Spirit for his people. Christ suffered the curse for their lawbreaking and gained the blessing by his law keeping "that we might receive the promise of the Spirit through faith" (Gal. 3:10–14). The Spirit who now works in God's children is the Spirit of the crucified Lord. They "walk in the Spirit" and bear "the fruit of the Spirit" because "they that are Christ's have crucified the flesh with the affections and lusts" (5:22–25). Flavel said, "If Christ had not died, the Spirit of God, by which you now mortify the deeds of the body, could not have been given unto you."[49]

God raised Christ from the dead by the power of the Holy Spirit. Paul says, "If the Spirit of him that raised up Jesus from the dead dwell in you, he that raised up Christ from the dead shall also quicken your mortal bodies by his Spirit that dwelleth in you" (Rom. 8:11).[50] Now Christ lives in the fullness of the Spirit's power. Christ was "determined the Son of God with power, according to [*kata*] the spirit of holiness, by the resurrection from the dead" (1:4 KJV mg.).[51] This verse presents a contrast with "made of the seed

45. Owen, *Pneumatologia*, in *Works*, 3:180.
46. Horton, *Rediscovering the Holy Spirit*, 103.
47. Owen, *The Death of Death in the Death of Christ*, in *Works*, 10:163.
48. Bickersteth, *The Holy Spirit*, 81.
49. Flavel, *The Method of Grace*, in *Works*, 2:147.
50. While Rom. 8:11 does not explicitly say that God gave life *to Jesus* by the Spirit, it identifies the Spirit with God's resurrection power toward us, which is the same power by which he raised Christ (Eph. 1:19–20).
51. The word translated as "declared" (*horizō*) in the KJV and ESV means "determined, ordained, appointed" (Luke 22:22; Acts 2:23; 10:42; 11:29; 17:26, 31; Heb. 4:7). This does not mean that Christ was "appointed" to be the Son of God, but that the incarnate Son was "appointed to be the Son of God *with power*" in his state of exaltation.

of David according to [*kata*] the flesh" (v. 3), a contrast not of two natures in Christ but of the two states or historical stages of his incarnate existence. In his risen, exalted state, Christ no longer lives according to the weakness of human flesh but according to the power of the Holy Spirit (cf. 6:9–10; 1 Cor. 15:43–44).[52] He was "put to death in the flesh but made alive in the Spirit" (1 Pet. 3:18, authors' translation).[53] The eternal life given by the Holy Spirit permeates and characterizes the glorious existence of the risen Lord Jesus.

Though the Spirit filled Christ throughout his life (Luke 4:1; cf. John 1:14), Christ received a greater fullness when he ascended into heaven and sat down at God's right hand. Peter explained at Pentecost, "This Jesus hath God raised up, whereof we all are witnesses. Therefore being by the right hand of God exalted, and having received of the Father the promise of the Holy Ghost, he hath shed forth this, which ye now see and hear" (Acts 2:32–33). Irenaeus said, "The Lord, receiving this as a gift from His Father, does Himself also confer it upon those who are partakers of Himself, sending the Holy Spirit upon all the earth."[54]

God gave to Christ "all spiritual blessings" that he purchased on the cross, so that all those in union with Christ might share those riches by the same Spirit (Eph. 1:3, 7, 13–14).[55] Novatian (d. c. 258) said that the Holy Spirit is "dwelling in Christ full and entire . . . but with His whole overflow copiously distributed and sent forth, so that from Him others might receive some enjoyment of His graces: the source of the entire Holy Spirit remaining in Christ, so that from Him might be drawn streams of gifts and works, while the Holy Spirit dwelt affluently in Christ."[56] All in Christ is for us. Yet God has so ordered grace and glory that in all things Christ has the preeminence, for all the fullness dwells in him (Col. 1:18–19). Flavel said,

> Whatever spiritual grace or excellency is in Christ, it is not appropriated to himself, but they [his people] do share with him: for indeed he was filled with the fulness of the Spirit, for their sakes and use: as the sun is filled with light, not to shine to itself, but to others; so is Christ

52. John Murray, *The Epistle to the Romans*, The New International Commentary on the New Testament, 2 vols. (Grand Rapids, MI: Eerdmans, 1968), 1:7, 11.

53. Greek: *thanatōtheis men sarki zōopoiētheis de pneumati*. Compare 1 Tim. 3:16, "was manifest in the flesh, justified in the Spirit" (*ephanerōthē en sarki, edikaiōthē en pneumati*). The latter may refer to the resurrection, or it could refer to a complex of ways by which the Spirit vindicated Christ as God's righteous servant.

54. Irenaeus, *Against Heresies*, 3.17.2, in *ANF*, 1:445.

55. See Smeaton, *The Doctrine of the Holy Spirit*, 130.

56. Novatian, *Treatise Concerning the Trinity*, chap. 29, in *ANF*, 5:641.

> with grace. . . . Making Christ the first receptacle of grace, who first and immediately is filled from the fountain, the Godhead: but it is for his people, who receive and derive from him, according to their proportion. . . . But then, whatever dignity is ascribed herein to the saints, there is, and still must be, a pre-eminency acknowledged and ascribed to Christ.[57]

The Holy Spirit and Christ's Exalted Reign

The Lord revealed through Isaiah that the Holy Spirit would rest upon Christ with sevenfold grace: "The spirit of the LORD shall rest upon him, the spirit of wisdom and understanding, the spirit of counsel and might, the spirit of knowledge and of the fear of the LORD" (Isa. 11:2). Consequently, this Son of David (v. 1) would judge the world with righteousness and power (vv. 3–5), and establish his kingdom in peace and the knowledge of God (vv. 6–9). Therefore, the Spirit is the divine agent by whom Christ, "the mighty God" born as a child in Israel, reigns from "the throne of David" to build God's kingdom of peace and justice forever (9:6–7).

The sevenfold Spirit of Isaiah 11 appears again in the visions of Revelation as the "seven Spirits" before God's throne (Rev. 1:4; 4:5).[58] Christ is the Mediator of the sevenfold virtues of the Spirit, for he identifies himself as "he that hath the seven Spirits of God" (3:1). In the vision of the heavenly throne, John saw that there "stood a Lamb as it had been slain, having seven horns and seven eyes, which are the seven Spirits of God sent forth into all the earth" (5:6). Horns represent power (1 Sam. 2:10); eyes portray presence and knowledge (Prov. 15:3). The Holy Spirit is the omnipresent executive of Christ's power and knowledge throughout the world. Therefore, by the Spirit, Christ takes possession of those whom he redeemed by his blood and makes them into priest-kings who will reign with him forever (Rev. 5:9–10). The Spirit is the divine executive of the kingdom of God and Christ (Rom. 14:17). Ambrose of Milan said, "The work is one, the judgment one, the temple one, the lifegiving one, the sanctification one, and the kingdom also of the Father, Son, and Holy Spirit one."[59]

57. Flavel, *The Method of Grace*, in *Works*, 2:142.

58. The deity of the "seven Spirits" is evident in that John invokes grace and peace upon the churches "from him which is, and which was, and which is to come; and from the seven Spirits which are before his throne; and from Jesus Christ" (Rev. 1:4–5). To include angels with God and Christ as the source of grace and peace would be blasphemy; this language is fitting only for a fully divine person.

59. Ambrose, *Of the Holy Spirit*, 2.2.25, in *NPNF*[2], 10:118.

The Spirit is the living link between Christ and his redeemed (1 Cor. 6:17, 19).[60] The Heidelberg Catechism (LD 18, Q. 49) tells us that this is one of the great benefits of Christ's ascension into heaven, "that He sends us His Spirit as an earnest, by whose power we 'seek the things which are above, where Christ sitteth on the right hand of God, and not things on earth.'" The catechism (LD 19, Q. 51) says that Christ's being seated at God's right hand profits us because "by His Holy Spirit He pours out heavenly graces upon us His members."[61] Herman Witsius (1636–1708) said, "If through the Spirit we are Christ's, whatever belongs to Christ, belongs also to us."[62]

The Spirit of God acts on Christ's behalf as the Lord administers the new covenant. Paul says that the saints are "the epistle of Christ ministered by us, written not with ink, but with the Spirit of the living God; not in tables of stone, but in fleshy tables of the heart" (2 Cor. 3:3). Paul alludes to the prophetic promises of the new covenant (Jer. 31:33; Ezek. 36:26–27). In the metaphor, believers are a living epistle, Christ is the author, Paul is the scribe, the Spirit is the ink, and the heart is the parchment on which Christ writes.[63]

So closely allied are the risen Christ and the Spirit in their work that Paul can say, "The Lord is that Spirit" (2 Cor. 3:17). As Paul says elsewhere, "The last Adam was made a quickening spirit" (1 Cor. 15:45)—that is, "the Spirit who gives life" (*pneuma zōopoioun*). Sinclair Ferguson says that we cannot read these statements as "a denial of the distinction in personal existence between the Son and the Spirit," but rather should understand that "the Son and the Spirit share an identity of ministry." He adds, "With respect to his economic ministry to us, the Spirit has been 'imprinted' with the character of Jesus."[64] Herman Ridderbos (1909–2007) said, "As Christ in the present and future power of his redemptive work can be known only from the all-embracing renewal and consummation of the Spirit of God, so on the other hand the promise of the Spirit and of his life-giving power receives its fulfillment,

60. On mystical union with Christ by the Spirit, see chap. 10.

61. *The Three Forms of Unity*, 83–84. See also Polyander, Walaeus, Thysius, and Rivetus, *Synopsis Purioris Theologiae*, 28.20 (2:171).

62. Herman Witsius, *Sacred Dissertations on the Apostles' Creed*, 2 vols. (1823; repr., Grand Rapids, MI: Reformation Heritage Books, 2010), 23.38 (2:339).

63. Colin G. Kruse, *2 Corinthians: An Introduction and Commentary*, Tyndale New Testament Commentaries 8 (Downers Grove, IL: InterVarsity Press, 1987), 91.

64. Ferguson, *The Holy Spirit*, 54–55. See also Bavinck, *Reformed Dogmatics*, 3:436; 4:88.

its form, and its prospect only in the person of Christ as the exalted and coming Lord."[65]

In this new covenant work, Christ does not merely give his commands to his covenant people; he gives them life by the Holy Spirit (2 Cor. 3:6). As a result, there is great "glory" to the ministry of the Spirit, even greater than the visible glory of the ministry of Moses (vv. 7–9), for the Holy Spirit grants the transforming spiritual sight of Christ's glory that shapes his people into his image, changing them "from glory to glory" (v. 18). By the Spirit, God causes the light of his glory in Christ to shine in the hearts of formerly blind sinners (4:4–6). The Spirit of Christ is now the "spirit of faith" in God's people, just as he was before Christ came in the flesh (v. 13).[66] Though they are not outwardly glorious but "earthen vessels" that are perishing (vv. 7, 16), they carry within themselves treasure, power, and the life of Jesus, even an eternal weight of glory (vv. 7, 10–11, 17).

Implications of the Spirit of Christ for the Christian Life

If we love Jesus Christ, then we must also love the Holy Spirit and treasure his work in our lives. The Heidelberg Catechism (LD 21, Q. 54) says, "The Son of God from the beginning to the end of the world, gathers, defends, and preserves to Himself [his church] by His Spirit and Word."[67] Wherever we encounter the grace of Christ, we find the power of the Spirit. The quintessence of Christ's kingdom is the dynamic activity of the Holy Spirit. Whenever we pray, "Thy kingdom come," we are asking the Father to work by the Word and Spirit.[68] From regeneration to resurrection, all that is in Christ for us is of God the Spirit.

Perhaps surprisingly, the main application of the doctrine of the Holy Spirit is that we must exercise faith in Jesus Christ. Indeed, the inseparability of the Spirit from the Son is the very reason why Jesus is called the Christ or "Anointed," as the Heidelberg Catechism (LD 12, Q. 31) says: "He is ordained of God the Father, and anointed with the Holy Ghost, to be our chief Prophet and Teacher . . . and to be our only High Priest . . .

65. Herman Ridderbos, *Paul: An Outline of His Theology*, trans. John Richard de Witt (Grand Rapids, MI: Eerdmans, 1975), 88.

66. On the Holy Spirit as "the same spirit of faith" (2 Cor. 4:13), see the section on the evidence of the grace promised in the new covenant in chap. 3.

67. *The Three Forms of Unity*, 85. See Polyander, Walaeus, Thysius, and Rivetus, *Synopsis Purioris Theologiae*, 28.26, 31 (2:173, 177).

68. The Heidelberg Catechism (LD 48, Q. 123), in *The Three Forms of Unity*, 112.

and also to be our eternal King, who governs us by His Word and Spirit, and who defends and preserves us in (the enjoyment of) that salvation, He has purchased for us."[69]

Conversely, whenever we perceive any spiritual need in ourselves or our churches, we must go to Christ, in whom the fullness of the Spirit dwells, to meet that need. It is not easy for us to acknowledge this; our pride and self-sufficiency militate against it. Sibbes said, "Let us labour, then, to see where to have supply in all our wants. We have a full treasury to go to. All treasure is hid in Christ for us." The tendency of people to worship idols and trust in man arises from this. Sibbes wrote, "They conceive not aright of the fulness of Christ, wherefore he was ordained, and sent of God; for if they did, they would not go to idols and saints, and leave Christ."[70]

This doctrine rebukes Christians for spiritual weakness and lack of comfort. Sibbes said, "Men live as if Christ were nothing, or did nothing concerning them, as if he were a person abstracted from them, as if he were not a head or husband, as if he had received the Spirit only for himself and not for them, whereas all that is in Christ is for us."[71] Let us, therefore, stir ourselves up to take hold of Christ by faith, and in grasping Christ to receive the Spirit of God for our every need. Then we will be able to say, "I can do all things through Christ which strengtheneth me" (Phil. 4:13).

If we truly know the Spirit of Christ, we will walk in increasing holiness in the image of Christ. The Heidelberg Catechism (LD 32, Q. 86) says, "Christ, having redeemed and delivered us by His blood, also renews us by His Holy Spirit after His own image; that so we may testify, by the whole of our conduct, our gratitude to God for His blessings, and that He may be praised by us; also, that every one may be assured in himself of his faith by the fruits thereof; and that by our godly conversation [conduct] others may be gained to Christ."[72]

You are studying the doctrine of the Holy Spirit. Do not be only a hearer of the Word and not also a doer. Live the doctrine that you are learning. Follow Christ in faith, prayer, suffering, and obedience by the power of the Spirit. Look to Christ daily as the Mediator of the Spirit. And

---

69. *The Three Forms of Unity*, 78.
70. Sibbes, *A Description of Christ*, in *Works*, 1:20–21.
71. Sibbes, *A Description of Christ*, in *Works*, 1:21.
72. *The Three Forms of Unity*, 98.

have great hope, for the Savior is superabundantly full of the Spirit for all who call upon his name.

Sing to the Lord

The Father, the Son, and the Spirit

Come, thou Almighty King,
Help us thy Name to sing,
Help us to praise:
Father, all-glorious,
O'er all victorious,
Come and reign over us, Ancient of Days.

Come, thou Incarnate Word,
Gird on thy mighty sword,
Our prayer attend:
Come, and thy people bless,
And give thy Word success;
Spirit of Holiness,
On us descend.

Come, Holy Comforter,
Thy sacred witness bear
In this glad hour:
Thou who almighty art,
Now rule in every heart,
And ne'er from us depart,
Spirit of pow'r.

To the great One in Three
Eternal praises be,
Hence evermore.
His sovereign majesty
May we in glory see,
And to eternity
Love and adore.

Anonymous
Tune: Trinity
Trinity Hymnal—Baptist Edition, No. 89

Questions for Meditation or Discussion

1. What evidence does the Bible give that the Holy Spirit is the revealer of Christ, both before and after his coming in the flesh?
2. How was the Holy Spirit involved in the conception of Christ in Mary's womb?
3. Why should we forever praise the Spirit of God for the incarnation of Christ?
4. What is the significance of the Spirit's descent on Christ at his baptism?
5. How does the experience of God's children, as described in Romans 8:14–17, find its prototype in Jesus?
6. What does the Bible teach regarding the Spirit and Christ's healings of people and casting out of demons?
7. What reasons can be given that the "eternal Spirit" in Hebrews 9:14 is the Holy Spirit?
8. What Scripture passages indicate that the Holy Spirit raised Christ from the dead?
9. How is the Holy Spirit engaged in the ministry of Christ as he sits at God's right hand?
10. How has this chapter and its practical implications challenged you regarding your spiritual life? What action should you take in response?

Questions for Deeper Reflection

11. Why might someone think that the Spirit's empowerment of Christ to work miracles implies that Jesus was a mere man? How would you respond to this idea?
12. What difference should it make in Christian piety to know that the Holy Spirit was directly involved in Christ's sacrificial death and resurrection to life?

5

Pentecost and the Paraclete

Baptized with the Spirit

During the celebration of Pentecost after Christ's ascension, an extraordinary event took place that marked a new advance in redemptive history. God poured out the Holy Spirit with such power that the church in Jerusalem grew in one great surge from 120 members to more than three thousand. The book of Acts chronicles how subsequently the Lord worked to spread the Word of God from Judea to Rome. How shall we explain this remarkable multiplication of God's people into an international movement? Christ had promised that "the Comforter . . . shall testify of me" (John 15:26) and had said to his apostles, "Ye shall receive power . . . and ye shall be witnesses unto me . . . unto the uttermost part of the earth" (Acts 1:8).

Christ's outpouring of the Spirit inaugurated a new era in God's mighty works. The "age of the Spirit," so to speak, is the mediatorial reign of the exalted Christ. Herman Bavinck said, "The first activity Christ performs after his exaltation, therefore, consists in the outpouring of the Holy Spirit." After the creation and the incarnation with its attendant accomplishments, "the outpouring of the Holy Spirit is the third great work of God."[1]

1. Bavinck, *Reformed Dogmatics*, 3:499–500.

In this new age, the Spirit continues to do all his great works but in more profound ways and on a much larger scale. For so long the Spirit worked in hidden ways among a chosen few. Now he works powerfully in the lives of many, causing the kingdom of faith, love, and holiness to fill the earth. He does this in the name of Christ—on his behalf and for his glory.[2]

Christ's Baptism of His People with the Spirit at Pentecost

The biblical term for this outpouring of grace is baptism with the Spirit. It was revealed through the prophets, actualized at Pentecost, and explained by the apostle Paul.

The Expectation of the Prophets

John the Baptist foretold the outpouring of the Holy Spirit by the Lord of glory: "I baptize you with water, but he who is mightier than I is coming, the strap of whose sandals I am not worthy to untie. He will baptize you with the Holy Spirit and fire" (Luke 3:16 ESV). The Gospels emphasize Christ's divine majesty as the giver of this great gift (cf. Matt. 3:11; Mark 1:7–8).

Baptism with the Spirit is figurative language for inundation with heavenly grace. The word translated as "baptize" (*baptizō*) is rare in the Greek Septuagint version of the Old Testament, but its literal meaning is clear enough in examples of people bathing in water.[3] John the Baptist compared baptism with the Spirit with his baptizing of people in the Jordan River, implying an outpouring of the Spirit like abundant water.[4] Cyril of Jerusalem said, "This grace was not in part, but His power was in full perfection; for as he who plunges into the waters and is baptized is encompassed on all sides by the waters, so were they also baptized completely by the Holy Ghost. The water however flows round the outside only, but the Spirit baptizes also the soul within, and that completely."[5]

2. This paragraph is adapted from Joel R. Beeke, "The Age of the Spirit and Revival," *Puritan Reformed Journal* 2, no. 2 (July 2010): 37–38 (full article, 32–51). Used by permission.

3. 4 Kingdoms [2 Kings] 5:14; Judith 12:7; Sir. 34:25 LXX (cf. Num. 19:19). The word *baptizō* is used figuratively in Isa. 21:4 LXX of an overwhelming experience.

4. The parallel is clear, for the words translated as "water" and "Spirit" are both in the dative case, modifying "baptize": John baptized "with water" (*en hydati*, Matt. 3:11; John 1:26; *hydati*, Mark 1:8; Luke 3:16; Acts 1:5) and Christ would baptize "with the Holy Spirit" (*en pneumati hagiō*, Matt. 3:11; Mark 1:8; Luke 3:16; John 1:33; Acts 1:5).

5. Cyril of Jerusalem, *Catechetical Lectures*, 17.14, in *NPNF*², 7:127.

The setting of this promise is eschatological and covenantal. John the Baptist moved seamlessly from Spirit baptism to judgment day, when Christ will destroy his enemies with unquenchable fire (Luke 3:16–17). Baptism "with the Holy Ghost and with fire" (v. 16) thus "involves nothing less than the eschatological judgment with its dual outcomes of salvation or destruction," as Richard Gaffin says.[6] John warned his fellow Israelites that physical descent from Abraham did not make a person a true member of the covenant people, for God raises up "children unto Abraham" by his supernatural power (v. 8), and they must show their identity by repentance that produces practical fruit in mercy and justice or fall under God's judgment (vv. 9–14). Therefore, the baptism of the Spirit is God's grace to his true people in the last times.

John echoed ancient prophecy, just as his own ministry was foretold by the prophets (Luke 3:4–5, citing Isa. 40:3–4). The Lord had said, "Fear not, O Jacob, my servant; and thou, Jesurun, whom I have chosen. I will pour water upon him that is thirsty, and floods upon the dry ground: I will pour my spirit upon thy seed, and my blessing upon thine offspring: and they shall spring up as among the grass, as willows by the water courses" (Isa. 44:2–4). The gift of the Spirit functions as a defining mark of God's renewed covenantal people, for it moves each of them to confess, "I am the Lord's," and to call himself by "the name of Israel" (v. 5). In the context, the Lord commissioned his people to be his "witnesses" that he alone is God (v. 8). In a similar promise in Joel 2:28, the Lord said, "I will pour out my spirit upon all flesh." The context locates this outpouring in a time of salvation prior to the day of the Lord (vv. 30–32).

Shortly after John compared his baptizing with water to Christ's future baptizing with the Spirit, John baptized Jesus, and then the Spirit descended upon Christ (Luke 3:16, 21–22). God had said to John, "Upon whom thou shalt see the Spirit descending, and remaining on him, the same is he which baptizeth with the Holy Ghost" (John 1:33). Christ's anointing and Pentecost are linked as "two stages in the communication of the Spirit," George Smeaton noted, the first "to equip the Redeemer for entering on his office" and the second to supply the church with "various gifts, by which it efficiently exercises the spiritual life for the advancement of Christ's cause."[7]

---

6. Richard B. Gaffin, *Perspectives on Pentecost: New Testament Teaching on the Gifts of the Holy Spirit* (Phillipsburg, NJ: Presbyterian and Reformed, 1979), 15.

7. Smeaton, *The Doctrine of the Holy Spirit*, 240.

The Events of Pentecost

After Jesus Christ had died and risen from the dead, he told his disciples that they would be his "witnesses" to "all nations, beginning at Jerusalem" and commanded them to wait in Jerusalem until "I send the promise of my Father upon you . . . until ye be endued with power from on high" (Luke 24:47–49; cf. Acts 1:4). The Spirit is called "the promise" of the Father because God's covenantal promises are summed up and fulfilled in baptism with the Spirit.[8] Christ explained, "For John truly baptized with water; but ye shall be baptized with the Holy Ghost not many days hence. . . . But ye shall receive power, after that the Holy Ghost is come upon you: and ye shall be witnesses unto me both in Jerusalem, and in all Judaea, and in Samaria, and unto the uttermost part of the earth" (Acts 1:5, 8). The words "not many days hence" show that Christ referred here to the outpouring of the Spirit at Pentecost (Acts 2).[9]

The calling of the apostles to serve as "witnesses" to the risen Lord Jesus is a central theme in Acts as it traces the fulfillment of God's promises in the expansion of Christ's church.[10] "Witness" language is legal and judicial, drawing on Isaiah's theme of God's "lawsuit" against idolaters, in which he calls for witnesses to demonstrate that he alone is God and Savior (Isa. 43:8–13; 44:8–9; 45:20–25). Christ's focusing of the witness on himself implies his deity and sole mediation of salvation. The Spirit is the divine agent to empower the apostolic witness so that people are brought to trust in Christ for the glory of God alone.

After Christ ascended into heaven, the disciples gathered in Jerusalem, seeking God in prayer and waiting for the baptism of the Spirit as the Lord had commanded.[11] The day of Pentecost arrived, or literally "was fulfilled" (*symplēroō*, Acts 2:1), language suggesting the coming of a major event in redemptive history (Luke 9:51). As was the case with Christ's incarnation and birth, so the coming of the Holy Spirit was "accompanied by miraculous signs."[12] There was "a sound from heaven as of a rushing mighty wind" that filled the house and "tongues like as of fire . . . [that] sat upon each of them. And they were all filled with the Holy Ghost, and began to speak with other tongues, as the Spirit gave them utterance" (Acts

8. Acts 2:31, 33; Gal. 3:8, 14, 16; Eph. 1:3, 13.
9. Anthony A. Hoekema, *Holy Spirit Baptism* (Grand Rapids, MI: Eerdmans, 1972), 18.
10. Acts 1:8, 22; 2:32; 3:15; 4:33; 5:32; 10:39, 41; 13:31; 22:15, 18; 23:11; 26:16, 22.
11. Luke 24:49–53; Acts 1:4–5, 12–15; 2:1.
12. Thomas, *The Holy Spirit*, 113.

2:2–4).[13] Filled by the power of the Spirit, Peter preached Christ in the very city where Jesus had been crucified, and three thousand were converted (v. 41). Peter explained that God was fulfilling his promise through the prophet Joel to pour out his Spirit on all flesh because the last days had begun (v. 17).

In the audible and visible theophany of Pentecost, "wind" (*pnoē*) showed the presence of the "Spirit" (*pneuma*). Flaming tongues suggested that the Spirit fills people so that their hearts burn with love for God and they speak the word of Christ to inflame the hearts of others.[14] The wind's filling "all the house" and the flames' resting "upon each of them" showed that the Spirit comes to the church collectively and individually to each one in it.[15] The combination of wind and fire from heaven may have alluded to the Lord sending fire upon Elijah's altar to evoke the worship of unfaithful Israel and sending wind to bring the rain of covenantal blessing after a drought (1 Kings 18:38–39, 45). Later, God caught up Elijah to heaven in a "whirlwind" and "fire," and gave Elijah's "spirit" to Elisha (2 Kings 2:9–12, 15–16), a foreshadowing of Christ's ascension and outpouring of the Spirit on the apostolic church.[16]

Pentecost was an annual feast in the Jewish calendar. Occurring on the "fiftieth day" (Greek *pentēkostē hēmera*) after the Passover, it was known as "the feast of weeks," when Israel brought the firstfruits of the wheat harvest to the Lord.[17] The salvation of Jews from many places during this feast after the outpouring of the Spirit suggests that Christ gathered the firstfruits of a great harvest from the nations (cf. Rom. 16:5; 1 Cor. 16:15) by the power of the Spirit (Luke 24:47–49; Acts 1:8). The supernatural ability given to the disciples to declare the glory of God in the tongues of many nations was a reversal of Babel, where God supernaturally divided humanity by confusing their tongues because people sought their own glory (Gen. 11:1–9). Through Jesus Christ, the Seed of Abraham, and those united to him, God was beginning to fulfill his purpose to bless all the families of the earth.[18]

---

13. It is not clear from Acts 2 whether those filled with the Spirit to speak in tongues were only the apostles or all of the 120 disciples. The immediate context explicitly focuses on the apostles (Acts 1:2, 26; 2:14, 37). However, hearing them speak in tongues affected a "multitude," and Joel's prophecy spoke of men and women (2:4–6, 17–18).

14. Gregory the Great, cited in Stanley M. Burgess, *The Holy Spirit: Medieval Roman Catholic and Reformation Traditions (Sixth–Sixteenth Centuries)* (Peabody, MA: Hendrickson, 1997), 14.

15. Pink, *The Holy Spirit*, 39–40.

16. Gerald Bilkes, "Precursors to Pentecost," in *The Beauty and Glory of the Holy Spirit*, ed. Joel R. Beeke and Joseph A. Pipa (Grand Rapids, MI: Reformation Heritage Books, 2012), 59–65.

17. Ex. 23:16; 34:22; Lev. 23:15–22; Deut. 16:9–12.

18. Gen. 12:1–3; 22:18; Gal. 3:8, 17, 26–29.

The baptism of the Spirit signaled the inauguration of God's kingdom. Luke situates Christ's promise of Spirit baptism (Acts 1:5) in the context of his "speaking of the things pertaining to the kingdom of God" (v. 3). The restoration of the kingdom to Israel in the open glory of the Son of David had to await the time hidden in God's decree (v. 6). However, Christ said that the power of the Holy Spirit would enable the disciples to be his witnesses "both in Jerusalem, and in all Judaea, and in Samaria, and unto the uttermost part of the earth" (v. 8). This is not a program for our involvement in missions, beginning with our community ("our Jerusalem"), for Jerusalem was not the home of the apostles, who were Galileans (Acts 1:11; 2:7). Instead, the mission "beginning at Jerusalem," a great theme of the Old Testament (Luke 24:44–47), lay in God's covenant to establish the monarchy of David's kingdom and the house of the Lord on Mount Zion.[19] Jerusalem is "the city of David."[20] Therefore, the beginning of the apostles' mission in Jerusalem signified the initiation of the messianic kingdom (Acts 2:29–36; 15:14–17).[21] Gaffin concludes that baptism with the Holy Spirit at Pentecost is "closely connected with the epochal, climactic events of Christ's work, especially his resurrection and ascension," for the kingdom has "already" come though it is "not yet" in open glory.[22]

By baptizing his church in Jerusalem with the Holy Spirit, Christ began the work of drawing individuals from all nations into one covenant people (cf. Eph. 2:18–19). The Jews who heard the gospel of Christ came from "every nation under heaven" (Acts 2:5). The Spirit was poured out on "all flesh" (v. 17). Though God kept his promise in Jerusalem, the kingdom now centered on a throne in heaven (v. 34). The gift of the Spirit was still offered to the Jews and their children, but also "to all that are afar off, even as many as the Lord our God shall call" (v. 39). After the Spirit was poured out, people of many nations lived together in remarkable unity as one church (vv. 44, 46). Later, the Spirit directed Peter to preach the gospel to Gentiles (10:19; 11:12), and the Spirit fell on them before Peter finished his sermon. Peter later said, "Then remembered I the word of the Lord, how that he said, John indeed baptized with water; but ye shall be baptized with the Holy Ghost. Forasmuch then as God gave them the like gift as he did unto us, who believed on the Lord Jesus Christ; what was I,

19. 1 Kings 11:13, 32, 36; 15:4; 2 Kings 21:7; 2 Chron. 6:6; Ps. 132:11–18.
20. 2 Sam. 5:7, 9; 6:10, 12, 16; three dozen times in Kings and Chronicles.
21. Isa. 2:1–5; 4:2–6; 11:9; 12:6; 18:7; 24:23; 28:16; 40:9; 46:13; 52:7; 59:20; 62:1–5.
22. Gaffin, *Perspectives on Pentecost*, 17.

that I could withstand God?" (vv. 16–17). The same baptism of the Spirit that launched the mission also bound together Jews and Gentiles as one people in Christ.

Since Pentecost, Christ grants the baptism of the Holy Spirit to the whole church and to every true member of it. Peter said, "Repent, and be baptized every one of you in the name of Jesus Christ for the remission of sins, and ye shall receive the gift of the Holy Ghost" (Acts 2:38). The same Spirit baptism that Christ gave his entire church is also granted to those who are converted and join that church. The same word translated as "gift" (*dōrea*) is used elsewhere in Acts for the baptism or outpouring of the Spirit.[23] The normative experience of the church is that all the saints are baptized with the Spirit, though not all are filled with the Spirit (Eph. 5:18).[24]

The Explanation of Paul

Outside of Acts, the only other mention of baptism with the Holy Spirit occurs in Paul's words: "For as the body is one, and hath many members, and all the members of that one body, being many, are one body: so also is Christ. For by one Spirit are we all baptized into one body, whether we be Jews or Gentiles, whether we be bond or free; and have been all made to drink into one Spirit" (1 Cor. 12:12–13).[25] The latter statement indicates that the Spirit irrigates all believers' souls with the heavenly graces of Christ.[26] The body of Christ is the oasis of the Holy Spirit in the barren wilderness of this world. Athanasius said, "When we are made to drink of the Spirit, we drink of Christ (1 Cor. 10:4)."[27] In this context, Paul speaks of the Spirit's empowerment of each member to serve the body (12:4–11) so that every member contributes to its life (vv. 14–27).

The baptism of the Spirit unites all those who belong to Christ. Though the Corinthian church was marred by immaturity (1 Cor. 3:1–3), Paul did not command its members to be baptized with the Spirit, but taught them that they already shared in this baptism as members of Christ's body. Just

23. Acts 8:19–20; 10:45; 11:16–17. See Stott, *Baptism and Fullness*, 25.

24. On the filling of the Spirit, see chap. 32.

25. Other texts sometimes interpreted as teaching Spirit baptism are Rom. 6:3–4; Gal. 3:27; Eph. 4:5; Col. 2:12. However, these texts more likely refer to the sacrament or ordinance of baptism as a sign of union with Christ.

26. The verb translated as "made to drink" (*potizō*, cf. Rom. 12:20) may also be used of watering plants (1 Cor. 3:6–8), and thus is used of God's pouring out of the Spirit like water in a dry land to give drink to the animals (Isa. 43:20 LXX; cf. Num. 20:8; Ps. 35:9 [36:8] LXX).

27. Athanasius, *The Letters of Saint Athanasius concerning the Holy Spirit*, 1.19 (112).

as believers are "one Spirit" with Christ (6:17), so they are united by "one Spirit" with each other in Christ (12:13; Eph. 2:18; 4:4).

Though they do not use the words "baptize" or "baptism," other texts in Paul's epistles also speak of the Spirit and his influences being "shed" or "poured out" (*ekcheō*), the same verb used of the Pentecostal outpouring of the Spirit.[28] Paul wrote to Titus that the Holy Spirit had been "shed on us abundantly through Jesus Christ our Saviour" (Titus 3:6). The "us" in this text refers to those who have been regenerated (v. 5) and justified (v. 7)—all believers in Christ. This was not merely the personal experience of Paul and Titus, but a truth to be taught to the church (v. 8). Similarly, Paul wrote to the Roman saints, "Hope does not put us to shame, because God's love has been poured into our hearts through the Holy Spirit who has been given to us" (Rom. 5:5 ESV).

Though Paul gives us several commands regarding our duty with respect to the Holy Spirit,[29] not once does he command us to be baptized with the Spirit.[30] Therefore, we conclude that since Pentecost, God gives the baptism or outpouring of the Spirit to all believers.

Summary: Baptized with the Spirit

At Pentecost, Christ baptized his people with the Holy Spirit, and he continues to incorporate each new convert into his church by the same baptism with the Spirit. This baptism arises from Christ's office as the mediatorial Lord of the Spirit. Gaffin says, "The gift (baptism, outpouring) of the Spirit is the crowning achievement of Christ's work. It is his coming in exaltation to the church in the power of the Spirit."[31] Christ received the Spirit's fullness at his baptism and an even greater measure of fullness at his session at God's right hand that he might share the Spirit with those in union with him. The Spirit baptism of the church at Pentecost was a unique redemptive-historical event, marking the initiation of the kingdom of the ascended Son of David. Richard Sibbes said, "Therefore, the church is fuller of grace, and grace hath been more spread and diffused since the ascension of Christ than before."[32] By baptizing his people with the Spirit, Christ floods them with an abundance of grace, empowers them all to

28. Acts 2:17–18, 33; cf. 10:45–47.
29. For example, see Gal. 5:16; Eph. 4:30; 5:18; 1 Thess. 5:19.
30. Stott, *Baptism and Fullness*, 50.
31. Gaffin, *Perspectives on Pentecost*, 20.
32. Sibbes, *A Description of Christ*, in *Works*, 1:23.

serve him for the building of his church, and unites them as one people. Therefore, baptism with the Spirit is not identical to regeneration, which the Spirit has worked through the ages.[33] However, it belongs to all of God's children.

The doctrine of baptism with the Spirit displays the great spiritual advance that God granted to his people by the humiliation and exaltation of his Son. Formerly the Spirit usually worked among godly Israelites in relatively hidden ways; now the Holy Spirit inundates the people of God. Once the Spirit empowered only a limited number of people, especially covenantal officers, to serve God's kingdom; now the Spirit of Christ empowers every saint to build up the body. In previous times, the Spirit focused his activity upon the nation of Israel; now he powerfully evangelizes and unites individuals from all nations and social classes to form one body in Christ. Pentecost was the D-Day of Christ's worldwide assault upon Satan's kingdom. It challenges us to ask ourselves, "Is it my passion that the nations will glorify God through the gospel?"[34]

The Claims of Pentecostalism

Contrary to our conclusions, some teachers assert that baptism with the Holy Spirit or the gift of the Spirit is a second blessing distinct from the grace given initially in salvation.[35] In Roman Catholicism, this grace corresponds to the sacrament of confirmation, in which the baptized faithful receive the full anointing of the Spirit.[36] Some theologians in Protestant traditions, including but not limited to Pentecostalism, also teach a baptism of the Spirit that grants greater holiness and power to believers.[37] The theological roots of Pentecostalism lie in the Wesleyan-Arminian doctrine of Christian perfection and the various holiness and higher-life movements to which it gave birth, matters that we will discuss under the doctrine of

33. Calvin identified the baptism of the Spirit with regeneration granted before Pentecost. Calvin, *Commentaries*, on Matt. 3:11; Acts 1:5. However, Calvin recognized that at Pentecost Christ poured out the Spirit with unprecedented "plenty" upon a "multitude." *Commentaries*, on Acts 2:17.

34. Steven J. Cole, sermon of October 8, 2000, cited in Thomas, *The Holy Spirit*, 129.

35. On the false doctrine of a second blessing, see chap. 28.

36. Thomas Aquinas, *Summa Theologica*, trans. Fathers of the English Dominican Province (London: R. & T. Washbourne, 1915), Part 3, Q. 72, Art. 1, Reply Obj. 1; Art. 2, Obj. 1 and Reply Obj. 1; Art. 6; and *Catechism of the Catholic Church* (New York: Doubleday, 1994), secs. 1285–89, 1294–95. The sacraments of the Roman Catholic Church are a topic to be considered under ecclesiology in *RST*, vol. 4 (forthcoming).

37. R. A. Torrey, *The Baptism with the Holy Spirit* (Chicago: The Bible Institute Colportage Association, 1895), 11–12, 16; and D. Martyn Lloyd-Jones, *The Baptism and Gifts of the Spirit*, ed. Christopher Catherwood (Grand Rapids, MI: Baker, 1994), 23, 42, 105–19, 133, 271, 273.

sanctification.[38] Here we focus on the Pentecostal doctrine of subsequence: that baptism with the Spirit is distinct from salvation and often received after conversion.

Introduction to the Pentecostal and Charismatic Movements

The doctrine of a subsequent baptism with the Spirit figures most prominently in the Pentecostal and charismatic movements, which teach that God still grants gifts of miraculous knowledge and power to the church. This doctrine is often coupled with the belief that God is restoring the church to its New Testament vitality in a "latter rain" of the Spirit before the end of the age (cf. Joel 2:23; James 5:7).[39] Modern Pentecostalism can be traced back to unusual events in 1901 among the students of Charles F. Parham (1873–1929) and a series of meetings led by William J. Seymour (1870–1922) beginning in 1906 at Azusa Street in Los Angeles, California.[40] These meetings gave birth to Trinitarian Pentecostal churches such as the Assemblies of God and to the anti-Trinitarian movement of oneness Pentecostalism.[41] In the 1960s Pentecostal teaching penetrated Protestant churches and the Roman Catholic Church, resulting in the "charismatic" movements (from the Greek *charisma*, "gift").[42] It should also be noted that some Christians who affirm the continuation of charismatic gifts differ from classic Pentecostalism in its doctrine of subsequence by teaching that all believers are baptized by the Spirit.[43]

The Assemblies of God denomination confesses the classic doctrine of Pentecostalism:

> All believers are entitled to and should ardently expect and earnestly seek the promise of the Father, the baptism in the Holy Spirit and fire,

38. See chap. 28.

39. Donald W. Dayton, *Theological Roots of Pentecostalism* (Grand Rapids, MI: Zondervan, 1987), 26–28.

40. Parham taught Pentecostal doctrine to Seymour, but later harshly criticized Seymour's services at Azusa Street. On the history, see Vinson Synan, *The Holiness-Pentecostal Tradition: Charismatic Movements in the Twentieth Century*, 2nd ed. (Grand Rapids, MI: Eerdmans, 1997), 90–103.

41. On oneness Pentecostalism, see *RST*, 1:924. For the affirmation of the doctrine of the Trinity by the Assemblies of God, see its "Statement of Fundamental Truths," no. 2, https://ag.org/Beliefs/Statement-of-Fundamental-Truths.

42. See Chad Owen Brand, introduction to *Perspectives on Spirit Baptism: Five Views*, ed. Chad Owen Brand (Nashville: B&H Academic, 2004), 12–13.

43. Rich Nathan and Ken Wilson, *Empowered Evangelicals: Bringing Together the Best of the Evangelical and Charismatic Worlds*, rev. ed. (Boise, ID: Ampelon, 2009). This perspective is associated with what Peter Wagner called the "third wave." C. Peter Wagner, *The Third Wave of the Holy Spirit: Encountering the Power of Signs and Wonders Today* (Ann Arbor, MI: Servant, 1988). However, it is held by a variety of Pentecostals and charismatics.

according to the command of our Lord Jesus Christ. This was the normal experience of all in the early Christian Church. With it comes the enduement of power for life and service, the bestowment of the gifts and their uses in the work of the ministry (Luke 24:49; Acts 1:4, 8; 1 Cor. 12:1–31). This experience is distinct from and subsequent to the experience of the new birth (Acts 8:12–17; 10:44–46; 11:14–16; 15:7–9).

The baptism of believers in the Holy Spirit is witnessed by the initial physical sign of speaking with other tongues as the Spirit of God gives them utterance (Acts 2:4). The speaking in tongues in this instance is the same in essence as the gift of tongues, but is different in purpose and use (1 Cor. 12:4–10, 28).[44]

The Arguments of Pentecostal and Charismatic Theology

Pentecostal and charismatic theologians present the following arguments.

First, they argue that many Christians have received authentic *spiritual experiences of a baptism with power after conversion*. Indeed, they claim that this experience of Spirit baptism is self-illuminating, for it "gives the interpreter of relevant Biblical texts an experiential presupposition which transcends the rational or cognitive presuppositions of scientific exegesis, and furthermore, results in an understanding, empathy, and sensitivity to the text."[45]

In reply, we acknowledge that the spiritual experience of true faith in Christ brings an illumination to the meaning of Scripture not found in the highest intellectual exercises of unbelievers (1 Cor. 2:14–16). However, to elevate a particular experience as a presupposition for biblical exegesis is the road to mysticism and elitism. Experiences must always be tested and interpreted according to God's written Word, not vice versa.[46]

How do we explain the experiences of those who claim they have been baptized with the Holy Spirit? Spiritual experiences come from a variety of sources. Satan is active in the church and the world (2 Cor. 11:13–15; 1 John 4:1–6). Human nature can produce strong psychological and physical responses to human stimuli (1 Sam. 25:37), and even responses to God that are not of his saving grace (Mark 4:16–17; John 18:6). Furthermore,

44. Assemblies of God, "Statement of Fundamental Truths," no. 7, https://ag.org/Beliefs/Statement-of-Fundamental-Truths#7. The Assemblies of God affirmed essentially the same words in its original statement of 1916. Stanley M. Horton, "A Pentecostal Perspective," in *Perspectives on Spirit Baptism*, ed. Brand, 54–55.

45. Roger Stronstrad, cited in Stanley Horton, "A Pentecostal Perspective," in *Perspectives on Spirit Baptism*, ed. Brand, 56.

46. Walter C. Kaiser Jr., "Response" to a Pentecostal perspective, in *Perspectives on Spirit Baptism*, ed. Brand, 96–97.

people may misinterpret regeneration, a fresh filling of the Spirit, or progressive sanctification as Spirit baptism. For example, both Pentecostals and non-Pentecostals have experienced growth in assurance of God's love that empowers them to serve the Lord more effectively (Ps. 51:12–13).[47] Christians may have transforming experiences of communion with the Holy Spirit when he powerfully witnesses with their spirits that they are children of God (Rom. 8:16). Finally, an event in a believer's life may arise from a combination of demonic, human, and/or divine factors (Matt. 16:15–23; Mark 9:2–6). Therefore, it is possible that an authentic experience of the Holy Spirit may be combined with other manifestations that are not from him.

Second, Pentecostals may argue that *Paul and Luke are not speaking of the same gift*. It is said that in Paul's theology, the Spirit baptizes us into Christ, whereas Luke says that Christ baptizes us with the Spirit.[48]

In reply, we note that Paul uses the same Greek words and grammatical syntax to describe Spirit baptism as in other references to it in the Gospels and Acts.[49] Gordon Fee, a Pentecostal scholar, concludes that Paul presents the Spirit as "the element 'in which' one is baptized."[50] Paul's teaching about the Spirit in 1 Corinthians 12 corresponds to that in the book of Acts, where baptism with the Spirit empowered ministry and unity (Acts 2:17–18, 44–46; 11:16–17).

Third, Pentecostals and charismatics may object that Paul's teaching in 1 Corinthians 12:13 indicates only *the extraordinary experience of the early church*, in which everyone was baptized with the Spirit.[51] This is not the case for many Christians today, but God has now brought charismatic renewal.[52]

---

47. J. I. Packer, *Keep in Step with the Spirit* (Old Tappan, NJ: Fleming H. Revell, 1984), 197, 225.

48. *NIDPCM*, 355. This objection may be made based on the KJV's rendering of 1 Cor. 12:13: "*by* one Spirit are we all baptized." That translation may have arisen from the early modern association of this text with the sacrament of baptism. Calvin, *Commentaries*, on 1 Cor. 12:13; Anonymous [Westminster Divines], *Annotations upon All the Books of the Old and New Testament* (London: Evan Tyler, 1657), on 1 Cor. 12:13; Anonymous [Dutch Reformed Divines], *The Dutch Annotations upon the Whole Bible*, trans. Theodore Haak (London: by Henry Hills, for John Rothwell, Joshua Kirton, and Richard Tomlins, 1657), on 1 Cor. 12:13; and Poole, *Annotations upon the Holy Bible*, 3:583, on 1 Cor. 12:13.

49. Compare *en heni pneumati . . . ebaptisthēmen* (1 Cor. 12:13) with *en pneumati hagiō* (Matt. 3:11; Mark 1:8; Luke 3:16; John 1:33; Acts 1:5). See Stott, *Baptism and Fullness*, 40; Grudem, *Systematic Theology*, 767–68; and J. Rodman Williams, *Renewal Theology*, 3 vols. (Grand Rapids, MI: Zondervan, 1990), 2:199.

50. Fee, *God's Empowering Presence*, 181.

51. Stanley Horton, "A Pentecostal Perspective," in *Perspectives on Spirit Baptism*, ed. Brand, 67; and Lloyd-Jones, *The Baptism and Gifts of the Spirit*, 38.

52. Williams, *Renewal Theology*, 2:327.

In reply, we argue that the assertion that *all* first-century Christians were baptized with the Spirit seems contradictory to Pentecostalism's doctrine that God ordinarily gives this gift in response to believers' praying with expectant faith while obediently submitting to God.[53] Did all early Christians do this? Did all the saints in Corinth, a church sharply rebuked for its immaturity, do this? Furthermore, Paul's statement gives every indication that Spirit baptism is granted to all believers in Christ. He does not say "you" were baptized, but "we all" (1 Cor. 12:13). The baptism pertains to the "one body"—a point that would be lost if it applied only to a segment of those in Christ. The words "Jews or Gentiles" and "bond or free" echo what Paul teaches elsewhere regarding the radical unity shared by all in union with Christ (Gal. 3:28; Col. 3:11).

Fourth, based on *the historical narratives of Acts*, Pentecostal theologians argue that believers often received the baptism of the Spirit after conversion.[54]

In reply, we assert that we cannot build a doctrine of a subsequent baptism with the Holy Spirit with speaking in tongues on the narratives in Acts because, as John Stott (1921–2011) observed, "there is no consistency about them."[55] Table 5.1 below shows that there is no indication that Luke intended to present a normative pattern concerning the relation between Spirit baptism and conversion, water baptism, laying on of hands, and speaking in tongues.

Coming of the Spirit	Timing of Conversion	Timing of Water Baptism	Laying On of Hands	Speaking in Tongues
Pentecost Event (Acts 2:1–4)	Long before Filling with Spirit	Not Mentioned	Not Mentioned	Yes
Pentecost Sermon (Acts 2:38)	Closely Linked to Gift of Spirit	Closely Linked to Gift of Spirit	Not Mentioned	Not Mentioned
Samaritans (Acts 8:12–17)	Days before Receiving Spirit	Days before Receiving Spirit	Yes	Not Mentioned

53. Williams, *Renewal Theology*, 2:271–72, 295–306; and Stanley Horton, "A Pentecostal Perspective," in *Perspectives on Spirit Baptism*, ed. Brand, 91–92.

54. *NIDPCM*, 356–57; Williams, *Renewal Theology*, 2:273–76; and Stanley Horton, "A Pentecostal Perspective," in *Perspectives on Spirit Baptism*, ed. Brand, 56–67.

55. Stott, *Baptism and Fullness*, 30.

Coming of the Spirit	Timing of Conversion	Timing of Water Baptism	Laying On of Hands	Speaking in Tongues
Saul of Tarsus (Acts 9:17–18)	Shortly before Filling with Spirit	Shortly after Filling with Spirit	Yes	Not Mentioned
Peter and Cornelius I (Acts 10:44–48)	Simultaneous with Gift of Spirit	Shortly after Gift of Spirit	Not Mentioned	Yes
Peter and Cornelius II (Acts 11:15–18)	Simultaneous with Gift of Spirit	Not Mentioned	Not Mentioned	Not Mentioned
Peter and Cornelius III (Acts 15:7–9)	Simultaneous with Gift of Spirit	Not Mentioned	Not Mentioned	Not Mentioned
Men in Ephesus (Acts 19:5–6)	Unclear	Shortly before Coming of Spirit	Yes	Yes

Table 5.1. Elements Accompanying the Initial Coming of the Spirit on People in Acts

Furthermore, there were special circumstances surrounding these events. The baptism of Christ's disciples with the Spirit at Pentecost involved those already saved experiencing the fulfillment of God's promise to David through Christ's resurrection, ascension, and session at God's right hand—the beginning of "the last days" (Acts 2:17, 25–36). Sinclair Ferguson says, "Their experience is epoch-crossing, and consequently atypical."[56] The mission to the Samaritans, a significant step in the expansion of Jewish-Christian witness (1:8), bridged a gap of tremendous ethnic hostility.[57] The delay of the baptism with the Spirit until the Jewish apostles came and laid hands on the Samaritan converts formed a strong bond to maintain the unity of the church.[58] The conversion of Saul of Tarsus was a unique event with massive implications for the Gentile mission. When God sent the gospel to the Gentiles of Cornelius's house, the outward sign of speaking in tongues impressed

56. Ferguson, *The Holy Spirit*, 80.
57. Matt. 10:5; Luke 9:52; 10:33; 17:16–18; John 4:9; 8:48.
58. Though the word translated as "baptize" (*baptizō*) is not used of the Spirit in Acts 8, the verb translated as "fall upon" (*epipiptō*, 8:16) is used of Spirit baptism elsewhere (11:15–16).

upon the Jews that believing Gentiles truly received the same Pentecostal Spirit and belonged to the same people of God. The disciples in Ephesus may not have been saved prior to meeting Paul, for they were ignorant of even John the Baptist's message about the Spirit, and Paul administered Christian baptism to them for the first time.[59] Furthermore, they might function as an example of the gospel reaching the Gentiles at "the ends of the earth" (1:8; 13:47) to include them with Israel, as their number "twelve" suggests (19:7).[60] Therefore, the experiences recorded in Acts do not offer biblical support for the doctrine of a distinct baptism of the Spirit after conversion.

Examining Table 5.1 also shows the impossibility of grounding on the book of Acts the doctrine that speaking in tongues is the normative initial evidence of being baptized with the Spirit. Among the several accounts of the initial coming of the Spirit, Luke mentions speaking in tongues in only three texts. In his epistles, Paul does not identify tongues as a sign of any special level of spiritual grace or empowerment, but one among many gifts that the Spirit distributes as he wills (1 Cor. 12:10–11). Paul implies, through a series of rhetorical questions, that it is not God's will that all members have any one gift: "Are all apostles? Are all prophets? Are all teachers? Are all workers of miracles? Have all the gifts of healing? Do all speak with tongues? Do all interpret?" (vv. 29–30). The answer is no.[61] This paves the way for Paul's argument that tongues, though good, is a lesser gift (14:5, 19).

Fifth, Pentecostals and charismatics argue that the verb translated as "believed" in Acts 11:17 and 19:2 has a *particular grammatical form* (aorist participle), which shows that its action precedes the action of the main verbs. Hence, believing precedes the giving and receiving of the Spirit.[62]

In reply, we assert that this argument is at best a dubious basis for the doctrine. The grammatical form under consideration sometimes implies

59. It might be argued that by calling them "disciples" (*mathētēs*), Luke indicates that they were Christians. However, the term "disciples" was also used of followers of John and the Pharisees (Luke 5:33; 7:18–19; 11:1). Furthermore, even if they professed to be "disciples" of Christ, the reality might have been otherwise.

60. Horton, *Rediscovering the Holy Spirit*, 195. Of course, the gospel reached the Gentiles long before this event.

61. Stanley Horton seeks to evade the force of this argument by asserting a distinction between speaking in tongues as an initial evidence of Spirit baptism and the regular gift of tongues. The latter alone is said to be implied in the present tense Greek verb translated as "speak" (*lalousi*, 1 Cor. 12:30). Horton, "A Pentecostal Perspective," in *Perspectives on Spirit Baptism*, ed. Brand, 76. However, it seems overly subtle to expect that the Corinthians would pick up on this nuance if all of them could say, "But I *did* speak in tongues!" Earlier, Paul speaks of God giving to some "various kinds of tongues" (*genē glōssōn*, vv. 10, 28) without anything that would distinguish a one-time exercise from a continuing gift.

62. Stanley Horton, "A Pentecostal Perspective," in *Perspectives on Spirit Baptism*, ed. Brand, 63, 65–66.

sequence in time, but it often does not when both verbs are in the same tense (aorist), as is the case here.[63] Also, an aorist participle may further describe the same event as the main verb.[64] Thus, when Paul asked if the Ephesian disciples literally had "received believing" (*elabete pisteusantes*), he may well have been referring to one act of receiving the Spirit when they trusted in Christ (cf. Gal. 3:1–2, 14).[65]

We conclude, then, from the testimony of Scripture that the baptism of the Holy Spirit refers to a richness of grace given to all of God's people at conversion as a consequence of Christ's exaltation to God's right hand (Acts 2:33). It is not biblical to say that believers should seek another baptism of the Spirit that evidences itself in speaking in tongues. This baptism is ours in Christ. If Christ has been raised up for all his people, and they all are in union with him (Eph. 2:6; Col. 3:1), how could this Spirit baptism be granted to some but not to others? Our shared baptism with the Spirit unites all members of Christ's body (1 Cor. 12:13).

Rather than dividing Christians into different levels of spirituality, the baptism of the Spirit unites them as participants in Christ by "one Spirit" (Eph. 4:4). This doctrine reminds us that even when we are not entirely of one mind and spirit with our brethren, we are united by the strongest of bonds: God himself, the Holy Spirit of Christ. Let us, therefore, labor to conduct ourselves with all humility, patience, and love toward one another (Eph. 4:1–3) and strive with open Bibles to attain "the unity of the faith, and of the knowledge of the Son of God" (v. 13). We should pray with the same mindset as the writer of the medieval hymn that Martin Luther embraced:

> Come, Holy Ghost, God and Lord,
> With all Thy graces now outpoured
> On each believer's mind and heart;
> Thy fervent love to them impart.

---

63. "When the aorist participle is related to an aorist main verb, the participle will often be contemporaneous (or simultaneous) to the action of the main verb." Daniel B. Wallace, *Greek Grammar beyond the Basics: An Exegetical Syntax of the New Testament* (Grand Rapids, MI: Zondervan, 1996), 624.

64. F. Blass and A. Debrunner, *A Greek Grammar of the New Testament and Other Early Christian Literature*, trans. and ed. Robert W. Funk (Chicago: The University of Chicago Press, 1961), sec. 339 (175). Examples appear in the context of the very Scripture passages cited in the argument: "believed [aorist participle *pisteusasin*], and turned unto the Lord" (Acts 11:21); "persuaded [aorist participle *peisas*] and turned away much people" (19:26).

65. Furthermore, Acts 11:17 may not follow a syntactical pattern that would allow for this argument to work, for the participle translated as "believed" may be attributive, modifying a pronoun ("us, who believed," *hēmin pisteusasin*), and not be adverbial to modify the verb *edōken*, which has a different subject ("God gave").

Lord, by the brightness of Thy light
Thou in the faith dost men unite
Of every land and every tongue;
This to Thy praise, O Lord, be sung.[66]

Christ's Promise of the Paraclete

If baptism with the Holy Spirit is a gift characteristic of the new age inaugurated by Christ's exaltation, then what is distinctively new about the Spirit's work in this age? We argued in a previous chapter that the Holy Spirit regenerated and indwelt people under the old covenant so that they could live by faith and please the Lord with good works.[67] If that is the case, then in what meaningful sense can we say that the Holy Spirit has come in greater fullness?

We find an answer to this question in Christ's teaching on the Holy Spirit in his extended discourse in the Gospel of John. There he richly describes the coming and ministry of the *paraklētos*, the "Comforter" or "Helper" (ESV), sometime anglicized as "Paraclete."

The Sending of the Paraclete

The Lord Jesus, looking ahead to his death, resurrection, and ascension, said, "I will pray the Father, and he shall give you another Comforter, that he may abide with you for ever; even the Spirit of truth" (John 14:16–17). This gift of the Spirit belongs to those who love Christ and keep his commandments (v. 15). Therefore, Christ promised that as a consequence of his going away to the Father and beginning a ministry of intercession, the Spirit would come to his disciples in a new capacity: "Comforter" and "Spirit of truth." The Spirit's ministry is inseparably linked to Christ, who is the truth (v. 6) and reveals the divine word of truth (17:17; 18:37).

As "another Comforter," the Spirit's mission extends and applies the mission of the Son. Tertullian (fl. 200) said that the Holy Spirit is the "Vicar of Christ,"[68] where "vicar" (Latin *vicarius*) means "substitute" or "representative." The sending of the Spirit from the Father and the Son parallels the sending of the Son from the Father (Gal. 4:4–6). Athanasius said,

66. This prayer was popular in Latin and German before the Reformation and has appeared in various forms in Lutheran hymnbooks since 1524. See The Free Lutheran Chorale-Book, "Come, Holy Ghost, God and Lord," https://www.lutheranchoralebook.com/texts/come-holy-ghost-god-and-lord/.

67. See the section on the Spirit of piety in chap. 3.

68. Tertullian, *On Prescription against Heretics*, chap. 28, in *ANF*, 3:256; cf. *On the Veiling of Virgins*, chap. 1, in *ANF*, 4:27; and Owen, *Pneumatologia*, in *Works*, 3:193.

> The Son is sent from the Father; for he says, "God so loved the world that he gave his only begotten Son" (John 3:16). The Son sends the Spirit; "If I go away," he says, "I will send the Paraclete" (16:7). The Son glorifies the Father, saying: "Father, I have glorified thee" (17:4). The Spirit glorifies the Son; for he says: "He shall glorify me" (16:14). The Son says: "The things I heard from the Father speak I unto the world" (8:26). The Spirit takes of the Son; "He shall take of mine," he says, "and shall declare it unto you" (16:14). The Son came in the name of the Father. "The Holy Spirit," says the Son, "whom the Father will send in my name" (14:26).[69]

The Title of the Paraclete

Paraklētos has received various interpretations. The translation "Comforter" derives from the meaning of related words rendered "comfort" (verb *parakaleō*, Matt. 2:18; noun *paraklēsis*, Acts 9:31). This is an ancient interpretation,[70] though in the old sense of comfort as strength, not the new sense of emotional support. However, this interpretation has little contextual support, for neither of these Greek words appears in John 14–16 or elsewhere in John's writings. Furthermore, it is not based on the usage of the term itself, but only its cognates.

The translation "Helper" (ESV) derives from the etymology of the term, which may be analyzed as one "called alongside" (*klētos para*). It may be supported by the breadth of the Spirit's activities described in this discourse, leading some scholars to say that the Spirit's work as "another Helper" includes all that Jesus was to his disciples as their helper and encourager.[71] However, Christ described the Spirit as both Paraclete and the Spirit of truth, which allows for a broader work while keeping a focused meaning for the first term.

The word *paraklētos* has a distinct meaning; it is used in ancient Greek literature for an "advocate" (Latin *advocatus*), not necessarily a legal expert or attorney but a person of social standing who is called upon to

69. Athanasius, *The Letters of Saint Athanasius concerning the Holy Spirit*, 1.20 (117–18). On the Trinitarian "order of operation" revealed in John 16:13–15, see Owen, *Pneumatologia*, in *Works*, 3:199.

70. Origen, *De Principiis*, 2.7.4, in *ANF*, 4:286. The text is uncertain, deriving from a Latin translation of a somewhat dubious Greek manuscript of Origen's work. Lochlan Shelfer, "The Legal Precision of the Term '*parakletos*'," *Journal for the Study of the New Testament* 32, no. 2 (2009): 132 (full article, 131–50).

71. Andreas J. Köstenberger, *A Theology of John's Gospel and Letters* (Grand Rapids, MI: Zondervan, 2009), 396–97; and Paul A. Rainbow, *Johannine Theology: The Gospel, the Epistles, and the Apocalypse* (Downers Grove, IL: IVP Academic, 2014), 237, 245.

speak on behalf of another in court.[72] Tertullian defined a paraclete as an advocate (*advocatus*) who persuades a judge by entreaties.[73] Eusebius (c. 260–c. 340) referred to a man as the "advocate" (*paraklētos*) of the Christians because he sought to testify in court on their behalf, for he had the "Advocate" (*paraklētos*) in himself, the Holy Spirit.[74] The same word is used of Christ as the "advocate" who intercedes for his people with the Father on the basis of his sacrifice for their sins (1 John 2:1–2).[75] Just as Christ is the Advocate in heaven on behalf of his people, so the Holy Spirit is the Advocate on earth on behalf of God.[76]

Therefore, Christ promised to send the Spirit as the legal Advocate to testify to men. We have already observed that the baptism of the Spirit empowers Christ's witnesses as God prosecutes his legal case against sinners. The context of Christ's teaching about the Spirit-Advocate is Christ's imminent arrest, trial, and sentencing to death by the wicked world (John 18–19). Christ explains that the world unjustly hates him and his disciples because he, as the Father's representative, exposes the world's sin (15:18–25). God and the world are like two contenders in court, each asserting his own righteousness and the sin of the other. God sends first the Son and then the Spirit as advocates to testify in this cosmic trial or divine lawsuit.[77] The legal setting is reinforced by Christ's saying that the Advocate "shall testify of me" when the apostles "bear witness" (vv. 26–27).

The Work of the Paraclete

Jesus said the Spirit would come as Paraclete to "reprove the world," specifically "of sin, and of righteousness, and of judgment: of sin, because they believe not on me; of righteousness, because I go to my Father, and ye see me no more; of judgment, because the prince of this world is judged" (John

72. *TDNT*, 5:800–803; and Shelfer, "The Legal Precision of the Term '*parakletos*'," 134–45. For examples in the New Testament era, see Philo of Alexandria, *Flaccus*, secs. 22, 151, in *The Works of Philo: Complete and Unabridged*, trans. C. D. Yonge, new ed. (Peabody, MA: Hendrickson, 1995), 727, 738; and *Didache*, 5.2, in J. B. Lightfoot, *The Apostolic Fathers*, ed. J. R. Harmer (London: Macmillan and Co., 1912), 231. Leon Morris cautiously suggested that the idea in John may be "friend at court" or "legal helper." Leon Morris, *The Gospel according to John*, The New International Commentary on the New Testament (Grand Rapids, MI: Eerdmans, 1995), 665–66.

73. Tertullian, *On Fasting*, chap. 13, in *ANF*, 4:111.

74. Eusebius, *Church History*, 5.1.9–10, in *NPNF*[2], 1:212–13.

75. On Christ's priestly intercession, see *RST*, 2:1088–99.

76. Berkhof, *Systematic Theology*, 401. Somewhat similarly, Christ intercedes in heaven for his people, and the Holy Spirit intercedes on earth within his people (Rom. 8:26–27, 34).

77. Köstenberger, *A Theology of John's Gospel and Letters*, 438–39; and Andrew T. Lincoln, *Truth on Trial: The Lawsuit Motif in the Fourth Gospel* (Peabody, MA: Hendrickson, 2000), 113–14.

16:7–11). Regarding the first, the revelation of Christ unmasks sin, for the unrepentant react against the light of Christ and reveal the depth of their enmity against God (3:19–20; 15:22–25). Regarding the second, Christ's ascension to glory brought to a conclusion his accomplishment of righteousness—the righteousness that the sinful world needs and cannot make for itself but must receive from God (3:16–18; 5:24). Regarding the third, Christ's unjust crucifixion reveals the world's domination by the Devil (8:40–44; 13:2), and Christ's obedience to the Father unto death on the cross reveals his victory over the world and its future judgment (12:27–31; 14:30–31).[78] Therefore, the Spirit is an Advocate not in the general operations of conscience in all mankind, but in the preaching of Christ through the gospel.

Christ's teaching on the Holy Spirit should shape the worship and evangelistic ministry of the church. Geoff Thomas says,

> If the work of the Spirit is to bring the world to conviction of sin, let us be coworkers with the Spirit. Let us abandon every ploy to make people think they are safe, every device of the professing church, whether by sumptuous ritual or psychological manipulation or enhancing the feel-good factor of religiosity, to tell people they are Christians. . . . Our responsibility by the cross of Christ and the power of the Spirit is to plant conviction in the hearts of people of their lostness and Christ's loveliness, which can be theirs for eternity.[79]

The antithesis between God and the world runs through Christ's discourse,[80] forming the background of the Advocate's ministry to Christ's disciples. The election of Christ and indwelling of the Spirit separate them from the world (John 14:17; 15:19) and make them, too, the object of its hostility and persecution (15:18–20; 16:1–3). However, as the world contends against them with its accusations, even claiming that killing them is an act of service to God (16:2), God and Christ send the Advocate to them to vindicate them. By the Spirit's presence in them (14:16–17), the Father and the Son come to them and dwell in them (vv. 20–21, 23), so that they are not "orphans" (plural *orphanos*) after Christ's ascension (v. 18, KJV mg., ESV).[81] They are not of this world, but they are not

78. Warfield, *The Holy Spirit*, 20–21.
79. Thomas, *The Holy Spirit*, 106.
80. John 14:17, 19, 22, 27, 30, 31; 15:18, 19; 16:8, 11, 33.
81. The word translated as "comfortless" (plural *orphanos*, John 14:18) or "orphans" (KJV mg., ESV) refers to the fatherless (Ex. 22:21–23 [22–24]; Lam. 5:3 LXX; James 1:27). It is not related to the word rendered "Comforter" (*paraklētos*).

abandoned; the Spirit makes their hearts into God's "home" (v. 23 ESV).[82] By sending the Advocate, Christ leaves heavenly peace with his disciples that fortifies them against their fears because Christ has overcome the world (v. 27; 16:33).

Hence, "Comforter," though not the best translation of the word *paraklētos*, is a fitting description of the Paraclete's work in believers. The Advocate of God has come with new power to assure God's children as "the Spirit of adoption" while they suffer in union and communion with Christ (Rom. 8:15–17). In the metaphor of the courtroom, he not only testifies of their justification, but also of their adoption into God's family as his sons and heirs (Gal. 4:6–7).

The Advocate in Christ's disciples always works as the Spirit of truth. Christ called him "another Comforter" (John 14:16), implying that the Spirit would continue the work of Christ to testify to the truth and establish the spiritual reign of God through reception of the truth (8:31–36; 18:36–37).[83] The Father sends the Advocate in Christ's name to teach and retain in their minds the truths revealed by Christ (14:26). This promise has special reference to the apostles. The Spirit of truth will teach them truths that Christ had not revealed in his earthly ministry because his disciples could not receive them yet (16:12–13). However, the Spirit does not teach truth apart from Christ. Jesus said, "He shall glorify me: for he shall receive of mine, and shall shew it unto you. All things that the Father hath are mine" (vv. 14–15). Therefore, one facet of the newness of the Spirit's ministry arises directly from the newness of Christ's revelation of glory in his incarnation (1:14) and climactic work of obedient suffering and exaltation (13:31–32; 17:1–5). The Spirit has always been the revealer of Christ (1 Pet. 1:11), but in his mission as the Advocate his work has greater glory because Christ has come, died, and been lifted up to the Father. One consequence of the Advocate's new work is the production of the New Testament, the covenantal document that permanently crystallizes the new revelation through God incarnate by which the Lord governs his church today.[84]

82. The word translated as "mansion" (*monē*, John 14:2) or "abode" (v. 23) means a dwelling or place of residence.

83. The language of witness or testimony is prominent in this Gospel. See John 1:7–8, 15, 19, 32, 34; 2:25; 3:11, 26, 28, 32, 33; 4:39, 44; 5:31–39; 7:7; 8:7, 13–14, 17–18; 10:25; 12:17; 13:21; 15:26–27; 18:23, 37; 19:35; 21:24.

84. On John 14:25–26; 16:12–14 as promises specifically applying to the apostles that were fulfilled in the production of the New Testament, see *RST*, 1:325–26.

The Time of the Paraclete

When did Christ send this Spirit-Advocate? Someone might propose that, according to John, it was the day of the resurrection, when Christ appeared to his disciples (John 20:19–20). John writes, "Jesus said to them again, 'Peace be with you. As the Father has sent me, even so I am sending you.' And when he had said this, he breathed on them and said to them, 'Receive the Holy Spirit. If you forgive the sins of any, they are forgiven them; if you withhold forgiveness from any, it is withheld'" (vv. 21–23 ESV). However, it is best to see this event as John's account of the Great Commission (cf. Matt. 28:18–20; Luke 24:44–49), with a blessing of the Spirit that anticipated the outpouring that would take place later. Christ's breathing upon them and saying, "Receive the Holy Spirit," might correspond to his giving instruction to the apostles "through the Holy Ghost" after his resurrection and before his ascension (Acts 1:2).

Christ indicated that he would send the Advocate after his ascension to heaven: "Now I go my way to him that sent me. . . . It is expedient for you that I go away: for if I go not away, the Comforter will not come unto you; but if I depart, I will send him unto you" (John 16:5, 7). This had not yet taken place on the day of Christ's resurrection, for he said, "I have not yet ascended to the Father" (20:17 ESV).[85]

Therefore, Christ's promise that he would send the Holy Spirit to be the Advocate and the Spirit of truth was fulfilled on the day of Pentecost. The very things Christ promised that the Paraclete would do, God accomplished through Peter's preaching of Christ after the Spirit was poured out at Pentecost. Consider the parallels in Table 5.2 below.[86]

In his promise of the Advocate, Christ linked the Spirit's witness to Christ with the apostles' witness to Christ (John 15:26–27). From Pentecost onward, the Spirit filled Christ's formerly fearful disciples with unprecedented boldness to bear witness to Christ in the face of their persecutors (Acts 2:14; 4:8, 13, 31). When Peter said to the Jewish high council, "We are his witnesses of these things [Christ's exaltation]; and so is also the Holy Ghost, whom God hath given to them that obey him" (5:32), he epitomized Christ's teaching about the Advocate (John 14:15–16; 15:26–27). Therefore, Christ sent the promised Paraclete at Pentecost.

85. Ferguson, *The Holy Spirit*, 65.

86. On the "close relationship" between John 16:8–11 and Acts 2, see Ferguson, *The Holy Spirit*, 69–70.

Christ's Promise of the Paraclete	Peter's Preaching at Pentecost
The Advocate will convict the world of sin, because of its unbelief in Jesus (John 16:8–9).	They had crucified the Lord, and Christ pierced them to the heart so that they cried, "What shall we do?" (Acts 2:36–37).
The Advocate will convict the world of righteousness because it will no longer see Jesus after he goes to the Father (John 16:10).	Jesus is God's "Holy One," whom he raised from the dead and exalted to pour out the Holy Spirit (Acts 2:27, 31–33).
The Advocate will convict the world that judgment has fallen on its ruler (John 16:11).	Christ's death was foreordained by God, issuing in his victory over death and exaltation to God's right hand (Acts 2:22–24, 34).

Table 5.2. Parallels between Christ's Promise of the Paraclete and Peter's Preaching at Pentecost

Summary: The Privilege of the Paraclete's Presence

In summary, Christ promised to give the Holy Spirit with greater fullness after the Lord's ascension into heaven. The distinctive marks of the Spirit's ministry during the reign of the exalted Mediator may be summarized by the words "Advocate" and "Spirit of truth." Christ's coming brought to a head the legal dispute between God and the world, and the Holy Spirit testifies on behalf of Christ and his people in order to propagate his spiritual kingdom by the truth. Whereas in former ages God allowed the world to walk largely in unchallenged darkness, the Paraclete now witnesses to the world about Christ through the truth revealed to the apostles and convicts the world of its sin and unbelief. By this means, Christ draws people to himself from all nations to form a people distinct from the world and hated by it. Yet the Paraclete is with them to testify that they are God's children in Christ and that God dwells in them in love. Even as the Spirit generates conflict between them and the world, he also assures them of their adoption in more powerful ways than ever before.

The ministry of the Advocate is rightly associated with the last days before the end of the age. Christ has come and accomplished redemption, and his Advocate brings the truth of Christ to his own. The Advocate brings the day of judgment near to the consciences of men by the gospel of Jesus Christ. Through God's truth, the Paraclete powerfully manifests

God's righteousness in Christ, both to the condemnation of the world and to the joy of the justified.

Do you know the ministry of the Advocate in your life? Without the Holy Spirit, people may follow a religion of reasonable beliefs, emotional experiences, and moral behavior, but they will not have the power of godliness within them. Has the Holy Spirit ever touched your conscience and awakened you to see that you not only do bad things, but have badness in your very heart—yes, that your heart is entirely bad until Christ saves you? Has the evil of your heart been exposed in your slowness to fully trust in Jesus Christ for all that he is? Have you come to see that Christ is the only righteousness of God that can make you righteous with God? Do you realize that the world is under the power of Satan, but Christ conquered the Devil at the cross? Has the truth of God's word come to you in a manner that you see the glory of God's Son? Having believed in Jesus, do you have a sense that God the Father is your Father and that you are his dear child? These are the works of the Paraclete, the Spirit of truth.

Sing to the Lord

Spirit of Pentecost, Spirit of Missions

O Spirit of the living God,
In all thy plenitude of grace,
Where'er the foot of man hath trod,
Descend on our apostate race.

Give tongues of fire and hearts of love
To preach the reconciling word;
Give pow'r and unction from above,
Whene'er the joyful sound is heard.

Be darkness, at thy coming, light;
Confusion, order in thy path;
Souls without strength inspire with might;
Bid mercy triumph over wrath.

Baptize the nations; far and nigh
The triumphs of the cross record;
The Name of Jesus glorify,
Till every kindred call him Lord.

James Montgomery
Tune: Mendon
Trinity Hymnal—Baptist Edition, No. 253

Questions for Meditation or Discussion

1. What can we learn about the baptism of the Holy Spirit from John the Baptist's words?
2. What ancient prophecies were fulfilled in the baptism of the Spirit?
3. What is the meaning of the Spirit's miraculous outpouring in Acts 2?
4. How does Paul explain the meaning of the baptism or outpouring of the Spirit?
5. What is the distinctive teaching of Pentecostal and charismatic theology regarding baptism with the Holy Spirit?
6. What arguments do Pentecostal and charismatic theologians make for this doctrine?
7. How can each of these arguments be answered? What reasons are there to believe that Christ baptizes all members of his body from the moment of their conversion?
8. According to Christ's teaching in John 14–16, how does the Holy Spirit work as the Paraclete and Spirit of truth?
9. What practical implications does the doctrine of baptism with the Holy Spirit have for missions? For the unity of God's church?

Questions for Deeper Reflection

10. Someone says to you, "After being a Christian for years, I received the baptism of the Holy Spirit and spoke in tongues. I know it's truly from God, for I have never experienced so much joy, love, and power before." How do you respond?
11. What is new about the Spirit's work since Pentecost? What is not new?
12. What arguments could be made for each of the following translations of the Greek word *paraklētos* as applied to the Spirit: "Comforter," "Helper," and "Advocate"? Which is the best translation? Why?

6

The Gifts of the Spirit in the Church

The baptism of the Holy Spirit is the "gift" of God.[1] However, with that gift come many spiritual "gifts" that the ascended Christ shares with men (Eph. 4:8). Thus, Paul says that his ministry as an apostle arose from "the gift of the grace of God given unto me by the effectual working of his power" (3:7). He also affirms, "Unto every one of us is given grace according to the measure of the gift of Christ" (4:7). John Owen said, "These gifts are from Christ, not as God absolutely, but as mediator, in which capacity he received all from the Father in a way of free donation. Thus, therefore, he received the Spirit as the author of all spiritual gifts."[2]

These gifts empower the church for its ministry, both in the ministry of the Word (Eph. 4:11–14) and the ministry of every member one to another (v. 16), so that Christ "might fill all things" with his glory (v. 10). Although these gifts are a vital part of the church's life and could be treated under the locus of ecclesiology, their power comes from the Holy Spirit poured out through Christ. Hence, we will discuss the spiritual gifts under pneumatology.

The Gifts of the Holy Spirit in General

The New Testament refers to Spirit-worked abilities as "gifts," using a few different Greek words,[3] particularly the word *charisma*,[4] which identifies

1. Acts 2:38; 8:20; 10:45; 11:17; cf. Heb. 6:4. On the baptism of the Spirit, see the previous chapter.

2. Owen, "A Discourse of Spiritual Gifts," in *Pneumatologia*, in *Works*, 4:422.

3. "Gift" translates *dōrea* in Eph. 3:7; 4:7; and *doma* in Eph. 4:8. In Heb. 2:4, "gifts of the Holy Ghost" is literally "divisions" or "distributions" (plural *merismos*; cf. 4:12) of the Spirit.

4. Rom. 12:6; 1 Cor. 1:7; 12:4, 9, 28, 30, 31; 1 Tim. 4:14; 2 Tim 1:6; 1 Pet. 4:10. The term *charisma* may also be used of salvation (Rom. 5:15–16; 6:23); the ability to live righteously in celibacy

these abilities as "grace" (*charis*) freely given by God.[5] Owen said, "They are free, undeserved gifts."[6] Paul parallels "gifts" with "administrations" or "ministries" (plural *diakonia*) and "operations" or "powerful workings" (plural *energēma*), for God works through the gifts to empower ministry (1 Cor. 12:4–6). The gifts are "spiritual gifts" (*pneumatika*), literally "spiritual things" (1 Cor. 12:1; 14:1). Owen wrote, "They are neither natural nor moral. . . . Their author is the Holy Spirit; their nature is spiritual; and the objects about which they are exercised are spiritual things."[7] Each gift is "the manifestation of the Spirit" (12:7), a display of his presence and power.[8] While some gifts are miraculous, others are the Spirit's supernatural empowerment of ordinary human activities to produce spiritual effects. What characterizes all gifts is their power to serve "to profit withal" (1 Cor. 12:7), literally "for the profiting/benefit" (*eis to sympheron*), the latter term referring to the edification of the church (6:12; 10:23). Therefore, a spiritual gift is a gracious divine endowment to empower a person to build up Christ's church by the activity of the Holy Spirit.

Though the gifts are grace in the sense of being undeserved mercies from God, Owen said, "These gifts are not saving, sanctifying graces. . . . There is something of the divine nature in the least grace, that is not in the most glorious gift."[9] Spiritual gifts, even miraculous gifts, may be exercised by wicked hypocrites such as Judas Iscariot whom Christ will condemn on the last day (Matt. 7:21–23; 10:1–8). Yet they are precious gifts. Owen said: "Although they are not [saving] grace, yet they are that without which the church cannot subsist in the world, nor can believers be useful to one another and the rest of mankind, unto the glory of God, as they ought to be."[10]

Both saving grace and spiritual gifts arise from Christ's mediatorial work, are worked by the power of the Holy Spirit, and serve for the good of the church.[11] However, saving grace is the fruit of the Spirit in a new

(1 Cor. 7:7–9); and perhaps spiritual blessing in general (Rom. 1:11). Thus, it is not a technical term for spiritual gifts for service. See D. A. Carson, *Showing the Spirit: A Theological Exposition of 1 Corinthians 12–14* (Grand Rapids, MI: Baker, 1987), 20–21.

5. Note "gift" (*charisma*) and "grace" (*charis*) in Rom. 12:3, 6; 1 Cor. 1:4, 7; 1 Pet. 4:10.
6. Owen, "A Discourse of Spiritual Gifts," in *Pneumatologia*, in *Works*, 4:423.
7. Owen, "A Discourse of Spiritual Gifts," in *Pneumatologia*, in *Works*, 4:424.
8. Roy E. Ciampa and Brian S. Rosner, *The First Letter to the Corinthians*, The Pillar New Testament Commentary (Grand Rapids, MI: Eerdmans; Nottingham, England: Apollos, 2010), 571.
9. Owen, "A Discourse of Spiritual Gifts," in *Pneumatologia*, in *Works*, 4:420.
10. Owen, "A Discourse of Spiritual Gifts," in *Pneumatologia*, in *Works*, 4:420–21.
11. Owen, "A Discourse of Spiritual Gifts," in *Pneumatologia*, in *Works*, 4:425–28.

nature; spiritual gifts are merely effects on men. Saving grace comes from God's election of a person to be his beloved child; the gifts come from God's choice of a person for some work or office. Saving grace transforms the whole soul, producing faith, love, and holiness so that Christ dwells in the heart; gifts merely give new knowledge to the mind or the operation of new powers to work.[12]

A spiritual gift is a divine endowment to an individual so that he or she can exercise a regular ministry by the Spirit's empowerment according to God's will. As an endowment, a gift consists of more than a mere event. The association of "gift" (*charisma*) with the working of divine energy (1 Cor. 12:6, 11) led James Dunn (1939–2020) to conclude, "Charisma is an event, an action enabled by divine power; charisma is divine energy accomplishing a particular result (in word or deed) through an individual."[13] The plurals in what literally reads "gifts of healings" (v. 9) are said to show that "the charisma is not a healing power which is effective for all (sorts of) illnesses; it is the actual healing itself. As there are many (different) illnesses, so there are many (different) healing charismata."[14] However, as D. A. Carson points out, Paul says that people "have" (*echō*) or possess gifts (Rom. 12:6; 1 Cor. 12:30), which implies that a *charisma* is not merely a particular divine act but a divine endowment bestowed on a person.[15] A gift is a spiritual stewardship in which the Master entrusts some of his resources to his servants: "As each has received a gift, use it to serve one another, as good stewards of God's varied grace" (1 Pet. 4:10 ESV). Furthermore, Paul explains "gifts" (Rom. 12:6) with the metaphor that the church of Christ is a body with "many members, and the members do not all have the same function" (v. 4 ESV), comparing individuals to eyes, ears, hands, and feet (1 Cor. 12:14–21). This implies that a spiritual "gift" is the Spirit's empowerment of a Christian to perform a kind of service that characterizes his organic relationship to the rest of the body.

Every Christian has a spiritual gift. Paul says, "Unto every one of us is given grace according to the measure of the gift of Christ" (Eph. 4:7). Peter writes, "As every man hath received the gift, even so minister the same one to another" (1 Pet. 4:10). Paul explains that this is a privilege

12. Owen, "A Discourse of Spiritual Gifts," in *Pneumatologia*, in *Works*, 4:428–38.

13. James D. G. Dunn, *Jesus and the Spirit: A Study of the Religious and Charismatic Experience of Jesus and the First Christians as Reflected in the New Testament* (Grand Rapids, MI: Eerdmans, 1975), 39.1 (209).

14. Dunn, *Jesus and the Spirit*, 39.3 (211).

15. Carson, *Showing the Spirit*, 21–22.

granted to the entire body of Christ since Christ baptized his church: "The manifestation of the Spirit is given to every man. . . . All these worketh that one and the selfsame Spirit, dividing to every man severally as he will. For as the body is one, and hath many members, and all the members of that one body, being many, are one body: so also is Christ. For by one Spirit are we all baptized into one body" (1 Cor. 12:7, 11–13).

The possession of a gift by every member of the body logically implies that each person receives at least one gift immediately upon conversion. However, that does not rule out the possibility that further gifts might be added or present gifts might be strengthened (or weakened) over the course of the Christian life. For example, since tongues did not edify the body apart from interpretation, Paul said that the one who spoke in tongues should "pray that he may interpret" (1 Cor. 14:13). Timothy evidently received a new or increased gift at his ordination, for Paul said, "Neglect not the gift that is in thee, which was given thee by prophecy, with the laying on of the hands of the presbytery" (1 Tim. 4:14). Paul also said, "Stir up the gift of God, which is in thee by the putting on of my hands" (2 Tim. 1:6).[16] Paul's exhortation suggests that Paul imparted a gift to Timothy after his conversion. "Stir up" (*anazōpyreō*)—literally "rekindle" or "relight the flame"—implies that a gift can decrease or increase in intensity.

Paul stresses the diversity of the gifts that flow from the unity we have in the one God (1 Cor. 12:4–6). He illustrates that diversity by listing several gifts (vv. 8–10), a list that we can supplement from other Scripture passages, as shown in Table 6.1 below.

We observe from this list that there is a significant pattern of order for three gifts: apostle, prophet, and teacher. Paul makes the order explicit in 1 Corinthians 12:28: "God hath set some in the church, *first* apostles, *secondarily* prophets, *thirdly* teachers." In his epistle to the Ephesians, Paul lists only apostles, prophets, evangelists, and pastors and teachers—all ministers of the Word, which directs and supports the life of the church as Christ rules it. However, we also observe that apart from apostles, prophets, and teachers, there does not seem to be any order to the other gifts, except for the placement of tongues (and interpretation) at the end of all three lists in 1 Corinthians 12, which suggests that Paul was correcting an overemphasis on that gift.

16. George W. Knight III, *The Pastoral Epistles: A Commentary on the Greek Text*, The New International Greek Testament Commentary (Grand Rapids, MI: Eerdmans; Carlisle, Cumbria, England: Paternoster, 1992), 208–9, 370–71.

Rom. 12:6–8	1 Cor. 12:8–10	1 Cor. 12:28	1 Cor. 12:29–30	Eph. 4:11	1 Pet. 4:10–11
prophecy	word of wisdom	apostles	apostles	apostles	speaking
ministry	word of knowledge	prophets	prophets	prophets	ministering
teaching	faith	teachers	teachers	evangelists	
exhortation	gifts of healing	miracles	workers of miracles	pastors and teachers	
giving	working of miracles	gifts of healing	gifts of healing		
ruling	prophecy	helps	speaking with tongues		
mercy	discerning of spirits	govern-ments	interpreta-tion		
	kinds of tongues	diversities of tongues			
	interpreta-tion of tongues				

Table 6.1. Lists of Spiritual Gifts in Original Order

The Specific Gifts of the Holy Spirit

In our discussion of the spiritual gifts, we will handle them in nine categories. Apostles and prophets were discussed in the first volume of *Reformed Systematic Theology* under the topic of special revelation, so we will treat them more briefly here.[17]

1. Apostleship

Though Paul does speak of "apostleship" (*apostolē*),[18] in the lists of spiritual gifts he always speaks concretely of "apostles" (plural *apostolos*). The word means someone whom one "sends" (*apostellō*), and it is most

17. On the apostolic office and its uniqueness, see *RST*, 1:422–30. On the cessation of prophecy, see *RST*, 1:433–57.
18. Rom. 1:5; 1 Cor. 9:2; Gal. 2:8.

often used in the New Testament in the technical sense of a special group of men directly appointed by Jesus Christ. The apostles were extraordinary ministers, for Christ gave them authority to heal, cast out demons, proclaim the gospel, serve as eyewitnesses that he was risen from the dead, receive new revelation from God by the Spirit, and establish the new covenant church.[19] The apostles also functioned as spiritual shepherds and teachers,[20] but unlike pastors and elders today their authority was not limited to a particular local church, but was universal in scope.[21] There are no apostles today.[22]

2. Prophecy and Discerning of Spirits

Paul writes of the gift of "prophecy" (*prophēteia*) as a contemporary activity,[23] and he lists "prophets" (plural *prophētēs*) second after apostles among the spiritual gifts.[24] A prophet is a messenger from God. As in the Old Testament, prophets received and proclaimed the word of the Lord by the inspiration of the Holy Spirit.[25] Prophets spoke truth directly "revealed" to them by God (1 Cor. 14:29–31; Eph. 3:5), though it might not have been a prediction of the future so much as an inspired message to exhort or comfort (1 Cor. 14:3). Just as Old Testament prophets often said, "Thus saith the Lord," so we read of a New Testament prophet saying, "Thus saith the Holy Ghost" (Acts 21:11). No one may speak in this way unless he speaks the infallible word of God that will most certainly come true (Deut. 18:21–22; 1 Kings 22:28). After Christ's coming, the new revelations of the apostles and prophets concerning Christ and his body laid a foundation for the church (Eph. 2:20; 3:5). With the end of the apostolic age, God ceased giving prophecy.

Paul also lists "discerning of spirits" among the spiritual gifts (1 Cor. 12:10). The word translated as "discerning" (*diakrisis*) refers to judging,

19. Matt. 10:1–8; Luke 6:13; Acts 1:21–26; 2:43; 5:12; 1 Cor. 9:1; 15:7–9; 2 Cor. 12:12; 13:3–4; Gal. 1:1, 11–12; Eph. 2:18–20; 3:5–6. *Apostolos* also may have the weaker sense of "messenger" (e.g., 2 Cor. 8:23; Phil. 2:25).

20. John 21:15–17; Acts 6:2, 4; 1 Pet. 5:1–2.

21. Luke 24:33, 47–48; Acts 1:2, 8; 9:17; 14:22–23. Thus, the apostles wrote authoritative epistles to many churches.

22. Regarding the twelve apostles, the number "twelve" likely alludes to the twelve tribes of Israel (Matt. 19:28; Luke 22:30; Rev. 21:12, 14). Calvin, *Commentaries*, on Matt. 10:1.

23. Rom. 12:6; 1 Cor. 12:10; 13:2, 8; 14:6, 22; 1 Thess. 5:20; 1 Tim. 1:8; 4:14.

24. 1 Cor. 12:28–29; Eph. 4:11; cf. 2:20; 3:5.

25. On the continuity of the new covenant prophets with the old covenant prophets, see the use of the term "prophet" for both in the same contexts: Luke 11:49–50; Acts 2:17–18, 30; 13:1, 15; 15:15, 32.

such as distinguishing between good and evil (Heb. 5:14). Paul uses the cognate verb later in 1 Corinthians for the need to "judge" (*diakrinō*) after prophets speak in the church (1 Cor. 14:29; cf. 1 Thess. 5:19–22). "Spirits" (plural *pneumata*) is used of prophetic activity (1 Cor. 14:32; cf. 1 John 4:1). Therefore, we define discerning of spirits as the gift of recognizing the source of a prophecy.[26]

The gifts of the apostles and the prophets were amazing graces from our Lord, for which we should be deeply grateful. God communicated through them the new revelation of Christ, founded the church among Israel and the nations, and gave us the Scriptures of the New Testament. Whenever we read God's Word and enjoy participating in the church of Christ, we benefit from the ministry of Christ's apostles and prophets.

3. *The Gift of Evangelists*

The Scriptures include "evangelists" (plural *euangelistēs*) only once among the lists of spiritual gifts (Eph. 4:11), where its placement after apostles and prophets but before pastors and teachers implies a particular kind of minister of the Word. The word appears in only two other texts. After exhorting Timothy to "preach the word," Paul writes, "Do the work of an evangelist" (2 Tim. 4:2, 5). This may refer to Timothy's special office as a companion and delegate of the apostle,[27] or it might simply mean "preach the gospel."[28] The term "evangelist" is also used of Philip (Acts 21:8), a man "full of the Holy Ghost and wisdom," whom the church in Jerusalem appointed to diaconal service (6:3, 5) but who later undertook an itinerant ministry of preaching the gospel with great effect, casting out demons, and healing the sick under supernatural direction from God (8:5–7, 26–40). Luke distinguishes him from the apostles (vv. 14–17), but his ministry resembled that of the seventy whom Christ sent out (Luke 10:1, 9, 17)—traditionally called the seventy evangelists. That group may have been precursors to the evangelists Christ gave to the church after his ascension (Eph. 4:11).[29] Based on this (sparse) usage, we tentatively define an "evangelist" as a person

26. Owen, "A Discourse of Spiritual Gifts," in *Pneumatologia*, in *Works*, 4:471–72.

27. On Timothy's ministry, see Acts 16:1–5; 17:14–15; 18:5: 19:22; 20:4; Rom. 16:21; 1 Cor. 4:17; 16:10; 2 Cor. 1:19; 1 Thess. 3:6; 1 Tim. 1:3; and many of the greetings in Paul's epistles. There is some evidence that Timothy had an extraordinary gift, given with prophecy and the laying on of Paul's hands (1 Tim. 1:18; 4:14; 2 Tim. 1:6).

28. Paul elsewhere writes of Timothy's labors in the "gospel" (*euangelion*, Phil. 2:22; 1 Thess. 3:2; 2 Tim. 1:8).

29. Owen, "A Discourse of Spiritual Gifts," in *Pneumatologia*, in *Works*, 4:445–46.

extraordinarily gifted by the Lord to preach the gospel and confirm it with miracles in conjunction with the ministry of the apostles. Thus, we distinguish between an "evangelist" and the work of evangelism, the work of all Christians to tell the gospel to others.

The New Testament gives us no reason to think this extraordinary gift continues today, giving the church no direction to recognize those truly qualified and called to serve as evangelists. John Calvin understood "evangelist" to refer to an extraordinary minister of the Word, not part of the regular ministry of the church, but wondered if God raised up evangelists in special seasons of great need in the church.[30] William Ames said, "The prophets, apostles, and evangelists were extraordinary ministers. Wyclif, Luther, Zwingli, and the others who were the first restorers of the gospel were not, strictly speaking, extraordinary ministers." Ames added, however, that the Reformers "are not wrongly called extraordinary by some" for their unusually great gifts and uncommon course of action to restore the church.[31]

4. Teaching, Exhorting, Word of Wisdom, Word of Knowledge, and Pastoring

Paul writes of a "teacher" (*didaskalos*), one who "teaches" (*didaskō*), and the work of "teaching" (*didaskalia*).[32] Christ was called "Teacher" (often translated as "Master," as in Matt. 8:19). Paul, too, was a teacher (1 Tim. 2:7; 2 Tim. 1:11). Of course, teaching involves instructing people in the knowledge of the truth (2 Tim. 2:24–25). Yet in Scripture a teacher is more than a communicator of information; he exercises authority over his disciples, and they become like him (Matt. 10:24–25; Luke 6:40). Christ said that as the church engages in its mission to "make disciples," one aspect of its work is "teaching them to observe all that I have commanded you" (Matt. 28:19–20 ESV). Teaching addresses not merely the mind but also the heart and the life with one's duties before God. Thus, to "teach" can be synonymous with preaching.[33] However, though teaching and admonishing go together,[34] Paul can distinguish between the gifts of "teaching" and "exhorting" (Rom. 12:7–8), which suggests that some people are more gifted in instruction in the truth and others in urging people to act on the truth.[35]

30. Calvin, *Institutes*, 4.3.4; *Commentaries*, on Eph. 4:11.
31. Ames, *The Marrow of Theology*, 1.33.37–39 (185).
32. Rom. 12:7; 1 Cor. 12:28–29; Eph. 4:11; cf. Acts 13:1.
33. Matt. 5:2; 7:29; 13:54; Mark 1:21–22; 2:13; 4:1; Luke 13:22; Acts 20:20; 2 Tim. 2:2.
34. 1 Tim. 4:13; 6:2; 2 Tim. 4:2; Titus 1:9; cf. Col. 1:28; 3:16.
35. See "exhort" or "beseech" in Acts 2:40; 11:23; 14:22; Rom. 12:1.

Nuances in the teaching gift may lie behind Paul's intriguing references to what he calls "word of wisdom" and "word of knowledge" (1 Cor. 12:8). It is possible that these gifts, listed only here, refer to the reception and declaration of new special revelation from God,[36] in which case they overlap with "prophecy" (v. 10). However, the term translated as "word" (*logos*) is commonly used for ordinary speech (4:19–20). The most natural interpretation of these phrases is that they refer to gifts used to communicate wisdom and knowledge.[37] The only list in which these gifts appear does not mention teaching (12:8–10), but the immediately following lists omit these gifts and do include teaching (vv. 28–30). The difference between "word of wisdom" and "word of knowledge" is hard to discern (cf. 1:24; 2:7; 8:1–4).[38]

Pastors and teachers are closely associated with each other. Paul groups the two together under the same definite article ("the pastors and teachers," Eph. 4:11).[39] All pastors must be teachers.[40] However, the Scriptures do not say that all teachers must be pastors. For example, Apollos "taught" the Scriptures (Acts 18:24–25), but he traveled from place to place and does not appear to have been a pastor in a particular church.[41] Therefore, it is best to interpret Paul as saying that Christ gave to the church "pastors" as part of a larger group of "teachers."[42]

Who among us has not benefitted from faithful teachers of God's Word? It is painful to imagine how immature and confused we would be if God had left us to study the Bible entirely on our own. Let us bless God for pastors, teachers, and writers who have blessed us. Let us recognize

36. Thus, Williams, *Renewal Theology*, 2:350–51, 355–56.

37. Anthony C. Thiselton, *1 Corinthians: A Shorter and Pastoral Commentary* (Grand Rapids, MI: Eerdmans, 2006), 198; and Kim Riddlebarger, *First Corinthians*, The Lectio Continua Expository Commentary on the New Testament (Powder Springs, GA: Tolle Lege, 2013), 324.

38. On knowledge and wisdom, see *RST*, 1:58, 731–33. Owen proposed that "word of wisdom" is the Spirit-given ability to skillfully and effectively defend the gospel against its adversaries (Luke 21:15; Acts 6:10). Owen, "A Discourse of Spiritual Gifts," in *Pneumatologia*, in *Works*, 4:454–55, 460.

39. Greek: *tous de poimenas kai didaskalous*. When used with plural nouns, the syntax of article-noun-*kai*-noun may indicate two distinct but united groups, two overlapping groups, either group as a subset of the other group, or one group described with two words. This syntactical pattern is distinguished from the Granville-Sharp rule, which applies to singular nouns (cf. Titus 2:13; 2 Pet. 1:1). Daniel B. Wallace, "The Semantic Range of the Article-Noun-*Kai*-Noun Plural Construction in the New Testament," *Grace Theological Journal* 4, no. 1 (1983): 72–78 (full article, 59–84), https://www.biblicalstudies.org.uk/pdf/gtj/04-1_059.pdf.

40. The word translated as "pastor" (*poimēn*) means "shepherd" (John 10:11; 1 Pet. 2:25), which is the function of the overseers of the church who "shepherd" (*poimainō*) God's flock (Acts 20:28; 1 Pet. 5:2). Overseers, also known as elders, must be "apt to teach" (1 Tim. 3:2; cf. Titus 1:9).

41. Acts 18:24–19:1; 1 Cor. 1:12; 3:4–6; 16:12; Titus 3:13.

42. Wallace, "The Semantic Range," 83. On elders, ministers, and professors of theology, see *RST*, vol. 4 (forthcoming).

that teachers, as imperfect as they are, still are gifts from the Lord Christ by the empowerment of the Holy Spirit. We should love and esteem those who teach us. We also should pray for them regularly, for they can do nothing of spiritual value apart from the Spirit of Christ.

5. Working of Miracles

In the lists of spiritual gifts that Paul wrote to the Corinthians, he speaks of "the working of miracles" (1 Cor. 12:10) and "miracles" (vv. 28–29).[43] The word translated as "working" (*energēma*) is the same as that translated as "operations" (v. 6), cognate to the verb "worketh" (*energeō*, v. 11). It emphasizes the divine activity in miracles. The word translated as "miracles" (plural *dynamis*) literally means "powers" and is a common biblical term for miracles, drawing attention to the supernatural power that they exhibit. Almost all the miracles worked through Christ's servants in the New Testament consist of healing diseases and disabilities, speaking in tongues, and casting out demons.[44] Since the first two gifts appear elsewhere in the same lists as miracles (vv. 9–10, 28–30), it may be that casting out demons is especially in view here. We will discuss signs and wonders in more detail in the next chapter.

Paul also lists "faith" (*pistis*) as a spiritual gift (1 Cor. 12:9). The same word is used of saving faith in Jesus Christ (2:5), but that cannot be in view here. Paul says, "Though I have all faith, so that I could remove mountains, and have not charity, I am nothing" (13:2). Christ also taught that "if ye have faith," you can move a "mountain" (Matt. 17:20; 21:21). If the mountain is to be taken literally, then this is faith to work miracles, such as the faith of Stephen (Acts 6:8).[45] This would link the gift of faith to healing and miracles, which follow it in Paul's list in 1 Corinthians 12:8–10. However, there is no record in the Scriptures of anyone transporting a mountain. Moving a mountain is also figurative language for overcoming obstacles to God's kingdom.[46] "Faith," then, might be the

43. In 1 Cor. 12:29, "workers of miracles" translates the single word that is often rendered as "miracles" (plural *dynamis*).

44. Healing and casting out demons: Matt. 7:22; 10:1; Mark 3:14–15; 6:7, 13; 9:38–40; 16:17; Luke 9:1–2, 49–50; 10:1, 9, 17; Acts 3:6–8; 4:16, 22; 5:16; 8:6–7, 13; 9:17–18, 32–35; 14:8–10, 19–20; 16:18; 19:11–12; 28:1–9. Tongues: Mark 16:17; Acts 2:1–13; 10:44–46; 19:6. Rarer miracles include the following. Being transported a distance away: Acts 8:39. Causing death: Acts 5:1–11. Inflicting blindness: Acts 13:9–12. Raising the dead: Acts 9:40; 20:9–12. Some accounts do not specify the signs and wonders performed: Acts 2:43; 5:12; 6:8; 14:3; 15:12.

45. Chrysostom, *Homilies on 1 Corinthians*, 29.5, in *NPNF*[1], 12:172; Calvin, *Commentaries*, on 1 Cor. 12:8–10; and Fee, *God's Empowering Presence*, 168.

46. Isa. 40:4; Jer. 51:25; Zech. 4:6–7. See Williams, *Renewal Theology*, 2:360. Christ's teaching on moving mountains takes place in the context of his cursing of a fig tree as prophetic symbolism

gift of extraordinary confidence in God to overcome obstacles, perhaps expressed in effectual prayer (Matt. 17:21; 21:22). This interpretation would link the gift of faith to the "word" gifts that precede it in the list. If so, then the gift transcends miracles and encourages the church to boldly persevere through persecution by faith in God's promises.[47]

6. *Healing*

Paul also writes to the Corinthians of "gifts of healing" (1 Cor. 12:9, 28, 30). Two Greek word groups are mainly used to express healing in the New Testament.[48] The two verbs (*iaomai* and *therapeuō*), translated as "heal," "cure," or "make whole," are used virtually interchangeably and almost always refer to physical healing.[49] To heal may also be expressed with the verb meaning to "save" (*sōzō*), often rendered "make whole."[50] The Scriptures also use the expression to become "whole" or "healthy" (*hygiēs*).[51]

Healing in the New Testament consists of supernatural restoration of the body to healthy functioning. Jesus healed all kinds of diseases and illnesses, and gave his apostles the power to do the same (Matt. 9:35; 10:1). Christ healed such serious maladies as lame legs, blind eyes, deaf ears, leprosy, a withered hand, serious fever, long-term hemorrhaging, and a severed ear.[52] The apostles healed three men who had been lame for years (Acts 3:1–8; 9:32–35; 14:8–10). While Paul was in Ephesus, cloths that had touched his body were taken to the sick, and they were healed

---

for God's judgment on Israel for its opposition to him (Matt. 21:12, 23, 43). See Gerald M. Bilkes, *Mercy Revealed: A Cross-Centered Look at Christ's Miracles* (Grand Rapids, MI: Reformation Heritage Books, 2015), 149–50.

47. See Owen, "A Discourse of Spiritual Gifts," in *Pneumatologia*, in *Works*, 4:461–62; Smeaton, *The Doctrine of the Holy Spirit*, 53; and Thiselton, *1 Corinthians: A Shorter and Pastoral Commentary*, 199.

48. The first word group consists of "healing" (*iama*, 1 Cor. 12:9, 28, 30), a related noun *iasis* (Luke 13:32; Acts 4:22, 30), and the verb *iaomai* (twenty-eight times in the New Testament). The second word group is primarily found in uses of the verb *therapeuō* (forty-four times). The noun *therapeia* appears in Luke 9:11 for miraculous healing and in Rev. 22:2 for eschatological healing; it is used with the meaning of "household" in Matt. 24:45 and Luke 12:42. In classical Greek, this root meant to "serve," and thus can be used for servants, worship, and medical assistance/healing.

49. On their interchangeability, see Matt. 8:7–8; Luke 6:18–19; 9:1–2; John 5:10, 13; Acts 28:8–9. The verb *therapeuō* always refers to physical healing, except once when it means "worship" (Acts 17:25). The verb *iaomai* refers to physical healing, except for six occasions when it is used metaphorically for spiritual healing, always in connection to citations from the Greek Old Testament. See Matt. 13:15 (Isa. 6:10); Luke 4:18 (Isa. 61:1); John 12:40 (Isa. 6:10); Acts 28:27 (Isa. 6:10); Heb. 12:12–13 (cf. Prov. 4:26 [LXX]; Isa. 35:3, 5–6); 1 Pet. 2:24 (Isa. 53:5).

50. Matt. 9:21–22; Mark 3:4; 5:23, 28, 34; 6:56; 10:52; Luke 6:9; 17:19; 18:42; Acts 4:9; 14:9; James 5:15. See the similar use of *diasōzō* in Matt. 14:36; Luke 7:3.

51. Matt. 12:13; 15:31; Mark 3:5; 5:34; Luke 6:10; John 5:4, 6, 9, 11, 14, 15; 7:23; Acts 4:10.

52. Matt. 9:27–30; 11:5; 15:30; Mark 3:1–5; Luke 4:38–39; 8:43–44; 22:51.

(19:11–12). Paul later healed a man of fever and dysentery (28:8). These clear restorations of health demonstrated the power of the living God.

The relationship between healing and faith in the New Testament is complex. In some cases, people received healing for themselves through their own faith in Christ.[53] In other cases, the faith that was instrumental in obtaining healing did not belong to the sick person but to someone else who sought the Lord on his behalf.[54] Sometimes God withheld miracles due to the unbelief of a people (Matt. 13:53–58; Mark 6:1–6).[55] At other times, Christ or his servants ministered to large crowds, and there was no discrimination between those who had faith and those who did not; the texts simply say that they healed them all.[56] God granted healing according to his free mercy.

The bestowal of gifts of healing did not mean that faithful Christians would live in uninterrupted health, not even in the apostolic age. Tabitha was "full of good works" but became "sick, and died" (Acts 9:36–37). It may be that Paul suffered from chronic physical ailments (2 Cor. 12:7–10; Gal. 4:15). When Paul says, "Our outward man is wasting away" (2 Cor. 4:16 ESV mg.), he does not offer a very positive outlook on the Christian's prospects of good health, especially as one grows older.[57] Epaphroditus became so sick that he nearly died, much to Paul's distress (Phil. 2:25–27). Timothy frequently was sick, including stomach problems, for which Paul prescribed not supernatural healing but "a little wine" (1 Tim. 5:23). Paul's last recorded words include the statement "Trophimus have I left at Miletum sick" (2 Tim. 4:20).

Healing in this life is not the right of every Christian on the basis of the promise "With his stripes we are healed" (Isa. 53:5). Isaiah speaks of

53. Matt. 9:22, 29; Mark 5:34; 10:52; Luke 8:48; 17:19; 18:42; Acts 14:9. In Acts 3:16, it is not clear whether the "faith" by which the lame man was healed (vv. 1–8) was his own or, more likely, that of Peter (note v. 12).

54. Matt. 8:13; 9:2; 15:28; Luke 7:9–10.

55. Mark 6:5–6 says, "He could there do no mighty work, save that he laid his hands upon a few sick folk, and healed them. And he marvelled because of their unbelief." Though Christ, literally, "was not able," we should not conclude that God's omnipotence to work was limited by their unbelief. Rather, Christ was not able because the incarnate Mediator acted in submission to the Father and dependence on the Spirit, who did not grant power because it was not God's will to bless those people who had hardened their hearts against Christ.

56. Matt. 8:16; 12:15; Luke 4:40; 6:17–19; Acts 5:16. Note also the healing of "many" (Acts 8:7) and "the rest of the people on the island who had diseases" (28:8–9 ESV).

57. The verb translated as "is wasting away" (*diaphtheiretai*) is in the present tense, as is the verb Paul parallels with it, "is being renewed" (2 Cor. 4:16 ESV). This implies a continuing or repeated process. The former verb means to ruin, corrupt, or destroy (Luke 12:33; Rev. 8:9). Our bodies are being destroyed by disease, deterioration, injury, etc. This is our condition as those with mortal bodies in a fallen world (cf. *phthora* in Rom. 8:21; 1 Cor. 15:42, 50). See Richard B. Gaffin Jr., "A Cessationist View," in *Are Miraculous Gifts for Today?*, ed. Wayne A. Grudem, Counterpoints (Grand Rapids, MI: Zondervan, 1996), 58–59.

healing as a comprehensive "peace" or well-being given to those whom God reconciles to himself (57:19–21). Peter quotes Isaiah 53:5 and applies it to the spiritual conversion of sinners (1 Pet. 2:24–25). The healing accomplished in the atonement includes the body (cf. Matt. 8:16–17), but the physical aspects of that healing await "the redemption of our body" when Christ returns (Rom. 8:23; cf. Rev. 22:1–3).

We may certainly pray for healing, even miraculous healing, as we will discuss in the next chapter. However, we will argue there that God did not intend to establish a perpetual ministry of supernatural healing in the church, but gave gifts of healing as signs that God's kingdom has come in Christ, though it has not yet arrived in glory. Christ gave healing to some (John 5:8) in order to show to all that he is the Son of God (vv. 17–20) and has life in himself to raise the dead, now spiritually (vv. 21, 24–26) and forever in glory (vv. 28–29). Therefore, let us contemplate the healings reported in the Bible, see in them signs of eternal life, and rejoice in hope in the healer who is the resurrection and the life of his people.

7. Helps, Ministry, Giving, and Mercy

Paul names the gift of "helps" (plural *antilēmpsis*, 1 Cor. 12:28). The word does not appear elsewhere in the New Testament, but it means help, assistance, or strength.[58] This gift empowers people to serve members of the body who are weaker, less honorable, or suffering (vv. 22–23, 26). The meaning of "helps" may be illuminated by the use of the related verb in Paul's words in Acts 20:33–35: "I have coveted no man's silver, or gold, or apparel. Yea, ye yourselves know, that these hands have ministered unto my necessities, and to them that were with me. I have shewed you all things, how that so labouring ye ought to support [*antilambanomai*] the weak, and to remember the words of the Lord Jesus, how he said, It is more blessed to give than to receive." Thus, "helps" likely refers to spiritual gifts by which a person gives practical assistance and encouragement to other Christians who are poor, sick, and needy.

In the parallel list of gifts in Romans, Paul names three gifts that may be subsets of "helps." One is the gift of "ministry" (*diakonia*, Rom. 12:7). This word, directly related to the word translated as "servant" (*diakonos*), can be used generally of all ministry or service (1 Cor. 12:5; Eph. 4:12). However, it may also be used specifically of the ministry of the Word (Acts

58. Pss. 21:20[22:19]; 82:9[83:8]; 83:6[84:5]; 88:19[89:18]; 107:9[108:8] LXX.

6:4; 2 Cor. 5:18) or of practical works such as household tasks (Luke 10:40), distributing food to widows (Acts 6:1), or giving money for famine relief.[59] Given that Paul distinguishes it from teaching and exhortation, "ministry" refers to the gift of doing good works that meet physical needs of the church and its members. Similarly, Peter distinguishes between gifts to "speak" and gifts to "minister" (*diakoneō*, 1 Pet. 4:11). Christians with the gift of ministry would serve well as "deacons" (plural *diakonos*) or as helpers under diaconal supervision (cf. Phil. 1:1; 1 Tim. 3:8, 12).

A second gift related to helps is the gift of giving (Rom. 12:8). The verb translated as "give" (*metadidōmi*) means to share (1:11; 1 Thess. 2:8), such as sharing one's material possessions (Luke 3:11). All Christians have the duty to give to help those in need (Eph. 4:28) and to financially support the ministry of God's Word (1 Cor. 9:6–14; Gal. 6:6), especially those elders who labor in that ministry (1 Tim. 5:17–18). However, Paul speaks here of a special gift in which the Holy Spirit empowers a member of Christ's body to give in an extraordinary way. This gift may be connected with wealth (Acts 4:34–37). However, the Scriptures also highlight giving that is extraordinary not in quantity but in self-sacrifice from those with few resources (Luke 21:1–4; 2 Cor. 8:1–5). As Paul says, central to the exercise of this gift is "simplicity" (*haplotēs*, Rom. 12:8), which may mean sincerity (2 Cor. 1:12; 11:3) or generosity (8:2; 9:11, 13).

Third, Paul speaks of the gift of mercy (Rom. 12:8). Mercy (verb *eleeō*, noun *eleos*) is compassionate kindness toward the weaknesses and needs of others (Matt. 9:27).[60] The showing of mercy is a character quality of all who will receive mercy on judgment day (5:7; James 2:13). Yet here Paul identifies it as a spiritual gift, teaching us that the Holy Spirit gives some Christians a much larger capacity to show mercy to people in misery. Since Paul has already listed ministry and giving, mercy likely highlights the gift of inner compassion and sympathy. Thus, it must be used "with cheerfulness" (Rom. 12:8). The gift of mercy empowers the saints to minister the comfort that enables suffering Christians to endure with hope knowing that they are not alone—just as the Lord comforts his people by his mercy.[61] Thus, by the gift of ministry the Holy Spirit enables people to do practical works of service, giving provides the resources necessary for that service, and mercy causes that service to manifest the compassion of God.

59. Acts 11:29; 12:25; 2 Cor. 8:4; 9:1, 12, 13.
60. On God's mercy and compassion, see *RST*, 1:784–85, 861–71.
61. Isa. 49:13–16; 54:4–10; Lam. 3:21–24; 2 Cor. 1:3–6.

It might be objected that these activities are entirely natural and do not require the empowerment of the Holy Spirit. However, that is not the case. The execution of practical ministry with God-glorifying, effective excellence requires great skill and wisdom, which are gifts of the Spirit (Ex. 31:3; Isa. 11:2). Anyone who has served as a deacon can testify how complicated and difficult such ministry can be. Caring for people requires empathetic insight into their deepest needs, as our Spirit-filled High Priest exhibits in his ministry (Heb. 4:15–16). Only the Spirit can take practical ministry and make it effective to advance God's kingdom.

Therefore, those who serve Christ in the area of practical helps must devote themselves to prayer that God would bless their efforts for his glory. When the apostles instructed the church in Jerusalem to select men to oversee the ministry to widows, they told the church to find men "full of the Holy Ghost and wisdom" (Acts 6:3). We must not be satisfied with less in our churches' diaconal ministries today.

8. Governments and Ruling

Paul says that among other gifts that God has set in the church, there is "governments" (plural *kybernēsis*), a term used only once in the New Testament (1 Cor. 12:28). Literally it refers to the steering or piloting of a ship; its figurative meaning is government, such as the government of a city or state.[62] It may be used of wise "counsels" necessary for success or victory.[63] This, then, is the gift of providing wise direction for a church or group of Christians serving together.

Paul also speaks of a leadership gift in terms of ruling: "he that ruleth, with diligence" (Rom. 12:8). The verb translated as "rule" (*proïstēmi*) means, among other things, to "lead, direct, govern" and to "care for, protect."[64] Both elements—authority and care—coincide in the New Testament teachings on leadership. Paul uses this term when he writes, "We beseech you, brethren, to know them which labour among you, and are over you [*proïstēmi*] in the Lord, and admonish you; and to esteem them very highly in love for their work's sake" (1 Thess. 5:12–13). A man must "rule" (*proïstēmi*) his household well or he is not qualified to "take care

62. *TDNT*, 3:1035–36. Compare "master," "pilot," or "helmsman" (*kybernētēs*) in Ezek. 27:8, 27; Acts 27:11; Rev. 18:17. The word *cybernetics* (the study of automatic control systems) was coined from this Greek root.

63. Prov. 1:5; 11:14; 24:6 LXX.

64. *TDNT*, 6:700–702. It can also mean "devote oneself to" (Titus 3:8, 14) and "put before" (not found in the New Testament).

of the church of God" as one of its elders (1 Tim. 3:4–5; cf. 5:17). So also must deacons (3:12).

It does not appear that government and ruling, appearing in different lists, express different gifts, but that they are different descriptions of the same kind of gifts. These gifts are intimately connected with the office bearers in the church. However, leadership gifts may be given to church members outside of the offices of ministers, elders, and deacons, for churches often need skillful leadership over specific ministries and activities that the elders and deacons oversee but cannot directly lead as they care for the congregation as a whole.

The difficulties and discouragements that attend the work of leadership and the great energy it requires are reflected in Paul's command that those who lead must do so "with diligence" (Rom. 12:8) or "zeal" (ESV; cf. v. 11). Let us thank God for the leaders whom he has provided for the church in the past and present, intercede for those who lead us now, that they may serve well, and petition him that by his Spirit he will raise up gifted leaders for the future.

9. Tongues and Interpreting Tongues

Paul speaks of the gift of "kinds of tongues"[65] and those who "speak with tongues" (*laleō glōssais*, 1 Cor. 12:10, 28, 30).[66] The word translated as "tongue" (*glōssa*) can refer to the muscular organ in the mouth (Mark 7:33), the act of speech (James 1:26; 1 John 3:18), or a particular language spoken by a people (Gen. 10:5; 11:7 LXX; Rev. 5:9; 7:9). To "speak" in or with a "tongue" (*laleō* with the dative of *glōssa*) means to speak in a particular language.[67] Therefore, this gift consisted not in unintelligible noises but in the supernatural ability to speak in other languages, whether "Persian," "Syriac," or some "other foreign tongue," as John Chrysostom said.[68]

Johannes Behm (1883–1948), representing a viewpoint commonly held among scholars in the early twentieth century, argued that speaking in

65. The phrases "divers kinds of tongues" (1 Cor. 12:10) and "diversities of tongues" (v. 28) translate the same Greek phrase (*genē glōssōn*).

66. From this phrase is derived the term *glossolalia*, coined in the nineteenth century, which refers to speaking in languages unknown to the speaker or in meaningless babble as a manifestation of ecstasy or religious fervor.

67. Isa. 19:18 LXX; Acts 2:11. Compare "speak" (*laleō*) in a "language" (dative *dialektos*, Acts 2:6) and the dative *dialektos* modifying other verbs of speech in Acts 1:19; 2:8; 21:40; 22:2; 26:14.

68. Chrysostom, *Homilies on 1 Corinthians*, 35.5, 36.3, in *NPNF*[1], 12:211, 218.

tongues produced inarticulate sounds without meaning.[69] His argument had three main bases. First, Paul compared tongues to making indistinct sounds with musical instruments (1 Cor. 14:7–8). But this is an analogy or illustration, not a description or definition of tongues. Second, Behm compared speaking in tongues to the ecstatic babble of pagan oracles. However, Paul strongly differentiated between Christian experiences of God and pagan experiences of idols and demons (1 Cor. 10:19–22; 12:2–3). If the gift of tongues was essentially the same as pagan ecstatic speech, it would not have been a sign of the true God to the Corinthians. Third, Behm explained the use of terms closely associated with intelligible languages by reference to "the 'language of the Spirit,' a miraculous language which is used in heaven between God and the angels (1 Cor. 13:1)."[70] However, Paul's words "though I speak with the tongues of men and of angels" cannot be used to define the gift of tongues, for the examples he gave in that passage are hyperbolic and extreme, such as having "all knowledge" and "all faith" (vv. 1–3).[71] Our understanding of tongues must be derived from the terms Paul used and what he said about its activity, which both point toward real human languages.[72] Whereas the babble view of tongues reduces it to a humanly explicable phenomena—an approach congenial to theological liberalism—the interpretation of tongues as real, unlearned languages maintains the character of the gift as truly miraculous.[73]

Speaking in tongues produced words that the speaker did not understand, and many hearers perhaps did not understand (1 Cor. 14:2). Another person might have been able to "interpret" (*diermēneuō*) them for the edification of the church (v. 5), a verb that means to explain (Luke 24:27 ESV) or, more specifically, to translate from one language to another (Acts 9:36).[74] The words spoken in tongues were not babble or nonsense, but consisted of praying, blessing, and thanking God in a manner that

69. *TDNT*, 1:722–26. Somewhat similar is Anthony Thiselton's view that the gift of tongues is "the language of the unconscious," releasing the praise and yearnings of the heart with groanings beyond words (Rom. 8:26). *1 Corinthians: A Shorter and Pastoral Commentary*, 203–4; and *The First Epistle to the Corinthians*, The New International Greek Testament Commentary (Grand Rapids, MI: Eerdmans; Carlisle, Cumbria, England: Paternoster, 2000), 988.

70. *TDNT*, 1:726.

71. Other hyperbolic references to angels appear in Gal. 1:8; 4:14.

72. Robert H. Gundry, "'Ecstatic Utterance' (N.E.B.)?," *The Journal of Theological Studies*, New Series, 17, no. 2 (October 1966): 299–307.

73. Smeaton, *The Doctrine of the Holy Spirit*, 51.

74. The idea of translating from one language to another is strongly associated with this root in the New Testament, as may be seen in related verbs: *hermēneuō* in John 1:38, 42; 9:7; Heb. 7:2; and *methermēneuō* in Matt. 1:23; Mark 5:41; 15:22, 34; John 1:41; Acts 4:36; 13:8.

would elicit an "Amen" from others if translated into speech they could understand (1 Cor. 14:15–16). When Paul said, "He that speaketh in an unknown tongue . . . speaketh mysteries" (v. 2), he meant hidden divine truths revealed for human understanding.[75]

Since speaking in tongues communicated truth in foreign languages, Paul taught that it had value in the public meetings of the church if there was someone there with the gift of "interpretation" (*hermēneia*, 1 Cor. 12:10; 14:26). With interpretation, the message spoken in tongues was understandable and edifying (14:5); without interpretation, ten thousand words in tongues were less helpful than five words in an understandable language (vv. 13–19). Therefore, the gift of interpretation was the Spirit-empowered ability to translate messages declared through the exercise of the gift of tongues.

It is not entirely clear how "he that speaketh in an unknown tongue edifieth himself" (1 Cor. 14:4; cf. v. 18). If he understood the meaning of what he said, he did not need to pray for the gift of interpretation (v. 13) and his mind would not have been unfruitful (v. 14). Apparently, the speaker was conscious that he was praising and thanking God (v. 17), though he spoke without "understanding" the specific content of his words (v. 19). This implies that both the content and the language came from the Holy Spirit. Tongues did not consist of the ability to communicate one's mind in a new language, but to speak a word from God—a kind of prophecy. However, the speaker was not in an ecstatic state but could control when he spoke (vv. 27–28).

Paul regulated speaking in tongues in the congregation for the sake of maintaining peace and order, and pursuing what would build up Christ's body (1 Cor. 14:26, 33, 40). If everyone had spoken in tongues simultaneously, the confusion of noise would have caused unconverted visitors to the church to think the believers were insane (v. 23). Speaking in tongues was not the language of corporate prayer or praise. Rather, a few people spoke in tongues, one at a time with interpretation; without an interpreter, they were to be quiet (vv. 26–28).

Speaking in tongues was a sign of judgment and salvation. In 1 Corinthians 14:21, Paul quoted Isaiah 28:11, in which the Lord said that he would speak to Israel in the foreign language of its conquerors because the people mocked his word as childish gibberish (vv. 9–10,

75. See *mysterion* in 1 Cor. 2:7; 4:1; 13:2; 15:51.

13).[76] Addressing Israel by a nation whose tongue the Hebrews could not understand was a covenantal curse (Deut. 28:49; Jer. 5:15). That prophecy of Isaiah stands in close proximity to the promise of Christ, the cornerstone that God would lay in Zion for the salvation of believers (Isa. 28:16), but a stone of stumbling for many in Israel (8:14; cf. Rom. 9:33; 1 Pet. 2:6–7). Gentiles in Corinth (like all people today) needed to learn from God's covenantal curses upon Israel that the Lord is faithful to carry out his threats against the wicked and unbelieving (1 Cor. 10:1–11). They also needed to learn that God has given salvation in Christ to believers from all nations.[77]

Paul's teaching about the gift of tongues corresponds with what Luke reports in the three instances of tongues in Acts.[78] At Pentecost, the disciples "were all filled with the Holy Ghost, and began to speak with other tongues, as the Spirit gave them utterance" (Acts 2:4). The infinitive verb translated as "utterance" (*apophthengomai*)—literally to "declare"—does not connote babble but is used elsewhere for clear and rational preaching (v. 14; 26:25). These "tongues" were foreign languages, understood by people who had come for the festival from many nations (2:5–11): "Every man heard them speak in his own language" (v. 6). Speaking in tongues at Pentecost did not provide a means of overcoming a language barrier for evangelism; the people who heard it were all "Jews" (v. 5), and Peter preached to them all in a common language, whether Greek or Aramaic (v. 14). The words spoken in tongues had intelligible content that glorified God: "We do hear them speak in our tongues the wonderful works of God" (v. 11). The same was true of Gentiles in the home of Cornelius: "They heard them speak with tongues, and magnify God" (10:46). Peter said that speaking in tongues was a fulfillment of God's promise to pour out the Spirit so that people "shall prophesy" (2:17–18), implying that tongues was a form of prophecy or closely connected to it. We read that the twelve disciples at Ephesus "spake with tongues, and prophesied" (19:6). When many people spoke in tongues at Pentecost, some observers charged them with being drunk (2:13–15), but those who understood the

76. Edward J. Young, *The Book of Isaiah*, 3 vols. (Grand Rapids, MI: Eerdmans, 1969), 2:277–78.

77. O. Palmer Robertson, "Tongues: Sign of Covenantal Curse and Blessing," *Westminster Theological Journal* 38, no. 1 (January 1975): 44–49 (full article, 43–53).

78. For a comparison of Luke's and Paul's presentations of tongues, see Craig S. Keener, *Acts: An Exegetical Commentary*, vol. 1, *Introduction and 1:1–2:47* (Grand Rapids, MI: Baker Academic, 2012), 813–15.

languages spoken saw it as a supernatural sign (v. 12). That is similar to Paul's teaching that tongues was a sign to unbelievers (1 Cor. 14:21–22), but they might think the congregation crazy if many spoke in tongues simultaneously (v. 23). Just as Paul linked tongues with God's covenantal curse on Israel (1 Cor. 14:21), so speaking in tongues in Acts was a sign that Israel had crucified its Messiah (Acts 2:23, 36) and the gospel of salvation was going out to the Gentile nations (2:39; 10:44–47). Sinclair Ferguson says, "What marks the reversal of Babel and indicates the universality of the new covenant also signals judgment on the covenant people for the rejection of Christ."[79] Thus, the gift of tongues is bound up with the great transition in redemptive history from a focus on national Israel to the mission to the world. As we will argue in the next chapter, tongues, together with the gifts of miracles and healing, has passed away.

Therefore, when we consider the gift of tongues in the New Testament, we should take to heart both God's severity and mercy. God judged his ancient covenant people, Israel, when many of them rejected his Son. We should not think that God will spare us if we do the same. On the other hand, the gift of tongues reminds us that even when God was judging Israel, his love overflowed in the mission to all nations. Christ is the Savior of the world (John 4:42), and he will receive the praise of people from every nation and tongue, for he redeemed them by his blood (Rev. 5:9).

Conclusion to the Study of Specific Spiritual Gifts

In summary, our analysis of the particular spiritual gifts listed in the Bible has led us to nine general kinds of giftedness poured out with the Spirit at Pentecost. Three of these gifts involved extraordinary ministers of the Word: apostles, prophets, and evangelists (Eph. 4:11). Three granted the ability to perform signs and wonders: miracles, healing, and tongues (1 Cor. 12:8–10, 28–30). As we noted earlier, we will discuss signs and wonders in more detail in the next chapter.

The last three categories of giftedness pertain to the ordinary ministry of the church through all ages: teachers, governments, and helps (and possibly faith). Peter deftly summarizes them as "one who speaks" and "one who serves" (1 Pet. 4:11 ESV; cf. Acts 6:1–4). It is notable that these gifts correspond to the offices of the church: ministers and elders on the one hand and deacons on the other. Thus, church officers should lead the

79. Ferguson, *The Holy Spirit*, 213.

way in the exercise of the gifts. That is not to say that such gifts belong exclusively to office bearers. Every believer in Christ has a spiritual gift. Paul has reminded us that the multiplicity of ways that Christians instruct, exhort, direct, rule, assist, serve, give, and show mercy displays the presence of God's Spirit in the church. Still, the biblical lists of spiritual gifts may not provide an exhaustive description of every nuance of giftedness, for God shapes and equips each individual according to his unique identity.

Extraordinary Ministers of the Word	Signs and Wonders	Ordinary Ministry
Apostles	Miracles (perhaps with faith)	Teaching (with exhortation, word of knowledge, word of wisdom, pastoring, speaking, and perhaps faith)
Prophets (with discerning of spirits)	Healing	Governing (with ruling)
Evangelists	Tongues (with interpretation)	Helping (with serving, giving, and mercy)

Table 6.2. Spiritual Gifts by Category

Our Duty regarding Spiritual Gifts

The doctrine of spiritual gifts is by no means theoretical but has significant practical implications for our responsibilities as Christians and members of the church.

1. *Judge your gifts with humble, sober realism.* Paul says, "For I say, through the grace given unto me, to every man that is among you, not to think of himself more highly than he ought to think; but to think soberly, according as God hath dealt to every man the measure of faith" (Rom. 12:3). Examine yourself and how God has used you in the past. Ask for counsel from wise, godly people who know you. Think clearly. What are your gifts? Avoid both proud self-exaltation and the false humility of denying that you are gifted by the Spirit. Instead, acknowledge the gifts you have as God's unmerited grace to you.

2. *Employ your gifts in active church membership.* Christians are members of one another in the body and have different functions (Rom. 12:4–5). They must put their gifts into active exercise—not half-heartedly

but with "generosity," "zeal," and "cheerfulness" (vv. 6–8 ESV). Be "fervent in spirit; serving the Lord" (v. 11). Start somewhere and do not be ashamed to do the most menial tasks. Even if you are not sure what your gifts are, the best way to discern them is to serve as best you know how and see how God works. Do not be like dead wood in a tree, but do what you can by your gifts to build up the church of your Savior. Then the body of Christ will be able to recognize and affirm your gifts for future service.

3. *Cherish the other gifts and rely on the other members of the body.* Paul teaches, "The eye cannot say unto the hand, I have no need of thee: nor again the head to the feet, I have no need of you" (1 Cor. 12: 21). Cast off foolish self-sufficiency and a judgmental spirit toward those who are different from you. Admire the gifts belonging to others. Place yourself under their ministry so you might benefit from their gifts. Learn to say, "Please help me. I need you."

4. *Treasure and pursue love above any spiritual gift.* Beware of confusing giftedness with godliness or thinking that rich gifts make up for poor holiness. Paul tells us that if we have the greatest gifts imaginable but lack love, then we are "nothing" (1 Cor. 13:1–3). Nothing! Meditate often on the genuine acts of love, how it patiently endures irritation, shows kindness to others, and does not envy, boast, magnify self, or insist on getting what it wants (vv. 4–5). Consider the purity of true love, how it does not rejoice in sin but rejects it with revulsion and rejoices in what is good and true (v. 6; Rom. 12:9). Then, "pursue love" (1 Cor. 14:1 ESV).

5. *Control your gifts for peace, order, and edification in the church.* Paul says, "Let all things be done unto edifying. . . . For God is not the author of confusion, but of peace, as in all churches of the saints. . . . Let all things be done decently and in order" (1 Cor. 14:26, 33, 40). The importance of using your gifts is never an excuse for dividing, disrupting, or destroying the church of Jesus Christ. Practice humble self-restraint for the purpose of love.

6. *Submit your gifts to the direction of the Lord Christ through his Word.* Christ ascended far above the heavens that he might fill all things, and gave the ministers of the Word to equip the saints (Eph. 4:10–12). Don't use your gifts as a maverick. Only when the members of the body are receiving the wisdom and grace of the ascended Lord through the Word are they ready to use their gifts rightly. From Christ is "the whole body fitly joined together," so that by "the effectual working in the measure of every

part," the body grows "unto the edifying of itself in love" (v. 16). Spiritual gifts are not given for solo performances but for a symphony.

7. *Serve as a steward of God's grace for his glory*. Peter says, "As every man hath received the gift, even so minister the same one to another, as good stewards of the manifold grace of God . . . that God in all things may be glorified through Jesus Christ, to whom be praise and dominion for ever and ever" (1 Pet. 4:10–11). We are but stewards of the Lord's riches. We serve for his glory in Jesus Christ. Therefore, we must not use our gifts for worldly success and grandeur in ministry, but with an eye on the eternal kingdom. The Lord will judge his servants according to the gifts he gives them. Whether you have great gifts or the least, the greatest honor and joy on earth cannot compare with what Christ will give you if you are faithful.

Sing to the Lord

God's Power, Victory, and Gifts in Christ

A mighty Fortress is our God,
A Bulwark never failing;
Our Helper he amid the flood
Of mortal ills prevailing.
For still our ancient foe
Doth seek to work us woe;
His craft and pow'r are great;
And armed with cruel hate,
On earth is not his equal.

Did we in our own strength confide,
Our striving would be losing;
Were not the right Man on our side,
The Man of God's own choosing.
Dost ask who that may be?
Christ Jesus, it is he,
Lord Sabaoth his Name,
From age to age the same,
And he must win the battle.

And though this world, with devils filled,
Should threaten to undo us,
We will not fear, for God hath willed
His truth to triumph through us.

The prince of darkness grim,
We tremble not for him;
His rage we can endure,
For lo! His doom is sure;
One little word shall fell him.

That Word above all earthly powers,
No thanks to them, abideth;
The Spirit and the gifts are ours
Through him who with us sideth;
Let goods and kindred go,
This mortal life also;
The body they may kill:
God's truth abideth still;
His kingdom is forever.

Martin Luther
Tune: Ein' Feste Burg
Trinity Hymnal—Baptist Edition, No. 81

Questions for Meditation or Discussion

1. What are the major terms used in the New Testament for spiritual gifts? What do those terms teach us about the nature of the gifts?
2. What is the difference between calling a gift an event or an endowment? Which is the biblical view of spiritual gifts? Why?
3. What are the distinctive qualities of the apostles?
4. What is a prophet?
5. Someone says, "I believe that healing is the birthright of every child of God, for Christ died for us, and 'with his stripes we are healed' (Isa. 53:5)." How do you respond?
6. For each of the following gifts, provide a brief definition and offer some examples of how someone with that gift might serve for the edification of Christ's church.
   - teaching
   - exhorting
   - ministering
   - giving
   - mercy
   - governments/ruling

7. Based on the practical applications at the end of this chapter and your own reflections, write your own "Ten Commandments regarding Spiritual Gifts," each beginning, "Thou shalt not . . ."
8. After reading this chapter, what do you think is your spiritual gift? Why? How are you using your gift to build up Christ's church?

Questions for Deeper Reflection

9. What is the relationship between teaching and exhorting? Can they ever be completely separated? Can they be distinguished in any way?
10. Why do many Christians tend to think, or at least to act, as if pastors were the only people with spiritual gifts? How can we remedy this error?
11. You have been asked to present a thirty-minute talk to high school students on the topic "What is the gift of tongues in the New Testament?" Prepare a detailed outline.

7

The Signs and Wonders of the Spirit

Among the many effects that the Holy Spirit produced, some of the most visible were works of supernatural power: "Many wonders and signs were done by the apostles" (Acts 2:43). The narrative of Acts is replete with miracles.[1] Paul speaks of what Christ "wrought by me . . . by word and deed, through mighty signs and wonders, by the power of the Spirit of God" (Rom. 15:18–19).

In this chapter, we will explore the reality and relevance of miracles. Signs and wonders reveal that God is the sovereign and supernatural Lord of heaven and earth, and that his kingdom has been inaugurated in Christ. However, though God does not change, we will argue that he willed that miraculous gifts should cease in the life of the church.

Introduction to Miracles

It is helpful for us to clarify what miracles are before discussing the miraculous gifts of the Spirit. The English word *miracle* (from Latin *miraculum*) refers to an event that evokes wonder. Thus, if a man walks away from a serious car accident, someone might say, "It's a miracle that you are alive." More specifically, people use *miracle* for an extraordinary event that shows God's activity in human history.[2]

1. Acts 2:1–13, 43; 3:6–8; 4:16, 22, 30–31; 5:1–11, 12, 16, 19; 6:8; 8:6–7, 13, 39; 9:17–18, 32–35, 40; 10:44–46; 12:6–11, 23; 13:9–12; 14:3, 8–10, 19–20; 15:12; 16:18, 26; 19:6, 11–12; 20:9–12; 28:1–9. This list does not include references to divine visions and other forms of special revelation.

2. See *Merriam-Webster's Collegiate Dictionary*, 11th ed. (Springfield, MA: Merriam-Webster, 2003).

New Testament Terminology for Miracles

Three Greek words dominate references to miracles in the New Testament. "Sign" (*sēmeion*),[3] sometimes translated as "miracle" or "wonder," identifies a supernatural event as an indication that a person is an authorized representative of a supernatural being.[4] "Wonder" (*teras*), always joined with "sign" in the New Testament, refers to a supernatural act as an event that produces amazement and awe in its observers.[5] "Powers" (plural *dynamis*), sometimes translated as "mighty works" or "miracles," highlights God's power demonstrated in these acts (Acts 2:22). Some Scripture passages use all three terms, "signs," "wonders," and "powers," to jointly describe miracles.[6]

Several other Greek words are also used of miracles. A miracle may be called a "mighty thing" (*kratos*, Luke 1:51, literally "he did *a mighty thing* by his arm"). Also, a miracle is sometimes referred to as a "work" (*ergon*), especially in the Gospel of John, where the great works of Christ serve as a witness to his divinity and mission.[7] Another adjective (*megaleios*) and the related noun (*megaleiotēs*) identify miracles as great or magnificent things.[8] Yet another adjective (*thaumasios*) is used to describe miracles as amazing, marvelous things (Matt. 21:15).

A Theological Definition of a Miracle

The following definition may be offered based on the Holy Scriptures: *A miracle is an extraordinary, observable event according to God's sovereign will that evokes awe at his powerful presence because it confirms and fulfills his word of salvation and judgment.*[9]

3. The word translated as "sign" (*sēmeion*) may be used of a miracle, an ordinary signal (Matt. 26:48), or another visible mark or observable event (24:3, 30; Luke 2:12; Rom. 4:11; 2 Thess. 3:17).

4. Edward N. Gross, *Miracles, Demons, and Spiritual Warfare: An Urgent Call for Discernment* (Grand Rapids, MI: Baker, 1990). For examples, see John 2:11, 18, 23; 3:2; 6:14; 7:31; 20:30–31; Acts 2:22; 8:6, 13; 14:3; Rom. 15:19; 2 Cor. 12:12; Heb. 2:4. Note also the working of "signs" by the servants of evil, supernatural powers (Mark. 13:22; 2 Thess. 2:9; Rev. 13:13–14; 16:14).

5. Matt. 24:24; Mark 13:22; John 4:48; Acts 2:19, 22, 43; 4:30; 5:12; 6:8; 7:36; 14:3; 15:12; Rom. 15:19; 2 Cor. 12:12; 2 Thess. 2:9; Heb. 2:4. The sense of "wonder" is well illustrated in Acts 2:43; 5:11–12.

6. Acts 2:22; 2 Cor. 12:12; 2 Thess. 2:9; Heb. 2:4; cf. singular "power" in Acts 6:8; Rom. 15:19; 2 Thess. 2:9.

7. Matt. 11:2; Luke 24:19; John 5:20, 36; 7:21; 9:3–4; 10:25, 32–33, 37; 14:10–12; 15:24; Acts 7:22.

8. *Megaleios*: Luke 1:49; Acts 2:11. *Megaleiotēs*: Luke 9:43; 2 Pet. 1:16.

9. Our definition may be compared to that of Sam Waldron: "A miracle is a redemptive, revelatory, extraordinary, external, astonishing manifestation of the power of God." Samuel E. Waldron, *To Be Continued? Are the Miraculous Gifts for Today?* (Merrick, NY: Calvary Press, 2005), 100.

Miracles are *extraordinary* acts of God, not regular displays of his glory in creation and providence, such as majestic mountains or the birth of a child. The extraordinary display of God's power in signs and wonders does not rule out his use of natural means, such as wind (Ex. 10:13, 19) or medicine (2 Kings 20:1–7), to accomplish his will. Even in such cases, however, the events were highly unusual. What sets apart an event as a miracle is not whether means are used, but whether God works with power to do what no man could do.

Miracles in the Bible are *observable* to the senses. The Lord "shows" people a "sign," and they "see" it.[10] Though the new birth and spiritual growth may be called miracles in a broad sense because they come from supernatural power and should evoke our praise, the Bible does not include them in what it calls signs, wonders, and powers.

God works miracles *according to his sovereign will*, just as salvation itself arises from the free decree of God's will (Rom. 9:15). The miracle-working God is the King over his creation (Ps. 74:12–17). He does all that he pleases in heaven and earth (135:6, 9). Miracles are not human manipulations of the world and its spiritual powers. The miracles of Christ and his servants do not involve divination, casting spells, or conjuring spirits, methods typical of ancient sorcery (Lev. 20:27; Deut. 18:9–11). Christ often worked miracles by a simple command, and his servants did so by invoking his name with faith.[11] Miracles are the works of the sovereign "Lord," the "I am" (Ex. 3:14–15; 10:2).

Miracles *evoke awe at God's powerful presence*, giving those who observe them a sense that the majestic, glorious Lord is near. God sent his plagues on Egypt "to the end thou mayest know that I am the Lord in the midst of the earth" (Ex. 8:22). After Jesus raised a young man from the dead, "There came a fear on all: and they glorified God, saying, That a great prophet is risen up among us; and, That God hath visited his people" (Luke 7:16).

Signs from God communicate that sense of God's presence *because they confirm and fulfill his word*. God gave Moses the power to work signs so that Israel would believe that the Lord had sent him (Ex. 4:8–9; 14:31). When Elijah raised a widow's son from the dead, the woman said, "Now by this I know that thou art a man of God, and that the word of the Lord in thy mouth is truth" (1 Kings 17:24). When the Lord healed Naaman

10. Deut. 4:34; 7:19; Ps. 95:9; Matt. 12:38; 16:1; John 2:18.
11. Luke 9:49; 10:17; Acts 3:6, 16; 4:10, 30; 16:18.

of his leprosy, he said, "Now I know that there is no God in all the earth, but in Israel" (2 Kings 5:15). The miracles of the New Testament confirm God's word through Christ and his messengers.[12]

Miracles fulfill God's word of *salvation and judgment*. They are not for private entertainment, personal promotion, or vengeance.[13] Miracles advance God's redemptive purposes to save and sustain his people and destroy their enemies. The miracles of the exodus both confirmed God's word through Moses and fulfilled God's promises to Abraham that God would redeem his people. The repeated references to "signs" and "wonders" in Acts echo the same terms used of God's plagues upon Egypt,[14] confirming the accomplishment of a new and greater exodus in Christ.[15] Christ's ministry of casting out demons shows that "the kingdom of God is come unto you" (Matt. 12:28).

Therefore, miracles are acts of God designed to manifest the glorious reality of his salvation and judgment revealed in the gospel of Christ. John Calvin said that the aim of miracles is "to confirm the doctrine of the gospel" (cf. Mark 16:20; Acts 14:3), and "the legitimate use of miracles, accordingly, is, to receive them as seals of the doctrine of the gospel (Rom. 15:19), and in that way make them subservient to the glory not of men and angels, but of God only, as Peter said (Acts 3:12, 16)."[16] John Owen said that the world was "asleep in sin and security, satisfied with their lusts and idolatries . . . [but miracles] awakened the dull, stupid world unto a consideration of the doctrine of the gospel, which otherwise they would have securely neglected and despised."[17]

Miracles, Skepticism, and Modern Science

The rationalism of the Enlightenment promoted skepticism toward all claims of supernatural events.[18] Scientists such as Robert Boyle (1627–1691) and

12. Luke 7:18–23; John 5:36; Acts 8:6; Heb. 2:3–4.

13. Here we see the contrast between biblical miracles and those attributed to the child Jesus in apocryphal writings, such as making birds out of clay and bringing them to life, or cursing children who annoyed him. *The Infancy Gospel of Thomas*, secs. 2–4, in *The Apocryphal New Testament: Being the Apocryphal Gospels, Acts, Epistles, and Apocalypses*, ed. Montague R. James, rev. ed. (Oxford: Oxford University Press, 1953), 49–50.

14. Ex. 7:3; 11:9–10; Deut. 4:34; 6:22; 7:19; 11:3; 26:8; 29:2; 34:11; Pss. 77(78):43; 104(105):27; 134(135):9; Jer. 39(32):20–21 LXX. See also Acts 7:36.

15. See David W. Pao, *Acts and the Isaianic New Exodus* (Eugene, OR: Wipf and Stock, 2016).

16. John Calvin, *Articles Agreed upon by the Faculty of Sacred Theology at Paris, with the Antidote*, Art. 11, in *Tracts Relating to the Reformation*, trans. Henry Beveridge, 3 vols. (Edinburgh: Calvin Translation Society, 1844), 1:92–93. See Calvin, *Institutes*, 4.19.6; and *Commentaries*, on Matt. 10:1.

17. Owen, "A Discourse of Spiritual Gifts," in *Pneumatologia*, in *Works*, 4:484–85.

18. On the Enlightenment and the Word of God, see *RST*, 1:287–95.

Isaac Newton (1642–1727) made remarkable progress in describing natural phenomena with mathematical laws. While Boyle and Newton were devout believers in God and the Bible, other philosophers used the success of the new science (or "natural philosophy" as it was called) to undergird the belief that all reality can be explained by rational principles. Subjugating divine revelation to human reason, Baruch Spinoza (1632–1677) viewed the Bible as a book of legends.[19] Not all Enlightenment thinkers embraced this skepticism. John Locke (1632–1704), a physician and philosopher considered to be a father of modern civil liberties, affirmed that belief in miracles is quite rational and that faith may be given to divine revelation with complete assent.[20]

Objections to miracles typically appeal to the laws of nature. Voltaire (Francois-Marie Arouet, 1694–1778) said, "A miracle is the violation of mathematical, divine, immutable, eternal laws. By the very exposition itself, a miracle is a contradiction in terms." Voltaire compared the universe to an "immense machine" that God must "derange" and "disfigure" in order to produce a miracle.[21] David Hume (1711–1776) said, "A miracle is a violation of the laws of nature; and as a firm and unalterable experience has established these laws, the proof against a miracle, from the very nature of the fact, is as entire as any argument from experience can possibly be imagined." As examples of "the laws of nature," Hume offered "that all men must die; that lead cannot, of itself, remain suspended in the air; that fire consumes wood, and is extinguished by water." In the same fashion, he said, "that a dead man should come to life . . . has never been observed, in any age or country."[22]

In reply, we note that these arguments are circular: the conclusion against miracles is based on a belief in "immutable, eternal laws" and "unalterable experience," thereby assuming that miracles can never be experienced because of unchangeable patterns in nature. But that is begging the question; it is precisely the point that the Bible contains many

19. On Spinoza, see *RST*, 1:288, 591.

20. John Locke, *An Essay concerning Human Understanding*, 4th ed. (London: Awnsham and John Churchil; and Samuel Manship, 1700), 4.16.13–14 (403); and *Discourse of Miracles*, in *The Works of John Locke*, 9 vols., 12th ed. (London: For C. and J. Rivington et al., 1824), 256–65.

21. Voltaire, *A Philosophical Dictionary*, vol. 7, s.v. "miracles," in *The Works of Voltaire*, ed. Tobias Smollett, rev. trans. William F. Fleming, intro. Oliver H. G. Leigh, 22 vols. (Paris: E. R. DuMont, 1901), 11:272–73; cf. 281–82.

22. David Hume, *An Enquiry Concerning Human Understanding*, chap. 10, in *Essays and Treatises on Several Subjects*, vol. II, new ed. (London: A. Millar et al., 1768), 133–34. See Colin Brown, *Miracles and the Critical Mind* (Exeter, England: Paternoster; Grand Rapids, MI: Eerdmans, 1984), 79–100.

testimonies of miracles, including several resurrections from the dead that have "been observed."

The objector might insist that science proves the laws of nature, which rule out the possibility of miracles. However, the laws of nature are patterns that God ordained, sustains, and directs by his sovereign word. They are not powers independent of God.[23] They cannot constrain his will, but are the effects of his will. Rather than viewing the universe as a machine that exists of itself without God (atheism) or that was created by God but left to run by itself (deism), we should see it as a created system constantly upheld and directed by God as he chooses (Ps. 135:5–7; Heb. 1:3).[24] This is not to deny that parts of creation act upon one another as real secondary causes, but it is to subordinate the system of secondary causes to the primary cause, the will of the Creator. Thomas Aquinas said, "He is not subject to the order of secondary causes; but, on the contrary, this order is subject to Him, as proceeding from Him, not by a natural necessity, but by the choice of His own will."[25] Therefore, miracles are not, strictly speaking, divine interventions or interference in the world, but variations in God's providence.[26]

God ordinarily controls the universe in observable patterns that allow us to live wisely. This is the basis of science, for without a wise Creator and Lord we have no reason to expect the universe to act in a regular and predictable manner.[27] However, God has the power and authority to work miracles, and it is good that he does so when it helps to advance his kingdom among men. Therefore, there is no logical or scientific reason why we should not believe in miracles.

Biblical Miracles, Divine Testimony, and Faith

Miracles have a complex relationship to faith and godliness. How do miracles function to evoke and nurture faith? What authority do they grant to those who work them? How does that authority relate to the Holy Scriptures, which testify to miracles in their historical narratives?

An apparent miracle, by itself, is not sufficient to establish the divine authority of someone's message. Sorcerers and false prophets can work

---

23. These two sentences are quoted from *RST*, 1:1083. See the discussion of providence and nature in 1:1082–85.

24. For an exposition of the Bible's teaching on providence, see *RST*, 1:1058–80 (chap. 52).

25. Aquinas, *Summa Theologica*, Part 1, Q. 105, Art. 6, Answer. On creatures as secondary causes in God's providence, see *RST*, 1:1070–76.

26. Grudem, *Systematic Theology*, 355.

27. For biblical principles regarding empirical science, see *RST*, 1:221–28.

signs and wonders.[28] It is not clear to what extent such miracles are illusions or supernatural events, but the Scriptures do attribute signs and wonders to Satan (2 Thess. 2:9; Rev. 16:14).[29] The Devil has power to do great works by God's permission, including igniting fire by lightning, sending destructive wind, afflicting people with disease, and giving people superhuman strength and knowledge.[30]

Miracles attest to God's messengers when they are observed in conjunction with hearing his word. After healing a man who had been lame for thirty-eight years, Christ Jesus said that the "works" he did were a "witness" (*martyria*) or "testimony" (ESV) "that the Father hath sent me" (John 5:36; cf. 10:25). Yet this testimony does not stand alone: other witnesses to Christ include the Old Testament Scriptures (5:39; cf. 1:45), the prophecies of John the Baptist (5:33, 36; cf. 1:7–8, 15), Christ's own words (8:13–18; 18:37), and the Spirit-empowered words of the apostles (15:26–27; 19:35; 21:24). Ultimately, all testimony to Jesus comes from the Father, the God who is true (3:32–33; 5:31–37). Therefore, God works miracles as one component in a mutually reinforcing complex of testimonies to Christ by the Word and Spirit. The mighty works of God do not function independently of God's words or the God-revealing character of his Son (14:7–11).

Miracles have significance for faith not merely as abstract works of power—which could prove only the presence of a superhuman force—but as acts of the Redeemer's grace proclaimed by the gospel of the kingdom. When John the Baptist asked Jesus for confirmation that he was the One to come, Christ did not merely point to works of power, but acts of compassion and grace: "The blind see, the lame walk, the lepers are cleansed, the deaf hear, the dead are raised, to the poor the gospel is preached" (Luke 7:22). When some people accused Christ of casting out demons by the power of Satan, Jesus responded by pointing to the gracious, redemptive character of his ministry: he did not build up Satan's kingdom, but tore it down by rescuing people from it (11:15–22). Apart from an understanding of the gospel, miracles lead to superstition and idolatry (Acts 14:8–13). Miracles confirm God's word, but the word must explain miracles.

---

28. Ex. 7:11–12, 22; 8:7, 18–19; Deut. 13:1–5; Matt. 24:24; Mark 13:22; Acts 8:10; Rev. 13:13–14; 19:20.

29. Paul says that Satan works "lying" (*pseudos*) signs and wonders (2 Thess. 2:9), but it is not clear whether this indicates that the miracles are fake or that they are used to confirm the "lie" (*to pseudos*, v. 11).

30. Job 1:12, 16, 19; 2:6–7; Mark 5:2–4; Luke 13:11, 16; Acts 16:16; 19:13–16. See *RST*, 1:1141–46.

The vital interconnection between miracles, the word, and God's grace in Christ helps to explain the Bible's ambiguity toward faith in signs and wonders. When the people of Israel saw the Lord's mighty work at the Red Sea, they "believed" him and sang his praise (Ex. 14:31–15:1; Ps. 106:12). However, they soon demonstrated their unconverted hearts by bitter grumbling, disobedience, and idol worship. People challenged Christ to show them a sign even as they exhibited unbelief and hostility toward him and received his rebuke.[31] Belief in Christ that arises from miracles often is not saving faith.[32] Seeking after mighty signs does not accord with faith in Christ crucified, for God's greatest display of his power is found in the cross (1 Cor. 1:22–25).

When we read of miracles in the Holy Scriptures today, they function as part of God's Word to reveal salvation in Christ. Alexander Bruce (1831–1899) said that miracles "enter into the very substance of revelation, and are not merely signs confirmatory of its truth."[33] It is true that "because they [miracles] exceed nature, they cannot but lay a foundation for accepting a force superior to nature," as Petrus van Mastricht (1630–1706) said.[34] However, God has woven miracles inseparably into the gospel of Christ. Signs and wonders say, as it were, "Behold your God," and, "Thy God reigneth!" (Isa. 40:9; 52:7; cf. Ex. 14:13; 15:18). Bruce said that it is the "Pharisaic method" to focus on miracles themselves; whereas the disciples focused on the living person of Jesus and "saw in all His acts, miraculous or otherwise, the self-manifestation of the Christ, the Son of the living God."[35]

Through miracles, God has testified that he is really present in human history through Christ with his infinite power to save and to judge. Signs and wonders feed our hope that God will redeem his people from all evil through Jesus Christ our Lord. Conversely, biblical miracles intensify God's warnings to those in danger of rejecting the faith or falling away. Those who witness miracles are all the more liable to God's punishment if they reject the word of Christ (Luke 10:13–15; Heb. 2:1–4). Thus, through miracles both salvation and judgment draw near.

31. Matt. 12:38–39; 16:1–4; Mark 8:11–12; John 2:18; 6:30, 36, 41–42.
32. John 2:23–24; 3:1–3; 4:48; 5:14–16; 6:26–27.
33. Alexander B. Bruce, *The Miraculous Element in the Gospels* (New York: A. C. Armstrong and Son, 1902), 285.
34. Petrus van Mastricht, *Theoretical-Practical Theology*, vol. 2, trans. Todd M. Rester, ed. Joel R. Beeke (Grand Rapids, MI: Reformation Heritage Books, 2019), 1.2.11 (50).
35. Bruce, *The Miraculous Element in the Gospels*, 289.

Miraculous Gifts of the Holy Spirit Today

We turn now from a general consideration of signs, wonders, and miracles to the miraculous gifts of the Holy Spirit poured out by the ascended Christ. This focuses our study on the period beginning at Pentecost and on the topic of the granting of authority to individuals to work miracles as their ministry to help evangelize the lost and build up the church.

Views of Miraculous Gifts Today

In the previous chapter, we studied the spiritual gifts and identified some of them as the Spirit-worked ability to perform signs and wonders. The question we will address in this section is, "What should we expect from God regarding miraculous gifts in the church today as compared to what we read in Acts?" Here we focus on "gifts" of the Spirit, which implies an endowment of authority and power to regularly perform signs and wonders. (The related question of whether God continues to work miracles apart from such gifts will be addressed later in this chapter.)

Answers to this question range across a spectrum of many nuanced positions. One side of the spectrum is defined by the belief that we should expect God to continue to provide many if not all of the miraculous gifts recorded in the Gospels and Acts. That cluster of positions is called *continuationism*. In the middle of the spectrum are the positions of those who are *open but cautious* regarding miraculous gifts. Some people in this category may allow for a limited, occasional use of such gifts in the life of the church. On the other end of the spectrum is the group of positions broadly labeled *cessationism* because they teach that God has ceased giving miraculous gifts to the church.

However, there is some complexity and overlap among positions on this question, as the table below shows. Some continuationists are cessationist regarding the apostles. Some open but cautious people allow for occasional uses of the miraculous gifts, but many are functionally cessationist in their practice. Some cessationists deny that any miracles occur today, but others, like us, think that only the miraculous gifts have ceased, not miracles themselves.

This debate had significant ramifications for the Reformation. Scholars in the Roman Catholic Church argued that one of the marks of the true church is its miracles, which they claimed their saints had worked in abundance. However, Reformed theologians denied that continuing miracles are a mark of the true church. Calvin said, "In demanding miracles of us, they act dishonestly. For we are not forging some new gospel, but are retaining the very gospel whose truth all the miracles that Jesus Christ and his disciples ever wrought serve to confirm."[36] Johannes Wollebius (1586–1629) said, "The gifts of miracles and prophecy were extraordinary ones, given for the confirmation of the gospel, and they have passed away."[37]

Continuationist		*Open but Cautious*		*Cessationist*	
All Gifts Available	All Gifts but Apostles Available	Occasional Continu-ationist	Functional Cessationist	No Miracu-lous Gifts; Open but Cautious to Miracles Themselves	No Miracles

Table 7.1. Some Positions in the Spectrum of Views on Miraculous Gifts Today

Arguments against Cessationism Answered

Though the debate among the various positions on miraculous gifts is very wide-ranging exegetically, historically, and theologically, we will present here major objections before presenting a positive case for our position. As the footnotes will show, some of these points have already been discussed in prolegomena under the topic of special revelation.[38]

Anti-Cessation Argument 1: Christian experience recorded throughout history. There are many reports of miracles and miracle workers throughout Christian history and today. For example, Basil the Great (c. 330–379) said that Gregory Thaumaturgus ("Wonder-Worker," d. 270) cast out

36. Calvin, *Institutes*, pref. 3.

37. Johannes Wollebius, *Compendium Theologiae Christianae*, 1.25.xxix.12, in *Reformed Dogmatics: Seventeenth-Century Reformed Theology through the Writings of Wollebius, Voetius, and Turretin*, ed. and trans. John W. Beardslee III (Grand Rapids, MI: Baker, 1965), 141. Henceforth cited as *Compendium*. See also Turretin, *Institutes*, 18.13.43–49 (3:114–16).

38. When discussing special revelation under the locus of prolegomena, we addressed several arguments often made for continuationism. See *RST*, 1:412–22. Rather than simply repeat that material here, we focus our interaction especially on particular arguments against cessationism presented in Jon Mark Ruthven, *On the Cessation of the Charismata: The Protestant Polemic on Post-Biblical Miracles*, Word and Spirit Monograph Series 1, rev. ed. (Tulsa, OK: Word & Spirit, 2011). Ruthven's book seeks to refute B. B. Warfield, *Counterfeit Miracles* (1918; repr., Edinburgh: Banner of Truth, 1972). However, it takes aim at the whole modern Reformed cessationist tradition, of which Warfield was a prominent exponent a century ago. In some cases, we cite Warfield's writings to defend him against charges made particularly against him.

demons, changed the course of rivers at his command, dried up a lake, and predicted the future—"a second Moses."[39] Augustine reported several miraculous healings, though he acknowledged that miracles were much less prominent in his day than in the times of Christ and the apostles.[40]

In reply, we do not deny that God continues to work miracles, but that he continues to give miracle workers to the church. Furthermore, one must be careful in evaluating claims to miracles. Stories of events are often embellished over time, and legends are uncritically accepted. Augustine and Gregory the Great (c. 540–604) told slightly different versions of the same miracle account, both theologians claiming to have personally received testimony from an eyewitness—though they lived more than a century apart and the story can be traced to a pagan legend that originated centuries earlier.[41] Accounts of miracles are often influenced by man's tendency to superstition. Augustine ascribed many of the miracles cited in the previous paragraph to the relics of martyrs—that is, their physical remains or other personal items collected after their deaths. Finally, toward the end of his life, Augustine said that although many miracles still take place, apostolic miracles such as speaking in tongues or healing by the shadow of a preacher (Acts 5:15) no longer occur—"even though such things happened at that time, manifestly they ceased later."[42]

Anti-Cessation Argument 2: Christian theology distorted by rationalistic philosophy. Reformed Christians, particularly those such as B. B. Warfield in the American Presbyterian tradition, have been accused of allowing the philosophy of Scottish common sense realism to make them hypercritical of miracle accounts.[43] Even though they believe in biblical miracles, their approach to postbiblical miracles is said to be "thoroughly skeptical," "demythologized" and "rationalistic," like "[Adolf] Harnack's rationalistic liberalism."[44]

In response, we say that a critical approach to reports of miracles in the early church is consistent with the early Reformed theologians. Calvin said that Roman Catholic theologians "allege miracles," but such pretended miracles are "foolish and ridiculous," "vain and false."[45] Wil-

39. Basil, *On the Spirit*, 28.74, in *NPNF*², 8:46–47.
40. Augustine, *The City of God*, 22.8, in *NPNF*¹, 2:485–91.
41. Warfield, *Counterfeit Miracles*, 77–84.
42. Augustine, *Retractions*, 1.12, cited in Brown, *Miracles and the Critical Mind*, 8.
43. Ruthven, *On the Cessation of the Charismata*, 33–40.
44. Ruthven, *On the Cessation of the Charismata*, 69, 73, 76.
45. Calvin, *Institutes*, pref. 3.

liam Perkins called for critical discernment regarding claims to miracles.[46] Owen said that we lack "any undoubted testimony that any of those gifts which were truly miraculous, and every way above the faculties of men, were communicated unto any after the expiration of the generation of them who conversed with Christ in the flesh, or those who received the Holy Ghost by their ministry." He blamed "the superstition and folly" of people for the invention of "innumerable miracles false and foolish" and commended diligent investigation of claims to miracles to see if they were truly supernatural.[47] If a church claimed to prove its divine authority by miracles, Owen said, "Let us see them," and called for "evidence."[48] He wrote these things before Thomas Reid (1710–1796), the father of Scottish common sense realism, was even born. Therefore, it is historically naive to condemn the critical sifting of miracle reports by Reformed theologians as rooted in the antisupernatural rationalism of the Enlightenment.

Anti-Cessation Argument 3: The supposed inactivity of the risen Lord Jesus. The charge is made that, according to Reformed cessationism, the exalted Christ is presently doing nothing while he waits for the church to complete its evangelistic mission.[49]

In response, we must say that this is an astonishing claim. Reformed theology presents a robust doctrine of Christ's threefold office—Prophet, Priest, and King—in both his states of humiliation and exaltation.[50] Christ is presently at work with sovereign power to illuminate people with the knowledge of the truth and conquer the powers of evil that enslave them. Christ is on the throne, reigning over all powers for the sake of his church.[51]

Anti-Cessation Argument 4: The restricting of the Holy Spirit to the work of salvation. It is alleged that Reformed cessationism limits the Holy Spirit today to "the Calvinistic steps of salvation," focusing its doctrine

46. Perkins, *A Reformed Catholic*, in *Works*, 7:113; and *A Warning against the Idolatry of the Last Times*, in *Works*, 7:454.

47. Owen, "A Discourse of Spiritual Gifts," in *Pneumatologia*, in *Works*, 4:475; and *The Duty of Pastors and People Distinguished*, in *Works*, 13:34.

48. Owen, *A Vindication of the Animadversions on Fiat Lux*, in *Works*, 14:268.

49. "The exalted Christ seems presently inactive, waiting, it appears, for the preaching of Calvinistic soteriology to accomplish its task in the world." Ruthven, *On the Cessation of the Charismata*, 98.

50. The Westminster Shorter Catechism (Q. 23–26), in *Reformed Confessions*, 4:356. On Christ's threefold office, see *RST*, 2:869–1168 (chaps. 43–55).

51. B. B. Warfield, *The Saviour of the World: Sermons Preached in the Chapel of Princeton Theological Seminary* (New York and London: Hodder and Stoughton, 1913), 165, 170, 186.

of the Spirit almost entirely on the doctrines of the Trinity, regeneration, and sanctification.[52]

In response, we assert that Reformed theologians do not teach any such limitation.[53] Reformed Christianity celebrates the Spirit's works in common grace throughout creation. The Reformed doctrine of the Spirit is a doctrine of kingdom and mission. Warfield said that "the Spirit of God is poured out upon all flesh with the end of extending the bounds of God's Kingdom until it covers the earth"; we live in "a missionary age; and it is because it is the dispensation of the Spirit that missions shall make their triumphant progress until earth passes at last into heaven."[54]

Anti-Cessation Argument 5: The stripping of power from the kingdom. Christ brought the kingdom not only in words but "in deed and word" (Luke 24:19). Paul says that the kingdom is not mere words but miraculous "power" (1 Cor. 4:20). Reformed cessationism purportedly neglects the biblical teaching that Christ has brought the kingdom in miraculous power and that this charismatic power continues to the end of the age.[55]

In response, we answer that God signaled the inauguration of his kingdom by miracles, but these are not the essence of the kingdom. The gift of the Spirit is the firstfruits of the eschatological kingdom (Rom. 8:23; cf. Eph. 1:14), for he produces the love that is of the essence of the new creation (Gal. 5:5–6, 22; 6:15). However, the *gifts* of the Spirit are not essential to the kingdom, as love is, but are "provisional and partial" tools by which God establishes and builds the kingdom, but which cease when their purpose is fulfilled (1 Cor. 13:8–13).[56] When Paul speaks of the kingdom consisting "not in word, but in power," he refers to the power of Christ exercised through church discipline (1 Cor. 4:19–20; 5:4). The defining marks of the kingdom as it resides in God's people are not signs and wonders, which may be done by the wicked, but the character qualities produced by supernatural grace (Matt. 5:3–12; 7:21–23; Rom. 14:17). Though we may not minimize the importance of power for ministry (Col.

52. Ruthven, *On the Cessation of the Charismata*, 98–99.

53. With respect to Warfield, we must appreciate that though his articles and sermons address a variety of topics, he never wrote a systematic theology or comprehensive treatment of the Spirit's work in the church today. It is notable that Warfield wrote the preface to Abraham Kuyper's broad-ranging treatise *The Work of the Holy Spirit*, which includes sections on the Spirit's work in creation, human abilities, spiritual gifts, church ministry, etc. In our response to this argument, we are grateful for the assistance of Fred Zaspel (personal correspondence).

54. B. B. Warfield, *Faith and Life: 'Conferences' in the Oratory of Princeton Seminary* (New York and London: Longmans, Green, and Co., 1916), 144–45.

55. Ruthven, *On the Cessation of the Charismata*, 100–107, 176.

56. Gaffin, *Perspectives on Pentecost*, 44.

1:29; 1 Thess. 1:5), the greatest power the church needs is that of persevering godliness, boldness, and communion with God.[57]

Anti-Cessation Argument 6: The cessation of all gifts only at Christ's coming. God gave every "gift" (*charisma*) to the church in order to "confirm you unto the end, that ye may be blameless in the day of our Lord Jesus Christ" (1 Cor. 1:7–8).[58] The cessation of all spiritual gifts is contingent upon the arrival of the "perfect" (*teleion*) when Christ returns (13:8–13; Eph. 4:11–13).[59] Jon Ruthven says that even apostles must continue to the end as the church repeatedly "reduplicates the original revelatory experience about Christ."[60]

In response, we argue that Paul does not teach that God uses the miraculous gifts to "confirm" the church until Christ's return (1 Cor. 1:8), but that God uses the gospel of Christ, God's "testimony," to establish his people by the power of Christ crucified (vv. 6, 18, 24; 2:1–4). Only by faith in the gospel will they be "blameless" before God (1:8; cf. Col. 1:22–23).

As to 1 Corinthians 13:8–13, there is a stream of interpretation that reads the text to indicate that miraculous gifts will cease when the church emerges from its infancy and receives God's complete special revelation.[61] The word translated as "perfect" (*teleion*, v. 10) may refer to maturity attainable in this life (2:6; 14:20; Phil. 3:15). The "childhood" of the church need not refer to the spiritual immaturity of individual members, but to the relative amount of revelation given at a stage in redemptive history (cf. Gal. 4:1–3).[62] Paul's phrase "face to face" alludes to Numbers 12:6–8, in which the Lord contrasts his revelations to prophets by dreams, visions, and "dark speeches" with his clear and open revelation to Moses, with whom he spoke "mouth to mouth" or "face to face"

---

57. Rom. 15:13; 1 Cor. 16:13; 2 Cor. 12:9; Eph. 3:16; 6:10; Col. 1:11; 2 Tim. 1:7–8; 2:1; 3:5, 17; 4:17.

58. Ruthven, *On the Cessation of the Charismata*, 112–13.

59. Ruthven, *On the Cessation of the Charismata*, 114–40.

60. Ruthven, *On the Cessation of the Charismata*, 198. Ruthven attempts to soften this claim by saying that "apostleship is no guarantee of infallibility or 'inerrancy,'" but that undermines the doctrine of Scripture.

61. Edwards, "Extraordinary Gifts of the Spirit Are Inferior to Graces of the Spirit," in *WJE*, 25:280–84; *Charity and Its Fruits*, in *WJE*, 8:362; Walter J. Chantry, *Signs of the Apostles: Observations on Pentecostalism Old and New*, 2nd ed. (Edinburgh: Banner of Truth, 1976), 49–54; Robert L. Reymond, *What about Continuing Revelations and Miracles in the Presbyterian Church Today?* (Nutley, NJ: Presbyterian and Reformed, 1977), 32–36; and (cautiously) Ferguson, *The Holy Spirit*, 226–28. For a grammatical argument that the future middle Greek verb translated as "shall cease" (*pausontai*) means that tongues will "die out" without any direct intervention, see Wallace, *Greek Grammar beyond the Basics*, 422–23.

62. Edwards, "Extraordinary Gifts of the Spirit Are Inferior to Graces of the Spirit," in *WJE*, 25:283–84.

(Ex. 33:11; Deut. 34:10).[63] When the full revelation of Christ, of whom Moses was a type, was granted and the new covenant documents completed, then the need for prophecy, tongues, and supernaturally granted knowledge ceased.

Other cessationists, including us, find it more plausible that Paul contrasts our present knowledge in this age with that in the kingdom of glory.[64] Paul includes himself ("we," "I") in this transition, and it is difficult to think that Paul's knowledge of Christ was childish compared to what is contained in the whole New Testament. Rather, Paul compares his present understanding with what he will receive in glory: "Then shall I know even as also I am known" (1 Cor. 13:12). Moses was "face to face" with God through a visible theophany—he saw God's glory and heard his voice (Ex. 33:9–11). This will be our experience when Christ returns.

However, this great eschatological transition does not mean that *all* the spiritual gifts will continue until Christ returns in glory. In 1 Corinthians 13, Paul focuses on the cessation of our present mode of "knowledge" (vv. 10–13). He does not explicitly say when prophecy and tongues will cease, only that they will do so because they are incomplete (vv. 8–9). The location of the "perfect" at Christ's future coming does "not necessarily mean that a charismatic gift or gifts could not have been withdrawn earlier than the parousia," as D. A. Carson says.[65] Paul's point is not the timing of the gifts but the supremacy of love over all spiritual gifts (vv. 8, 13).[66]

Ruthven's assertion that apostles who receive special revelations from God continue today is devastating for faith and life. It shifts the basis of Christian knowledge and practice off the written Word of God and suspends it on present experience. That is precisely Ruthven's agenda: to correct the supposed error of the Reformers in making "the exposition of Scriptures" central to the life of the church and convince people to pursue the true mandate "to hear God's immediate voice."[67] This is a path away

63. The word translated as "darkly" (*ainigma*, 1 Cor. 13:12) is the same as "dark speeches" (Num. 12:8 LXX).

64. Calvin, *Commentaries*, on 1 Cor. 13:9–12; Anonymous [Westminster Divines], *Annotations upon all the Books of the Old and New Testament*, on 1 Cor. 13:8–13; and Poole, *Annotations upon the Holy Bible*, 3:586–87, on 1 Cor. 13:8–13.

65. Carson, *Showing the Spirit*, 70.

66. On 1 Cor. 13:8–13 and cessationism, see *RST*, 1:413–14.

67. Jon Mark Ruthven, *What's Wrong with Protestant Theology?* (Tulsa, OK: Word & Spirit, 2013), 2. He says that the "central theme of the Bible" is "the word of God as directly and normatively revealed in the human heart that demands obedience" (300).

from faith in God's Word toward fanaticism. Martin Luther warned, "God gives no one his Spirit or grace apart from the external Word which goes before. We say this to protect ourselves from the enthusiasts. . . . God does not want to deal with us human beings, except by means of the external Word and sacrament."[68] As Calvin said, people who seek the direction of the Spirit apart from the Word try "to fly without wings."[69] We hope that Christians, Pentecostal or otherwise, will not heed the siren call of new revelation, but will cling to the Holy Scriptures as their only divine rule of faith and obedience.

Arguments for the Cessation of Miraculous Gifts

We have presented answers to arguments against cessationism. What positive case can be made for cessationism? We present the following arguments that extraordinary ministers, such as apostles and prophets, and miraculous gifts, such as healing, miracles, and tongues, have ceased.[70] We are not arguing that miracles have ceased, but that God has ceased giving miraculous "gifts" to the members of Christ's church. A spiritual gift is not an individual act or event, but, as we noted earlier, is a divine endowment given to a person so that he or she can serve the church in a regular manner with spiritual effectiveness by the activity of the Holy Spirit.[71]

---

68. The Smalcald Articles, 3.8.3, 10, in *The Book of Concord*, 322–23. Enthusiasm is the belief that one is so indwelt by a deity that one's thoughts or actions come directly from God.

69. Calvin, *Commentaries*, on Isa. 30:1. Calvin said, "If it be objected, that the Scriptures do not contain everything, and that they do not give special answers on those points of which we are in doubt, I reply, that everything that relates to the guidance of our life is contained in them abundantly. If, therefore, we have resolved to allow ourselves to be directed by the word of God, and always seek in it the rule of life, God will never suffer us to remain in doubt, but in all transactions and difficulties will point out to us the conclusion. Sometimes, perhaps, we shall have to wait long, but at length the Lord will rescue and deliver us, if we are ready to obey him."

70. We are not attempting to set a date for the cessation of miraculous gifts. It is possible that some miracle workers associated with the apostles in the latter part of their ministry lived several decades after the apostles died. See Owen, "A Discourse of Spiritual Gifts," in *Pneumatologia*, in *Works*, 4:474–75.

71. Rom. 12:4–8; 1 Cor. 12:4–30. See the general introduction to spiritual gifts in chap. 6. Sam Storms objects to the idea that a "gift" involves a regular ministry. He notes that Paul literally writes of "gifts of healings" (*charismata iamatōn*, 1 Cor. 12:9) and argues that the plural indicates a specialized or occasional ability to heal, even to the point that a person "may be gifted to heal only one person at one particular time of one particular disease." Sam Storms, "A Third Wave View," in *Are Miraculous Gifts for Today?*, ed. Grudem, 212. However, the Gospels and Acts offer no support for a specialized or occasional gift of healing. As to Paul's doctrine, the grammatical plural also appears in other gifts in Paul's list: literally, "workings of miracles," "discernings of spirits," and "kinds of tongues" (1 Cor. 12:10). The interpretation of plurals as specialization would make no sense in "discernings of spirits" (a gift to discern some kinds of spirits but not others?). Furthermore, the plural "gifts of healings" is given by God to the singular "another" (*allō*), and likewise we read "to another [singular] workings of miracles." Paul's point is that each gift enables an individual to do multiple acts/kinds of healings or miracles—the opposite of what Storms claims. See Williams, *Renewal Theology*, 2:375.

1. *Concentrations of miracles.*[72] God's Word reveals a pattern in which God has concentrated his miracles in certain periods of history, such as the time of the redemption of Israel from Egypt through Moses, the period when Elijah and Elisha confronted Israel's covenant breaking, and the ministries of Jesus Christ and his apostles. Outside of those periods, miracles are relatively rare in biblical history, and few, if any, people can be considered to be miracle workers.[73] Miracles in the New Testament are closely associated with Christ and the apostles. Of the miracles that Luke reports in Acts, almost all are performed by the apostles.[74] When Tabitha died in Joppa, the disciples sent for Peter—evidently because they could not help her but knew that an apostle could—and he raised her from the dead (Acts 9:36–42). Stephen (6:8) and Philip (8:6–7, 39) worked miracles, but the apostles had laid hands on them (6:5–6). Ananias healed Saul of his blindness (9:17–18), and Barnabas did miracles as he ministered alongside Paul (Acts 14:3; 15:12). This pattern creates the expectation that the gifts of miracles would pass away with the apostles. Luther said, "The day of miracles has passed."[75] Thus, as Jonathan Edwards noted, the "apostolic age" is called "the age of miracles." He explained that Christianity was "established through so great a part of the known world by miracles," and now "these miracles stand recorded in those writings as a standing proof and evidence of the truth of the Christian religion to all ages."[76]

2. *The uniqueness of the apostles.*[77] The apostles of Jesus Christ were a unique group of men who had no successors. The apostles were directly appointed by Christ to work miracles and declare his word as directly revealed to them by God.[78] They were eyewitnesses that he had risen from the dead.[79] They left behind no instructions for ordaining further apostles

72. See *RST*, 1:424–26.

73. See *NIDNTTE*, 4:285. Apart from the signs performed by Moses, Elijah, and Elisha, miracles worked through God's servants or in direct answer to their prayers in the Old Testament include those granted to Joshua (Josh. 3:7–17; 10:12–14), Gideon (Judg. 6:19–22, 36–40), Samson (Judg. 15:18–19), Samuel (1 Sam. 7:9–10; 12:16–18), an unnamed man of God sent to Bethel (1 Kings 13:1–6), Hezekiah (2 Kings 19:15–19, 35; 20:1–11), and Daniel and his Hebrew friends in Babylon (Dan. 3:21–27; 4:31–34; 5:5–6; 6:16–24). None of these men manifested a "gift" for regular miracles, but received a few miracles on special occasions.

74. Acts 2:43; 3:6–8; 4:16, 22; 5:1–11, 12, 16; 9:32–35, 40; 13:9–12; 14:3, 8–10, 19–20; 15:12; 16:18, 26; 19:11–12; 20:9–12; 28:1–9.

75. Luther, *Sermons on the Gospel of St. John*, in *LW*, 24:79.

76. Edwards, *A History of the Work of Redemption*, in *WJE*, 9:365. See *Charity and Its Fruits*, in *WJE*, 8:357.

77. See *RST*, 1:422–24.

78. Matt. 10:1–8, 20; Luke 6:13; Acts 2:43; 5:12; Gal. 1:1, 11–12; 1 Cor. 14:37; 2 Cor. 12:12.

79. Acts 1:22; 5:31–32; 1 Cor. 9:1; 15:7–8.

but instead instituted an order of ordinary elders to direct the churches by the word already revealed.[80]

3. *The foundational function of apostles and prophets to the church.*[81] The ministry of the apostles and prophets was foundational to the church (Eph. 2:20; Rev. 21:14), grounding it forever on the truth of Christ our cornerstone (Isa. 28:16; cf. 1 Cor. 3:10–11). A "foundation" (*themelios*) is a substructure of rock (cf. Matt. 7:25) on which a building is constructed (Rom. 15:20; 1 Cor. 3:10–12). A builder does not lay the foundation a second time unless there is a serious error in it (Heb. 6:1). The metaphor of a foundation is set in a redemptive-historical context (Eph. 2:11–22; 3:4–5). Therefore, it signals the unique place of the apostles and new covenant prophets in history.[82] Their special function consisted in receiving new revelation by the Spirit concerning Christ's work and its implications for the people of God in the new covenant (2:12–13; 3:5–6).[83] Our responsibility is not to augment but to guard the apostolic deposit of truth (1 Tim. 6:20; 2 Tim. 1:14), "the faith which was once delivered unto the saints" (Jude 3).

The gift of tongues was either a form of prophecy or closely associated with prophecy (Acts 2:4, 17–18; 19:6). If coupled with the gift of interpretation, tongues functioned as prophesy, for it brought a message from God to the congregation (1 Cor. 14:5, 13). Since God has ceased giving new prophetic revelation, the gift of tongues has also ceased.[84]

4. *The miraculous gifts and new special revelation.* As we saw, miracles are often called "signs" because they show that the miracle worker is an authorized representative of a supernatural being. The gift of working miracles caused people to recognize Moses and Elijah as the bearers of

---

80. Acts 14:23; 20:17, 28–32; Phil. 1:1; 1 Tim. 3:1–7; 5:17; Titus 1:5–9; James 5:14; 1 Pet. 5:1–5.

81. See *RST*, 1:436–41.

82. Ruthven objects that Christ is depicted as the *last* stone added to a structure, and thus these stone/foundation texts cannot represent the foundational position of Christ and the apostles and prophets in the sequence of history. *On the Cessation of the Charismata*, 215. However, the background of the term translated as "cornerstone" (*akrogōniaios*, Eph. 2:20) is likely found in Isa. 28:16 LXX, where it pictures Christ as the foundational cornerstone of God's spiritual Zion. See *RST*, 2:747n47.

83. Ruthven argues that the "foundation" is the apostolic confession of Christ (cf. Peter in Matt. 16:16–19), "which is revealed to and confessed by all Christians at all times. . . . This revealed confession unlocks the kingdom to the confessor," which includes the Gentiles. *On the Cessation of the Charismata*, 209–11. However, Paul's discussion of the work of the apostles and prophets does not focus on *how* to enter the kingdom but the revelation *that* the Gentiles are now included as equal partners and fellow heirs with believing Israel (Eph. 3:5–6; cf. 2:11–13, 17–19). Neither is Paul looking back to Peter's confession, but to his own calling as an apostle to the Gentiles (3:1–4, 7–8).

84. Waldron, *To Be Continued?*, 88–90.

divine revelation.[85] The books of Ruth and Esther report no prophecies and no miracles, for their narratives describe God's ordinary works of providence. At one point in Israel's history, the people complained, "We see not our signs: there is no more any prophet" (Ps. 74:9). Signs are linked to prophecy, and a lack of miracles to a lack of new revelations from God. Signs "signify the reality of the gospel of Christ," as George Knight says (Acts 2:22; 8:6; 14:3).[86] Edwards said, "The thing chiefly designed by the extraordinary gifts [of the Spirit] was to introduce and establish that standing revelation of the mind and will of God by his word, as the grand means of grace and standing rule of faith and practice through all ages." But when that rule of faith was complete, "then those extraordinary influences of the Spirit of God withdrew and vanished away. . . . They are no more to be expected in the Christian church."[87]

5. *The completion of special revelation in Christ.*[88] The climactic revelation of God in his Son implies both the conclusion of prophecy and the end of miraculous gifts. Christ's once-for-all accomplishment of eternal redemption (Heb. 9:12, 26, 28) also brought the final revelation of God's covenantal grace: "God, who at sundry times and in divers manners spake in time past unto the fathers by the prophets, hath in these last days spoken unto us by his Son, . . . [the] heir of all things," who "purged our sins [and] sat down" at God's right hand (1:1–3).

Christ's final revelation was divinely attested by miracles: "How shall we escape, if we neglect so great salvation; which at the first began to be spoken by the Lord, and was confirmed unto us by them that heard him; God also bearing them witness, both with signs and wonders, and with divers miracles, and gifts ["distributions," KJV mg.] of the Holy Ghost, according to his own will?" (Heb. 2:3–4).[89] Calvin said, "It was fitting that the new preaching of the gospel and the new kingdom of Christ should be illumined and magnified by unheard-of and extraordinary miracles."[90]

85. Ex. 4:1–9; 14:31; 19:9; Num. 16:28; 1 Kings 17:24; 18:36–37; cf. 1 Kings 13:1–6.

86. George W. Knight III, "The Cessation of the Extraordinary Spiritual Gifts," in *The Beauty and Glory of the Holy Spirit*, ed. Beeke and Pipa, 96.

87. Edwards, "Extraordinary Gifts of the Spirit Are Inferior to Graces of the Spirit," in *WJE*, 25:285, 287. See Owen, *The Duty of Pastors and People Distinguished*, in *Works*, 13:31–32.

88. See *RST*, 1:434–36.

89. "Signs and wonders," "divers miracles," and "gifts of the Holy Ghost" (Heb. 2:4) appear to be three ways of describing the same extraordinary acts: various awe-inspiring works of divine power distributed by the Holy Spirit among his servants. These items are joined by a series of uses of "and" (*kai*) without other grammatical features: signs and wonders *kai* diverse miracles *kai* gifts of the Holy Spirit. Signs and wonders are joined by *te kai*, which pairs them together as one phrase (cf. "gifts and sacrifices," 5:1; "prayers and supplications," v. 7).

90. Calvin, *Institutes*, 4.19.6.

This text does not refer to the continuing ministry of the Word, but to the special ministry of those who saw Christ and "heard him" in the apostolic generation. Since the redemption and revelation of Christ are full and final, it is reasonable to conclude that these miraculous gifts were also a unique divine testimony that needs no repetition after those human eyewitnesses died. Robert Reymond (1932–2013) said, "It is nonrepeatable historical events of redemption which call forth special revelatory explanation; it is special revelation in turn which calls forth miraculous authentication."[91]

6. *The difference between biblical gifts and modern "gifts."* What are claimed to be continuations or restorations of the miraculous gifts prove to be pale shadows of the biblical realities. The biblical prophets and apostles declared the infallible word of God.[92] The very term translated as "miracles" (*dynamis*) indicates extraordinary acts of power, not merely the coordination of ordinary events with surprising and helpful timing. The apostles and evangelists healed long-term disabilities.[93] Speaking in tongues consisted of the ability to declare the glory of God in languages unknown to the speaker but understandable to those who ordinarily communicated in those languages (Acts 2:6, 8, 11).[94] The evidence for such miracles was substantial and verifiable. Even people hostile to the gospel had to say, "What shall we do to these men? For that indeed a notable miracle hath been done by them is manifest to all . . . and we cannot deny it" (4:16).

However, this is not the case for miracle workers today. Instead, prophecies prove false. Some people who claim to perform miracles are liars and frauds,[95] using the tricks of professional swindlers and methods similar to those of illusionists and hypnotists. Many illusionists openly state that they have no supernatural power and have proven quite helpful in exposing false miracle workers.[96] Hypnosis leads people into a state of uncritical mental suggestibility; it can produce effects such as a reduced response to

91. Robert L. Reymond, *A New Systematic Theology of the Christian Faith* (Nashville: Thomas Nelson, 1998), 413.

92. See *RST*, 1:426–28, 441–55.

93. Acts 3:6–8; 8:7; 9:32–35; 14:8–10.

94. See the discussion of the nature of tongues in chap. 6.

95. Even in the ancient world, Josephus spoke of "imposters and deceivers" who falsely claimed that they could work "wonders and signs." Flavius Josephus, *Antiquities of the Jews*, 20.167–68, in *The Works of Josephus: Complete and Unabridged*, trans. William Whiston, new ed. (Peabody, MA: Hendrickson, 1987), 536.

96. For example, consider the illusionists/authors André Kole and Dan Korem. See Norman L. Geisler, *Miracles and the Modern Mind: A Defense of Biblical Miracles* (Grand Rapids, MI: Baker, 1992), 114–15.

pain.[97] God often grants remarkable healing in answer to prayer, but the spiritual gift of healing involves a regular ministry of supernatural healing. Thomas Schreiner says, "If the signs and wonders of the apostles have returned, we should see the blind receiving their sight, the lame walking, and the dead being raised. . . . If people truly have the gift of healing and miracles today, they need to demonstrate such by performing the kinds of healings and miracles found in the Bible."[98]

"Tongues" in the Bible refers to a supernatural ability to speak in foreign languages,[99] but studies done on people who claim to speak in tongues have not identified their speech as a language with an intelligible message, but a sequence of disorganized sounds that is linguistically "meaningless" and bears "no systematic resemblance to any natural language, living or dead."[100] Such "glossolalia" can be produced by young children and people of non-Christian religions.[101] It may express sincere religious devotion but is not a manifestation of the Spirit, for it is sometimes taught by encouraging audiences to make noises or repeat a syllable or word.[102]

In summary, God's Word reveals a pattern in history in which most miracles were concentrated in special seasons when God sent miracle workers to his people. One such season was the time of the apostles, who had a unique ministry. Together with the prophets sent by Christ, the apostles were the foundation of the church in bringing new covenant revelation. God used miraculous gifts to confirm new special revelation. Since Christ brought the completion of redemption and revelation, God also testified to them in a "grand finale" of miracles. However, those miraculous ministries will not be repeated any more than the redemption and revelation in Christ. The cessation of the miraculous gifts is confirmed by an exami-

97. David G. Benner and Peter C. Hill, *Baker Encyclopedia of Psychology and Counseling*, 2nd ed. (Grand Rapids, MI: Baker, 1999), 594. For a critical analysis of faith healing techniques by comparison to hypnosis, see Philip Foster, "Suggestibility, Hysteria, and Hypnosis," in *The Signs and Wonders Movement—Exposed*, ed. Peter Glover (Epsom, Surrey, UK: Day One, 1997), 61–82.

98. Thomas Schreiner, "Why I Am a Cessationist," *The Gospel Coalition*, January 22, 2014, https://www.thegospelcoalition.org/article/cessationist/.

99. See the section on tongues in the previous chapter.

100. William J. Samarin, *Tongues of Men and Angels: The Religious Language of Pentecostalism* (New York: Macmillan; London: Collier-Macmillan, 1972), 2. See David Hilborn, "Glossolalia as Communication—A Linguistic-Pragmatic Perspective," in *Speaking in Tongues: Multi-Disciplinary Perspectives*, ed. Mark J. Cartledge, Studies in Pentecostal and Charismatic Issues (Eugene, OR: Wipf and Stock, 2006), 116.

101. *NIDPCM*, 671, 675; and E. Mansell Pattison, "Behavioral Science Research on the Nature of Glossolalia," *Journal of the American Scientific Affiliation* 20 (September 1968): 73–86, available at https://www.asa3.org/ASA/PSCF/1968/JASA9-68Pattison.html.

102. Victor Budgen, *The Charismatics and the Word of God: A Biblical and Historical Perspective on the Charismatic Movement*, 2nd ed. (Darlington, England: Evangelical Press, 1989), 65–67.

nation of modern claims to such gifts, for we do not see people making infallible prophecies or having ministries of miracles that match the signs reported in the book of Acts. Hence, we conclude, as John Chrysostom did sixteen centuries ago, that such gifts have had a "cessation, being such as then used to occur but now no longer take place."[103]

Pastoral Prayer for Healing

Christ and the apostles regularly ministered to the sick. Though the gifts of healing have ceased, is there any parallel to this pattern in present pastoral ministry? According to James, prayer for healing should be a regular part of congregational life. James says, "Is any sick among you? Let him call for the elders of the church; and let them pray over him, anointing him with oil in the name of the Lord: and the prayer of faith shall save the sick, and the Lord shall raise him up; and if he have committed sins, they shall be forgiven him" (James 5:14–15). In this text, James envisions a case of serious illness, for the elders must be called to the person and pray "over" him, suggesting he is lying in bed.[104] James promises that "the prayer of faith" offered up by the elders "shall save the sick," and he will "be healed."

What is the significance of anointing with olive oil? Though olive oil can promote healing in some cases (Isa. 1:6; Luke 10:34), members of the household or a doctor should administer medicine, not the elders. Anointing with soothing, often fragrant, oil was a common cultural gesture in the ancient world, displaying joy.[105] The physical touch of anointing another person expresses love and acceptance,[106] somewhat like extending the hand of fellowship (Gal. 2:9) and greeting the brethren with a holy kiss.[107] Touching a sick person was especially significant among Jewish Christians brought up with a strong revulsion against the ceremonial uncleanness associated with illness (Leviticus 15). Jesus often touched those whom he healed, even lepers, which surely communicated mercy and love.[108] Anointing with oil may also symbolize the work of the Holy

103. Chrysostom, *Homilies on 1 Corinthians*, 29.1, in *NPNF*[1], 12:168.

104. Douglas J. Moo, *The Letter of James*, The Pillar New Testament Commentary (Grand Rapids, MI: Eerdmans, 2000), 238. This passage does not refer to spiritual healing, but to bodily healing (236–37).

105. Pss. 45:7–8; 104:15; Dan. 10:3; Matt. 6:17.

106. Ezek. 16:9; Mark 16:1; Luke 7:38, 46; John 11:2; 12:3.

107. Rom. 16:16; 1 Cor. 16:20; 2 Cor. 13:12; 1 Thess. 5:26.

108. Matt. 8:3, 15; 9:25, 29; 20:34; Mark 1:31, 41; 5:41; 6:5; 7:32–33; 8:23, 25; 9:27; Luke 4:40; 5:13; 8:54; 13:13; 22:51; John 9:6. People also touched Jesus: Matt. 9:20–21; 14:36; Mark 3:10; 5:27–31; 6:56; Luke 6:19; 8:44–47.

Spirit,[109] but there is no warrant for reading a consecration or sacrament into this text.[110] An equivalent today would be elders praying for a person's healing and spiritual growth while laying hands on his head or shoulder or holding his hand.

Is healing an absolute promise, provided that the elders came and prayed with faith? This, Douglas Moo observes, "is ultimately the question of how the prayers of human beings interact with the sovereign purposes of God."[111] When James says, "The prayer of faith shall save the sick" (James 5:15), or when the Lord Jesus says, "What things soever ye desire, when ye pray, believe that ye receive them, and ye shall have them" (Mark 11:24), they are not making promises without exceptions, but speaking in generalizations about the relation of faith and effective prayer.[112] This principle must be balanced with James's teaching that we do not know what tomorrow will bring, for we must always say, "If the Lord will, we shall live, and do this, or that" (James 4:14–15). Calvin said, "That gift of healing, like the rest of the miracles, which the Lord willed to be brought forth for a time, has vanished away"; however, "the Lord is indeed present with his people in every age; and he heals their weaknesses as often as necessary."[113]

Faith and Miracles Today

While the miraculous gifts passed away with the apostles and prophets, the Lord God Almighty has not passed away. He remains as omnipotent as ever, fully capable of doing whatever he wills. He will demonstrate that power with unspeakable glory when his Son returns. What then should be our approach to miracles at this time as we await the return of our Lord?

Be cautious about giving full credence to everything that is claimed to be a miracle from God. Ask questions: Is the alleged miracle and any teach-

109. Calvin, *Institutes*, 4.19.18. Note the anointings for consecration to Spirit-empowered office in 1 Sam. 10:1, 6; 16:13; 1 Kings 19:15–16.

110. Neither Mark 6:13 nor James 5:14 gives an adequate basis for the Roman Catholic sacrament of the anointing of the sick or extreme unction, which uses holy oil blessed by a bishop to give spiritual renewal to the sick and preparation for possible death. J. A. Motyer, *The Message of James: The Tests of Faith* (Downers Grove, IL: InterVarsity Press, 1985), 190–92. See *Catechism of the Catholic Church*, secs. 1499, 1510–23, 1532.

111. Douglas Moo, "Divine Healing in the Health and Wealth Gospel," *Trinity Journal* 9, no. 2 (Fall 1988): 208 (full article, 191–209).

112. The epistle of James is notably similar to Christ's Sermon on the Mount and the Proverbs. All of them present truth in the form of aphorisms, concise sayings that forcefully declare principles of ethics or wisdom without explaining all the various exceptions to the rules.

113. Calvin, *Institutes*, 4.19.19.

ing associated with it consistent with what God has revealed in his Word? What is the evidence that it took place? Can it be adequately explained by natural causes?[114] It is not unbelief to exercise discernment. Some miracles are virtually inconceivable today, such as raising the dead, turning the sea into dry land, or walking on water. Such would be signs that a great prophet is among us.

However, do not be skeptical if you hear credible reports that God has answered the prayers of his people in marvelous ways, such as delivering someone from serious illness, need, or danger, or demonstrating the power of the true God against idols. Too often we are like the church members praying for Peter's release from prison (Acts 12:1–17), who did not believe it when Peter appeared on their doorstep! Rather, give thanks and rejoice in the Lord's goodness (Psalm 107).

Pray big prayers. Gladys Aylward (1902–1970) was serving as a missionary in China in the 1930s when war broke out with Japan. She led one hundred children on a long trek to escape the invading armies. However, they came to an impassible barrier, the Yellow River, and Aylward began to lose hope. One of the children reminded her that God divided the Red Sea so that Moses led the people safely across. Aylward replied, "I am not Moses." The girl said, "But God is always God." They prayed together. Then a Chinese military officer discovered them and kindly arranged for them to cross the river by boat.[115] In the same way, we should not pretend to be miracle workers like Moses, but we can pray for God to help us and trust that nothing is impossible for him.

However, set your mind not on miracles but on Christ and his heavenly glory (Col. 3:1–2). Christ says, "Seek ye first the kingdom of God, and his righteousness; and all these things shall be added unto you" (Matt. 6:33). While we may pray for our personal needs and desires, our most fervent petitions should seek the glory of God's name, the advance of his kingdom, the doing of his will, and the salvation of our souls (vv. 9–13).

Augustine said of Christ, "It is more important that He healed the faults of souls, than that He healed the weaknesses of mortal bodies. . . . For that which is the real health of bodies, and which is looked for from the Lord, will be at the end, in the resurrection of the dead. What shall live then shall no more die; what shall be healed shall no more be sick;

114. Gross, *Miracles, Demons, and Spiritual Warfare*, 75–81.

115. Noël Piper, *Faithful Women and Their Extraordinary God* (Wheaton, IL: Crossway, 2005), 96–98.

what shall be satisfied shall no more hunger and thirst; what shall be made new shall not grow old."[116] Just as signs and wonders attested to Christ and the inauguration of his kingdom, so should the biblical accounts of miracles stir up our longing for Christ's return to establish his kingdom in glory forever.

Sing to the Lord

God's Signs and Wonders

O praise the Lord, His deeds make known,
And call upon His name;
Sing ye to Him, His praises sing,
His wondrous works proclaim.

God sent His servant Moses then,
And Aaron, whom He chose;
Great signs and wonders they displayed
To terrify their foes.

In darkness they were taught to fear
God's great and holy Name;
On man and beast, on vine and field,
His awful judgment came.

His sacred word to Abraham
He kept, though waiting long,
And brought His chosen people forth
With joy and thankful song.

Psalm 105
Tune: Boardman
The Psalter, No. 289

Questions for Meditation or Discussion

1. What can we learn from the New Testament terminology for miracles?
2. What is the authors' definition of a miracle? Explain it in your own words.

116. Augustine, *Tractates on the Gospel of St. John*, 17.1, in *NPNF*[1], 7:111.

3. Someone says to you, "I don't believe in miracles. Science has proven them impossible." How do you respond?
4. How do miracles function to evoke and confirm faith?
5. What is continuationism? The open but cautious view? Cessationism?
6. How do the authors answer the following objections to cessationism?
   - Christians have experienced miracles throughout history.
   - Cessationists are rationalistic and skeptical of the supernatural.
   - If there are no miracle workers today, then Christ is doing virtually nothing.
   - Cessationists limit the Holy Spirit to saving souls.
   - If there are no apostles, prophets, miracle workers, healers, or tongues today, then the kingdom of God has no power.
   - Paul teaches that all the gifts will cease only at Christ's coming (1 Cor. 13:8–13).
7. What positive arguments can be made for cessationism?
8. After reading this chapter, where would you place yourself on the spectrum of views presented in Table 7.1? Why? How did reading this chapter affect your view?
9. What encouragement does James 5 give to us to pray for God's healing? What is a wise approach to the promise of James 5:15?

Questions for Deeper Reflection

10. What effects would it have on the church if someone were received as a modern miracle worker? How should a pastor respond if someone claiming to have such powers comes to town?
11. A friend of yours has a child who is severely disabled. Your friend tells you that she continues to pray for God to heal the child completely but lately has questioned whether it is right to ask God for a miracle. How would you counsel this person and encourage her faith in the Lord?

8

The Holy Spirit and the New Creation

God the Holy Spirit is the Creator, Lord, and giver of life. We first encounter the Spirit of God in the Bible in the work of creation, hovering over the newly made world in its initial state of formlessness in order to give order and life (Gen. 1:2).[1] The Spirit's work appears implicitly when God personally breathes into the first man the breath of life (2:7; cf. Job 33:4). Since man plunged himself and the world around him into an accursed state due to sin, the Spirit has acted as the Re-Creator of fallen creation and the restorer of life. Herman Bavinck said, "Just as the creation is a trinitarian work, so also the re-creation was from the start a project of the three persons. All the grace that is extended to the creation after the fall comes to it from the Father, through the Son, in the Holy Spirit."[2] The Spirit effects the new creation by indwelling and empowering the people of God through Christ. Adam of St. Victor (d. 1146) wrote, "Come, Creator Spirit, Spirit Recreator . . . Thou art the Gift; Thou art the Giver."[3]

The Holy Spirit's works in Israel, Christ, and the church aim at producing and forming the new creation where God dwells in his glory. The specific acts of grace by which the Spirit does this are discussed in the next part of this book. However, to conclude our study of pneumatology and

1. On the work of the Spirit in creation, see chap. 2.
2. Bavinck, *Reformed Dogmatics*, 3:215.
3. "*Veni, Creator Spiritus / Spiritus recreator / . . . / Tu donum, tu donator.*" Adam of St. Victor, "De Spiritu Sancto," in F. A. March, ed., *Latin Hymns, with English Notes* (New York: Harper & Brothers, 1896), 137.

soteriology in the history of salvation and pave the way for the order of salvation, we will examine what the Bible teaches about the Spirit's work of making the new creation in general. This is a rich theme, rooted in Genesis and blossoming especially in the prophecy of Isaiah. It is a message of hope that can fill our hearts with joy and peace.

The Spirit and the Tabernacle of God's Renewed Presence

We begin by returning to the Spirit's works in the Old Testament period. John Owen reminded us, "Whatever the Holy Spirit wrought in an eminent manner under the Old Testament, it had generally . . . a respect unto our Lord Jesus Christ and the gospel; and so was preparatory unto the completing of the great work of the new creation in and by him."[4]

One of the Spirit's works in the old covenant era was the construction of the tabernacle and later the temple. The Lord filled his chosen craftsmen with the Spirit of God so that they had the wisdom and skill to make the tabernacle according to his design (Ex. 31:3; 35:31). The tabernacle was a place where God spoke with his people, and its design featured trees, cherubim, gold, precious stones, and large supplies of water.[5] All of these elements appear in the description of the garden of Eden and the surrounding region (Gen. 2:8–17; 3:24).[6] Thus, the Lord indicated that his tabernacle was like a restored garden of Eden, the beginning of a new creation he was initiating among his covenant people. The type of the tabernacle reveals that the Spirit is the divine agent who empowers the construction of the new creation. This pattern continues through redemptive history. David received the plan for the temple by a revelation of the Spirit (1 Chron. 28:12, 19). In the new covenant, God's temple is the church of Jesus Christ, built by gifted workers empowered by the Holy Spirit (1 Cor. 3:9–10; 12:4–11).

The Holy Spirit is not only the divine agent to construct God's new creation, but also the divine resident who manifests God's presence in that temple. The Spirit was with the people of Israel when the Lord dwelt in their midst in the fiery cloud (Isa. 63:11, 14). God always fulfilled his promise to be with his people by the Spirit (Hag. 2:1–5).[7] Today, the church is God's temple because the Holy Spirit dwells in his people (1 Cor. 3:16; Eph. 2:21–22).

4. Owen, *Pneumatologia*, in *Works*, 3:126.
5. Ex. 25:1–26:37; 28:9, 17–20; 30:17–21.
6. See *RST*, 2:136–37, 275–76.
7. See the discussion of the Spirit's work to manifest God's presence with Israel in chap. 3.

The Spirit's work of forming the new creation and filling it with God's presence centers on Jesus Christ. God's promise of his renewed presence with his people focuses on the virgin-born "Immanuel" or "God with us" (Isa. 7:14; cf. Matt. 1:23). The child is God himself come to dwell with his people in his wisdom, power, eternity, and peace (Isa. 9:6). As the angel Gabriel explained to Mary, this virginal conception took place by the supernatural agency of the Spirit: "The Holy Ghost shall come upon thee, and the power of the Highest shall overshadow thee: therefore also that holy thing which shall be born of thee shall be called the Son of God" (Luke 1:35). The incarnate Christ is God dwelling in his living tabernacle or temple (John 1:14; 2:21).[8] Christ's humanity is the magnum opus of the Holy Spirit, for in Christ not only does man reenter paradise, but paradise is now a man.

Therefore, our longing for paradise, our spiritual hunger to dwell with God in a place full of his glory, reveals our need for the Holy Spirit. We thirst for the living water that only he can supply. This should drive us to pray earnestly for the Father to give us more of the Spirit's work through Christ. Conversely, our possession of the Holy Spirit as God dwelling within us is the firstfruits and pledge of our future inheritance in Christ. Every motion of the Spirit to make us holy gives us a sign that Christ is ours and that one day we will see him face to face and walk with him in the gardens of the new Jerusalem. Let God's children, therefore, rejoice in hope.

The Spirit and the Kingdom of God's Renewed Reign

Another major theme of creation is God's reign or kingdom. God created man as his image bearer in order that man might rule the earth as God's representative (Gen. 1:26–28). Man's rebellion against God's commandment disrupted this delegated divine kingdom, and Satan began to erect his kingdom of darkness in the world. One facet of the new creation is that God's "throne" is reestablished in human life and his people who bear his image "reign" over his world (Rev. 21:1–2; 22:1–5).

The Holy Spirit supplies the power to restore God's kingdom among his covenantal people. The work began in Israel. The Spirit came mightily upon the judges and kings of Israel so that they led the nation in justice and

8. On the tabernacle/temple motif in John 1:14 and Luke 1:35, see *RST*, 2:787–88, 792–93.

victory.[9] The Spirit rallied David's mighty men to give their wholehearted allegiance to their king (1 Chron. 12:18). Christ, the Son of David, was anointed by the Spirit after his baptism and immediately went to fight against the Tempter to whom the first Adam had surrendered the kingdom (Matt. 1:1; 3:16–4:1). Christ said, "If I cast out devils by the Spirit of God, then the kingdom of God is come unto you" (12:28). Therefore, the Holy Spirit acts to overthrow the domain of Satan and restore the kingdom of God through the Lord's sons and daughters on earth.

Just as was the case with the tabernacle, the Spirit's work to make a new creation in which God reigns centers on the person of the incarnate Christ. Christ is not merely an instrument or servant of the kingdom. He is the King and the epitome of the kingdom, for he is "the Man of the Spirit."[10] A major prophecy linking Christ, the Spirit, and the kingdom of God appears in Isaiah 11:1–2, which says, "There shall come forth a shoot from the stump of Jesse, and a branch from his roots shall bear fruit. And the Spirit of the Lord shall rest upon him, the Spirit of wisdom and understanding, the Spirit of counsel and might, the Spirit of knowledge and the fear of the Lord" (ESV). Jesse was David's father; the text hence refers to the promised Son of David (9:7). The multiplication of words associated with the Spirit shows the fullness of spiritual graces given to this King. Bede (c. 672–735) said that this sevenfold fullness of the Spirit can be attributed only to "the mediator between God and humanity, the man Jesus Christ," for the saints "receive from his fulness only as the Spirit grants it."[11] The qualities of "wisdom and understanding," "counsel and might," and "knowledge and the fear of the Lord" are essential to good and successful government by kings (Prov. 8:12–16). Therefore, all the gifts of the Spirit needed for the advance of God's kingdom are gathered together and deposited in Christ. The kingdom rests entirely in his capable hands (Isa. 9:6), and through him righteousness and justice will prevail with eternal, infallible, and invincible power (9:7; 11:3–5).

Christians should not be surprised to find themselves engaged in strife and conflict with evil, both within their souls and with the powers around

9. Judg. 3:10; 6:11–24, 27, 34–35; 11:29, 32; 14:6, 19; 15:14–15; 1 Sam. 10:1, 6; 11:6; 16:13–14. See chap. 3.

10. Ferguson, *The Holy Spirit*, 52.

11. Bede, *Homilies on the Gospels*, 1.2, in *ACCS/OT*, 10:102. See also Young, *The Book of Isaiah*, 1:381.

them. The Spirit of God has invaded the satanic kingdom of this world and is reestablishing God's kingdom over his creation. Just as Adam once stood as God's servant-king over the earth, so Jesus Christ now reigns as the Mediator of God's kingdom. Christ exercises his kingdom through the Spirit and gives each of his people the graces and gifts of the Spirit. John Calvin commented, "He received the gifts of the Spirit, that he might bestow them upon us. And this is the anointing from which he receives the name of Christ, which he imparts to us; for [which cause] are we called Christians."[12] As a result, we are the anointed servants through whom the Spirit advances the kingdom. We must expect that the Devil will fight back, but we need not fear: "Greater is he that is in you, than he that is in the world" (1 John 4:4).

The Spirit and the New Creation in Cosmic Perspective

It might be questioned whether we have warrant to speak of the Spirit's work to construct God's tabernacle and kingdom among men as a "new creation." However, God's promises have an expansive scope that far exceeds Israel and even mankind to reach the whole world.

Peace between Man and Beast

The prophecy of the King we just examined concludes with this remarkable promise:

> The wolf also shall dwell with the lamb, and the leopard shall lie down with the kid; and the calf and the young lion and the fatling together; and a little child shall lead them. And the cow and the bear shall feed; their young ones shall lie down together: and the lion shall eat straw like the ox. And the sucking child shall play on the hole of the asp, and the weaned child shall put his hand on the [adders'][13] den. They shall not hurt nor destroy in all my holy mountain: for the earth shall be full of the knowledge of the LORD, as the waters cover the sea. (Isa. 11:6–9)

By the Spirit, Christ will establish a kingdom that will release this world from its curse. Fierce animals may figuratively represent wicked people (Ezek. 22:27; Zeph. 3:3). Calvin said that the prophet describes "the character and habits of those who have submitted to Christ, . . .

12. Calvin, *Commentaries*, on Isa. 11:2. "Which cause" is "why" in the original translation.
13. "Adders" is the reading in the KJV margin. The KJV text reads "cockatrice."

[but his] discourse looks beyond this; for it amounts to a promise that there will be a blessed restoration of the world."[14] The text may point to a literal pacification of wild animals, for it alludes to the condition of the pristine creation when man ruled the beasts, man and beast ate only plants, and there was no enmity between man and serpents (Gen. 1:28–30; 2:19; 3:14–15).[15] The kingdom of the Spirit-empowered Messiah will restore the earth to the peace in which God first created it. Gregory of Elvira (fl. 375) said, "In his kingdom, God will recreate the world as wonderfully as it was made at the beginning, before the first man sinned."[16]

Israel hoped for a kingdom of universal peace and prosperity (Mic. 4:3–4). One of the curses on the Israelites for breaking the covenant consisted in God sending wild animals to kill them (Lev. 26:6, 22; Deut. 32:24). However, God promised to remove such dangers when he saved his people (Ezek. 34:25; Hos. 2:18). Instead, the Lord would give abundant rain, plentiful crops, strong livestock, and glorious sunshine (Isa. 30:23–26; Amos 9:13). Such promises are not "a descent into a materialistic bonanza," Alec Motyer (1924–2016) commented, but "the outpouring of creation's bounty" formerly restrained by God's curse, and so are signs "of the end of sin and the curse and of the return of Eden."[17]

The Blossoming of the Wilderness

God will heal the earth through the outpouring of the Spirit, bringing changes that are "far-reaching and all-embracing."[18] God's curses upon rebellious Israel manifested the broader curse for Adam's transgression, for mankind had "broken the everlasting covenant" (Isa. 24:5).[19] The judgments declared in Isaiah transcend national catastrophes and point ultimately to the dissolution of the cosmos (34:4). Even in this age, the Lord will cause "thorns and briers" to come in the land of his people (32:13; cf. Jer. 12:13; Hos. 10:8), manifestations of the curse on the earth that God spoke to Adam for his disobedience (Gen. 3:17–18). However, God promised that these judgments would last "until the Spirit is poured upon

---

14. Calvin, *Commentaries*, on Isa. 11:6.
15. Young, *The Book of Isaiah*, 1:390–91; and J. Alec Motyer, *The Prophecy of Isaiah: An Introduction and Commentary* (Downers Grove, IL: InterVarsity Press, 1993), 124.
16. Gregory of Elvira, in *ACCS/OT*, 10:107–8.
17. Motyer, *The Prophecy of Isaiah*, 251.
18. Young, *The Book of Isaiah*, 1:399.
19. On the covenant of works with Adam, see *RST*, 2:265–321 (chaps. 14–16).

us from on high, and the wilderness becomes a fruitful field, and the fruitful field is deemed a forest. Then justice will dwell in the wilderness, and righteousness abide in the fruitful field. And the effect of righteousness will be peace, and the result of righteousness, quietness and trust forever" (Isa. 32:15–17 ESV; cf. 29:17). The prophecy describes this "peace" in comprehensive terms, both physical effects on the earth and spiritual effects among people, especially "righteousness." Peter may have Scripture passages such as this in view when he says, "We, according to his promise, look for new heavens and a new earth, wherein dwelleth righteousness" (2 Pet. 3:13).

Isaiah also speaks of the desert blossoming as a rose when God's glory is revealed; the healing of the blind, deaf, lame, and dumb; and the redeemed walking on the way of holiness with great joy (Isaiah 35). That promise found partial fulfillment in Jesus's ministry of physical healing (Matt. 11:5; cf. Acts 3:8), but complete fulfillment will come in the heavenly city of God, where there will be no sorrow or sin (Isa. 35:8, 10; Rev. 21:4, 27). Graham Cole says, "God's concerns are not limited to the human domain. Nothing less than the wider creation provides his palette. And the poured out Spirit is the brush that returns color to the canvas."[20]

New Creation, New Eden

This transformation by the Spirit is a work of new creation. The Lord will cause rivers and springs to flow in the dry land and trees to grow in the desert, and people will know that "the Holy One of Israel hath created it" (Isa. 41:17–20). Water and trees are prominent in the account of the garden of Eden (Gen. 2:8–15); thus, this is a picture of "the future age of blessing," a work of God that is "fundamentally new and marvelous, a new creation," as Edward Young (1907–1968) said.[21] The Lord says, "Drop down, ye heavens, from above, and let the skies pour down righteousness: let the earth open, and let them bring forth salvation, and let righteousness spring up together; I the LORD have created it" (Isa. 45:8). He will do "new things," and "they are created now, and not from the beginning" (48:6–7). The Lord will comfort "Zion" and "make her wilderness like Eden, and her desert like the garden of the LORD; joy and gladness shall be found therein, thanksgiving, and the voice of melody" (51:3). This implies both the abundance of good and the removal of the

20. Cole, *He Who Gives Life*, 141.
21. Young, *The Book of Isaiah*, 3:93, 95.

curse due to sin.[22] The Lord says, "For, behold, I create new heavens and a new earth: and the former shall not be remembered, nor come into mind" (65:17). The verb translated as "create" (*bara'*) in these texts is the same verb used for God's original act of creation.[23] Combined with "heavens" and "earth," "create" constitutes a definite reference to the original work of creation (Gen. 1:1; 2:4), but now made new. The promise of the new creation includes the enjoyment of houses, food, and long life—and the repetition of the promise that the wolf and the lamb will feed together (Isa. 65:21–25).

The new creation will be a new home for God's people. The return of Israel from exile foreshadowed the return of man to a land of abundance. The Lord said to Israel through the prophet Ezekiel, "Ye shall dwell in the land that I gave to your fathers; and ye shall be my people, and I will be your God. I will also save you from all your uncleannesses: and I will call for the corn, and will increase it, and lay no famine upon you. And I will multiply the fruit of the tree, and the increase of the field, that ye shall receive no more reproach of famine among the heathen" (Ezek. 36:28–30). Consequently, the Promised Land is the new Eden. "And they shall say, This land that was desolate is become like the garden of Eden" (v. 35). As does Isaiah, Ezekiel links this promise of a renewed land with the outpouring of the Spirit: "Then shall they know that I am the Lord their God, which caused them to be led into captivity among the heathen: but I have gathered them unto their own land, and have left none of them any more there. Neither will I hide my face any more from them: for I have poured out my spirit upon the house of Israel, saith the Lord God" (39:28–29).

God gave Ezekiel a vision of the transformation of the land by a river that flows from the house of God and waters trees full of nourishing fruit and healing foliage (Ezek. 47:1–12; cf. Joel 3:18; Zech. 14:8–9), an Edenic image that reappears in John's vision of the new Jerusalem (Rev. 22:1–2). It is likely that the river symbolizes the work of the Holy Spirit (John 7:37–39), who, as we have seen, is depicted like water poured out upon the world.[24] While the river represents God's life-giving grace for the salvation of individuals, the vision emphasizes the healing of the land where they dwell with God.

22. Motyer, *The Prophecy of Isaiah*, 404.
23. Gen. 1:1, 21, 27; 2:3–4; 5:1–2; 6:7; Isa. 40:26, 28; 42:5; 45:12, 18.
24. Prov. 1:23; Isa. 32:15; 44:3; Ezek. 39:29; Joel 2:28–29.

Hope Directed toward a Person and a Place

Therefore, the promises of God direct our hope to nothing less than the restoration of all things, the glorious inheritance of which Canaan was a type. Owen said, "The great work whereby God designed to glorify himself ultimately in this world was that of the new creation, or of the recovery and restoration of all things by Jesus Christ (Heb. 1:1–3; Eph. 1:10)."[25]

When Christians overspiritualize their faith, they forget that God created man as a union of body and soul, and placed him in a physical world to live, eat, and work. God made us not only for relationships with other people but also for a place. It is there that God manifests his glorious presence through the beauty and delights of his creation. We were meant to know God's goodness by tasting the sweetness of fresh fruit and to perceive his greatness by gazing upon the skies far above us. Consequently, the Spirit's work of renewal has cosmic proportions—and so should our hope. Before his ascension, Christ said, "I go to prepare a place for you . . . that where I am, there ye may be also" (John 14:2–3). We should pant to join him in the new creation. Until that happens, we are strangers and pilgrims away from our homeland.

The Spirit and the New Creation in the People of God

While the Spirit's work of new creation has a cosmic scope, it also has a human focus that centers on the renewed inner life and flows outward into relationships of justice. We have already observed that the new creation by the Spirit is characterized by "righteousness."[26] Just as the apex of the first creation was man, created in God's image, so the heart of the new creation is the new man in Christ, re-created in his image (Eph. 2:10; 4:24; Col. 3:10).

The Re-Creation of Justice

David hints at this new creation of the inner man in his penitential prayer: "Create [*bara'*] in me a clean heart, O God, and renew a right spirit within me. Cast me not away from your presence, and take not your Holy Spirit from me" (Ps. 51:10–11 ESV). As we argued in an earlier chapter, David is speaking of the Spirit's work in reference not merely to official empow-

25. Owen, *Pneumatologia*, in *Works*, 3:157.
26. Isa. 11:1–5; 32:15–17; 45:8; 2 Pet. 3:13.

erment to serve, but also to moral sanctification.[27] David seeks salvation from the corruption he has multiplied in his inner man by his sinful acts. He prays for "a clean heart," a mindset and disposition that are pleasing and acceptable to the Holy One;[28] and a "right spirit," one of settled faithfulness to God and his covenant.[29] This grace of a clean and a right spirit is a divine work of creation and renewal. Therefore, the work of new creation had already begun in Old Testament saints as the Holy Spirit repeatedly brought moral and spiritual renewal to their souls.

Isaiah's prophecies also join spiritual renewal and new creation. The Lord who promised to place "my Spirit [*ruakh*]" on his Servant to bring "justice" to the nations is the God "who created the heavens and stretched them out" and "gives breath to the people on [the earth], and spirit [*ruakh*] to those who walk in it" (Isa. 42:1, 5 ESV). The repetition of the word "spirit" binds together the creation of man by God and the transformation of man through Christ. "Justice" refers to attitudes, actions, and relationships rightly ordered according to the will of the Judge.[30]

The Lord names himself the "Creator of Israel," but this act of creation consisted of his calling, redeeming, and consecrating a people for his glory (Isa. 43:1–7, 15). Matthew Poole (1624–1679) said that God had "created" them when he made them "his people, and that in so miraculous a manner, as if he had created [them] a second time out of nothing."[31] Israel's creation as a redeemed nation foreshadowed the re-creation of man in Christ by the Spirit, a new and greater exodus (vv. 2–4, 16–17). The nation's deliverance from exile in Babylon (v. 14) would be surpassed by the deliverance of God's elect from the guilt and power of their sins so that they would live for God's glory (vv. 7, 10, 25).

Life and Light Rekindled

God says, "I will do a new thing . . . rivers in the desert, to give drink to my people, my chosen. This people have I formed for myself; they shall shew forth my praise" (Isa. 43:19–21). What are these rivers? The Maker

27. On Ps. 51:11, see the discussion of the Spirit of piety in the Old Testament in chap. 3.

28. People who were ceremonially unclean could not have contact with holy things without offending God (Lev. 22:3–4). Thus, here "a clean heart" describes an inner cleanness consistent with divine holiness (cf. Ps. 24:3–4).

29. The word translated as "right" (*kun*) means "established" and is used of covenant faithfulness in Ps. 78:8, 37.

30. On "judgment" or "justice" (*mishpat*), see *RST*, 1:812, 818.

31. Poole, *Annotations upon the Holy Bible*, on Isa. 43:1 (2:421).

of Israel says, "I will pour water on the thirsty land, and streams on the dry ground; I will pour my Spirit upon your offspring, and my blessing on your descendants. They shall spring up among the grass like willows by flowing streams. This one will say, 'I am the LORD's,' another will call on the name of Jacob, and another will write on his hand, 'The LORD's,' and name himself by the name of Israel" (44:3–5 ESV). Motyer commented, "Rain from heaven figures all those reviving, life-giving agencies of grace whereby the Lord, through his Spirit, transforms the desert of his people's lives," so that "new life imparted" becomes "new life displayed."[32] God re-creates his people by the Holy Spirit, who gives them spiritual life to confess the Lord as their God and declare their allegiance to him as his people. The Spirit provides the inner, vital reality of man's faithful response to the covenant (2 Cor. 3:3, 6).

Further promises of the Spirit (Isa. 59:21; 61:1) bracket the promise that the light of God's glory will dawn upon the world in darkness (60:1–3, 19–20). This, too, is a picture of new creation, for just as God said, "Let there be light" (Gen. 1:3), so he causes the light of his glory in Christ to shine in the hearts of men and renew his image in them (2 Cor. 3:18; 4:6; 5:17). The seed of the new creation is the "new heart" and "new spirit" given by God together with the indwelling of his Spirit (Ezek. 36:26–27).

Though this re-creation of God's people begins with conversion, it is not complete until the conquest of all evil: "Be ye glad and rejoice for ever in that which I create: for, behold, I create Jerusalem a rejoicing, and her people a joy. And I will rejoice in Jerusalem, and joy in my people: and the voice of weeping shall be no more heard in her, nor the voice of crying" (Isa. 65:18–19). Not only will God's people have complete joy, but God will have complete delight in them, for all that displeases him will be removed. The first creation's "God saw every thing that he had made, and, behold, it was very good" (Gen. 1:31) is met and surpassed by the new creation, in which God exuberantly rejoices in his people (cf. Isa. 62:5; Zeph. 3:17).[33]

The prophecy of Isaiah welds together the doctrine of creation and new creation through the Spirit. Though they are distinct works, they are the works of the same God. The Creator of heaven and earth is the Re-Creator of his redeemed covenant people. Abraham Kuyper said, "The Holy Spirit, who in regeneration kindles the spark of eternal life, has already kindled

32. Motyer, *The Prophecy of Isaiah*, 342.
33. Motyer, *The Prophecy of Isaiah*, 530.

and sustained the spark of natural life." To be sure, the Spirit's works of new creation surpass his works of the original creation and are more prominent in the Bible. "But," Kuyper said, "however different the measures of operation and of energy, the Holy Spirit remains in creation and re-creation the one omnipotent Worker of all life and quickening, and is therefore worthy of all praise and adoration."[34]

The Magnificent Scope of Salvation

The theme of new creation by the Spirit shows us the grandeur of salvation. Salvation is not merely a matter of obtaining personal peace and more moral and loving lives. Our rebirth and resurrection with Christ make us participants in the eternal inheritance of Christ (Eph. 2:6–7; 1 Pet. 1:3–4). In salvation, the new creation enters our lives by union with Christ.[35] Herman Ridderbos said that Paul's reference to the new creation in 2 Corinthians 5:17 "is not meant merely in an individual sense ('a new creature'), but one is to think of the new world of the re-creation that God has made to dawn in Christ, and in which everyone who is in Christ is included. . . . It is a matter of two worlds, not only in a spiritual, but in a redemptive-historical, eschatological sense."[36] Andrew Lincoln comments, "The new creation, which in its widest sense includes the summing up of all things in Christ . . . has already begun as a movement in history in the lives of men and women."[37]

That does not mean that Christians are now the agents to transform the earth into the new creation in this present age. The transformation of the world awaits Christ's return; the new creation is now beginning as the seed of the kingdom takes root in human lives. Michael Horton says, "Every believer is a microcosm of the renewed cosmos."[38] The new creation is not cultural influence or ecological care—as valuable as those endeavors are while God's people function as salt and light in a fallen world—but a supernatural work of the Holy Spirit to manifest the glory of God in Christ. Horton writes, "This is hardly the picture of a gradual conquest of the nations and cultures of this age. On the contrary, the installment of the new creation that dominates this present age is the regeneration of

34. Kuyper, *The Work of the Holy Spirit*, 46–47.
35. 2 Cor. 5:17; Gal. 6:15; Eph. 2:10, 15 (Greek); 4:24; Col. 3:10.
36. Ridderbos, *Paul*, 45.
37. Andrew T. Lincoln, *Ephesians*, Word Biblical Commentary 42 (Dallas, TX: Word, 1990), 114.
38. Horton, *Rediscovering the Holy Spirit*, 178.

sinners and their incorporation through Spirit-given faith into the body of Christ, his church."[39]

The Spirit's work to make a people holy to the Lord is nothing less than an omnipotent renewal of creation. When Paul wrote that God "saved us, by the washing of regeneration, and renewing of the Holy Ghost" (Titus 3:5), he used the same word that Jesus Christ did when he spoke of "the regeneration when the Son of man shall sit in the throne of his glory" (Matt. 19:28). The word translated as "regeneration" (Greek *palingenesia*) is literally "genesis again" and points to the new heaven and new earth. Thus, Paul says that God gave us regeneration so that "we should be made heirs according to the hope of eternal life" (Titus 3:7). Regeneration begins a process that will end only in the full acquisition of eternal life in glory. Sinclair Ferguson says, "Paul sees regeneration within a broader context as a share in the renewal-resurrection which has been inaugurated by the Spirit in Christ. . . . [It] is, therefore, not merely an inner change; it is the incursion of a new order into the present order of reality."[40] Bavinck said, "Thus rebirth encompasses the entire scope of re-creation from its very first beginning in the heart of people to its ultimate completion in the new heaven and new earth."[41]

What a glorious hope belongs to those who have the Holy Spirit! If the Spirit of Christ dwells in you, then you already possess the glory of the new heaven and new earth in your heart. You are a citizen of the new creation. You are one of the many sons and daughters whom God is bringing to glory through Jesus Christ, the last Adam. The Spirit of Christ who dwells in you is leading you through afflictions into the very glory of the resurrected Christ.[42] Ferguson writes, "The Spirit is given to glorify us . . . to transform the very constitution of our being so that we become glorious."[43] Therefore, lift up your head, child of God. The Spirit Re-Creator lives in you, and you will glorify and enjoy God forever.

Sing to the Lord

Spirit Creator and Re-Creator

Come, O Creator Spirit blest,
And in our hearts take up thy rest;

---

39. Horton, *Rediscovering the Holy Spirit*, 186–87.
40. Ferguson, *The Holy Spirit*, 118.
41. Bavinck, *Reformed Dogmatics*, 4:53.
42. See Rom. 8:9, 11, 14, 17.
43. Ferguson, *The Holy Spirit*, 249.

Spirit of grace, with heav'nly aid
Come to the souls whom thou hast made.

Thou art the Comforter, we cry,
Sent to the earth from God Most High,
Fountain of life and Fire of love,
And our Anointing from above.

Bringing from heav'n our sev'nfold dow'r,[44]
Sign of our God's right hand of pow'r,
O blessed Spirit, promised long,
Thy coming wakes the heart to song.

Make our dull minds with rapture glow,
Let human hearts with love o'erflow;
And, when our feeble flesh would fail,
May thine immortal strength prevail.

Anonymous, Latin, 10th century
Tune: Grace Church
Trinity Hymnal—Baptist Edition, No. 251

Questions for Meditation or Discussion

1. How did the tabernacle reveal God's intention to make a new creation? How was the Holy Spirit involved in the tabernacle and temple?
2. How was God's kingdom revealed in the original creation? How has the Holy Spirit worked to renew God's kingdom since man's fall?
3. What does Isaiah 11:1–9 teach us about the Holy Spirit, Christ, and the new creation?
4. What effects does the Holy Spirit produce, according to Isaiah 32:15–17? How is this transformation further described in Isaiah 35?
5. What Scripture passages in the prophets promise a new "Eden"? What is the significance of these promises?

44. A "dower" (abbreviated "dow'r") is money or property given upon marriage or upon the death of a spouse.

6. What does David mean when he prays that God will "create" in him a new heart (Ps. 51:10)? How is the Holy Spirit (v. 11) involved?
7. How would you explain the meaning of Isaiah 44:1–5 to a class of high school students?
8. How does the biblical theme of the new creation shed new light on the doctrine of regeneration in Titus 3:5?
9. How has reading this chapter increased your hope and desire for the new creation?
10. How has reading this chapter increased your desire to pray for the work of the Holy Spirit in your life, family, and church? If it has not had that effect on you, why not?

Questions for Deeper Reflection

11. How are the biblical themes of the tabernacle and the kingdom fulfilled in the full glory of the new creation?
12. Why is it important in our theology that we recognize that the Holy Spirit is both the Creator of the creation and the Re-Creator of the new creation? What difference would it make if we deny or neglect the truth that the Re-Creator is first the Creator?
13. How can the reader discern whether prophetic descriptions of a transformed earth apply to physical changes in the world, spiritual changes in people, or both? After explaining some principles to guide the reader, show how these descriptions could be used to interpret Isaiah 32:15–17; 43:19–21; and 44:1–5.

Section B

The Holy Spirit and the Order of Salvation (Ordo Salutis)

9

Union with Christ by the Spirit, Part 1

Biblical Themes

The Spirit applies salvation by uniting people with Christ.[1] In the mind of the apostle Paul, to be "without Christ" is to have "no hope" and to be "without God in the world" (Eph. 2:12). But "in Christ" we have "all spiritual blessings" (1:3). John writes, "God hath given to us eternal life, and this life is in his Son. He that hath the Son hath life; and he that hath not the Son of God hath not life" (1 John 5:11–12). The Christian can have the joy of knowing that the Holy Spirit is "given me, to make me by a true faith, partaker of Christ and all His benefits."[2]

God saves sinners by a constellation of interconnected graces that theologians describe as the "order of salvation." This second section of our book will describe those graces, but we must first address the summary grace that undergirds all others: union with Christ. John Calvin wrote, "As long as Christ remains outside of us, and we are separated from him, all that he has suffered and done for the salvation of the human race remains useless and of no value for us. Therefore, to share with us what he has received from the Father, he had to become ours and to dwell within us.

1. The Westminster Shorter Catechism (Q. 30), in *Reformed Confessions*, 4:357.
2. The Heidelberg Catechism (LD 20, Q. 53), in *The Three Forms of Unity*, 84.

. . . The Holy Spirit is the bond by which Christ effectually unites us to himself."[3]

We may distinguish between *union* and *communion*. Union with Christ is the oneness, bond, and established relationship between him and his people. Communion with God is the active exercise and enjoyment of the graces of that union—living fellowship with God. As John Owen said, our communion with God consists in his sharing himself with us and our obedient response through the union we have with him in Jesus Christ.[4] However, since union with Christ involves God's saving power and personal love, union and communion are inseparable.

In placing union first in our discussion of the order of salvation, we are not saying that union with Christ is the first stage of God's saving work in an individual. On the contrary, it is the basis and great means by which God applies all blessings. Some theologians use the term *union with Christ* to refer specifically to spiritual, vital union.[5] However, the biblical doctrine is broader. Union with Christ is not one portion of the bridge by which God brings many sons to glory, but the entire structure that "underlies every step of the application of salvation," as John Murray (1898–1975) said.[6] Sinclair Ferguson says, "The dominant motive and architectonic principle of the order of salvation should therefore be union with Christ in the Spirit."[7]

Corporate Solidarity in the Last Adam

The writings of John and Paul are our primary sources for the doctrine of Christ's union with his people, but the building blocks of this doctrine appear as early as the book of Genesis.[8] Before the fall of man into sin, God had prepared types of Christ that would help sinners after the fall to look forward with hope in Christ. The first and most basic type of the

3. Calvin, *Institutes*, 3.1.1.

4. "Our communion, then, with God consisteth in his communication [sharing] of himself unto us, with our returnal unto him of that which he requireth and accepteth, flowing from that union which in Jesus Christ we have with him." Owen, *Communion with God*, in *Works*, 3:8.

5. For example, see Bruce Demarest, *The Cross and Salvation: The Doctrine of Salvation*, Foundations of Evangelical Theology (Wheaton, IL: Crossway, 1997), 323–24.

6. John Murray, *Redemption Accomplished and Applied* (Grand Rapids, MI: Eerdmans, 1955), 161. Murray placed his treatment of union with Christ after his chapters on the blessings of salvation, but we place it first to highlight its foundational place.

7. Ferguson, *The Holy Spirit*, 100.

8. Portions of this chapter are adapted from Joel R. Beeke and Paul M. Smalley, "Images of Union and Communion with Christ," *Puritan Reformed Journal* 8, no. 2 (2016): 125–36. Used by permission.

union between Christ and his people appears in the corporate solidarity of mankind in Adam.

1. Christ stands like Adam as *the one head of his people.* God created the entire human race in a single man so that from him came every other human being in the world, including his wife, created by a supernatural act of God.[9] Adam, whose very name means "Man," stood as mankind's representative in God's first covenant (Gen. 2:16–17) and fathered children in his image just as God had created man in his image (5:1–3). Our purpose here is not to discuss the nature and fall of man, topics that belong to the locus of anthropology, not soteriology.[10] However, we see in Adam a foreshadowing of Christ, what Paul calls "the figure [literally type] of him that was to come" (Rom. 5:14). Just as Adam's transgression resulted in mankind's condemnation and death, much more Christ stands as the Head of his people so that his righteousness becomes their justification and life (vv. 15–19).

Herman Ridderbos wrote, "Christ and Adam stand over against one another as the great representatives of the two aeons [ages], that of life and that of death."[11] Just as Adam's sin did not pertain to him alone but brought sin and death to "all men, which by a common generation have been and are born of him," Girolamo Zanchi (1516–1590) said, "so likewise that the righteousness of Christ and the eternal life due unto him is not held in Christ alone, but is derived into all those, who by the regeneration of the Holy Spirit are made one with him. . . . All our salvation and life is placed in him, as in our head, that it may indeed be bestowed and communicated upon all the elect of God which are united unto him."[12]

2. Christ is *the covenant officer with whom God's people are one.* As we saw in Romans 5, Adam acted not as a private individual but in a public, official capacity as the representative of others in a solemn legal arrangement between God and mankind—a covenant. God gave us further pictures of the church's union with Christ in the officers whom he appointed in his covenant with Israel. Just as Adam was the first prophet,

9. Gen. 2:7, 22; 3:20; 1 Chronicles 1.

10. On Adam as the representative of all his natural descendants in the covenant of works, see *RST*, 2:265–305 (chaps. 14–15). On Adam's transgression and the state of sin that ensued for mankind, see *RST*, 2:365–416 (chaps. 19–21).

11. Ridderbos, *Paul*, 57.

12. Girolamo Zanchi, *De Religione Christiana Fides—Confession of Christian Religion*, vol. 1, ed. Luca Baschera and Christian Moser, Studies in the History of Christian Traditions (Leiden: Brill, 2007), 12.1 (231). We have slightly modernized the 1599 translation.

priest, and king, so God appointed these offices in Israel, for Christ is our Prophet, Priest and King.[13]

In these offices, we see echoes of the corporate solidarity between Adam and his people. Moses appealed to God for mercy upon Israel on the basis of the Lord's favor to his prophet (Ex. 33:7–17). When the high priest ministered in the holy places of the tabernacle, he bore the names of the twelve tribes on his shoulders and over his heart (28:9–12, 21, 29). David's victory over Goliath was the victory of Israel over the Philistines (1 Sam. 16:13; 17:51–52). When the king sinned, God's judgment fell on the nation (2 Sam. 24:10–15; 1 Kings 9:4–7). As the nation was God's son (Ex. 4:22; Hos. 11:1), so the king was God's son (2 Sam. 7:14; Ps. 89:26–27). God designed the covenant officers of Israel to foreshadow Christ in his unity with his people. He is God's servant, and they are God's servant (Isa. 42:1; 43:10). He is Israel, yet he came to save Israel (49:3, 6). God has bound Christ and his people together in the bundle of life (cf. 1 Sam. 25:29).

3. Christ is *in his people, and they are in him and with him.* John writes of Christ and his people being and abiding "in" each another.[14] Paul develops this idea at length, writing frequently of being "in Christ."[15] Anthony Hoekema (1913–1988) wrote, "This expression ["in Christ" or *en Christō*], together with cognate expressions such as 'in the Lord' (*en Kyriō*) or 'in him' (*en autō*), occurs 164 times in Paul's epistles."[16] Paul links his doctrine of being in Christ with Christ's identity as the last Adam. He says, "For since by man came death, by man came also the resurrection of the dead. For as *in Adam* all die, even so *in Christ* shall all be made alive" (1 Cor. 15:21–22). God's Son is the Image of God, and by his Spirit we are transformed into the same image, for he is the last Adam.[17] Ridderbos said, "Christ is thereby designated as the Inaugurator of the new humanity."[18] When Paul writes of Adam and Christ as the "first man" and "second man" (v. 47), it is as if no one else ever lived: all other human beings are

13. On the threefold office in Adam as the man created in God's image and made God's representative by his covenantal word, see *RST*, 2:162–68, 274–76. The threefold office of Christ is the theme of *RST*, 2:869–1168 (chaps. 43–55).

14. John 6:56; 14:20; 15:4–10; 17:21, 23; 1 John 2:6, 28; 3:6; cf. abiding with respect to Christ's word, Spirit, etc. in John 8:31; 14:16–17; 1 John 2:10, 14, 24, 27; 3:15, 17, 24; 4:12–16; 2 John 2, 9.

15. For some examples, see Rom. 3:24; 6:11, 23; 8:1–2; 1 Cor. 1:2, 30; 15:22; 2 Cor. 5:17; Gal. 2:17; 3:14; Eph. 1:3, 20; 2:6–7, 10; Phil. 3:14; 4:19; Col. 1:28; 1 Thess. 4:16; 1 Tim. 1:14; 2 Tim. 1:9, 13; 2:1.

16. Anthony A. Hoekema, *Saved by Grace* (Grand Rapids, MI: Eerdmans, 1989), 65.

17. Rom. 8:29; 1 Cor. 15:45–49; 2 Cor. 3:17–18; 4:4–6.

18. Ridderbos, *Paul*, 56.

bound up in Adam or in Christ. Richard Sibbes wrote, "So then we see we have in Christ, 'the second Adam,' whatsoever we lost in the first root . . . and more than all we lost, he being God-man."[19]

Paul also writes of being "with Christ" in his redemptive works. He says, "I am crucified with Christ" (Gal. 2:20); "therefore we are buried with him" (Rom. 6:4); "even when we were dead in our trespasses, [God] made us alive together with Christ—by grace you have been saved—and raised us up with him and seated us with him in the heavenly places in Christ Jesus" (Eph. 2:5–6 ESV); and we shall "be also glorified together" with Christ (Rom. 8:17). Our union with Christ is so complete that when he was crucified, we were crucified; when he died, we died; when he was buried, we were buried; when he was raised from the dead, we were raised; and when he ascended into heaven and sat down at the right hand of the Father, we were also glorified.

Images of Union and Communion with God in Christ

To help us to receive this doctrine with faith and joy, God has given us several delightful word pictures of our union with Christ rooted in Adam's experience in the garden of Eden.

God's Temple in Christ

The garden of Eden was the first temple, where Adam and Eve experienced God's special presence and offered him priestly service.[20] After the fall of man, God gave Israel the tabernacle and temple as a sign that he would dwell with his people again in grace despite the uncleanness of their sins (Ex. 29:42–46; 1 Kings 8:12–13). The Lord said that if Israel kept his commandments, "I will set my tabernacle among you: and my soul shall not abhor you. And I will walk among you, and will be your God, and ye shall be my people" (Lev. 26:11–12). Robert Peterson says, "The primary way that God identifies with his people, uniting himself to them, is by his commitment to be present with them. . . . God desires to be united to his people in covenant relationship."[21] Even after the sins of Israel provoked God to remove his presence from them and destroy his temple, he promised to restore his sanctuary among them forever (Ezek. 37:23–28).

19. Sibbes, *The Hidden Life*, in *Works*, 5:210. See *The Spiritual Jubilee*, in *Works*, 5:225.
20. On the garden of Eden as God's temple, see *RST*, 2:136–37.
21. Robert A. Peterson, *Salvation Applied by the Spirit: Union with Christ* (Wheaton, IL: Crossway, 2015), 22.

In the new covenant, God makes his people into his temple by their union with Christ in the Holy Spirit. Paul writes, "Know ye not that ye are the temple of God, and that the Spirit of God dwelleth in you?" (1 Cor. 3:16). The "ye" indicates a plural subject: the church as a body is God's temple where he dwells. Paul explains that believers in Christ are joined to Christ as the parts of a temple are joined to its cornerstone (Eph. 2:19–22).[22] Peter likewise describes Christ as "a living stone," the cornerstone on whom believers are built "like living stones" into "a spiritual house, to be a holy priesthood, to offer spiritual sacrifices" for the glory of him who called them "out of darkness into his marvelous light" (1 Pet. 2:4–5, 9 ESV). Peterson says, "They have come into contact with the living stone and receive spiritual life from him. . . . When joined to the living stone they become living stones and immediately are joined to all other living stones. . . . Christians are both temple and priesthood, and therefore union with Christ serves the worship of God through his Mediator."[23] The ultimate hope of believers is that God will dwell with his people, and they will be like a magnificent temple-city that needs no holy buildings because God is there through Jesus Christ (Rev. 21:3, 9–23).[24]

How can human beings be God's temple? Believers are joined to the Lord Jesus Christ by the Holy Spirit, and therefore the Holy Spirit dwells in their bodies as God's temple for his glory (1 Cor. 6:17–20). Christ is the temple of God (John 1:14; 2:19–22), for in him the "fullness" of deity dwells in a bodily form (Col. 2:9). The church in union with him is indwelt and increasingly filled by his fullness until his glory fills all things in the new creation.[25] Grant Macaskill writes, "The logic of this image . . . is that this mediatorial function of Christ involves nothing less than a giving of himself. . . . The glorification spoken of, then, can only be understood in relational or even personal terms: it is the giving of one person to others, who are thereby glorified by his presence, while remaining distinct from him."[26]

The biblical image of a temple teaches us that union with Christ joins believers permanently to him so that they become the home of God's spe-

22. On Christ as "cornerstone," see *RST*, 2:747n47.

23. Peterson, *Salvation Applied by the Spirit*, 239–40.

24. The vision of the new Jerusalem in Revelation 21 is patterned on the temple with its lavish use of gold, cube-shaped Most Holy Place, angels at the gates, and gemstones like those on the high priest's garments.

25. Eph. 1:23; 3:17–19; 4:10–13; cf. Isa. 6:1, 3.

26. Grant Macaskill, *Union with Christ in the New Testament* (Oxford: Oxford University Press, 2013), 151.

cial presence, to behold his glory and offer up their praises forever. Since Christ is the cornerstone, believers rest on him by faith, and he bears the full weight of God's temple by his wisdom, righteousness, and power.

God's Fruit Bearers in Christ

The garden of Eden was an orchard, for "out of the ground made the LORD God to grow every tree that is pleasant to the sight, and good for food," including "the tree of life" (Gen. 2:9). These trees were for the delight and nourishment of man, as we will discuss shortly. However, Genesis tells us that God also delighted in the goodness of his creation, including fruitful trees (Gen. 1:12). Furthermore, the language of fruitfulness is applied to mankind's multiplication of offspring in God's commission to his image bearers and his covenant with Abraham and Israel.[27]

The Holy Scriptures also apply this picture of fruitfulness to living in righteousness. In the tabernacle, the golden lampstand had the form of an almond tree (Ex. 25:33), a sign of the fruitful life found through the priestly ministry of Christ (Num. 17:8). The righteous flourish like trees planted in the house of God to declare his perfection (Ps. 92:12–15). The person who trusts in the faithful love of God is "like a green olive tree in the house of God" (52:8). The righteous are a "tree of life" that produces fruit for the blessing of other people (Prov. 11:30; 15:4).

God compared Israel to a vine that he had planted and nurtured to impressive size, but which he gave over to destruction.[28] Like the trees of Eden, the vineyard of Israel was planted by God to bear good fruit: justice and righteousness (Isa. 5:1–7). The vine of Israel proved corrupt (Jer. 2:21), but God promised that he would bless his vineyard again so that Israel would fill the world with fruit (Isa. 27:2–6). God would heal their backsliding and "be as the dew unto Israel" so that the nation would grow as a beautiful olive tree, for from the Lord comes Israel's fruit (Hos. 14:4–8).

Christ said, "I am the vine, ye are the branches: he that abideth in me, and I in him, the same bringeth forth much fruit: for without me ye can do nothing" (John 15:5). Thus, he identified himself as the true Israel, the fulfillment of what God's people were meant to be. God's judgment was

27. Gen. 1:28; 9:1, 7; 17:6; 28:3; 35:11; 48:4; Lev. 26:9.

28. Ps. 80:8–19; Ezek. 15:6; 17:6; 19:10. In the Bible, a vine is not sharply distinguished from a tree, but is considered a woody plant "among the trees of the forest" (Ezek. 15:6) and may be depicted as growing to a great height with a mass of branches (19:11).

going to fall again on those who would not offer good fruit to God (Matt. 21:33–44; cf. John 15:6). The only way for people to bear fruit pleasing to God is to have a living, organic, abiding union with Christ as branches to a vine. In him alone can we be the true Israel of God, the delightful garden of the Lord. The image is not of a vine clinging to a tree, but a branch drawing its life from a vine, as John Flavel observed.[29] Zanchi said, "As a branch can draw no vital sap from the vine . . . [unless it is] joined to the vine . . . even so men cannot receive any salvation or life from Christ (in whom alone it is placed), unless they are grafted into him and joined in a true and real union, and being joined abide in him."[30]

The image of branches on the vine has immense practical significance. The Christian life is impossible apart from union with Christ. William Bridge (1600–1671) said, "Our spiritual life, it doth arise from our union with Christ; and though a man may have many moral virtues . . . yet if not united to Christ by the Spirit, he is but a dead man."[31] Furthermore, the exercise of the Christian life requires continual dependence on Christ. Rowland Stedman (d. 1673) said, "If they have strength and ability to work the works of God, it is imparted through him. For they are branches in him, and he is the vine, so that we have no cause to boast of ourselves, nor is there any ground for self-confidence, or trusting in ourselves. But the whole life that we live, should be by faith on the Son of God."[32]

God's Guests at the Feast in Christ

Though the trees of Eden served as pictures of God's fruitful people in union with Christ, in the historical garden they functioned primarily to nourish the life of Adam and his wife (Gen. 2:9, 16; 3:22). Genesis emphasizes the verdant setting by directing attention to the river that watered the garden before issuing into four great rivers (Gen. 2:10). To the Israelites who had left the Nile to wander in the dry wilderness, this must have been a picture of overwhelming blessing. Living in the well-watered garden, the first man and woman enjoyed a daily feast in the presence of the Lord God.

Partaking of food and drink depicts the life-giving communion of God's saints with him. Israel ate manna in the wilderness (Exodus 16),

29. Flavel, *The Method of Grace*, in *Works*, 2:38–39.

30. Zanchi, *De Religione Christiana Fides*, 12.3 (1:233).

31. William Bridge, *The Spiritual Life and In-Being of Christ in All Believers*, in *The Works of the Rev. William Bridge*, 5 vols. (London: Thomas Tegg, 1845), 1:301.

32. Rowland Stedman, *The Mystical Union of Believers with Christ* (London: by W. R. for Thomas Parkhurst, 1668), 247.

the bread from heaven (Ps. 78:24; John 6:31). The elders of Israel had a taste of table fellowship with God on Mount Sinai (Ex. 24:9–11). Christ appears in Proverbs as the Wisdom who is "a tree of life" to all who take hold of him (Prov. 3:18). Wisdom prepares a rich banquet and calls foolish humanity to come and eat (9:1–12). The Lord calls sinners to return to him so that they may eat and drink without money and without price (Isa. 55:1–2). God is the best of hosts (Ps. 23:5–6). The Lord is the fountain of living water who alone can satisfy the thirsty soul (Jer. 2:13; 17:5–8, 13). Feasting on God as one's satisfying food and drink is especially associated with God's temple as the place of his special presence.[33] The temple was the location of Israel's feasts, and it was there that Israel ate the meat of the sacrifices (Deut. 12:5–7, 17–18).

Christ drew upon this rich Old Testament background when he compared union and communion with him to eating and drinking. Christ alone gives the living water that eternally satisfies (John 4:14), the heavenly streams of the Holy Spirit (7:37–39). Jesus himself is the Bread of Life on whom we feed by faith (6:35). Christ shockingly said that we must eat his flesh and blood to have eternal life and dwell in him (vv. 48–58). "Flesh and blood" is language used of human life (Heb. 2:14) and of sacrifice (Lev. 17:11). Calvin said, "As the eternal Word of God is the fountain of life (John 1:4), so his flesh, as a channel, conveys to us that life which dwells intrinsically, as we say, in his divinity."[34] Christ's discourse "does not relate to the Lord's supper," which he had not yet instituted; rather, "he now speaks of the perpetual and ordinary way of eating the flesh of Christ, which is done by faith only."[35] Christ said we must eat his flesh to indicate that we must trust in him as the sacrificed God-man, for "the only bond of union by which he becomes one with us is when our faith relies on his death."[36]

Eating Christ is a metaphor for entering into a deep union with him by faith so that the incarnate Mediator becomes our life as we commune with him. Michael Barrett writes, "As we believe Christ and His gospel, we receive life and enter into a mutual bond with Christ: 'He that eateth my flesh, and drinketh my blood, dwelleth in me, and I in him' [John 6:56]. We must have a regular, daily diet of eating the Bread of Life and drinking

33. Pss. 36:8; 42:1–4; 46:4–5; 63:1–5; cf. 27:4; 43:3–4; 65:4; 84:1–2.
34. Calvin, *Commentaries*, on John 6:51.
35. Calvin, *Commentaries*, on John 6:53–54.
36. Calvin, *Commentaries*, on John 6:56.

the Living Water if we are going to grow in grace and in the knowledge of God."[37]

God's Clothing in Christ

Clothing originated in the garden of Eden. Adam and Eve made puny attempts to cover their nakedness in their shame after the fall (Gen. 3:7). However, God in his mercy clothed them with the skins of animals (v. 21), which was mankind's first exposure to physical death and a sign of the sacrifices by which their guilt and shame would be covered.[38]

In the temple, the priests wore holy garments for beauty and glory so that they would not die in God's holy presence (Exodus 28). Clothing became a symbol of salvation itself: "I will greatly rejoice in the LORD, my soul shall be joyful in my God; for he hath clothed me with the garments of salvation, he hath covered me with the robe of righteousness, as a bridegroom decketh himself with ornaments, and as a bride adorneth herself with her jewels" (Isa. 61:10).[39] The Lord puts on clothing when he goes forth to fight for his people: the armor of righteousness, salvation, and judgment (59:16–18). The Lord desired for Israel to cling to him like a man's clothes "that they might be unto me for a people, and for a name, and for a praise, and for a glory" (Jer. 13:11). The Lord will be their "crown of glory," and they shall be the same unto him (Isa. 28:5; 62:3).

In the New Testament, clothing is an image of union and communion with Christ. Paul says, "Put ye on the Lord Jesus Christ, and make not provision for the flesh, to fulfil the lusts thereof" (Rom. 13:14). John Murray commented, "To put on Christ is to be identified with him not only in his death but also in his resurrection. It is to be united to him in the likeness of his resurrection life [cf. Rom. 6:1–10]."[40] Being clothed with Christ is not only an imperative, but also an indicative true of all believers: "For as many of you as have been baptized into Christ have put on Christ" (Gal. 3:27).[41] Just as in conversion they have "put off"

37. Michael P. V. Barrett, *Complete in Him: A Guide to Understanding and Enjoying the Gospel*, 2nd ed. (Grand Rapids, MI: Reformation Heritage Books, 2017), 103.

38. On the significance of Adam and Eve's fig leaves and leather clothing, see *RST*, 2:352–53, 362.

39. See also Ps. 132:9, 16; Zech. 3:4.

40. Murray, *The Epistle to the Romans*, 2:170.

41. Texts such as this are sometimes used to argue that union with Christ is effected through the sacraments. *Catechism of the Catholic Church*, secs. 1131, 1997. However, reading these Scripture passages in context shows that vital union with Christ is coupled with faith in him (Rom. 6:3–4,

the "old man" of Adam, so they have "put on the new man" of Christ (Eph. 4:22–24; Col. 3:9–10). Remarkably, their union with Christ is so close that believers may clothe themselves in the very armor of God, for they fight in the strength of the Lord (Eph. 6:10–11).[42] God clothes them with power by the Holy Spirit (Luke 24:49). One day, when the trumpet sounds, they will be clothed with immortality by their union with the risen Lord Jesus (1 Cor. 15:53–54). In all his graces, the Lord Jesus is as close to them as their own garments.

Christ's Bride

One of the most amazing pictures of union with Christ is that of a bride and bridegroom. This, too, is rooted in Eden, where God made the first woman from Adam's side and presented her to him as his wife (Gen. 2:18–25). Marriage is a covenant or solemn promise (Mal. 2:14; cf. Gen. 2:23), so it serves as an image of the covenantal love between the Lord God and man.[43]

Through the prophets, the Lord repeatedly used the image of marriage to describe his love for Israel and to call her to faithfulness toward him. God's relationship with his people is a love story in which his undeserved kindness is repaid by their infidelity, until his grace breaks their hearts and brings them home again to live in covenant with him (Ezekiel 16). Backsliders in Israel must repent, said the Lord, "for I am married unto you" (Jer. 3:14). Though Israel had committed spiritual adultery, God would renew the marriage covenant based on his own righteousness, faithfulness, love, and compassion (Hos. 2:19–20). The Lord spoke to Israel as to a barren woman, promising her a vast number of children: "For thy Maker is thine husband; the Lord of hosts is his name; and thy Redeemer the Holy One of Israel; the God of the whole earth shall he be called" (Isa. 54:5). The Lord promises to rejoice over his people as a bridegroom rejoices over his bride (62:5). Greater love has never been seen than the love between the divine Bridegroom and his beloved bride.

17; Gal. 3:26–27; Col. 2:12). It is possible to receive the Spirit of Christ before baptism (Acts 10:44–48) or to be baptized while not yet saved (8:13, 18–23). A full discussion of the sacraments or ordinances of public worship and their relationship to salvation belongs to the theological locus of ecclesiology. See *RST*, vol. 4 (forthcoming).

42. See also Rom. 13:12; 1 Thess. 5:8.

43. On the covenantal overtones of "the Lord God" and the institution of marriage in Genesis 2, see *RST*, 2:132, 138–41.

Against this background, we can only consider Christ's reference to himself as the Bridegroom of his people to be a claim to deity (Matt. 9:15; 25:6). Ministers of the gospel are mere friends of the Bridegroom, and their hearts long for the church to be fully devoted to Christ (John 3:29; 2 Cor. 11:2). Paul compares the spiritual union of the Bridegroom and his bride to the one-flesh union of man and woman.[44] Macaskill writes, "The two do not meld or melt, their beings are not confused. They are, instead, united and any transfer of properties of one to the other must be spoken of in terms of inter-personal communication, not hybridization."[45]

Union with Christ as our heavenly Bridegroom should move the church to exult, "I am my beloved's, and my beloved is mine" (Song 6:3). Edward Pearse (c. 1633–1673) wrote that the spiritual marriage of Christ and his people consists of "a giving of themselves to each other" in "a near and intimate union" that enables "full and lasting communion" with each other in "strong and ardent affections" of love, resulting in "mutual rest" and "great delight" in each other forever.[46]

The hope of the church is that her covenant betrothal will one day come to fruition at the "marriage supper of the Lamb," and for this she prepares herself by grace by making a wedding dress of righteous deeds (Rev. 19:7–9). Indeed, she can produce good deeds only by her marital union with the risen Lord (Rom. 7:1–6). Joined together as spiritual lovers, Christ and his church live in a union and communion of which the intimacy of sexual union is a faint shadow at best. The union of the church to her heavenly Bridegroom gives her greater honor and dignity than the angels themselves. Flavel said, "They are as the barons and nobles in his kingdom, but the saints as the dear spouse and wife of his bosom."[47]

Christ's Body

When Adam received his wife from God in the garden of Eden, the Lord added these words to explain the relevance of this for mankind: "Therefore shall a man leave his father and his mother, and shall cleave unto his

44. 1 Cor. 6:16–17; Eph. 5:31–32; both citing Gen. 2:24.
45. Macaskill, *Union with Christ in the New Testament*, 156.
46. Edward Pearse, *The Best Match: The Soul's Espousal to Christ*, ed. Don Kistler (Grand Rapids, MI: Soli Deo Gloria, 1994), 4–17. We have summarized the main headings of Pearse's chapter.
47. Flavel, *The Method of Grace*, in *Works*, 2:42.

wife: and they shall be one flesh" (Gen. 2:24). Paul interprets this according to his inspired Adam-Christ typology, writing, "For no man ever yet hated his own flesh; but nourisheth and cherisheth it, even as the Lord the church: for we are members of his body, of his flesh, and of his bones. For this cause shall a man leave his father and mother, and shall be joined unto his wife, and they two shall be one flesh. This is a great mystery: but I speak concerning Christ and the church" (Eph. 5:29–32).

Therefore, just as a husband and wife are one flesh, so the church is Christ's body, joined to him as closely as his hands and feet. He is the Head of the body.[48] Barrett writes, "The head is the command center for all the operations of life. From the head flow all the impulses and instructions for the body to function. A headless body is lifeless. It is only in union with its head that a body can live."[49]

Christ has great tenderness for the members of his body (Eph. 5:29–30). Whatever affects them also involves him, and therefore they must conduct themselves in holiness (1 Cor. 6:13–17). Christ told his suffering people that whoever touches them touches the apple of his eye—the most sensitive part of his body (Deut. 32:10; Zech. 2:8). The risen Lord rebuked a persecutor of the church, saying, "Why persecutest thou me?" (Acts 9:4).

Christ's union with his body transcends the union between any earthly husband and wife because he lives in his body by the Holy Spirit (1 Cor. 6:15, 17; 12:12–13). Christ promised to send the Spirit to dwell in his people, and said, "I will come to you. . . . Because I live, ye shall live also" (John 14:17–19). "The Spirit of Christ" dwells in those who belong to him (Rom. 8:9). Through this spiritual and organic connection, Christ shares his life with his body so that it grows and builds itself up (Eph. 4:15–16; Col. 2:19). Though we may perish physically in our afflictions, yet we shall live forever, for already we are joined to Christ in his resurrection and are "his body, the fullness of him that filleth all in all" (Eph. 1:19, 23). Even when Christians are dead, they are "the dead in Christ" and will rise again at his coming (1 Thess. 4:16).

The church is not a collection of isolated individuals, but "one new man" in Christ, reconciled to God "in one body" (Eph. 2:15–16). Paul writes, "So we, being many, are one body in Christ, and individually

48. 1 Cor. 11:3; Eph. 4:15; 5:23; Col. 1:18; 2:19.
49. Barrett, *Complete in Him*, 104.

members of one another" (Rom. 12:5). Though we are diverse, every member of the church belongs to the body, and every member is needed (1 Cor. 12:12–30). We are one body with one Lord, and therefore must labor to maintain the unity Christ has given us (Eph. 4:1–6). Union with Christ has massive implications for how we relate to other Christians.

The union of Christ with the church as his body far exceeds anything found in the first Adam. In this regard, we must recognize that the last Adam is more than a man—he is the Lord. As God the Son, Christ is essentially one with the Spirit and has union with his Spirit-indwelt people in a manner that transcends the types and shadows of the Old Testament and brings us into the most intimate union with God that is possible for created beings. The metaphors for union with Christ that we have examined in this section communicate the close, life-giving, organic connection between Christ and his people.

Summary and Application

The union of God's chosen people with Christ arises from his unique office as the last Adam of the new creation. In corporate solidarity with Christ as their Prophet, Priest, and King in the covenant, believers are one with him in his person, work, and blessings. They are living stones built on the cornerstone of Christ in the temple where God dwells; branches abiding in the vine of Christ to bear the fruit of the true Israel; guests eating at God's table, where Christ is the spiritual food and their glorious clothing; the beloved bride of the Son of God; and the body of Christ, joined to him as their living Head in the Holy Spirit.

Since union with Christ is the heart of salvation, we must examine ourselves to see if we are truly united to him. Paul writes, "Examine yourselves, whether ye be in the faith; prove your own selves. Know ye not your own selves, how that Jesus Christ is in you, except ye be reprobates?" (2 Cor. 13:5). True religion is not merely a matter of true beliefs, moral behavior, and participation in the ordinances of worship, although it includes all these. It is a supernatural relationship with Jesus Christ, such that you are in him and he is in you.

Union with Christ produces good fruit, including humility, love, purity, and good works. Thomas Boston (1676–1732) said, "They that are barren may be branches of Christ by profession, but not by real implantation. All who are united to Christ bring forth the fruit of gospel-obedience and true holiness."[50] Most of all, union with Christ reorients a person's whole life toward Jesus Christ.

Are you in union with Jesus Christ? Do you belong to him? If you must answer in the negative, then you are in a desperate condition. Regardless of how religious or moral you may be, you are lost and dead in your sins. You are an enemy of God, under God's wrath, and without hope in the world. However, even as you read this book, God in his mercy is patiently calling you to come to his Son. Why will you die? Come, there is a banquet prepared in Christ for sinners—without cost to you because he paid the price. By grace, come and eat by a Spirit-worked faith. Receive Christ, and you will discover that you have been born again by God's sovereign grace to a living hope, and Christ is yours forever.

If you are in Christ, then you have much for which to be grateful. The thought that Christ has united himself so very closely to Christians should overwhelm us with his love for us. God overcame all our enmity and resistance against him and gave us the Spirit of faith so that we take hold of him who has taken hold of us. As Owen said, the Christian should exclaim, "What am I, poor, sinful dust and ashes, one that deserves to be lightly esteemed by the whole creation of God, that I should be thus united unto the Son of God, and thereby become his son by adoption?"[51] Wilhelmus à Brakel said that believers should meditate on "the unsearchable grace and goodness of God that such wretched and sinful men may be so intimately united with the Son of God," for such meditations "will most wondrously set the heart aflame with love."[52] Therefore, Brakel said, "arise, satisfy and fill yourself with Him, rejoice in Him and His benefits."[53] Our mouths should be full of songs of praise that the almighty Lord would join himself to such as us. Our hearts should swell with desire to enjoy intimate fellowship with the God who has so desired to be near to us.

Charles Spurgeon (1834–1892) quoted the favorite expression of a recently deceased Christian: "Lord Jesus, we are one with thee. We feel that we have a living, loving, lasting union with thee." Spurgeon said, "Those three words have stuck by me; and ever since he has gone, I have found

50. Thomas Boston, *Human Nature in Its Fourfold State* (Edinburgh: Banner of Truth, 1964), 302.
51. Owen, *An Exposition of the Epistle to the Hebrews*, 4:149.
52. Brakel, *The Christian's Reasonable Service*, 2:91.
53. Brakel, *The Christian's Reasonable Service*, 2:93.

myself repeating them to myself involuntarily—'a living, loving, lasting union.' He owed everything to that."[54] So also do we.

Sing to the Lord

God Dwells with His People

God is our refuge and our strength,
Our ever present aid,
And, therefore, though the earth remove,
We will not be afraid;
Though hills amidst the seas be cast,
Though foaming waters roar,
Yea though the mighty billows shake
The mountains on the shore.

A river flows whose streams make glad
The city of our God,
The holy place wherein the Lord
Most High has His abode;
Since God is in the midst of her,
Unmoved her walls shall stand,
For God will be her early help,
When trouble is at hand.

Psalm 46
Tune: Materna
The Psalter, No. 125
Trinity Hymnal—Baptist Edition, No. 37

Questions for Meditation or Discussion

1. Why do the authors discuss union with Christ first in the section on the order of salvation?
2. How is the union between Christ and his people foreshadowed in Adam?
3. What are several examples from the writings of John and Paul saying that Christ and his people are "in" each other? What does this language teach us?

54. C. H. Spurgeon, *The Metropolitan Tabernacle Pulpit*, 57 vols. (Edinburgh: Banner of Truth, 1969), 38:98.

4. How does the biblical theme of God's dwelling place or temple illuminate union with Christ and communion with God through him?
5. What does Christ's parable of the vine and the branches (John 15:1–10) teach us about union with Christ?
6. A Roman Catholic friend of yours says, "I have union with Christ by celebrating the Eucharist, for Jesus said, 'He that eateth my flesh, and drinketh my blood, dwelleth in me, and I in him'" (John 6:56). How would you explain this Scripture passage to your friend?
7. What Scripture passages compare our union with the Lord to wearing clothing? What can we learn from this comparison?
8. What are the practical implications of knowing that the church is the bride of Christ?
9. What does it mean that the church is the "body" of Christ?
10. Are you in union with Jesus Christ? Why do you say so? What difference does it make?

Questions for Deeper Reflection

11. You are asked to speak to an adult class on the subject "What is union with Christ?" Write a definition and a detailed outline proving each part of the definition from the Holy Scriptures.
12. Of the six biblical images of union with Christ, which does your church most need to hear right now? Why?

10

Union with Christ by the Spirit, Part 2

Theological and Practical Considerations

There is a glorious richness to the church's union with Christ. Even the word *union* cannot capture the full range and dynamic of this doctrine. Constantine Campbell proposes that we use "four terms: union, participation, identification, and incorporation." He explains, "*Union* gathers up faith union with Christ, mutual indwelling, trinitarian, and nuptial notions. *Participation* conveys partaking in the events of Christ's narrative. *Identification* refers to believers' location in the realm of Christ and their allegiance to his lordship. *Incorporation* encapsulates the corporate dimensions of membership in Christ's body."[1] We would add to Campbell's list the word *representation*, for as we saw in the last chapter, union with Christ pertains to him being the last Adam, the representative of his people in their covenantal relationship with God.[2]

In this chapter, we will continue our study of union with Christ by examining the meaning of that union as God decrees salvation in eternity and executes that decree in stages through history; correcting false conceptions

1. Constantine R. Campbell, *Paul and Union with Christ: An Exegetical and Theological Study* (Grand Rapids, MI: Zondervan, 2012), 413.
2. Cf. Campbell, *Paul and Union with Christ*, 345–46.

of union with Christ; and making practical applications of this doctrine for the Christian life.

The Modes of Union with Christ at Various Stages of History

The true nature of union with Christ is illuminated by tracing that union from God's decree through its execution in various stages of redemptive history. Many of Paul's "in Christ" statements pertain to a vital union between Christ and the church by his Spirit. Thus, Paul wrote that certain believers "were in Christ before me" (Rom. 16:7). In a very important sense, no one is in Christ who is not converted and indwelt by the Spirit. However, other uses of Paul's "in Christ" and "with Christ" language indicate a union that precedes a person's conversion, even his birth, and reaches back into the eternal counsels of God.

There is a beautiful complexity to how God unites us with Christ at different points in eternity and time. Thomas Goodwin taught that union with Christ includes God's grace in *eternity*, "when Christ did but undertake for us" to be our representative in God's eternal "covenant" and "secret purpose"; in *history*, "when in the fullness of time he had performed what he undertook," so that "when Christ died and rose again, we were in him by representation"; and in *personal application*, "when Christ by his Spirit knits us to him, and works faith in us," so that we are "made one with him actually."[3] We will trace this complexity in five steps.

Union with Christ in the Father's Eternal Election

God has blessed us with every spiritual blessing in Christ "according as he hath chosen us in him before the foundation of the world, that we should be holy and without blame before him in love" (Eph. 1:4).[4] Our election "in Christ" does not mean that God chose us because he foreknew that we would follow Christ in faith and obedience.[5] Rather, it means that God united his chosen ones with Christ in his "purpose and grace . . . before the world began" (2 Tim. 1:9). This plan took the form of an eternal "promise" made within the Trinity when no one else existed (Titus 1:1–2). Herman Bavinck said, "A bond was already forged

3. Goodwin, *The Object and Acts of Justifying Faith*, in *Works*, 8:138–39. See Beeke and Jones, *A Puritan Theology*, 482.
4. The doctrine of election is presented in *RST*, 1:979–1057 (chaps. 49–51).
5. On foreknowledge with respect to God's decree, see *RST*, 1:963–64, 1036–38.

between the mediator and those who were given him by the Father in eternity, in election, and more precisely in the pact of salvation (*pactum salutis*)."[6] Eternal union with Christ is federal (from Latin *foedus*, covenant) in nature. The Westminster Larger Catechism (Q. 31) says, "The covenant of grace was made with Christ as the second Adam, and in him with all the elect as his seed."[7]

John Gill wrote, "He is the representative-head of his church, or of all the elect of God; they were all considered in him, and represented by him, when he covenanted with his Father for them; all that he engaged to do and suffer, was not only on their account, but in their name and stead; and all that he received, promises and blessings, were not only for them, but he received them as personating [representing] them."[8] Marcus Johnson says, "In some ineffable way, those whom God has chosen as his own have always been 'in Christ,' . . . [which shows] that the initiative of our salvation always rests with God—he loved us in Christ before we were born and will always love us so!"[9]

In its eternal aspect, union with Christ is not a vital, transforming relationship. Neither does it imply a righteous status for the elect before their conversion, for all unbelievers are under the wrath of God for their sins.[10] The elect are in Christ at this stage only with respect to the plan, decree, and purpose of God. However, this covenantal union is the foundation of all other aspects of union with Christ, for in them God executes his eternal decree.

Union with Christ in His Incarnation

Christ joined himself to us when he took to himself human nature.[11] "For both he that sanctifieth and they who are sanctified are all of one: for which cause he is not ashamed to call them brethren" (Heb. 2:11). Since "the children are partakers of flesh and blood, he also himself likewise took part of the same" (v. 14). Christ's incarnation gives him a common nature with all human beings, but his incarnational union joins him

6. Bavinck, *Reformed Dogmatics*, 3:523. On the eternal counsel of peace, see *RST*, 2:584–609 (chap. 30).
7. *Reformed Confessions*, 4:305.
8. Gill, *Body of Divinity*, 228.
9. Marcus Peter Johnson, *One with Christ: An Evangelical Theology of Salvation* (Wheaton, IL: Crossway, 2013), 36.
10. John 3:18, 36; Rom. 1:18; Eph. 2:3.
11. The doctrine of the incarnation is presented in *RST*, 2:783–865 (chaps. 39–42).

particularly to the "brethren" and "children" whom God gave to him to save. He took our flesh to serve as our kinsman-redeemer, who made propitiation, provides justification, and intercedes sympathetically for "the people" (vv. 17–18).[12]

God's covenant with his people is "I am with you."[13] Christ is not merely God *for* us but also God *with* us, "Immanuel" (Isa. 7:14). As Robert Letham notes, Christ's incarnation fulfills the central promise of God's covenant: "God is our God in Jesus Christ . . . [and] in Christ we are God's people."[14] The God-man is the fulfillment of all the promises of God (2 Cor. 1:20), and he is the very heart and soul of the covenant of grace (Isa. 42:6; 49:8). Letham writes, "The incarnation is the indispensable basis for union with Christ. Since Christ has united himself to us in the incarnation, we can be united to him by the Holy Spirit."[15] Thus, the "Emmanuel knot of union" joins us to the One in whom "all things are possible" (Matt. 19:26).[16]

Union with Christ is not direct union between our human persons and God; we are united to the incarnate Lord, and through him to the triune God. The church is therefore enabled to have the closest communion with God because God has united himself to human nature. This Christ-centered doctrine preserves both the transcendence of God and his intimate relation with his children. J. Todd Billings says, "Intimate communion with God is possible, but it is communion with a God who is inherently other and inherently mysterious to human beings. . . . So let the adopted children of God adore his mystery by focusing their hearts and minds on Jesus Christ, who will always be 'in the middle.'"[17] We are united to the Son who, though the radiance of God's infinite glory and the exact image of his Father, has shared in our weakness, suffering, and temptation (Heb. 1:3; 2:18; 4:15). Through Jesus Christ, God is able to connect with us in a fully divine yet truly human way.

---

12. On Christ as our kinsman-redeemer (*goel*), see *RST*, 2:860–61. See Turretin, *Institutes*, 16.3.5 (2:647).
13. Gen. 26:3, 24; 28:13–15; 31:3; Isa. 41:10; 43:1–3; Jer. 42:11; 46:28; Hag. 1:13; 2:4; Matt. 28:20.
14. Robert Letham, *Union with Christ: In Scripture, History, and Theology* (Phillipsburg, NJ: P&R, 2011), 36–37. See Gen. 17:7–8; Ex. 6:7; 29:45–46; Lev. 26:12; Deut. 29:13; Isa. 40:1; Jer. 7:23; 11:4; 24:7; 30:22; 31:33; 32:38; Ezek. 36:28; Joel 2:27; 2 Cor. 6:16; Rev. 21:3, 7.
15. Letham, *Union with Christ*, 40.
16. A. J. Gordon, *In Christ; Or, The Believer's Union with His Lord* (Boston: Gould and Lincoln, 1872), 10.
17. J. Todd Billings, *Union with Christ: Framing Theology and Ministry for the Church* (Grand Rapids, MI: Baker Academic, 2011), 93–94.

Union with Christ in His Death, Resurrection, and Ascension

"Christ died for our sins" (1 Cor. 15:3). This statement is so familiar that we rarely marvel at how it could be possible. How does one person become the substitute for many (Mark 10:45) and their surety before God (Heb. 7:22, 27)? The answer is that he is one with them in the covenant of grace. They are his covenant "seed," and therefore he bore their sins (Isa. 53:10, 12). As Letham notes, many objections to substitutionary atonement fall to the ground as soon as we recognize the union between Christ and his people, for God made the sins of his people to belong to Christ (v. 6) and his righteousness to belong to them (v. 11) when he ordained that they belong to one another and should be "regarded as one."[18] This great exchange takes place by union, for God accomplished reconciliation "in Christ," and "he hath made him to be sin for us, who knew no sin; that we might be made the righteousness of God *in him*" (2 Cor. 5:19, 21).[19]

The Bible says not only that Christ died for his people, but that they died with him—yes, and were buried with him in the tomb, rose with him from the grave, and are seated with him in heavenly places.[20] All of the believer's present experiences of saving grace flow through his union with Christ in these great events. What Christ accomplished and received as the Mediator belongs to every one of his people, and we should count it as our possession: "to be dead indeed unto sin, but alive unto God through Jesus Christ our Lord" (Rom. 6:11). Herman Ridderbos noted that by death and resurrection Paul is not describing moments of elevated spiritual experience, "but rather an abiding reality determinative for the whole of the Christian life," and so "we have to do here with the church's 'objective' state of salvation."[21]

Our union with Christ in the great acts of redemption is a matter not just of present sanctification but also of historical fact. Paul says, "One has died for all, therefore all have died; and he died for all, that those who live might no longer live for themselves but for him who for their sake died and was raised" (2 Cor. 5:14–15 ESV). Behind the present reality that believers live unto God is the past reality that they "died" with Christ millennia ago upon the cross. This is possible only because they were already in Christ

18. Letham, *Union with Christ*, 64.

19. On substitutionary atonement through covenantal union, see *RST*, 2:1028–30.

20. Rom. 6:1–14; 7:4–6; Gal. 2:19–20; 5:24; 6:14; Eph. 2:4–7; Col. 2:13, 20; 3:1–4; 2 Tim. 2:11; cf. 1 Pet. 2:24.

21. Ridderbos, *Paul*, 59.

by a decretal and incarnational union. Bavinck wrote, "The whole church, comprehended in him as its head, has objectively been crucified, has died, been resurrected, and glorified with him. All the benefits of grace therefore lie prepared and ready for the church in the person of Christ."[22]

We should never isolate the saving and sanctifying work of the Spirit from the finished work of Jesus Christ. All that the Spirit brings to God's elect in the application of salvation springs directly from the accomplishment of salvation by the Son. One practical implication of this connection is that we ever live by faith in the Son of God. His work at the cross and empty tomb must never leave our sight, for all grace and glory flow to us through our union with him.

Union with Christ in the Spirit's Works of Personal Salvation

The Spirit applies to us the redemption purchased by Christ by establishing us in a vital union with Christ. "There is therefore now no condemnation to them which are in Christ Jesus," and they have been emancipated by "the Spirit of life in Christ Jesus" (Rom. 8:1–2). Fallen mankind is in a state of death and hatred against God, but "the Spirit of Christ" gives "life and peace" to those who belong to Christ (vv. 6–9). Thus, "if Christ be in you, the body is dead because of sin; but the Spirit is life because of righteousness" (v. 10). Geerhardus Vos said, "The life of Christ exercises a secret action on the life of the regenerate sinner."[23] Christ personally dwells in believers by the Spirit. William Bridge said, "Christ that is in a believer, is not the habit of grace only, which the saints have in their souls, but Christ himself by his Spirit."[24]

Christ becomes one with his people by the Holy Spirit. Paul says, "He that is joined unto the Lord is one spirit" (1 Cor. 6:17). The term translated as "join" (*kollaō*), literally "glue together," is used earlier for the union of a man and a woman (v. 16).[25] However, the believer is not joined to Christ in a physical manner, but as "one spirit," which in context refers to the Holy Spirit (vv. 11, 19). Paul says, "Now if any man have not the Spirit of Christ, he is none of his" (Rom. 8:9).

Every person of the Trinity must do his part for God's people to have eternal life, which is life in communion with the triune God. John Flavel

22. Bavinck, *Reformed Dogmatics*, 3:523.
23. Vos, *Reformed Dogmatics*, 4:25–26.
24. Bridge, *The Spiritual Life and In-Being of Christ in All Believers*, in *Works*, 1:363.
25. Cf. *proskollaō* in Gen. 2:24 LXX; Matt. 19:5; Mark 10:7; Eph. 5:31.

explained, "All divine and spiritual life is originally in the Father, and cometh not to us, but by and through the Son (John 5:26). To him hath the Father given to have an *autozōe* [self-life]—a quickening, enlivening power in himself; but the Son communicates this life which is in him to none but by and through the Spirit (Rom. 8:2)."[26] This, however, is not merely an act of the Trinity upon the soul, but the personal indwelling of the Trinity in each redeemed person. Philip Melanchthon (1497–1560) said, "The Father and the Son are actually present, breathing the Holy Spirit into the heart of the believer. This presence and indwelling is what is called spiritual renewal."[27] Therefore, spiritual union with Christ enables fellowship with the whole Trinity, fellowship on a human level analogous with the eternal communion in the triune God (John 17:20–23).[28]

In Spirit-applied union with Christ, the roots of federal and representative union bear fruit in the elect. Paul says, "Therefore if any man be in Christ, he is a new creature: old things are passed away; behold, all things are become new" (2 Cor. 5:17). Lewis Smedes (1921–2002) said, "The classic passage on the new creature in Christ begins with a 'therefore,' and this word refers back to the crucifixion [vv. 14–15]. The event that changed things for people is the death of Jesus. . . . The crucial moment is a moment in past history."[29] By vital union with the last Adam, we are caught up in the new creation inaugurated by his death and resurrection. Smedes wrote, "Being in Christ, we are part of a new movement by His grace, a movement rolling on toward the new heaven and new earth where all things are made right and where He is all in all."[30]

As a result, what Christ accomplished outside of us and apart from us is now applied to us. Paul says, "But of him are ye in Christ Jesus, who of God is made unto us wisdom, and righteousness, and sanctification, and redemption" (1 Cor. 1:30). Richard Sibbes said, "We can have no communion without union with him—when we are one with him once by faith, we have life from Christ."[31] He added, "Whatsoever Christ hath, or is, or

---

26. Flavel, *The Method of Grace*, in *Works*, 2:37.

27. Cited in J. V. Fesko, "Union with Christ," in *Reformation Theology: A Systematic Summary*, ed. Matthew Barrett (Wheaton, IL: Crossway, 2017), 430. "*Praesentes Pater et Filius spirant Spiritus S. in cor credentis. Et haec praesentia et habitatio est hoc, quod dicitur novitas spiritualis.*" Philip Melanchthon, Epistolarum, "*Iudicium de Osiandro*," in *CR*, 8:582.

28. Johnson, *One with Christ*, 42. On communion with the triune God, see *RST*, 1:944–52.

29. Lewis Smedes, *All Things Made New: A Theology of Man's Union with Christ* (Grand Rapids, MI: Eerdmans, 1970), 104.

30. Smedes, *All Things Made New*, 127–28.

31. Sibbes, *The Hidden Life*, in *Works*, 5:209.

hath done or suffered, it is mine by reason of this union with him by faith, which is the grace of union that knits us to Christ, and the first grace of application."[32] Rowland Stedman described union with the Mediator as "that special relation . . . arising from their close and intimate conjunction with him: whereupon they are accounted as one with Christ, their spiritual state is fundamentally changed, and the benefits of redemption are effectually applied unto their souls."[33]

Central to vital union is faith in Jesus Christ, for Christ dwells in the heart by faith (Eph. 3:17). By faith we receive him as our Savior (John 1:12). Christ described faith as coming to him as a result of being drawn to him by God (6:35, 37, 44). Therefore, spiritual union with Christ is union through a Spirit-worked faith. Stedman said, "The Lord Christ, by his Spirit, taketh possession of them, and dwelleth in them; and believers through faith of the operation of the Spirit, take hold of Christ, and get into him; and so they are knit together and become one."[34]

The image of union as the cleaving of husband and wife to each other (Eph. 5:24, 30–32) reminds us that our union with Christ by a Spirit-worked faith is the bond of love. William Ames wrote, "There are three chains of union that are used in our conjunction with God in Christ: the Spirit, faith, and love. The Spirit is the chain by whom Christ lays hold of us and binds us to Himself. Faith is the chain by which we lay hold of Christ and we apply Him to ourselves. Love is a chain through which we hand over and consecrate our all to Christ."[35]

All of the glorious pictures of union with Christ discussed in the last chapter are actualized in the life of each believer through spiritual union. The Christian is part of God's holy temple built on Christ, a fruitful branch organically abiding in Christ the vine, an eating and drinking guest at the spiritual banquet where Christ is both host and food, and a member of the body of Christ, his beloved bride, under his nurturing headship and clothed in his righteousness, holiness, and glory. We may say with Vos that union with Christ by the Spirit is an "organic" unity, a unity of "life," a "spiritual" unity, a "reciprocal" unity, a "personal and corporate" unity, and a "transforming and conforming" unity.[36]

32. Sibbes, *The Spiritual Jubilee*, in *Works*, 5:242.
33. Stedman, *The Mystical Union of Believers with Christ*, 55.
34. Stedman, *The Mystical Union of Believers with Christ*, 121
35. Ames, *A Sketch of the Christian's Catechism*, 38.
36. Vos, *Reformed Dogmatics*, 4:25–28.

As we noted earlier, our union with Christ by the Spirit presupposes Christ's union with us by the incarnation. Therefore, union with Christ does not mean our humanity dissolves into the divine infinity, but that a real bond exists between us and Jesus Christ humanly seated at God's right hand in heaven (Eph. 2:6; Col. 3:1–4). Though mystical union with Christ is spiritual, "yet it is true and real," as Girolamo Zanchi said, for "by the Spirit of Christ we, although remaining on the earth, yet are truly and really joined to the body, blood, and soul of Christ, reigning in heaven."[37] Our union is indeed with God the Son, but with him as incarnate, for, as John Calvin noted, in Christ's humanity we find "a fountain, open to us . . . in the person of the Mediator" that would otherwise "lie unprofitably hidden in that deep and hidden spring" of the divine nature.[38] The Spirit enriches Christ's "human nature" so that "he might enrich us with his wealth."[39] Therefore, though this union is formed and energized by the omnipresent and infinite Holy Spirit, it bears a very human quality. In other words, being "in Christ" does not divorce our spiritual lives from our earthly lives, but empowers us to live unto God as human beings in this world just as Jesus did.

Union with Christ in the Glory of God Forever

The Christian hope is that Christ will appear in glory and that believers will share in his glory (Rom. 8:17). We will be like Christ, for we will see him as he is (1 John 3:2). Paul says, "Our citizenship is in heaven, and from it we await a Savior, the Lord Jesus Christ, who will transform our lowly body to be like his glorious body, by the power that enables him even to subject all things to himself" (Phil. 3:20–21 ESV). The last Adam will come to raise up his bride, and by his blood-bought grace she will be glorious, holy, and without any blemish (Eph. 5:27).

When Christ returns, the exaltation that we already share by virtue of our covenantal union with him will become ours in actual possession. Just as God has "raised us up" already with Christ and caused us to sit with Christ in heavenly glory by virtue of our union with him, so God will spend the ages to come displaying "the exceeding riches of his grace in his kindness toward us through Christ Jesus" (Eph. 2:6–7). Then the union

37. Zanchi, *De Religione Christiana Fides*, 12.8 (1:237, 239).
38. Calvin, *Institutes*, 3.11.9.
39. Calvin, *Commentaries*, on Isa. 11:2.

already established will come to fruition in our glorious communion with God through Christ.

In the symbolic language of Revelation, we will return to the garden of Eden to drink the living water and eat of the tree of life in the presence of God as the bride of the last Adam, "the Lamb" of God: "And there shall be no more curse: but the throne of God and of the Lamb shall be in it; and his servants shall serve him: and they shall see his face; and his name shall be in their foreheads. And there shall be no night there; and they need no candle, neither light of the sun; for the Lord God giveth them light: and they shall reign for ever and ever" (Rev. 22:3–5).

The Federal and Spiritual Dimensions of Union with Christ

Our sketch of the modes of union with Christ through the ages highlights the two distinct dimensions of that union. Archibald A. Hodge (1823–1886) observed that union with Christ has two "aspects," the first being "federal and representative" and the second "spiritual and vital."[40] The latter is *mystical union* with Christ, so called because Paul describes it as a "mystery," a reality we never would have imagined unless God had revealed it to us in his Word.[41] Hodge explained that it is "'mystical,' because it so far transcends all the analogies of earthly relationships, in the intimacy of its communion, in the transforming power of its influence, and in the excellence of its consequences."[42] William Perkins said, "Therefore we must rather labor to feel it by experience in the heart, than to conceive it in the brain."[43]

Whereas the earlier stages of union with Christ in God's election and Christ's incarnation and redemptive work consisted of the decretal and covenantal aspects, the stage of mystical union by the Spirit's works of application takes these up and adds the relational, transformational, and experiential aspects. In earlier stages, Christ was appointed and acted as the Prophet, Priest, and King for his people, but here they are anointed to perform the duties and enjoy the privileges of being subordinate prophets, priests, and kings in union with him.[44]

It is important to maintain the order. Christ's covenantal union with his people, where *he acted for them*, is the ground and cause of his mystical

40. Archibald A. Hodge, *Outlines of Theology*, rev. ed. (New York: Robert Carter and Brothers, 1879), 482.

41. Eph. 3:3–6; 5:31–32; Col. 1:26–27.

42. Hodge, *Outlines of Theology*, 483.

43. Perkins, *An Exposition of the Symbol*, in *Works*, 5:368.

44. Hodge, *Outlines of Theology*, 485.

union with them, by which *he lives in them*. John Brown of Haddington said that "legal union" is the covenantal cause and "mystical union" is the spiritual effect.[45] Bavinck said, "This mystical union between Christ and believers is an essential and indispensable constituent in the work of salvation. Yet it is not the only and the first relation that exists between Christ and his own. In Scripture, this relation is built on the federal relation. Romans 6–8 follows Romans 3–5."[46]

In terms of the marriage analogy, by forming the federal union God selects and secures the bride for Christ just as the Lord arranged for Abraham's servant to bring Rebekah to Isaac, but the spiritual union begins when "Isaac brought her into his mother Sarah's tent, and took Rebekah, and she became his wife; and he loved her" (Gen. 24:67). The legal and covenantal framework of betrothal forms the structure by which the marriage is personally initiated and in which the relationship of love and fellowship takes place and is preserved.

Union with Christ has as many dimensions as Christ has graces for his people. It consists of far more than a relationship with a friend. It transcends moral imitation. It cannot be exhausted by the imputation of righteousness that we receive in justification by faith alone. Yet it cannot be reduced to experiences of Christ's love, presence, and power. This union is a cord of many strands: legal, covenantal, vital, spiritual, ethical, and relational. In short, God has made Christ to be everything to the believer. Christ does not merely dispense his benefits, but gives himself to us, and in him we have all.

False Views of Union with Christ

Outside of the relations among the divine persons in the Trinity, our union with Christ is the closest union possible between persons. However, there are also important ways in which we are *not* united to the Lord.

Pantheism and Panentheism: Confusion of Essences

Pantheism identifies God with his creation; panentheism joins the world to God as if it were his body and he were its animating soul.[47] Such views are similar to a confusion of God's providence in all creation through God

45. John Brown of Haddington, *Questions and Answers on the Shorter Catechism* (Grand Rapids, MI: Reformation Heritage Books, 2006), 142.

46. Bavinck, *Reformed Dogmatics*, 3:405. See also Vos, *Reformed Dogmatics*, 4:23.

47. On pantheism and panentheism, see *RST*, 1:590–98.

the Son (Heb. 1:3) with God's presence through Christ as the Mediator of saving grace.[48] Millard Erickson explains that in this confusion, "Christ is one with us and is in us by virtue of creation rather than redemption."[49] Some people speak of the cosmic Christ who indwells all people and all things. Matthew Fox says, "The mystical awakening that foreshadows a global healing is presented as a cosmic awakening . . . to a Cosmic Christ alive and vital in all creatures and in all humans."[50]

However, our spirits are not God's Spirit but remain distinct even when he dwells in us. Thus, the Spirit "beareth witness with our spirit" (Rom. 8:16). We are not God, but God's temple. When the Bible speaks of union with Christ, it does not imply that we are God or part of God, for he is the Creator and we are creatures. Calvin wrote, "We hold ourselves to be united with Christ by the secret power of his Spirit. . . . But we deny that Christ's essence is mixed with our own."[51] Stedman said, "A sincere convert is one with the person of the Mediator, but they are not thereby made one person: as some have vented their blasphemies, that they are Christed with Christ, and Godded with God."[52] Our union with God is not a direct apprehension of the divine being, but union first with Christ the incarnate Mediator (John 1:18), and then with God through Christ in the Spirit (Eph. 2:18). Furthermore, not all people have a vital union with Christ, but many have no part in him because they are part of Satan's kingdom (2 Cor. 6:14–16).

Unbiblical Mysticism: Confusion of Persons

By unbiblical mysticism, we refer to the absorption of the individual consciousness into God, implying or tending to the loss of one's distinct personality.[53] Such a loss of individual personality is not consistent with the picture of union as marriage; we do not become the Bridegroom, but we become his bride.

Mysticism can also arise from depersonalizing the Lord Christ. New Testament scholar Gustav Adolf Deissmann (1866–1937) said that the apostle Paul taught a moralistic mysticism in which Christ became an inward energy that empowered religious action. Deissmann explained

48. Vos, *Reformed Dogmatics*, 4:24.
49. Erickson, *Christian Theology*, 879.
50. Matthew Fox, *The Coming of the Cosmic Christ* (New York: HarperCollins, 1988), 5.
51. Calvin, *Institutes*, 3.11.5.
52. Stedman, *The Mystical Union of Believers with Christ*, 58.
53. Berkhof, *Systematic Theology*, 451.

Paul's view of Christ as a universal Spirit by comparison to the air we breathe, such that he is in us and we are in him. Christ thus permeates and surrounds us in a mystical fashion, giving us life and acting through us.[54] Such mysticism tends to divorce Christ from the historical person Jesus of Nazareth.

Unbiblical mysticism can result in a passive approach to holiness, at least when one attains a certain level of spiritual experience. Meister Eckhart von Hochheim (c. 1260–1328) said, "Relax and let God operate you and do what he will with you. . . . Praying, reading, singing, watching, fasting, and doing penance—all these virtuous practices were contrived to catch us and keep us from strange, ungodly things. . . . But when a person has a true spiritual experience, he may boldly drop external disciplines . . . as long as that experience lasts."[55]

When Paul wrote, "I have been crucified with Christ. It is no longer I who live, but Christ who lives in me," he did not claim that all his thoughts and acts were Christ's and he had no distinct mind or will anymore, for he proceeded to say, "And the life I now live in the flesh I live by the faith of the Son of God, who loved me, and gave himself for me" (Gal. 2:20). Communion with Christ is not letting go and letting God, but the active exercise of faith in Christ as he reveals himself in the Word of God. It is not an emptying of the mind, but the filling of the mind with the gospel of Christ. It is not union with a nebulous spirit, but a relationship with the historical Jesus Christ who died on the cross and rose physically from the dead.

Perkins explained that our conjunction with Christ is not a union of one substance, such as is shared by the three persons of the Trinity in the one substance or essence of the deity. Neither is it a union of one person, such as joins the divine and human natures of Christ together in one person. It is the union of one Spirit. Perkins wrote, "The very same Spirit of God that dwells in the manhood of Christ and fills it with all graces above measure is derived thence and dwells in all the true members of the church and fills them with the like graces in measure. And therefore St. John says, 'Hereby we know that we dwell in him and he in us, because he hath given us of his Spirit' [1 John 4:13]."[56]

54. Smedes, *All Things Made New*, 84; Campbell, *Paul and Union with Christ*, 32.

55. Meister Eckhart, "Sermon on the Eternal Birth," in *Late Medieval Mysticism*, ed. Ray C. Petry, The Library of Christian Classics 13 (Philadelphia: Westminster, 1957), 182–84.

56. Perkins, *An Exposition of the Symbol*, in *Works*, 5:368.

Deification: Confusion of Glories

Deification (*theōsis* or *theiōsis*) is the doctrine that Christ became a man in order to make men into participants in the glory and energies of God.[57] Athanasius said, "For He was made man that we might be made gods."[58] Despite first impressions based on such strong language, deification is not pantheism or polytheism. The fathers used the language of deification to communicate the wonder of our adoption by union with Christ. Psalm 82:6 says, "Ye are gods; and all of you are children of the most High." Irenaeus commented, "For it was for this end that the Word of God was made man, and He who was the Son of God became the Son of man, that man, having been taken into the Word, and receiving the adoption, might become the son of God."[59] Augustine said, "If we have been made sons of God, we have also been made gods: but this is the effect of grace adopting, not of nature generating . . . not born of His substance, that they should be the same as He, but that by favour they should come to Him, and be fellow-heirs with Christ."[60] Thus, deification is a manner of describing our glorification with Christ.

According to medieval Catholicism, in deification the natural properties of humanity are replaced by the glory of God. Bernard of Clairvaux (1090–1153) spoke of such an absolute submission to God that "the soul is deified," for "as a small drop of water appears lost if mixed with wine, taking its taste and colour; and as, when plunged into a furnace, a bar of iron seems to lose its nature and assume that of fire . . . so it is with the natural life of the Saints; they seem to melt and pass away into the will of God. For if anything merely human remained in man, how then should God be all in all? It is not that human nature will be destroyed, but that it will attain another beauty, a higher power and glory."[61]

As developed in late medieval Eastern Orthodoxy, deification is the gracious gift of participation in the uncreated energies of God. Gregory Palamas (c. 1296–1359) distinguished between God's unknowable essence

57. For a rebuttal of the idea that Christ's humanity was deified in his incarnation, see *RST*, 2:847–50.

58. Athanasius, *On the Incarnation of the Word*, 54.3, in *NPNF*[2], 4:65. The cited translation reads "that we might be made God," but the verb *theopoieō* means "make into a god, deify." G. W. H. Lampe, ed., *A Patristic Greek Lexicon* (Oxford: Oxford University Press, 1961), 630.

59. Irenaeus, *Against Heresies*, 3.19.1, in *ANF*, 1:448; cf. the preface to book 5, in *ANF*, 1:526.

60. Augustine, *Psalms*, 50.2, in *NPNF*[1], 8:178.

61. Bernard of Clairvaux, *The Love of God*, trans. Marianne Caroline and Coventry Patmore, 2nd ed. (London: Burns and Oates, 1884), chap. 10 (45). See also the fourteenth-century mystics Meister Eckhart, John Tauler, and Henry Suso, cited in Demarest, *The Cross and Salvation*, 315–16.

and his uncreated divine energies, the latter of which can illuminate human nature and make it radiant with the same divine glory.[62] This deification through the uncreated light of God, by which we are said to become "partakers of the divine nature" (2 Pet. 1:4), is the heart of Eastern Orthodox mysticism.[63]

However, the Holy Scriptures do not teach the existence of an uncreated divine energy or light that is distinct from God's essence. In the divine simplicity, God is light and love (1 John 1:5; 4:8). If God's light and love were different from his essence, it would be impossible to know God as he truly is. However, we can have a true, albeit limited knowledge of God fitting to creatures who bear his image (5:20).[64]

Deification is said to fulfill Christ's prayer "As thou, Father, art in me, and I in thee, that they also may be one in us" (John 17:21).[65] However, the grammatical structure "as . . . also" in Christ's prayer implies a comparison or similarity; our union with God is not identical to Christ's union with the Father, which is unique and divine (John 10:30–31).[66] Bruce Demarest writes that the two unions are "both unions of life and love," but the Son's union with the Father is ontological or a union of being (John 10:38), whereas the believer's union with Christ is not.[67]

While the Bible does speak of the image of God, conformity to the likeness of Christ, and glorification with Christ (Rom. 8:17, 29), it speaks of men as "gods" only in a figurative and sometimes ironic sense: "I have said, Ye are gods . . . but ye shall die like men" (Ps. 82:6–7). Peter writes of being "partakers of the divine nature" when speaking of gaining virtue,

62. Gregory Palamas, *The Triads*, ed. John Meyendorff, trans. Nicholas Gendle, The Classics of Western Spirituality (New York: Paulist, 1983), 3.2.5–7 (93–96); and Stanley M. Burgess, *The Holy Spirit: Eastern Christian Traditions* (Peabody, MA: Hendrickson, 1989), 70–72. Burgess claims that Palamas's distinction can be found in the fourth century in Basil, Letter 234, in *NPNF*², 8:274. However, while Basil does distinguish between God's incomprehensible essence and his attributes revealed in his operations, he does not speak in that epistle of *uncreated* energies, merely God's operations or acts. Burgess's citations of Athenagoras and Irenaeus are also unconvincing.

63. Vladimir Lossky, *The Mystical Theology of the Eastern Church* (Crestwood, NY: St. Vladimir's Seminary Press, 1976), 9–10, 67–90.

64. On divine simplicity, see *RST*, 1:624–37 (chap. 33). On our ability to know God by his revelation while the infinite depths of his glory remain incomprehensible to us, see *RST*, 1:69–72, 504–6, 641–45.

65. Symeon Lash, "Deification," in *The Westminster Dictionary of Theology*, ed. Alan Richardson and John Bowden (Philadelphia: Westminster Press, 1983), 147–48; and Timothy Ware, *The Orthodox Church*, new ed. (London: Penguin, 1997), 231–32.

66. For a comparison of the mystical union between Christ and believers with the substantial union of persons in the Trinity and the hypostatic union of two natures in the one person of Christ, see Thomas Manton, *Sermons upon John 17*, in *The Works of Thomas Manton*, 22 vols. (London: James Nisbet, 1873), 11:33–36.

67. Demarest, *The Cross and Salvation*, 328.

godliness, and love (2 Pet. 1:2–7)—the moral image of God, not participation in his inherent glory.

Therefore, we do not have biblical warrant to speak of our union with Christ as deification. Insofar as such language is used to describe the church's participation in the manifest glory of the triune God on the level of adopted image bearers and not deity, there is a kernel of truth in it.[68] However, the term *deification* is too easily misunderstood to be useful. God's people are indeed glorified with the incarnate Christ, but that is with the manifest, created glory of the temple, not the eternal, uncreated glory of the Trinity.

The biblical doctrine of union with Christ presents that union as the conjunction of distinct persons through a covenantal and spiritual bond through which God's glory is manifested in and among people in a manner accommodated to human life, not a divine emanation or spiritual ascent that causes people to participate directly in God's infinite life. Grant Macaskill summarizes,

> The union between God and humans is covenantal, presented in terms of the formal union between God and Israel. The concept of the covenant underlies a theology of representation, by which the story of the one man (Jesus) is understood to be the story of his people. Their identification with him, their participation in his narrative, is realised by the indwelling Spirit, who constitutes the divine presence in their midst and is understood to be the eschatological gift of the new covenant. Reflecting this covenantal concept of presence, the union is commonly represented using temple imagery. The use of temple imagery maintains an essential distinction between God and his people, so that her glorification is understood as the interpersonal communication of a divine property [glory or fullness], not a mingling of essence.[69]

Union with Christ and Reformed Theology

The Reformed tradition has long recognized the necessity and centrality of union with Christ for eternal life. Calvin wrote, "That joining together of Head and members, that indwelling of Christ in our hearts—in short, that mystical union—are accorded by us the highest degree of importance, so

68. For a sympathetic discussion of deification in Eastern Orthodoxy, see Letham, *Union with Christ*, 91–100.

69. Macaskill, *Union with Christ in the New Testament*, 1.

that Christ, having been made ours, makes us sharers with him in the gifts with which he has been endowed."[70]

In Reformed theology, union with Christ holds together the distinct but inseparable graces of justification and sanctification. Calvin said, "Christ was given to us by God's generosity, to be grasped and possessed by us in faith. By partaking of him, we principally receive a double grace: namely, that being reconciled to God through Christ's blamelessness, we may have in heaven instead of a Judge a gracious Father; and secondly, that sanctified by Christ's spirit we may cultivate blamelessness and purity of life."[71] Francis Turretin wrote,

> Just as Christ sustains a twofold relation to us of surety and head (of surety, to take away the guilt of sin by a payment made for it; of head, to take away its power and corruption by the efficacy of the Spirit), so in a twofold way Christ imparts his blessings to us, by a forensic imputation, and a moral and internal infusion. The former flows from Christ as surety and is the foundation of our justification. The latter depends upon him as head, and is the principle of our sanctification.[72]

However, despite this rich heritage, some scholars have recently accused Reformed orthodox theologians of disintegrating the unity of our saving relationship with Christ by splitting union with Christ into the sequence of benefits in the order of salvation, and particularly of creating an artificial bifurcation between justification and sanctification. As a result, the criticism asserts, the federal and forensic dimension of union with Christ has been separated from the spiritual and transformative dimension.[73] At root, this criticism appears to be another attempt to elevate some aspect of Calvin's theology as central to Reformed Christianity and then pass judgment on later Reformed writers as if they were sub-Calvinian.[74]

70. Calvin, *Institutes*, 3.11.10; cf. 3.2.24.

71. Calvin, *Institutes*, 3.11.1.

72. Turretin, *Institutes*, 16.3.6 (2:647).

73. William B. Evans, *Imputation and Impartation: Union with Christ in American Reformed Theology*, Studies in Christian History and Thought (Milton Keynes, UK: Paternoster, 2008), 81–82; "Déjà Vu All over Again? The Contemporary Reformed Soteriological Controversy in Historical Perspective," *Westminster Theological Journal* 72, no. 1 (Spring 2010): 135–51; and "Three Current Reformed Models of Union with Christ," *Presbyterion* 41, nos. 1–2 (Fall 2015): 12–30. See J. V. Fesko, "Methodology, Myths, and Misperceptions: A Response to William B. Evans," *Westminster Theological Journal* 72, no. 2 (Fall 2010): 391–402; and Evans's reply (403–14).

74. "Unfortunately, we are moving not so much beyond such fallacious argumentation as into a new phase of the same: as the language of christocentrism has worn old, the new centrism has tried to impose a model of union with Christ on Calvin's theology and then to make the same sort of negative claim about later 'Calvinists': now that Calvin can be seen to focus on union with Christ,

In response to this criticism, we declare that Reformed orthodox theologians connected every part of the order of salvation to the one Christ. This principle is notably illustrated in the diagram that accompanied Perkins's *Golden Chain*, in which each aspect of the order of salvation has a line drawn from it to Christ's redeeming work at the center. Ames said, "Not all are saved by Christ, but only those who are united or engrafted into Christ."[75] The Westminster Larger Catechism (Q. 65–66) introduces the graces of effectual calling, justification, adoption, sanctification, assurance, and glory by saying, "The members of the invisible church by Christ enjoy union and communion with him in grace and glory. The union which the elect have with Christ is the work of God's grace, whereby they are spiritually and mystically, yet really and inseparably, joined to Christ as their head and husband; which is done in their effectual calling."[76] Turretin wrote, "From this union of persons arises the participation in the blessings of Christ, to which (by union with him) we acquire a right (to wit, justification, adoption, sanctification and glorification)."[77] Turretin said that though justification and sanctification "should be distinguished and never confounded," they must "never be torn asunder," for "as Christ is given to no one as a surety to whom he is not given for a head, so no one is justified by the merit of the surety (Christ) who is not sanctified by the efficacy of Christ (the head) after his image."[78]

According to Reformed orthodoxy, spiritual union with Christ is the channel through which other graces flow. Herman Witsius said, "True saving benefits are bestowed on none of the elect, before effectual calling, and actual union to Christ by a lively faith."[79] John Owen said that vital union with Christ "is the first and principal grace, in respect of causality and efficacy. . . . Hence is our adoption, our justification, our sanctification, our fruitfulness, our perseverance, our resurrection, our glory."[80] For this reason, the Scriptures can sum up all gospel blessings that believers

his thought can be radically separated from the later Calvinists who purportedly never thought of the concept." Richard A. Muller, *Calvin and the Reformed Tradition: On the Work of Christ and the Order of Salvation* (Grand Rapids, MI: Baker Academic, 2012), 63.

75. Ames, *A Sketch of the Christian's Catechism*, 37. See the Heidelberg Catechism, LD 7, Q. 20, in *The Three Forms of Unity*, 73.

76. *Reformed Confessions*, 4:312. See also Irish Articles (Art. 33), in *Reformed Confessions*, 4:95–96.

77. Turretin, *Institutes*, 15.8.9 (2:563).

78. Turretin, *Institutes*, 17.1.15, 17 (2:691–92).

79. Herman Witsius, *The Economy of the Covenants between God and Man*, 2 vols. (1822; repr., Grand Rapids, MI: Reformation Heritage Books, 2010), 2.7.8 (1:237).

80. Owen, *An Exposition of the Epistle to the Hebrews*, 4:149–50.

enjoy in the present and hope for in the future by the statement "We are made partakers of Christ" (Heb. 3:14).[81]

Practical Implications of Spiritual Union with Christ

Though the benefits of union with Christ are too many to enumerate, we do well to end these chapters with a brief discussion of its practical implications. Here we refer to the implications of vital, spiritual, mystical union with Christ, for until the Spirit joins us to Christ by God's effectual calling, no saving benefits accrue to the elect.

First, union with Christ lays the foundation for *communion with God.* After promising to send the Holy Spirit so that Christ would share his life with his disciples and be in them (John 14:16–20), Jesus said, "He that hath my commandments, and keepeth them, he it is that loveth me: and he that loveth me shall be loved of my Father, and I will love him, and will manifest myself to him" (v. 21). He also promised, "My Father will love him, and we will come to him, and make our abode with him" (v. 23). What amazing love! We should crave to know this love more and fellowship more deeply with our God in Christ—a potent motive for obedience.

Second, union with Christ initiates and perpetuates *spiritual transformation.* By union with him in his death and resurrection, Christians have undergone a tremendous change in their basic orientation in life: they no longer live for themselves but for the One who died and rose again for them (Rom. 14:7–9; 2 Cor. 5:15). They have crucified the flesh with its evil desires and now engage in a Spirit-led war against their remaining sins (Gal. 5:17, 24).

Like branches of the vine, Christians bear fruit pleasing to God by abiding in Christ (John 15:1–16), and therefore should "seek fruitfulness in union," as Demarest says.[82] Michael Barrett reminds us, "Fruit does not procure union; instead, it reveals the fact of union" (vv. 2, 6, 8).[83] However, God desires much fruit, for it glorifies him (v. 8). Flavel wrote, "We are married to Christ 'that we should bring forth fruit unto God' (Rom. 7:4)."[84] We do so by consciously depending on Christ as the One apart from whom we can do nothing, by using the means of the Word and prayer, by humbly receiving the Father's purifying discipline,

81. Owen, *An Exposition of the Epistle to the Hebrews*, 4:146.
82. Demarest, *The Cross and Salvation*, 341.
83. Barrett, *Complete in Him*, 107.
84. Flavel, *The Method of Grace*, in *Works*, 2:41.

and by keeping Christ's commandments, especially his commandment to love one another.[85]

Third, union with Christ causes *participation in Christ's sufferings*. Paul wrote that he aimed to "be found in him [Christ] . . . that I may know him, and the power of his resurrection, and the fellowship of his sufferings, being made conformable unto his death" (Phil. 3:9–10). Through the mystical union, both the sufferings and the consolations of Christ overflow to believers, and their lives are marked by both his death and resurrection power (2 Cor. 1:5; 4:10–11). As he went to the cross, so they must take up their crosses and follow him (Matt. 16:21, 24). We must suffer with him if we would be glorified with him (Rom. 8:17).

Fourth, union with Christ confers *a new and noble identity*. Stedman wrote, "If believers are united unto Christ . . . then hence I gather, that they are the most honorable and most excellent persons upon the face of the earth."[86] Joined to the King, poor sinners become members of the royal family. In union with the Son, we are sons and daughters of God.

Sinclair Ferguson lists a number of practical effects this truth can have on us:

- Great dignity: "As I look at myself I see failure, sin, sometimes shame and disgrace. But that is neither the ultimate nor the whole truth about me as a Christian. No! I am united to Christ, a joint heir of his riches, a child of God."
- Confidence in prayer: "If I am united to Christ, then all that is his is mine. So long as my heart, will and mind are one with Christ's in his word, I can approach God with the humble confidence that my prayers will be heard and answered."
- Strength in temptation: We are members of the holy Son of God. "I am united to the Lord Jesus Christ. How can I, of all people, commit this sin?"[87]

Fifth, union with Christ connects us to each other as *members of one body*. Christians are not isolated individuals, but their lives are organically intertwined with those of other believers. This should spur us to depend on each other for our needs, value the weakest believers in the church (1 Cor.

85. John 15:2, 5, 7, 10, 12.
86. Stedman, *The Mystical Union of Believers with Christ*, 268.
87. Sinclair B. Ferguson, *The Christian Life: A Doctrinal Introduction* (Edinburgh: Banner of Truth, 1989), 113, punctuation modified.

12:21–22), and serve as active members in local churches that the whole body might grow (Eph. 4:16). Christ taught us that whatever we do for the least of his brothers, we have done for him (Matt. 25:35–40), for the weakest Christian is one with Christ. It should also motivate us to walk carefully in humility and patience, lest we disrupt the precious unity that Christ has given us in his Spirit and so wound his dear body (Eph. 4:1–3).

Sixth, union with Christ empowers pastors with *bold fidelity in ministry*. The apostle Paul said, "For we are not as many, which corrupt the word of God: but as of sincerity, but as of God, in the sight of God speak we *in Christ*" (2 Cor. 2:17). Gospel preachers speak the Word in union with Christ. Albert Martin writes of the effect that this truth should have on our ministry:

- Fidelity in our message: "If He is the Head, the great anointed One, the great Prophet . . . how dare we then speak in His name, in union with Him, and speak anything other than His Word?"
- Boldness: Even preachers who are naturally quiet and mild in personality can preach with authority and must do so when they speak in Christ the Lord.
- Holy optimism: "In union with Christ there is no defeat." We must learn to say in faith with Paul, "Now thanks be unto God, which always causeth us to triumph in Christ, and maketh manifest the savour of his knowledge by us in every place" (2 Cor. 2:14). God is working his will through the Mediator, and we are the instruments of the victorious, risen Lord.[88]

Seventh, union with Christ grants to all Christians *hope in trials and temptations*. Flavel, who buried more than one wife and often fled for his own life in the troubled times of seventeenth-century England, said, "The mystical union is an indissoluble union; there is an everlasting tie betwixt [between] Christ and the believer . . . death dissolves the dear union betwixt the husband and wife, friend and friend, yea, betwixt soul and body, but not betwixt Christ and the soul."[89] Thomas Boston said, "None can untie this happy knot."[90]

Therefore, we may exult with the apostle Paul,

> Who shall separate us from the love of Christ? Shall tribulation, or distress, or persecution, or famine, or nakedness, or peril, or sword?

88. Albert N. Martin, *Union with Christ* (Toronto: Toronto Baptist Seminary, 1978), 117.
89. Flavel, *The Method of Grace*, in *Works*, 2:40.
90. Boston, *Human Nature in Its Fourfold State*, 256.

> . . . Neither death, nor life, nor angels, nor principalities, nor powers, nor things present, nor things to come, nor height, nor depth, nor any other creature, shall be able to separate us from the love of God, which is in Christ Jesus our Lord. (Rom. 8:35, 38–39)

While we wait and persevere, we know that the Lord of all is as tender to us as a man is to his own body (Eph. 5:28–29). He will give us what we need. He will use all our sufferings as a person uses harsh medicines and strong exercises when necessary for the health of his body. He will care for us and bring us to glory. If the Head is in heaven, then the body will follow!

Sing to the Lord

Union with Christ

'Twixt[91] Jesus and the chosen race
Subsists a bond of sovereign grace,
That hell, with its infernal train,
Shall ne'er dissolve, or rend in twain!

This sacred bond shall never break,
Though earth should to her center shake;
Rest, doubting saint, assured of this,
For God has pledged his holiness.

Hail, sacred union, firm and strong!
How great the grace! How sweet the song!
That rebel worms should ever be
One with incarnate Deity!

One in the tomb; one when he rose;
One when he triumphed o'er his foes;
One when in heaven he took his seat,
While seraphs sung at hell's defeat.

This sacred tie forbids their fears,
For all he is or has is theirs;
With him, their Head, they stand or fall—
Their Life, their Surety, and their All.

91. "Twixt," a contraction of "betwixt," means "between."

John Kent
Tune: Long Meter. May be sung to Old Hundredth (cf. *The Psalter*, No. 268; *Trinity Hymnal—Baptist Edition*, No. 1)
William Gadsby, comp., *A Selection of Hymns for Public Worship* (Harpenden, England: Gospel Standard Strict Baptist Trust, 1978), No. 405

Questions for Meditation or Discussion

1. What five terms could be used to describe the saints' connection to Christ? What does each imply about that connection?
2. In what sense can God's people be said to be "in Christ" from eternity? What Scripture passages teach this truth?
3. How did Christ's incarnation contribute to our union with Christ?
4. Where does the Bible teach that Christians died, rose, and ascended with Christ? What do such statements mean? Why is this crucial for our salvation?
5. How does the Holy Spirit make union with Christ into a vital, fruitful relationship?
6. What will be the benefits of union with Christ in God's glorious kingdom forever?
7. Explain the following terms:
   - federal union
   - mystical union
8. How might people confuse union with Christ with us becoming God (pantheism or panentheism) or losing our distinct personality in Christ (unbiblical mysticism)? How could you show that this is not what the Bible means?
9. Of the several practical implications listed at the end of this chapter, select one as particularly helpful to you. What will you do to apply it to your life as effectively as you can?

Questions for Deeper Reflection

10. What is the doctrine of "deification"? Offer constructive criticism of this doctrine from biblical, doctrinal, experiential, and practical perspectives.
11. What are the dangers of emphasizing the legal and covenantal aspect of union with Christ to the neglect of the spiritual and relational aspect? What are the dangers of doing the opposite?

11

The Order of the Application of Salvation

How does the Spirit apply Christ's redemption to individuals? Some Christians would respond by simply quoting Acts 16:31: "Believe on the Lord Jesus Christ, and thou shalt be saved." Of course, faith in Christ is necessary unto salvation (John 3:16, 18, 36). Nevertheless, we must not reduce the application of redemption to "faith," as did Julius Kaftan (1848–1926).[1] To say that, given Christ's death and resurrection, each person's salvation depends merely on his choice to trust in Christ would be to fall into Pelagianism.[2] Sinners are "dead" in their sins; God must make them alive in Christ—they must be "saved" (passive voice, Eph. 2:5). This raises the question, "What gracious works does God do to apply Christ's redemption to people?"[3]

Though there is a simplicity to the gospel that makes it possible for a child to understand and receive it, there are "unsearchable riches" in Christ (Eph. 3:8), a host of spiritual blessings found in union with him (1:3–14). The application of redemption to elect sinners involves a complex of interrelated works of grace called the "order of salvation" (Latin *ordo salutis*).[4]

1. Julius Kaftan, *Dogmatik* (Tübingen: J. C. B. Mohr, 1920), sec. 69 (651–56), cited in Berkhof, *Systematic Theology*, 416. Kaftan based faith on the authority of divine revelation, but located revelation not in God's written Word but in the historical events that the Scriptures fallibly present and interpret. This led Kaftan to critique both orthodoxy and theological liberalism. George B. Foster, "Kaftan's Dogmatik," *The American Journal of Theology* 2, no. 4 (October 1898): 819–22 (full article, 802–27). In some ways, Kaftan's historical approach anticipated the twentieth-century "biblical theology" movement and Wolfhart Pannenberg. See *RST*, 1:309–13.

2. On Pelagianism, see *RST*, 1:1003; 2:366–68.

3. See Reymond, *A New Systematic Theology of the Christian Faith*, 704.

4. On the term's history and usage, see Richard A. Muller, *Dictionary of Latin and Greek Theological Terms: Drawn Principally from Protestant Scholastic Theology*, 2nd ed. (Grand Rapids, MI: Baker Academic, 2017), 250.

Herman Bavinck said, "Which is the road that leads to the eternal blessed life? Or, as Luther once put it: How do I find a gracious God? It is the order of salvation, the order or way of salvation (*ordo* or *via salutis*) that seeks to answer that question. For by it one must understand the manner and order in which, or the road whereby, the sinner obtains the benefits of grace acquired by Christ."[5]

Arguments for an Order of Salvation

No single text in the Bible lists a full order of salvation. However, there are reasons for us to think of salvation in terms of an order of interrelated acts.

1. *Salvation resembles a story in that it has a beginning, middle, and end.* Christ completely accomplished redemption for his people; however, those who belong to him are not immediately and completely given their inheritance.[6] Louis Berkhof (1873–1957) said, "God does not impart the fulness of His salvation to the sinner in a single act."[7] Rather, God applies salvation to people in a process involving a series of acts. The Bible speaks of salvation in the past as an accomplished fact for believers. They literally "have been saved" (perfect of *sozō*, Eph. 2:5, 8)—that is, placed in a state of salvation. In other Scripture passages, salvation is described as a present and continuing process for believers: they "are being saved" (present of *sozō*, 1 Cor. 1:18; 15:2). Salvation is also portrayed as a future event when believers "will be saved" (future of *sozō*, Rom. 5:9–10). Salvation has a complexity that warrants discussing it in distinct acts.

2. *Salvation involves distinct divine acts that stand in relation to each other.* The classic text on the order of salvation, Romans 8:30, says, "Whom he did predestinate, them he also called: and whom he called, them he also justified: and whom he justified, them he also glorified." The grammar links these acts together to depict God bringing the same group of people through the execution of his plan for salvation. Paul lists distinct acts here; predestination took place in eternity and the others take place in time. John Murray said, "When we think of the application of redemption we must not think of it as one simple and indivisible act. It comprises a series of acts and processes. . . . Each has its own distinct meaning, function, and purpose in the action and grace of God."[8]

5. Bavinck, *Reformed Dogmatics*, 3:565.
6. Bavinck, *Reformed Dogmatics*, 3:566.
7. Berkhof, *Systematic Theology*, 416.
8. Murray, *Redemption Accomplished and Applied*, 79–80.

3. *Salvation is a work of the God of order.* Paul says that "God is not the author of confusion, but of peace," and therefore commands, "Let all things be done decently and in order" (1 Cor. 14:33, 40). The Lord did not create the world in a haphazard fashion, but followed an order from day one through day six (Genesis 1). Salvation is a work of new creation (2 Cor. 5:17) and also exhibits "a divine order," even a "divine logic."[9] Johannes Polyander (1568–1646) said, "The election unto salvation . . . is carried out through certain steps and means whereby God has determined that those whom he has chosen for himself should be blessed with his saving grace in this age and with his eternal glory in the age that is to come."[10]

4. *The knowledge of the order of salvation preserves us from error.* For example, if we believe that faith has priority over regeneration, then we imply that salvation is not under the power of God but is sovereignly determined by the will of man. If we sever repentance from saving faith, we may be prone to grant assurance of salvation to people who continue to live in bondage to their sins. If we do not distinguish justification from sanctification and give justification logical priority over good works, we will probably think that our standing before God in some way depends on the merit of our good works. Such errors dishonor God and harm souls.

5. *God wills for his people to meditate on and experience each distinct blessing.* He could have planned and executed the salvation of his chosen people without revealing much to them about it. However, though man could not conceive "the things which God hath prepared for them that love him . . . God hath revealed them unto us by his Spirit" (1 Cor. 2:9–10). God desires that his people not only know these blessings in their minds, but that they also experience them in their hearts, so as to glorify him (Gal. 4:4–6; Eph. 1:16–20). Therefore, we should study them.

Historical Development of the Reformed *Ordo Salutis*

The concept of an order of salvation is very old. Augustine said that the church is, first, predestinated; second, called; third, justified; and fourth, glorified.[11] Our "justification" is not preceded by any merit in us but only by God's prevenient grace.[12] Augustine said, "By the law is the knowledge

9. Murray, *Redemption Accomplished and Applied*, 82.

10. Polyander, Walaeus, Thysius, and Rivetus, *Synopsis Purioris Theologiae*, 30.1 (2:209).

11. Augustine, *Homilies on the Gospel of John*, 26.15, in *NPNF*[1], 7:173. See also Epistle 145.3, in *NPNF*[1], 1:496.

12. Augustine, *Expositions on the Book of Psalms*, 6 vols. (Oxford: John Henry Parker; London: F. and J. Rivington, 1847), 32.2.1 (1:278). For Augustine, "justification" meant becoming righteous, including moral renewal.

of sin, by faith the acquisition of grace against sin, by grace the healing of the soul from the disease of sin, by the health of the soul the freedom of the will, by free will the love of righteousness, by love of righteousness the accomplishment of the law," identifying these as "the stages which I have here connected together in their successive links."[13] Medieval Catholic theologians continued to analyze the logical and causal relationship among the graces.[14]

The modern use of the term *ordo salutis* first appeared in the writings of Reformed theologians during the sixteenth century.[15] Martin Bucer (1491–1551) commented on Paul's epistle to the Ephesians, "He describes the order of our salvation [*ordinem salutis nostrae*]. First of all, there is election: then an effective and regenerating call through the gospel. [Then] faith and hope, to which love is joined."[16] Girolamo Zanchi wrote, "The *ordo salutis* must be observed. The first step is election. The Father gives us to Christ. Second is faith in Christ. For we come to Christ, drawn, by faith given from the Father. Third, we are united to Christ, and eternal salvation."[17] One source of the Reformed order of salvation was "meditations on the text of Romans 8:28–30" that viewed it as containing a "golden chain" of God's saving acts.[18]

The sequence of salvation appears early in the Reformed confessional tradition. John Calvin's Catechism (1545) treats the doctrine of faith in

13. Augustine, *On the Spirit and the Letter*, 52.30, in *NPNF*[1], 5:106.

14. Peter Lombard, *The Sentences*, trans. Giulio Silano, 4 vols. (Toronto: Pontifical Institute of Mediaeval Studies, 2007–2010), 3.24.8–9; 3.26.1 (3:102–3, 111); and Aquinas, *Summa Theologica*, Part 2.1, Q. 113, Art. 8.

15. As early as the ninth century, theologians used the phrase *ordo salutis* for God's plan of salvation in Christ, but not with the technical sense of the process of applying grace to individuals. Jaroslav Pelikan, *The Christian Tradition: A History of the Development of Doctrine*, 5 vols. (Chicago: University of Chicago Press, 1978), 3:108. For references to the *ordo salutis* or golden chain in early Reformed theology, see J. V. Fesko, "Romans 8.29–30 and the Question of the *Ordo Salutis*," *Journal of Reformed Theology* 8 (2014): 41–50 (full article, 35–60).

16. Martin Bucer, *Praelectiones Doctiss. in Epistolam D. P. ad Ephesios . . . Anno MD.L. & LI* (Basileae: Apud Petrum Pernam, 1562), 27A. English translation in N. Scott Amos, *Bucer, Ephesians and Biblical Humanism: The Exegete as Theologian*, Studies in Early Modern Religious Tradition, Culture and Society (New York: Springer, 2015), 126. This usage is much earlier than that claimed to be the earliest by Reinhold Seeburg: the 1723 Lutheran orthodox dogmatics of Johann Franciscus Buddeus (1667–1729). R. Seeberg, "Order of Salvation," in *The New Schaff-Herzog Encyclopedia of Religious Knowledge*, ed. Samuel Macauley Jackson, 13 vols. (New York; London: Funk & Wagnalls, 1908–1914), 8:252.

17. Girolamo Zanchi, *De Tribus Elohim* (1589), 4.3.4, cited in J. V. Fesko, *Beyond Calvin: Union with Christ and Justification in Early Modern Reformed Theology (1517–1700)*, Reformed Historical Theology 20 (Göttingen: Vandenhoek and Ruprecht, 2012), 80.

18. Muller, *Calvin and the Reformed Tradition*, 166. Examples include Ulrich Zwingli (167–68), Zacharias Ursinus (189–90), and Caspar Olevianus (192). See the reference to Rom. 8:30 as a "golden chain" (*auream . . . catenam*) in Robert Rollock, *In Epistolam S. Pauli Apostoli ad Romanos*, rev. ed. (Genevae: Apud Franc. le Preux, 1595), 176.

this order: the Spirit's work to apply God's promises to the heart, faith, justification, and good works pleasing to God by union with Christ through the Spirit.[19] The articles of the Church of England (1552/1562) present a sequential listing of God's works of grace that suggests an order of salvation: calling, response to calling, justification, adoption, conformity to Christ, good works, and everlasting happiness.[20] Craig's Catechism (1581), an early Scots Presbyterian confession, traces a sequence of election, effectual calling, faith, union with Christ, communion in his graces, justification, continual sanctification, victorious spiritual warfare against Satan, and assurance of election and glorification.[21]

The order of salvation also appeared in early Reformed polemics against Roman Catholicism. William Whitaker (1548–1595) appealed to the golden chain to refute the claim that no one can be certain of eternal life without a special revelation from God. Whitaker said, "You cut the sinews of God's everlasting decree. For seeing God's predestination is certain and unchangeable, it causes our calling, justifying, and glorifying to be as certain as itself. For is it in your power to dissolve and break that golden chain of the apostle (Rom. 8:30)? And to whom can his own perseverance be doubtful, seeing God testifies his perpetual good will toward us?"[22]

William Perkins described the "golden chain" as election, then union with Christ by effectual calling, the latter of which God executes by means of the preaching of the Word, softening the heart, and faith that apprehends Christ, leading to justification and adoption, then sanctification, glorification, and blessedness in heaven.[23]

Though trained in the Reformed tradition, Jacob Arminius (1560–1609) hinged salvation on the human will, the choices of which God merely foreknows.[24] Man can always resist God's grace, but if he uses it well, then God

19. Calvin's Catechism of 1545 (Q. 111–126), in *Reformed Confessions*, 1:483–85.

20. The Forty-Two Articles (Art. 17); and the Thirty-Nine Articles (Art. 17), in *Reformed Confessions*, 2:6, 760.

21. Craig's Catechism, in *Reformed Confessions*, 3:602–3.

22. William Whitaker, *Responsionis ad Decem Illas Rationes, Quibus Fretus Edmundus Campianus . . . Defensio contra Confutationem Ioannis Duraei* (London: Excudebat Henricus Midletonus impensis Thomae Chardi, 1584), 8.47 (626). English translation adapted from William Whitaker, *An Answere to the Ten Reasons of Edmund Campian . . . [and] the Sum of the Defence of Those Reasons by John Duraeus*, trans. Richard Stocke (London: by Felix Kyngston, for Cuthbert Burby and Edmund Weaver, 1606), 234n1.

23. Perkins, *A Golden Chain*, chaps. 36–38, 48, 50, in *Works*, 6:172–75, 181, 184, 186, 212, 216. See Perkins's chart in that treatise. Cf. Ames, *The Marrow of Theology*, 1.26–30 (157–74).

24. Jacob Arminius, *Declaration of Sentiments*, in *The Works of James Arminius*, trans. James Nichols and William Nichols, 3 vols. (Grand Rapids, MI: Baker, 1991), 1:653–54.

will give more grace.[25] The order of salvation is, first, calling; second, faith; third, justification and regeneration; and fourth, adoption and sanctification—with the possibility of attaining the perfect keeping of God's law: not sinless perfection, but perfection in the eyes of divine mercy.[26] Others followed in Arminius's steps, notably John Wesley (1703–1791), who taught a sequence of prevenient grace, convicting grace, repentance and faith, justifying grace, regenerating grace, sanctifying grace, and the possibilities of falling away or attaining entire sanctification or perfect love in this life.[27]

At the Synod of Dort, the Reformed churches rejected the Arminian elevation of man's will to the pivotal position in the plan of salvation, stating that the logical order of salvation's application for the elect is effectual calling, faith, justification, sanctification, preservation, and glorification.[28] The Westminster Confession of Faith (3.6) presents the following sequence: effectual calling, faith, justification, adoption, sanctification, preservation.[29] The Westminster Larger Catechism (Q. 65–90) expands on each element in this sequence, placing it all under union with Christ accomplished through effectual calling.[30] The Westminster catechisms also coordinate faith with repentance as two sides of a saving response to the gospel.[31]

Modern Criticisms of the *Ordo Salutis*

Some theologians have criticized the very notion that there is an *ordo salutis*—though few theologians operate with no order of their own. Here are the major concerns they raise.

1. *The Scriptures do not teach an order of salvation.* Karl Barth (1886–1968) said, "The Bible does not offer any such schema," and if confronted with the distinctions of later theologians, "surely the Reformers must have turned over in their graves."[32] G. C. Berkouwer (1903–1996) said that

25. Arminius, *Apology*, Art. 17; and *Certain Articles*, Art. 17, in *Works*, 2:20, 722.

26. Arminius, *Nine Questions*, No. 9; *Private Disputations*, Arts. 45–49; *Certain Articles*, Arts. 20–21; and *Friendly Conference . . . with Mr. Francis Junius*, in *Works*, 2:68, 401–10, 724–25; 3:22–23.

27. *John Wesley's Sermons: An Anthology*, ed. Albert C. Outler and Richard P. Heitzenrater (Nashville: Abingdon, 1991), 336, 488–89; and Thomas C. Oden, *John Wesley's Scriptural Christianity: A Plain Exposition of His Teaching on Christian Doctrine* (Grand Rapids, MI: Zondervan, 1994), 323.

28. The Canons of Dort (Head 1, Art. 7), in *The Three Forms of Unity*, 122.

29. *Reformed Confessions*, 4:238–39.

30. *Reformed Confessions*, 4:312–18.

31. The Westminster Larger Catechism (Q. 153); and the Shorter Catechism (Q. 85–87), in *Reformed Confessions*, 4:339–40, 364–65.

32. Karl Barth, *Church Dogmatics*, ed. G. W. Bromiley and T. F. Torrance, 4 vols. in 14 (London: T&T Clark, 1936–1977), IV/3.2, sec. 71.2 (506–7).

Romans 8:30 does not teach an order but merely expresses the richness of God's grace. If Paul meant to communicate an order, he would not have omitted sanctification, and he would not have used a different order in texts such as 1 Corinthians 6:11.[33]

In reply, we point out that the sequence of Romans 8:30—beginning with eternal predestination, moving through calling and justification in time, and ending with glorification forever, all linked by the grammatical construction "whom he . . . them he also"—does communicate an order of God's acts.[34] As to 1 Corinthians 6:11, though Paul lists "sanctification" between washing and justification, it is likely that he is referring to definitive sanctification, not progressive sanctification.[35] Therefore, this objection does not stand.

2. *An order of salvation distracts us from salvation by grace alone through Christ alone.* Barth said, "It directs our attention away from that which in this process is done on and in man by God, by Jesus Christ and by the Holy Spirit. It turns abstractly . . . to his Christian experiences and states."[36] Berkouwer argued that the order of salvation obscures salvation by faith in Christ alone much as the medieval Roman Catholic view of salvation did.[37]

We answer that the biblical order of salvation protects both the doctrines of salvation by grace alone and in Christ alone. The subject of every verb in Romans 8:30 is God, grounding the *ordo salutis* in his grace alone. The progress of the order from divine foreknowledge and predestination confirms that justification and glorification arise from divine grace and not human merit. The immediately preceding context (v. 29) centers the order on Christ and union with him as the "Son" who is "the firstborn among many brethren."

This biblical linking of every element in the order of salvation to Christ and his redemptive work is reflected in Reformed theology. Robert Letham says, "The paramount placement of union with Christ, far from requiring that we dispense with the *ordo salutis*, preserves and enhances it by pointing to its integrating feature. The Westminster divines knew this when combining a logical *ordo salutis* in the WCF [Westminster Confession of

33. G. C. Berkouwer, *Faith and Justification*, Studies in Dogmatics (Grand Rapids, MI: Eerdmans, 1954), 31–32.
34. MacArthur and Mayhue, eds., *Biblical Doctrine*, 568.
35. On definitive sanctification as God's act of placing people in a state of holiness, see chap. 27.
36. Barth, *Church Dogmatics*, IV/3.2, sec. 71.2 (507).
37. Berkouwer, *Faith and Justification*, 32–33.

Faith], 9–18, with the same topics as aspects of union and communion with Christ in WLC [Westminster Larger Catechism], 65–90."[38]

However, this objection raises a legitimate concern. Sinclair Ferguson writes, "When expressed in terms of the model of a chain of causes and effects, the traditional *ordo salutis* runs the danger of displacing Christ from the central place in soteriology."[39] The remedy is to constantly remember that Christ is not only the source of salvation and the glory of heaven, but he is "the way" we must travel (John 14:6). Berkouwer rightly said, "To walk in the way of salvation can only mean to live in and through Him."[40] Otherwise, we may fall into the error of pietistic experientialism and shift the focus of faith "from the objective to the subjective work of salvation," as Bavinck warned, so that "instead of being directed toward Christ," people become "directed toward themselves" and the conditions they must fulfill for salvation.[41]

3. *An* ordo salutis *fails to acknowledge Paul's redemptive-historical theology*. Herman Ridderbos said that the idea of an order arose from a loss of emphasis on Christ due to "the influence of pietism, mysticism, and moralism."[42] Ridderbos wrote that Paul's letters contain "no such thing as a systematic development of the *ordo salutis*," primarily because "his viewpoint is a different one," for he focuses on God's works of redemption in history instead of individual regeneration.[43] Richard Gaffin cautions, "The center of Paul's teaching is not found in the doctrine of justification by faith or any other aspect of the *ordo salutis*. Rather, his primary interest is seen to be in the *historia salutis* [history of salvation] as that history has reached its eschatological realization in the death and especially the resurrection of Christ."[44] Gaffin states that Paul's concept of the "tension between resurrection realized and yet to be realized is totally foreign to the traditional *ordo salutis*."[45] Rather than speaking of regeneration as a major category of soteriology, Gaffin asserts, we should speak of resurrection with Christ.[46]

---

38. Robert Letham, *Systematic Theology* (Wheaton, IL: Crossway, 2019), 616.
39. Ferguson, *The Holy Spirit*, 99.
40. Berkouwer, *Faith and Justification*, 34.
41. Bavinck, *Reformed Dogmatics*, 3:567–68.
42. Ridderbos, *Paul*, 14.
43. Ridderbos, *Paul*, 206.
44. Richard B. Gaffin Jr., *Resurrection and Redemption: A Study in Paul's Soteriology*, 2nd ed. (Phillipsburg, NJ: Presbyterian and Reformed, 1987), 13.
45. Gaffin, *Resurrection and Redemption*, 138.
46. Gaffin, *Resurrection and Redemption*, 140–41.

Here again, we can learn much from this criticism, for we should never discuss the order of salvation in us apart from the history of salvation in Christ. It is possible to become man-centered and overly experiential in a way that leads to spiritual paralysis or pride. However, we must not set up a false dichotomy between the objective history of salvation and the subjective order of salvation. It does not help us to so emphasize the accomplishment as to neglect the application. The Scriptures speak amply of both. We can guard ourselves from separating them by emphasizing the doctrines of the Trinity and union with Christ.

4. *The modern evangelical use of the order of salvation focuses on the individual to the neglect of the church.* Letham explains, "For Rome, the church and sacraments have priority, with personal salvation tacked on at the end. . . . Protestantism adopts a reverse procedure. The *ordo salutis* relates to the salvation of the individual, with church and sacraments considered later and separately. . . . At grassroots level, church membership is effectively a de facto optional extra."[47] This is a very real problem, especially in a society that elevates individualism and personal autonomy as supreme values.

However, as Letham observes, in this regard contemporary evangelicalism has departed from historic Reformed Christianity, which joined together Christ, the church, and salvation.[48] The Westminster Larger Catechism opens its discussion of the order of salvation with the statement "The members of the invisible church by Christ enjoy union and communion with him in grace and glory" (Q. 65). Spiritual union with Christ is given by effectual calling (Q. 66), which issues in communion in the benefits of "justification, adoption, sanctification, and whatever else, in this life, manifests their union with him" (Q. 69).[49] What does salvation have to do with the visible church? The catechism (Q. 154) says, "The outward and ordinary means whereby Christ communicates to his church the benefits of his mediation, are all his ordinances; especially the word, sacraments, and prayer; all which are made effectual to the elect for their salvation."[50] God implements the order of salvation through the ministry of the church. Thus, outside the visible church "there is no ordinary possibility of salvation."[51]

47. Letham, *Systematic Theology*, 616.
48. Letham, *Systematic Theology*, 617–18.
49. *Reformed Confessions*, 4:312.
50. *Reformed Confessions*, 4:340.
51. The Westminster Confession of Faith (25.2), in *Reformed Confessions*, 4:264.

Therefore, despite these criticisms and concerns, we may construct an order of salvation that reflects God's way of bringing perishing sinners to glory through Jesus Christ. Such an *ordo salutis* will be profitable to us insofar as it is based on God's Word. John MacArthur and Richard Mayhue say, "To speak of logical order or priority is not to unnaturally foist 'human logic' on the text of Scripture. Instead, it is to read out of the text the divine logic and order that the Spirit of God himself has plainly revealed."[52]

Developing a Biblical Order of Salvation

Though no single text of Scripture furnishes us with an entire *ordo salutis*, a systematic examination of several biblical passages yields an order of application.

A Basic Biblical Order of Salvation by Union with Christ

We begin with Romans 8:28–30: "And we know that all things work together for good to them that love God, to them who are the called according to his purpose. For whom he did foreknow, he also did predestinate to be conformed to the image of his Son, that he might be the firstborn among many brethren. Moreover whom he did predestinate, them he also called: and whom he called, them he also justified: and whom he justified, them he also glorified."

Those who love God are "the called" (Rom. 8:28), not merely in the general sense that they have heard the gospel, but in a special sense that defines those who belong to Jesus Christ as his people (1:6–7; 1 Cor. 1:2). The call of God is "according to his purpose." Murray said, "That purpose provides the pattern or plan according to which calling takes place. Therefore, the purpose is prior to the calling."[53] This purpose is God's free choice (Rom. 9:11), formed before the creation of the world (Eph. 1:4–5; 2 Tim. 1:9). Paul unpacks the divine purpose in two divine acts: God foreknew and predestinated those who are called (Rom. 8:29).

People are "called" when they hear the gospel (2 Thess. 2:14), for God's Word invites them to salvation, regardless of how they respond.[54]

52. MacArthur and Mayhue, eds., *Biblical Doctrine*, 567.
53. Murray, *Redemption Accomplished and Applied*, 83.
54. Prov. 1:20–27; 8:1–6; 9:1–6; Isa. 58:1; Jonah 1:2; 3:2; Matt. 22:1–14; Rom. 10:21.

The *preaching of the Word* is necessary for salvation, for "faith cometh by hearing, and hearing by the word of God" (Rom. 10:16–17). Yet Paul means more than this when he speaks of calling. "The called" are those not merely informed but transformed by God's grace so that they see the glory of Christ in the gospel and believe in him (1 Cor. 1:22–24). We speak of this as *effectual calling* because God makes it effective in the heart. This is confirmed when Paul writes that those whom God "called, them he also justified" (Rom. 8:30). *Justification* is by faith in Christ (3:28), so calling must result in faith. Paul also teaches that *faith* is the instrument of receiving justification and hence is logically prior to justification: "We have believed in Jesus Christ, that we might be justified" (Gal. 2:16).[55]

Next, Paul writes, "whom he justified, them he also glorified" (Rom. 8:30). In the context, *glorification* refers to the gift of perfect freedom and conformity to Christ that God's children will enjoy when Christ returns (vv. 17–18, 29). Here again we see that there is an order to what Paul writes; as Murray said, "Glorification could not be prior to calling and justification."[56] However, in Paul's teaching, "glory" has already begun by the inward transformation of believers by the Spirit (2 Cor. 3:18). Thus, glorification may include progressive *sanctification*.[57] Paul speaks earlier in Romans 8 of the Spirit's present work in those who belong to Jesus Christ in order to lead them to put sin to death and to obey God's law (vv. 4, 9–14). It is important to distinguish sanctification and the good works it produces from justification—a key difference between Roman Catholic and Reformation orders of salvation.[58]

Therefore, we can summarize a basic order of application as follows: the general call of the gospel, effectual calling, faith, justification, sanctification, and glorification. We might visualize this framework as depicted in Table 11.1 below:

→	→	→	→	→	→
General Gospel Call	Effectual Calling	Faith	Justification	Sanctification	Glorification

Table 11.1. A Basic Biblical Order of Salvation by Union with Christ

55. See Berkhof, *Systematic Theology*, 417.
56. Murray, *Redemption Accomplished and Applied*, 84.
57. Turretin, *Institutes*, 17.1.11 (2:691).
58. Vos, *Reformed Dogmatics*, 4:8–9.

A Fuller Biblical Order of Salvation by Union with Christ

However, matters become more complicated when we survey all of Romans 8 and the rest of Scripture for teaching on salvation. Each of the terms between the hearing of the gospel and final glorification has other biblical terms that stand in relation to it, and we must consider how these other terms fit into the *ordo salutis*. Let us survey them here, realizing that a fuller discussion will have to wait until future chapters.

In other epistles, the apostle writes of another aspect of salvation, "the washing of regeneration and renewing of the Holy Ghost" (Titus 3:5). *Regeneration* is a new birth by the Spirit (Gal. 4:23, 29; cf. John 3:1–8; 1 Pet. 1:23) or a new creation (2 Cor. 5:17; Gal. 6:15). We use "regeneration" here in its narrow sense of the beginning of spiritual life, not its broad sense as the whole work of renovating God's image.[59] From the new birth spring Christian righteousness, repentance of sin, love, and faith in Christ (1 John 2:29; 3:9; 4:7; 5:1).[60] Therefore, it is prior to faith and is coordinated and closely connected to effectual calling.

Paul addresses Christians as "the sons of God," implying that all believers have received the grace of *adoption* (Rom. 8:14). He writes, "For ye are all the children of God by faith in Christ Jesus" (Gal. 3:26), which teaches us that adoption takes place through faith in the same way as justification.[61] Paul uses "adoption" once with respect to our eschatological hope of glory (Rom. 8:23), but elsewhere speaks of adoption as a grace already received by believers (Gal. 4:5), for they are the "sons" of God.[62] Similarly, John 1:12 says, "But as many as received him, to them gave he power [*exousia*, literally "authority"] to become the sons of God, even to them that believe on his name." Robert Reymond said, "Faith in Christ is the necessary logical (not chronological) precondition to adoption, just as it is to justification."[63]

The work of sanctification presupposes that Christians already have fundamentally turned from sin back toward God (Rom. 8:12–13), so they no longer are the slaves of sin but the willing servants of God and righteousness, and are now ashamed of their former lives (6:15–23). Paul calls this *repentance*, without which no one will escape God's wrath (Rom. 2:4–5;

59. Kersten, *Reformed Dogmatics*, 2:362.

60. On the causal connections between the new birth and these graces in John's epistle, see Reymond, *A New Systematic Theology of the Christian Faith*, 709.

61. Cf. *dia [tēs] pisteōs* in Rom. 3:22, 30; Gal. 2:16; Phil. 3:9.

62. Rom. 8:14, 19; Gal. 3:26; 4:6.

63. Reymond, *A New Systematic Theology of the Christian Faith*, 708.

cf. 1 Thess. 1:9–10). Repentance is coupled with faith in the preaching of the gospel (Mark 1:15; Acts 20:21; 26:18, 20). As Reymond said, this evidence indicates that faith and repentance are "interdependent graces, each occurring in conjunction with the true and proper exercise of the other."[64]

Paul also speaks much of our *perseverance* through sufferings in the hope that nothing can separate us from God (Rom. 8:17, 25). This perseverance is undergirded by God's grace of *preservation*, for his constant love makes us more than conquerors (vv. 35–39).

On the basis of these observations, we present a fuller *ordo salutis* in this table:

→ General Gospel Call	→ Effectual Calling	→ Faith	→ Justification	→ Sanctification	→ Glorification
	→ Regeneration	→ Repentance	→ Adoption	→ Preservation and Perseverance	

Table 11.2. A Fuller Biblical Order of Salvation by Union with Christ

Explanation and Clarification of the Fuller Order

The elements in this table are not all in the same relationship with those they follow and precede. The preaching of the Word and conviction do not cause effectual calling, but effectual calling takes place through the instrumentality of the Word, and God often precedes it with conviction. Effectual calling produces faith and repentance. Justification does not cause sanctification, but sanctification presupposes the grace of a reconciled God who causes his justified people to walk in holy fellowship with him. Sanctification does not cause glorification, but it is the God-ordained path to glory. The complexity of relationships cautions us against treating the *ordo salutis* as if each element caused the next element in the sequence. God is the cause of all: the sequence represents the order of his operations (Rom. 8:30).

The order represents a logical sequence more than a temporal sequence, for effectual calling, the birth of faith, justification, and adoption take

64. Reymond, *A New Systematic Theology of the Christian Faith*, 706.

place in the first moment of the application of salvation to an individual. It is true that we may group the elements of the order as referring to past salvation for the Christian ("I have heard the Word, been effectually called, justified by faith, adopted, and indwelt by the Spirit"), present salvation ("I am being sanctified and preserved"), and future ("I will be glorified"). However, effectual calling, faith, and justification are not sequential in time, but take place in the same moment. Furthermore, faith and repentance are not past events for the Christian, but continuing graces in present exercise. Thus, J. van Genderen and W. H. Velema say, "We do not want to turn it into a sequence of experiences, i.e., a chronological order. Our interest is in the theological coherence of the benefits."[65] The order shows how the graces fit together in the execution of God's plan.

The acts in this order are not all of the same kind. The order of salvation combines three kinds of divine acts, as Gisbertus Voetius (1589–1676) observed. Some acts present moral motives to persuade people without directly transforming their hearts (Word and conviction). There are also acts that change our status and relation to God (justification and adoption). Other acts involve real changes in people's hearts and lives (effectual calling, glorification, etc.).[66] Furthermore, the order includes human acts (faith, repentance, and perseverance).

The reader will also note that we have placed several of these graces in parallel to each other rather than in sequence. When we discuss each grace more extensively, we will examine the relationships among them; for example, between calling and regeneration or between justification and adoption. Different theologians will come to different conclusions about the exact arrangement of the *ordo salutis*, and we must not be dogmatic about all the details. The wonderful complexity of salvation cannot be fully represented in a linear series, but involves multidimensional sets of relationships. However, the basic sequence represented by the top row of Table 11.2 (general call, effectual call, faith, justification, sanctification, glorification) is clearly taught in Scripture.

The ten items listed in Table 11.2 provide a good summary of the doctrine of salvation. Of course, we could add more to this chart, and we will address other biblical descriptions of the Spirit's work. We could add dying and rising with Christ (Rom. 6:1–4), but we have already explored

65. Van Genderen and Velema, *Concise Reformed Dogmatics*, 577.
66. Gisbertus Voetius, as summarized in Vos, *Reformed Dogmatics*, 4:4–5.

union with Christ as the great theme that flies like a banner over the entire *ordo*.[67] This order provides the basic categories that we will focus on as we explore the application of salvation in Christ. We will reserve glorification until our discussion of eschatology in the fourth and final volume of *Reformed Systematic Theology*, although we will end this volume with a brief consideration of the hope of glory.

Practical Applications of the Order of Salvation

Each item in the order has many applications to the Christian life, which we will explore as we consider every doctrine in its place. However, the whole topic of the *ordo salutis* has sweet and helpful implications for life that we will summarize here.

First, God has provided *complete salvation in Christ for all our needs.* Robert Culver (1916–2015) noted in his discussion of the order of salvation, "Since the human malady of sin is 'systemic' the remedy must be systemic."[68] When we survey the order of salvation, we discover a salvation in which God has grace for every need at every step of life, from the state of sin to the state of glory. This reminds us that we need look to nothing outside of Jesus Christ to meet all our spiritual needs. Christ and Christ alone is sufficient.

Second, God has given *abundant and amazingly generous grace in Christ.* Murray observed that God filled his creation with "good things to satisfy the needs of man and beast" (cf. Psalm 104), then commented, "The provision which God has made for the salvation of men is even more strikingly manifold. For this provision has in view the manifoldness of man's need and exhibits the overflowing abundance of God's goodness, wisdom, grace, and love."[69] Let us, therefore, marvel at the Father's kindness, rejoice in his love, and give him the praise that he so richly deserves. The *ordo salutis* should make us exclaim, "God is good!"

Third, God has exhibited his *divine wisdom in ordering his grace for his glory.* For example, the priority of effectual calling before faith means that we must thank God for every drop of saving faith we encounter in mankind. The place of justification before sanctification shows us that

67. See chaps. 9–10, especially the discussion in chap. 10 of union with Christ in his death and resurrection.

68. Robert Duncan Culver, *Systematic Theology: Biblical and Historical* (Fearn, Ross-shire, Scotland: Christian Focus, 2005), 653.

69. Murray, *Redemption Accomplished and Applied*, 79.

our righteousness resides in Christ alone and not in our good works, so that we may boast in nothing in ourselves but must boast in the Lord. The place of effectual calling and sanctification before glorification shows us that if men desire to have any basis for hope that they will inherit eternal life, they must honor God with their obedience in this life. Therefore, we should take up the order of salvation and learn to live all our lives for the glory of God alone.

Fourth, God has laid *a foundation for eternal hope*. We have no direct access to God's eternal decree and await the future judgment day. However, the golden chain of grace, with each link joined to those around it, allows the Christian, by the Spirit's applying grace, to grasp his salvation with assurance. He may say, "I have been effectually called to Christ, for by the Spirit's grace I see in my life a living faith in the Lord Jesus and the fruit of union with him. Therefore, I know that God predestined me and will glorify me. I am bound up with Jesus Christ in the purposes of God, and all things work together to bring me into conformity with his image as one of Christ's brethren." Glorious hope! May a growing understanding of the Holy Spirit's application of salvation by union with Christ produce an increasing holiness and a deepening assurance in God's children.

Sing to the Lord

God's Manifold Saving Grace

Amazing grace, how sweet the sound,
That saved a wretch like me.
I once was lost, but now am found,
'Twas blind, but now I see.

'Twas grace that taught my heart to fear,
And grace my fears relieved;
How precious did that grace appear
The hour I first believed!

Through many dangers, toils, and snares,
I have already come;
'Tis grace hath brought me safe thus far,
And grace will lead me home.

And when this flesh and heart shall fail,
And mortal life shall cease,

I shall possess within the veil
A life of joy and peace.

When we've been there ten thousand years,
Bright shining as the sun,
We've no less days to sing God's praise
Than when we've first begun.

John Newton
Tune: Amazing Grace
Trinity Hymnal—Baptist Edition, No. 402

Questions for Meditation or Discussion

1. What is an "order of salvation" (*ordo salutis*)?
2. What key text in the Holy Scriptures is used as the basis for an order of salvation?
3. What arguments may be presented for the validity of constructing an order of salvation?
4. What is the earliest known use of the phrase *ordo salutis* in its modern sense?
5. How did early Reformed theologians speak of an order?
6. What order has been proposed by Arminianism and Wesleyanism?
7. According to Reformed orthodoxy, what is the basic *ordo salutis*?
8. Based on Romans 8:29–30, what basic order of salvation in Christ may be deduced? How is this order justified from this text and others?
9. What full order of salvation is proposed by the authors? How do they justify the placement of each element added to the basic order?
10. After reading this chapter, do you believe that it is helpful to Christian life to teach an order of the application of salvation in Christ? Why or why not? What practical benefits could it have?

Questions for Deeper Reflection

11. Is it possible to discuss the application of salvation without any order of salvation? Why or why not? How would it affect our treatment of soteriology if we tried to avoid an order?
12. Of the criticisms and concerns about an order of salvation that the authors list, which seems most significant to you? Why? How can we avoid the problems highlighted by that objection?

12

General Calling, Part 1

The Free Offer of the Gospel

When the apostle Paul came to the city of Thessalonica on the Aegean coast of Macedonia, he went to the local synagogue and taught the people about Christ from the Scriptures. Some believed the gospel, but others stirred up the city against the Christians, forcing Paul and Silas to leave (Acts 17:1–10). In Paul's letters to the church in Thessalonica, he marveled at the grace of God that had converted the believers there (1 Thess. 1:1–10; 2 Thess. 1:3–5). All glory for the establishment of this church had to go to God. Paul said, "We are bound to give thanks alway to God for you, brethren beloved of the Lord, because God hath from the beginning chosen you to salvation through sanctification of the Spirit and belief of the truth: whereunto he called you by our gospel, to the obtaining of the glory of our Lord Jesus Christ" (2 Thess. 2:13–14).

The doctrine of divine calling highlights the centrality of the word of the Lord in all his works. Herman Bavinck wrote, "God produces both creation and new creation by his Word and Spirit. By his speech he calls all things into being out of nothing (Gen. 1; Ps. 33:6; John 1:3; Heb. 1:3; 11:3); by the word of his almighty power he again raises up the fallen world."[1] Therefore, the study of God's call is crucial to our understanding of salvation, reflection upon our own conversion, and our practice of evangelism.

1. Bavinck, *Reformed Dogmatics*, 4:33.

Terminology and Definitions of Calling

The language of calling comes from two very common verbs used in the Bible (Hebrew *qara'*; Greek *kaleō*).[2] The basic idea of these verbs is to speak out loud, and among their meanings, such as to give a name or to cry out for help, is the sense of "to summon or invite."[3] God's call initiated his covenant relationship with Abraham: "Look unto Abraham your father, and unto Sarah that bare you: for I called him alone, and blessed him, and increased him" (Isa. 51:2; cf. Heb. 11:8). God's call on Israel reflected his election of that nation to be his people and his servant in the world in order to make known his glory (Isa. 41:8–9; 43:1, 7).

Theologians distinguish God's calling as the external calling (*vocatio externa*) by the hearing of the Word and the internal calling (*vocatio interna*) by the inward work of the Spirit to apply the Word. Augustine said, "When, therefore, the gospel is preached, some believe, some believe not; but they who believe at the voice of the preacher from without, hear of the Father from within, and learn; while they who do not believe, hear outwardly, but inwardly do not hear nor learn; that is to say, to the former it is given to believe; to the latter it is not given."[4] John Calvin referred to the "inner call," saying that "it consists not only in the preaching of the Word but also in the illumination of the Spirit."[5] Theologians also distinguish between ineffective calling (*vocatio inefficax*), which offers nothing more than moral persuasion that men may reject; and effectual calling (*vocatio efficax*),[6] which transforms the heart and saves the sinner.[7]

2. Reformed theologians distinguish God's call as the real call (*vocatio realis*)—which sounds forth "through nature, history, environment, various leadings, and experiences" to impress upon us the principles of God's law—and the verbal call (*vocatio verbalis*), which comes through the Word of God. Bavinck, *Reformed Dogmatics*, 4:33–34. Cf. "universal calling" (*universalis vocatio*) and "special calling" (*specialis vocatio*) in Polyander, Walaeus, Thysius, and Rivetus, *Synopsis Purioris Theologiae*, 30.2–7 (2:206–11). The real or universal call is common grace (see chap. 2) through general revelation (see *RST*, 1:185–86, 195–212). The verbal or special call is a function of special revelation (*RST*, 1:187–89, 264–79), and it is our focus here. We are not aware of any instance in Scripture where the words translated as "call" (*qara'*, *kaleō*) refer to God's general revelation.

3. Geoffrey W. Bromiley, ed., *The International Standard Bible Encyclopedia*, rev. ed., 4 vols. (Grand Rapids, MI: Eerdmans, 1979–1988), 1:580.

4. Augustine, *On the Predestination of the Saints*, 15.8, in *NPNF*[1], 5:506. On Augustine's view of calling and his own conversion experience, see Demarest, *The Cross and Salvation*, 211–13.

5. Calvin, *Institutes*, 3.24.2

6. On the Latin terms, see Muller, *Dictionary of Latin and Greek Theological Terms*, 396–97.

7. Some theologians include in the internal calling the common operations of the Spirit, which are not effectual. Thus, internal calling may be effectual or ineffectual. See Calvin, *Institutes*, 3.24.8, 17; Polyander, Walaeus, Thysius, and Rivetus, *Synopsis Purioris Theologiae*, 30.32, 34–38 (2:221, 223); Turretin, *Institutes*, 15.3.5 (2:511); and Samuel Willard, *A Compleat Body of Divinity* (1726; facsimile repr., New York: Johnson Reprint, 1969), 441. Other theologians include the common operations of the Spirit in the external call and use "inward calling" to refer exclusively to

In the Old Testament, God's call sometimes consisted of an authoritative summons and gracious invitation by his word that people might obey but could ignore or reject. Divine Wisdom "crieth [*qara'*] in the chief place of concourse, in the openings of the gates: in the city she uttereth her words, saying, How long, ye simple ones, will ye love simplicity? And the scorners delight in their scorning, and fools hate knowledge? Turn you at my reproof" (Prov. 1:20–23; cf. 8:1, 4; 9:3). The Lord's prophets would "cry" or "call" to Israel with words of both grace and judgment (Isa. 40:2–3, 6; 58:1). God sent Jonah to call Nineveh to repentance lest the city be destroyed (Jonah 1:2; 3:2). The verb rendered as "call" (*qara'*) may be translated as "proclaim," as in the proclamation of the good news of God's grace (Isa. 61:1–2).

However, at times "call" may express an effectual act of God. The Lord calls forth the generations from the beginning of time, sovereignly summoning each generation into existence (Isa. 41:4). The fatherly calling of the Lord drew Israel out of bondage: "When Israel was a child, then I loved him, and called my son out of Egypt" (Hos. 11:1). Here "called" refers not to an invitation for the nation to relocate but to God's effectual salvation of the people of Israel when he brought them out of the house of bondage with mighty acts of power.

Similarly, in the New Testament, the verb translated as "call" (*kaleō*) is used in both senses. Bruce Demarest writes that God's call may refer to "an invitation or command to salvation that may be sinfully disregarded" or to "God's work of evoking or drawing into a saving relation" in which "the outcome is assured; the calling according to divine purpose always proves effectual."[8] Calling may refer to God's effective summons that creates a saved and holy people.[9] J. I. Packer (1926–2020) wrote, "The developed biblical idea of God's calling is of God summoning men by his word, and laying hold of them by his power, to play a part in and enjoy the benefits of his gracious redemptive purposes."[10] Effectual calling will be the subject of later chapters.[11]

---

effectual calling. Brakel, *The Christian's Reasonable Service*, 2:194, 209; Witsius, *The Economy of the Covenants*, 3.5.7, 25 (1:345–46, 355–56); and Kersten, *Reformed Dogmatics*, 2:366, 372–73.

8. Demarest, *The Cross and Salvation*, 217–18. For the former, he cites Matt. 9:13; 22:3–4, 8, 14; Mark 2:17; Luke 5:32; 14:16–17, 24. For the latter (effectual calling), he cites Acts 2:39; Rom. 8:30; 9:11; 1 Cor. 1:9, 26; 7:20; Gal. 1:15; 2 Thess. 2:14; 1 Tim. 6:12; 2 Tim. 1:9; Heb. 3:1; 9:15; 1 Pet. 2:9; 2 Pet. 1:3; Jude 1; Rev. 17:14; 19:9.

9. Rom. 1:6–7; 8:28, 30; 9:11, 24; 1 Cor. 1:2, 9, 24; Gal. 1:15; 4:1, 4; Col. 3:15; 1 Thess. 2:12; 4:7; 5:24; 2 Thess. 2:14; 1 Tim. 6:12; 2 Tim. 1:9; Heb. 9:15; 1 Pet. 1:15; 2:9, 21; 3:9; 5:10; 2 Pet. 1:3; Jude 1; Rev. 17:14.

10. J. I. Packer, "Call, Calling," in *The Evangelical Dictionary of Theology*, ed. Walter A. Elwell (Grand Rapids, MI: Baker, 1984), 184.

11. See chaps. 15–16.

In this chapter, we will give our attention to the divine calling that goes forth through the Word and may or may not result in salvation. For example, Christ said, "I am not come to call the righteous, but sinners to repentance" (Matt. 9:13; cf. Mark 2:17; Luke 5:32). The same Greek term is used for God's invitation to come and eat his feast (Matt. 22:3–9, 14; Luke 14:16–24). This call is God's gracious invitation to receive Christ as he is offered in the gospel.[12]

Although the grace of God saves sinners by a powerful life-giving work in the soul, we have no expectation of such a work taking place apart from the hearing or reading of the gospel. As Samuel Willard (1640–1707) observed, the gospel is God's appointed means of salvation (Rom. 1:16). Through the gospel, God deals with men as he created them: as reasonable creatures with minds, wills, and affections that act according to persuasion and conscience (2 Cor. 4:2; 5:11). Faith in Christ must involve knowledge of him whom we trust (2 Tim. 1:12), and this knowledge can come only by hearing or reading the Word of God (Rom. 10:14–17). Hence, the gospel of the Scriptures must be preached so that people may become wise unto salvation by faith in Christ (2 Tim. 3:15–4:2).[13]

The Characteristics of the Gospel Call

In Christ's parable of the wedding banquet (Matt. 22:1–14), the king has prepared a lavish feast to honor his son at his wedding. He sends out his servants with the good news that people are invited to join the celebration. Those invited surprisingly reject the generous invitation and abuse the king's servants, provoking him to send his soldiers to destroy these wicked men and burn their city. The king, however, is not discouraged, but sends out his servants into the highways to gather all kinds of people into the feast. When the king discovers that one of the guests is not dressed in a wedding garment, the king has him arrested and punished for gross contempt at such a dignified event. This parable, which uses Greek words translated as "call" (*kaleō*) or "called" (*klētos*) six times in fourteen verses,[14] illustrates many aspects of how God calls sinners through his word.

12. Berkhof, *Systematic Theology*, 458.
13. Willard, *A Compleat Body of Divinity*, 436–37.
14. Matt. 22:3, 4, 8, 9, 14. "Call" (*kaleō*) is often translated as "bid" or "bidden" in the KJV.

1. God calls sinners through his *scriptural* word. In the parable, the call goes forth through the mouths of the king's servants, who represent the messengers of the Lord. The first part of Christ's parable resembles the Lord's sending of his prophets to Judah:

> The Lord, the God of their fathers, sent persistently to them by his messengers, because he had compassion on his people and on his dwelling place. But they kept mocking the messengers of God, despising his words and scoffing at his prophets, until the wrath of the Lord rose against his people, until there was no remedy. Therefore he brought up against them the king of the Chaldeans. . . . And they burned the house of God and broke down the wall of Jerusalem and burned all its palaces with fire and destroyed all its precious vessels. (2 Chron. 36:15–17, 19 ESV)

The parable also has similarities to Christ's sending of the apostles to Israel, the rejection of Christ by its leaders and many of its people, the judgment of God against Jerusalem, and the expansion of the apostles' mission to Jews and Gentiles (cf. Matt. 21:33–46). Therefore, the call of God goes out through the Spirit-inspired words of his prophets and apostles, the writers of the Holy Scriptures (2 Pet. 1:20–21; 3:2, 16). If we want to hear and disseminate that call today, we must do so through the reading and preaching of the Bible. The call is a message from God.

2. God calls sinners through his *official* word. In the parable, the call is brought to people by the servants of a king, and their message bears the trustworthiness and the authority of the one who sends them. The chief officer and apostle of the gospel is Jesus Christ himself (Heb. 3:1), who spoke not his own words but the words of the Father who sent him.[15] The church does not speak of its own authority but as the representatives of the Lord, commissioned to bring his teaching (Matt. 28:18–20). Preachers are ambassadors sent by Christ and entrusted with the gospel, and so they speak from God as his servants, in the sight of God as his stewards, and in union with Christ.[16] John Flavel said, "The preaching of the gospel by Christ's ambassadors is the means appointed for the reconciling and bringing home of sinners to Christ."[17] The words translated as "preach"

15. John 3:34; 7:16; 8:28; 12:49; 14:10, 24.
16. 1 Cor. 4:1–2; 2 Cor. 2:17; 5:20; 1 Thess. 2:4.
17. Flavel, *The Method of Grace*, in *Works*, 2:50.

(*kēryssō*) or "preacher" (*kēryx*) literally refer to a herald,[18] an official of the royal court who raised his voice to publicly "declare official decrees and announcements," with a message that "does not originate from them," but "behind it stands a higher power."[19] The call is a message of authority.

3. God calls sinners through his *evangelical* word. In the parable, the servants announce the joyful occasion of the wedding of the king's son and the abundant feast prepared for all who come. In reality, God's servants announce the "good news" (*euangelion*) that the Son of God has become a man, died on the cross, and risen from the dead (1 Cor. 15:3–4), so that the "Lord over all is rich unto all that call upon him" (Rom. 10:12). The call is not an exhortation for a more disciplined effort to save ourselves, but good news of great joy for sinners (Luke 2:10; 5:32). It brings peace and moves people to sing of their Savior (Isa. 52:7–9). The call is a message of grace.

4. God calls sinners through his *judicial* word. Christ's parable is not about an invitation from a private person, but from a king who relates to people as his subjects under the justice of his court (Matt. 22:2, 7, 11, 13). Therefore, though the call invites the unworthy to a feast, it also exposes the rebellion of the king's enemies and brings just judgment upon them (vv. 5–7). For this reason, God's call has the nature of "testimony" by his "witnesses."[20] The gospel itself declares that those who reject Christ in unbelief bring upon themselves the condemnation and wrath of God (John 3:18, 36).

As the Heidelberg Catechism (LD 31, Q. 84) says, the gospel opens the kingdom to believers in the proclamation that if men "receive the promise of the gospel by a true faith, all their sins are really forgiven them of God for the sake of Christ's merits"; however, the gospel shuts the kingdom to the unbelieving and unrepentant, for "they stand exposed to the wrath of God and eternal condemnation, so long as they are unconverted,"[21] or as the Latin version reads, "as long as they persist in their sins."[22] The call is a message of judgment, either of forgiveness or condemnation.

18. See Matt. 4:23; 24:14; Mark 1:14; Luke 4:18; 24:47; Acts 8:5; 9:20; Rom. 10:14; 1 Cor. 1:23; 2 Cor. 4:5; 1 Thess. 2:9; 1 Tim. 2:7; 2 Tim. 1:11; 4:2.

19. *TDNT*, 3:686–88.

20. Luke 9:5; 21:13; 24:48; John 1:7–8, 15; 3:11, 26, 28, 32–33; 5:31–39; 7:7; 8:17–18; 10:25; 15:26–27; 18:31; 21:24; Acts 1:8, 22; 2:32, 40; 3:15; 4:33; 5:32; 8:25; 10:39–43; 13:31; 14:3, 17; 15:8; 18:2; 20:21; 22:15, 18; 23:11; 26:16, 22; 28:23. See the Lord's court case against the nations in Isa. 43:8–13; 44:6–9.

21. *The Three Forms of Unity*, 97.

22. Latin: *dum in suis sceleribus perseverant.* See E. V. Gerhart et al., eds., *The Heidelberg Catechism, in German, Latin, and English: With an Historical Introduction* (New York: Charles Scribner, 1863), 222.

5. God calls sinners through his *general* word. The breadth of the call appears in the parable, for the king commands his servants, "Go ye therefore into the highways, and as many as ye shall find, bid [call or invite] to the marriage" (Matt. 22:9). The servants obey and call "all" whom they find (v. 10). The call goes out to "many," though "few" prove to be elect and are saved (v. 14). James Durham (1622–1658) said, "We make this offer to all of you, to you who are atheists, to you that are graceless, to you that are ignorant, to you that are hypocrites, to you that are lazy and lukewarm . . . come to the wedding."[23] In a similar parable in Luke, the master tells his servant to invite the poor, crippled, and blind, and when there is more room at the banquet, to "go out into the highways and hedges" (Luke 14:23).

Johannes Wollebius said, "Common calling is the act by which all persons whatsoever are invited to the state of grace or participation in Christ the mediator."[24] The call appeals to all who hear it to respond: "Ho, every one that thirsteth, come ye to the waters, and he that hath no money; come ye, buy, and eat; yea, come, buy wine and milk without money and without price" (Isa. 55:1; cf. John 7:37). Christ said, "Come unto me, all ye that labour and are heavy laden, and I will give you rest" (Matt. 11:28). One of the last statements of the Bible is "And the Spirit and the bride say, Come. And let him that heareth say, Come. And let him that is athirst come. And whosoever will, let him take the water of life freely" (Rev. 22:17). The call is a message of open invitation.

6. God calls sinners through his *merciful* word. Christ depicted the king in his parable as a man of great patience. When those first invited insult him by refusing to come, the king responds by sending the servants again with sweet words about how good the feast is (Matt. 22:3–4).[25] After they prove to be violent traitors, the king extends the invitation to others both "bad and good" (v. 10). God's mercy shows itself in how he amazingly stoops to plead with wicked rebels. "Say to them, As I live, declares the Lord God, I have no pleasure in the death of the wicked, but that the wicked turn from his way and live; turn back, turn back from your evil ways, for why will you die, O house of Israel?" (Ezek. 33:11

23. Cited in Sinclair B. Ferguson, *The Whole Christ: Legalism, Antinomianism, and Gospel Assurance—Why the Marrow Controversy Still Matters* (Wheaton, IL: Crossway, 2016), 111.

24. Wollebius, *Compendium*, 1.20 (115).

25. Craig L. Blomberg, *Matthew*, The New American Commentary 22 (Nashville: Broadman & Holman, 1992), 327.

ESV). Preachers must warmly plead with sinners with "the meekness and gentleness of Christ" (2 Cor. 5:20; 10:1). Packer said that the apostle Paul did not "preach the gospel in a harsh, callous way, putting it before his neighbor with a contemptuous air, . . . [for] love made Paul warm-hearted and affectionate in his evangelism."[26] The call is a message of compassion.

7. God calls sinners with his *resistible* word. Though the host of the banquet in the parable is a mighty king, his invited guests not only turn down the invitation but treat his royal hospitality with contempt (Matt. 22:5–6). It is "completely unnatural" to refuse an invitation to such a feast, showing the irrationality of unbelief.[27] The Scriptures speak of men commonly rejecting God's call. God's Wisdom says, "I have called, and ye refused; I have stretched out my hand, and no man regarded" (Prov. 1:24). The Lord says, "I have spread out my hands all the day unto a rebellious people, which walketh in a way that was not good, after their own thoughts. . . . When I called, ye did not answer; when I spake, ye did not hear; but did evil before mine eyes, and did choose that wherein I delighted not" (Isa. 65:2, 12; cf. 66:4). The martyr Stephen declared, "Ye stiffnecked and uncircumcised in heart and ears, ye do always resist the Holy Ghost: as your fathers did, so do ye" (Acts 7:51). The call is a message of responsibility.

8. God calls sinners through his *sacrificial* word. The servants of the king give their time, energy, and patience to bring the invitation to people in many places, and they suffer contempt, abuse, and death (Matt. 22:5–7). Christ elsewhere said that this is a characteristic of God's prophets and apostles: "Therefore also said the wisdom of God, I will send them prophets and apostles, and some of them they shall slay and persecute: that the blood of all the prophets, which was shed from the foundation of the world, may be required of this generation" (Luke 11:49–50; cf. Matt. 23:34–36). No one suffered more to proclaim the truth than God's Son, Jesus Christ, who said shortly before he was crucified, "To this end was I born, and for this cause came I into the world, that I should bear witness unto the truth" (John 18:37). In union with him, his gospel preachers experience both Christ's sufferings and power (2 Cor. 1:3–6; 4:12). Missionary work is a sacrifice offered to God (Phil. 2:17; 2 Tim. 4:6), and

26. J. I. Packer, *Evangelism and the Sovereignty of God* (Downers Grove, IL: InterVarsity Press, 1976), 51–52.

27. Leon Morris, *The Gospel according to Matthew*, The Pillar New Testament Commentary (Grand Rapids, MI: Eerdmans; Leicester, England: Apollos, 1992), 548.

those who financially support missions offer a pleasing sacrifice (Phil. 4:18). Though we do not suffer to accomplish redemption, we must suffer in order to proclaim redemption. The call is a message delivered through dedicated servants.

9. God calls sinners through his *successful* word. Christ concluded his parable with the saying, "For many are called, but few are chosen" (Matt. 22:14). Surprisingly, after the parable described most people's choice to reject the king's call, Christ said that the few who responded rightly did so because of God's choice of them. God's word of calling accomplishes God's will (Isa. 55:1, 10–11). The general call is resistible, but this does not imply that God's purpose for an individual is thwarted when that sinner rejects Christ. Wilhelmus à Brakel said, "God's objective in causing the gospel to be proclaimed to the non-elect is to proclaim and acquaint man with the way of salvation, to command man to enter this way, and to display His goodness. . . . It is also God's objective to convict man of his wickedness in his refusal to come upon such a friendly invitation."[28] In the end, God will be glorified. The call is a message of glory.

The Contents of the Gospel Call

When the Lord Jesus rose from the dead and appeared to his apostles and other disciples, he gave them further illumination to understand the Old Testament and his own teachings (Luke 24:33–36, 44–45). He then commissioned them to be his witnesses and promised them the power of the Holy Spirit to take the scriptural message to the nations (vv. 48–49). What was the message? Christ said, "Thus it is written, that the Christ should suffer and on the third day rise from the dead, and that repentance for the forgiveness of sins should be proclaimed in his name to all nations, beginning from Jerusalem" (vv. 46–47 ESV). We observe three basic components: the doctrine of Christ, the command of repentance, and the promise of forgiveness.

The apostles' gospel contains the same three elements: doctrine about Christ, requirement of faith, and promise of forgiveness. Peter said, "God anointed Jesus of Nazareth with the Holy Ghost and with power . . . whom they slew and hanged on a tree: him God raised up the third day. . . . Through his name whosoever believeth in him shall receive remission of sins" (Acts 10:38–43). Paul writes, "I declare unto you the gospel . . . by

28. Brakel, *The Christian's Reasonable Service*, 2:206.

which also you are saved, if you hold fast that word which I preached to you . . . that Christ died for our sins according to the scriptures, and that he was buried, and that he rose again the third day according to the scriptures: and that he was seen by Cephas, then by the twelve" (1 Cor. 15:1–5).

Therefore, we may summarize the essential elements of the gospel as follows: (1) the doctrine of the good news, or the facts of the gospel about Christ and redemption; (2) the summons to repent and believe in Christ; and (3) the promise of salvation for all those who, by grace, have repented of sin and trusted in Christ alone.[29]

1. The Doctrine of the Good News

The gospel is not merely an invitation to action but a teaching revealed by God. Paul says, "But God be thanked, that ye were the servants of sin, but ye have obeyed from the heart that form of doctrine which was delivered you" (Rom. 6:17). He writes of the "sound doctrine" that is "according to the glorious gospel of the blessed God" (1 Tim. 1:10–11). Christ's preaching of the gospel was accompanied by teaching wherever he went (Matt. 4:23; 9:35). The charge to every preacher is to "preach the word . . . with all long suffering and doctrine" (2 Tim. 4:2).

The first doctrine involved in the call of God is the doctrine of man's sin against his God. This is the bad news before the good news, the law before the gospel. Paul's greatest writing on the gospel is the epistle to the Romans (Rom. 1:1, 9, 16; 16:25), and he devotes much of the first three chapters to the bad news that man refuses to honor the Creator whose glory shines in all things (1:21). Of course, this assumes man's knowledge of the Creator through general revelation (vv. 19–20). Man's ungodliness provokes God's wrath (v. 18) and brings man into spiritual darkness and slavery to all kinds of evil (vv. 21–31). Even outwardly religious people are guilty of self-righteousness, hypocrisy, and refusal to repent of their sins, so God's wrath will fall on all sinners on judgment day (2:1–16). Though the people of Israel had many blessings and privileges from God, apart from God's grace they were no better than the Gentiles (2:17–3:8). Therefore, Paul concludes, "As it is written, There is none righteous, no, not one: there is none that understandeth, there is none that seeketh after God. They are all gone out of the way, they are together become unprofitable; there is none that doeth good, no, not one" (vv. 10–12). In this way,

29. Cf. Berkhof, *Systematic Theology*, 459–60.

the moral law accompanies the gospel in God's call in order to reveal sin and expose sinners to the wrath of God (3:19–20; 4:15).

The moral law is not the gospel.[30] However, the moral law reveals our need for the gospel. Thus, we find law and gospel mixed in evangelistic preaching. In calling sinners to Christ on Pentecost, Peter rebuked them for murdering the Messiah—and they were cut to the heart for their sin (Acts 2:36–37). When Paul preached the gospel to the Gentiles, he not only offered Christ to them, but also reproved them for worshiping idols and called them to repent (14:15–16; 17:24–31). Paul spoke to Felix and Drusilla of faith in Christ and also righteousness, self-control, and the judgment to come, so that "Felix trembled" (24:24–25). Therefore, we must distinguish between law and gospel, but we must preach the law so that sinners may see their need for God's Son, understand the significance of repentance, and, once converted, live in a manner pleasing to God. However, God calls sinners to himself by the gospel, not the law.

What is the doctrine of the gospel? Broadly, it is the good news of Christ (Mark 1:1; Rom. 1:1, 3). Based on Paul's epistle to the Romans, evangelistic sermons in Acts, and the usage of the words translated as "gospel" (*euangelion*) and "preach the gospel" (*euangelizomai*) in the New Testament, we may summarize the basic gospel doctrine as follows:

- God has revealed himself by speaking to men "the gospel of God" (Rom. 1:1).[31]
- The one true God and Creator of all things is good to sinful men (Rom. 2:4).[32]
- God is sovereignly working out his plan revealed in Scripture (Rom. 1:2).[33]
- God sent his Son, Jesus Christ, through the line of King David (Rom. 1:3).[34]
- Christ lived a perfectly righteous life of obedience to God's law (Rom. 5:18–19).[35]

30. We write here specifically of the *moral* law. However, when "law" refers to the entire Old Testament, including the promises of Christ and the types of the ceremonial law, it does bear witness to the gospel (Rom. 3:21).

31. Rom. 15:16; 2 Cor. 11:7; Gal. 1:11–12; 1 Thess. 2:2, 8–9; 1 Pet. 4:17 (*euangelion* in all).

32. Acts 14:15–17 (*euangelizomai*); 17:24–25.

33. Acts 13:17–22, 27, 29, 32 (*euangelizomai*), 33; 1 Cor. 15:1–4 (*euangelion* and *euangelizomai*).

34. Acts 13:23; 2 Tim. 2:8 (*euangelion*). Thus, the preaching that the kingdom of God has arrived in Christ is central to the gospel (Mark 1:14–15; cf. Isa. 52:7).

35. Acts 3:14; 4:27; 7:52; 22:14.

- Christ died on the cross to satisfy God's justice for our sins (Rom. 3:24–26).[36]
- Christ rose from the dead for our salvation (Rom. 1:4; 4:25; 5:10).[37]
- Christ will come again to judge all mankind (Rom. 2:16).[38]

When viewed as a whole, the doctrine of God's call may be encapsulated in four words: God, sin, Christ, and salvation.

2. *The Summons to Repent and Believe*

The gospel call does not consist merely in the teaching of doctrine, but also in an exhortation and appeal to respond to that doctrine by turning to God. The Lord says, "Look unto me, and be ye saved, all the ends of the earth: for I am God, and there is none else" (Isa. 45:22). The gospel call does not merely describe the response, but commands, urges, exhorts, admonishes, warns, pleads, and appeals for such a response.[39]

The response demanded by the gospel may be summarized in the words *repentance* and *faith*.[40] Christ said, "The time is fulfilled, and the kingdom of God is at hand: repent ye, and believe the gospel" (Mark 1:15). Paul said that in his public and private teaching he was constantly "testifying both to the Jews, and also to the Greeks, repentance toward God, and faith toward our Lord Jesus Christ" (Acts 20:21). When the disciples of Christ were scattered by persecution, some preached Christ to the Gentiles, "and the hand of the Lord was with them: and a great number believed, and turned unto the Lord" (11:21).[41]

Both repentance and faith are obligations, duties required by God of all who hear the gospel. When Christ said, "Repent ye, and believe the gospel" (Mark 1:15), he used imperative verbs.[42] Through the gospel, Paul says, God "commandeth all men every where to repent" (Acts 17:30). John says, "This is his commandment, That we should believe on the name of his Son Jesus Christ, and love one another, as he gave us commandment" (1 John 3:23). To refuse to believe God's promises concerning his

36. 1 Cor. 1:17 (*euangelizomai*); 15:2–3 (*euangelion*). The references in Acts to Christ dying on a "tree" (Acts 5:30; 10:39; 13:29) imply dying under God's curse against sin as sinners' substitute (Deut. 21:23; Gal. 3:13; 1 Pet. 2:24).

37. 1 Cor. 15:2–4 (*euangelion*), 21; 2 Tim. 2:8 (*euangelion*).

38. Acts 10:42; 17:31.

39. We have already observed this in Isa. 55:1; Matt. 11:28; John 7:37; Rev. 22:17.

40. We will explore the nature of these two graces in more detail in chaps. 19–21 on conversion.

41. At times one is emphasized and the other assumed. See Luke 5:32; John 12:36; 14:1; Acts 2:38; 16:31; 26:20.

42. See also John 12:36; 14:1; Acts 2:38; 16:31; 26:20.

Son is "a dreadful sin," as Brakel said, because "he that believeth not God hath made him a liar" (1 John 5:10).[43]

3. The Promise of Salvation

In order to encourage people to repent and believe, and to give assurance to those who do, God attached promises to a right response to the gospel. Perhaps the most famous is "everyone who calls on the name of the Lord shall be saved" (Joel 2:32 ESV; cited in Acts 2:21; Rom. 10:13). Christ said, "For God so loved the world, that he gave his only begotten Son, that whosoever believeth in him should not perish, but have everlasting life" (John 3:16). The Lord Jesus also said, "Verily, verily, I say unto you, He that heareth my word, and believeth on him that sent me, hath everlasting life, and shall not come into condemnation; but is passed from death unto life" (5:24). Peter said, "Repent ye therefore, and be converted, that your sins may be blotted out" (Acts 3:19). He preached that "whosoever believeth in him shall receive remission of sins" (10:43). The gospel message couples repentance and forgiveness (Luke 24:47; Acts 5:31), repentance and life (Acts 11:18), and repentance and salvation (2 Cor. 7:10).

The promise of salvation communicates to all who hear the gospel the warrant to receive Christ as the Savior from sin, along with all his benefits. Sinners need not search themselves for some qualification before they can come to Christ. All are invited and commanded to come immediately, and therefore have the right and authorization from God to do so. That is not to say that all men have the ability to come, for apart from God's grace no one can come to Christ (John 6:44). It is to say, however, that all who come to Christ with true faith will be saved. Jesus promised, "All that the Father giveth me shall come to me; and him that cometh to me I will in no wise cast out" (John 6:37). "In no wise" translates a Greek double negative: "I will certainly never cast them out." As the Scottish "Marrow men" said, "Although we believe the purchase and application of redemption to be peculiar to the elect, who were given by the Father to Christ in the counsel of peace, yet the warrant to receive him is common to all."[44] Samuel Rutherford (1600–1661) wrote, "Nor have the reprobate ground to quarrel at the decrees of God, though they be not chosen, yet they are

43. Brakel, *The Christian's Reasonable Service*, 2:204.

44. "Queries Agreed unto by the Commission of the General Assembly," Query 10, in Edward Fisher, *The Marrow of Modern Divinity* (Fearn, Ross-shire, Scotland: Christian Focus, 2009), 371.

called, as if they were chosen, and . . . they have as fair a revealed warrant to believe, as the elect have; they are men, sinners of the world, to whom Christ is offered."[45]

Controversies Concerning the Free Offer of the Gospel

The gospel call has been a point of controversy regarding its relation to the sovereignty of God. Since the Bible teaches on the one hand the sovereign particularity of God's will to save only some sinners—indeed, many sinners (but not all)—from their deserved punishment, and on the other hand that God calls all who hear the gospel to salvation, Christians have sometimes erred by pitting one side of the biblical testimony against the other. This is a form of rationalism in which we use our limited human reasoning to dismiss one side of biblical truth because we cannot see how it fits with another side. The solution is to accept both by faith and to humble our minds beneath the majesty of the incomprehensible God.

1. *The Objection against Sovereign Grace*

Jacob Arminius taught that when God calls sinners through the gospel, he has no other will than that they all repent and believe.[46] The Arminian Remonstrance of 1610 (Art. 2) says, "Jesus Christ, Savior of the world, has died for each and every man, and through His death on the cross has merited reconciliation and forgiveness of sins for all."[47] In modern Arminianism, it is viewed as an essential part of evangelism to tell unrepentant, unbelieving sinners that "Christ died for you." Therefore, Arminians charge Reformed Christians with either denying the gospel call or "incredible double talk."[48] David Allen writes, "Without belief in the universal saving will of God and a universal extent in Christ's sin-bearing, there can be no well-meant offer of the salvation from God to the non-elect who hear the gospel call."[49]

In response to such charges, the Reformed theologians at the Synod of Dort taught that although God intended Christ's death to effectively

45. Samuel Rutherford, *Christ Dying and Drawing Sinners to Himselfe* (London: by J. D. for Andrew Crooke, 1647), 442.

46. Arminius, *Certain Articles*, Art. 17, in *Works*, 2:721.

47. *Reformed Confessions*, 4:43.

48. Terry L. Miethe, "The Universal Power of the Atonement," in *The Grace of God and the Will of Man*, ed. Clark H. Pinnock (Minneapolis: Bethany House, 1989), 83.

49. David L. Allen, "The Atonement: Limited or Universal?," in *Whosoever Will: A Biblical-Theological Critique of Five-Point Calvinism*, ed. David L. Allen and Steve W. Lemke (Nashville: Broadman & Holman, 2010), 95.

save "all the elect" and "them alone," his sacrifice was "of infinite worth and value, abundantly sufficient to expiate the sins of the whole world."[50] Likewise, the Canons of Dort strongly affirm the general call of the gospel to all men: "As many as are called by the gospel are unfeignedly called. For God hath most earnestly and truly declared in His Word what will be acceptable to Him; namely, that all who are called, should comply with the invitation. He, moreover, seriously promises eternal life and rest to as many as shall come to Him and believe on Him."[51]

There is no contradiction between God's eternal election and his gospel call. The first is God's decision; the second is our duty.[52] Wollebius wrote, "He calls both [the elect and the non-elect] in earnest and without any deceit," for even the reprobate "are called in earnest, and salvation is offered them on condition of faith."[53] Matthew Barrett explains that there is no inconsistency between the unconditional election of some and the gospel call to all, for the gospel offer "is the very means by which God converts sinners"; furthermore, "God never makes a promise in the gospel offer that he does not keep."[54] Barrett notes, "The well-meant offer is just as problematic . . . for the Arminian," for, as Bavinck said, "in that case, God also offers salvation to those whom he infallibly knows will not believe."[55]

As to the mistaken belief that we must tell unbelievers "Christ died for you" in order to properly evangelize them, we reply that Reformed evangelists have preached the gospel warmly and fruitfully for centuries without providing any such formula. Packer wrote,

> The fact is that the New Testament never calls on any man to repent on the ground that Christ died specifically and particularly for him. The basis on which the New Testament invites sinners to put faith in Christ is simply that they need Him, and He offers Himself to them, and that those who receive Him are promised all the benefits that His death secured for His people. . . . Our task in evangelism is to reproduce as faithfully as possible the New Testament emphasis.[56]

---

50. The Canons of Dort (Head 2, Arts. 3, 8), in *The Three Forms of Unity*, 134, 136.
51. The Canons of Dort (Head 3/4, Art. 8), in *The Three Forms of Unity*, 143.
52. Owen, *A Display of Arminianism*, in *Works*, 10:47–48.
53. Wollebius, *Compendium*, 1.20.7 (116).
54. Matthew Barrett, *Salvation by Grace: The Case for Effectual Calling and Regeneration* (Phillipsburg, NJ: P&R, 2013), 76.
55. Barrett, *Salvation by Grace*, 77, citing Bavinck, *Reformed Dogmatics*, 4:37.
56. Packer, *Evangelism and the Sovereignty of God*, 68.

The confidence that Christ died for you is the basis for unfailing hope that you will never be condemned or separated from the love of God: "He that spared not his own Son, but delivered him up for us all, how shall he not with him also freely give us all things? Who shall lay any thing to the charge of God's elect? It is God that justifieth. Who is he that condemneth? It is Christ that died, yea rather, that is risen again, who is even at the right hand of God, who also maketh intercession for us. Who shall separate us from the love of Christ?" (Rom. 8:32–35). This confidence does not belong to unbelievers. To affirm that the Son of God "loved me, and gave himself for me" is at the heart of my assurance that I am in union with Christ (Gal. 2:20), not the first act of saving faith to take hold of Christ. Brakel explained, "Everyone is obligated to come to Christ and to receive Him in order to be justified, sanctified, preserved, and glorified. One must not interpret this to mean that everyone is under obligation to believe that Christ has died for him and is his Savior. . . . Faith is not assurance; for assurance is a consequence of faith."[57]

2. *The Objection against the Gospel Call*

Just as some people have so emphasized the general gospel call as to severely downplay God's sovereign election, others have so emphasized election as to minimize the gospel call. The various forms of this error are often called *hyper-Calvinism*. However, we must acknowledge that this label has difficulties. Often it is wrongly applied to legitimate forms of historic Reformed doctrine, such as unconditional election or eternal reprobation. The term is also misleading because, as Iain Murray writes, "Too often it has been supposed that the difference between Calvinism and Hyper-Calvinism is simply a question of degree."[58] The problem is not too high a view of divine sovereignty but the denial of other biblical doctrines.

Some advocates of sovereign grace deny that the gospel call is an *offer* of Christ. The most relevant meaning of the verb *offer* in this case is "to present for acceptance or rejection."[59] John Gill wrote, "The gospel is indeed ordered to be preached to every creature to whom it is sent and comes"; however, he also said, "That there are universal offers of grace and salvation made to all men I utterly deny; nay, I deny that they are made

57. Brakel, *The Christian's Reasonable Service*, 2:204.

58. Iain H. Murray, *Spurgeon and Hyper-Calvinism: The Battle for Gospel Preaching* (Edinburgh: Banner of Truth, 1995), 40.

59. *Merriam-Webster's Collegiate Dictionary*, s.v. "offer."

to any; no, not to God's elect; grace and salvation are provided for them in the everlasting covenant, procured for them by Christ, published and revealed in the gospel, and applied by the Spirit."[60] Yet we note that Gill could preach as follows: "Come to the Lord as humble penitents . . . let sensible sinners come to the person, blood and righteousness of Christ for justification and salvation."[61] Gill also encouraged preachers "fervently" and "boldly" to "set forth the lost and miserable estate and condition of men by nature, the danger they are in, the necessity of regeneration and repentance, and of a better righteousness than their own, and of faith in Christ; which things are blessed for the turning of men from darkness to light."[62] He commended preaching that is "very moving . . . striking . . . spiritual, savory, and evangelical having a tendency to awaken the minds of sinners to a sense of sin and danger, and to relieve and comfort the distressed."[63] However, it does appear that Gill held to a mild form of hyper-Calvinism that discouraged churches from freely calling and commanding lost sinners to come to Christ, believe in him, receive him, and be saved.[64]

The language of the free offer expresses biblical truth. Faith is receiving of Christ (John 1:11–12; Col. 2:6), but it is difficult to understand how Christ could be received if he were not offered to people in the gospel. Grace is a gift that must be received for salvation (John 1:16; Rom. 5:17). Christ offers the Spirit to the thirsty, and sinners receive the Spirit by faith

60. John Gill, *The Doctrine of Predestination Stated, and Set in Scriptural Light: In Opposition to Mr. Wesley's Predestination Calmly Considered*, in *Sermons and Tracts* (1815; repr. Streamwood, IL: Primitive Baptist Library, 1981), 3:117–18.

61. John Gill, *The Watchman's Answer to the Question, What of the Night?*, in *Sermons and Tracts*, 1:59; cf. John Gill, *The Glory of God's Grace Displayed, In Its Abounding over the Aboundings of Sin* (London: Aaron Ward, 1724), 38.

62. Gill, *Body of Divinity*, 931–32.

63. John Gill, funeral sermon for Samuel Wilson (1750), cited in S. H. Cone, "Biographical Sketch of the Author," in Samuel Wilson, *A Scripture Manual or a Plain Representation of the Ordinance of Baptism*, in *The Baptist Library: A Republication of Standard Baptist Works*, ed. Charles G. Sommers, William R. Williams, and Levi L. Hill, 3 vols. (Prattsville, NY: Robert H. Hill, 1843), 1:29–30.

64. Gill said that the gospel obligates men to historical faith—that is, to assent that the historical events reported in the gospel are true— but does not obligate them to saving faith in Christ. John Gill, *The Cause of God and Truth* (1855; repr., Paris, AK: The Baptist Standard Bearer, 1992), 31–32. Therefore, it is not man's immediate duty to trust in Christ upon hearing the gospel. "Though I think the judgment should still be surrounded with cautions and caveats, there may be compelling evidence that Gill held to the distinctive hyper-Calvinist tenet." Tom J. Nettles, "John Gill and the Evangelical Awakening," in *The Life and Thought of John Gill (1697–1771): A Tercentennial Appreciation*, ed. Michael A. G. Haykin (Leiden: Brill, 1997), 153n60. "Gill was shaped by the rationalism of his day. . . . Gill's theology did hamper passionate evangelism and outreach." Michael A. G. Haykin, "Remembering Baptist Heroes: The Example of John Gill," in *Ministry by His Grace and for His Glory: Essays in Honor of Thomas J. Nettles*, ed. Thomas K. Ascol and Nathan A. Finn (Cape Coral, FL: Founders, 2011), 29.

in Christ (John 7:37–39; Gal. 3:1–2). The Spirit in his operations upon the believer is a "gift" that repentant sinners "receive."[65]

The free offer is affirmed in Reformed confessional statements. Calvin's Catechism of 1537 (Art. 12) says, "Just as the merciful Father offers us the Son through the word of the Gospel, so we embrace him through faith and acknowledge him as given to us. It is true that the word of the Gospel calls all to participate in Christ, but a number, blinded and hardened by unbelief, despise such a unique grace. Hence, only believers enjoy Christ; they receive him as sent to them; they do not reject him when he is given, but follow him when he calls them."[66] The Genevan Confession (Art. 11) states, "We believe the promises of the gospel and receive Jesus Christ as He is offered to us by the Father and described to us by the Word of God."[67] The Canons of Dort (Head 3/4, Art. 9) say, "It is not the fault of the gospel, nor of Christ offered therein, nor of God, who calls men by the gospel and confers upon them various gifts, that those who are called by the ministry of the Word refuse to come and be converted."[68]

The Westminster Standards affirm the same. The Shorter Catechism (Q. 31) says that Christ is "freely offered to us in the gospel."[69] The Larger Catechism (Q. 68) speaks of how God justly leaves in unbelief the wicked for "their willful neglect and contempt of the grace offered to them."[70] The Westminster Confession of Faith (7.3) says, "The Lord was pleased to make . . . the covenant of grace; wherein He freely offereth unto sinners life and salvation by Jesus Christ; requiring of them faith in Him, that they may be saved."[71]

The free offer of the gospel expresses God's sincere desire for sinners to repent and be saved. Another relevant meaning of the word *offer* is "to declare one's readiness or willingness."[72] The Word reveals the goodness of God to all people. God "is kind unto the unthankful and to the evil"

65. Acts 2:38; 8:19–20; 10:45, 47; 11:17.
66. *Reformed Confessions*, 1:365–66.
67. *Reformed Confessions*, 1:397–98.
68. *The Three Forms of Unity*, 143. On the meaning of *offero* in the Canons of Dort and other Reformed orthodox writings, see R. Scott Clark, "Janus, the Well-Meant Offer of the Gospel, and Westminster Theology," in *The Pattern of Sound Doctrine: Systematic Theology at the Westminster Seminaries, Essays in Honor of Robert B. Strimple*, ed. David VanDrunen (Phillipsburg, NJ: P&R, 2004), 169–73.
69. *Reformed Confessions*, 4:357. See also Q. 86 on "faith in Jesus Christ" (4:365).
70. *Reformed Confessions*, 4:312.
71. *Reformed Confessions*, 4:242–43.
72. *Merriam-Webster's Collegiate Dictionary*, s.v. "offer."

because of his "merciful" character (Luke 6:35–36; cf. Matt. 5:44–48).[73] When the gospel comes to people, he expresses his good desires for them in saying, "O that there were such an heart in them, that they would fear me, and keep all my commandments always, that it might be well with them, and with their children for ever!" (Deut. 5:29).

In Ezekiel 18:23, we read, "Have I any pleasure at all that the wicked should die? saith the Lord GOD: and not that he should return from his ways, and live?" The words "have I any pleasure at all" render a grammatical construction that repeats the same Hebrew root for emphasis. Calvin said, "God desires nothing more earnestly than that those who were perishing and rushing to destruction should return into the way of safety. . . . And this is the knowledge of salvation, to embrace his mercy which he offers us in Christ."[74] This is a revelation of the heart of God. Johannes Polyander said, "The impelling cause [of the gospel call], whereby God is moved internally by himself, is God's grace, his good pleasure and favorably-inclined will to offer, in Christ, his salvation to wretched sinners."[75]

Does this teaching overthrow the Reformed doctrine of election? Herman Hoeksema said that to teach a "general love of God and desire to save sinners" is "Arminianism and Pelagianism."[76] There is some tension in the Bible at this point, but no surrender of the doctrines of sovereign grace. In one sense, God desires all men to repent. In another sense, he desires to punish the wicked, and he sometimes gives them up to a hard and unrepentant heart. When Eli corrected his wicked sons, the Scriptures say that they did not listen and repent "because the LORD would slay them" (1 Sam. 2:25). Literally the verse says the Lord "was pleased to cause them to die," using the same verb translated as "please" (*khapets*) as is used in Ezekiel 18:23.

Therefore, one text says that God is not pleased that sinners do not repent and so die; another text says that some sinners did not repent because God was pleased that they should die. How can we understand both of these texts together?

The answer lies in the manifold and complex display of God's goodness to fallen sinners. God's gracious character shows itself in his goodness and compassion to all his creation (Ps. 145:8–9). Therefore, he calls all who

73. See chap. 2.
74. Calvin, *Commentaries*, on Ezek. 18:23.
75. Polyander, Walaeus, Thysius, and Rivetus, *Synopsis Purioris Theologiae*, 30.12 (2:213).
76. Hoeksema, *A Triple Breach in the Foundation of the Reformed Truth*, 32.

hear the gospel to repent and live, and desires that they do so. As John Murray said, "The full and free offer of the gospel is a grace bestowed upon all. Such grace is necessarily a manifestation of love or lovingkindness in the heart of God."[77] However, God is also the sovereign and righteous King (vv. 13, 17). He is free to work as he sees fit (115:3) and always works consistently with his righteousness (33:4–5). The same goodness by which he delights in mercy (Mic. 7:18) is that by which he delights in justice (Jer. 9:24). In his sovereign freedom, he has chosen to be good to all people in temporal blessings, to graciously call many people to eternal joy, and to actually save only some (Matt. 22:14). He is patient and good to many in this life whom he has destined for destruction for their sins (Rom. 2:4–5; 9:22). This is the doctrine of reprobation.[78]

Moïse Amyraut (1596–1664) misunderstood this to indicate two wills in God,[79] but Calvin spoke more wisely when he said that "his will is one and simple; but since our minds do not penetrate the abyss of secret election, in accommodation to the capacity of our weakness, the will of God is exhibited to us in two ways."[80] Francis Turretin explained, "Now in calling God indeed shows that he wills the salvation of the called by the will of precept and good pleasure (*euarestias*), but not by the will of decree.... It teaches what is pleasing and acceptable to God and in accordance with his own nature (namely, that the called should come to him); but not what he himself has determined to do concerning man."[81] Therefore, we do not preach a two-faced God or a God of duplicity, but one God whose wisdom and will are infinitely beyond our understanding (Rom. 11:33–34), knowable only in part and then by his revelation alone.[82] God's purpose is not to confuse us but to assure us that he gladly receives every repentant sinner (Luke 15) and to call us to praise him for our salvation, for it is entirely of his gracious will (Eph. 1:3–6).

77. *Collected Writings of John Murray*, 4 vols. (Edinburgh: Banner of Truth, 1982), 4:132. This article (pp. 113–32) was a committee report authored by Murray for the General Assembly of the Orthodox Presbyterian Church. It is available at http://www.opc.org/GA/free_offer.html.

78. On God's good delight in repentance and retribution, see *RST*, 1:845–46. On reprobation, see *RST*, 1:989–97.

79. On Amyraldianism, see *RST*, 1:1024, 1026.

80. Calvin, *Commentaries*, on Matt. 23:37. On Calvin and Amyraut's misinterpretation of him, see Muller, *Calvin and the Reformed Tradition*, 107–25.

81. Turretin, *Institutes*, 15.2.15 (2:507). On God's preceptive will and decretive will, see *RST*, 1:764–67.

82. On the importance of recognizing the vast difference between God's theology (archetypal) and our theology (ectypal) as image bearers, particularly our theology as pilgrims on earth who have not arrived, see Clark, "Well-Meant Offer," in *The Pattern of Sound Doctrine*, ed. VanDrunen, 149–68, 174–79.

The combination of human responsibility, divine sovereignty, and the free offer of the gospel appears most beautifully in Jesus Christ, the perfect Image of God. The Lord Jesus Christ said of the Jews in Jerusalem who would soon kill him, "How often would I have gathered [you] together, even as a hen gathereth her chickens under her wings, and ye would not" (Matt. 23:37). Both occurrences of "would" translate the same Greek verb (*thelō*), which means to desire, to will, or to decide.[83] Christ was willing, but they were not willing.

Again, Christ said to a group of Jews, "These things I say, that ye might be saved" (John 5:34). The grammatical syntax (*hina* plus a subjunctive verb) indicates purpose. Hence, the Son of God made known his desire and the intention behind the message he communicated: that those who heard him would come to him by faith and have eternal life (v. 24)—though they were not willing to do so (v. 40). Christ's words clarify matters for everyone who hears the gospel. Jesus wants them to be saved by faith in him; if they are unsaved, it is because of their unwillingness to come to him.[84]

Similarly, in Matthew 11 we hear that Christ condemned the cities of Galilee for their rejection of the gospel and called everyone who was burdened to come to him and find rest (Matt. 11:20–24, 28–30). Yet sandwiched between these declarations of human responsibility and the free offer, we read that God has hidden the truth from some people according to his good pleasure, and that no one can know the Father except those to whom Christ chooses to reveal him (vv. 25–27). The Lord Jesus shows us that man's responsibility for his sins, God's sovereignty in saving whom he chooses, and the free offer of the gospel belong together.

The Canons of Dort (Head 1, Art. 5) say, "The cause or guilt of this unbelief, as well as of all other sins, is no wise in God, but in man himself; whereas faith in Jesus Christ and salvation through Him is the free gift of God."[85] Calvin said,

> If we see and acknowledge, therefore, the principle on which the doctrine of the Gospel offers salvation to all, the whole sacred matter is settled at once. That the Gospel is, in its nature, able to save all I by no means deny. But the great question lies here: Did the Lord by His

83. *TDNT*, 3:44–46.
84. Willard, *A Compleat Body of Divinity*, 438. On John 5:34, see Samuel E. Waldron, *The Crux of the Free Offer of the Gospel* (Greenbrier, AR: Free Grace Press, 2019), 19–34.
85. *The Three Forms of Unity*, 121.

eternal counsel *ordain* salvation for *all men?* It is quite manifest that all men, without difference or distinction, are *outwardly called* or invited to repentance and faith. It is equally evident that the same Mediator is set forth before all, as He who alone can reconcile them to the Father. . . . The mercy of God is offered equally to those who believe and to those who believe not, so that those who are not divinely taught within are only rendered inexcusable, not saved.[86]

The Motivations for Missions and Evangelism

Reformed Christianity is a missionary faith because the Bible is a missionary book. The gospel proclaims the mission of Christ to save the world and the mission of the church to preach the gospel to the world (John 3:16–17; 17:18; 20:21). The Canons of Dort (Head 1, Art. 3), citing Romans 10:14–15, say, "That men may be brought to believe, God mercifully sends the messengers of these most joyful tidings to whom He will and at what time He pleaseth; by whose ministry men are called to repentance and faith in Christ crucified."[87]

The gospel should not be preached with limitations on whom it calls, and neither should sinners try to discern whether they are chosen by God before coming to Christ. The Canons (Head 2, Art. 5) say, "Moreover, the promise of the gospel is, that whosoever believeth in Christ crucified, shall not perish, but have everlasting life. This promise, together with the command to repent and believe, ought to be declared and published to all nations, and to all persons promiscuously [without restriction or discrimination] and without distinction, to whom God out of His good pleasure sends the gospel."[88]

The sound doctrines of the Holy Scriptures give us powerful motives to engage in the costly work of missions and evangelism. They include:

- *The universality of original sin.* All mankind lies under the dreadful darkness of corruption, sin, alienation from God, and enmity toward him (Rom. 3:10–12; 8:7).
- *The despondency of the human condition.* Human beings are in a hopeless condition without Jesus Christ, dead in their sins and under God's wrath (Eph. 2:1–3, 12).

86. John Calvin, *On Eternal Predestination*, in *Reformed Confessions*, 1:751, emphasis original.
87. *The Three Forms of Unity*, 120–21.
88. *The Three Forms of Unity*, 135.

- *The reality of God's love.* Even though the world hates God and Christ, God still loved the world so much that he sent his Son to save sinners (John 3:16–19).
- *The insufficiency of general revelation.* Though God's creation reveals his glory, it is only the word of the Lord that saves souls (Psalm 19; Rom. 1:16, 20).
- *The indispensability of the blood of Christ.* There is only one Mediator between God and man: Jesus Christ, who gave himself as a ransom for all (1 Tim. 2:5–6).
- *The necessity of faith in Jesus Christ.* Christ's death does not save people automatically, but they must hear of him, believe him, and call upon his name (Rom. 10:13–15).
- *The authority of the risen Lord.* Christ rose with all authority; his commission impels and authorizes the church to make disciples of all nations (Matt. 28:19–20).
- *The urgency of the times.* Sinners must seek the Lord while he may be found; today is the day of salvation, but the day will come to an end (Isa. 55:6; 2 Cor. 6:2).
- *The sovereignty of God's grace.* While we are powerless to change sinners, the Lord can make the dead come to life so that our labors are not in vain (2 Cor. 3:5; Eph. 2:4–5).
- *The ultimacy of the glory of God.* God will be glorified in the salvation and damnation of men, and his glory is our highest love and aim (Rom. 9:22–24; 11:36).

What great reasons we have to bring the gospel to all nations! Let us therefore give our time, energy, money, skills, children, and our very lives to bring the gospel to the world.

Furthermore, we must not only preach the gospel, but we must pray for the raising up and empowerment of gospel preachers (Matt. 9:38; Eph. 6:19–20) and for the conversion of lost sinners (Rom. 10:1). The Reformers and Puritans taught Christians to pour out their earnest prayers for the propagation of the gospel and the advance of Christ's kingdom in all nations, for the conversion of the Jews, and for the fullness of the Gentiles to be brought in.[89] Let us give ourselves with all diligence so that the gospel call may go out to sinners and the effectual call may bring elect sinners to Christ by a living faith.

89. See Beeke and Jones, *A Puritan Theology*, 761–69.

Sing to the Lord

The Call to the Nations

O sing a new song to the Lord, sing all the earth to God;
In daily praises bless His Name and tell His grace abroad.
Among the nations far and wide His glory celebrate;
To all the peoples of the earth His wondrous works relate.

The Lord is great above all gods, let glad hosannas rise;
The heathen gods are idols vain; Jehovah made the skies.
Great honor is before His face, and majesty divine;
Within His holy dwelling-place both strength and beauty shine.

Let all the peoples of the earth give glory to the Lord,
Give Him the glory due His name and strength to Him accord;
With offerings come ye to His courts, in holy beauty bow,
Let all the earth with reverence come and serve Jehovah now.

To all the nations of the earth the blessed tidings bring;
Tell all the world Jehovah reigns, the universal King.
The world shall therefore stand unmoved, established by His might;
And just is He to judge the wrong and vindicate the right.

Let heaven and earth and sounding sea to Him glad tribute bring;
Let field and wood and all therein before Jehovah sing;
For, lo, He comes to judge the earth, and all the world shall see
His everlasting faithfulness, His truth and equity.

Psalm 96
Tune: St. Leonard
The Psalter, No. 257

Questions for Meditation or Discussion

1. What are the various senses in which theologians speak about God's "call" to salvation?
2. Why is the gospel call important?
3. For each of the following characteristics of the gospel call, give a brief explanation of its meaning and scriptural basis:
   - scriptural
   - official

- evangelical
- judicial
- general
- merciful
- resistible
- sacrificial
- successful

4. What three things form the basic contents of the gospel call?
5. How do some people use the free and sincere offer of the gospel to try to refute the sovereignty of God's saving grace? How can we answer them?
6. How do other people use the sovereignty of God's saving grace to try to refute the free and sincere offer of the gospel? How can their charge be answered?
7. What motivations does the Bible provide for missions and evangelism?
8. How could the truths taught in this chapter increase your personal motivation to practice and support evangelism? How will you make use of those truths to grow in this way?

Questions for Deeper Reflection

9. Someone says that Christ offers salvation only to those convicted that they are sinners and burdened by their sins (Matt. 9:13; 11:28). How would you answer him? What is the meaning of those statements by our Lord, and what is their implication for the free offer of the gospel?
10. What lessons can preachers learn from the nine characteristics of the gospel call listed in this chapter? Write them in the form of a guide for how the church can pray for its pastors, and then use that guide in your regular prayers.

13

General Calling, Part 2

Preparatory Grace and the Spirit of Conviction

In the gospel, the Lord calls out, "Ho, every one that thirsteth, come ye to the waters, and he that hath no money; come ye, buy, and eat; yea, come, buy wine and milk without money and without price" (Isa. 55:1). The free and full offer of Christ and his grace goes out to all who hear the good news of the Holy Scriptures. Jesus says, "Come unto me, all ye that labour and are heavy laden, and I will give you rest" (Matt. 11:28).

What, however, are these references to the thirsty, the poor without money, and those who are weary and burdened? They do not speak of qualifications or worthiness, but of need and helplessness. Christ said, "They that are whole need not a physician; but they that are sick. I came not to call the righteous, but sinners to repentance" (Luke 5:31–32). Jesus was not saying that he limits his calls to certain people—as if some are righteous and do not need him—but that his call addresses men as sinners, and only those convinced of their sin will respond.

Reformed and Puritan writers of the sixteenth through the eighteenth centuries regularly spoke of this matter as part of their treatment of spiritual experience. William Perkins said, "No man can heartily say, 'I believe Jesus Christ to be my Savior,' before he feel that in himself he is utterly lost and castaway without His help."[1] John Preston (1587–1628) said, "We preach Christ generally unto all, that whosoever will, may receive Christ, but men will not receive him—till they be humbled, they think they stand in no need of Christ."[2]

In this chapter, we will explore the doctrine of preparatory grace, the common operation of the Holy Spirit to awaken sinners to their need for Christ. A balanced view of preparatory grace is necessary to avoid legalism, reject all human merit in salvation, and appreciate that salvation is by the work of the Holy Spirit from beginning to end.

A Definition of the Doctrine and Dangers of Its Distortion

What is preparatory grace? It is God's work to show unbelievers their sin and need for Christ. We may define it as follows: preparatory grace is a common yet supernatural operation of the Holy Spirit upon unbelievers through the Word of God by which he illuminates the mind and convicts the conscience. By this common grace, the Spirit prepares a person to rationally consider the gospel and his need for salvation. Preparatory grace often produces temporary effects in a person's beliefs, affections, and actions, but not so that the person exercises the smallest degree of justifying faith, pleasing submission to God's will, or holy love. This preparation does not merit salvation in any way or give certain hope of salvation. Rather, the person prepared by God is more aware of his need for salvation by the grace of God in Jesus Christ.

We call this conviction *grace* because it is a mercy to sinners who deserve to be given over to total blindness and hardness.[3] We call it *preparatory* grace because it ordinarily precedes regeneration but does not necessarily lead to regeneration, for it is one of the common operations of the Holy Spirit. As we discuss preparation, we must bear in mind that "the soul in one moment passes from death to life," but that "some are converted in a very gradual fashion," as Wilhelmus à Brakel said, and that in a great variety of ways.[4]

1. Perkins, *An Exposition of the Symbol*, in *Works*, 5:101. Portions of this chapter are adapted from Joel R. Beeke and Paul M. Smalley, *Prepared by Grace, for Grace: The Puritans on God's Ordinary Way of Leading Sinners to Christ* (Grand Rapids, MI: Reformation Heritage Books, 2013). Used by permission.

2. John Preston, "Pauls Conversion. Or, The Right Way to Be Saved," in *Remaines of That Reverend and Learned Divine, John Preston* (London: for Andrew Crooke, 1634), 187.

3. On common grace, see chap. 2.

4. Brakel, *The Christian's Reasonable Service*, 2:238–39.

The doctrine of preparatory grace can be misunderstood or twisted into a kind of legalism known as *preparationism*. Charles Spurgeon vividly expressed concern about this idea by means of a fictitious spiritual physician whom he labeled "Dr. Preparation," who says, "The way to be saved is to prepare yourselves for Christ, and if you prepare yourself and make yourselves fit for Jesus Christ, then you will obtain peace."[5] Preparationism makes people think that they cannot come to Christ until they have experienced sufficient grief and humiliation over their sins—as if that makes them worthy or fit for God's grace.

We must not let the danger of preparationism become the occasion to throw out the biblical and healthy doctrine of preparatory grace. Reformed orthodox theologians carefully distinguished the two and affirmed the latter.[6] Spurgeon himself said, "Self-despair is a blessed preparation for faith in Jesus!"[7] He added,

> Many preachers of God's gospel . . . have sown on the unbroken fallow ground, and forgotten that the plough must break the clods. We have seen too much of trying to sew without the sharp needle of the Spirit's convincing power. . . . It is our duty to preach Jesus Christ even to self-righteous sinners, but it is certain that Jesus Christ will never be accepted by them while they hold themselves in high esteem. Only the sick will welcome the physician. It is the work of the Spirit of God to convince men of sin, and until they are convinced of sin, they will never be led to seek the righteousness which is of God by Jesus Christ. I am persuaded, that wherever there is a real work of grace in any soul, it begins with a pulling down.[8]

Augustinian Preparatory Grace versus Semi-Pelagian Preparation

When people criticize preparatory grace as preparationism, they often confuse the Augustinian and Reformed doctrine of preparation with that of the Roman Catholic Church in its semi-Pelagian tendencies. At the heart of Augustinianism is the belief that man is dead in sin and God's grace sovereignly and effectively changes the hearts of those he has chosen. Augustine analyzed grace as a series of steps from unbelief to glory:

5. Spurgeon, *The Metropolitan Tabernacle Pulpit*, 14:474.
6. Polyander, Walaeus, Thysius, and Rivetus, *Synopsis Purioris Theologiae*, 32.6 (2:279).
7. Spurgeon, *The Metropolitan Tabernacle Pulpit*, 45:341.
8. Spurgeon, *The Metropolitan Tabernacle Pulpit*, 17:376.

preparing grace to give a knowledge of sin, operating grace to create faith, cooperating grace to join with the renewed will to produce good works, and perfecting grace to enable perseverance.[9] God uses his law "to alarm the unrighteous, so that . . . they may in faith flee for refuge to the grace that justifies," a justification that takes place "on account of no antecedent merits of his own works."[10] Similarly, Thomas Aquinas said that man cannot prepare himself to receive grace except by the grace of God preparing him, whether that preparation takes place in an instant or step by step over time.[11]

As we have noted in our studies of predestination and human sin, Pelagianism denied that Adam's transgression brought mankind into bondage to sin and asserted that people can choose to serve God by their natural abilities. According to semi-Pelagianism, sinners can choose God only if he first helps them by grace, but he gives grace to all and leaves it to them to decide how to respond. As developed by some later medieval theologians, semi-Pelagianism issued in the idea that unregenerate sinners could attain "congruent merit" with God by doing the best they could to prepare themselves for his saving grace.[12]

The Reformers reacted strongly against the semi-Pelagian notion of preparation. John Calvin said that fallen man cannot produce the smallest impulse toward God, and free will cannot contribute any preparation for saving grace (Gen. 6:5; 8:21; John 6:44–45).[13] However, the Council of Trent rejected the Reformation, reasserted the medieval view of preparation by free will, and left the door open to the nominalist view of preconversion merit by denying that all works done before regeneration are sin. The decrees of Trent state that adults must prepare themselves for salvation by freely cooperating with "the illumination of the Holy Ghost" instead of rejecting "the prevenient grace of God."[14]

---

9. Philip Schaff, *History of the Christian Church*, 8 vols., 3rd ed. (New York: Charles Scribner's Sons, 1891), 3:849. These distinctions about grace were later appropriated by Reformed theologians. See Muller, *Dictionary of Latin and Greek Theological Terms*, 141–42.

10. Augustine, *On the Spirit and the Letter*, chap. 16, in *NPNF*[1], 5:89–90; cf. *On Grace and Free Will*, chap. 33, in *NPNF*[1], 5:458; *The Enchiridion on Faith, Hope, and Love* (Washington, DC: Regnery, 1996), chap. 32 (39); and Letter 145, in *NPNF*[1], 1:496. For more citations of Augustine on this use of the law, see Calvin, *Institutes*, 2.7.9.

11. Aquinas, *Summa Theologica*, Part 2.1, Q. 109, Art. 6; Q. 112, Art. 2.

12. On Pelagianism and semi-Pelagianism, see *RST*, 1:1003–11; 2:366–70.

13. Calvin, *Institutes*, 2.2.27; 2.3.7; *Commentaries*, on John 6:45.

14. The Canons and Decrees of the Council of Trent, Session 6, Chap. 5, and Canons 7, 9, in Philip Schaff, ed., *The Creeds of Christendom*, rev. David S. Schaff, 3 vols. (Grand Rapids, MI: Baker, 1983), 2:92, 112.

Modern Roman Catholicism continues to teach the same doctrine.[15] Since the Second Vatican Council (Vatican II), Roman Catholicism has affirmed a universal illumination of all mankind by God's grace so that even those who do not have the gospel may find salvation if they seek God and do good by the power of their free will.[16] Furthermore, as Sinclair Ferguson says, in the Roman Catholic system of salvation, not just before conversion, but "the whole *ordo* was, in fact, a preparation for a future justification," for Roman Catholicism denies a definite justification and assurance of salvation for most people in this life apart from special revelation from God.[17] The principle of *more grace for him who does what he can* permeates the Roman Catholic system from the cradle to the grave. The same principle was later affirmed by Jacob Arminius regarding cooperation with prevenient grace.[18]

Reformed and Puritan theologians have consistently repudiated this idea of preparation by free will and works of congruity.[19] The Westminster Confession of Faith (9.3) denies that man is "able, by his own strength, to convert himself, or to prepare himself thereunto (John 6:44, 65; Eph. 2:2–5; 1 Cor. 2:14; Titus 3:3–5)."[20] William Ames said that all "dispositions" in the unconverted that Roman Catholics considered "meritorious, whether out of condignity, or out of congruity . . . either only from free will, or partly also from grace, have been justly rejected." However, this does not "remove all preparatory affections and motions" by which God makes a way in sinners for conversion.[21] Calvin taught that God

15. Ludwig Ott, *Fundamentals of Catholic Dogma*, ed. James C. Bastible, trans. Patrick Lynch (Cork: Mercier, 1962), 268; *Catechism of the Catholic Church*, secs. 2001, 2002, 2009, 2010.

16. Vatican II, *Lumen Gentium*, sec. 16, http://www.vatican.va/archive/hist_councils/ii_vatican_council/documents/vat-ii_const_19641121_lumen-gentium_en.html; *Gaudium et Spes*, sec. 17, http://www.vatican.va/archive/hist_councils/ii_vatican_council/documents/vat-ii_const_19651207_gaudium-et-spes_en.html. Even Joseph Ratzinger said in 1969 that some of these statements by Vatican II are "downright Pelagian," though later as Pope Benedict XVI he stated his agreement with the conciliar document. John L. Allen Jr. *Pope Benedict XVI: A Biography of Joseph Ratzinger* (London: Continuum, 2000), 81.

17. Ferguson, *The Holy Spirit*, 131.

18. Arminius, *Apology*, Art. 17, in *Works*, 2:19–20.

19. See the Thirty-Nine Articles of the Church of England (Arts. 10, 13), in *Reformed Confessions*, 2:758; the Irish Articles (Arts. 25–26), in *Reformed Confessions*, 4:94; William Pemble, *Vindiciae Gratiae*, in *The Workes of the Late Learned Minister of God's Holy Word, Mr William Pemble*, 4th ed. (Oxford: by Henry Hall for John Adams, 1659), 56; and John Cotton, *The Way of Life, Or, Gods Way and Course, in Bringing the Soule into, and Keeping It in, and Carrying It on, in the Ways of Life and Peace* (London: by M. F. for L. Fawne and S. Gellibrand, 1641), 182–85.

20. *Reformed Confessions*, 4:246.

21. William Ames, *Praeparatione peccatoris ad conversionem*, "On the Preparation of a Sinner for Conversion," trans. Steven Dilday, theses 1–2, cited in Beeke and Smalley, *Prepared by Grace, for Grace*, 264.

"prepareth our hearts to come unto him to receive his doctrine."[22] He compared the heart to a rough piece of stone that must be made smooth before God writes his laws upon it. Calvin said, "We cannot do this of our own self-moving, but he must direct us thereto by his Holy Spirit. . . . Before men are brought to the faith . . . they have some good preparative aforehand. . . . It is God's working in their hearts, who maketh that preparation there by the grace of his Holy Spirit."[23]

William G. T. Shedd (1820–1894) said, "The term 'preparative' as used by the Augustinian and Calvinist, is very different from its use by the Semi-Pelagian and Arminian. The former means by it, conviction of sin, guilt, and helplessness. . . . In the Semi-Pelagian use, a 'preparative' denotes some faint desires and beginnings of holiness in the natural man."[24]

Similarly, Herman Bavinck noted that "one can speak of 'preparatory grace' in a sound sense."[25]

The Biblical Doctrine of Preparatory Grace

The doctrine of preparatory grace teaches that the Holy Spirit often works in a supernatural but nonsaving manner through the Word to illuminate minds and convict consciences so that people, as rational but corrupt bearers of God's image, begin to consider the gospel of Christ.

The Word, the Spirit, and Common Grace

Preparatory grace is common grace, an influence of the Holy Spirit through God's Word that does not in itself save sinners. In the parable of the sower, our Lord Jesus Christ taught that the Word of God may have effects on men's souls without producing the fruit of saving conversion (Mark 4:3–9).[26] According to Christ's interpretation of the parable, the broad sowing of seed illustrates the proclamation of the gospel to all who hear the Word of God, and there are various responses to that offer.[27] From a farmer's perspective, the sole purpose of sowing seed is to produce a harvest, and therefore, the three cases of fruitless-

22. John Calvin, *Sermons on Deuteronomy* (1583; facsimile repr., Edinburgh: Banner of Truth, 1987), 423.
23. Calvin, *Sermons on Deuteronomy*, 422.
24. William G. T. Shedd, *Dogmatic Theology*, 2 vols. (New York: Charles Scribner's Sons, 1888), 2:511–12.
25. Bavinck, *Reformed Dogmatics*, 4:39.
26. Polyander, Walaeus, Thysius, and Rivetus, *Synopsis Purioris Theologiae*, 30.34–38 (2:223).
27. James A. Brooks, *Mark*, The New American Commentary 23 (Nashville: Broadman & Holman, 1991), 79.

ness must be understood to mean that these people did not partake of the kingdom of God and were not saved from the coming judgment.[28] In some people's hearts, the sower's labors bear fruit (v. 20), and a potentially hundredfold harvest indicates God's supernatural blessing (Gen 26:12).[29] However, despite the opposition of Satan, the hardness of men's hearts, and the temptations of the world, the Word still has an influence upon the lives of some who remain unsaved, which Jesus pictured as seed that germinates and produces a plant but no fruit (Mark 4:16–19). This influence includes a temporary profession of faith with joy (v. 16) in contrast to a complete lack of interest and understanding (Matt. 13:19).

Christ also taught that the Holy Spirit may act upon people in a way that temporarily delivers from Satan's influences in some measure but does not save them. Christ told the parable of an unclean spirit that goes out of a man and later returns with seven other spirits (Matt. 12:43–45). In the context, the departure of an evil spirit is caused by Christ's powerful work through the Holy Spirit (v. 28). While wandering, the unclean spirit still refers to the person as "my house" (v. 44), indicating that the person is not yet delivered by Christ from Satan's kingdom (v. 29). The condition of such people is linked to the following parable of the sower by Christ's statement that their nature must be changed to produce good "fruit" (v. 33). Though this parable especially illustrates deliverance from demonic possession, Jesus applied its message broadly to "this wicked generation" (v. 45), the many people in Israel who had experienced his ministry of word and deed by the Spirit (vv. 41–42). Great crowds had been attracted to Jesus (13:1), and no doubt he had influenced them in various ways, but they had not become obedient members of God's family (12:50). When Christ taught in Jerusalem, "the common people [*ho polus ochlos*, literally the great crowd] heard him gladly" (Mark 12:37), but a short time later "the people" (*ho ochlos*) cried out for his crucifixion (15:11–14).

We conclude that Christ works among sinners with two effects, both produced by the Word and Spirit but with distinct results. The first

28. Craig L. Blomberg, *Interpreting the Parables*, 2nd ed. (Downers Grove, IL: IVP Academic, 2012), 289, 294. Christ used a lack of "fruit" to illustrate this very truth in other sayings (Matt. 7:17–20; 12:33–37; 21:43; Luke 13:1–9; John 15:5–6, 8).

29. James R. Edwards, *The Gospel according to Mark*, The Pillar New Testament Commentary (Grand Rapids, MI: Eerdmans, 2002), 129. A good harvest in ancient Palestine was probably ten or twentyfold. Brooks, *Mark*, 79.

temporarily reduces Satan's influence, restrains sin, and creates a kind of short-term openness to God's Word, but does not save. The second brings people to a new kingdom, nature, family, and fruitfulness.

We find a similar teaching, also using agricultural images, in Hebrews 6:4–8, a classic text on the apostasy of professing Christians.[30] Some people have been "enlightened" or illuminated by the influences of the Word and the Holy Spirit (vv. 4–5). Yet they are like land that receives the rain, but instead of producing a good harvest, bears only "thorns and briers" and will be burned under God's curse (vv. 7–8). However, others respond with the fruit of genuine Christian love, the "things that belong to salvation" (vv. 9–10 ESV).

Therefore, in addition to the saving works of the Spirit, there are "common operations of the Spirit."[31] They are called "common," Brakel said, "because the elect and the impenitent are partakers of them."[32] Spurgeon said that the Spirit of God works in two ways upon the soul: he provides grace that effectively saves forever or grace that places temporary restraint on the sins of depraved men so that they tremble at the Word. This is no insult to God's power. Just as a strong man need not use all his physical power but merely may touch something with his finger, so the omnipotent Spirit may work in a manner that men may resist insofar as he wills.[33]

The Romans Road: The Law, the Gospel, and the Spirit

Paul's epistle to the Romans presents "the gospel of God" with crystalline clarity (Rom. 1:1). Before Paul expounds the good news, he spends a significant part of his epistle on the bad news: sixty-four verses on wrath, sin, darkness, depravity, hypocrisy, and judgment (Rom. 1:18–3:20). Why does Paul not go straight to Christ and his grace? We find the answer in Paul's transitional statement from his treatment of wrath to his treatment of grace:

> Now we know that what things soever the law saith, it saith to them who are under the law: that every mouth may be stopped,

30. On this text and the doctrine of the perseverance of the saints, see chaps. 30–31.
31. The Westminster Confession of Faith (10.4) and Larger Catechism (Q. 68), in *Reformed Confessions*, 4:247, 312.
32. Brakel, *The Christian's Reasonable Service*, 2:240.
33. C. H. Spurgeon, *The New Park Street Pulpit*, 6 vols. (repr., Pasadena, TX: Pilgrim, 1975), 4:53.

> and all the world may become guilty before God. Therefore by the deeds of the law there shall no flesh be justified in his sight: for by the law is the knowledge of sin. But now the righteousness of God without the law is manifested, being witnessed by the law and the prophets; even the righteousness of God which is by faith of Jesus Christ. (Rom. 3:19–22)

Paul presents the law in order that people may know that God is righteous in his judgment ("every mouth may be stopped . . . before God," cf. Rom. 3:4–5), they have sinned against God ("the knowledge of sin," cf. vv. 9–10), and they cannot be "justified in his sight" by obedience to the law (cf. 2:12–13). R. C. Sproul wrote, "The law has the capacity to bring inward conviction, dread, guilt and shame . . . as such the law functions as a forerunner of Christ, preparing for the reception of the good news of the gospel."[34] Bavinck said, "The gospel always presupposes the law and also needs it in its administration."[35]

The use of the law to humble sinners is an important part of Reformed experiential Christianity. Calvin said, "Because they are too full of their own virtue or of the assurance of their own righteousness, they are not fit to receive Christ's grace unless they first be emptied. Therefore, through the recognition of their own misery, the law brings them down to humility in order thus to prepare them to seek what previously they did not realize they lacked."[36] Johannes Wollebius wrote, "The law is that teaching, by which God has shown what he wants done by us . . . in order that we, knowing that we cannot satisfy his demands upon us, may be led to seek Christ."[37] The Westminster Larger Catechism (Q. 95–96) summarizes this use of the law as follows:

> Q. Of what use is the moral law to all men?
> A. The moral law is of use to all men, to inform them of the holy nature and will of God (Lev. 11:44–45; 20:7–8; Rom. 7:12), and of their duty, binding them to walk accordingly (Mic. 6:8; James 2:10–11); to convince them of their disability to keep it, and of the sinful pollution of their nature, hearts, and lives (Ps. 19:11–12;

34. R. C. Sproul, *The Gospel of God: An Exposition of Romans* (Fearn, Ross-shire, Scotland: Christian Focus, 1994), 72; cf. Charles Hodge, *Commentary on the Epistle to the Romans*, rev. ed. (Philadelphia: Alfred Martien, 1873), 133.
35. Bavinck, *Reformed Dogmatics*, 4:454.
36. Calvin, *Institutes*, 2.7.11.
37. Wollebius, *Compendium*, 13(1).4 (75).

> Rom. 3:20; 7:7): to humble them in the sense of their sin and misery (Rom. 3:9, 23), and thereby help them to a clearer sight of the need they have of Christ (Gal. 3:21–22), and of the perfection of his obedience (Rom. 10:4).
>
> Q. What particular use is there of the moral law to unregenerate men?
> A. The moral law is of use to unregenerate men, to awaken their consciences to flee from the wrath to come (1 Tim. 1:9–10), and to drive them to Christ (Gal. 3:24); or, upon their continuance in the estate and way of sin, to leave them inexcusable (Rom. 1:20; 2:15), and under the curse thereof (Gal. 3:10).[38]

Paul returns to the subject of the law later in Romans, where he says that we must not accuse God's law of being evil, for it is holy, just, and good—again vindicating God from the accusations of the wicked (Rom. 7:7–13). The law functions to reveal the great sinfulness of sin, corruption so deep that when confronted by God's law it rebels even more. Thus, the law produces death, though God ordained it for life (cf. 10:5), because it causes sinners who formerly lived in complacency to taste something of the death coming upon them for their sins.

John Flavel said that Paul teaches us two key truths in Romans about the law of God: he is "denying to it a power to justify us," but he is also "ascribing to it a power to convince us, and so prepare us for Christ."[39] Flavel believed such legal preparation was necessary because "unregenerate persons are generally full of groundless confidence and cheerfulness, though their condition be sad and miserable."[40]

It may be asked how the law can be effective for such a task when so many people who know God's law live complacently in hypocrisy (Rom. 2:1, 17–24). How did the law have such an impact on Paul? He had lived as a self-righteous Pharisee all his life (Acts 22:3; Phil. 3:6), but Paul writes of a change in his experience: formerly he was "alive without the law," but then "the commandment came . . . and I died" (Rom. 7:9). The best explanation is that the Holy Spirit applied the law in a powerful way to Paul's unconverted heart. Though Paul opposes the dominion of the law over the wicked to the new life of the Spirit (vv. 1–6), he also affirms

38. *Reformed Confessions*, 4:319–20.
39. Flavel, *The Method of Grace*, in *Works*, 2:287.
40. Flavel, *The Method of Grace*, in *Works*, 2:288.

that "the law is spiritual" (v. 14)—that is, produced and energized by the Holy Spirit.[41]

It is possible that Paul is referring to this convicting operation of the Spirit in Romans 8:15, where he says, "For ye have not received the spirit of bondage again to fear; but ye have received the Spirit of adoption, whereby we cry, Abba, Father." Many modern interpreters view "the spirit of bondage" not as the Holy Spirit, but as a human "spirit" or as a rhetorical device to contrast slavery to the reception of the Spirit by the sons of God.[42] However, the Puritans commonly interpreted the phrase to refer to the work of the Holy Spirit prior to conversion. Ames said, "Some servile fear is a gift of the Holy Spirit; as nearly all interpreters gather from Romans 8:15, 'the spirit of bondage again to fear.'"[43] As Thomas Goodwin noted, it is unlikely that the "spirit of bondage" refers specifically to Israel's bondage under the law, for many of the Roman believers were Gentiles (1:14–16); or that it refers to natural conscience, for it is something "received," and it is not received by the children of God, who may indeed still have an accusing conscience.[44] Thus, he concludes that this phrase refers to an operation of the Holy Spirit. Other arguments for this interpretation include: (1) the word *spirit* is used in Romans 8 only once for the human spirit (v. 16), but repeatedly for the Holy Spirit; (2) the parallel "Spirit of adoption" is the Holy Spirit, as the parallel with Galatians 4:6 shows; (3) the word *again* implies that people generally do experience this fearful bondage before God adopts them as his children; (4) such bondage is not identical with slavery to sin because that is a willing slavery (Rom. 6:15–23), whereas this is a bondage "to fear"; (5) fearful bondage is an apt way to describe the experience of death under the law of which Paul writes (7:7–13); (6) as we already noted, Paul associates the law with the Spirit (7:14); and (7) other Scripture passages associate the Spirit with powerful conviction of sin.[45]

Therefore, the moral law of God prepares sinners for the gospel by revealing his righteousness as Lawgiver and Judge, their guilt before God

41. Fee, *God's Empowering Presence*, 509–10; and Hodge, *Commentary on the Epistle to the Romans*, 358.

42. Fee, *God's Empowering Presence*, 565; Murray, *The Epistle to the Romans*, 1:296–97; and Douglas J. Moo, *The Epistle to the Romans*, The New International Commentary on the New Testament (Grand Rapids, MI: Eerdmans, 1996), 500.

43. Ames, "Preparation of a Sinner," thesis 12, cited in Beeke and Smalley, *Prepared by Grace, for Grace*, 266; cf. Brown, *Systematic Theology*, 252.

44. Goodwin, *The Work of the Holy Ghost in Our Salvation*, in *Works*, 6:363.

45. Mic. 3:8; John 16:8; Acts 2:4, 37; 7:54–55.

as sinners, and the impossibility of saving themselves by good works. In this function, the law is spiritual, inspired and applied by the Holy Spirit to awaken sinners, silence the enemies of God, and stir up a sense of need for salvation by the righteousness of another. Though the law and wrath of God are often omitted from evangelistic presentations, they are in fact the first part of the Romans road to salvation.

The Spirit of Preparation and Conviction in the Gospels and Acts

We find another strand of biblical evidence for preparatory grace in the history of God's dealings with mankind. The Lord testified through the centuries against Israel's sins through his Spirit (Neh. 9:30; Ezek. 3:24–27), yet the people resisted the Spirit and persecuted the prophets through whom he spoke (Acts 7:51–52). The greatest of the prophets was John the Baptist, a man filled with the Holy Spirit from his mother's womb to be like a second Elijah who would confront the people for their covenant breaking (Luke 1:15–17; 7:28). Through John, the Spirit prepared the way for the Lord Jesus. John threatened the coming of God's wrath, called sinners to repentance, and gave them specific rebukes for sins peculiar to their various callings in life (3:3, 7–18). Jesus came to seek and save the lost (19:10), but the Spirit saw fit to prepare the lost for the Savior by a messenger of law and judgment. Theologians have seen John's ministry of preaching not only as a step in God's plan for Israel's history but as a model for how God typically works to prepare people to receive the Lord Jesus Christ.[46]

The Gospels explicitly highlight the *preparatory* quality of John's ministry through their citation of Isaiah 40:3–5, which begins, "The voice of him that crieth in the wilderness, Prepare ye the way of the LORD."[47] They also cite Malachi 3:1, "Behold, I will send my messenger, and he shall prepare the way before me."[48] The context in Isaiah 40 instructs us about the nature of this preparation. Isaiah 40:6–8 compares fallen mankind ("flesh") to grass that withers "because the spirit of the LORD bloweth upon it," but "the word of our God shall stand for ever." The Spirit comes to address not only man's mortality but his morality: the "flower" that fades under the Spirit's blowing is man's "goodliness," literally his

46. Preston, "Pauls Conversion," in *Remaines*, 185; Sargent Bush Jr., ed., *The Correspondence of John Cotton* (Chapel Hill: University of North Carolina Press, 2001), 111–12; Goodwin, *The Work of the Holy Ghost in Our Salvation*, in *Works*, 6:362–63; *The Dutch Annotations upon the Whole Bible*, on Isa. 40:4, 6; Matt. 11:12; and Edwards, *Religious Affections*, in *WJE*, 2:154–55.

47. Cited in Matt. 3:3; Mark 1:3; Luke 3:4–6; John 1:23.

48. Cited in Matt. 11:10; Mark 1:2; Luke 7:27.

"faithful love" (*khesed*). God would not wither authentic love in man; the picture is of a false, superficial love that has no endurance.[49] This image of a hot, withering wind is particularly striking because Isaiah compared the salvation brought by the Spirit to waters poured out on the desert to make it blossom and bear fruit (32:15–17; 44:1–5). Alec Motyer said that the Spirit is both "the Lord, and giver of life" and "the Lord, and giver of death" through "divine judgment."[50] Next we hear the call to preach good news because the Good Shepherd is coming (40:9–10). Therefore, the order in which God brings comfort to his people (vv. 1–2) is to prepare them by the flesh-withering preaching of the Word in the power of the Spirit of judgment, and then to renew them with the good news.

The power and limitations of preparatory grace are illustrated in John's effect on Herod Antipas. Mark 6:20 says, "For Herod feared John, knowing that he was a just man and an holy, and observed him; and when he heard him, he did many things,[51] and heard him gladly." The Spirit-filled life and preaching of John thus produced respect, fear, a kind of joy in hearing the word, and some religious actions in a wealthy ruler. Charles Hodge noted that the general operations of the Spirit may produce in sinners a "conviction of the truth" about God and his Word, a "conviction of sin" and man's "entire helplessness" to save himself, and a "joy" and "temporary faith" in the Word, which mindset "often leads to reformation, and to an externally religious life."[52] However, in Herod's case, it did not result in repentance, and Herod murdered John in order to appease his wife and impress his colleagues (vv. 21–28).

When the Lord Jesus came, he was anointed with the power of the Holy Spirit to preach good news to the poor and brokenhearted (Luke 4:14, 18). He called sinners to come to him and find life and peace (Matt. 11:28; John 7:37). Yet his preaching of the gospel contained a large amount of law and wrath as well. He who offered the living water to the Samaritan woman also said, "Go, call thy husband," in order to convict her of her immorality (John 4:14–18). Christ's Sermon on the Mount not only declares God's

49. Cf. Hos. 6:4, "Your goodness [*khesed*] is as a morning cloud, and as the early dew it goeth away."

50. Motyer, *The Prophecy of Isaiah*, 301.

51. Some translations read "he was greatly perplexed" instead of "he did many things," reflecting the textual variant *ēporei* instead of *epoiei*. The former reading is attested only by Aleph, B, family 13, and a few other manuscripts; the latter has strong attestation in A, C, D, family 1, and the vast majority of manuscripts. The reading "perplexed" may have arisen by assimilation with *diēporei* in Luke 9:7.

52. Hodge, *Systematic Theology*, 2:671–73.

blessing and instructs the faithful in pleasing their Father, but also exposes the sins of the heart, religious hypocrisy, and worldly materialism as liable to the divine judgment of hellfire (Matthew 5–7). Christ excoriated the scribes and Pharisees, and said that they were sons of hell (Matthew 23). We would not present an imbalanced view of Christ's life and ministry, which was full of mercy to sinners (Luke 15). However, we must not overlook his efforts to expose sin and awaken a fear of divine judgment.

Jesus said, "Thou art not far from the kingdom of God" to a man who understood that to love the Lord with all one's heart and one's neighbor as oneself is much more important than outward ceremonies of worship (Mark 12:32–34). There is such a vast gap between spiritual death and life that conversion is impossible apart from God's supernatural grace (10:26–27). However, a person is more subjectively prepared for conversion when he loses his satisfaction with outward religion and realizes the depth of what God's law demands. A superficial view of the law leads to a damning confidence in man's goodness (vv. 17–20).

When the Lord Jesus prepared his disciples for his return to the Father, he promised that their witness to him would be accompanied by the witness of the Holy Spirit (John 15:26–27). He explained the Spirit's testimony to the hostile world as follows: "When he is come, he will reprove the world of sin, and of righteousness, and of judgment: of sin, because they believe not on me; of righteousness, because I go to my Father, and ye see me no more; of judgment, because the prince of this world is judged" (16:8–11). The word translated as "reprove" (*elenchō*) could also be rendered as "expose," "convince," or "convict"; it means "to show someone his sin."[53] This conviction is not the universal operation of natural conscience, but the exposure of sin and Satan that accompanies the preaching of the gospel of Christ.[54] Graham Cole writes, "The world is on trial. The Holy Spirit will continue the prosecution begun by Jesus."[55] In conviction, judgment day draws near. Jonathan Edwards said, "When sinners are the subjects of great convictions of conscience, and a remarkable work of the law; 'tis only a transacting the business of the day of judgment, in the conscience beforehand."[56]

53. *TDNT*, 2:474. The article adds, "and to summon him to repentance," but notes that it can be used with respect to judgment day (Jude 15), where there is no call to repentance, but a conviction unto a sentence of punishment.

54. Regarding John 16:8–11, see the work of the Paraclete as discussed in chap. 5.

55. Cole, *He Who Gives Life*, 188.

56. Edwards, "True Grace, Distinguished from the Experience of the Devils," in *WJE*, 25:621.

The first great manifestation of this ministry of the Spirit appeared on the day of Pentecost, when the Spirit came with fiery power upon Christ's prophetic witnesses (Acts 2:1–4, 17–18). Ferguson writes, "There is a close relationship between the promise of John 16:8–11 and the events described in Acts 2."[57] The Spirit did not work immediately upon the crowds, but through the preaching of the Holy Scriptures. Both law and gospel played their part as Peter unfolded the promises of the crucified and exalted Messiah and accused his hearers of the most heinous murder in history. The Westminster Larger Catechism (Q. 155) says, "The Spirit of God maketh the reading, but especially the preaching of the word, an effectual means of enlightening, convincing, and humbling sinners; of driving them out of themselves, and drawing them unto Christ."[58] The results were astonishing: "Now when they heard this, they were pricked in their heart, and said unto Peter and to the rest of the apostles, Men and brethren, what shall we do?" (Acts 2:37). The word translated as "pricked" (*katanyssō*) means to pierce; it is of the same root used for the soldiers' piercing (*nyssō*) of Christ's side with a spear (John 19:34). The only explanation for such a response is the power of the Holy Spirit. However, Peter did not answer their question by assuring them that they were already saved by the Spirit; instead, he called them to repentance and salvation. Conviction of sin in itself is not identical with repentance unto life.

The link between Christ's exaltation and the conviction of sinners at Pentecost shows that preparation is a work of the messianic King. Caspar Olevianus (1536–1587) explained that the elect are "prepared" by "Christ the King" before he "generates faith in them" by his work of showing them "that all people are under sin," "what a great evil sin is," "that the nature of God is righteous and that therefore He curses all sinners," and that God will execute "righteousness and judgment against the impenitent and unbelieving."[59] In the poetic language of the Psalms, the King rides forth to war "because of truth and meekness and righteousness," and his "arrows are sharp in the heart of the king's enemies; whereby the people fall under thee" (Ps. 45:4–5).

57. Ferguson, *The Holy Spirit*, 69.

58. *Reformed Confessions*, 4:340.

59. Caspar Olevianus, *An Exposition of the Apostles' Creed*, trans. Lyle D. Bierma (Grand Rapids, MI: Reformation Heritage Books, 2009), 11–13. On this Reformer's view of "preparation for faith" through "horrors of conscience" by the law, see R. Scott Clark, *Caspar Olevian and the Substance of the Covenant* (Edinburgh: Rutherford House, 2005), 194–95.

We find a similar situation among the Gentiles when an earthquake broke open the prison where Paul and Silas were kept after they preached in Philippi (Acts 16:26–34). The prison guard awoke to open doors and, assuming that the prisoners had escaped, drew his sword to commit suicide. When Paul compassionately told him not to harm himself, the man ran in trembling, fell down before them, escorted them out, and said, "What must I do to be saved?" (v. 30). As before, they did not assure him of salvation based on his fears and concerns, but preached the gospel of salvation by faith in Jesus Christ, and he and the members of his household believed, rejoiced, and were baptized. The Lord may use circumstances with the Word to prepare sinners. Brakel wrote, "The Lord generally uses some internal and external preparations, such as poverty, tragic occurrences, loss of property or loved ones, earthquakes, war, pestilence, danger of death, illness, or other things. This causes the person to become unsettled; he begins to contemplate repentance, the Word of God takes hold, he is convinced of sin, and he begins to perceive what eternal condemnation is."[60]

We must note, however, that not all conviction results in conversion. Peter and the other apostles preached Christ to the leaders of Israel, and they were "cut to the heart," but their response was to plan how to kill the apostles (Acts 5:33). When Stephen preached to the angry mob in Jerusalem, he did so as a man filled with the Holy Spirit, and again his hearers were "cut to the heart" (7:54–55), but they covered their ears and murdered him. The verb in both cases (*diapriō*) means to cut deeply—profound conviction. Paul spoke to Felix and Drusilla about faith in Christ, righteousness, self-control, and judgment day, and "Felix trembled" before his prisoner and spoke with him often (24:25–26), but he remained a slave of his greed instead of becoming a servant of Christ. These men were profoundly affected as the Holy Spirit applied the Word to their consciences, but they were not saved.

In summary, we have seen from the Gospels and Acts that the Holy Spirit works through the preaching of God's Word to illuminate sinners to the truths of God's Word and to convince them of their guilt. This stirs them to fear, to ask questions, and to listen to the answers of God's servants. This work of conviction is not the natural activity of conscience, but a supernatural agitation of conscience by the Spirit through the Word of Christ. The Spirit does not use preparatory grace to make men more worthy of salvation, but to convince them of their worthiness of damnation. At

60. Brakel, *The Christian's Reasonable Service*, 2:210.

times, this mighty work issues in the conversion of sinners. However, there is no necessary connection between conviction and conversion. Conviction may provoke a guilty sinner to respond with intensified persecution against God's people.

The Qualitative Difference between Preparatory Grace and Saving Grace

Preparatory illumination brings truth to a person who still loves sin: "And this is the condemnation, that light is come into the world, and men loved darkness rather than light, because their deeds were evil" (John 3:19). Flavel said that such light shines through God's Word and is "common, and intellectual only, to *conviction*," in contrast to the "special and efficacious light" that shines in the soul, "bringing the soul to Christ in true *conversion*." Such light, Flavel wrote, "may actually shine into the consciences of men . . . and convince them of their sins, and yet men may hate it, and choose darkness rather than light."[61]

However, the Scriptures also teach another kind of illumination by the Spirit. Saving illumination transforms people into new creations so that they see the glory of Christ, and the same glory indwells them and conforms them to his image (2 Cor. 3:18; 4:6). Such illumination causes the heart to burn with love (Luke 24:32). Edward Reynolds (1599–1676) said that it gives the heart "a due taste and relish of the sweetness of spiritual truth."[62] Saving illumination makes a person into a child of the light—that is, someone whose very nature is light so that he loves what is good, right, and true (John 12:36; Eph. 5:8).[63] Flavel wrote that Christ not only "breaks in upon the understanding and conscience by powerful convictions and compunctions," but also opens "the door of the heart"—that is, "the will"—conquering it and making it willing "by a sweet and secret efficacy."[64]

We will explore the nature of effectual calling in later chapters; the point here is that preparatory illumination, though powerful, does not confer spiritual life in the least degree. Brakel wrote, "In all preparatory exercises man is and remains dead, however, and his deeds cannot please

61. Flavel, *The Method of Grace*, in *Works,* 2:440–41, emphasis original.

62. Cited in Flavel, *A Fountain of Life*, in *Works,* 1:133. See Edward Reynolds, *Animalis Homo*, in *The Works of the Right Rev. Edward Reynolds*, 6 vols. (1826; repr., Morgan, PA: Soli Deo Gloria, 1998), 4:368.

63. Cf. Luke 16:8; 1 Thess. 5:5.

64. Flavel, *A Fountain of Life*, in *Works,* 1:137.

God, however virtuous they may seem. The soul receives the very first principle of life simultaneously with the first act of faith. . . . There is no spiritual life apart from union with Christ, who is the life of the soul."[65] Neither does preparation always lead to spiritual life. Ames said that there is no "certain and definite connection" between preparation and salvation.[66]

In preparation, God rearranges the thoughts and feelings of the unconverted so that they may rationally consider the gospel without yet granting them spiritual life. Ames compared preparation to God forming Adam's body out of the dust before breathing life into it (Gen. 2:7) or the act of assembling and putting flesh on the dry bones in Ezekiel's vision before the Spirit raised them to life (Ezek. 37:1–14). The formed body was still completely dead until God added the gift of life, but it was materially rearranged to receive life. Just as Adam's formed body was as passive as a corpse in receiving the breath of life from God, so sinners prepared by the Spirit's convictions are passive in receiving the gift of faith.[67]

We cannot insert preparatory grace into Romans 8:30 to say, "Whom he did predestinate, *them he also prepared; and whom he prepared*, them he also called." As Ames illustrated, preparation does not introduce a disposition that if increased would result in regeneration, like heating wood until it catches fire, but instead reduces some obstacles to conversion, "as dryness of wood tends to fire" though it remains cold.[68] This doctrine does not introduce a "middle state between men regenerate and unregenerate," but recognizes "a great latitude" within the state of spiritual death, where some are plunged into ignorance and stupefied by sin, whereas others, though no less dead in sin, have some knowledge and moral sense.[69]

Theological Implications of Preparatory Grace

Having surveyed the biblical testimony regarding preparatory grace, we will draw out some implications of this doctrine for our theology of God, man, and salvation.

65. Brakel, *The Christian's Reasonable Service*, 2:245; cf. Owen, *An Exposition of the Epistle to the Hebrews*, 4:146.

66. Ames, "Preparation of a Sinner," question 1, cited in Beeke and Smalley, *Prepared by Grace, for Grace*, 270.

67. Ames, "Preparation of a Sinner," theses 16, 18, cited in Beeke and Smalley, *Prepared by Grace, for Grace*, 268–69.

68. Ames, "Preparation of a Sinner," thesis 6, cited in Beeke and Smalley, *Prepared by Grace, for Grace*, 265.

69. Ames, "Preparation of a Sinner," thesis 17, cited in Beeke and Smalley, *Prepared by Grace, for Grace*, 268.

1. *Preparatory grace honors God as Creator and Redeemer.* Mankind is dead in sin (Eph. 2:1). Apart from God's gift of life through the risen Christ, people are unable to repent and believe in Christ (John 6:44; Rom. 8:7). The doctrine of preparatory grace honors the Redeemer by drawing a clear line between conviction and regeneration. However, mankind's fall did not destroy people's created faculties of thinking, feeling, and choosing. In preparatory grace, God deals with sinners according to their created natures even while their souls remain spiritually dead in sin. Ames wrote that it is "crude" to treat an unbeliever as if he were a mere "stone."[70] Samuel Willard said, "The Spirit of God, in the work of application, treats with men as reasonable creatures."[71] God remains their Creator and Lord even when they are in the state of sin.

2. *Preparatory grace assists the free offer of the gospel.* As we have seen, God calls out in the gospel, "Ho, every one that thirsteth, come ye to the waters, and he that hath no money; come ye, buy, and eat" (Isa. 55:1). The gospel freely offers salvation to all, but only those who feel their need for a Savior ("every one that thirsteth") and understand that they cannot merit it or save themselves ("he that hath no money") will receive it. The Westminster Shorter Catechism (Q. 31) says that the first work by which God "doth persuade and enable us to embrace Jesus Christ, freely offered to us in the gospel . . . [is] convincing us of our sin and misery."[72] The doctrine of preparation does not limit the warrant of all sinners to come to Christ, but explains how God prepares their souls with rational motives to flee the wrath to come. Robert Purnell (1606–1666) said, "I know no qualifications and preparations that are so required, as that without it we *should* not come, but there be some, without which we *will* not come."[73]

3. *The doctrine of preparation teaches dependence on the Spirit.* God gives sinners the new birth and justifying faith through the hearing of the Word of God.[74] However, many people will not even listen to the Word of God because of their prejudices. This can be deeply discouraging to God's people, for how else will sinners be saved? God's mighty power breaks down the strongholds of men's minds and casts down lies that stand against the

70. Ames, "Preparation of a Sinner," corollary, cited in Beeke and Smalley, *Prepared by Grace, for Grace*, 271.

71. Willard, *A Compleat Body of Divinity*, 432.

72. *Reformed Confessions*, 4:357.

73. Robert Purnell, *The Way Step by Step to Sound and Saving Conversion, With a Clear Discovery of the Two States, Viz: Nature, and Grace* (London: by T. Childe, and L. Parry, for Edw. Thomas, 1659), 26, emphasis added.

74. Rom. 10:17; James 1:18; 1 Pet. 1:23.

knowledge of God (2 Cor. 10:4–5). Purnell wrote, "Whatsoever preparations and qualifications there is required in any before conversion, they are wrought in us by the finger of God."[75] We must therefore pray frequently and fervently to the Father for the Spirit of conviction to awaken sinners.

4. *The doctrine of preparation engages sinners with the law but not with legalism.* The law and the gospel work together in perfect harmony, the first diagnosing the disease and the latter prescribing the cure (Rom. 3:19–21). Paul explains this use of the law when he writes, "The law is not made for a righteous man, but for the lawless and disobedient," proceeding to list various violations of the Ten Commandments and then writing that this is "according to the glorious gospel of the blessed God" (1 Tim. 1:9–11). Perkins wrote, "First, the law prepares us by humbling us; then comes the gospel, and it stirs up faith."[76] We need not fear promoting legalism if we preach the law as Christ did, with heart-searching application, and also preach the gospel. As Edwards pointed out, a superficial view of the law tends to engender self-righteousness, but the searching preaching of the law tends to destroy self-righteousness.[77]

5. *Preparatory grace is through Christ and to Christ.* Christ's promise about the Spirit of conviction is "I will send him unto you" (John 16:7; cf. 15:26). The Spirit of Pentecost who moved sinners to cry out, "What shall we do?" is the Spirit poured out by the Lord who is seated at God's right hand (Acts 2:33, 37). To the proud, self-satisfied, and independent, Christ comes knocking and calling for them to turn to him as the giver of spiritual sight and riches (Rev. 3:17–20, 22). The tendency of legal conviction is to lead sinners to Christ (Gal. 3:24), and therefore we may rejoice in it for the glory of Christ.

The Proper Use of the Doctrine of Preparation

The doctrine of preparatory grace describes the work of the Holy Spirit, not man's work by the power of his free will or the preacher's skill in the pulpit. However, this doctrine has practical implications for our spiritual lives, especially with respect to the practice of evangelism.

1. *Pastors must preach the law and the gospel.* The Holy Spirit uses the law to convict sinners of their need for Christ, but the moral law is not

75. Purnell, *The Way Step by Step to Sound and Saving Conversion*, 27.
76. Perkins, *Commentary on the Galatians*, in *Works*, 2:205.
77. Edwards, "Pressing into the Kingdom of God," in *WJE*, 19:284–85.

sufficient to lead people to salvation. The Holy Spirit uses the gospel to reveal the Savior of sinners, but no one will count himself a helpless sinner without the application of the law. Therefore, evangelism requires both the law and the gospel over the course of the regular preaching ministry of the church.

2. *Sermons should discriminate between believers and unbelievers.* Christ said that the Spirit would convict the world "of sin, because they believe not on me" (John 16:9). Too much modern preaching muddies the waters by failing to distinctly address either believers or unbelievers. We should not dangle the children of God over the flames of hell, and neither should we communicate false assurance to the unrepentant.

3. *Preachers should avoid teaching speculative schemes of preparation.* Though the Scriptures reveal the preparatory work of the Holy Spirit, God has not revealed either a detailed scheme of steps that one must follow to be prepared or a degree of conviction that is necessary for faith in Christ. Edwards said, "'Tis to be feared that some have gone too far towards directing the Spirit of the Lord, and marking out his footsteps for him, and limiting him to certain steps and methods."[78] Brakel wrote, "There is a wondrous diversity in the Lord's dealings."[79] John Newton (1725–1807) warned against teachers who "abound with distinctions" in their experiential teachings, "which are suited to cast down those whom the Lord would have comforted," including the requirement of profound submission to God *before* trusting in Christ.[80] However, Newton also expressed the simplicity of preparatory grace and regenerating grace:

> 'Twas grace that taught my heart to fear,
> And grace my fears relieved;
> How precious did that grace appear,
> The hour I first believed.[81]

4. *Preachers must address the consciences of unbelievers.* As witnesses under the lordship of the Holy Spirit, the preachers of the Word must seek to convince people of their violation of God's law, the corruption of their

78. Edwards, *Religious Affections*, in *WJE*, 2:161–62.

79. Brakel, *The Christian's Reasonable Service*, 2:246.

80. John Newton, *Wise Counsel: John Newton's Letters to John Ryland, Jr.*, ed. Grant Gordon (Edinburgh: Banner of Truth, 2009), 119–20.

81. "Amazing Grace," first published under the title "Faith's Review and Expectation," in John Newton and William Cowper, *Olney Hymns* (London: W. Oliver, J. Buckland, and J. Johnson, 1779), 53–54.

hearts, their guilt under the justice of God, the horrible wickedness of refusing to trust in Christ, and the coming judgment. This effort relies not on sheer emotionalism but on the impassioned preaching of rational truth from the Scriptures to the consciences of those who hear. This need not be done with a proud and condemning spirit, for God convicts sinners in mercy and grace. It can be done with tears (Acts 20:19, 31).

5. *We cannot always distinguish experientially between preparatory grace and the first motions of saving grace.* Since the converted are characterized by poverty of spirit and mourning over sin (Isa. 57:15; Matt. 5:3–4), they are often more aware of their remaining sin than their inward graces of faith, repentance, hope, love, and so forth. Therefore, it may be difficult to discern the point at which conviction of sin becomes repentance unto life. The method of the new birth is mysterious (John 3:8; cf. Eccles. 11:5).[82] Perkins said that faith may begin not in confidence but in a desire to be reconciled to God through Christ (though it does not begin in a mere desire to escape judgment).[83] Brakel wisely observed, "If he were to begin with the first serious conviction, in all probability he did not have faith yet. If he were to begin with the moment when, for the first time, he exercised faith consciously and in a most heartfelt manner, he would reckon too late, for in all probability he already had faith."[84] This mystery calls pastors to exercise patience and cautious discernment when dealing with people strongly convicted by the preaching of the Word.

6. *Sinners must be exhorted to use the means of grace.* The Holy Spirit uses human means to convict and convert, and therefore the lost should be pressed to attend them diligently. John Cotton (1584–1652) answered the question "What preparation is there in a blind man to see?" by urging sinners to listen to the Word, apply it to themselves, and pray for God's grace just as the blind man cried after our Savior (Mark 10:47–48), and though the people rebuked him, he cried until he received sight.[85] Flavel said, "Why cannot those feet carry thee to the assemblies of the saints, as well as to an ale-house?"[86]

7. *Sinners must not be allowed to rest in conviction but must be pressed to receive and rest upon Christ.* Preparation must never become a goal; it

82. Edwards, *Religious Affections*, in *WJE*, 2:160–61.
83. Perkins, *An Exposition of the Symbol*, in *Works*, 5:14.
84. Brakel, *The Christian's Reasonable Service*, 2:245.
85. Cotton, *The Way of Life*, 184–85.
86. Flavel, *England's Duty under the Present Gospel-Liberty*, in *Works*, 4:53.

is only God's ordinary way of bringing sinners to Christ. We must not let unbelievers turn conviction into a condition they must fulfill before coming to Christ, and then excuse their unbelief because they have not experienced enough conviction. Neither may we let sinners find confidence because of their sense of guilt and remorse. God's promises of grace are given only to those who repent and believe in Christ. Nothing short of faith and repentance is satisfactory, for otherwise people are lost. Calvin warned that the fear of God's wrath against sin may produce some outward moral reformations but prove to be "nothing but a sort of entryway of hell."[87] Christ alone can save sinners, and he does so through faith.

8. *The church must pray for the power of the Holy Spirit.* Without the Spirit, no one will really listen to the ministry of the Word, much less be converted by it. Flavel observed that, due to Satan's power, all the thunders of the moral law pronounced against an unbeliever "make no more impression than a tennis-ball against a wall of marble." Similarly, though the gospel sings a song of grace in the ears of sinners, "these gospel-melodies only dispose them to a more quiet sleep in sin."[88] Therefore, the church must take up the promise of John 16:8 and pray for the Spirit to come with power and convict the world. The Spirit can shatter the proud self-confidence of any sinner. Spurgeon said, "By nature, the sinner does not dread the wrath of God. . . . No sooner, however, is he awakened by God's Spirit, than fear takes possession of his heart, the arrows of the Almighty drink up his spirit, the thunders of the law roll in his ears."[89]

Let us therefore pray for God to awaken sinners and not hesitate to apply to their souls the painful medicines of God's convicting truth. This is the way of the great Physician of souls. As Calvin said, "He wounds that he may cure, and slays that he may give life."[90]

Sing to the Lord

Conviction and the Call of the Gospel

Come, ye sinners, poor and wretched,
Weak and wounded, sick and sore;
Jesus ready stands to save you,
Full of pity joined with power.

87. Calvin, *Institutes*, 3.3.4.
88. Flavel, *England's Duty*, in *Works*, 4:48.
89. Spurgeon, *The New Park Street Pulpit*, 3:326.
90. Calvin, *Commentaries*, on Ezek. 18:23.

He is able, he is able, he is able,
He is willing; doubt no more.

Come, ye needy, come and welcome,
God's free bounty glorify;
True belief and true repentance,
Every grace that brings you nigh,
Without money, without money, without money,
Come to Jesus Christ and buy.

Come, ye weary, heavy laden,
Bruised and broken by the fall;
If you tarry till you're better,
You will never come at all:
Not the righteous, not the righteous, not the righteous—
Sinners Jesus came to call.

Let not conscience make you linger,
Nor of fitness fondly dream;
All the fitness he requireth
Is to feel your need of him;
This he gives you, this he gives you, this he gives you;
'Tis the Spirit's rising beam.

Joseph Hart
Tune: Caersalem
Trinity Hymnal—Baptist Edition, No. 393

Questions for Meditation or Discussion

1. What is the definition of preparatory grace?
2. How does the Reformed doctrine of preparatory grace differ from the Roman Catholic doctrine of preparation?
3. What are some biblical evidences that God's Spirit works through the Word in some people in a manner that does not result in their salvation?
4. What implications does the order of the epistle to the Romans have for the function of the law in our evangelism of unbelievers?
5. How can Christ's statement "Thou art not far from the kingdom of God" (Mark 12:34) be understood in a manner consistent with the truth that sinners are dead (Eph. 2:1)?

6. What can we learn from the book of Acts about the Spirit's work of conviction?
7. What is the difference between preparatory illumination and saving grace?
8. How do Adam's body and the dry bones in Ezekiel's prophecy illustrate preparatory grace?
9. What has been your experience of preparatory illumination and conviction?
10. Why is the doctrine of preparatory grace a call for the church to pray?

Questions for Deeper Reflection

11. Someone says to you that the doctrine of preparation is against the Reformed doctrine of human depravity, for the Westminster Confession of Faith (9.3) says that man is not able to prepare himself for conversion. How do you respond?
12. What is the error of "preparationism"? How can preachers preach so that they may be used by the Spirit of conviction and yet avoid preparationism?

14

General Calling, Part 3

Resisting, Testing, and Blaspheming the Holy Spirit

When the general call of the gospel goes out to sinners, many respond to the message of God's mercy by aggravating and increasing their rebellion against him. The Spirit's conviction, which tends to awaken sinners to their need to repent and receive Christ, becomes the occasion of greater displays of defiance and further hardening of heart. The light of Christ shines on them in grace, but hating the light, they react by hiding deeper in darkness (John 3:19–20).

The Holy Scriptures describe sins committed against the light of the gospel as resisting, testing, and blaspheming the Holy Spirit. All unbelievers under the ministry of the Word resist the Holy Spirit so long as they refuse to repent and believe the gospel. People who engage in gross hypocrisy in the church test or tempt the Holy Spirit. Those who blaspheme the Holy Spirit irreversibly harden themselves against the gospel of Christ.

Resisting the Holy Spirit

At the conclusion of his sermon to a crowd of unbelievers in Jerusalem, the martyr Stephen said, "Ye stiffnecked and uncircumcised in heart and ears, ye do always resist the Holy Ghost: as your fathers did, so do ye.

Which of the prophets have not your fathers persecuted? And they have slain them which shewed before of the coming of the Just One; of whom ye have been now the betrayers and murderers: who have received the law by the disposition of angels, and have not kept it" (Acts 7:51–53).

The Meaning of Resisting the Spirit

The verb translated as "resist" (*antipiptō*) in Acts 7:51 literally means to collide or fall upon, and figuratively to resist, oppose, or be in conflict against.[1] It is rare in biblical writings,[2] but it is used to describe Israel's striving against the Lord at Meribah in the wilderness (Num. 27:14 LXX).[3] "Meribah" is a transliteration of a Hebrew word for "contention" used to name two locations where Israel strove against the Lord over the lack of water during its wilderness wandering (Ex. 17:7; Num. 20:13). The name became proverbial for Israel's hard-hearted refusal to trust God's word (Pss. 95:7–8; 106:32 ESV; cf. Heb. 3:8). Since Stephen spoke of Israel's rebellion in the wilderness (Acts 7:39–41), he likely had Meribah in mind. This makes his rebuke particularly ominous, since Meribah was associated with being excluded from God's rest (Ps. 95:8, 11). Likewise, by calling his hearers "stiffnecked," or stubbornly rebellious and unbelieving,[4] Stephen alluded to Israel's making of the golden calf that he spoke of earlier in this speech (Acts 7:39–41), an incident that would have resulted in Israel's destruction but for the intercession of Moses.[5] By resisting the Holy Spirit and refusing to turn to Jesus, the new and greater Moses (v. 37), Stephen's hearers provoked divine judgment and excluded themselves from the inheritance of the saints (cf. 26:18).

Given that the Holy Spirit is an invisible, incorporeal, and infinite being, what does it mean to resist him? First, it means *rejecting the Spirit's Word*.[6] Stephen said that the people rebelled against "the law" and "the prophets" as their ancestors did (Acts 7:52–53). He may have been

1. Henry George Liddell and Robert Scott, *A Greek-English Lexicon*, rev. Henry Stuart Jones et al. (Oxford: Oxford University Press, 1996), 161.

2. The word translated as "resist" (*antipiptō*) appears only in Acts 7:51 in the New Testament, twice in the tabernacle instructions for pieces set opposite each other (Ex. 26:5, 17 LXX), and once in Num. 27:14 LXX, as discussed above.

3. Though the Lord's words in Num. 27:14 are directed to Moses, the plural ("ye") refers to the nation of Israel.

4. Deut. 31:27; 2 Kings 17:14; Neh. 9:16–17; Prov. 29:1; Isa. 48:4; Jer. 7:26; 17:23; 19:15.

5. See the references to Israel's stiff neck in Ex. 32:9; 33:3, 5; Deut. 9:6–13.

6. Calvin, *Commentaries*, on Acts 7:51; and David G. Peterson, *The Acts of the Apostles*, The Pillar New Testament Commentary (Grand Rapids, MI: Eerdmans; Nottingham, England: Apollos, 2009), 264.

alluding to the confession of the returned exiles: "They turned a stubborn shoulder and stiffened their neck and would not obey. Many years you bore with them and warned them by your Spirit through your prophets. Yet they would not give ear" (Neh. 9:29–30 ESV).[7] The Holy Spirit is the author of the prophetic word (2 Pet. 1:20–21). To respond to God's Word with unbelief and disobedience is to resist the Spirit.

Second, it often entails *fighting the Spirit's conviction.* The Spirit who gave God's word to the prophets also gave them "power" to preach against sin (Mic. 3:8).[8] In other words, resisting the Spirit involves rejecting both the truth he reveals in his word and the persuasive force with which he presses that truth on the conscience.[9] Stephen's preaching exemplified the empowerment of the Spirit: he was "a man full of faith and of the Holy Spirit," and "they could not withstand the wisdom and the Spirit with which he was speaking" (Acts 6:5, 10 ESV; cf. Luke 12:11–12; 21:15).[10] Stephen's preaching caused sinners to be "cut to the heart," but they responded with ferocious hatred (Acts 7:54).

Third, resisting the Spirit often expresses itself in *persecuting the Spirit's messengers.* One cannot harm the infinite Spirit, but one can hurl angry words, slander, and violence against his flesh-and-blood servants. Stephen accused the Spirit-resisters of his day of following their forefathers who persecuted and murdered the prophets and God's righteous Son (Acts 7:52). Again, he may have been alluding to the postexilic confession: "They were disobedient, and rebelled against thee, and cast thy law behind their backs, and slew thy prophets which testified against them to turn them to thee, and they wrought great provocations" (Neh. 9:26). Stephen's hearers confirmed his words by making him the first Christian martyr (Acts 7:54–60).

Fourth, resisting the Spirit arises from *lacking the Spirit's inner circumcision.* Stephen identified the reason why people resist the Spirit: they are "stiffnecked and uncircumcised in heart and ears." His hearers were uncircumcised not in the physical sense of lacking the sign of the covenant, but in their settled orientation of heart as proud rebels and covenant

---

7. Compare "stiff-necked" (*sklērotrachēloi*) and "ears" (*ōsin*) in Acts 7:51 to "stiffened their neck" (*trachēlon autōn esklērunan*) and "they would not give ear" (*ouk ēnōtisanto*) in Neh. 9:29–30 LXX; cf. Jer. 7:26; 19:15.

8. On Mic. 3:8, see the section on the Spirit of prophecy in chap. 3.

9. Diodati, *Pious and Learned Annotations upon the Holy Bible*, on Acts 7:51; and Henry, *Commentary on the Whole Bible*, 2093 (on Acts 7:51).

10. David Martyn Lloyd-Jones, *Triumphant Christianity*, Studies in the Book of Acts, vol. 5 of 6 (Wheaton, IL: Crossway, 2006), 231–32.

breakers.[11] Though outwardly circumcised, their spiritual state was no different than that of uncircumcised pagans.[12] As the prophet Zechariah said, "They made their hearts diamond-hard lest they should hear the law and the words that the LORD of hosts had sent by his Spirit through the former prophets. Therefore great anger came from the LORD of hosts" (Zech. 7:12 ESV). Their actions displayed that they lacked the inner circumcision, the grace of God that causes sinners to hear his Word, love him, and keep his commandments by the indwelling Spirit (Deut. 29:4; 30:6; Ezek. 36:26–27). In other words, people resist the Spirit because they lack the Spirit (cf. Rom. 8:7–9).

The Implications of the Doctrine of Resisting the Spirit

Stephen's statement about resisting the Spirit is often used as an argument against the sovereignty of God's grace.[13] It is said that if grace can be resisted, then salvation ultimately depends on man's will, not God's will. However, that argument assumes that God's grace can do nothing more than teach and convict—factors from outside the heart that seek to persuade sinners to repent and believe. Stephen's words show that the root of all resistance is an internal factor: being "uncircumcised in heart." The circumcision of the heart is a grace of Christ worked by the Spirit (Rom. 2:29; Col. 2:11), and when it is granted, it overcomes the reigning disposition to resist God by implanting love for God in the heart. Unlike mere persuasion, the Spirit performs this work with omnipotent power, for it is a work of spiritual resurrection and new creation. John Brown of Haddington said, "His influences and evidences in the declarations of the prophets and apostles, and his common operations may be effectually resisted, quenched, and despitefully used—but his special and saving influences cannot."[14]

The doctrine of resisting the Spirit implies a severe warning to unbelievers, a comfort for believers, and an exhortation for preachers.

Unbelievers, when you fight against God's Word and its preachers, you are not fighting against man but God. You are acting like those people in Israel who rejected the prophets, Jesus Christ, and his apostles, bringing down terrible judgment. Be warned, unbelievers! You have taken a stand

11. Lev. 26:41; Deut. 10:16; Jer. 4:4; 6:10. On the significance of circumcision, see the discussion of the covenant with Abraham in *RST*, 2:618–19, 621–23.
12. Peterson, *The Acts of the Apostles*, 264.
13. On effectual calling, see chaps. 15–16.
14. Brown, *Systematic Theology*, 353–54.

against the almighty Lord of heaven and earth. You are resisting the God who gives you life, breath, and all things pertaining to this life. You are opposing the Judge of all the earth. Every time you hear the gospel and walk away unrepentant, you are showing your heart's hostility to the Lord. If you persist in this wickedness, you will be shut out of the inheritance, losing the enjoyment of all good forever, and will be cast into the lake of fire to suffer unceasing punishment from the God whom you have rejected.

Why would you resist the Holy Spirit? Is he not your good and loving Creator, who daily sustains your body and soul in existence? Is he not the Spirit of Jesus Christ, the kind and loving Savior? Jonathan Edwards said, "'Tis a great sin to resist the Holy Ghost because of the mercifulness of his motions and operations. All the inward operations of the Holy Spirit tend to the good of those that are the subjects of them."[15] Will you resist the God who offers to save you and make you happy forever in him? James Greendyk says, "How much longer will you trifle with your precious soul, despise God's goodness as revealed in Jesus Christ, and cast aside His warnings? God is as sincere in the offers of His mercy as He is in His threatenings."[16]

Believers, this doctrine summons you to consider your conversion and ongoing faith and repentance. Why is it that you are not resisting the Spirit today? Before you were converted you always resisted the Spirit. Why are you no longer an enemy of God? Believers, rejoice! God has saved you from your uncircumcised heart. He has rescued you from ears that did not hear. He has saved you from resisting the Spirit by placing the Spirit in your hearts, so that now your good will is his work. Therefore, praise and thank the Savior forever. And do not resist the Spirit today as he addresses you in the Word. Why would you act like an unbeliever again?

Preachers, this doctrine exhorts you to soberly consider your vocation to bring the Word of God to sinners. On the one hand, you must expect rejection and persecution. Perhaps you will be killed by the wicked for your faithfulness. If you preach the Word inspired by the Spirit, you certainly will be resisted by those who resist the Spirit. On the other hand, recognize that when men turn an indifferent ear and a cold shoulder to you or raise an angry voice and a violent hand against you, they are not really fighting

15. Edwards, Sermon 355, on Acts 7:51, in *Works of Jonathan Edwards Online*, vol. 50, *Sermons, Series II, 1735*, ed. Jonathan Edwards Center (New Haven, CT: Yale University, 2008), sig. L 3r, http://edwards.yale.edu/archive?path=aHR0cDovL2Vkd2FyZHMueWFsZS5lZHUvY2dpLWJpbi9uZXdwaGlsby9nZXRvYmplY3QucGw/Yy40ODo2LndqZW8=.

16. J. Greendyk, "The Danger of Resisting the Holy Spirit (1)," in *The Banner of Sovereign Grace Truth* 5, no. 5 (May/June 1997): 115 (full article, 115–16).

you. They are fighting God. Therefore, they cannot win. Stay the course, keep the faith, and finish the race of your ministry.

Testing the Holy Spirit

Whereas most people who are resisting the Holy Spirit remain outside of the church's membership, those testing the Holy Spirit have insinuated themselves into the church. We learn of this sin from a time when some disciples sold houses and lands, and gave the money to the apostles to help the poor (Acts 4:34–37). Ananias and his wife Sapphira likewise sold some property and brought a benevolence gift to the apostles but secretly kept back part of the money from the sale (5:1–2).

Much to their surprise, Peter rebuked them, not for keeping some of the money—for it was theirs (Acts 5:4)—but for pretending to give the whole amount. Evidently their intent was to make a name for themselves in the church, and they lied to accomplish it. Behind this act of hypocrisy was contempt for God the Holy Spirit, who dwells in his church and acts powerfully through its officers, ministries, and members (1:8; 2:4, 17–18, 38; 4:8, 31). Christians should conduct themselves with holy fear in God's presence in the church. John Calvin said, "We ought to know we do not come here to parade ourselves before men, but to present ourselves before the majesty of . . . our Master and our Sovereign King. . . . Hypocrisy is out of place here."[17] Ananias and Sapphira's sin against God and the danger it posed to the church were so great that God struck them both dead when they appeared before the apostles.

The Meaning of Testing the Holy Spirit

Peter's words to Ananias and Sapphira are sobering and instructive: "Why hath Satan filled thine heart to lie to the Holy Ghost. . . . Thou hast not lied unto men, but unto God. . . . How is it that ye have agreed together to tempt the Spirit of the Lord?" (Acts 5:3–4, 9). The verb translated as "tempt" (*peirazō*) may also be rendered "test"; it alludes to the people of Israel putting the Lord to the test by their unbelief in the wilderness, thus provoking his wrath.[18] Testing the Lord is the opposite of humbly trusting his goodness and submitting to his preceptive will; it comes from a heart

17. John Calvin, *Sermons on the Acts of the Apostles: Chapters 1–7*, trans. Rob Roy McGregor (Edinburgh: Banner of Truth, 2008), 199.

18. See *peirazō* in Ex. 17:2, 7; Num. 14:22; Pss. 77[78]:56; 105[106]:14 LXX; Acts 15:10; Heb. 3:9; *ekpeirazō* in Deut. 6:16; Ps. 77[78]:18 LXX; Matt. 4:7; Luke 4:12; 1 Cor. 10:9.

that demands that God act according to our will and, if he does not, insolently says, "Is the Lord among us, or not?" (Ex. 17:7).[19] Ananias's and Sapphira's hypocrisy was a challenge to the Spirit's presence in the church, an implicit denial of his perfect power, knowledge, or righteousness. His holy response vindicated all three of these glorious attributes.

It appears that Ananias and Sapphira not only acted hypocritically in this instance, but were hypocrites—wicked people who claimed to be righteous followers of Christ. To be "filled" by "Satan" (Acts 5:3) is the polar opposite of being "filled" with the Holy Spirit (13:52).[20] This implies heinous inward corruption comparable to that of the satanically driven hypocrite Judas Iscariot[21] or the Jewish sorcerer and false prophet Barjesus, an enemy of the gospel (vv. 6–10).

The sudden deaths of this couple imply that their presence in the church was an offense to God's holiness. They lied to the *Holy* Spirit (Acts 5:3). Calvin said, "God cannot abide this unfaithfulness, when as bearing a show of holiness where there is none, we do mock him contemptibly."[22] In the past, the Lord had struck dead two priestly sons of Aaron for failing to honor him as holy (Lev. 10:1–7) and on more than one occasion had killed people who violated the holiness of the ark of the covenant, the symbol of God's presence in the tabernacle (1 Sam. 6:19–20; 2 Sam. 6:1–9). Similarly, the hypocrisy of Ananias and Sapphira made them "an unclean presence" that had to be banished from the presence of the Holy Spirit dwelling in the church.[23] The idea of uncleanness may explain why the disciples buried them so quickly (Acts 5:6, 10)—that is, to remove defilement from the holy just as the corpses of Aaron's sons were taken away outside of the camp (Lev. 10:3–5).[24] When unrepentant sinners masquerade as godly worshipers, their outward acts of worship are an abomination to the Lord (Prov. 15:8; 28:9).

This warning against testing the Spirit should not be misinterpreted to mean that God will kill every hypocrite in the church (Gal. 2:4) or that anyone in the church who dies unexpectedly is a hypocrite (Isa. 57:1–2).

19. William Hendriksen, *Exposition of the Gospel according to Matthew*, New Testament Commentary (Grand Rapids, MI: Baker, 1979), 230.

20. Darrell L. Bock, *Acts*, Baker Exegetical Commentary on the New Testament (Grand Rapids, MI: Baker Academic, 2007), 222; and Keener, *Acts*, 2:1189.

21. Luke 22:3–6; John 6:70–71; 12:4–6; 13:2, 27.

22. Calvin, *Commentaries*, on Acts 5:1.

23. Bock, *Acts*, 225.

24. On excluding unclean people and things outside the camp, see Lev. 13:46; 16:27–28; Num. 5:1–4; 31:19–20.

Rather, it reveals that the Holy Spirit knows and abhors any members of the church whose godliness is a shell that conceals an evil heart. Just as the Holy Spirit acted to protect the holiness of the church in this instance,[25] we can expect him to act to defend the holiness of Christ's body today.

The Implications of the Warning against Testing the Holy Spirit

This Scripture passage presents three points of application. First, *the fear of the Lord*: "Great fear came upon all the church, and upon as many as heard these things" (Acts 5:11). We should fear the living God and show him great reverence in the church. The Spirit of the Lord sees all our secrets, including the depths of our hearts. He is the Holy Spirit and he hates all sin. He has taken the church—not the building but the people—as his holy temple. Do not defile the temple of the Spirit by unrepented sin. If the church becomes aware of hypocrites in its midst, it must act to lovingly reprove them and, if they refuse to repent after repeated appeals, to remove them from church membership. "Put away from among yourselves that wicked person" (1 Cor. 5:13). If the church refuses to discipline its members, then the Lord may discipline the church (Rev. 2:18–23).

Second, *the warning to unbelievers*: "None of the rest dared join them" (Acts 5:13 ESV). The word translated as "join" (*kollaō*) here refers to joining the membership of the church as a professing disciple of Christ (9:26; cf. 17:34). Calvin explained, "The people recognized a majestic presence of God and were frightened by it. . . . [This] led them to say, 'God is in the midst of these people.'"[26] It is one thing to attend the services of the church to hear the Word of God though you are not a professing Christian—that is a proper use of the means of grace. It is quite another thing, however, to profess to be a Christian while your heart is ruled by some self-seeking motive instead of faith and love toward God. If you are living a lie, you are testing the Holy Spirit and should immediately repent and confess your former hypocrisy to the pastors.

Third, *the encouragement to believers*: "More than ever believers were added to the Lord, multitudes of both men and women" (Acts 5:14 ESV). If you repent of sin and believe in Jesus Christ, then you should not hesitate to profess your faith and join the church. The Holy Spirit gladly dwells in you, for you are forgiven of all your sins because of Christ's death on the

25. Keener, *Acts*, 2:1183.
26. Calvin, *Sermons on the Acts of the Apostles: Chapters 1–7*, 225.

cross (2:38; 5:30–31). Rejoice and be glad, for the Lord dwells with you in grace and love (Zeph. 3:14–17)! This truth is not incompatible with a childlike fear of God: "Serve the LORD with fear, and rejoice with trembling" (Ps. 2:11). Reverence in the church helps unbelievers to consider Christ, for people recognize the plausibility and urgency of the gospel only in the light of God's holiness.

Blaspheming the Holy Spirit

Sadly, some people respond to the free offer of the gospel call by so hardening their hearts that they close the door to their own salvation. Christ said, "All manner of sin and blasphemy shall be forgiven unto men: but the blasphemy against the Holy Ghost shall not be forgiven unto men. And whosoever speaketh a word against the Son of man, it shall be forgiven him: but whosoever speaketh against the Holy Ghost, it shall not be forgiven him, neither in this world, neither in the world to come" (Matt. 12:31–32; cf. Mark 3:28–30; Luke 12:10).

The Meaning of Blasphemy against the Holy Spirit

Blasphemy against the Holy Spirit is a reaction against the Spirit's powerful work to make known God's grace in Christ, in which an unconverted sinner wholeheartedly condemns Christ and the Spirit as if they were demonically evil. It is an extreme form of resisting the Spirit, severely aggravated by sinning against one's own knowledge and conviction, and by treating God's mercy as if it were Satan's malice.

The word translated as "blasphemy" (*blasphēmia*, or as a verb, *blasphēmeō*) refers to strong speech against someone (Mark 15:29), such as slandering him as an evil person (Rom. 3:8; 14:16; Titus 3:2). Blasphemy against God could involve claiming to be God, which is an insult to the Lord (Mark 2:7; 14:64; John 10:33), or could entail speaking evil of the Lord.[27] In Matthew 12, Christ warned against speaking evil of the Holy Spirit because certain scribes had said that Christ "hath an unclean spirit" (Mark 3:30). Christ was casting demons out of people by the power of the Holy Spirit, but the scribes and Pharisees accused him of doing so by the power of Satan (Matt. 12:17–30). They blasphemed the *Holy* Spirit by speaking of him as if he were an *evil* spirit.

27. 4 Kingdoms [2 Kings] 19:4, 6, 22 LXX; James 2:7; Rev. 13:6; 16:9, 11, 21.

Christ's teaching in its context provides four clarifications to the meaning of this blasphemy. First, blasphemy against the Spirit is directed not so much against his person (such as denying his deity or personality) as against his operations to manifest the grace of Christ.[28] Herman Bavinck said, "The context makes it clear that the sin against the Holy Spirit has to consist in a conscious, deliberate, intentional blasphemy of the—clearly recognized yet hatefully misattributed to the devil—revelation of God's grace in Christ by the Holy Spirit."[29]

Second, blasphemers react not only to the Spirit's miracles, such as casting out demons, but also to his testimony through the Word. The context affirms the Spirit's holistic empowerment of Christ, including his preaching (Matt. 12:18). The scribes and Pharisees were not merely rejecting Christ's miracles as satanic, but his message of grace as contrary to their interpretation and application of the law (9:3; 12:1–14; 15:1–2).

Third, merely saying certain words does not constitute blasphemy against the Holy Spirit. Rather, such blasphemy expresses an inner disposition of extreme hostility and obstinate rebellion. In the context, the Lord discerned their thoughts and taught that the heart is the source of a man's words and works (Matt. 12:25, 33–37). William Perkins said that such blasphemy is caused by "a set and obstinate malice against God and against His Christ." He concluded, "Therefore, when a man does in the time of persecution either for fear or rashly deny Christ, he does not commit this sin against the Holy Ghost, as may appear by the example of Peter, who denied Christ (Matt. 26:73–75)."[30]

Fourth, as Wilhelmus à Brakel said, blasphemy against the Holy Spirit is not merely a "lack of repentance," which may be forgiven if later reversed, but a special sin not "commonly committed by the unconverted," which places the sinner in a position where he can never be pardoned by God.[31]

Bavinck said,

> The blasphemy against the Holy Spirit, therefore, does not simply consist in unbelief, nor in resisting and grieving the Holy Spirit in general, nor in denying the personality or deity of the Holy Spirit, nor in sinning

28. Perkins, *A Golden Chain*, chap. 53, in *Works*, 6:245; and Brakel, *The Christian's Reasonable Service*, 1:400.
29. Bavinck, *Reformed Dogmatics*, 3:155–56.
30. Perkins, *A Golden Chain*, chap. 53, in *Works*, 6:245.
31. Brakel, *The Christian's Reasonable Service*, 1:401.

> against better knowledge and to the very end without qualification. Nor is it a sin solely against the law, but also a sin specifically against the gospel, and that against the gospel in its clearest manifestation. There is much, therefore, that precedes it: objectively, a revelation of God's grace in Christ, the nearness of his kingdom, a powerful working of the Holy Spirit; and subjectively, an illumination and conviction of the mind so intense and powerful that one cannot deny the truth of God and has to acknowledge it as being divine.[32]

The Magnitude of Blasphemy against the Holy Spirit

Why is blasphemy against the Spirit the unpardonable sin? It is not because of the dignity of the divine person insulted, for Christ said that blasphemy in general can be forgiven, even blasphemy against Christ himself (Matt. 12:31–32).[33] Therefore, people should not despair of salvation because they have formerly spoken evil of God or any person in the Trinity. Paul was once a blasphemer, but Christ saved him (1 Tim. 1:13–15).

The heinousness and danger of blasphemy against the Spirit consists in its fierce condemnation of the grace of God in Jesus Christ as disclosed powerfully by the Spirit. Paul's blasphemy was done "ignorantly in unbelief" (1 Tim. 1:13), like that of many Jews at his time (Acts 3:17; 13:27), whereas blaspheming the Spirit is done directly against the illumination of the Spirit.[34] Calvin said, "By detracting from the grace and power of God, we make a direct attack on the Spirit, from whom they proceed, and in whom they are revealed to us. Shall any unbeliever curse God? It is as if a blind man were dashing against a wall. But no man curses the Spirit who is not enlightened by him. . . . Those only are blasphemers against the Spirit, who slander his gifts and power, contrary to the conviction of their own mind."[35]

By calling the highest good (God's grace in Christ by the Spirit) the deepest evil (Satan's work), these blasphemers permanently harden their hearts to the salvation offered in the gospel. Calvin said, "They must be desperate who turn the only medicine of salvation into a deadly venom."[36] This is why

32. Bavinck, *Reformed Dogmatics*, 3:155.

33. Christ's reference to himself as the "Son of man" in Matt. 12:32, a title that sometimes refers to Christ in his human suffering (8:20; 17:12, 22), suggests that he was referring to those who blaspheme him in ignorance that he is the Son of God (Acts 3:17). Poole, *Annotations upon the Holy Bible*, 3:57, on Matt. 12:31–32; and R. T. France, *Matthew*, Tyndale New Testament Commentaries 1 (Downers Grove, IL: InterVarsity Press, 1985), 214.

34. Perkins, *A Golden Chain*, chap. 53, in *Works*, 6:245–46.

35. Calvin, *Commentaries*, on Matt. 12:31. See *Institutes*, 3.3.22–24.

36. Calvin, *Commentaries*, on Matt. 12:31.

they cannot be saved, for, as Leon Morris (1914–2006) commented, "there is no way to forgiveness other than by the path of repentance and faith."[37]

The Modern Implications of Blasphemy against the Holy Spirit

Some have argued that blasphemy against the Holy Spirit was committed in a unique redemptive historical situation and cannot be committed today. Certainly those who heard Christ and saw his miracles were even more guilty if they did not repent (Matt. 11:20–24) than others who did not hear and see him. However, the inclusion of this warning in the canonical Scriptures indicates that it has continuing relevance. As we saw, Christ issued this warning in the context of the Spirit's empowerment of his whole ministry, including the ministry of the Word. It was not limited to those who saw his miracles. We read similar warnings in the Epistles about sin that has no remedy (1 John 5:16), particularly apostasy and gross rebellion against the light of the Word and Spirit (Heb. 6:4–6; 10:26–27). Therefore, we conclude that this sin remains possible today.[38]

People with sensitive consciences may feel great anxiety over whether they have blasphemed the Holy Spirit. Some may even fall into deep despair of ever being saved. However, we must exhort them to base their beliefs and expectations on the Word of God, not their feelings. The unforgiveable sin does not consist in rebellious thoughts or words against God. As Augustine pointed out, everyone involved in paganism, Judaism, or Christian heresy has sinned against the Holy Spirit in some fashion.[39] Such sins may be forgiven.

Blasphemy against the Spirit, according to Christ's words, takes place when an unrepentant sinner so hardens himself against Christ and the Spirit that he regards God's grace as demonically evil. This blasphemer does not view Christ as the Savior, but as a satanic impostor. He comes to this position despite the Spirit's work to convince him otherwise through the Word. It is impossible for a person to have such an attitude and still desire Christ to save him by the Spirit. Matthew Henry (1662–1714) commented, "We have reason to think that none are guilty of this sin, who believe that Christ is the Son of God, and sincerely desire to have part in his merit and mercy: and those who fear they have committed this sin, give

37. Morris, *The Gospel according to Matthew*, 318–19.
38. Poole, *Annotations upon the Holy Bible*, 3:57, on Matt. 12:31–32.
39. Augustine, *Sermons on Selected Lessons of the New Testament*, 21.3.5, in *NPNF*[1], 6:319–20.

a good sign that they have not."[40] Therefore, no one who fears damnation and wishes to be saved through Christ should exclude himself from the possibility of salvation. Instead, he should flee to Christ and rest in him.

The reality that there is an unforgiveable sin does not give us warrant to cease calling unbelievers to repentance. Christ did not state this verdict as a pronouncement on all the scribes and Pharisees, telling them that they had no hope, but phrased the warning as the indefinite singular "whoever may" (*hos an*, Matt. 12:32; Mark 3:29). The fact that Christ reasoned with them to demonstrate how irrational it was to think he was conquering Satan's kingdom by Satan's power suggests that some of them had not yet committed this grave sin and could yet be saved (Matt. 12:25–27). We likewise should continue to reason with sinners and exhort them to repent, even when they display great hardness of heart against the gospel.

We should also warn unbelievers that there is a point of no return in one's rejection of Christ. Though the free offer of the gospel will continue to give them the obligation and warrant to come to Christ, they can become so opposed to the Holy Spirit's testimony to Christ that they will never repent and never escape from the fury that is going to fall on God's adversaries. Let no one deceive himself to minimize the evil of this poisonous attitude. Bavinck said that this blasphemy is motivated purely by "conscious and intentional hatred against God," and it expresses the pinnacle of human sin: "putting God in the place of Satan and Satan in the place of God."[41] Though God mercifully offers them Christ and strives with their consciences, they "spit in his face when he shines evidently before us," as Calvin said. Consequently, God rightly "punishes contempt of his grace, by hardening the hearts of the reprobate, so that they never have any desire towards repentance."[42] Therefore, we should urge people not to persist in resisting the Spirit, but to repent and believe now, lest they settle their choice on Satan and receive his fate.

Concluding Applications regarding Sinful Responses to the Gospel Call

The general call of the gospel is a remarkable display of God's goodness, generosity, and grace. However, God's best draws out man's worst. Even as

40. Henry, *Commentary on the Whole Bible*, 1674, on Matt. 12:31–32.
41. Bavinck, *Reformed Dogmatics*, 3:156.
42. Calvin, *Commentaries*, on Matt. 12:31.

the Lord condescends to plead with sinners to receive the grace offered to them in Christ, many of them respond by resisting his Spirit, persecuting his messengers, entering the church under a cloak of hypocrisy, or going to the extreme of blaspheming the Spirit by treating the grace of Christ as if it were the evil of Satan. As we contemplate the horror of man's common reaction to the gospel, the Word of God calls us to respond in the following ways.

First, *we should humble ourselves for our sin.* The doctrines of resisting the Spirit, testing the Spirit, and blaspheming the Spirit show how profoundly corrupt, stubbornly rebellious, and foolishly deceitful the human race is. We should marvel and grieve over the sinfulness of our hearts. What have we become, that those created in the image of God now respond to him in such a manner—and that when he speaks to us in mercy? Neither do we have the right to hide behind bigotry toward the Jews as if they were worse than other peoples. When the Pharisees opposed Jesus, our non-Jewish ancestors were bowing before idols, worshiping demons, and living in violence and immorality. The story of man's resistance to the Spirit is our story, and it reveals the depths to which humanity has fallen away from God. Therefore, let us humble ourselves and view our nature, once made by God to be his palace and temple, to be broken into ruins and filled with all manner of unclean things. Man has become the enemy of God, and our hatred against him is displayed nowhere more starkly than in our response to his love.

Second, *we should acknowledge our need for inward, transforming grace.* The old Pelagian error tells us that all we need to attain salvation is our free will, knowledge of the truth, and the offer of forgiveness by the blood of Christ. The reality is that in our fallen state we choose to resist the truth and scorn the blood of Christ—we always have and always will until God circumcises our hearts. Let the words of Stephen sink into our minds: "Ye stiffnecked and uncircumcised in heart and ears, ye do always resist the Holy Ghost: as your fathers did, so do ye" (Acts 7:51). The clear light of the truth and powerful conviction of the Spirit are not sufficient to produce faith and repentance. Indeed, some people respond to such truth and conviction by blaspheming the Holy Spirit. We need new hearts and new spirits, a new birth by the Holy Spirit, so that we will trust in the Lord Jesus Christ and be saved.

Third, *we should thank God with grateful hearts if he has saved us.* Our souls should overflow with warm gratitude. Did God patiently bear with us when we resisted the Holy Spirit in the preaching of the gospel? It was sheer mercy, for he could have justly destroyed us instead. Did God strip us of our illusions of godliness so that we could find true godliness? He had every right to judge us for our hypocrisy. Did God restrain us from blindly rushing to damnation by hardening ourselves against Christ and blaspheming the Holy Spirit? It was only his kindness that kept him from giving us over to the darkness we deserved. If the Lord has saved you, then you ought to rejoice with trembling at his grace to you, for he saved you despite your resistance. Give him the praise and glory for your salvation, and never take it for granted.

Sing to the Lord

Man's Resistance against God's Mercies

My people, give ear, attend to my word,
In parables new deep truths shall be heard;
The wonderful story our fathers made known
To children succeeding by us must be shown.

Let children thus learn from history's light
To hope in our God and walk in His sight,
The God of their fathers to fear and obey,
And ne'er like their fathers to turn from His way.

The story be told, to warn and restrain,
Of hearts that were hard, rebellious and vain,
Of soldiers that faltered when battle was near,
Who kept not God's covenant nor walked in His fear.

He gave them to drink, relieving their thirst,
And forth from the rock caused water to burst;
Yet faithless they tempted their God, and they said,
Can He Who gave water supply us with bread?

Psalm 78
Tune: Chios
The Psalter, No. 213, stanzas 1, 3, 4, 6
Or Tune: Hanover (Croft)
Trinity Hymnal—Baptist Edition, No. 301, stanzas 1, 3, 4, 7

Questions for Meditation or Discussion

1. What key text in the Holy Scriptures speaks of resisting the Holy Spirit?
2. What is the meaning of resisting the Holy Spirit?
3. What implications does this doctrine have for unbelievers, believers, and preachers?
4. In what event in biblical history do we read of tempting or testing the Holy Spirit?
5. What does it mean to test the Spirit?
6. What implications does this doctrine have for the church?
7. What does it mean to blaspheme the Holy Spirit?
8. Why is blasphemy against the Holy Spirit the unpardonable sin?
9. What implications does this doctrine have for people today?
10. Of the applications offered at the end of this chapter, which speaks most powerfully to your heart? Why? What practical actions can you take in response?

Questions for Deeper Reflection

11. During a conversation with you about God's sovereignty in salvation, a friend argues that Acts 7:51 proves that God's grace is always resistible. How do you answer him?
12. Someone attending your church comes to you in great distress, convinced that she has committed blasphemy against the Holy Spirit because some years ago she heard the gospel and mocked Jesus and the Holy Spirit. How do you respond?

15

Effectual Calling, Part 1

Biblical Teaching

Many of those who hear the call of the gospel respond with indifference, hostility, or a superficial acceptance that neither changes them deeply nor lasts through trials. However, some do respond with true faith and repentance, bear fruit, and persevere to the end. How are we to explain the difference?

Charles Spurgeon said, "I remember sitting one day in the house of God . . . when a thought struck my mind—how came I to be converted? I prayed, thought I. Then I thought how came I to pray? I was induced to pray by reading the Scriptures. How came I to read the Scriptures? . . . And then, in a moment, I saw that God was at the bottom of all, and that he was the author of faith."[1] Although our conversion involves our trusting in Christ and turning from sin to God, it arises from God's activity in the soul. God saves sinners *by grace alone*, a central component of which is the grace of effectual calling.

Herman Witsius said, "The first immediate fruit of eternal election, and the principal act of God by which appointed salvation is applied, is effectual calling. Of which the apostle [says]: 'whom he did predestinate them he also called' (Rom. 8:30). And this calling is that act by which

1. Spurgeon, *The New Park Street Pulpit*, 1:384.

those, who are chosen by God and redeemed by Christ, both externally and internally are sweetly invited and effectually brought from a state of sin to a state of communion with God."[2]

This calling does not bypass or destroy the human will but saves the will by the grace of God.[3] Effectual calling is not coercion but sovereign persuasion of the mind, conscience, and will. Thomas Hooker (1586–1647) said, "The will must be effectually persuaded by the Spirit of the Father."[4] He went on to say, "The soul must be enlightened . . . for though faith be above reason, yet it is with reason." Hooker explained that this rational faith in Christ is not obtained by mere reasoning, but takes place when "the Lord calls us to come and enables us to come," for the Spirit of the Lord brings into the heart "the prevailing sweetness in the promise," and "it sinks into the heart's roots, and it comes to take possession of the soul." The heart then says, "Away with profit and the world and all, let me have the Lord and his grace."[5]

A Basic Explanation of Effectual Calling

At the heart of the doctrine of effectual calling is the idea that God calls his elect so powerfully that they are saved. Frequently in the New Testament Epistles, to be called is to be saved.[6] Thus, in the New Testament, "call" (*kaleō*) is often "a technical term for the process of salvation."[7] This calling is not merely an offer but a powerful act of God that applies redemption.

Paul teaches the doctrine of effectual calling: "All things work together for good to them that love God, to them who are the called according to his purpose," for "whom he did predestinate, them he also called: and whom he called, them he also justified: and whom he justified, them he also glorified" (Rom. 8:28, 30).[8] Matthew Barrett

2. Witsius, *The Economy of the Covenants*, 3.5.1 (1:344), punctuation and word order adjusted.

3. Bernard of Clairvaux, *Concerning Grace and Free Will*, trans. and ed. Watkin W. Williams (London: Society for Promoting Christian Knowledge, 1920), chap. 1 (4–5). See *RST*, 1:1010–11.

4. Thomas Hooker, *The Soules Vocation or Effectual Calling to Christ* (London: by John Haviland, for Andrew Crooke, 1638), 284.

5. Hooker, *The Soules Vocation or Effectual Calling to Christ*, 287, 290–91.

6. The terms pertinent to effectual calling include the "called" (*klētoi*), Rom. 1:6, 7; 8:28; 1 Cor. 1:2, 24; Jude 1; Rev. 17:14; "calling" (*klēsis*), Rom. 11:29; 1 Cor. 1:26; 7:20; Eph. 1:18; 4:1, 4; Phil. 3:14; 2 Thess. 1:11; 2 Tim. 1:9; Heb. 3:1; 2 Pet. 1:10; and "call" (*kaleō*), Rom. 8:30; 9:11, 24; 1 Cor. 1:9; Gal. 1:6, 15; 5:8, 13; Eph. 4:1, 4; Col. 3:15; 1 Thess. 2:12; 4:7; 5:24; 2 Thess. 2:14; 1 Tim. 6:12; 2 Tim. 1:9; Heb. 9:15; 1 Pet. 1:15; 2:9, 21; 3:9; 5:10; 2 Pet. 1:3. Also "call to" (*proskaleō*), Acts 2:39.

7. *TDNT*, 3:489.

8. On Rom. 8:30, see chap. 11.

observes, "Paul has the same exact group of people in mind throughout his entire description of the chain of salvation, which also means that he does indeed affirm an unbreakable chain, one in which each link leads inevitably to the next."[9] The calling in view cannot be the general gospel call, for many who hear the gospel are not justified. This calling must produce faith, for we are justified by faith in Christ (3:28). Paul does not say, "whom he called, *and who chose to believe*, them he also justified." Rather, he says, "whom he called, them he also justified." This indicates that all the called are justified. Therefore, God's effectual calling always produces faith.

Theologians offer various definitions of effectual calling. In the Augustinian and Reformed tradition, effectual calling has often been defined according to its internal power to change the heart to respond rightly to the external preaching of the Word.[10] Johannes Wollebius said, "This calling is the act by which God calls the elect, who are in themselves still wretched and corrupt, to participation in the grace of salvation, externally by the word of the gospel, internally by enlightening their minds and changing their hearts."[11] The Westminster divines defined it as that powerful work of the Holy Spirit to enlighten the mind and renew and reorient the will toward God so that people willingly embrace Christ as he is offered to them in the gospel.[12] Some more recent theologians have focused on the nature of the divine call as the Father's sovereign summons that brings people into union with Christ through faith in the gospel.[13]

The Definition and Doctrine of Effectual Calling

We present the following definition of effectual calling, which we will unpack point by point in our doctrinal exposition: *Effectual calling is the sovereign summons of the triune God, by which, according to his eternal election of individuals, through undeserved grace he produces gospel faith and repentance in them to create a new people in spiritual*

9. Barrett, *Salvation by Grace*, 87.

10. On external calling and internal calling, see the discussion of the terminology of calling in chap. 12.

11. Wollebius, *Compendium*, 1.28.(1).2 (158–59).

12. The Westminster Confession of Faith (10.1); the Westminster Larger Catechism (Q. 67); and the Westminster Shorter Catechism (Q. 31), in *Reformed Confessions*, 4:246–47, 312, 357; cf. Demarest, *The Cross and Salvation*, 221.

13. Murray, *Redemption Accomplished and Applied*, 89–94; and Grudem, *Systematic Theology*, 693; cf. Reymond, *A New Systematic Theology of the Christian Faith*, 718.

union with Christ, who live in holiness while God infallibly brings them to glory.

1. Effectual calling is the *sovereign summons* of God. The word translated as "call" (*kaleō*) can refer to an invitation (Luke 14:13, 16), but it may also bear the more forceful sense of a summons (Matt. 4:19–22), as from a master or a king (22:1–3).[14] When that King is God, his call comes with sovereign authority, and to refuse it is to bring down divine judgment (Isa. 65:12; 66:4 LXX).

The Lord may choose to "call" people with sovereign power that cannot be refused. God may be said to "call" people when he sends his word with effectual power to save them, as when the Lord called Israel out of Egypt (Hos. 11:1). For the Lord to "have called" Israel is the equivalent of his creating them as a nation, redeeming them from Egypt, and taking them as his people (Isa. 43:1). The Lord is said to "call" people even when this call is not a function of his spoken or written word but his secret providence that summons people or things to do his will.[15]

Wayne Grudem observes that the New Testament often speaks of "calling" in a way that shows "that no powerless, merely human calling is in view," but rather a "'summons' from the King of the universe . . . [that] has such power that it brings about the response that it asks for in people's hearts."[16] Peter says to God's "chosen" that God "hath called you out of darkness into his marvellous light," in contrast to those who continue to "stumble at the word, being disobedient" (1 Pet. 2:8–9). This calling consists of removing his elect people from the kingdom of unbelief and sin ("darkness") and bringing them into the kingdom of Christ ("light").[17] The sovereignty of this calling is exhibited in its nature as an act of new creation and its fruit of faith and repentance, themes we will develop below.

2. Effectual calling is the summons *of the triune God*. The Father, the Son, and the Holy Spirit act together as one God in calling sinners.[18] In a manner of speaking, the Father is the author who originates the call, the

14. Cf. Gen. 12:18; 20:9; Ex. 1:18; 1 Sam. 22:11; 2 Sam. 9:2, 9; 14:33; 1 Kings 1:28, 32; 2 Kings 6:11, etc. LXX.

15. Isa. 40:26; 45:3–4; 46:11; 48:13–15; Jer. 1:15; Lam. 1:15; Ezek. 38:21; Amos 5:8 LXX.

16. Grudem, *Systematic Theology*, 692.

17. Acts 26:18; 2 Cor. 6:14; Eph. 5:8, 11–14; Col. 1:12–13; 1 Thess. 5:4–5; 1 John 2:8–10.

18. Thomas Hooker, *The Application of Redemption, by the Effectual Work of the Word, and Spirit of Christ, for the Bringing Home of Lost Sinners to God. The First Eight Books* (London: Peter Cole, 1656), 402.

incarnate Son is the living Word he speaks, and the Spirit is the life-giving breath that accompanies the Word.[19]

God the Father is the primary author of effectual calling.[20] Paul writes that Christians are "beloved of God, called to be saints," where God is "our Father" (Rom. 1:7). Just as the Scriptures highlight the Father as the author of election, so they prominently feature him as the author of the call. God the Father predestined his people "to be conformed to the image of his Son," and those "whom he did predestinate, them he also called" (8:29–30). The Father has called his people into the fellowship of his Son (1 Cor. 1:9), calling each one at the time he appointed to reveal his Son in him (Gal. 1:14–16). Paul says that the God who has "chosen you to salvation through sanctification of the Spirit" also "called you by our gospel, to the obtaining of the glory of our Lord Jesus Christ" (2 Thess. 2:13–14). God "called us with an holy calling" according to his eternal grace "in Christ Jesus" (2 Tim. 1:9). The Father must draw and teach people inwardly for them to come to Christ (John 6:44–45). John Murray said, "It is God the Father specifically and by way of eminence who calls effectually by his grace."[21]

The Scriptures also indicate that God the Son acts in the call. He is the living Word or Revelation of God (John 1:1, 18). The Son raises sinners from spiritual death by the power of his speech: "The hour is coming, and now is, when the dead shall hear the voice of the Son of God: and they that hear shall live" (5:25). Yet this life originates in the Father (v. 26), and the Son gives it according to the Father's initiative (v. 19). Christ is the Good Shepherd, and "the sheep hear his voice: and he calleth his own sheep by name, and leadeth them out" (10:3). The Shepherd says, "Other sheep I have, which are not of this fold: them also I must bring, and they shall hear my voice. . . . My sheep hear my voice, and I know them, and they follow me" (vv. 16, 27). Just as the Father draws people to the Son, so Christ draws people to himself (12:32). When Peter speaks of "him that hath called us to glory and virtue," the antecedent to "him" seems to be both "God" and "Jesus our Lord" (2 Pet. 1:2–3). Christ mediates all saving illumination to men as their Prophet, obtains all saving grace

19. Cf. the citations of Kevin Vanhoozer and Martin Luther in Jonathan Hoglund, *Called by Triune Grace: Divine Rhetoric and the Effectual Call*, Studies in Christian Doctrine and Scripture (Downers Grove, IL: IVP Academic, 2016), 183, 189. Hoglund uses biblical exegesis, Reformed theology, and speech-act theory to construct an intriguing approach to effectual calling as "triune rhetoric" in which the Father is the authoritative caller, the Son is the convincing argument, and the Spirit is the creator of a responsive audience (189–205).

20. Reymond, *A New Systematic Theology of the Christian Faith*, 714.

21. Murray, *Redemption Accomplished and Applied*, 90.

for them as their Priest, and exercises all saving power as their King.[22] The Heidelberg Catechism (LD 21, Q. 54) says, "The Son of God from the beginning to the end of the world, gathers, defends, and preserves to Himself by His Spirit and Word, out of the whole human race, a Church chosen to everlasting life."[23]

Although Paul never explicitly speaks of the Holy Spirit calling people, he closely associates the Spirit with our calling.[24] When the word of God comes with the power of salvation it is because the Spirit applies it to the elect of God (1 Thess. 1:3–5). The voice speaking in the Scriptures is the voice of the Holy Spirit.[25] The Lord Jesus said that the life-giving operations of his words are inseparable from his Spirit: "It is the spirit that quickeneth; the flesh profiteth nothing: the words that I speak unto you, they are spirit, and they are life" (John 6:63). The Spirit unites us to Christ by faith (1 Cor. 6:17). The Heidelberg Catechism (LD 25, Q. 65) says, "Since then we are made partakers of Christ and all His benefits by faith only, whence doth this faith proceed? From the Holy Ghost, who works faith in our hearts by the preaching of the gospel, and confirms it by the use of the sacraments."[26] John Brown of Haddington said, "The Holy Ghost is the effectual applier of redemption to us, in and by whom Christ and his Father work in us."[27]

Therefore, the effectual call is the undivided operation of the whole Trinity to summon people to himself. Augustine said, "The Father is heard, and teaches to come to the Son. Engaged herein is also the Son Himself, because He is His Word by which He thus teaches. . . . Herein engaged, also, at the same time, is the Spirit of the Father and of the Son; and He, too, teaches, and does not teach separately, since we have learned that the workings of the Trinity are inseparable."[28]

3. Effectual calling is according to God's *eternal election*. God executes his eternal decree by calling his elect people to his Son. God "hath saved us, and called us with an holy calling, not according to our works, but according to his own purpose and grace, which was given us in Christ Jesus before the world began" (2 Tim. 1:9). The people "whom he did

---

22. On Christ's illumination of sinners according to his prophetic office, see *RST*, 2:970–73. On his ministry as King to build up the church through conversion, see *RST*, 2:1151.

23. *The Three Forms of Unity*, 85.

24. Eph. 4:4; 1 Thess. 4:7–8; 2 Thess. 2:13–14; 2 Tim. 1:7–9.

25. 2 Sam. 23:2; Acts 1:16; Heb. 3:7–8; 10:15–17.

26. *The Three Forms of Unity*, 88.

27. Brown, *Systematic Theology*, 337.

28. Augustine, *On the Predestination of the Saints*, 13.8, in *NPNF*[1], 5:504.

predestinate, them he also called" (Rom. 8:30). They are "called according to his purpose" to create a spiritual family "conformed to the image of his Son" (vv. 28–29). William Perkins said that the first step of God's manifesting his eternal love to a sinner is "an effectual calling whereby a sinner being severed from the world is entertained into God's family, . . . [resulting in] that admirable union or conjunction which is the engrafting of such as are to be saved into Christ."[29]

Therefore, in effectual calling God implements in our experience what he purposed in eternity. John Calvin said, "God by his call manifests the election, which he otherwise holds hidden within himself."[30] To be sure of one's calling is to be sure of one's election by God (2 Pet. 1:10; cf. Rom. 8:30). Paul thanked God "because God hath from the beginning chosen you to salvation . . . whereunto he called you by our gospel" (2 Thess. 2:13–14). It is a discriminating calling because it executes God's purpose to punish some sinners as "vessels of wrath fitted for destruction" and save others as "vessels of mercy, which he had afore prepared unto glory," and only the latter are those "whom he hath called" (Rom. 9:22–24). The link between calling and election gives priority to God's choice over man's choice in the application of salvation. Paul explains why Jacob was called but Esau was not: "For the children being not yet born, neither having done any good or evil, that the purpose of God according to election might stand, [it was] not of works, but of him that calleth" (Rom. 9:11). God's effectual call does not come to save people because of anything good in them or that they will do, but only because of "the purpose of God according to election." Then, by grace, they respond willingly to the gospel.

4. Effectual calling is God's summons to chosen *individuals*. Though most references to the "called" are plural, it is clear that God calls them as individuals. This calling does not refer to that of an entire nation or ethnic group, but to that individual "whom he hath called, not of Jews only, but also of the Gentiles" (Rom. 9:24). All those who have heard the evangelistic preaching of the gospel fall into one of three categories: Jews who reject the gospel, Greeks who reject the gospel, and the "called, both Jews and Greeks," who trust in Christ (1 Cor. 1:22–24). Bruce Ware notes that "the called" are a group taken "out

29. Perkins, *A Golden Chain*, chap. 36, in *Works*, 6:172.
30. Calvin, *Institutes*, 3.24.1.

of the broader, general group of all the Jews and Gentiles."[31] Not all people are effectually called.

Paul writes that he was individually called to salvation "when it pleased God, who separated me from my mother's womb, and called me by his grace" (Gal. 1:15). Although Paul's calling to preach the gospel is in view (v. 16), his emphasis falls on how God saved him from legalism (vv. 13–14) and brought him into vital union with Christ (v. 16). Paul's point is that the gospel that he preached could not have originated from him or any man, but must have come from God (vv. 11–12), because Paul was an enemy of the gospel until God changed him by the sovereign grace of the call.

The personal nature of effectual calling is beautifully illustrated by Christ's parable of the good shepherd. He said, "He calleth his own sheep by name, and leadeth them out. . . . and the sheep follow him: for they know his voice" (John 10:3–4). Therefore, although this calling comes through the general preaching of the gospel, it is not a general broadcast but a specific summons when Christ applies the Word to the souls of individual sinners, calling each "by name."

5. Effectual calling is *undeserved grace*. Though God calls some individuals and not others effectively to Christ, the difference is not based on any superiority in those called. Paul wrote to the Corinthians, "For ye see your calling, brethren, how that not many wise men after the flesh, not many mighty, not many noble, are called: but God hath chosen the foolish things of the world to confound the wise; and God hath chosen the weak things of the world to confound the things which are mighty" (1 Cor. 1:26–27).

Rooted in God's unconditional election, effectual calling is not based on any moral worthiness, goodness, or responsiveness in a person, but arises entirely from God's merciful will (Rom. 9:11, 16). As we noted earlier, Paul says that God "called us with an holy calling, not according to our works, but according to his own purpose and grace" (2 Tim. 1:9). William Ames wrote, "The calling does not depend on the dignity, honesty, industry, or any endeavor of the ones called, but only upon the election and predestination of God."[32]

Therefore, effectual calling gives us no basis to boast in ourselves but ample reason to glory in the free grace of God. As Paul says (1 Cor. 4:7),

31. Bruce A. Ware, "The Place of Effectual Calling and Grace in a Calvinist Soteriology," in *The Grace of God, the Bondage of the Will*, ed. Thomas R. Schreiner and Bruce A. Ware (Grand Rapids, MI: Baker, 1995), 2:358.

32. Ames, *The Marrow of Theology*, 1.26.6 (157).

who makes us differ from anyone? What do we have that we have not received? God's calling of the weak has the purpose "that no flesh should glory in his presence," but that "he that glorieth, let him glory in the Lord" (1:29, 31; citing Jer. 9:23–24).

6. In effectual calling, God *produces gospel faith and repentance* in the elect. As we said earlier, this is the clear implication of Paul's statement "Moreover whom he did predestinate, them he also called: and whom he called, them he also justified" (Rom. 8:30), for we are justified by faith.

Paul identified effectual calling as the crucial factor that explains why some believe but others reject the gospel. He said, "We preach Christ crucified, unto the Jews a stumblingblock, and unto the Greeks foolishness; but unto them which are called, both Jews and Greeks, Christ the power of God, and the wisdom of God" (1 Cor. 1:23–24). It is not ethnicity or cultural background that determines whether a person sees divine glory in the gospel of Christ and so comes to him; rather, the influence of God's call opens the sinner's eyes and saves him. This is the work particularly attributed to the Holy Spirit (2:12–16), without whom no one can confess Jesus as Lord (12:3), the basic profession of saving faith (Rom. 10:9). Calvin said that Christ "unites himself to us by the Spirit alone. By the grace and power of the same Spirit we are made his members, to keep us under himself and in turn to possess him. . . . Faith is the principal work of the Holy Spirit."[33] The Belgic Confession (Art. 22) states, "The Holy Ghost kindleth in our hearts an upright faith, which embraces Jesus Christ with all His merits, appropriates Him, and seeks nothing more besides Him."[34]

Faith and repentance are gifts of God through Jesus Christ, as is plain from the book of Acts. God sent the risen Christ to bless sinners by "turning away every one of you from his iniquities" (Acts 3:26). God also exalted Christ to his right hand "to give repentance to Israel, and forgiveness of sins" (5:31). After Peter's successful visit to the Gentiles in the home of Cornelius, the Christian Jews praised God because he had "also to the Gentiles granted repentance unto life" (11:18). When believers were scatted by persecution, "preaching the Lord Jesus" to Gentiles, "the hand of the Lord was with them: and a great number believed, and turned unto the Lord (vv. 20–21). When sinners heard the word of the Lord, "as many as were ordained to eternal life believed" (13:48). While Paul preached

33. Calvin, *Institutes*, 3.1.3–4.

34. *The Three Forms of Unity*, 39.

to Lydia, the Lord opened her heart so that she became a faithful disciple and received baptism (16:14–15). Christ works through the preaching of the word to Jews and Gentiles "to open their eyes, and to turn them from darkness to light, and from the power of Satan unto God, that they may receive forgiveness of sins" (26:18). No book of the Bible is more focused on missions than Acts, and no book is clearer that faith and repentance are gifts from God.

Saving faith is not something that resides in all humanity to some degree and, therefore, just needs to be stirred up or directed to the proper object. Paul writes, "All men have not faith" (2 Thess. 3:2). Godliness and eternal life belong to those who have "the faith of God's elect" (Titus 1:1). Saving faith is not common among men, but the special possession of those whom God has chosen.

Paul says, "For by grace are ye saved through faith; and that not of yourselves: it is the gift of God" (Eph. 2:8). The pronoun translated as "that" (*touto*) is in the neuter gender and does not agree with the preceding nouns "grace" (*charis*) or "faith" (*pistis*), both being feminine. Andrew Lincoln concludes that it refers "to the preceding clause as a whole, and thus to the whole process of salvation it describes, which of course includes faith as its means."[35] James White adds, "This would mean that all the elements of the work of salvation by grace through faith are not human in origin."[36] That faith is the gift of God is also clear from the context in Ephesians. Man is dead in sin until God grants him a spiritual resurrection through Christ (vv. 1, 5). Believers are God's new creation in Christ, "his workmanship" (v. 10). Therefore, any motion of a sinner toward God, including faith, must be from God's grace and for God's glory. This explains why Paul thanked God constantly for the Ephesians' "faith in the Lord Jesus, and love unto all the saints" (1:15–16).[37] Paul not only glorified God for giving them faith and love, but prayed for these gifts: "Peace be to the brethren, and love with faith, from God the Father and the Lord Jesus Christ" (6:23). Faith and love are gifts of the triune God (1 Tim. 1:14; 2 Tim. 1:13–14).

7. Effectual calling is powerful *to create a new people*. Christ raises the spiritually dead by the power of his voice, just as he raised Lazarus from the grave by his mighty command (John 5:25; 11:43–44). God's speech

35. Lincoln, *Ephesians*, 112.

36. James R. White, *The God Who Justifies* (Minneapolis: Bethany House, 2001), 324.

37. See also Rom. 1:8; Col. 1:3–4; 1 Thess. 1:2–5; Philem. 4–5.

has the power to accomplish what he wills. Herman Ridderbos wrote that it is "the word of divine power by which God calls into being that which does not exist and by which he works what he commands."[38] Creation is an act of divine calling. The Lord says, "Mine hand also hath laid the foundation of the earth, and my right hand hath spanned the heavens: when I call unto them, they stand up together" (Isa. 48:13). God "calls into existence the things that do not exist" (Rom. 4:17 ESV). By his word and Spirit he created the universe, "for he spake, and it was done" (Ps. 33:6, 9). Charles Hodge said that "this form of expression" implies that "God is the author or cause of the effect, which occurs in consequence of his call," and "the efficiency [effective power] to which the effect is due is not in second causes," but simply the power of God.[39]

God exercises the same creative omnipotence in effectual calling. Just as "God said, Let there be light: and there was light" (Gen. 1:3), so "God, who commanded the light to shine out of darkness, hath shined in our hearts, to give the light of the knowledge of the glory of God in the face of Jesus Christ" (2 Cor. 4:6). God's almighty word creates a divine and supernatural light in the soul. Previously, sinners were blind and perishing in utter darkness (vv. 3–4; cf. Eph. 4:17–18; 5:8). The shining of God's face gives salvation.[40] Thus, God is not only active but manifestly present in his glory when he saves the soul through the Word.

The inward and effectual illumination of sinners by the glory of Christ is necessary for them to trust in him. James Fisher (1697–1775), Ebenezer Erskine (1680–1754), and Ralph Erskine (1685–1752) wrote, "What is the necessity of this illumination, [in] order to the embracing of Christ? Because, without it, there can be no discerning of his matchless excellency, inexhaustible sufficiency, and universal suitableness, the saving knowledge of which is necessary to the comfortable embracing of him—'They that know thy name, will put their trust in thee' (Ps. 9:10)."[41] All these truths are revealed in the gospel, but the wicked remain blind to them apart from the work of new creation.

Samuel Willard reflected on how God's saving illumination, described in 2 Corinthians 4:6, transforms the mind and will so that the person ex-

38. Ridderbos, *Paul*, 235.

39. Hodge, *Systematic Theology*, 2:641.

40. Pss. 4:6; 31:16; 44:3; 67:1; 80:3, 7, 19; 89:15; 119:135.

41. James Fisher et al., *The Assembly's Shorter Catechism Explained* (Lewes, East Sussex, UK: Berith, 1998), 31.41 (173).

ercises faith in Christ. God "lets in a divine light into the understanding, by which it is renewed. He doth not put a new faculty into the man, but he restores the image of God to it." God brings the knowledge of Christ into the understanding in glorious brightness so that the person, who perhaps formerly could talk about the gospel, now sees the beauty and glory of Christ. This light convinces the mind, for light needs no other evidence or argument but makes reality plainly visible. The person perceives the "incomparable excellency" in Christ and becomes ready to trust him for eternal life and happiness. "Now not only is the mind irradiated with these discoveries, so as to subscribe to the truth of them; but there is with it put into the heart an appreciation of him [Christ]: he is made to it exceeding precious." God effectively moves the person to the spontaneous, free, and willing "choice of Christ, as the object of his trust," and "he puts a new spring into the affections, by infusing the habits of grace into them, suitable to their operations" to flee evil and pursue good.[42]

When God calls into being the response of faith and repentance, he energizes the human heart with light and life where it was once darkness and death. The sinner's faculties of understanding and will, once set against God, now become responsive to him. God changes the sinner so that the unwilling "come most freely, being made willing by his grace."[43] Wilhelmus à Brakel wrote, "In the internal call God works in a manner which is consistent with man's nature."[44] Brown wrote, "Doth God renew our will by force? No; he sweetly changes it, by means of the pleasant and attracting discoveries [disclosures] he makes of Christ."[45]

Effectual calling displays the infinite power of the Creator over his creatures, even in their rebellion against him. Thomas Watson said, "God rides forth conquering in the chariot of his gospel; he conquers the pride of the heart, and makes the will, which stood out as a fort-royal, to yield and stoop to his grace. . . . God puts forth a divine energy, nay, a kind of omnipotence."[46] However, divine omnipotence does not call by coercive force but by effectual wooing. Francis Turretin wrote of "the supernatural power of grace . . . which so sweetly and at the same time powerfully

42. Willard, *A Compleat Body of Divinity*, 452–53, 456.

43. The Westminster Confession of Faith (10.1), in *Reformed Confessions*, 4:246–47.

44. Brakel, *The Christian's Reasonable Service*, 2:209.

45. Brown, *Questions and Answers on the Shorter Catechism*, 151. The terminology of sweetness in descriptions of God's grace is found frequently in the writings of Augustine, Bernard of Clairvaux, Martin Luther, and John Calvin. See I. John Hesselink, "Calvin, Theologian of Sweetness," *Calvin Theological Journal* 37 (2002): 318–32.

46. Watson, *A Body of Divinity*, 223.

affects the man that he cannot (thus called) help following God who calls and being converted."[47]

By God's creative power, he initiates the new creation in Christ by forming a new people (Isa. 65:17–18; 2 Cor. 5:17). The Lord who calls each generation into existence is also the Redeemer who calls his chosen people (Isa. 41:4, 9). In this regard, he calls them not only out of nonexistence, but out of contrary existence as members of this wicked world. This was foreshadowed in the old covenant. The Lord called Abraham out of his pagan homeland (Acts 7:2–4) to follow him to blessing and an inheritance (Isa. 51:2; Heb. 11:8). He called Israel, his beloved son, out of idolatrous Egypt (Hos. 11:1). In the prophecy of Isaiah, the Lord reminded the Israelites that they were his chosen, redeemed, and called people (Isa. 43:1; 48:12).

Saving illumination creates a new humanity in Christ. Paul alludes to our union with Christ as our last Adam, for the Lord Jesus is "the image of God" (2 Cor. 4:4). When the Spirit opens our eyes, he creates such a conjunction between us and the last Adam that we begin to be "changed into the same image" (3:17–18). The light of Christ illuminates sinners who formerly were darkness so that they become light in union with the Lord (Eph. 5:8, 14).

The identity of Israel as God's chosen and called people finds its typological fulfillment in the calling of elect Jews and elect Gentiles into the church of Christ (1 Pet. 2:9).[48] They are "called to be saints" (Rom. 1:7; 1 Cor. 1:2; cf. Jude 1). Those who are called have a new identity that transcends all human distinctions; they are the holy church of Christ, the spiritual Israel of God, one family under one Father, sharing one Spirit, in union with one Lord. They no longer belong to this world but are pilgrims here.

8. Effectual calling creates a people in *spiritual union with Christ.* There is no salvation apart from union with Christ by the Holy Spirit.[49] God forms this spiritual union by effectual calling. The saints are "called unto the fellowship of his Son Jesus Christ our Lord" (1 Cor. 1:9). They believe in Christ because of God's "calling," and because of him they are in union with Christ (vv. 24, 26, 30). Christ is the true Israel, the Servant "called" by God to be the light that glorifies God by illuminating fallen

47. Turretin, *Institutes*, 15.4.10 (2:510); cf. 15.4.18–22 (2:524–26).
48. Ridderbos, *Paul*, 332–33.
49. See chaps. 9 and 10 on union with Christ.

mankind (Isa. 42:6–7; 49:1, 3, 6). His calling is the basis of our calling, and his light illuminates and transforms us (9:2; 60:1–3). As Ames pointed out, effectual calling initiates spiritual union with the Lord Jesus so that we may partake of his saving benefits.[50] Turretin wrote, "Calling is an act of the grace of God in Christ by which he calls men dead in sin and lost in Adam through the preaching of the gospel and the power of the Holy Spirit, to union with Christ and to the salvation obtained in him."[51]

Saving illumination makes us God's dwelling place in Christ. When Paul says that God "hath shined in our hearts, to give the light of the knowledge of the glory of God in the face of Jesus Christ" (2 Cor. 4:6), he alludes to God's glory dwelling in his temple (Ex. 40:34–38; 1 Kings 8:10–11)—imagery of covenantal union and communion (2 Cor. 6:14–16). The priests at the tabernacle and temple blessed Israel with the words "The LORD make his face shine upon thee, and be gracious unto thee" (Num. 6:25). This grace aimed at the glory of God among all nations (Ps. 67:1–3). Peter says that the called obtain the privileges of God's people by their union with Jesus Christ, for they are joined to him like stones built upon the cornerstone, and thus the marvelous light of God's glory illuminates them as his living temple (1 Pet. 2:4–6, 9).

We may ask whether effectual calling is logically prior to union with Christ or union is prior to calling. To answer this question, we draw on a distinction that we made earlier: federal versus spiritual union.[52] *Federal union* with Christ is prior to our calling, for Christ was called first in God's counsels (Isa. 42:6), and God determined to give us grace and eternal life in Christ before time began (2 Tim. 1:9; Titus 1:2). Hodge said, "There is a federal union with Christ which is antecedent to all actual union, and is the source of it."[53] However, effectual calling is causally prior to *spiritual union* with Christ because God effectively calls us to come to Christ through a Spirit-worked faith. The Westminster Shorter Catechism (Q. 30) says, "The Spirit applieth to us the redemption purchased by Christ, by working faith in us, and thereby uniting us to Christ in our effectual calling."[54]

9. Effectual calling creates a people obligated and motivated to live in *holiness*. Though God's call is not based on good works, it is a "holy

50. Ames, *The Marrow of Theology*, 1.26.1–3 (157); cf. the Westminster Larger Catechism (Q. 66); and the Westminster Shorter Catechism (Q. 30), in *Reformed Confessions*, 4:312, 357.

51. Turretin, *Institutes*, 15.1.2 (2:501).

52. See chap. 10.

53. Charles Hodge, *Ephesians* (1856; repr., Edinburgh: Banner of Truth, 1991), 9.

54. *Reformed Confessions*, 4:357.

calling" (2 Tim. 1:9), and those who partake of it are "holy brethren" (Heb. 3:1) and "saints" or holy people (Rom. 1:7; 1 Cor. 1:2). God's call brings believers into relationship with him and obligates them to walk with him in holiness. Peter says, "As he which hath called you is holy, so be ye holy in all manner of conversation; because it is written, Be ye holy; for I am holy" (1 Pet. 1:15–16). Paul writes, "God hath not called us unto uncleanness, but unto holiness" (1 Thess. 4:7). He exhorts Christians "that ye would walk worthy of God, who hath called you unto his kingdom and glory" (2:12).

Since God's calling forms a new people in union with Christ, its ethical implications include the obligation to support the health and unity of the body of Christ, the living church. Paul exhorts believers "that ye walk worthy of the vocation [calling] wherewith ye are called," especially to treat one another with humility, meekness, patience, and love, for "there is one body, and one Spirit, even as ye are called in one hope of your calling" (Eph. 4:1–4). Rather than being peace breakers, Christians must "let the peace of God rule in your hearts," to which they "are called in one body" (Col. 3:15).

Our calling to Christ implies that we are called to suffer with him for the glory of God. Peter says, "If, when ye do well, and suffer for it, ye take it patiently, this is acceptable with God. For even hereunto were ye called: because Christ also suffered for us, leaving us an example, that ye should follow his steps" (1 Pet. 2:20–21). Christ modeled holiness and integrity, submitting to authorities even when they were unfair, responding to insults with quietness and confidence in God's judgment, and suffering so that others may find restoration and return to God (vv. 18–25). Christians must live in unity, compassion, love, mercy, and courtesy, and return blessings for curses, knowing that to this they were "called" (3:9). Our suffering "as strangers and pilgrims" in this wicked world is not meaningless but an inevitable part of our mission to "shew forth the praises of him who hath called you out of darkness into his marvellous light" so that those who see our good works may glorify God (2:9, 11–12). Bruce Demarest writes, "Christ has called us to a life of proclamation and praise."[55]

Christians must continue to answer God's call. God's calling in one sense is a past event for Christians: they "which are called [perfect tense]" (Heb. 9:15). However, God continues to call them forward in holiness

55. Demarest, *The Cross and Salvation*, 231.

until they reach glory: God "calls [present tense] you into his own kingdom and glory" (1 Thess. 2:12 ESV). Paul's ambition, as should be true of every mature Christian, was to "press toward the mark for the prize of the high calling of God in Christ Jesus" (Phil. 3:14).

Hence, effectual calling is knowable in its internal and external effects. Effectual calling creates faith and repentance, and therefore launches the Christian on a trajectory of holiness. Effectual calling is a divinely powerful cause that produces effects. On the basis of these effects, believers may come to a solid assurance that they are called by God and so are justified and will be glorified (Rom. 8:30).

The most basic effect of effectual calling is faith in Christ, an inward knowledge of his beauty and glory that transforms the heart (2 Cor. 4:6). A living faith motivates the believer to pursue Christ and his will, and this pursuit assures us of our calling. Peter applies this principle when he exhorts believers to increase in faith, virtue, knowledge, self-control, patience, godliness, brotherly love, and Christlike love (2 Pet. 1:5–7). It is possible for Christians to backslide into unfruitfulness and so lose their assurance that their sins are forgiven (vv. 8–9). Therefore, Peter exhorted the brothers to "give diligence to make your calling and election sure," for those who have such graces and grow in them may be confident that they will never fall away, but will enjoy the eternal kingdom of Christ (vv. 10–11).

In order to avoid legalism at this point, we must remember not to reverse the order of cause and effect. God has called us to virtue (2 Pet. 1:3). He did not call us because of our virtue. Our godliness does not establish our calling, but establishes our knowledge of our calling, just as effects are evidence of their cause. John says, "Hereby we do know that we know him, if we keep his commandments" (1 John 2:3). Furthermore, our godliness does not arise from ourselves, but from God's power as we look by faith to the "exceeding great and precious promises" given to us in the gospel of Christ (2 Pet. 1:4). When we seek assurance, we must not only examine ourselves but fix our eyes upon Christ, the Priest who sacrificed himself for our sins and intercedes even now for us in heaven (1 John 2:1–2). Our calling is always to Christ.

10. Through effectual calling and its continuing effects on the called, *God infallibly brings them to glory*. Paul states the general principle that the call cannot fail: "For the gifts and the calling of God are irrevocable"

(Rom. 11:29 ESV).[56] Though Paul specifically addresses the national calling of Israel, he does so in the context of the personal salvation of God's elect by faith in the gospel (vv. 26–28). God's national call upon Israel is irrevocable in part because God elected individuals within Israel to be saved by grace (vv. 1–6). How much more, then, is God's call upon the elect individual irrevocable?

The Holy Scriptures ground the assurance of believers upon God's faithfulness to his call. God will establish the saints to the end when Christ returns, for "God is faithful, by whom ye were called" (1 Cor. 1:8–9). Paul prays that God will sanctify and preserve believers until the coming of Christ, and promises, "Faithful is he that calleth you, who also will do it" (1 Thess. 5:24). Peter assures suffering Christians, "The God of all grace, who hath called us unto his eternal glory by Christ Jesus, after that ye have suffered a while, make you perfect, stablish, strengthen, settle you" (1 Pet. 5:10). Once God has effectually called a person, that person's destiny is clear, for those "whom he called . . . them he also glorified" (Rom. 8:30).

Effectual calling is heavenly and glorious in its ultimate aim. The goal of effectual calling is not just conversion but complete sanctification and glorification. God has "called us to glory" (2 Pet. 1:3; cf. 1 Pet. 5:10). The children of God are "partakers of the heavenly calling" (Heb. 3:1). Christ died so that "they which are called might receive the promise of eternal inheritance" (Heb. 9:15). Our calling is closely associated with our hope (Eph. 1:18; 4:4). We are "called" to "eternal life," and in response we "fight the good fight of the faith" (1 Tim. 6:12).

Just as God's call brings unconverted sinners to Christ and conforms them to Christ's holiness and sufferings in this life, so it effectively brings them to the glory of Christ. These are not distinct callings, but facets of one calling in Christ. God "called you by our gospel, to the obtaining of the glory of our Lord Jesus Christ" (2 Thess. 2:14). The effectual call through the gospel summons sinners into the glorious kingdom of God (1 Thess. 2:12).

Effectual calling is a wondrous grace and privilege. Watson said, "God calls them to glory, as if a man were called out of a prison to sit upon a throne."[57] The Philadelphia Baptist Association reminded its churches in 1784 that "the way to advance in durable riches and righteousness, to

56. The word translated as "irrevocable" (*ametamelētos*, Rom. 11:29 ESV) means without change of mind or purpose, here referring to God's unchangeable purpose (cf. Heb. 7:21).

57. Watson, *A Body of Divinity*, 222.

live on high, live above the vanities and pomp of this trifling world and to shame those who walk unworthily, is to regain a sense of our heavenly vocation."[58] Let us never forget that we are called by the heavenly King to share in his holy kingdom.

Applications of the Doctrine of Effectual Calling

As our study of effectual calling has shown, this doctrine is of immense significance to our lives. Its applications are rich and manifold, and we will highlight a few to conclude this chapter.

1. *The church must preach the gospel for the salvation of sinners.* God's ordinary method of saving sinners does not bypass their minds but calls sinners to Christ through the word. The very terminology of the "call" reminds us that God's voice comes to us in words. Therefore, we must not wait for God to strike the unconverted with salvation like lightning from a blue sky. We must be faithful to deliver the gospel call and pray for God to deliver the effectual call.

2. *A person must be effectually called to be saved.* Apart from God's effectual call, no amount of education or moral reformation can save a sinner. Have you been effectually called to Christ? Your eternal happiness or sorrow hinges upon this question. Examine yourself, we implore you, to seek to determine whether you are in the faith. Has God supernaturally caused the light of Christ to shine in your heart? Does your life indicate that you have been called into God's glorious light? Do not delay. If God has not called you, then call upon him to save you before you close this book.

3. *A person's election makes itself known in his calling.* The golden chain of salvation shows that God brings salvation to the elect through effectual calling (Rom. 8:30). We cannot peer back into God's secret decree, and we should not try. The only way a person can know for sure in this life that he is chosen by God for salvation is to see that he has been called by God to Christ. If you lack assurance, then make your calling and election sure in your conscience. By grace, take hold of God's promises and strive to grow in holiness.

4. *Christians should glorify God alone for their conversion.* Though no one is a Christian unless he exercises faith and repentance, no saving faith

58. "The Circular Letter of the Philadelphia Baptist Association for 1784," in Terry Wolever, *The Life of John Gano, 1727–1804: Pastor-Evangelist of the Philadelphia Association*, Philadelphia Association Series (Springfield, MO: Particular Baptist Press, 2012), 489. Gano was the letter's primary author.

or repentance arises from the will of fallen man. It is all the gift of God. If you are among the called, then give thanks to the Father daily for rescuing you from the power of darkness and transferring you into the kingdom of his beloved Son (Col. 1:12–13). Stir up your heart with the thought that, despite your sins, God sovereignly summoned you to Christ and his glory. Declare his glory in every way that you can.

5. *The called must pursue practical holiness.* God's call does not terminate upon conversion but draws us into the way of holiness. Abraham Booth (1734–1806) said, "Happy are you, reader, if you know by experience what it is to be called by grace. If such be your state, it becomes your indispensable duty to walk worthy of your calling, for it is high, holy, heavenly. Yes, believer, your calling is truly noble." He concluded, "The consideration of these things, as a noble incentive to obedience, should fire your mind with godly zeal, should fill your heart with Christian gratitude, should direct your feet in the paths of duty, and manifest its constraining influence through your whole conduct."[59] Remember, Christian, you are one of the called!

6. *The called must cultivate the unity of the church.* Christian, you are not alone in your calling. God's calling joins you to his Son and his church. Do not act like an isolated individual, for that would contradict your very identity as one of the called. View yourself as part of a caravan of pilgrims summoned by the King to his celestial city and traveling together on the narrow road. Of what local church are you a member? How are you loving and serving your brothers and sisters there?

7. *The called should joyfully hope in a happy future.* If you received tickets in the mail to a dream vacation next year, all expenses paid, wouldn't you look forward to it with glad anticipation? If you became sad about your present circumstances, you might look at pictures of where you are going to brighten your day. How much more should Christians look at the promises of God's kingdom of glory and rejoice. God has called you to the glory of Christ. He is faithful, and he will do it. Booth said, "What shall I say? You are called from the slavery of sin, to the practice of holiness; into a state of grace here, and to the enjoyment of glory hereafter. In short, it is the High God that called you, it is the way of holiness in which you are called to walk, and it is an unfading inheritance, an eternal kingdom, you are called to enjoy."[60] Rejoice, Christian, for you are called by God!

59. Abraham Booth, *The Reign of Grace, from Its Rise to Its Consummation*, 1st American ed. (New York: T. Allen, 1793), 92–93.

60. Booth, *The Reign of Grace*, 93.

The hope of our heavenly calling should motivate us to seek heavenly treasure. Since we are citizens of heaven, Thomas White (d. 1672) said, "maintain a constant trade and traffic" with heaven and "expect returns" in incorruptible rewards. "Be always preparing for your passage" to your homeland, and you will receive a rich welcome there.[61]

Sing to the Lord

Celebrating God's Effectual Call

I was a wandering sheep, I did not love the fold;
I did not love my Shepherd's voice, I would not be controlled.
I was a wayward child, I did not love my home;
I did not love my Father's house, I loved afar to roam.

The Shepherd sought his sheep, the Father sought his child;
They followed me o'er vale and hill, o'er deserts waste and wild:
They found me nigh to death, famished and faint and lone;
They bound me with the bands of love, they saved the
wandering one.

Jesus my Shepherd is; 'twas he that loved my soul,
'Twas he that washed me in his blood, 'twas he that made me
whole;
'Twas he that sought the lost, that found the wandering sheep,
'Twas he that brought me to the fold, 'tis he that still doth keep.

I was a wandering sheep, I would not be controlled;
But now I love my Shepherd's voice, I love, I love the fold.
I was a wayward child, I once preferred to roam;
But now I love my Father's voice, I love, I love his home.

Horatius Bonar
Tune: Lebanon
Trinity Hymnal—Baptist Edition, No. 396

Questions for Meditation or Discussion

1. What do theologians mean by *effectual* calling?
2. What definition of effectual calling is presented in this book?

61. Thomas White, "Of Effectual Calling," in *Puritan Sermons, 1659–1689*, ed. James Nichols, 6 vols. (repr., Wheaton, IL: Richard Owen Roberts, 1981), 5:283.

3. How is each person in the Trinity active in effectual calling? Support your answer from Scripture.
4. How would you prove that effectual calling is extended to particular individuals chosen by God before the creation of the world?
5. Someone says, "The thing I can't stand about the idea of effectual calling is that God plays favorites. It's no wonder that Calvinists are so arrogant and look down on others." How do you respond?
6. What is the meaning of 2 Corinthians 4:6, and what are its implications for the doctrine of effectual calling?
7. How does effectual calling affect a person's relationship to Jesus Christ?
8. What Scripture passages show that faith and repentance are gifts of God?
9. What are the practical implications of God's call for holiness, church membership, and suffering?
10. A friend confides in you that the doctrines of election and calling make him nervous because he can't be sure if he is chosen and called. What do you say to him?
11. Are you effectually called? What evidence of calling is in your life?

Questions for Deeper Reflection

12. Why does the doctrine of effectual calling logically imply the doctrine of election, unless one believes that God saves everyone?
13. What theological problems might arise from the assertion that union with Christ is logically prior to effectual calling? That effectual calling is logically prior to union with Christ? What solution do the authors propose to this conundrum? How satisfying is that solution?

16

Effectual Calling, Part 2

Theological Controversy

The Scriptures give clear testimony that God's work of grace is free and effective in transforming sinners into repentant believers. However, the sovereignty of God's grace has been disputed. Therefore, in this chapter we address objections and questions concerning the doctrine of God's effectual call.

The primary dispute pertains to man's freedom to respond to God's grace. Referring to those who oppose the doctrine of divine sovereignty in salvation, Herman Bavinck wrote, "Their primary objection is always that the doctrine of efficacious and insuperable grace introduces a 'natural' coercion into the spiritual life, militates against the nature of rational beings, renders humans totally passive, and undermines moral freedom and responsibility."[1]

Terminology and Proper Framing of the Theological Issue

It is common to frame this issue according to the question of *irresistible grace* versus *resistible grace*—that is, whether God's saving call can be successfully resisted by man's will.[2] However, the term *irresistible grace*

1. Bavinck, *Reformed Dogmatics*, 4:84.

2. On TULIP, the popular (but relatively recently coined) summary of the Reformed doctrines of grace, in which the letter "I" stands for irresistible grace, see *RST*, 1:116–17.

was not originally chosen by Reformed divines, but was used by others to attack Reformed doctrine.[3] It was Jacob Arminius who said, "The whole controversy reduces itself to the solution of this question, 'Is the grace of God a certain irresistible force?'"[4]

The Canons of Dort do not use the term *irresistible grace*, but say, "This grace of regeneration does not treat men as senseless stocks and blocks, nor takes away their will and its properties, neither does violence thereto; but spiritually quickens, heals, corrects, and at the same time sweetly and powerfully bends it; that where carnal rebellion and resistance formerly prevailed, a ready and sincere spiritual obedience begins to reign."[5]

The term *irresistible grace* can be misunderstood, so whoever uses it should carefully explain that it does not involve coercion or violation of the human will, which freely resists God prior to salvation but freely embraces Christ when liberated from sin and given a new disposition by saving grace.[6] Johannes Polyander noted that nothing about God's effectual calling is "forced or impetuous [*violentus*], but sweet and suitably applied to turning the crooked will of the one who is moved for the better, so that from [being] unwilling he becomes willing."[7] Augustine said, "Therefore he is drawn in wondrous ways to will, by Him who knows how to work within the very hearts of men. Not that men who are unwilling should believe, which cannot be, but that they should be made willing from being unwilling."[8]

Another common way to frame the discussion is the distinction of *monergism* versus *synergism*. *Monergism* (from Greek *monos*, "alone," and *ergon*, "work") means that God's grace alone acts to save. *Synergism* (from *syn*, "with, together," and *ergon*, "work") means that God's grace and man's will cooperate toward salvation.

However, the distinction between monergism and synergism must be rightly applied. All true Christians (as opposed to Pelagians) agree that God's grace alone takes the first step to attract and draw sinners, for God always initiates with man. Furthermore, they agree that salvation involves

---

3. Turretin, *Institutes*, 15.6.3 (2:547); Edwards, *Efficacious Grace*, in *WJE*, 21:249; and Bavinck, *Reformed Dogmatics*, 4:82.

4. Arminius, *Declaration of Sentiments*, in *Works*, 1:664.

5. The Canons of Dort (Head 3/4, Art. 16), in *The Three Forms of Unity*, 147.

6. Augustus H. Strong, *Systematic Theology*, 3 vols. (Philadelphia: Griffith and Rowland, 1909), 3:792–93; and Hoekema, *Saved by Grace*, 105. See Joel R. Beeke, *Living for God's Glory: An Introduction to Calvinism* (Lake Mary, FL: Reformation Trust, 2008), 104.

7. Polyander, Walaeus, Thysius, and Rivetus, *Synopsis Purioris Theologiae*, 30.42 (2:225).

8. Augustine, *Against Two Letters of the Pelagians*, 1.37.19, in *NPNF*[1], 5:389.

the acts of both God and man, for human beings must believe in Christ and repent of sin. Soteriological monergism, or the Augustinian and Reformed doctrine of salvation, is distinguished by the belief that God's grace alone produces saving faith and vital union with Christ, for effectual grace overcomes man's unbelief and resistance against the gospel. According to synergism, man must cooperate with God by not resisting his grace in order for that grace to bring man to faith and salvation. The difference lies in the effectual power of grace.

Therefore, this debate is clarified by the distinction of *effectual grace* versus *necessary grace*.[9] *Effectual grace* means that God's saving call is an act of divine power that effectively produces salvation in all to whom God sends it. Hence, John Calvin referred to God's drawing of sinners to Christ as "effectual calling" (*efficax vocatio*).[10] Effectual calling does not save apart from human dispositions and acts. Rather, by this calling God creates the human dispositions and acts necessary to receive salvation. The Canons of Dort (Heads 3/4, Art. 12) say, "The will thus renewed is not only actuated and influenced by God, but in consequence of this influence, becomes itself active. Wherefore also, man is himself rightly said to believe and repent, by virtue of that grace received."[11] By contrast, *necessary grace* means that God gives to people what they need for their conversion, but their progress to faith and repentance is contingent on something in them that God's grace does not effectively produce.

The doctrine of effectual calling makes sense only in the context of the biblical doctrine of sin. Therefore, the divines at the Synod of Dort addressed both doctrines together. Different views of the power of God's call correlate to the distinction of *total inability* versus *natural or restored ability* among the unsaved to respond rightly to the gospel call.[12] Those who reject the doctrine of effectual calling believe either that fallen

9. Hodge, *Systematic Theology*, 2:675. Hodge noted that it is not properly called "effectual" because of its results when people choose to believe and are saved, but because of its inherent power to infallibly produce salvation. Sometimes what we have called "necessary" grace is called "sufficient." See the view rebuked in the Canons of Dort (Heads 3/4, Art. 10), in *Reformed Confessions*, 4:137. However, technically speaking, if grace were "sufficient" to produce faith and repentance, it would be effectual in doing so. Hooker, *The Application of Redemption . . . The First Eight Books*, 427–35; and Barrett, *Salvation by Grace*, 85.

10. Calvin, *Commentaries*, on 1 Cor. 1:9; cf. *Commentaries*, on 1 Pet. 1:1–2; *Canons and Decrees of the Council of Trent, with the Antidote*, in *Tracts Relating to the Reformation*, 3:121 (cf. the use of "effectual" in 111, 113, 155); and *On the Eternal Predestination of God*, in *Reformed Confessions*, 1:709, 714, 765, 798 (citing Augustine).

11. *The Three Forms of Unity*, 145.

12. Reymond, *A New Systematic Theology of the Christian Faith*, 714; MacArthur and Mayhue, eds., *Biblical Doctrine*, 576–77; and Letham, *Systematic Theology*, 656–57.

mankind retains some spiritual ability to respond well to God or that God has restored a measure of spiritual ability to people before saving them so that they can respond and believe. By contrast, the Canons of Dort say that men "are neither able nor willing to return to God," and so the fact that some "who are called by the gospel obey the call and are converted is not to be ascribed to the proper exercise of free will . . . but it must be wholly ascribed to God."[13]

Augustinian and Reformed theologians believe that God's calling must be effectual because nothing less would save people enslaved to sin. We need an effectual calling that, as Thomas White said, is "the real separation of the soul unto God; and a clothing it with such gracious abilities, whereby it may be enabled to repent of its sins, and to believe in his Son"; a calling that accomplishes "our translation from the state of nature—which is a state of sin, wrath, death, and damnation—to a state of grace, which is a state of holiness, life, peace, and eternal salvation."[14] Such a calling is monergistic grace, the work of God alone, for it is "a spiritual resurrection of the soul" and "a new creation of the soul" (cf. Eph. 1:19; 2:5, 10).[15] In this work, the Canons of Dort (Heads 3/4, Art. 11) explain, the Holy Spirit "opens the closed, and softens the hardened heart, and circumcises that which was uncircumcised, infuses new qualities into the will, which though heretofore dead, He quickens; from being evil, disobedient, and refractory, He renders it good, obedient, and pliable; actuates and strengthens it, that like a good tree, it may bring forth the fruits of good actions."[16]

Various Views of God's Grace in Relation to the Sinner's Will

The Scriptures teach that man has a will and is responsible for his decisions and actions; they also teach that God is sovereign and free in the gift of salvation. However, theologians have differed sharply in how to put these truths together without nullifying either one. Under other theological loci we have already considered the doctrines of predestination, original sin, and the free choice of the will.[17] Here we focus on how different theological traditions have viewed God's saving grace in the calling of sinners so that they willingly come to Christ.

13. The Canons of Dort (Heads 3/4, Arts. 3, 10), in *The Three Forms of Unity*, 141, 143.
14. White, "Of Effectual Calling," in *Puritan Sermons, 1659–1689*, 5:272.
15. White, "Of Effectual Calling," in *Puritan Sermons, 1659–1689*, 5:274–75.
16. *The Three Forms of Unity*, 144.
17. On predestination, see *RST*, 1:979–1057 (chaps. 49–51). On original sin and the free choice of the will, see *RST*, 2:365–434 (chaps. 19–22).

Natural Ability (Pelagianism)

The most optimistic view of human ability is that taught by Pelagius (fl. 380–420). At the core of Pelagianism is the belief that after Adam's sin, man retained the natural ability to obey God completely by human free will.[18] God's grace consists of creating us with the freedom of the will to choose good, giving us the truth of the Word to cast off sinful habits, and granting the promise of forgiveness by Christ's blood.[19] Therefore, the only grace needed to respond rightly to God's law and gospel is that contained in human nature. A synod of bishops meeting in Carthage in 418 condemned Pelagianism as inconsistent with the Christian faith.[20]

The Pelagian view of freedom and grace has reappeared in modern theological liberalism, with its denial of original sin, affirmation of human goodness, and application of the theory of evolution to human progress.[21] Thus, salvation is activating the potential already latent in all people. Friedrich Schleiermacher said that "the essence of redemption" is "that the God-consciousness already present in human nature, though feeble and repressed, becomes stimulated and made dominant by the entrance of the living influence of Christ."[22] Tendencies toward Pelagianism may also appear in evangelical churches through the influence of theologians such as Charles Grandison Finney (1792–1875), who said that a sinner is passive only with respect to the Holy Spirit's giving "the perception of the truth," but the sinner is the active agent in regeneration, and so "regeneration consists in the sinner changing his ultimate choice."[23]

18. Pelagius, "The Christian Life and Other Essays," trans. Ford Lewis Battles (Pittsburgh: s.n., 1972), 55–56, 61, 64; cf. G. F. Wiggers, *An Historical Presentation of Augustinism and Pelagianism from the Original Sources*, trans. and ed. Ralph Emerson (Andover, MA: Gould, Newman, and Saxton, 1840), 83–88; Robert F. Evans, *Pelagius: Inquiries and Reappraisals* (New York: Seabury, 1968), 100–101, 104; and Karen C. Huber, "The Pelagian Heresy: Observations on Its Social Context" (PhD diss., Oklahoma State University, 1979), 59–60.

19. Pelagius, "The Christian Life," 65; Evans, *Pelagius*, 108–11; and Huber, "The Pelagian Heresy," 64–65.

20. Wiggers, *An Historical Presentation of Augustinism and Pelagianism*, 171–73.

21. Demarest, *The Cross and Salvation*, 205. He cites Lyman Abbott (1835–1922), an influential Congregational pastor. See J. Gresham Machen, *Christianity and Liberalism* (1923; repr., Grand Rapids, MI: Eerdmans, 1992), 64–68.

22. Schleiermacher, *The Christian Faith*, 2:476. This God-consciousness or "feeling of absolute dependency" is "a universal element of life" embedded in human nature (1:133–34), and thus Schleiermacher's view of salvation is the stirring up of what is already in man by creation, though hindered by sin.

23. Charles G. Finney, *Lectures on Systematic Theology: Embracing Lectures on Moral Government, Together with Atonement, Moral and Physical Depravity, Regeneration, Philosophical Theories, and Evidences of Regeneration* (Oberlin, OH: James M. Fitch, 1846), 497, 500; cf. Demarest, *The Cross and Salvation*, 289.

Restored Ability by Universal Necessary Grace (Roman Catholicism and Arminianism)

Many professing Christians reject the baldly heretical assertions of Pelagianism that no grace beyond nature is necessary for conversion, but still preserve a central function for man's will in determining his salvation—synergism. God restores the human will to its ability to either receive or resist his saving grace by giving a universal, necessary grace, called *prevenient grace* because it "comes before" (Latin *praevenio*) man's response.

The official doctrine of Roman Catholicism follows this trajectory, though theologians of that church have proposed a variety of views, ranging from Augustinianism to semi-Pelagianism. John Eck (1483–1543) said, "We assert the pull of the Father through prevenient and cooperating grace [John 6:44], but to assent to that pull, and not to harden our hearts, if we have heard his voice—this is of free will."[24] The Council of Trent declared that a sinner becomes righteous when "by his own free will" he cooperates with the unmerited "prevenient grace of God."[25] Bitter debates about the efficacy of grace erupted between the Dominicans and the Jesuits (both orders in the Roman Catholic Church), which the papacy could not resolve except by prohibiting further discussion. The question exploded again during the Jansenist controversy of the seventeenth century, in which the Roman Catholic Church condemned the doctrine that there is an effectual grace of God that cannot be successfully resisted by man.[26] By condemning the doctrines of Cornelius Jansenius (1585–1638), the church unwittingly rejected Augustine's own soteriology.[27] The denial of "irresistible" grace continues in modern Roman Catholicism, which

24. John Eck, *Enchiridion of Commonplaces: Against Luther and Other Enemies of the Church*, trans. Ford Lewis Battles (Grand Rapids, MI: Baker, 1979), 218.

25. Council of Trent, Session 6, Chap. 5, in *The Creeds of Christendom*, ed. Schaff, 2:92.

26. On the controversies involving Michael Baius, Leonard Lessius, Domingo Bañez, Luis de Molina, Robert Bellarmine, and Cornelius Jansenius, see Wim François and Antonio Gerace, "The Doctrine of Justification and the Rise of Pluralism in the Post-Tridentine Catholic Church," in *More than Luther: The Reformation and the Rise of Pluralism in Europe*, ed. Karla Boersma and Herman J. Selderhuis, Refo500 Academic Studies 55 (Göttingen: Vandenhoeck & Ruprecht, 2019), 15–40.

27. "Good arguments may be advanced to show that both sides were right in their accusations. Jansenists were on firm ground in saying they were faithful to the Augustinian teaching, and quite justified in scenting Pelagian errors in the Jesuit theology. The Jesuits were no less right in demonstrating the fundamental conformity of Jansenist tenets with Calvin's theory of predestination. This amounts to saying that, by condemning Jansenius, the Church was in effect condemning—without, of course, saying it explicitly—Augustine himself, its own greatest theological authority." Leszek Kolakowski, *God Owes Us Nothing: A Brief Remark on Pascal's Religion and the Spirit of Jansenism* (Chicago: University of Chicago Press, 1995), 5. See Owen, *Pneumatologia*, in *Works*, 3:300–301.

teaches that the cooperation of human free will is necessary to render God's grace effective.[28]

Though Arminian theologians significantly differ from the Roman Catholic Church in many doctrines, they, too, teach universal prevenient grace. Against Pelagius, Arminius taught that man's free will cannot do any "true and spiritual good" without an internal work of prevenient grace.[29] However, he said that all sinners have received "sufficient grace" to be saved if they so choose, or God's justice could not condemn them.[30] Arminius said, "All unregenerate persons have freedom of will, and a capacity of resisting the Holy Spirit, of rejecting the proffered grace of God."[31] He further affirmed, "To him who does what he can by the primary grace already conferred upon him . . . God will bestow further grace."[32] God's call and witness go out to all men through general revelation; if the gospel is not preached to them, it is their fault for suppressing the truth, but this truth will lead to salvation by grace "if rightly used."[33] Though there are various theologies that might be called "Arminian," evangelical Arminianism insists that original sin makes all men unable to respond rightly to God apart from prevenient grace, as Thomas Summers (1812–1882) asserted.[34]

Necessary but Not Effectual Grace with the Word (Lutheranism)

A third option is to reject universal grace, but to affirm internal grace that always accompanies the preaching of God's Word. The promise itself contains God's power. Though proponents of this view reject synergism, they also reject the idea that God's grace is inherently effectual to save God's elect. Rather, the promise is universal and grace comes to all who hear the Word, but God saves according to how people respond.

---

28. *Catechism of the Catholic Church*, secs. 2001–2002. For a pre-Vatican II approach, see Ott, *Fundamentals of Catholic Dogma*, 246. For a post-Vatican II Roman Catholic perspective modeled after Karl Rahner, see Roger Haight, "Sin and Grace," in *Systematic Theology: Roman Catholic Perspectives*, ed. Francis Schüssler Fiorenza and John P. Galvin, 2 vols. (Minneapolis: Fortress, 1991), 2:117–26.

29. Arminius, Letter to Hippolytus a Collibus, sec. 4, in *Works*, 2:700.

30. Arminius, *Certain Articles*, 17.12, in *Works*, 2:721–22; cf. *The Arminian Confession of 1621*, trans. and ed. Mark A. Ellis, Princeton Theological Monograph Series (Eugene, OR: Pickwick, 2005), 6.2 (59).

31. Arminius, *Certain Articles*, 17.5, in *Works*, 2:721.

32. Arminius, *Apology*, Art. 17, in *Works*, 2:20. On these points, see the Arminian Remonstrance (Arts. 3–4), in *Reformed Confessions*, 4:43.

33. Arminius, *An Examination . . . of a Treatise, Concerning the Order and Mode of Predestination and the Amplitude of Divine Grace by Rev. William Perkins*, in *Works*, 3:484.

34. Thomas Summers, *Systematic Theology: A Complete Body of Wesleyan Arminian Divinity*, ed. John J. Tigert, 2 vols. (Nashville: Publishing House of the Methodist Episcopal Church, South, 1888), 2:34–35, 54–55. See Barrett, *Salvation by Grace*, 241–42.

This is the view of historic Lutheranism, which frames the question according to Martin Luther's distinction between law (human responsibility) and gospel (sovereign, unconditional grace).[35] The Lutheran churches confess, "Through Adam's fall human nature and our essence are completely corrupted."[36] Though people are not blocks of wood without thought or volition, the unregenerate human mind is "blind in spiritual matters," and the will is "God's enemy."[37] This view denies that fallen human beings can complete or even initiate their conversion apart from God's grace.[38] God saves sinners by grace alone (*sola gratia*): "They are and remain God's enemy until by his grace alone, without any contribution of their own, they are converted, made believers, reborn, and renewed by the power of the Holy Spirit through the Word as it is preached and heard."[39] However, those who hear the Word of God—and "in this Word the Holy Spirit is present"—must "not plug their ears."[40] Those who despise God's Word are "blocking the Holy Spirit's ordinary path, so that he cannot carry out his work in them."[41]

The Formula of Concord states, "The Holy Spirit most certainly wills to be present, effective, and active through the Word when it is preached, heard, and considered. . . . [God foreordained] that he would harden, reject, and condemn all those whom he called through the Word when they spurn the Word and resist and persist in resisting the Holy Spirit, who wants to exercise his power in them and be efficacious through the Word. This is why 'many are called and few are chosen.'"[42] Lutheran theologians attribute every good motion to the grace of God, but, as Martin Chemnitz (1522–1586) said, "When prevenient grace, that is the first beginnings of faith and conversion are given to a man, immediately the battle between the flesh and the Spirit begins," and throughout this process "the will of man . . . can resist the Holy Spirit . . . and it can destroy the work of

35. On Martin Luther's affirmation of both God's total responsibility for all things and man's total responsibility for human actions, including evil, see Robert Kolb, *Bound Choice, Election, and the Wittenberg Theological Method: From Martin Luther to the Formula of Concord* (Minneapolis: Fortress, 2017), 31–65.

36. Formula of Concord (Epitome, 1.8), in *The Book of Concord*, 488–89.

37. Formula of Concord (Epitome, 2.1–2), in *The Book of Concord*, 491–92.

38. Formula of Concord (Epitome, 2.9–10), in *The Book of Concord*, 493. See Martin Chemnitz, *Loci Theologici*, I.6.5, trans. J. A. O. Preus, in *Chemnitz's Works* (St. Louis, MO: Concordia, 2008), 7:429, 437.

39. Formula of Concord (Solid Declaration, 2.5), in *The Book of Concord*, 544.

40. Formula of Concord (Epitome, 2.3), in *The Book of Concord*, 492 cf. Epitome, 11.8, in *The Book of Concord*, 517.

41. Formula of Concord (Epitome, 11.12), in *The Book of Concord*, 518.

42. Formula of Concord (Solid Declaration, 11.39–40), in *The Book of Concord*, 647.

God."[43] Nevertheless, as Heinrich Mueller (1631–1675) said, "To the degree that we ascribe something to ourselves in the process of conversion, to that degree we rob God, deny His glory and the power of Christ's death."[44] Carl F. W. Walther (1811–1887) explained, "If you willfully resist, you cannot be converted. Yes, it is alone God's work if a human being is converted; but it is man's sole doing if he is not converted."[45]

Particular and Effectual Saving Grace (Augustinianism and Reformed Theology)

The last view of God's saving grace affirms that God issues a general call to all who hear the Word of God. It also affirms that if a person is informed by the Word and awakened by the Spirit, but still resists the Spirit and rejects Christ, it is entirely the sinner's fault. So far, it agrees with the Roman Catholic, Arminian, and Lutheran teachings on this topic. However, according to this view, God gives effectual grace to some people so that they willingly repent and believe.

Salvation by effectual inward grace was the teaching of Augustine. He said, "It is not by law and teaching uttering their lessons from without, but by a secret, wonderful, and ineffable power operating within, that God works in men's hearts not only revelations of the truth, but also good dispositions of the will."[46] He added that God speaks in the effectual call not to the ear but to the heart, and this grace "is rejected by no hard heart, because it is given for the sake of first taking away the hardness of the heart."[47] Augustine wrote,

> Since it is not a good will that precedes a call but a call that precedes a good will, it is rightly ascribed to God who calls that we will what is good. . . . For the effectiveness of God's mercy cannot be in man's power, so that he would be merciful to no avail if man were unwilling, because, if he should will to have mercy even on those persons . . . he could call them in such a way as would be appropriate for them, so that they would be moved and would understand and would follow.[48]

---

43. Chemnitz, *Loci Theologici*, I.6.7, in *Works*, 7:449, 452.

44. Cited in C. F. W. Walther, *Walther's Works: All Glory to God* (St. Louis, MO: Concordia, 2016), 155.

45. Walther, *All Glory to God*, 158.

46. Augustine, *On the Grace of Christ*, 25.24, in *NPNF*[1], 5:227.

47. Augustine, *On the Predestination of the Saints*, 13.8, in *NPNF*[1], 5:505. Calvin cites this statement in *Institutes*, 3.24.1.

48. Augustine, *Miscellany of Questions in Response to Simplician*, 1.2.12–13, trans. Boniface Ramsey, ed. Raymond Canning, in *The Works of Saint Augustine: A Translation for the 21st Century*, 42 vols. (Hyde Park, NY: New City, 1995–2015), 1/12:194–95.

This is also the teaching of Reformed theologians. The Canons of Dort (Head 3/4, Art. 12) note that the Bible compares this grace to a spiritual resurrection and new creation, and say,

> This is in no wise effected merely by the external preaching of the gospel, by moral suasion [attempt at persuasion by appeal to the mind],[49] or such a mode of operation, that after God has performed His part, it still remains in the power of man to be regenerated or not, to be converted or to continue unconverted; but it is evidently a supernatural work, most powerful . . . so that all in whose heart God works in this marvelous manner are certainly, infallibly, and effectually regenerated, and do actually believe.[50]

The Westminster Confession of Faith (10.2) says, "This effectual call is of God's free and special grace alone, not from any thing at all foreseen in man, who is altogether passive therein, until, being quickened and renewed by the Holy Spirit, he is thereby enabled to answer this call, and to embrace the grace offered and conveyed in it."[51]

In summary, we might imagine asking four professing Christians, "Why are you saved?" They all answer that they are saved by trust in Christ, who died for their sins and rose again. The next question is posed: "Why did you trust in Christ?" The Pelagian answers, "I came to Christ by my own free will." The other three say, "I came to Christ because the grace of God drew me." Another question is posed to these three: "Why did you come to Christ when many who hear the gospel do not?" The Arminian Christian says, "I cooperated with the grace that God gives to everyone." The Lutheran Christian responds, "I did not resist the grace that God's Word brings to all who hear it." The Reformed Christian answers, "God overcame my resistance and sweetly inclined my heart to believe God's Word, so that I willingly came to Christ."[52]

The Effectual Power of God's Saving Grace

Sinners, no matter how much they are informed in mind and awakened in conscience, are still in a state of spiritual darkness such that they hate God

---

49. Compare John Owen's remark: "By *suasion* we intend such a persuasion as may or may not be effectual; so absolutely we call that only *persuasion* whereby a man is actually persuaded." *Pneumatologia*, in *Works*, 6:301, emphasis original.

50. *The Three Forms of Unity*, 144–45.

51. *Reformed Confessions*, 4:247.

52. Cf. Demarest, *The Cross and Salvation*, 206, 208, 210, 216.

and love sin (John 3:19–20; 15:18–25). Adam's sin has placed all his natural descendants under the power of sin so that no one is righteous, seeks God, or does good (Rom. 3:9–12; 5:12). Human beings lacking the Holy Spirit are dead in sin (Eph. 2:1) and are so hostile to God that they cannot submit to his law (Rom. 8:5–8). They are enslaved to sin (John 8:34) and subjected to the corrupting power of Satan (v. 44; 12:31). They are totally unable to perceive or enter God's kingdom (3:3, 5), come to Christ (6:44, 65), hear Christ's word (8:43), believe in Christ (12:39), receive the Holy Spirit (14:17), or bear fruit glorifying to God (15:5, 8).[53]

In order to save them, the Lord must effectually call them so that they have spiritual eyes to see the glory of Christ (1 Cor. 1:23–24; 2 Cor. 4:6) and exercise justifying faith (Rom. 8:30). John Brown of Haddington wrote, "An almighty, invincible, or as others term it, irresistible, influence of the Holy Ghost is therefore absolutely necessary in and with the outward call of the gospel in order to apply it to men's hearts, so as to translate them from their state of sin and misery into a state of union to, and fellowship with Christ."[54]

In our study of what the Bible teaches concerning God's effectual call in the previous chapter, we saw that his saving grace powerfully and infallibly produces faith and repentance.[55] To be saved by grace is to be raised from the dead and made a new creation (Eph. 2:1, 5, 10)—both of which involve omnipotent, effectual, divine power.

One of the clearest statements of the effectual power of God's saving grace comes directly from our Lord Jesus Christ, who teaches, "No man can come to me, except the Father which hath sent me draw him: and I will raise him up at the last day. It is written in the prophets, And they shall be all taught of God. Every man therefore that hath heard, and hath learned of the Father, cometh unto me" (John 6:44–45). To come to Christ is to trust him with saving faith (v. 35), but no one is spiritually able to exercise faith in Jesus Christ apart from a powerful work of God. The word translated as "draw" (*helkuō*) literally means to move by pulling, such as pulling fish in a net or dragging a man somewhere.[56] Here it

53. See the discussion of total depravity and total inability in *RST*, 2:400–416 (chap. 21).

54. Brown, *Systematic Theology*, 350.

55. See the discussion in chap. 15 of Acts 3:26; 5:31; 11:18, 20–21; 13:48; 16:14–15; 26:18; Rom. 8:30; 1 Cor. 1:23–24; 12:3; Eph. 1:15–16; 2:8; 6:23; 1 Tim. 1:14; 2 Tim. 1:13–14.

56. For the common use of *helkuō* or *helkō* to refer to moving objects or people by physical force, see Deut. 31:3; 2 Kingdoms (2 Sam.) 22:17; Ps. 9:30 (10:9); Isa. 10:15; Jer. 45(38):13; Hab. 1:15 LXX; John 18:10; 21:6, 11; Acts 16:19; 21:30; James 2:6. See also Sirach 28:19; 3 Macc. 4:7; 5:49; 4 Macc. 11:9 LXX. The term can also be used for summoning a military force under one's

refers to God effectively drawing a person spiritually toward Christ in willing faith. This drawing is so effective that Christ says that everyone thus taught and drawn will come to him and be raised up on the last day. Therefore, the drawing is no mere attraction but powerful action resulting in spiritual change.[57]

Christ also says, "All that the Father giveth me *shall come* to me," and, "No man *can come* unto me, except it were given unto him of my Father" (John 6:37, 65). Bruce Ware summarizes, "First, all those drawn to Christ by the Father do in fact come and are in fact saved (6:37, 39, 45). Second, only those drawn to Christ by the Father can in fact come (6:44, 65). Both of these points are derived directly from Jesus's own teaching within the context of continued unbelief (6:36, 64)." We may conclude, then, that this drawing is "effectual" and "selective."[58]

Consider what we would have to change in John 6:37 in order for the verse to fit the doctrine of resistible saving grace. The text reads, "All that the Father giveth me shall come to me; and him that cometh to me I will in no wise cast out." Christ's words would need to be adjusted to read, "*Some people* that the Father giveth me shall come to me; and him that cometh to me I *might later* cast out." That is a far cry from what our Lord said.

Objections to Effectual Calling

Although the Scriptures plainly teach that God's saving call is effectual to draw people to Christ, theologians raise a number of objections to the doctrine, which they believe require its modification. Some objections to effectual grace are aimed against other doctrines, such as election and human depravity and inability. These we have addressed under their proper loci.

---

command (1 Macc. 10:82). Its use in "draw me" (Song 1:4) is poetic and metaphorical, parallel to "the king hath brought me into his chambers." The Lord says, "I drew you with compassion" (Jer. 38[31]:3 LXX) in the context of the new covenant, where God promises to write his laws on the heart (vv. 31–34). That is an interesting parallel to John 6:44, but it is not clear if the LXX correctly renders the Hebrew word (*mashak*), which may mean to "prolong, continue" here (cf. Ps. 36:10).

57. It is objected that the word translated as "draw" (*helkuō* or *helkō*) can also mean "attract." Roger E. Olson, *Against Calvinism* (Grand Rapids, MI: Zondervan, 2011), 163. However, this meaning is secondary and less common, and even then "attract" refers to powerful forces such as magnetism and magical spells that are said to produce action. Liddell and Scott, *A Greek-English Lexicon*, II.8 (535). Plato used the phrase "to persuade and constrain" (*pros to peithein te kai helkein*), but constraint here has the sense of innate, natural "necessity." *The Republic*, vol.1, *Books 1–5*, trans. Paul Shorey, rev. ed., Loeb Classical Library 237 (Cambridge, MA: Harvard University Press, 1937), 5.7.458d (1:456–59).

58. Ware, "The Place of Effectual Calling and Grace in a Calvinist Soteriology," in *The Grace of God, the Bondage of the Will*, ed. Schreiner and Ware, 2:356.

However, there are other objections brought specifically against effectual calling.

Objection 1: God calls all people to Christ through the gospel. The king says to his servants, "Invite to the wedding feast as many as you find" (Matt. 22:9 ESV). John Miley (1813–1895) wrote that this biblical truth cannot be reconciled with the idea that God wills to call only some effectively to salvation: "They were not given to the Son to be redeemed, because it was not the pleasure of the Father that they should be saved. How then can the offer of salvation be made to them?"[59] William Pope (1822–1903) said that "there is no trace in Scripture" of any distinction between the external call of the gospel and "effectual calling."[60]

In reply, we teach that God's general call goes out through the gospel, but Scripture also speaks of God's saving call as a grace given only to some. Believers in Christ are "the called" in distinction from unbelievers (1 Cor. 1:23–24). If this calling referred to the general call of the gospel, then "the called" would refer to all who heard it.

An Arminian counterargument is that believers are designated "the called" only because they have received a place in God's church, which, like Israel, is God's corporately chosen and called people.[61] Or, "call" is said to mean "name" in such texts, as in giving those in Christ the name of God's people (Rom. 9:7, 25–26).[62] However, in the texts that pertain to our topic, calling is not just conferring a new status or name, but an act of God on people by which he brings them out of the darkness into his light (1 Pet. 2:9), draws them into fellowship with Christ (1 Cor. 1:9), and summons them to his kingdom and glory.[63]

Objection 2: Obligation implies ability. Since people who hear the gospel have the obligation to repent and believe in Christ, they must have the ability to do so without special help from God. Though Arminian Christians use this argument, it is a Pelagian device, for it implies that all people have the ability to keep God's law perfectly, love God with all their being, and avoid all sin—because such is our obligation. It certainly rules out the need for supernatural grace. Bavinck noted, "If humans are by nature capable of meeting those conditions [such as faith and repentance],

59. John Miley, *Systematic Theology*, 2 vols. (New York: Eaton and Mains, 1892, 1894), 2:267.
60. William Pope, *A Compendium of Christian Theology*, 3 vols. (London: Wesleyan Conference Office, 1877), 2:345.
61. Pope, *A Compendium of Christian Theology*, 2:346.
62. Thus, Brian Abasciano, cited in Hoglund, *Called by Triune Grace*, 53–57.
63. 1 Thess. 2:12; 2 Thess. 2:14; 1 Pet. 5:10.

they are in fact so good that there is no need whatever for regeneration in a scriptural sense. In that case, a moral upbringing and self-improvement are more than sufficient."[64]

This objection fails to distinguish between different kinds of ability. Certainly, ethical obligation presumes created faculties, such as the mind to understand, the will to choose, and the physical capacity to perform the duty. However, obligation does not require that people have the inward goodness necessary to do the good demanded of them, particularly if previous sin has rendered them wholly inclined toward evil. Since Adam's disobedience, men are dead in sin, ruled by Satan, and unable to do any spiritual good. They are "by nature" objects of God's wrath, and so we may speak of man's *natural inability* to please God since the fall (Eph. 2:1–3).

There are grave problems with the idea that people are free and worthy of praise or blame only if they have the inner ability to choose either good or evil. Brown wrote, "Hath God then no freedom of choice, no liberty? Are all his attributes and works unworthy of praise, because his infinite and unchangeable perfection of nature cannot admit his doing any thing base or sinful?" He also asked, "Are the act of devils no sins, because their inclination is fixed on mischief?"[65] God's Word teaches both the obligation and the inability of fallen men to do good (Rom. 3:12, 19; 8:7–8). Sin is deeply engraved upon men's hearts (Jer. 17:1), and God must take away their hearts of stone and give them hearts of flesh (Ezek. 11:19).

Objection 3: God gives prevenient grace to all people through Christ. It is written in John 1:9, "That was the true Light, which lighteth every man that cometh into the world." The verb translated as "lighteth" (*photizō*) can be used for the spiritual illumination of the heart (Eph. 1:18). Thus, some conclude that Christ's light shines within the soul of every human being in the world. John Wesley said this light is grace that can lead to salvation: "This light, if man did not hinder, would shine more and more to the perfect day."[66] He added, "There is a measure of free will supernaturally restored to every man, together with that supernatural light which 'enlightens every man that cometh into the world.'"[67] Roger Olson says,

64. Bavinck, *Reformed Dogmatics*, 4:84.

65. Brown, *Systematic Theology*, 347.

66. John Wesley, *Explanatory Notes upon the New Testament*, 2nd ed. (London, 1757), on John 1:9 (222).

67. John Wesley, *Predestination Calmly Considered*, sec. 45, in *The Works of John Wesley*, 10 vols., 3rd ed. (1872; repr., Grand Rapids, MI: Baker, 1979), 10:230.

"Because of Jesus Christ and the Holy Spirit no human being is actually in a state of absolute darkness and depravity. . . . No human being actually exists in that natural state."[68] Instead, Olson posits an "intermediate stage" between being unregenerate and regenerate, a spiritual condition in which Christ's grace has brought a sinner's soul "to a point where it can respond freely to the divine call" but also "is able to resist and spurn the prevenient grace of God by denying the gospel."[69]

In response, we note that contrary to the claim that Christ's light partially illuminates the hearts of unbelievers so that they may choose the Lord, Christ said of the unbeliever, "There is no light in him" (John 11:10). Though the light of God's truth may shine upon a sinner and even have some effect on his mind and conscience, that influence does not change the state of his heart from blindness and darkness until God saves him.[70]

What, then, does John 1:9 mean when it says that Christ "lighteth every man"? One interpretation, found in early Reformed exegesis, is that this illumination refers to Christ's work as Creator and Lord (vv. 1–3) to give the power of reasoning and the testimony of conscience to every human being.[71] However, against this interpretation it must be observed that the metaphor of "light" in the Gospel of John is constantly linked to Christ's incarnate mission to bring eternal life into this dark and dead world, not his work as the Creator and Sustainer of the universe.[72]

Another, more likely, interpretation recognizes that the verb translated as "lighteth" can mean to teach, as one man instructs others.[73] In the context of John 1, this enlightenment refers to the objective truth made known by the incarnate Word (John 1:1, 14, 18). Christ compared John the Baptist to a light that shone upon those who heard his preaching, though many of them did not repent (5:35). In a similar manner, Matthew's Gospel cites the prophecy of Isaiah concerning the shining of divine light in the darkness and applies it to Christ's preaching in Galilee (Isa. 9:2; Matt. 4:12–17). D. A. Carson comments, "Inner illumination then is not in view. . . . What is at stake, rather, is the objective revelation, the 'light' that comes into the

68. Roger E. Olson, *Arminian Theology: Myths and Realities* (Downers Grove, IL: InterVarsity Press, 2006), 154.

69. Olson, *Arminian Theology*, 164–65.

70. See John 9:39–41; 12:35, 40, 46; Acts 26:18; 2 Cor. 4:4; 6:14; Eph. 4:18; 5:8; Col. 1:13.

71. Calvin, *Commentaries*, on John 1:9; and Anonymous [Dutch Reformed Divines], *The Dutch Annotations upon the Whole Bible*, on John 1:9.

72. John 1:4–5, 7–9; 3:19–21; 5:35; 8:12; 9:5; 11:9–10; 12:35–36, 46.

73. 2 Kings 12:2; 17:27, 28; Ps. 118[119]:130 LXX; Eph. 3:9.

world by the incarnation of the Word."[74] John 1:9 teaches that no one receives the knowledge of salvation apart from the Word revealed by Christ.

Arminian theologians object that John 1:9 speaks of the enlightenment of "every man." Grant Osborne (1942–2018) wrote, "The stress is on God's universal salvific will in drawing 'all men' to himself."[75] In response to Christ's statement "I, if I be lifted up from the earth, will draw all men unto me" (12:32), Osborne said, "The predestinarian passages [in the Gospel of John] must be balanced with such statements as this," for it shows that "all people are equally drawn to the Father."[76] Osborne interpreted the drawing to refer to "God's universal salvific love."[77]

However, this interpretation loads too much freight into the word *all*, which commonly refers to many or all kinds, but not necessarily everyone without exception (John 2:10; 3:26).[78] Paul said that he was "warning every man, and teaching every man" (Col. 1:28), but did not claim a worldwide ministry to every human being. John 1:9 most likely refers to Christ's revelation of God's grace and truth to everyone who hears the gospel. As to "all men" in John 12:32, in the context we read that Gentiles were seeking Christ (12:20–22). Matthew Barrett writes, "When Jesus says he will draw all people to himself, he is not referring to all without exception, but rather to all without distinction, Jew and Greek alike."[79] Christ applies the accomplishment of his death by effectually drawing many people from all nations.

There is no biblical basis for the doctrine of universal prevenient grace that enables all mankind to choose salvation.[80] Arminian theologian Ben Witherington admits, "Wesley's concept of prevenient grace is frankly weakly grounded if we are talking about proof texts from the Bible. . . . Prevenient grace certainly comports with the character of a gracious God and his desire that none should perish, but one should not hang one's entire

74. D. A. Carson, *The Gospel according to John*, The Pillar New Testament Commentary (Grand Rapids, MI: Eerdmans, 1991), 124.

75. Grant R. Osborne, "Soteriology in the Gospel of John," in *The Grace of God and the Will of Man*, ed. Pinnock, 244.

76. Osborne, "Soteriology in the Gospel of John," in *The Grace of God and the Will of Man*, ed. Pinnock, 252, 256.

77. Grant R. Osborne, "Exegetical Notes on Calvinist Texts," in *Grace Unlimited*, ed. Clark H. Pinnock (Minneapolis: Bethany House, 1975), 171.

78. On universal terms such as *all* and *world* in the Bible and their implications for God's grace, see *RST*, 2:1071–76.

79. Barrett, *Salvation by Grace*, 256.

80. Thomas R. Schreiner, "Does Scripture Teach Prevenient Grace in the Wesleyan Sense?," in *The Grace of God, the Bondage of the Will*, ed. Schreiner and Ware, 2:365–82.

theology about what sinners can do by free choice on such an exegetically weakly supported notion."[81]

This doctrine also involves a number of theological problems. As Johannes Wollebius said, "It is absurd to suppose that this grace of calling is extended to all," when not even the call of the gospel "reaches all men."[82] Another problem is that this view of prevenient grace makes man's total depravity and total inability merely theoretical, for grace is said to restore mankind's will to a measure of freedom. However, Barrett observes that the Bible does not present man as theoretically dead in sin, but as actually dead until raised with Christ.[83]

Francis Turretin said, "To innumerable persons neither a heart to understand is given, nor eyes to see (Deut. 29:4)."[84] He argued that the idea of sufficient grace that does not effectively produce salvation is incoherent and logically unstable, for those with sufficient grace will not trust in Christ unless either their own wills add something not given to them by God's grace (which is Pelagianism, contrary to 1 Cor. 4:7) or God gives them further grace, which means that the first grace is not sufficient (the Reformed view).[85]

The objection that God's grace is never "irresistible" involves a strange inconsistency for those who believe in prevenient grace. The first act of prevenient grace is unfailingly effectual in raising fallen sinners to a level where they can then choose not to resist God. Such prevenient grace must overcome the ruling power of their sinful resistance against God by nature and do so without their consent. Arminian prevenient grace may be called "irresistible."[86] Bavinck rightly asked, if God effectually renews sinners "to the extent that they can choose for the gospel," then why would he not completely overcome their sinful resistance and save them?[87]

Furthermore, such a view of grace dishonors the sovereignty of God and magnifies the independent power of free will.[88] Evangelical Arminian Christians want to glorify God alone for their salvation, but their theology

81. Ben Witherington III, *The Problem with Evangelical Theology: Testing the Exegetical Foundations of Calvinism, Dispensationalism and Wesleyanism* (Waco, TX: Baylor University Press, 2005), 207, 209.
82. Wollebius, *Compendium*, 1.28.7 (159).
83. Barrett, *Salvation by Grace*, 248–52.
84. Turretin, *Institutes*, 15.3.18 (2:514).
85. Turretin, *Institutes*, 15.3.14–17 (2:513–14).
86. Barrett, *Salvation by Grace*, 223–24.
87. Bavinck, *Reformed Dogmatics*, 2:84–85.
88. Turretin, *Institutes*, 15.3.10 (2:512).

is inconsistent with the noble desire of their hearts. Elisha Coles (c. 1608–1688) said that if a medicine were compounded out of several ingredients, but one ingredient made all the others effective, such that apart from it the medicine would not heal, then we would rightly say that that ingredient was the principal part of the cure. In the same way, this doctrine attributes the crucial factor in salvation to man, not to God.[89] Wilhelmus à Brakel said, "Free will remains lord and master, having ultimate power to either accept or reject."[90] Tom Hicks writes that according to the Arminian doctrine of grace, "everyone who hears the gospel receives the same enabling resistible grace from God, which means that the determining difference or decisive (deciding) factor in human salvation is not God's grace alone.... Some men go to heaven for all eternity because they made a better choice than other men."[91] How is this consistent with giving all the glory to God for our salvation?

Objection 4: People can and do resist God's call in the gospel. There are numerous texts and examples available to prove this sad truth, such as Proverbs 1:24: "I have called, and ye refused." The most common Scripture passage cited is Acts 7:51: "Ye stiffnecked and uncircumcised in heart and ears, ye do always resist the Holy Ghost: as your fathers did, so do ye." Therefore, it is argued that "the influence of the Holy Spirit is resistible."[92]

What is puzzling about this objection is that Reformed theologians also teach human resistance against God.[93] We have given extensive treatment to the sin of resisting the Holy Spirit.[94] However, the Holy Spirit is free to act according to his will (John 3:8), which includes what kind of power he exercises and whether it transforms hostility into faith and repentance. Brown said, "Opposition doth not necessarily infer actual prevalence over his strongest efforts."[95] God exercises his effectual power only in his call upon the elect.

One Arminian counterargument is that Acts 7:51 refers to God's chosen people, Israel, and therefore this must be God's effectual call upon his

89. Elisha Coles, *A Practical Discourse of God's Sovereignty* (London: Nath. Hiller, 1699), 211.
90. Brakel, *The Christian's Reasonable Service*, 2:215.
91. Tom Hicks, "Understanding Effectual Calling," in *Ministry by His Grace and for His Glory*, ed. Ascol and Finn, 166.
92. Steve W. Lemke, "A Biblical and Theological Critique of Irresistible Grace," in *Whosoever Will*, ed. Allen and Lemke, 117–18.
93. The Westminster Larger Catechism (Q. 105), in *Reformed Confessions*, 4:323.
94. See chap. 14.
95. Brown, *Systematic Theology*, 353.

elect.[96] This counterargument fails to recognize the difference between national election in the old covenant and individual election to salvation. Paul writes that "they are not all Israel, which are of Israel," but God's effectual call comes upon those individual Jews and Gentiles whom God elected (Rom. 9:6, 11).

Objection 5: Sinners can defeat God's purpose to save them. Isaiah told a parable about a farmer who planted a vineyard and did everything that a farmer could do to make it fruitful, only for it to produce bad fruit (Isa. 5:1–7). The Lord then said of Israel and Judah, "What more was there to do for my vineyard, that I have not done in it?" (v. 4 ESV). Therefore, it is argued, God did everything he could to bring sinners to repentance, but they rejected him.[97]

In reply, we observe that in Isaiah's parable of a farmer and his vineyard, God spoke of himself "after the manner of men," as Turretin said, and demonstrated his patience with Israel and his justice in condemning the people for rebellion after all God did for them.[98] The Lord was speaking of the external blessings granted to Israel in the old covenant, such as his protection (Isa. 5:5) and prophetic word (v. 24). James Boyce (1827–1888) said that God's Word "meets with no success because of the willful sinfulness of man, although, in itself, it has all the elements which should secure its acceptance."[99] God was not speaking here of the inward work of saving grace, which he told Isaiah was denied to many in Israel (Isa. 6:10). Brown said, "God may do all that is possible or proper in the bestowal of outward means of salvation upon men, without success (Isa. 5:1–4); but not all that he can do, in the exertion of his spiritual influence."[100]

Moses recognized that God had not granted most of Israel inward, effectual grace, writing in Deuteronomy 29:4, "Yet the Lord hath not given you an heart to perceive, and eyes to see, and ears to hear, unto this day." However, God can "circumcise thine heart, and the heart of thy seed, to love the Lord thy God" (30:6). God was not defeated by Israel's

96. Lemke, "Critique of Irresistible Grace," in *Whosoever Will*, ed. Allen and Lemke, 119.

97. Brian Abasciano, "The FACTS of Salvation: A Summary of Arminian Theology/the Biblical Doctrines of Grace," under the heading, "Freed to Believe by God's Grace (the F in FACTS)," http://evangelicalarminians.org/wp-content/uploads/2013/10/Abasciano.-The-FACTS-of-Salvation.pdf.

98. Turretin, *Institutes*, 15.3.19 (2:515).

99. James P. Boyce, *Abstract of Systematic Theology* (1887; repr., Cape Coral, FL: Founders, 2006), 367. He includes among the gospel's "elements which should secure its acceptance" the sufficiency of the way of salvation revealed in Scripture, the fact of sin, the free offer of the gospel, and the trustworthiness of God (369).

100. Brown, *Systematic Theology*, 353.

resistance, but saved his elect ones from among the people by the effectual grace of his call (Rom. 9:6–16).

The objector might appeal to the statement "the Pharisees and the lawyers rejected the purpose of God for themselves" (Luke 7:30 ESV), arguing that this proves that men can frustrate God's saving purpose for them and make his call ineffectual.

However, the word translated as "purpose" (*boulē*; rendered as "counsel" in the KJV) may refer either to the decretive will of God—his plan for what will happen (Acts 2:23)—or the preceptive will of God—his word to us about what we should do (20:27), including our duty to repent and believe (v. 21). The context of Luke's statement shows that the Pharisees rejected the preaching of both John the Baptist and the Lord Jesus Christ (Luke 7:31–34). The term translated as "rejected" (*atheteō*, v. 30) can mean "frustrate" or "nullify" (Gal. 2:21; 3:15), but it is also used of men despising and rejecting God's Word (Mark 7:9; Luke 10:16). Therefore, this text speaks of men rejecting God's Word and is no evidence against the effectual grace God gives to those he has decreed to save.

Objection 6: Entrance into the kingdom is harder for some than others. Christ said, "How difficult it is for those who have wealth to enter the kingdom of God!" (Luke 18:24 ESV). It is argued that if the doctrine of irresistible grace were true, Christ never would have said that it is more difficult for some people to enter the kingdom than for others.[101]

In reply, we acknowledge that some people experience more obstacles against their coming to Christ than others. Though all unconverted people are spiritually dead (Eph. 2:1), some have a clearer understanding of God's Word than others (Mark 12:34). Some have consciences "seared with a hot iron" (1 Tim. 4:2). Some are so entangled by the riches of this world that it is humanly impossible for them to seriously consider following Christ (Luke 18:22–25). Obstacles to faith and repentance must be overcome for people to be saved, for they are rational and volitional beings. However, these Scripture passages do not teach man's ability to convert himself or God's inability to save whom he pleases. When the disciples asked, "Who then can be saved?" Christ answered, "The things which are impossible with men are possible with God" (vv. 26–27). Salvation is humanly impossible, but God's omnipotent power can save whom he wills.

101. Lemke, "Critique of Irresistible Grace," in *Whosoever Will*, ed. Allen and Lemke, 121.

Objection 7: God promises the Spirit of life to those who believe. Christ said that "he that believeth on me" shall receive "rivers of living water"—that is, "the Spirit" (John 7:38). Therefore, it is argued, faith clearly precedes the Spirit's work of giving new life.[102]

In reply, we agree that the Spirit is received by faith in Christ (Gal. 3:2, 14). However, the Spirit has more than one operation (consider, for example, his works of conviction, the new birth, indwelling, and baptism). To identify one work of the Spirit as logically subsequent to faith does not require all his works to be so. The Holy Spirit works powerfully on sinners prior to their believing—as advocates of the doctrine of prevenient grace acknowledge.[103] Therefore, the reception through faith of one work by the Spirit is no objection against a prior work by the Spirit that leads to faith. And the Spirit does work faith, for apart from the Spirit no one can receive the truths of God or confess that Jesus is Lord (1 Cor. 2:14; 12:3).[104]

However, the objector may insist that God promises the gift of eternal life to those who believe (John 3:15–16). Therefore, it is argued, the grace of inner renewal is a consequence of faith; faith is not the result of inner renewal by effectual calling and regeneration.[105]

In reply, we say that it is an exegetical mistake to identify "life" or "eternal life" with effectual calling and regeneration, defined as the initial application of Christ's redemption for salvation. In the Bible, eternal life refers to the life of the age to come. In many Scripture passages, "life" or "eternal life" particularly denotes that resurrection life that is yet future.[106] To be sure, by faith we already participate in that life in this age (John 1:4; 3:15–16; 5:24; 1 John 5:11–13). However, one cannot argue from this that faith is prior to effectual calling and regeneration, for the Scriptures also teach that justification is prior to eternal life (Titus 3:7) and that sanctification leads to eternal life (Rom. 6:22; Gal. 6:8). Christians are exhorted to fight the good fight of faith and do good works in order to "lay hold on eternal life" (1 Tim. 6:12, 19). God gives "life" to his children whenever he restores them to repentance after they sin (1 John 5:16). The giving of eternal life, like salvation itself, takes place

102. Lemke, "Critique of Irresistible Grace," in *Whosoever Will*, ed. Allen and Lemke, 139.

103. Lemke, "Critique of Irresistible Grace," in *Whosoever Will*, ed. Allen and Lemke, 137–38.

104. For further discussion of the relations among faith, eternal life, and regeneration, see the next chapter.

105. See the summary of this argument in Barrett, *Salvation by Grace*, 289–90.

106. Dan. 12:2; Matt. 7:14; 18:8–9; 19:29; 25:46; Mark 9:43, 45; 10:30; Luke 18:30; John 5:28; 12:25; Rom. 2:7; 6:22; 2 Cor. 5:4; Gal. 6:8; Col. 3:3–4; James 1:12; Jude 21.

in stages.[107] We cannot equate life with effectual calling or regeneration. Paul says that God "saved us, by the washing of regeneration, and renewing of the Holy Ghost" so that "we should be made heirs according to the hope of eternal life" (Titus 3:5, 7).[108] It is better to interpret promises of believers' present possession of eternal life to indicate that faith is instrumental to vital union with Christ, who is our life (John 11:25; 14:6; 1 John 5:20). Effectual calling, however, is the act by which God creates that faith union.

Objection 8: God is love. This is without doubt the teaching of the Scriptures (1 John 4:8), but in arguments for universal saving grace, this truth is set against God's sovereign and particular election and calling. It is argued that a deity that "intentionally saves just a few" is not the God of love revealed in the Bible.[109] Wesley said that God's love meant that, regardless of what else the Bible says, he could never believe in sovereign, particular grace: "No Scripture can mean that God is not love, or that his mercy is not over all his works."[110]

The Arminian argument at this point is that if God has the power to save everyone by effectual calling, then he must do so because he is good and loving. But not all are saved. Therefore, it is said, God does not have the power to call sinners effectually. A good and loving human being would relieve all the suffering that he has the power to stop, and since we are created in God's image, he would do the same.[111]

This argument is a form of the problem of evil, which argues that if God does not prevent evil, then he is either not perfectly good or not all-powerful.[112] The problem with the Arminian use of this argument is that, if valid, it releases a skeptical acid that dissolves the doctrines of God's omnipotence and providence entirely. The argument applies not only to hell but to all forms of suffering in this world. We would have to conclude that God lacks the power not only to effectually call sinners but also to prevent diseases, disabilities, and disasters. Some Arminians respond that God remains sovereign "by right" and omnipotent by nature ("he could control everything"), but not sovereign "in actuality" in this present age because he limits himself. This, they say,

107. On salvation as past, present, and future, see the first argument for an order of salvation in chap. 11.

108. Barrett, *Salvation by Grace*, 298–300.

109. Lemke, "Critique of Irresistible Grace," in *Whosoever Will*, ed. Allen and Lemke, 149.

110. John Wesley, *Free Grace, A Sermon Preach'd at Bristol* (Bristol: S. & F. Farley, 1739), 25.

111. Olson, *Against Calvinism*, 166.

112. On the problem of evil, see *RST*, 1:1091–97.

relieves God of the problem of evil, because he only permits it.[113] But they are wrong, for if God has the omnipotence to prevent or quickly defeat evil, then according to their own argument he must do so or he is not good.

The solution is to reject the argument because it is contrary to Scripture, logical reasoning, and the humility befitting mere men. The Bible teaches that God is entirely good, that all his gifts are good (James 1:17), and that he controls all things, including evil, according to his good purposes (Rom. 8:28).[114] The logical problem of evil fails to account for the fact that the all-powerful God has all-good reasons for ordaining evil (Gen. 50:20). Men's demand to fully understand and evaluate God's reasons by their own wisdom is inappropriate, for though they are his image bearers, they are merely creatures and he is the Creator (Isa. 45:9; Rom. 9:20). If God is truly God, then he has the liberty to exercise his love as he chooses (Ex. 33:19).

Polyander said of those who change God's effectual calling into universal grace, "They mix up God's love towards humanity (whereby God embraces all people as his own creatures) with the love whereby He has ordained to take into His grace a select number of people from the common crowd of sinners who are perishing for their own wickedness, and to guide them in Jesus Christ, the Son in whom He delights. And in so doing, they also rob God, who is beholden to no-one, of all His freedom to set apart some whom He chooses."[115]

We wholeheartedly affirm that God is love, but human understanding of divine love must be defined by the whole doctrine of God revealed in Scripture. A reduction of God to a single attribute is the pathway to doctrinal compromise. God is love, but God is also "light" or absolute righteousness (1 John 1:5). Due to his righteousness, his wrath burns against sinners (Rom. 1:18). It is entirely within the rights of his justice to condemn the entire human race (Pss. 130:3; 143:2).

Goodness does not require God to give the same grace to everyone, for grace is not a matter of debt but a free gift (Rom. 3:24; 4:4; 5:15).[116] God's goodness to his creation does not necessitate that he do all within his omnipotent power to save every wicked rebel. His goodness, eternal mercy, and faithful love are displayed not only in salvation but also in

113. Olson, *Against Calvinism*, 100.
114. On God's providence and his control of all things, see *RST*, 1:1065–70.
115. Polyander, Walaeus, Thysius, and Rivetus, *Synopsis Purioris Theologiae*, 30.27 (2:218–19).
116. On divine freedom and distributive justice, see *RST*, 1:815.

destroying his enemies (Ps. 136:1, 10–22). Far be it from us to raise the least complaint against the goodness of God! Instead, let us be filled with wonder that he called us out of the darkness into his marvelous light, and let us declare his excellencies forever.[117]

Objection 9: People are responsible for their choice to believe or disbelieve. Faith in Christ is commanded by God, just as God commands us to love one another (1 John 3:23). John 3:18 says, "He that believeth on him is not condemned: but he that believeth not is condemned already." If people are unable to exercise faith without God's effectual call, and if that call certainly brings them to faith, then this nullifies their responsibility and treats them as robots without free will, whereas God relates to them personally, not mechanically.[118] If Judas's betrayal of Jesus was predestined, then he had no moral responsibility for his actions.[119]

One problem with that argument appears in Christ's words: "Truly the Son of man goeth, as it was determined: but woe unto that man by whom he is betrayed!" (Luke 22:22). Christ said that the events leading to his crucifixion, including his betrayal by Judas (v. 21), were all predetermined by God (cf. Acts 2:23; 4:28). What God had spoken in his Word about Christ had to come to pass (Luke 22:37). However, Christ did not conclude from this that Judas was not to be blamed, but rather that God's righteous judgment would fall on him. Judas voluntarily betrayed Jesus (v. 6). Therefore, Christ taught both God's sovereign predestination and the responsibility of sinners for the sins that they commit by the free choices of their wills.[120]

Another problem with this argument is that it overlooks man's condition in the state of sin, in which people freely choose only what is evil in God's sight until God saves them. We must beware the Pelagian temptation to view each person as if he stands between spiritual good and evil, with the freedom to choose one or the other. There is no neutrality. Neither are we like Adam in the garden. Instead, mankind exists in fallen Adam, under condemnation, slavery, and inability to save himself from either (Rom. 3:9–19; 8:7–8). The only deliverance is found in Jesus Christ, the

117. On the false charge that the doctrine of reprobation contradicts God's goodness, see *RST*, 1:1018–21.

118. Clark H. Pinnock, "Responsible Freedom and the Flow of Biblical History," in *Grace Unlimited*, ed. Pinnock, 97.

119. Jeremy A. Evans, "Reflections on Determinism and Human Freedom," in *Whosoever Will*, ed. Allen and Lemke, 262.

120. On the free choice of the will, see *RST*, 2:417–34 (chap. 22).

last Adam (5:12–19), to whom God must join us by his effectual call. If we are in Adam, we are lost; if we are called in Christ, then we are saved.[121]

Furthermore, we do not deny that people are responsible to exercise faith in Christ, for faith involves the right disposition and free choice of the will. However, effectual calling does not force people to do something against their wills, but supernaturally renews and redirects their wills through the application of God's Word with divine power. When the Father draws people to Christ, he draws their hearts by giving them a delightful knowledge of his Son's beauty, glory, and sufficiency for their needs. Augustine said, "Do not think that you are drawn against your will. The mind is drawn also by love."[122] Turretin said, "When man learns from God, he is not indeed drawn with a twisted neck, but is conquered by the truth and vanquished by a triumphant delight, than which nothing is sweeter, nothing more efficacious."[123]

Evangelism by Faith in Effectual Grace through the Word

We close this chapter with some instruction and exhortation regarding a biblical approach to evangelism, for it is in evangelism that this matter of God's sovereignty and human responsibility most directly touches our lives.

The doctrine of effectual calling does not in the least diminish the importance of preaching the Word of God. The gospel is "the power of God unto salvation to every one that believeth" (Rom. 1:16). Faith comes "by hearing, and hearing by the word of God" (10:17). However, God must add to the operation of the Word upon the mind the work of the Spirit upon the heart in order to save the person.[124] Turretin wrote, "Although the Spirit in effectual calling does not act without the word, still he does not act only mediately through the word; but he also acts immediately with the word, so that the calling necessarily produces its effect."[125]

We must evangelize the lost. We are beset with influences undermining the necessity of evangelism. On one side, the false teaching of inclusivism tells us that people may be saved through non-Christian religions and good works. To the contrary, J. I. Packer wrote, "they must be told of Christ

121. See Brown, *Systematic Theology*, 346–47.
122. Augustine, *Tractates on the Gospel of John*, 26.4, in *NPNF*[1], 7:169, language modernized.
123. Turretin, *Institutes*, 15.6.13 (2:550).
124. Bavinck, *Reformed Dogmatics*, 4:81.
125. Turretin, *Institutes*, 15.4.23 (2:526). See his vindication and discussion of this principle, 2:526–52.

before they can trust Him, and they must trust Him before they can be saved by Him. Salvation depends on faith, and faith on knowing the gospel" (cf. Rom. 10:13–14).[126] Therefore, "repentance and remission of sins should be preached in his [Christ's] name among all nations, beginning at Jerusalem" (Luke 24:47). Like the apostle Paul, churches must strive to send the gospel to places where Christ is not yet named (Rom. 15:20), for there is no other name under heaven revealed to mankind by which we must be saved (Acts 4:12).

On the other side, it is often assumed that those who grow up in the church are saved. Bruce Demarest warns, "Don't trust Christian parentage or baptism for new life."[127] Christ gives life through his Word and Spirit (John 6:63). There is great danger in presuming that the children of believers are saved.[128] Archibald Alexander (1772–1851) wrote, "The education of children should proceed on the principle that they are in an unregenerate state, until evidences of piety clearly appear."[129] Brakel said that young children may pray and behave according to their parents' instruction merely from natural affections and the common operations of the Spirit.[130] Therefore, we must speak the gospel to children, call them to faith and repentance, and teach them the distinctive marks of a true Christian—the fruit of effectual calling.

When we speak the gospel, we should call people to Christ with urgency and genuineness. We should have the same earnestness in our evangelism as the Lord, who said, "Except ye repent, ye shall all likewise perish," and the same compassion as him who longed to gather the people of Jerusalem as a hen gathers her chicks under her wings (Luke 13:5, 34). As Packer said, our calling is not to try to discern the elect in the unconverted world but to love our neighbors as ourselves.[131]

The doctrine of effectual calling, far from discouraging evangelism, should steel us with courage, hope, and resolve to preach the gospel to the worst pagans and the most self-righteous Pharisees. Packer wrote, "The sovereignty of God in grace gives us our only hope of success in

126. Packer, *Evangelism and the Sovereignty of God*, 97.

127. Demarest, *The Cross and Salvation*, 306.

128. On hypercovenantalism, see William Young, "Historic Calvinism and Neo-Calvinism (Part 1)," in *Westminster Theological Journal* 36, no. 1 (Fall 1973): 48–64; "Part 2" in issue 36, no. 2 (Winter 1974): 156–73.

129. Archibald Alexander, *Thoughts on Religious Experience* (repr., Edinburgh: Banner of Truth, 1967), 13.

130. Brakel, *The Christian's Reasonable Service*, 2:249.

131. Packer, *Evangelism and the Sovereignty of God*, 99.

evangelism."[132] We need not fear that men's hardness or opposition will stop God from saving those on whom his merciful heart is set. Paul wrote that, though he was in chains for the gospel, "the word of God is not bound," and "therefore I endure all things for the elect's sakes, that they may also obtain the salvation which is in Christ Jesus with eternal glory" (2 Tim. 2:9–10).

The doctrine of effectual grace equips God's servants with meekness and gentleness to bear patiently with those who oppose the truth, for God may well give them repentance so that they are saved from the snare of the Devil (2 Tim. 2:24–26). He will act in his time. We need not fret when our message falls on deaf ears, for it is not our task to give repentance unto life, but the Lord's (Acts 11:18). We are to be faithful servants, and he will grant us his reward. We should not worry that we are not adequate but are mere jars of clay (2 Cor. 4:7). John Piper writes, "God's aim is that his own power through the gospel, not ours, be exalted."[133]

The doctrine of effectual calling should encourage us to pray. We can plant the seeds and water them, but only God can make the seed sprout, grow, and bear fruit (1 Cor. 3:6–7). Since only God can effectually call sinners to Christ, let us bathe the ministry of the Word with prayer. Let it be true of us as Paul says in the very place he gives his clearest teaching on predestination and calling: "My heart's desire and prayer to God . . . is, that they might be saved" (Rom. 10:1).

Sinners laboring under a sense of their corruption and enslavement to sin can find great encouragement in the knowledge that God is able to call men with effectual power. Thomas Hooker said that the sinner may say, "Though my prayers, my endeavors, my heart, my hopes fail me, yet God can do it. . . . Though you may be in the mouth of hell . . . yet God is able to call you from there."[134] Christians, too, may rejoice in this doctrine when they face spiritual difficulties, distresses, darkness, or desertion: "If God the Father has once drawn them to his Christ when they did nothing but oppose this work, all the powers of hell shall never be able to withdraw them from the Lord Jesus when they desire to cleave to him and to be his."[135]

---

132. Packer, *Evangelism and the Sovereignty of God*, 106.

133. John Piper, *Finally Alive: What Happens When We Are Born Again* (Fearn, Ross-shire, Scotland: Christian Focus, 2009), 182.

134. Hooker, *The Application of Redemption . . . The First Eight Books*, 437–38, grammar and punctuation modernized.

135. Hooker, *The Application of Redemption . . . The First Eight Books*, 441, grammar and punctuation modernized.

Sing to the Lord

Praising God for Calling Us to Himself

Praise waits for Thee in Zion;
All men shall worship there
And pay their vows before Thee,
O God Who hearest prayer.
Our sins rise up against us,
Prevailing day by day,
But Thou wilt show us mercy
And take their guilt away.

How blest the man Thou callest
And bringest near to Thee,
That in Thy courts forever
His dwelling place may be;
He shall within Thy temple
Be satisfied with grace,
And filled with all the goodness
Of Thy most holy place.

O God of our salvation,
Since Thou dost love the right,
Thou wilt an answer send us
In wondrous deeds of might.
In all earth's habitations,
On all the boundless sea,
Man finds no sure reliance,
No peace, apart from Thee.

Psalm 65
Tune: Mendebras
The Psalter, No. 170
Or Tune: Nyland
Trinity Hymnal—Baptist Edition, No. 306

Questions for Meditation or Discussion

1. What is the main controversy concerning effectual calling?
2. How would you explain and clarify the following theological distinctions?

- irresistible grace versus resistible grace
- monergism versus synergism
- effectual grace versus necessary grace
- total inability versus natural or restored ability

3. What is the Pelagian view of how God's grace leads us to conversion?
4. According to official Roman Catholic doctrine and the teachings of classic Arminianism, what is God's prevenient grace and how does it relate to the human will?
5. How has historic Lutheranism explained the operations of God's grace through the Word?
6. You are explaining effectual calling to someone. She objects, "That can't be true because people resist the Spirit and frustrate God's purpose to save them." What do you say?
7. How is the doctrine of effectual calling consistent with the truth that God is love?
8. Someone says, "God's call cannot be effectual, because people have free will and are responsible for their choices." How do you respond?
9. How does the doctrine of effectual calling encourage you to tell people the gospel? What can you do to make personal use of this doctrine to strengthen your evangelistic motivation?

Questions for Deeper Reflection

10. What other doctrines stand in close relation to effectual calling? If we were to deny effectual calling, how would our denial tend to affect our understanding of those doctrines?
11. Imagine that you are invited to be the main speaker at a question-and-answer session on the topic of effectual calling with students at a Christian university. Prepare an outline for how you would answer each of the objections in this chapter if they were raised.

17

Regeneration, Part 1

Biblical Teaching

One night a Pharisee came to Jesus and said, "Rabbi, we know that thou art a teacher come from God: for no man can do these miracles that thou doest, except God be with him" (John 3:2). Surprisingly, Christ replied, "Except a man be born again, he cannot see the kingdom of God. . . . Ye must be born again" (vv. 3, 7). With a few words, Jesus denied that men may be saved by rigorous devotion, religious education, right beliefs, or personal reformation—they must have a miraculous new life from God.

This message, "Ye must be born again," has been a divine instrument of awakening, conversion, and revival. George Smeaton noted that the Puritans taught "that the regeneration of the nature is not less important than the justification of the person" and saw the Holy Spirit work to regenerate many, for "it was a period also of great awakenings, when villages and towns were simultaneously brought under deep religious impressions."[1] George Whitefield (1714–1770) said that "the doctrine of our regeneration, or new birth in Christ Jesus . . . [is] one of the most fundamental doctrines of our holy religion . . . [and] the very hinge on which the salvation of each of us turns," yet many professing Christians seldom think about it and have no experiential knowledge of it or its ef-

1. Smeaton, *The Doctrine of the Holy Spirit*, 337.

fects in their lives.[2] The doctrine of the new birth remains a crucial piece in the theology and practical ministry of the church.

Clarification of Theological Terminology

Theologians speak of this doctrine with the words *regenerate* and *regeneration*. The Heidelberg Catechism (LD 3, Q. 8) says, "Are we then so corrupt that we are wholly incapable of doing any good, and inclined to all wickedness? Indeed we are; except we are regenerated [*regeneremur*] by the Spirit of God."[3] This terminology comes from the Latin translation of the Bible: "beget again" (*regenero*, 1 Pet. 1:3 Vulgate) and "rebirth" (*regeneratio*, Titus 3:5 Vulgate).

As a theological term, *regeneration* has been used with a spectrum of meanings. In its most narrow sense, it refers to God's initial act to renew a sinner's heart. In a somewhat broader sense, it has to do with both initial divine renewal and resulting human conversion when a sinner actively turns to the Lord. In its broadest sense, it refers to the whole process of renewing a man in the image of God that continues through life.[4] These various meanings for regeneration can be found in the writings of John Calvin and sixteenth-century Reformed confessions.[5]

Many Reformed theologians from the seventeenth century onward reserved *regeneration* for the initial gift of life to the heart, as we see in the Canons of Dort and Westminster Confession of Faith.[6] The doctrine of regeneration was sometimes subsumed in theological systems under the

---

2. George Whitefield, "On Regeneration," in *Sermons of George Whitefield*, ed. Lee Gatiss, 2 vols. (Wheaton, IL: Crossway, 2012), 2:275. Originally published as *The Nature and Necessity of Our New Birth in Christ Jesus* (London: C. Rivington, 1737), this sermon "could almost be regarded as the manifesto of the movement" during the Great Awakening. Arnold Dallimore, *George Whitefield: The Life and Times of the Great Evangelist of the 18th Century Revival*, 2 vols. (Edinburgh: Banner of Truth, 1970, 1980), 1:345.

3. *The Three Forms of Unity*, 70. See *The Heidelberg Catechism, in German, Latin, and English*, 138.

4. Petrus van Mastricht, *Theoretico-Practica Theologia*, new ed., 2 vols. (Trajecti ad Rhenum: Thomae Appels, 1699), 6.3.5 (2:659–60); English translation: *A Treatise on Regeneration* (New Haven, CT: Thomas and Samuel Green, 1770), 16–17. The former set of books is being translated as *Theoretical-Practical Theology* and published by Reformation Heritage Books in seven volumes; the latter book was modernized and published by Soli Deo Gloria in 2002.

5. Calvin, *Institutes*, 2.3.6; 2.7.11; 3.3 title; 3.3.9; *Commentaries*, on John 1:13; 3:5; Titus 3:4–7; Calvin's Catechism of 1537 and 1538 (Art. 18), and French Confession (Art. 22), in *Reformed Confessions*, 1:370, 423; 2:148; and Belgic Confession (Arts. 24 and 35), in *The Three Forms of Unity*, 41.

6. The Canons of Dort (Heads 3/4, Arts. 11–12, 16, etc.), in *The Three Forms of Unity*, 144–45, 147; and the Westminster Confession of Faith (13.1), in *Reformed Confessions*, 4:249. However, note the ambivalence of "regeneration" in the writings of Wilhelmus à Brakel, who at one point said that "man does not cooperate in the initial moment of regeneration, but is passive," but later said that faith has a logical and causal priority over regeneration. *The Christian's Reasonable Service*, 2:223, 233, 245, 261.

topic of effectual calling,[7] a pattern found in the Westminster Standards.[8] The emphasis on calling may have been due to "a desire to stress the close connection between the Word of God and the operation of His grace."[9] Other Reformed orthodox divines gave regeneration distinct attention in their systems, as we are doing here.[10]

The tendency of many Reformed orthodox theologians to subsume regeneration under effectual calling should not be misunderstood as a neglect of the doctrine of the new birth. William Whately (1583–1639), Thomas Goodwin, John Owen, George Swinnock (1627–1673), Thomas Cole (c. 1627–1697), Ezekiel Hopkins (1634–1690), Stephen Charnock (1628–1680), and Thomas Boston gave extensive treatments to the doctrine of regeneration in separate treatises.[11] Smeaton said, "The result was the introduction of a new phase of theology . . . a theology of regeneration cultivated and expanded as a topic by itself."[12]

Biblical Descriptions of Regeneration

Although the language of being "born again" is familiar in modern evangelical Christianity, we must not assume that people have a right under-

---

7. Ames, *The Marrow of Theology*, 1.26.19 (159); Wollebius, *Compendium*, 1.28.i (158); Turretin, *Institutes*, 15.5.2, 10 (2:542, 544); Johann Heidegger, *The Concise Marrow of Christian Theology*, trans. Casey Carmichael, intro. Ryan Glomsrud, Classic Reformed Theology 4 (Grand Rapids, MI: Reformation Heritage Books, 2019), 21.7 (147); and Thomas Boston, *An Illustration of the Doctrines of the Christian Religion*, in *The Whole Works of the Late Rev. Thomas Boston*, ed. Samuel M'Millan, intro. Joel R. Beeke and Randall J. Pederson, 12 vols. (repr., Stoke-on-Trent, England: Tentmaker, 2002), 1:558.

8. The Westminster Confession of Faith (10.1; 13.1), in *Reformed Confessions*, 4:246, 249. *Regenerate* and *regeneration* appear only incidentally in the Larger Catechism and not at all in the Shorter Catechism.

9. Berkhof, *Systematic Theology*, 470.

10. Witsius, *The Economy of the Covenants*, 3.6 (1:356–72); van Mastricht, *Theoretico-Practica Theologia*, 6.3 (2:657–74); *A Treatise on Regeneration*, 9–51; Brakel, *The Christian's Reasonable Service*, 2:233–60; and Wilhelmus Schortinghuis, *Essential Truths in the Heart of a Christian*, trans. Harry Boonstra and Gerrit W. Sheeres, ed. James A. De Jong, Classics of Reformed Spirituality (Grand Rapids, MI: Reformation Heritage Books, 2009), 23.1–10 (87–88). Antonius Walaeus treated regeneration in conjunction with repentance after his treatment of calling. Polyander, Walaeus, Thysius, and Rivetus, *Synopsis Purioris Theologiae*, 32.2–27 (2:277–91).

11. William Whately, *The New Birth* (London: Joane Man and Benjamin Fisher, 1635); Goodwin, *The Work of the Holy Ghost in Our Salvation*, in *Works*, 6:73–116, 151–230, 359–520; Owen, *Pneumatologia*, in *Works*, 3:207–28, 297–366; George Swinnock, *The Door of Salvation Opened by the Key of Regeneration*, in *The Works of George Swinnock*, 5 vols. (1868; repr., Edinburgh: Banner of Truth, 1992), 5:1–261; Thomas Cole, *A Discourse of Regeneration, Faith and Repentance* (London: Thomas Cockerill, 1689); Ezekiel Hopkins, *The Nature and Necessity of Regeneration; or, the New-Birth*, in *The Works of Ezekiel Hopkins*, ed. Charles W. Quick, 3 vols. (Philadelphia: Leighton Publications, 1874), 2:221–98; Stephen Charnock, *The Necessity of Regeneration*, *A Discourse of the Nature of Regeneration*, *A Discourse of the Efficient of Regeneration*, and *A Discourse of the Word, the Instrument of Regeneration*, in *The Complete Works of Stephen Charnock*, 5 vols. (Edinburgh: James Nichol, 1864), 3:7–335; and Boston, *Human Nature in Its Fourfold State*, 203–52.

12. Smeaton, *The Doctrine of the Holy Spirit*, 337.

standing of what the Bible means by that phrase. Therefore, we begin by looking at the terms translated as "regeneration" and "born again," as well as other complementary descriptions of how God saves lost sinners.

Salvation by Spiritual Rebirth

When the Lord Jesus says, "Ye must be born again" (John 3:7), the word translated as "born" (passive *gennaō*) takes the literal sense of a father who "begets" or "fathers a child" or a mother who "bears" or "gives birth to a child" in the active voice,[13] and, frequently, "be conceived" or "be born" in the passive.[14] The second word (*anōthen*) in the phrase translated as "born again" (vv. 3, 7) can mean "from the beginning" (Luke 1:3; Acts 26:5), "from above" (John 19:11; James 1:17), or "again" (Gal. 4:9). Either of the last two meanings would fit in our Lord's discourse, for the new birth is like a "second" birth (John 3:4) and is from the heavenly influence of "the Spirit" (vv. 5–6) given through the Son who "cometh from above" (vv. 31, 34).[15] It may be that Christ spoke with a double meaning: a new birth from heavenly, divine influences.[16]

The idea of being "born" (passive *gennaō*) of God appears in several places in the Holy Scriptures.[17] Paul writes of how he has "begotten" (active *gennaō*) children in the Lord through his ministry (1 Cor. 4:15; Philem. 10), although the metaphor focuses on his relationship with converts, not their becoming children of God. James uses another term when he writes that God "of his own will begat [*apokueō*] . . . us with the word of truth" (James 1:18), this word meaning to bring forth a child (cf. v. 15). Peter says that God the Father "hath begotten us again unto a lively hope (1 Pet. 1:3) and that we have been "born again . . . by the word of God" (v. 23), using a verb (*anagennaō*) that means begotten or born again.[18] Peter also speaks of Christians as "newborn [*artigennētos*] babes" (2:2).

---

13. Matt. 1:2–16; Luke 1:13, 57; 23:29; John 16:21; Acts 7:8, 29; Gal. 4:24 [in a maternal allegory]. Metaphorically, the verb in the active voice can mean "to produce" (2 Tim. 2:23). See also Ps. 2:7 LXX; Acts 13:33; Heb. 1:5; 5:5.

14. Matt. 1:20; 2:1, 4; 19:12; 26:24; Mark 14:21; Luke 1:35; John 3:4; 8:41; 9:2, 19–20, 32, 34; 16:21; 18:37; Acts 7:20; 22:3; Rom. 9:11; Gal. 4:23; Heb. 11:12, 23; 2 Pet. 2:12. It can be used with reference to one's native language or citizenship—a condition or culture into which one is "born" (Acts 2:8; 22:28).

15. Cf. "above" (*epanō*, twice in John 3:31) and "from above" (*ek tōn anō*, 8:23).

16. Van Mastricht, *Theoretico-Practica Theologia*, 6.3.3 (2:658); *A Treatise on Regeneration*, 11–12.

17. John 1:13; 1 John 2:29; 3:9; 4:7; 5:1, 4, 18; cf. Gal. 4:29.

18. *NIDNTTE*, 1:563.

Paul also says that God saved us by "the washing of regeneration, and renewing of the Holy Ghost" (Titus 3:5). Paul is describing not an ongoing work but one that God performed in those who were "once foolish, disobedient, led astray, slaves" (v. 3 ESV) but who now are saved by grace (vv. 4–5). "Regeneration" (*palingenesia*) and "renewing" (*anakainōsis*) are best taken as describing the same act of salvation.[19] The first word, which literally means "genesis again," appears elsewhere in the New Testament only in Christ's reference to the "regeneration" when he will reign in glory (Matt. 19:28). Thus, it may be used eschatologically for the regeneration of the world. The root word (*genesis*) means "birth"[20] or "generation," as often in biblical genealogies.[21] Therefore, "regeneration" (*palingenesia*) also means rebirth. Ancient writers used the term for rebirth individually, nationally, or cosmically.[22] Paul's latter word, translated as "renewing" (*anakainōsis*), is used for the renewal of the mind to discern God's will (Rom. 12:2), and the related verb (*anakainoō*) is used for the renewal of the inner man (2 Cor. 4:16) and the renewal of the image of God, an allusion to creation (Col. 3:10).

Other Biblical Descriptions of Regeneration

The language of new birth, which itself is metaphorical, is augmented in the Bible with other vivid images of this tremendous change that God works in salvation.

One image of salvation that corresponds to regeneration is *washing*. God saves sinners by a "washing" (*loutron*, Titus 3:5; cf. Eph. 5:26) that decisively purifies them of their previous sins (Titus 3:3). Several other New Testament texts speak of salvation as washing.[23] Christ's words "born of water and of the Spirit" (John 3:5) also suggest washing. Though washing would later be pictured in Christian baptism (Acts 22:16), the background for this image lies in the Old Testament rituals of washing with water to cleanse away ceremonial defilement and allow for access to God's holy

19. In the phrase "washing of regeneration, and renewing of the Holy Ghost" (Titus 3:5), the conjunction "and" (*kai*) is likely epexegetical, so that the sense is "washing of regeneration, that is, renewing by the Holy Spirit."

20. Gen. 40:20; Ruth 2:11; Hos. 2:5(3); Ezek. 16:3–4 LXX.

21. Gen. 5:1; 10:1, etc. LXX; Matt. 1:1.

22. *TDNT*, 1:673, 687–88; Marcus Varro, *On the Origin of the Roman People*, cited in Augustine, *The City of God*, 22.28.1, in *NPNF*[1], 2:506; and Philo of Alexandria, *On the Eternity of the World*, 3.8–9, in *Works*, 708.

23. On salvific washing, see the use of *louō* in John 13:10; Heb. 10:22; Rev. 1:5 (Majority Text); and *apolouō* in Acts 22:16; 1 Cor. 6:11.

presence, especially for the priests (Heb. 10:22).[24] Of course, physical washing cannot remove spiritual evil (Jer. 2:22), so the Lord promised an effectual spiritual washing: "Then will I sprinkle clean water upon you, and ye shall be clean: from all your filthiness, and from all your idols, will I cleanse you" (Ezek. 36:25).

The Jews associated nothing more closely with birth than *circumcision*, the sign of the Abrahamic covenant (Gen. 17:9–14).[25] Pride and rebellion reign in "uncircumcised hearts" (Lev. 26:41)—that is, hearts lacking covenantal faithfulness to God. The Israelites needed to circumcise their hearts and repent of their sinful stubbornness (Deut. 10:16; Jer. 4:4). However, Israel lacked a heart to understand (Deut. 29:4); the people's sin was engraved on their hearts as on stone tablets (Jer. 17:1). Therefore, the Lord himself had to circumcise their hearts so that they would love him (Deut. 30:6). This inward circumcision is worked by the Spirit of Christ, who cuts away pride, sin, and man-pleasing to form a worshiper of God (Rom. 2:29; Col. 2:11; cf. Phil. 3:3).

A new birth produces a new man, and a circumcised heart involves inner transformation, both of which imply a *new heart and new spirit*, just as the Lord promised Israel (Ezek. 11:19; 36:26). Christ alluded to this promise when he said that a person must be "born of water and of the Spirit" (John 3:5), for God had bracketed his promise of a new heart with the promises of cleansing with water and indwelling by his Spirit (Ezek. 36:25, 27).[26] Paul alludes to this promise when he writes that Christian converts are "the epistle of Christ ministered by us, written not with ink, but with the Spirit of the living God; not in tables of stone, but in fleshy tables of the heart" (2 Cor. 3:3).[27] As with inward circumcision, the new heart constitutes a new people who live in covenantal faithfulness to the Lord (Jer. 32:39–40; cf. 31:31–34).

A heart of stone is dead, and so the gift of a new heart implies a *resurrection from the dead* in the inner person so that he becomes alive toward God. Ezekiel prophesied the resurrection of Israel from the dead, depicting God transforming dry bones into a living army (Ezek. 37:1–10).

24. Ex. 19:10, 14; 29:4; 30:18–21; 40:31–32; Lev. 8:6; 14:8–9; Num. 8:7, 21; 19:17–19; etc.

25. On the meaning of circumcision, see the discussion of the Abrahamic covenant in *RST*, 2:618–19, 621–23.

26. Carson, *The Gospel according to John*, 192–95.

27. Paul's words translated as "of stone" (*lithinos*), "fleshy" (*sarkinos*), and "heart" (*kardia*) in 2 Cor. 3:3 are the same words used in Ezek. 11:19; 36:26 LXX for the removal of the old heart and gift of a new heart.

The Lord said, "I will put my Spirit within you, and you shall live" (v. 14 ESV). This promised resurrection by the Spirit correlates with the Spirit's work to renew the heart for obedience to God's law (36:25–27). The New Testament frequently speaks of present salvation in terms of resurrection or giving life to the dead, for God's people have been raised with Christ.[28] Sharing in Christ's resurrection is broader than regeneration,[29] but at times regeneration is in view, as when Paul says that God, "even when we were dead in our trespasses, made us alive together with Christ—by grace you have been saved" (Eph. 2:5 ESV).

In the Bible, the resurrection of the body belongs to the coming age of glory (Dan. 12:2; John 5:28), and therefore, spiritual resurrection entails a *new creation*. The prophets closely connect the work of the Spirit with the theme of God re-creating his world.[30] That renewal includes the transformation of sinners into people who keep God's covenant (Isa. 44:1–5). God promises, "I create new heavens and a new earth . . . I create Jerusalem a rejoicing, and her people a joy. And I will rejoice in Jerusalem" (65:17–19). The New Testament teaches that God's new creation in Christ has already penetrated this fallen world in the regeneration of sinners.[31]

The Definition and Doctrine of Regeneration

We may briefly define regeneration as *supernatural rebirth into spiritual life by which God begins salvation.*[32] Regeneration is not a change in the substance of human nature as body and soul, a change merely in feelings or beliefs, or a change into sinless moral perfection. Rather, it is God's initial gift of new spiritual life.[33] Regeneration is a mystery that transcends complete human understanding. However, we may more fully describe regeneration as *the supernatural rebirth or re-creation of a sinner by God in which he applies the life of the risen Christ to produce conversion in the*

28. Luke 15:24, 32; John 5:21, 24–25; 6:63; Rom. 5:17, 21; 6:4, 11; 7:4–6; 8:2, 6–10; 1 Cor. 15:45; 2 Cor. 3:6; 5:15; Eph. 2:5–6; 5:14; Col. 2:12–13; 3:1; 1 John 3:14; cf. 1 Pet. 1:3.

29. See the discussion of Christ's resurrection in *RST*, 2:901–3, 1128–32.

30. See chap. 8.

31. 2 Cor. 5:17; Gal. 6:15; Eph. 2:10, 15 (Greek); cf. 2 Cor. 3:18; 4:6; Eph. 4:24; Col. 3:10.

32. To assert the supernatural quality of the birth, Reformed orthodox divines sometimes referred to regeneration as a "physical" act versus a "moral" act, not in the sense of involving physical matter or bodily force, but as a life-giving change in human "nature" (Greek *physis*) versus a mere attempt to persuade the mind through arguments. See Owen, *Pneumatologia*, in *Works*, 3:307; and Ferguson, *The Holy Spirit*, 123. They also called it "hyperphysical" (Latin *hyperphysica*), which means "supernatural." Witsius, *The Economy of the Covenants*, 3.6.4 (1:357).

33. Berkhof, *Systematic Theology*, 468.

inner man for the renewal of God's image and definitive cleansing from sin—all only because of his mercy and love.

Supernatural Rebirth

John introduces the doctrine of the new birth at the very beginning of his Gospel, where he speaks of Christ's incarnation: "He came to his own, and his own people did not receive him. But to all who did receive him, who believed in his name, he gave the right to become children of God, who were born, not of blood nor of the will of the flesh nor of the will of man, but of God" (John 1:11–13 ESV). Faith is the instrument of receiving "the right [*exousia*] to become children of God," the grace of adoption. However, there is another aspect of salvation related but not identical to adoption: being "born of God."[34] John makes a threefold denial regarding the cause of this spiritual birth. It is possible to interpret all three negations as pertaining to natural childbirth,[35] for that is the meaning of "born, not of blood."[36] The second phrase, "nor of the will of the flesh," could refer to physical desire (cf. Eph. 2:3). The third, "nor the will of man," could refer to the will of a father.[37] If so, John is merely saying that no one is naturally born into God's family.

However, the word translated as "will" (*thelēma*) appears in two of the three negations (John 1:13). It would be strange for John to contrast the new birth with natural birth in this manner, for the Bible teaches that natural conception and birth are not by human will but by the will of God alone.[38] Furthermore, the terms translated as "flesh" (*sarx*) and "man" (*anēr*) can be used generally for human beings (vv. 14, 30; 6:10; 17:2). Therefore, it is possible that the last two negations are roughly synonymous, both denying

---

34. On the distinction between adoption through faith and regeneration in John 1:12–13, see Barrett, *Salvation by Grace*, 163–67.

35. William Hendriksen, *Exposition of the Gospel according to John*, New Testament Commentary (Grand Rapids, MI: Baker, 1953), 1:82; and Carson, *The Gospel according to John*, 126. The syntax "not . . . nor . . . nor" (*ou . . . oude . . . oude*) may be used to present a list of distinct items (Lev. 26:1; Num. 20:5, 17; Deut. 29:22[23]; Judg. 1:27; 3 Kingdoms [1 Kings] 13:8, 16; Hos. 3:4 LXX; John 1:25; 1 Thess. 2:3; Rev. 7:16) or emphatically to reinforce a single idea (Gen. 21:26; Ps. 130[131]:1; Isa. 5:27; 13:20; 23:4; 42:2 LXX; Matt. 12:19).

36. Note the association of birth with blood in Lev. 12:4–5, 7; Ezek. 16:4–6; cf. Wisdom 7:1–2: "In my mother's womb [I] was fashioned to be flesh . . . being compacted in blood."

37. The word translated as "man" (*anēr*) in "nor of the will of man" (John 1:13) is not the generic term for a human being (*anthrōpos*, vv. 4, 6, 9), but the more gender-specific "male human being," sometimes meaning "husband" (Matt. 1:16–19; Mark 10:12; Luke 2:36; 16:18; John 4:16–18, etc.).

38. Gen. 4:1; 20:18; 25:21; 29:31; 30:1–2, 22; 33:5; 1 Sam. 1:5–6; Pss. 127:3–5; 128:3; 139:13–16.

that the new birth proceeds from human will.[39] If so, the text says that no one becomes God's child by natural birth or human will. Or it may be that the three negations address three ways in which people falsely claim to be part of God's family:[40] first, by physical birth; second, by human choice; or third, by the choice of a father or religious leader.[41]

Christ gave concentrated teaching on regeneration in his encounter with the Pharisee Nicodemus. John sets up the context by reporting that even when men saw Christ's miracles and responded by believing in him, "Jesus did not commit himself unto them, because he knew all men" (John 2:23–25). Nicodemus likewise said, "Rabbi, we know that thou art a teacher come from God: for no man can do these miracles that thou doest, except God be with him" (3:2). This man was the flower of human religion, being a devout Jew and a highly educated student of the Old Testament. However, Christ admonished him, "except a man be born again, he cannot see the kingdom of God" (v. 3). When Nicodemus protested, Jesus insisted, "Except a man be born of water and of the Spirit, he cannot enter into the kingdom of God" (v. 5).

Christ asserted man's inability to attain salvation apart from a supernatural rebirth—an inability emphasized by the repeated use of "cannot" (John 3:3, 5). Christ's interactions with Nicodemus demonstrated that this inability cripples the very mind of man. Christ said that, unregenerate man "cannot see the kingdom." Some interpreters take "cannot see" as roughly synonymous with "cannot enter" (cf. "shall not see life," v. 36). However, in John's writings, vision can represent spiritual perception.[42] Though Nicodemus said, "We know" (v. 2), Christ said that though he was "the teacher of Israel," he did "not understand" (v. 10 ESV). Nicodemus came at "night" (v. 1–2; 7:50; 19:39) and remained in the "darkness" of this world (3:19–20).[43]

Christ said, "That which is born of the flesh is flesh; and that which is born of the Spirit is spirit" (John 3:6). Christ ruled out all human agency

39. Calvin, *Commentaries*, on John 1:13.

40. Cf. Gerald L. Borchert, *John 1–11*, The New American Commentary 25A (Nashville: Broadman & Holman, 1996), 118.

41. J. C. Ryle, *Expository Thoughts on John*, 2 vols. (New York: Robert Carter & Brothers, 1879), 1:23. "All the power of regenerate men in the world joined together cannot renew another." Charnock, *The Efficient of Regeneration*, in *Works*, 3:169.

42. See *eidon* in John 3:3; 12:40; *theōreō* in John 6:40; 14:17, 19; *horaō* in John 14:7, 9; 1 John 3:6.

43. Cf. Christ's metaphorical use of "night" (John 11:10) and John's double meaning at Judas's departure: "and it was night" (13:30; cf. Luke 22:53).

in the new birth, for "flesh" (*sarx*) refers not merely to the body (6:51–56) but to humanity considered holistically (1:14; 17:2). When contrasted to God, "flesh" emphasizes man's powerlessness to produce life (6:63), as well as opposition to God's righteousness (8:15).[44] Therefore, "that which is born of the flesh is flesh" means that human nature is dead and depraved, and can produce only more death and depravity. William Hendriksen (1900–1982) paraphrased, "Sinful human nature produces sinful human nature."[45] Charnock said, "The highest morality without a new creation is but flesh."[46]

When Christ said, "That which is born of the Spirit is spirit" (John 3:6), what did he mean by "spirit"? John Murray said it "is human nature under the dominance of the Holy Spirit."[47] Goodwin explained that it is not "the communication of the Holy Spirit himself" to indwell us, but "an effect or work of the Spirit in us." Also, "it is not a communication of the Godhead to us" to make us divine, for the divine nature is "indivisible" and "eternal," but this "spirit . . . is born in time."[48] This "spirit" born of the Holy Spirit is "all those gracious and heavenly dispositions" that make the soul fit for spiritual things.[49] D. A. Carson comments that it is "a new nature . . . related to the sphere of God and things divine."[50] Therefore, "spirit" refers to an inner life fit to glorify God in response to his truth, to "worship him in spirit and truth" (4:23–24; cf. "spiritual" in 1 Cor. 2:14–15).

Jesus compared this work of the "Spirit" (*Pneuma*) to the blowing of the "wind" (*pneuma*) to illustrate the divine sovereignty, efficacy, and mystery of regeneration: "The wind bloweth where it listeth, and thou hearest the sound thereof, but canst not tell whence it cometh, and whither it goeth: so is every one that is born of the Spirit" (John 3:8). Jesus literally said that the wind blows "where it chooses" (*hopou thelei*), and

44. Murray, *Collected Writings*, 2:185. The contrast between "flesh" and the "Spirit" that makes Christ's "words" to be "life" (John 6:63) is played out in the contrast between unbelief and faith when many turned away from Christ but Peter said, "Lord, to whom shall we go? Thou hast the words of eternal life." Consider, too, Christ's statements: "Judge not according to the appearance, but judge righteous judgment" (7:24); "Ye judge after the flesh; I judge no man. And yet if I judge, my judgment is true: for I am not alone, but I and the Father that sent me" (8:15–16). Therefore, "flesh," when opposed to God in John's Gospel, connotes unbelief and unrighteousness.

45. Hendriksen, *Exposition of the Gospel according to John*, 134.

46. Charnock, *The Nature of Regeneration*, in *Works*, 3:132.

47. Murray, *Collected Writings*, 2:185.

48. Goodwin, *The Work of the Holy Ghost in Our Salvation*, in *Works*, 6:158.

49. Goodwin, *The Work of the Holy Ghost in Our Salvation*, in *Works*, 6:162. He notes that "spirit" is often used for an inward disposition, such as whoredom (Hos. 4:12), jealousy (Num. 5:14), meekness (Gal. 6:1), fear (2 Tim. 1:7), or prayer (Zech. 12:10).

50. Carson, *The Gospel according to John*, 196.

in a similar way the Holy Spirit cannot be controlled or manipulated, but grants the new birth as God wills (cf. James 1:18). The effects of the wind are plain to the senses, and the new birth produces new life that shows itself in the actions of the regenerate. However, the wind is invisible and untraceable, and we cannot comprehend the Spirit's act of regeneration (cf. Eccles. 11:5).

Re-Creation of a Sinner

Regeneration is "genesis again" (*palingenesia*, Titus 3:5), the personal equivalent of the renewal of the world (Matt. 19:28). Just as God created all things through his living and eternal Word (John 1:1–3), so his gift of regeneration is a work of new creation through the incarnate Word (vv. 13–14). Although the participation of the saints in the new creation only begins with regeneration, nevertheless it may be said already that "if anyone is in Christ, he is a new creation" (2 Cor. 5:17 ESV), and such people "no longer live for themselves but for him who for their sake died and was raised" (v. 15 ESV).

God's work of creation did not consist of rearrangement of existing materials by the operation of natural forces, but the creation of new materials and energies out of nothing and the supernatural formation of them into new cosmic structures and new living creatures by his word, culminating in the creation of man in God's image (Genesis 1). Although regeneration does not add new components to created human nature (such as mind, spirit, etc.), it does bring graces that had no prior existence in a sinner, such as living hope and love (1 Pet. 1:3, 22–23). God also brings a new order to the faculties of the person's soul so that his thoughts, affections, and choices, formerly darkened and corrupted, are illuminated and directed by the word of truth (Eph. 4:20–24). Regeneration produces the putting off of the "old man" of malice and lies, and the putting on of the "new man" of love and knowledge, which is "renewed . . . after the image of him that created him" in Christ Jesus (Col. 3:8–12). Those made alive in Christ have been "created in Christ Jesus unto good works" (Eph. 2:10).

Salvation is not attainable by religious activities but requires this new creation. Paul says, "For in Christ Jesus neither circumcision availeth any thing, nor uncircumcision, but a new creature" (Gal. 6:15)—that is, "faith which worketh by love" (5:6). David Clarkson (1622–1686) said, "Except a man be a new creature, no privilege or religious duty will avail him anything, as to acceptation with God or salvation." Just as was the case with circumcision in the old covenant, "so baptism, and hearing the word, and prayer, they are privileges and duties commanded by God and necessary to be observed, yea, and many ways profitable; but as to acceptation with God and salvation of the observer, they avail nothing, except he be a new creature."[51]

As an act of new creation, regeneration prepares a man to live in God's kingdom in the new heaven and new earth (Titus 3:5–7; 1 Pet. 1:3–4). Justification gives the right to eternal life, but regeneration gives a fitness to enter and enjoy it, for the new creation is a holy place irradiated by the glory of the holy God (Rev. 21:23, 27). It would be more appropriate to bring a hog straight out of a pigpen into a king's dining room than to bring an unregenerate sinner into God's holy kingdom.[52] If one did so, neither the hog nor the king would be pleased. Whitefield said, "Can anyone conceive how a filthy, corrupted, polluted wretch can dwell with an infinitely pure and holy God, before he is changed and rendered in some measure like him?"[53] But the regenerate have the essence of heaven formed in their hearts, so their entrance into the kingdom of glory will be their homegoing, delightful to them and to the Lord. John Piper says, "So when you think of your new birth, think of it as the first installment of what is coming. Our body and the whole world will one day take part in this regeneration."[54]

Application of the Life of the Risen Christ

Regeneration is an inward resurrection by the life of the resurrected Christ. Paul says, "But God . . . even when we were dead in sins, hath quickened us together with Christ" (Eph. 2:4–5). The word translated as "quicken together" (*syzōopoieō*) or "made . . . alive together" (ESV) is a term for raising the dead to life.[55] The phrase "with Christ" indicates that this resurrection engages us in vital union with God's incarnate Son in his redemptive acts.[56] Charles Hodge said that because Christ and his people

51. David Clarkson, *The New Creature*, in *The Works of David Clarkson*, 3 vols. (1864; repr., Edinburgh: Banner of Truth, 1988), 2:6.

52. Swinnock, *The Door of Salvation Opened by the Key of Regeneration*, in *Works*, 5:38–39.

53. Whitefield, "On Regeneration," in *Sermons*, 2:280.

54. Piper, *Finally Alive*, 89.

55. The word *syzōopoieō* is a compound of *syn* ("with, together") and *zōopoieō* ("make alive"). See *zōopoieō* in 2 Kings 5:7 LXX; John 5:21; 6:63; Rom. 4:17; 8:11; 1 Cor. 15:21–22; 1 Pet. 3:18.

56. Lincoln, *Ephesians*, 108. See the discussion of union with Christ in his resurrection in chap. 10.

are one, "his death was their death, his life is their life."[57] Just as Christ rose from the dead to enter into his glory, so regeneration is the beginning of eternal life and glory in the midst of this age of death. Sinclair Ferguson says, "Here then, in the deep structures of New Testament thought, the eschatological nature of regeneration is underscored."[58]

As a spiritual resurrection from the dead, regeneration is an extraordinarily powerful exercise of divine power, for the saints believe "according to the working of his mighty power, which he wrought in Christ, when he raised him from the dead" (Eph. 1:19–20). They were spiritually dead (2:1), empty of spiritual life, indeed "alienated from the life of God" (4:18). Robert Rollock (c. 1555–1599) commented that Paul does not call them "half dead, or sick and infirm, but wholly dead, destitute of any ability to think or do good."[59] Mere morality may clean up dead sinners, but it cannot raise them to life: "An embalmed carcass is as much dead as a putrefied one," Charnock said.[60] Death also implies corrupting evil, which Paul identifies as the Devil and disobedient desires, and offensive uncleanness, which provokes the condemning wrath of God (2:2–3). The application of Christ's resurrection delivers sinners from all these evils, for it raises them up with Christ in victory over all powers (1:21; 2:6), secures for them an unending future under God's kindness (2:7), and makes them alive as new creations to perform good works (vv. 5, 10). The latter of these blessings pertains particularly to regeneration.

Similarly, Paul writes, "You, being dead in your sins and the uncircumcision of your flesh, hath he quickened together with him" (Col. 2:13). Here spiritual death is compared to "uncircumcision"—that is, a state of rebellion against God's covenant (Gen. 17:14). By giving them life, God "circumcised" these covenant breakers "with a circumcision made without hands" so that they became covenant keepers (Col. 2:11).

The life of the risen Lord comes to people through the gospel and gives them eternal spiritual life. Peter says, "Blessed be the God and Father of our Lord Jesus Christ, which according to his abundant mercy hath begotten us again unto a lively hope by the resurrection of Jesus Christ from the

57. Hodge, *Ephesians*, 73. See Col. 3:1, 4.
58. Ferguson, *The Holy Spirit*, 119.
59. "*Non vocat hic semimortuos, aut agrotos ac infirmos, sed prorsus mortuos, omni facultate bene cogitandi aut agenda destitutos.*" Robert Rollock, *In Epistolam Pauli Apostoli ad Ephesios* (Edinburgh: Robertus Waldegrave, 1590), on Eph. 2:1 (57). English translation adapted from Flavel, *The Method of Grace*, in *Works*, 2:86.
60. Charnock, *The Nature of Regeneration*, in *Works*, 3:131.

dead" (1 Pet. 1:3). Regeneration produces hope in the future inheritance (v. 4), hope that is "lively" or "living" because God causes hope to spring forth by Christ's resurrection. This implies that it is not merely the message of the resurrection, but the life of the risen Christ that causes regeneration. "By him," God's elect "do believe in God, that raised him up from the dead, and gave him glory; that your faith and hope might be in God" (v. 21), for they have been "born again . . . by the word of God, which liveth and abideth for ever" (v. 23).

As the change from spiritual death to spiritual life, regeneration is an instantaneous act of God. There is no middle ground between death and life. The person whom "the Son quickeneth" passes "from death unto life" (John 5:21, 24). This distinguishes regeneration from the experience of conversion, which is often a process of learning and struggle leading to repentance and faith over time. Regeneration is a secret work of God perceived only by its fruits: the action of the invisible "wind" of God known by its effects (3:8).[61]

Regeneration is the supernatural re-creation of a sinner by God in which he brings the life of the risen Christ to dead sinners. Death and life represent two states of mankind with respect to God. Goodwin said, "There are two vastly differing states of sin and damnation, of grace and salvation, which the new birth is the passage between."[62] Just as the resurrection of the body endows it with a new kind of life, possessing new qualities of incorruption, glory, and power that endure forever (1 Cor. 15:42–44), so being made alive with Christ in this age gives the soul a new kind of life with permanent new qualities in the understanding and will.[63]

Power That Produces Conversion in the Inner Man

Regeneration consists particularly in the working of a change of the inner man. God said, "A new heart also will I give you, and a new spirit will I put within you: and I will take away the stony heart out of your flesh, and I will give you an heart of flesh" (Ezek. 36:26). The Lord had required the people of Israel to make themselves "a new heart and a new spirit" by turning from sin back to him (18:30–32). However, the hearts of the

61. Berkhof, *Systematic Theology*, 468–69.
62. Goodwin, *The Work of the Holy Ghost in Our Salvation*, in *Works*, 6:75.
63. Goodwin, *The Work of the Holy Ghost in Our Salvation*, in *Works*, 6:194.

people were stubborn (2:4; 3:7) and fixed on whoring with idols (6:9; 20:16). Therefore, the Lord promised to change them himself, asserting that he would be the sole cause of this change by his repeated "I will" (36:25–27).[64]

The Lord's promise of a new heart means that God gives a new disposition to the soul's faculties that causes people to turn to him, know him, and love him.[65] The "heart" in the Scriptures consists of the inner man, the command center from which all of a person's life flows in his thoughts, affections, choices, and actions (Prov. 4:23; Mark 7:21–23). The heart is the seat of faith: "With the heart man believeth" (Rom. 10:10). The heart is also the center of faithfulness (Neh. 9:8). It is with the heart that people both fear and love the Lord (Deut. 5:29; 10:12). God says, "I will give them one heart . . . that they may fear me for ever . . . I will put my fear in their hearts" (Jer. 32:39–40). In this text, "fear" is both a quality that God puts in people's hearts and an action that they take as a result.

Franciscus Gomarus (1563–1641), using "conversion" in a broad sense, said, "For the grace of conversion is twofold: habitual and actual [*habitualis et actualis*]," meaning that it involves a change of both disposition and action. Gomarus explained, "The former is that by which a human is regenerated by the power of the Holy Spirit or is given the powers of faith and love. The latter is that by which the already-regenerate person, with the aid of God's word and Spirit, exercises these powers in the activity of believing and loving."[66]

Regeneration is not a work that merely alters a person's behavior or changes his beliefs. Just as Elisha threw salt into a poisonous spring and God miraculously made the water healthy and good (2 Kings 2:19–22), so in the new birth the Lord purifies and sweetens the deepest wells of human motivation. As Augustine said, God works by "a secret, wonderful, and ineffable power" to produce goodness in the will.[67]

---

64. "I will sprinkle . . . I will cleanse . . . I will give . . . I will put . . . I will remove . . . [I] will give . . . I will put . . . [I will] cause" (Ezek. 36:25–27 ESV). Charnock, *The Efficient of Regeneration*, in *Works*, 3:169.

65. Polyander, Walaeus, Thysius, and Rivetus, *Synopsis Purioris Theologiae*, 32.2 (2:277). On the faculties of the soul and their spiritual disposition, see *RST*, 2:255–59.

66. Franciscus Gomarus, *De Gratia Conversionis*, in *Opera Theologica Omnia*, 2 vols. (Amsterdam: Joannis Janssonii, 1644), 1:135. English translation in Bavinck, *Reformed Dogmatics*, 4:150 (misattributed to the *Synopsis Purioris Theologiae*). See also Turretin, *Institutes*, 15.4.13–17 (2:522–24).

67. Augustine, *On the Grace of Christ*, 25.24, in *NPNF*[1], 5:227. The full quotation was given earlier in the discussion of Augustine's view of God's grace in chap. 16.

Regeneration is a comprehensive work on the whole inner man. In the new creation, "all things are become new" (2 Cor. 5:17). Boston said, "Original sin infects the whole man; and regenerating grace, which is the cure, goes as far as the disease."[68] Charnock said, "Because there was an universal depravation [corruption] by the fall, regeneration must answer it in its extensiveness in every faculty. Otherwise it is not the birth of the man, but of one part only. . . . Sin hath rooted itself in every part; ignorance and error in our understandings; pride, and self-love, and enmity in our wills; all must be unrooted by a new grace, and the triumphs of sin spoiled [taken captive] by a new birth."[69]

The new birth is a powerful work that infallibly produces changes in people. Christ tersely said, "That which is born of the Spirit is spirit" (John 3:6). Regeneration produces:

- Righteousness in one's conduct: "If ye know that he is righteous, ye know that every one that doeth righteousness is born of him" (1 John 2:29).
- Love for one's brothers: "Beloved, let us love one another: for love is of God; and every one that loveth is born of God, and knoweth God" (1 John 4:7).
- Persevering faith in Jesus Christ: "Whosoever believeth that Jesus is the Christ is born of God. . . . For whatsoever is born of God overcometh the world: and this is the victory that overcometh the world, even our faith" (1 John 5:1, 4).

In each case, the verb translated as "is born" (*gegennētai*) is in the perfect tense, indicating a completed past action or the state that it produces, preceded by a present participle, so that these Scripture passages mean that "everyone who is believing in Christ, loving, and doing righteousness has been born of God." Regeneration is the cause of these graces.

We must distinguish the divine act of initial regeneration from the human acts of conversion. Charnock said, "Conversion is related to regeneration, as the effect to the cause. Life precedes motion, and is the cause of motion." He added, "In regeneration, man is wholly passive; in conversion, he is active."[70] James Boyce said, "Regeneration is the work

68. Boston, *Human Nature in Its Fourfold State*, 208.
69. Charnock, *The Necessity of Regeneration*, in *Works*, 3:26–27.
70. Charnock, *The Nature of Regeneration*, in *Works*, 3:88–89; cf. Turretin, *Institutes*, 15.5.9–12 (2:544–45).

of God, changing the heart of man by his sovereign will, while conversion is the act of man turning towards God with the new inclination thus given to his heart."[71]

Renewal of God's Image

The "new man" is "after the image of him that created him" (Col. 3:10). John's description of the new birth's effects implies that regeneration renews the image of God in sinful men.[72] The one born of God does righteousness because God "is righteous" (1 John 2:29). The one born of God loves because "God is love" (4:7–8). The idea of the divine image is implied in the very words "beget" and "born," for a father begets a child in his own likeness (Gen. 5:3; cf. 1 Pet. 1:3, 15).[73]

Regeneration accomplishes the renewal of God's image by uniting people to Christ, for he is the Image of God (Rom. 8:29; Col. 1:15). As Athanasius said, "the Image of the Father" came "to renew man once made in His likeness" so that we can be "born again . . . born and created anew in the likeness of God's image."[74]

In the gospel, God's glory radiates from Christ, the Image of God, but Satan blinds men from seeing and appreciating this splendor (2 Cor. 4:4). However, by the work of new creation, God causes that light to shine in the hearts of sinners (v. 6). Satan's work is defeated, and sinners are saved. As a result, they are now being "changed into the same image from glory to glory" (3:18).[75] Peter boldly calls this being made "partakers of the divine nature" (2 Pet. 1:4). It is called "nature," Goodwin explained, because it consists of dispositions "inherent in us," and "divine" because it "bears a likeness to God's nature" in "holy dispositions wrought in us," as we see by its contrast to "the corruption that is in the world through lust" (v. 4).[76] And just as the image of God is holistic, imprinted on all of man's nature, activity, and relations, so regeneration begins a process that progressively sanctifies the whole man, body and soul (2 Cor. 7:1; 1 Thess. 5:23).[77]

---

71. Boyce, *Abstract of Systematic Theology*, 374.

72. See the section on the renewed image of God in *RST*, 2:170–72.

73. Goodwin, *The Work of the Holy Ghost in Our Salvation*, in *Works*, 6:152.

74. Athanasius, *On the Incarnation of the Word*, sec. 14, in *NPNF*², 4:43–44.

75. On saving illumination, see the point in chap. 15 on effectual calling's power to create a new people.

76. Goodwin, *The Work of the Holy Ghost in Our Salvation*, in *Works*, 6:153. Against the misinterpretation of 2 Pet. 1:4 as deification, see the discussion of the topic in chap. 10.

77. Van Mastricht, *Theoretico-Practica Theologia*, 6.3.16 (2:662); *A Treatise on Regeneration*, 27. On the holistic scope of God's image in man, see *RST*, 2:194–200.

The new birth initiates spiritual warfare between the soul and the forces of the Devil. The one "born of God overcometh the world" (1 John 5:4). In the new birth, the cosmic conflict between Christ and Satan enters the soul, for "he that committeth sin is of the devil; for the devil sinneth from the beginning. For this purpose the Son of God was manifested, that he might destroy the works of the devil" (3:8). Therefore, Whately said, one of the principal effects of regeneration is "spiritual combat" against Satan. Whately explained, "No sooner does a Christian begin to draw the breath of this new life, but he finds himself called to fighting. . . . He stands in a pitched field of enemies, so soon as he can go upon the feet of his soul, and there he must never cease giving and taking blows, till he cease to be in this lower world."[78]

Definitive Cleansing from Sin

The Lord exhorted his people to "wash" their hearts from wickedness so that they would escape the curses coming on their nation (Jer. 4:14), but they could no more wash themselves than a man can wash away the natural color of his skin (13:23). Sinners need an inner miracle akin to the physical healing granted to the leper from Syria, Naaman, who at Elisha's command dipped himself seven times in the Jordan River "and his flesh came again like unto the flesh of a little child, and he was clean"—physically born again, as it were (2 Kings 5:14).

The decisive spiritual washing necessary for salvation takes place in the new birth by the Holy Spirit. Paul says, "For we ourselves were once foolish, disobedient, led astray, slaves to various passions and pleasures, passing our days in malice and envy, hated by others and hating one another," but God "saved us . . . by the washing of regeneration" (Titus 3:3, 5 ESV). One of the primary corruptions from which regeneration washes us is hatred and malice. Murderous, merciless hatred characterizes the Devil and his children (John 8:44). Demonic "wisdom" is full of "bitter envying and strife," but the wisdom "from above" brings "meekness" and makes men "gentle" (James 3:13–18). Richard Sibbes said, "It is an eminent and infallible mark of regeneration to have the violence and fierceness of our cruel nature taken away."[79] Consequently, those born again must devote themselves to good works, practice submission to proper authorities, and show gentleness to all men (Titus 3:1–2, 8).

78. Whately, *The New Birth*, 46, language modernized.
79. Sibbes, *The Touchstone of Regeneration*, in *Works*, 7:130.

Paul warns that "the unrighteous shall not inherit the kingdom of God," listing several kinds of sinners, but says, "Such were some of you: but ye are washed, but ye are sanctified, but ye are justified in the name of the Lord Jesus, and by the Spirit of our God" (1 Cor. 6:11). Here "washed" refers to the definitive cleansing from sin granted in salvation, accompanied by being definitively "sanctified," or consecrated to God, and being "justified," or declared righteous.

The Lord Jesus Christ offered a tangible illustration of this spiritual cleansing when he washed the feet of his disciples, telling them that they (except Judas) were already "washed" and "clean" (*katharos*), and warning that anyone whom he does not "wash" has no part with him (John 13:8, 10–11). Participation in Christ's kingdom requires a one-time spiritual bath, which need not be repeated, though a disciple needs regular partial cleansing comparable to the washing of his feet (vv. 9–10). Later, Christ again told the disciples in the context of the parable of the vine and the branches, "Ye are clean [*katharos*] through the word which I have spoken unto you" (15:3). Given that the context pertained to sharing in Christ's life and bearing fruit, the cleansing in view is best understood to refer not to forgiveness but to regeneration.

Just as the flow of clean water washes away much filth, so the spiritual life introduced by regeneration cleanses from sin. Thomas Chalmers (1780–1847) spoke of "the expulsive power of a new affection," for no demonstration or explanation of the foolishness and evil of worldly desires will help a person conquer them, but only the addition of a new and greater love, for "it is then that the heart, brought under the mastery of one great and predominant affection, is delivered from the tyranny of its former desires."[80]

Peter says that when God saved the Gentiles he "cleansed their hearts by faith" (Acts 15:9 ESV). The verb translated as "cleanse" (*katharizō*) can be used of forgiveness (Heb. 9:14; 1 John 1:9), but by making the object of cleansing the "heart," Peter indicates that he is speaking of an inner purification. This cleansing of the heart makes people capable of holy fellowship with God (Ps. 24:3–4; Matt. 5:8) and his saints (Acts 10:14–15, 28; 2 Tim. 2:22).

John writes, "Whosoever is born of God doth not commit sin; for his seed remaineth in him: and he cannot sin, because he is born of God" (1 John 3:9). Christians still sin even after they are born again and should acknowledge that they do so (1:8–10). However, the present-tense verb

80. Thomas Chalmers, *The Expulsive Power of a New Affection* (London: Hatchard and Co., 1861), 12.

translated as "doth not commit sin" indicates an end of the continuous pattern of rebellion against God's law that characterizes the children of the Devil (3:4–8). The cause of this repentant spirit is the living principle ("seed") of holiness that regeneration plants in the soul.[81] This new life is not a transient effect of the Spirit on the soul, but an abiding life that continues to preserve the soul from the reign of sin.[82] God has put holy fear in the heart so that his people will not depart from him (Jer. 32:40). Boston said, "It is a lasting change. . . . The life given in regeneration, whatever decays it may fall under, can never be utterly lost."[83]

However, the regenerate must maintain a realistic view of their state. As we noted above, though believers are definitively washed, they still have much remaining sin that they must put to death and weakness of grace that they must stir into a lively, mature exercise. Therefore, an internal war ensues upon the new birth. Though Peter tells believers that they have been "born again" (1 Pet. 1:23), he also warns them to "abstain from fleshly lusts, which war against the soul" (2:11). Whately said, "Thus, the regenerate finds himself strangely divided within and against himself."[84] Johann Heidegger (1633–1698) said, "Regeneration is imperfect in this life," resulting in spiritual "struggle."[85] This inner conflict is not evidence against regeneration but evidence for it, because the Spirit has begun to produce holy desires that are contrary to the desires of sin (Gal. 5:17).[86]

Grace Given Because of God's Mercy and Love

Since by regeneration God saves people from a state of sin and guilt, the new birth is entirely undeserved, being granted contrary to their worthiness of damnation because of God's grace alone. After writing that "love is of God; and every one that loveth is born of God, and knoweth God . . . for God is love," John says, "We love him, because he first loved us" (1 John 4:7–8, 19).

81. The exact identity of this "seed" (*sperma*) that "remaineth" (*menō*) in the one born of God (1 John 3:9) is unclear. The best interpretation of "seed" may be the new life produced by regeneration, which is a vital, Spirit-worked knowledge and love that "abides" (*menō*) in believers (2:14, 27; 4:12–17). Poole, *Annotations upon the Holy Bible*, 3:935, on 1 John 3:9; John R. W. Stott, *The Letters of John: An Introduction and Commentary*, Tyndale New Testament Commentaries 19 (Downers Grove, IL: InterVarsity Press, 1988), 129–30; and Daniel L. Akin, *1, 2, 3 John*, The New American Commentary 38 (Nashville: Broadman & Holman, 2001), 148–49.

82. Goodwin, *The Work of the Holy Ghost in Our Salvation*, in *Works*, 6:193.

83. Boston, *Human Nature in Its Fourfold State*, 209.

84. Whately, *The New Birth*, 50.

85. Heidegger, *The Concise Marrow of Christian Theology*, 21.9 (148).

86. Schortinghuis, *Essential Truths in the Heart of a Christian*, 23.7 (88).

We were dead, empty of the life that pleases God and stained by the corruption that offends him, "but God, who is rich in mercy, for his great love wherewith he loved us, even when we were dead in sins, hath quickened us together with Christ (by grace ye are saved)" (Eph. 2:4–5). Therefore, no one can boast (v. 9). Salvation is "to the praise of the glory of his grace" (1:6). The Christian should say, "Why am I spiritually alive? God made me alive with Christ. Why did he do that? Not because of anything in me—for I was worthy of nothing but wrath—but only because he chose to look upon me with saving mercy and love."

Paul reminds God's children that they were once like all men: "foolish, disobedient, deceived, serving divers lusts and pleasures, living in malice and envy, hateful, and hating one another" (Titus 3:3). God regenerated them because of his "kindness and love . . . not by works of righteousness which we have done, but according to his mercy" (vv. 4–5). We should let that settle into our minds, root out of our hearts every proud assumption that God saved us because of anything we have done, and marvel at the kindness, love, and mercy that God showed when he regenerated us.

The doctrine of regeneration prepares believers for worship. It teaches them to say with Peter, "Blessed be the God and Father of our Lord Jesus Christ, which according to his abundant mercy hath begotten us again" (1 Pet. 1:3). It is profitable for us to meditate on each word about God in these texts and praise him for it:[87]

- "Love" (*agapē*, Eph. 2:4; 1 John 4:7)—Praise God for his great benevolence that led him to generously do good to us by giving us life when we were dead in sin.
- "Grace" (*charis*, Eph. 2:5)—Praise God because, though he owed us nothing, he chose to show us favor and powerfully save us by regeneration.
- "Mercy" (*eleos*, Eph. 2:4; Titus 3:5; 1 Pet. 1:3)—Praise God that he not only considered what we deserved but had tender compassion on us in our misery.
- "Kindness" (*chrēstotēs*, Titus 3:4)—Praise God for his great goodness toward us when we were evil by giving us a radical new beginning to become his heirs.

87. On God's goodness and kindness, mercy, grace, and benevolent love, see *RST*, 1:783–87, 794–96.

- "Love toward man" (*philanthrōpia*, Titus 3:4)—Praise God that he chose to be friendly to men when we were his enemies and changed us to be his friends.[88]

The doctrine of regeneration magnifies the glory of God, for in the new birth the Lord supernaturally brings the resurrection life of Christ into the inner man of a lost sinner, so that he becomes a new creation who trusts Christ, repents of sin, and loves God and man. Although regeneration only begins the application of salvation, it is an amazingly gracious and powerful act of God. The regenerate will praise God forever for it.

Sing to the Lord

The Spirit, Our Regenerator

Come, Holy Spirit, come;
Let thy bright beams arise;
Dispel the darkness from our minds,
And open all our eyes.

Convince us of our sin;
Then lead to Jesus' blood,
And to our wond'ring view reveal
The secret love of God.

'Tis thine to cleanse the heart,
To sanctify the soul,
To pour fresh life in every part,
And new create the whole.

Dwell, therefore, in our hearts;
Our minds from bondage free;
Then we shall know and praise and love
The Father, Son, and Thee.

Joseph Hart
Tune: Camberwell
Trinity Hymnal—Baptist Edition, No. 254

88. Though *philanthrōpia* may be used of human friendliness to one's neighbor, as when the people of Malta gave heat and shelter to the shipwrecked (Acts 28:2, the only other New Testament use), it also referred to the benevolence of gods and kings to those under their friendly care. *TDNT*, 9:107–10.

Questions for Meditation or Discussion

1. In what ways have Reformed theologians used the term *regeneration* over the centuries?
2. What images and descriptions does the Bible use for regeneration?
3. How do the authors define regeneration?
4. What is the meaning of the triple negation in John 1:13?
5. What truths can we learn from Jesus's teaching in John 3:3–8?
6. What does it mean that regeneration is a new creation?
7. How does regeneration relate to the resurrection of Jesus Christ?
8. What does regeneration produce in the soul?
9. What Scripture passages link regeneration to the renewal of God's image?
10. In what Scripture passages is regeneration compared to washing? What does this mean?
11. What is the only reason why God regenerates a sinner? How does that affect you personally?

Questions for Deeper Reflection

12. How should we interpret the meaning of "flesh" in John 3:6? Why? How does that interpretation affect how we view the necessity of the new birth?
13. A Christian friend says, "I don't believe that regeneration happens in an instant. It took years of questioning and struggling before I found peace with God." How do you respond?
14. At a conference where many speakers will address regeneration, you have been invited to present a break-out session on "Regeneration and the Coming Glory." Prepare a detailed outline for your forty-minute teaching on regeneration and eschatology.

18

Regeneration, Part 2

Theological Questions and Practical Applications

When Christ compares the new birth by the Holy Spirit to the blowing of the wind, he admonishes us to respect the mystery of this divine work (John 3:8). We do not even completely understand our own spirits, for they are not objects of our senses, so can we expect to comprehend their supernatural renewal by the infinite and invisible God?

However, God has revealed regeneration to us for our faith and godliness. Therefore, God's Word calls us to reflect on the theological and practical implications of this doctrine. Such reflections will both protect us from error and motivate us to live in humility and gratitude toward God the Holy Spirit, our Lord and life giver.

Theological Questions about Regeneration

In order to deepen our understanding of the new birth, we will consider how this doctrine relates to other doctrines in our theological system.

Regeneration in Relation to the Trinity

Who causes regeneration—God the Father, God the Son, or God the Holy Spirit? Regeneration is Trinitarian grace, involving the Father, the Son, and the Holy Spirit in one divine act.[1] It is often ascribed to God the Father, to whom the regenerate relate as his children. The expression that believers are born "of God" (*ek [tou] theou*) identifies him as the cause of their regeneration.[2] The Father begets them anew (1 Pet. 1:3) and brings them forth (James 1:17–18).

God the Son is the Mediator of the new birth, for the Father sends the Spirit of regeneration "through Jesus Christ our Saviour" (Titus 3:4–6). God has made his children alive together with the risen Lord Jesus (Eph. 2:5; Col. 2:13) and begotten them again through his resurrection (1 Pet. 1:3). The victorious last Adam rose as "a quickening spirit" (1 Cor. 15:45)—that is, with the power to give life by the Spirit. Christ was not passive in his resurrection but actively raised himself (John 2:19; 10:17–18), and in a similar way he actively gives life to the spiritually dead (5:21, 25). Christ washes his people so that they are clean (13:8–10).

God the Holy Spirit is the divine agent sent from the Father and the Son to regenerate sinners. The new birth is "of" (*ek*) the Spirit (John 3:5–7, 8), just as Christ's supernatural conception in a virgin was "of [*ek*] the Holy Spirit" (Matt. 1:20). God saves sinners "by the washing of regeneration, and renewing of the Holy Ghost" (Titus 3:5–6).

Regeneration in Relation to God's Sovereignty

Is regeneration a sovereign and effectual work of God's grace alone? Yes, it is. Although we have already presented arguments that God's saving call is effectual grace,[3] it is helpful to collect evidence from our study of regeneration in the previous chapter to show that it is a monergistic and effectual work that infallibly produces salvation.

First, regeneration is not of human will but of God: believers have been "born, not of blood, nor of the will of the flesh, nor of the will of man, but of God" (John 1:13). John Murray said, "God is the agent or begetter without cooperation or collusion on the side of man. . . . John piles up negatives to exclude human determination."[4] Robert Culver said, "God and God alone is the author of the new birth."[5]

1. Van Mastricht, *Theoretico-Practica Theologia*, 6.3.7 (2:660); *A Treatise on Regeneration*, 19–20.
2. John 1:13; 1 John 3:9; 4:7; 5:1, 4, 18; cf. the use of *gennaō ek* to designate a person's mother (Matt. 1:16; Gal. 4:23) or fornication as the cause of illegitimate birth (John 8:41).
3. See chap. 16, where we also address objections to effectual grace.
4. Murray, *Collected Writings*, 2:193.
5. Culver, *Systematic Theology*, 695.

Second, regeneration is a new birth from the Holy Spirit (John 3:3–8). J. I. Packer said, "Infants do not induce, or cooperate in, their own procreation and birth," so the new birth is "not caused or induced by any human efforts."[6]

Third, human nature is unable to produce the new birth, which must come from God the Holy Spirit. Christ said, "That which is born of the flesh is flesh; and that which is born of the Spirit is spirit" (John 3:6).

Fourth, God grants regeneration according to his free and sovereign will. Christ illustrates, "The wind blows where it wishes" (John 3:8 ESV). James says, "Of his own will he brought us forth" (James 1:18 ESV). James Boyce wrote, "The Scripture attributes the birth to the will of God exclusively."[7]

Fifth, regeneration is an act of new creation (2 Cor. 5:17; Eph. 2:10). Creation is God's work, and he does it alone (Isa. 44:24). William Perkins said, "The conversion of a sinner is a creation, and no creature can prepare itself to his own creation."[8]

Sixth, in regeneration, God takes people dead in sin and makes them alive in Christ—a spiritual resurrection by grace (Eph. 2:5). Therefore, sinners contribute no more to their initial regeneration than a corpse contributes to its resurrection. Regeneration is entirely God's work in Christ.

Seventh, God's Word describes regeneration as the removal of a stony heart and the implantation of a heart of flesh (Ezek. 11:19; 36:26). John Owen pointed out that this implies effectual grace, for a "stony heart" is set in "an obstinate, stubborn opposition" to God, but a "heart of flesh," by contrast, is marked by "a principle of all holy obedience unto God." To remove the one and give the other is to overcome man's sinful resistance and replace it with submission. To argue that God promises to do this if we do not resist his grace is to make the promise of a new heart into nonsense, for to not resist is to trust and submit. Owen showed the folly of that argument: "So, then, God promiseth to convert us, on condition that we convert ourselves; to work faith in us, on condition that we do believe; and a new heart, on condition that we make our hearts new ourselves."[9]

6. J. I. Packer, "Regeneration," in *The Evangelical Dictionary of Theology*, ed. Elwell, 925. See Barrett, *Salvation by Grace*, 151–53.

7. Boyce, *Abstract of Systematic Theology*, 375.

8. Perkins, *A Treatise on God's Free Grace and Man's Free Will*, in *Works*, 6:417.

9. Owen, *Pneumatologia*, in *Works*, 3:326–28. See Perkins, *A Treatise on God's Free Grace and Man's Free Will*, in *Works*, 6:418–19.

Eighth, the new birth produces repentance, faith, love, righteous deeds, and victory over the world (1 John 2:29; 3:9; 4:7; 5:1, 4). Therefore, the new birth is the cause of conversion; men do not receive the new birth by first converting themselves. Murray wrote, "Regeneration is the beginning of all saving grace in us, and all saving grace in exercise on our part proceeds from the fountain of regeneration. We are not born again by faith or repentance or conversion; we repent and believe because we have been regenerated."[10]

Hence, we see the absolute necessity of the new birth for salvation. Without regeneration, the glorious offer of the gospel will not save a single soul. It would be of no help that "God so loved the world, that he gave his only begotten Son, that whosoever believeth in him should not perish, but have everlasting life" unless God also saves the sinner from his stubborn unbelief by which he "hateth the light, neither cometh to the light" (John 3:16, 20). William Whately said, "If Christ should come and die for one man ten thousand times, all those deaths should profit that one man nothing at all for his salvation, unless he be made a new creature."[11] That is why one great fruit of Christ's death is the gift of regeneration—the new creation so that those who have lived for themselves begin to live for him (2 Cor. 5:15, 17).

Regeneration in Relation to Baptism

What is the relationship between the new birth and the sacrament of baptism? Some people might see them as having no relationship at all, taking an individualistic view of salvation divorced from the church and its ordinances. The Roman Catholic Church, the Lutheran churches, and, according to some interpretations, the confessions and liturgies of the Anglican, Episcopal, and Methodist churches teach that regeneration takes place through baptism, though each church has its own understanding of what this means.[12]

Reformed churches teach that baptism is a sign and seal of regeneration.[13] As such, it is a means of grace to be received by faith. However,

10. Murray, *Redemption Accomplished and Applied*, 103.

11. Whately, *The New Birth*, 13, punctuation modernized.

12. *Catechism of the Catholic Church*, sec. 683; Small Catechism, The Sacrament of Holy Baptism, secs. 9–10, in *The Book of Concord*, 359; the Thirty-Nine Articles, Art. 27, in *Reformed Confessions*, 2:763; and *The United Methodist Hymnal* (Nashville: The United Methodist Publishing House, 1989), 39, 42. See Demarest, *The Cross and Salvation*, 281–85.

13. The Westminster Confession of Faith (28.1); and the Westminster Larger Catechism (Q. 165), in *Reformed Confessions*, 4:266, 342. See the Belgic Confession (Art. 34); and the Heidelberg Catechism (LD 27, Q. 72–73), in *The Three Forms of Unity*, 54–56, 91.

some Reformed divines have taught that God ordinarily regenerates the elect offspring of believers when they are baptized—not by any virtue residing in or communicated through baptism, but on account of the covenant of grace.[14] The Westminster Confession of Faith (28.6) left the timing of regeneration open: "The efficacy of Baptism is not tied to that moment of time wherein it is administered; yet, notwithstanding, by the right use of this ordinance, the grace promised is not only offered, but really exhibited, and conferred, by the Holy Ghost, to such (whether of age or infants) as that grace belongeth unto, according to the counsel of God's own will, in His appointed time."[15]

We cannot here explore the doctrine of the sacraments in any depth; that pertains to the locus of ecclesiology.[16] However, at this point we do need to clarify the relationship between regeneration and baptism.

The New Testament closely connects baptism to union with Christ, especially in his death, burial, and resurrection.[17] However, the Bible indicates that people can be saved and receive the Holy Spirit before baptism—simply by hearing the gospel (Acts 10:44–48). People may be baptized but remain the slaves of sin (8:13, 20–23; cf. 1 Cor. 10:1–5). Paul said, "Christ sent me not to baptize, but to preach the gospel" (1 Cor. 1:17), which would be inconceivable if baptism were the ordinary means of regeneration. Therefore, baptism does not confer regeneration.

In favor of baptismal regeneration, it is often argued that Christ taught that we must be "born of water and of the Spirit" in order to enter his kingdom (John 3:5).

Some respond to this argument by saying that "water" and "Spirit" refer to natural birth and spiritual birth respectively. However, the fluids of natural birth are better described as "blood" (1:13). Furthermore, the syntax uses one verb and one preposition to describe not two births

14. Herman Witsius said, "I find four distinct opinions among theologians. Some think that regeneration takes place at different periods of time—it may be before, it may be at, or it may be after baptism [Zanchi, Ames, Spanheim]. Others place it uniformly before baptism [Calvin, Voetius, Burgess, *Synopsis Purioris Theologiae*, Witsius, and van Mastricht]. Others teach that infants are baptized unto future regeneration, being incapable of it at the time [Amyraut]. Indeed, many contend that God usually confers regeneration upon infants in the very act and moment of baptism [Le Blanc, Cocceius]." Herman Witsius, "The Efficacy and Utility of Baptism," sec. 23, trans. William Marshall and J. Mark Beach, ed. J. Mark Beach, *Mid-America Journal of Theology* 17 (2006): 142 (full article, 121–90). See van Mastricht, *Theoretico-Practica Theologia*, 6.3.31 (2:668–69); *A Treatise on Regeneration*, 45–49.

15. *Reformed Confessions*, 4:267.

16. On the sacraments or ordinances, see *RST*, vol. 4 (forthcoming).

17. Rom. 6:3–4; Gal. 3:27; Col. 2:12; 1 Pet. 3:21.

but one: literally "born of water and Spirit" (*gennēthē ex hydatos kai pneumatos*).

Another response to this argument from John 3:5 for baptismal regeneration is to say that "water" does refer to baptism, but only as a sign of rebirth, not a means of regeneration. However, if "water" refers to baptism, then we must acknowledge that God regenerates by or through baptism, for the phrase "born of" identifies the cause of regeneration.[18]

The best approach is to interpret "water" in this text to refer to the inner cleansing by God and not baptism. In the background of Christ's teaching was the prophecy that God would cleanse the people of Israel from idolatry with "clean water," give them a new heart, and put his Spirit in them (Ezek. 36:25–27).[19] When Christ proceeded to further describe regeneration, he spoke only of the Spirit, not of water or of baptism (John 3:6, 8). If we take "water and Spirit" to mean "water, that is, the cleansing work of the Holy Spirit," then the passage makes good sense. The Greek text, literally "of water and Spirit" (*ex hydatos kai pneumatos*), links the two words. Christ, like the prophets before him, elsewhere compared the work of the Spirit to flowing water.[20] The imagery of this text, like many others that speak of salvation as a washing (e.g., Eph. 5:26; Titus 3:5), uses the types of the Mosaic ceremonial washings to refer to salvation in Christ by the Spirit.[21]

It may be further argued in favor of baptismal regeneration that Ananias told Paul, "Arise, and be baptized, and wash away thy sins, calling on the name of the Lord" (Acts 22:16).

However, this Scripture passage contains two commands, each modified by a participle, so that it may very literally be translated, "Arising, be baptized, and wash away your sins, calling on the name of the Lord." In the second command, cleansing (probably forgiveness) is directly linked not to baptism but to calling on the Lord in faith. Similarly, when Paul joins baptism and salvation, in the context he makes it clear that salvation is by faith in Christ (Gal. 3:27; Col. 2:12).

---

18. "If we regard *hudōr* [water] as baptism then we shall have to give to baptism an efficiency coordinate with *Pneumatos* (Spirit)." Murray, *Collected Writings*, 2:181.

19. Carson, *The Gospel according to John*, 192–95. It is sometimes argued that Nicodemus could not have identified "water" with baptism, but baptism by John and Jesus's disciples is present in the context (John 3:22–23, 26).

20. John 4:14; 7:37–39; cf. Isa. 44:3–4 and references to the pouring out of the Spirit in Joel 2:28–29, etc.

21. Poole, *Annotations upon the Holy Bible*, 3:290, on John 3:5.

The doctrine of baptismal regeneration, applied to infant baptism, logically implies that God's saving grace is not powerfully effective to rescue people from sin, for that doctrine asserts that the millions of infants taken to the church font were all born again. Where is the righteousness, love, faith, and victory over this world that regeneration produces?[22] It is not merely a question of whether the regenerate persevere (an important doctrinal point in itself), but whether they ever show evidences of saving grace at all. Many children who receive the sacrament in professing Christian churches do not, proving that they have not been regenerated. Thomas Watson said, "It is not baptism [which] makes a Christian; many are no better than baptized heathens. The essential part of religion lies in the new creature."[23]

If we are speaking of adults, then the doctrine of baptismal regeneration implies that regeneration is not necessary for repentance and faith. We note that in the book of Acts, the baptism of adults followed their repentance and faith (Acts 2:38, 41; 8:12). However, Luke ascribes repentance and faith to God's grace (11:18, 21). For example, God opened Lydia's heart, she became a disciple, and then she was baptized (16:14–15). Again, "many of the Corinthians hearing believed, and were baptized" (18:8). If baptism were God's ordinary means to give regeneration, then faith and repentance would follow baptism. Baptismal regeneration implies that people have the power to repent and believe apart from God's regenerating grace—but this is impossible because they are dead in sin (Eph. 2:1). To say baptism is the means of regeneration for infants but not adults is to posit two fundamentally different ways of salvation and, thus, to prove that baptism is not necessary for regeneration at all.

Why, then, is baptism so closely associated with new life in Christ if it is not the means or occasion of regeneration? The biblical answer is to identify baptism as one of the covenantal signs that God instituted in order to visibly represent his promises, such as the rainbow, circumcision, and keeping the Sabbath (Gen. 9:9–17; 17:9–14; Ex. 31:13–17). These signs were not instruments by which God saved his people; rather, they were external reminders of his covenantal promises to strengthen faith. Similarly, baptism is the new covenant sign of union with Christ—not the effective means of regeneration but the outward mark of regeneration.

22. John 3:6; Titus 3:3–5; 1 John 2:29; 3:9; 4:7; 5:1, 4.

23. Thomas Watson, "Who Are in Christ Are New Creatures," in *A Body of Practical Divinity . . . with a Supplement of Some Sermons* (London: Thomas Parkhurst, 1692), 984 [pagination error beginning at 545].

Regeneration in Relation to People Unable to Understand the Gospel

It might be objected that if God does not regenerate people through baptism, then what hope do we have for our children who die in infancy or who never attain the mental capacity to understand the gospel of Christ? They, too, are subject to the power of sin and death.[24]

Reformed Christians confess that God is able to save whom he pleases, but that he always saves through the grace of Jesus Christ applied by the Holy Spirit. The Westminster Confession of Faith (10.3) says, "Elect infants, dying in infancy, are regenerated, and saved by Christ, through the Spirit, who worketh when, and where, and how He pleaseth: so also are all other elect persons who are uncapable of being outwardly called by the ministry of the Word."[25] While we cannot know whom God has elected, the Canons of Dort (Head 1, Art. 17) state that, based on the Reformed doctrine that God sets apart "the children of believers" in the covenant of grace, "godly parents have no reason to doubt of the election and salvation of their children whom it pleaseth God to call out of this life in their infancy."[26]

The Holy Scriptures show us evidence that God is able to save people in infancy, which implies that he also can save the mentally underdeveloped and those who suffer severe brain injuries. The clearest example appears in John the Baptist. The angel told John's father, "He shall be filled with the Holy Ghost, even from his mother's womb" (Luke 1:15). When Mary visited Elizabeth, then pregnant with John, Elizabeth exclaimed, "Why is this granted to me that the mother of my Lord should come to me? For behold, when the sound of your greeting came to my ears, the baby in my womb leaped for joy" (vv. 43–44 ESV). This event implies that God granted John a supernatural prophetic revelation so that he recognized by Mary's voice the presence of the Lord's mother. It also implies that John already loved Christ, for he responded with exuberant joy. Since these events are explicitly linked to the ministry of the Holy Spirit, we conclude that John was regenerated.

There are some other biblical references to people who knew the Savior from their youngest days. David said, "But thou art he that took me out of the womb: thou didst make me hope when I was upon my mother's

---

24. Gen. 8:21; Pss. 51:5; 58:3; Rom. 5:14. See the Belgic Confession (Art. 15), in *The Three Forms of Unity*, 32.

25. *Reformed Confessions*, 4:247.

26. *The Three Forms of Unity*, 127. The relation of the infant seed of believers to the covenant of grace and the church of Christ will be explored under the locus of ecclesiology in *RST*, vol. 4 (forthcoming).

breasts. I was cast upon thee from the womb: thou art my God from my mother's belly" (Ps. 22:9–10). The verb translated as "hope" (*batakh*) is that used for the trust that the godly place in the Lord to deliver them from evil (vv. 4–5). This psalm is a prophecy of Christ and may have little or no reference to David's life.[27] Therefore, it may not be a direct proof of infant regeneration. However, the incarnate Son is truly human in body and soul. Therefore, the text at least proves that an infant human being is capable of hoping in the Lord as his covenant God. God called Christ "from the womb" to be his faithful servant (Isa. 49:1, 5). Therefore, we conclude that God is capable of calling other elect infants in a manner unknown to us so that they trust in him as their God and Savior.

We read elsewhere in the Psalms, "For thou art my hope, O Lord God: thou art my trust from my youth. By thee have I been holden up from the womb: thou art he that took me out of my mother's bowels: my praise shall be continually of thee" (Ps. 71:5–6). The verb translated with the passive "have I been holden up" (*niphal* of *samak*) has the reflexive sense of "to support oneself" or "lean," often by trusting in someone.[28] Thus, the psalmist says that he has trusted in God from the womb. It might be objected that the Psalms also speak of animals looking to God for their food (Pss. 104:27; 145:15–16), not because beasts have faith in the Creator but as a personification of their need for his provision. However, Psalm 71 speaks of a believer's infantile leaning on God as an early expression of his present trust in the Lord—not the fact of dependence but the attitude. This passage gives some justification to those who can honestly say that they have known and trusted God as long as they can remember.

The salvation of infants is a profound mystery. Children think in childish ways (1 Cor. 13:11), and infants lack discernment and the ability to communicate verbally (Isa. 7:15–16; 8:4). Very young children cannot understand God's Word (Neh. 8:2–3). They cannot hear the gospel and exercise faith in its promises, which is God's ordinary way to save sinners (Rom. 10:13–17). However, the examples given above show that the undeveloped condition of a human being's mind does not prevent him from possessing and exercising faith and love toward God. This implies that God is able to reveal himself to infants and those with mental disabilities, and to regenerate them. This doctrine should give great comfort to Christians

27. Compare Ps. 22:1, 7–8, 18 to Matt. 27:35, 39, 43, 46, and Ps. 22:22 to Heb. 2:12.
28. 2 Kings 18:21; 2 Chron. 32:8; Isa. 36:6; 48:2; cf. Judg. 16:29 (KJV mg.).

that the Lord can save his elect even if a disability or early death cuts them off from understanding the Word.

However, we must be cautious not to distort this wonderful truth into false teachings and harmful applications. God does not save babies because they are inherently pure and good. The biblical doctrine of original sin teaches us that all mankind is sinful and can be saved only by God's grace in Christ applied through the Holy Spirit. Neither may we presume that children have been regenerated apart from any evidence of faith and repentance in them. Some godly Christians have trusted in Christ as long as they can remember, but as Murray said, a regenerated child exhibits that regeneration by his love for God and righteousness.[29]

Goodwin said that among Christian adults, "some few will be found sanctified from their infancy, insomuch as they dare not say but they had workings of grace on them ever since they can remember." However, Scripture passages such as Titus 3:3–7 show that God "generally and ordinarily" ordains that his elect be regenerated "when grown up to years of discretion."[30]

God's ordinary way to save people is through the preaching of the gospel. The Bible gives us no examples of adults saved apart from faith in Jesus Christ, but warns that "there is none other name under heaven given among men, whereby we must be saved" (Acts 4:12). Though there are examples of infant godliness in the Holy Scriptures, those examples are rare, and the exhortations to repent and believe God's Word in order to be saved are many.[31] Those examples of godliness from early childhood consist of individuals who exhibited the reality of their early faith by persevering in faith in God's promises and living for God's glory through many trials (cf. Psalm 71). Let no one claim regeneration as an infant who does not do the same.

Regeneration in Relation to the Call of the Gospel

If God ordinarily saves through the gospel, then what is the relationship between regeneration and the gospel call? God calls sinners to faith and

29. Murray, *Collected Writings*, 2:199–201.

30. Goodwin, *The Work of the Holy Ghost in Our Salvation*, in *Works*, 6:87.

31. As far as we know, there are no other clear examples of infant salvation in the Bible in addition to those we have cited from Psalm 22, Psalm 71, and Luke 1. God's statement that he knew and sanctified Jeremiah in the womb (Jer. 1:5) might refer to infant salvation, but might refer to God's setting apart of Jeremiah in his purpose, just as Paul wrote that God set him apart while he was still in his mother's womb, long before his conversion (Gal. 1:13–16).

repentance in the gospel, but he does not command them to be born again. Rather, the Lord teaches that all people need to be born again (John 3:7) so that sinners will despair of saving themselves by their own works (Titus 3:5) and believers will give him the glory for their conversion (1 Pet. 1:3). Regeneration is not of human will (John 1:13), but of God, "of his own will" (James 1:18). Conversion is man's duty (Ezek. 18:31), but the grace to produce conversion is God's work (36:26).

It may be asked, however, what the Scriptures mean when they say that God brought us forth "with the word of truth" (James 1:18). Evidently, this word is the seed of regeneration, for James goes on to write of the "engrafted" (*emphytos*, literally "implanted") word (v. 21).[32] We are "born again, not of perishable seed but of imperishable, through the living and abiding word of God" (1 Pet. 1:23 ESV). The latter phrase uses a preposition translated as "through" or "by" (*dia* with genitive) that identifies the word as God's instrument in regeneration. Peter contrasts "corruptible seed" with "the word of God, which liveth and abideth forever," quoting Isaiah 40:6–8, which contrasts man as mortal "flesh" with the everlasting "word"—that is, "the gospel" (1 Pet. 1:24–25). Therefore, the seed of regeneration is the word of God.[33]

A controversy arose among Reformed theologians in the late nineteenth century as to whether regeneration is *immediate*, not in the sense of taking place instantaneously, but in the sense that it operates apart from human means, particularly the means of the preached word to persuade the mind to believe.[34] If regeneration is immediate, then one might object that this contradicts the Scriptures (James 1:18; 1 Pet. 1:23) and some statements in Reformed confessions,[35] as well as rendering the preaching of the gospel superfluous for salvation. If, on the other hand, God regenerates

32. Cf. "plant" (*phyteuō*) in Matt. 15:13; 21:33; Mark 12:1, etc.

33. Thomas R. Schreiner, *1, 2 Peter, Jude*, The New American Commentary 37 (Nashville: Broadman & Holman, 2003), 94–95. Contra Vos, *Reformed Dogmatics*, 4:44.

34. On the controversy following the union of 1892 and the formation of the *Gereformeerde Kerken in Nederland* (Reformed Churches in the Netherlands), see J. Mark Beach, introduction to Herman Bavinck, *Saved by Grace: The Holy Spirit's Work in Calling and Regeneration*, trans. Nelson D. Kloosterman, ed. J. Mark Beach (Grand Rapids, MI: Reformation Heritage Books, 2008), xii–xlvii.

35. "True faith" is "wrought in man by the hearing of the Word of God and the operation of the Holy Ghost." The Belgic Confession (Art. 24), in *The Three Forms of Unity*, 41. "As the almighty operation of God, whereby He prolongs and supports this our natural life, does not exclude, but requires the use of means, by which God of His infinite mercy and goodness hath chosen to exert His influence, so also the beforementioned supernatural operation of God, by which we are regenerated, in no wise excludes or subverts the use of the gospel, which the most wise God has ordained to be the seed of regeneration and food of the soul." The Canons of Dort (Heads 3/4, Art. 17), in *The Three Forms of Unity*, 147.

through the word, then one may object that this reduces regeneration to mere persuasion that depends on the response of the hearer.[36]

The way to resolve this problem is to recognize that regeneration may be considered as immediate *and* as taking place through the instrumentality of the Word *in different respects*, and hence, there is no logical contradiction. This resolution may take different forms.

Louis Berkhof and Murray proposed that regeneration is immediate in the initial generation of spiritual life (1 Pet. 1:3), but it is by means of the word in the bringing forth of that already created life into the activity of conversion (James 1:18; 1 Pet. 1:23).[37] This proposal makes good sense theologically. However, it runs into some difficulty in its interpretation of the relevant Scripture passages. Peter has just asserted that the new birth is an act of begetting (active *anagennaō*) that produces a living hope (1 Pet. 1:3), so it is quite strained to say that his subsequent reference to being born again (passive *anagennaō*) has to do not with regeneration per se but with the conversion it produces. James 1:18 emphasizes that God brought us forth "of his own will"; the text does not speak of man's faith and repentance.[38]

We propose that regeneration, being the renewal of the entire heart in all its faculties, operates on the mind by means of the Word to produce an informed faith (Rom. 10:17) but on the will immediately so that it freely chooses to believe, love, and obey the Word.[39] In regeneration, Christ simultaneously acts both as Prophet to cause people to know the Lord by his Word (Matt. 11:27) and as King to cause them to turn to him in faith and repentance (Acts 5:31; 11:21). Sinclair Ferguson writes,

> For the New Testament writers, however, there is no hint of a threat to divine sovereignty in the fact that the word is the instrumental cause of regeneration, while the Spirit is the efficient cause. . . . Since the Spirit's work in regeneration involves the transformation of the whole

36. Vos, *Reformed Dogmatics*, 4:41–42.

37. Berkhof, *Systematic Theology*, 465, 467, 469, 475; and Murray, *Collected Writings*, 2:197.

38. It might be objected that James 1:15 distinguishes between the act to "conceive" (*syllambanō*) and the act to "bring forth" (*apokueō*), the verb James uses later in v. 18 for regeneration. However, a closer reading of the text shows that the distinction is between "conceive" and "bring forth" or "birth" (*tiktō*). Both are metaphorical descriptions of the acts of lust in producing sin. Then sin is said to "bring forth" (*apokueō*) death.

39. This should not be viewed in a crude manner as if the mind and will were different components in the soul and that God touches one only indirectly but the other directly; the faculties are not parts of the soul but its capabilities for thinking, feeling, and choosing. God is infinitely present with the soul in all its acts.

> man, including his cognitive and affective powers, the accompanying of the internal illumination of the Spirit by the external revelation of the word (and vice versa) is altogether appropriate. Since faith involves knowledge, it ordinarily emerges in relationship to the teaching of the gospel found in Scripture. Regeneration and the faith to which it gives birth are seen as taking place not by revelationless divine sovereignty, but within the matrix of the preaching of the word and the witness of the people of God (cf. Rom. 10:1–15). Their instrumentality in regeneration does not impinge upon the sovereign activity of the Spirit. Word and Spirit belong together.[40]

When saying that God regenerates through the word, it is important to guard the truth that in regeneration God acts directly upon the will.[41] John Cameron (1579–1625) said that in conversion God directly persuades the mind, and the will necessarily follows—as if it were free to do so apart from regenerating grace. On the contrary, Andreas Rivetus (1572–1651) rightly taught that the triune God "enlightens the mind and moves or bends the will" so that faith arises from divine action "that immediately affects the will and influences it into its movement and action," whereas "the ordinary instrumental cause of faith is the word."[42] Owen said, "We grant that in the work of regeneration, the Holy Spirit, towards those that are adult, doth make use of the word, both the law and the gospel, and the ministry of the church in the dispensation of it, as the ordinary means thereof." However, there is an "immediate operation of the Spirit, by his power and grace, or his powerful grace, upon the minds or souls of men in their regeneration. . . . And hence the work of grace in conversion is constantly expressed by words denoting a real internal efficiency; such as creating, quickening, forming, giving a new heart."[43]

Thus, the Synod of Utrecht (1905) concluded regarding "immediate regeneration" that "this term may be used in a good sense," for "regeneration is not effected through the Word or the Sacraments as such, but through the almighty and regenerating operation of the Holy Spirit."

40. Ferguson, *The Holy Spirit*, 125–26.

41. For the same point framed in terms of effectual calling, see Turretin, *Institutes*, 15.4.23 (2:526–27).

42. Polyander, Walaeus, Thysius, and Rivetus, *Synopsis Purioris Theologiae*, 31.9–10 (2:237, 239; on Cameron, see editorial comment at 2:237n15).

43. Owen, *Pneumatologia*, in *Works*, 3:316–17.

However, "this regenerating operation of the Holy Spirit" must not be "divorced from the preaching of the Word," for though God can save children who die in infancy, "in the case of adults the regenerating operation of the Holy Spirit accompanies the preaching of the gospel."[44]

Regeneration in Relation to Effectual Calling

What is the relationship between regeneration and effectual calling? Reformed and evangelical theologians have proposed various ways to relate regeneration to effectual calling. One approach is to see them as distinct and separable, especially in young children who are said to be regenerated but not called and converted.

Petrus van Mastricht said that regeneration creates the power to trust, repent, and love, but not the dispositions or acts of faith, repentance, and love, which may arise much later. He said, "One truly regenerate may, both as to habit and act, be for a time an unbeliever, destitute of repentance and walking in sin."[45] Abraham Kuyper said, "The new life is present, but dormant . . . like seed-grain in the ground in winter; like a spark glowing under the ashes, but not kindling the wood; like a subterranean stream coming at last to the surface."[46] This secret work of regeneration in some cases "precedes the inward call" and "the preaching of the Word." Regeneration, he says, runs in three stages: first, "when the Lord plants new life in the dead heart"; second, "when a new-born man comes to conversion"; and third, "when conversion merges into sanctification." The first and second stages are "frequently separated . . . by an interval of many days."[47] The second grace of effectual calling, Kuyper said, is given to those already regenerate: "This calling of the Holy Spirit proceeds in and through the preaching of the Word, and calls the *regenerated* sinner to arise from death."[48]

However, we have no biblical warrant to speak of unconverted people as regenerate. The new birth produces righteousness, repentance, love, and faith. Stephen Charnock said, "How so active a principle as a spiritual life should lie dead, and asleep for so long, even many years which intervene

44. Conclusions of Utrecht, in J. L. Schaver, *The Polity of the Churches*, 3rd ed., 2 vols. (Chicago: Church Polity Press, 1947), 2:36 (also available in the appendix to Bavinck, *Saved by Grace*, 170–71).
45. Van Mastricht, *Theoretico-Practica Theologia*, 6.3.17 (2:663); *A Treatise on Regeneration*, 28.
46. Kuyper, *The Work of the Holy Spirit*, 295.
47. Kuyper, *The Work of the Holy Spirit*, 318, 320.
48. Kuyper, *The Work of the Holy Spirit*, 342, emphasis original.

between baptism and conversion, is not easily conceivable."[49] Murray said, "The regenerated infant is not under the dominion of sin, is not a child of wrath, but a child of God and a member of his kingdom. . . . We must not, therefore, conceive of the regenerate infant as regenerated in infancy and then converted when he reaches years of understanding and discretion. No, not at all! When the infant is regenerated, that infant is converted . . . the heart and mind—germinal and rudimentary though they be—are turned towards God."[50] Hence, as G. H. Kersten said, "Calling and regeneration occur at the same time."[51]

A second approach to the relation of regeneration to effectual calling, proposed by some recent evangelical theologians who teach a modified version of Reformed theology, presents a causal order first of effectual calling; second, faith; and third, regeneration. They acknowledge that man's spiritual death in sin makes him unable to trust in Christ until God effectually calls him, but argue that regeneration must follow faith because the Scriptures say we believe in order to be saved and receive the Holy Spirit and eternal life (John 3:15; Acts 2:38; 16:31).[52]

However, this approach suffers from significant exegetical and theological problems. Exegetically, one cannot restrict salvation or eternal life to regeneration, for the former terms have a broad scope that are used to refer to various aspects of the application of redemption from beginning to end.[53] Otherwise, how shall we interpret texts such as "Work out your own salvation" (Phil. 2:12) or "He shall receive an hundredfold now in this time . . . and in the world to come eternal life" (Mark 10:30)? The reception of the Holy Spirit by faith pertains to his indwelling and empowerment, not to regeneration.

Theologically, this approach entails confusion, even contradiction, in the doctrines of effectual calling and regeneration. Effectual calling is presented as incomplete, a grace that "stops short of effecting the complete transformation of life commonly represented by the term regeneration."[54] Yet it is also presented as the powerful act "by which the Spirit illumines darkened minds, softens stubborn wills, and inclines

49. Charnock, *The Nature of Regeneration*, in *Works*, 3:94.
50. Murray, *Collected Writings*, 2:200.
51. Kersten, *Reformed Dogmatics*, 2:375.
52. Erickson, *Christian Theology*, 863–64; and Demarest, *The Cross and Salvation*, 221, 227, 289, 291. See the discussion in Barrett, *Saved by Grace*, 285–92.
53. See our response to the objection that "God promises the Spirit of life to those who believe" in chap. 16.
54. Demarest, *The Cross and Salvation*, 265.

contrary affections toward the living God."[55] Matthew Barrett says, "What is left to take place in regeneration?"[56] Therefore, this approach is inconsistent and unstable, tending to collapse into Arminian prevenient grace.

The same theologians who propose this second view say that regeneration is God's giving life to the dead, putting a new heart into a person, and causing "a whole reversal of the person's natural tendencies."[57] Regeneration changes blind and ignorant sinners into those able to know God and his ways, and releases the will from bondage to sin.[58] If this is the case, then how can anyone repent and believe prior to regeneration, when they are still blind and enslaved? In order to sustain this proposal, one must weaken regeneration into a giving of eternal life to those already converted, whereas in the Scriptures regeneration is the living root of all repentance, faith, love, and obedience (1 John 2:29; 3:9; 4:7; 5:1).

A third approach to regeneration and effectual calling, favored by some Reformed theologians, is to identify regeneration as the divine act that makes effectual calling effectual. Murray said, "The call that comes through the Word—the effectual call—is logically prior even to regeneration, and the grace wrought by regeneration is but the grace inwardly wrought by the Spirit in order that the appropriate response to the efficacious call may be elicited in us. Regenerative grace is carried to us in the bosom of the effectual call."[59] Robert Reymond wrote that regeneration is "the effecting force in God's effectual summons," for "the Father's effectual summons . . . is effectual through the regenerating work of the Spirit of God."[60]

However, the effectual call is depicted in the Bible as inherently effectual, for it is the sovereign execution of God's eternal decretive will (Rom. 8:30). The conversion of some individuals when others in the same group hear the gospel but remain unconverted can be explained by saying that the former were "called" (1 Cor. 1:23–24). Therefore, the saving call is not the general call plus effectual regeneration; the saving call is effectual in itself.

---

55. Demarest, *The Cross and Salvation*, 221.
56. Barrett, *Saved by Grace*, 296.
57. Erickson, *Christian Theology*, 872–73.
58. Demarest, *The Cross and Salvation*, 298.
59. Murray, *Collected Writings*, 2:197.
60. Reymond, *A New Systematic Theology of the Christian Faith*, 716–17.

We propose that effectual calling and regeneration are distinct perspectives on the same act of God. William Ames, Johannes Wollebius, Johann Heidegger, and Wilhelmus Schortinghuis (1700–1750) rightly noted that regeneration or rebirth is another name for effectual calling in the Bible.[61] The Holy Scriptures use the terms *calling* and *rebirth* to describe God's initial work of individual salvation in Christ as a gracious, effectual act of new creation in the heart that produces faith and holiness. The overlap between the two doctrines makes it difficult, if not impossible, to consider effectual calling and regeneration as different divine acts. David Dickson (c. 1583–1662) said that "regeneration" is "one in effect with effectual calling."[62] Herman Bavinck said, "Regeneration in the active sense, the regenerative activity of God [as distinct from the human acts of conversion], is only another name for the call: the efficacious call of God."[63]

However, rather than subsuming regeneration under effectual calling, we also see distinct emphases that would be lost if we neglect either doctrine, for each offers its own perspective on this mysterious work that informs our understanding. Both are analogical descriptions of an incomprehensible act of God. The commonalities and distinctions of effectual calling and regeneration are summarized in Table 18.1 below.

The last distinction in the table helps us to understand how the initial application of salvation relates to union with Christ. On the one hand, effectual calling describes this from the perspective of God powerfully calling people to Christ to unite them with him by faith (1 Cor. 1:9, 24, 26, 30; cf. John 6:37, 44). On the other hand, Christ must regenerate them to new life by his resurrection so that they become new creations and live by faith in him (Eph. 2:5, 8, 10). John Flavel described this as the double bond of union with Christ: "The Spirit, on Christ's part, quickening us with spiritual life, whereby Christ first takes hold of us; and faith on our part, when thus quickened, whereby we take hold of Christ."[64]

61. Ames, *The Marrow of Theology*, 1.26.19 (159); Wollebius, *Compendium* 1.28.i (158); Heidegger, *The Concise Marrow of Christian Theology*, 21.6 (147); and Schortinghuis, *Essential Truths in the Heart of a Christian*, 22.8 (86). A comparison of Schortinghuis's discussions of internal calling and regeneration shows that they have the same characteristics and effects (chaps. 22–23 [85–88]).

62. David Dickson, *Therapeutica Sacra, Shewing Briefly the Method of Healing the Diseases of the Conscience, concerning Regeneration* (Edinburgh: Evan Tyler, 1664), 10.

63. Bavinck, *Reformed Dogmatics*, 4:77.

64. Flavel, *The Method of Grace*, in *Works*, 2:85.

Doctrine	Effectual Calling	Regeneration
Core Definition	Summons by Word	Rebirth by Power
Common Elements	God's Grace	God's Grace
	An Effectual, Saving Act	An Effectual, Saving Act
	In Christ	In Christ
	New Creation	New Creation
	Centered on the Heart	Centered on the Heart
	Produces Faith and Holiness	Produces Faith and Holiness
Distinct Emphases	Linked to Order of Salvation from Election to Glorification	Focused on Crucial Act of Giving Life That Initiates Salvation
	Viewed as Divine Speech Acting from Outside In	Viewed as Divine Renewal Acting from Inside Out
	Often Framed Corporately: "The Called [Plural]"	Often Framed Individually: "He Who Has Been Born Again"
	Beginning of Union with Christ	Energized by Christ's Resurrection

Table 18.1. Effectual Calling and Regeneration Compared

Practical Applications of the Doctrine of Regeneration

As the initiation of the application of salvation, regeneration is a very practical doctrine, with many implications for both the evangelism of the lost and the edification of the saints.[65]

It might be thought that the doctrine of regeneration would discourage *evangelism*, but the opposite is true, for there is a very real sense in which we are born again through the word of God, the gospel. Therefore, if we desire for our family members, friends, and neighbors—yes, even our enemies—to be born again, then we must labor and pray for them to hear the gospel, that the seed of regeneration might be sown in them. Since we may plant the seeds of truth but only God can cause them to grow, we may do evangelism released from the need to make something happen by

65. Extensive applications or "uses" of this doctrine are found in the conclusions of each of Charnock's treatises on regeneration in *Works*, 3:57–81, 128–65, 289–306, 319–35.

our own wisdom or skill, resting in the goodness and love of God. If he can raise the dead, which he has already done in Jesus Christ, then he has the power to save the lost. Flavel said, "This speaks encouragement to ministers and parents, to wait in hopes of success at last, even upon those that yet give them little hope of conversion at the present."[66]

Even as the doctrine of the new birth encourages us to speak the gospel, it promotes *humble prayer*. The wind blows where it wishes, and we cannot control it. Why, then, do men think that they can control God the Holy Spirit and force his hand to produce conversions and revival as they choose? Far be it from us to think we can schedule the Spirit's work and put it on a calendar and manipulate it in our meetings. Instead, let us devote ourselves to earnest prayer for the Holy Spirit to blow upon the hearts of dead sinners and raise them up into life.

In evangelism, the doctrine of the new birth is a powerful *weapon to overthrow self-righteousness*. Man is helpless to see or enter the kingdom of God. The Lord Jesus says to sinners that despite all their learning and religion, "Ye must be born again" (John 3:7). It may seem ludicrous to tell the unconverted of a work that they are unable to do for themselves, but it might be exactly what God uses to awaken them to their desperate condition. Some proud sinners may rejoice to hear John 3:16 because they think it an easy matter for them to believe in Christ and be saved. They then manufacture a kind of belief in Jesus that he rejects (2:23–25). They must also hear the message of John 3:3–8 to challenge their self-confidence and make them hunger after true saving grace.

John Calvin compared the doctrine of regeneration to the sharp edge of a plough:

> For as it is useless to sow seed in a field which has not been prepared by the labours of the husbandman [farmer], so it is to no purpose to scatter the doctrine of the Gospel, if the mind has not been previously subdued and duly prepared for docility and obedience. Christ saw that the mind of Nicodemus was filled with many thorns, choked by many noxious herbs, so that there was scarcely any room for spiritual doctrine. This exhortation, therefore, resembled a ploughing to purify him, that nothing might prevent him from profiting by the doctrine.[67]

66. Flavel, *The Method of Grace*, in *Works*, 2:99.
67. Calvin, *Commentaries*, on John 3:3.

The doctrine of regeneration also provides a *counter to intellectual pride*. Who had more reason to be proud about his knowledge than he who was "the teacher of Israel" (John 3:10 ESV)? Yet Christ warned Nicodemus that unless he was born again he could not see the kingdom (v. 3). Neither may we scoff at the Pharisees while repeating their arrogance with our evangelical doctrines. Charnock said, "An evangelical head will be but drier fuel for eternal burning, without an evangelical impression upon the heart and the badge of a new nature."[68] Bible knowledge cannot save us, but will only puff us up apart from the new birth that creates love in our hearts.

However, for sinners awakened to the stubborn wickedness and unbelief of their hearts, the doctrine of the new birth offers a *reason to hope in Christ*. Yes, their flesh can produce only more flesh, but the Spirit can give birth to spiritual life. No matter how corrupt they are and how long they have persisted in their sins, God can give them a radical new beginning. Humbled under a sense of their sins, they can pray, "Thou hast chastised me, and I was chastised, as a bullock unaccustomed to the yoke: turn thou me, and I shall be turned" (Jer. 31:18). Like blind Bartimaeus, they cannot heal themselves of their spiritual darkness, but they can cry, "Son of David, have mercy on me," to the One who is able to heal them (Mark 10:47). Just as unregenerate Nicodemus spoke to Jesus and heard his teaching, so the unregenerate should pray to the Lord for mercy and listen to his Word, that they may be born again.[69]

Those who trust in Christ and repent of their sins find in this doctrine a *potent, God-glorifying comfort*. As they look back on their conversion, they see that "the kindness and love of God our Saviour toward man appeared, not by works of righteousness which we have done, but according to his mercy he saved us, by the washing of regeneration, and renewing of the Holy Ghost" (Titus 3:4–5). They ask, "Why am I saved?" Regeneration answers, "Not because of anything good in you or done by you, but only because God loved you and the Holy Spirit made you new." And they respond, "Then all glory be to God alone!"

If God has given you this gift, then he will give you all good forever. Every blessing written in the Bible is your birthright if you are born of God. In this world, all the providences of God are profitable to you. Even

68. Charnock, *The Necessity of Regeneration*, in *Works*, 3:59.

69. Van Mastricht, *Theoretico-Practica Theologia*, 6.3.38 (2:673); *A Treatise on Regeneration*, 61.

if earthly possessions are few, they are perfumed with love. And if God so loved you when you were dead and loathsome in your sins, how much more will he show his love to you in the ages to come now that you are alive in Christ? Then he will give you perfect holiness and complete happiness in the presence of God and Christ,[70] for in giving regeneration to you, God has given you to Christ, and in Christ you have everything.

Understanding the new birth cultivates an attitude of *continual dependence on the Spirit*. Believers may learn from regeneration that their spiritual life does not come from themselves but from the Lord. Though they are active in the life that has been given to them, they must never think that disciplines and ordinances give life. Richard Sibbes said,

> I beseech you, in your daily practice, all learn this, that you trust not too much to any outward performance or task, to make idols of outward things. People when they would change their dispositions and be better, they take a great deal of pains in hearing, and reading, and praying. All these are things necessary, but they are dead things without the Spirit of Christ. Therefore in the use of all those outward things, whatsoever they be, look up to Christ . . . that sends the Spirit into our hearts. . . . He laboureth in vain that relieth not wholly upon the Spirit of God, that trusts not to a higher strength than his own.[71]

The doctrine of regeneration spurs God's children to do *good works*. This is the emphasis of Paul's teaching on this matter to Titus. Paul begins his discourse on regeneration by saying, "Put them in mind to be subject to principalities and powers, to obey magistrates, to be ready to every good work," and ends, "This is a faithful saying, and these things I will that thou affirm constantly, that they which have believed in God might be careful to maintain good works. These things are good and profitable unto men" (Titus 3:1, 8). But if God regenerated us apart from "works of righteousness which we have done" (v. 5), why would this doctrine motivate us to do works now? First, regeneration displays the remarkable love of God to change his enemies into his friends. If God has so loved us as to give us this new beginning and make us into new creations, shall we not love him in return and serve him well? Second, regeneration shows us that authentic salvation includes not only justification but also transformation.

70. Adapted from Swinnock, *The Door of Salvation Opened by the Key of Regeneration*, in *Works*, 5:144–45, 160–62.

71. Sibbes, *The Excellency of the Gospel above the Law*, in *Works*, 4:295.

Shall we claim to be justified when our lives are barren of the fruits of regeneration? Third, this doctrine shows us that the way to glorify the God of regeneration is to "adorn the doctrine of God our Saviour" with an honorable life of doing good (2:10). We tell the world that we have been born again and that they must be born again. Let us, therefore, show the beauty of the new birth in a life of holy love.

In particular, the doctrine of regeneration is a solid basis to exhort believers to conduct themselves with *patience and gentleness toward the wicked*, for we were not saved by our religion or righteousness, but only because God did a supernatural work of grace to lift us out of the pit of our corruption. Paul exhorts believers "to speak evil of no man, to be no brawlers, but gentle, shewing all meekness unto all men. For we ourselves also were sometimes foolish, disobedient, deceived, serving divers lusts and pleasures, living in malice and envy, hateful, and hating one another. But . . . according to his mercy he saved us, by the washing of regeneration, and renewing of the Holy Ghost" (Titus 3:2–5). The strongest advocates of the doctrine of sovereign regeneration should be the meekest and most merciful of men.

Lastly, what God has revealed to us about regeneration shows us *his unspeakable glory*. Van Mastricht observed that the new birth requires in God "infinite power, a superabundant greatness of power, as great, and if possible, even greater, than was exercised in creation," because regeneration must both overcome the power of sin and create new life; it requires in God "infinite or exhaustless goodness and mercy," for he gives eternal life to those who by their sins have earned eternal death; and it requires his "infinite, or the more absolute sovereignty," for "passing by whom he will, he bestows the spiritual life on whom he pleases."[72] Therefore, we should contemplate regeneration with awe and wonder, and worship its author, for he is God.

Sing to the Lord

Rejoicing in Our Spiritual Birth

Zion, founded on the mountains,
God, thy Maker, loves thee well;
He has chosen thee, most precious,

72. Van Mastricht, *Theoretico-Practica Theologia*, 6.3.33 (2:669–70); *A Treatise on Regeneration*, 51.

He delights in thee to dwell;
God's own city, God's own city,
Who can all thy glory tell?

Heathen lands and hostile peoples
Soon shall come the Lord to know;
Nations born again in Zion
Shall the Lord's salvation show,
God Almighty, God Almighty
Shall on Zion strength bestow.

When the Lord shall count the nations,
Sons and daughters He shall see,
Born to endless life in Zion,
And their joyful song shall be,
"Blessed Zion, blessed Zion,
All our fountains are in thee."

Psalm 87
Tune: Regent Square
The Psalter, No. 238
Or Tune: Caersalem
Trinity Hymnal—Baptist Edition, No. 369

Questions for Meditation or Discussion

1. How does the Bible tell us that each person in the Trinity is involved in regeneration?
2. What arguments may be given that regeneration is an effectual work of God alone?
3. How do some theologians argue that God regenerates sinners through baptism?
4. How can we refute the doctrine of baptismal regeneration?
5. What evidence is there in God's Word that God can regenerate infants?
6. What cautions do we need to make about applying the doctrine of infant regeneration?
7. Someone says, "Obviously regeneration cannot be an immediate work of God on the heart, for the Bible says God regenerates through the word (James 1:18; 1 Pet. 1:23)." What do you say?

8. What practical applications does the doctrine of regeneration have for the evangelization of unbelievers?
9. How can the doctrine of regeneration strengthen the spiritual lives of believers?
10. How has studying regeneration affected your spiritual life? What are a couple of practical actions that you could take to deepen the impact of this doctrine on your life?

Questions for Deeper Reflection

11. A friend writes to you and says, "I heard that you think that the new birth changes sinners into believers. But that just doesn't make sense, because we are saved through faith, and we believe as a choice of our free will." Write a response that opens up the Bible's teachings about regeneration and answers this friend's objections.
12. What difference will it make in our churches, families, and individual lives if we believe that God ordinarily regenerates the elect children of believers while they are infants? What if we believe that God ordinarily regenerates them by their hearing and understanding of the gospel?
13. How have theologians related regeneration to effectual calling? What do you think is the best approach, and why?

19

Conversion, Part 1

Repentance unto Life

In this chapter, we introduce the human response to God's saving grace. So far in our consideration of the order of salvation, we have focused on the Holy Spirit's acts toward us by the Word. In so doing, we have struck a strongly monergistic note: salvation is by grace alone, with no contribution from the wisdom, merit, or power of fallen men. All things in salvation are from God through Christ by his Spirit. However, God's saving call upon us produces spiritual life within us that results in gracious acts from us. Our response consists of "the manifestations and the results" of God's saving work in us, as Martyn Lloyd-Jones said.[1]

Introduction to Conversion

John Gill said, "Effectual vocation is the call of men out of darkness to light; and conversion answers to that call, and is the actual turning of men from the one to the other."[2] Anthony Hoekema wrote, "Conversion may be defined as the conscious act of a regenerate person in which he or she turns to God in repentance and faith."[3]

1. Lloyd-Jones, *Great Doctrines of the Bible*, 2:117.
2. Gill, *Body of Divinity*, 545.
3. Hoekema, *Saved by Grace*, 113.

Theological Terminology of Conversion

The words *convert* and *conversion* in English (from the Latin *conversio*, "turning around") refer to the turning of sinners to God.[4] Theologians make distinctions to clarify what kind or aspect of turning is in view.[5] The first distinction pertains to whether *conversion* refers to God's initial turning of sinners' hearts or their consequent and willing turning to him (cf. Jer. 31:18–19; Lam. 5:21). "Habitual or passive conversion" is the Holy Spirit's work of giving a new heart, in which man is the passive recipient of grace. "Actual or active conversion" is the activity of the new heart, the acts of faith and repentance, in which man actively works by God's grace. The former is more properly called regeneration; the latter, conversion.[6]

Theologians further distinguish actual conversion into first, second, and continual conversion. The "first actual conversion" is the person's first activity of turning from sin to God. Theologians also speak of a "second actual conversion," in which a backslidden believer renews his repentance (cf. Psalm 51; Luke 22:32). "Continual actual conversion," or sanctification, is the progressive work of increasingly putting sin to death and living to God by union with Christ.

In our discussion of conversion, we focus on the first actual conversion, having treated regeneration already and reserving progressive sanctification for later chapters, though much of what we have to say here also pertains to continual conversion and regular repentance.

Variety in Conversion

Herman Bavinck wrote, "Although true conversion is always the same in essence, yet, in the manner and the time when it occurs, there are all sorts of differences."[7] Manasseh turned to the Lord as an adult (2 Chron. 33:11–13), but Obadiah feared the Lord from his youth (1 Kings 18:12). Christ saved Paul in a crisis of confrontation (Acts 9), but Timothy's faith may have arisen more quietly (16:1; 2 Tim. 1:5; 3:15).

The converted come from all kinds of spiritual backgrounds. Paul was a devout Pharisee (Acts 26:5). Mary Magdalene was inhabited by seven

4. In the KJV, "convert" is used for turning or repentance in Ps. 51:13; Isa. 1:27; 6:10; Matt. 13:15; 18:3; Mark 4:12; Luke 22:32; John 12:40; Acts 3:19; 28:27; James 5:19–20. See "conversion" in Acts 15:3.

5. Bavinck, *Reformed Dogmatics*, 4:150–52.

6. Turretin, *Institutes*, 15.4.13 (2:522); and Willard, *A Compleat Body of Divinity*, 794–95.

7. Bavinck, *Reformed Dogmatics*, 4:153.

demons until the Lord cast them out and she followed Christ (Luke 8:2). Zacchaeus was a rich tax collector until, stirred by the Spirit, he sought and found Christ (19:1–10).

God's method of drawing a sinner to Christ varies. Some people pass through piercing convictions of sin before coming to faith in Christ (Acts 2:37). The experience of others may be a quieter illumination combined with a less profound conviction of sin, as Lydia's experience seems to have been (16:14–15). Others may go through a battle of will until they are brought humbly to submit to God's holy ways, such as Naaman (2 Kings 5). Wilhelmus à Brakel observed that although "the soul in a moment passes from death unto life," people often are "converted in a very gradual fashion, with much vacillation between sorrow and joy."[8] In such people's cases, seasons of conviction and fear may come and go over a span of years.[9]

What is most important in conversion is not the manner or sequence of experiences, but the presence of genuine repentance and faith. When calling sinners to Christ, we must not demand any one pattern of conversion. Instead, we should teach the fundamental principles about repentance and faith, and call sinners to Christ.

The Two Sides of Conversion: Repentance and Faith

The call of the gospel invites and commands sinners to a twofold response: repentance and faith.[10] Faith and repentance stand in essential unity, as two sides of the one saving response to the Word of God. In the Bible, conversion is sometimes described simply as repentance[11] or as faith in Christ.[12] In other Scripture passages, faith and repentance appear together.[13]

Repentance from sin and faith in God's mercy are joined in an organic relationship. Hosea taught Israel to "turn to the Lord" with a prayer of dependence on him as the only Savior and God of mercy (Hos. 14:2–3). Isaiah wrote, "Let the wicked forsake his way, and the unrighteous man his thoughts: and let him return unto the Lord, and he will have mercy upon him; and to our God, for he will abundantly pardon" (Isa. 55:7).

8. Brakel, *The Christian's Reasonable Service*, 2:238.
9. See chap. 13 on preparatory grace and conviction of sin.
10. See chap. 12 on the general call of the gospel.
11. Matt. 4:17; Luke 5:32; 24:47; Acts 2:38; 26:20.
12. John 1:12; 3:15–18; Acts 10:43; 16:31.
13. 2 Kings 17:13–14; Ps. 78:32–34; Isa. 10:20–22; 30:15; Jonah 3:5, 8; Mark 1:15; Acts 11:21; 17:30–34; 20:21; Heb. 6:1.

Joel called out to the people, "Turn unto the LORD your God: for he is gracious and merciful" (Joel 2:13). John Owen said that the essence of true repentance, "without which it is not acceptable," lies "in its performance according to the gospel rule"—that is, "with faith" in God's mercy.[14] Therefore, saving faith and true repentance are so intertwined as to never exist apart from each other, but, as John Calvin said, "are held together by a permanent bond."[15]

Faith and repentance, however, are not identical. The immediate object of faith is Jesus Christ, the Mediator between God and man (John 3:16; Gal. 2:16), whereas the immediate object of repentance is God (1 Thess. 1:9). Thus, Paul says that he preached "repentance toward God, and faith toward our Lord Jesus Christ" (Acts 20:21). By faith, we receive Christ and justification, adoption, and life in him (John 1:12; Rom. 5:1). By repentance, we turn from disobedience against God and begin to obey his commandments (Matt. 21:28–31).[16]

Though faith and repentance appear simultaneously in all the saved, is there a causal priority or logical order between them? Calvin and several Reformed orthodox divines said that, though guilty fears and some moral reformation may precede faith, saving repentance logically follows faith and depends on it as its cause.[17] John Colquhoun (1748–1827) observed the order in Acts 11:21, that they "believed, and turned unto the Lord."[18] An important concern of these divines was that we must not bind sinners to perform good works or feel deep penitence before they may come to Christ.[19]

However, one can argue just as cogently that faith depends on repentance. Samuel Willard acknowledged, "Without repentance, there can be no faith. . . . For no man can choose his sins and Christ too."[20] A person who still hates God will not trust in Christ to reconcile him to God. Those who love the darkness and hate the light because their deeds are evil will

14. Owen, "Greater Catechism," 20.4, in *Two Short Catechisms*, in *Works*, 1:488.
15. Calvin, *Institutes*, 3.3.5.
16. Willard, *A Compleat Body of Divinity*, 795–96.
17. Calvin, *Institutes*, 3.3.1, 4; Ames, *The Marrow of Theology*, 1.26.31 (160); Polyander, Walaeus, Thysius, and Rivetus, *Synopsis Purioris Theologiae*, 32.40–42 (2:297); Willard, *A Compleat Body of Divinity*, 795; and Fisher et al., *The Assembly's Shorter Catechism Explained*, 87.13–20 (369–71).
18. John Colquhoun, *Repentance* (London: Banner of Truth, 1965), 105–7; cf. Fisher et al., *The Assembly's Shorter Catechism Explained*, 87.15 (370).
19. Calvin, *Institutes*, 3.3.2; Colquhoun, *Repentance*, 111–15; and Fisher et al., *The Assembly's Shorter Catechism Explained*, 87.20 (370–71).
20. Willard, *A Compleat Body of Divinity*, 783.

not come to the light (John 3:19–20). Will a person look to Christ to save him from his sins if he still loves those sins? As to their order, in some Scripture passages, repentance appears first and faith second.[21]

Some recent Reformed theologians have argued that neither faith nor repentance is prior, but that they are interdependent graces, distinct but inseparable, the twin effects immediately produced by regeneration.[22] John Murray said, "There is no priority. The faith that is unto salvation is a penitent faith and the repentance that is unto life is a believing repentance."[23] Such an approach reflects the fluidity with which the Holy Scriptures describe conversion, the interdependence of repentance and faith, and the gospel call that presses sinners to both believe and repent without delay.

Repentance unto Life

Faith will be the topic of the next two chapters. In the remainder of this chapter, we will explore the biblical doctrine of repentance, with a special focus on a sinner's initial repentance unto life.

Biblical Terminology of Repentance

The Scriptures use several words to describe the grace of repentance. The most common term for repentance in the Old Testament is translated as "turn" (Hebrew *shub*), occurring in this sense over a hundred and forty times.[24] The idea is "doing a turnabout," setting a new direction away from evil and toward the Lord.[25] Its negative side with respect to sin can be expressed with the word translated as "forsake" (*'azab*).[26] We read of the necessity of "departing" (*sur*) from evil, an idea closely connected to the fear of the Lord.[27] People must "put away" (*hiphil* of *sur*) false gods and idols.[28] Another term used a few times of man's repentance can be

21. Mark 1:15; Acts 20:21; Heb. 6:1.

22. Hoekema, *Saved by Grace*, 123; and Reymond, *A New Systematic Theology of the Christian Faith*, 706.

23. Murray, *Redemption Accomplished and Applied*, 113.

24. Demarest, *The Cross and Salvation*, 251. For examples, see Deut. 4:30; 30:2; 1 Kings 8:33, 35, 48; 13:33; 2 Chron. 15:4; 30:9; Neh. 9:26, 35; Job 22:23; Pss. 51:13; 116:7; Prov. 1:23; Isa. 1:27; 6:10; 10:21–22; 19:22; 31:6; 55:7; 59:20; Jer. 3:7, 12, 14, 22; 4:1; 5:3; 15:7; 18:8; Ezek. 3:19; 13:22; 14:6; 18:32; Hos. 3:15; 5:4; 6:1; 7:10, 16; 11:5; 14:1–2; Amos 4:9–11; Joel 2:12; Mal. 3:7.

25. *NIDOTTE*, 4:57.

26. Ps. 37:8; Prov. 28:13; Isa. 55:7.

27. 2 Kings 3:3; 13:2, 11; 14:24; 15:9, 18, 24, 28; Job 1:1, 8; 2:3; 28:28; Pss. 34:14; 37:27; Prov. 3:7; 4:27; 13:19; 14:16; 16:6, 17; cf. 1 Pet. 3:11.

28. Gen. 35:2; Josh. 24:14, 23; Judg. 10:16; 1 Sam. 7:3–4; 1 Kings 15:12; 2 Kings 23:19; 2 Chron. 14:3, 5; 17:6; 30:14; 33:15; 34:33; Jer. 4:1.

rendered as "grieve, be sorry, change one's mind" (*nakham*).[29] Of course, repentance can be expressed with other words as well, such as "cease to do evil; learn to do well" (Isa. 1:16–17).

The New Testament refers to repentance with a word meaning "turn" (Greek *epistrephō*), used eighteen times of turning from sin to the Lord.[30] Almost sixty references to repentance in the New Testament employ a term meaning to "change one's mind" (*metanoeō*)[31] or its cognate noun (*metanoia*).[32] Other terms for repentance include to feel remorse (*metamelomai*, Matt. 21:29, 32), to sorrow (*lupeō*, *lupē*, 2 Cor. 7:9–11), and to mourn (*pentheō*).[33]

The Definition of Saving Repentance

A sinner may feel remorse over his sins that does not turn him to God but leads him to despair and death (Matt. 27:3; 2 Cor. 7:10) or to a return to the filth of sin (2 Pet. 2:20–22). Sinners may tremble at God's Word (Acts 24:25), humble themselves (1 Kings 21:27), and respond positively to God's preachers for a time (Mark 4:16–17; 6:20) but still not be saved. Willard said, "There is a legal repentance, which is so called, because it proceeds from the terrors of the law, and is produced by convictions and terrors of conscience. . . . It produceth a worldly sorrow, and often it drives men to an outward reformation of their lives." However, there is also "evangelical repentance," called "repentance unto life" (Acts 11:18).[34]

How should we define saving repentance? James Ussher (1581–1656), echoing William Perkins, said that genuine repentance is "an inward and true sorrow for sin, especially that we have offended so gracious a God, and so loving a Father; together with a settled purpose of heart, and a careful endeavor to leave all our sins, and to live a Christian life, according to all God's commandments."[35] The Westminster Shorter Catechism (Q. 87)

29. Job 42:6; Jer. 8:6; 31:19.

30. Matt. 13:15; Mark 4:12; Luke 1:16–17; 17:4; 22:32; Acts 3:19; 9:35; 11:21; 14:15; 15:19; 26:18, 20; 28:27; 2 Cor. 3:16; 1 Thess. 1:9; James 5:19–20; 1 Pet. 2:25.

31. Matt. 3:2; 4:17; 11:20–21; 12:41; Mark 1:15; 6:12; Luke 10:13; 11:32; 13:3, 5; 15:7, 10; 16:30; 17:3–4; Acts 2:38; 3:19; 8:22; 17:30; 26:20; 2 Cor. 12:21; Rev. 2:5, 16, 21–22; 3:3, 19; 9:20–21; 16:9.

32. Matt. 3:8, 11; 9:13; Mark 1:4; 2:17; Luke 3:3, 8; 5:32; 15:7; 24:47; Acts 5:31; 11:18; 13:24; 19:4; 20:21; 26:20; Rom. 2:4; 2 Cor. 7:9–10; 2 Tim. 2:25; Heb. 6:1, 6; 12:17; 2 Pet. 3:9.

33. Matt. 5:4; 1 Cor. 5:2; James 4:9.

34. Willard, *A Compleat Body of Divinity*, 794. On the law and preparatory, common grace, see chap. 13.

35. Ussher, *A Body of Divinity*, 31st head (299). See Perkins, *The Foundation of Christian Religion*, in *Works*, 5:504.

says, "Repentance unto life is a saving grace, whereby a sinner, out of a true sense of his sin, and apprehension of the mercy of God in Christ, doth, with grief and hatred of his sin, turn from it unto God, with full purpose of, and endeavour after, new obedience."[36]

True repentance is a saving grace, given freely by God to sinners by his effectual calling and regeneration.[37] Repentance is both turning from sin (1 Kings 8:35; Isa. 59:20) and turning to God (2 Chron. 15:4; 36:13), turning "from darkness to light, and from the power of Satan unto God" (Acts 26:18).[38] After describing the depravity of the nations (Eph. 4:17–19), Paul writes, "But ye have not so learned Christ; if so be that ye have heard him, and have been taught by him, as the truth is in Jesus: that ye put off concerning the former conversation the old man, which is corrupt according to the deceitful lusts; and be renewed in the spirit of your mind; and that ye put on the new man, which after God is created in righteousness and true holiness" (vv. 20–24). Calvin said, "Repentance can thus well be defined: it is the true turning of our life to God, a turning that arises from a pure and earnest fear of him; and it consists of the mortification of our flesh and of the old man, and in the vivification of the Spirit."[39]

Repentance constitutes the willing movement of the soul toward God's gracious purpose to restore his image in fallen man. Putting off the old man and putting on the new in Christ are two sides of the process of being "renewed in knowledge after the image of him that created him" (Col. 3:9–10; cf. 2 Cor. 3:18). God created man in his image (Gen. 1:26–27), but this image was severely damaged when man fell into sin. In Christ, God's Son, God provided us with the perfect image (2 Cor. 4:4; Col. 1:15) to which he intends to conform his elect (Rom. 8:29). Calvin said that the aim of repentance "is to restore in us the image of God that has been disfigured and all but obliterated through Adam's transgression."[40]

Since the two greatest commandments of God's law mandate love for God and love for our neighbors (Matt. 22:37–39), the central thrust of repentance is turning from the defiling dominance of our self-love to love the Lord with all our hearts (Deut. 30:6) and to love our neighbors as ourselves (Luke 3:10–14). People often think of repentance with regard to

36. *Reformed Confessions*, 4:365.
37. Acts 3:26; 5:31; 11:18, 20–21; 26:18; 2 Tim. 2:25–26. See the earlier chapters on effectual calling and regeneration.
38. Polyander, Walaeus, Thysius, and Rivetus, *Synopsis Purioris Theologiae*, 32.33 (2:293).
39. Calvin, *Institutes*, 3.3.5.
40. Calvin, *Institutes*, 3.3.9.

sins of commission, but repentance may inflame our deepest grief over sins of omission, especially our horrifying failure to love our God and fellow human beings as we should.

The Comprehensiveness of Repentance

Some theologians, particularly those adhering to certain forms of dispensationalism, have argued that "repent" merely means to change one's mental beliefs. Lewis Sperry Chafer denied that repentance involved any element of sorrow for sin, but argued that it simply consisted of the change from not believing in Christ to believing in him, and that in the Scriptures it may serve "as a synonym for the word *belief.*"[41] Charles Ryrie (1925–2016) wrote that "repent" (Acts 2:38) means to change what one thinks about Jesus Christ.[42]

However, the Scriptures represent repentance as a turning of the whole person from sin to God. God calls out, "Turn ye even to me with all your heart" (Joel 2:12). The requirement for experiencing God's deliverance is "If ye do return unto the Lord with all your hearts" (1 Sam. 7:3). Though the Greek verb commonly translated as "repent" (*metanoeō*) means to "change one's mind," this change is not restricted to the intellect, for feelings and volitional commitments are also aspects of the meaning of the Greek root translated as "mind" (*nous*).[43] Hoekema said, "It involves a change in the entire person, and in his or her outlook on life."[44] People do not merely repent of their false beliefs but "repent of their deeds" (Rev. 2:22).

Repentance involves a change in every aspect of human life, inward and outward.

1. *Intellectual change*: turning the mind. Turning people to the Lord involves turning "the disobedient to the wisdom of the just" (Luke 1:16–17). To "repent" requires that people "be persuaded" (16:30–31). Spiritual blindness and a lack of understanding prevent conversion (Matt. 13:15). Sinners turn to God when Christ opens their eyes (Acts 26:18). The prodigal son's foolish life brought many sorrows upon him, but his return home began "when he came to himself" and thought on the kindness of his

41. Chafer, *Systematic Theology*, 3:372–74, 377.
42. Charles C. Ryrie, *So Great Salvation: What It Means to Believe in Jesus Christ* (Wheaton, IL: Victor, 1989), 96.
43. *TDNT*, 4:976–77. See the use of *nous* in Rom. 1:28; 7:22–23; Col. 2:18; 2 Thess. 2:2; 1 Tim. 6:5; 2 Tim. 3:8.
44. Hoekema, *Saved by Grace*, 125.

father (Luke 15:17). Repentance often involves a time of reflection when people "call to mind" their experiences (Deut. 30:1–2; 2 Chron. 6:37).[45] God gives to some who oppose his Word "repentance to the acknowledging [literally knowledge] of the truth" (2 Tim. 2:25). Once their mindset was fleshly and hostile to God (Rom. 8:7), but now they no longer view Christ or other people according to the flesh (2 Cor. 5:16). Furthermore, the frequent link between repentance and forgiveness of sins implies that repentance involves a change of mind such that one recognizes his sins and need for forgiveness.[46] Thus, Archibald A. Hodge taught that repentance is based upon a new spiritual sense given in God's saving illumination of the soul, including "(1) sense of the hatefulness of sin, (2) sense of the beauty of holiness, (3) apprehension of the mercy of God in Christ."[47]

2. *Emotional change*: turning the affections. Before conversion, man "drinketh iniquity like water" (Job 15:16), but when he is converted, his sins make him ashamed (Ezek. 16:63; 20:43; Rom. 6:21). Thomas Watson said, "Heaven is never longed for till sin be loathed."[48] Through repentance, sinners "flee from the wrath to come" (Luke 3:7–8). In the ancient world, people expressed their grief outwardly by tearing their clothes, but when someone turns to God, he tears his heart (Joel 2:12–13). Jesus said that if Tyre and Sidon had seen his miracles, "they would have repented long ago in sackcloth and ashes" (Matt. 11:21), cultural expressions of grief (Jer. 6:26). At the root of "repentance to salvation" is "godly sorrow" (2 Cor. 7:10). Thus, James calls upon proud and worldly people to "be afflicted, and mourn, and weep: let your laughter be turned to mourning, and your joy to heaviness" (James 4:9). This wholehearted departing from evil comes from the fear of the Lord (Prov. 16:6). Conversion also brings new joy in God.[49] When God calls this wicked world to submit to Christ the King, he says, "Serve the LORD with fear, and rejoice with trembling" (Ps. 2:11). As Gerard Wisse (1873–1957) said, repentance is a "sweet dying" and "affectionate sorrow."[50]

3. *Volitional change*: turning the will. Mere beliefs and feelings are insufficient for saving repentance; it requires an act of choice (Deut. 30:19–

45. Mark J. Boda, *'Return to Me': A Biblical Theology of Repentance*, New Studies in Biblical Theology (Downers Grove, IL: InterVarsity Press, 2015), 156.

46. Mark 1:4; Luke 3:3; 17:3, 4; 24:47; Acts 2:38; 3:19; 5:31; 8:22.

47. Hodge, *Outlines of Theology*, 487.

48. Thomas Watson, *The Doctrine of Repentance*, Puritan Paperbacks (Edinburgh: Banner of Truth, 1987), 45.

49. Matt. 13:44; Acts 13:48; 1 Thess. 1:6.

50. G. Wisse, *Godly Sorrow* (St. Thomas, ON: Free Reformed, 1998), 21–22.

20; Josh. 24:15). Unconverted sinners are not willing to come to Christ (Matt. 22:3; 23:37; John 5:40), but his disciples have a reoriented will: "If any man will come after me, let him deny himself, and take up his cross, and follow me" (Matt. 16:24).[51] One great effect of the death of Christ is the change of the fundamental direction of their lives: "He died for all, that they which live should not henceforth live unto themselves, but unto him which died for them, and rose again" (2 Cor. 5:15). God works in his people "to will" for them to obey him (Phil. 2:12–13). The people who have an everlasting place in God's temple are those who by grace "choose the things that please me" (Isa. 56:4).

4. *Behavioral change*: turning the conduct. The Lord exhorted Israel, "Wash you, make you clean; put away the evil of your doings from before mine eyes; cease to do evil; learn to do well; seek judgment [justice], relieve the oppressed, judge [give justice to] the fatherless, plead for the widow" (Isa. 1:16–17). It is not only confessing but forsaking sin that leads to mercy from God (Prov. 28:13). John the Baptist called Israel to produce fruit fitting for repentance, comparing them to trees that must either bear fruit or be cut down and burned (Luke 3:8–9). Repentance requires caring for the poor instead of oppressing them (vv. 10–14). Christ's calling of "sinners to repentance" is his call to "follow me" (5:27, 32). Paul preached to all people "that they should repent and turn to God, and do works meet [fitting] for repentance" (Acts 26:20). Wayne Grudem says, "Repentance is a heartfelt sorrow for sin, a renouncing of it, and a sincere commitment to forsake it and walk in obedience to Christ."[52]

The Spiritual Exercise of Repentance

Repentance is an active grace. The Holy Scriptures give us rich descriptions of the experiential exercises of repentance in Psalms 32 and 51, Jeremiah 3:22–4:2, Hosea 14, and Luke 15:11–32.[53]

Repentance involves *turning from sin to the merciful God*. David's penitential psalm begins strikingly with the words "Blessed is he whose transgression is forgiven, whose sin is covered. Blessed is the man unto whom the LORD imputeth not iniquity, and in whose spirit there is no

51. In Matt. 16:24; 22:3; 23:37; and John 5:40, "will" or "would" renders the Greek word translated as "to will" (*thelō*).

52. Grudem, *Systematic Theology*, 713.

53. For a practical exposition of Hosea 14 with respect to backsliders, see Joel R. Beeke, *Getting Back in the Race: The Cure for Backsliding* (Adelphi, MD: Cruciform, 2011), 41–102.

guile" (Ps. 32:1–2). Psalm 51 opens with the same thought framed as a petition: "Have mercy upon me, O God, according to thy lovingkindness: according unto the multitude of thy tender mercies blot out my transgressions. Wash me throughly from mine iniquity, and cleanse me from my sin" (Ps. 51:1–2). Hosea called the people to turn to the Lord as their only hope for mercy (Hos. 14:1, 3).

There can be no turning to God without trust in his goodness, forgiveness, and love in Christ. The prodigal son returned to his father when he remembered his father's goodness (Luke 15:17), but the older son remained alienated from his father out of unbelief toward his goodness—though quite sure of his own worthiness (vv. 29–30). Judas felt remorse for betraying Christ, confessed his sin to the priests, and returned the money he had been paid, but he gave himself over to despair instead of turning back to the love and mercy of God, and so was lost forever (Matt. 27:3–5). As the Shorter Catechism (Q. 87) says, true repentance involves "an apprehension of the mercy of God in Christ."[54] John Brown of Haddington explained that this is "a sight of him as merciful in pardoning our sins, and saving our souls through Christ," and it is necessary "to melt our heart for sin, and keep us from despair."[55] Hodge said, "Out of Christ God is a consuming fire, and an inextinguishable dread drives the soul away." We must be attracted by mercy. Also, "a sense of the amazing goodness of God to us in the gift of his Son . . . is necessary to excite in the repentant soul the proper shame and sorrow for sin as committed against God."[56]

Repentance involves *heartfelt confessing of sins against the righteous God*. David's failure to own his sins brought God's conviction heavily upon him, but then, "I said, I will confess my transgressions unto the Lord; and thou forgavest the iniquity of my sin" (Ps. 32:3–5). Repentance is not a merely formal or outward confession of sin, but a heartfelt grieving and forsaking of it. David said, "For I acknowledge my transgressions" (51:3), which implies that he confessed specific acts of rebellion against God's law. David continued, "And my sin is ever before me," which indicates distress and shame over sin. Jeremiah wrote, "We lie down in our shame . . . for we have sinned against the Lord our God" (Jer. 3:25). Watson said, "A

54. *Reformed Confessions*, 4:365.
55. Brown, *Questions and Answers on the Shorter Catechism*, 296.
56. Hodge, *Outlines of Theology*, 488.

woman may as well expect to have a child without pangs as one can have repentance without sorrow."[57]

David said, "Against thee, thee only, have I sinned" (Ps. 51:4). David did not overlook his crimes against people, but confessed that he had committed treason against God.[58] David also confessed that God was "justified" or shown to be righteous when he judged David (v. 4). David's confession also speaks to two aspects of sin that many people ignore: that David was sinful by nature from his conception as an infant (v. 5) and that he needed not only a change of behavior but inward change (v. 6). While sophisticated theological understanding of the doctrine of sin is not necessary for saving repentance, the sinner must see that his problem is not just what he does but *who he is*. As a result of this new self-assessment, the penitent believer confesses that he is "no longer worthy" of blessing (Luke 15:19 ESV).

Repentance motivates *praying for saving grace*. Though our sins and misery are like "floods of great waters," the repentant one may grasp hold of God in prayer as "my hiding place," and the Lord will surround him with "songs of deliverance" (Ps. 32:6–7). David prayed for the cleansing and joy of God's forgiveness (51:7–9), alluding to the ritual use of "hyssop" to ceremonially cleanse an unclean person, even a healed leper, so that he might draw near to God again (Lev. 14:4–7; Num. 19:18–20). David also prayed for the renewal of his heart so that he might live in joy and freedom (Ps. 51:10–12). He said, "Create in me a clean heart, O God" (v. 10). Derek Kidner (1913–2008) commented, "With the word *create* he asks for nothing less than a miracle. It is a term for what God alone can do."[59]

Therefore, repentance longs for both forgiveness and holiness by grace alone. It moves sinners to pray for both "pardon of sins" and "profound inner renewal," as Bruce Demarest says.[60] This is no mercenary claim on forgiveness so that the sinner can further pursue sin, but a true turning to the Lord for justification and sanctification. God's invitation to repentance is backed by his promise, "I will heal their backsliding, I will love them freely" (Hos. 14:4).

---

57. Watson, *The Doctrine of Repentance*, 19.
58. Derek Kidner, *Psalms 1–72: An Introduction and Commentary on Books I and II of the Psalms*, Tyndale Old Testament Commentaries (Downers Grove, IL: InterVarsity Press, 1973), 190.
59. Kidner, *Psalms 1–72*, 192.
60. Demarest, *The Cross and Salvation*, 253.

Repentance often shows itself in *declaring God's salvation to others.* To turn to the Lord is to resolve to live for his glory by calling others to him. The penitent David boldly addressed his readers, "I will instruct thee and teach thee in the way which thou shalt go: I will guide thee with mine eye. Be ye not as the horse, or as the mule, which have no understanding: whose mouth must be held in with bit and bridle, lest they come near unto thee" (Ps. 32:8–9). David said, "Then will I teach transgressors thy ways; and sinners shall be converted unto thee" (51:13).

This does not fill the penitent's mouth with proud scolding—David had admitted his own stubbornness (Ps. 32:3–4)—but with humble praises to the Lord. God is now the "God of my salvation: and my tongue shall sing aloud of thy righteousness. . . . And my mouth shall shew forth thy praise" (51:14–15). Jeremiah said of those who return to the Lord, "Thou shalt swear, The LORD liveth, in truth, in judgment, and in righteousness; and the nations shall bless themselves in him, and in him shall they glory" (Jer. 4:2). The repentant sinner is not self-centered but desires all men to know that salvation is of the Lord.

Repentance leads people into *worshiping God with his penitent church.* There is a social dimension to repentance, for the penitent separates himself from the wicked world and joins God's people in worshiping the Lord. David said, "Many sorrows shall be to the wicked: but he that trusteth in the LORD, mercy shall compass him about. Be glad in the LORD, and rejoice, ye righteous: and shout for joy, all ye that are upright in heart" (Ps. 32:10–11). Repentance qualifies the converted person to worship, for "the sacrifices of God are a broken spirit: a broken and a contrite heart, O God, thou wilt not despise" (51:16–17). Sinclair Ferguson writes, "It is a spirit in which self-sufficiency and self-defense have been penetrated and broken down."[61]

This is the paradox of penitence. The repentant sinner returns to God in brokenness over his sin but discovers that God embraces him as his loving Father and brings him into his house for a feast (Luke 15:22–24). The funeral for sin becomes the celebration of reconciliation, for the unworthy sinner "was dead, and is alive again; and was lost, and is found" (v. 32).

Repentance should engage the whole covenantal community in seeking God's grace. Solomon foresaw this as a major function of the temple: God's people suffer divine discipline, return to the Lord, seek him in prayer

61. Ferguson, *The Holy Spirit*, 137.

at his holy place, and obtain forgiveness for their sins (1 Kings 8:33, 35, 47–48).[62] The prayers of God's people after the exile reflect a corporate penitence that consciously confesses Israel's failure to repent and the Lord's righteousness in judging them (Neh. 9:1–37; cf. Dan. 9:1–19). The risen Lord Jesus Christ calls entire churches or groups within churches to repent or face the consequences (Rev. 2:5, 16, 21–22; 3:3, 19). Lamenting over sin, turning from it to the Lord, and trusting in his forgiveness should be regular components in the church's worship, and there may be times when the pastors should call for a special emphasis on repentance, such as seasons of special conviction or calamity.

True Repentance Discerned by Its Character and Fruit

Some conversions prove to be false conversions. Christ told us of people who receive the word "with gladness" but "have no root in themselves, and so endure but for a time" until troubles wither their profession of faith (Mark 4:16–17). Others hear the word, but its influence in their lives is choked out by the reigning power of worldly fears and desires (v. 19). Simon Magus stands as a sad example of those who have a kind of faith in the gospel and are baptized but remain in the slavery of sin—hypocrites (Acts 8:5–24). Herman Kuiper (1889–1963) wrote, "It happens time and again that men whose hearts remain strangers to God's saving grace make a break with their past wickedness and embark upon the road of virtue in such a fashion that their change of conduct bears a marked resemblance to the changed manner of living which accompanies true conversion."[63]

How do we distinguish between true repentance and its counterfeits? Paul gave us a litmus test of repentance in his contrast between two different kinds of sorrow over sin: "godly sorrow," which "worketh repentance," versus "the sorrow of the world" (2 Cor. 7:10). Worldly sorrow is so called because it grieves over sin's consequences based on the wisdom of this world, which is man-centered, treasuring the ability, riches, and honor of man (1 Cor. 1:20–22, 27–29). David Garland writes, "Worldly grief is caused by the loss or denial of something we want for ourselves. It is self-centered."[64] Worldly sorrow "worketh death" (2 Cor. 7:10) because

62. Boda, *'Return to Me,'* 55–56.
63. Herman Kuiper, *By Grace Alone: A Study in Soteriology* (Grand Rapids, MI: Eerdmans, 1955), 82.
64. David E. Garland, *2 Corinthians*, The New American Commentary 29 (Nashville: Broadman & Holman, 1999), 355.

it is the rebellious response of sinners to God's law (cf. Rom. 7:13),[65] the law received without the life-giving Spirit (2 Cor. 3:3, 6). Worldly sorrow over sin is but a foretaste of hell.

However, "godly sorrow" (2 Cor. 7:10), literally "sorrow according to God" (*lupē kata theon*), grieves over sin because it dishonors and displeases God, and so this grief produces "repentance to salvation."[66] Brown wrote, "In legal repentance, we are affected chiefly with the guilt of sin, and with gross sins; but in repentance unto life, we are affected chiefly with the filth of sin, the dishonor done to God by it, and with secret and beloved sins."[67] Godly sorrow is driven by a new sense of God's glory and love for him and his laws—even above our temporal happiness. The repentant believer says, "Before I was afflicted I went astray: but now have I kept thy word. Thou art good, and doest good; teach me thy statutes. . . . It is good for me that I have been afflicted; that I might learn thy statutes. The law of thy mouth is better unto me than thousands of gold and silver" (Ps. 119:67–68, 71–72). Willard said, "In repentance this love is kindled and rendered inexpressibly great. . . . And that service which was before a burden, is now a recreation."[68]

Wisse wrote, "We do not turn to God because we are pessimistic, tired of the world, or have reached our saturation point with the world. Instead, we turn from the world because we have met with God"—giving us "an inner glimpse of the loveliness of God" so that we hate sin.[69] Here is a method to test our motives. Are you sad merely because your sins hurt you and other people, or because your sins offend God?

Paul also teaches some distinguishing effects of true godly sorrow: "For behold this selfsame thing, that ye sorrowed after a godly sort, what carefulness it wrought in you, yea, what clearing of yourselves, yea, what indignation, yea, what fear, yea, what vehement desire, yea, what zeal, yea, what revenge! In all things ye have approved yourselves to be clear in this matter" (2 Cor. 7:11). Thus, true repentance produces:

- *Carefulness*: The Greek work (*spoudē*) means eagerness, diligence, and earnestness. True repentance engages the soul in a sincere effort to rid itself of sin and to please God.

65. Peter Naylor, *A Study Commentary on 2 Corinthians*, EP Study Commentary (Darlington, England: Evangelical Press, 2002), 1:324.

66. Polyander, Walaeus, Thysius, and Rivetus, *Synopsis Purioris Theologiae*, 32.38 (2:295).

67. Brown, *Questions and Answers on the Shorter Catechism*, 295.

68. Willard, *A Compleat Body of Divinity*, 804.

69. Wisse, *Godly Sorrow*, 17–18.

- *Clearing*: The word (*apologia*) means answer or defense, not here an attempt to excuse ourselves, but a conscientious demonstration that we have truly repented.
- *Indignation*: This term (*aganaktēsis*) communicates displeasure and outrage at sin, at oneself for sinning, and at anyone who refuses to repent of this sin.[70]
- *Fear*: The fear (*phobos*) of God is to depart from evil (Job 28:28). It may refer to the fear of losing fellowship with God through unrepented sin (2 Cor. 6:14–7:1).
- *Vehement Desire and Zeal*: Real repentance engages the soul in a strong longing (*epipothēsis*) and burning desire (*zēlos*) to restore relationships injured by sin.[71]
- *Revenge*: Out of a concern for justice (*ekdikēsis*) where wrong has been done, we humbly accept consequences for our sins and make appropriate restitution.[72]

These are the fruits of God-centered repentance that demonstrate that repentance is true. There are certainly degrees of true repentance, and the mature height of godly repentance is not necessary for salvation. However, the acorn has the same genetic code as the mighty oak, and repentance unto life bears this same character wherever it is found, even as a seed.

The Necessity of Repentance

There is no salvation apart from repentance. When the preaching of Christ crucified and risen again cut the crowds in Jerusalem to the heart and they cried, "What shall we do?" Peter said, "Repent" (Acts 2:38) and promised forgiveness only to those who did so. Peter preached, "Repent ye therefore, and be converted, that your sins may be blotted out" (3:19).[73] The Westminster Confession of Faith (15.3) says, "Although repentance be not to be rested in, as any satisfaction for sin, or any cause of the pardon thereof, which is the act of God's free grace in Christ; yet is it of such necessity to all sinners, that none may expect pardon without it."[74]

70. The word is *hapax legomenon* in the New Testament, but its cognate verb appears in Matt. 20:24; 21:15; 26:8; Mark 10:14, 41; 14:4; Luke 13:14.

71. Paul used these same two words in 2 Cor. 7:7 about the Corinthians' attitude toward him, reflecting their earnest desire to be reconciled to the apostle whom they had wronged.

72. Charles Hodge, *An Exposition of the Second Epistle to the Corinthians* (New York: A. C. Armstrong & Son, 1891), 184–86.

73. The verb translated as "blot out" (*exaleiphō*) in Acts 3:19 is the same used of God's forgiveness in the Greek translation of Ps. 51:1, 9 (50:3, 11 LXX).

74. *Reformed Confessions*, 4:251.

Those dispensationalist theologians who define repentance as a mere change of belief oppose telling sinners that they must turn from sin to God in order to be saved. Chafer asserted, "Next to sound doctrine itself, no more important obligation rests on the preacher than that of preaching the Lordship of Christ to Christians exclusively, and the Saviorhood of Christ to those who are unsaved."[75] Ryrie said that we must "distinguish salvation from discipleship."[76]

However, Christ said, "if any man will come after me, let him deny himself, and take up his cross daily, and follow me. For whosoever will save his life shall lose it: but whosoever will lose his life for my sake, the same shall save it" (Luke 9:23–24). The issue here is not mere rewards but gaining or losing your very self or soul ("life" translates the Greek *psychē*, v. 24) in the day of judgment (v. 26).

Zane Hodges (1932–2008), another dispensationalist theologian, rejected Chafer's and Ryrie's limitation of repentance to mental beliefs,[77] but took another pathway to essentially the same view of saving conversion by postponing repentance to a second stage after salvation. Hodges wrote, "The call to faith represents the call to eternal salvation. The call to repentance is the call to enter into harmonious relations with God."[78]

On the contrary, Ferguson writes, "Repentance is as necessary as faith for salvation. Salvation is salvation from sin. It involves more than forgiveness. It includes our sanctification. It must therefore engage those who are saved in the turning away from sin which is involved in repentance."[79] John MacArthur and Richard Mayhue say, "Scripture is unmistakably clear: repentance is not an optional element but is an essential component of the true gospel."[80]

Repentance is *necessary for salvation*. John the Baptist warned sinners of "the wrath to come" and exhorted them, "Bring forth therefore fruits meet for repentance" (Matt. 3:7–8). He compared them to trees that, if

75. Chafer, *Systematic Theology*, 3:387.

76. Charles C. Ryrie, *Basic Theology: A Popular Systematic Guide to Understanding Biblical Truth* (Wheaton, IL: Victor, 1986), 339.

77. Zane C. Hodges, *Absolutely Free! A Biblical Reply to Lordship Salvation* (Grand Rapids, MI: Zondervan, 1989), 146, 224n10–12.

78. Hodges, *Absolutely Free!*, 145.

79. Ferguson, *The Holy Spirit*, 134.

80. MacArthur and Mayhue, eds., *Biblical Doctrine*, 595–96. For two critical responses to the teaching that a person can be saved without repentance from sin and submission to Christ's lordship, see John MacArthur Jr., *The Gospel according to Jesus: What Is Authentic Faith?*, rev. ed. (Grand Rapids, MI: Zondervan, 2008); and Michael S. Horton, ed., *Christ the Lord: The Reformation and Lordship Salvation* (Eugene, OR: Wipf and Stock, 1992).

failing to produce good fruit, will be cut down "and cast into the fire" (v. 10). What is this wrath and fire? John explained that Christ was coming to separate his people from others and cast the latter into "unquenchable fire" (v. 12). The Lord Jesus preached, "Repent: for the kingdom of heaven is at hand" (Matt. 4:17). He warned, "Every tree that bringeth not forth good fruit is hewn down, and cast into the fire" (7:19). This is the fire of hell (5:22). Without fruitful repentance, sinners go to hell. Only those who do God's will are on the narrow road to life (7:13–14, 21; cf. 12:50). Christ said, "Except ye repent, ye shall all . . . perish" (Luke 13:3, 5).

One argument brought against the necessity of repentance is that the Gospel of John promises eternal life through faith in Christ (John 3:16; 20:31), but never uses the words *repent* or *repentance*.[81]

In reply, we answer that as already noted, in the Scriptures the gospel call is sometimes to faith, sometimes to repentance, and sometimes to both—indicating the essential unity and inseparability of faith and repentance.[82] Furthermore, by the same argument, we would have to conclude that the Gospels of Matthew and Mark do not teach salvation by grace, since the word *grace* (Greek *charis*) does not appear in either book.[83] Doctrines are taught not just with specific words, but with ideas.

In John's Gospel, Jesus does teach repentance, albeit in other words. No one comes to the light of Christ unless he also ceases loving darkness and sin (John 3:19–21). Jesus said to a man whom he healed after decades of being handicapped, "Sin no more, lest a worse thing come upon thee" (5:14). Christ said that he would call forth all mankind from their graves, "they that have done good, unto the resurrection of life; and they that have done evil, unto the resurrection of damnation" (v. 29). Christ called men to discipleship as the way to eternal life: "He that loveth his life shall lose it; and he that hateth his life in this world shall keep it unto life eternal. If any man serve me, let him follow me; and where I am, there shall also my servant be: if any man serve me, him will my Father honour" (12:25–26). Jesus warned that those who outwardly adhere to him but bear no fruit will be cast into the fire (15:5–6).

81. Chafer, *Systematic Theology*, 3:376; and Hodges, *Absolutely Free*, 26.

82. See the discussion above in this chapter on the two sides of conversion.

83. These Gospels do teach salvation by grace alone, for Jesus came to save his people from their sins (Matt. 1:21; 18:11), a salvation that is impossible with men but possible with God (19:25–26; Mark 10:26–27), for Christ gives rest to the weary and heavily loaded who come to him (Matt. 11:28), not the righteous, but sinners (9:13; Mark 2:17)—that is, those who deserve to go to hell even for sins of the heart (Matt. 5:22, 29–30).

Paul also preaches repentance as necessary for salvation (Acts 26:18–20), declaring that, in light of judgment day, all men must repent (17:30–31). He teaches that "the goodness of God leadeth thee to repentance" and warns those who remain unrepentant that they are storing up wrath for themselves on judgment day (Rom. 2:4–5). Union with Christ includes dying to sin and rising to a new life of obedience (6:1–14). The saved are no longer slaves of sin, but willing servants of righteousness who are ashamed of sin and now obey the truth (vv. 17–18, 21). Paul writes, "They that are Christ's have crucified the flesh with the affection and lusts" (Gal. 5:24). Christ's true church submits to her Head (Eph. 5:23–24), but those ruled by immorality, greed, or disobedience will receive God's wrath, not his kingdom (vv. 5–6).

"Repentance from dead works" is a doctrine foundational to true Christianity (Heb. 6:1). Owen said, "Without this, whatever notions men may have of reconciliation with God, they will find him in the issue as 'devouring fire,' or 'everlasting burnings.' All doctrines, notions, or persuasions that tend to alleviate the necessity of that personal repentance . . . or would substitute any outward penance . . . are pernicious [deadly] to the souls of men."[84]

Therefore, we conclude that repentance is necessary for salvation. Though adorned with phrases such as "faith alone" and "grace alone," theology that denies the necessity of repentance for salvation is a tragic betrayal of the Bible and the Reformation. Ferguson says, "The idea that it is possible to receive justification without sanctification, to trust in a Savior who does not actually or presently save, to receive a new birth that does not actually give life, or to have a faith that is not radically repentant despite uniting us to a crucified and risen Christ simply did not find a place in Reformation theology."[85]

Have you repented of your sins? Let no one deceive you with empty words. Satan has long led mankind astray with his soul-damning lie: "Ye shall not surely die" (Gen. 3:4). God says, "The wages of sin is death" (Rom. 6:23). Turn, therefore, from the sins that will ruin you forever; turn to the Lord who gives eternal life through Jesus Christ. Tear your heart over your sins; mourn before the Lord. Judgment day is coming. Bring forth the fruit of repentance, or you will be found outside of Christ, outside of life, and outside of all hope.

---

84. Owen, *An Exposition of the Epistle to the Hebrews*, 5:26.
85. Sinclair Ferguson, *The Grace of Repentance* (Wheaton, IL: Crossway, 2010), 42.

Repentance is also *necessary for growth and perseverance.* The repentance of new converts is sincere, but it is far from perfect. Confessing and grieving over sin is necessary even for the godly when they commit wickedness (Psalms 32 and 51). A Christian might need to repent seven times a day for sins committed against a brother (Luke 17:3–4). Some of Christ's most poignant calls to repentance were addressed to Christian churches (Rev. 2:5, 16; 3:3, 19). The opposite of repentance is hardness of heart, and if we allow the deceitfulness of sin to harden our hearts, then we will fall away from the faith and prove that we have not been partakers of Christ (Heb. 3:8, 12–14).

Repentance is not merely a gateway into the Christian life, but the pathway we must follow all our lives until we reach the kingdom of glory. Martin Luther famously wrote in his Ninety-Five Theses, "When our Lord and Master Jesus Christ said, 'Repent' (Matt. 4:17), he willed the entire life of believers to be one of repentance."[86] Calvin said that we must "give attention to continual repentance."[87] He wrote, "This warfare will end only at death."[88] We must repent of our vain thoughts, evil lusts, worldliness, backslidings from God, failing to use our talents for his glory, ingratitude, unbelief, and a host of other sins. Just as we must live by faith (Gal. 2:20), so each step forward in the Christian life is a further turning from sin to God. Hoekema said that our lifelong repentance and sanctification is "a pilgrimage from the mind of the flesh to the mind of Christ, a putting off of the old self and a putting on the new."[89] Samuel Davies (1723–1761) said, "Every true penitent is a critic upon his own heart; and there he finds constant cause for repentance while in this imperfect state."[90]

Motives for Unbelievers to Repent

Many obstacles stand in the way of a sinner's repentance. There is the general thoughtlessness and vanity of mind that hinders many from considering eternity. Some are dimly aware of the coming judgment but are held in the icy grip of spiritual lethargy. Caricatures of true religion prejudice many minds against repentance. Pride and presumption carry others comfortably to the gates of hell. Some distort the sovereignty of God into

86. Luther, *Ninety-Five Theses*, in *LW*, 31:25.
87. Calvin, *Institutes*, 3.3.20.
88. Calvin, *Institutes*, 3.3.9.
89. Hoekema, *Saved by Grace*, 131.
90. *Sermons by the Rev. Samuel Davies*, 3 vols. (Philadelphia: Presbyterian Board of Publication, 1864), 2:391.

a reason for sin as if the almighty King were not also the righteous Judge. Some put off repentance to another day, foolishly banking on a future that might suddenly be cut off, while hardening their hearts against each gospel offer. Ultimately, the obstacle beneath all obstacles is people's hatred for God and love for sin, such that they would prefer to perish as God's enemies than repent of their wickedness (Rev. 9:20–21).

Despite this stubbornness and hardness of sinners, God's Word presents strong motives toward repentance for those who have ears to hear. Thomas Boston reminded us of several, and we close this chapter with them both to exhort you to repent if you are unconverted and to equip you to speak to your unconverted friends.[91]

1. *God's command* obligates you to repent (Acts 17:30). If there were no other reason in the world to repent, God's absolute authority and clear command are enough.

2. *God's mercies* lead you to repent (Rom. 2:4). Every day God shows you his goodness and preserves your life while calling you to him. Will you not turn to this good God?

3. *The evil of sin* drives you to repent (Isa. 57:21). All sin's pleasures are bait on a deadly hook. Sin offers no lasting peace, and its pleasure will turn to bitterness.

4. *The inevitability of death* urges you to repent (Heb. 9:27). Are you prepared to face the living God? Once you die, it is too late to repent and find forgiveness of sins.

5. *The justice of God's judgment* demands that you repent (2 Cor. 5:10–11). The Lord will most certainly judge you according to his perfect justice. What if Christ returned today?

6. *The sufferings of Christ* should draw you to repent (Zech. 12:10). Look upon the cross and see how dreadful God's wrath is against sin, as well as how much God loves sinners. Are you so hard-hearted that you can consider the sin-bearing Son of God and not repent?

7. *The wrong of your sins against God* should move you to repent (Ps. 51:4). Sin disregards God's all-seeing eye, defies his justice, opposes his holiness, tramples on his laws, despises his Son, grieves his Spirit, and defaces the Father's image.

8. *The consequences of whether you repent* should convince you to repent. If you do not repent, you will perish (Luke 13:3). "It is a fearful

91. Boston, *The Necessity of Repentance*, in *Works*, 6:431–45.

thing to fall into the hands of the living God" (Heb. 10:31). However, if you repent, you will never perish (Isa. 55:7). Boston said, "There is mercy for thee, if thou wilt repent, and come to Christ. Good news, sinners, if ye repent, all your sins shall be blotted out, ye shall be embraced in the wide and warm arms of mercy."[92]

In light of such great motives, let us not fail to turn from sin to the Lord. Today is the day of grace; make good use of the opportunity. Indeed, make your entire life a continuous exercise of repentance, that your life may be a continuous act of drawing closer to God.

Sing to the Lord

Returning to the God of Mercy

God be merciful to me,
On Thy grace I rest my plea;
Plenteous in compassion Thou,
Blot out my transgressions now;
Wash me, make me pure within,
Cleanse, O cleanse me from my sin.

My transgressions I confess,
Grief and guilt my soul oppress;
I have sinned against Thy grace
And provoked Thee to Thy face;
I confess Thy judgment just,
Speechless, I Thy mercy trust.

I am evil, born in sin;
Thou desirest truth within.
Thou alone my Saviour art,
Teach Thy wisdom to my heart;
Make me pure, Thy grace bestow,
Wash me whiter than the snow.

Broken, humbled to the dust
By Thy wrath and judgment just,
Let my contrite heart rejoice
And in gladness hear Thy voice;

92. Boston, *The Necessity of Repentance*, in *Works*, 6:443–44.

From my sins O hide Thy face,
Blot them out in boundless grace.

Psalm 51
Tune: Ajalon
The Psalter, No. 140
Trinity Hymnal—Baptist Edition, No. 415

Questions for Meditation or Discussion

1. How would you define the following terms? Which is the focus of this chapter?
   - habitual or passive conversion
   - actual or active conversion
   - first actual conversion
   - second actual conversion
   - continual actual conversion
2. What are the dangers of insisting that all first conversions must fit a certain form?
3. What is the relationship between faith and repentance?
4. What is the Westminster Shorter Catechism's definition of repentance? How is each part of that definition supported by the Word of God?
5. How did Chafer and Ryrie define repentance? Is that biblical? Why or why not?
6. Why is a view of God's mercy in Christ essential for the exercise of repentance?
7. How can we discern true repentance from nonsaving remorse for sin?
8. What scriptural statements or truths show that turning from sin to God is necessary for salvation?
9. Of the motives for repentance, which seem most compelling to you? Why?
10. Have you repented? How do you know?

Questions for Deeper Reflection

11. Someone says, "I reject the legalism of demanding that people repent and do good works in order to be counted true children

of God. I believe in the pure gospel of salvation by grace alone through faith alone." How do you respond?

12. One reason why early Reformed theologians said that faith is causally prior to repentance is to protect the church against the false teaching that sinners must first repent *before* coming to Christ in faith. Why is this such a grave danger? Do theologians who say that neither faith nor repentance is prior to the other successfully evade this danger? Why or why not?

20

Conversion, Part 2

Faith in Jesus Christ

There is a richness to faith in Jesus Christ that excels all explanation. Faith in Christ is the heart of a relationship with God. Romans 5:1 says, "Therefore being justified by faith, we have peace with God through our Lord Jesus Christ." In unbelief we are cut off, but by faith we stand (11:20). Faith is the heart of life itself: "The just shall live by faith" (1:17). Christians live by faith in the Son of God, who loved us and gave himself for us (Gal. 2:20). Christian theology expresses the pattern of sound doctrine revealed in the Scriptures, and we can "hold fast the form of sound words" only "in faith and love which is in Christ Jesus" (2 Tim. 1:13). All the lines of the order of salvation converge upon faith in Christ.[1]

J. C. Ryle (1816–1900) compared faith to "the hand of the soul," by which the drowning man grasps Christ and is saved (Heb. 6:18); "the eye of the soul," by which the sinner looks to Christ, just as the Israelites bitten by the snakes looked to the bronze serpent and were healed (John 3:14–15); "the mouth of the soul," by which the perishing eat the bread of life (6:35); and "the foot of the soul," by which the one pursued by a deadly enemy flees to the strong tower and is safe (Prov. 18:10).[2]

1. Kuiper, *By Grace Alone*, 92.
2. J. C. Ryle, *Old Paths*, 2nd ed. (London: William Hunt and Co., 1878), 228–29.

In this chapter, we will open the biblical doctrine of saving faith, which, like repentance, is the fruit of God's effectual calling of sinners to Christ.

Biblical Terminology of Faith

In the Old Testament, to exercise faith is often expressed with a verb meaning "make firm, establish, be faithful, reliable" (Hebrew *aman*), and thus to "believe" (*hiphil* of *aman*).[3] The relationship between the two meanings appears in the play on words in Isaiah 7:9: "If ye will not believe [*hiphil* of *aman*], surely ye shall not be established [*niphal* of *aman*]" (cf. 2 Chron. 20:20). B. B. Warfield wrote that the root is applied in Scripture to "whatever holds, is steady, or can be depended on," whether a solid wall or a trustworthy person.[4] From this root is derived the word *amen*, which means "truly" or "let it be so" (Jer. 28:6). To believe (*aman*) is man's response to God's faithfulness (*emunah*), his absolute reliability in all he says and does.[5] Faithfulness is the direct opposite of deception (Prov. 12:22).[6] The Lord's people believe in his "truth" (*emet*),[7] for he is "the God of truth," literally "the God of amen" (Isa. 65:16). To "hear" (*shem'a*) him rightly is to believe him.[8]

Another term is "trust" (*batakh*), often used in the Psalms of trusting the Lord.[9] "Trust" is sometimes used in parallel with "believing" (*aman*), showing their close interrelation.[10] Nouns related to this verb mean "confidence, security, or safety" (*betakh*, *mibtakh*).[11] Trusting in the Lord is explained as "leaning" (*sha'an*), a verb that means to rest one's weight and find support (Judg. 16:26), and so used to describe resting and relying on the Lord.[12] Another vivid image of trusting in the Lord is provided in the

3. Gen. 15:6; Ex. 4:5, 31; 14:31; Num. 14:11; 20:12; Deut. 1:32; 9:23; 2 Kings 17:14; 2 Chron. 20:20; Pss. 27:13; 78:22, 32; 106:12, 24; 116:10; 119:66; Isa. 7:9; 28:16; 43:10; 53:1; Jonah 3:5; Hab. 1:5.

4. Benjamin B. Warfield, "The Philological Expression of Faith," in *Biblical and Theological Studies*, ed. Samuel G. Craig (Philadelphia: Presbyterian and Reformed, 1968), 429.

5. Deut. 32:4; Pss. 33:4; 36:6; 40:11; 88:12; 89:2, 3, 6, 9, 25, 34, 50; 92:3; 96:13; 98:3; 100:5; 119:75, 86, 90, 138; 143:1; Isa. 11:5; 25:1; Hos. 2:22; Lam. 3:23.

6. *NIDOTTE*, 1:431.

7. For example, see Gen. 32:10; Ex. 34:6; Pss. 57:3; 71:22; 86:15; 91:4; 111:7–8; Mic. 7:20.

8. Ex. 4:1, 5, 8–9; Deut. 9:23; 2 Kings 17:14; 2 Chron. 20:20; Ps. 106:24–25; Isa. 55:2–3.

9. 2 Kings 18:5, 22, 30; 19:10; 1 Chron. 5:20; Pss. 4:5; 9:10; 13:5; 21:7; 22:4–5, 9; 25:2; 26:1; 27:3; 28:7; 31:6, 14; 32:10; 33:21; 37:3, 5; 40:3; 52:8; 55:23; 56:3–4, 11; 62:8; 78:22; 84:12; 86:2; 91:2; 115:8–11; 118:8–9; 119:42; 125:1; 143:8; Prov. 3:5; 16:20; 28:25; 29:25; Isa. 12:2; 26:4; 36:7, 15; 37:10; 51:10; Jer. 17:7; 39:18; Zeph. 3:2.

10. Job 39:11–12; Ps. 78:22; Mic. 7:5.

11. For example, see Ps. 65:5; Prov. 14:26; Isa. 30:15; 32:17.

12. 2 Chron. 13:18; 14:11; 16:7–8; Prov. 3:5; Isa. 10:20; 50:10; Mic. 3:11.

verb "take refuge" (*khasah*)—that is, to seek shelter and protection, as when people hide in a fortress or chicks run under the wings of the hen.[13]

Faith is expressed in the New Testament through the Greek verb translated as "believe" (*pisteuō*), used 248 times, and its cognate noun "faith" (*pistis*) and adjective "faithful" or "believing" (*pistos*), used 244 times and sixty-seven times respectively. In classical Greek, this word group was used of beliefs about the gods but not of trust in them, for they were not viewed as beings of faithful love.[14] However, this word group was commonly used in the Septuagint to translate the Hebrew root "believe" (*aman*), and so in the New Testament it carries the idea of faith in the trustworthiness of the Lord. Hebrews 11:11 says, "Through faith [*pistis*] Sara herself received strength . . . because she judged him faithful [*pistos*] who had promised." The noun translated as "faith" (*pistis*) in some instances can also mean "faithfulness" (Rom. 3:3; Gal. 5:22), and in others it means the content of faith—that is, the doctrines believed.[15]

The New Testament uses the phrase "believe into" (*pisteuō eis*),[16] an expression not ordinarily found in secular Greek or the Septuagint.[17] Warfield observed that this construction appears "some forty-nine times" and posited that it expresses "an absolute transference of trust from ourselves to another"—namely, to Christ.[18] Geerhardus Vos found in it the idea of a "movement of the will into Christ" to abandon self-reliance and rely on him, "a relocation of the resting point of life."[19] However, this construction may also be used of nonsaving faith, so we must be cautious not to overinterpret its meaning.[20]

Another word (*peithō*) means to persuade or convince, and thus in some places to believe, have confidence in, or trust.[21] This verb in its perfect, passive form (*pepoithenai*) was often used in the Septuagint to translate the Hebrew verbs rendered as "trust" (*batakh*) and "take refuge in"

13. Ruth 2:12; 2 Sam. 22:3, 31; Pss. 2:12; 5:11; 7:1; 11:1; 16:1; 17:1; 18:2, 30; 25:20; 31:1, 19; 34:8, 22; 36:7; 37:40; 57:1; 61:4; 64:10; 71:1; 91:4; 118:8–9; 141:8; 144:2; Prov. 14:32; 30:5; Isa. 14:32; 57:13; Nah. 1:7; Zeph. 3:12.

14. Vos, *Reformed Dogmatics*, 4:75.

15. Gal. 1:23; Eph. 4:13; 1 Tim. 1:19; 3:9; Jude 3.

16. For examples of "believe into" (*pisteuō eis*), see Matt. 18:6; John 1:12; 2:23; 3:15, 16, 18; 7:31, 38–39; 8:30; 10:42; 11:25, 26, 45; 12:11, 36, 37, 42, 44, 46; 14:1, 12; 16:9; 17:20; Acts 10:43; Gal. 2:16.

17. *NIDNTTE*, 3:765.

18. Warfield, "The Philological Expression of Faith," in *Biblical and Theological Studies*, 438–39.

19. Vos, *Reformed Dogmatics*, 4:80.

20. Bavinck, *Reformed Dogmatics*, 4:107. See *pisteuō eis* in John 2:23; 7:31; 8:30; 11:45; 12:42.

21. For example, see Matt. 27:43; Luke 16:31; Acts 13:43; 17:4; 18:4; 19:8, 26; 26:28; 28:23.

(*khasah*).[22] It can be used of being persuaded of some truth (Rom. 14:14) or of the Christian's confidence in the reliability and victory of God's grace in Christ.[23]

Therefore, the biblical words for faith communicate the idea of trust in the faithfulness of God, pictured as resting on him and hiding in him, so that one's confidence is in the Lord.

Kinds of Faith That Do Not Save

Though God gives many promises to those who believe in his Son, he also warns that there are kinds of faith that do not result in salvation. This is not because such faith is not strong enough or does not last long enough, but because it lacks the essential qualities of saving faith. Faith that does not unite us to Christ in salvation appears in various forms.[24]

1. Saving faith is not *mere mental belief*. Theologians often call this *historical faith* because it bears the same nature as belief that an event truly happened in history. William Perkins referred to it as "knowledge of God's Word and assent."[25] Robert Sandeman (1718–1771) said that the "sole requisite" for justification is "the work finished by Christ in His death," and, "everyone who understands this report to be true, or is persuaded that the event actually happened as testified by the apostles, is justified."[26] However, if that were so, men could be justified and remain as wicked as the Devil (James 2:19). Herman Kuiper wrote, "They believe that the Word of God is true . . . but these truths do not become a living power within them, directing them Godward and heavenward."[27] Justifying faith is no "easy-believism," but a living reliance upon Christ that results in good works (vv. 14–17). An example of such mental belief is seen when Paul said to Herod Agrippa, "Believest thou the prophets? I know that thou believest," yet Agrippa was no Christian (Acts 26:27). Watson said, "There may be an assent to divine truth, and yet no work of grace on the heart."[28]

---

22. The Septuagint also translates *batakh* with "hope" (*elpizō*), but not with "believe" (*pisteuō*). *TDNT*, 2:521; and *NIDNTTE*, 3:686.
23. Rom. 8:38–39; 2 Cor. 1:9; Phil. 1:6; 2 Tim. 1:12; Heb. 11:13.
24. On the first three categories, see Perkins, *An Exposition of the Symbol*, in *Works*, 5:9–11; and Polyander, Walaeus, Thysius, and Rivetus, *Synopsis Purioris Theologiae*, 31.3 (2:231).
25. Perkins, *An Exposition of the Symbol*, in *Works*, 5:9.
26. Cited in D. M. Lloyd-Jones, *The Puritans: Their Origins and Successors* (Edinburgh: Banner of Truth, 1987), 174.
27. Kuiper, *By Grace Alone*, 61.
28. Watson, *A Body of Divinity*, 215.

2. Saving faith is not *transient emotional commitment*. It is possible to "receive the word with joy" and "for a while believe," but later "fall away" (Luke 8:13). Israel "believed" God's word and "sang his praise" by the Red Sea, but "they soon forgat his works" and later "believed not his word" (Ps. 106:12–13, 24). Such a response may clean up a person's life temporarily, though he later returns to the filth of his sin (2 Pet. 2:20). Theologians often refer to this as *temporary faith*, though it is not saving faith that only lasts for a time, but a different kind of faith, one that merely excites the emotions for a period of time without transforming the heart.

Christians may be troubled over whether they possess mere temporary faith or true saving faith. However, the two differ not only in duration but in nature, allowing each person to discern which kind of faith he has. As Christ noted in the parable of the soils, in temporary faith, the seed of the word has no root in the heart (Luke 8:13). It is superficial because it is seated only in the emotions, causing rejoicing in the benefits of Christ (Matt. 13:20), whereas saving faith is rooted in a new heart (Luke 8:15) given by divine regeneration (Ezek. 36:26), causing rejoicing in God himself (Deut. 30:6; Rom. 5:1–2, 11). Temporary faith lacks humility and self-knowledge of sin's enslaving power (John 8:30–34); saving faith evokes true self-abhorrence because of sin (Ezek. 16:62–63). Temporary faith has a different aim and end than saving faith, for the former loves the glory of man but the latter the glory of God (John 5:44; 12:42–43). Superficial, temporary faith grows rapidly at first (Matt. 13:5), but saving faith usually grows step by step through trials and inward struggles against temptation (1 Tim. 6:12; James 1:3–4). Temporary faith withers under persecution (Matt. 13:21), but saving faith perseveres and grows purer and stronger through persecution (Heb. 11:24–26; 1 Pet. 1:5–7). This is because saving faith draws life from Christ and communes with him in the power of his death and resurrection (Gal. 2:20). Saving faith receives Christ (John 1:12). Wilhelmus à Brakel said, "Temporary believers know of no union with Christ by faith."[29]

3. Saving faith is not *confidence in miracles*. Theologians sometimes call this type *faith of miracles* or *miraculous faith*. In the New Testament, people received miracles from Christ and his apostles through faith in God's power.[30] However, faith of miracles is not saving faith. When Christ

29. Brakel, *The Christian's Reasonable Service*, 2:292.
30. Matt. 9:28–30; Mark 6:5–6; Acts 14:9.

was in Jerusalem, "many believed in his name, when they saw the miracles, which he did"; however, "Jesus did not commit himself unto them, because he knew all men," but told one of them that he must be "born again" (John 2:23–3:3). Christ will reject many miracle workers on judgment day with the horrifying words "I never knew you" (Matt. 7:22–23). Judas was commissioned as an apostle to work miracles (10:1–4, 8), but he was a wicked man (John 6:70). Paul complained that Jews looked for miracles, but said that saving faith belongs to those who trust in Christ crucified by the call of God (1 Cor. 1:22–24).[31]

4. Saving faith is not *blind submission to church leaders*. Faith rests in the gospel revealed by God, not the traditions of men (Gal. 1:11–14). The Lord warns, "In vain they do worship me, teaching for doctrines the commandments of men" (Matt. 15:9). Some representatives of medieval and Counter-Reformation Roman Catholicism fell into this error through the doctrine of *implicit faith* (*fides implicita*).[32] Medieval theologians taught that simple people need not understand Christian theology, but have only a basic faith in God and Christ while submitting to the church's guidance.[33] The doctrine of implicit faith originated in a legitimate distinction between the understanding required of pastors and the simple faith needed for salvation, but it resulted in abuse of authority, neglect of biblical teaching, and dependence on the sacraments for salvation.[34] Pope Innocent IV (d. 1254) went so far as to say that it is sufficient "for the simple, and perhaps, for all laymen" to "believe that God is, and that he is the rewarder of all the good," and otherwise to believe "implicitly" that "everything which the Catholic Church believes is true."[35] It is hard to see how such

31. On miracles and their relation to faith, see chap. 7.

32. Muller, *Dictionary of Latin and Greek Theological Terms*, 122; cf. Vos, *Reformed Dogmatics*, 4:95.

33. Lombard, *The Sentences*, 3.25.2 (3:108); and Aquinas, *Summa Theologica*, Part 2.2, Q. 2, Arts. 5–8. This was based on Gregory the Great's allegorical interpretation of "the oxen were plowing, and the asses feeding beside them" (Job 1:14) to refer to the dependence of simpleminded people on the understanding of the wise. Gregory the Great, *Morals on the Book of Job*, 3 vols. (Oxford: John Henry Parker, 1844), 1.2.49, on Job 1:14–15 (1:100).

34. Turretin, *Institutes*, 15.9 (2:564–68).

35. "Simplicibus, & etiam forte omnibus laicis . . . credere quia Deus est, & quod est remunerator omnium bonorum . . . implicite . . . credere verum esse, quicquid credit ecclesia catholica." Innocent IV, *Super Libros Quinque Decretalium* (Frankfurt, 1570), 1.1; English translation adapted from Reinhold Seeberg, *Text-Book of the History of Doctrines*, trans. Charles E. Hay, 2 vols., rev. ed. (Philadelphia: Lutheran Publication Society, 1905), 2:90. See also the statement of Gabriel Biel, "I believe as the church believes." Gabriel Biel, *Sacri Canonis Missae*, lect. 12B, cited in Seeberg, *Text-Book of the History of Doctrines*, 2:196. Such implicit faith was exemplified by the story of a charcoal maker ("collier") who, when asked about his faith, replied that he believed what the church believes, and this faith supposedly proved to be enough to defeat the Devil. Christopher Fowler, "The Scripture Was Written for the Use of the Laity, and Should

faith could be called faith in Jesus Christ. Counter-Reformation theologians, in their zeal to attack the Reformers' translation of the Bible into the languages of the common people, promoted a devotion based on ignorance.[36] However, John Calvin said, "faith rests not on ignorance, but on knowledge.... We do not obtain salvation . . . because we are prepared to embrace as true whatever the church has prescribed."[37] Authentic "implicit faith" consists in receiving whatever God's Word says with a teachable spirit (James 1:21).[38] People with poor understanding and memory may have genuine faith, but we cannot remove knowledge from the essence of faith and reduce faith to mere assent to the church.[39] Ignorance of the Lord destroys souls (Hos. 4:6).

5. Saving faith is not *claiming earthly blessings with confidence*. Preachers such as E. W. Kenyon (1867–1948) and Kenneth Hagin (1917–2003) attempted to turn faith into a supernatural law for obtaining health and wealth, even the power to bring such blessings into reality by one's words.[40] Hagin said, "Faith is laying hold of the unrealities of hope and bringing them into the realm of reality."[41] On the contrary, faith is not power to control our circumstances, but dependence on the Lord to save us and bring us to glory. Job lost his health and wealth, but said, "Though he slay me, yet will I trust in him" (Job 13:15). Paul says, "We were pressed out of measure, above strength, insomuch that we despaired even of life: but we had the sentence of death in ourselves, that we should not trust in ourselves, but in God which raiseth the dead" (2 Cor. 1:8–9).

Be Translated into Known Tongues, That They May Understand It; And Should Be Heard and Read by Them," in *Puritan Sermons, 1659–1689*, 5:572–73. See Albertus Pighius, *Hierarchiae Ecclesiasticae* (Coloniae Agrippinae [Cologne or Köln], Germany: Arnoldi Birckmanni, 1572), 1.5 (38D–39A).

36. Henry Cole (c. 1500–c. 1579) allegedly said in a 1559 disputation, "Ignorance is the mother of devotion." *The Works of John Jewel*, ed. Richard William Jelf, 8 vols. (Oxford: Oxford University Press, 1848), 1:32, 125, 156; 3:305, 485–87. The Douay-Rheims Bible counseled a Roman Catholic, if pressed by Protestants over his faith, simply to say that he was "a Catholic man" and leave the reasons to the Roman Catholic Church. It was said to be better for the common people to hear the Mass and repeat prayers in Latin even though they did not understand the language. *The New Testament of Jesus Christ, Translated Faithfully into English out of the Authentical Latin . . . in the English College of Rhemes* (Rhemes [Rheims or Reims], France: John Fogney, 1582), on Luke 12:11 and 1 Corinthians 14 (177, 462–63).

37. Calvin, *Institutes*, 3.2.2.

38. Calvin, *Institutes*, 3.2.5; and Ames, *The Marrow of Theology*, 2.5.34–37 (244).

39. Perkins, *A Reformed Catholic*, in *Works*, 7:122, 124.

40. Kate Bowler, *Blessed: A History of the American Prosperity Gospel* (Oxford: Oxford University Press, 2013), 45–49.

41. Kenneth E. Hagin, *What Faith Is*, 5th ed. (Tulsa, OK: Hagin Evangelistic Association, 1972), 3. Virtually the same statement appears in E. W. Kenyon, *The Two Kinds of Faith: Faith's Secret Revealed* (Lynnwood, WA: Kenyon's Gospel Publishing, 1998), Kindle ebook, chap. 2.

6. Saving faith is not merely *saying a prayer or making a physical motion*. Paul wrote that "with the heart man believeth unto righteousness" (Rom. 10:10). No one is saved by physical action. Some modern evangelistic practices by well-meaning but mistaken preachers may lead people to think that faith in Christ means raising one's hand in a meeting, standing up, walking to the front of a room, or repeating the words of a prayer.[42] This error amounts to little more than evangelical sacramentalism, no different in essence than the belief that eating bread and drinking wine confers eternal life. The Lord warned against drawing near to him outwardly without turning to him with the heart (Matt. 15:8–9).

The Object of Saving Faith

The saving power of faith lies not in faith itself but in the object of faith. The object of saving faith consists of the invisible God as he reveals himself in his word through the Mediator, Jesus Christ. Faith particularly takes as its object what cannot be known by the senses because it is invisible or future: "Faith is the substance of things hoped for, the evidence of things not seen" (Heb. 11:1). By faith people live "as seeing him who is invisible" (v. 27) and pursue his promised blessing, "not having received the promises, but having seen them afar off" (v. 13). They please God by faith, for they "believe that he is, and that he is a rewarder of them that diligently seek him" (v. 6). Augustine said, "We believe in order that we may know, we do not know in order that we may believe. For what we shall yet know, neither eye hath seen, nor ear heard, nor hath it entered the heart of man. For what is faith, but believing what you see not?"[43]

The words translated as "substance" (*hypostasis*) and "evidence" (*elenchos*) in Hebrews 11:1 indicate that faith gives a present and proven reality in the heart to things not yet experienced by the senses. Perkins commented, "Saving faith has this power and property to take that thing in itself invisible and never yet seen and so lively to represent it to the heart of the believer and to the eye of his mind as that after a sort he presently sees and enjoys that invisible thing and rejoices in that sight and enjoying of it."[44] Vos explained that faith "imparts to us proof and reality" of "things that one does not yet possess," and faith is like evidence because

42. Iain Murray, *The Invitation System* (Edinburgh: Banner of Truth, 1967), 3–6, 26–30.
43. Augustine, *Tractates on the Gospel of John*, 40.9, in *NPNF*[1], 7:228.
44. Perkins, *A Cloud of Witnesses*, on Heb. 11:1, in *Works*, 3:8.

"by my faith I am assured of an invisible entity, as I am assured of something by a proof."[45] Francis Turretin argued that faith is so described "not only because it makes future goods subsist speculatively in the intellect by assent, but especially practically in the heart by trust and hope . . . as the examples of Noah, Abraham, Moses, and others prove" in Hebrews 11.[46] Hence, Paul says, "we are always confident. . . . For we walk by faith, not by sight" (2 Cor. 5:6–7).

The hoped-for but presently unseen object of saving faith is Jesus Christ and the salvation and glory that he brings. This is a great theme of the writings of John.[47] The call of the gospel is "Believe on the Lord Jesus Christ, and thou shalt be saved" (Acts 16:31). Paul preaches of "faith toward our Lord Jesus Christ" and "faith in Christ" (20:21; 24:24). He writes of "faith of Jesus Christ" (Rom. 3:22; Gal. 2:16; 3:22) and "faith of Christ" (Phil. 3:9), identifying not faith's origin but its object. Peter writes of "the appearing of Jesus Christ: whom having not seen, ye love; in whom, though now ye see him not, yet believing, ye rejoice with joy unspeakable and full of glory: receiving the end of your faith, even the salvation of your souls" (1 Pet. 1:7–9).[48]

Though Christ is the immediate object of faith, in grasping Christ, faith apprehends God (Acts 16:31, 34; Titus 3:8), for Christ is God's Mediator in his revelation, redemption, and reign. The Lord Jesus said, "He that believeth on me, believeth not on me, but on him that sent me" (John 12:44).[49] Faith in Christ does not take the eyes of believers off God, but instead focuses them on God, because God is in Christ and Christ is in God (14:11; 2 Cor. 5:19). William Ames explained, "Christ as redeemer is the mediate but not the ultimate object of faith, for we believe through Christ in God."[50] Those redeemed by Christ's blood "by him do believe in God, that raised him up from the dead, and gave him glory; that your faith and hope might be in God" (1 Pet. 1:21). In the "act of faith," the person called by God "wholly leans upon Christ as his Savior and through Christ upon God" (John 3:15–16; 1 Pet. 1:21),[51] for faith looks to Christ as the One

45. Vos, *Reformed Dogmatics*, 4:77–78.
46. Turretin, *Institutes*, 15.10.11 (2:570).
47. John 1:12; 3:15–18, 36; 6:29, 35, 40, 47, 69; 9:35; 11:27; 14:1; 17:20; 20:31; 1 John 3:23; 5:1, 5, 10, 13, etc.
48. On Christ as the special object of faith, see also Acts 10:43; 11:17; 19:4; Rom. 10:9; Gal. 2:16; Phil. 1:29; Col. 1:4; 2:5; 1 Tim. 1:16; 2 Tim. 3:15; 1 Pet. 2:6.
49. On believing in him who "sent" Christ, see also John 5:24; 6:29; 11:42; 17:8, 21.
50. Ames, *The Marrow of Theology*, 1.3.8 (81).
51. Ames, *The Marrow of Theology*, 1.26.26 (159).

sent by God.[52] This is not to place Christ in a subordinate position to God, for Christ is God, the second person of the Trinity (John 1:1). Rather, it is to recognize that Christ is the only Mediator. Samuel Willard said that the "ultimate object of our faith can be no other than God alone. . . . For he alone can save us from all misery and confer upon us complete felicity." However, "the immediate object of our faith is . . . Jesus Christ, God-man, Mediator," for "it is certain that no sinful man can come to God in any other way but by him" (cf. John 14:6).[53]

Faith rests in the Lord God as our supreme good (Pss. 4:5–7; 27:4, 13). Ames said, "Our true and highest good consists in the union and communion we have with God. . . . He actually communes with us personally, according to the well-known formula of the covenant, 'I will be your God.'"[54] Saving faith engages the soul with trust that the Lord is the Savior from all evil and "the overflowing fountain of all good," to quote the Belgic Confession (Art. 1).[55] In one early Protestant confession of faith, Wolfgang Capito (1478–1541) and Martin Bucer wrote that "believing the gospel" we are "fully satisfied with one God," the perpetual fountain of blessing that abundantly overflows into our lives.[56]

Faith looks to God as the only One who is all-sufficient to save and satisfy. Ames wrote, "Faith is the resting of the heart on God, the author of life and eternal salvation."[57] He noted that saving faith is properly "trust" or, in other biblical terminology, to "lean upon and rely on," and so "to believe in God, therefore, is to cling to God by believing, to lean on God, to rest in God as our all-sufficient life and salvation."[58]

The Threefold Nature of Saving Faith

Wilhelmus Schortinghuis said that "genuine faith" consists of "a literal, and especially an experiential knowledge of the truths of the Gospel, God, oneself, Christ, and the way of grace; of a warm-hearted and willing assent; and of a trust that finds refuge with God in Christ."[59] These are not three kinds of faith, but three interwoven aspects of saving faith.

52. John 5:24, 37–38; 6:29; 11:42; 12:44; 17:8, 21.
53. Willard, *A Compleat Body of Divinity*, 786.
54. Ames, *A Sketch of the Christian's Catechism*, 8.
55. *The Three Forms of Unity*, 17.
56. Tetrapolitan Confession, chap. 4, in *Reformed Confessions*, 1:144. The original translation reads "the perennial fountain of blessings that is copiously effluent."
57. Ames, *The Marrow of Theology*, 1.3.1 (80).
58. Ames, *The Marrow of Theology*, 1.3.13–15 (82).
59. Schortinghuis, *Essential Truths in the Heart of a Christian*, 24.4 (89).

Historical Background: Saving Faith Is More Than Assent

Over the course of Christian history, the church has matured in its understanding of the doctrine of faith, especially with respect to faith's relation to assent. Augustine said, "Belief itself is nothing else than to think with assent."[60] This may suggest that faith is an act entirely of the intellect, but he also says that "faith . . . is in the will of man," for it involves the choice of the will as moved by grace.[61] Faith in the Word of God is foundational to love, both because a man "cannot love what he does not believe to exist,"[62] and because "faith obtains the Spirit in fuller measure, the Spirit sheds love abroad in us, and love fulfils the law."[63]

Peter Lombard (c. 1096–1160) taught the doctrine of unformed faith (*fides informis*)—that is, that faith consists of mental assent to God's revelation and lacks saving life and merit until God infuses love into the soul as the "form" of faith.[64] Thomas Aquinas, citing Augustine, defined faith as "to think with assent."[65] Faith, in Aquinas's teaching, definitely resides in the intellect but attains completion only when accompanied by love in the will.[66] Faith is meritorious when it is "accompanied by charity" or love, because then "the act of believing is an act of the intellect assenting to the divine truth at the command of the will moved by the grace of God."[67] Aquinas added, "Charity is called the form of faith because it quickens the act of faith"—that is, brings it to life.[68] Aquinas believed that "lifeless faith" (faith that produces no works, James 2:20) is essentially the same intellectual disposition as "living faith," but cannot save because the will lacks love.[69] Against the Reformers, the Council of Trent declared that we cannot be united to Christ or justified by faith alone; love also must be infused into the heart as our righteousness.[70]

---

60. Augustine, *On the Predestination of the Saints*, 5.2, in *NPNF*[1], 5:499.
61. Augustine, *On the Predestination of the Saints*, 10.5, in *NPNF*[1], 5:503.
62. Augustine, *On Christian Doctrine*, 1.37.41, in *NPNF*[1], 2:533.
63. Augustine, Letters, 145.3, in *NPNF*[1], 1:496.
64. Lombard, *The Sentences*, 3.23.4–5 (3:99). On unformed faith, see James T. Bretzke, *Consecrated Phrases: A Latin Theological Dictionary, Latin Expressions Commonly Found in Theological Writings*, 3rd ed. (Collegeville, MN: Liturgical Press, 2013), 82; *Catechism of the Catholic Church*, secs. 1815, 1827; Wollebius, *Compendium*, 1.29.10 (163); Turretin, *Institutes*, 15.13.1–4 (2:580–81); and Bavinck, *Reformed Dogmatics*, 4:109.
65. Aquinas, *Summa Theologica*, Part 2.2, Q. 2, Art. 1.
66. Aquinas, *Summa Theologica*, Part 2.2, Q. 4, Arts. 2–3.
67. Aquinas, *Summa Theologica*, Part 2.2, Q. 2, Art. 9, Reply Obj. 1, Answer.
68. Aquinas, *Summa Theologica*, Part 2.2, Q. 4, Art. 3, Reply Obj. 1.
69. Aquinas, *Summa Theologica*, Part 2.2, Q. 4, Art. 4.
70. Council of Trent, session 6, chap. 7 and canons 11–12, in *The Creeds of Christendom*, ed. Schaff, 2:96, 112–13. See *Catechism of the Catholic Church*, sec. 1991.

Saving faith will never be without love (Gal. 5:6; 1 John 5:1–5). Faith without love is worthless (1 Cor. 13:2), and "faith, if it hath not works, is dead" (James 2:17). However, saving faith is not mere belief in the mind that must be supplemented by love, but a living trust that breathes the grace of the Holy Spirit in all its operations. The Reformers and their heirs explained faith in terms of a combination of elements to highlight the fact that faith is more than mere assent to the truth but involves the trust of the whole heart.[71] Petrus van Mastricht said, "Saving faith consists neither in the intellect alone nor in the will alone, but in the whole spiritual life of a person."[72]

A simple but comprehensive analysis of faith that many theologians have used helpfully presents faith in three dimensions: knowledge (*notitia*), assent (*assensus*), and confident trust (*fiducia*).[73] Warfield said, "No true faith has arisen unless there has been a perception of the object to be believed or believed in, an assent to its worthiness to be believed or believed in, and a commitment of ourselves to it as true and trustworthy."[74] John Murray wrote, "As *assensus* is cognition passed into conviction, so *fiducia* is conviction passed into confidence. Herein resides the unique and distinguishing character of this faith."[75]

In describing saving faith in this threefold manner, we must avoid a bifurcation of faith into saving and nonsaving elements, as if saving faith consisted of historical faith in knowledge and assent plus saving

71. Philip Melanchthon, *The Chief Theological Topics: Loci Praecipui Theologici 1559*, trans. J. A. O. Preus, 2nd ed. (St. Louis, MO: Concordia, 2011), 152; Perkins, *An Exposition of the Symbol*, in *Works*, 5:11, 13–14; Ames, *The Marrow of Theology*, 1.3.2–3, 18–19; 2.5.12–16 (80–81, 241); John Preston, *The Breast-plate of Faith and Love* (1634; facsimile repr., Edinburgh: Banner of Truth, 1979), 1:40–41; Witsius, *The Economy of the Covenants*, 3.7.26 (1:384); Brown, *Questions and Answers on the Shorter Catechism*, 289; and Gill, *Body of Divinity*, 742.

72. Van Mastricht, *Theoretical-Practical Theology*, 1.2.1.22 (2:15). On faith as an act of the heart, see Pss. 28:7; 112:7; Prov. 3:5; Rom. 10:9–10.

73. Perkins, *An Exposition of the Symbol*, in *Works*, 5:18; Ames, *The Marrow of Theology*, 2.5.12 (241); Wollebius, *Compendium*, 1.29.7 (162); Turretin, *Institutes*, 15.8.3 (2:561); Brakel, *The Christian's Reasonable Service*, 2:270–82; van Mastricht, *Theoretical-Practical Theology*, 1.2.1.41 (2:31); Gill, *Body of Divinity*, 736; Hodge, *Outlines of Theology*, 466; Warfield, "On Faith in Its Psychological Aspects," in *Biblical and Theological Studies*, 402–3; Vos, *Reformed Dogmatics*, 4:115; Murray, *Collected Writings*, 2:257–59; Berkhof, *Systematic Theology*, 503–5; Grudem, *Systematic Theology*, 709–10; Ferguson, *The Christian Life*, 63–67; Reymond, *A New Systematic Theology of the Christian Faith*, 726–29; Michael S. Horton, *The Christian Faith: A Systematic Theology for Pilgrims on the Way* (Grand Rapids, MI: Zondervan, 2011), 583; Demarest, *The Cross and Salvation*, 259–60; and Letham, *Systematic Theology*, 672–73. For a Lutheran view of faith, see Chemnitz, *Loci Theologici*, II.13.2, in *Works*, 8:931. Later Lutheran orthodox writers appear to have adopted the threefold description of faith. Heinrich Schmid, *The Doctrinal Theology of the Evangelical Lutheran Church, Verified from the Original Sources*, rev. Charles A. Hay and Henry E. Jacobs (Philadelphia: Lutheran Publication Society, 1889), 419–20.

74. Warfield, "On Faith in Its Psychological Aspects," in *Biblical and Theological Studies*, 402.

75. Murray, *Collected Writings*, 2:258.

trust.[76] Turretin wrote, "For in justifying faith, knowledge is deep, cleaving to the inmost heart; experimental, not derived from hearing alone, but confirmed by the sense of experience (1 Pet. 2:3; Phil. 1:9); 'living and practical,' bearing with it not only light, but also heat (1 John 2:4)." He said that the assent of justifying faith "is certain and solid . . . so as to be carried into the things to be believed by an action as it were intuitive."[77] Turretin added, "Trust is so of the essence of faith that it cannot be called faith which is destitute of such trust."[78] Alexander Comrie (1706–1774) embraced the threefold model but wisely "rejected the definition of saving faith as historical knowledge *plus* assent and trust."[79] He asserted that saving faith possesses "a supernatural [spiritual] knowledge which the Holy Spirit, by means of the Word, works in the hearts of the elect when effectually calling them," so that "the objects of faith . . . are unveiled by divine light."[80] For Comrie, "Assent is faith's 'amen' as it embraces spiritual knowledge. . . . By spiritual assent, the believer 'takes refuge' in Christ to embrace Him and to find rest only in Him."[81] Although knowledge of the Scriptures and historical faith often precede saving faith, the difference between them is not a matter of "measure or degree" but "principle and essence," Herman Bavinck said. This is so because in saving faith, knowledge and assent have a different character than those possessed by the unregenerate, being seen in "another light" and embraced in a more personal, spiritual manner.[82]

Saving Faith as Experiential Knowledge of God

Faith must start with the knowledge of God as he reveals himself in the Holy Scriptures. Paul writes, "How then shall they call on him in whom they have not believed? And how shall they believe in him of whom they have not heard? And how shall they hear without a preacher? . . . So faith cometh by hearing, and hearing by the word of God" (Rom. 10:14, 17). John MacArthur and Richard Mayhue say, "The biblical conception of faith is not an existential leap in the dark or a sentimental, wish-upon-a-star

76. Kersten, *Reformed Dogmatics*, 2:400–402.
77. Turretin, *Institutes*, 15.15.6 (2:589).
78. Turretin, *Institutes*, 15.10.5 (2:569).
79. Joel R. Beeke, *The Quest for Full Assurance: The Legacy of Calvin and His Successors* (Edinburgh: Banner of Truth, 1999), 228.
80. Cited in Beeke, *The Quest for Full Assurance*, 228.
81. Beeke, *The Quest for Full Assurance*, 229.
82. Bavinck, *Reformed Dogmatics*, 4:127.

kind of hope. . . . True faith is based in knowledge; it has its sure and solid foundation in the knowledge of divinely revealed truth."[83]

Christian faith cannot subsist on personal feelings about spiritual matters, no matter how sincere. Such a faith would amount to "empty superstitions," Robert Reymond said, and would "fatally wound Christianity in the heart."[84] Anyone who rests his faith on spiritual experience without standing on the clear teachings of the written Word remains in utter darkness (Isa. 8:20). We must not follow our own hearts (Num. 15:39). Though it may be popular to be "spiritual but not religious" and to follow one's inner light as if it were the leading of the Spirit, the results are disastrous, for everyone will naturally do what is right in his own eyes (Judg. 21:25).[85] G. K. Chesterton (1874–1936) said, "Of all conceivable forms of enlightenment the worst is what these people call the Inner Light. Of all horrible religions the most horrible is the worship of the god within. . . . That Jones shall worship the god within him turns out ultimately to mean that Jones shall worship Jones."[86]

The division between faith and the written Word of God is further encouraged by the tendency in modern theology to reduce faith to an existential encounter with God. Friedrich Schleiermacher spoke for modern liberalism when he denied that faith in Christ is founded on the authority of the Bible and instead taught that faith arises from man's universal sense of dependence on God.[87] Karl Barth defined faith as "the gift of meeting" between God and man,[88] consistent with his teaching that God's Word is not the Bible but instead God's act through the fallible human writings in the Bible.[89]

Faith cannot stand on personal experience but must have an objective basis in the revealed truth of God. We are saved through "belief of the truth" (2 Thess. 2:13). Christ rebuked people for being "slow of heart to

83. MacArthur and Mayhue, eds., *Biblical Doctrine*, 596.

84. Reymond, *A New Systematic Theology of the Christian Faith*, 727.

85. A recent study of young adults showed that those identifying as "spiritual but not religious" are more likely to commit crimes than people in any other category, including those who reject all spirituality. Sung Joon Jang and Aaron B. Franzen, "Is Being 'Spiritual' Enough without Being Religious? A Study of Violent and Property Crimes among Emerging Adults," *Criminology* 51, no. 3 (August 2013): 595–627, available at http://www.baylorisr.org/wp-content/uploads/Jang Franzen-2013.pdf.

86. G. K. Chesterton, *Orthodoxy* (New York: John Lane, 1908), 138.

87. Schleiermacher, *The Christian Faith*, 2:591, 593; cf. 1:33–34.

88. Karl Barth, *Dogmatics in Outline*, trans. G. T. Thomson (New York: Harper and Row, 1959), 15.

89. On Barth's view of divine revelation, see *RST*, 1:304–9.

believe all that the prophets have spoken" (Luke 24:25). He prayed to his Father, "Thy word is truth" (John 17:17). The pathway to faith in Christ is to search the Scriptures (5:39; Acts 17:11). We need nothing else, and nothing else will persuade us if we refuse to believe the Bible (Luke 16:27–31). Calvin said, "This, then, is the true knowledge of Christ, if we receive him as he is offered by the Father: namely, clothed with his gospel."[90]

Though the knowledge of God's Word is essential to salvation, this knowledge must surpass information in the head and penetrate to the heart. God's wrath falls on those who refuse to know him even when they have his Word.[91] Those who do not know God hate him, his Son, and his people (John 15:19, 21; 16:3). The knowledge of God is the greatest treasure, more valuable than wisdom, power, or wealth (Jer. 9:23–24), and God promises in his covenant that his people will know him by the supernatural work of his grace (31:34; Hos. 2:20; cf. Isa. 11:9). Paul said, "I count all things but loss for the excellency of the knowledge of Christ Jesus my Lord" (Phil. 3:8). He said this because, as Christ explained, such knowledge is not merely information but the very essence of eternal life (John 17:3). This is a knowledge that liberates sinners from their slavery to sin (8:32, 34). Those who know God listen to his Word, repent of sin, keep his commandments, and love God and one another.[92] The experiential knowledge of God is the root of all spiritual life and godliness (2 Pet. 1:2–3; 3:18). A. W. Pink said, "A theoretical knowledge of Christ is not sufficient," but "there must be a spiritual and supernatural knowledge of Christ imparted by the Holy Spirit."[93]

There is a close relationship between faith and the knowledge of God (Isa. 43:10–11; John 17:6–8). Psalm 9:9–10 says, "The LORD also will be a refuge for the oppressed, a refuge in times of trouble. And they that know thy name will put their trust in thee: for thou, LORD, hast not forsaken them that seek thee." Calvin said, "Now we shall possess a right definition of faith if we call it a firm and certain knowledge of God's benevolence towards us, founded upon the truth of the freely given promise in Christ, both revealed to our minds and sealed upon our hearts through the Holy Spirit."[94] He clarified that faith "is more of the heart than of the brain, and more of the disposition than of the understanding."[95]

---

90. Calvin, *Institutes*, 3.2.6.
91. Ps. 79:6; Jer. 9:3, 6; 10:25.
92. 1 John 2:3–4, 13–14; 3:6; 4:6–8.
93. Arthur W. Pink, *Studies on Saving Faith* (Swengel, PA: Reiner, 1974), 78, 80.
94. Calvin, *Institutes*, 3.2.7.
95. Calvin, *Institutes*, 3.2.8.

The Bible compares this inward knowledge to an inward sense of God. Psalm 34:8 says, "O taste and see that the LORD is good: blessed is the man that trusteth in him" (cf. 1 Pet. 2:2–4). A dietitian may understand the chemical components of a particular food and its interactions with the human body, but if he has a medical condition that prevents his tongue and stomach from operating correctly, he cannot taste and digest the food. Faith acts from a spiritual sense of God's goodness, a real relish of God that no unregenerate man has.[96] Salvation is called seeing God in Christ.[97] Thomas Goodwin said that this knowledge is of a different kind than what the natural man sees in his sin-darkened mind. The unbeliever is like a deaf man who can study the principles of music but never hears the beauty of its harmonies—but the soul of the regenerate has new eyes and ears.[98] Bavinck wrote, "To the regenerate person, believing in God or in Christ as such is just as natural as it is for everyone to believe in the world of the senses."[99]

We exercise faith, Paul explains, because the light of God's glory not only shines on us externally in the gospel but "hath shined in our hearts, to give the light of the knowledge of the glory of God in the face of Jesus Christ" (2 Cor. 4:6).[100] Those who see this divine light recognize that God is the all-sufficient One. They know him and trust him (Ps. 36:7–10). Jonathan Edwards said that such illumination consists of "a true sense of the divine and superlative excellency of the things of religion: a real sense of the excellency of God, and Jesus Christ, and of the work of redemption, and the ways and works of God revealed in the gospel."[101] The light of Christ in the soul effectively transforms the person (2 Cor. 3:18). Edwards wrote, "It will turn the heart to God as the fountain of good, and to choose him for the only portion. This light, and this only, will bring the soul to . . . Christ."[102] Thus, Vos said that "in saving faith there is something different and more than the old knowledge of historical faith. . . . A new knowledge arises—completely different and to be compared with nothing else—which only a true believer, regenerated by God's Spirit, knows."[103]

96. Hoeksema, *Reformed Dogmatics*, 2:75.
97. John 1:14; 6:40; 12:44–46; 14:9; 1 John 3:6; 3 John 11; cf. 2 Cor. 4:4, 6.
98. Goodwin, *The Object and Acts of Justifying Faith*, in *Works*, 8:259.
99. Bavinck, *Reformed Dogmatics*, 4:101.
100. See the discussion in chap. 15 of saving illumination as an act of new creation by vital union with Christ.
101. Edwards, *A Divine and Supernatural Light*, in *WJE*, 17:413. See Edwards, *Religious Affections*, in *WJE*, 2:272.
102. Edwards, *A Divine and Supernatural Light*, in *WJE*, 17:424.
103. Vos, *Reformed Dogmatics*, 4:100.

Experiential knowledge of God brings with it a humbling knowledge of ourselves as those created in God's image but ruined by sin. As Calvin said, until we raise our thoughts to God, "we flatter ourselves most sweetly, and fancy ourselves all but demigods." However, gazing on God is like looking at the brilliance of the sun: God dazzles us and fills us with "dread and wonder" at our wickedness, foolishness, and weakness.[104] We cry out, "Woe is me! for I am undone; because I am a man of unclean lips, and I dwell in the midst of a people of unclean lips: for mine eyes have seen the King, the LORD of hosts" (Isa. 6:5). Though God often grants a conviction of the guilt of sin and the soul's liability to damnation prior to saving faith,[105] the evil of sin only appears when our eyes are opened to see the beauty of God by faith. However, faith's preoccupation is not with self or even with the evil of sin, but with the glory of God. Brakel said that faith's objective is to glorify God: "In exercising faith one glorifies God in all His perfections, as they shine forth in the face of Jesus Christ."[106]

Saving Faith as Submissive Assent to God's Word

The immediate object of saving faith is the word of God. All who do not believe the truth of the gospel are damned, but God has chosen his people for salvation through a Spirit-worked belief in the truth (2 Thess. 2:12–13). Philip Melanchthon said, "Faith is constant assent to God's every word, and it does not exist outside of God's Spirit renewing and enlightening our hearts."[107] Faith involves an intellectual submission to the gospel.[108] As we noted earlier in our discussion of the biblical terminology of faith, faith in God's word rests upon his power and faithfulness to do what he promises (Rom. 4:21; Heb. 11:11). Ames said, "Faith is the virtue by which, clinging to the faithfulness of God, we lean upon him, so that we may obtain what he gives to us."[109]

Faith in Christ embraces the doctrines of the Bible with the assent of belief. Faith assents to the Word because it is God's testimony in Christ, and God is true (John 3:33–34). We must never set faith in Christ against

104. Calvin, *Institutes*, 1.2.2–3.

105. See chap. 13 on preparatory grace.

106. Brakel, *The Christian's Reasonable Service*, 2:290.

107. Philip Melanchthon, *Commonplaces: Loci Communes 1521*, trans. Christian Preus (St. Louis, MO: Concordia, 2014), 119.

108. Donald Macleod, *A Faith to Live By: Understanding Christian Doctrine*, rev. ed. (Fearn, Ross-shire, Scotland: Christian Focus, 2002), 173.

109. Ames, *The Marrow of Theology*, 2.5.11 (241).

faith in the propositions of the Word. Christ said to Martha, "I am the resurrection, and the life: he that believeth in me, though he were dead, yet shall he live: and whosoever liveth and believeth in me shall never die. Believest thou this?" (11:25–26). He gave her propositional truth and asked her if she believed it. She responded, "Yea, Lord: I believe that thou art the Christ, the Son of God, which should come into the world" (v. 27). God gave us the Word so that we may "believe that" (*pisteuō hoti*) his teachings are true.[110]

Saving assent to the truth is not a mere idea in the mind but hearty *submission* to the word of God. Paul wrote of the "obedience of faith" (Rom. 1:5, Greek; 16:26). His ministry aimed at bringing the nations to obedience (15:18), which is submissive imitation of Christ (Phil. 2:5–13; cf. Heb. 5:8–9). The gospel demands obedience, and those who do not obey the gospel are not saved.[111] What did Paul mean by obedience to the gospel? He described it in Romans 6:17: "But God be thanked, that ye were the servants of sin, but ye have obeyed from the heart that form of doctrine which was delivered you." Prior to conversion, the human mind is hostile to God's truth (1:18; 8:7). By God's grace, Christians have been converted from being slaves of sin to people who submit to the word of God. It is clear that Paul had submission to authority in view because in this context he wrote of servants obeying their masters (6:16). Paul's use of the term "obedience of faith" indicates "that true obedience to God is inseparable from faith and that true faith inevitably issues in obedience—indeed, the very act of faith is viewed as an expression of obedience."[112]

The assent of faith is sometimes expressed in the verb translated as "hear" (Hebrew *shama'*; Greek *akouō*). Though to "hear" may mean merely to detect sound or gain information by one's ears (Gen. 3:8; Matt. 2:3), it may also take the sense of agreeing with the speaker and acting according to what he says (Gen. 3:17; 37:27 [KJV mg.]; Matt. 18:15–16).[113] Moses said, "Hear, O Israel, the statutes and judgments which I speak in your ears this day, that ye may learn them, and keep, and do them" (Deut. 5:1). The Father says, "This is my beloved Son, in whom I am well pleased; hear ye him" (Matt. 17:5). An essential part of rightly hearing God is as-

110. For example, see John 11:42; 13:19; 20:31; Heb. 11:6.

111. Rom. 10:16; 2 Thess. 1:8; cf. John 3:36 (Greek); Gal. 3:1; 5:7; 1 Pet. 1:22; 4:17.

112. *NIDOTTE*, 4:550.

113. To "hear" (*shama'*) someone's "voice" or "word" often means to obey him. Gen. 22:18; 26:5; Ex. 19:5; Josh. 1:18; Jer. 11:3, 8, etc.

senting to his word—the "hearing of faith" (Gal. 3:2, 5). Christ says to the children of the Devil, "Ye cannot hear my word. . . . Because I tell you the truth, ye believe me not" (John 8:43, 45). He adds, "Ye believe not, because ye are not of my sheep. . . . My sheep hear my voice, and I know them, and they follow me" (10:26–27). Caspar Olevianus wrote, "Once we know the will of God, faith is to assent to Him in the whole of His Word as one who is true and omnipotent. It is thus to give Him glory and not to give consideration to anything in ourselves or other creatures that appears contrary to His Word."[114]

As we said earlier when discussing faith as knowledge, the Bible calls faith not only hearing but also seeing, the result of an inward spiritual illumination by which the believer perceives the glory of God and Christ (2 Cor. 4:6). Physical vision gives an assurance of the reality of what we see—seeing is believing. Goodwin said that since faith "is a spiritual sight and a spiritual sense, it hath a certainty joined with it." Thus, faith is called "assurance" (1 Thess. 1:5; Heb. 10:22; cf. Rom. 4:21), not that it always entails assurance of one's salvation, but it does entail "an assured persuasion" of what is believed.[115] Edwards said that this spiritual sight of divine realities brings with it "a conviction of the truth and reality of them." It does so by removing "the prejudices that are in the heart" and engaging "the attention of the mind" with the beauty of God and his will, and also by displaying to the heart the superlative divine glory of God. The light shining in the gospel "is a kind of intuitive and immediate evidence," so that those effectually called "believe the doctrines of God's Word to be divine, because they see divinity in them."[116] Supernatural illumination produces supernatural assent.

Saving faith tastes God's goodness (Ps. 34:8) and sees his grace and truth in Christ (John 1:14). Thus, it not only engages the believer's assent to the truth of the gospel but also to the beauty and delightfulness of Christ. The gospel, as Thomas Manton (1620–1677) said, presents its message of salvation "not only as true, but good," and consequently "not only an intellectual assent is required, but a practical assent"—that is, "consent to choose it for my portion and happiness" and "confidence and dependence upon Christ for it."[117] Johann Heidegger said that this

114. Olevianus, *An Exposition of the Apostles' Creed*, 16.
115. Goodwin, *The Object and Acts of Justifying Faith*, in *Works*, 8:265.
116. Edwards, *A Divine and Supernatural Light*, in *WJE*, 17:414–15.
117. Manton, "The Excellency of Saving Faith," in *Several Discourses Tending to Promote Peace and Holiness among Christians*, in *Works*, 2:145.

"practical assent" is a "trusting (*fiducialis*) assent" because it assents to the gospel of Christ as "most worthy of all love and devotion."[118] Thus, faith even as "practical assent" is not "free from trust."[119]

Therefore, though we call this aspect of faith "assent to the truth," the assent of saving faith is essentially different from the assent of the unsaved to some truths of God. In the assent of the believer, he submits to Christ's goodness and authority as Lord (Rom. 10:9; Eph. 5:22–24), whereas the wicked may acknowledge the truth to some extent but remain rebels and enemies (James 2:19). As Brakel pointed out, unbelievers may assent to the truth of the words of the Bible, but they do not have the mind of Christ, a spiritual understanding found in union with Christ (1 Cor. 2:14–16; Eph. 4:20). They do not receive the word so that it is rooted deeply in a good and honest heart (Luke 8:13, 15) granted in regeneration (Ezek. 36:26).[120] Turretin wrote, "It sticks to the uppermost surface of the soul (to wit, the intellect); it does not penetrate to the heart, nor does it have true trust in Christ." However, "justifying faith is rooted intimately in the heart, consisting in a deep, most internal, vital, friendly and efficacious impression by which the word becomes implanted (*emphyton*) and tempered with faith (James 1:21; Heb. 4:2).[121]

Through the submission of assent, faith permanently integrates the word of God into the heart of man. Christ taught that true disciples abide in God's word and the word abides in true disciples (John 8:31; 15:7–8). Only then does the word of God bring salvation from the slavery of sin (8:32, 36). When people receive the word with a living faith, that word sanctifies them (17:8, 17). Calvin said, "For the Word of God is not received by faith if it flits about in the top of the brain, but when it takes root in the depth of the heart."[122]

Saving Faith as Confident Trust in Christ

Saving trust in the Lord particularly focuses on Christ as the only Mediator of grace. The Westminster Shorter Catechism (Q. 86) says, "Faith in Jesus Christ is a saving grace (Heb. 10:39), whereby we receive and rest upon

118. Heidegger, *The Concise Marrow of Christian Theology*, 21.17 (151).
119. Heidegger, *The Concise Marrow of Christian Theology*, 21.20 (152).
120. Brakel, *The Christian's Reasonable Service*, 2:292–93.
121. Turretin, *Institutes*, 15.15.4 (2:588).
122. Calvin, *Institutes*, 3.2.36.

him alone for salvation, as he is offered to us in the gospel (John 1:12; Isa. 26:3–4; Phil. 3:9; Gal. 2:16)."[123]

As we have seen, the biblical vocabulary for faith communicates the idea of confident trust in the Lord. To believe is to treat something as firm, established, and reliable, like a solid rock on which we can build our lives and hopes (Isa. 28:16). Faith in the Lord is leaning on him as our sole support and strength: "Trust in the LORD with all thine heart; and lean not unto thine own understanding" (Prov. 3:5). Faith is hiding oneself or taking refuge in the Lord as one's fortress against danger (Ps. 18:2).

Saving faith is particularly reliance on Jesus Christ. As Turretin explained, the "general" object of faith is "the whole word of God" in all its teachings, but "the special and proper object" is "the evangelical promise concerning Christ, the Mediator, and the special mercy granted in him to believers and penitents."[124] In a manner of speaking, the divine light shining in our hearts through the gospel is the radiance of Jesus's face (2 Cor. 4:6). Brakel said, "Faith is a heartfelt trust in Christ—and through Him in God—in order to be justified, sanctified, and glorified, leaning upon Christ's voluntary offer of Himself and upon His promises that He will perform this to all who receive Him and rely upon Him to that end."[125]

We must not divide faith between Christ and the word, as if faith had two different objects. We believe in Christ through his word, written through the prophets and apostles (John 4:41; 5:46; 17:20). The Lord Jesus says, "Verily, verily, I say unto you, He that heareth my word, and believeth on him that sent me, hath everlasting life, and shall not come into condemnation; but is passed from death unto life" (5:24). If we do not believe in Christ, then his word is not abiding in us (v. 38). We cannot separate Christian discipleship from devotion to the word. Christ says, "If ye continue in my word, then are ye my disciples indeed" (8:31). Brakel said, "Faith does not focus on the Word alone, but proceeds by means of the Word to Christ, the Surety and Mediator."[126]

Saving faith in Christ involves *receiving* him. John writes, "He came unto his own, and his own received him not. But as many as received him, to them gave he power to become the sons of God, even to them that

123. *Reformed Confessions*, 4:365. Similarly, the Westminster Confession of Faith (11.2) and the Larger Catechism (Q. 72) speak of faith as receiving and resting on Christ. *Reformed Confessions*, 4:248, 313.

124. Turretin, *Institutes*, 15.11.13; 15.12.2 (2:574, 576).

125. Brakel, *The Christian's Reasonable Service*, 2:295.

126. Brakel, *The Christian's Reasonable Service*, 2:274.

believe on his name" (John 1:11–12). The word "name" refers to God's glory in Christ as revealed in Christ's words and works.[127] Christ is the living Word that reveals God, the light of his glory (vv. 1, 9). Therefore, saving faith is not accepting Christ merely as one's friend, but receiving him as the glorious Lord of grace and truth (v. 14).

Paul wrote to the converts in Colossae, "As ye have therefore received Christ Jesus the Lord, so walk ye in him: rooted and built up in him, and stablished in the faith, as ye have been taught, abounding therein with thanksgiving" (Col. 2:6–7). Receiving Christ implies receiving the word of God ("as ye have been taught") in contrast to relying on human wisdom (v. 8). Paul further explained, "For in him dwelleth all the fullness of the Godhead bodily. And ye are complete in him, which is the head of all principality and power" (vv. 9–10). We receive Christ by faith (and continue to walk in him by faith) through a heartfelt conviction that he is the all-sufficient Lord, and thus the only Savior on whom we are to depend.

Receiving Christ is pictured for us in the various images of union with Christ given in the Bible.[128] Receiving Christ is compared to eating bread (John 6:35), drinking water (7:37), and putting on clothing (Rom. 13:12, 14). Perkins compared faith to a hand by which we "apprehend" or take hold of Christ.[129] It is the empty hand of a beggar. John Brown of Haddington wrote that faith is "called a receiving of Christ . . . because it takes hold of him as God's great gift."[130]

Saving faith in Christ may also be described as *resting* on him alone for salvation. Christ is our foundation (1 Cor. 3:11). Isaiah 28:16 says, "Therefore thus saith the Lord GOD, Behold, I lay in Zion for a foundation a stone, a tried stone, a precious corner stone, a sure foundation: he that believeth shall not make haste [or flee in panic]." Peter cites this text (with Ps. 118:22) to show that Christ is the cornerstone of God's temple, and Christians rest on him by faith (1 Pet. 2:6–7). James Fisher and the Erskines said that "faith is called resting on Christ" because "he is revealed in the word as a firm foundation (Isa. 28:16), on which we may lay the weight of our everlasting concerns, with the greatest confidence and satisfaction (Ps. 116:7)."[131] Resting on Christ is illustrated in the biblical

127. Cf. John 5:43–44; 12:28; 17:6, 11–12, 26.
128. See chap. 9 on images of union with Christ.
129. Perkins, *An Exposition of the Symbol*, in *Works*, 5:12–14, 207.
130. Brown, *Questions and Answers on the Shorter Catechism*, 290.
131. Fisher et al., *The Assembly's Shorter Catechism Explained*, 86.21 (361).

pictures of union with Christ as God's temple built on the cornerstone and as branches abiding in the vine (John 15:1–8). Believers are those who lean on Christ, the mighty God who alone can support them in all their needs, including times of great personal darkness (Isa. 9:6; 10:20–21; 50:10).

Faith is receiving and resting on Christ *as he is offered to us in the gospel.* The gospel offers Christ in the fullness of his threefold office.[132] Faith receives Christ as the divine Prophet to teach us the authoritative truth (Acts 3:22–23); as the divine Priest to give us forgiveness and reconciliation with God by his one sacrifice and perpetual intercession (Heb. 7:25; 10:10); and as the divine King to rescue us from sin and Satan, and to rule us by his Spirit through his Word (Psalm 2; Acts 5:31–32).[133] By faith, we receive the whole Christ. His teaching heals our blindness and ignorance; his blood and intercession take away our guilt and punishment; his power delivers us from sin and misery. To attempt to receive a partial Christ would be to grasp an incomplete salvation, which is a sure damnation.

If we would receive Christ by the hand of faith, then that hand must be empty. We receive Christ in his offices because we trust in no other to do what he was promised to do. Brown wrote, "What must we renounce in receiving Christ as our prophet? Our own wisdom and knowledge, as ignorance and folly (1 Cor. 3:18; Prov. 30:2–3). What must we renounce in receiving him as our priest? Our own righteousness as filthy rags. What must we renounce in receiving him as our king? Our own strength, will, and pleasure [doing whatever we please]."[134]

However, in renouncing ourselves, we gain all in Christ. If we seek wisdom to overcome our foolishness, in him "are hid all the treasures of wisdom and knowledge" (Col. 2:3). If we seek power to overcome the problems of our fallen human condition, in him "dwelleth all the fullness of the Godhead bodily," and he is "the head of all principality and power" (vv. 9–10). If we seek mercy to overcome our guilt, in him "we have redemption through his blood, the forgiveness of sins, according to the riches of his grace" (Eph. 1:7). Brakel said, "In Christ there is a fullness to meet all your needs and fulfill all your desires."[135]

---

132. Willard, *A Compleat Body of Divinity*, 792; and Boston, *An Illustration of the Doctrines of the Christian Religion*, in *Works*, 2:403.

133. The threefold office of Christ receives extensive attention in *RST*, 2:869–1168 (chaps. 43–55).

134. Brown, *Questions and Answers on the Shorter Catechism*, 294.

135. Brakel, *The Christian's Reasonable Service*, 2:298.

Sing to the Lord

Trusting in Christ Alone

Not what my hands have done can save my guilty soul;
Not what my toiling flesh has borne can make my spirit whole.
Not what I feel or do can give me peace with God;
Not all my prayers and sighs and tears can bear my awful load.

Thy work alone, O Christ, can ease this weight of sin;
Thy blood alone, O Lamb of God, can give me peace within.
Thy love to me, O God, not mine, O Lord, to thee,
Can rid me of this dark unrest, and set my spirit free.

Thy grace alone, O God, to me can pardon speak;
Thy power alone, O Son of God, can this sore bondage break.
No other work, save thine, no other blood will do;
No strength, save that which is divine, can bear me safely through.

I bless the Christ of God; I rest on love divine;
And with unfaltering lip and heart, I call this Saviour mine.
His cross dispels each doubt; I bury in his tomb
Each thought of unbelief and fear, each lingering shade of gloom.

Horatius Bonar
Tune: Leominster
Trinity Hymnal—Baptist Edition, No. 403

Questions for Meditation or Discussion

1. What are the main words used in the Old Testament for faith? What does each communicate?
2. What might the New Testament mean by "believe into" (*pisteuō eis*)?
3. What are several kinds of faith that do not save? How does each fall short?
4. In your church background, which of the kinds of nonsaving faith were people most likely to confuse with saving faith? How did that affect people's lives?
5. What is the definition of saving faith? What are its three dimensions?
6. Why is it necessary to know some truths of the Bible in order to have saving faith?

7. How does faith relate to a heart knowledge of God? How is this different from head knowledge?
8. Does faith include submission to God's word? Prove it from Scripture.
9. How does the Westminster Shorter Catechism define saving faith? How would you prove each part of that definition from the Bible?
10. When you reflect on the meaning of saving faith as discussed in this chapter, do you see such faith in your own heart and life? If not, what is holding you back? If so, how can you grow?

Questions for Deeper Reflection

11. What is the Roman Catholic doctrine of "unformed" and "formed" faith? Is that doctrine biblical? Why or why not?
12. Demons know God's Word (Matt. 4:6) and assent to its truth, at least in some important doctrines (James 2:19). What, then, are the differences between demonic faith and saving faith?

21

Conversion, Part 3

The Exercise and Necessity of Faith

Too often, people consider faith to be either a mere belief in the mind or a feeling of confidence.[1] Such faith would be a weak, fragile thing. Saving faith is a supernatural gift from God, an effect of divine power no less than the resurrection of Christ from the dead (Eph. 1:19–20). The apostle Paul says that the only thing that counts is a faith that energetically works through love (Gal. 5:6). James says that the only faith that saves is a living faith that produces good works of mercy and self-renunciation (James 2:14–26). Thus, Martin Luther said, "Faith is not the human notion and dream that some people call faith. . . . Faith, however, is a divine work in us. . . . O it is a living, busy, active, mighty thing, this faith. It is impossible for it not to be doing good works incessantly."[2]

Faith is, at its core, a dynamic relationship with Christ. Geerhardus Vos wrote that faith is "not a lifeless mirror that catches what is placed before it, but a stream of living water . . . incessantly in motion." Faith is not just *about* Christ, but it unites the soul *to* him in a living union. Vos said, "To believe, then, is not to have a conviction concerning the Mediator as

1. Portions of this chapter are adapted from Joel R. Beeke, "Justification by Faith Alone: The Relation of Faith to Justification," in *Justification by Faith Alone: Affirming the Doctrine by Which the Church and the Individual Stands or Falls*, ed. Don Kistler (Morgan, PA: Soli Deo Gloria, 1995), 70–77. Used by permission.

2. Luther, *Preface to Romans*, in *LW*, 35:370.

a third party based on the testimony of God, but to be engaged with the Mediator Himself as a living person, to go to Him, to take in His image as it is delineated by Scripture, and to feast on beholding Him."[3]

In the previous chapter, we developed the doctrine of faith in terms of what it is: its terminology, definition, and three dimensions. However, there remain crucial questions about faith. How does it exercise itself in the activities of the soul? How important is faith for salvation and spiritual growth?

Faith's Experiential Exercise

Although faith is a gift of God, it is also the disposition and activity of the regenerate soul. Faith, therefore, manifests itself in exercises and operations. We explore five of its major exercises below. The following is not a sequence of acts, though the acts might be experienced sequentially. Rather, it is an analysis of faith's acts that cohere in every believing soul.

Faith Empties Us of Self

The gospel call teaches us how to view ourselves by faith: "All ye that labour and are heavy laden" (Matt. 11:28); "every one that thirsteth . . . and he that hath no money" (Isa. 55:1); "not . . . the righteous, but sinners" (Luke 5:32). To lay hold of Christ and to treasure his righteousness necessitates letting go of one's own righteousness. Faith teaches utter humility, the total emptiness of all within the sinner when viewed outside of Christ.[4] Faith means the utter despair of everything except Christ to be our righteousness, salvation, and eternal life.

To that end, faith makes a sinner conscious of the desperate situation he is in and the tragic judgment he deserves. Sin must become sin in his estimation if grace is to become grace. Far from being a work of merit, faith makes him realize his demerit, negates all hope of merit, and makes him cling entirely to the hope of divine mercy. John Calvin said, "Faith cannot be truly preached, without wholly depriving man of all praise by ascribing all to God's mercy."[5] J. van Genderen and W. H. Velema say, "There is no faith without repentance, inner brokenness, and awareness of guilt," which arise "when man is reborn in humility before God."[6]

3. Vos, *Reformed Dogmatics*, 4:120.
4. Berkouwer, *Faith and Justification*, 172–75.
5. Calvin, *Commentaries*, on Rom. 3:27.
6. Van Genderen and Velema, *Concise Reformed Dogmatics*, 595.

Faith breeds a large view of Christ and a small view of self. Jacob prayed, "I am not worthy of the least of all the mercies, and of all the truth [faithfulness], which thou hast shewed unto thy servant" (Gen. 32:10). A Roman centurion told Christ, "Lord, I am not worthy that thou shouldest come under my roof: but speak the word only, and my servant shall be healed. For I am a man under authority, having soldiers under me: and I say to this man, Go, and he goeth; and to another, Come, and he cometh; and to my servant, Do this, and he doeth it." Christ responded, "Verily I say unto you, I have not found so great faith, no, not in Israel" (Matt. 8:8–10).

The law must condemn us for our willful failure to love God and our neighbors (Rom. 3:19–20) if we are to appreciate the beauty of the Savior who perfectly obeyed the law and bore the penalty of sin (5:6–10). Our unrighteousness must be uncovered if Christ's righteousness is to be discovered as our only righteousness (Ps. 71:16).

Thomas Watson said that saving faith is "self-renunciation." He explained,

> Faith is going out of one's self, being taken off from our own merits, and seeing we have no righteousness of our own. "Not having my own righteousness" (Phil. 3:9). . . . Repentance and faith are both humbling graces; by repentance a man abhors himself; by faith he goes out of himself. . . . The sinner behind sees God's justice pursuing him for sin, before, hell ready to devour him; and in this forlorn condition, he sees nothing in himself to help, but he must perish unless he can find help in another.[7]

Faith renounces self precisely because it embraces Christ. The self-denying character of faith cannot be separated from its taking hold of Christ as one's only hope and righteousness. William Gurnall (1616–1679) said, "Faith hath two hands; with one it pulls off its own righteousness and throws it away . . . with the other it puts on Christ's righteousness over the soul's shame, as that in which it dares alone see God or be seen of him."[8]

Faith Comes to Christ and Receives Him

Christ calls sinners to "come unto me" (Isa. 55:3; Matt. 11:28; John 7:37). This is not a physical motion, but a spiritual action. To come to Christ is

7. Watson, *A Body of Divinity*, 215–16.

8. William Gurnall, *The Christian in Complete Armour*, 2 vols. in 1 (1864; repr., Edinburgh: Banner of Truth, 2002), 2:15.

to receive him for the satisfaction of our ultimate needs and deepest desires (John 6:35; 7:37). This coming arises from an inward conviction that Christ is suitable and sufficient for us, so that the soul cries out, "Lord, to whom shall we go? Thou hast the words of eternal life. And we believe and are sure that thou art that Christ, the Son of the living God" (6:68). In believing in Christ, the soul receives Christ (1:12). It is an active appropriation of him. As the Westminster Larger Catechism (Q. 73) says, faith "is an instrument by which he receiveth and applieth Christ and his righteousness."[9]

As we have seen, faith is not mere intellectual assent. Rather, faith believes from the heart what the Scriptures teach about our sin, the holiness of God, and the saving work of Christ. Before God's holiness, faith repudiates self-righteousness and brings the sinner to know his need for Christ as revealed by the Spirit through the Scriptures. Faith abandons all self-generated merit as it is increasingly allured to Christ and his merits. Calvin wrote, "Faith is not a distant view, but a warm embrace of Christ, by which he dwells in us, and we are filled with the divine Spirit."[10]

The believer finds his warrant and liberty to receive Christ in the promises of Christ. Wilhelmus à Brakel wrote, "He knows himself to be destitute, and he perceives Jesus as suitable, fully sufficient, willing, truthful, offering Himself, and promising that no one will be cast out who comes to Him. . . . 'Yes,' he continues, 'Jesus is willing, yes, more willing than I am, for He Himself takes the initiative, presents Himself, invites me, and He Himself draws me.'"[11]

By faith, the Christian surrenders to the gospel and falls into the outstretched arms of God. John Gill wrote that in faith there is "a casting or throwing themselves into the arms of Christ" to be carried by him as an infant is carried by his father.[12] As G. C. Berkouwer said, "The act of faith is as much being held by God as holding Him; the power of faith is exercised as much in capitulation as in conquering—the faith that overcomes the world is capitulation to Christ's great victory."[13] Faith looks away from self to Christ, moving entirely from

9. *Reformed Confessions*, 4:313.
10. Calvin, *Commentaries*, on Eph. 3:17.
11. Brakel, *The Christian's Reasonable Service*, 2:287.
12. Gill, *Body of Divinity*, 737.
13. Berkouwer, *Faith and Justification*, 190.

and in grace. Faith flees with all the soul's poverty to Christ's riches. It moves with all the soul's guilt to Christ as reconciler, with all the soul's bondage to Christ as liberator.

Faith confesses with Augustus Toplady (1740–1778):

> Nothing in my hand I bring,
> Simply to thy cross I cling;
> Naked, come to thee for dress;
> Helpless, look to thee for grace;
> Foul, I to the fountain fly;
> Wash me, Saviour, or I die.[14]

Saving faith lays hold of Christ and his righteousness, and experiences pardon and a peace that passes understanding (Rom. 5:1; Phil. 4:7). Faith is nothing more than the means that unites a sinner with his Savior. As Calvin said, faith "justifies in no other way but in that it leads us into fellowship with the righteousness of Christ."[15] Theodore Beza (1519–1605) said, "Our salvation is not only established on our faith (although without faith none can be saved), but upon him whom we apprehend by faith, i.e., Jesus Christ."[16]

Faith does not receive saving benefits in abstraction from Christ, but receives Christ as the One in whom all saving benefits are given (Eph. 1:3; 1 John 5:11–12). John Preston explained, "First remember that you must take Christ himself, and then other things that we have by him. . . . Faith doth not leap over Christ, and pitch upon the promises of justification and adoption, but it first takes Christ. . . . It is an adulterous affection for a wife not to think of the person of her husband, but to think only what commodity she shall have by him, what honors, what riches, what conveniences."[17]

Faith grasps Christ in a believing embrace, surrendering all of self, clinging to his Word, and relying on his promises. Christ is not only the object of faith but is himself present in faith. Gill said that in receiving Christ, the believer receives:

- "Christ in all his offices."
- "Christ, and all the blessings of grace along with him."

14. *Trinity Hymnal—Baptist Edition*, No. 421.
15. Calvin, *Institutes*, 3.11.20.
16. Theodore Beza's Confession (4.20), in *Reformed Confessions*, 2:270.
17. Preston, *The Breast-plate of Faith and Love*, 1:45.

- "Christ . . . as a free gift; he is the gift of God."
- "Christ in preference to all others . . . as the one Lord and Head, as the one Mediator, between God and man, and as the one and only Saviour of sinners."[18]

Faith rests in the person of Christ—coming, hearing, seeing, trusting, taking, embracing, knowing, rejoicing, loving, and triumphing. It leaves its case in the hands of Christ as the great Physician, taking his prescriptions, following his directions, and trusting in his finished work and ongoing intercession. Luther said, "Faith takes hold of Christ and has Him present, enclosing Him as the ring encloses the gem."[19] Faith wraps the soul in Christ's righteousness. It appropriates with a believing heart the perfect righteousness, satisfaction, and holiness of Christ. It counts the efficacy of Christ's obedience and blood as the righteousness of God himself.[20] It weds the soul to Christ, experiences divine pardon and acceptance in the Beloved, and makes the soul partake of every covenant mercy.

Christ grants us a special opportunity to exercise faith in him in the Lord's Supper. George Swinnock wrote, "There is a threefold act of faith to be put forth at a sacrament. First, faith must look out for Christ; secondly, faith must look up to Christ for grace; thirdly, faith must take Christ down, or receive him and grace."[21] To look out for Christ is to not allow our minds to rest in the bread and cup, but to look farther to Christ as the sacrifice. "Look up to Christ as a treasury of grace for the supply of all thy necessities, and put thy hand of faith into this treasury, and thou shalt take out unsearchable riches."[22] We must receive him and all his benefits through the Word and sacraments into our souls. Swinnock urged, "Oh make haste to receive him, and make him a feast by opening the doors of thy soul, that the King of glory may enter in."[23]

Faith Lives out of Christ

Being united to Christ by faith, the believer possesses all of Christ's benefits and experiences them abundantly as the Spirit applies them. In the eyes of faith, Christ is chief among ten thousand, altogether lovely (Song 5:10,

18. Gill, *Body of Divinity*, 739.
19. Luther, *Lectures on Galatians*, on Gal. 2:16, in *LW*, 26:132.
20. Rom. 3:21–25; 5:9; 6:7; 2 Cor. 5:18–21.
21. Swinnock, *The Christian Man's Calling*, in *Works*, 1:203.
22. Swinnock, *The Christian Man's Calling*, in *Works*, 1:204.
23. Swinnock, *The Christian Man's Calling*, in *Works*, 1:206.

16). Faith can say, when gazing and feasting on his blessed person and benefits, as was said of Solomon, "Behold, the one half of the greatness of thy wisdom was not told me: for thou exceedest the fame that I heard" (2 Chron. 9:6). Faith then exclaims, "Christ is all!" (Col. 3:11).

This Christ-centeredness is the hallmark of faith. It is the very nature and fountain of faith. Faith does not look at itself. Many today are too preoccupied with looking at their faith rather than looking at faith's object. The Reformers spoke much about faith, but their concern was object-centered rather than subject-centered. It was Christocentric rather than anthropocentric, theological rather than psychological. It was not faith in our faith, faith in the faith, or faith in Christ's benefits, but faith in Christ. B. B. Warfield said, "It is, accordingly, solely from its object that faith derives its value. . . . The saving power of faith resides thus not in itself, but in the Almighty Saviour on whom it rests. . . . It is not, strictly speaking, even faith in Christ that saves, but Christ that saves through faith."[24]

Faith is obedience to Christ's command "Abide in me" (John 15:4). Christ abides in us through his word only insofar as we embrace him by faith (5:38). Faith depends on Christ's support and draws from Christ the life of the soul: "I am the vine, ye are the branches: he that abideth in me, and I in him, the same bringeth forth much fruit: for without me ye can do nothing" (15:5). Richard Sibbes wrote, "Having the Spirit of Christ, faith fetches all strength from Christ."[25]

Faith lives out of Christ because faith roots itself especially in the death and resurrection of Christ for us, which are the heart of the gospel (1 Cor. 15:1–5). Paul says, "For I through the law am dead to the law, that I might live unto God. I am crucified with Christ: nevertheless I live; yet not I, but Christ liveth in me: and the life which I now live in the flesh I live by the faith of the Son of God, who loved me, and gave himself for me" (Gal. 2:19–20).

God is pleased with faith because faith is pleased with Christ. Christ is faith's only object and expectation. Faith enables the soul to enjoy the whole salvation of Christ, for by faith Christ becomes the soul's wisdom, righteousness, sanctification, and redemption (1 Cor. 1:30). Faith commits the total person of the sinner to the total person of Christ.

---

24. Warfield, "Faith," in *Biblical and Theological Studies*, 423–25.
25. Sibbes, *The Life of Faith*, in *Works*, 5:367.

Faith Strives against Obstacles

Saving faith is fighting faith. Paul writes, "Fight the good fight of faith, lay hold on eternal life, whereunto thou art also called" (1 Tim. 6:12). A. W. Pink warned, "The Lord Jesus did not teach that saving faith was a simple matter. Far from it. Instead of declaring that the saving of the soul was an easy thing, which many would participate in, He said: 'Strait is the gate, and narrow the way, which leadeth unto life, and few there be that find it' (Matt. 7:14)."[26]

Faith must overcome the onslaught of unbelieving fear (2 Tim. 1:7; 1 John 4:18). It moves the Christian to cry, "Lord, I believe; help thou mine unbelief" (Mark 9:24). Though some people arrive quickly at assurance in Christ, others cling to him in a storm of doubts. The submissive assent of saving faith to God's promises is no easy matter, but a supernatural victory sometimes accompanied by much striving. Brakel described the first motions of saving faith in terms of longing, tears, wrestling, being tossed about by fear, and yet clinging to Christ as one's only hope.[27] William Perkins said, "We must consent to the Word of God, resisting all doubt." He explained that faith may be weak, but it still joins us to Christ in a saving way if it includes "a serious desire to believe," so that our hearts will "strive with doubtfulness and distrust, and endeavor to put their assent to the sweet promises made in the gospel."[28] He added, "Even strong faith is assaulted with temptations and doubtings."[29] As Bruce Demarest notes, just as the life of the body requires "a constant struggle to ward off disease," so the life of faith engages the soul in a battle to fight off doubt and unbelief.[30]

Faith in Christ must battle against misplaced worldly trust. Some sinners trust in wealth (1 Tim. 6:17). Christ said, "How hard it is for them that trust in riches to enter into the kingdom of God!" (Mark 10:24). Other sinners have "trusted in themselves that they [are] righteous," and Christ calls them to humble themselves and call out, "God be merciful to me a sinner" (Luke 18:9–14). Still other sinners trust in the glory of man and the honors this world bestows, which is a deadly enemy of saving faith. Christ exclaimed, "How can ye believe, which receive honour one of another, and seek not the honour that cometh from God only?" (John

26. Pink, *Studies on Saving Faith*, 38.
27. Brakel, *The Christian's Reasonable Service*, 2:287–88.
28. Perkins, *A Golden Chain*, chap. 36, in *Works*, 6:178–79.
29. Perkins, *An Exposition of the Symbol*, in *Works*, 5:17.
30. Demarest, *The Cross and Salvation*, 273. He cites Alister E. McGrath, *The Sunnier Side of Doubt* (Grand Rapids, MI: Zondervan, 1990), 27.

5:44). Saving faith wages war against one's cursed, God-abandoning trust in man so that it may draw living water from the Lord alone (Jer. 17:5–8).

Faith not only fights against unbelief and false trust, but against all sin. With faith, the Holy Spirit initiates the inward battle of Spirit against flesh (Gal. 5:17). Faith conquers by the victory of Christ. The apostle John said, "For whatsoever is born of God overcometh the world: and this is the victory that overcometh the world, even our faith. Who is he that overcometh the world, but he that believeth that Jesus is the Son of God?" (1 John 5:4–5). Watson said, "Love is the crowning grace in heaven, but faith is the conquering grace upon earth."[31] Sibbes said that for those who live by faith in Christ for their sanctification, "there will be courage to set upon any duty, to encounter and resist any sin."[32]

Faith strives against proud unbelief and various temptations that arise when trouble and persecution fall upon the godly. The Lord revealed to Habakkuk that judgments would strike Israel by the hand of Babylon, and the prophet said, "The just shall live by his faith" (Hab. 2:4). John Owen commented, "What this text teaches us is, that in the approaches of overwhelming calamities . . . we ought, in a peculiar manner, to live by faith."[33] Such faith will deliver us from sinful fear of man and will give instead "a reverential fear of God in his judgments" (cf. 3:16; Heb. 11:7). By faith God's people will take refuge in the "ark" of safety from all the floods of divine judgment, which is Jesus Christ and his righteousness.[34] And when the calamity is reproach and persecution from the wicked, "faith will give us such an experience of the power, efficacy, sweetness, and benefit of gospel ordinances and gospel worship," together with an experiential "sense of the authority of Jesus Christ" to direct his church and rule over the greatest magistrate on earth, that we will gladly choose to worship with God's people according to his Word rather than have the favor of the whole world.[35]

Even in its warfare, faith never loses its character of Christ-centered dependence. Faith hides in Christ and fights from that position of safety. The Belgic Confession (Art. 29) says,

> With respect to those who are members of the Church, they may be known by the marks of Christians, namely, by faith; and when they

31. Watson, *A Body of Divinity*, 217.
32. Sibbes, *The Life of Faith*, in *Works*, 5:370.
33. Owen, "The Use and Advantage of Faith in a Time of Public Calamity," in *Works*, 9:491.
34. Owen, "The Use and Advantage of Faith in a Time of Public Calamity," in *Works*, 9:493–95.
35. Owen, "The Use of Faith under Reproaches and Persecutions," in *Works*, 9:501–2.

> have received Jesus Christ the only Savior, they avoid sin, follow after righteousness, love the true God and their neighbor, neither turn aside to the right or left, and crucify the flesh with the works thereof. But this is not to be understood as if there did not remain in them great infirmities; but they fight against them through the Spirit all the days of their life, continually taking their refuge in the blood, death, passion, and obedience of our Lord Jesus Christ, in whom they have remission of sins through faith in Him.[36]

Satan has erected innumerable obstacles to faith in Christ, and faith hacks its way through them all on its way to the city of God.[37]

Faith Produces Good Works

Though God justifies sinners by faith alone, he does not justify them by a faith that is alone. Saving faith is God's means to cleanse the heart and sanctify the life (Acts 15:9; 26:18). Faith that does not bring good works is not saving faith, but a dead faith (James 2:14, 17). Thus, Paul writes of the "work of faith" (1 Thess. 1:3; 2 Thess. 1:11). He says, "For in Jesus Christ neither circumcision availeth any thing, nor uncircumcision; but faith which worketh by love" (Gal. 5:6). Faith engages love to produce good works, for faith looks upon the love of God in Christ, and "we love him, because he first loved us" (1 John 4:16, 19).

Watson wrote that we see "the preciousness of faith . . . in its having influence upon all the graces, and setting them to work: not a grace stirs till faith sets it to work. . . . If faith did not feed the lamp of hope with oil, it would soon die. Faith sets love to work. . . . Believing the mercy and merit of Christ causes a flame of love to ascend."[38] "Call forth first that commander-in-chief," George Swinnock said, "and then the private soldiers, the other graces, will all follow."[39]

Faith not only ventures *to* Christ with the demanding law at its heels and ventures *on* Christ with all the soul's guilt, but also ventures *for* Christ despite all difficulties and discouragements. "Without faith it is impossible to please God" (Heb. 11:6). By faith God's people throughout time have walked in courageous obedience, hoping in the invisible God. Abel pleased

36. *The Three Forms of Unity*, 49–50.
37. For eight obstacles against coming to Christ, see Beeke and Jones, *A Puritan Theology*, 518–23.
38. Watson, *A Body of Divinity*, 217.
39. Swinnock, *The Christian Man's Calling*, in *Works*, 1:202.

God in his worship, Abraham obeyed God's calling, Sarah received power to bear a child in her old age, Isaac and Jacob declared the Lord's blessing on their offspring, and Moses chose the reproach of Christ over the riches of Egypt—all by faith (vv. 4–26).

Furthermore, as Sibbes said, "the life of faith orders our prosperity. How? Not to abuse those good blessings bestowed on us, not to be puffed up by them, not to disdain, but to relieve others by them. Faith causes us to think of them as they are set forth in the word. It causes that we delight not too much in them, shows us better and more lasting riches, friends, and the like."[40] Faith leads those wealthy in this world to be wealthy in works: "Charge them that are rich in this world, that they be not highminded, nor trust in uncertain riches, but in the living God, who giveth us richly all things to enjoy; that they do good, that they be rich in good works, ready to distribute, willing to communicate [share]" (1 Tim. 6:17–18).

Faith, Thomas Manton reminded us, spurs believers to pursue the everlasting enjoyment of God in glory, and toward that end, "to forsake all things in this world." Faith makes them like the merchant in Christ's parable, who sells all he has to gain the pearl of great price (Matt. 13:45–46).[41] Faith makes people into children of Abraham and Sarah, who lived as "strangers and pilgrims on the earth" so that they might gain the city of God (Heb. 11:13–16).

By faith, the spiritual warrior can stand against the temptations by which Satan attempts to pierce and ignite his soul (Eph. 6:16). By faith, believers persist in doing many works of love even while they endure the pain of persecution (2 Thess. 1:3–5). By faith, they rejoice in God's promises and are filled with hope (Rom. 15:13). By faith, believers draw near to God and enjoy his holy presence mediated through the great High Priest (Heb. 10:19–22). By faith, the prayers of God's children call the power of God down from heaven (James 5:15–16). By faith, Christians speak to others the word that they themselves believe (2 Cor. 4:13). By faith, ministers are empowered by the Holy Spirit for faithful and effective ministry (Acts 6:6, 8; 11:24).

Do you have saving faith in Christ? Faith is known in its exercises in the soul and practical results in life. Examine yourself to see if you are in the faith and if faith is in you.

---

40. Sibbes, *The Life of Faith*, in *Works*, 5:378.
41. Manton, "The Excellency of Saving Faith," in *Several Discourses*, in *Works*, 2:157–58.

- Does your faith in Christ puff you up with pride or place you on your face before a holy God? Is your faith coupled with a spirit of self-righteousness or self-denial?
- Does your faith bring you to Christ hungering and thirsting for him, and receiving him as your life?
- Does your faith live out of Christ on a daily basis? Is your faith like the abiding of a branch in the vine to draw life from him and bear fruit for his glory?
- Does your faith lead you into spiritual warfare against unbelief and sin? Is your faith a shield dented and scratched from conflict or a dusty trophy on a shelf?
- Does your faith produce good works of service to the Master? Is your faith a living, energetic motion of your heart or a dead thing in your brain?

Hypocrites, be warned, for the weakest saving faith is as different from nonsaving faith as a living seed is from a dead stone. If all you have is dead faith, then you may expect to receive salvation as much as a farmer can expect to grow a crop after sowing gravel in his field.

Weak believers, be encouraged, for the smallest seed of faith is sufficient to bring you to heaven. However, the stronger your faith, the more it will bring heaven into you.

Strong believers, press on and keep watch over your souls. You are doing well, but do not grow careless, lest you fall. Seek always to increase your faith, for you have not yet attained the full riches of Christ Jesus. As Augustine said, "You should always be dissatisfied with yourself for what you are, if you wish to arrive at what you are not yet; for where you are satisfied, there you remain."[42]

The Necessity of Faith in Christ

Faith in the Lord is a holy command, a personal necessity, and a pressing urgency (2 Kings 17:14, 18). John Flavel wrote, "The soul is the life of the body, faith is the life of the soul, and Christ is the life of faith."[43] Faith is not an option to enhance one's spiritual life, but a necessity for salvation, spiritual life, communion with God, fruitfulness in our daily walk, deliverance from hell, and eternal glory and happiness.

42. Cited in van Mastricht, *Theoretical-Practical Theology*, 1.2.1.51 (2:38).
43. Flavel, *The Method of Grace*, in *Works*, 2:104.

The Necessity for Salvation of the Lost

Faith in Christ is indispensable. Without faith there is only damnation (Mark 16:16). John writes, "He that believeth on him is not condemned: but he that believeth not is condemned already, because he hath not believed in the name of the only begotten Son of God. . . . He that believeth on the Son hath everlasting life: and he that believeth not the Son shall not see life; but the wrath of God abideth on him" (John 3:18, 36).

It is not just that faith is necessary, but that faith *in Christ* is necessary. It is not faith that saves, but *Christ* who saves through faith. Faith must unite us to God's Son, for he alone is the Mediator of eternal life (John 14:6). John says, "This is the record, that God hath given to us eternal life, and this life is in his Son. He that hath the Son hath life; and he that hath not the Son of God hath not life. These things have I written unto you that believe on the name of the Son of God; that ye may know that ye have eternal life, and that ye may believe on the name of the Son of God" (1 John 5:11–13).

Paul warns that when Christ is revealed from heaven, he will come "in flaming fire taking vengeance on them that know not God, and that obey not the gospel of our Lord Jesus Christ" (2 Thess. 1:8). Both those ignorant of God and those who hear the gospel but reject it will be damned. Paul says that it is God's intent "that they all might be damned who believed not the truth, but had pleasure in unrighteousness," but God has chosen some for "salvation through sanctification of the Spirit and belief of the truth" (2 Thess. 2:12–13).

Everyone who would be saved must hear the gospel and respond to it with saving faith in Jesus Christ. Paul unfolds this necessity in the sequence of divine logic in Romans 10:13–14:

- Whosoever shall call upon the name of the Lord shall be saved.
- How shall they call on him in whom they have not believed?
- How shall they believe in him of whom they have not heard?
- How shall they hear without a preacher?

The Westminster Larger Catechism (Q. 60) concludes,

> Q. Can they who have never heard the gospel, and so know not Jesus Christ, nor believe in him, be saved by their living according to the light of nature?

> A. They who, having never heard the gospel (Rom. 10:14), know not Jesus Christ (2 Thess. 1:8–9; Eph. 2:12; John 1:10–12), and believe not in him, cannot be saved (John 8:24; Mark 16:16), be they never so diligent to frame their lives according to the light of nature (1 Cor. 1:20–24), or the laws of that religion which they profess (John 4:22; Rom. 9:31–32; Phil. 3:4–9); neither is there salvation in any other, but in Christ alone (Acts 4:12), who is the Saviour only of his body the church (Eph. 5:23).[44]

Trusting Christ as the only Savior glorifies him. As John Dagg pointed out, the necessity of faith in Christ highlights his incomparable greatness. No one other than the Lord could say, "If ye believe not that I am he, ye shall die in your sins" (John 8:24). Dagg wrote, "If we believe in Christ, according to the Scriptures, we fully justify all that he claimed for himself, and all that his apostles claimed for him; and we rejoice to render to him all honor and praise."[45]

The Necessity for Growth in the Saved

Christ's apostles said to him, "Increase our faith" (Luke 17:5). Though Christ extolled the power of a tiny seed of faith (v. 6), he also rebuked his disciples for being people of "little faith." Smallness of faith leads to anxiety in daily needs, terror in crises, doubts about the power of God, and weakness in understanding God's word.[46] On the other hand, the Lord Jesus commended the centurion and the Canaanite woman for their great faith (Matt. 8:10; 15:28). Paul thanked God for the believers in Thessalonica, "because that your faith groweth exceedingly" (2 Thess. 1:3). Some godly Christians, in the manner of Stephen and Barnabas, are full of faith (Acts 6:5, 8; 11:24). When believers grow in their faith, it not only blesses them but also expands the missionary growth of the kingdom of Christ (2 Cor. 10:15).

Therefore, Christians should seek to grow in their faith in the Lord. Even young believers can exercise "full assurance of faith" (Heb. 10:22), and there are always more riches of assurance for us to attain in Christ (Col. 2:2). Faith does not increase by sheer willpower but in the same manner in which it was first created—that is, by the Holy Spirit

---

44. *Reformed Confessions*, 4:311.
45. Dagg, *Manual of Theology*, 1:178.
46. Matt. 6:30; 8:26; 14:31; 16:8; Luke 12:28.

working through means of grace to open our eyes to Christ's glory in God's Word.

Take hold of Christ in the Word. To grow in our faith, we do not need more *than* Christ, but more *of* Christ grasped in our knowledge, assent, and trust. Paul writes, "As ye have therefore received Christ Jesus the Lord, so walk ye in him" (Col. 2:6–7). Meditate on Christ in the Word, and you will feed your soul. To enable this, read the Word regularly and sit under the experiential preaching of the Word.

Pray for the grace of the Spirit (Luke 11:13). Ask the covenant God of our Lord Jesus Christ, the Father of glory, to reveal himself more to you by the Holy Spirit (Eph. 1:17). Pray for the Father to strengthen you in your inner man so that Christ dwells in your heart by faith—more and more unto the fullness of God (3:16–19).

Cling to Christ when sorrows come. Suffering is the school of faith (James 1:2–3). Pain is the refining fire that proves and purifies the gold of our faith (1 Pet. 1:7). When the sorrows of Christ overflow into your life, go to the river of living water and draw forth more of the comfort of Christ, both for yourself and others (2 Cor. 1:3–6). Remember that God has called us to know Christ in "the power of his resurrection, and the fellowship of his sufferings" (Phil. 3:10).

Grow in your faith by fellowshipping with Christ every day. Remember that saving faith is a relationship with a living person. Brakel said, "Give diligence to increase in faith. . . . Setting your heart upon Jesus; giving yourself and your salvation into the hands of Jesus; entrusting yourself to Him and relying upon Him; resting and leaning upon Him . . . that He may justify, sanctify, and save your soul, since He is omnipotent, faithful, true, and wise. What can be more appropriate, safer, and Christ-glorifying than that?"[47]

Live by faith in the Son of God, and you will live unto God (Gal. 2:20).

Sing to the Lord

Trusting in the Lord

To Thee I lift my soul, in Thee my trust repose;
My God, O put me not to shame before triumphant foes.

47. Brakel, *The Christian's Reasonable Service*, 2:304–5.

None shall be put to shame that humbly wait for Thee,
But those that willfully transgress, on them the shame shall be.

Show me Thy paths, O Lord, teach me Thy perfect way,
O guide me in Thy truth divine, and lead me day by day.

For Thou art God that dost to me salvation send,
And patiently through all the day upon Thee I attend.

Recall Thy mercies, Lord, their tenderness untold,
And all Thy lovingkindnesses, for they have been of old.

Psalm 25
Tune: Dennis
The Psalter, No. 60

Questions for Meditation or Discussion

1. Martin Luther said, "It is a living, busy, active, mighty thing, this faith." Prove this statement from the Holy Scriptures.
2. Why does faith in Christ necessarily involve rejecting our pride and self-righteousness?
3. Someone says, "My cousin went to a religious meeting and heard the preacher say he should come to Jesus, so he went up to the front to pray. What does it mean to 'come to Jesus'?" What do you say?
4. What must a person perceive by faith in Jesus Christ in order to come to him?
5. What does it mean to live by faith in the Son of God?
6. Why must saving faith strive and fight against opposition?
7. What Scripture passages show that saving faith will produce good works?
8. How would you answer someone who claims that anyone will go to heaven if he has faith in a higher power of some kind?
9. Why should Christians zealously pursue growth in their faith?
10. What is a practical step that you can take in order to strengthen and grow your faith in Christ?

Questions for Deeper Reflection

11. A friend from church tells you, "I am not sure whether I really have saving faith in Christ. I do believe in him, but frankly I'm scared

because I have so many doubts, too. How can I tell whether my faith is saving faith or just the dead belief of a lost sinner?" What do you say?

12. You have an opportunity to address a group of Christians who are suffering painful trials. Prepare a detailed outline on the topic "Growing in Faith While in the Fire."

22

Justification, Part 1

Biblical Teaching

At the heart of the gospel is the promise of justification by faith alone (Latin *sola fide*). Paul says that God is "the justifier of him which believeth in Jesus" (Rom. 3:26). Justification answers the crucial question of salvation: "How can a sinful human being be righteous with the just and holy God?" (cf. Job 9:2; 25:4).

The doctrine of justification may not seem relevant to people who think that God is unconditional love to the exclusion of justice. The good news of justification presupposes the justice of God (Gen. 18:25).[1] The Lord undergirded the judicial system of Israel with his declaration "I will not justify the wicked" (Ex. 23:7). Leon Morris wrote, "The thoughts of righteousness, justification and the rest are inextricably bound up with other concepts like those of judgment, pleading in the law court, and, especially, law itself," noting that in the biblical perspective, God is "a God of law."[2] John Owen said that we will think rightly about justification only by "a continual regard" to God's "greatness, majesty, holiness, and sovereign authority."[3]

---

1. On God's legal and penal justice, see *RST*, 1:814–16, 819–20.
2. Leon Morris, *The Apostolic Preaching of the Cross*, 3rd ed. (Grand Rapids, MI: Eerdmans, 1965), 253.
3. Owen, *The Doctrine of Justification by Faith*, in *Works*, 5:13.

The need for justification comes into sharp focus when we consider the guilt of sinful mankind before God (Rom. 3:9–18). John Calvin wrote that we cannot speak of justification properly without a sense of the majesty of divine justice and man's "guilt before the heavenly Judge." Only then can we understand the psalmist's cry, "If thou, LORD, shouldest mark iniquities, O Lord, who shall stand?" (Ps. 130:3).[4] Owen said, "A clear apprehension and due sense of the greatness of our apostasy from God, of the depravation [corruption] of our natures thereby, of the power and guilt of sin, of the holiness and severity of the law, are necessary unto a right apprehension of the doctrine of justification."[5]

The Nature of Justification: Terminology and Definition

Though our English words *justify* and *righteousness* come from different roots, the ideas are bound together in a single root in both Hebrew (*hiphil* of *tsadeq*, *tsedeq*) and Greek (*dikaioō*, *dikaiosunē*). In the Hebrew Old Testament, the verb translated as "justify" (*hiphil* of *tsadeq*) has a predominantly judicial and legal meaning as the act of a judge to declare a person to be in the right according to the principles of legal justice. For example, we read, "If there be a controversy between men, and they come unto judgment, that the judges may judge them; then they shall justify [*hiphil* of *tsadeq*] the righteous, and condemn the wicked" (Deut. 25:1). This verb is used similarly of the Lord in his judicial actions: "Then hear thou in heaven, and do, and judge thy servants, condemning the wicked, to bring his way upon his head; and justifying [*hiphil* of *tsadeq*] the righteous, to give him according to his righteousness" (1 Kings 8:32).

Geerhardus Vos said,

> That the meaning of the word is strictly judicial and nothing else appears most clearly from Proverbs 17:15, "The one who justifies the godless and the one who condemns the righteous are both indeed an abomination to the LORD." Were one now to maintain that here "justify" means "to change someone into an upright person by infusing good qualities," one would then get the result that to make an evil person into a good one is an abomination to God.[6]

4. Calvin, *Institutes*, 3.12.1.
5. Owen, *The Doctrine of Justification by Faith*, in *Works*, 5:20.
6. Vos, *Reformed Dogmatics*, 4:133.

In these texts, the Septuagint renders the Hebrew verb in question as the Greek word translated as "justify" (*dikaioō*), a term commonly used for receiving a favorable verdict from a judge.[7] In secular Greek literature, it apparently never refers to changing someone's moral character.[8] In the New Testament, "justify" (*dikaioō*) also bears this twofold meaning of rendering a judicial verdict of righteous[9] or publicly demonstrating someone to be righteous.[10] Antonius Thysius said that the Greek term translated as "justify," like the Hebrew term it renders, "is strictly speaking nearly always a forensic term denoting a forensic act of judgment by a judge."[11]

The vast majority of New Testament references to God justifying people are found in the epistles of Paul, though there are a few elsewhere.[12] Most of Paul's uses appear in the epistles to the Romans (fourteen times) and the Galatians (eight times).[13] From the New Testament usage, we observe the following:

1. Justification is *a gracious forensic declaration by God*. We have seen that one primary meaning of the word *dikaioō* pertains to the verdict of a judge regarding a person's standing according to the law. This is precisely the situation Paul sets forth in Romans, anticipating "the day of wrath and revelation of the righteous judgment of God; who will render to every man according to his deeds" (Rom. 2:5–6). Paul's great exposition of justification in Christ is prefaced by the words "Now we know that what things soever the law saith, it saith to them who are under the law: that every mouth may be stopped, and all the world may become guilty before God. Therefore by the deeds of the law there shall no flesh be justified in his sight: for by the law is the knowledge of sin" (Rom. 3:19–20). Therefore, justification is a legal verdict given to those who have no legal claims; it is a gift of grace in the courtroom of God.

---

7. See *dikaioō* in Gen. 44:16; 2 Chron. 6:23; Pss. 81(82):3; 142(143):2; Isa. 5:23; 43:9, 26; 50:8 LXX. This Greek term is also used for pleading for another person's legal rights in court (Isa. 1:17; Mic. 7:9 LXX, translating the Hebrew *rib*) or for publicly demonstrating someone's righteousness (Job. 33:32; Jer. 3:11; Ezek. 16:51–52 LXX, translating the Hebrew *piel* of *tsadeq*).

8. Morris, *The Apostolic Preaching of the Cross*, 253. Only once in the Septuagint (Ps. 72[73]:13) does "justify" (*dikaioō*) render "wash" (*zacah*), and the latter verb may be translated as "count as pure" in a legal sense (Mic. 6:11).

9. Luke 18:14; Rom. 2:13; 3:26; 8:33; 1 Cor. 4:4.

10. Matt. 11:19; Luke 7:29, 35; 10:29; 16:15; Rom. 3:4; 1 Tim. 3:16; James 2:21, 24–25.

11. Polyander, Walaeus, Thysius, and Rivetus, *Synopsis Purioris Theologiae*, 33.2 (2:305). See Demarest, *The Cross and Salvation*, 366. "Forensic" means "pertaining to a court of law."

12. Luke 18:14; Acts 13:39; James 2:21, 24, 25; Rev. 22:11 (Textus Receptus, but not in Majority Text).

13. Rom. 2:13; 3:20, 24, 26, 28, 30; 4:2, 5; 5:1, 9; 6:7; 8:30 (2x), 33; Gal. 2:16–17 (4x); 3:8, 11, 24; 5:4. See also 1 Cor. 6:11; Titus 3:7.

2. Justification involves *forgiveness of guilt and freedom from condemnation.* Paul says in Acts 13:38–39, "Be it known unto you therefore, men and brethren, that through this man is preached unto you the forgiveness of sins: and by him all that believe are justified from all things, from which ye could not be justified by the law of Moses." Paul sets justification in Christ over against condemnation in Adam (Rom. 5:16). He writes, "Who shall lay any thing to the charge of God's elect? It is God that justifieth. Who is he that condemneth? It is Christ that died, yea rather, that is risen again, who is even at the right hand of God, who also maketh intercession for us" (8:33–34). God's verdict for those in Christ is "no condemnation" (v. 1).

3. Justification involves *a judicial reckoning of faithful obedience to God's law.* This is the common meaning of "justify" as an act of a judge. Louis Berkhof explained that in salvation justification has a "negative element" and a "positive element."[14] Just as justification removes the negative reckoning of guilt against sinners, so it also grants them a positive standing of righteousness. In the midst of Paul's discussion of justification, he describes it as a legal reckoning or imputation of righteousness, picking up the language of Genesis 15:6 in Romans 4:3–6:

> For what saith the scripture? Abraham believed God, and it was counted unto him for righteousness. Now to him that worketh is the reward not reckoned of grace, but of debt. But to him that worketh not, but believeth on him that justifieth the ungodly, his faith is counted for righteousness. Even as David also describeth the blessedness of the man, unto whom God imputeth righteousness without works.

The Greek word translated as "count," "reckon," or "impute" (*logizomai*) has the general meaning of "consider,"[15] but it may also be used more specifically of legal and financial accounting, as we can see in Paul's reference to paying wages to "him that worketh" as a "debt" (Rom. 4:4). In contrast to those against whose record God counts their sins (v. 8; 2 Cor. 5:19), God counts righteousness to those whom he justifies. This righteousness is the status of one who has obeyed God's commandments (Rom. 5:18–19). Therefore, when God the sovereign Judge justifies a person, he graciously declares that person to be reckoned as obedient to God's law.

14. Berkhof, *Systematic Theology*, 514–15.
15. Rom. 14:14; 1 Cor. 13:11; Phil. 4:8.

In light of the biblical terminology and its theological context, we may summarize the meaning of justification in this definition: *Justification is God's gracious forensic declaration that guilty sinners are forgiven (and thus freed from condemnation) and reckoned as obedient to the law (and thus worthy of eternal life), both on the basis of the finished work of Jesus Christ received by faith alone.* William Ames said, "Justification is the gracious judgment of God by which he absolves the believer from sin and death, and reckons him righteous and worthy of life for the sake of Christ apprehended in faith."[16] Since justification is a forensic and judicial declaration, it is not a process but "an instantaneous legal act of God."[17]

Justification is a dramatic reversal of the legal status of a sinner. Zechariah vividly illustrated this reversal in his vision of Joshua the high priest standing before the Lord wearing filthy garments while Satan accused him. The Lord commanded that the filthy garments be taken away and that clean, beautiful clothing be given to him (Zech. 3:1–5). In the same way, Christians "have put on Christ" and are "justified by faith" (Gal. 3:24, 27).

Justification is also a reversal of human expectations, for it is granted not to the righteous but to sinners. Christ illustrated this in the parable of the Pharisee and the publican, which he told to people who "trusted in themselves that they were righteous, and despised others." The Pharisee boasted before God about his good works, but the tax collector cried out in contrition, "God be merciful to me a sinner." Christ said, "I tell you, this man went down to his house justified [*dikaioō*] rather than the other: for every one that exalteth himself shall be abased; and he that humbleth himself shall be exalted" (Luke 18:9–14). How can this be?

The Basis of Justification: The Righteousness of God in Christ

In Paul's discussion of justification in Christ in his epistle to the Romans, he speaks of "the righteousness of God" and of righteousness being "imputed" to believers. To understand how God "justifieth the ungodly" (Rom 4:5), we must examine Paul's use of these two expressions in this context more carefully.

16. Ames, *The Marrow of Theology*, 1.27.6 (161). To absolve is to set free from an obligation or penalty.

17. Grudem, *Systematic Theology*, 723.

The Righteousness of God

Paul's discussion of justification is closely connected to "the righteousness of God." Paul writes, "For therein [in the gospel] is the righteousness of God revealed from faith to faith: as it is written, The just shall live by faith" (Rom. 1:17). He adds, "But now the righteousness of God without the law is manifested, being witnessed by the law and the prophets; even the righteousness of God which is by faith of Jesus Christ unto all and upon all them that believe: for there is no difference" (3:21–22). He proceeds to explain how sinners can be "justified freely by his grace through the redemption that is in Christ Jesus" (v. 24). For Paul, "the righteousness of God" can be shorthand for the gospel message (10:3). Though the term "the righteousness of God" could refer to God's attribute of righteousness, righteousness from God, or righteousness approved by God, John Murray argued that, like "the power of God" in Romans 1:16, "the righteousness of God" in verse 17 refers to "a righteousness of divine properties and characterized by divine qualities. It is a 'God-righteousness'. . . . contrasted not only with human unrighteousness but with human righteousness."[18] James Buchanan (1804–1870) wrote, "It is brought in as divine righteousness, only when all human righteousness has been shut out."[19]

Paul's language is rooted in the Old Testament usage of the expression "the righteousness of God."[20] For example, the Lord announced, "My righteousness is near; my salvation is gone forth . . . my salvation shall be for ever, and my righteousness shall not be abolished" (Isa. 51:5–6). God's righteousness is not merely a synonym for salvation or God's covenant faithfulness—we may not replace the lexical meaning of righteousness with its salvific and covenantal application in certain contexts.[21] God has resolved to glorify himself in his holiness, righteousness, and justice (5:16). He will not set aside his law with its righteous requirements, but will honor his law (42:21). Rather, the righteousness of God is a shorthand description of how God exercises and glorifies his righteousness in the salvation of sinners.[22] He satisfied his just demands through Christ's righteous life and substitutionary

18. Murray, *The Epistle to the Romans*, 1:31.

19. James Buchanan, *The Doctrine of Justification* (1867; repr., Grand Rapids, MI: Baker, 1955), 316.

20. On the righteousness of God in justification, see *RST*, 1:820–22.

21. See Charles Lee Irons, *The Righteousness of God: A Lexical Examination of the Covenant-Faithfulness Interpretation*, Wissenschaftliche Untersuchungen Zum Neuen Testament, 2/386 (Tübingen: Mohr Siebeck, 2015).

22. Demarest, *The Cross and Salvation*, 370.

death for the sins of his people (53:6, 11). In union with the Lord, they are justified (45:24–25). God clothes them in righteousness as with a beautiful robe (61:10). As a result, God promises his people, "No weapon that is formed against thee shall prosper; and every tongue that shall rise against thee in judgment thou shalt condemn. This is the heritage of the servants of the Lord, and their righteousness is of me, saith the Lord" (54:17).

The satisfaction of divine justice by Christ does not in the least contradict the truth that sinners are "justified freely by his grace" (Rom. 3:24). As Ames pointed out, God's method of justification in Christ magnifies God's grace because, first, "God has not prosecuted His own right against us and against our sins according to the rigor of the law and of avenging justice"; second, God willingly planned and executed "the means of this reconciliation, although He was the offended party"; third, God "did not spare His own, only begotten Son for the sake of procuring that reconciliation"; and fourth, we are not justified because of any merit in us, but only because God "engrafts us into His own Son . . . and thus He makes us partakers of the reconciliation that is in Him."[23]

The Imputation of Christ's Righteousness

What is this divine righteousness that now belongs to justified believers? It is the righteousness of Christ's passive and active obedience—that is, his suffering of the penalty of God's law and his doing of what God commands.[24] Isaiah 53 teaches that Christ suffered as the substitute for his people ("the Lord hath laid on him the iniquity of us all . . . for the transgression of my people was he stricken," vv. 6, 8). It also emphasizes Christ's sinlessness ("he had done no violence, neither was any deceit in his mouth," v. 9), God's pleasure in him (v. 10), and his righteousness (v. 11). The passage especially links Christ's personal righteousness with the justification of his people when it says, "My righteous servant [shall] justify many" (v. 11), which is even more plain in the Hebrew text, for it immediately couples "justify" and its cognate noun "righteous" (*yatsdiq tsadiq*). Therefore, there is an exchange of sin and righteousness in view: the people's sins are placed on him so that he suffers for them, and his righteousness is counted to them so that they share in his vindication.

23. Ames, *A Sketch of the Christian's Catechism*, 118.

24. On Christ's saving obedience, which is both passive and active, see *RST*, 2:1033–57 (chap. 50).

As Paul says in 1 Corinthians 1:30, Christ has become our righteousness, and it is ours only if we are "in Christ Jesus." John Brown of Haddington explained that God can legally count us as "perfectly righteous . . . only as we are one with Christ."[25] Justification is not a mechanical or impersonal event, but a benefit of union with Christ. Believers are "justified in Christ" (Gal. 2:17 ESV).[26] Christians are "justified freely by his grace through the redemption that is in Christ Jesus" (Rom. 3:24).

Paul speaks of the exchange of the people's sin for divine righteousness when he says, "For he hath made him to be sin for us, who knew no sin; that we might be made the righteousness of God in him" (2 Cor. 5:21). Wilhelmus à Brakel said, "Believers are thus made righteous in Him, as He has in like manner been made sin for them. Here is a mutual transfer from one to the other."[27] To make Christ sin was not to cause him to become sinful or commit sin, but rather to count him as a sinner (though he knew no sin) so as to not count his people's sins against them (v. 19). Similarly, our being "made the righteousness of God in him" is not God's transformation of sinners into better people, but his counting them as righteous by imputing Christ's obedience to them. William Perkins explained that justification is "a kind of translation of the believer's sins to Christ and again Christ's righteousness to the believer, by a reciprocal or mutual imputation."[28]

Therefore, just as mankind was condemned by the disobedience of one man, the first Adam, so God's people are justified by the obedience of one man, Jesus Christ, the last Adam (Rom. 5:15–19). Where Paul writes, "by the obedience of one shall many be made righteous" (v. 19), the verb translated as "made" (*kathistēmi*) commonly means to appoint to a status or position.[29] In this context, Paul repeatedly writes of how Adam's sin brought condemnation and death on those in him, whereas Christ's righteousness brought justification and life to those who are in him. Therefore, "made righteous" does not refer to the sanctification of many people's character, but to their justification in the courtroom of God. Christ's obedience is their righteousness.

---

25. Brown, *Questions and Answers on the Shorter Catechism*, 158.

26. The KJV reads "justified by Christ." The Greek preposition (*en*) can mean "in," "with," or "by," but Paul commonly speaks of union with Christ with this expression (*en Christō*).

27. Brakel, *The Christian's Reasonable Service*, 2:352.

28. Perkins, *A Golden Chain*, chap. 37, in *Works*, 6:182.

29. Matt. 24:45, 47; 25:21, 23; Luke 12:14, 42, 44; Acts 6:3; 7:10, 27, 35; 17:15; Rom. 5:19; Titus 1:5; Heb. 2:7; 5:1; 7:28; 8:3; James 3:6; 4:4; 2 Pet. 1:8.

This is the solid ground upon which the believer stands, as Paul says, "not having mine own righteousness, which is of the law, but that which is through the faith of Christ, the righteousness which is of God by faith" (Phil. 3:9). Francis Turretin said that Christ's righteousness alone is the "meritorious cause" of God's verdict over us, "so that for no other reason does God bestow the pardon of sin and the right to life than on account of the most perfect righteousness of Christ imputed to us and apprehended by faith." This is not a matter of mere academic dispute, but one that we properly perceive only "when the conscience is placed before God . . . that supreme Judge . . . by whose brightness the stars are darkened; at whose strength the mountains melt." In his presence, nothing in us will suffice to answer God's holy law; the beginnings of holiness within us cannot deliver us from condemnation for our sins. Only "the righteousness and obedience of Christ alone imputed to us" will save us from wrath and carry us to heaven.[30]

The Execution of Justification: From Eternity to Glory

When we discussed union with Christ, we traced the implementation of this union from its conception in God's eternal counsels to the bringing of God's people to the glory of Christ.[31] Since justification is a benefit of union with Christ, it too may be viewed in the perspective of different moments in eternity and history.

1. *God decreed justification in eternity through Christ.* God's salvation is "not according to our works, but according to his own purpose and grace, which was given us in Christ Jesus before the world began" (2 Tim. 1:9). God "hath chosen us in him before the foundation of the world, that we should be holy and without blame before him in love" (Eph. 1:4). Christ is "the Lamb slain from the foundation of the world" (Rev. 13:8), the Redeemer "foreordained before the foundation of the world" (1 Pet. 1:20). Therefore, God decreed the justification of his elect ones in Christ before he created anything.

However, the elect are not thereby always justified. The person who does not believe in Christ is presently under God's condemnation (John 3:18), whether or not he is elect. "He that believeth on the Son hath everlasting life: and he that believeth not the Son shall not see life; but the

30. Turretin, *Institutes*, 16.2.6–8 (2:639–40).
31. See chap. 10.

wrath of God abideth on him" (3:36). Until God makes them alive with Christ, the elect are "children of wrath, even as others" (Eph. 2:3), "having no hope, and without God in the world," and so "far off" from God and his people (vv. 12–13). Brown asked, "In what state are the elect before justification?" and answered, "Though God loves them with an everlasting love, and his providence secretly makes way for their union to Christ; yet, in respect of the law, and of God as a judge, they are in a state of wrath and condemnation."[32]

2. *God accomplished justification by Christ's obedience, death, and resurrection.* Paul says that Christ "was delivered for our offences, and was raised again for our justification" (Rom. 4:25). He adds, "By the obedience of one shall many be made righteous" (5:19), referring to their "justification" (v. 18). When Paul writes that the incarnate God was "justified in the Spirit" (1 Tim. 3:16), he appears to refer to Christ's resurrection (cf. Rom. 1:4; 8:11). Christ was vindicated of all charges against him and declared righteous by God's raising him from the dead. In raising the Surety of his people from the grave, God raised and representatively justified all whom he had given to his Son as well. Thus, we may speak of our virtual or representative justification in Christ's great redeeming work, for Christ could say in his dying breath, "It is finished" (John 19:30).

3. *God promises justification in the gospel of Christ.* The evangelical promise announces "the forgiveness of sins" and that "all that believe are justified" (Acts 13:38–39). Romans 8:1 declares, "There is therefore now no condemnation to them which are in Christ Jesus." Whenever the good news is preached, God declares the justification of believers.

4. *God grants actual justification by faith in Christ.* Though justification is decreed in eternity, accomplished by Christ in history, and proclaimed in the gospel through the ages, it is applied and actualized only when a person is regenerated and trusts in Christ alone for salvation. Paul's repeated refrain is that we are justified by faith in Jesus Christ.[33] Paul locates justification after predestination and calling in the order of salvation (Rom. 8:30). The moment of actual justification appears clearly in Paul's words "We have believed in Jesus Christ, that we might be justified" (Gal. 2:16). The word translated as "that" (*hina*) expresses the purpose or re-

32. Brown, *Questions and Answers on the Shorter Catechism*, 156.

33. Acts 13:39; Rom. 1:17; 3:22–25, 28; 4:5, 9, 11, 13; 5:1; 9:30; 10:6; Gal. 3:8, 11, 16, 24; Phil. 3:9; cf. Heb. 11:7.

sult. Murray wrote of this text, "Faith in Christ is in order to justification, and is therefore regarded as antecedent to it."[34]

5. *God imparts a subjective sense of justification in the conscience.* The Puritans spoke of the "court of conscience," for God has set up the conscience in the soul to give a sense of his judgment on each person and his actions (Rom. 2:15; 9:1).[35] The justifying "blood of Christ" not only changes the believer's status before God, but when applied by faith to the heart can "purge your conscience from dead works to serve the living God" (Heb. 9:14)—that is, convey an inward sense of being clean and acceptable before God so that the believer can draw near to God with "boldness" (10:19, 22). This sense of justification is an aspect of the Spirit's work of assurance, which Paul describes with legal language: "The Spirit itself beareth witness with our spirit, that we are the children of God" (Rom. 8:16). Owen said this is an allusion "to judicial proceedings in point of titles and evidences," carried out not in court but "conscience."[36] He added, "The promise of the gospel, conveyed unto the soul by the Holy Spirit, and entertained by faith, completes the justification of a believer in his own conscience, and gives him assured peace with God."[37] Consequently, the objectively justified believer becomes subjectively assured of his righteousness before God. This will be explored more fully under the topic of assurance.[38]

Recognizing the distinctions between these five points guards us against the error often known as "eternal justification," in which justification by faith is seen merely as a person's recognition that God has already, indeed always, justified him. The Westminster Confession of Faith (11.4) says, "God did, from all eternity, decree to justify all the elect, and Christ did, in the fulness of time, die for their sins, and rise again for their justification: nevertheless, they are not justified, until the Holy Spirit doth, in due time, actually apply Christ unto them."[39]

We must reject the false doctrine that all the elect are already justified and that faith is only the realization of what has always been true. First,

34. Murray, *Redemption Accomplished and Applied*, 129.

35. Sibbes, *A Commentary upon the First Chapter of the Second Epistle of St Paul to the Corinthians*, in *Works*, 3:211. On justification in the court of conscience in the theology of Owen and Alexander Comrie, see Beeke, *The Quest for Full Assurance*, 182–85, 240.

36. Owen, *Communion with God*, in *Works*, 2:241.

37. Owen, *An Exposition of the Epistle to the Hebrews*, 3:300.

38. On assurance of salvation, see chaps. 33–34.

39. *Reformed Confessions*, 4:248. See also the Conclusions of the Synod of Utrecht (1905), in Schaver, *The Polity of the Churches*, 2:35.

as Thomas Goodwin said, justification by faith is not "only in respect to the court of my own conscience," for then "a man was as much justified before he believed as after, and his faith would add nothing new to his state, but his own apprehension of it; whereas the Scripture speaks of a man's justification by faith as of a real thing, and as a thing done anew."[40] Second, this doctrine would sever justification from sanctification. If the elect are justified apart from vital union with Christ, then how can we say with Paul, "What shall we say then? Shall we continue in sin, that grace may abound? God forbid. How shall we, that are dead to sin, live any longer therein?" (Rom. 6:1–2). We could be justified and yet not dead to sin. Third, we may not confuse the decree of God with the execution of that decree without overthrowing human responsibility and God's sovereign use of means to accomplish his ends. Fourth, locating actual justification in eternity would undermine evangelistic urgency. While we glorify God for his election and look to Christ because of his finished work, we must proclaim to condemned sinners the gospel message that God justifies only those people who trust in his Son. Murray said, "Justification by faith is the jubilee trumpet of the gospel."[41]

6. *God will publicly justify believers on judgment day.* Christ speaks of his people being "justified" on "the day of judgment" (Matt. 12:36–37). Paul says that God "will render to every man according to his deeds," eternal life to those who persevere in doing good in hope of God's promise of glory, and wrath and anguish to those who do not obey God's truth but do evil, and in that eschatological context he says, "The doers of the law shall be justified" (Rom. 2:6–10, 13). The final judgment cannot be by faith alone because of its very nature as a public demonstration of God's glory and righteousness (v. 5). On judgment day, our works will glorify God, who produced them through Christ (Phil. 1:9–11; 2 Thess. 1:9–12). They will show that we are truly children of God (Matt. 25:34–40). However, our works could never deliver us from the wrath of God—only Christ can do that by his righteousness (Rom. 5:9; 1 Thess. 1:10). On the basis of his redeeming death, God's people will "receive the promise of eternal inheritance" (Heb. 9:15).

Due to the grace of justification by faith, the believer's experience of judgment day will be fundamentally different from that of the unbeliever.

40. Goodwin, *The Object and Acts of Justifying Faith*, in *Works*, 8:214.
41. Murray, *Collected Writings*, 2:217.

Johannes Wollebius said that God will judge the wicked "in accordance with their works and on account of their works," but he will judge the righteous "according to the works of faith, but not on account of works." He noted that in the imagery of Revelation 20:12, two kinds of books are opened on judgment day, the book of works and the book of life, "so that we may know that the salvation of the righteous depends not on works but on the eternal grace of God."[42] Even the rewards God will give to us for our good works are from his fatherly mercy (Luke 12:32–33). The Belgic Confession (Art. 24) says, "We do good works, but not to merit by them. . . . We do not deny that God rewards our good works, but it is through His grace that He crowns His gifts."[43] The Heidelberg Catechism (LD 24, Q. 63) concurs: "This reward is not of merit, but of grace."[44]

Paul's expectation that all people will be judged by Christ according to their works (2 Cor. 5:10) did not lead him to call men to do works, but first and foremost to be reconciled to God through the forgiveness of their sins and the imputation of Christ's righteousness (vv. 18–21). Only the reconciled can please God with their works done by the Spirit's sanctifying grace.

The Means of Justification: By Faith in Christ

In Genesis 15:6, we read of Abraham, "He believed in the LORD, and he counted it to him for righteousness." This text was Paul's key to unlock the doctrine of justification by faith (Rom. 4:3; Gal. 3:6). Abraham was commonly viewed in ancient Judaism as a man whose faithfulness merited blessing for himself and his offspring.[45] In contrast, Paul uses Abraham as an example of how God "justifieth the *ungodly*" (Rom. 4:5) by imputing a "righteousness without works" (v. 6) before Abraham had received circumcision (vv. 9–12). Therefore, Abraham is "the father of all them that believe, though they be not circumcised; that righteousness might be imputed unto them also" (v. 11). Abraham was not justified by works of the law, and neither are Christians today, because the law can only bring

42. Wollebius, *Compendium*, 1.35.11 (184).
43. *The Three Forms of Unity*, 42.
44. *The Three Forms of Unity*, 63.
45. See the Prayer of Manasseh (v. 8) and Jubilees 23:10, in *Apocrypha and Pseudepigrapha of the Old Testament in English*, ed. R. H. Charles, 2 vols. (Oxford: Clarendon, 1913), 1:622; 2:48. See Richard N. Longenecker, *Galatians*, Word Biblical Commentary 41 (Nashville: Thomas Nelson, 1990), 110–11; and William Hendriksen, *Exposition of Paul's Epistle to the Romans*, vol. 1, *Chapters 1–8*, New Testament Commentary (Grand Rapids, MI: Baker, 1980), 145.

God's wrath on those who transgress it (vv. 13–15). Just as Abraham believed in God's promise of a supernaturally provided seed through whom God would bless the world (vv. 17–22)—which seed of blessing was Christ (Gal. 3:14, 16)—so also we today trust in the God who "raised up Jesus our Lord from the dead; who was delivered for our offences, and was raised again for our justification" (Rom. 4:23–25). Therefore, faith in the promises about Christ is God's ancient and only way of justifying sinners.

Habakkuk 2:4 rebukes the proud but promises, "The just shall live by his faith." Habakkuk's phrase "by faith," as rendered into Greek by the Septuagint (*ek pisteōs*), became a crucial expression for Paul to declare the function of faith in justification.[46] Paul says, "Therefore being justified by faith, we have peace with God through our Lord Jesus Christ" (Rom. 5:1). He also uses the phrase "through faith" (*dia pisteōs*).[47] Paul writes of "the righteousness of God which is by faith of Jesus Christ unto all and upon all them that believe" (3:22). At times, Paul uses the two prepositions interchangeably (vv. 25–26, 30). He writes in Galatians 2:16, "Knowing that a man is not justified by [*ex*] the works of the law, but by the faith [*dia pisteōs*] of Jesus Christ, even we have believed in Jesus Christ, that we might be justified by the faith [*ek pisteōs*] of Christ, and not by [*ex*] the works of the law: for by [*ex*] the works of the law shall no flesh be justified." This concurrent use of the two prepositions shows that the preposition *ek* should not be understood to designate the source or ground of justification, but, like *dia*, indicates the means or instrument through which God bestows it and men receive it. Paul also uses the dative case of faith (*pistei*) without a preposition to express the same idea of instrumentality.[48]

Where the Bible speaks of the "faith of Christ" (Phil. 3:9), it does not refer to faith exercised *by* Christ (subjective genitive) but to faith exercised *toward* Christ (objective genitive). Paul uses the phrase "the faith [*pistis*] of Jesus Christ" in Galatians 2:16 in a parallel manner with "we have believed [*pisteuō*] in Jesus Christ." Similarly, he speaks of the righteousness "by faith of Jesus Christ" for all who "believe" (Rom. 3:22; cf. Gal. 3:22). Paul never writes of Christ exercising faith. The use of the phrase "faith of

---

46. Rom. 1:17; 3:26, 30; 4:16; 5:1; 9:30, 32; 10:6; 14:23; Gal. 2:16; 3:7, 8, 9, 11, 12, 22, 24; 5:5. Paul cites Hab. 2:4 in Rom. 1:17; Gal. 3:11.

47. For examples of the phrase *dia pisteōs* being used of obtaining justification or salvation, see Rom. 3:22, 25; Gal. 2:16; Eph. 2:8; Phil. 3:9; 2 Tim. 3:15; Heb. 6:12; cf. 2 Cor. 5:7; Heb. 11:33; 1 Pet. 1:5.

48. Rom. 3:28; 5:2; 11:20; Phil. 3:9. The simple dative of *pistis* is used through Hebrews 11 for "by faith"; cf. the construction *en pistei* in Gal. 2:20; 2 Thess. 2:13.

Christ" is so interwoven with references to our trusting in Christ that it is clear Paul intends to communicate faith in Christ.

We are justified by faith in Christ. Faith, therefore, is not our righteousness, but the means through which we receive the righteousness of God in Christ. Paul never says that God justifies us *because of* faith or *on the basis of* faith. Berkhof said, "Scripture never says that we are justified *dia tēn pistin*, on account of faith. This means that faith is never represented as the ground of our justification."[49] Faith does not fulfill any condition of divine justice to make us acceptable to God. Faith does not become our merit instead of our good works. On the contrary, faith always looks outside of itself for righteousness in another—namely, Jesus Christ, the Righteous One. Thomas Watson said, "The dignity is not in faith as a grace, but relatively, as it lays hold on Christ's merits."[50] Justifying faith may be weak and full of imperfections, but it rests in the perfect righteousness of Christ. The Heidelberg Catechism (LD 23, Q. 61) says, "Why sayest thou that thou art righteous by faith only? Not that I am acceptable to God, on account of the worthiness of my faith, but because only the satisfaction, righteousness, and holiness of Christ, is my righteousness before God; and that I cannot receive and apply the same to myself any other way than by faith only."[51]

James Fisher and the Erskines said that faith is the instrument of justification "to show that our justification is wholly of grace; it being the nature of faith to take the gift of righteousness freely, without money, and without price; 'therefore it is of faith, that it might be by grace' (Rom. 4:16)." They explained that faith "is merely the hand that receives and applies the righteousness of Christ, by which we are justified."[52] Therefore, faith "is nothing else than a solemn declaration of our poverty and nakedness; and . . . therefore, it is our duty to glory only in Christ Jesus, saying, 'Surely—in the Lord have we righteousness and strength' (Isa. 45:24)."[53]

Reformed theologians have spoken of faith as a *condition* of the covenant and participation in Christ.[54] Some have gone further and

49. Berkhof, *Systematic Theology*, 520–21. See Bavinck, *Reformed Dogmatics*, 4:211.

50. Watson, *A Body of Divinity*, 227.

51. *The Three Forms of Unity*, 87.

52. Fisher et al., *The Assembly's Shorter Catechism Explained*, 33.56–57 (182).

53. Fisher et al., *The Assembly's Shorter Catechism Explained*, 33.66 (183).

54. Theodore Beza said in his Confession (4.5–6), "He has given His only-begotten Son, upon this condition, that whosoever embraces Him by faith will not perish. . . . Faith embraces and appropriates Jesus Christ to itself and all that is in Him (John 17:20–21), since He is given us on the condition that we believe in Him." The Westminster Larger Catechism says that God made "a covenant of life" with Adam "upon condition of personal, perfect, and perpetual obedience"

spoken of faith as the condition of justification. Stephen Charnock said, "Faith is the condition God requires to justification."[55] Others have firmly rejected the term *condition* with respect to justification. Robert Traill (1642–1716) said, "A man is justified by faith . . . only as a mere instrument receiving the imputed righteousness of Christ . . . this faith, in the office of justification, is neither condition nor qualification, nor our gospel-righteousness, but in its very act a renouncing of all such pretenses."[56] Owen wrote,

> Some do plead that faith is the condition of our justification, and that otherwise it is not to be conceived of. As I said before, so I say again, I shall not contend with any man about words, terms, or expressions, so long as what is intended by them is agreed upon. And there is an obvious sense wherein faith may be called the condition of our justification; for no more may be intended thereby, but that it is the duty on our part which God requireth, that we may be justified. And this the whole Scripture beareth witness unto.[57]

Owen proceeded to say that faith may be called a condition in the limited sense of being "the instrument whereby we apprehend or receive Christ and his righteousness." However, he recognized that the word *condition* is ambiguous and tends to confusion and strife. It also can provide an opening for men to distort faith into some kind of righteousness or something that we must pay or perform to procure grace.[58]

We will not criticize those who speak of faith as a condition of justification if the word *condition* is rightly defined, but it seems wiser to speak of faith as the "instrument with which we embrace Christ our Righteousness," as the Belgic Confession (Art. 22) says.[59] Calvin compared faith to an empty vessel or open mouth to receive Christ.[60]

(Q. 20), and made the covenant of grace with Christ and the elect, "requiring faith as the condition to interest them in him" (Q. 32). *Reformed Confessions*, 2:253–54; 4:303, 305.

55. Charnock, *The Existence and Attributes of God*, in *Works*, 2:214.

56. Robert Traill, *A Vindication of the Protestant Doctrine Concerning Justification . . . from the Unjust Charge of Antinomianism*, in *The Works of Robert Traill*, 4 vols. (1810; repr., Edinburgh: Banner of Truth, 1975), 1:277.

57. Owen, *The Doctrine of Justification by Faith*, in *Works*, 5:113.

58. Owen, *The Doctrine of Justification by Faith*, in *Works*, 5:113–16. Owen believed that the covenant of grace itself is unconditional, based on the promise of the new covenant (Jer. 31:31–34; cf. Hebrews 8).

59. *The Three Forms of Unity*, 39.

60. Calvin, *Institutes*, 3.11.7.

Wollebius wrote, "Faith justifies, not as a work or because of its worthiness, but simply as the instrument that apprehends Christ."[61]

Justification by Faith Alone and the Place of Good Works

The Westminster Confession of Faith (11.2) says, "Faith, thus receiving and resting on Christ and His righteousness, is the alone instrument of justification (John 1:12; Rom. 3:28; 5:1): yet it is not alone in the person justified, but is ever accompanied with all other saving graces, and is no dead faith, but worketh by love (James 2:17, 22, 26; Gal. 5:6)."[62] The tension between "faith alone" and "faith that is not alone" requires more attention to clarify the relationship between justification, faith, and good works.

First, justification by faith is *the opposite of justification by works of obedience to the law*. Paul writes, "Therefore by deeds of the law there shall no flesh be justified in his sight: for by the law is the knowledge of sin" (Rom. 3:20). The sins Paul has just pointed out from the law are moral offenses such as not doing good, not seeking God, wicked speech, violence, and lack of fear of God (vv. 9–18). Therefore, it is plain that Paul intends to exclude not only ceremonial "deeds of the law," but works of the moral law as well—neither can justify us. Paul says, "Therefore we conclude that a man is justified by faith without the deeds of the law" (v. 28). Paul often says that salvation comes to us not by our works, but by grace.[63]

Paul's doctrine of justification by faith alone apart from works stands in apparent contradiction to James 2:21–24, which says,

> Was not Abraham our father justified by works, when he had offered Isaac his son upon the altar? Seest thou how faith wrought with his works, and by works was faith made perfect? And the scripture was fulfilled which saith, Abraham believed God, and it was imputed unto him for righteousness: and he was called the Friend of God. Ye see then how that by works a man is justified, and not by faith only.

However, the contradiction is only apparent, for James uses the word translated as "justify" (*dikaioō*) in a different sense than Paul. When Paul

61. Wollebius, *Compendium*, 1.30.10 (166).
62. *Reformed Confessions*, 4:248.
63. In addition to Romans 3–4 and Galatians 2–3, see Rom. 9:11; 11:6; Eph. 2:8–9; 2 Tim. 1:9; Titus 3:5.

writes of justification by faith, "justify" has its forensic sense of a judge declaring a person righteous in the court of justice. In James, however, "justify" has the other sense that we noted earlier when discussing the terminology of justification: to declare or demonstrate publicly that a person is righteous.[64] In the same way, James says that Abraham had a right relationship with God when he trusted in God's promise (Gen. 15:6), but Abraham publicly demonstrated that he was in such a relationship with God by a living faith when he obeyed God's command to sacrifice his son Isaac (22:9–12). James's concern is how we show that our faith is real and living (James 2:14, 17, 26). Paul's concern is how we are counted righteous by God.[65]

Second, justification by faith is *the inseparable companion of the grace of sanctification.* While justification is a declarative act regarding the believer's legal status with God, it is always preceded by God's effectual calling of the sinner (Rom. 8:30) and is immediately followed by progressive sanctification in a believer's life. Paul anticipates that his gospel of justification by faith alone will provoke some to say, "Why not sin all the more, that grace may abound?" Paul's answer is the believer's union with Christ. Everyone with justifying faith is united to Christ in his death and resurrection, and therefore has died to sin and become alive to God. Sin cannot reign over them any longer (Rom. 6:1–14).

Christ is the wisdom, righteousness, sanctification, and redemption of those in union with him (1 Cor. 1:30). Wisdom pertains to receiving the gospel by faith, and redemption probably looks forward to deliverance from all evil. Between them lie the two great benefits enjoyed by believers in this life: righteousness (justification) and sanctification. Based on their appearance together in this text, Calvin inferred, "We cannot be justified freely through faith alone without at the same time living holily. For these fruits of grace are connected together, as it were, by an indissoluble tie, so that he who attempts to sever them does in a manner tear Christ in pieces."[66]

Both Paul and James teach that saving faith produces the works of love (Gal. 5:6; James 2:17). Martin Luther said, "Faith always justifies and makes alive; and yet it does not remain alone, that is, idle. Not that it does not remain alone on its own level and in its own function, for it always

64. Matt. 11:19; Luke 7:29, 35; 10:29; 16:15; Rom. 3:4; 1 Tim. 3:16; James 2:21, 24–25.

65. Berkhof, *Systematic Theology*, 521; Grudem, *Systematic Theology*, 731; and Joel R. Beeke and Steven J. Lawson, *Root and Fruit: Harmonizing Paul and James on Justification* (Conway, AR: Free Grace Press, 2020).

66. Calvin, *Commentaries*, on 1 Cor. 1:30; cf. *Institutes*, 3.11.6.

justifies alone. But it is incarnate and becomes man; that is, it neither is nor remains idle or without love."[67]

Justification and sanctification are inseparable but distinct graces in Christ. John Brown of Wamphray (c. 1609–1679) compared the two graces as follows:[68]

Justification	Sanctification
Change in relation to God and his law	Change in nature
Judicial act of God acquitting believers	Continual building up
Complete and not of various degrees	Growing work of many degrees
Perfect at the first moment	Not perfect until death
Equal in all	Not the same in all believers
Cannot be lost	Degrees may be lost
Instantaneous	Progressive
Removes guilt and liability to penalty	Kills the being and power of sin
Man accepted and righteousness imputed	Grace infused and the Spirit given
Gives the right to life	Gives fitness to share inheritance
By faith alone	Requires exercise of all graces

Table 22.1. Justification and Sanctification Contrasted

Both justification and sanctification are necessary for salvation, for each addresses a crucial problem of the sinner. John Angell James (1785–1859) wrote,

> Conceive of a man in prison under sentence of death, and at the same time dangerously ill of the jail fever. If the monarch pardons him, this is not enough for his safety and happiness, for he will die soon of his disease, unless it be cured. On the other hand, if the physician cures his disease, it is of little consequence unless the monarch gives him a

67. Luther, *Lectures on Galatians*, on Gal. 3:12, in *LW*, 26:272. Luther proceeded to compare faith's relationship with good works to Christ's two natures—they are inseparable but distinct.

68. John Brown of Wamphray, *The Life of Justification Opened* (N.p.: 1695), 268. See Joel R. Beeke, "John Calvin and John Brown of Wamphray on Justification," in *Reformed Orthodoxy in Scotland: Essays on Scottish Theology, 1560–1775*, ed. Aaron Clay Denlinger (London: Bloomsbury T&T Clark, 2015), 191–211. A similar comparison was made by J. C. Ryle, cited in J. I. Packer, *Faithfulness and Holiness: The Witness of J. C. Ryle* (Wheaton, IL: Crossway, 2002), 134.

reprieve; for though he get well of his disorder, he must soon suffer the penalty of the law; but if he be both pardoned and cured, he will be completely saved.[69]

The Experiential and Practical Benefits of Justification by Faith Alone

Although justification by faith alone is an invisible transaction regarding a person's legal status before God, it has massive implications for the Christian life. The faith that apprehends Christ for righteousness thereby grasps hold of a host of blessings in him.

1. *Peace of conscience.* Paul says, "Therefore being justified by faith, we have peace with God through our Lord Jesus Christ" (Rom. 5:1). The gospel is the preaching of peace (Acts 10:36), and Christ is our peace (Eph. 2:14). This is objective peace with God, but it bears fruit in subjective peace (1:2; 6:23). As faith increases, so do boldness and confidence in the presence of God (3:12). The divine verdict of righteousness pronounced in the heavenly courts is read, rejoiced in, and treasured in the earthly court of human conscience. A deep knowledge of peace with God through Christ gives solid ground on which to stand in the spiritual battle (6:15). Bruce Demarest says, "The righteous God has pardoned, cleansed, and freed true believers from the burden of sin and guilt. Overly scrupulous Christians need to celebrate this glorious reality."[70]

2. *Joyful communion with the reconciled God.* Though justification is a legal doctrine, it is not a dry, intellectual truth, but the opening of the door for a sweet relationship with the righteous God. Sin separates people from God (Isa. 59:2) and provokes him to anger (Rom. 1:18). Justification removes both guilt and wrath, so that nothing can separate believers from the love of God in Christ (8:33–39). Paul writes that as those "justified by his blood, . . . we also joy in God through our Lord Jesus Christ, by whom we have now received the atonement [literally reconciliation]" (5:9, 11). Through Christ, believers have access to the Father in one Spirit (Eph. 2:18). John exults, "Truly our fellowship is with the Father, and with his Son Jesus Christ" (1 John 1:3).

3. *Liberty to confess our sins and seek God's fatherly forgiveness.* The church enjoys the holy fellowship of walking in God's light, for "the blood

69. John Angell James, *Pastoral Addresses, Chiefly on the Subject of Christian Duty* (New York: Robert Carter and Brothers, 1852), 319.

70. Demarest, *The Cross and Salvation*, 380.

of Jesus Christ his Son cleanseth us from all sin" (1 John 1:6–7). This involves regular confession, repentance, experience of God's forgiveness through Christ, and renewal of their resolve to keep God's commandments (1:8–2:3). Christians may pray, "Forgive us our debts," knowing that we address not an angry Judge but a reconciled Father, even "our Father," as Christ taught us to pray (Matt. 6:9, 12). Therefore, in confession of sins, believers do not need repeated justification, but look to the God who has already justified them to receive their confession and repentance, and renew his gracious fellowship with them.[71] Brown of Haddington explained that "every day they live" believers "need a fatherly, but no new legal pardon," for the legal pardon is an act of God the Judge to release them from "eternal wrath," but the "fatherly pardon is an act of God as a Father," by which he "frees from chastisement."[72]

4. *The gift of eternal life and blessing.* The righteous shall "live" by faith (Hab. 2:4; Rom 1:17). Just as the condemnation of sin brought death on every level of existence, so Paul writes of the "justification of life," for those who receive "the gift of righteousness shall reign in life" through Jesus Christ (Rom. 5:17–18). Brown of Wamphray commented, "This life, whereof believers are made partakers, is begun, continued and carried on by faith, and therefore it is not by the works of the law, but by faith, that they arc justified and brought into a state of life."[73] Delivered from the curse of the law by Christ's redemption, believers receive the blessing promised to Abraham, the Spirit of life (8:1–3; Gal. 3:10–14). God is not against them, but for them, and so all things work together for their good (Rom. 8:28, 31).

5. *Freedom of conscience from human judgments.* God's verdict over believers is authoritative and final, so there is no condemnation for them (Rom. 8:1). Paul writes, "Who shall lay any thing to the charge of God's elect? It is God that justifieth" (v. 33). Wisdom still requires believers to listen to rebuke and correction lest they bring sorrow and shame on their lives (Prov. 13:18; 15:5). The church has the right and responsibility to hold believers accountable for their behavior and even remove the unrepentant from church membership (Matt. 18:15–18). However, when they do sin, they need not whip themselves, receive absolution from a human

71. On the contrary idea of repeated, daily justification, see Brakel, *The Christian's Reasonable Service*, 2:381–91.

72. Brown, *Questions and Answers on the Shorter Catechism*, 157.

73. Brown, *The Life of Justification Opened*, 9.

priest, or try to make satisfaction for sins, but must look to the Righteous One, Jesus Christ, who is the propitiation for their sins and their intercessor with God (1 John 2:1–2).

6. *Grounds for assurance of salvation.* If justification were by works, even in part, then people could never know in this life if they had done well enough to be accepted by God. Justification before God would be a never-ending quest of the anxious conscience. However, since Christians are "justified by faith" and "have peace with God" by the finished work of Christ, they "stand" in the status of divine grace (Rom. 5:1–2). Though good works and perseverance are important evidences of salvation (vv. 3–5), if we attempt to rest upon them we will soon find them to fail us. Justification by an imputed righteousness apart from works is solid ground for the trembling saint. Augustus Toplady wrote,

> From whence this fear and unbelief?
> Hath not the Father put to grief
> His spotless Son for me?
> And will the righteous Judge of men,
> Condemn me for that debt of sin,
> Which, Lord, was charg'd on Thee?
>
> Complete atonement Thou hast made,
> And to the utmost farthing paid
> Whate'er Thy people ow'd;
> Nor can His wrath on me take place,
> If shelter'd in Thy righteousness,
> And sprinkled with Thy blood.[74]

7. *Hope of glory.* Paul says that the consequence of "being justified by faith" is that we "rejoice in hope of the glory of God" (Rom. 5:1–2). The anticipation of judgment day no longer should fill believers with dread, because they are counted righteous in Christ. The crimson stains of their wickedness are washed away (Isa. 1:18), and they no longer owe outstanding debts crying out for punishment from God. Christ has satisfied the law's requirement and penalty. While the thought of Christ's judgment should fill believers with holy awe, it is an awe mingled with joy, for their Judge has justified them by his blood.

74. *Hymns and Sacred Poems, on a Variety of Divine Subjects, Comprising the Poetical Remains of the Rev. Augustus M. Toplady* (London: Daniel Sedgwick, 1860), 155.

Sing to the Lord

Singing of Christ's Saving Righteousness

Jesus, thy blood and righteousness
My beauty are, my glorious dress;
'Midst flaming worlds, in these arrayed,
With joy shall I lift up my head.

Bold shall I stand in thy great day;
For who aught to my charge shall lay?
Fully absolved through these I am
From sin and fear, from guilt and shame.

When from the dust of death I rise
To claim my mansion in the skies,
Ev'n then this shall be all my plea,
Jesus hath lived, hath died, for me.

Jesus, be endless praise to thee,
Whose boundless mercy hath for me—
For me a full atonement made,
An everlasting ransom paid.

Count Nikolaus Ludwig von Zinzendorf, trans. John Wesley, with alterations
Tune: Germany
Trinity Hymnal—Baptist Edition, No. 439

Questions for Meditation or Discussion

1. Why is it crucial for us to know God's justice and our sin in order for us to understand and appreciate justification?
2. What do the Hebrew and Greek words translated as "justify" mean?
3. What are the negative and positive aspects of the gift of justification?
4. What does "the righteousness of God" mean in Romans 1:17?
5. How does 2 Corinthians 5:21 teach a mutual imputation between Christ and believers?
6. How does justification by faith differ from the justification of the elect in God's eternal plan?
7. What does it mean to say that we are justified by faith alone?

8. What did James mean when he wrote that "by works a man is justified, and not by faith only" (2:24)?
9. How do justification and sanctification differ?
10. Which of the benefits of justification listed above is most precious to you now? Why?

Questions for Deeper Reflection

11. How does the believer's present justification by faith alone provide the basis for his future justification by the judgment according to works?
12. What are the possible implications of describing faith as the "instrument" or "condition" of justification? Which is the best term to use, and why?

23

Justification, Part 2

Historical and Polemical Theology (Ancient to Reformation)

The doctrine of justification has been the subject of much controversy, for the Devil and human self-righteousness militate against it. Martin Chemnitz, the "other Martin" of the Lutheran Reformation, said that restoring the doctrine of justification to light after it had been buried under false teaching was "a labor far greater than those of Hercules," and it would have been quite impossible "if the Holy Spirit had not led the way in kindling the light of the Word." Therefore, Chemnitz said, as heirs of the Reformation, "we must devote far more effort to retaining the genuine meaning and apostolic purity of the doctrine of justification, to handing it on to our posterity, and to preventing its being torn away from us or being adulterated by sophistic trickery or fraud."[1]

In this chapter, we will address the theological controversies that swirled about justification during the Reformation in the sixteenth century. However, in order to understand them, we must begin long before the Reformation and consider the ancient and medieval teaching of the church on this topic.

1. Martin Chemnitz, *Loci Theologici*, introductory remarks to loci on justification, in *Justification: The Chief Article of Christian Faith as Expounded in* Loci Theologici, trans. J. A. O. Preus, ed. Delpha H. Preus (St. Louis, MO: Concordia, 1985), 12.

The Early Church Fathers on Justification

The theologians of the early church were largely preoccupied with questions of the person of Christ and the doctrine of the Trinity, so they gave less attention to justification. However, from the earliest ages of the church, Christians have proclaimed and celebrated the gospel of salvation by grace alone apart from our works. Clement of Rome (d. 99) said in the first century, "We, too, being called by His will in Christ Jesus, are not justified by ourselves, nor by our own wisdom, or understanding, or godliness, or works which we have wrought in holiness of heart; but by that faith through which, from the beginning, Almighty God has justified all men; to whom be glory for ever and ever. Amen."[2] In the second century AD, an anonymous Christian exulted in the "sweet exchange" of the punishment we deserved for the righteousness that Christ accomplished.[3]

Theodoret of Cyr (c. 393–466) commented on Paul's statement "By grace ye are saved" (Eph. 2:5), saying, "For it is not because of the excellence of our lives that we have been called but because of the love of our Savior."[4] Marius Victorinus (fl. c. 355) said, "He did not make us deserving, since we did not receive these things by our own merit but by the grace and goodness of God."[5] The same author wrote that salvation "is the gift of God. It is not from your works, but it is God's grace as God's gift, not from anything you have deserved."[6]

John Chrysostom said, "What then is Paul saying? Not that God has forbidden works but that he has forbidden us to be justified by works. No one, Paul says, is justified by works, precisely in order that the grace and benevolence of God may become apparent!"[7] Chrysostom commented on the justification of Abraham by faith apart from works (Rom. 4:1–2): "For a person who had no works, to be justified by faith, was nothing unlikely. But for a person richly adorned with good deeds, not to be made just from hence, but from faith, this is the thing to cause wonder, and to set the power of faith in a strong light."[8] Preaching on Romans

2. Clement, *First Epistle*, chap. 32, in *ANF*, 1:13.

3. Anonymous, *Epistle to Diognetus*, chap. 9, in *ANF*, 1:28. The text is quoted in *RST*, 2:1013–14.

4. Theodoret, Epistle to the Ephesians, 2.4–5, in *ACCS/NT*, 8:132. We are indebted for the references in this paragraph and the next to Thomas C. Oden, *The Justification Reader* (Grand Rapids, MI: Eerdmans, 2002), 44–46, 59.

5. Marius Victorinus, Epistle to the Ephesians, 1.2.7, in *ACCS/NT*, 8:132.

6. Marius Victorinus, Epistle to the Ephesians, 1.2.9, in *ACCS/NT*, 8:134.

7. Chrysostom, Homilies on Ephesians, 4.2.9, in *ACCS/NT*, 8:134.

8. Chrysostom, Homilies on Romans, Homily 8, in *NPNF*[1], 11:385.

8:33–34, he said, "He does not say, it is God that forgave our sins, but what is much greater, 'It is God that justifieth.' For when the Judge's sentence declares us just, and a Judge such as that too, what signifieth the accuser? . . . Who then is to condemn us, since God crowns us, and Christ was put to death for us, and not only was put to death, but also after this intercedeth for us?"[9] On Paul's words in 2 Corinthians 5:21, Chrysostom said that Christ "suffered as a sinner to be condemned, as one cursed"; we become the righteousness of God "when we are justified not by works (in which case it were necessary that not a spot even should be found), but by grace, in which case all sin is done away." He compared salvation to a king's substitution of his beloved son for a criminal: the king "transferred the death and the guilt as well, from him to his son . . . that he might both save the condemned man and clear him from his evil reputation," and consequently advance him to "great dignity" and "glory unspeakable."[10]

However, the early church fathers also planted seeds that would lead to grave confusion about justification, not least of which was the term *merit* (Latin *meritum*).[11] Tertullian said, "We affirm that a judgment has been ordained by God according to the merits of every man."[12] He wrote, "A good deed has God as its debtor, just as an evil has too; for a judge is a rewarder of every cause."[13] Tertullian said that repentance before baptism is the price and compensation God requires for the forgiveness of sins, and repentance after baptism is the satisfaction for further sins.[14] Cyprian (d. 258) wrote that the blood of Christ washes away the sins committed before baptism, but good works must cleanse us from the guilt of later sins: "By works of righteousness God is satisfied."[15]

Merit theology reached its pinnacle in Pelagius, who taught that God loves the saints according to the merit of their righteousness.[16] His disciple Celestius (fl. 400–430) said, "God's grace is given in

9. Chrysostom, Homilies on Romans, Homily 15, in *NPNF*[1], 11:455.

10. Chrysostom, Homilies on 2 Corinthians, 11.5–6, in *NPNF*[1], 12:334–35.

11. Alister E. McGrath, *Iustitia Dei: A History of the Christian Doctrine of Justification*, 2 vols. (Cambridge: Cambridge University Press, 1986), 1:23.

12. Tertullian, *Ad Nationes*, 1:19, in *ANF*, 3:127; cf. *Against Marcion*, 5.12, in *ANF*, 3:456.

13. Tertullian, *On Repentance*, chap. 2, in *ANF*, 3:658. See Johann Heinz, *Justification and Merit: Luther vs. Catholicism* (Berrien Springs, MI: Andrews University Press, 1981), 114–15.

14. Tertullian, *On Repentance*, chaps. 6–7, in *ANF*, 3:661, 663.

15. Cyprian, *On Works and Alms*, chaps. 1–5, in *ANF*, 5:476–77.

16. Pelagius, "The Christian Life," 18.

proportion to our deserts; because were he to give it to sinful persons, he would seem to be unrighteous."[17] Pelagius said that baptism justifies sinners so that their past sins are forgiven if they seriously intend to obey from then onward. After their baptism, however, Christians must merit the kingdom of God by the right use of their free will to do good works. According to Pelagius, justification apart from works means apart from ceremonial works of the Jewish law, not apart from works of obedience.[18]

Augustine led the church in opposing Pelagianism and defended salvation by grace. He said, "He, then being made sin, just as we are made righteousness (our righteousness being not our own, but God's, not in ourselves, but in Him); He being made sin, not His own, but ours, not in Himself, but in us."[19] Augustine added that we are "justified in the blood of Christ" because Christ suffered "that He might pay for us debtors that which He Himself did not owe" to set us free from the Devil.[20] The blood of the sinless One "was poured out for the remission of our sins" because the only bond by which Satan held us was that we were "guilty of sin," but now in Christ we are released from God's wrath and reconciled to him.[21]

However, Augustine understood *justify* as "make righteous," broadly including both forgiveness and transformation by grace apart from prior works.[22] Augustine said, "Works do not precede justification. . . . Justification does not subsequently accrue to them as doers of the law, but justification precedes them as doers of the law. For what else does the phrase 'being justified' signify than 'being made righteous,' by Him, of course, who justifies the ungodly man, that he may become a godly one instead?"[23] In part, the problem of interpreting "justification" is linguistic. Unlike the Hebrew and Greek words translated as "justify" in the Bible, which refer to one's legal and judicial status,[24] the

17. Cited in Pelagius, "The Christian Life," 65.

18. Evans, *Pelagius*, 109, 113–14, 119; Pelagius, *Commentary on Romans*, on Rom. 3:28, in *ACCS/NT*, 6:105.

19. Augustine, *Enchiridion*, chap. 41 (52).

20. Augustine, *On the Trinity*, 15.14.18, in *NPNF*[1], 3:177.

21. Augustine, *On the Trinity*, 15.15.19; 15.16.21, in *NPNF*[1], 3:177, 179.

22. See David F. Wright, "Justification in Augustine," in *Justification in Perspective: Historical Developments and Contemporary Challenges*, ed. Bruce L. McCormack (Grand Rapids, MI: Baker Academic, 2006), 55–72.

23. Augustine, *On the Spirit and the Letter*, chap. 45, in *NPNF*[1], 5:102. See Michael Horton, *Justification*, 2 vols., New Studies in Dogmatics (Grand Rapids, MI: Zondervan, 2018), 1:88–89.

24. On the biblical terminology for justification, see chap. 22.

Latin verb *justifico* can mean "to act justly, do justice" or "to make just, forgive, or vindicate."[25] Augustine's discussions of justification tended to focus on the infusion of inward grace to overcome original sin.[26] For Augustine, justification was an unmerited gift of forgiveness and a new disposition of love that produces good works.[27] He also used the language of merit for the virtues of those saved by grace, but emphasized that this merit was by grace: "When God crowns our merits, he crowns nothing but his own gifts."[28] Augustine acknowledged that even for those whose faith "worketh by love" (Gal. 5:6), their "righteousness, too, though true in so far as it has respect to the true good, is yet in this life of such a kind that it consists rather in the remission of sins than in the perfecting of virtues." They must continually pray, "Forgive us our debts" (Matt. 6:12), for "however well one maintains the conflict, and however thoroughly he has subdued these enemies, there steals in some evil thing, which, if it do not find ready expression in act, slips out by the lips, or insinuates itself into the thought."[29]

While we recognize that the early church fathers made an important point in linking good works with authentic godliness that will receive God's blessing on judgment day, we do not believe that Christians should speak of the merit of one's works with God, even when clarifying that such merit is produced by God's grace. In Latin, *meritum* can refer to something's worth or value; however, it often connotes earning or deserving a reward.[30] Even if we obeyed God perfectly, we would merit nothing, for servants owe obedience to their master (Luke 17:7–10). As we are in our fallen condition, if God should judge us according to the strict requirements of his law, who could stand (Ps. 130:3)? Paul rejects the notion that we merit anything when he writes, "Now to him that worketh is the reward not reckoned of grace, but of debt. But to him that worketh not, but believeth on him that justifieth the ungodly, his faith is counted for righteousness" (Rom. 4:4–5). Our justification is a free gift from God (3:24), as is eternal life, for the

25. Charlton T. Lewis and Charles Short, eds., *A New Latin Dictionary* (New York: Harper & Brothers; Oxford: Clarendon, 1879), s.v. *justifico* (1020).

26. Augustine, *On the Merits and Forgiveness of Sins, and on the Baptism of Infants*, 1.9.10, in *NPNF*[1], 5:18–19. See McGrath, *Iustitia Dei*, 1:14–15, 30–31.

27. Augustine, *Expositions on the Book of Psalms*, 111.3 (5:258–59).

28. Augustine, Epistle 194, cited in McGrath, *Iustitia Dei*, 1:28. See Augustine, *Enchiridion*, chaps. 30–32, 94, 109–10, in *NPNF*[1], 3:247–48, 267, 272.

29. Augustine, *The City of God*, 19.27, in *NPNF*[1], 2:419.

30. Lewis and Short, eds., *A New Latin Dictionary*, s.v. *mereo* (1136).

only wages that we can merit is death (6:23). Christ alone is our merit before God, and our good works can receive no reward apart from his righteousness.

The Medieval Catholic Theologians on Justification

The medieval church in the West continued to follow the trajectory of defining justification as inward transformation by the grace of Christ and the forgiveness of sins, which enables a life by grace and the gaining of merit.[31] Peter Abelard (1079–1142) said that we are justified by love, faith being the means by which God stirs up love for him in us by revealing his love for us in Christ.[32] Peter Lombard wrote, "Christ's death justifies us, as by it charity [Christian love] is kindled in our heart" and we "are released from the devil's bonds."[33] Thomas Aquinas said that God's sanctifying grace justifies a man by making him pleasing to God through the infusion of a new habit into the soul and the forgiveness of sins.[34] Aquinas emphasized the free and sovereign nature of divine grace as the cause of all movements toward God.[35] However, William of Ockham (d. 1347) and Gabriel Biel (d. 1495) went so far as to forge a semi-Pelagian ladder of merit from the depths of man's fall all the way to heaven. At each rung of the ladder, a person was promised that he could ascend another step as long as he merited it by doing what he could for God by the free choice of his will.[36]

Although merit was part of medieval theology, the piety of medieval theologians did not encourage Christians to rely on their merits but on Christ. Anselm of Canterbury (c. 1033–1109) prayed for God to perfect

31. For a study of justification in the teachings of Peter Lombard, Thomas Aquinas, John Duns Scotus, William of Ockham, and Gabriel Biel, see Horton, *Justification*, 1:93–162.

32. Peter Abelard, *Exposition of the Epistle to the Romans*, on Rom. 3:21–26, in *A Scholastic Miscellany: Anselm to Ockham*, ed. Eugene R. Fairweather, Library of Christian Classics 10 (Philadelphia: Westminster, 1956), 278–79.

33. Lombard, *The Sentences*, 3.19.1.1–3 (3:78–79).

34. Aquinas, *Summa Theologica*, Part 2.1, Q. 111, Art. 1, Reply Obj. 1; Art. 2, Answer; Q. 113, Art. 8.

35. "God does not justify us without ourselves, because whilst we are being justified we consent to God's justification by a movement of our free-will. Nevertheless this movement is not the cause of grace, but the effect; hence the whole operation pertains to grace." Aquinas, *Summa Theologica*, Part 2.1, Q. 111, Art. 2, Reply Obj. 2.

36. Heiko Oberman, *The Dawn of the Reformation: Essays in Late Medieval and Early Reformation Thought* (Edinburgh: T&T Clark, 1986), 213; *The Harvest of Medieval Theology: Gabriel Biel and Late Medieval Nominalism* (Durham, NC: Labyrinth, 1963), 132; and Steven E. Ozment, *The Age of Reform (1250–1550): An Intellectual and Religious History of Late Medieval and Reformation Europe* (New Haven, CT: Yale University Press, 1980), 234. See the discussion of semi-Pelagian preparationism in chap. 13.

his salvation "not according to my deserts but out of your kindness that came first to me."[37] He counseled a dying sinner,

> Put all thy confidence in this [Christ's] death alone, place thy trust in no other thing. . . . And if God would judge thee, say, "Lord, I place the death of our Lord Jesus Christ between me and thy judgment; and otherwise I will not contend or enter into judgment with thee." And if he shall say unto thee that thou art a sinner, say, "I place the death of our Lord Jesus Christ between me and my sins." If he shall say unto thee that thou hast deserved damnation, say, "Lord, I put the death of our Lord Jesus Christ between thee and all my sins; and I offer his merits for my own, which I should have, and have not."[38]

Bernard of Clairvaux said, "Perhaps I have committed some great sin, my conscience is troubled, but I do not despair, because I remember the wounds of my Lord. . . . The pitying mercy of the Lord is, then, all my merit. . . . Shall it be my own righteousness that I celebrate? Nay, O Lord; I will make mention of Thy righteousness, even of Thine only (Ps. 71:16). For that is mine also, since Thou Thyself hast become my Righteousness."[39] Bernard spoke of God's gift of an "alien righteousness" to those who lack their own, and he spoke of justification by Christ's blood.[40]

John Owen cited many such theologians—including Counter-Reformation Roman Catholic theologians—who denied any place to our merits and rested on Christ alone for righteousness,[41] and commented, "I had rather learn what some men really judge about their own justification from their prayers than their writings."[42] Therefore, the Reformers believed that the true doctrine of justification was present in seed form in the ancient and medieval church, but that it was obscured by other teachings that had to be

---

37. *The Prayers and Meditations of St. Anselm*, trans. Benedicta Ward (Harmondsworth, England: Penguin, 1973), 94.

38. Cited in Owen, *The Doctrine of Justification by Faith*, in *Works*, 5:16–17. See Anselm, *Admonitio Morienti*, in J. P. Migne, ed., *Patrologia Latina* (Paris, 1865), 158:687, cited in Oden, *The Justification Reader*, 58.

39. Bernard of Clairvaux, *Sermons on the Song of Songs*, 61.3, 5, in *The Life and Works of Saint Bernard, Abbot of Clairvaux*, ed. John Mabillon, trans. Samuel J. Eales, 4 vols. (London: John Hodges, 1896), 4:367–68. For this citation of Bernard, we are indebted to Calvin, *Institutes*, 3.12.3.

40. Anthony N. S. Lane, *Bernard of Clairvaux: Theologian of the Cross*, Cistercian Studies Series 248 (Collegeville, MN: Liturgical Press, 2013), 91 (Bernard's epistle against Abelard, 6.15), 218–19.

41. Owen, *The Doctrine of Justification by Faith*, in *Works*, 5:16–18, 32–33, 36–40.

42. Owen, *The Doctrine of Justification by Faith*, in *Works*, 5:18.

cleared away so that justification by faith in Christ alone could be clearly seen and defended.

The Reformers on Justification

Despite attempts to reinterpret his teaching by modern theologians,[43] Martin Luther remains a great champion of justification by faith alone.[44] He rejected all merit outside of Christ and justification by the infusion of love into the soul.[45] Luther said, "For by His Word God has revealed to us that He wants to be a merciful Father to us. Without our merit—since, after all, we cannot merit anything—He wants to give us forgiveness of sin, righteousness, and eternal life for the sake of Christ."[46] He added, "We are pronounced righteous solely by faith in Christ, not by the works of the Law or by love."[47] Luther further explained, "Christ who is grasped by faith and who lives in the heart is the true Christian righteousness, on account of which God counts us righteous and grants us eternal life. Here there is no work of the Law, no love; but an entirely different kind of righteousness."[48]

Luther spoke of an "alien righteousness" given to believers, "the righteousness of another." As a result, the Christian can say, "Mine are Christ's living, doing, and speaking, his suffering and dying, mine as much as if I had lived, done, spoken, suffered, and died as he did." Luther explained this in terms of the union of a bridegroom and his bride so that they share all things—"so Christ and the church are one spirit." He said, "Through

43. Beginning in the late 1970s, a group of Finnish Lutherans led by Tuomo Mannermaa (1937–2015) argued that Martin Luther did not teach justification as a forensic declaration but a deifying union with God and participation in divine love. Veli-Matti Kärkkäinen, "Deification View," in *Justification: Five Views*, ed. James K. Beilby, Paul Rhodes Eddy, and Steven E. Enderlein (Downers Grove, IL: InterVarsity Press, 2011), 219–28. See Tuomo Mannermaa, *Christ Present in Faith: Luther's View of Justification* (Minneapolis: Fortress, 2005); and Kurt E. Marquart, "Luther and Theosis," *Concordia Theological Quarterly* 64, no. 3 (July 2000): 182–205. This interpretation has been criticized by other Lutheran scholars because of the lack of evidence that deification is the central idea of Luther's doctrine of justification, it does not fit with many of Luther's statements, it fails to appreciate Luther's rhetorical manner of expressing himself, and it ignores Luther's ontology of the Creator and his creation by the word. Robert Kolb, "Contemporary Lutheran Understandings of the Doctrine of Justification," in *Justification: What's at Stake in the Current Debates*, ed. Mark Husbands and Daniel J. Treier (Downers Grove, IL: InterVarsity Press, 2004), 153–56; and Robert Kolb and Charles P. Arand, *The Genius of Luther's Theology: A Wittenberg Way of Thinking for the Contemporary Church* (Grand Rapids, MI: Baker Academic, 2008), 48n65.

44. On Luther's doctrine of justification and its development, see R. Scott Clark, "*Iustitia Imputata Christi*: Alien or Proper to Luther's Doctrine of Justification?," *Concordia Theological Quarterly* 70 (2006): 269–310.

45. Luther, *Lectures on Galatians*, on Gal. 2:16, in *LW*, 26:124–29.

46. Luther, *Lectures on Galatians*, on Gal. 2:16, in *LW*, 26:127.

47. Luther, *Lectures on Galatians*, on Gal. 2:16, in *LW*, 26:137.

48. Luther, *Lectures on Galatians*, on Gal. 2:16, in *LW*, 26:130.

faith in Christ, therefore, Christ's righteousness becomes our righteousness and all that he has becomes ours; rather, he himself becomes ours."[49]

Shortly after Luther began teaching justification by faith alone and distinguishing between the law and the gospel, the Reformation faced a false teaching that discarded the use of the law in Christian spirituality. Luther rejected good works only "as the basis for justification," but emphasized "the importance of good works in the life of faith."[50] However, John Agricola (1494–1566) broke from Luther and Philip Melanchthon by insisting that the law of God has no place in the Christian life and pertains only to civil government. Agricola wrote, "If they sin, they run to Christ and shake their sins on him. If they do something good, then it is not theirs but his. They need no law." Agricola went so far as to say to believers, "If you sin, be happy; it should have no consequence."[51] Luther called this perspective *antinomianism* and firmly rejected it.[52] Melanchthon complained in 1527, "Nowadays many teach faith and the remission of sins, but they do not teach *poenitentia* [repentance]. But without *poenitentia* faith is nothing but a foolish dream."[53]

Like Luther, John Calvin also taught justification by faith alone through the imputed righteousness of Christ. He said "that our righteousness is not in us but in Christ, that we possess it only because we are partakers in Christ."[54] God justifies people by faith because faith "binds us to Christ, so that, made one with him, we may enjoy participation in his righteousness."[55] Calvin denied that God counts a man righteous "because by Christ's righteousness he shares the Spirit of God," but taught that God gives righteousness by the imputation of Christ's obedience: "Our righteousness is not in us but in Christ. . . . To declare that by him alone we are accounted righteous, what else is this but to lodge our righteousness in Christ's obedience, because the obedience of Christ is reckoned to us as if it were our own?"[56]

---

49. Luther, *Two Kinds of Righteousness*, in *LW*, 31:297–98.
50. David Steinmetz, cited in Mark Jones, *Antinomianism: Reformed Theology's Unwelcome Guest?* (Phillipsburg, NJ: P&R, 2013), 5.
51. Cited in Timothy J. Wengert, *Law and Gospel: Philip Melanchthon's Debate with John Agricola of Eisleben over* Poenitentia, Texts and Studies in Reformation and Post-Reformation Thought (Grand Rapids, MI: Baker, 1997), 85, 87.
52. On the controversy, see the introduction to Luther, *Against the Antinomians*, in *LW*, 47:101–6.
53. Cited in Wengert, *Law and Gospel*, 23.
54. Calvin, *Institutes*, 3.11.23.
55. Calvin, *Institutes*, 3.17.11.
56. Calvin, *Institutes*, 3.11.23.

Calvin wrote, "Man, accordingly, has no works in which to glory before God; and hence, stripped of all help from works, he is justified by faith alone." He defined justification as follows: "The sinner, received into communion with Christ, is reconciled to God by his grace, while, cleansed by Christ's blood, he obtains forgiveness of sins, and clothed with Christ's righteousness as if it were his own, he stands confident before the heavenly judgment seat."[57]

Calvin argued that the fathers unwisely introduced the term *merit* when other words would have better served to describe the value of good works, for the fathers asserted that salvation was entirely of grace.[58] He remarked,

> For when Augustine says anything clearly, Lombard obscures it, and if there was anything slightly contaminated in Augustine, he corrupts it. The schools have gone continually from bad to worse until, in headlong ruin, they have plunged into a sort of Pelagianism. For that matter, Augustine's view, or at any rate his manner of stating it, we must not entirely accept. For even though he admirably deprives man of all credit for righteousness and transfers it to God's grace, he still subsumes grace under sanctification, by which we are reborn in newness of life through the Spirit.[59]

Against antinomianism, Calvin asserted that Christ gives a "double grace" to all in him: they are counted righteous by imputation and are progressively made holy by the Spirit of God.[60] Calvin said, "As Christ cannot be torn into parts, so these two which we perceive in him together and conjointly are inseparable—namely, righteousness and sanctification."[61]

This doctrine of justification by faith alone is clearly affirmed in the Reformation confessions and catechisms. The Augsburg Confession (Art. 4) states "that we cannot obtain forgiveness of sin and righteousness before God through our merit, work, or satisfactions, but that we receive forgiveness of sin and become righteous before God out of grace for Christ's sake through faith."[62]

The Heidelberg Catechism (LD 23, Q. 60) says,

57. Calvin, *Institutes*, 3.17.8.
58. Calvin, *Institutes*, 3.15.2. He cited Chrysostom, Augustine, and Bernard.
59. Calvin, *Institutes*, 3.11.15.
60. Calvin, *Institutes*, 3.11.1.
61. Calvin, *Institutes*, 3.11.6.
62. *The Book of Concord*, 38, 40.

> Q. How art thou righteous before God?
> A. Only by a true faith in Jesus Christ; so that, though my conscience accuse me, that I have grossly transgressed all the commandments of God, and kept none of them, and am still inclined to all evil; notwithstanding, God, without any merit of mine, but only of mere grace, grants and imputes to me the perfect satisfaction, righteousness and holiness of Christ; even so, as if I never had had, nor committed any sin; yea, as if I had fully accomplished all that obedience which Christ has accomplished for me, inasmuch as I embrace such benefit with a believing heart.[63]

The Westminster Shorter Catechism (Q. 33) asks, "What is justification?" and answers, "Justification is an act of God's free grace, wherein he pardoneth all our sins (Rom. 3:24–25; 4:6–8), and accepteth us as righteous in his sight (2 Cor. 5:19, 21), only for the righteousness of Christ imputed to us (Rom. 5:17–19), and received by faith alone (Gal. 2:16; Phil. 3:9)."[64] The catechism refers to justification as an act and not a work "because, like the sentence of a judge, it is completed at once, and not carried on gradually like a work of time," James Fisher and the Erskines wrote.[65] The Westminster Confession of Faith (11.1) clarifies,

> Those whom God effectually calleth, He also freely justifieth (Rom. 8:30; 3:24): not by infusing righteousness into them, but by pardoning their sins, and by accounting and accepting their persons as righteous; not for any thing wrought in them, or done by them, but for Christ's sake alone; nor by imputing faith itself, the act of believing, or any other evangelical obedience to them, as their righteousness; but by imputing the obedience and satisfaction of Christ unto them (Rom. 4:5–8; 2 Cor. 5:19, 21; Rom. 3:22, 24–25, 27–28; Titus 3:5, 7; Eph. 1:7; Jer. 23:6; 1 Cor. 1:30–31; Rom. 5:17–19).[66]

In summary, the Reformation view of justification is that God freely grants to a sinner a righteousness not his own, but the righteousness of Jesus Christ, forgiving that sinner of all his sins and imputing to him the obedience of Christ through faith alone. Calvin called this doctrine "the main hinge on which religion turns," apart from which a person has no

63. *The Three Forms of Unity*, 87.
64. *Reformed Confessions*, 4:357.
65. Fisher et al., *The Assembly's Shorter Catechism Explained*, 33.10 (177).
66. *Reformed Confessions*, 4:247.

"foundation on which to establish your salvation" or "build piety toward God."[67]

The Council of Trent and Modern Roman Catholicism on Justification

At first, Roman Catholic responses to the Reformers' doctrine of justification were mixed. At the Regensburg Colloquy (1541), some Roman Catholic theologians showed remarkable openness to affirm that righteousness "is imputed to us on account of Christ and his merit, not on account of the worthiness or perfection of the righteousness imparted to us in Christ."[68] Cardinal Gasparo Contarini (1483–1542), a papal legate at the colloquy, said that Christians do have "a righteousness inherent in us," but we must rest in Christ's perfect righteousness imputed to us, "and on account of it alone we must believe that we are justified before God."[69]

Pope Paul III (1468–1549) convened the Council of Trent in the mid-sixteenth century to respond to the challenges of the Reformers, and Trent gave particular attention to the doctrine of justification in its sixth session (1547).[70] Roman Catholic historian Hubert Jedin (1900–1980) wrote, "The Tridentine decree on justification is the Church's authoritative answer to the teaching of Luther and the *Confessio Augustana* [the Augsburg Confession] on grace and justification."[71] Whatever ambiguity and openness there may have been among Roman Catholics toward the Reformers' doctrine of justification, at Trent the battle lines were drawn. Unfortunately, the council's decrees often caricatured Reformation teachings or mingled them with ideas that the Reformers also condemned. However, the canons and decrees of Trent make it clear that the Roman Catholic Church rejects justification by faith alone.[72]

67. Calvin, *Institutes*, 3.11.1.

68. The Regensburg Agreement (5.4), in Anthony N. S. Lane, *Justification by Faith in Catholic-Protestant Dialogue: An Evangelical Assessment* (London: T&T Clark, 2002), 235. The colloquy foundered on differences over the authority of the church and the nature of the Eucharist. Calvin thought the statement on justification to be acceptable though in need of further clarification; Luther rejected it (46–60). See also Anthony N. S. Lane "A Tale of Two Imperial Cities: Justification at Regensburg (1541) and Trent (1546–1547)," in *Justification in Perspective*, ed. McCormack, 119–45.

69. Gasparo Contarini, *De Justificatione*, in *Gasparis Contareni Cardinalis Opera* (Paris: Apud Sebastinanum Nivellium, 1571), 592; English translation in Turretin, *Institutes*, 16.2.18 (2:643–44).

70. Council of Trent, Decree on Justification, in *The Creeds of Christendom*, ed. Schaff, 2:89–118.

71. Hubert Jedin, *A History of the Council of Trent*, trans. Dom Ernest Graf, 2 vols. (Edinburgh: Thomas Nelson, 1957), 2:307.

72. Council of Trent, Decree on Justification, canons 9, 11, in *The Creeds of Christendom*, ed. Schaff, 2:112–13.

According to Trent, justification "is not remission of sins merely, but also the sanctification and renewal of the inward man, through the voluntary reception of the grace."[73] Justification is not a forensic act of God, but his gift of a righteousness "inherent in us," having been "infused into us of God, through the merit of Christ,"[74] granted through the "instrumental cause" of baptism.[75] Adults must prepare themselves for justification by cooperating with prevenient grace through believing God's promises, loving him, hating their sins, and resolving to keep God's commands.[76] After being justified, Christians "are still further justified" as their personal virtue increases in a life of faith and good works.[77] Thus, the first justification of regeneration leads to the second justification of meritorious works. Through mortal sin, "the received grace of justification is lost," but those persevering in love and the use of the sacraments may hope that God may reward "their good works and merits" with eternal life.[78]

R. C. Sproul observed, "It is slanderous to Rome to charge them with a pure Pelagianism that teaches justification by works. Rome has a view of justification by faith." However, Sproul noted that in the Roman Catholic view, faith is not the instrument by which we are justified—that, they say, is baptism and later penance—and we are not justified by faith alone, for love must be added by God's renewing grace so that we really are righteous in our hearts.[79] In other words, the Roman Catholic Church means something quite different by justification than the forensic, judicial justification taught by the Reformers.

The doctrine of Trent continues to be the official stance of the Roman Church. At the beginning of the Second Vatican Council (1962), Pope John XXIII (1881–1963) said of the church's doctrines, "What was, still is."[80] The 1994 *Catechism of the Catholic Church* affirms the doctrine of

73. Council of Trent, Decree on Justification, chap. 7, in *The Creeds of Christendom*, ed. Schaff, 2:94.
74. Council of Trent, Decree on Justification, chap. 16, in *The Creeds of Christendom*, ed. Schaff, 2:108–9.
75. Council of Trent, Decree on Justification, chap. 7, in *The Creeds of Christendom*, ed. Schaff, 2:94–95.
76. Council of Trent, Decree on Justification, chaps. 5–6, in *The Creeds of Christendom*, ed. Schaff, 2:92–93.
77. Council of Trent, Decree on Justification, chap. 10, in *The Creeds of Christendom*, ed. Schaff, 2:99.
78. Council of Trent, Decree on Justification, chaps. 15–16, in *The Creeds of Christendom*, ed. Schaff, 2:106–7. The fallen are said to be restored through the sacrament of penance (2:139–58).
79. R. C. Sproul, "The Forensic Nature of Justification," in *Justification by Faith Alone*, ed. Kistler, 32.
80. Cited in *Congregation for the Doctrine of the Faith: Responses to Some Questions Regarding Certain Aspects of the Doctrine of the Church*, June 29, 2007, Vatican, http://www.vatican.va

justification by infused righteousness, quoting Trent with approval.[81] It says, "Justification entails the sanctification of his whole being," which God works by the "deifying grace received in Baptism."[82]

The Roman Catholic Church also continues to teach salvation by meritorious works, though it carefully qualifies the meaning and function of merit in order to simultaneously say that salvation is by grace. Though "with regard to God, there is no strict right to any merit on the part of man," nevertheless, God's children can obtain "true merit" through their good works produced by grace.[83] The catechism says, "Moved by the Holy Spirit and by charity, we can then merit for ourselves and for others the graces needed for our sanctification, for the increase of grace and charity, and for the attainment of eternal life."[84] Ludwig Ott (1906–1985) said, "A just man merits for himself through each good work an increase of sanctifying grace, eternal life (if he dies in a state of grace) and an increase of heavenly glory."[85] However, the Catholic catechism says that all merit comes from Christ through one's union with him in love, so that the saints have always known "that their merits were pure grace."[86] Merit arises from the free initiative of God's grace, joined with "man's free acting through his collaboration, so that the merit of good works is to be attributed in the first place to the grace of God, then to the faithful."[87]

The Eastern Orthodox Church also holds a view of justification by regeneration at baptism, but with an emphasis on salvation by participation in the divine energies, not merit. The *Orthodox Study Bible* says that salvation depends "upon the grace and mercy of God," but rejects justification by faith alone, saying that justification by faith refers to being "gradually transformed internally and externally into His likeness."[88] John Meyendorff (1926–1992) said, "Communion in the risen body of Christ; participation in divine life; sanctification through the energy of God, which penetrates true humanity and restores it to its 'natural' state, rather than

/roman_curia/congregations/cfaith/documents/rc_con_cfaith_doc_20070629_responsa-quaestiones_en.html#_ftnref1.

81. *Catechism of the Catholic Church*, secs. 1987–1991.
82. *Catechism of the Catholic Church*, secs. 1995, 1999.
83. *Catechism of the Catholic Church*, secs. 2007–2009.
84. *Catechism of the Catholic Church*, sec. 2010.
85. Ott, *Fundamentals of Catholic Dogma*, 267.
86. *Catechism of the Catholic Church*, sec. 2011.
87. *Catechism of the Catholic Church*, sec. 2008.
88. *The Orthodox Study Bible: New Testament and Psalms*, ed. Joseph Allen et al. (Nashville: Thomas Nelson, 1993), 346, 348.

justification, or remission of inherited guilt—these are at the center of Byzantine understanding of the Christian Gospel."[89] However, there are witnesses to justification by faith in the Greek/Eastern tradition. We have already noted the statements of Chrysostom about justification. We also note that Theophylact of Ohrid (c. 1050–c. 1109), whose commentaries often quoted Chrysostom, spoke of justification as being counted righteous, the opposite of condemnation and curse, and as accomplished by faith apart from works.[90]

Objections to Justification by Faith Alone

We have already argued that the Holy Scriptures speak of a forensic justification in which God declares a sinner to be righteous through faith in Christ apart from any good works.[91] Some Roman Catholic biblical scholars, such as Joseph Fitzmyer (1920–2016), have acknowledged that Paul's use of "justify" is forensic and judicial.[92] Here we will address some other Roman Catholic objections to the Reformation doctrine of justification by faith alone.

Objection 1: God's word is always effective. If God declares a person righteous, then that declaration actually transforms a person, because God's word always accomplishes what God declares.[93] Therefore, God's judicial verdict that the sinner is righteous is also his act of renewing that sinner with inward grace so that he actually becomes righteous.

In reply, we agree that God's word is always effective to accomplish what he intends: "It shall accomplish that which I please" (Isa. 55:11). However, the argument begs the question: What does God intend by justification? The Scriptures represent justification as God's declaration of a new legal status. His sovereign declaration accomplishes exactly that.

Objection 2: Biblical justification is regeneration. According to Ott, the Bible "represents justification as a re-birth from God, that is, as a

89. John Meyendorff, *Byzantine Theology: Historical Trends and Doctrinal Themes*, 2nd ed. (New York: Fordham University Press, 1979), 146.

90. Nick Needham, "The Evolution of Justification: Justification in the Medieval Traditions," in *The Doctrine on Which the Church Stands or Falls: Justification in Biblical, Theological, Historical, and Pastoral Perspectives*, ed. Matthew Barrett (Wheaton, IL: Crossway, 2019), 618–21.

91. On the meaning of "justify" and James's statement that we are not justified only by faith alone, see chap. 22.

92. Joseph A. Fitzmyer, "Pauline Theology," secs. 68–70, in *The New Jerome Biblical Commentary*, ed. Raymond E. Brown, Joseph A. Fitzmyer, and Roland E. Murphy (Englewood Cliffs, NJ: Prentice Hall, 1990), 1397–98.

93. Gerald O'Collins, Roman Catholic response to the traditional Reformed view, in *Justification: Five Views*, ed. Beilby, Eddy, and Enderlein, 127.

generation of a new, supernatural life in the former sinner."[94] Two texts alleged to prove this argument are Titus 3:5–7: "He saved us, by the washing of regeneration, and renewing of the Holy Ghost . . . that being justified by his grace, we should be made heirs"; and 1 Corinthians 6:11: "But ye are washed, but ye are sanctified, but ye are justified in the name of the Lord Jesus, and by the Spirit of our God."

In reply, we note that the Scriptures sometimes list benefits of salvation together without identifying them with each other. In 1 Corinthians 1:30, Paul writes that Christ has become our wisdom, righteousness, sanctification, and redemption, but that does not prove that wisdom is the same thing as redemption. In the same way, Titus 3 and 1 Corinthians 6 do not identify justification with regeneration or sanctification, but link them together as aspects of salvation by grace alone. Furthermore, Paul distinguishes between effectual calling and justification (Rom. 8:30), and as we have seen, effectual calling and regeneration are two ways of describing the same gracious act of God.[95] Therefore, we should see justification according to the forensic and judicial idea that the word *justify* denotes and thus distinguish it from regeneration.

Objection 3: God speaks no lies. Ott wrote, "It would be incompatible with the veracity and sanctity of God that He should declare the sinner to be justified, if he remains in reality sinful."[96] This is sometimes called the "legal-fiction argument," for it claims that justification apart from any consideration of our goodness would be a lie on the part of God. Such would be a serious violation of God's justice, for he declares, "I will not justify the wicked" (Ex. 23:7).

In reply, we answer that God's declaration of sinful believers as "righteous" is not a lie. Neither does it contradict God's assessment of believers as still sinful and in need of continuing transformation (Rev. 2:4). Herman Bavinck said, "A person is ungodly in an *ethical* sense, but on account of the righteousness of Christ that person becomes righteous in a *juridical* sense. . . . Justification is as real as sanctification, and imputation is no less real than infusion. The only difference is this: in justification righteousness is granted to us in a juridical sense, while in sanctification it becomes ours in an ethical sense."[97]

94. Ott, *Fundamentals of Catholic Dogma*, 251.
95. On regeneration's relation to effectual calling, see chap. 18.
96. Ott, *Fundamentals of Catholic Dogma*, 251.
97. Bavinck, *Reformed Dogmatics*, 4:213, emphasis original.

We also assert with Paul that God does indeed justify the ungodly by counting them righteous apart from their own merit (Rom. 4:5–6). However, God does not do so as an arbitrary act, much less an unjust, lawless act. Rather, God declares the believing sinner righteous because of the legal reality of his union with Christ, who has satisfied God's justice by his obedience and death according to the eternal counsel of peace that constitutes Christ as the surety of his people.[98] Robert Reymond wrote, "To the contrary, the justified sinner is in fact righteous in God's sight because of the 'in Christ' relationship in which he stands (2 Cor. 5:21), in which relationship the righteousness of Christ is actually imputed to him."[99] Antonius Thysius said, "It is abominable in the sight of God that the wicked is justified by the judgment of men (Ex. 23:1; Deut. 25:1; Prov. 17:15), because it happens contrary to the Law. In the case that God justifies the ungodly, the judgment is in harmony with righteousness, because it happens according to the Law while Christ intervenes with a righteousness whereby he makes satisfaction to the Law, and that righteousness becomes our own by imputation and faith."[100] Union with Christ thus changes the believer's legal relationship to God. Millard Erickson says, "When looking at the believer, God the Father does not see him or her alone. He sees the believer together with Christ."[101]

Objection 4: Only some works are excluded from justification. For example, it is said that Paul rejects the justifying value of works as "works of the law of the Old Testament, for example, circumcision."[102] Similarly, it is said that Paul rejects works done before regeneration. Therefore, it is alleged, Paul's polemical statements that justification is by faith apart from works of the law does not exclude works of love done by grace in obedience to the law of Christ.

In reply, we argue that Paul not only denies a place for "works of the law" in our salvation, but "works" without further qualification.[103] Salvation is "not of works, lest any man should boast" (Eph. 2:9). God saved us "not by works of righteousness which we have done" (Titus 3:5). When Paul says that "by the deeds of the law there shall no flesh be justified in

98. Bavinck, *Reformed Dogmatics*, 4:214. On the counsel of peace, see *RST*, 2:584–609 (chap. 30).
99. Reymond, *A New Systematic Theology of the Christian Faith*, 753.
100. Polyander, Walaeus, Thysius, and Rivetus, *Synopsis Purioris Theologiae*, 33.31 (2:323).
101. Erickson, *Christian Theology*, 886.
102. Ott, *Fundamentals of Catholic Dogma*, 254.
103. Rom. 3:27; 4:2, 6; 9:11; 11:6.

his sight: for by the law is the knowledge of sin" (Rom. 3:20), he has "all the world" in view, and cites the law about *moral* violations by Jews and Gentiles (vv. 9–18). Paul's polemic against justification by works addresses the entire law (Gal. 5:3), for violating any commandment of God, moral or ceremonial, brings God's curse (3:10). Paul presents regenerate believers such as Abraham and David as examples of justification "without works" (Rom. 4:1–8).[104] Therefore, when Paul teaches that believers are justified apart from works of the law, he excludes all works, even good works done by Christians in love, from our justification.[105]

Objection 5: Faith cannot justify without love. It is argued that justification cannot be by faith alone, for Paul says that "though I have all faith . . . and have not charity [love], I am nothing" (1 Cor. 13:2).[106] Therefore, when Paul says we are justified by faith, it is alleged, he means "faith which worketh by love" (Gal. 5:6), such that faith alone is not the instrument of justification but the meritorious works of love.

In reply, we note that Paul's statement in 1 Corinthians 13 is not addressed to the topic of justification, but to the importance of love in the Christian life. Furthermore, it appears that the faith in view in that text is not saving faith, but the faith of miracles, for Paul writes, "Though I have all faith, so that I could remove mountains" (v. 2). We agree that justifying faith is always accompanied by love, but that does not prove that love is part of justification. Paul nowhere teaches that we are justified by love.

Objection 6: "Faith alone" is antinomian. If we are justified merely for believing in Jesus, then many people are justified because they intellectually agree that Christ died for sinners even though they live in unrepentant wickedness and rebellion against God.[107]

In reply, we point out that the Reformation doctrine of faith is not bare assent, but knowledge, assent, and trust—a living, experiential faith that transforms the life by union with Christ.[108] Calvin said, "It is therefore faith alone which justifies, and yet the faith which justifies is not alone."[109]

---

104. Turretin, *Institutes*, 16.2.12 (2:641). Turretin also notes that Lombard and Aquinas state in their commentaries on Romans 3:27 that Paul excludes not only ceremonial works but also obedience to the moral law from our justification. *Institutes*, 16.2.11 (2:641).

105. See Thomas Schreiner, *Faith Alone: The Doctrine of Justification* (Grand Rapids, MI: Zondervan, 2015), 100–111.

106. Joseph Pohle, "Justification," in *The Catholic Encyclopedia* (New York: Robert Appleton, 1910), 8:574, http://www.newadvent.org/cathen/08573a.htm.

107. On this charge by Robert Bellarmine, see Turretin, *Institutes*, 16.2.4 (2:638).

108. See chap. 20.

109. Calvin, *Canons and Decrees of the Council of Trent, with the Antidote*, in *Tracts Relating to the Reformation*, 3:152.

Rather, justifying faith is always accompanied by love. Justifying faith unites believers to Christ so that he is both their justification and their sanctification (1 Cor. 1:30). Paul says, "They that are Christ's have crucified the flesh with the affections and lusts. If we live in the Spirit, let us also walk in the Spirit" (Gal. 5:24–25). Those whose lives are characterized by the works of the flesh instead of the fruit of the Spirit will not inherit the kingdom of God (vv. 19–23).

Antinomianism is a real danger. As Mark Jones points out, antinomianism has never been a monolithic movement, but may involve a variety of errors, imbalances, or infelicitous expressions that minimize the importance of obedience to God's law, collapse sanctification into justification, or speak as if there were virtually no distinction between the believer and Christ in their status and activity.[110] A common core shared by antinomians is that "they stripped away a number of biblical truths and attempted to give justification by faith alone an all-controlling place in the life of the Christian" in order to grant assurance of salvation to as many as possible.[111] The answer to antinomianism, however, is not to embrace the Roman Catholic Church's confusion of justification and sanctification. Rather, the best defense against antinomianism is to recognize the centrality of Christ and union with him to salvation, and to receive justification and sanctification as distinct but inseparable graces of the one Christ.

The Practical Importance of *Sola Fide*: *Soli Deo Gloria*

We have already discussed the practical applications of justification by faith alone (*sola fide*).[112] Here we would close this polemical survey by noting the greatest reason why it is important to defend the true doctrine of justification: the giving of glory to God alone (*soli Deo gloria*).

The apostle Paul stresses in a number of places that God has so designed our salvation to exclude all human boasting and direct us to glorify him alone. Paul says that God has chosen to save the unworthy for this very purpose: "That no flesh should glory in his presence. But of him are ye in Christ Jesus, who of God is made unto us wisdom, and righteousness,

110. Jones, *Antinomianism*, 7–9. An example of collapsing sanctification into justification so that the former consists of nothing more than a growing appreciation of one's status in Christ may be found in Tullian Tchividjian, *Jesus + Nothing = Everything* (Wheaton, IL: Crossway, 2011), 78, 94–96, 103. See the critique in David Murray, "Does Jesus + Nothing = Everything?," http://headhearthand.org/blog/2011/12/12/does-jesus-nothing-everything/.

111. Jones, *Antinomianism*, 127.

112. See chap. 22.

and sanctification, and redemption: that, according as it is written, He that glorieth, let him glory in the Lord" (1 Cor. 1:29–31). He drew here from the great declaration of Jeremiah 9:23–24 (cf. Isa. 45:22–25).

Paul connects this theme of *soli Deo gloria* explicitly to his contrast of faith and works to show that God designed justification to silence human boasting:

- "Where is boasting then? It is excluded. By what law? of works? Nay: but by the law of faith. Therefore we conclude that a man is justified by faith without the deeds of the law" (Rom. 3:27–28).
- "For if Abraham were justified by works, he hath whereof to glory; but not before God" (Rom. 4:2).
- "For by grace are ye saved through faith; and that not of yourselves: it is the gift of God: not of works, lest any man should boast" (Eph. 2:8–9).

God saves his chosen people "to the praise of the glory of his grace . . . to the praise of his glory . . . unto the praise of his glory" (Eph. 1:6, 12, 14).

This should be the grand motive that drives our preaching and teaching of justification by faith in Christ alone—that our theology should result in doxology. Locating any part of our righteousness before God in anything in ourselves or what we do brings the grave danger that we will grasp hold of some of the glory that belongs to God alone.[113] If the reason why we are counted worthy of entering God's kingdom resides in us in any way, then we have cause to boast. But if the only reason why we are deemed worthy of glory lies in Christ Jesus, then we will spend all eternity glorifying him. Justification by faith alone is the heartbeat of the soul that cries, "Worthy is the Lamb that was slain!"

God has planned and arranged justification so that it is a grand revelation of his glory. Mark Thompson says, "The justification of the ungodly, on the basis of the propitiation provided by God himself in and through the person of the Son, is equally an expression of his righteousness and his love. It is a wide-open window into the character and being of the triune God. If justification were not by faith only, we would have to recast our understanding not only of God's promises and purposes but also of God's being and character. God has acted in perfect freedom,

113. Calvin, *Institutes*, 3.13.1–2.

grace, righteousness, and love because this is what he is like through and through."[114]

We conclude, then, with the affirmation of the Belgic Confession (Art. 23): "Therefore we always hold fast this foundation, ascribing all the glory to God, humbling ourselves before Him, and acknowledging ourselves to be such as we really are, without presuming to trust in any thing in ourselves or in any merit of ours, relying and resting upon the obedience of Christ crucified alone, which becomes ours when we believe in Him."[115]

Sing to the Lord

Rejoicing in Justification

How blest is he whose trespass hath freely been forgiv'n,
Whose sin is wholly covered before the sight of heav'n.
Blest he to whom Jehovah imputeth not his sin,
Who hath a guileless spirit, whose heart is true within.

While I kept guilty silence my strength was spent in grief,
Thy hand was heavy on me, my soul found no relief;
But when I owned my trespass, my sin hid not from Thee,
When I confessed transgression, then Thou forgavest me.

So let the godly seek Thee in times when Thou art near;
No whelming flood shall reach them, nor cause their hearts to fear.
In Thee, O Lord, I hide me, Thou savest me from ill,
And songs of Thy salvation my heart with rapture thrill.

Psalm 32
Tune: Rutherford
The Psalter, No. 83
Or Tune: Prysgol
Trinity Hymnal—Baptist Edition, No. 462

Questions for Meditation or Discussion

1. What did the early church fathers say about justification apart from works?

114. Mark Thompson, "The Theology of Justification by Faith: The Theological Case for *Sola Fide*," in *The Doctrine on Which the Church Stands or Falls*, ed. Barrett, 426.
115. *The Three Forms of Unity*, 40–41.

2. How did the fathers cloud the basis of our salvation with the term *merit*?
3. Owen said, "I had rather learn what some men really judge about their own justification from their prayers than their writings." What did he mean? What evidence did the authors present that medieval theologians looked to Christ's righteousness alone, not their own merit?
4. What did the Reformers teach about justification?
5. How did the Roman Catholic Church, at the Council of Trent, respond to the Reformation doctrine of justification by faith alone?
6. On what basis do some people say that justification in the Bible is regeneration? How can we show this claim to be incorrect?
7. How do the Holy Scriptures show that justification apart from works means *all* works, including works of love done by Christians through the grace of God?
8. Someone says, "Obviously we are not justified by faith alone, but by faith working through love (Gal. 5:6), for Paul says that he could have all faith but without love he is nothing (1 Cor. 13:2)." How do you respond?
9. Why does the doctrine of justification by faith alone not encourage people to live in a lawless manner, sinning as much as they please?
10. What is the connection between *sola fide* and *soli Deo gloria*? How can you use the doctrine of justification by faith alone to move yourself to more frequent and fervent praise to God?

Questions for Deeper Reflection

11. How did the use of Latin instead of studying the Bible in Hebrew and Greek contribute to the doctrinal confusion regarding justification? How does this illustrate the importance of studying the Bible in its original languages?
12. How does the doctrine of union with Christ answer the objection that justification by faith alone is a legal fiction? Write your answer as if you were addressing young people who had asked, "How can God truthfully declare sinners perfectly righteous when they are not?"

24

Justification, Part 3

Historical and Polemical Theology (Modern)

One reason why the doctrine of justification is crucial to Christianity is that our view of justification is inseparable from our view of Christ and his work. Do we believe that God justifies us because of Christ alone? Or is our righteousness before God based on something that is in us or that we do? Justification by faith alone exalts Christ alone. Guy Waters says, "Nothing that we have done, are doing, or will do contributes to the basis of God's verdict 'justified.' God does not look on our activity when He justifies us. Instead, He looks only to the perfect work of Jesus. He does not justify us because of what we do. He justifies us because of what Christ did."[1]

The Reformation debate over justification by faith alone does not exhaust the controversies surrounding this doctrine. In this chapter, we will survey some other significant controversies, such as the Wesleyan-Arminian denial of the imputation of Christ's righteousness, the universalist view of justification in Barthian theology, and the ecclesiological justification of the New Perspective on Paul.

1. Guy Waters, *A Christian's Pocket Guide to Being Made Right with God: Understanding Justification* (Fearn, Ross-shire, Scotland: Christian Focus, 2012), 20–21.

Arminian and Other Evangelical Denials of the Imputation of Christ's Righteousness

Theologians of the Arminian tradition have often denied the imputation of Christ's righteousness to believers. The extent to which Jacob Arminius agreed with Reformed orthodoxy on justification is a matter of debate. He affirmed forensic justification by grace through faith apart from works, but he also taught that faith is imputed as the righteousness of believers.[2] A later Arminian Remonstrant, Philip Limborch (1633–1712), clearly asserted that Christ's righteousness is not imputed to believers, and that God counts their faith as their righteousness.[3]

John Wesley said that "we are justified by faith alone."[4] He also said that justification "is not the being actually made just and righteous," for "this is sanctification," which is "a distinct gift of God, and of a totally different nature." Wesley added, "The plain scriptural notion of justification is pardon, the forgiveness of sins."[5] Faith in Christ is "the only instrument" of justification, and "there is no justification without it."[6] However, Wesley did not like the phrase "the righteousness of Christ" because of his concern that antinomians would abuse it to excuse themselves from obeying God's commands.[7] He viewed "the righteousness of God" to be "the mercy of God," or particularly "God's method of justifying sinners."[8] Wesley taught that Christ's work is the "sole meritorious cause, both of our justification and sanctification," in that he purchased them.[9] However, he balked at saying that Christ's obedience is imputed to believers. Thomas Oden (1931–2016)

2. Arminius, *Private Disputations*, 48.2, 5, Cor. 1, in *Works*, 2:406–7; Witsius, *The Economy of the Covenants*, 3.8.51 (2:411–12); Aza Goudriaan, "Justification by Faith and the Early Arminian Controversy," in *Scholasticism Reformed: Essays in Honour of Willem J. van Asselt*, ed. Maarten Wisse, Marcel Sarot, and Willemien Otten (Leiden: Brill, 2010), 155–78; Keith D. Stanglin, *Arminius on the Assurance of Salvation: The Context, Roots, and Shape of the Leiden Debate, 1603–1609*, Brill's Series in Church History 27 (Leiden: Brill, 2007), 105–10; Keith D. Stanglin and Thomas H. McCall, *Jacob Arminius: Theologian of Grace* (Oxford: Oxford University Press, 2012), 167–69; and Olson, *Arminian Theology*, 202–8; cf. *The Arminian Confession of 1621*, 18.3 (111).

3. Olson, *Arminian Theology*, 209; John Mark Hicks, "The Righteousness of Saving Faith: Arminian versus Remonstrant Grace," *Evangelical Journal* 9 (Spring 1991): 27–39; and Philip Limborch, *Theologia Christiana* (Amsterdam, 1686), 6.4, cited in John Mark Hicks, "The Theology of Grace in the Thought of Jacobus Arminius and Philip van Limborch: A Study in the Development of Seventeenth-Century Dutch Arminianism" (PhD diss., Westminster Theological Seminary, 1985), 207–8, 213–16, 221.

4. Wesley, *Remarks on a Defense of Aspasio Vindicated*, in *Works*, 10:349.

5. Wesley, *Justification by Faith*, 1.2, 5, in *Sermons*, 114–15.

6. Wesley, *Justification by Faith*, 4.2–5, in *Sermons*, 118–19.

7. Wesley, *Thoughts on the Imputed Righteousness of Christ*, in *Works*, 10:312–15.

8. Wesley, *Thoughts on the Imputed Righteousness of Christ*, secs. 2–3, in *Works*, 10:312–13.

9. Wesley, *Thoughts on the Imputed Righteousness of Christ*, secs. 2–3, in *Works*, 10:312–13; and *The Lord Our Righteousness*, 1.4, 2.9, in *Sermons*, 384, 387.

wrote, "Wesley affirmed that Christ is 'our substitute as to penal sufferings' but not as a substitute for our personal acts of obedience."[10]

Richard Watson (1781–1833), an influential systematizer of Wesleyan Methodist thought, wrote that "the imputation of righteousness" consisted of "the non-imputation of sin"—that is, "the non-punishment, or pardon of sin."[11] Watson, however, denied that faith has any merit with God, but is only the necessary condition for forgiveness.[12] Other Arminians, such as Roger Olson, advocate a return to the Reformation doctrine of imputation, which he believes was the view of Arminius.[13]

A number of other theologians have recently criticized or rejected the doctrine of Christ's obedience imputed to believers. Mark Seifrid, who in many ways is an advocate for justification by faith alone, characterizes the classic Reformed doctrine of the imputation of Christ's obedience as an understandable attempt to formulate forensic justification in reaction to Roman Catholicism, but nevertheless sees it as deficient and misleading as a biblical interpretation.[14] Rich Lusk, a representative of the Federal Vision or Auburn Avenue Theology, says that believers are righteous by virtue of their union with Christ, but "this justification requires no transfer or imputation of anything"; rather, the believer shares in the vindication of the risen Lord Jesus as long as he abides in Christ because righteousness is a covenant relationship, not a matter of "abstract justice."[15]

Robert Gundry rejects the doctrine of the imputation of Christ's righteousness to believers.[16] He believes that the righteousness imputed to us is our faith, not the obedience of Christ.[17] Gundry accordingly denies that Adam's sin was counted against his descendants.[18] Gundry summarizes the

10. Oden, *John Wesley's Scriptural Christianity*, 210.

11. Richard Watson, *Theological Institutes*, 2 vols. (New York: Lane and Scott, 1851), 2:241.

12. Watson, *Theological Institutes*, 2:242.

13. Olson, *Arminian Theology*, 220. He cites Thomas Oden as another example.

14. Mark A. Seifrid, *Christ, Our Righteousness: Paul's Theology of Justification*, New Studies in Biblical Theology (Downers Grove, IL: InterVarsity Press, 2000), 174–75. Seifrid sees justification not as an event in the personal application of salvation, but as God's act in Christ when he was crucified and raised from the dead.

15. Rich Lusk, "A Response to 'The Biblical Plan of Salvation,'" in *The Auburn Avenue Theology, Pros and Cons: Debating the Federal Vision*, ed. E. Calvin Beisner (Fort Lauderdale, FL: Knox Theological Seminary, 2004), 142, 147.

16. Robert H. Gundry, "Why I Didn't Endorse The Gospel of Jesus Christ: An Evangelical Celebration," *Books and Culture* 7, no. 1 (January/February 2001): 6–9, http://www.booksandculture.com/articles/2001/janfeb/1.6.html.

17. Robert H. Gundry, *Commentary on the New Testament: Verse-by-Verse Explanations with a Literal Translation* (Peabody, MA: Hendrickson, 2010), 583 (Rom. 4:1–3), 601 (Rom. 8:28–30).

18. Robert H. Gundry, "The Nonimputation of Christ's Righteousness," in *Justification: What's at Stake in the Current Debates*, ed. Husbands and Treier, 27–29.

two sides of justification as follows: "Negatively, God does not count our sins against us. Jesus took them away. Positively, God counts our faith as righteousness."[19] One practical benefit of denying the imputed righteousness of Christ, Gundry says, is the opportunity to emphasize our obedience against the error of antinomians.[20]

Arguments for the Imputation of Christ's Righteousness

The Reformed orthodox doctrine of justification includes "the imputation of alien righteousness," not any righteousness that is "inherent" in believers. "This alien righteousness of Christ becomes our own, and so we are made righteous in the presence of God," as Antonius Thysius said.[21] We have already presented a positive case that the Holy Scriptures teach the imputation of Christ's obedience to believers.[22] Here we offer specific arguments for that doctrine in light of objections made against it.

First, *Paul teaches it in 2 Corinthians 5:21*, saying, "For he hath made him to be sin for us, who knew no sin; that we might be made the righteousness of God in him." This is a plain statement of the imputation of our sins to Christ and his righteousness to us.

Gundry argues, however, that "made [*ginomai*] the righteousness of God" should be interpreted according to "made [*ginomai*] a curse for us" (Gal. 3:13). He argues that the latter means "became the object of God's curse," and so the former means "become the objects of his salvifically active righteousness."[23]

In reply, we believe that "made the righteousness of God in him" in 2 Corinthians 5:21 should be interpreted not according to a distant parallel in Galatians 3:13 but to the parallel in the same verse, "he hath made him to be sin for us." This does not mean that God made Christ the object of our sin, but that God counted our sin against Christ so that he would not count it against us (v. 19). In parallel with "made him to be sin for us," the clause "that we might be made the righteousness of God in him" means that God counted Christ's righteousness to us. It may be objected that

19. Gundry, "Nonimputation," in *Justification: What's at Stake in the Current Debates*, ed. Husbands and Treier, 25.

20. Gundry, "Nonimputation," in *Justification: What's at Stake in the Current Debates*, ed. Husbands and Treier, 44.

21. Polyander, Walaeus, Thysius, and Rivetus, *Synopsis Purioris Theologiae*, 33.5, 21 (2:307, 315).

22. See chap. 22 on justification and the righteousness of God in Christ.

23. Gundry, "Nonimputation," in *Justification: What's at Stake in the Current Debates*, ed. Husbands and Treier, 41; cf. Gundry, *Commentary on the New Testament*, 706 (2 Cor. 5:20–21).

Paul wrote, "that we might be made the righteousness of God," not the righteousness of Christ. However, as Richard Philips observes, Paul wrote "the righteousness of God *in him*"—that is, "in Christ."[24] Paul called it "the righteousness of God" to emphasize that "God was in Christ" (v. 19), accomplishing this righteousness through the obedience of the Son.

Second, *the justification of sinners requires it*. The indictment of man's unrighteousness and the imputation of righteousness to sinners imply the crediting of something to our account that is not our right, nature, or possession. The Hebrew verb translated as "count" (*khashab*) in Genesis 15:6 can refer to regarding a daughter as a stranger (31:15), counting silver as of no value (1 Kings 10:21; cf. Job 41:27, 29), crediting the value of a sacrifice to a person (Lev. 7:18), and considering something to be the legal or spiritual equivalent of something else (Lev. 25:31; Num. 18:27). Based on such parallels, O. Palmer Robertson writes that the imputation of righteousness in Genesis 15:6 means to "account to him a righteousness that does not inherently belong to him."[25]

Gundry makes an objection based on Romans 2:26, in which Paul says, "Therefore if the uncircumcision [an uncircumcised Gentile] keep the righteousness of the law, shall not his uncircumcision be counted for [*logizomai eis*] circumcision?" Gundry says, "Now it is hard, if not impossible, to think that Romans 2:26 presents a Gentile law-keeper's uncircumcision as the instrument by which an alien circumcision is received."[26]

In reply, we note that the grammar of Romans 2:26 illustrates the Reformation idea of imputation. The idea here is reckoning A as if it were B, not because of A, but on account of C. God reckons this Gentile's uncircumcision (A) as the equivalent of circumcision (B), not because of uncircumcision itself (A), but on account of his obedience (C). In a similar manner, God reckons faith (A) as if it were righteousness (B), not because of faith (A), but on account of Christ's obedience (C).

Third, *the righteousness that God imputes to believers was objectively accomplished in Christ*. Herman Bavinck said, "The righteousness of God in terms of which he acquits believers is objectively revealed in the gospel,

24. Richard D. Philips, "A Justification of Imputed Righteousness," in *By Faith Alone: Answering the Challenges to the Doctrine of Justification*, ed. Gary L. W. Johnson and Guy P. Waters (Wheaton, IL: Crossway, 2006), 94.

25. O. Palmer Robertson, "Genesis 15:6: New Covenant Expositions of an Old Covenant Text," *Westminster Theological Journal* 42, no. 2 (Spring 1980): 265 (full article, 259–90).

26. Gundry, "Nonimputation," in *Justification: What's at Stake in the Current Debates*, ed. Husbands and Treier, 21.

apart from the works of the law and before faith (Rom. 1:17; 3:21). . . . For God has put Christ forward as a propitiatory sacrifice . . . and this Christ was handed over to death for our trespasses . . . and was thus raised for our justification (Rom. 4:25), because we were or had to be justified in him. He, therefore, is our righteousness (1 Cor. 1:30)."[27] In other words, the justifying righteousness already wrought by God the Son incarnate is part of the announcement of the gospel, whereas faith is our response to the gospel.

Fourth, *justification involves the imputation of righteousness as a gift of free grace*. If faith is our righteousness, then the counting of it as such can hardly be considered a gift of grace to a sinner because it is based on the person's disposition and activity. However, imputation of righteousness is "of grace" to "the ungodly" (Rom. 4:4–5). The fact that Paul refers to Abraham and others whom God justifies as "ungodly" shows that God does not count any virtue or action of theirs to be their righteousness—including their faith. John Piper writes, "Paul's conceptual framework is that the thing imputed to us is external to us. . . . Faith receives the gift of righteousness."[28]

Fifth, *the idea that God counts faith itself as our righteousness raises serious questions about God's justice and law*. If God does not impute the righteousness of Christ's obedience to sinners, then on what other basis can he justify them? Is God's law an arbitrary standard, such that he can make anything the condition of being righteous in his sight? What, then, of the justice of God? The doctrine of Christ's imputed righteousness glorifies God because it affirms his unchanging justice as expressed in his moral law. Justification by faith does not abolish God's law but establishes it (Rom. 3:31).[29]

Sixth, *our righteousness is not depicted as our faith but as the result of believing*. Jews and Gentiles believe in Christ "that righteousness might be imputed unto them" (Rom. 4:11). When people exercise faith in Christ, they receive righteousness as a gift from God (5:17). Paul says, "For with the heart man believeth unto righteousness; and with the mouth confession is made unto salvation" (10:10). Just as confession itself is not our salvation, so faith is not our righteousness, but the means by which we lay

27. Bavinck, *Reformed Dogmatics*, 4:210.

28. John Piper, *Counted Righteous in Christ: Should We Abandon the Imputation of Christ's Righteousness?* (Wheaton, IL: Crossway, 2002), 60.

29. Heidegger, *The Concise Marrow of Christian Theology*, 22.9 (155).

hold of Christ our righteousness. Our righteousness is not our faith, but "the righteousness [or righteous work] of one"—that is, "the obedience of one" man, Jesus Christ (5:18–19).

Seventh, *justification includes the grant of the right to eternal life*, or the enjoyment of God's glory in the age to come (Rom. 5:1–2; Titus 3:7). If we are justified only by Christ's substitutionary sufferings and not by the imputation of Christ's obedience, then justification addresses only the penalty of the law for disobedience, and not the law's requirement of obedience in order to be counted righteous. As William Perkins pointed out, Christ's sufferings by themselves would deliver us from hell but would not grant us a right to eternal life.[30]

Eighth, *the imputation of Christ's obedience does not remove the reason for Christian obedience*. One of the most common objections to the imputation of Christ's obedience to believers is that it would destroy all reason and motive for us to obey.

Our answer to this objection is that Christ died to fulfill the law for our justification, and it is true that believers no longer need to obey God in order to be justified. However, we are still bound to obey God for other reasons, not least of which is thankfulness for God's mercies to us.[31] As John Owen explained, Christ fulfilled the law for us as the condition for life ("Do this, and live"). In Christ, we are freed from obeying to fulfill that condition, but "we are not freed from obedience, as a way of walking with God."[32]

This objection turns the evangelical order of obedience on its head, for it assumes that the law's rigor will motivate good works. R. Scott Clark writes, "The law word of Scripture, 'do this and live' (Luke 10:28), is neither designed nor has the power to produce sanctity. This much is evident from the structure of Paul's epistles. He typically speaks the imperative (i.e. the law) after and on the basis of the indicative (i.e. the gospel)."[33]

Ninth, *God has given believers perfect righteousness*. If faith is our righteousness, then our justification is not complete, but will grow or decline according to the strength of our faith (and perhaps the works it produces). However, justification is given to believers as a complete and

30. Perkins, *Galatians*, on Gal. 2:15–16, in *Works*, 2:115.
31. Perkins, *Galatians*, on Gal. 2:15–16, in *Works*, 2:115.
32. Owen, *Communion with God*, in *Works*, 2:163.
33. R. Scott Clark, "Do This and Live: Christ's Active Obedience as the Ground of Justification," in *Covenant, Justification, and Pastoral Ministry*, ed. R. Scott Clark (Phillipsburg, NJ: P&R, 2007), 253.

perfect grant based on Christ, not our faith. Romans 8:1 says, "There is therefore now no condemnation" for those united to Christ. Our justification has nullified every accusation that might condemn us: "Who shall lay any thing to the charge of God's elect? It is God that justifieth" (v. 33). God has forgiven us "all trespasses" (Col. 2:13). We are granted "the righteousness of God" (Rom. 3:22; 2 Cor. 5:21), not the merely human and deeply flawed righteousness consisting of our faith. Thysius said that with respect to our justification, "faith is judged not by its own worthiness but by the worthiness of its object."[34] Archibald A. Hodge said, "Justifying faith terminates on or in Christ, in his blood and sacrifice, and in the promises of God; in its very essence, therefore, it involves trust, and, denying its own justifying value, affirms the sole merit of that on which it trusts."[35]

On the basis of these arguments and previously presented biblical exegesis, we conclude that God indeed imputes the obedience of Jesus Christ to all who trust in him. Christ is our righteousness. Bavinck said, "In order to stand before the judgment of God, to be acquitted of all guilt and punishment, and to share in the glory of God and eternal life, we must have Christ, not something of Him, but Christ Himself. . . . And then we can stand before His presence as though we had never had sin, or done sin, indeed, as though we had ourselves achieved the obedience which Christ has achieved for us."[36]

Karl Barth on Universal Justification

Karl Barth's doctrine of justification exemplifies his attempt to rework Reformed theology according to his own peculiarly Christocentric manner of asserting the lordship of God.[37] Barth did view justification as a judicial act of God that restores man from the wrong relationship with God that he had obtained by sin. It is grace to sinners from the God who is the epitome of law and order[38] and God's solution to the problem of sinful man standing in the presence of the Holy One.[39] God declares "a verdict which disowns and renounces," but that verdict has not fallen on

34. Polyander, Walaeus, Thysius, and Rivetus, *Synopsis Purioris Theologiae*, 33.30 (2:321).
35. Hodge, *Outlines of Theology*, 504.
36. Herman Bavinck, *The Wonderful Works of God*, trans. Henry Zylstra (Glenside, PA: Westminster Seminary Press, 2019), 436.
37. See Fred H. Klooster, "Aspects of the Soteriology of Karl Barth," *Journal of the Evangelical Theological Society* 2, no. 2 (Spring 1959): 6–14, http://www.etsjets.org/files/JETS-PDFs/2/2-2/BETS_2-2_6-14_Klooster.pdf.
38. Barth, *Church Dogmatics*, IV/1, sec. 61.1 (528–29).
39. Barth, *Church Dogmatics*, IV/1, sec. 59.3 (290).

sinful man but "has fallen instead on Jesus Christ," for "in his place Jesus Christ has suffered the death of a malefactor. The sentence on him as a sinner has been carried out."[40] In Christ, God also declares "a verdict which recognizes and accepts" man, for "in his place Jesus Christ rendered that obedience which is required of the covenant partner of God."[41]

However, Barth tended to reduce soteriology to Christology, and the application of redemption to a realization of what Christ has already done for all mankind, though they may not subjectively accept it.[42] Barth wrote, "God's verdict and direction and promise have been pronounced over all. To that extent, objectively, all are justified, sanctified, and called. But the hand of God has not touched all."[43] Fred Klooster (1922–2003) commented, "There is no backtracking from the universalism asserted in this connection."[44] Justification, Barth said, is "unconditionally pronounced and unconditionally valid" in "the central event of all human history."[45] Justifying faith, according to Barth, is "man's recognition, acknowledging and acceptance of this verdict."[46] Thus, for Barth, justification by faith is not a change of legal status effected in an individual through the divine gift of faith, but the awakening of a person to what Christ has already done for him and for all.[47]

Barth's universalistic interpretation of justification was not embraced by all other neoorthodox theologians. For example, Emil Brunner (1889–1966) recognized Barth's universalism but rejected it as contrary to the New Testament.[48]

Contrary to Barth, as we observed when discussing eternal justification and the instrumental funcion of faith, actual justification takes place only when a person exercises faith in Jesus Christ.[49] We are justified by faith, and we believe "that we might be justified" (Gal. 2:16). It might be argued, on the contrary, that just as Adam's offense brought judgment "upon all men to condemnation," so also Christ's righteousness brought

40. Barth, *Church Dogmatics*, IV/1, sec. 58.2 (93).
41. Barth, *Church Dogmatics*, IV/1, sec. 58.2 (94).
42. Barth, *Church Dogmatics*, IV/1, sec. 58.4 (147).
43. Barth, *Church Dogmatics*, IV/1, sec. 58.4 (148).
44. Klooster, "Aspects of the Soteriology of Karl Barth," 8.
45. Barth, *Church Dogmatics*, IV/1, sec. 61.2 (568).
46. Barth, *Church Dogmatics*, IV/1, sec. 58.2 (93).
47. Bruce L. McCormack, "*Justitia Aliena*: Karl Barth in Conversation with the Evangelical Doctrine of Imputed Righteousness," in *Justification in Perspective*, ed. McCormack, 179.
48. Emil Brunner, *Dogmatics*, vol. 1, *The Christian Doctrine of God*, trans. Olive Wyon (Philadelphia: The Westminster Press, 1950), 348–49.
49. See chap. 22.

"justification of life" to "all men" (Rom. 5:18).[50] However, the "all" in this text refers to all those in union with either Adam or Christ (cf. 1 Cor. 15:21–22).[51] Justification is not a universal gift that we must simply recognize as already given. Justification is given to those who "receive abundance of grace and of the gift of righteousness" in Christ (Rom. 5:17).

The New Perspective on Paul and Ecclesiological Justification

The New Perspective on Paul is a reinterpretation of Paul's teaching that arose in the latter half of the twentieth century. Krister Stendahl (1921–2008) said that the Reformation doctrine of justification by faith owed more to the anguished consciences of Augustine and Martin Luther than to the teaching of the apostle Paul, whom Stendahl said was concerned not so much with individual salvation as the inclusion of Gentiles into the church.[52] E. P. Sanders argues that, contrary to the Reformers' interpretation, ancient Judaism was not a legalistic religion of salvation by works, but a religion of covenantal grace in which works served as the means to maintain the covenantal relationship, a system Sanders called "covenantal nomism."[53] According to Sanders, Paul teaches, "Salvation is by grace but judgment is according to works; works are the condition of remaining 'in,' but they do not earn salvation."[54]

In the New Perspective, justification is not about one's standing before God so much as one's standing in the community of faith. James Dunn said that in Paul's polemic, the "works of the law" are those "boundary markers" that set Israel apart from the nations—the ceremonial laws on such matters as circumcision, cleanliness and uncleanliness, and the Sabbath.[55] Justification by faith, according to the New Perspective, nullifies reliance on ethnicity (as Jews) or cultural markers (such as circumcision) and declares acceptance of all who acknowledge Christ's lordship as equal

50. Karl Barth, *Christ and Adam: Man and Humanity in Romans 5*, trans. T. A. Smail (Eugene, OR: Wipf and Stock, 1956), 19.

51. On the meaning of "all" in Rom. 5:18 and similar texts, see *RST*, 2:1071–76.

52. Guy Prentiss Waters, "Introduction: Whatever Happened to *Sola Fide?*," in *By Faith Alone*, ed. Johnson and Waters, 24–25.

53. E. P. Sanders, *Paul and Palestinian Judaism: A Comparison of Patterns of Religion* (Philadelphia: Fortress, 1977), 422. See James D. G. Dunn, "New Perspective View," in *Justification: Five Views*, ed. Beilby, Eddy, and Enderlein, 181; and Alister E. McGrath, "Justification," in *Dictionary of Paul and His Letters*, ed. Gerald F. Hawthorne, Ralph P. Martin, Daniel G. Reid (Downers Grove, IL: InterVarsity Press, 1993), 517.

54. Sanders, *Paul and Palestinian Judaism*, 543.

55. Dunn, "New Perspective View," in *Justification: Five Views*, ed. Beilby, Eddy, and Enderlein, 190–92.

members in the church.[56] Dunn also suggested that Paul offers a form of covenantal nomism: salvation by a gracious covenant that requires us to do works of obedience in order to abide in God's favor forever.[57]

N. T. Wright states that Paul used the verb "justify" not for all of salvation and not for moral transformation, but "as a declaration which grants [a person] a status."[58] However, Wright argues, the saving righteousness of God is not "a legal transaction," which Wright considers "a cold business, almost a trick of thought."[59] He says that God's righteousness is his covenantal faithfulness to vindicate Christ and Christ's people.[60] In Christ, "their sins are no longer accounted against them and they stand on resurrection ground," having received "Spirit-given membership of the family of God's renewed covenant," the sign of which is faith.[61] Justification "is not 'how you become a Christian,' so much as 'how you can tell who is a member of the covenant family.'"[62] It is "the verdict of God himself as to who really is a member of his people."[63] Wright says that in Galatians 2, "to be justified" does not mean "to be granted free forgiveness of your sins" or "to come into a right relation with God," but "to be reckoned by God to be a true member of his family, and hence with the right to share table fellowship."[64] He adds, "In standard Christian theological language, it wasn't so much about soteriology as about ecclesiology; not so much about salvation as about the church."[65] Thus, we may label this view ecclesiological justification.

The New Perspective has provoked criticism from a number of Reformed and evangelical scholars.[66] We have already argued in the previous

56. Thomas R. Schreiner, "Works of the Law," in *Dictionary of Paul and His Letters*, 976; and Moo, *The Epistle to the Romans*, 213.

57. Dunn, "New Perspective View," in *Justification: Five Views*, ed. Beilby, Eddy, and Enderlein, 199–200.

58. N. T. Wright, *Justification: God's Plan and Paul's Vision*, new ed. (Downers Grove, IL: InterVarsity Press, 2016), 90–91.

59. N. T. Wright, *What Saint Paul Really Said: Was Paul of Tarsus the Real Founder of Christianity?* (Grand Rapids, MI: Eerdmans, 1997), 110.

60. Wright, *Justification*, 99–100.

61. Wright, *Justification*, 251.

62. Wright, *What Saint Paul Really Said*, 122.

63. Wright, *Justification*, 121.

64. Wright, *Justification*, 116.

65. Wright, *What Saint Paul Really Said*, 119. We note here that Wright does not entirely deny the vertical dimension, but places strong emphasis on the horizontal.

66. For an overview of the controversy, see Paul Rhodes Eddy, James K. Beilby, and Steven E. Enderlein, "Justification in Contemporary Debate," in *Justification: Five Views*, ed. Beilby, Eddy, and Enderlein, 57–67. For a specific critique of Sanders's view of Judaism and Paul, see Peter T. O'Brien, "Was Paul a Covenantal Nomist?," in *Justification and Variegated Nomism: A Fresh Appraisal of Paul and Second Temple Judaism*, vol. 2, *The Paradoxes of Paul*, ed. D. A. Carson, Peter T. O'Brien, and Mark A. Seifrid (Grand Rapids, MI: Baker Academic, 2004), 249–96.

chapter that justification is a forensic concept pertaining to a person's standing according to God's legal justice, and that the righteousness of God is not identical to his covenant faithfulness, but is the obedience and substitutionary suffering of Christ imputed to believers. If these truths are established from Scripture, then much of the New Perspective's criticisms of Reformed theology falls to the ground. In addition, we would add the following arguments.

First, the doctrine of justification by faith in Christ alone certainly has implications for social acceptance, as Paul forcefully reminded Peter in Antioch (Gal. 2:11–16). Justification by faith places people of every gender, nationality, and social status on an equal standing before God if they are united with Christ (3:24–28). However, it is a fallacy of reasoning to identify something with its implications. Michael Horton says, "Wright simply makes the effect the definition of the cause itself."[67] Justification is not social acceptance, but acceptance by God the Judge, which then implies that believers should accept each other. The Greek word group associated with justification is bound up with the idea of justice and righteousness, as D. A. Carson points out.[68] Douglas Moo says that Wright's attempt to turn justification into church membership "illegitimately privileges context over semantics," adding that "there is no need to collapse the two concepts into one."[69] J. V. Fesko surveys several texts in the book of Job and the Psalms, and concludes, "Throughout the O[ld] T[estament], righteousness is not a term that means covenant membership, contra Wright. Rather, righteousness, when referring to people, is usually the status of righteousness demonstrated by obedience to Torah."[70]

Second, it may well be that first-century Judaism ascribed much to God's grace. For that matter, so does Roman Catholicism. In the Reformation debate on justification, it was not grace versus no grace, but whether or not grace justified us by faith in Christ alone or by faith plus our love and good works. Horton writes of Sanders's book, "By the end of the book, I was convinced that at least the streams of Judaism he described (election based on foreseen obedience, the 'merit of the fathers,' the 'weighing of merits,' . . .)

67. Horton, *Justification*, 2:296.

68. D. A. Carson, "The Vindication of Imputation," in *Justification: What's at Stake in the Current Debates*, ed. Husbands and Treier, 51.

69. Douglas J. Moo, "Justification in Galatians," in *Understanding the Times: New Testament Studies in the Twenty-First Century; Essays in Honor of D. A. Carson*, ed. Andreas J. Köstenberger and Robert W. Yarbrough (Wheaton, IL: Crossway, 2011), 173–74.

70. J. V. Fesko, *Justification: Understanding the Classic Reformed Doctrine* (Phillipsburg, NJ: P&R, 2008), 223.

bore striking resemblances to the 'covenantal nomism' of late medieval (especially nominalist) theology."[71] Waters similarly observes that in theological terms, we may consider large portions of "ancient rabbinic Judaism" to be "a semi-Pelagian religion," evidenced by the statement by first-century Rabbi Akiba, "The world is judged by grace, and yet all is according to the amount of work."[72] The New Perspective has also been criticized for oversimplifying the great variety of beliefs present in first-century Judaism.[73] Therefore, observations about the function of grace in first-century Judaism do not threaten the Reformation doctrine of justification.

Third, while Jewish identity markers such as circumcision had a significant part in Paul's debate with Judaizers in the church, Paul's polemic against justification by works of the law included obedience to the whole law, especially the moral law. We have already discussed this point in our response to Roman Catholic arguments.

Fourth, the New Testament indicates that self-righteousness and merit theology were indeed an issue among the Jews. Christ told the parable of the Pharisee and the publican to "certain which trusted in themselves that they were righteous" (Luke 18:9). The Pharisee in the parable thanks God that he is not a gross sinner, but a devout and religious person, implying that he credits God's grace for making him so. However, Christ still depicts the Pharisees as boasting in their moral superiority and good works. Fesko observes, "In this parable Christ describes the Pharisee, not in Wright's terms of loyalty to the covenant badges, circumcision, food laws, and Sabbath observance, but in terms of the general commands of Torah: thievery, injustice, adultery, fasting, and tithing."[74] In contrast to this confidence in moral self-righteousness, Christ declares that God justifies the man who humbles himself as a sinner and looks to God's propitiating, sacrificial grace as his only hope.

We have an inspired perspective on first-century Judaism in the testimony of a first-century Jew, one Saul of Tarsus, later known as Paul, the apostle of Jesus Christ. Referring to his "kinsmen according to the flesh" (Rom. 9:3), Paul writes, "I bear them record that they have a zeal of God, but not according to

---

71. Michael S. Horton, "Traditional Reformed Response" to New Perspective View, in *Justification: Five Views*, ed. Beilby, Eddy, and Enderlein, 202.

72. Guy Prentiss Waters, *Justification and the New Perspectives on Paul: A Review and Response* (Phillipsburg, NJ: P&R, 2004), 152.

73. See the extensive studies in *Justification and Variegated Nomism: A Fresh Appraisal of Paul and Second Temple Judaism,* vol. 1, *The Complexities of Second Temple Judaism*, ed. D. A. Carson, Peter T. O'Brien, and Mark A Seifrid (Grand Rapids, MI: Baker Academic, 2001). For a summary, see 543–48.

74. Fesko, *Justification*, 236.

knowledge. For they being ignorant of God's righteousness, and going about *to establish their own righteousness*, have not submitted themselves unto the righteousness of God" (10:2–3). Paul saw the Judaism he had left behind not as a grace-centered faith, but as a fatal misreading of God's Word.

Like his Lord, Paul contrasts two principles of justification in Romans 4:4–5, works and faith, and the way of works is the seeking of a reward like the earning of wages. Though we may not separate faith and works in the Christian life, Paul teaches us that we must maintain the polarity between faith and works in justification.[75] To those who object that with respect to justification by faith, faith includes works, we respond that though faith includes submission to God's Word and trust in Christ, and so is the root of good works, faith itself is not good works, and good works are not the instrument or cause of justification in any way. Moo writes, "Faith is the disposition of the will necessary for works to be done in a way pleasing to God; but faith does not include in itself those works."[76] Rather, faith alone is the instrument because faith is the inward grace that receives Christ in his perfect righteousness.

Therefore, we conclude that the New Perspective has misunderstood the New Testament, both in its inspired assessment of Judaism and in its doctrine of justification.[77] The acceptance of all believers, Jews and Gentiles, into the church is an important implication of the gospel, but it is not the message of justification itself. Justification pertains to a far greater question than where we stand with mere men. Justification is God-centered, and therefore, justification is primarily about our relationship with a just and holy God. There is no better news than that God counts believers as righteous for Christ's sake.

The Confidence That Arises from the Imputation of Christ's Obedience to Believers

The imputation of Christ's obedience to those who trust in him gives cause for believers to rejoice in the Lord with great confidence. Bavinck said,

75. Rom. 3:20–22, 27; 9:32; Gal. 2:16; 3:10–12.

76. Moo, "Justification in Galatians," in *Understanding the Times*, ed. Köstenberger and Yarbrough, 184.

77. For other interactions with the New Perspective, see Cornelis P. Venema, *The Gospel of Free Acceptance in Christ: An Assessment of the Reformation and New Perspective on Paul* (Edinburgh: Banner of Truth, 2006); John Piper, *The Future of Justification: A Response to N. T. Wright* (Wheaton, IL: Crossway, 2007); and *Jesus, Paul, and the People of God: A Theological Dialogue with N. T. Wright*, ed. Nicholas Perrin and Richard B. Hays (Downers Grove, IL: InterVarsity Press, 2011).

"The believer who is justified in Christ is the freest creature in the world. At least, so it ought to be."[78] Thus, in concluding this chapter, we will consider the confidence that belongs to justified believers, with the prayer that God will make these realities experiential blessings for his people in Christ.

1. *Confidence that their persons are pleasing to God.* Justification does not merely remove the guilt of believers' sins, leaving them in a state of neutrality before God with the possibility that their good works might gain his blessing. Rather, justification by the imputed righteousness of Christ causes their persons to be fully pleasing to God because he views them in union with Christ and thus clothed with his perfect righteousness (Isa. 61:10; 62:5).[79] The Lord takes pleasure in his people who hope in his mercy (Pss. 147:11; 149:4). Christians have the smile of God upon them. The law that demands perfect obedience in order for people to receive life and blessing has been satisfied by Christ's mediatorial obedience in their place (Gal. 3:10–14). Even when their sins provoke God's fatherly displeasure and discipline (Heb. 12:5–6), he still delights in them as his people and rejoices to bless them forever (Jer. 32:41; Zeph. 3:17). The more their consciences are directed by the knowledge that God counts them righteous because of Christ, the more confidence and courage they will have in all things: "The wicked flee when no man pursueth: but the righteous are bold as a lion" (Prov. 28:1).

2. *Confidence that their good works are pleasing to God.* The forgiveness of sins and imputation of righteousness granted in justification make it possible for God's children to truly please their Father with their obedience even though their good works fall short of the full demands of his holy law. By faith, they please God (Heb. 11:5–6), and their good works please him (13:16). The fact that their Father sees what they do in secret, while forming in them a healthy fear of him, need not produce bondage to guilt, but rather encourages them to know that their forgiving Father will reward them for any good he finds in their works (Matt. 6:4, 6, 12, 18). This is not a reward based on any merit, for God's servants owe all their obedience to him and merit no reward (Luke 17:7–10). Yet, so great is God's pleasure in the imperfect obedience of his children that he will reward them a hundredfold, even with eternal, heavenly treasures (Matt. 6:20; 19:29). Amazingly the Lord will give "praise" to his people (Rom.

78. Bavinck, *The Wonderful Works of God*, 450.

79. See the discussion and figures in Grudem, *Systematic Theology*, 725–26.

2:29), saying to each of them, "Well done, thou good and faithful servant" in light of the works he has done (Matt. 25:21). Truly, God gives the reward of grace to his justified children.

3. *Confidence that their obedient worship and prayers are pleasing to God.* Christians offer their worship to God through Christ (Heb. 13:15). Hence, though their praises and prayers are imperfect in motive and execution, they are presented to God covered in the righteousness of Christ. God forgives the flaws of their worship and delights in whatever conforms to his Word. Otherwise, nothing that sinners offer to God pleases him. Proverbs 15:8 says, "The sacrifice of the wicked is an abomination to the LORD: but the prayer of the upright is his delight." Clothed in the righteousness of Christ, God's people worship him as holy priests, offering spiritual sacrifices in which God delights (1 Pet. 2:4–6).[80]

4. *Confidence that their entrance into glory is pleasing to God.* God does not merely tolerate justified sinners coming into his holy presence, but welcomes them with joy. The King will say, "Come, ye blessed of my Father, inherit the kingdom prepared for you from the foundation of the world" (Matt. 25:34). The imputed righteousness of Christ gives believers the right to anticipate an eternal reward in the inheritance of the Lord. Thysius observed that by forgiveness of sins "we are set free from guilt and condemnation, and delivered from eternal death," and by the imputation of Christ's active righteousness "we are deemed worthy even of a reward, and we receive the right to life eternal, which is awarded to us." These are inseparable, for "the one entails the other."[81] Yet, without the doctrine of imputed righteousness, believers may lose sight that God not only delivers them from hell but gladly confers on them the right to enjoy unending happiness in his glory.

This magnificent and manifold confidence should transform how the saints relate to one another. They should train their minds so that they view other Christians as people forgiven of all their sins and perfectly righteous in God's sight. Consequently, Christians should not judge each other. This does not mean failing to exhort one another in love (Lev. 19:17–18; Heb. 3:13), for justification does not negate sanctification but upholds and enables it. However, it does mean that Christians should not condemn one

80. On the priesthood of believers, see *RST*, 2:1103–8.

81. Polyander, Walaeus, Thysius, and Rivetus, *Synopsis Purioris Theologiae*, 33.8 (2:307).

another for their faults, but "receive ye one another, as Christ also received us to the glory of God" (Rom. 15:7). They should rejoice and give thanks for any faith, hope, and love they observe in each other, no matter how imperfect (1 Thess. 1:2–3).

It should be noted, however, that this confidence belongs only to the people united to Christ by a living faith. The unrepentant unbeliever has no right to these promises, but "the wrath of God abideth on him" (John 3:36). He must flee to Christ and take refuge in his righteousness, and until he does so God views him as filthy, guilty, and accursed (Isa. 64:6). When a sinner receives Christ, though, he may rejoice, for God has delivered him from his wrath and brought him into justifying union with his beloved Son.

Sing to the Lord

Christ's Perfect Righteousness for His People

Fountain of never-ceasing grace,
Thy saints' exhaustless theme,
Great object of immortal praise,
Essentially supreme;
We bless thee for the glorious fruits
Thine incarnation gives;
The righteousness which grace imputes,
And faith alone receives.

In thee we have a righteousness
By God himself approved;
Our rock, our sure foundation this,
Which never can be moved.
Our ransom by thy death was paid,
For all thy people giv'n,
The law thou perfectly obeyed,
That they might enter heav'n.

As all, when Adam sinned alone,
In his transgression died,
So by the righteousness of one
Are sinners justified;
We to thy merit, gracious Lord,

With humblest joy submit,
Again to Paradise restored,
In thee alone complete.

Augustus Toplady
Tune: St. Matthew
Trinity Hymnal—Baptist Edition, No. 440

Questions for Meditation or Discussion

1. What position did John Wesley take on the imputation of Christ's righteousness to believers? Why?
2. What is Robert Gundry's interpretation of 2 Corinthians 5:21, and why is it incorrect?
3. Why does the justification of sinners require the imputation of Christ's obedience to them?
4. How do the Holy Scriptures show that our imputed righteousness is not our faith?
5. Why does the grant of the right to eternal life imply the imputation of Christ's righteousness?
6. If Christ's obedience is counted to believers, then why should they obey God?
7. What did Karl Barth teach about justification?
8. What does the New Perspective on Paul claim about justification?
9. What criticisms do the authors present of the New Perspective?
10. What confidence can the doctrine of imputation give to believers? How has reading this chapter affected your own confidence in the Lord?

Questions for Deeper Reflection

11. How important is the imputation of Christ's obedience for the doctrine of justification? What consequences follow if we deny imputation?
12. If believers and their good works are pleasing to God because of their justification, then why do believers often lack confidence and courage? How could this be remedied?

25

Adoption, Part 1

Biblical Theology

While justification by faith in Christ alone is the foundational blessing of union with Christ, adoption in Christ may be the highest blessing of all.[1] The apostle John marveled, "Behold, what manner of love the Father hath bestowed upon us, that we should be called the sons of God" (1 John 3:1). In justification, God declares sinners righteous in the court of his legal justice. In adoption, God takes justified believers into his household to be his children—the grant of a new legal relationship. John Murray called adoption "the apex and epitome of grace."[2]

The Westminster Shorter Catechism (Q. 34) gives a concise definition of this blessing: "Adoption is an act of God's free grace, whereby we are received into the number, and have a right to all the privileges of the sons of God."[3] Adoption is called an *act* (like justification, Q. 33) in contrast to a work (as are effectual calling and sanctification, Q. 31, 35), because adoption is a change of relation and status, not a change in nature.[4] A work may take time to complete, but an act is "done in a

1. On the history of the doctrine of adoption in Reformed theology, see Tim J. R. Trumper, "An Historical Study of the Doctrine of Adoption in the Calvinistic Tradition" (PhD diss., University of Edinburgh, 2001); and Joel R. Beeke, *Heirs with Christ: The Puritans on Adoption* (Grand Rapids, MI: Reformation Heritage Books, 2008).
2. Murray, "Adoption," in *Collected Writings*, 2:229; cf. 233.
3. *Reformed Confessions*, 4:358.
4. Willard, *A Compleat Body of Divinity*, 484.

moment."[5] As an act of free grace, adoption is not based on any merit in the person, but only on God's mercy exercised toward sinners as he wills. Neither does adoption arise out of any unfulfilled need in God, who is fully sufficient in his triune glory; it is a gift. When God adopts a sinner, he counts him to be one of his legal *sons* and heirs. Johann Heidegger said, "Adoption is the gracious sentence of God whereby He adopts those justified and reconciled to God by faith through and on account of Christ above, and as sons and heirs, coheirs with Christ."[6] Theologians sometimes describe the result of adoption as a "filial" relationship (from Latin *filius*, "son"). This grace is not given to one child, but to a number of them, even "a great multitude" (Rev. 7:9).[7]

Adoption grants to believers in Christ a high status beyond comparison, and few have meditated as deeply on the topic as it deserves. William Perkins said that for "such rebels to be made the sons of God—it is a wonderful privilege and prerogative, and no dignity like unto it."[8] Thomas Watson reflected on our nature by creation and by sin, and concluded, "It were much for God to take a clod of dust, and make it a star; it is more for him to take a piece of clay and sin, and adopt it for his heir."[9]

The more a Christian is conscious of his adoption, the more peace, stability, and joy he will have. Samuel Willard said,

> The time is coming when every man's foundation shall be tried; he only that is built upon the Rock shall then stand. To be able in an evil day to sit still with an undaunted courage and calm serenity upon our spirit, is a great felicity. The only way to do this is to be able to trust in the Lord, and with all grounded confidence to rely upon his power, goodness, and fidelity. This is no common thing, but the privilege of only a few, and those such whom God (having set his love upon them in Christ) hath taken to be his possession, and listed in the number of his children.[10]

Willard went on to say, "Could we draw all the water out of this well, it would make us to think ourselves in heaven before we come there. But the

5. Brown, *Questions and Answers on the Shorter Catechism*, 145.
6. Heidegger, *The Concise Marrow of Christian Theology*, 22.18 (159).
7. Willard, *A Compleat Body of Divinity*, 487.
8. Perkins, *An Exposition of the Symbol*, in *Works*, 5:33.
9. Watson, *A Body of Divinity*, 233.
10. Samuel Willard, Epistle "To the Reader," in *The Child's Portion: or the Unseen Glory of the Children of God, Asserted, and Proved: Together with Several Other Sermons* (Boston: Samuel Green, 1684), no pagination, punctuation modernized.

well is deep, and our line too short, and our bucket too shallow, whence they are but sips and small draughts we here obtain." It is our hope that God's children might find some sips of living water in this chapter and the next that will refresh their souls.[11]

The Cultural Background of Adoption in the Ancient World

There is evidence for the practice of adoption in the ancient Near East as early as the second millennium BC in the Code of Hammurabi at Babylon and documents of the Hurrian community at Nuzi. The effects of such adoptions included raising slave offspring to the status of legitimate sons, securing the care of elderly parents and their proper burial, perpetuating the family line, and creating relationships for the legal sale of family land.[12]

Among the Israelites, we have the record of Moses being taken by Pharaoh's daughter and raised as her son (Ex. 2:1–10; cf. Acts 7:20–22; Heb. 11:24). A form of adoption appears in the complaint of Abram that with no child of his own, his steward, Eliezer, stood to inherit his estate (Gen. 15:1–4), an arrangement that had a parallel in Hurrian culture.[13] Another practice with adoptive overtones was the making of a father's child by a slave woman into a legitimate son, even counted as the son of his legal wife (16:2)—hence Rachel's words to Jacob about Bilhah: "Behold my maid Bilhah, go in unto her; and she shall bear upon my knees, that I may also have children by her" (30:3; cf. 50:23). The law of Moses contains no provision for adoption, perhaps because the need for an heir was often met either by polygamy (cf. 1 Sam. 1:1–8) or levirate marriage (Deut. 25:5–10). Nevertheless, the Jews did sometimes practice adoption, as when Mordecai "took" his cousin Esther "for his own daughter" after her parents died; he brought her up, and she obeyed him (Est. 2:7, 10, 15, 20).[14]

Adoption is also attested in ancient Greek and Roman societies. It involved the transfer of a son or daughter from one family to another in order to become the heir of the new father and take care of his proper burial. It often involved a public ceremony involving other citizens or

11. Willard, Epistle "To the Reader," in *The Child's Portion*, no pagination.

12. Allen Mawhinney, "*Yiothesia* in the Pauline Epistles: Its Background, Use and Implications" (PhD diss., Baylor University, 1982), 33–38.

13. Derek Kidner, *Genesis: An Introduction and Commentary*, Tyndale Old Testament Commentaries 1 (Downers Grove, IL: InterVarsity Press, 1967), 134.

14. Another example of ancient Jewish adoption is a fifth century BC contract found at Elephantine, Egypt, by which a man named "Uriah" adopted "Yedoniah" as his son. Mawhinney, "*Yiothesia* in the Pauline Epistles," 51.

civil rulers. Adoption might be effected through the father's last will and testament, and so occur at his death. Adoption under Roman law emphasized the bringing of a person and his possessions under his new father's absolute authority (*patria potestas*). The specific form of adoption varied from people to people.[15]

Another important cultural background for the doctrine of adoption is the divine sonship ascribed to ancient kings. The king of Egypt was regarded as the son of a god, and himself a divine being. The king of Babylon was also considered the son of a god, but only a human representative and servant of the deity.[16] The divine sonship of kings also appears in the Holy Scriptures. Human kings are called "sons of the Most High" (Ps. 82:6 ESV). However, this description appears in an ironic context, for these so-called sons exploit their power for injustice (v. 2) and die as mere men (v. 7). They have no true familial relationship with the just Judge (v. 8). "Sons of the Most High" in this passage likely is a use of the Hebraic formula "sons of" to denote people who bear some quality or characteristic, here the majesty and authority by which these rulers represent something of God's kingship, albeit in a morally distorted fashion. This leads us to consider a biblical theology of sonship, beginning with the image of God.

God's Adoption of Sons in the Book of Moses

The biblical theme of divine sonship is rooted in God's creation of man "in our image, after our likeness" (Gen. 1:26). Adam in turn fathered a son "in his own likeness, and after his image" (5:1–3). A son is the living image of his father, and man is created in God's image to reveal and represent him on earth. A son should live for the honor of his father by doing his will, and God's created image bearers exist for the glory of the Creator.[17]

Man's privileged status as God's son in his original state also appears in the threefold covenantal office—prophet, priest, and king—conferred on him in the garden of Eden (Gen. 2:15–19).[18] A prophet hears and speaks

15. William Smith, ed., *A Dictionary of Greek and Roman Antiquities*, 2nd ed. (London: Walton and Maberly, 1859), s.v. *adoptio* (14–16); and Mawhinney, "*Yiothesia* in the Pauline Epistles," 10–33. In classical Greek, adoption was called *poiēsis* or *thesis*, and in Latin, *adoptio* or *adrogatio*. There is some distinction between the latter two terms, *adrogatio* referring to the adoption of a man who was no longer under a father's authority but legally stood on his own.

16. Henri Frankfort, *Kingship and the Gods: A Study of Ancient Near Eastern Religion as the Integration of Society & Nature* (Chicago: University of Chicago Press, 1948), 36–47, 237, 252, 299–300.

17. On these facets of being created in God's image, see *RST*, 2:167.

18. On the threefold office in the garden of Eden, see *RST*, 2:274–76.

God's word, just as a son learns by listening to his father and repeating what he says. A priest has special access to and communion with God, just as a son may enjoy an intimate friendship with his father. Divinely appointed kings share a measure of God's authority to rule over his kingdom, just as a son may share in his father's authority over his land and possessions, and enjoy them as his inheritance. Since the Lord God made man out of the dust of the earth (v. 7), this sonship was a gift of grace, not a relationship by nature.

However, it is notable that Genesis 1–3 never calls Adam the son of God (though see Luke 3:38). This might be because of the conditional arrangement that God made with our first father, whose disobedience to the covenant forfeited mankind's blessed estate. Though created to be God's sons, mankind cast aside that great privilege when Adam and Eve denied God's word, defiled themselves by giving their hearts to the creature rather than the Creator, and failed to defend God's kingdom against the evil intruder who tempted them.

There are hints of adoption in the rest of Genesis. The debated reference to "the sons of God" (Gen. 6:2, 4) may suggest that divine sonship continues among the righteous, exemplified by Enoch and Noah, who "walked with God" (5:21–24; 6:9).[19] There are suggestions of restored sonship in God's covenant with Abraham and his seed, in which he pledges to be their God and to take them as his people (17:7–8). God promised that they would "inherit" the land, using the same terminology as that for a father's grant of property to his "heir."[20]

The redemption of Israel from Egypt displays God's fatherly love for Abraham's offspring. The book of Exodus emphasizes God's compassion for his people and faithfulness to his covenant with their fathers.[21] God sent Moses to Pharaoh, saying, "Thus saith the LORD, Israel is my son, even my firstborn: and I say unto thee, Let my son go, that he may serve me: and if thou refuse to let him go, behold, I will slay thy son, even thy firstborn" (Ex. 4:22–23). The Lord's covenant with Abraham evidently implied the corporate adoption of his seed to be God's "son."

19. The other interpretive options for "the sons of God" in Gen. 6:2, 4 are angels or powerful men. However, angels, though called "sons of God" (Job 1:6; 2:1; 38:7), do not marry or procreate (Matt. 22:30), and it is unlikely that powerful men would be designated as "sons of God" when they are noted for behavior offensive to God (Gen. 6:2–3).

20. See *yarash* in Gen. 15:3–4, 7–8; 21:10; 22:17; 24:60; 28:4. This same verb is used for Israel's taking possession of the land that is the Lord's *gift* to them (Deut. 1:8; 3:18, 20; 4:1; 5:31; 9:6, 23; etc.).

21. Ex. 2:23–25; 3:6–9; 6:4–5.

As God's "firstborn," Israel had the right to preeminent blessing and royal honor.[22]

Divine adoption defined the relationship between the Lord and Israel. Moses told the people that "in the wilderness . . . the LORD your God carried you, as a man carries his son" (Deut. 1:31 ESV). Moses also said, "As a man disciplines his son, the LORD your God disciplines you" (8:5 ESV). This adoption had practical implications: "Ye are the children [literally "sons"] of the LORD your God: ye shall not cut yourselves, nor make any baldness between your eyes for the dead. For thou art an holy people unto the LORD thy God, and the LORD hath chosen thee to be a peculiar people unto himself, above all the nations that are upon the earth" (14:1–2). This is a rare instance where the people of Israel are called God's "sons" (plural) and not the collective "son" (singular).

Individual participation in Israel's national adoption was conditional upon repentance, faith, and evangelical obedience, and did not belong to those who showed themselves to be God's enemies: "They have dealt corruptly with him; they are no longer his children because they are blemished; they are a crooked and twisted generation. Do you thus repay the LORD, you foolish and senseless people? Is not he your father, who created you, who made you and established you?" (Deut. 32:5–6 ESV). John Calvin commented, "Moses, therefore, declares that they are not children, because they are a perverse nation. For although their adoption always stood firm, still its efficacy was restricted to the elect part of them, so that God, without breaking His covenant, might reject the general body."[23]

God's Adoption of Sons in the Monarchy and Latter Prophets

The Lord brought his adoptive grace to a focal point when he promised regarding David's seed, "I will be his father, and he shall be my son. If he commit iniquity, I will chasten him with the rod of men, and with the stripes of the children of men: but my mercy shall not depart away from him, as I took it from Saul, whom I put away before thee" (2 Sam. 7:14–15). God adopted the son of David, pledging himself to be his "father," and making him God's "firstborn, higher than the kings of the earth" (Ps. 89:26–27). Here adoption takes on a decidedly royal flavor, implying exaltation to

22. Gen. 27:19, 27–29; 49:3; Deut. 31:15–17; Ps. 89:27.
23. Calvin, *Commentaries*, on Deut. 32:5.

great authority. The Lord adopted Solomon, "for I have chosen him to be my son, and I will be his father" (1 Chron. 28:6). The adoption extended to David's royal descendants after Solomon (cf. Ps. 89:28–37). However, God's adoption of royal sons of the line of David foreshadowed and was fulfilled in David's greatest descendant (Luke 1:32), who was not adopted by God but was already God's Son at birth (v. 35), for he is the eternal, only begotten Son (John 3:16; 17:5, 24).

God's adoption of the godly in Israel also continued under the Davidic monarchy. David rejoiced in God's love for his people, saying, "As a father shows compassion to his children, so the LORD shows compassion to those who fear him" (Ps. 103:13 ESV). Solomon exhorted, "My son, despise not the chastening of the LORD; neither be weary of his correction: for whom the LORD loveth he correcteth; even as a father the son in whom he delighteth" (Prov. 3:11–12). The children of God in these texts were not the Israelites as a nation but "individual Israelites" who were the objects of God's special love, as Robert Peterson observes.[24]

The Hebrew prophets made use of the doctrine of divine adoption both to press upon Israel its duties to God and to exult in the wonder of God's love. The Lord complained, "I have nourished and brought up children, and they have rebelled against me" (Isa. 1:2), and, "If then I be a father, where is mine honour?" (Mal. 1:6). Yet Isaiah prayed on behalf of the godly remnant, "Doubtless thou art our father, though Abraham be ignorant of us, and Israel acknowledge us not: thou, O LORD, art our father, our redeemer; thy name is from everlasting" (Isa. 63:16; cf. 64:8). Through this text, the prophet assured Israel that, though God disciplined Israel severely, "the banishment shall not be perpetual," Calvin said, "for God, being a most indulgent Father, moderates his chastisements in such a manner, that he always forgives his children."[25] God would restore his covenantal family. The Lord said, "Bring my sons from far, and my daughters from the ends of the earth; even every one that is called by my name: for I have created him for my glory" (43:6–7).[26]

Though the pagans regarded their gods as fathers and mothers in the sense of being their makers (Jer. 2:27), the prophets of the Lord declared

24. Robert A. Peterson, *Adopted by God: From Wayward Sinners to Cherished Children* (Phillipsburg, NJ: P&R, 2001), 23–24.

25. Calvin, *Commentaries*, on Isa. 44:22.

26. Isaiah refers to Christ as "the everlasting Father" (Isa. 9:6). However, this does not refer to divine adoption but to Christ's status as the covenantal progenitor of a new race, like Abraham: "He shall see his seed" (53:10).

that God's fatherhood is not merely as Creator but also as Savior.[27] God's intention in his covenant had long been adoptive: "I said, How shall I put thee among the children, and give thee a pleasant land, a goodly heritage of the hosts of nations? And I said, Thou shalt call me, My father; and shalt not turn away from me" (3:19).[28] Jeremiah's book of consolation records these words of God in the context of the new covenant: "I am a father to Israel, and Ephraim is my firstborn. . . . Is Ephraim my dear son? . . . I will surely have mercy upon him" (31:9, 20). Though the Israelites' sins would provoke God to reject them, yet "it shall be said unto them, Ye are the sons of the living God" (Hos. 1:10). This was because the Lord loved Israel from its beginning and called his "son out of Egypt" (11:1). God will punish the wicked, but as for those who fear him, "they shall be mine, says the LORD of hosts, in the day when I make up my treasured possession, and I will spare them as a man spares his son who serves him" (Mal. 3:17 ESV).

Therefore, we observe in the Old Testament that God revealed his adoptive love, first for mankind as a whole as those created in his image, and then after the fall brought ruin to his image bearers, to the covenant seed of Abraham, the nation of Israel. Adoption is not exclusively a New Testament doctrine. However, the focus of adoption in the Old Testament is primarily on the covenant people as God's corporate "son" and secondarily on the son of David as God's royal "son." The Old Testament does not fully develop a piety of personal adoption for individual believers. In the Psalms, we find God addressed with many magnificent and beautiful titles, but nowhere do we find the psalmist crying out to "our Father."

God's Adoption of Sons in the Gospels

With the coming of God the Son incarnate, the Lord revealed his adoption in a far greater way. Few words are more characteristic of Christ's teaching about God than "Father." Christ refers to God as "Father" no less than forty-four times in the Gospel of Matthew, most of which have to do with God as the Father not specifically of Christ but of all who are one with

27. Peterson, *Adopted by God*, 16–17.

28. Israel calls the Lord "my Father" (Jer. 3:4, 19), but this relationship is also described as that between a wife and her husband (v. 1). This led F. B. Huey to comment, "A wife sometimes called her husband 'Father' in the [ancient Near East] as acknowledgment of his authority and protection." F. B. Huey Jr., *Jeremiah, Lamentations*, The New American Commentary 16 (Nashville: Broadman & Holman, 1993), 72n. However, sonship seems to be in view, for the Lord said, literally, "I will set you among the sons" (v. 19).

Christ in faith and obedience. Christ's faithful disciples will one day be openly acknowledged to be the "sons of God" (Matt. 5:9 ESV; cf. v. 45),[29] and Jesus already tells them that God is "your Father which is in heaven" (vv. 16, 45, 48; 6:1; 7:11), even the singular "*thy* Father" (6:4, 6, 18).

Christ infused his doctrine of piety with the fatherhood of God toward his people. The highest ideal of his ethic for his disciples is imitation of their Father in his love and perfection (Matt. 5:43–48). Calvin said, "God would have those whom he has adopted, as he is to them a kind and indulgent Father, to bear and exhibit his image on the earth."[30] Christ teaches his disciples to regularly address God as "our Father which art in heaven" (6:9). They must not call anyone else their spiritual father, "for one is your Father, which is in heaven" (23:9). Jesus reveals God as the *attentive* Father who notices how his children serve him in secret and will reward them (6:4, 6, 18), the *caring* Father who knows what they need before they ask (v. 8), the *providing* Father who gives to them all that they need (vv. 25–32), and the *responsive* Father who delights to answer his children's prayers (7:9–11).

The Lord Jesus does not use the term *adoption*, but that does not mean he taught that all people are God's children by nature. The sons of God have a distinctive character. They are peacemakers and love their enemies (Matt. 5:9, 44–45). Christ says that only the obedient belong to the family of God: "Whosoever shall do the will of my Father which is in heaven, the same is my brother, and sister" (12:50). Given that Christ's message was fundamentally a call for sinners to repent (4:17; 9:13), his description of God's children as people who do God's will and love one another implies that only those who repent of their sins and turn to God have the right to call themselves his children.

While Christ's parable of the prodigal son (Luke 15:11–32) does not explicitly involve adoption, it resonates with the theme of adoption and links it to repentance and restoration. The younger son in the parable treats his father as if he were already dead when he demands his inheritance and begins to spend it (vv. 11–12). When he comes to his senses, he realizes that he has forfeited all rights to sonship in his father's family and resolves to say, "Father, I have sinned against heaven, and before thee, and am no more worthy to be called thy son: make me as one of thy hired servants" (v. 18).

29. In Matt. 5:9, 45, the word translated in the KJV as "children" is more literally "sons" (plural *huios*).

30. Calvin, *Commentaries*, on James 2:13.

However, when he returns home in repentance, his father receives him with "great love and affection," as Matthew Henry noted: "Here were eyes of mercy, and those eyes were quick-sighted.... Here were bowels of mercy... he had compassion.... Here were feet of mercy, and those feet quick-paced: He ran.... Here were arms of mercy... to embrace him.... Here were lips of mercy.... He kissed him."[31] The father gives his penitent son "the best robe" and puts "a ring on his hand" (v. 22), signs of honor and authority.[32] The father calls for a feast (v. 23), something that one would expect for the birth and weaning of a new son (Gen. 21:8). The father explains, "For this my son was dead, and is alive again; he was lost, and is found" (Luke 15:24, cf. v. 32). He had ceased to be a son, but now is restored to sonship again by his father's grace. The elder son also shows that despite staying at home and slaving away at his work, as he thinks (v. 29), he is alienated from his father (v. 30) and needs repentance and reconciliation. This parable illustrates the restoration of repentant sinners into God's family, especially for those already external members of God's covenantal son, Israel.

Christ's teaching concerning the children of God has an eschatological orientation, being an aspect of his preaching of God's kingdom. Jesus says, "Blessed are the peacemakers: for they shall be called [future tense] the children of God" (Matt. 5:9). In context, this refers to the time when they shall also "inherit the earth" and "see God" (vv. 5, 8). When Christ returns and sends his angels to cast lawbreakers into the fire of judgment, "then shall the righteous shine forth as the sun in the kingdom of their Father" (13:41–43). The glory of their sonship will then be manifested, no matter how lowly and afflicted they were in this life (cf. 25:35–40). Christ comforts them, saying, "Fear not, little flock; for it is your Father's good pleasure to give you the kingdom," which includes "treasure in the heavens that faileth not" (Luke 12:32–33). Only at "the resurrection from the dead" are they fully revealed as "sons of God" (20:35–36 ESV). Therefore, their present privilege as God's children is an example of God's kingdom already coming in hidden spiritual form to this world.

The Gospel of John links becoming God's child with faith in Jesus Christ, for he is God's Son by nature. In so doing, it sharply critiques those who would rely upon their physical descent from Abraham to have a place in God's family. John writes, "He came to his own, and his own

31. Henry, *Commentary on the Whole Bible*, 1879, on Luke 15:11–32.
32. Gen. 41:42; Est. 8:2, 8, 10, 15; cf. 1 Macc. 6:15.

people did not receive him. But to all who did receive him, who believed in his name, he gave the right to become children of God" (John 1:11–12 ESV).[33] This may be the clearest statement of adoption by God in the Gospels, for "right" (*exousia*) implies a legal authority, liberty, or privilege.[34] A believer does not receive power to make himself into a child of God (by sanctification), but receives the privilege of being counted a child of God. This shows that becoming God's child is the grant of a new legal status in relation to God. Yet becoming God's child requires a new birth that changes one's nature (v. 13; 3:3–8). The child of God stands in new spiritual relationships with God and Christ on the one hand and with the Devil on the other. Christ said to his fellow Jews, "I know that ye are Abraham's seed," but warned them, "If God were your Father, ye would love me: for I proceeded forth and came from God. . . . Ye are of your father the devil, and the lusts of your father ye will do" (8:37, 42, 44).

Becoming God's child, according to John, is a gift of God's grace through union with Christ in his death and exaltation. As such, it extends far beyond ethnic Israel. The high priest unwittingly prophesied that "Jesus should die for that nation; and not for that nation only, but that also he should gather together in one the children of God that were scattered abroad" (John 11:51–52). Christ dwells "in" his disciples, and he prayed to the Father, "Thou hast sent me, and hast loved them, as thou hast loved me" (17:23). This is an astonishing statement of the union between the Son and his people as the object of the Father's love. After Christ died and rose from the dead, he sent this message to his disciples: "I ascend unto my Father, and your Father; and to my God, and your God" (20:17)—and that after they all had forsaken him! By his ascension, he lifted up his people to be the children of the living God.

God's Adoption of Sons in Paul's Epistles

The doctrine of the saints' adoption into God's family is an integral part of the message of the New Testament Epistles, especially those written by

---

33. The word *tekna* is more accurately translated as "children" than "sons" (John 1:12; 1 John 3:1–2 KJV).

34. Poole, *Annotations upon the Holy Bible*, 3:279, on John 1:12; and Carson, *The Gospel according to John*, 126. For examples of *exousia* as authority, right, or liberty, see Matt. 8:9; 9:6; Mark 13:34; Luke 19:17; Acts 5:4; 9:14; 26:10, 12; cf. *exousiazō* in 1 Cor. 7:4. See also *TDNT*, 2:562–69. The word *exousia* can also refer to power (Luke 12:5), a ruler (Rom. 13:1; Eph. 1:21), and a dominion (Acts 26:18; Col. 1:13), and sometimes it is used in a manner that may involve both power and authority (John 5:27; 19:10–11).

Paul. In the openings of ten of Paul's epistles, he invokes "God our Father," together with Christ, to bless his saints with grace and peace.[35] Christ "gave himself for our sins, that he might deliver us from this present evil world, according to the will of God and our Father" (Gal. 1:4).

Paul alone among the New Testament writers uses the word translated as "adoption" (*huiothesia*), always in reference to God's grace to his people.[36] The word is a composite of roots meaning "placement as a son" (from *huios* and *tithēmi*).[37] In ancient secular literature, the term refers to the legal act of designating someone as one's son and heir by transferring him from one family to another.[38] Similarly, divine adoption, as Francis Turretin observed, is "a juridical act of God," in which he "admits us into his own family . . . and gives us the dignity of sons."[39] Thomas Boston said, "Adoption is not a real change of the sinner's nature; but as justification a relative change of his state." As such, "it is done in an instant, not carried on by degrees."[40] Somewhat more precisely, "adoption" (*huiothesia*) can refer to both the *act of adopting* and the *relation of sonship* that results from the act.[41] However, we should distinguish between the status of adopted sons, which is presently granted to all in Christ, and the results of adoption, which develop over time.

Scholars debate whether "adoption" (*huiothesia*) in Paul's theology takes its meaning primarily from the Old Testament or from Greco-Roman culture. Since Paul says that "the adoption" belongs to the "Israelites" (Rom. 9:4), we must see this doctrine as growing out of God's covenantal dealings with the offspring of Abraham, dealings that reach their pinnacle in Christ (cf. Gal. 3:24–4:6).[42] We have observed that the Holy Scriptures provide a rich theme of divine sonship that is rooted in Adam, developed in Israel, focused on David's seed, and fulfilled in Jesus Christ and his church. David Garner notes that the great covenantal teachings of the Old Testament form the "foundational" elements of Paul's gospel,

35. Rom. 1:7; 1 Cor. 1:3; 2 Cor. 1:2; Gal. 1:3; Eph. 1:2; Phil. 1:2; Col. 1:2; 2 Thess. 1:1–2; 1 Tim. 1:2; Philem. 3.

36. Rom. 8:15, 23; 9:4; Gal. 4:5; Eph. 1:5. The term does not appear in the LXX.

37. Compare *nomothesia* (Rom. 9:4), which means "legislation"—that is, the putting forth or making of a law (*nomon tithēmi*)—and *horothesia* (Acts 17:26), a "boundary" or the result of placing a "boundary line" (*horion*).

38. *TDNT*, 8:397–98. The word *huiothesia* is extant from the late third or second century BC.

39. Turretin, *Institutes*, 16.6.2–3 (2:667).

40. Boston, *An Illustration of the Doctrines of the Christian Religion*, in *Works*, 1:615–16.

41. David B. Garner, *Sons in the Son: The Riches and Reach of Adoption in Christ* (Phillipsburg, NJ: P&R, 2016), 49–50.

42. Hodge, *Commentary on the Epistle to the Romans*, 470.

and it is the gospel of Christ that determines Paul's concept of adoption.[43] However, Garner also observes that we cannot ignore that fact that Paul uses a term well known to Greek and Roman readers to communicate and illustrate this teaching. Garner says, "He seizes *huiothesia* from its familiar Greco-Roman context, and amasses to it Old Testament messianic and covenantal concepts, and then imbues it with . . . eschatologically realized (New Testament) theological content."[44]

However, we are not to consider the saving grace of adoption in Christ to be identical with the national, corporate adoption of Abraham's descendants, but rather as standing in continuity with the individual adoption of believers in Israel: "They which are the children of the flesh, these are not the children of God" (Rom. 9:8). Whether we consider people in ethnic Israel or among the Gentiles, it is only those who are chosen and called who are personally adopted as "the children [literally "sons," plural *huios*] of the living God" (v. 11, 23–26).

Paul teaches that God adopts those who trust in Christ: "For ye are all the children [plural *huios*] of God by faith in Christ Jesus" (Gal. 3:26). This is a benefit of union with Christ ("in Christ"), which redefines the status of believers by giving them a new identity that transcends all earthly categories (vv. 27–28). Willard said, "Our sonship is properly an act of our communion or fellowship with Christ. . . . Our union with Christ is the true and proper ground of our communion with him in all his benefits."[45] Hence, the adoption of Christians in Christ "far excels" the status of Adam as God's son, Roger Drake (1608–1669) observed, for Adam "indeed was God's son by similitude and dependence; but not by special union and communion with Christ, the natural Son of God, as we now are."[46]

The adoption of Christians (Gal. 3:26) is not radically different from that of old covenant saints, but is an aspect of their ingrafting into Israel, for "if ye be Christ's, then are ye Abraham's seed, and heirs according to the promise" (v. 29). However, God has brought his people into a new phase of redemptive history. Paul explains that Israel, though God's "heir," was like a child under restrictive authority before reaching adulthood (4:1–3). However, God sent his Son to "redeem them that were

43. Garner, *Sons in the Son*, 45–46.
44. Garner, *Sons in the Son*, 49.
45. Willard, *The Child's Portion*, 12.
46. Roger Drake, "The Believer's Dignity and Duty Laid Open, In the High Birth Wherewith He Is Privileged, and the Honorable Employment To Which He Is Called," in *Puritan Sermons, 1659–1689*, 5:332.

under the law, that we might receive the adoption of sons" (v. 5). Consequently, the believer in Christ is elevated to the status of "a son; and if a son, then an heir of God through Christ" (v. 7). Paul implies that the adoption of believers in Christ is of one piece with God's grace under the covenant with Abraham (cf. 3:14), but the status of the adopted sons has arrived at a greater liberty because Christ accomplished redemption.[47] Calvin commented that "the fathers under the Old Testament . . . were partakers of the same adoption" but "did not so fully as yet enjoy their privilege."[48] The transition is redemptive-historical and eschatological, for Christ came "in the fulness of time" (4:4).

The transition from being minor sons implies that in this age God's sons already enjoy the inheritance to some extent because Christ accomplished redemption and rose from the dead. Paul says, "Because ye are sons, God hath sent forth the Spirit of his Son into your hearts, crying, Abba, Father" (Gal. 4:6). The Spirit's work in God's sons is the down payment of their inheritance (2 Cor. 1:22; 5:5; Eph. 1:14). Though adoption is a legal act, it has immediate implications for the experiential and practical life, for the Spirit comes as "the Spirit of adoption" (Rom. 8:15). He is "the Spirit of Christ" (v. 9), the risen Lord who now reigns as "the Son of God with power, according to the spirit of holiness" (1:4). Garner writes, "The resurrection life of the Son of God comprehensively shapes the believer's state, outlook, and identity," and "the Spirit of adoption's dynamic presence bonds the redeemed to the resurrected Son."[49]

The gift of the Spirit of adoption is distinct from adoption itself and is a consequence of it, given "because ye are sons" (Gal. 4:6). However, there is no adoption without sanctification and comfort, for "as many as are led by the Spirit of God, they are the sons of God," and "the Spirit itself beareth witness with our spirit, that we are the children of God" (Rom. 8:14, 16). The Spirit of adoption forms within God's adopted sons a childlike "affection and confidence" in response to their knowing God's fatherly love for them. Adoption confers the rights of sonship; the Spirit of adoption cultivates the enjoyment of those rights and the performance of the corresponding obligations.[50]

---

47. Jeremiah Burroughs, *The Saints' Happiness, Together with the Several Steps Leading Thereunto: Delivered in Divers Lectures on the Beatitudes* (1867; repr., Ligonier, PA: Soli Deo Gloria, 1992), 193; and Witsius, *The Economy of the Covenants*, 3.10.15–26 (1:447–50).

48. Calvin, *Commentaries*, on Gal. 4:1, 5.

49. Garner, *Sons in the Son*, 107.

50. Murray, "Adoption," in *Collected Writings*, 2:229.

The eschatological "already/not yet" orientation of adoption implies that God's children have not entered their glory in Christ. They are "joint-heirs with Christ," but must presently "suffer" in union with him (Rom. 8:17). Their status is hidden, but there is coming a "manifestation" (*apokalypsis*), literally a "revelation" of who they are, when all creation "shall be delivered from the bondage of corruption into the glorious liberty of the children of God" (vv. 19, 21). Though already adopted legally, God's children wait for their public recognition, "the adoption . . . the redemption of our body" (v. 23). Then they will be released from their bondage to all evils in order to enjoy the glory of God forever.

Adoption is sovereign grace from God. Paul teaches that adoption, like all blessings in Christ, is rooted in God's eternal election and predestination. God "hath chosen us in him before the foundation of the world . . . having predestinated us unto the adoption of children by Jesus Christ to himself, according to the good pleasure of his will, to the praise of the glory of his grace" (Eph. 1:4–6). The Pauline doctrine of adoption reveals that the heart of the electing God is that of a loving Father who desires to take the unworthy as his sons and daughters. This predestination centers on Christ and, when executed in time, creates a spiritual family transformed into "the image of his Son" and united around him as the "firstborn among many brethren" (Rom. 8:29).

As a relational and covenantal blessing, adoption has significant implications for the Christian life, according to Paul's theology. We may summarize these implications with the words *consecration*, *imitation*, and *distinction*.

Paul writes that since God has said, "I will dwell in them, and walk in them; and I will be their God, and they shall be my people," Christians should pursue *consecration* to God by separating from the world's sins: "Come out from among them, and be ye separate, saith the Lord, and touch not the unclean thing; and I will receive you. And will be a Father unto you, and ye shall be my sons and daughters, saith the Lord Almighty. Having therefore these promises, dearly beloved, let us cleanse ourselves from all filthiness of the flesh and spirit, perfecting holiness in the fear of God" (2 Cor. 6:16–7:1). Paul's allusions to Old Testament texts in these words (cf. Lev. 26:12; Isa. 52:11) remind us of the continuity of adoption and its ethical implications through the ages.

Paul says that adoption calls us to *imitation*: "Therefore be imitators of God, as beloved children. And walk in love, as Christ loved us and gave himself up for us, a fragrant offering and sacrifice to God" (Eph. 5:1–2 ESV). Children naturally mimic their parents; God's adopted children must learn to trust their Father's love and imitate his character by living like his Son.

Finally, we note that adoption implies that Christians must conduct themselves in *distinction* from this world. This, too, is by faith. Paul says, "Do all things without grumbling or disputing, that you may be blameless and innocent, children of God without blemish in the midst of a crooked and twisted generation, among whom you shine as lights in the world" (Phil. 2:14–15 ESV).

God's Adoption of Sons in the Other Epistles

While the sonship of believers is not as prominent in the other New Testament Epistles as it is in those written by Paul, it remains an important theme.

The epistle to the Hebrews assumes adoption when it speaks of God's intent of "bringing many sons unto glory" (Heb. 2:10). To this end, Christ counts his people as his "brethren," even "the children which God hath given me" (vv. 11–13). Since "the children are partakers of flesh and blood, he also himself likewise took part of the same" so he could save them by his death (v. 14). In order to save those who "obey him," Christ, "though he were a Son, yet learned he obedience by the things which he suffered" (5:8–9). Our salvation as God's sons depended on the eternal Son bringing his human nature into an experiential submission to God—Christ's tested and perfected human sonship to God is the foundation of our sonship. Likewise, God tests his people as a father disciplines his beloved sons so that they may share in his holiness (12:5–6, 10). Millard Erickson notes, "He is our heavenly Father, not our heavenly Grandfather. Thus, discipline is one of the features of our adoption."[51] Here Hebrews cites the wisdom of Solomon (Prov. 3:11–12), another indication that God's people through the ages share a common relationship to God as their Father.[52]

Peter exhorts God's chosen, redeemed, and born-again people to conduct themselves "as obedient children," for they "call on the Father, who

51. Erickson, *Christian Theology*, 894.

52. Hebrews 12:23 refers to the heavenly church as the "firstborn" (plural *prōtotokos*). This could mean that all believers are firstborn sons of God, like Israel (Ex. 4:22), but the plural more likely alludes to the "firstborn" in Israel who were saved by the blood of the Passover lamb, claimed by God, and later exchanged for the Levites (Ex. 13:15; Num. 3:41, 45–46, 50; 8:16–18 LXX).

without respect of persons judgeth according to every man's work" (1 Pet. 1:14, 17). This accords with God's command, "Be ye holy; for I am holy" (v. 16; citing Lev. 11:44), an obligation that, as we saw earlier, coordinated with the status of Israel as God's special, adopted people (Deut. 14:1–2).

John often addresses the recipients of his first epistle with the affectionate title "little children" (*teknia*).[53] He also writes of them or other Christians with the terms "brethren" or "brother" (*adelphos*),[54] language commonly used throughout the New Testament for one's fellow saints.[55] This language reminds us that God's adoption of sinners as his children creates a special ethos in the church, knitting people from diverse backgrounds together as one family. John strongly distinguishes God's children from the rest of the world: "In this the children of God are manifest, and the children of the devil: whosoever doeth not righteousness is not of God, neither he that loveth not his brother" (1 John 3:10; cf. 5:1–2).

Becoming God's child is a gift of God's marvelous love. John exclaims, "Behold, what manner of love the Father hath bestowed upon us, that we should be called the sons [*teknon*] of God" (1 John 3:1). William Ames noted the "difference between human adoption and divine. . . . Human adoption was introduced when there were no, or too few, natural sons. But divine adoption is not from any want but from abundant goodness."[56] John Cotton said, "God would have every child of his to behold his love," and this first, "for his own glory," second, "that we might better support our spirits against the discouragements we meet with," and third, "that so we might be persuaded to love God, and strengthened to doing and suffering." John's "behold what manner of love" corrects men's "squint lookings," Cotton said, for "they do not look at God's love, but into themselves."[57]

As we have seen in other writers, John regards this sonship as eschatological and not yet complete: "Beloved, now are we the sons of God, and it doth not yet appear what we shall be: but we know that, when he shall

53. 1 John 2:1, 12, 28; 3:7, 18; 4:4; 5:21. However, at times this is "my little children," and so this language is familial without directly alluding to adoption by God.

54. 1 John 2:7, 9–11; 3:10, 12–17; 4:20–21; 5:16.

55. Believers are addressed as "brethren" or "brothers" about 170 times in Acts through Revelation. By comparison, the word "saints" appears about sixty times in all New Testament uses. "Christian" appears only three times (Acts 11:26; 26:28; 1 Pet. 4:16).

56. Ames, *The Marrow of Theology*, 1.28.15 (166).

57. John Cotton, *A Practical Commentary, or an Exposition with Observations, Reasons, and Uses upon the First Epistle Generall of John* (London: by R. I. and E. C. for Thomas Parkhurst, 1656), 219, on 1 John 3:1.

appear, we shall be like him; for we shall see him as he is" (1 John 3:2). The result is that God's children have "hope" (v. 3). Cotton compared this hope to a ship's anchor, "that God's children might not be tossed and hurried up and down," but "kept from dashing against rocks, and sands." This hope not only steadies the believer, but "every man that hath this hope in him purifieth himself, even as he is pure" (v. 3). Thus, God's children have "a lively fruitful hope."[58]

In the book of Revelation, the doctrine of adoption is closely related to the glorification of God's people at the end of the age. Christ says, "He that overcometh, and keepeth my works unto the end, to him will I give power over the nations: and he shall rule them with a rod of iron; as the vessels of a potter shall they be broken to shivers: even as I received of my Father" (Rev. 2:26–27). Here the Lord quotes the ancient promise that the Lord made to "my Son" and extends it to those who follow him to the end, implying their adoption as royal sons (Ps. 2:7–9). Christ also says, "To him that overcometh will I grant to sit with me in my throne, even as I also overcame, and am set down with my Father in his throne" (Rev. 3:21). The kingly privileges of the incarnate Son will be shared with those who conquer by his redemptive victory on the cross (5:5, 9–10; 12:11; 17:14). The adoption implicit in these texts is openly stated toward the end of the book: "He that overcometh shall inherit all things; and I will be his God, and he shall be my son" (21:7). These words blend the promises of the covenant with Abraham (Gen. 17:7) and the covenant with David (2 Sam. 7:14). Watson said, "Adoption ends in coronation."[59] Just as God originally created man to be his son, as we saw in Genesis, so God will restore those redeemed by the Lamb to live as his children in a renewed paradise where they will serve as his prophets, priests, and kings forever (Rev. 22:1–5; cf. 1:6; 5:10; 20:6).

Sing to the Lord

God's Fatherly Love for His Children

The tender love a father has
For all his children dear,
Such love the Lord bestows on them
Who worship Him in fear.

58. Cotton, *A Practical Commentary . . . upon the First Epistle Generall of John*, 229, 231, on 1 John 3:3.

59. Watson, *A Body of Divinity*, 234.

The Lord remembers we are dust,
And all our frailty knows;
Man's days are like the tender grass,
And as the flow'r he grows.

The flow'r is withered by the wind
That smites with blighting breath;
So man is quickly swept away
Before the blast of death.

Unchanging is the love of God,
From age to age the same,
Displayed to all who do His will
And reverence His Name.

Those who His gracious covenant keep
The Lord will ever bless;
Their children's children shall rejoice
To see His righteousness.

Psalm 103:13–18
Tune: Avondale
The Psalter, No. 278
Trinity Hymnal—Baptist Edition, No. 85

Questions for Meditation or Discussion

1. How was adoption practiced in the different cultures of the ancient Near East and Greco-Roman world?
2. How is God's adoption of sons rooted in his creation of Adam?
3. What did God say about the nation of Israel regarding its adoption?
4. How does the Old Testament reveal God's adoption of individual believers?
5. What does God's covenant with David contribute to our understanding of adoption?
6. How does the Lord Jesus infuse his teachings on piety with the fatherhood of God?
7. What does Paul mean by "adoption" (*huiothesia*)? How is adoption related to the Spirit of adoption?
8. According to Paul, how has the progress of redemptive history and the coming of Christ affected the sonship of God's people?

9. What do the other New Testament Epistles (besides those written by Paul) reveal about the privileges and obligations implied by being the children of God?
10. How has reading this chapter enriched your understanding of what it means to be a child of God? How can you live more fully in the light of this doctrine?

Questions for Deeper Reflection

11. Two of your friends are having a friendly debate. One says that individual believers were not adopted sons of God until Christ rose from the dead, and the other says that all believers throughout the ages have enjoyed the exact same grace of adoption. What do you say?
12. Prepare a detailed outline for a forty-minute talk to an adult class on "What did the apostle Paul teach about the adoption of sons in Christ?"

26

Adoption, Part 2

Systematic and Relational Considerations

Adoption, as John Gill observed, is an act of "surprising" grace, especially when one considers that it is the King of kings who adopts and miserable sinners whom he takes as his children.[1] This is well illustrated in the story of Mephibosheth (2 Samuel 9). By all accounts, this man was in a sorry state: he was lame in his feet and a direct descendant of the wicked King Saul, who had persecuted David. He considered himself to be as worthless as "a dead dog" (v. 8; cf. 1 Sam. 24:14; 2 Sam. 16:9). However, David, out of his love for Mephibosheth's father, Jonathan, restored the inheritance of Saul's house and his servants to Mephibosheth and invited the lame man to eat with David at his "table, as one of the king's sons" (2 Sam. 9:11). Though not a formal adoption, David's action was a type of God's marvelous mercy that brings the weak and unworthy to sit as the King's sons at his table.

Adoption enfolds many rich benefits for God's people. The Westminster Confession of Faith (chap. 12) says,

> All those that are justified, God vouchsafeth [graciously grants], in and for His only Son Jesus Christ, to make partakers of the grace of adoption, by which they are taken into the number, and enjoy the liberties and privileges

1. Gill, *Body of Divinity*, 523.

> of the children of God, have His name put upon them, receive the spirit of adoption, have access to the throne of grace with boldness, are enabled to cry, Abba, Father, are pitied, protected, provided for, and chastened by Him as by a Father: yet never cast off, but sealed to the day of redemption; and inherit the promises, as heirs of everlasting salvation.[2]

The Westminster divines recognized that adoption is a grace distinct from justification but like it in that adoption arises from union with Christ. They traced the effects of adoption throughout the Christian life and into glory itself.

Having surveyed a biblical theology of adoption in the previous chapter, in this one we will consider adoption from three angles: as a unique privilege for the people in union with Christ, as a perspective on all of salvation, and as a transformation of every relationship we have.

Adoption as a Privilege Unique to Those in Christ

In order to appreciate the surpassing greatness of God's grace in adoption, we must see that it is a privilege that belongs only to those who are united to Christ by a living faith. God dispenses honors and blessings liberally among his creatures, but adoption confers a unique status; there is simply no other privilege in the created realm that can compare.

In many ways, the highest order of beings that God created are the angels, but the adopted children of God have a dignity that even the angels do not enjoy. Angels are called "sons of God" a few times in the Holy Scriptures,[3] but this may be a Hebraic expression for a major characteristic of angels—that is, their close association with God in dwelling in his presence, reflecting his glory, and doing his will.[4] There is no evidence of a father-son relationship between God and the angels, and the Scriptures tend to reserve sonship to Christ and his people.[5] Even if angels are sons of God in some sense, it is not by union with God the Son incarnate. Christians are heirs with Christ (Rom. 8:17), and thus enjoy a status far above the angels (1 Cor. 3:21–23; 6:3).

Adoption in Christ distinguishes not only men from angels, but also God's redeemed people from other human beings. We cannot say that all

2. *Reformed Confessions*, 4:249.
3. Job 1:6; 2:1; 38:7; cf. Ps. 89:6.
4. See *RST*, 1:1113. Compare the expressions "son of strength" and "son of wickedness" (see the Hebrew text of 1 Sam. 14:52; 1 Chron. 17:9).
5. Grudem, *Systematic Theology*, 738.

people are children of God simply because God loves them. One of the central falsehoods of liberal modernism is the universal fatherhood of God. Everyone is said to be the child of God.[6] It might be argued in favor of this idea that Christ taught all people to view God as their Father (as, allegedly, in Matthew 5–7). In the parable of the prodigal son (Luke 15), Christ presents God as the father of both the rebellious son and the proud, resentful son. Paul says that there is "one God and Father of all, who is above all, and through all, and in you all" (Eph. 4:6). This teaching of God's universal fatherhood implies that all people will be saved, regardless of their faith or life.[7]

In reply, we observe that the doctrine of universal salvation fails to account for the pervasive biblical theme of God's final judgment on the wicked, taught clearly and forcefully by Christ himself.[8] The teachings of the Lord Jesus about God as the heavenly Father identify the Father's children as people who exhibit a distinctive righteousness that many people do not possess.[9] Two kinds of people take two ways to two destinations—destruction or life (Matt. 7:13–14). The first way leads to "a furnace of fire: there shall be wailing and gnashing of teeth"; the second leads to a place where "the righteous shine forth as the sun in the kingdom of their Father" (13:42–43).

Thus, in light of Christ's overall teaching about salvation and sonship, we should not interpret the parable of the prodigal son to mean that God is the Father of unrepentant sinners. Instead, we recognize that parables make illuminating comparisons, and here the point of comparison is God's love for sinners and willingness to gladly receive them when they repent. It should also be noted that Christ told this parable to his fellow Jews, all of whom shared in the corporate adoption granted to old covenant Israel, and in that sense were God's children (Deut. 14:1).

As to Paul's statement about "one God and Father of all" (Eph. 4:6), he writes concerning the body of Christ, the people who have the Spirit and faith in Christ (vv. 4–5), not about all humanity. The "all" is "all the saints" (3:18).

Only those saved by grace through faith in Jesus Christ can rightly claim to be God's children and to have God as their heavenly Father (Gal. 3:26).

---

6. On the liberal modernistic doctrine of Albrecht Ritschl and Adolf Harnack, see *RST*, 1:291.
7. On religious pluralism, see *RST*, 1:299–304.
8. For example, note the teachings of Jesus Christ in Matt. 5:22, 29–30; 7:13–14; 8:12; 10:28; 18:9; 22:13; 23:15, 33; 24:51; 25:30, 41–46. Similar teachings appear throughout the New Testament.
9. Matt. 5:9, 16, 19, 44–45; 6:1–4.

We see again the contrast between two groups of people in John's words: "He came to his own, and his own people did not receive him. But to all who did receive him, who believed in his name, he gave the right to become children of God" (John 1:11–12 ESV). One group does not trust in Christ; the other receives him by faith, and it is they alone who are the children of God.

That is not to say, however, that there is no sense in which God is the Father of mankind. Luke writes that Adam, the father of the whole human race, was "the son of God" (Luke 3:38). Paul says that all human beings are God's "offspring" (Acts 17:28), for he created and sustains them (vv. 24–25), and they bear some likeness to him that cannot be found in the rocks of the earth (v. 29). The Scriptures sometimes use the title "Father" for God to mean that he is the Creator, such as "the Father of lights" (James 1:17) and perhaps "the Father of spirits" (Heb. 12:9; cf. Num. 27:16).

However, the fall broke mankind's relationship with the Creator. Rarely do the Holy Scriptures speak of God's fatherhood toward all men; the vast majority of references to divine sonship pertain to God's saving grace toward his redeemed people.[10] As we saw in our biblical theology of adoption,[11] being God's child or having God as one's Father is a special, covenantal grace granted corporately to Israel and individually to believers in Christ. Adoption by God is not by creation but by covenant.[12] Furthermore, Israel's sonship involved national privileges and redemption from physical slavery (Ex. 4:22; Hos. 11:1) but not salvation from sin, for many Israelites remained covenant breakers and enemies of God (Mal. 1:6; 2:10). Christ denied that all the descendants of Abraham were children of God in any vital and spiritual sense, saying, "If God were your Father, ye would love me. . . . Ye are of your father the devil, and the lusts of your father ye will do. He was a murderer from the beginning, and abode not in the truth, because there is no truth in him. When he speaketh a lie, he speaketh of his own: for he is a liar, and the father of it" (John 8:42, 44). If this is true of unbelievers in Israel, how much more the Gentiles? Christ sent Paul to the nations "to turn them from darkness to light, and from the power of Satan unto God" (Acts 26:18).

Roger Drake said, "Unbelievers, being not children of God, can expect nothing from God as a Father. . . . They are orphans."[13] Indeed, God has

10. Murray, *Redemption Accomplished and Applied*, 135.
11. See chap. 25.
12. On adoption as a covenantal theme, see *RST*, 2:711–12.
13. Drake, "The Believer's Dignity and Duty," in *Puritan Sermons, 1659–1689*, 5:339–40.

great pity on natural orphans (Ps. 68:5), but spiritual orphans are such because of sin, and thus are "children of wrath" (Eph. 2:3), the objects of God's just anger (Rom. 1:18). They are not God's children, but his "enemies" (5:10; Col. 1:21). However, their dire condition shows the greatness of God's love when he saves and adopts them. It is a "mystery" that no man could have conceived apart from the gospel, Jeremiah Burroughs (c. 1600–1646) said, that "every man or woman that is a child of God now, certainly was a child of wrath before."[14] Adoption is not our natural right, but a gift of salvation.

Samuel Willard said, "This truth may afford potent arguments to encourage unbelievers to seek after faith, and to believe in Jesus Christ. . . . Receive him by a true faith, and he will make you, not only friends, but children unto God."[15] Unbeliever, are you not ashamed of your fallen, sinful condition that makes you an orphan in God's world? Do you desire honor and riches that will last? Do you want God's protection and care? Isn't it better to be a child of God than to be a child of the Devil? Then do not refuse God's sincere offer of Christ in the gospel.[16]

Adoption as a Systematic Perspective on Salvation

Believers would do well to consider how adoption colors the whole gospel. Stephen Marshall (c. 1594–1655) said, "Though sometimes in the Holy Scriptures our sonship is but one of our privileges, yet very frequently in the Scripture all that believers do obtain from Christ in this world and the world to come, here and to eternity, all is comprehended in this one, that they are made the children of God."[17] Sinclair Ferguson says that "sonship" may be employed as "an organising principle for understanding salvation," for it is covenantal, develops as a theme through redemptive history, expresses the "already/not yet" tension of New Testament eschatology, and centers on Jesus Christ.[18] Adoption is a lens through which we can view salvation in its entirety, from its conception in God's decree to its completion in glory.

14. Burroughs, *The Saints' Happiness*, 192.

15. Willard, *The Child's Portion*, 37.

16. Willard, *The Child's Portion*, 37–42.

17. Stephen Marshall, "The High Priviledg [*sic*] of All True Believers to be the Sons of God," in *The Works of Mr Stephen Marshall . . . The First Part* (London: Peter Cole and Edward Cole, 1661), 37. He cited Rom. 8:23; 2 Cor. 6:18; Gal. 4:4–5; Eph. 1:5 (38).

18. Sinclair B. Ferguson, "The Reformed Doctrine of Sonship," in *Pulpit & People: Essays in Honour of William Still on His 75th Birthday*, ed. Nigel M. de S. Cameron and Sinclair B. Ferguson (Edinburgh: Rutherford House, 1986), 86–87.

However, we have treated adoption as an element in the order of salvation because God actually adopts people only when they exercise faith in Christ. Adoption is a grace distinct from regeneration, justification, and other elements of the application of salvation.[19] This raises the question of how adoption relates to other elements, beginning with the divine election and predestination that God executes through the *ordo salutis*.[20]

1. *Election and predestination are the planning of adoption.* In election, God chose whom he would adopt; in predestination, he determined their destiny beforehand to become his sons through Christ's mediation (Eph. 1:4–5). The doctrine of election shows that adoption ultimately comes because of God's will; the Father chose people to be his children. Adoption is one way of summarizing the goal of God's eternal decree of salvation and reveals its fatherly affection.

Some theologians have treated adoption as an eternal act that is immanent in God's mind.[21] However, Paul distinguishes predestination from adoption when he says that God "predestinated us *unto* [*eis*] the adoption of children" (Eph. 1:5). We must not confuse God's eternal decree with the execution of that decree in time. Willard said, "Here it may be inquired, Whether it be an immanent and eternal or transient and temporary act? . . . To this it may be replied, that the foundation for this [adoption] was laid in the eternal decree of God which is an immanent act . . . so that it cannot fail. . . . But the adoption itself by which we are put among children, and made actual heirs of God, is a transient temporary act, and is applied upon our believing in Christ. Before this time we were aliens, enemies."[22]

2. *Incarnation is Christ's taking a nature suitable for our adoption.* The first step of God's accomplishing adoption was sending his Son, "made of a woman" (Gal. 4:4–5). Christ took "flesh and blood" because that was the nature of his "brethren" whom he came to save and bring to glory (Heb. 2:10–15).[23] Irenaeus said, "For it was for this end that the Word of God

19. See Murray, *Redemption Accomplished and Applied*, 132–33; and Beeke, *Heirs with Christ*, 25–33.

20. The order of salvation (*ordo salutis*) is the topic of chap. 11.

21. Thus, Gill, *Body of Divinity*, 201–3; and Anne Dutton, *A Discourse Concerning God's Act of Adoption. To Which Is Added, a Discourse upon the Inheritance of the Adopted Sons of God*, in *Selected Spiritual Writings of Anne Dutton: Eighteenth-Century, British-Baptist, Woman Theologian*, ed. JoAnn Ford Watson, 7 vols. (Macon, GA: Mercer University Press, 2003–2015), 4:222, 224.

22. Willard, *A Compleat Body of Divinity*, 485. He used "temporary" in the sense of "temporal, in time," not in the modern sense of lasting only for a time and then ceasing.

23. On the incarnate Son's brotherly relation to God's people, see *RST*, 2:818–19.

was made man, and He who was the Son of God became the Son of man, that man, having been taken into the Word, and receiving the adoption, might become the son of God."[24] Adoption as sons is a blessing of union with God's Son, and if human beings were to be adopted, then the Son had to take to himself human nature and become one with them, experiencing the suffering and temptation that they do (v. 18). The incarnation implies that our adoption does not transport us into a deified realm, but sets the stage for us to become fully human sons and daughters of God. Christ's incarnation was also necessary so that he could "make propitiation for the sins of the people" (v. 17 ESV)—that is, accomplish "redemption" so that "they which are called might receive the promise of eternal inheritance" (9:15).

3. *Redemption by Christ's blood is the objective accomplishment of adoption.* Christ kept God's law and suffered its penalty of death in order to redeem lawbreakers so that they would become God's sons (Gal. 4:4–5). Apart from redemption in Christ, God's elect would have remained under the law's curse (3:10, 13), and thus estranged from the Father (Eph. 2:12–13). Christ's sacrifice reveals the infinite price that God was willing to pay in order to adopt sinners. Thomas Watson said, "It was no easy thing to make heirs of wrath, heirs of the promise. . . . For when God was about to make us sons and heirs, he could not seal the deed but by the blood of his own Son."[25] Michael Barrett asks, "How much did our adoption cost?" and answers, "It cost Christ everything—His life and His death."[26] Furthermore, adoption shows the marvelous intimacy of the reconciliation Christ accomplished between sinners and God by his death (v. 16), for "strangers and foreigners" become "the household of God" (v. 19).

4. *Resurrection and ascension are the incarnate Son's exaltation as the Mediator of adoption.* Paul says that the gospel of God is "concerning his Son Jesus Christ our Lord, which was made of the seed of David according to the flesh; and declared to be the Son of God with power, according to the spirit of holiness, by the resurrection from the dead" (Rom. 1:3–4). The word translated as "declared" (*horizō*) is more literally rendered "appointed" (cf. Acts 17:31). This is not indicating that Christ was not the Son of God until God raised him from the dead and adopted him—the heresy

24. Irenaeus, *Against Heresies*, 3.19.1, in *ANF*, 1:448.
25. Watson, *A Body of Divinity*, 235.
26. Barrett, *Complete in Him*, 180.

of adoptionism.[27] Christ was already the Son when God sent him into the world to become a man and redeem sinners (Rom. 8:3, 32; Gal. 4:4). In Romans 1:4, Paul is teaching that at Christ's resurrection, the Father appointed him to a new, exalted function as Mediator, not merely "the Son of God" but "the Son of God with power."[28] This state of exaltation manifests the divine glory that the Son has always possessed and authorizes him to save his people from all nations (Matt. 28:18–20; John 17:2). He ascended to *his* "God" and "Father" to secure the adoption of his people by *their* "God" and "Father" (John 20:17). He went "to prepare a place" for them in the "Father's house" (14:2). The Son has entered into his glory so that believers can be "joint-heirs with Christ" (Rom. 8:17). Barrett says, "What Christ inherits, we inherit."[29]

Some theologians, while affirming that Christ is the eternal Son and disavowing the heresy of adoptionism, have maintained that God did adopt the incarnate Son at his resurrection.[30] These theologians argue that we should refer to Christ's exaltation as an adoption because in it Christ attained "human sonship," a prerequisite for our adoption into human sonship.[31] A significant passage of Scripture in this discussion is Psalm 2:7, "I will declare the decree: the Lord hath said unto me, Thou art my Son; this day have I begotten thee," which is cited and applied to Christ's resurrection in Acts 13:33 (cf. Heb. 1:3–5). However, this text is best interpreted to refer to God's public acknowledgement of his Son at his enthronement (cf. Ps. 2:6), not God's adoption of Christ. God's Word never says that God adopted Jesus or that Jesus became God's Son. Jesus was God's Son when yet a child (Matt. 2:15; Luke 2:49). Though Christ had to develop his holy humanity through many trials in order to save sinners, he did not do this to attain sonship; as the Scriptures say, "Though he were a Son, yet learned he obedience by the things which he suffered" (Heb. 5:8).[32] The application of the term *adoption* to God the Son incarnate is not biblically warranted and obscures Christ's eternal identity as the Son of the Father in the Trinity. One cannot appeal to the doctrine of Christ's two natures in one person to justify speaking of his adoption,

27. On Christological adoptionism, see *RST*, 2:825–26.

28. See Murray, *The Epistle to the Romans*, 1:9–10; and Trevor J. Burke, *Adopted into God's Family: Exploring a Pauline Metaphor*, New Studies in Biblical Theology (Downers Grove, IL: InterVarsity Press, 2006), 102–7.

29. Barrett, *Complete in Him*, 186.

30. Peterson, *Adopted by God*, 59–63; and Garner, *Sons in the Son*, 173–207.

31. Garner, *Sons in the Son*, 194.

32. See the section on the power of Christ's victory in *RST*, 2:1123–25.

for legal adoption does not pertain to a nature but to a person, and the person of Christ has always been God's Son.[33] Christ was not adopted by God, but was raised and exalted to heaven so that his people in union with him may enjoy the full rights of sons. Adoption is the application to unworthy sinners of the privileges apprehended by the worthy Son when God exalted him.

5. *Calling is the effectual summons to Christ for adoption.* God takes those "whom he hath called, not of the Jews only, but also of the Gentiles," and brings them from being "not my people" to "be called the children of the living God" (Rom. 9:24–26). The effectual call draws people to Christ and joins them to him by faith (1 Cor. 1:9, 22–24, 30). As a result, they are "in the beloved"—that is, in union with God's beloved Son (Eph. 1:6). Adoption is a grand benefit of that union with Christ that effectual calling creates.

6. *Regeneration is God's giving sinners a nature suitable to live in the relationships granted by adoption.* Drake said, "Every true believer is a child of God by regeneration and adoption."[34] Regeneration and adoption are "distinct" but "never separated as to the subject."[35] Adoption is an unmerited gift of a new status and relationship to God, received by faith alone (Gal. 3:26), but it would not be fitting to grant this relationship to those who are yet children of the Devil and enemies of God's Son (John 8:42, 44). It is not that the renewed image of God merits sonship or makes people God's sons; rather, God works regeneration "so that the adopted may be imbued with a disposition which is consonant with the responsibilities and privileges and prerogatives belonging to the status of adoption," as John Murray said.[36]

Regeneration implants new life into men so that they trust in Christ and have a disposition to hate sin and love God's children (1 John 3:9–10, 14; 5:1). Watson said, "When a man adopts another for his son and heir, he may put his name upon him, but he cannot put his disposition into him; if he be of a morose rugged [sullen and harsh] nature, he cannot alter it; but whom God adopts he sanctifies; he not only gives a new name but

33. The doctrines of Christ's deity and incarnation are treated extensively in *RST*, 2:757–865 (chaps. 38–42).

34. Drake, "The Believer's Dignity and Duty," in *Puritan Sermons, 1659–1689*, 5:329.

35. Drake, "The Believer's Dignity and Duty," in *Puritan Sermons, 1659–1689*, 5:338, contra Archibald Hodge, who endorsed "a complex view" of adoption, "including the change of nature together with the change of relation," so that adoption consists of regeneration and justification. Hodge, *Outlines of Theology*, 516.

36. Murray, "Adoption," in *Collected Writings*, 2:228.

a new nature (2 Pet. 1:4)."[37] Adoption is the granting of the legal status of sons to those to whom God has given a trusting, childlike heart by regeneration. Adoption and regeneration are closely connected but not identical, for adoption is through faith in Christ (John 1:12; Gal. 3:26), whereas regeneration is causally prior to faith (1 John 5:1).[38] Robert Letham says, "John 1:12–13 illustrates this point. There is a sequence; first comes regeneration, being 'born . . . of God,' then faith or receiving him . . . and, as a direct consequence, adoption as children of God, *tekna theou*. This is simultaneous, a logical sequence, not a temporal one."[39]

7. *Repentance is a sinner's turning to the Father for adoption.* Sinners are restored to the Father's household when they come to him in repentance over their sins and discover the magnitude of his grace (Luke 15:21–22). By grace, they have become obedient to Christ's Father and thus show the marks of belonging to Christ's family (Matt. 12:50). Adoption is the Father's gift to repentant sinners, in which he not only forgives and receives them, but elevates them to the honored position of his favored sons and daughters.

8. *Faith is the human instrument of receiving adoption.* Those who believe in Jesus Christ are granted the right to be counted God's children (John 1:12). People are God's children "by faith" (*dia tēs pisteōs*, Gal. 3:26), the same way that they are justified (Rom. 3:30) and saved as a free gift apart from their works (Eph. 2:8–9). Adoption is bound up in their union with Christ, for by faith they receive Christ himself (John 1:12), and by faith, outwardly expressed in baptism, they "put on Christ" (Gal. 3:27). John Brown of Haddington said, "How is faith the instrument of adoption? It unites us to Christ, in whom we become heirs of God."[40] Thus, the Father brings people into his family by union with his Son as their Bridegroom.[41] Herman Witsius said, "We become children of God by marriage with the Lord Jesus; for when we become his spouse, then we pass with him into his Father's family."[42]

9. *Justification is the legal prerequisite of adoption.* Only when people are justified by faith do they have peace with God—a reconciled relation-

37. Watson, *A Body of Divinity*, 233.
38. Willard, *The Child's Portion*, 13. On regeneration and faith, see chap. 18.
39. Letham, *Systematic Theology*, 731–32.
40. Brown, *Questions and Answers on the Shorter Catechism*, 163.
41. On union with Christ and spiritual marriage with him, see chap. 9. On the covenant of grace as the church's marriage to the Lord, see *RST*, 2:712–15.
42. Witsius, *The Economy of the Covenants*, 3.10.12 (1:445). See also Willard, *A Compleat Body of Divinity*, 488; and Brakel, *The Christian's Reasonable Service*, 2:420.

ship (Rom. 5:1, 11). Until they are justified, divine justice condemns them to suffer divine wrath. However, in justification, God ceases to impute to them the guilt of their sins and instead imputes to them the righteousness of Jesus Christ.[43] Some theologians have identified adoption as part of justification—namely, the imputation of Christ's obedience for the right to eternal life.[44] Adoption, however, is an even greater blessing than justification. In justification, God graciously counts sinners to be righteous servants and confers on them the right to eternal life. In adoption, God grants them the legal status of his sons. William Ames said that justification gives people a title to heaven, but "adoption adds to it excellence and dignity."[45] Willard said, "It is one thing to be adjudged righteous, and another to be put among children; one thing to have God accept us as a Judge, another to do so as a Father."[46] Adoption elevates the status of God's people beyond justification, for adoption grants them greater intimacy with God ("Abba, Father") and higher privilege in his kingdom ("heirs," Gal. 4:6–7). However, adoption depends on justification, for they must be "justified" in order to be "made heirs according to the hope of eternal life" (Titus 3:7). As Ames said, "Adoption of its own nature requires and presupposes the reconciliation found in justification."[47]

Adoption may be compared to justification by considering the status of God's adopted vis-à-vis the angels. Both the holy angels and the saints will live forever in God's glory. Both are counted by God as his righteous servants. However, the world to come will not be subjected to angels, whereas it will be subjected to human beings brought to glory as God's "sons" through Jesus Christ (Heb. 2:5, 9–10). They are heirs because God appointed his Son to be the mediatorial "heir" (*klēronomos*) of the universe (1:2). The incarnate Son inherited (*klēronomeō*) a name greater than that of the angels when God exalted him to his right hand, not for his own sake, but as the Mediator for the sake of his brethren (vv. 3–5). God has ordained that the angels be the servants of those who will inherit

---

43. See chaps. 22–24 on justification and imputation.

44. "The other part of justification is adoption or the bestowal of a right to life, flowing from Christ's righteousness.... Adoption is included in justification itself as a part which, with the remission of sins, constitutes the whole of his benefit." Turretin, *Institutes*, 16.6.1, 7 (2:666, 668). See also Brakel, *The Christian's Reasonable Service*, 2:415; Hodge, *Systematic Theology*, 3:129, 164; Bavinck, *Reformed Dogmatics*, 4:226–27; and Vos, *Reformed Dogmatics*, 4:155–56.

45. Ames, *The Marrow of Theology*, 1.28.7–8 (165).

46. Willard, *A Compleat Body of Divinity*, 482–83.

47. Ames, *The Marrow of Theology*, 1.28.6 (165). On adoption as a blessing distinct from justification, see also Buchanan, *The Doctrine of Justification*, 262–64; and Boyce, *Abstract of Systematic Theology*, 407–9.

(*klēronomeō*) salvation (v. 14). What is the difference? Angels are righteous servants of God, but believers are adopted sons in the Son.

10. *Sanctification is the practical outworking of adoption.* Those who are predestined to adoption are also elected to be holy (Eph. 1:4–5). The Holy Spirit has come to God's adopted sons as the Spirit of adoption, the Spirit of God's Son (Rom. 8:15; Gal. 4:6). Since believers in Christ are "the sons of God," they are "led by the Spirit" to conduct themselves as sons (Rom. 8:14). Thomas Manton said, "The Spirit giveth us life, motion, and direction. . . . His leading consisteth in his restraining motions, for the mortifying of sin, or the avoiding of sin. . . . checks of conscience, by which he seeketh to humble us for sin, and to reclaim us from sin. . . . [and] his inviting and quickening motions, to bring us in a way of holiness. . . . The Spirit inclineth and presseth us to that which is good." As a result, God's children become like God's incarnate Son: "Jesus was led by the Spirit continually. . . . We are always bound to depend upon the Holy Ghost; the Spirit must still lead us and move us in all our operations."[48]

Adoption itself offers motives for sanctification. The promises of adoption and fellowship with the Father should motivate adopted sons to separate themselves from sin and pursue holiness (2 Cor. 6:16–7:1). Having been begotten again by the Father, they must learn to live "as obedient children" (1 Pet. 1:3, 14). They must pray, give, and fast, knowing that they do all things in the presence of their Father (Matt. 6:1–18). They must work out their salvation by faith and obedience so that they become in practical life who they are by adoption: children of God (Phil. 2:12–15). Their aim is to attain the purpose of their predestination: "to be conformed to the image of his Son, that he might be the firstborn among many brethren" (Rom. 8:29). Knowing that we are God's children gives us hope that "we shall be like him; for we shall see him as he is. And every man that hath this hope in him purifieth himself, even as he is pure" (1 John 3:2–3).

11. *Preservation and perseverance are the school of adoption.* Through perseverance, believers mature as God's children, develop a deeper experiential knowledge of their Father, and confirm their sonship by repeatedly passing the tests that call them to repent, believe, and obey. The sorrows of this life are not designed by God to destroy his children, but are the "chastening" (*paideia*) of their Father (Heb. 12:5–6), a word that refers

48. Manton, *Sermons upon Romans VIII*, on Rom. 8:14, in *Works*, 12:92–97.

to difficult training given to children to make them mature.[49] They endure this training because God deals with them "as with sons"; he disciplines his children "for our profit, that we might be partakers of his holiness" (vv. 7, 10). John Calvin said, "In the very harshness of tribulations we must recognize the kindness and generosity of our Father toward us, since he does not even then cease to promote our salvation."[50] In these trials, the Father's born-again children experience his powerful preservation to sustain them through faith as he brings them to their imperishable inheritance (1 Pet. 1:3–7). Adoption is the legal initiation of a process that brings God's people through many trials to enter the kingdom.

12. *Glorification is the completion of the aims of adoption.* Christ ascended into heaven to prepare a place for his disciples in "my Father's house" (John 14:2). Believers are "heirs of God, and joint-heirs with Christ," and they "suffer with him" so that they will "be also glorified together with him" (Rom. 8:17). For this, Paul says, we "groan within ourselves" as we hope and wait for what we do not see (vv. 23–24). Mark Johnston says, "For those who are God's children, there is a deep, mysterious longing to go to our everlasting home in heaven."[51]

Glorification and liberation from all evil are so intimately tied to sonship in Christ that glorification can be called "adoption" (Rom. 8:21, 23). "Then shall the righteous shine forth as the sun in the kingdom of their Father" (Matt. 13:43). Adoption, then, is nothing less than glorification begun on earth—the gift of a legal title to inherit the glory of God in Christ as one's portion forever. No wonder that John exclaims over the marvelous love of God, that he should call us his children, for we will see him and be like him (1 John 3:1–2).

David Garner takes "adoption" (*huiothesia*) to refer to a complex of graces that includes both parts of the *duplex gratiae*, justification and sanctification, and reaches to glorification.[52] Garner explains this according to the inaugurated eschatology of the New Testament, saying, "By the Spirit we have already received our 'adoption' as God's children, but what is *already* is also *not yet*."[53] Paul can use *huiothesia* for the final glorification of God's children (Rom. 8:23), which is the consummation

49. See the discussion of God's fatherly purposes for affliction in *RST*, 2:484–90.

50. Calvin, *Institutes*, 3.8.6.

51. Mark Johnston, *Child of a King*, Focus on Faith (Fearn, Ross-shire, Scotland: Christian Focus, 1997), 165.

52. Garner, *Sons in the Son*, 71–75, 141–44, 305, 308.

53. Garner, *Sons in the Son*, 108, emphasis original.

of sanctification, when God will realize his purpose that "whom he did foreknow, he also did predestinate to be conformed to the image of his Son" (v. 29). Elsewhere, Paul speaks of the purpose of predestination as simply "adoption" (Eph. 1:5), which suggests that adoption might include sanctification and glorification.[54] However, Paul also views adoption as an already established status for believers: "You *are* all sons of God" (Gal. 3:26 ESV) and "As many as are led by the Spirit of God, they *are* the sons of God" (Rom. 8:14; cf. Eph. 5:1; Phil. 2:15). It is important not to press the eschatological perspective so as to obscure the decisive adoption of believers into God's family, for their adoption is not a progressive work but a judicial act done with the first exercise of faith. It is because of that status of adoption—"because ye are sons"—that believers enjoy the comforting, sanctifying, and ultimately glorifying influences of "the Spirit of his Son" (Gal. 4:6; cf. Rom. 8:11–17). When Paul looks ahead to "the adoption . . . the redemption of our body" (Rom. 8:23), he speaks of the realization of the full effects of adoption and redemption, not adoption and redemption per se. Geerhardus Vos said, "Because the resurrection is a revelation of sonship . . . it can be also called the 'adoption of sons' (*huiothesia*)."[55]

Adoption fills the everlasting rewards that God gives to his people with fatherly grace. The rewards that Christians will receive on judgment day come from "thy Father" (Matt. 6:4, 6, 18–20). Though Christ will reward his people for their faithful service, he says that these rewards come to those "blessed of my Father," who "inherit the kingdom prepared . . . from the foundation of the world" (25:34). Even a reward for a believer's diligent and loving service is called "mercy of the Lord in that day" (2 Tim. 1:16–18). Calvin commented, "When God rewards us, it is not on account of our merits or of any excellence that is in us"; rather, he reveals "himself to be, not a stern judge, but a kind and indulgent Father."[56] Knowing him as Father and being acknowledged as his sons and daughters in Christ will be believers' greatest reward.

Adoption as the Transformation of Relationships

Adoption brings the believer into a new sphere of relationships as a child of God. The primary orientation of adoption is Godward. However, being

54. Garner, *Sons in the Son*, 75.
55. Geerhardus Vos, *The Pauline Eschatology* (Princeton, NJ: Geerhardus Vos, 1930), 198–99.
56. Calvin, *Commentaries*, on 2 Tim. 2:18.

adopted as God's son or daughter has massive implications for all of one's relationships.[57] Consequently, the believer also has a new set of obligations to live as befits a child of God.

A Transformed Relationship to the Triune God

Though we immediately think of the Father when considering adoption, this gracious act of God involves all three persons of the Trinity, but in different ways. The result is that the adopted children of God have new relationships with the Father, the Son, and the Holy Spirit.

First, adoption is initiated by *God the Father*. The Father predestined his chosen people to adoption before he created the world (Eph. 1:4–5). It was his eternal will that they be his children. At the pinnacle of history, the Father sent the Son to redeem them so that they would receive the adoption of sons (Gal. 4:4–5). This adoption becomes theirs when they are effectually called (Rom. 9:24–26), and the Father is the author of that call (1:7; 8:29–30).

Just as God the Father initiates adoption on every level, so his grace brings his adopted children into a new relationship with him as their Father. He "predestinated us unto the adoption of children by Jesus Christ *to himself*" (Eph. 1:5).[58] The result of their adoption is that by grace they call on him as "Abba, Father" (Rom. 8:15; Gal. 4:6), "abba" being the Aramaic word that a child would use to address his father in the home—a notable choice of terms given that Paul was writing in Greek to churches including many Gentiles. It was the word Jesus used to pray to the Father in his deepest distress (Mark 14:36), which implies that God draws his people into the same kind of relationship with him that Jesus has with the Father through his human nature. Indeed, it suggests that the Son himself dwells in them by his Spirit, stirring them to call upon his Father as "our Father," as Athanasius said.[59] We should meditate on the love behind such an adoption and marvel at it. William Perkins said, "Let all such as fear God enter into a serious consideration of the unspeakable goodness of God, comforting themselves in this, that God the Father has vouchsafed [granted] by His own Son to make them of vassals of Satan to be His own dear children."[60]

57. See Joel R. Beeke, *The Epistles of John* (Darlington, England: Evangelical Press, 2006), 115–20.

58. Although early editions of the ESV did not include "to himself" in Eph. 1:5, the phrase was added to the ESV in its 2016 revision. The Greek phrase *eis auton* is an undisputed part of the Greek text.

59. Athanasius, *Four Discourses against the Arians*, 4.22, in *NPNF*², 4:441.

60. Perkins, *An Exposition of the Symbol*, in *Works*, 5:114.

Although adoption brings believers into a gracious relation with each person in the Trinity, it is particularly God the Father who adopts them as their heavenly Father (1 John 3:1). Their Father is not the Son or the Holy Spirit, but the Father of the Son (2 Cor. 1:2–3; Eph. 1:2–3). Christ refers to the same person when he speaks of "my Father, and your Father" (John 20:17).[61]

The adopted children of God should relate to the Father in a manner fitting to his being their perfect divine Father. God's children should trust their heavenly Father in everything. Their Father knows what they need before they ask (Matt. 6:7, 32). Will not the God who cares for all the birds and flowers in the world take care of his own children (vv. 26–30)? God's sons and daughters should revere their Father with childlike fear, reflect his holy character in their lives, and obey his commands (1 Pet. 1:14–17). They should seek to honor him in all that they do, especially their acts of worship, for he is the great King (Mal. 1:6, 14). God invites them to seek all good things from his hand and promises that his fatherly heart delights to give good gifts to his children when they pray (Matt. 7:7–11). He also calls them to display his goodness and mercy by loving their fellow men, even those who hate them (5:44–48). They must be imitators of their Father, loving others because he has loved them in his Son, Jesus Christ (Eph. 4:32–5:2).

When their heavenly Father sends hard and painful trials into their lives, they should neither despise his discipline nor despair, but receive it humbly and soberly as his loving and wise method of making them holy like him (Heb. 12:5–11). They can hope in his reward, for he sees even their secret works of devotion and will surely reward them for every good deed (Matt. 6:4, 6, 18). They must be patient, for the heavenly Father gives heavenly treasure (vv. 19–21), and they cannot live for him and for earthly riches at the same time (v. 24). Yet they should not fear that they will lose anything by doing their Father's will; it is his good pleasure to give them the kingdom, and his rewards will never fade, be lost, or spoil (Luke 12:32–33; cf. 1 Pet. 1:3–4). They may know that God, whom they call "our Father," is "the Father of mercies, and the God of all comfort," and his comfort overflows to them in Christ to help them endure all their troubles and comfort one another (2 Cor. 1:2–4). Brown said, "God's fatherly eye is still on them, his arms about them, and his angels surround them."[62]

61. Murray, *Redemption Accomplished and Applied*, 137–40.
62. Brown, *Questions and Answers on the Shorter Catechism*, 164.

Second, adoption is accomplished by *God the Son* and in union with him. The Father chose his people "in" Christ, predestined them for adoption "by" him, and gave them redemption "in" him "through his blood" (Eph. 1:4–5, 7). Human beings can be adopted into God's family because God's Son became their brother who partakes of their flesh and blood (Heb. 2:12–14). So great is his love for them that "he is not ashamed to call them brethren" (v. 11). Thomas Houston (1803–1882) said, "Christ is the Elder Brother of those that are adopted into God's family.... Christ regards His saints with the love of a brother's heart. He takes the tenderest interest in all their concerns, and He never ceases to do them good."[63]

Christ died under God's curse to redeem his people so that they would receive God's blessing and adoption (Gal. 3:13–14; 4:5). The Son of God mediates their sonship to them, and they are adopted when they trust in Christ as the Mediator (John 1:12; Gal. 3:26). The Father loves them "as" he has loved the Son (John 17:23). They are being conformed to the image of the Son (Rom. 8:29). They will receive their inheritance as God's sons as joint heirs with Christ in glory (v. 17). In every respect, their adoption revolves around God the Son incarnate, "the firstborn among many brethren" (v. 29).

On the one hand, there is an infinite difference between Christ's sonship and ours, for he is the only begotten Son of God, and God the Father is Christ's Father in a way that is "immanent, eternal, and exclusive."[64] Calvin said, "We are the children of God not by nature, but only by adoption and grace, in that God wills to regard us as such (Eph. 1:5). But the Lord Jesus who was begotten of the substance of His Father, and is of one essence with Him, is rightly called the only Son of God (John 1:14; Heb. 1:2) for there is no other who is God's Son by nature."[65] On the other hand, the sonship of God the Son incarnate, particularly as exercised and experienced in his human nature, is the ground of our sonship. We are "sons in the Son."[66]

---

63. Thomas Houston, *The Adoption of Sons, Its Nature, Spirit, Privileges, and Effects: A Practical and Experimental Treatise* (Paisley: Alex. Garner et al., 1872), 58.

64. Murray, "Adoption," in *Collected Writings*, 2:223. On Christ as the Son of God, see *RST*, 2:750–51.

65. Calvin's Catechism of 1545 (Q. 46), in *Reformed Confessions*, 1:474. See also the Heidelberg Catechism (LD 13, Q. 33), in *The Three Forms of Unity*, 79. Compare the words of Athanasius: "Although there be one Son by nature, True and Only-begotten, we too become sons, not as He in nature and truth, but according to the grace of Him that calleth." Athanasius, *Four Discourses against the Arians*, 3.25.19, in *NPNF*[2], 4:404.

66. As is the title of David Garner's already cited book, *Sons in the Son*.

God's children should align their purposes with God's revealed purpose that centers on his Son (Col. 1:16). Paul says, "For whom he did foreknow, he also did predestinate to be conformed to the image of his Son, that he might be the firstborn among many brethren" (Rom. 8:29). They should strive to become like Christ, imitating his filial obedience to the Father's will and purging themselves of all sin. They should seek Christ's honor and good name in all they do, for he is the "firstborn," and so God wills that Christ always be preeminent in his family (cf. Col. 1:18; 3:17). They should labor to win converts to Christ and build up Christ's church, for the Father is pleased that his Son be "the firstborn among *many* brethren," for his glory and honor.

Third, adoption is applied and progressively realized through *God the Holy Spirit*. He is the Spirit of regeneration (Titus 3:5), by whom sinners are brought to trust in Christ (1 Cor. 12:3) and thus to be adopted (Gal. 3:26). He is "the Spirit of life in Christ Jesus," who vivifies his people (Rom. 8:2, 10) and leads the sons of God to put sin to death and walk in paths of obedience (vv. 13–14). He is the Spirit of adoption, whom God sends into men's hearts crying, "Abba, Father," and witnessing with their spirits that they are the children of God (vv. 15–16). He is the Spirit of resurrection, who will give life to their mortal bodies on the last day (v. 11).

The Holy Spirit is the divine agent of the communion that God's children enjoy with the loving Father and the grace-filled Son (2 Cor. 13:14). God's Spirit is "the Spirit of his Son" (Gal. 4:6), coming to God's people in Christ's name and for Christ's glory with the riches of grace given to Christ by the Father (John 14:26; 16:13–15). Through Christ, believers "have access by one Spirit unto the Father" (Eph. 2:18). In the Spirit, they have fellowship with one another as the family of God, for there is "one Spirit," "one Lord," and "one God and Father of all" (4:4–6). Adoption is God's provision for the church to have communion with the triune God.[67]

Christians should cherish the ministry of the Holy Spirit in their lives. How precious is the work of the Spirit of adoption, through whom they know assurance of God's fatherly love for them! Let the children of God walk carefully so as never to grieve the Spirit or forfeit any of his comforting, sanctifying, and empowering blessings. Neither should they ever fear

67. On communion with the triune God, see *RST*, 1:944–52.

the Holy Spirit; he is "the Spirit of your Father" (Matt. 10:20), and his ministry is no alien power but the Father's blessing on his beloved children.

The believer's relationship with the triune God is a treasure of infinite glory and felicity. Wilhelmus à Brakel said, "The excellency of the children of God is so great that it exceeds all comprehension, . . . [for God] has all glory within Himself, is above all praise, and has made everything . . . and all that He is, He is for His children." Consequently, "a godly beggar is a thousand times more exalted and glorious than the greatest monarch who has ever been in the world."[68] Therefore, Willard said, "love God with a filial affection. He deserves your best love, who hath shown you such love as this."[69]

A Transformed Relationship to Oneself

Just as an adopted child takes a new family name and receives a new identity, so adoption by God should change how the Christian views himself. God gives his child a "new name"—that is, God's own name written on his adopted and beloved image bearer.[70] We may use Paul's teaching in Galatians 3:26–29 to guide us as we consider this new identity that a Christian may embrace as his new self-image.

First, and most obviously, the believer should view himself or herself as *God's son or daughter*. Paul says, "For ye are all the children of God by faith in Christ Jesus" (Gal. 3:26). The word translated as "children" is literally "sons" (*huioi*). Paul uses the masculine "sons" not to exclude women, but to include them as equal heirs with the full spiritual rights of adult sons, something not often granted to women in ancient cultures. Though people are afflicted by spiritual bondage, when God adopts them, he gives them freedom: "Thou art no more a servant, but a son" (4:7; cf. John 8:34–36). All believers have been exalted to the liberty and nobility of being God's prophets, priest, and kings in Christ.[71] Martin Luther spoke of "the inestimable grace and glory that we have in Christ Jesus, namely, that we miserable sinners, by nature children of wrath (Eph. 2:3), may arrive at this honor, that through faith in Christ we are made children and heirs of God and fellow heirs with Christ (Rom. 8:17), lords of heaven

68. Brakel, *The Christian's Reasonable Service*, 2:417–18.

69. Willard, *The Child's Portion*, 42.

70. Isa. 43:6–7; 62:2–5; Rev. 2:17; 3:12; 14:1; 22:4.

71. Ames, *The Marrow of Theology*, 1.28.25–27 (167); and Drake, "The Believer's Dignity and Duty," in *Puritan Sermons, 1659–1689*, 334. On Christian participation in the threefold office, see *RST*, 2:978–85, 1103–8, 1157–67.

and earth. . . . No tongue, either of men or of angels (1 Cor. 13:1), could proclaim the glory of this magnificently enough."[72] If David considered it a great honor to be the son-in-law of a human king (1 Sam. 18:23), much more should we count ourselves honored to be adopted by the King of kings.[73] And if the children of earthly kings must learn to act like royalty, how much more should Christians say, "I am a son or daughter of the King and must conduct myself accordingly."

Second, the believer should count himself to be *one with the Son of God*. Paul says, "As many of you as have been baptized into Christ have put on Christ" (Gal. 3:27). The image of putting on clothing communicates close union with Christ.[74] The Son is now the believer's, and the believer belongs to the Son. All the blessings that the Son of God has obtained as the Mediator are also his (Eph. 1:3). The Christian's life is now bound up in him whom the Father embraces as his beloved Son (v. 6). The child of God has been raised with Christ and is seated with him in the heavenly places (2:6). Consequently, those raised with Christ should "seek those things which are above, where Christ sitteth on the right hand of God" (Col. 3:1). As God's adopted children in union with the Son, our lives have a purpose, meaning, and destiny bound up with the kingdom of God and Christ, and our treasures and our hearts should be there.

Third, the believer should know that he has *an identity that transcends earthly categories*. Paul says, "There is neither Jew nor Greek, there is neither bond [slave] nor free, there is neither male nor female: for ye are all one in Christ Jesus" (Gal. 3:28). The categories that Paul lists are part of our identities: we are to some extent defined by ethnicity, social status, liberty, and gender. The Bible does not deny these things or the ways that they shape our relationships. However, Paul says that the adopted son of God has an identity that trumps all these factors and unifies him with all those in Christ. Ferguson says, "Our self-image, if it is to be biblical, will begin just here. God is my Father (the Christian's self-image always begins with the knowledge of God and who He is!); I am one of his children (I know my real identity); His people are my brothers and sisters (I recognize the family to which I belong, and have discovered my deepest 'roots')."[75]

---

72. Luther, *Lectures on Galatians*, on Gal. 3:26, in *LW*, 26:352.
73. Burroughs, *The Saints' Happiness*, 194.
74. On images of union with Christ, see chap. 9.
75. Sinclair B. Ferguson, *Children of the Living God* (Colorado Springs, CO: NavPress, 1987), 18–19.

Fourth, the believer should see himself as *an heir of God's promises.* Paul says, "If ye be Christ's, then are ye Abraham's seed, and heirs according to the promise" (Gal. 3:29). All the promises of God's covenant of grace are his if he belongs to Christ. He is not cursed but blessed by God (vv. 13–14; cf. Gen. 12:1–3). Therefore, let the believer in Christ no longer judge himself in a fleshly or worldly manner (2 Cor. 5:16). Though perhaps poor in this world, the child of God is rich in grace (James 2:5; Rev. 2:9) and will be magnificently rich in glory, when God will "show the immeasurable riches of his grace in kindness toward us in Christ Jesus" (Eph. 2:7 ESV).

A Transformed Relationship to the World

When a child is adopted, his adoption often requires the termination of parental rights to sever him legally from his birth family. Likewise, sinners do not come to God as mere orphans, but as children of the Devil (John 8:44; 1 John 3:10). Therefore, adoption breaks their former relationship with the kingdom of darkness and brings them into the kingdom of light.

First, adoption and the other grace it entails, such as sanctification, imply *the formation of an antithesis with the world.* John says, "Behold, what manner of love the Father hath bestowed upon us, that we should be called the sons of God: therefore the world knoweth us not, because it knew him not" (1 John 3:1). In this context, "the world" refers to the dominion of Satan and sin (v. 8). God's children have been born again into a new life so that they repent of sin and do what is right (2:29; 3:9). The world does not "know" them, just as it does not "know" God—that is, it has no spiritual relationship with him, as is evident by its lack of love and obedience (cf. 2:3–4, 13–14). John concludes, "Marvel not, my brethren, if the world hate you" (3:13). The adopted sons of God are loved by their heavenly Father but hated by the world and its spiritual ruler. Therefore, while adoption is a comforting doctrine, it also teaches us to anticipate persecution from the ungodly. Christ laid these two beatitudes beside each other: "Blessed are the peacemakers: for they shall be called the children of God. Blessed are they which are persecuted for righteousness' sake: for theirs is the kingdom of heaven" (Matt. 5:9–10).

Second, adoption also implies a *call to maintain distinctiveness from the world.* The world constantly pressures God's children to conform, but they must instead be "transformed by the renewing of [their] mind" (Rom.

12:2). They must not rest in being God's adopted children, but must labor to be "blameless and innocent, children of God without blemish in the midst of a crooked and twisted generation, among whom [they] shine as lights in the world" (Phil. 2:15 ESV). Paul alludes here to Moses's rebuke of Israel: "They have dealt corruptly with him [God]; they are no longer his children because they are blemished; they are a crooked and twisted generation" (Deut. 32:5 ESV). In God's covenant with Israel, he adopted the nation corporately, but many among the people were not children of God—and their corrupt lives showed it. By contrast, God's true children must show that they are not hypocrites only wearing the badge of the covenant; instead, they must be salt and light in the world (cf. Matt. 5:14–16). The distinctive godliness of God's children is essential for them to bring glory to God and to be winsome witnesses to perishing sinners. Though the distinctiveness of God's children certainly involves avoiding gross violations of the Ten Commandments, Paul highlights a subtler and yet more potent distinction: "Do all things without murmurings and disputings" (Phil. 2:14). Few qualities set Christians apart from the world more than their trust in the Lord, contentment, diligent service, and patient endurance of hardship instead of bitter complaining and grumbling. It was this very quality that contrasted the faith of Joshua and Caleb with the unbelieving Israelites (Num. 14:1–9).

Third, adoption enables God's children to have a *peaceable and kind heart toward enemies in the world.* Christ says, "Blessed are the peacemakers: for they shall be called the children of God" (Matt. 5:9). The sons and daughters of God show their spiritual identity by being people of peace who promote reconciliation and harmony. Jesus teaches his disciples, "Love your enemies, bless them that curse you, do good to them that hate you, and pray for them which despitefully use you, and persecute you; that ye may be the children of your Father which is in heaven: for he maketh his sun to rise on the evil and on the good, and sendeth rain on the just and on the unjust" (vv. 44–45). Burroughs said, "They look upon their Father, that is a God of peace, and this moves them to peace, and the sweet satisfaction that their souls have in the fatherly love of God, in those privileges they enjoy as the children of God . . . makes them to be of peaceable dispositions."[76] People who "know God to be their Father, and enjoy those sweet and blessed privileges of God's children" have

76. Burroughs, *The Saints' Happiness*, 190.

peace in their hearts and tend to live at peace with others "let the world do what they will—for the world must be the world, and wicked men must be wicked men."[77]

Fourth, adoption grants God's children *participation in the Son's mission to the world*. On the day of Christ's resurrection, his message to the apostles was this: "I am ascending to my Father and your Father, to my God and your God," and "as the Father has sent me, even so I am sending you" (John 20:17, 21 ESV).[78] Having been incorporated into the Father's family by union with his Son, Christ's disciples now participate in the extension of the Son's mission throughout the world by their proclamation of his Word (17:18, 20). God's only begotten Son is the great missionary, and God's adopted sons share in his mission. Christ says, "He that receiveth whomsoever I send receiveth me; and he that receiveth me receiveth him that sent me" (13:20). The gospel must reach "the children of God . . . scattered abroad" for whom Christ died (11:51–52)—that is, those among the nations not yet adopted by faith (1:12) but given to the Son by the Father in God's decree for him to give them eternal life (10:16, 29; 17:2). Therefore, the mission of the gospel is a family enterprise: initiated by the Father, accomplished by the Son, and applied by the Spirit through the service of God's children. Adoption shapes missions by reminding the church that it cannot fulfill the Great Commission apart from vital union with the Son, the great missionary. The church functions as God's adoption agency, arranging for the Father's family to grow through the mediation of the Son by the power of the Holy Spirit. When the Christian looks at perishing sinners, he should see potential brothers and sisters who, by grace, may join him at the Father's table.

A Transformed Relationship to the Church

When a person is adopted by God, he not only gains a new Father but also a new family. Adoption creates an ethic of brotherhood among believers that should shape their whole lives. For example, the epistle of James, a very practical letter about the Christian life, refers to the "brethren" or one's "brother" (plural or singular *adelphos*) nineteen times, often in

77. Burroughs, *The Saints' Happiness*, 190–91.

78. Although the KJV reads "my Father" in John 20:21, the Greek text says "the Father" (*ho patēr*). Given Christ's words "my Father and your Father" in v. 17, the phrase "the Father" may point to God's fatherhood toward both his Son and his adopted sons whom Christ now commissions.

affectionate expressions such as "my brethren" or "my beloved brethren." While we cannot fully explore the Bible's teachings about this relationship in the scope of this chapter, we can trace some of the major duties that arise from becoming a brother or sister in the family of God.

First, God's adopted child must count himself to have *true membership in God's family with his brothers and sisters*. As we discussed earlier, the believer in Christ has a new identity as a child of God. This is not an individualistic identity to be cultivated in isolation, but an identity rooted in a network of family relations. God's people should say, "Have we not all one Father?" (Mal. 2:10 ESV). Yes, there is "one God and Father of all" the people of God (Eph. 4:6). Jesus speaks of the members of his spiritual family who do the Father's will as "my brother, and sister, and mother" (Matt. 12:50). Christians should count one another as brothers, sisters, and mothers.

Second, God's adopted child must recognize his *fundamental spiritual equality with his brothers and sisters*. The believer in union with Christ has become united to all people in him, regardless of their ethnic, social, or gender diversity (Gal. 3:28). Watson noted that women are sometimes excluded from the world's honors, "but of spiritual privileges, females are as capable as males."[79] Paul says, "There is neither Greek nor Jew, circumcision nor uncircumcision, Barbarian, Scythian, bond nor free: but Christ is all, and in all" (Col. 3:11). Robert Peterson writes, "As the family of God, the church is God's answer to fear and bigotry," and though "many churches fall short of the ideal, . . . the family of God should welcome with open arms people of every 'tribe and language and people and nation' (Rev. 5:9)."[80] Equality calls believers to humility. Although Christians may have legitimate authority over each other in the domestic, economic, ecclesiastical, and political structures of this age, no Christian is the lord of another, and all Christians are fellow heirs of eternal life (1 Tim. 6:2; 1 Pet. 3:1, 7).

79. Watson, *A Body of Divinity*, 232. It might be objected that the very term translated as "adoption" (*huiothesia*), or "adoption as sons," is gender-biased because it is specific to a male "son" (*huios*). However, this fails to recognize that Paul is including both males and females in the privileges of union with Christ, who is the "Son" (*huios*). Garner warns against muddling "this verbally poignant Son/sons solidarity," and writes, "Since Christ is not *teknon* [child], the chosen conception for filial grace is not *teknothesia* [adoption as children]." Garner adds, "In fact, at times Paul speaks of the *huioi* as *tekna* (e.g., Rom. 8:15–17); we can be assured that Paul's choice of *huiothesia* and *huioi* representing both sexes perpetuates no gender bias and divulges no misogyny. With its etymological composition, *huiothesia* prominently serves his pervasive *in Christ* soteriology." Garner, *Sons in the Son*, 52.

80. Peterson, *Adopted by God*, 148.

Third, God's adopted child must maintain *harmonious relationships with his brothers and sisters.* The Lord Jesus rebukes anyone who is sinfully "angry with his brother" or who insults "his brother," and urges everyone to go quickly to "be reconciled to thy brother" if one realizes that "thy brother hath ought against thee" (Matt. 5:22–24). If one Christian sins against another, Christ counsels the one who is wronged, "If thy brother shall trespass against thee, go and tell him his fault between thee and him alone: if he shall hear thee, thou hast gained thy brother" (18:15). Brethren must be quick to forgive each other when they repent (Luke 17:3–4).

Fourth, God's adopted child must give *sacrificial service to his brothers and sisters.* Believers should not exploit their status as sons and daughters of God in order to assert their rights in selfishness and mutual contention. Paul says, "For, brethren, ye have been called unto liberty; only use not liberty for an occasion to the flesh, but by love serve one another" (Gal. 5:13). Paul points out that we have a special duty to our brethren: "As we have therefore opportunity, let us do good unto all men, especially unto them who are of the household of faith" (6:10). John warns, "He that loveth not his brother abideth in death" (1 John 3:14). Such love is Christlike in sacrificing oneself for others: "Hereby perceive we the love of God, because he laid down his life for us: and we ought to lay down our lives for the brethren" (v. 16). Brotherly love requires practical action to help those in need, not mere words (vv. 17–18). The King will say on judgment day, "Inasmuch as ye have done it unto one of the least of these my brethren, ye have done it unto me" (Matt. 25:40).

Fifth, God's adopted child must share in *giving and receiving exhortation among his brothers and sisters.* Mutual admonition in the family of God is the royal law of love: "You shall not hate your brother in your heart, but you shall reason frankly with your neighbor, lest you incur sin because of him. You shall not take vengeance or bear a grudge against the sons of your own people, but you shall love your neighbor as yourself: I am the LORD" (Lev. 19:17–18 ESV). Though not all are teachers (1 Cor. 12:29), all the brothers are "able also to admonish one another" (Rom. 15:14). While this practice is foreign to cultures that elevate privacy and individualism to the highest level, regular mutual exhortation is crucial for the perseverance of God's saints, for sin is exceedingly deceitful (Heb. 3:12–13).

The mutual service and admonition enjoined in the last two points imply that every child of God should be an active member of a local church. It is impossible to know the needs of one's brothers and sisters well enough to perform these duties without regularly meeting together for worship and fellowship with the same congregation week after week (Heb. 10:24–25).

Sixth, God's adopted child must sweeten *ministry with familial affection to his brothers and sisters*. Peter regarded colleagues in ministry as faithful and beloved brothers (1 Pet. 5:12; 2 Pet. 3:15). Paul did not regard his partners in ministry as mere coworkers, but as family members. He wrote of "Epaphroditus, my brother, and companion in labour, and fellowsoldier" (Phil. 2:25) and "Tychicus, a beloved brother and faithful minister in the Lord" (Eph. 6:21; cf. Col. 4:7). Being part of God's family also shaped how Paul related to those under his ministry, for he not only taught them but loved them like a nursing mother and gave them both an example and exhortation to follow like a good father (1 Thess. 2:7–12). Paul instructed Timothy, "Do not rebuke an older man but encourage him as you would a father, younger men as brothers, older women as mothers, younger women as sisters, in all purity" (1 Tim. 5:1–2 ESV).

Seventh, God's adopted child must engage in *communication with his brothers and sisters*. It is one mark of a healthy family that its members share information and love with each other, though great distances may separate them. Much of the New Testament consists of epistles written between Christians. These are not merely theological and ethical treatises, but letters expressing greetings and warm affection between members of one family (Rom. 16:14, 23). Paul closes one epistle, "All the brethren greet you. Greet ye one another with an holy kiss" (1 Cor. 16:20). Likewise, God's children should hold each other in such esteem and affection that though they may be separated "in presence," they will not be so "in heart" (1 Thess. 2:17). They should communicate with each other through various media—though they would prefer to meet face to face (2 John 12).

Although adoption by God is an invisible, heavenly transaction, it transforms every relationship that believers have. God brings them to himself as his sons and daughters, and commits himself to them as their heavenly Father. He unites them to his Son, so that Christ becomes their elder brother and his inheritance of blessing becomes theirs. God sends them the Spirit of his Son to assure them and guide them on the holy highway to their inheritance. He gives them a new identity as his children, which is more important and enduring than anything else about them. God separates them from the world and sets them in antithesis to it, so that while they suffer its persecution, they will escape the damnation that will fall on it. Finally, he makes them part of a family, so that all the redeemed of all nations and eras become their brothers and sisters. Adoption changes everything.

Sing to the Lord

The Amazing Privilege of Adoption

Behold th'amazing gift of love
The Father hath bestowed
On us, the sinful sons of men,
To call us sons of God!

Concealed as yet this honor lies,
By this dark world unknown,
A world that knew not when he came,
E'en God's eternal Son.

High is the rank we now possess;
But higher we shall rise;
Though what we shall hereafter be
Is hid from mortal eyes:

Our souls, we know, when God appears,
Shall bear his image bright;
For then his glory, as he is,
Shall open to our sight.

A hope so great and so divine
May trials well endure,
And purify our souls from sin,
As Christ himself is pure.

Isaac Watts/Scottish Paraphrase
Tune: St. Stephen
Trinity Hymnal—Baptist Edition, No. 442 (lacking last stanza)

Questions for Meditation or Discussion

1. You are talking with your family after attending a funeral at another church where the pastor repeatedly said, "Everyone is a child of God." How would you explain in what limited sense that statement is true and in what sense it is false, even dangerously misleading?
2. What is the relationship between predestination and adoption?
3. How were Christ's incarnation, death, and resurrection important for God to adopt people as his children?
4. What is the difference between regeneration and adoption? Why must people be regenerated in order to be God's adopted sons and daughters?
5. Why does Paul call the glorification of the saints their "adoption" (Rom. 8:23)?
6. How does adoption transform one's relationship to God the Father?
7. How are God the Son and God the Holy Spirit involved in adoption?
8. You have a friend who is a Christian but often feels unloved and unlovable, little better than human trash. How could she use the doctrine of adoption to form a new self-image?
9. How does adoption by God affect a person's relationship to the unbelieving world?
10. What is one way that this chapter has helped you to see your relationship to other Christians in a new light? What should you do about it?

Questions for Deeper Reflection

11. The authors argue that adoption is not identical to justification, sanctification, glorification, or a combination of them, but is a distinct grace. Do you agree? Why or why not?
12. How would the life of the local church be changed if it wholeheartedly embraced the doctrine of adoption? How might you help your church to take a step in that direction?

27

Sanctification, Part 1

Biblical Teaching

Holiness is the lifeblood of Christianity. When holiness declines, believers are left anemic and weak. Without holiness, professing Christians are no better than corpses. With holiness comes spiritual vitality, warmth, energy, and God-pleasing activity. For this reason, the Scriptures place an absolute premium on the holiness of God's people.

Holiness is often misunderstood and caricatured. For some, the word *holy* implies outdated backwardness. For others, holiness smacks of moralistic legalism with a long list of good things a person is not allowed to do. Still others associate holiness with an ugly pride that says, "I am better than you." However, in the Bible, *holiness* is a beautiful word; in fact, the Bible speaks of the beauty of holiness.[1] Jonathan Edwards said, "Holiness is a most beautiful, lovely thing. Men are apt to drink in strange notions of holiness from their childhood, as if it were a melancholy, morose, sour, and unpleasant thing; but there is nothing in it but what is sweet and ravishingly lovely."[2]

Sanctification is the work of God by which he makes people holy. Though difficult to recognize in English, this meaning is found in the etymology of the very word *sanctification* (Latin *sanctus*, "holy," plus *facere*,

1. 1 Chron. 16:29; 2 Chron. 20:21; Pss. 29:2; 96:9; 110:3.
2. Edwards, "The Way of Holiness," in *WJE*, 10:478.

"make").[3] Reformed and evangelical theologians distinguish between justification and sanctification, as we have seen, identifying the former as a change in legal status and the latter as a change in heart and life.[4] Sanctification is the extension of repentance across the duration of the Christian life, and thus a continued conversion.[5]

The Biblical Terminology of Sanctification

Although the English language uses two distinct roots for *holiness* and *sanctification*, in the Old Testament, the same Hebrew root is employed for both. The Hebrew term for "holy" (*qadesh*) is closely related to the word translated as "sanctify" (*piel* or *hiphil* of *qadash*), also rendered as "consecrate" and "hallow." The basic meaning of the term is to be or make sacred, set apart from what is ordinary and set against what is unclean (Lev. 10:10; 11:44). God is inherently and superlatively holy: "Holy, holy, holy, is the Lord of hosts" (Isa. 6:3). His holiness is his being set apart from all creation by his majestic glory (vv. 1–2) so that he wills to manifest his glory in all creation (v. 3). God is set against all that dishonors him and fails to reflect his perfection according to its created purpose (v. 5). Human holiness is not merely keeping rules, but dedication to God as the Supreme Being, and thus the supreme purpose for which we live as his image bearers.[6]

Objects and people are sanctified or consecrated when they are set apart for divine service, such as holy garments for priests (Ex. 28:2), a holy assembly for worship (12:16), or the holy Sabbath (16:23); or when they are made sacred by his presence, such as holy ground (3:5) or the tabernacle that the Lord said was "sanctified by my glory" because "I will dwell" there (29:43, 45). Moses said to Israel, "For thou art an holy people unto the Lord thy God: the Lord thy God hath chosen thee to be a special people unto himself, above all people that are upon the face of the earth" (Deut. 7:6). This national sanctification brought with it the duty of personal separation from ceremonially unclean things, for if the holy and the unclean come into contact, either judgment or atonement must intervene.[7] The holiness of Israel entailed not only ritual, external

3. Hoekema, *Saved by Grace*, 193.

4. See the discussion of justification and good works in chap. 22, especially Table 22.1. On the question of whether justification is the "cause" of sanctification, see Letham, *Systematic Theology*, 736–37.

5. See chap. 19 on conversion and repentance.

6. Hoekema, *Saved by Grace*, 194. On the meaning of holiness, see *RST*, 1:567–70.

7. Lev. 10:10; 16:16; 22:3; Num. 19:13, 20; Deut. 23:14; Isa. 35:8; 52:1; Ezek. 22:26; 44:23.

purity, but also moral holiness in the duties of reverence, turning from idols, showing mercy to the poor, and walking in integrity and love (Lev. 19:1–18; Ps. 24:3–4).

The New Testament uses the Greek words translated as "holy" (*hagios*, 240 times), "sanctify" (*hagiazō*, twenty-nine times), and "sanctification" or "holiness" (*hagiasmos*, ten times).[8] This word group generally translates the aforementioned Hebrew root (*qadash*) in the Septuagint.[9] The New Testament shares in the perspective of the Hebrew prophets that holiness belongs supremely and essentially to the Lord.[10] One of the predominant uses of the adjective "holy" (*hagios*) in the New Testament is in the title "Holy Spirit" (ninety-four times).[11]

The New Testament stresses the moral-ethical dimension of holiness rather than ritual holiness (Rom. 6:19; 1 Thess. 4:3, 7). The earthly center of holiness is God's presence in his holy temple, but now that temple is not a building but the people of the church who are indwelt by God's Spirit.[12] Therefore, the New Testament calls for a separation from the world not in terms of the priestly rituals and ceremonial cleanness emphasized by the law of Moses, but moral righteousness and spiritual worship of the true God (2 Cor. 6:14–7:1).

Holiness, however, is not just a way of life, but the identity of God's people in union with Christ. More than sixty times, the adjective *holy* functions nominally, translated as "saints" (*hagioi*), people made holy by God.[13] Paul wrote to "the church of God which is at Corinth, to them that are sanctified in Christ Jesus, called to be saints, with all that in every place call upon the name of Jesus Christ our Lord, both theirs and ours" (1 Cor. 1:2). They were sanctified "in Christ"; indeed, Christ was their "sanctification" (v. 30). They were separated from the polluted realm of

8. Rarer forms of this root in the New Testament are "holiness" (*hagiōsunē*, three times; Rom. 1:4; 2 Cor. 7:1; 1 Thess. 3:13) and "holiness" (*hagiotēs*, once; Heb. 12:10).

9. Occasionally, "holy" or "holiness" translates another Greek word group (*hosi-*) in the New Testament that is never used in the Septuagint to translate *qadosh* or *tsadiq*, but renders the Hebrew root for faithful love (*khesed* or *khasid*). This family of Greek terms is perhaps better understood as "faithful" or "pious" (*hosios*, or negatively, *anosis*), "piously" (*hosiōs*), or "piety" (*hosiotēs*). *TDNT*, 5:490–91. See Luke 1:75; Acts 2:27; 13:34–35; Eph. 4:24; 1 Thess. 2:10; 1 Tim. 1:9; 2:8; 2 Tim. 3:2; Titus 1:8; Heb. 7:26; Rev. 15:4. This word group is clearly related to the concept of sanctification, but it is semantically distinct from the terminology of "holy" (*hagios*).

10. John 17:11; 1 Pet. 1:15–16; Rev. 3:7; 4:8; 6:10. However, the New Testament does not speak of God's holiness as often as the Old Testament, except with respect to the Holy Spirit.

11. This includes those instances in the KJV where the phrase is translated as "Holy Ghost." See chap. 1 on the names of the Holy Spirit.

12. 1 Cor. 3:16–17; 6:19–20; Eph. 2:21–22; 1 Pet. 2:4–5.

13. Compare "saints" (plural *qadish*; rendered *hagioi*, LXX) in Pss. 16:3; 34:9; 89:5, 7; Dan. 7:18, 21, 22, 25, 27.

sin and brought into the sacred realm of the divine by union with Christ. For a Christian "to be sanctified" is "to be made a saint, or a holy person set apart for a holy use."[14]

Though holiness is commonly regarded as moral purity, it is crucial that we understand it according to its God-centered orientation. Geerhardus Vos said, "Holiness means a relationship with God, a dedication to God. To be holy never means something that one is in himself, apart from God." Holiness cannot be understood if one "starts with man and assumes that to sanctify is to make someone better." Holiness always "serves for God's glorification."[15]

The Theological Definition of Sanctification

William Ames said, "Sanctification is the real change in man from the sordidness of sin to the purity of God's image." He explained that just as justification frees the believer from the "guilt of sin," so sanctification frees him from the "stain of sin" to restore him to the purity of the image of God.[16] Johannes Wollebius wrote that sanctification "is the free act of God, by which the faithful, who are engrafted into Christ through faith and justified through the Holy Spirit, are progressively set free from their innate sinfulness and restored to his image, so that they may be made fit to glorify him by good works."[17]

Perhaps the best concise definition of sanctification is found in the Westminster Shorter Catechism (Q. 35): "Sanctification is the work of God's free grace, whereby we are renewed in the whole man after the image of God, and are enabled more and more to die unto sin, and live unto righteousness."[18]

In this definition, sanctification is called a *work* and not an act because it involves a real change in a person's nature effected over time, not merely the grant of a new legal or relational status. The "God of peace . . . [is] working in you that which is wellpleasing in his sight, through Jesus Christ; to whom be glory for ever and ever" (Heb. 13:20–21).

This divine work is of *God's free grace*, for it is not based on any merit in the person sanctified but flows from God's unconditional elec-

14. Fisher et al., *The Assembly's Shorter Catechism Explained*, 35.1 (188).
15. Vos, *Reformed Dogmatics*, 4:188.
16. Ames, *The Marrow of Theology*, 1.29.4–5 (168).
17. Wollebius, *Compendium*, 1.31.(1).2 (171).
18. *Reformed Confessions*, 4:358.

tion in Christ for the praise of his glory (Eph. 1:4, 6). Paul says, "We are bound to give thanks alway to God for you, brethren beloved of the Lord, because God hath from the beginning chosen you to salvation through sanctification of the Spirit and belief of the truth" (2 Thess. 2:13). In the broader context of the Westminster Standards, it is clear that the grace of sanctification, like all saving grace, is "purchased by Christ" and given by the Spirit's work of "uniting us to Christ."[19] Evangelical sanctification differs as much from legalistic holiness as evangelical justification differs from legalistic self-righteousness, for the gospel reveals both justification and sanctification "in Christ."[20]

By God's grace, *we are renewed*. Sanctification is the outworking and development of the new creation in human life, the continual putting on of the "new man" (Eph. 4:24). Paul says, "Be ye transformed by the renewing of your mind" (Rom. 12:2). Francis Turretin said that sanctification is not merely a change in conduct, but "a change and renovation of the nature itself (corrupted by original sin)."[21]

Sanctification involves the renewal of *the whole man*, body and spirit (2 Cor. 7:1). Paul prays, "The very God of peace sanctify you wholly; and I pray God your whole spirit and soul and body be preserved blameless unto the coming of our Lord Jesus Christ" (1 Thess. 5:23).

This holistic renewal is according to *the image of God* (Eph. 4:22–24). By the Spirit, the person being sanctified increasingly beholds the glory of Christ and is "changed into the same image from glory to glory" (2 Cor. 3:18). Thomas Watson said, "It is a principle of grace savingly wrought, whereby the heart becomes holy, and is made after God's heart. A sanctified person bears not only God's name, but his image."[22] The restoration of God's image links sanctification to glorification (Rom. 8:17–18, 21, 29; 2 Cor. 4:4, 16). Thus, Richard Sibbes said, "Grace is glory begun, and glory is grace perfected."[23] Watson said, "Sanctification is glory in the seed, and glory is sanctification in the flower."[24]

The work of sanctification is never completed in this life but progresses *more and more* as the saints "press toward the mark for the prize of the

19. The Westminster Shorter Catechism (Q. 29–30, 32), in *Reformed Confessions*, 4:357. See also the Westminster Larger Catechism (Q. 65–69), in *Reformed Confessions*, 4:311–12.
20. Bavinck, *Reformed Dogmatics*, 4:248.
21. Turretin, *Institutes*, 17.1.4 (2:690).
22. Watson, *A Body of Divinity*, 241.
23. Sibbes, *The Excellency of the Gospel above the Law*, in *Works*, 4:288.
24. Watson, *A Body of Divinity*, 242.

high calling of God in Christ Jesus" (Phil. 3:12–14). The God who has "begun a good work" in them will bring it to completion (1:6). Ames said that sanctification is a "real change" consisting in "degrees of beginning, progress, and completion, . . . [for] the inward man is renewed day by day" (2 Cor. 4:16).[25]

Sanctification has negative and positive sides, so that God's people increasingly *die unto sin* and *live unto righteousness.* This arises from believers' union and communion with Christ, an important biblical theme that we will explore later in this chapter.

The Necessity of Sanctification

When the Bible says that without holiness "no man shall see the Lord" (Heb. 12:14), it indicates the absolute necessity of sanctification in order for a person to behold God's glory in the eternal kingdom (Matt. 5:8; 1 John 3:2–3). The kingdom is "the holy city," and nothing unclean "that defileth" will be permitted into it (Rev. 21:2, 10, 27). Our appreciation for holiness deepens when we consider the reasons for this necessity.

First, *God's people must be sanctified because he is holy* (1 Pet. 1:14–16). The holiness of God is his incomparable glory. Moses said, "Who is like unto thee, O Lord, among the gods? Who is like thee, glorious in holiness, fearful in praises, doing wonders?" (Ex. 15:11). God reigns forever (v. 18). His holiness shines forth in his infinite majesty and moral perfection as the supreme King (Ps. 99:1–5). The Lord expresses the demands of holiness in his holy law (Rom. 7:12). Therefore, men must fear God, humble themselves, and keep his commandments in order to honor the Holy One and dwell in his holy presence (Isa. 5:24; 57:15).[26] For the Holy One to allow unsanctified people to dwell with him would be to deny that he is God.

Second, *God's people must be sanctified because they are his image bearers.* God created man in his image, according to his likeness (Gen. 1:26–27). Though that image includes dominion over the creatures (v. 28), at its core is moral likeness to God in knowledge, righteousness, and holiness (Eph. 4:24; Col. 3:10).[27] Holiness, then, is at the heart of God's created purpose for mankind. For people, to be holy is to be fully human.

25. Ames, *The Marrow of Theology*, 1.29.1–2 (167–68).
26. See the exposition of the doctrine of God's holiness in *RST*, 1:570–82.
27. On the image of God, see *RST*, 2:161–206 (chaps. 8–10).

Rocks, trees, and animals need not be morally excellent because God did not create them to reflect his personal character. However, if human beings are not holy, they fail to fulfill their created purpose and "come short of the glory of God" (Rom. 3:23). Consequently, without holiness men cannot exercise dominion in God's kingdom, but with holiness they will reign with him eternally (Rev. 21:2, 27; 22:4–5). Only through holiness will men glorify God and enjoy him forever.

Third, *God's people must be sanctified because they are born in the state of sin.* Since the fall of man, every human being is conceived in sin (Ps. 51:5) and "estranged from the womb: they go astray as soon as they be born, speaking lies" (58:3). David sums up the human condition: "The LORD looked down from heaven upon the children of men, to see if there were any that did understand, and seek God. They are all gone aside, they are all together become filthy: there is none that doeth good, no, not one" (14:2–3).[28] Therefore, we may ask, "Can any have a sanctified life, who have not a renewed nature?" and answer, "No; for a corrupt tree cannot bring forth good fruit (Matt. 7:18)."[29] A mighty work of grace must come to their lives for people to have holiness that pleases the Lord. Apart from sanctification, mankind is unclean, an offense to God's holiness, and the object of his displeasure.

Fourth, *God's people must be sanctified because morality and religiosity are not holiness.* Sinners have the power to refrain from much outward sin, such as gross rebellion against authority, murder, adultery, and theft. They may also engage in acts of religious devotion such as prayer and fasting (Luke 18:9–12). However, apart from a supernatural work of divine grace, sin is engraved on their hearts (Jer. 17:1; 31:33) and they remain under its reigning power (Rom. 3:9; 6:14, 17). Watson warned, "Civility is but nature refined; there is nothing of Christ there, and the heart may be foul and impure."[30] John Gill said that "moral virtue" was "exercised by some of the heathen philosophers to a very great degree, and yet they had not a grain of holiness in them; but were full of the lusts of envy, ambition, pride, revenge," and so on.[31] The essence of holiness is love for the one true God, which comes from an inward work of divine grace (Deut. 6:4–5; 7:9; 30:6). Despite all the morality and religion in the

28. On the state of sin, or original sin, see *RST*, 2:386–416 (chaps. 20–21).
29. Fisher et al., *The Assembly's Shorter Catechism Explained*, 35.24 (190).
30. Watson, *A Body of Divinity*, 243.
31. Gill, *Body of Divinity*, 552.

world, Paul says, "there is none righteous . . . there is none that seeketh after God" (Rom. 3:10–11). Hence, sanctification is not merely man's work, but "has a supernatural character."[32]

Fifth, *God's people must be sanctified because regeneration is only the beginning of holiness.* The new birth of God introduces righteousness and love, and breaks the ruling pattern of sin (1 John 2:29; 3:9; 4:7).[33] However, Peter says to those who are "born again" that since "ye have purified your souls in obeying the truth through the Spirit unto unfeigned love of the brethren, see that ye love one another with a pure heart fervently" (1 Pet. 1:22–23). What regeneration implanted, believers must cultivate and grow. They have become partakers of "the divine nature," but Peter exhorts them to press on, "giving all diligence," to increase in every virtue (2 Pet. 1:3–7). Such progress is not by human power; rather, believers must "grow in grace, and in the knowledge of our Lord and Saviour Jesus Christ" (3:18). Christians experience a battle between sinful desires of the flesh and holy desires produced by the Spirit.[34] Believers also have worldly thoughts in minds that must be renewed (Rom. 12:2). Though they are "light in the Lord" (Eph. 5:8), the saints need more of the Spirit's work for their "understanding" to be "enlightened" so that they may "know" the truth in a more spiritual and experiential manner (1:18; cf. Col. 1:9). Due to the reality of indwelling sin, believers need a continuing work of grace so that they grow in holiness.

Sixth, *God's people must be sanctified because salvation demands the response of holy love.* Having been forgiven much, the saints love much—a love that moves them to honor Christ with tears, self-abasement, and costly devotion (Luke 7:36–50). Paul says, "I beseech you therefore, brethren, by the mercies of God, that ye present your bodies a living sacrifice, holy, acceptable unto God, which is your reasonable service" (Rom. 12:1). To "live and die happily," the Heidelberg Catechism (LD 1, Q. 2) says, people must not only know how great their sins and miseries are and how to be delivered from them, but also how they can show their "gratitude to God for such deliverance."[35] Therefore, the catechism (LD 32, Q. 86) says, "Christ, having redeemed and delivered us by His blood, also renews

32. Vos, *Reformed Dogmatics*, 4:194–97.

33. On regeneration, see chaps. 17–18.

34. Rom. 7:14–15; Gal. 5:17; James 1:14–15; 1 Pet. 2:11. See the next chapter on the man in Rom. 7:14–25.

35. *The Three Forms of Unity*, 68.

us by His Holy Spirit after His own image; that so we may testify, by the whole of our conduct, our gratitude to God for His blessings, and that He may be praised by us."[36]

Seventh, *God's people must be sanctified because good works demonstrate the reality of their salvation by faith*. God saves people through faith apart from works.[37] However, faith is an invisible act of the soul. A living faith in Christ becomes visible by the works it generates through love (Gal. 5:6). James says, "Faith, if it hath not works, is dead, being alone," and so, "I will shew thee my faith by my works" (James 2:17–18). Sanctification is necessary to prove to God's people and to those around them that they are truly united to Christ by a genuine faith. The Westminster Confession of Faith (16.2) says,

> These good works, done in obedience to God's commandments, are the fruits and evidences of a true and lively faith: and by them believers manifest their thankfulness, strengthen their assurance, edify their brethren, adorn the profession of the gospel, stop the mouths of the adversaries, and glorify God, whose workmanship they are, created in Christ Jesus thereunto, that, having their fruit unto holiness, they may have the end, eternal life.[38]

The Trinitarian Grace of Sanctification

All true holiness is by God's grace. This grace is divine and Trinitarian, proceeding from the Father through the Son by the Spirit.

Election unto Holiness by the Father

The deepest root of sanctification reaches back to before time began. Paul says, "He hath chosen us in him before the foundation of the world, that we should be holy and without blame [*hagious kai amōmous*] before him in love" (Eph. 1:4). God did not choose us because of any holiness in us, but in order that we would become holy. Paul uses the same words again to describe the final result of Christ's death: "That he might present it to himself a glorious church, not having spot, or wrinkle, or any such thing; but that it should be holy and without blemish [*hagia kai amōmos*]" (5:27). The repetition of this phrase shows that the Father accomplished

36. *The Three Forms of Unity*, 98.
37. John 1:12; Gal. 2:16; Eph. 2:8–9.
38. *Reformed Confessions*, 4:251–52.

the sanctifying purpose of his election through his Son's sanctifying accomplishment of redemption. God's election unto holiness involves the decree of initial sanctification by the Holy Spirit at conversion (2 Thess. 2:13). God's predestination aims ultimately at the elect being "conformed to the image of his Son, that he might be the firstborn among many brethren" (Rom. 8:29).

Therefore, all glory for our holiness must be given to God, for all our choices to be holy flow from his eternal choice of us. Man's practical holiness is a response to God's will: "For this is the will of God, even your sanctification, that ye should abstain from fornication: that every one of you should know how to possess his vessel in sanctification and honour. . . . For God hath not called us unto uncleanness, but unto holiness" (1 Thess. 4:3–4, 7).

Union with Christ in His Death and Resurrection

Christ's name "Jesus" testifies to the fact that "he shall save his people from their sins" (Matt. 1:21). As the Mediator of the new covenant, Christ administers the promised grace to his people so that God's law is written on their hearts, they know him, and he forgives all their sins (Heb. 8:6–12). Sanctification is so inseparably tied to Christ's ministry that one passage of Scripture refers to Christ "the Lord" (*ho Kyrios*) simply as "he that sanctifieth" (*ho hagiazōn*) his brethren (2:3, 11). The expression is especially striking in the light of God's declaration ten times in the Old Testament that he is "the Lord who sanctifies" his people.[39]

Christ's saving work came to a climax in his death and resurrection, so much so that the gospel may be summarized in this twofold event (1 Cor. 15:3–4). Christ "was delivered for our offences, and was raised again for our justification" (Rom. 4:25). However, Christ is not only the "righteousness" but also the "sanctification" of those who are "in Christ Jesus" (1 Cor. 1:30). Thomas Boston said, "Union with Christ is the only way to sanctification."[40]

Christ's death has the power to convert sinners and produce in them a life of zealous obedience (Titus 2:14). As Peter says, Christ "bare our sins in his own body on the tree, that we, being dead to sins, should live

39. Greek *egō kyrios ho hagiazōn* (Ex. 31:13; Lev. 20:8; 21:8, 15; 22:16, 32; Ezek. 20:12 LXX); *egō eimi kyrios ho hagiazōn* (Lev. 21:23; Ezek. 37:28 LXX); or *egō kyrios ho theos ho hagiazōn* (Lev. 22:9 LXX). These are all the uses of *hagiazōn* in the LXX.

40. Boston, *An Illustration of the Doctrines of the Christian Religion*, in *Works*, 2:9.

unto righteousness: by whose stripes ye were healed. For ye were as sheep going astray; but are now returned unto the Shepherd and Bishop of your souls" (1 Pet. 2:24–25). Herman Bavinck wrote, "By this act, he not only won for them the forgiveness of sins; his self-offering, his death, was also a total consecration to the Father, a perfect act of obedience to his will, a sanctification of himself that by his word they too might be sanctified in the truth (John 17:17, 19)."[41]

Paul expounds this theme of our union with Christ in his death and resurrection.[42] Our justification by union with Christ does not encourage us to sin, for by that same union with Christ we have died to sin and been raised with him to walk in a new life (Rom. 6:1–4). We have been crucified with Christ and live with him unto God (Gal. 2:19–20). Sinclair Ferguson writes, "Redemptive-historically this crucifixion took place at Calvary; existentially its significance and implications are realized in us by the Spirit in regeneration, repentance, and faith. This latter realization is rooted in the historicity of the former."[43]

Before our conversion, the law could only provoke our fallen nature to more sin; united with Christ like a bride to her husband, we have left behind that old reality and now bear fruit for God through our relationship with the risen Lord (Rom. 7:1–6). Grafted into Christ, we share in his redemptive accomplishments so that the reigning power of sin has been crucified and we are alive unto God (6:5–10).

Christ's crucifixion has decisively separated us from the controlling power of sin and this world (Gal. 5:24; 6:14; Col. 2:20), though sinful desires still remain in us (Gal. 5:17) and must be put to death (Rom. 8:12–13; Col. 3:5). Christ's resurrection has made us alive with him (Eph. 2:4–5), and the risen Christ who sits at God's right hand is our very life (Col. 3:1–4). This is not something that believers need to seek to attain, but is an established fact for all in Christ. We Christians must embrace this truth by faith in order to find the strength to resist sin's motions in us and surrender ourselves in the service of God (Rom. 6:11–14).

Christians should not view themselves as slaves under the reigning power of sin or the condemnation of God's law. Paul says, "For sin shall not have dominion over you: for ye are not under the law, but under grace" (Rom. 6:14). God has set them free from the mastery of sin (v. 18). Neither

41. Bavinck, *Reformed Dogmatics*, 4:233.
42. See chap. 10 on union with Christ in his death, resurrection, and ascension.
43. Ferguson, *The Holy Spirit*, 147.

should believers in Christ see themselves as divided between two centers, the "old man" and the "new man," like a nation divided in civil war with two competing capital cities. Paul says, "Our old man is crucified with him" (v. 6). He adds, "Ye have put off the old man with his deeds, and have put on the new man, which is renewed in knowledge after the image of him that created him" (Col. 3:9–10).[44] Richard Melick comments, "The old self and new self are never described as coexisting in anyone. . . . The old self is never a proper description of a believer."[45] Even the translation "old self" can be misleading, for the contrast is between the spiritual states of those outside of Christ and those in Christ ("the new man").[46] John Murray said, "The old man is the unregenerate man; the new man is the regenerate man created in Christ Jesus unto good works. It is no more feasible to call the believer a new man and an old man, than it is to call him a regenerate man and an unregenerate."[47]

No part of our lives is enslaved to sin if we are in union with Christ. If we would correct the political metaphor, we are like a nation united under one king reigning from one capital city (the heart), but with cells of enemy soldiers scattered across the land and engaging in guerrilla warfare against our souls. By the victory of Christ, we can and must kill the internal enemies of remaining sin. When we put off the sins of the old man and put on the obedience of the new man (Eph. 4:22–24), we are not fighting for our freedom, but fighting because we are already free in Christ, and he is implementing his victory progressively in us. Christians may rejoice with Paul: "God be thanked, that ye were the servants of sin, but ye have obeyed from the heart that form of doctrine which was delivered you. Being then made free from sin, ye became the servants of righteousness" (Rom. 6:17–18).

Therefore, we have been ransomed by Christ from the futile way of life of our unbelieving forefathers (1 Pet. 1:18–19). The Heidelberg Catechism (LD 32, Q. 86) captures the immense value of this grace from Christ:

---

44. In Col. 3:9, "lie" is in the present tense, but "put off" and "put on" are in the aorist tense, for which reason the translators have treated the latter two acts as events already done. This interpretation is confirmed by the fact that Paul immediately proceeds to describe their new identity as defined by Christ (v. 11).

45. Richard R. Melick, *Philippians, Colossians, Philemon*, The New American Commentary 32 (Nashville: Broadman & Holman, 1991), 295.

46. The precedent for "new man" in Eph. 4:24 is 2:15, where it refers to our corporate unity in Christ: "to make in himself of twain [the two groups of Jews and Gentiles] one new man."

47. John Murray, *Principles of Conduct: Aspects of Biblical Ethics* (Grand Rapids, MI: Eerdmans, 1957), 218; cf. *Epistle to the Romans*, 1:219–20.

> Because Christ, having redeemed and delivered us by His blood, also renews us by His Holy Spirit after His own image; that so we may testify, by the whole of our conduct, our gratitude to God for His blessings, and that He may be praised by us; also, that every one may be assured in himself of his faith by the fruits thereof; and that by our godly conversation [conduct] others may be gained to Christ.[48]

The Supernatural Agency of the Holy Spirit

God applies the accomplishment of Christ's death and resurrection to the sanctification of his elect people by the Holy Spirit. When the Mediator of the covenant writes God's law on men's hearts, he does so "not with ink, but with the Spirit of the living God," the Lord and life giver (2 Cor. 3:3, 6). Therefore, we are "sanctified by the Holy Ghost" (Rom. 15:16). Wollebius said, "The efficient cause [of sanctification] is the entire Holy Trinity in its essential oneness, but especially the Holy Spirit, whom Christ has sent for this purpose."[49]

Just as Paul highlights the death and resurrection of Jesus Christ in Romans 6 as the great divine work of sanctification *for* us, so he highlights the indwelling of the Holy Spirit in Romans 8 as the great divine work of sanctification *within* us. The Spirit of God is "the Spirit of life in Christ Jesus" because he liberates us from sin and death (v. 2). The wicked hate God and cannot submit to his law (vv. 5–8), but those who belong to Christ "are not in the flesh, but in the Spirit," who comes to them as "the Spirit of Christ" (v. 9). Already, though our bodies still suffer the mortal effects of man's fall into sin, the Holy Spirit is giving life to us because of Christ's imputed righteousness (v. 10). The Holy Spirit leads us to wage war against our sin to put it to death and to walk as obedient sons of God (vv. 13–14).

Therefore, the Holy Spirit applies the dying and rising of Christ to his people so that they progressively die to sin and live to righteousness. William Perkins wrote, "Sanctification has two parts: mortification and vivification."[50] "Mortification" means putting to death; "vivification" or "quickening" means bringing to life. Samuel Willard said, "Mortification is a work of the Spirit, in which he crucifieth original sin in us, by applying

48. *The Three Forms of Unity*, 98.
49. Wollebius, *Compendium*, 1.31.3 (172).
50. Perkins, *A Golden Chain*, chap. 38, in *Works*, 6:186. See also Ames, *The Marrow of Theology*, 1.29.17–26 (170).

to it the death of Christ. . . . Vivification is a work of the Spirit, by which he restores in us our lost righteousness, by the application of the resurrection of Christ."[51]

The divine agency in sanctification, particularly the supernatural work of the Holy Spirit applying the finished work of Christ, refutes the heresy of Pelagianism. Pelagius believed that Adam's sin did not diminish man's ability to obey God.[52] Humanity retains the power in its free will to choose to sin or not to sin. Thus, God's sanctifying grace to us consists merely of the created power of the will and the influence of God's word to persuade us to do what is right. It is theoretically possible in this view for a man to never sin.[53] However, the sanctifying work of the Spirit shows that man cannot become holy without an internal, powerful work of grace.

The Holy Spirit's presence in the believer is his great power to fight sin. When God's people are tempted to sin, Paul reminds them that those who practice sexual immorality, homosexuality, idolatry, theft, substance abuse, or oppression will not inherit the kingdom; furthermore, "such were some of you: but ye are washed, but ye are sanctified, but ye are justified in the name of the Lord Jesus, and by the Spirit of our God" (1 Cor. 6:11). We must not sin and cannot continue in sin, for "he that is joined unto the Lord is one spirit" (v. 17). The living union between Christ and his people by the Holy Spirit is both a motive to pursue holiness and the strength to actualize it. Paul says, "What? Know ye not that your body is the temple of the Holy Ghost which is in you, which ye have of God, and ye are not your own? For ye are bought with a price: therefore glorify God in your body, and in your spirit, which are God's" (vv. 19–20).

Therefore, to live by faith in the Son of God (Gal. 2:20) is to "walk in the Spirit" (5:16, 25).[54] To obey God's law is to cooperate with the Spirit in rejecting the wicked works of the flesh and producing the fruit of love and self-control—"the fruit of the Spirit" (vv. 19–24). The Christian who is living and growing in holiness is a "spiritual" person (1 Cor. 2:15; Gal. 6:1)—that is, a person whose life is pervasively influenced by the Holy Spirit.

---

51. Willard, *A Compleat Body of Divinity*, 497–98.

52. On Pelagianism, see *RST*, 2:367.

53. Pelagius, "The Christian Life," 55–56, 61, 64–65; Wiggers, *An Historical Presentation of Augustinism and Pelagianism*, 83–88; Evans, *Pelagius*, 100–101, 104, 108–11; and Huber, "The Pelagian Heresy," 59–60, 64–65.

54. The meaning of walking in the Spirit and being led by him will be further discussed in chap. 32.

The primary and essential means by which the Spirit sanctifies people is God's Word. Christ said that his "words" are "spirit" and "life" (John 6:63). He told those who abide in his "word" that "ye shall know the truth, and the truth shall make you free" (8:32). Christ prayed to the Father, "Sanctify them through thy truth: thy word is truth" (17:17). The Word gives life to the soul (Ps. 119:50). Treasuring up the Word in the heart and taking heed to it cleanses our ways and fortifies us against temptation in our heart (vv. 9, 11). God's Word imparts understanding and stirs hatred of all false ways (v. 104). Through the revealed knowledge of God, he has provided "all things that pertain unto life and godliness" (2 Pet. 1:3).[55] James Boyce noted that the truths of the Holy Scriptures are so central to sanctification that all other means "are not only secondary, but actually subordinate means to the word of God. . . . In themselves they have no efficacy, and only accomplish the end of sanctification by bringing the believer into connection with the truth of God."[56]

The Christian may move forward in the spiritual battle of sanctification with these bold assertions ringing in his ears: "God chose me and decreed my holiness before time began. I died with Christ and rose again with him, so that I am dead to sin and alive to God. The Holy Spirit works in me even now so that I can put my remaining sins to death and live in increasing holiness." Anthony Hoekema wrote, "One important implication of this teaching is that believers should have positive images of themselves. . . . We are indeed new creatures in Christ."[57]

The Divine Implementation of Sanctification

The language of sanctification is used in different senses in the New Testament. Occasionally, to "sanctify" refers to consecrating someone or something in ceremonial holiness, with a backward glance at the rituals of the old covenant (Matt. 23:17, 19; Heb. 9:13). More commonly, sanctification denotes one of the chief parts and benefits of salvation in Christ. However, even with regard to salvation, sanctification can refer either to an initial, definitive work that God has done for all the saints or to a continuing work that God is doing in them that elicits their cooperation.

---

55. Boyce, *Abstract of Systematic Theology*, 418.
56. Boyce, *Abstract of Systematic Theology*, 419.
57. Hoekema, *Saved by Grace*, 214.

Definitive Sanctification

As we noted in our discussion of terminology, the New Testament refers to Christians more than sixty times as "saints" or "holy ones" (*hagioi*). All believers, therefore, are in a state of holiness before the Lord. Referring to the members of the church, Paul says, "The temple of God is holy" (1 Cor. 3:17; cf. Eph. 2:21). According to Peter, they are a "holy priesthood" and a "holy nation" (1 Pet. 2:5, 9). Comparing the people of God through the ages to a tree, Paul writes, "If the root be holy, so are the branches" (Rom. 11:16). Even as Paul exhorts "the elect of God" to "put on" or practice the spiritual virtues of Christlikeness, he says they are already "holy" (Col. 3:12). The family of God consists of "holy brethren" (1 Thess. 5:27; Heb. 3:1).

The same truth appears in the use of the verb translated as "sanctify" (*hagiazō*) in the perfect tense to communicate that Christians have been sanctified or are in a state of holiness. The Word of God is able to give them "an inheritance among all them which are sanctified" (Acts 20:32). Paul wrote "unto the church of God which is at Corinth, to them that are sanctified in Christ Jesus, called to be saints" (1 Cor. 1:2). Though the Corinthian church had many moral and spiritual problems, Paul still addressed the believers there as those in a state of holiness (cf. 6:11, also in the perfect tense). Similarly, Jude wrote "to them that are sanctified by God the Father, and preserved in Jesus Christ, and called" (Jude 1).

The Lord Jesus Christ sent Paul to open the eyes of sinners so that they might turn to God and "receive forgiveness of sins, and inheritance among them which are sanctified [perfect *hagiazō*] by faith" in Christ (Acts 26:18). Unlike justification, however, sanctification does not consist merely in a new status before God without any actual renewal of the soul, but is worked in believers through the operation of the Holy Spirit to make them obedient (Rom. 15:16 [perfect *hagiazō*], 18; 1 Pet. 1:2 [*hagiasmos*]). This is not an imputation of holiness, but a new spiritual state and inward condition. It is the decisive transfer of a person from the kingdom where sin reigns to the kingdom where grace reigns, a transfer that happens when the person is united to Christ (Rom. 5:21; 6:14; Col. 1:13).

Since the latter half of the twentieth century, Reformed theologians have called this act of God *definitive sanctification* in order to distinguish it from the Spirit's continuing work in the lives of sinners. Murray said that, in this sense, sanctification is "a decisive and definitive breach with the power and service of sin" for those who have "come under the control" of "grace."[58] Earlier Reformed theologians sometimes spoke of *initial sanctification*, referring either to regeneration or to regeneration and conversion.[59]

How is definitive sanctification related to effectual calling, regeneration, and conversion? Definitive sanctification is closely associated with effectual calling, though viewed from the perspective of consecration to a state of holiness. Effectual calling is named a "*holy* calling" (2 Tim. 1:9), and believers are "called to be saints" (Rom. 1:7; 1 Cor. 1:2).[60]

However, definitive sanctification also overlaps with conversion: Paul says in Acts 26:18 that God's people are "sanctified *by faith*,"[61] for Christ has worked to "*turn* them from darkness to light, and from the power of Satan unto God." Peter notes that God saves Gentiles just as he does Jews, "purifying their hearts by faith" (15:9). Faith and repentance are the effects of effectual calling, which from another perspective is described as regeneration.[62] Paul associates these concepts with one another when he writes that "God hath from the beginning chosen you to salvation through *sanctification* of the Spirit and *belief* of the truth: whereunto he *called* you by our gospel" (2 Thess. 2:13–14). Therefore, it seems best to consider definitive sanctification to encompass effectual calling, regeneration, and conversion.

Definitive sanctification is outwardly signified by baptism. Paul writes, "How shall we, that are dead to sin, live any longer therein? Know ye not, that so many of us as were baptized into Jesus Christ were baptized into his death?" (Rom. 6:2–3). The Heidelberg Catechism (LD 26, Q. 69–70) says that "Christ appointed this external washing with water" to assure the Christian that he is "washed by His blood and Spirit," the first washing referring to the forgiveness of sins and the latter to being "renewed by the Holy Ghost, and sanctified to be members of Christ, that so we may more

58. Murray, *Collected Writings*, 2:280.

59. Boston, *An Illustration of the Doctrines of the Christian Religion*, in *Works*, 1:655; John Newman, *The Popish Doctrine of Merit and Justification Considered*, 3rd ed. (London: R. Ford and R. Hett, 1735), 38; John Colquhoun, *Sermons, Chiefly on Doctrinal Subjects* (Edinburgh: J. & D. Collie, 1836), 170; and Robert Shaw, *An Exposition of the Confession of Faith of the Westminster Assembly of Divines*, 8th ed. (Glasgow: Blackie and Son, 1857), 143.

60. See the connection between calling and holiness/sanctification in 1 Thess. 4:7; Heb. 3:1; 1 Pet. 1:15; 2:9; Jude 1.

61. This assumes that "by faith" (*pistei*) modifies "sanctified" (*hēgiasmenois*), its immediate antecedent, and not "receive" (*labein*).

62. See chaps. 15–18.

and more die unto sin, and lead holy and unblameable lives."[63] Definitive sanctification at the beginning of the Christian life paves the way for progressive sanctification throughout this life.

Given that Christians are "saints," having been definitively sanctified by Christ through the Spirit, we must regard holiness as essential to true Christianity. John Sheffield (d. 1680) observed, "To imagine a Christian without holiness, is . . . to imagine a sun without light, and fire without heat: which is a pure contradiction."[64]

Progressive Sanctification

After Paul reminds believers of their decisive death to sin and coming alive to God by union with Christ, he goes on to call them to pursue increasing holiness of life, saying,

> As ye have yielded your members servants to uncleanness and to iniquity unto iniquity; even so now yield your members servants to righteousness unto holiness. For when ye were the servants of sin, ye were free from righteousness. What fruit had ye then in those things whereof ye are now ashamed? For the end of those things is death. But now being made free from sin, and become servants to God, ye have your fruit unto holiness, and the end everlasting life. (Rom. 6:19–22)

Sanctification, then, is both the present state of believers (they are sanctified in Christ) and their progressive growth (they are being sanctified by Christ), for which they must engage their effort by faith in God's promises. Paul says, "Having therefore these promises, dearly beloved, let us cleanse ourselves from all filthiness of the flesh and spirit, perfecting holiness in the fear of God" (2 Cor. 7:1). The woman who is devoted to the Lord aims "that she may be holy both in body and in spirit" (1 Cor. 7:34). "Be ye holy; for I am holy" remains God's command to his obedient children in the new covenant, and they must carry it out in reverent fear of their Father (1 Pet. 1:14–17). The call to holiness requires believers to give attention to their obedience to specific laws of God, such as the seventh commandment (1 Thess. 4:3–7). To despise God's holy law is to despise God's Holy Spirit, a blasphemous contempt incongruous with the saving knowledge of God (v. 8).

63. *The Three Forms of Unity*, 90.

64. John Sheffield, "Of Holiness," in *Puritan Sermons, 1659–1689*, 5:432.

Believers who do not actively pursue holiness are in grave danger of sinning in a way that wounds their spiritual lives and stains their reputations. Some of the most exemplary believers in the Holy Scriptures, such as David and Peter, fell into grievous sins because of a lack of watchfulness and progress in holiness. As we noted earlier, continued repentance is necessary for believers for their growth and perseverance in the Christian life.[65]

Although progressive sanctification requires the work of regenerate men, it is also a grace that flows from the election of the Father, the finished work of Christ, and the ongoing work of the Holy Spirit. The success of this work of sanctification depends on God so that believers will be found holy at "the coming of our Lord Jesus Christ," but they can be confident, for "faithful is he that calleth you, who also will do it" (1 Thess. 5:23–24).

Therefore, progressive sanctification is cooperative, requiring human willing and working. The Westminster Confession of Faith (16.3) says,

> Their ability to do good works is not at all of themselves, but wholly from the Spirit of Christ. And that they may be enabled thereunto, besides the graces they have already received, there is required an actual influence of the same Holy Spirit, to work in them to will, and to do, of His good pleasure: yet are they not hereupon to grow negligent, as if they were not bound to perform any duty unless upon a special motion of the Spirit; but they ought to be diligent in stirring up the grace of God that is in them.[66]

Louis Berkhof said "that man must cooperate with the Spirit of God" in sanctification is plainly evident from "the repeated warnings against evils and temptations . . . [and] the constant exhortations to holy living" in the Bible. He added, "These imply that the believer must be diligent in the employment of the means at his command for the moral and spiritual improvement of his life."[67]

Perhaps the clearest statement of the cooperation of God and man in sanctification is Philippians 2:12–13: "Wherefore, my beloved, as ye have always obeyed, not as in my presence only, but now much more in my absence, work out your own salvation with fear and trembling. For it is God which worketh in you both to will and to do of his good pleasure."

65. See the discussion of the necessity of repentance in chap. 19.
66. *Reformed Confessions*, 4:252.
67. Berkhof, *Systematic Theology*, 534.

On the one hand, Paul commanded these children of God to "work" at their obedience and to do so with an awe-filled sense of the salvation and judgment to be revealed when all the world beholds Jesus Christ and confesses that he is Lord (Phil. 2:9–11). Paul said they must work out their salvation "now," indicating that sanctification is the daily duty of the believer. Peter O'Brien writes, "[This] is a demand to make that salvation fruitful in the here and now as the graces of Christ or the fruit of the Spirit (Gal. 5:22–23) are produced in their lives. It involves continually living in a manner worthy of the gospel of Christ (Phil. 1:27) or 'the continual translating into action of the principles of the gospel that they had believed.'"[68]

On the other hand, in Philippians 2:13 Paul assured his readers that God "worketh" in them. They acted by the invisible "supply of the Spirit of Jesus Christ" (1:19). All the "fruits of righteousness" that they bore came "by Jesus Christ" (v. 11). God's work rules over man's work, for God gives the believer "both to will and to do," both the heart and the hand of obedience. Paul did not say that God worked in them so that it was possible for them to work if they so willed, but that God worked both their willing and their working. Paul could address these people as those who "have always obeyed" because he knew that God had "begun a good work" in them and would carry that work on to its completion in glory (v. 6).

Murray explained the delicate balance of Philippians 2:12–13:

> God's working in us is not suspended because we work, nor our working suspended because God works. Neither is the relation strictly one of co-operation as if God did his part and we did ours so that the conjunction or coordination of both produced the required result. God works in us and we also work. But the relation is that *because* God works we work. All working out of salvation on our part is the effect of God's working in us . . . both the willing and the doing.[69]

Wilhelmus à Brakel noted that in both natural life and spiritual life, "man is the cause of his actions . . . albeit that in his being and motions he is dependent upon God." All the power and activity of spiritual life is from God, activated and energized by the "continual influence" of the Holy Spirit. Yet it is man who loves God, hates sin, and performs good works in obedience to God's law. Brakel said, "Man, being thus moved

68. Peter T. O'Brien, *The Epistle to the Philippians*, The New International Greek Testament Commentary (Grand Rapids, MI: Eerdmans, 1991), 279.
69. Murray, *Redemption Accomplished and Applied*, 148–49.

by the influence of God's Spirit, moves, sanctifies himself, engages in that activity which his new nature desires and is inclined toward, and does that which he knows to be his duty."[70]

Consequently, we may take great encouragement in our striving after holiness, for our work is evidence that God works in us. Murray wrote, "The more persistently active we are in working, the more persuaded we may be that all the energizing grace and power is of God."[71]

Sing to the Lord

A Prayer for Sanctifying Grace

Teach me, O Lord, Thy way of truth,
And from it I will not depart;
That I may steadfastly obey,
Give me an understanding heart.

In Thy commandments make me walk,
For in Thy law my joy shall be;
Give me a heart that loves Thy will,
From discontent and envy free.

Turn Thou my eyes from vanity,
And cause me in Thy ways to tread;
O let Thy servant prove Thy word
And thus to godly fear be led.

Turn Thou away reproach and fear;
Thy righteous judgments I confess;
To know Thy precepts I desire,
Revive me in Thy righteousness.

Psalm 119:33–40
Tune: Bishop
The Psalter, No. 325

Questions for Meditation or Discussion

1. What Hebrew and Greek words are used in the Bible for sanctification? What do they mean?

70. Brakel, *The Christian's Reasonable Service*, 3:5.
71. Murray, *Redemption Accomplished and Applied*, 149.

2. How does the Westminster Shorter Catechism define sanctification? Explain the significance of each part of the definition and offer some biblical support.
3. How is the necessity of sanctification grounded in both God's nature and human nature?
4. Someone says, "I don't see why we need a supernatural work of God to sanctify us. People should simply make better choices." How do you respond?
5. If God's children are already born again, then why do they need the grace of sanctification?
6. Why are good works a crucial part of the Christian life?
7. How is God the Father involved in sanctification?
8. What did Christ accomplish for our sanctification by his death and resurrection?
9. How does the Holy Spirit work our sanctification?
10. What does Philippians 2:12–13 teach about progressive sanctification?

Questions for Deeper Reflection

11. Explain how our sanctification takes the form of gratitude—that is, love for God that answers to his love for us. Give specific directions for how to stir up this gratitude into holy action.
12. Examine the passages of Scripture that pertain to "definitive sanctification" and make an argument for how definitive sanctification relates to effectual calling, regeneration, faith, and repentance.

28

Sanctification, Part 2

Theological Controversies

Though the doctrine of sanctification has not been the focal point of such intense controversy as the doctrine of justification, a number of erroneous ideas about it have challenged the church.[1] Misunderstanding the doctrine of sanctification has serious results for the Christian life, somewhat like the repercussions of a soldier not knowing how to use his armor and weapons.

A common error about sanctification is the idea that there are two levels of Christianity: ordinary Christians and an elite group of spiritual people. This distinction sometimes involves the teaching of Christian *perfection* as an attainable state in this life.

Several passages of Scripture warn against thinking that any mere man can attain sinless perfection in this life.[2] Paul implies as much when he says that he has not attained the goal but still presses on (Phil. 3:12–14). Someone might object that John writes, "Whosoever abideth in him sinneth not: whosoever sinneth hath not seen him, neither known him. . . . Whosoever is born of God doth not commit sin; for his seed remaineth in him: and he cannot sin, because he is born of God" (1 John 3:6, 9). However, John is not describing a perfection belonging to some children

1. Portions of this chapter are adapted from Joel R. Beeke and Michael P. V. Barrett, *A Radical, Comprehensive Call to Holiness* (Fearn, Ross-shire, Scotland: Christian Focus, 2020), 379–96. Used by permission.

2. 1 Kings 8:46; Prov. 20:9; Eccles. 7:20; James 3:2; 1 John 1:8, 10.

of God, but the state of all those "born of God." Louis Berkhof said, "He is contrasting two states . . . as to their essential nature and principle."[3] By using the Greek present tense, John indicates that regeneration breaks the continuous, habitual pattern of sin and replaces it with a prevailing, though imperfect, pattern of obedience.[4] He also warns, "If we say that we have no sin, we deceive ourselves, and the truth is not in us" (1:8).

Since God's Word clearly testifies of the continuing sinfulness of all men on earth, few people who affirm a doctrine of perfection would claim that absolute sinlessness is possible; rather, they teach a qualified perfection. In this chapter, we will examine and refute various claims to Christian perfection or a higher spiritual life.

Celibacy, Poverty, and Asceticism (Roman Catholicism)

The Roman Catholic Church teaches that the high road to holiness is that of virginity or celibacy—abstinence from sexual activity. Christ himself is said to be the "model" of celibacy, and "from the very beginning of the Church there have been men and women who have renounced the great good of marriage to follow the Lamb wherever he goes, to be intent on the things of the Lord, to seek to please him, and to go out to meet the Bridegroom who is coming."[5] Virginity for the kingdom is thus a "powerful sign" of God's grace and union with Christ.[6] Apart from Christ, Mary is the highest exemplar of this virtue, remaining a perpetual virgin and "full of grace" for the church, of which she is the spiritual mother by her faith and obedience.[7] Furthermore, "all the ordained ministers" (except permanent deacons) of the Roman Catholic Church are ordinarily required to be celibate, for they are "called to consecrate themselves with undivided heart to the Lord."[8] Though matrimony is one of the seven sacraments, it is "better and more blessed to remain in virginity, or in celibacy, than to be united in marriage."[9]

The self-denial of sexual intimacy in marriage is part of a larger pattern of severe treatment of the body that is believed necessary to master one-

3. Berkhof, *Systematic Theology*, 539.
4. Grudem, *Systematic Theology*, 751.
5. *Catechism of the Catholic Church*, sec. 1618. It uses the language of Matt. 25:6; 1 Cor. 7:32; and Rev. 14:4.
6. *Catechism of the Catholic Church*, sec. 1619.
7. *Catechism of the Catholic Church*, secs. 496, 499, 508–11.
8. *Catechism of the Catholic Church*, sec. 1579.
9. Council of Trent, session 24, canon 10, in *The Creeds of Christendom*, ed. Schaff, 2:197.

self, perform satisfactory penance for sins, and progress in holiness.[10] This practice is called "asceticism" (Latin *ascesis* or Greek *askēsis*, "exercise, training"). It involves denying oneself food, sleep, sexual intimacy, human companionship, material possessions, or other goods; afflicting one's body with painful blows; wearing uncomfortable sackcloth; or kneeling for long periods of time on a hard surface.

Asceticism developed as Christians responded to persecution of the church by the world and later to the worldliness of the church whose members chose to be culturally acceptable. The early church greatly admired the martyrs for their courageous suffering for Christ in the hope that earthly losses would be more than compensated by treasure in heaven. The church then extended the ideal of martyrdom to self-imposed sufferings for purification from sins and separation from the world. This ascetic impulse led to the monastic movement, an attempt to separate from society in order to pursue perfection, exemplified in its early days by Antony (c. 251–356) and Pachomius (c. 287–346), given a theological basis by John Cassian (c. 360–c. 433), and directed with community rules such as those of Basil the Great and Benedict of Nursia (c. 480–c. 543).[11]

Asceticism is essential to the Roman Catholic pursuit of holiness. According to the Roman Catholic Church, monks, nuns, and members of other special orders who take vows of "chastity, poverty and obedience," which require the practice of "mortification" of the flesh, are "following Christ with greater freedom and imitating Him more closely."[12] Theirs is "a special consecration" that by "renouncing the world they may live for God alone."[13] Pope John Paul II (1920–2005) regularly slept on a bare floor instead of his bed and whipped himself with a belt—and these practices, when revealed, were commended by Roman Catholics as acts of self-mortification.[14] The Roman Catholic Church calls all its members to practice some form of asceticism during Lent, when "the Church unites

10. *Catechism of the Catholic Church*, secs. 1460, 1734, 2015, 2339–40.

11. Owen Chadwick, introduction to *Western Asceticism*, trans. and ed. Owen Chadwick, Library of Christian Classics 12 (Philadelphia: Westminster, 1958), 18–30.

12. Pope Paul VI, *Perfectae Caritatis* (Perfect Love), secs. 1, 12, decree on October 28, 1965, of Vatican II, http://www.vatican.va/archive/hist_councils/ii_vatican_council/documents/vat-ii_decree_19651028_perfectae-caritatis_en.html. See *Catechism of the Catholic Church*, secs. 914–33.

13. Pope Paul VI, *Perfectae Caritatis*, secs. 5, 12.

14. Collin Hansen, "Why Pope John Paul II Whipped Himself," *Christianity Today*, February 8, 2010, http://www.christianitytoday.com/ct/2010/februaryweb-only/16-11.0.html.

herself each year to the mystery of Jesus in the desert."[15] Ascetic ideas and practices are also promoted in Eastern Orthodoxy.[16]

The Roman Catholic Church teaches that "the life consecrated to God" is characterized by following Christ's "evangelical counsels" of "celibacy for the sake of the kingdom, poverty, and obedience."[17] They are called evangelical counsels (*consilia evangelica*) because they are not precepts mandatory for everyone,[18] but are found in some of Christ's teachings in the Gospels (hence "evangelical"), such as where he speaks of becoming "perfect" in love (Matt. 5:48) or tells the rich young ruler, "If you would be perfect, go, sell what you possess and give to the poor, and you will have treasure in heaven; and come, follow me" (19:21 ESV). As Thomas Aquinas said, this perfection does not consist in loving God as much as we "possibly can," which is reserved for heaven, but in removing all mortal sin and other hindrances to love, which is possible in this life by following the evangelical counsels of Christ.[19]

In response, we note that the so-called evangelical counsels of Christ are calls to repentance. The rich young ruler came to Jesus Christ asking how to "have eternal life," not how to attain a higher level of consecration (Matt. 19:16). The word translated as "perfect" (*teleios*, v. 21) is best understood as "complete," the answer to the ruler's question, "What do I still lack?" (v. 20 ESV) in his quest for eternal life. "Perfect" may also have been somewhat ironic, since the man had just claimed that he had kept all of God's commandments (vv. 18–20). When Christ called him to give away his wealth, he did not teach poverty as a general principle of discipleship or a pathway to greater communion with God, but identified the false god that held that particular man back from following Christ and called him to renounce it in order to gain eternal life (v. 21). John Calvin commented that Christ spoke this way "to point out a particular disease, as if he were laying his finger on the sore."[20] One cannot worship money ("mammon") and God; repentance requires turning from one to the other (6:24). Hence,

15. *Catechism of the Catholic Church*, sec. 540; cf. 1438.

16. See Tito Colliander, *Way of the Ascetics: The Ancient Tradition of Discipline and Inner Growth*, trans. Katherine Ferré, intro. Kenneth Leech (Crestwood, NY: St. Vladimir's Seminary Press, 1985).

17. *Catechism of the Catholic Church*, sec. 915; cf. 944. See also *Code of Canon Law*, canons 573–606, http://www.vatican.va/archive/ENG1104/__P1Y.HTM.

18. Compare Tertullian's rendering of 1 Cor. 7:25: "I do not have a precept [*praeceptum*] of the Lord, but I offer advice [*consilium*]." Cited in Bavinck, *Reformed Dogmatics*, 4:239. Cf. Tertullian, *On Exhortation to Chastity*, chap. 4, in *ANF*, 4:52. See also 1 Cor. 7:25 Vulgate.

19. Aquinas, *Summa Theologica*, Part 2.2, Q. 184, Arts. 2–3.

20. Calvin, *Commentaries*, on Mark 10:21.

it is difficult for the rich to enter the kingdom of God (19:23–24), for their treasures capture their hearts (6:21). One sign that the rich have put their hope in God is that they are rich in giving money away (1 Tim. 6:17–19), and all the more if that is necessary to make restitution for ill-gotten gain (Luke 19:8–10). However, giving away one's possessions to the poor, even all one's possessions, is worth nothing unless it is done out of love (1 Cor. 13:3). Hence, Calvin commented, Paul "denies that man's perfection consists in renouncing all his goods."[21]

Christ's requirements to follow him are not optional counsels that lead to greater rewards, but the cost of ordinary discipleship. The Lord Jesus said, "He that loveth father or mother more than me is not worthy of me: and he that loveth son or daughter more than me is not worthy of me. And he that taketh not his cross, and followeth after me, is not worthy of me. He that findeth his life shall lose it: and he that loseth his life for my sake shall find it" (Matt. 10:37–39). Christ "demands everything," as Charles Hodge noted, even one's supreme love and total devotion.[22]

When our Lord commands his disciples, "Be ye therefore perfect, even as your Father which is in heaven is perfect" (Matt. 5:48), he is not offering a higher plane of sanctification to those already faithful and is not promising the attainability of perfection in this life. Rather, Christ is teaching all his disciples that they must strive to be like the Father in his perfect love.

Christ says that celibacy for the sake of the kingdom is an extraordinary gift given only to some, who are "eunuchs for the kingdom of heaven's sake" (Matt. 19:12). God's ordinary, creational pattern for sexual purity still holds: "For this cause shall a man leave father and mother, and shall cleave to his wife: and they twain shall be one flesh" (v. 5). Paul writes of celibacy as a "gift of God" and commends the unmarried state for those who would do ministry without the weighty responsibilities of family life (1 Cor. 7:7, 32–35), but he adds, "Nevertheless, to avoid fornication, let every man have his own wife, and let every woman have her own husband. . . . For it is better to marry than to burn" (vv. 2, 9). There is no biblical basis for thinking that celibacy is a higher pathway of holiness than married life or for restricting ministers of the Word from sexual activity in marriage. The apostle Peter was married (Mark 1:30), and he and other apostles brought their wives

21. Calvin, *Institutes*, 4.13.13.
22. Hodge, *Systematic Theology*, 3:236.

along with them (1 Cor. 9:5). To deny pastors the freedom to enjoy sexual intimacy with their wives is to open a door for strong sexual temptation (7:5).

As to self-denial and controlling the body, we agree that Christ commended fasting as a spiritual discipline while we wait and long for his return (Matt. 6:1–18; 9:15). We must not let our physical desires master us, but must bring them into subjection to God's will (1 Cor. 6:12). Calvin said that we must tame the body like a wild horse so that it is under our mastery.[23] This self-control is what Paul means when he says, "I keep under my body" (1 Cor. 9:27). The verb (*hypōpiazō*) means to give a black eye, but Paul is not speaking of literally bruising himself, for he is using the athletic metaphors of a runner and a boxer (vv. 24–26). "No boxer pummels himself with blows. . . . The expression is thus a figurative one."[24] Paul did not afflict his body to make satisfaction for his sins, for Christ's work of making atonement for sin was perfect and final.[25] Rather, Paul exercised self-discipline in order to accomplish his apostolic mission (v. 23) and to persevere in the Christian race until he reached immortal glory (vv. 24–25).

Self-denial is essential to Christian discipleship (Luke 9:23). However, this does not justify the ascetic abuse of the body or mandatory abstinence from the common pleasures of God's creation. Though the Old Testament records a number of instances when people wore uncomfortable "sackcloth," this was a temporary expression of grief common in the ancient Near East, not an ordinary means of sanctification.[26] The Spirit of God warned the apostolic church that false teachers would forbid people to marry and to eat certain foods, but the truth is that God's creations are all good and can be received in holiness if used with prayer, thanksgiving, and obedience to God's Word (1 Tim. 4:1–5). The body itself is God's good creation, and a Christian's body is united to Christ and destined to share in his resurrection (1 Cor. 6:13–15). If God blesses us with wealth, then we must be "rich in good works," but we may legitimately enjoy God's material blessings, for God "giveth us richly

23. Calvin, *Commentaries*, on 1 Cor. 9:27.

24. *TDNT*, 8:591.

25. On the finality of Christ's sacrifice, see *RST*, 2:1063–66.

26. Gen. 37:34; 2 Sam. 3:31; 1 Kings 20:31–32; 21:27; 2 Kings 6:30; 19:1–2; 1 Chron. 21:16; Neh. 9:1; Est. 4:1–4; Job 16:15; Pss. 30:11; 35:13; 69:11; Isa. 3:24; 15:3; 20:2; 22:12; 37:1–2; 50:3; 58:5; Jer. 4:8; 6:26; 48:37; 49:3; Lam. 2:10; Ezek. 7:18; 27:31; Dan. 9:3; Joel 1:8, 13; Amos 8:10; Jonah 3:5–6, 8; Matt. 11:21; Luke 10:13; Rev. 6:12; 11:3.

all things to enjoy" (1 Tim. 6:17–18). Paul warns that asceticism may appear godly, but in fact it has no power to overcome inward sin; we conquer sin only by living in communion with Christ by faith in his death and resurrection (Col. 2:18, 23; 3:1). Therefore, we reject asceticism as a pathway to holiness.

Christian Perfectionism (Wesleyan Methodism)

The Reformers asserted the necessity of self-denial[27] but rejected monasticism as a false path to perfection.[28] Early Reformed theologians strongly advocated against any claim to perfection short of glorification.[29] However, the doctrine of perfection, in one sense or another, has persisted in various quarters of Protestantism, especially those influenced by Arminianism. In 1605, Jacob Arminius said that no man can keep the law perfectly according to the full rigor of its demands, but Christians can attain perfection according to the standard of God's "clemency" (*epieikeia*) insofar as they are empowered by Christ's grace.[30] The theological successor of Arminius, Simon Episcopius (1583–1643), taught that it is possible for men, when "assisted by divine grace," to love God with perfect wholeness of heart as measured "according to the covenant of grace."[31] Therefore, according to some Arminian theologians, evangelical perfection involves the fulfillment of an adjusted covenantal standard, a law modified by the gospel.

John Wesley taught that Christians could attain "perfection," though he did not refer to freedom from ignorance, intellectual mistakes, or weakness of mind.[32] He spoke of a perfection consisting in a freedom from

---

27. Calvin, *Institutes*, 3.7.1–3.

28. Luther, *The Judgment of Martin Luther on Monastic Vows*, in *LW*, 44:243–400; and Calvin, *Institutes*, 4.13.10–21; cf. the Augsburg Confession (16.4, 27.44–62), in *The Book of Concord*, 48, 88–90; and the Westminster Confession of Faith (22.7), in *Reformed Confessions*, 4:261.

29. Ames, *The Marrow of Theology*, 1.29.29 (170); Wollebius, *Compendium*, 1.31.xii (173); and Turretin, *Institutes*, 17.2 (2:693–702).

30. Arminius, *Nine Questions*, No. 9, in *Works*, 2:68. Francis Turretin also acknowledged an "evangelical perfection, which is with the covering of grace and with paternal forbearance (*epieikeia*) when all things are counted as done, when what is not done is pardoned (viz., covered by the righteousness of Christ, in whom we are said to be perfect, Col. 2:10)." Turretin, *Institutes*, 17.2.4 (2:694). However, Arminius did not mention the imputed righteousness of Christ (he considered the act of faith to be the Christian's righteousness; see chap. 24), but spoke of perfection only in terms of the "evangelical covenant" and "proportionate" power given to believers to keep its demands.

31. Cited in George Peck, *The Scripture Doctrine of Christian Perfection Stated and Defended: With a Critical and Historical Examination of the Controversy, Ancient and Modern*, 3rd ed. (New York: Lane & Scott, 1848), 134.

32. John Wesley, *Christian Perfection*, I.1–9, in *Sermons*, 70–73.

voluntary violations of God's laws, "loving God with all the heart, so that every evil temper is destroyed and every thought and word and work springs from and is conducted to that end by the pure love of God and our neighbor."[33] Wesley denied that "all Christians do, and must commit sin, as long as they live."[34]

Some theologians in the Wesleyan Methodist tradition qualify perfection as less than sinless fulfillment of the full extent of God's law while retaining the idea of "entire sanctification" consisting in perfect love and an end of the inner battle against indwelling sin.[35] Thomas Oden called this condition "sustained radical responsiveness to grace"[36] and marshalled the following arguments to support it. First, God would not command holiness, perfection, and blamelessness in this life if it were impossible (Gen. 17:1; Matt. 5:48). Second, God would not promise full salvation and holiness without blemish if it were not possible (Ps. 119:1–3; 1 Thess. 5:23–24; 1 John 1:7, 9). Third, Scripture provides examples of complete consecration in Enoch, Noah, Job, Barnabas, and others.[37]

In response, we argue, first, it is a Pelagian argument to say that God's commands imply our spiritual ability, for it suggests that all mankind is capable of sinless obedience to God, a claim contradicted by Scripture (Rom. 3:9–18; 8:6–8).[38] Second, God promises full salvation from the presence of sin only in the life to come (Heb. 12:23; 1 John 3:2–3). In this present life, he promises believers deliverance from the enslaving power of sin (Rom. 6:14). However, believers must continue to confess their sins and pray for forgiveness (1 John 1:9), lean on Christ's death and intercession when they do sin (2:1–2), and pursue holiness (Heb. 12:14). Third, when the Bible refers to saints on earth as "perfect" (Hebrew *tamim*, Greek *teleios*), it refers to their life of holistic godliness, not to perfection of moral life and freedom from all known sins (Gen. 6:9; 1 Cor. 14:20; Phil. 3:15).[39] Noah got drunk on one occasion (Gen. 9:21). The Lord rebuked Job for contending against his ways, and Job repented (Job 40:1–5; 42:1–6). Paul confronted the

33. Quoted in Oden, *John Wesley's Scriptural Christianity*, 323.
34. Wesley, *Christian Perfection*, II.7, in *Sermons*, 75.
35. Hoekema, *Saved by Grace*, 215–16.
36. Thomas C. Oden, *Systematic Theology*, 3 vols. (Peabody, MA: Prince, 1992), 3:232.
37. Oden, *Systematic Theology*, 3:242–43.
38. See the second objection against effectual grace in chap. 16.
39. Erickson, *Christian Theology*, 901–2.

apostle Peter for being at fault when he allowed himself to be influenced by Jewish legalists and withdrew from eating with Gentiles (Gal. 2:11–16).

Therefore, we reject perfectionism, and we warn our fellow believers against the spiritual elitism that such teaching promotes. Biblical realism demands that we face the ugliness of our remaining sin. However, we must also reject a lazy compromise with sin. We must set our sights on the ideal of perfect obedience. Let us pursue holiness with all our might. Our prayer must be, "Search me, O God, and know my heart: try me, and know my thoughts: and see if there be any wicked way in me, and lead me in the way everlasting" (Ps. 139:23–24).

Modern Second-Blessing Theology

Wesley's doctrine of Christian perfection morphed into a number of forms in the nineteenth century.[40] While there is diversity among them, they shared the common idea that Christians must seek a further blessing after conversion that elevates them to a higher level of spirituality.

The Holiness Movement

Methodist writer Phoebe Palmer (1807–1874) and Oberlin College professors Charles Finney and Asa Mahan (1800–1889) promoted what came to be known as the Holiness Movement. These teachers linked the doctrine of perfection with a crisis experience of second blessing, which they called the baptism of the Holy Spirit, for victorious power in sanctification and ministry.[41] This doctrine gained an even wider following through the ministries of Adoniram J. Gordon (1836–1895), Dwight L. Moody (1839–1899), A. B. Simpson (1843–1919), and R. A. Torrey (1856–1928).[42]

Finney appears to have been one of the earliest to teach such a doctrine. He wrote in 1839 that believers must yield themselves to the Holy Spirit and thus receive him by faith after their conversion.[43] The promise in the new covenant of the sanctifying Holy Spirit was fulfilled at Pentecost, but

40. For a comprehensive study of nineteenth-century movements of this kind, see Benjamin B. Warfield, *Perfectionism*, 2 vols. (New York: Oxford University Press, 1931).

41. Richard Gilbertson, *The Baptism of the Holy Spirit: The Views of A. B. Simpson and His Contemporaries* (Camp Hill, PA: Christian Publications, 1993), 146–57.

42. Gilbertson, *The Baptism of the Holy Spirit*, 55, 62, 157–59, 167–76.

43. Charles G. Finney, "Lecture XIV: The Holy Spirit of Promise," *The Oberlin Evangelist* 1, no. 18 (August 14, 1839): 138 (full article, 137–38).

Christians must individually appropriate it by faith.[44] The promise of God writing his law on the heart (Jer. 31:33) is said to be nothing less than a promise of entire sanctification in this life.[45] Finney used the language of Spirit baptism to describe an overpowering experience of God that he reportedly felt shortly after his conversion in 1821, an experience that caused him and another man to bellow and laugh uncontrollably.[46] Finney later wrote, "I shall use . . . entire sanctification to designate a state of confirmed and entire consecration of body, soul and spirit or of the whole being to God . . . not in the sense that a soul entirely sanctified cannot sin, but that as a matter of fact, he does not and will not sin."[47]

Palmer wrote, "Jesus, your Redeemer, your Saviour, waits even now to sanctify you wholly; and I pray God that your whole spirit, and soul, and body be preserved blameless unto the coming of our Lord Jesus Christ."[48] Her words allude to 1 Thessalonians 5:23–24, a key text used in the Holiness Movement.[49]

The Higher Life Movement

Another form of Christian perfectionism, known as the Higher Life Movement, arose from the teachings of W. E. Boardman (1810–1886) and Hannah Whitall Smith (1832–1911) with her husband, Robert Pearsall Smith (1827–1898), both of whom had roots in the Quaker movement. They emphasized that entire sanctification is received by faith in Christ alone. This view of sanctification was summarized in the declaration by the Friends (Quakers) Conference at Richmond, Indiana, in 1887:

> Whosoever submits himself wholly to God, believing and appropriating His promises, and exercising faith in Christ Jesus, will have his heart continually cleansed from all sin, by His precious blood, and, through the renewing, refining power of the Holy Spirit, be kept in

44. Charles G. Finney, "Lecture XV: The Covenants," *The Oberlin Evangelist* 1, no. 19 (August 28, 1839): 146 (full article, 145–47).

45. Charles G. Finney, *Lectures on Systematic Theology: Embracing Ability, (Natural, Moral, and Gracious,) Repentance, Impenitence, Faith and Unbelief, Justification, Sanctification, Election, Reprobation, Divine Purposes, Divine Sovereignty, and Perseverance* (Oberlin, OH: James M. Fitch, 1847), 216.

46. Charles G. Finney, *An Autobiography* (1876; repr., Westwood, NJ: Fleming H. Revell, 1908), 20–21.

47. Finney, *Lectures on Systematic Theology, Embracing Ability . . . Perseverance*, 201.

48. Phoebe Palmer, *The Way of Holiness* (New York: Piercy and Reed, 1843), 40.

49. See also Palmer, *The Way of Holiness*, 47; and Finney, *Lectures on Systematic Theology, Embracing Ability . . . Perseverance*, 219–20.

> conformity to the will of God, will love Him with all his heart, mind, soul and strength. . . . Thus, in its full experience, sanctification is deliverance from the pollution, nature, and love of sin [citing Luke 1:74–75; Rom. 8:2; 1 Thess. 5:23–24].[50]

Boardman taught "a second experience," "a second conversion," and "a deeper work of grace" than one's initial regeneration.[51] The first and second experiences, Boardman said, reflect the two distinct blessings of justification and sanctification. Just as we receive Christ for justification, so justified believers must also receive Christ for sanctification.[52] Renouncing all of our resolutions and struggles for holiness, we are told to place our souls in the hands of Christ, and with that, "a new and higher level has been reached," the "starting point" for the true Christian race.[53] Boardman said that "there are Christians of two classes in the world," some truly converted but not delivered from the bondage of sin described in Romans 7, and others who have left behind Romans 7 and found the freedom of Romans 8 by receiving the Spirit of adoption.[54]

In the Higher Life view, sanctification is not a hard battle involving human striving and effort, but an experience of constant victory by faith. Robert Smith wrote, "I must freely own that this is my continuous experience. Day by day, as I walk in this way of faith and holiness, wonder and praise fill my heart for heavenly communion, inward purity, victory over the world, abounding peace, and the known presence of Jesus in my soul."[55] He claimed that temptations no longer rose up from within his heart, but only from Satan outside, and that as a Christian he now had power to quench all of Satan's fiery darts.[56] Hannah Smith said, "Man's part is to trust, and God's part is to work."[57] She said that "surrender and trust . . . is positively all the man can do," for all good works are "not

50. *A Declaration of Some of the Fundamental Principles of Christian Truth, as Held by the Religious Society of Friends; Adopted by Friends' Conference Held in Richmond, Indiana, U.S.A.* (Richmond, IN: Nicholson & Bro., 1887), 11. This declaration summarized the views of only some of the Friends at that time.

51. W. E. Boardman, *The Higher Christian Life* (Boston: Henry Hoyt, 1858), 47–48.

52. Boardman, *The Higher Christian Life*, 51–52.

53. Boardman, *The Higher Christian Life*, 59–60.

54. Boardman, *The Higher Christian Life*, 265–68.

55. Robert Pearsall Smith, *Holiness through Faith*, rev. ed. (New York: Anson D. F. Randolph & Co., 1870), 21.

56. Smith, *Holiness through Faith*, 26–27.

57. Hannah Whitall Smith, *The Christian's Secret to a Happy Life*, rev. ed. (Chicago: F. H. Revell, 1883), 24.

by us, but by Him. . . . We do not do anything, but He does it."[58] Sadly, the Smiths did not end their race well; both Robert and Hannah fell away from the faith.[59]

The Early Keswick Movement

Despite the tragic apostasy of the Smiths, the Higher Life Movement found a rallying point for sympathizers from many Christian denominations at the Keswick Convention in England, which the Smiths had helped to start in 1875.[60] The purpose of the annual conference, which continues today, has been to call Christians to a higher level of consecration by receiving the sanctifying work of the Holy Spirit, and then to launch them into service and missions.

Many prominent evangelicals of a century ago were connected with the Keswick Convention. These included H. C. G. Moule (1841–1920), F. B. Meyer (1847–1929), Andrew Murray (1828–1917), James Hudson Taylor (1832–1905), Frances Ridley Havergal (1836–1879), and Amy Carmichael (1867–1951).[61]

Charles Trumbull (1872–1941) summarized the classic Keswick view: "What are the conditions of this Victorious Life? Only two, and they are very simple. Surrender and faith. 'Let go, and let God.'"[62] Over the course of the twentieth century, the teachings presented at the Keswick Convention have shifted toward a more biblical view of sanctification.[63]

Classic Dispensationalism

Lewis Sperry Chafer, prominent early teacher of dispensationalism, taught that mankind consists of three groups: natural men, carnal Christians, and

58. Smith, *The Christian's Secret to a Happy Life*, 25–26.

59. Robert Smith was removed from public ministry in 1875, repeatedly committed adultery, and became an agnostic. Hannah was strongly feminist and independent from her husband, rejected orthodox Christianity, rejoined the Quakers, and embraced universal salvation. Andrew David Naselli, *Let Go and Let God? A Survey and Analysis of Keswick Theology* (Bellingham, WA: Lexham Press, 2010), 111–15.

60. "Keswick" is pronounced Keh-zick.

61. Andrew David Naselli, "Keswick Theology: A Survey and Analysis of the Doctrine of Sanctification in the Early Keswick Movement," *Detroit Baptist Seminary Journal* 13 (2008): 24–25 (full article, 17–67).

62. Cited in Naselli, "Keswick Theology," 32.

63. See Steven Barabas, *So Great Salvation: The History and Message of the Keswick Conference* (Chicago: Fleming H. Revell, 1952); and John C. Pollock and Ian Randall, *The Keswick Story: The Authorized Version of the Keswick Convention*, new ed. (Fort Washington, PA: CLC Publications, 2006). One factor in this return to a more biblical doctrine was the lectures of John Stott on Romans 5–8 at the 1965 Keswick Convention, published as John R. W. Stott, *Men Made New: An Exposition of Romans 5–8* (Downers Grove, IL: InterVarsity Press, 1966).

spiritual Christians (citing 1 Cor. 2:14–3:1).[64] The carnal Christian, Chafer said, lives "on the same plane" as the unsaved, though he is born again by the Holy Spirit.[65] Chafer differed from many of those whom we have surveyed thus far in that he said all Christians are baptized by the Holy Spirit, and he rejected terms such as "second blessing" and "higher life."[66] However, Chafer still taught a sharp distinction between carnal Christians and those filled with the Spirit. Only in the latter does the Spirit produce the fruit of Christian character, power for Christian service, illumination for Christian knowledge, and other blessings.[67] This doctrine corresponds to the teaching we observed earlier from some dispensational theologians that turning from sin to God is not necessary for salvation.[68] In order to become filled with the Spirit and remain so, Chafer taught, the Christian must confess all known sins for cleansing by the blood of Christ (1 John 1:9), yield his will and dedicate his entire life to God (Rom. 6:13; 12:1), and rely upon the power of the Holy Spirit.[69]

In Chafer's view, holiness is not obtained by "human resolution or struggle"; the only fight in which the believer must engage is the fight to "maintain an attitude of dependence on Him to do what He alone can do."[70] In fact, even the love of Christians is really not their own human activity created by grace, but instead God's love "passing through the heart of the believer out from the indwelling Spirit," as if Christians are passive conduits instead of people changed by God.[71] Since the life of holiness consists of God working instead of us working, the spiritual life is repeatedly called "superhuman"—a failure to recognize that restoration of the image of God in Christ is a return to true humanity.[72]

Broader Evangelicalism and Pentecostalism

Though we have highlighted specific movements, second-blessing theology has become very influential among evangelicals. A widely distributed

64. Lewis Sperry Chafer, *He That Is Spiritual*, rev. ed. (Philadelphia: Sunday School Times Co., 1919), 3–14. On Chafer and the teachings of dispensationalism regarding God's covenants, see *RST*, 2:554–58.

65. Chafer, *He That Is Spiritual*, 12–13.

66. Chafer, *He That Is Spiritual*, 35–37, 41. Chafer's refusal to use "baptism" for entrance into the higher life could reflect an attempt to distance himself from Pentecostalism, which he abhorred as satanic (58–59).

67. Chafer, *He That Is Spiritual*, 39, 45, 55, 60–61.

68. See chap. 19 on repentance.

69. Chafer, *He That Is Spiritual*, 82–85, 105–8, 119. On false claims about the aorist tense of the word translated as "yield" and "present" in Rom. 6:13 and 12:1, see footnote 16 in chap. 29.

70. Chafer, *He That Is Spiritual*, 121.

71. Chafer, *He That Is Spiritual*, 50–51.

72. Chafer, *He That Is Spiritual*, 65, 74, 125.

booklet written by Bill Bright (1921–2003) depicts the carnal Christian with self on the throne and "Christ dethroned and not allowed to direct the life," until the Christian desires the Spirit's help, confesses his sins, presents his whole life to God, and claims the filling of the Spirit by faith.[73]

In some respects, Pentecostalism is a further development of two-level Christianity, with its own version of the higher life by receiving the baptism of the Holy Spirit and speaking in tongues.[74] John Robertson McQuilkin (1927–2016) said that "glossolalia [tongues] aside . . . the position [on sanctification] of Assemblies of God spokesman Stanley Horton and much of the contemporary charismatic movement is not that far distant from the Keswick approach."[75]

Exegetical Response to the Carnal Christian Doctrine

A crucial issue in the controversy over second-blessing theology is the identity of the person described in Romans 7:14–25, which begins, "For we know that the law is spiritual, but I am of the flesh, sold under sin. For I do not understand my own actions. For I do not do what I want, but I do the very thing I hate" (vv. 14–15 ESV). Given Paul's expression of spiritual frustration here, some theologians understand the passage to be inconsistent with the freedom ascribed to those in Christ in Romans 8. To be "sold under sin" is the language of spiritual slavery (1 Kings 21:20, 25) or being given into the power of one's enemy (Deut. 32:30; Judg. 2:14). Therefore, Romans 7:14–25 is interpreted to refer either to an unbeliever (in continuity with vv. 7–13) or to a believer in a different spiritual state from that described in Romans 8—that is, a carnal Christian who lives in a state of spiritual defeat.

In response, we argue that it is best to interpret Romans 7:14–25 as describing a believer in Christ who is in the same spiritual state as that described in Romans 8. There are several reasons for this argument.

First, *Paul describes his present experience as a believer in Christ.* In Romans 7:14, Paul shifts from tenses associated with past events (mostly aorist, with pluperfect, perfect, and imperfect) to the present tense: "I am,"

73. Bill Bright, *Have You Made the Wonderful Discovery of the Spirit-Filled Life?* (Peachtree City, GA: Cru, 2018), 3, 10–11, available at https://crustore.org/media/Spirit-Filled-Life_English_.pdf.

74. "Baptism in the Holy Spirit has been the gateway into a new dimension of the Holy Spirit's presence and power." Williams, *Renewal Theology*, 2:200. On the claims of Pentecostalism and a biblical critique, see chap. 5.

75. J. Robertson McQuilkin, "Response to Horton," in Melvin Dieter et al., *Five Views on Sanctification*, Counterpoints (Grand Rapids, MI: Zondervan, 1987), 145.

"I do," and so on.[76] He presents himself as a man who trusts in Christ for salvation, saying, "Who shall deliver me from the body of this death? I thank God through Jesus Christ our Lord" (vv. 24–25).

Second, *to be "carnal" or fleshly (Rom. 7:14) is not the same as being "in the flesh" and thus lacking the Spirit* (8:9). Carnal need not mean unregenerate, but only fleshly in some respects, for Paul calls Christians "carnal" (1 Cor. 3:1, 3, 4).[77] As to being "sold under sin" (Rom. 7:14), while it does refer to a condition from which Paul cannot free himself (v. 23), it cannot be compared to Ahab's selling of himself to do evil (1 Kings 21:20, 25). Ahab willingly gave himself over to the sins that he loved, but the man in Romans 7:14–25 "is subjected to a power that is alien to his own will," as John Murray wrote.[78]

This man loves God's law and serves it willingly. In Romans 7:7–13, the law only provokes more evil desires, but in verses 14–25, Paul speaks of his holy desires that agree with and delight in the law as good (vv. 16, 19, 22). His inner man is no longer a willing slave of sin, but "I myself serve the law of God" (v. 25). This accords with the doctrine that converted people in union with Christ are "servants of righteousness" (6:17–18). Paul distinguishes between himself and the "sin that dwelleth in me" (7:17), the latter of which wages war against his "inward man" or "mind," which loves God's law (vv. 22–23). James Fraser of Alness (1700–1769) observed, "The prevailing habitual inclination and determination of his will was towards good."[79] If Romans 7:14–25 described an unconverted person, it would teach that a person can have a will characteristically inclined toward obeying God's law without being regenerated by the Holy Spirit. In sharp contrast, Paul teaches that the mindset of the flesh is "enmity against God: for it is not subject to the law of God, neither indeed can be" (8:7). This is the mindset of a person who does not have the Spirit of God dwelling in him (v. 9).[80]

Third, *inward conflict of holy desires and sinful desires is characteristic of true Christians*. Paul's description in Romans 7:14–25 finds a counterpart

76. Hendriksen, *Exposition of Paul's Epistle to the Romans*, 1:228.

77. James Fraser, *A Treatise on Sanctification: An Explication of Romans Chapters 6, 7, and 8:1–4*, rev. ed. (1897; repr., Audubon, NJ: Old Paths, 1992), 270–71. In the case of the Corinthians, Paul's calling them "carnal" is somewhat akin to telling a fifteen-year-old that he is acting like a two-year-old, not because he is no longer potty-trained or thinks and acts in every respect like a toddler, but because some of his attitudes and actions are immature.

78. Murray, *The Epistle to the Romans*, 1:261.

79. Fraser, *A Treatise on Sanctification*, 277.

80. Hendriksen, *Exposition of Paul's Epistle to the Romans*, 1:226; and Murray, *The Epistle to the Romans*, 1:258.

in Galatians 5:17: "For the flesh lusteth against the Spirit, and the Spirit against the flesh: and these are contrary the one to the other: so that ye cannot do the things that ye would." The latter text clearly describes a Christian who has the Holy Spirit but who must engage in inward wrestling against remaining sin. James says that believers experience an inner dynamic when tempted because temptation resonates with sinful desires that still reside in them: "Every man is tempted, when he is drawn away of his own lust, and enticed" (James 1:14). Peter writes, "Dearly beloved, I beseech you as strangers and pilgrims, abstain from fleshly lusts, which war against the soul" (1 Pet. 2:11).

The Westminster Confession of Faith (13.2) states, "This sanctification is throughout, in the whole man; yet imperfect in this life, there abiding still some remnants of corruption in every part; whence ariseth a continual and irreconcilable war, the flesh lusting against the Spirit, and the Spirit against the flesh."[81]

Fourth, Romans 7–8 evidences *no transition from defeat to victory*. Such a transition cannot be read into Paul's exclamation in Romans 7:25, "I thank God through Jesus Christ our Lord," because he does not follow it with a description of newly found victory, but with a restatement of the same condition of inward conflict: "So then with the mind I myself serve the law of God; but with the flesh the law of sin." His exclamation does not take him out of the state described in Romans 7, but shows that the Christian overcomes sin by faith in Christ while remaining in a state of inward conflict and frustration.

The experience of Romans 7:14–25 is summed up in the phrase "the body of this death," from which Paul longs for deliverance (v. 24). Here, "death" (*thanatos*) encompasses both physical mortality and the inward corruption of sin (8:6, 38)—"the law of sin which is in my members" (7:23). Paul uses very similar language in the surrounding chapters for the condition of believers: he speaks of the "mortal" (*thnētos*) body (6:12; 8:11) and says that "the body is dead [*nekros*] because of sin" (8:10). Therefore, the description of the Christian in Romans 8 is fundamentally the same as that in Romans 7—namely, enduring the inward corruption of sin in this present life of mortality.[82] The ultimate solution to indwelling sin

81. *Reformed Confessions*, 4:249.

82. The idea of the body of death should be distinguished from the "body of sin" (Rom. 6:6; cf. Col. 2:11), which refers to the controlling power of sin over a man's life. Murray, *The Epistle to the Romans*, 1:220–21. Note that Paul said that for the man in union with Christ, "the body of

will be granted when the Holy Spirit raises the believer from death to glorious life at the resurrection (8:11). The Spirit already leads him forward to conquer indwelling sin, not by translating him into a new spiritual state of ease, but by leading him in a battle to the death against "the deeds of the body" (v. 13). The influences of the Spirit do not release us from the painful struggles of Romans 7; rather, the Spirit causes us to "groan within ourselves, waiting for . . . the redemption of our body" (v. 23).

Fifth, Paul's frustration reflects *holy ambition for perfect love, not total failure to obey*. Paul writes with experiential intensity of his frustration with indwelling sin, but his statements should not be taken as absolute and all-encompassing. Though he says, "For the good that I would I do not: but the evil which I would not, that I do" (Rom. 7:19), this should not be understood as a complete lack of doing good or a total abandonment to commit sin. Those who live in unrepented sin are on the pathway to wrath and eternal death, not to life (2:5; 6:21–23; 8:13). Rather, Paul's delight in and inward subjection to the law (7:22, 25) as the holy, just, and good word of the Spirit (vv. 12, 14) imply that "the good that I would" is entire and perfect obedience, which he longs to give to God but is not able. This is not a condition of immaturity but the tension found in the highest levels of godliness. Murray wrote, "The more sanctified he becomes the more painful to him must be the presence in himself of that which contradicts the perfect standard of holiness."[83]

When Paul says, "For the good that I would I do not: but the evil which I would not, that I do" (Rom. 7:19), he does not imply that he continually engaged in sinful behaviors and never did good deeds. He speaks of the law here not in terms of external behavior, but as "spiritual" (v. 14)—that is, from the Holy Spirit and addressing matters of the human spirit.[84] In the larger context, Paul highlights a commandment that regulates inward desires—"Thou shalt not covet"—and complains of "concupiscence" or evil desire (vv. 7–8). Paul well understands that the soul of the law is the inner quality of love (13:10). Therefore, he describes his frustrated desire to live in perfect love and cast out all sinful lust. Fraser said, "He willed that the love of God should fill his heart, and prevail in it to the most intense degree; that his heart should be wholly

sin" is destroyed by Christ's crucifixion, but he still lives in his "mortal body" in which remaining sin still works and must be resisted (Rom. 6:6, 12).

83. Murray, *The Epistle to the Romans*, 1:258.

84. See Rom. 1:11; 15:27; 1 Cor. 2:13, 15; 9:11; cf. John 4:24.

spiritual and heavenly, in all its thoughts and affections . . . that vain thoughts, sin and sinful imperfections should never hold him short of such perfect attainment in his duty."[85]

Sixth, the contrast between Romans 7:14–25 and Romans 8 is between *the law's weakness and the Spirit's power, not two states* (carnal and spiritual). Even for the regenerate believer, the law does not supply the power needed to conquer sin, but only directs the believer to what is good, holy, and righteous. Therefore, the law can neither justify nor sanctify us. Rather, Paul teaches that Christians put sin to death and obey God's law only by the empowerment of the Holy Spirit received through Jesus Christ.

However, Paul does not know of a category of Christians who are not empowered by the Spirit: "For as many as are led by the Spirit of God, they are the sons of God" (Rom. 8:14). The only two states that he mentions are those of walking after the flesh and of belonging to Christ and having the Holy Spirit (vv. 4–9). Only those who walk in the pathway of suffering obedience and self-denial will enter eternal life and the glory of Christ (vv. 13, 17).

Therefore, we conclude that there is no special category of believers united to Christ who remain in a state of powerlessness, defeat, and enslavement to sin. Christians who feel discouraged or defeated do not need to be translated into a new state, but need to renew their faith in the finished work of Christ, repent of their sins, and press on in the battle. At the same time, there is also no category of believers on earth who have risen above the daily battle against indwelling sin. All members of the church militant must endure the frustration and struggle of Romans 7:14–25, and all may enjoy the hope and comfort of Romans 8.

Before we proceed to the next point, we must pause to warn of the great danger of considering yourself a Christian if you are not walking in obedience to God. John says, "Hereby we do know that we know him, if we keep his commandments. He that saith, I know him, and keepeth not his commandments, is a liar, and the truth is not in him" (1 John 2:3–4). John Owen wrote, "He will lead none to heaven but whom he sanctifies on the earth. The holy God will not receive unholy persons; this living head will not admit of dead members, nor bring men into the possession of a glory which they neither love nor like."[86]

85. Fraser, *A Treatise on Sanctification*, 278.
86. Owen, *An Exposition of the Epistle to the Hebrews*, 3:417.

Theological Response to Second-Blessing Christianity

We may summarize the teachings of two-level Christianity in the following principles. First, regeneration is insufficient to initiate the process of sanctification. Second, sanctification is separable from justification and sometimes begins later. Third, regenerate and justified believers can live defeated under the power of sin. Fourth, victory is found in a second blessing, typically described as a new experience of the Holy Spirit. Fifth, holiness is not attained by effort but in surrender and faith: "Let go and let God." Sixth, the higher life is superhuman in its divine quality.

In our response to second-blessing theology, we will address each of these teachings with points of our own.

First, *the new birth produces a new life*. One of the concerns driving many advocates of these views is the dismal conduct of many professing Christians. With this concern we greatly sympathize. Their solution, however, is unbiblical, for it denies that the new birth truly produces righteous conduct, turning from sin, Christlike love, and victory over the world (1 John 2:29; 3:9; 4:7; 5:4). The new birth is a supernatural, miraculous act of God, like raising the dead to life. We deny the biblical doctrine of regeneration and dishonor its divine author when we say that it fails to produce fruit.[87] We must never say that saving grace permits sin to reign so that a person may be saved without Christ seated, so to speak, on the throne of his life. William Hendriksen said, "Grace dethrones sin. It destroys sin's lordship."[88]

Second, *all in Christ are justified and sanctified*. Sanctification is distinct from justification, but it is never separated from justification, for the justified person is united to Christ by a Spirit-worked faith. If we break this connection, we open ourselves to the charge that justification by faith alone promotes sin. On the contrary, no one may rightly say that we can sin all the more so that justifying grace may abound, for believers have died with Christ to sin and risen with him to live unto God (Rom. 6:1–14; Gal. 2:16–20).

Third, *no one in Christ is a slave of sin*. While it may be true that some *professing* believers live under the power of sin, there is no biblical basis to say that true believers, those who are regenerate and justified, live under the power of sin. Paul's words in Romans 6 do not address an elite group

87. On the effective power of the new birth, see chaps. 17–18.
88. Hendriksen, *Exposition of Paul's Epistle to the Romans*, 1:203.

in the church, but all those effectually called to belong to Jesus Christ as his holy people (Rom. 1:6–7). Paul does not command them to die to sin by appropriating Christ's death, but to count themselves as already dead to sin because of the crucifixion of Christ (6:2, 6, 11).[89] He does not call them to come out of the dominion of sin, but promises that sin will not reign over them (v. 14), for they are no longer slaves of sin, but of righteousness (vv. 17–18). Those who belong to Christ have crucified the flesh with its evil desires (Gal. 5:24). By contrast, those ruled by sin do not belong to Christ. Those whose lives are characterized by unrepented sin are not on the road to heaven, and the only alternative is the wrath of God (1 Cor. 6:9–10; Gal. 5:19–21; Eph. 5:5–6). Murray commented on Romans 6:1–2, "This is the identity of the believer—he died to sin . . . a definitive act in the past. . . . A believer cannot therefore live in sin; if a man lives in sin he is not a believer."[90]

Fourth, *Christians do not need a "second blessing."* The Holy Scriptures do not teach the necessity of a second blessing distinct from conversion. Instead, they teach the necessity of a steady walk with God with new blessings of grace each day. The baptism of the Holy Spirit is already granted to all believers in Christ (1 Cor. 12:13).[91] It is the duty of all Christians to be "filled with the Spirit" (Eph. 5:18), but, like being filled with God's Word (Col. 3:16), this is not an entrance into another spiritual state, but a dynamic pattern of growth in grace in which we are more and more filled as we become more holy.

What about Paul's prayer for the entire sanctification of the Thessalonian saints? He wrote, "The very God of peace sanctify you wholly; and I pray God your whole spirit and soul and body be preserved blameless unto the coming of our Lord Jesus Christ. Faithful is he that calleth you, who also will do it" (1 Thess. 5:23–24). Certainly, Paul prayed for God to work holiness through every part of their lives, inward and outward (cf. 2 Cor. 7:1). His prayers for them sought great growth in their love, growth he hoped to see in this life (1 Thess. 3:11–12). We should likewise pray for our sanctification. However, Paul looked for the ultimate answer to these prayers at Christ's coming in glory (v. 13; 5:23). That is our entire sanctification and Christian perfection: when we see him as he is (1 John 3:2).

89. Murray, *The Epistle to the Romans*, 1:225–26.
90. Murray, *The Epistle to the Romans*, 1:213.
91. See chap. 5.

Fifth, *sanctification comes by our faith and work*. While it is certainly true that we are sanctified by faith in Jesus Christ, the principle of "Let go and let God" unwisely pits faith against the effort to do good works in sanctification. When Paul describes the duties of the Christian life, he does not simply tell the readers of his epistles to surrender so that the Spirit will carry them along in holiness, but gives them many practical commands to obey while continually calling them to rely on Christ. In this regard, sanctification is different from justification, which is by faith alone apart from works of the law (Rom. 3:28). Paul never says, "Work out your justification," but with regard to our obedience he does say, "Work out your salvation with fear and trembling" (Phil. 2:12). Owen wrote that the Holy Spirit "works in us and with us, not against us or without us; so that his assistance is an encouragement as to the facilitating of the work, and no occasion of neglect as to the work itself."[92]

Paul's solution for the carnal Corinthians (1 Cor. 3:1–3) was not to receive holiness by faith without any effort, but to repent of their glorying in man (v. 21). They needed to "be watchful, stand firm in the faith, act like men, be strong" (16:13–14 ESV). Paul compares the Christian life to an athletic competition in which believers must run, strive, fight, and discipline themselves in order to win the prize (9:24–27; cf. Heb. 12:1). To be sure, the spiritual battle can be won only by the strength believers find in Christ, but they must still "wrestle" with and "stand" against the forces pressing upon them if they would win (Eph. 6:10–14).

The second half of "Let go and let God" demeans the sovereignty of God, as if he cannot work unless people give him permission. Instead of teaching that God works only if we will, the Bible says that God works our willing (Phil. 2:13). Reversing this order too easily becomes the occasion of spiritual pride. Kenneth Prior warns, "There is a subtle danger of speaking of sanctification as essentially coming from our own effort or initiative. We can unconsciously do this even while acknowledging our need for the power of the Holy Spirit, by making the operation of that power dependent upon our surrender and consecration."[93]

Sixth, *the life of sanctification is not superhuman, but truly human*. We are not becoming gods but putting on the "new man" according to the human image of God (Eph. 4:24). Christ forged this new humanity as his human body and soul passed through the fires of suffering. God's

92. Owen, *Of the Mortification of Sin in Believers*, in *Works*, 6:20.

93. Kenneth Prior, *The Way of Holiness: A Study in Christian Growth* (Downers Grove, IL: InterVarsity Press, 1982), 42.

Spirit does not pour divine love through us like water through a conduit, but comes to us as "the Spirit of life in Christ Jesus" and "the Spirit of Christ"—that is, of Christ crucified for our sins (Rom. 8:2–3, 9). In this life, God's Spirit does not lift us up into a heavenly realm of divine omnipotence; he brings divine omnipotence down into the earthly realm of weakness and death, first in Christ, and through Christ in us.

Jesus obeyed God in a manner that involved profound struggle, suffering, tears, and cries to God—and Jesus was without sin (Heb. 2:18; 4:15; 5:7–8). How much more, then, is our pathway to holiness full of difficulty and tribulation, and yet also hope through the Holy Spirit (Rom. 5:3–5). Sanctification does not replace our human minds and wills with divine energy, but conforms us to the image of God's incarnate and crucified Son (8:17, 29). There is no resurrection without the cross, neither for Christ nor for those in union with him (Phil. 3:10–11). Martin Luther said that the Christian is "tempted to flee when fear overcomes him, or to yield to sinful desire when it entices him . . . but in the end, he does not surrender, even though it costs him utmost exertion and pain just barely to resist and to come out on top." Sanctification is finding life by losing it, for as Luther wrote, "The righteous man always resembles more a loser than a victor, for the Lord lets him be tested and assailed to his utmost limits as gold is tested in a furnace."[94] Yet it is in the furnace that gold is refined.

A superhuman view of sanctification may arise from a confused eschatology, as if we had already arrived in glory. Hendriksen said, "The Christian is living in an era in which two ages, the old and the new, overlap."[95] We no longer belong to this world, but we are still in it, and to some extent it is still in us. God's grace teaches that "denying ungodliness and worldly lusts, we should live soberly, righteously, and godly, in this present world; looking for that blessed hope, and the glorious appearing of the great God and our Saviour Jesus Christ" (Titus 2:12–13).

Practical Conclusion

Over the history of the Christian church, some people with defective views of sanctification have risen to high levels of holiness and performed notable works of service in the mission of the church. We would not in the least

94. Martin Luther, *Lectures on Romans*, ed. and trans. Wilhelm Pauck, Library of Christian Classics (Louisville: Westminster John Knox, 1961), 189 (Rom. 6:14).

95. Hendriksen, *Exposition of Paul's Epistle to the Romans*, 1:232.

deny this or fail to thank God for what Christ has done through them. However, doctrines make a difference in how we live, and false doctrines of sanctification can produce a great deal of confusion, sin, and sorrow in the lives of those who embrace them. We have seen in this chapter that both in Roman Catholicism and Protestant evangelicalism there has been a tendency to teach one such false doctrine—that there are two levels of Christians.

One of the great problems with this error is that it tends to excuse hypocrites from striving after a life of holiness while thinking they are in Christ and to confuse believers into thinking they have arrived at a high level of holiness when in fact they are just beginning. This teaching replaces the continual duty of spiritual combat with a crisis. The believer is then told that he has arrived at a high spiritual plane and his focus must be on maintaining it, often through a simplistic formula. Since such a doctrine often appeals to God's grace, the believer is made to feel that any questioning of this doctrine is doubting the sufficiency of Christ. People are then launched into Christian service and missions while still poorly equipped to face the reality of their remaining sin with the faith of a persevering spiritual warrior.

The beauty of the Reformed view of sanctification is that it grounds holiness on grace but also calls believers to obedient action on the basis of grace. Wilhelmus à Brakel said,

> There is a union between you and Christ indeed, and you are indeed one Spirit with Him (1 Cor. 6:17). You are indeed grafted into Him as into an olive tree and thus have become a partaker of His life and nature (Rom. 11:17). Should not then the same life of Jesus become manifest in us, and should we not then walk as He has walked? You are indeed the bride of the Lord Jesus. . . . Would a bride not adorn herself to make herself pleasant and charming to her bridegroom?[96]

Let us, therefore, cast off our sins and run the race that is set before us with our eyes fixed on Jesus. Let us press on in the upward call of Christ. Let us pursue holiness, without which no one will see the Lord.

Sing to the Lord

Seeking Sanctifying Grace

Teach me, O Lord, thy holy way,
And give me an obedient mind;

96. Brakel, *The Christian's Reasonable Service*, 3:25.

That in thy service I may find
My soul's delight from day to day.

Guide me, O Saviour, with thy hand,
And so control my thoughts and deeds,
That I may tread the path which leads
Right onward to the blessed land.

Help me, O Saviour, here to trace
The sacred footsteps thou hast trod;
And, meekly walking with my God,
To grow in goodness, truth, and grace.

Guard me, O Lord, that I may ne'er
Forsake the right, or do the wrong:
Against temptation make me strong,
And round me spread thy shelt'ring care.

Bless me in ev'ry task, O Lord,
Begun, continued, done for thee:
Fulfil thy perfect work in me;
And thine abounding grace afford.

William T. Mason
Tune: Penitence
Trinity Hymnal—Baptist Edition, No. 456

Questions for Meditation or Discussion

1. How can we know that no one can be sinless in this life?
2. What are the "evangelical counsels," according to Roman Catholicism?
3. What is asceticism? How can we refute its false teachings?
4. What did John Wesley teach about perfection?
5. Describe the following movements with respect to their teachings on sanctification: (a) the Holiness Movement; (b) the Higher Life Movement; (c) the early Keswick movement; (d) classic dispensationalism.
6. In what ways are the Pentecostal and the Keswick doctrines of sanctification alike?
7. Someone says, "The doctrine of a carnal Christian is clearly taught by Paul in 1 Corinthians 3:1–3." How do you respond?

8. How is second-blessing theology rooted in an inadequate view of regeneration?
9. How has the doctrine of two-level Christianity, whether Roman Catholic or evangelical, affected your life and your church?

Questions for Deeper Reflection

10. Prepare a detailed outline for a ten-page booklet on the subject "Biblical Self-Denial: A Practical Guide to Avoiding Materialism and Monasticism."
11. What spiritual problems are often caused by believing second-blessing theology? What practical steps can people take to overcome those problems after they have left behind such doctrine and embraced a more biblical view of sanctification?
12. Consider this statement: "Sanctification is by faith in Christ alone." How might that statement be understood in a way contrary to God's Word? How might it be understood in a way in agreement with God's Word?

29

Sanctification, Part 3

Practical Applications

Sanctification is the work of God's grace that produces the willing and working of man toward obedience.[1] Holiness is entirely of grace, but it engages the whole man, body and soul, in the most strenuous activity known in human history. Scripture compares the Christian life to running a race (Heb. 12:1) and fighting in a war (Eph. 6:10–18). Furthermore, holiness is a divine mandate upon us (1 Pet. 1:15–16), an absolute imperative that defines our calling and obligates us for all our lives.

J. C. Ryle said, "Holiness is the habit of being of one mind with God, according as we find His mind described in Scripture." Consequently, "a holy man will endeavour to shun every known sin, and to keep every known command . . . [and] will strive to be like our Lord Jesus Christ."[2] Sanctification requires a person to pursue "meekness, longsuffering, gentleness, kind tempers, government of his tongue . . . temperance and self-denial . . . charity and brotherly kindness . . . mercy and benevolence . . . purity of heart . . . the fear of God . . . humility . . . faithfulness in all the duties and relations of life . . . [and] spiritual mindedness."[3]

1. Portions of this chapter are adapted from Joel R. Beeke, "Cultivating Holiness," in *Puritan Reformed Spirituality: Historical, Experiential, and Practical Studies for the Whole of Life* (Darlington, England: Evangelical Press, 2020), 400–424. Used by permission.

2. J. C. Ryle, *Holiness: Its Nature, Hindrances, Difficulties, and Roots*, foreword by D. Martyn Lloyd-Jones (Cambridge: James Clarke & Co., 1956), 35. Obedience to the Ten Commandments is the topic of chaps. 37–40.

3. Ryle, *Holiness*, 36–38. The meaning of these Christian virtues is explored in chaps. 35–36.

The Call to Cultivate Holiness

Christians must cultivate holiness with all the effort of a farmer whose future prosperity depends on the crops he grows. Paul says, "Be not deceived; God is not mocked: for whatsoever a man soweth, that shall he also reap. For he that soweth to his flesh shall of the flesh reap corruption; but he that soweth to the Spirit shall of the Spirit reap life everlasting. And let us not be weary in well doing: for in due season we shall reap, if we faint not" (Gal. 6:7–9).

A Holistic Task

Personal holiness demands the engagement of the whole heart (Ps. 86:11; Jer. 32:39). Holiness of heart must be cultivated in every sphere of life: in privacy with God, in the confidentiality of our homes, in the competitiveness of our workplaces, in the pleasures of social friendships, in relation with our unevangelized neighbors and the world's hungry and unemployed, as well as in public worship on the Lord's Day. Everything, Paul tells us, is to be "sanctified"—that is, made holy (1 Tim. 4:4–5). Every pot and pan in our homes should be holy—dedicated to the glory of the Lord (Zech. 14:20–21). Horatius Bonar (1808–1889) wrote,

> Holiness . . . extends to every part of our persons, fills up our being, spreads over our life, influences everything we are, or do, or think, or speak, or plan, small or great, outward or inward, negative or positive, our loving, our hating, our sorrowing, our rejoicing, our recreations, our business, our friendships, our relationships, our silence, our speech, our reading, our writing, our going out and our coming in—our whole man in every movement of spirit, soul, and body.[4]

Heeding the call to holiness is a daily task. John Calvin said, "The whole life of Christians ought to be a sort of practice of godliness, for we have been called to sanctification."[5] It requires a whole-life commitment to "live unto God" (Gal. 2:19), to live and to die as one set apart to the lordship of Jesus Christ (Rom. 14:8–9). Thus, holiness must fill our entire heart and cover all of life. Paul prays, "The very God of peace sanctify you wholly; and I pray God your whole spirit and soul and body be preserved

4. Horatius Bonar, *God's Way of Holiness* (repr., Pensacola, FL: Mount Zion Publications, 1994), 16.
5. Calvin, *Institutes*, 3.19.2.

blameless unto the coming of our Lord Jesus Christ" (1 Thess. 5:23). Thomas Boston said, "Holiness is not one grace only, but all the graces of the Spirit; it is a constellation of graces. . . . Every part of man is sanctified, though no part is perfectly so."[6]

Sanctification does not change the essence of human nature but gives it a new spiritual life oriented toward God. As Samuel Willard said, just as unregenerate sinners are still human in "body and soul," with "human understanding, will, affections, conscience, memory, etc.," so sanctification does not add to or subtract from the human constitution, but renews all its faculties by putting into them "gracious qualities and principles."[7] William Perkins observed that sanctification reaches to the whole person, renewing the mind to discern good and evil, and to meditate on God's words and works; consecrating the memory to hold good things; quieting the conscience with Christ's blood and a good life; liberating the will to choose good and refuse evil; purifying the affections with hope, holy fear, sorrow over sin, and zealous love for God; and fitting the body to serve righteousness.[8]

An Impossible Task apart from Christ

Anyone who has read the Sermon on the Mount with a sensitive conscience has felt the weight of our Lord's commands. Even an angry word or a lustful thought is a sin worthy of the fires of hell (Matt. 5:22, 28–29). It is not enough to love our children, spouses, and friends, but we must love our enemies and do good to those who hate us (v. 44). Just as the Lord said in the law of Moses, "Ye shall be holy: for I the Lord your God am holy" (Lev. 19:2), so Christ said, "Be ye therefore perfect, even as your Father which is in heaven is perfect" (Matt. 5:48).

The call to holiness fit well with man in his original state as the flawless image of God (Gen. 1:27; Eccles. 7:29), but in our depravity and disorder not one of us can answer its high demands (1 Kings 8:46). Even when God taught and cared for Israel like a well-kept vineyard, the people still failed to produce good fruit (Isa. 5:1–7). Christ, however, comes to us and says, "I am the vine, ye are the branches: he that abideth in me, and I in him, the same bringeth forth much fruit: for without me ye can do nothing"

6. Boston, *Human Nature in Its Fourfold State*, 294.
7. Willard, *A Compleat Body of Divinity*, 493.
8. Perkins, *A Golden Chain*, chap. 38, in *Works*, 6:187–89.

(John 15:5). He is the last Adam and the true Israel, who alone fulfilled God's call to holiness in his perfect humanity, tested and proven through great trials.[9] Only by union with him and continual communion with him can we produce fruit pleasing to God. Just as Christ's obedience and death grant believers the legal status of righteousness before God, so Christ's holiness in the Spirit grants believers new life and spiritual productivity. This does not excuse us from careful and laborious obedience to God's law, but it shows that the way of obedience is wedded to faith in Christ.

Therefore, we can make no progress in holiness until we are joined to the holy Lord Jesus by faith. Walter Marshall (1628–1680) said, "We cannot attain to the practice of true holiness, by any of our endeavours, while we continue in our natural state, and are not partakers of a new state, by union and fellowship with Christ through faith."[10] Therefore, before we go further, ask yourself this crucial question: Am I in Christ? Am I trusting in Jesus Christ for salvation from the guilt and power of sin? Do I have Christ's Spirit in me? Without him, you have no holiness.

If you are not in Christ, then do not seek to become holy before coming to him, but come to him as you are, for Christ is the source of all holiness for sinners. Boston said, "Unholiness ought not to stop a sinner from coming to Christ, more than a disease ought to hinder a man to take the physician's help, or cold from taking the benefit of the fire."[11] Ryle said, "Would you be holy? Would you become a new creature? Then you must begin with Christ."[12]

The Life of Faith in Christ

It would be a huge mistake to look to Christ for justification but then move on to pursue holiness by human willpower and wisdom. Sanctification is the working out of our conversion through our entire lives. Therefore, sanctification is by Christ just as justification is by Christ. Paul writes, "As ye have therefore received Christ Jesus the Lord, so walk ye in him: rooted and built up in him, and stablished in the faith, as ye have been taught, abounding therein with thanksgiving" (Col. 2:6–7). Whatever spiritual

9. See the discussion of the power of Christ's victory in *RST*, 2:1123–25.

10. Walter Marshall, *The Gospel Mystery of Sanctification* (Grand Rapids, MI: Reformation Heritage Books, 1999), 53.

11. Boston, *An Illustration of the Doctrines of the Christian Religion*, in *Works*, 2:14.

12. Ryle, *Holiness*, 49.

needs we may have, we "are complete in him," for in him all God's fullness is granted to us in human form (vv. 9–10).

Depend on Christ in His Threefold Office

Having died and risen with Christ, we are to "live by faith in the Son of God" (Gal. 2:20 ESV). We run the race of sanctification "looking unto Jesus" (Heb. 12:2) according to his threefold office as Prophet, Priest, and King.[13]

In our sanctification, we look to Christ as the Prophet to make known to us God and his will. God has "spoken unto us by his Son," who is "the brightness of his glory, and the express image of his person" (Heb. 1:2–3). If we desire to know God and his purposes better, which is at the core of our spiritual growth (Col. 1:9–10), then we must depend upon him "in whom are hid all the treasures of wisdom and knowledge" (2:3). Christ is the light of the world (John 8:12) and the healer of the blind (Isa. 42:7). Therefore, our prayer must be "Open thou mine eyes, that I may behold wondrous things out of thy law" (Ps. 119:18).

In order to pursue holiness, we must depend upon Christ as the Priest who has once for all consecrated his people to God through his blood, making purification for our sins and sitting down at the right hand of God (Heb. 1:3). By God's will, "we are sanctified through the offering of the body of Jesus Christ once for all" (10:10); literally "we have been sanctified" (perfect *hagiazō*). From this definitive sanctification by the sacrifice of Christ flows the process of progressive sanctification: "For by one offering he hath perfected for ever them that are sanctified" (v. 14), literally "those who are being sanctified" (present participle *hagiazō*). Christ's priestly sacrifice brings us the double grace of justification and sanctification promised in the new covenant (vv. 15–17). Looking to Christ's present priestly ministry in heaven, the church may draw near to the Most Holy Place and receive grace to become more holy (vv. 19–25).

In the battle for sanctification, we need daily to draw upon the power and victory of Christ as the King. God's Son is the Lord and heir of all things, who preserves them by his word of power (Heb. 1:3). He is the Creator of heaven and earth (vv. 10–12), and therefore able to form the new creation in us. In order to bring "many sons to glory," our victorious

13. Christ's threefold office is extensively discussed in *RST*, 2:869–1168 (chaps. 43–55). Here we simply summarize some of its implications for progressive sanctification.

"captain" became our brother and suffered with and for us, "for both he that sanctifieth and they who are sanctified are all of one" (2:10–11). By his conquering death, we overcome the Devil (v. 14). To share in Christ's victory, we must submissively depend upon the Son who, though sinless, "learned he obedience by the things which he suffered" and so "became the author of eternal salvation unto all them that obey him" (5:8–9). We overcome every trial and temptation "by faith" in him, like the saints of old (11:1–38).

Count Yourself Dead to Sin and Alive to God

Christ has accomplished our full salvation by his death and resurrection, and we obtain it through our union with him.[14] We must exercise faith that his finished work has decisively broken the reigning power of sin over us and brought us into a new realm of grace and holiness (Rom. 6:1–14). Paul commands us to perform a sacred accounting in our minds: "Consider yourselves dead to sin and alive to God in Christ Jesus" (v. 11 ESV). William Hendriksen commented, "What has been established, namely, that believers are in principle dead to sin and alive to Christ, must become the abiding conviction of their hearts and minds, the take-off point for all their thinking, planning, rejoicing, speaking, doing. They must constantly bear in mind that they are no longer what they used to be."[15]

This accounting of faith does not replace the work of obedience, for Paul goes on to say, "Let not sin therefore reign in your mortal body, that ye should obey it in the lusts thereof. . . . But yield yourselves unto God . . . and your members as instruments of righteousness unto God" (Rom. 6:12–13). The word translated as "yield" (*paristēmi*) means to present or offer, and Paul uses it again of the Christian's offering himself as a "living sacrifice" to God (12:1), by which he does God's will in service, love, and mercy (vv. 2–21). This is our daily duty.[16]

14. See the discussion of our union with Christ in his death and resurrection in chaps. 9–10, and with regard to sanctification, in chap. 27.

15. Hendriksen, *Exposition of Paul's Epistle to the Romans*, 1:201.

16. It has been claimed that the aorist tense of the word translated as "yield" or "present" (6:13; 12:1) implies a once-for-all dedication or consecration, such as the crisis alleged by Higher Life and Keswick teachers to be the baptism or filling with the Holy Spirit. See the sources by Evan Hopkins, Lewis Sperry Chafer, John Walvoord, Charles Ryrie, Dwight Pentecost, Warren Wiersbe, and others cited in William W. Combs, "Romans 12:1–2 and the Doctrine of Sanctification," *Detroit Baptist Seminary Journal* 11 (2006): 13 (full article, 3–24). See also chap. 28. However, the aorist imperative does not imply a once-for-all action. Consider the aorist imperative used in commands to pray to God (Matt. 6:6), pay taxes (Rom. 13:7), glorify God (1 Cor. 6:20), and put off sin and

This command to "yield" is not a call to a passive surrender, but to an active fight to do what is right; the same word translated as "instruments" (plural *hoplon*, Rom. 6:13) is rendered elsewhere as "weapons" or "armour."[17] Paul is saying, "Count yourself as part of Christ's kingdom, and do not let the sin that remains in you move your bodies to fight on the wrong side of this spiritual war, but live as soldiers of Christ, using the members of your body as weapons of righteousness."

Counting ourselves dead to sin and alive to God by Christ empowers the battle of sanctification, for Paul next writes, "For sin shall not have dominion over you: for ye are not under the law, but under grace" (Rom. 6:14). We are not fighting to become free from the tyranny of sin but fighting because we are free. Our baptism testifies to us that our old man was buried with Christ and that Christ was raised so that "we also should walk in newness of life" (v. 4). John Murray said, "As surely as Christ rose from the dead so surely shall we walk in newness of life."[18] This mindset of faith enables us to press on in the hard labor of putting sin to death and performing acts of righteousness because we know that the victory is won in Christ.

The Pattern of Sanctification

The experiences of God's children vary widely as their Shepherd leads them in paths of righteousness for his name's sake. No Christian should take his past experience and make it a rule that others must follow. However, all believers strive after the same holiness, and the Holy Scriptures reveal a common pattern in God's ways with his people as he sanctifies them.

Covenantal Sanctification as the People of God

God's covenant with Israel illuminates God's pattern of sanctification in Christ, though Israel's sanctification was more focused on externals and only some in the nation of Israel were spiritually saved and sanctified. The life of holiness is rooted in faith in the promise of the covenant: "I am the Lord that doth sanctify you" (Ex. 31:13; cf. Lev. 20:8; 21:8). The call of the covenant is to separate from unclean things, for "I am the

---

put on godliness (Eph. 4:31; Col. 3:5, 8, 12). None of these are singular events, but duties calling for repeated action.

17. John 18:3; Rom. 13:12; 2 Cor. 6:7; 10:4; cf. Hendriksen, *Exposition of Paul's Epistle to the Romans*, 1:202–3.

18. Murray, *The Epistle to the Romans*, 1:216.

Lord your God; ye shall therefore sanctify yourselves, and ye shall be holy; for I am holy" (Lev. 11:44). The motive of sanctification is the fear of the Lord (19:2, 14, 30, 32). The pathway of sanctification is obedience to God's laws (20:7–8). The identity of God's holy ones is the people whom he has separated from the world to be his (v. 26). The holy people of God are the objects of his fatherly love, and he trains them through hardship to live in dependence, reverence, and obedience toward him (Deut. 7:6–8; 8:1–6).

The same themes appear in the New Testament. Sanctification is the effect of God's eternal, electing, covenantal grace: "Blessed be the God and Father of our Lord Jesus Christ . . . he hath chosen us in him before the foundation of the world, that we should be holy" (Eph. 1:3–4).[19] In the new covenant, God cleanses his people so that under Christ's reign "they shall also walk in my judgments, and observe my statutes, and do them. . . . And the heathen shall know that I the Lord do sanctify Israel" (Ezek. 37:24, 28). God's promise to be "their God" requires separation from the world and "perfecting holiness in the fear of God" (2 Cor. 6:16–7:1). Though the old covenant ceremonial laws are abolished, "the keeping of the commandments of God" remains essential to the Christian life (1 Cor. 7:19). Christians were once lawbreakers outside of God's kingdom, but, Paul says, "ye are washed, . . . ye are sanctified" (6:11), and "your body is the temple of the Holy Ghost which is in you, which ye have of God, and ye are not your own" (v. 19). They must live as "obedient children" of the holy Father (1 Pet. 1:14–17), and he disciplines them to train them in his righteous ways (Heb. 12:5–11).

Progressive Repentance in Its Positive and Negative Aspects

Just as Levitical holiness demanded negative separation or cleansing from the unclean and positive consecration to the holy God, so New Testament holiness has a double aspect that must be maintained lest we lose our spiritual balance. As we noted earlier, our communion with Christ in holiness consists of dying and coming to life, sometimes called "mortification" and "vivification," by virtue of Christ's death and resurrection applied by the Holy Spirit.[20]

The Heidelberg Catechism (LD 33) states:

19. On Eph. 1:3–6 and its implications for election, covenant, and holiness, see *RST*, 1:981–89.
20. See the discussion of the supernatural agency of the Holy Spirit in chap. 27.

Q. 88: Of how many parts doth the true conversion[21] of man consist?
A. Of two parts: of the mortification of the old, and the quickening [making alive] of the new man.

Q. 89: What is the mortification of the old man?
A. It is a sincere sorrow of heart that we have provoked God by our sins; and more and more to hate and flee from them.

Q. 90: What is the quickening of the new man?
A. It is a sincere joy of heart in God, through Christ, and with love and delight to live according to the will of God in all good works.[22]

Paul also communicates this twofold aspect of sanctification with the imagery of changing our clothing, expressed in the words "put off" and "put on."[23] This language is used of union with Christ (Gal. 3:27),[24] and also communicates the need to get rid of sinful attitudes and actions ("put off . . . anger, wrath, malice," Col. 3:8) and to do what is pleasing to God ("put on . . . kindness, humbleness," v. 12).

We must practice both sides. If we focus too much on putting off sin, we may grow morbid and fail to manifest the beautiful, happy virtues of our Lord. If we try to focus entirely on the positive, we will fail to deal with the bitter roots that poison our lives. Complete repentance requires a complete turn from the bad to the good.

The Imitation of God and Christ

As noted earlier, our capacity for holiness is grounded in our creation in God's image.[25] The holiness of God himself ought to be our foremost stimulus to cultivate holy living. We must seek to be like our Father in heaven. In the Spirit, we are to strive to think God's thoughts after him via his Word, to be of one mind with him, and to live and act as God himself would have us do. As Stephen Charnock concluded, "This is the prime way of honoring God. We do not so glorify God by elevated admirations,

---

21. The catechism here uses "conversion" to include the first actual conversion and continual actual conversion (sanctification). Note the "more and more" in Q. 89. See the discussion of terminology in chap. 19.

22. *The Three Forms of Unity*, 99.

23. Rom. 13:12, 14; Gal. 3:27; Eph. 4:22, 24–25; 6:11, 14; Col. 3:8, 10, 12; 1 Thess. 5:8; cf. Heb. 12:1; James 1:21; 1 Pet. 2:1.

24. On the comparison of union with Christ to clothing, see chap. 9.

25. On the necessity of holiness due to the holiness of God and his creation of man in his image, see chap. 27.

or eloquent expressions, or pompous services of him, as when we aspire to a conversing with Him with unstained spirits, and live *to* him in living *like* him."[26]

The imitation of God requires meditation on who he is, especially his attributes and affections of moral excellence.[27] As we read the Scriptures and hear the preaching of the Word, we should consider God's goodness, mercy, grace, patience, love, truth, faithfulness, righteousness and justice, jealousy for his glory, joy, wrath against sin, and compassion. This is our God and Father, and we should delight in his ways and become like him.

Such imitation arises from love, our love rising up in response to his love for us (Col. 3:12; 1 John 4:19). Sanctification is the formation and development of a heart that loves God supremely (Deut. 6:5; 30:6). This motivates us to seek to please him (Eph. 5:10). A. W. Pink wrote, "There must be a loving and delighting to do the will of God in a cheerful manner."[28] A desire to please the heavenly Father shows itself in imitating his ways: "Be imitators of God, as beloved children" (Eph. 5:1 ESV).

Imitating God implies following Christ, God's perfect image (cf. Eph. 5:2). Paul says,

> Let this mind be in you, which was also in Christ Jesus: who, being in the form of God, thought it not robbery to be equal with God: but made himself of no reputation, and took upon him the form of a servant, and was made in the likeness of men: and being found in fashion as a man, he humbled himself, and became obedient unto death, even the death of the cross. (Phil. 2:5–8)

Christ was humble, willing to give up his rights in order to obey God and serve sinners. If we would be holy, Paul is saying, we must be like-minded. Christ teaches us that the greatest in the kingdom are those who live in obedience to all of God's commands, in childlike humility before God, and in servanthood to others—among whom Christ is the supreme Servant (Matt. 5:19; 18:4; 20:25–28). If we would be like him, we must take up our crosses and follow him (16:24).

Christ is the way of sanctification—both the Mediator of holiness and the path of holiness. On the one hand, we should not aim for conformity

26. Charnock, *The Existence and Attributes of God*, in *Works*, 2:268.
27. God's moral attributes of holy love are discussed in *RST*, 1:781–875 (chaps. 41–44).
28. Arthur W. Pink, *The Doctrine of Sanctification* (Swengel, PA: Reiner, 1975), 25.

to Christ as a condition of acceptance with God, but rather trust in him to save us and justify us with his perfect righteousness. On the other hand, we must walk in this way and seek no other. Augustine wisely said that it is better to limp on the path than to run outside of it.[29] Ask in each situation, "How does God's Word call me to imitate Christ here and now?" Then trust him for holiness and press on to imitate him. You will often disappoint yourself, but he will not disappoint you.

Warfare against Temptation and Indwelling Sin

Christians must never forget that they are in a war.[30] Indeed, the Christian's soul is a battleground between the Spirit and indwelling sin.[31] There is also an enemy outside of them. Paul says, "For we wrestle not against flesh and blood, but against principalities, against powers, against the rulers of the darkness of this world, against spiritual wickedness in high places" (Eph. 6:12). In this one verse, Paul warns us that our spiritual enemies are powerful, numerous, invisible, evil, and personally attacking us.[32]

Though this war is invisible, it has a cost and consequences far beyond anything fought with bullets and bombs. William Gurnall said the "war between the saint and Satan . . . [is] so bloody a one, that the cruelest which ever was fought by men, will be found but sport and child's play to this. Alas, what is the killing of bodies to the destroying of souls?"[33]

If we would win, then we must fight. We must "strive" (Luke 13:24), "fight the good fight of faith," and "lay hold of eternal life" (1 Tim. 6:12). The remnant of our sinful flesh fights against every good motion of the Holy Spirit within us (Gal. 5:17). If we tolerate sin, it will not tolerate holiness in our lives but will progressively cast it out. Every bit of sin in its essence is hatred for God (Rom. 8:7), just as "every drop of poison is poison . . . and every spark of fire is fire," and therefore, sin cannot be reconciled to God, but "must be abolished and destroyed," as John Owen said.[34]

Live in present-tense, total commitment to God. Don't fall prey to the "one-more-time" syndrome. Postponed obedience is disobedience.

---

29. Augustine, *Expositions on the Book of Psalms*, 32.2.4 (1:282); and *Ennarationes in Psalmos*, 31.2.4, in *Patrologia Latina*, 36:260; cf. Calvin, *Institutes*, 1.6.3; 3.14.4.

30. On the Christian's combat against sin, see also *RST*, 2:474–75.

31. On Rom. 7:14–25 and related passages, see the exegetical response to the carnal Christian doctrine in chap. 28.

32. On Satan, the demons, and spiritual warfare, see *RST*, 1:1133–57 (chap. 55).

33. Gurnall, *The Christian in Complete Armour*, 1:2–3.

34. Owen, *The Nature, Power, Deceit, and Prevalency of the Remainders of Indwelling Sin in Believers*, in *Works*, 6:176–77.

Tomorrow's holiness is impurity now. Tomorrow's faith is unbelief today. Aim not to sin at all (1 John 2:1), asking for divine strength to bring every thought into captivity to Christ (2 Cor. 10:5), for Scripture indicates that thought life ultimately determines character: "For as he thinks within himself, so he is" (Prov. 23:7).

You must show no mercy to your sin but kill it by the Holy Spirit (Rom. 8:13). Owen wrote, "The vigour, and power, and comfort of our spiritual life depends on the mortification of the deeds of the flesh." He urged, "Make it your daily work; be always at it while you live; cease not a day from this work; be killing sin or it will be killing you."[35] Do not allow sin to have the least space in your heart. Owen said, "Rise mightily against the first actings [of sin], . . . suffer it not to get the least ground."[36] Though you are unable to completely destroy it, do not cease to fight it and strive to weaken it as much as possible. Resolve with Jonathan Edwards "never to give over, nor in the least to slacken my fight with my corruptions, however unsuccessful I may be."[37]

Obedience to the Law of God

Paul's strong polemic against justification by works of the law sometimes leaves people with the impression that the law has no function in guiding believers in righteous living. However, the moral law of God remains constant until heaven and earth pass away (Matt. 5:17–19).[38] If we love Christ, we will keep his commandments (John 14:15).

Our keeping of God's law is nothing less than the fulfillment of God's new covenant promise in Christ, as God writes his law on men's hearts and causes them to obey it by his indwelling Spirit (Jer. 31:33; Ezek. 36:27). Wilhelmus à Brakel wrote, "Sanctification is the efficacious operation of God in elect, called, regenerated, and justified sinners . . . causing them to live according to His will as expressed in the law of the ten commandments."[39]

Paul writes that we are "justified by faith without the deeds of the law" (Rom. 3:28) and that in Christ we are not "under the law" (6:14–15), but he affirms that we are "servants of righteousness" (v. 18). Therefore, to be released from being "under the law" does not remove our obligation to

35. Owen, *Of the Mortification of Sin in Believers*, in *Works*, 6:9.
36. Owen, *Of the Mortification of Sin in Believers*, in *Works*, 6:62.
37. Edwards, "Resolutions," no. 56, in *WJE*, 16:757.
38. On the abiding duty to obey God's moral law, see *RST*, 2:678–700 (chap. 34).
39. Brakel, *The Christian's Reasonable Service*, 3:4.

keep God's commandments, but sets us free from the state of condemnation, death, and enslavement to sin.[40] We must be saved from the law's condemnation, but we cannot be saved from obedience to God's commands, for this would destroy our very humanity, not to mention our redeemed identity as God's sons.

Therefore, Christian holiness is still defined by obedience to the moral law of God. The Holy Scriptures abound with statutes and commandments, and we will not progress in holiness if we neglect them. The pinnacle of wisdom is still "Fear God, and keep his commandments: for this is the whole duty of man. For God shall bring every work into judgment, with every secret thing, whether it be good, or whether it be evil" (Eccles. 12:13–14).

If sanctification is a work of demolition and construction, then the Word of God is the "rule and square" of this work—indeed, it is the "line," "measure," and "balance" by which all things must be "framed, ordered, measured, and pondered," as James Ussher said. This is because "as the law requireth obedience, so the gospel directeth the faithful how to perform it."[41]

Submission to Providential Suffering

Holiness is intertwined with adoption, and our sanctification comes to us as sons. God's Son passed through great sorrows in order to bring us to glory. Similarly, God's adopted sons and daughters must also pass through sorrows to come to glory, that they may bear the image of the Son (Rom. 8:17, 28–29).[42]

Therefore, an important aspect of our part in sanctification is submission to our Father's will as he trains us through suffering. Ussher is reported to have said, "Sanctification is nothing less than for a man to be brought to an entire resignation of his will to the will of God, and to live in the offering up of his soul continually in the flames of love, as a whole burnt-offering to Christ."[43] While that submission is incomplete in this life, it is the duty of every Christian in the pursuit of holiness (Rom. 12:1–2).

Hebrews 12:5–6 says, "Ye have forgotten the exhortation which speaketh unto you as unto children, My son, despise not thou the chastening

40. Murray, *The Epistle to the Romans*, 1:229.
41. Ussher, *A Body of Divinity*, 19th head (180–81).
42. See the discussion of the adopted child's relationship to the Father in chap. 26.
43. Cited in Gill, *Body of Divinity*, 554.

of the Lord, nor faint when thou art rebuked of him: for whom the Lord loveth he chasteneth, and scourgeth every son whom he receiveth." Such discipline is not necessarily a chastisement for a specific sin, though it may be (Ps. 32:3–5; 1 Cor. 11:30–32); rather, God's fatherly discipline is his training program to mature his children. His hand of discipline is a sign that we are truly part of his family (Heb. 12:7–8). He disciplines us "that we might be partakers of his holiness" (v. 10). Discipline is painful today, but we should humbly reverence our Father and look for the harvest of righteousness that it will bring to our lives (vv. 9, 11). In our darkest hours, we may look to his Son, who endured the cross itself (v. 2), and know that all our sorrows will be turned into glory and joy.[44]

God is the great launderer who is scrubbing the stains out of his children's clothes (Mal. 3:2). Gurnall said, "God would not rub so hard if it were not to fetch out the dirt that is ingrained in our natures. God loves purity so well he had rather see a hole than a spot in his child's garments."[45] Let us, therefore, patiently wear the ragged garments of our present sorrows, knowing that our Father will clothe us in glory greater than that of Solomon's golden days (Matt. 6:28–30).

Living unto God

The heart of holiness is the motive of the heart. All outward works of obedience are worthless if one's heart is not directed toward God (Matt. 15:8–9). The apostle Paul says, "Whether therefore ye eat, or drink, or whatsoever ye do, do all to the glory of God" (1 Cor. 10:31). The Westminster Shorter Catechism (Q. 1) says, "Man's chief end is to glorify God, and to enjoy him for ever."[46]

Paul calls this living unto God, indicating the direction of our love, hope, fear, and joy. He says, "For none of us liveth to himself, and no man dieth to himself. For whether we live, we live unto the Lord; and whether we die, we die unto the Lord: whether we live therefore, or die, we are the Lord's" (Rom. 14:7–8).[47]

Calvin expressed this eloquently:

44. For an exposition of Hebrews 12:1–13, see Burk Parsons, "The Father's Beautiful Hand of Blessed Chastisement," in *The Beauty and Glory of the Father*, ed. Joel R. Beeke (Grand Rapids, MI: Reformation Heritage Books, 2013), 127–37.

45. Gurnall, *The Christian in Complete Armour*, 1:417–18.

46. *Reformed Confessions*, 4:353.

47. On living unto the Lord, see *RST*, 2:1175–79.

> We are not our own: let not our reason nor our will, therefore, sway our plans and deeds. We are not our own: let us therefore not set it as our goal to seek what is expedient for us according to the flesh. We are not our own: in so far as we can, let us therefore forget ourselves and all that is ours. Conversely, we are God's: let us therefore live for him and die for him. We are God's: let his wisdom and will therefore rule all our actions. We are God's: let all the parts of our life accordingly strive toward him as our only lawful goal.[48]

Therefore, we must make it our great aim in all that we do to do it unto the Lord (Col. 3:23). His will must be our rule, his pleasure our delight, and his glory our reward. We must abhor and reject all that disobeys, displeases, and dishonors him. This is the essence of holiness: the consecration of our lives unto the glory of God's holy name.

Obstacles to Holiness

Indwelling sin opposes our sanctification like a many-headed hydra. In this section, we will discuss some of the more subtle ways in which it resists our progress in holiness. We must learn to recognize them in our souls and fight against every manifestation of sin as a deadly enemy.

Self-Centeredness

We are often more concerned about sin's consequences for ourselves than its offense to God. Avoiding pain becomes the hidden agenda of obedience. However, the cultivation of holiness necessitates hating sin as God hates it. Those who love God "hate evil" (Ps. 97:10). Paul says, "Let love be genuine. Abhor what is evil; hold fast to what is good" (Rom. 12:9 ESV). We must cultivate a view of sin as always and preeminently a wrong done against God (Ps. 51:4). William Plumer (1802–1880) said, "We never see sin aright until we see it as against God."[49]

"Wrong views about holiness are generally traceable to wrong views about human corruption," Ryle asserted. "If a man does not realize the dangerous nature of his soul's diseases, you cannot wonder if he is content with false or imperfect remedies."[50] Cultivating holiness demands a rejec-

48. Calvin, *Institutes*, 3.7.1.

49. William S. Plumer, *Studies in the Book of Psalms* (Philadelphia: J. B. Lippincott and Co., 1867), 557 (Ps. 51:4).

50. Ryle, *Holiness*, 1.

tion of the pride of life and the lusts of the flesh, as well as the willingness to pray, "Give me the single eye, Thy Name to glorify."[51]

We fail when we do not consciously live with our priorities centered on God's Word, will, and glory. In the words of the Scottish theologian John Brown of Edinburgh (1784–1858), "Holiness does not consist in mystic speculations, enthusiastic fervors, or uncommanded austerities; it consists in thinking as God thinks, and willing as God wills."[52] Those who are "lovers of their own selves" may produce an outward "form of godliness," but it will be a hollow shell of holiness without "power" (2 Tim. 3:2, 5).

Spiritual Lethargy

Our progress is hindered when we misunderstand living by faith (Gal. 2:20) to imply that no effort toward holiness is commanded of us. Sometimes we are even prone to consider human effort sinful or "fleshly." Ryle provided us with a corrective here:

> Is it wise to proclaim in so bald, naked, and unqualified a way as many do, that the holiness of converted people is by faith only, and not at all by personal exertion? Is this according to the proportion of God's Word? I doubt it. That faith in Christ is the root of all holiness . . . no well-instructed Christian will ever think of denying. But surely the Scriptures teach us that in following holiness the true Christian needs personal exertion and work as well as faith.[53]

We are responsible for holiness. Whose fault is it but our own if we are not holy? We need to implement a fight-or-flight attitude to sinful temptations. And sometimes we simply need to obey the plain injunction to "abstain" from sin (1 Thess. 4:3; 5:22; 1 Pet. 2:11). Isaiah did not mince words: "Cease to do evil; learn to do well" (Isa. 1:16–17).

If you have put off the old man and put on the new (Eph. 4:22–24), live accordingly (Col. 3:9–10). "Mortify therefore your members" and "seek those things which are above" (Col. 3:1, 5), not as a form of legalism, but as a repercussion of divine blessing in Christ (Col. 2:9–23).[54] If anything

51. *The Psalter*, No. 236 (Ps. 86:11).
52. John Brown of Edinburgh, *Expository Discourses on the First Epistle of the Apostle Peter* (New York: Robert Carter and Brothers, 1855), 94.
53. Ryle, *Holiness*, viii.
54. Sinclair Ferguson, "The Reformed View," in *Christian Spirituality: Five Views of Sanctification*, ed. Donald L. Alexander (Downers Grove, IL: InterVarsity Press, 1988), 64.

in your life causes you to stumble, cut it off (Matt. 5:30). Look the other way; walk the opposite way (Prov. 5:8). If necessary, run (Gen. 39:12).

Spiritual Pride

We also fail miserably when we take pride in our holiness and think that our exertions can somehow produce holiness apart from faith. From beginning to end, holiness is the work of God and his free grace. As the Westminster Confession of Faith (13.1, 3) states, believers are sanctified "through the virtue of Christ's death and resurrection," and it is only "through the continual supply of strength from the sanctifying Spirit of Christ" that they overcome sin and grow in grace.[55]

All our success in holiness should humble us and make us grateful. Richard Sibbes said, "There is not the least thought or affection to goodness in us, but it comes from God; we are what we are by his grace."[56] Both justification and sanctification come to us by sheer grace. Sibbes added, "By grace we are what we are in justification, and work what we work in sanctification. . . . Therefore in that respect there must be poverty of spirit."[57]

This does not deny that we must work, nor does it deny that there is a real change made in the disposition of the believer's heart by which he actively desires and labors after holiness. Pink wrote, "Mortification is a task to which every Christian must apply himself with prayerful diligence and resolute earnestness. The regenerate have a spiritual nature within that fits them for holy action, otherwise there would be no difference between them and the unregenerate."[58]

Nevertheless, self-sanctification, strictly speaking, is nonexistent. The Belgic Confession (Art. 24) says, "Therefore we do good works, but not to merit by them (for what can we merit?)—nay, we are beholden [indebted] to God for the good works we do and not He to us, since it is He that worketh in us both to will and to do of His good pleasure."[59] As Calvin explained, "Holiness is not a merit by which we can attain communion with God, but a gift of Christ which enables us to cling to him and to follow him."[60] Harriet Auber (1773–1862) said,

---

55. *Reformed Confessions*, 4:249.
56. Sibbes, *The Saint's Hiding Place in the Evil Day*, in *Works*, 1:410.
57. Sibbes, *The Rich Poverty; Or the Poor Man's Riches*, in *Works*, 6:245.
58. Arthur W. Pink, *Practical Christianity* (Grand Rapids, MI: Guardian Press, 1974), 143–44.
59. *The Three Forms of Unity*, 42.
60. John Calvin, *Golden Booklet of the True Christian Life*, trans. Henry J. Van Andel (Grand Rapids, MI: Baker, 1952), 13.

And every virtue we possess,
And every conquest won,
And every thought of holiness,
Are His alone.[61]

One of the tragic ironies of spiritual pride is that glorying in our progress makes us unwilling to confess our failures. Seeking the praise of men, we conceal sins that we deem shameful and cover backsliding with a false front. Over time, the toleration of secret sins leads to the eruption of scandalous sin that may devastate us, our families, and our churches. It is far better to confess and repent of our sins early and often. "He that covereth his sins shall not prosper: but whoso confesseth and forsaketh them shall have mercy" (Prov. 28:13).

Shirking Battle

We are prone to avoid the battle of daily spiritual warfare. No one likes war. Maintaining personal holiness in an unholy world with a heart prone to backslide necessitates a perpetual fight. When our timidity and laziness move us to shrink back from the fight, we must confront ourselves with the only alternative to battle: friendship with the world, the flesh, and the Devil.

There is no neutrality in this war. The Lord warns, "Ye adulterers and adulteresses, know ye not that the friendship of the world is enmity with God? Whosoever therefore will be a friend of the world is the enemy of God" (James 4:4). Samuel Rutherford said, "If there be any choice of devils, a raging and a roaring devil is better than a calm and sleeping devil. . . . The devil's war is better than the devil's peace."[62]

Hence, the wisest course is to "submit yourselves therefore to God. Resist the devil, and he will flee from you" (James 4:7). You will either stand against Satan in the strength of the Lord or you will fall before the Devil. "Wherefore take unto you the whole armour of God, that ye may be able to withstand in the evil day, and having done all, to stand" (Eph. 6:13). Do not fear the Devil when he comes like "a roaring lion," for the God of all grace has called you to eternal glory, and he will establish you

61. Harriet Auber, *The Spirit of the Psalms, or, a Compressed Version of Select Portions of the Psalms of David, Adapted to Christian Worship* (London: for T. Cadell and C. & J. Rivington, 1829), 148, emphasis added.

62. Samuel Rutherford, *The Trial and Triumph of Faith* (Edinburgh: The Assembly's Committee, 1845), 402–3.

(1 Pet. 5:8–10). Even if you must resist the Devil to the point of death, remember the words of Hugh Latimer (c. 1487–1555) to Nicholas Ridley (c. 1500–1555) as they went to be burned at the stake for their faith in Christ: "Be of good comfort, Master Ridley, and play the man. We shall this day light such a candle, by God's grace, in England, as I trust shall never be put out."[63]

Disciplines to Cultivate Holiness

The battle for holiness by faith in Christ requires the cultivation of basic Christian habits in one's life. Though these are but means of grace, they are means that we must use diligently if we desire to grow in holiness. The Word of God commands the Christian to "exercise thyself . . . unto godliness" (1 Tim. 4:7), using an athletic term for vigorous training (*gymnazō*), for as Thomas Lea writes, "Godly habits would not appear without determined human purpose and effort."[64]

First, *meditate on God's Word.* Know and love the Holy Scriptures. This is God's primary road to holiness and to spiritual growth—the Spirit as master Teacher blessing the reading and searching of God's Word. Jesus prayed, "Sanctify them through thy truth: thy word is truth" (John 17:17). Peter advises, "As newborn babes, desire the sincere milk of the word, that ye may grow thereby" (1 Pet. 2:2).

If you would not remain spiritually ignorant and impoverished, read through the entire Bible in regular cycles every one to three years. Memorize the Scriptures (Ps. 119:11), search them (John 5:39), think upon them (Ps. 1:2), and live and love them (19:10). Compare Scripture with Scripture; take time to study the Word. Jerry Bridges (1929–2016) observed that Proverbs 2:1–5 sets before us several principles for personal Bible study: "teachability" (receiving God's words), "intent to obey" (storing God's commandments), "mental discipline" (applying the heart), "prayerful dependence" (crying for knowledge), and "diligent perseverance" (searching for hidden treasure).[65] Do not expect growth in holiness if you spend little time alone with God and fail to take his Word seriously.

---

63. Cited in R. Demaus, *Hugh Latimer: A Biography*, rev. ed. (London: Religious Tract Society, 1881), 454.

64. Thomas D. Lea and Hayne P. Griffin, *1, 2 Timothy, Titus*, The New American Commentary 34 (Nashville: Broadman & Holman, 1992), 134.

65. Jerry Bridges, *The Practice of Godliness* (Colorado Springs, CO: NavPress, 1996), 41.

Develop from Scripture a mindset of discernment and wisdom by the regular application of biblical principles for a holy life (Heb. 5:14). Do not merely ask, Does the Bible explicitly forbid this action? Use biblical truth to evaluate the action in question with discernment. Ask probing questions: Is this beneficial to me (1 Cor. 6:12)? Does it bring me under any enslaving power (v. 12)? Does it put me in bondage to mere men instead of Christ (7:22–23)? Does it help others, especially toward their salvation (8:13; 10:33)? Is it consistent with godly examples (11:1)? Most importantly, does it glorify God (10:31)?

Second, *pray for more sanctifying grace*. Use Scripture as God's guidebook for praying that you will be sanctified. Hence, pray with David, "Create in me a clean heart, O God" (Ps. 51:10). Call upon God with the psalmist: "Give me understanding, and I shall keep thy law; yea, I shall observe it with my whole heart. Make me to go in the path of thy commandments; for therein do I delight. Incline my heart unto thy testimonies, and not to covetousness. Turn away mine eyes from beholding vanity; and quicken thou me in thy way" (119:34–37).

Meditate on the implications of the Lord's Prayer for sanctification using such means as the Westminster Shorter Catechism, and pray it for yourself and the church out of an illuminated understanding. Make use of Paul's prayers and blessings recorded in his epistles, for these are rich guides in praying for the spiritual growth of the saints.[66]

Frequently remind yourself of the necessity of prayer for spiritual growth because sanctification is by grace. The Heidelberg Catechism (LD 44, Q. 115) says that one reason why God uses his law to show his children that they never fully obey him is to prod us to "constantly endeavor and pray to God for the grace of the Holy Spirit, that we may become more and more conformable to the image of God, till we arrive at the perfection proposed to us in a life to come." The catechism (LD 45, Q. 116) also says that "prayer is necessary for Christians" because "it is the chief part of thankfulness which God requires of us; and also, because God will give His grace and Holy Spirit to those only, who with sincere desires continually ask them of Him, and are thankful for them."[67]

Third, *participate fully in the life of the church*. Make diligent use of the ministry of the Word, of prayer and praise in the congregation of

66. For example, see Paul's prayers and blessings in Rom. 15:13; 2 Cor. 13:14; Eph. 1:15–19; 3:14–21; Phil. 1:9–11; Col. 1:9–13; 1 Thess. 3:9–13; 5:23; 2 Thess. 1:11–12; 3:5.

67. *The Three Forms of Unity*, 109–10.

God's people, and of baptism and the Lord's Supper as means of grace to strengthen your faith in Christ and obedience to God. Seek fellowship in the body of Christ as an active member of the church (Eph. 4:16). Converse and pray with fellow believers whose godly walk you admire: "He that walketh with wise men shall be wise" (Prov. 13:20). Thomas Watson said, "Association begets assimilation."[68] A Christian life lived in isolation from other believers will be defective; usually such a believer will remain spiritually immature (Prov. 18:1). Recognize, too, that when you come together with God's people, you must not come merely to receive, but to give and to serve.[69]

The Belgic Confession (Art. 28) says of the true church that "all men are in duty bound to join and unite themselves with it, maintaining the unity of the Church; submitting themselves to the doctrine and discipline thereof; bowing their necks under the yoke of Jesus Christ; and as mutual members of the same body, serving to the edification of the brethren, according to the talents God has given them."[70]

Fourth, *flee worldliness as pilgrims on earth*. We must not let the world conform us to its image (Rom. 12:2). Though worldliness is expressed in how people talk, dress their bodies, array their possessions, and spend their time, we must remember that the core of worldliness lies in what people love. John warns, "Love not the world, neither the things that are in the world. If any man love the world, the love of the Father is not in him. For all that is in the world, the lust of the flesh, and the lust of the eyes, and the pride of life, is not of the Father, but is of the world. And the world passeth away, and the lust thereof: but he that doeth the will of God abideth for ever" (1 John 2:15–17). Rather than letting such defiling desires control our hearts, we must set our minds on whatever is honorable, just, pure, lovely, and virtuous (Phil. 4:8).

Christians must live as citizens of another world, "strangers and pilgrims" passing through this earth on their way to a better place (Heb. 11:13). "The citizens of the city of God," Augustine said, "sigh for the peace of their heavenly country."[71] Calvin said, "If heaven is our homeland, what else is the earth but our place of exile? . . . It is like a sentry

68. Watson, *A Body of Divinity*, 249.

69. For a brief overview of the blessings and responsibilities of church membership, see Joel R. Beeke, *A Faithful Church Member* (Darlington, England: Evangelical Press, 2011). Church life will be explored under the locus of ecclesiology in *RST*, vol. 4 (forthcoming).

70. *The Three Forms of Unity*, 48.

71. Augustine, *The City of God*, 15.6, in *NPNF*[1], 2:287.

post at which the Lord has posted us, which we must hold until he recalls us."[72] He added, "The present life is for his people as a pilgrimage on which they are hastening on toward the Heavenly Kingdom."[73] They hope in "new heavens and a new earth, wherein dwelleth righteousness" (2 Pet. 3:13).

Fifth, *fill your mind with the glory of God*. The knowledge of God casts down our pride and raises up God's image in us. Calvin observed that so long as we avoid thinking much about God, "we flatter ourselves most sweetly, and fancy ourselves all but demigods"; but when we "begin to raise our thoughts to God, and to ponder his nature, and how completely perfect are his righteousness, wisdom, and power," we are humbled and astonished.[74] To get a glimpse of God's incomparable holiness is to see how insignificant we and all our idols are (Isa. 40:12–26; Jer. 10:1–16). As Owen said, a sense of God's majesty shows how small and corrupt we are, which "strikes deep at the root of any indwelling sin."[75] Faith flourishes in an atmosphere of humility, and nothing humbles man like knowing the Holy One.

Our Lord taught us that the knowledge of God is our very life (John 17:3). Paul counted "the knowledge of Christ Jesus my Lord" as far more excellent than all things (Phil. 3:8). Man's intelligence, power, and wealth are not worth boasting about, but we should glory in knowing the Lord (Jer. 9:23–24). Such knowledge of God makes us like God, people of faithful love (Hos. 6:6) and workers of justice in an unjust world (Jer. 22:16).[76]

A particularly helpful way of setting your mind on the glory of God is to meditate on the Psalms. Though the Psalter contains different kinds of prayers, many of them focus on the glory of God and Christ.[77] Read them, pray them, and sing them in the presence of the Lord.

Sixth, *know your sinful heart*. Though the grace of regeneration gives people new hearts, their remaining sin still actively opposes the holy thoughts and desires that the Spirit produces. Sin no longer reigns in the Christian (Rom. 5:21; 6:14), but it does strive for control and must be constantly put down, lest Christians backslide from the Lord (6:12, 19).[78]

---

72. Calvin, *Institutes*, 3.9.4.
73. Calvin, *Institutes*, 3.10.1.
74. Calvin, *Institutes*, 1.1.2.
75. Owen, *Of the Mortification of Sin in Believers*, in *Works*, 6:63.
76. On our knowledge of God, see *RST*, 1:69–75, 501–17.
77. Consider Psalms 2, 7, 11, 16, 23, 24, 27, 29, 33, 36, 46, 62, 63, 72, 89, 90, 91, 96–99, 103, 104, 139, and 145.
78. On backsliding and its cure, see chap. 41. See also Beeke, *Getting Back in the Race*.

Believers must exhort each other against "the deceitfulness of sin" (Heb. 3:13). Sin tends to dull their minds to the Word so that they are in danger of drifting from it (2:1). They can lose the fervency of the love they first had (Rev. 2:4). They may become spiritually lazy, decline in their zeal, and even grow angry against the servants of God (2 Chron. 16:10). Therefore, keep watch over your heart (Prov. 4:23). "He that trusteth in his own heart is a fool" (28:26). Welcome admonitions from a loving brother, and say with David, "Let the righteous smite me; it shall be a kindness: and let him reprove me; it shall be an excellent oil" (Ps. 141:5).

Seventh, *look to the blood of Christ.* Though we have already spoken of the necessity of faith in Christ to walk in holiness, the great importance of this truth warrants speaking of it again. Owen said that all other disciplines for putting sin to death are merely "preparatory" to this work: "Set faith at work on Christ for the killing of thy sin. His blood is the great sovereign remedy for sin-sick souls. Live in this, and thou wilt die a conqueror; yea, thou wilt, through the good providence of God, live to see thy lust dead at thy feet."[79]

Believe that Jesus Christ has the fullness of grace for all your needs (John 1:16). Christ died and rose again so that you would die to self and live unto God with zeal for good works (2 Cor. 5:15; Titus 2:14). Say, "Behold, the Lord Christ, that hath all fulness of grace in his heart, all fulness of power in his hand, he is able to slay all these his enemies."[80] Watson said, "Get faith in Christ's blood. . . . Justifying faith does that in a spiritual sense which miraculous faith does, it removes mountains, the mountains of pride, lust, envy."[81]

Lift up your heart with hope that Christ will certainly help you. You cannot know when or how, but if you are his, and you look to him to do this, then he will certainly act. He is the merciful and faithful high priest who was appointed by God to help those in temptation (Heb. 2:17–18). He is a willing and compassionate Savior, and if we come to God trusting in him, we will "obtain mercy, and find grace to help in time of need" (4:15–16).[82]

Sing to the Lord

The Lord, Our Lawgiver and Sanctifier

Thou, Lord, hast dealt well with Thy servant,
Thy promise is faithful and just;

79. Owen, *Of the Mortification of Sin in Believers*, in *Works*, 6:79.
80. Owen, *Of the Mortification of Sin in Believers*, in *Works*, 6:79.
81. Watson, *A Body of Divinity*, 249.
82. Owen, *Of the Mortification of Sin in Believers*, in *Works*, 6:80–82.

Instruct me in judgment and knowledge,
For in Thy commandments I trust.

Before my affliction I wandered,
But now Thy good word I obey;
O Thou, Who art holy and gracious,
Now teach me Thy statutes, I pray.

The proud have assailed me with slander;
Thy precepts shall still be my guide;
Thy law is my joy and my treasure,
Though sinners may boast in their pride.

Affliction has been for my profit,
That I to Thy statutes might hold;
Thy law to my soul is more precious
Than thousands of silver and gold.

Psalm 119:65–72
Tune: Nilus
The Psalter, No. 329

Questions for Meditation or Discussion

1. How is the call to cultivate holiness a holistic task and one that is impossible apart from Christ?
2. How should we rely on Christ in his threefold office as we pursue holiness?
3. What are the positive and negative sides of sanctification as an exercise of repentance?
4. How does our sanctification require us to give attention to (a) the moral character of God and Christ; (b) indwelling sin; (c) the law of God; and (d) how we respond to affliction?
5. What does it mean to live unto God? How is that important for sanctification?
6. What are four subtle obstacles to growing in holiness?
7. How must Christians use God's Word so that they may be sanctified by means of it?
8. Why is it crucial to pray if we are to grow spiritually? What are some scriptural prayers we could use to seek greater sanctification?

9. Why is looking to the blood of Christ essential to sanctification? What does it mean to look to his blood for holiness?

Questions for Deeper Reflection

10. How would you explain to a group of eleven- or twelve-year-old children what it means to count yourself dead to sin and alive to God?
11. What can we learn about sanctification from God's covenantal relationship with Israel? How is Christian sanctification different from the holiness of the old covenant?
12. Someone says, "I am completely dedicated to pursuing holiness, but I have no need for the church. In fact, given all its hypocrisy and problems, the church would hinder me from sanctification." How do you respond?

30

Preservation and Perseverance, Part 1

Biblical Promises and Warnings

Does God preserve his people so that they all persevere in the faith to the end? The question is not whether all who profess to be Christians will enter the kingdom of God. Christ said that many who claim to be his disciples will hear him say to them on judgment day, "I never knew you: depart from me, ye that work iniquity" (Matt. 7:21–23). Others will fall away in this life under persecution or turn aside after false teachers (24:9–13, 24). Rather, the question is "whether effectually called, regenerated, Spirit-sealed, and justified believers can irrevocably fall from the state of grace and be condemned to eternal punishment."[1]

We will argue that God promises to preserve every true believer in Christ so that he will follow the Lord until he reaches eternal glory. The words *preservation*[2] and *perseverance*[3] summarize the two sides of this

1. Demarest, *The Cross and Salvation*, 432.

2. A few divines use the term *conservation* for preservation. Thus, Manton, *Sermons upon John 17*, in *Works*, 10:300; Witsius, *The Economy of the Covenants*, 3.13.2 (2:55); and Brown, *Systematic Theology*, 437.

3. Some theologians use the term *eternal security of believers* rather than *perseverance of the saints*. While the former term can be used in a true and biblical sense, Robert Letham notes that "the eternal security of the believer" tends to make the issue simply one of believing and may even suggest "carefree" comfort, "safe and secure from all alarms," whereas "the word *perseverance*

doctrine. On the one hand, God promises to preserve those whom he effectually calls: "Whom he called, them he also justified: and whom he justified, them he also glorified" (Rom. 8:30). On the other hand, believers must persevere to the end in order to attain glory: they are "heirs of God, and joint-heirs with Christ; if so be that we suffer with him, that we may be glorified together" (v. 17).

One could approach this topic by presenting a series of biblical and theological arguments for the Reformed doctrine of the perseverance of the saints and then answering objections and questions.[4] Such an approach would be particularly effective as a polemic against false doctrine. However, it is our intention to employ a more pastoral method. After setting the debate in its historical context to clarify the issues, we will alternate between the promised grace of preservation and the necessary duty of perseverance. These complementary truths work together to nurture Christian endurance energized by both confident hope and holy fear.

Historical Background of the Debate over Perseverance

The perseverance of the saints was not a matter that attracted much theological discussion prior to the Pelagian controversy.[5] The early church fathers recognized that some members of the church fall away from the faith. They pressed upon people the necessity of repentance of sins and warned of the damnation to fall on the unrepentant. For instance, Irenaeus said that the church in all places confesses one God, the Father Almighty, and one Christ Jesus, the Son of God, who will return from heaven in glory to judge the world and "confer immortality on the righteous, and holy, and those who have kept His commandments, and have persevered in His love."[6] Yet they also regarded saving faith to be "fruitful of virtue" and "firmly established,"[7] even "immoveable," because believers have been crucified with Christ.[8] Justin Martyr said, "My faith towards Him [the

conjures up the idea of struggle against a variety of obstacles, 'through many dangers, toils, and snares.'" Letham, *Systematic Theology*, 742–43.

4. A good example of this approach may be found in Turretin, *Institutes*, 15.16 (2:593–616).

5. On the historical theology of this doctrine, see John Jefferson Davis, "The Perseverance of the Saints: A History of the Doctrine," *Journal of the Evangelical Theological Society* 34, no. 2 (June 1991): 213–28.

6. Irenaeus, *Against Heresies*, 1.10.1, in *ANF*, 1:330–31. This is one version of the ancient rule of faith.

7. Clement, *First Epistle*, chap. 1, in *ANF*, 1:5.

8. Ignatius, *Epistle to the Smyrnaeans*, chap. 1, in *ANF*, 1:86.

Son] is stedfast, and my love to the Father immoveable, God bestowing both upon us."[9]

In his battle against Pelagianism, Augustine asserted that "the perseverance by which we persevere in Christ even to the end is the gift of God," but "it is uncertain whether any one has received this gift as long as he is still alive."[10] It is possible for men to be "justified" and "renewed" unto piety but to fall away, he said, for only those chosen in the secret predestination of God will persevere.[11] Augustine taught the perseverance of the elect but not the perseverance of all believers. He believed in baptismal regeneration,[12] and there is no denying that some of those who are baptized do fall away.

In contrast to Augustine, other theologians seeking an alternative to Pelagianism affirmed the power of man's will but still asserted the necessity of God's grace to assist the will in conversion and perseverance. John Cassian said that sometimes God "puts into us the very beginnings of holy desire, and grants both the commencement of a good work and perseverance in it."[13] However, sometimes God's grace is a response to the goodness of our wills: "Through the excellence of nature which is granted by the goodness of the Creator, sometimes the first beginnings of a good will arise, which however cannot attain to the complete performance of what is good unless it is guided by the Lord, the Apostle bears witness and says: 'For to will is present with me, but to perform what is good I find not' [Rom. 7:18]."[14] Even in later stages of maturity, "the persistence of the goodness already acquired" depends both on God and "the freedom of the will."[15]

The teaching that a regenerated believer might lose his salvation continued into the medieval period,[16] though often with the qualification that the elect will reach glory. Thomas Aquinas agreed with Augustine that

9. Justin Martyr, *Against Marcion* (no longer extant), cited in Irenaeus, *Against Heresies*, 4.6.2, in *ANF*, 1:468.

10. Augustine, *A Treatise on the Gift of Perseverance*, chap. 1, in *NPNF*[1], 5:526. See Henry Knapp, "Augustine and Owen on Perseverance," *Westminster Theological Journal* 62, no. 1 (Spring 2000): 65–87.

11. Augustine, *Gift of Perseverance*, chap. 21, in *NPNF*[1], 5:532; cf. *A Treatise on Rebuke and Grace*, chaps. 11–16, 42, in *NPNF*[1], 5:476–78, 489.

12. Augustine, *The Enchiridion*, chap. 42, in *NPNF*[1], 3:252.

13. John Cassian, *Conferences*, 13.17, in *NPNF*[2], 11:433. On the attempt by Cassian and others to find middle ground between Pelagius and Augustine, see *RST*, 1:1004–7.

14. Cassian, *Conferences*, 13.9, in *NPNF*[2], 11:427. In this quotation, Cassian's doctrine of prevenient grace, if we may so call it, conflates grace with creation.

15. Cassian, *Conferences*, 13.18, in *NPNF*[2], 11:434.

16. Peter Lombard taught that Christian love can perish, resulting in the loss of saving grace in the soul. Lombard, *The Sentences*, 3.31.1 (3:128–31).

perseverance is possible only by the continual assistance of God's grace, and the "gift of perseverance" is not given to all who receive saving grace.[17] Those who are predestined to eternal life though in themselves capable of dying in mortal sin, nevertheless will certainly and infallibly attain the crown of life.[18]

Lutheranism teaches that God desires to give perseverance to all in whom he has begun a good work of salvation, but if "they willingly turn themselves away," grieve the Spirit, and entangle themselves in sin, their last state is worse than the one they were in before their conversion.[19] When a saint commits gross sin, such as adultery or murder, then "at that point faith and the Spirit have departed."[20] However, those chosen in Christ before the foundation of the world "shall be eternally saved." Hence, believers are taught to confess, "We have a glorious comfort in this salutary teaching, that we know how we have been chosen for eternal life in Christ out of sheer grace, without any merit of our own, and that no one can tear us out of his hand."[21]

The Council of Trent stated the position of the Roman Catholic Church that perseverance is God's gift but no one who is "born again and justified" at the present can know apart from direct revelation that he is one of God's elect or that he will persevere to the end.[22] "The received grace of justification is lost, not only by infidelity whereby even faith itself is lost, but also by any other mortal sin whatever, though faith be not lost."[23] The fallen can be "again justified . . . through the sacrament of Penance," which is "a second plank after the shipwreck of grace lost."[24]

While the Augustinian tradition had long affirmed the perseverance of the elect, prominent early Reformed theologians taught the perseverance of all who have saving faith in Christ.[25] Ulrich Zwingli (1484–1531) said that

---

17. Aquinas, *Summa Theologica*, Part 2.1, Q. 109, Art. 10, Answer.
18. Aquinas, *Summa Theologica*, Part 1, Q. 23, Art. 6.
19. Formula of Concord (Solid Declaration, 11.42), in *The Book of Concord*, 647–48.
20. The Smalcald Articles (3.43), in *The Book of Concord*, 319.
21. Formula of Concord (Epitome, 11.7, 13), in *The Book of Concord*, 517–18.
22. Council of Trent, session 6, chap. 13, canons 15–17, in *Creeds of Christendom*, ed. Schaff, 2:103, 113–14.
23. Council of Trent, session 6, chap. 15, in *Creeds of Christendom*, ed. Schaff, 2:106; cf. canon 23 (2:115).
24. Council of Trent, session 6, chap. 14, in *Creeds of Christendom*, ed. Schaff, 2:104–5.
25. Though taught by early Reformed divines, the doctrine of the perseverance of the saints was not prominent in sixteenth-century Reformed confessions. Some early British Reformed confessional statements simply affirm the perseverance of *the elect*, such as the Thirty-Nine Articles (Art. 17) and the Lambeth Articles (Art. 5), in *Reformed Confessions*, 2:746, 759. See Jay T. Collier, *Debating Perseverance: The Augustinian Heritage in Post-Reformation England*, Oxford Studies in Historical Theology (Oxford: Oxford University Press, 2018). In other early

saving faith is given only to the elect, and so believers can know that they are chosen and secured to eternal life, and are not among those who will fall away from Christ.[26] Heinrich Bullinger, observing that Christ prayed for Peter "that thy faith fail not" (Luke 22:32), said that Christians look to the Lord for "his aid to keep us that we fall not from true faith." He added that the "root and substance of faith doth always remain, although it be at some time more, and at some time less."[27] John Calvin commended "a quiet reliance upon the Lord's promise, where he declares that all by whom he is received in true faith have been given to him by the Father, no one of whom, since he is their guardian and shepherd, will perish."[28]

Jacob Arminius said that it is possible for believers to fall away from Christ and lose their salvation by their own negligence, though he was noncommittal on whether they actually do so.[29] After Arminius died, the Arminians affirmed that some "believers" who are "elected, adopted, and justified" later desert the faith, and only those who persevere will be saved.[30]

The international Reformed movement decisively rejected the Arminian position in the Canons of Dort, the fifth head of which remains the most extensive Reformed confessional statement on the doctrine of perseverance.[31] Perhaps the best short statement of this doctrine is found in the Westminster Confession of Faith (27.1), which says, "They, whom God hath accepted in His Beloved, effectually called, and sanctified by His Spirit, can neither totally nor finally fall away from the state of grace, but shall certainly persevere therein to the end, and be eternally saved."[32] The words "neither totally nor finally" are important, for the confession does

Reformed confessions, the doctrine is not explicitly addressed. However, the Belgic Confession (Art. 35) rules out Augustine's belief that people may be godly but not elect when it asserts that the "spiritual and heavenly" life granted in "second birth" is "not common, but is peculiar to God's elect." *The Three Forms of Unity*, 57. See also the Second Helvetic Confession (chap. 10), in *Reformed Confessions*, 2:825–26. The Heidelberg Catechism (LD 21, Q. 54) implies the perseverance of the saints when it says, "I am and for ever shall remain, a living member" of God's elect church saved and preserved by Christ. *The Three Forms of Unity*, 85. See *The Commentary of Dr. Zacharias Ursinus on the Heidelberg Catechism*, trans. G. W. Williard, 2nd American ed. (Columbus: Scott & Bascom, 1852), 114–16.

26. Ulrich Zwingli, *On the Providence of God*, in *On Providence and Other Essays*, ed. William John Hinke (1922; repr., Durham, NC: Labyrinth, 1983), 197–99.

27. Bullinger, *The Decades*, 1:99.

28. Calvin, *Institutes*, 3.24.7.

29. Arminius, *Declaration of Sentiments*, in *Works*, 1:664–66; cf. Stanglin, *Arminius on the Assurance of Salvation*, 130–34.

30. *The Arminian Confession of 1621*, 18.6 (112–13).

31. *The Three Forms of Unity*, 153–63.

32. *Reformed Confessions*, 4:253.

not deny that believers can partly or temporarily fall away—but their faith does not completely and permanently fail.[33]

Christ's Promises of Eternal Life

The future happiness of those who trust in Christ is grounded on the promise that they have already received "eternal life" (John 3:15). Eternal life consists of participation in the kingdom of God by the resurrection from the dead (Dan. 12:2). Christ used "eternal life" and the "kingdom" almost interchangeably when referring to the future happiness of his people.[34] Therefore, believers already possess the everlasting life of God's glorious kingdom. This is an example of inaugurated eschatology, the appearance of realities belonging to the end of the age in this present world. Wayne Grudem writes, "Now if this is truly eternal life that believers have, then it is life that lasts forever with God."[35]

This conclusion is borne out in specific promises that the Lord Jesus Christ gives to his people. Christ says, "Whosoever drinketh of the water that I shall give him shall never thirst; but the water that I shall give him shall be in him a well of water springing up into everlasting life" (John 4:14). The Greek phrase rendered as "shall never thirst"[36] employs a double negative for emphasis, with the phrase meaning "forever": he will *certainly never* thirst (cf. John 6:35). Those who receive "everlasting life" will never be deprived of God's life-giving, heart-satisfying grace.

The Lord Jesus also says, "Verily, verily, I say unto you, He that heareth my word, and believeth on him that sent me, hath everlasting life, and shall not come into condemnation; but is passed from death unto life" (John 5:24). The word translated as "verily" (*amēn*) communicates certainty. Those who have eternal life in the present by faith in him will never be condemned.[37] They have already made the transition "from death unto life." Christ compares this to a present spiritual resurrection from the dead (vv. 25–26). He then looks ahead to the future physical resurrection, showing that the "condemnation" (*krisis*) from which believers are

33. See Wollebius, *Compendium*, 1.32.i, v (174).

34. Matt. 7:14, 21; Mark 9:45–47; 10:17, 23–25, 30; Luke 18:29–30.

35. Grudem, *Systematic Theology*, 790.

36. Greek: *ou mē dipsēsē eis ton aiōna*.

37. Someone might object that the verb translated as "shall not come" (*erchetai*) is in the present tense, not the future (John 5:24), which might mean that the believer is presently not condemned as long as he keeps believing. However, the same present-tense verb appears regarding the future coming (*erchetai*) of the resurrection of the dead (v. 28).

now delivered (v. 24) is the future "damnation" (*krisis*) of the wicked (vv. 28–29). D. A. Carson writes, "This is perhaps the strongest affirmation of inaugurated eschatology in the Fourth Gospel."[38]

Christ promises, "All that the Father giveth me shall come to me; and him that cometh to me I will in no wise cast out. For I came down from heaven, not to do mine own will, but the will of him that sent me. And this is the Father's will which hath sent me, that of all which he hath given me I should lose nothing, but should raise it up again at the last day" (John 6:37–39). As surely as the Son obeys the Father, Christ will lose not one of the people the Father gave to him, but will bring them all to the resurrection of glory. Calvin commented, "He is not the guardian of our salvation for a single day, or for a few days, but . . . he will take care of it to the end, so that he will conduct us, as it were, from the commencement to the termination of our course."[39] This is what it means to "have everlasting life" (v. 40).

Christ weaves these truths into his metaphor of a shepherd and his sheep, saying, "My sheep hear my voice, and I know them, and they follow me: and I give unto them eternal life; and they shall never perish, neither shall any man pluck them out of my hand. My Father, which gave them me, is greater than all; and no man is able to pluck them out of my Father's hand" (John 10:27–29). Since the Father gave them to the Son, and the Son gave them "eternal life," "they shall never perish" (again, the Greek emphatic double negative). This promise is backed by the divine power of the Father and the Son—one God in Trinity (v. 30). Calvin said, "The salvation of all the elect is not less certain than the power of God is invincible."[40] John Owen said, "He layeth their abiding with him as his sheep upon the omnipotence of God," for Christ promises "by his power and the power of his Father to preserve them . . . which power shall not, nor possibly can be, prevailed against. . . . By the almighty power of his Spirit and grace, he confirmeth his saints in a voluntary abiding with him all their days."[41]

Someone might object that this promise says nothing about a person removing himself from God's hand, but only pertains to external forces

38. Carson, *The Gospel according to John*, 256.
39. Calvin, *Commentaries*, on John 6:39.
40. Calvin, *Commentaries*, on John 10:28–29.
41. Owen, *The Doctrine of the Saints' Perseverance*, in *Works*, 11:284–85.

tearing him away.[42] In reply, we note, first, that any attempt to insert the possibility of damnation into this text contradicts Christ's promise, "They shall never perish." Second, Christ literally says that "no one [*oudeis*] is able" to take them from the Father, excluding all people and powers, even the person tempted to fall away. Third, the danger facing Christ's disciples was false teachers and persecutors such as the Pharisees (John 9:13–41), whom Jesus said were spiritual thieves, robbers, and wolves (10:1, 8, 10). Christ uses the same word for "pluck" (*harpazō*) or seize in these promises (vv. 28–29) that he used earlier of a wolf attacking the sheep (v. 12).[43] Therefore, Christ's promise that no one can snatch his sheep away means that God will preserve his elect people from falling away under the influence of wicked leaders who threaten, entice, or deceive.

Another objection against using these promises as evidence for the preservation of the saints is that Christ teaches man's responsibility to believe (John 6:35; 10:25–26).[44] Grudem explains, "Arminian theologians frequently assume that if they affirm human responsibility and the need for continuing in the faith they have thereby negated the idea that God's sovereign keeping and protection is absolutely certain and eternal life is guaranteed." He responds that such theologians, first, fail exegetically to provide convincing interpretations of these promises that show "why we should not take these words as absolute guarantees," and second, fail theologically by assuming that human responsibility negates God's sovereignty.[45] He concludes, "It seems better to adopt the Reformed position that says that God's sovereign protection is consistent with human responsibility, because it works through human responsibility and guarantees that we will respond by maintaining the faith that is necessary to persevere."[46]

The Necessity of Perseverance

Christ's promises of eternal life are solid and sure for all believers. However, we abuse them if we promise eternal security to people regardless of whether they continue to follow Christ in faith and obedience. John Mur-

42. Robert Shank, *Life in the Son: A Study of the Doctrine of Perseverance* (Minneapolis: Bethany House, 1989), 208.
43. Compare the references to false teachers and persecutors as "wolves" in Matt. 7:15; 10:16; Luke 10:3; Acts 20:29.
44. Osborne, "Soteriology in the Gospel of John," in *The Grace of God and the Will of Man*, ed. Pinnock, 249.
45. On the Reformed doctrine of the free choice of the will, see *RST*, 2:417–34 (chap. 22).
46. Grudem, *Systematic Theology*, 791n6.

ray said that the doctrine of the perseverance of the saints "is not at all that they will be saved irrespective of their perseverance or their continuance, but that they will assuredly persevere."[47]

The Lord Jesus insists that his disciples must persevere to the end to receive full and final salvation. Twice when speaking of the persecution that his disciples would face, Christ says, "The one who endures to the end will be saved" (Matt. 10:22; 24:13 ESV). In the parable of the soils, the distinguishing mark of good soil is that such people receive the word "in an honest and good heart . . . and bring forth fruit with patience [*hypomonē*]," literally "endurance" (Luke 8:15). Christ did not always rejoice over those who believed in him (John 2:23–25), but admonished them, "If ye continue in my word, then are ye my disciples indeed" (8:31).

The Lord Jesus Christ did not mean by this that ultimate salvation requires the avoidance of "mortal" sins.[48] Herman Bavinck noted, "Those who consider total apostasy a possibility have to make a distinction between the sins by which the grace of regeneration is lost and other sins by which it is not lost. In other words, they are compelled to resort to the Roman Catholic distinction between mortal and venial sins."[49] There is no such list to be found in the Scriptures, for every sin deserves death (Rom. 1:32; 6:23).

Perseverance will involve arduous repentance if one commits great and scandalous sins. Peter fell into public denial of Christ, yet his faith did not utterly fail, and he repented with many tears and was restored through deep humiliation.[50] Johannes Wollebius reminded us that perseverance in the faith does not mean "that the elect cannot fall into the gravest sin" or "that their faith does not ever reach the verge of collapsing"; indeed, their "faith may be lost as far as its full action is concerned," though not lost in its inward disposition (*habitus*).[51]

Christ calls men to deny themselves, take up their crosses, and follow him, for this is the only way to find life and vindication on judgment day (Luke 9:23–26). The doctrine of the perseverance of the saints is not a cause of laziness and does not injure godliness, morality, prayer, and other

47. Murray, *Redemption Accomplished and Applied*, 154–55.

48. See the discussion of degrees of actual sin in *RST*, 2:445–47.

49. Bavinck, *Reformed Dogmatics*, 4:268. He noted that it is logically possible to hold another position, that "grace is lost by every—even the most minor—sin." But few would hold such an extreme position.

50. Luke 22:31–34, 54–62; John 21:15–17.

51. Wollebius, *Compendium*, 1.32.1 (174); cf. Turretin, *Institutes*, 15.16.5 (2:594).

acts of devotion, but instills a hope that purifies (1 John 3:2–3), as the Canons of Dort (Head 5, Rejection 6) tell us.[52] The apostolic message demands that converts continue to cling to Christ and endure many tribulations to enter the kingdom (Acts 11:23; 14:22). Jude says, "Building up yourselves on your most holy faith, praying in the Holy Ghost, keep yourselves in the love of God, looking for the mercy of our Lord Jesus Christ unto eternal life" (Jude 20–21).

The doctrine of perseverance should never be construed to imply that the Christian life is one of easy victory. The Canons of Dort (Head 5, Art. 4) state,

> Although the weakness of the flesh cannot prevail against the power of God, who confirms and preserves true believers in a state of grace, yet converts are not always so influenced and actuated by the Spirit of God, as not in some particular instances sinfully to deviate from the guidance of divine grace, so as to be seduced by, and comply with the lusts of the flesh; they must, therefore, be constant in watching and prayer that they be not led into temptation. When these are neglected, they are not only liable to be drawn into great and heinous sins by Satan, the world and the flesh, but sometimes by the righteous permission of God actually fall into these evils. This the lamentable fall of David, Peter, and other saints described in Holy Scripture demonstrates.[53]

The Word of God even says that participation in the kingdom is conditional on perseverance. Paul wrote to a church tempted with false doctrine that God would present the people holy in his sight "*if ye continue* in the faith grounded and settled, and be not moved away from the hope of the gospel" (Col. 1:23). In another epistle, he wrote about his suffering and imprisonment, and said, "*If we suffer*, we shall also reign with him: if we deny him, he also will deny us" (2 Tim. 2:12). The epistle to the Hebrews states that we are Christ's house "*if we hold fast* the confidence and the rejoicing of the hope firm unto the end," and "we are made partakers of Christ, *if we hold* the beginning of our confidence stedfast unto the end" (Heb. 3:6, 14).

We sympathize with those who are offended by a doctrine that Christians have no need of "deliberately persevering in faith" because of their

52. *The Three Forms of Unity*, 161–62.
53. *The Three Forms of Unity*, 154.

"confidence in some past act or experience."[54] Salvation by grace does not guarantee heaven if we assent to a doctrine, pray a prayer, or have an emotional experience. Therefore, the mantra "once saved, always saved" needs to be qualified by the necessity of perseverance. We dare not say, as R. T. Kendall says, "Whoever once truly believes that Jesus was raised from the dead, and confesses that Jesus is Lord, will go to heaven . . . no matter what work (or lack of work) may accompany such faith." Such a statement implies that a professing believer who "falls into sin, stays in sin," and dies in that condition will "still go to heaven."[55] This contradicts the biblical doctrine of the necessity of perseverance. However, the solution is not to make Christ's promises of preservation conditional on our fluctuating wills, but to recognize that God preserves his people in eternal life by giving them effectual grace to willingly persevere.

The Warnings against Apostasy

The word *apostasy* derives from a Greek word (*apostasia*) meaning a departing from or a falling away—in this case, a forsaking of a previously held religion (Acts 21:21; 2 Thess. 2:3). The related verb, translated as "depart" (*aphistēmi*), is sometimes used in the same sense of a spiritual falling away (Luke 8:13; 1 Tim. 4:1; Heb. 3:12). At times, we read of people who "fall from" (*ekpiptō*) the grace of God or their former steadfastness in the faith (Gal. 5:4; 2 Pet. 3:17). The New Testament is full of warnings to Christians to guard against such a falling away.

Warnings in the Teachings of Our Lord

In the parable of the soils, the rocky soil represents people who, "when they hear, receive the word with joy . . . which for a while believe, and in time of temptation fall away" (Luke 8:13). Christ does not describe them as once being good soil and later falling from that condition. He says that they are "on the rock" and "have no root" (v. 13)—that is, they do not receive the word into the depths of their hard hearts, in contrast to the people represented by good soil, who receive the word with "an honest and good heart" (v. 15). Therefore, they do not have saving faith, but a temporary faith that consists of a transient emotional commitment.[56]

54. Shank, *Life in the Son*, 64.

55. R. T. Kendall, *Once Saved, Always Saved* (Carlisle, Cumbria, England: Paternoster, 1997), 19, 50–51.

56. See the discussion of saving faith and its counterfeits in chap. 20.

Wilhelmus à Brakel said, "All that is denominated as faith is not saving faith. Otherwise Agrippa would also have been a believer, for he believed the Holy Scriptures (Acts 26:27)."[57]

Christ also warns against apostasy in the parable of the vine (John 15), which draws from Isaiah's twofold depiction of Israel as a vineyard that produced only the bad fruit of injustice but one day would fill the world with good fruit (Isa. 5:1–7; 27:2–6). Christ is the true vine, and only by union with him can we be part of the true and fruitful Israel (John 15:1, 5). However, Jesus says, "If a man abide not in me, he is cast forth as a branch, and is withered; and men gather them, and cast them into the fire, and they are burned" (v. 6). To "cast" agricultural products into a "fire" is an image for the punishment of the wicked in hell for their failure to produce the fruit of righteousness.[58] In this parable, the picture is of outward adherence to Christ without drawing spiritual life from him as a branch does from the vine. Disciples in this condition prove themselves to be like ancient Israel in its apostasy from God. Those who fruitfully abide in Christ and his word are his true disciples who glorify God (vv. 7–8). They are different from the world because Christ has "chosen" them to bear fruit (vv. 16–18). Therefore, while apostasy is real, those who fall away are not God's elect who once were in vital union with his Son.

All of Christ's apostles fell away from him in varying degrees during his passion; Peter even denied knowing Christ three times (Mark 14:27–31). While the apostasy of the eleven was not total or final (Luke 22:31–32), their partial and temporary falling away is still a sobering warning to believers, who tend to have too high an estimation of their own fortitude (Rom. 11:20; 1 Cor. 10:12), as did Peter (Matt. 26:33). Though God's grace preserves believers from completely falling away, "they may, through the temptations of Satan and of the world, the prevalency of corruption remaining in them, and the neglect of the means of their preservation, fall into grievous sins; and, for a time, continue therein," as the Westminster Confession of Faith (27.3) says, so that true believers, while not apostatizing, nevertheless by their backsliding "incur God's displeasure, and grieve His Holy Spirit, come to be deprived of some measure of their graces and comforts, have their hearts hardened, and their consciences wounded; hurt and scandalize others, and bring temporal judgments upon themselves."[59]

57. Brakel, *The Christian's Reasonable Service*, 4:288.
58. Matt. 3:10; 7:19; 13:40, 42, 50; Luke 3:9; cf. Matt. 18:8–9; Mark 9:47.
59. *Reformed Confessions*, 4:253.

The preeminent example of complete apostasy is Judas. After years of ministry as one of the twelve apostles, he betrayed Christ for a sum of money, and later was filled with remorse and killed himself in despair.[60] Judas had been "a devil" for a long time before this betrayal (John 6:70; cf. 12:6). So skillful was his hypocrisy that not one of the other apostles suspected him (Matt. 26:21–25). Judas was accountable for his sin, but his apostasy fulfilled the decree of God revealed to the prophets.[61] Christ said, "Truly the Son of man goeth, as it was determined: but woe unto that man by whom he is betrayed!" (Luke 22:22). Thus, Judas's apostasy was not the frustration of God's grace by man's changeable will, but the fulfillment of God's will. Christ prayed, "While I was with them in the world, I kept them in thy name: those that thou gavest me I have kept, and none of them is lost, but the son of perdition; that the scripture might be fulfilled" (John 17:12). "Son of perdition" is a Hebraic idiom meaning a person destined to destruction (2 Thess. 2:3, 8). What Judas meant for evil, God planned for the salvation of many perishing sinners (cf. Gen. 50:20).

In summary, we find that our Lord Jesus gives strong warnings against apostasy. Those who appear to be faithful disciples, even prominent leaders, may fall away and be damned forever. However, Christ's doctrine of apostasy does not indicate that true believers fall away unto damnation. Rather, Christ warns that people with an attachment to him and his church but no real change of heart are in grave spiritual danger. Therefore, Christ calls his professing disciples to a deep, vital, fruitful, and lasting union and communion with him. The closer their walk with him, the less likely they are to fall even temporarily into scandalous sin.

Warnings in Acts and Paul's Epistles

A classic case of apostasy is recorded in Luke's account of the spiritual awakening in Samaria through the preaching of Philip (Acts 8:5–25). When Philip preached Christ, a famous sorcerer named Simon "believed also" and "was baptized" (v. 13), but later tried to pay the apostles for the power to confer the Holy Spirit on people (vv. 18–19). Peter replied, "Thy money perish with thee, because thou hast thought that the gift of God may be purchased with money. Thou hast neither part nor lot in this matter: for thy heart is not right in the sight of God. Repent therefore of

60. Matt. 10:4; 26:14–16, 47–49; 27:3–5.
61. Ps. 41:9, cited in John 13:18; Ps. 109:7–8, cited in Acts 1:20.

this thy wickedness, and pray God, if perhaps the thought of thine heart may be forgiven thee. For I perceive that thou art in the gall of bitterness, and in the bond of iniquity" (vv. 20–23). Simon's case demonstrates that men may have a kind of faith and be baptized, yet remain in a state of sin and attempt to corrupt the church by their hypocrisy.

The writings of the apostle Paul present examples of individuals who apostatized due to false doctrine, fear of persecution, or love of earthly goods. He spoke of "Hymenaeus and Alexander," who "concerning faith have made shipwreck" (1 Tim. 1:19–20). Literally the text says, "concerning *the faith*" (*peri tēn pistin*), referring to their turning away from biblical doctrine (cf. 3:9; 4:1). Paul later warned Timothy of "Hymenaeus and Philetus; who concerning the truth have erred, saying the resurrection is past already; and overthrow the faith of some" (2 Tim. 2:17–18). Demas, once part of Paul's missionary team (Col. 4:14; Philem. 24), forsook Paul, "having loved this present world" (2 Tim. 4:10). However, such apostasies did not shake Paul's confidence that "the Lord knoweth them that are his"; instead, it confirmed his conviction that everyone who calls upon Christ for salvation must "depart from iniquity" (2:19).

Paul wrote to the churches of Galatia, "I marvel that ye are so soon removed from him that called you into the grace of Christ unto another gospel" (Gal. 1:6). Though Paul continued to address them as "brethren" (v. 11) in hopes of their recovery, he warned anyone who clung to the false doctrine of justification by Christ plus works, "Christ is become of no effect unto you, whosoever of you are justified by the law; ye are fallen from grace" (5:4). James Montgomery Boice (1938–2000) commented, "The phrase ['fallen from grace'] does not mean that if a Christian sins, he falls from grace and thereby loses his salvation. There is a sense in which to sin is to fall into grace, if one is repentant. But to fall from grace, as seen by this context, is to fall into legalism. Or to put it another way, to choose legalism is to relinquish grace as the principle by which one desires to be related to God."[62] People may turn away from the gospel of salvation by grace alone through faith alone in Christ alone, in which case they abandon the only way to God and, if they do not repent, cast themselves into destruction.

62. James Montgomery Boice, "Galatians," in *The Expositor's Bible Commentary*, ed. Frank E. Gaebelein, 12 vols. (Grand Rapids, MI: Zondervan, 1976), 10:488.

Warnings in the Epistle to the Hebrews

No portion of the Bible has received such serious consideration with regard to the question of perseverance as the epistle to the Hebrews, for it is a "word of exhortation" (Heb. 13:22) to cling to Christ and not fall away. Two texts in Hebrews particularly describe apostasy. The first is Hebrews 6:4–6: "For it is impossible for those who were once enlightened, and have tasted of the heavenly gift, and were made partakers of the Holy Ghost, and have tasted the good word of God, and the powers of the world to come, if they shall fall away, to renew them again unto repentance; seeing they crucify to themselves the Son of God afresh, and put him to an open shame."

Those who teach that true believers may fall away and be lost forever argue that the spiritual experiences listed here can describe none other than true Christians. Grant Osborne wrote, "There is no more powerful or detailed description of the true Christian in the New Testament."[63] Ian Howard Marshall (1934–2015) said, "The conclusion is irresistible that real Christians are meant."[64] The apparent force of this argument has led some theologians to argue that this text refers to a hypothetical apostasy of believers that is in fact impossible because of God's grace.[65] It is true that while believers are prone to apostatize if left to themselves, the Lord will never allow his children to fall off that precipice. However, taking this text as only a hypothetical warning neglects the force of its admonition.

The case for seeing true believers here is not as strong as it might seem. The language that is used is consistent with the experience of people present with the worshiping church, including those not truly converted. Consider the fourfold experience attributed to these people:

- "Once enlightened" (Heb. 6:4). This refers to their first learning and assenting to the gospel (10:32). The Bible sometimes uses the metaphor of enlightenment for the saving grace of effectual calling (2 Cor. 4:6), but it may also refer to the knowledge of truth (Ps. 119:105; Prov. 6:23) granted by the preaching of the Word

63. Grant R. Osborne, "Soteriology in the Epistle to the Hebrews," in *Grace Unlimited*, ed. Pinnock, 149.

64. I. Howard Marshall, *Kept by the Power of God: A Study of Perseverance and Falling Away* (Minneapolis: Bethany Fellowship, 1969), 144.

65. Thomas Hewitt, *The Epistle to the Hebrews*, Tyndale New Testament Commentary (Grand Rapids, MI: Eerdmans, 1960), 110–11; and Homer Kent, *The Epistle to the Hebrews* (Grand Rapids, MI: Baker, 1972), 113–14; cf. Demarest, *The Cross and Salvation*, 458–60.

(Matt. 4:14–17).[66] One may be enlightened but still love sin and hate God (John 3:19–20).

- "Tasted of the heavenly gift" (Heb. 6:4). To "taste" (*geuomai*, here and in v. 5) means to experience. Though Osborne claimed it means "they had fully experienced the salvation blessings,"[67] the term does not determine the extent or intensity of the experience, for it can be used of eating a meal (Acts 20:11) or tasting a fluid but refusing to drink it (Matt. 27:34). The "heavenly gift" (used only here) likely refers to some effect of the Word on those assembled for worship (Heb. 12:22).
- "Made partakers of the Holy Ghost" (Heb. 6:4). The word translated as "partakers" (plural *metochos*) can be used of union with Christ (3:14), but it also can have the weaker meaning of "partners" who participate or accompany someone in an activity (Luke 5:7), as Grudem notes.[68] The Spirit is certainly present with the church (1 Cor. 3:16) and performs many common operations on the unsaved, such as convicting of sin (John 16:8) and granting spiritual gifts (1 Cor. 12:7–11; 13:1–2).
- "Tasted the good word of God, and the powers of the world to come" (Heb. 6:5). Here again is a description of an experience of biblical preaching that many find within Christian assemblies without necessarily being converted. The word rendered as "powers" (plural *dynamis*) is often translated as "miracles" (2:4) and refers to miraculous signs.

Therefore, this fourfold experience could be shared by unconverted members or visitors who attend the public worship of the church. The text says nothing about such people being regenerated, brought to faith in Christ, or justified. It stands in marked contrast to the section that follows it, in which the writer speaks of "things that accompany salvation," such as works of love, hope, imitation of the godly, and faith in the promises (Heb. 6:9–12).

The passage also says, "It is impossible . . . to renew them again unto repentance" (Heb. 6:4, 6). Though the word translated as "repentance"

66. For examples of "enlighten" (*photizo*) with the meaning of "teach" or "bring knowledge," see 2 Kings 12:2; 17:27, 28; Ps. 118[119]:130 LXX; John 1:9; Eph. 3:9. See the discussion of John 1:9 in the section on prevenient grace (objection 3 against effectual calling) in chap. 16.

67. Osborne, "Soteriology in the Epistle to the Hebrews," in *Grace Unlimited*, ed. Pinnock, 149.

68. Grudem, *Systematic Theology*, 798.

(*metanoia*) is often used for turning to God in a saving manner, it can refer to other changes of mind or activity (12:17).[69] When unconverted people fall away, they have no motivation to renew their profession of faith and rejoin the church, for they have already tasted and rejected the church's message about Christ.[70] It may be that "impossible" speaks of human inability but not a divine impossibility, just as Christ spoke of the impossibility of the rich being saved but added that "with God all things are possible" (Matt. 19:24–26). Geerhardus Vos argued that the implicit subject of the verb "renew" is the preachers of the Word, leaving open the possibility that God could grant renewal.[71] However, it may be that "impossible" closes the door to all hope for unconverted people who have hardened themselves to such an extent that they have sealed their consciences shut against the gospel of Christ after having experienced the convicting and confirming ministry of the Holy Spirit.

Further insight into Hebrews 6:4–6 arises from recognizing that Hebrews compares the present church to Israel in the wilderness.[72] When the people of Israel left Egypt, they initially "believed the Lord" by the Red Sea (Ex. 14:31), but soon forgot his works and turned away in the wilderness (Ps. 106:12–13). The language of Hebrews 6:4–5 reflects the wilderness experience:

- The Israelites were "enlightened" by the fiery pillar that led them (Ex. 13:21; Neh. 9:12, 19).[73]
- The Israelites "tasted of the heavenly gift" when they ate the manna (Ex. 16:4; Neh. 9:15), the "bread of heaven" (Ps. 105:40).
- The Israelites experienced the presence of the Holy Spirit (Isa. 63:10–14; Hag. 2:5), who rested upon Moses and other leaders (Num. 11:24–29; Neh. 9:20).

---

69. The verb translated as "repent" (*metanoeō*) can be used to refer to a man going back on his vow (Prov. 20:25 LXX) or of God changing his course of action (1 Kingdoms [1 Sam.] 15:29; Jer. 4:28; 18:10; Amos 7:3, 6; Joel 2:13–14; Jonah 3:9–10; 4:2; Zech. 8:14 LXX). As to Heb. 12:17, the clause "he found no place for repentance [*metanoia*]" could mean that Esau could not get his father (or God) to repent about giving the highest blessing to Jacob or that Esau repented of despising his birthright (v. 16; cf. Gen. 27:36) but his pleas were still rejected by his father (and God). Either way, such "repentance" is not turning from sin to God for salvation.

70. Grudem, *Systematic Theology*, 799–800.

71. Vos, *Reformed Dogmatics*, 4:225.

72. Heb. 3:7–11; 4:1–11; 11:14–16. See *The Reformation Heritage KJV Study Bible*, ed. Joel R. Beeke, Michael P. V. Barrett, Gerald M. Bilkes, and Paul M. Smalley (Grand Rapids, MI: Reformation Heritage Books, 2014), 1789.

73. The verb used in Heb. 6:4 for "enlighten" (*phōtizō*) is also rendered as "to give them light" (Neh. 9:12, 19 LXX).

- The Israelites tasted the "good word" of the promise-keeping God (Josh. 21:45; 23:15)[74] and the power of God in his plagues and miracles (Exodus 7–14; Neh. 9:10, 17).

The parallel with Israel reveals what kind of people the writer to the Hebrews had in mind. In the wilderness, Israel was not a godly nation that fell away from God, but consisted mostly of wicked people who sometimes had a superficial faith but displayed their hard hearts by rebelling against the Lord in unbelief and failing to enter the promised land (Numbers 13–14; Psalm 95). In the same way, the warning of Hebrews 6 pertains not to believers who lose their faith and salvation, but to those who are externally part of the church but prove themselves to be wicked enemies of Christ.

Hebrews 6:4–6 refers to people who have received much from God, but they do not respond rightly. This interpretation is confirmed by verses 7–8: "For the earth which drinketh in the rain that cometh oft upon it, and bringeth forth herbs meet for them by whom it is dressed, receiveth blessing from God: but that which beareth thorns and briers is rejected, and is nigh unto cursing; whose end is to be burned." We do not find here a field that produced good fruit and later was overgrown by weeds, but a field that responded to the rain of heaven only with the evil effects of Adam's fall: "thorns and briers."[75] As a result of this response, it stands under the imminent curse of God and ultimately fiery destruction. Grudem writes, "When we recall other metaphors in Scripture where good fruit is a sign of true spiritual life and fruitlessness is a sign of false believers (for example, Matt. 3:8–10; 7:15–20; 12:33–35), we already have an indication that the author is speaking . . . about people who are not genuinely Christians."[76] It will not do to conclude that "this is not a warning about loss of salvation but about loss of rewards," as Norman Geisler (1932–2019) said.[77] Believers may see some of their works "burned" on judgment day so that they lose rewards they might have obtained (1 Cor. 3:14–15). However, this warning in Hebrews says that the people themselves will be cursed and burned.

74. Compare "good word" (*kalon rhēma*, Heb. 6:5) to "good words" (*tōn rhēmatōn tōn kalōn*, Josh. 21:45; *ta rhēmata ta kala*, Josh. 23:15 LXX).

75. The same phrase, *akanthas kai tribolous*, appears in both Heb. 6:8 and Gen. 3:18 LXX.

76. Grudem, *Systematic Theology*, 796.

77. Norman L. Geisler, "A Moderate Calvinist View," in *Four Views on Eternal Security*, ed. J. Matthew Pinson, Counterpoints (Grand Rapids, MI: Zondervan, 2002), 100. Geisler said that one must have faith in Christ to be saved, but "one does not have to be a faithful Christian to get into heaven" (108). As Michael Horton points out (114), this so-called "moderate Calvinist" view is not Calvinism at all. See *RST*, 1:1036n13.

Another reason to regard the apostates as those who never respond to the gospel with saving faith and repentance is the way the text contrasts them to true believers. The writer refers to the people who fall away in the third person as "those" or "they" (Heb. 6:4–8), but then in the next passage switches to the second person ("your" and "you," vv. 9–12). This passage begins, "But, beloved, we are persuaded better things of you, and things that accompany salvation" (v. 9). The "better things" include saving faith, hope, and love (vv. 10–12). The writer particularly singles out "your work and labour of love" toward "the saints," which is such a clear evidence of salvation that he is sure God will vindicate them as his own (v. 10). By implication, the people addressed in the earlier section—those who fully fall away—lack these saving graces that are evident in at least some of the recipients of this letter.

Therefore, the description in Hebrews 6 of those who apostatize fits well with people who hear the gospel accompanied by the convicting, miracle-working Spirit; assent to the gospel; temporarily amend their ways to join the church; and even experience the passing joys of temporary faith, but lack saving grace and later fall away completely. Thomas Manton said, "Preparative grace may fail. . . . Plenty of blossoms do not always foretell store of fruit."[78]

We find a similar warning in Hebrews 10:26–27: "For if we sin wilfully after that we have received the knowledge of the truth, there remaineth no more sacrifice for sins, but a certain fearful looking for of judgment and fiery indignation, which shall devour the adversaries." In this context, the willful sin is the apostasy of forsaking Christ, the confession of his truth, and the assembly of his church (vv. 19–25). After coming to a "knowledge of the truth" revealed in the gospel, if a person rejects Christ there is no other sacrifice available for his sins, and he will fall under the righteous judgment of God. The writer describes the apostate as one "who hath trodden under foot the Son of God, and hath counted the blood of the covenant, wherewith he was sanctified, an unholy thing, and hath done despite unto the Spirit of grace" (v. 29). This extreme form of apostasy consists of an audacious contempt for Jesus Christ and his death on the cross as presented by the Holy Spirit in the gospel.

Those who reject the preservation of the saints argue that since the apostate was "sanctified" or made holy, he must have once been a true

78. Manton, *Sermons upon John 17*, in *Works*, 10:301. On preparatory grace, see chap. 13.

believer saved by Christ's blood (Heb. 10:10, 29). In response, we note that the phrase "he was sanctified" (v. 29) is somewhat ambiguous. It could be interpreted to mean that the apostate was formerly saved; to state a general principle that "one is sanctified" by Christ's blood (the gospel that the apostate rejects); or to refer to Christ's own consecration as the priest or sanctuary of his people.[79] Only the first of these three interpretations would militate against the doctrine of perseverance.

Complete apostasy from Christ is not the way that those united to Christ act. Hebrews 3:6 says that we are Christ's house, "if we hold fast the confidence and the rejoicing of the hope firm unto the end." Again, "We are made partakers of Christ, if we hold the beginning of our confidence steadfast unto the end" (v. 14) The verb translated as "are made" (*gegonamen*) is in the perfect tense and could be translated "have become," indicating our present state. Therefore, we demonstrate the reality of our present union with Christ by our future perseverance in the faith. If we are in Christ, we will persevere; those who do not persevere were never in Christ.

It may be objected that the doctrine of perseverance makes the warnings in Hebrews superfluous and ridiculous, for no true Christian apostatizes. In reply, we answer that such warnings stir up the members of the church to examine themselves and press on in sound doctrine and holiness. For any among them who are unconverted, such warnings may result in conviction and salvation so that they do not apostatize. For those who are converted, these warnings serve to make them more vigilant and diligent. Vos said, "They are intended and formulated precisely to cause believers to persevere. In this, too, God makes use of means by which He awakens us and causes us to persevere."[80] Thomas Watson said that such admonitions serve believers "as goads and spurs to quicken them to greater diligence in working out their salvation."[81]

The Divine Grace of Preservation

When God saves a sinner, God also guards him by grace so that he will continue in the faith. Brakel wrote, "Believers, when left to themselves, do not have sufficient strength to preserve themselves, their faith, or their

79. On the interpretation of Heb. 10:29, see *RST*, 2:1068–69.
80. Vos, *Reformed Dogmatics*, 4:222.
81. Watson, *A Body of Divinity*, 283.

spiritual life. They would succumb to the assault of the enemy. Nevertheless, they are preserved, but by a strength which comes from without."[82]

Preserving Grace Promised in the New Covenant

One of the great problems addressed by the prophet Jeremiah was the apostasy of Israel from her God (Jer. 2:11–13; 3:12, 14, 22). The hearts of the Israelites, like the hearts of all people since the fall of man, were like stone tablets with sin engraved upon them (17:1). Consequently, man's "heart departeth from the LORD" (v. 5). The Lord announced his remedy for this apostasy in the "new covenant" (31:31–32).[83] This covenant promises supernatural grace that overcomes man's covenant breaking. On the one hand, it transforms how people relate to God: "I will put my law in their inward parts, and write it in their hearts" (v. 33). The Lord says, "I will put my fear in their hearts, that they shall not depart from me" (32:40). God will put into the hearts of his people a permanent inclination to godliness so that they will never fall away.

On the other hand, the grace promised in the new covenant secures how God relates to his people: "For I will forgive their iniquity, and I will remember their sin no more" (Jer. 31:34). The blessed counterpart to "they shall not depart from me" is "I will make an everlasting covenant with them, that I will not turn away from them, to do them good" (Jer. 32:40). Therefore, no sin of theirs will break the relationship they have with the Lord.

The new covenant contains the promise of preservation and perseverance. It might be objected that God promises to grant his people perseverance if they so choose. We reply that this is absurd. As Francis Turretin said, "God would promise perseverance to man provided he perseveres," which is trifling, "for to what good would he promise him what he already has?"[84]

It might be further objected that this promise pertains only to the new covenant and did not apply to the saints under the old covenant. However, the grace promised to God's people in the new covenant had already been given to individuals whom God had saved in Israel under the old covenant, for there is one covenant of grace.[85] Though the

82. Brakel, *The Christian's Reasonable Service*, 4:275–76.

83. On the new covenant, see *RST*, 2:641–53.

84. Turretin, *Institutes*, 15.16.12 (2:597).

85. On the unity of the gospel and the covenant of grace throughout history, see *RST*, 2:565–83, 655–77 (chaps. 29, 33). On the new covenant in both its newness as a historical covenant and yet its continuity with the grace previously given to God's saved people, see *RST*, 2:645–46 (chap. 32).

inscription of God's law on the heart is a new covenant promise, David could already say of the righteous, "The law of his God is in his heart" (Ps. 37:31). His present spiritual state gave him confidence that God would preserve him to the end. David said, "Though he fall, he shall not be utterly cast down: for the LORD upholdeth him with his hand. . . . Depart from evil, and do good; and dwell for evermore. For the LORD loveth judgment, and forsaketh not his saints; they are preserved for ever" (vv. 24, 27–28). Therefore, David and all the godly at that time could rejoice confidently in their future: "Surely goodness and mercy shall follow me all the days of my life: and I will dwell in the house of the LORD for ever" (23:6).

Preserving Grace Promised in the New Testament Epistles

The New Testament confirms that Christ is the Mediator of the new covenant and of all the grace and glory that are promised to those whom God has called to himself (Heb. 8:6–13; 9:15). To them belongs the inward sanctification that overcomes the corruptions of their hearts; to them belongs the legal justification that wipes clean their record before God (10:15–17). God says, "I will never leave thee, nor forsake thee" (13:5).

Believers face many obstacles to their perseverance and final salvation. The Canons of Dort (Head 5, Art. 3) say, "By reason of these remains of indwelling sin, and the temptations of sin and of the world, those who are converted could not persevere in a state of grace if left to their own strength. But God is faithful, who having conferred grace, mercifully confirms and powerfully preserves them therein, even to the end."[86]

Paul teaches that the promises of divine preservation rest on the faithfulness of God. He writes, "I thank my God always on your behalf, for the grace of God which is given you by Jesus Christ . . . who shall also confirm you unto the end, that ye may be blameless in the day of our Lord Jesus Christ. God is faithful, by whom ye were called unto the fellowship of his Son Jesus Christ our Lord" (1 Cor. 1:4, 8–9). To "confirm" (*bebaioō*) is to establish or strengthen. Similarly, after praying for the entire sanctification of the saints in Thessalonica and their preservation in holiness until Christ comes, Paul says, "Faithful is he that calleth you, who also will do it" (1 Thess. 5:23–24). He writes, "All men have not

86. *The Three Forms of Unity*, 153–54.

faith. But the Lord is faithful, who shall stablish you, and keep you from evil. And we have confidence in the Lord touching you, that ye both do and will do the things which we command you" (2 Thess. 3:2–4). Brakel wrote, "The only cause of their steadfastness is the omnipotent and faithful God."[87]

Despite the necessity to keep watch against temptation and wage war against indwelling sin, the Christian may enjoy an assured hope. Paul wrote to the Philippian saints that he was thankful to God for them, "being confident of this very thing, that he which hath begun a good work in you will perform it until the day of Jesus Christ" (Phil. 1:6). Christians must work out their salvation, but both their willing and their working are produced by God (2:12–13). Like Paul, they must "press toward the mark of the high calling of God in Christ Jesus" (3:14). Yet they need not do so in anxiety over their future, but should "rejoice in the Lord always," yes, they should "rejoice" (4:4 ESV). Their boast in every circumstance is "I can do all things through Christ which strengtheneth me" (v. 13). Even if facing possible martyrdom, they can say, "I know that this shall turn to my salvation through your prayer, and the supply of the Spirit of Jesus Christ, according to my earnest expectation and my hope, that in nothing I shall be ashamed, but that with all boldness, as always, so now also Christ shall be magnified in my body, whether it be by life, or by death. For to me to live is Christ, and to die is gain" (1:19–21).

Peter says that those whom God has caused to be born again "are kept by the power of God through faith" even as they endure great trials—indeed, those trials are divinely designed to verify and purify their faith like gold refined by fire (1 Pet. 1:3, 5). The word translated as "kept" (passive *phroureō*) means guarded, as by a vigilant military garrison.[88] John Gill said, "The means by which they are kept is, the power of God, which is as a fortress to them . . . and so [they] are safe and secure."[89] Here we find preservation and perseverance in the faith, not preservation without faith or preservation conditional upon faith, but divine power preserving "through faith"—faith being the instrument that God created and sustains to save us to the end. Anthony Hoekema said, "The power of God, the strongest power in the universe, is ceaselessly protecting, guarding, and

87. Brakel, *The Christian's Reasonable Service*, 4:276.
88. See 2 Cor. 11:32 and Josephus, *Life of Flavius Josephus*, sec. 53, in *Works*, 4.
89. Gill, *Body of Divinity*, 564.

keeping us for the final stage of our salvation, which is ready to be revealed when Christ comes again."[90] Peter concludes that epistle by writing, "The God of all grace, who hath called us unto his eternal glory by Christ Jesus, after that ye have suffered a while, make you perfect, stablish, strengthen, settle you. To him be glory and dominion for ever and ever. Amen" (5:10–11). William Bridge said, "God's calling grace doth assure us of his confirming grace."[91]

John emphasizes in his epistles the importance of walking in righteousness and love if a person is to have any basis for calling himself a Christian (1 John 1:5–7; 2:4–6; etc.). He warns against the danger of following false teachers who contradict the doctrine of Christ, and exhorts, "Abide in him" (2:28). However, he also indicates that those who apostatize from the true church show that they never truly belonged to it: "They went out from us, but they were not of us; for if they had been of us, they would no doubt have continued with us: but they went out, that they might be made manifest that they were not all of us" (v. 19). The difference is that "ye have an unction from the Holy One,"[92] the anointing of the Holy Spirit, who sustains the spiritual knowledge of God in believers by his inward teaching (vv. 20–21, 27).

John describes regeneration as grace that produces a victorious life that overcomes sin. He says, "Whosoever is born of God doth not commit sin; for his seed remaineth in him: and he cannot sin, because he is born of God" (1 John 3:9). As we explained under the topic of regeneration, John is not claiming sinlessness for God's children, but asserting that it is impossible ("cannot") for those born of God to engage in a prolonged lifestyle characterized by unrepented sin.[93] Hence, they cannot fully fall away. John also says, "Whatsoever is born of God overcometh the world: and this is the victory that overcometh the world, even our faith" (5:4). Saving faith is conquering faith.

God's preserving grace should move Christians to praise and adore him. The preservation of the saints in their persevering faith is a glorious display of God's goodness, faithfulness, immutability, and power. Owen

90. Hoekema, *Saved by Grace*, 244.

91. Bridge, *The Good and Means of Establishment*, in *Works*, 4:263.

92. The emphatic *kai hymeis* that begins 1 John 2:20 distinguishes the saints to whom John wrote from those who departed from the church (v. 19), just as the *kai hymeis* that begins v. 27 distinguishes them from deceivers (v. 26).

93. See the discussion of 1 John 3:9 under the heading of definitive cleansing from sin in chap. 17.

said, "Though you take but weak and faint hold on Christ, he takes sure, strong, and unconquerable hold on you. Have you not often wondered, that this spark of heavenly fire should be kept alive in the midst of the sea?"[94] Hence, we close this chapter with the doxology of Jude: "Now unto him that is able to keep you from falling, and to present you faultless before the presence of his glory with exceeding joy, to the only wise God our Saviour, be glory and majesty, dominion and power, both now and ever. Amen" (Jude 24–25).

Sing to the Lord

Praising God for Preserving Grace

A debtor to mercy alone,
Of covenant mercy I sing;
Nor fear, with thy righteousness on,
My person and off'ring to bring.
The terrors of law and of God
With me can have nothing to do;
My Savior's obedience and blood
Hide all my transgressions from view.

The work which his goodness began,
The arm of his strength will complete;
His promise is Yea and Amen,
And never was forfeited yet.
Things future, nor things that are now,
Nor all things below or above,
Can make him his purpose forgo,
Or sever my soul from his love.

My name from the palms of his hands
Eternity will not erase;
Impressed on his heart it remains,
In marks of indelible grace.
Yes, I to the end shall endure,
As sure as the earnest is giv'n;
More happy, but not more secure,
The glorified spirits in heav'n.

94. Owen, "The Strength of Faith," in *Works*, 9:29.

Augustus Toplady
Tune: Llangristiolus
Trinity Hymnal—Baptist Edition, No. 99

Questions for Meditation or Discussion

1. What are the views on perseverance held by Augustine, Lutherans, the Roman Catholic Church, Arminians, and Reformed theologians?
2. Is perseverance in faith and obedience to the end necessary for final salvation? Demonstrate your answer from the Holy Scriptures.
3. Someone asks you, "Do you believe 'once saved, always saved'?" How do you answer?
4. What promises of divine preservation do we find in the Gospel of John? What do they mean?
5. What did Jesus Christ teach about apostasy in the parable of the soils?
6. Who are the people who "fall away" in Hebrews 6:4–6? How does Hebrews 6 reveal what their spiritual state was before they apostatized?
7. What does the new covenant (Jer. 31:31–34) imply for the preservation of the saints?
8. How does the apostle Paul ground the confidence of believers concerning their future preservation on the faithfulness of God?
9. What promises of preservation are found in the epistles of Peter, John, and Jude?
10. How does the doctrine of the preservation and perseverance of the saints glorify God?

Questions for Deeper Reflection

11. If no regenerate, justified believer falls away fully and finally, then what is the point of the biblical warnings against apostasy? How should ministers apply the warnings when preaching?
12. A thoughtful friend says, "It seems that if you focus on the necessity of persevering, then you will work hard at being a Christian but will live with anxiety about your future; but if you focus on the promise of preservation, you will have peace and joy but be lazy." How do you respond?

31

Preservation and Perseverance, Part 2

Resting and Running

In *The Pilgrim's Progress*, the allegory of the Christian life by John Bunyan (1628–1688), Interpreter shows Christian things that foreshadow what lies ahead of him on the difficult road to the Celestial City. In one scene, Christian sees a palace of eternal glory guarded by many armed soldiers ready to attack anyone who attempts to enter it. Though many pull back in fear, one brave man puts on armor, courageously assaults the gate, and receives many wounds, but presses forward into the palace, where he is welcomed and honored. Here Bunyan depicted the fierce battle that a Christian must fight if he would enter the glorious kingdom of Jesus Christ.

In another room of Interpreter's house, Christian sees a fire by a wall. A man pours large quantities of water on the fire, but it does not go out. Interpreter takes Christian to the other side of the wall, where he discovers a hidden man who continually pours oil into the fire. Bunyan thus portrayed how the Devil seeks to quench the Christian's faith, hope, and love, but Christ secretly and effectively sustains the souls of his people so that they persevere in the faith.[1]

1. John Bunyan, *Pilgrim's Progress*, in *The Works of John Bunyan*, ed. George Offor, 3 vols. (1854; repr., Edinburgh: Banner of Truth, 1991), 3:100.

These vignettes capture two essential elements found in the doctrine of perseverance: the demand for great endurance if we would enter glory and the provision of grace that infallibly produces endurance. Johann Heidegger said, "The perseverance of the saints is the grace or gift of God whereby He gives the elect justified by faith and sanctified unconquerable constancy as they persist to struggle against sin and the troubles of this age or even to rise from falls through repentance in grace once given until the day of their redemption."[2]

In a word, perseverance involves the hard work of running the Christian race. Happily, that running is grounded in resting on God's work of preservation. In this chapter, we expound these connected imperatives of resting in God's preservation and running with perseverance.

Resting in the Triune Preserver of Your Salvation

The Christian's comfort and hope are greatly strengthened by the doctrine of perseverance, but believers do not trust in a doctrine so much as in the triune God who preserves them. The Westminster Confession of Faith (27.2) summarizes the reason for the Christian's hope to persevere by the Trinitarian covenant of grace:

> This perseverance of the saints depends not upon their own free will, but upon the immutability of the decree of election, flowing from the free and unchangeable love of God the Father; upon the efficacy of the merit and intercession of Jesus Christ, the abiding of the Spirit, and of the seed of God within them, and the nature of the covenant of grace: from all which ariseth also the certainty and infallibility thereof.[3]

We have already examined the power of God's "seed" in the regenerate (1 John 3:9) and the implications of God's covenant regarding perseverance.[4] In this section, we will look at the involvement of each person of the Trinity in preservation in order to encourage believers to trust in God.

Immutable Election and Comforting Support by the Father

Christian, rest your hope for preservation in God the Father, for he loves you eternally. Paul says that God the Father blessed us in Christ, "as he

---

2. Heidegger, *The Concise Marrow of Christian Theology*, 24.1 (171).
3. *Reformed Confessions*, 4:253.
4. See the previous chapter.

hath chosen us in him before the foundation of the world, that we should be holy and without blame before him in love" (Eph. 1:4). Apart from the consideration of any goodness or worthiness in us, the Father lovingly chose us before time began to be saved and made perfect in his presence.[5]

Election unto holiness by God the Father implies that no one has the right to consider himself one of God's elect unless he is being sanctified by grace. The perseverance of the saints is not a doctrine to promote sinful security, but is properly used when it is a "real source of humility, filial reverence [childlike fear], true piety, patience in every tribulation, fervent prayers, constancy in suffering, and in confessing the truth, and of solid rejoicing in God," as the Canons of Dort (Head 5, Art. 12) state.[6]

However, election unto holiness also implies that God's sanctifying grace cannot fail in those in whom he has begun to work. God's purpose and plan can never fail (Num. 23:19; Ps. 33:10–11). He has demonstrated "the immutability of his counsel" by sealing his covenant with an oath (Heb. 6:17). He says to his elect, "I have loved thee with an everlasting love" (Jer. 31:3). His faithful love is "from everlasting to everlasting upon them that fear him" (Ps. 103:17).

Therefore, God's immutability or unchangeableness guarantees that those whom he elected and called will be preserved until they reach glory. "All things," good and bad, are decreed by God to make his beloved people "to be conformed to the image of his Son" (Rom. 8:28–29). This golden chain cannot be broken: "Whom he did predestinate, them he also called: and whom he called, them he also justified: and whom he justified, them he also glorified" (v. 30). John MacArthur and Richard Mayhue say, "The believer's security is grounded in the unchanging love, infinite power, and saving will of the Father."[7]

God the Father supports his chosen children with his mercies and powerful comfort. Paul says, "Blessed be God, even the Father of our Lord Jesus Christ, the Father of mercies, and the God of all comfort; who comforteth us in all our tribulation" with a comfort that not only provides emotional consolation but also strengthens the saints for "enduring" suffering (2 Cor. 1:3–4, 6). The Father strengthens them "with might by his Spirit in the inner man," and by "the power that worketh in us" he is "able to do exceeding abundantly above all that we ask or think" (Eph. 3:14,

5. On the doctrine of election as revealed in Eph. 1:3–6, see *RST*, 1:981–89.
6. *The Three Forms of Unity*, 157.
7. MacArthur and Mayhue, eds., *Biblical Doctrine*, 644.

16, 20). With and through his Son, he supplies them "peace," "love with faith," and "grace" (6:23–24). Therefore, God's children may say, "It is of the LORD's mercies that we are not consumed, because his compassions fail not. They are new every morning: great is thy faithfulness" (Lam. 3:22–23).

Perfect Redemption and Effective Intercession by the Son

Christian, rest your hope for preservation also in God the Son, because he is your willing and able Mediator. The Father sent his Son into the world not merely to make salvation possible if we add the crucial ingredients of our faith, obedience, and perseverance, but to accomplish and apply complete salvation to the elect, including our perseverance.

First, Christ's sacrifice accomplished complete redemption—not merely potential redemption, but effective redemption.[8] Hebrew 10:14 says, "For by one offering he hath perfected for ever them that are sanctified." They are still in the process of being "sanctified" (*hagiazomenous*, present participle), but his offering has already "perfected" (*teteleiōken*, perfect tense) them, where the verb "perfect" means to bring them all the way to their intended goal, even heavenly glory (12:23). Thus, although the calling and perseverance of vast numbers of saints had not yet taken place, Christ could say on the cross, "It is finished" (John 19:30).

The perfect righteousness of Christ, obtained by his obedience and death and imputed to believers in their justification, secures their future with God. Paul says, "Much more then, being now justified by his blood, we shall be saved from wrath through him" (Rom. 5:9). George Whitefield said, "I cannot think they are clear in the notion of Christ's righteousness, who deny the final perseverance of the saints," for justification "not only signifies remission of sins past but also a federal right to all good things to come. If God has given us his only Son, how shall he not also with him freely give us all things?"[9]

Furthermore, Christ's obedience unto death secured the sanctification and perseverance of his people. He bought them with the price of his own blood (1 Cor. 6:20). His redemption creates people who have died to sin and live to righteousness, being zealous for good works (Titus 2:14; 1 Pet.

8. See the discussion of the efficacy of Christ's perfect sacrifice in *RST*, 2:1066–71.

9. Whitefield, "Christ the Believer's Wisdom, Righteousness, Sanctification and Redemption," in *Sermons*, 2:222.

2:24–25). Christ's perseverance for them is the legal ground for God's perseverance with them and their perseverance to the end.[10] By satisfying the debt they owed to God's justice, Christ defeated Satan and his demonic forces and won the victory (Col. 2:13–15).

Christ obtained victory over Satan by obeying God perfectly through every trial (Matt. 4:1–11; John 12:27–33). He is "the author and finisher of our faith; who for the joy that was set before him endured the cross, despising the shame, and is set down at the right hand of the throne of God" (Heb. 12:2). Christ accomplished his perseverance in order to share it with those united to him, so that they, too, will persevere in the faith (3:14; 5:8–9). Geerhardus Vos said that "the principle error of those who teach the apostasy of the saints" is that "they confuse the state of believers in the covenant of grace with the state of Adam before the fall, as if these two were completely the same."[11] The Christian is not his own Adam but stands in union with the last Adam, who has conquered by his persevering obedience.

Second, Christ's intercession applies his complete redemption. "He is able also to save them to the uttermost that come unto God by him, seeing he ever liveth to make intercession for them. For such an high priest became us, who is holy, harmless, undefiled, separate from sinners, and made higher than the heavens" (Heb. 7:25–26). The words translated as "to the uttermost" (*eis to pantelēs*) indicate that Christ's intercession guarantees the salvation of his people "to the all completion." His intercession never ceases, for he lives forever. "Christ has stretched out his hand to us, that he may not desert us in the midst of the course," as John Calvin said.[12] His intercession never fails to obtain the Father's blessing, for he is perfectly pleasing to God and exalted by God to supreme authority. Furthermore, he intercedes as the "surety" (v. 22) who took the legal responsibility to pay his people's debts and has fulfilled the commission that God gave him (v. 21) by his once-for-all sacrifice of himself (v. 27).[13] Consequently, Christ mediates to his chosen people all the graces of the new covenant, including both justification and sanctification (8:1, 6–12).[14]

10. Fisher et al., *The Assembly's Shorter Catechism Explained*, Cat. Q. 36, "Perseverance," Q. 6 (201).

11. Vos, *Reformed Dogmatics*, 4:217.

12. Calvin, *Commentaries*, on John 6:39.

13. On Christ's priestly intercession, see *RST*, 2:1088–1103.

14. The new covenant and its significance for God's preservation of his saints are discussed in the previous chapter.

The faith of believers cannot fully and finally fail under Satan's temptations because God the Son incarnate intercedes for them. Christ said to Peter, "Behold, Satan hath desired to have you, that he may sift you as wheat: but I have prayed for thee, that thy faith fail not: and when thou art converted [literally turn back], strengthen thy brethren" (Luke 22:31–32). Christ intercedes with the same intent now as when he prayed, "Holy Father, keep through thine own name those whom thou hast given me" (John 17:11).

This invincible combination of Christ's redemption and intercession moved the apostle Paul to exult in the glorious hope belonging to all in Christ. Paul says, "Who shall lay any thing to the charge of God's elect? It is God that justifieth. Who is he that condemneth? It is Christ that died, yea rather, that is risen again, who is even at the right hand of God, who also maketh intercession for us" (Rom. 8:33–34). Therefore, nothing—not the persecution of men or the temptation of demons, not the present or the future, nothing at all—"shall be able to separate us from the love of God, which is in Christ Jesus our Lord" (vv. 35–39).

Powerful Sanctification and Incitement to Prayer by the Spirit

Christian, rest your hope for preservation in God the Holy Spirit, for he is the great divine agent who effectually works the graces promised in the covenant of grace. The Lord says, "I will put my spirit within you, and cause you to walk in my statutes, and ye shall keep my judgments, and do them" (Ezek. 36:27). The Holy Spirit will not fail to maintain the living principle of obedience in the souls of his own.

The Spirit will never abandon the work of sanctification. His indwelling presence in true disciples of Christ is guaranteed by the will of the Father and the intercession of the Son. Christ promised, "I will pray the Father, and he shall give you another Comforter, that he may abide with you for ever" (John 14:16). The promise is "for ever." The Spirit will never leave believers, for God has sealed them with the Spirit until the day of redemption.[15] Thomas Watson said, "Grace is compared to a river of the water of life (John 7:38). This river can never be dried up, because God's Spirit is the spring that continually feeds it."[16] Herman Witsius said, "So

15. 2 Cor. 1:22; Eph. 1:13–14; 4:30. On the sealing of the Spirit, see chap. 34.

16. Watson, *A Body of Divinity*, 281. See Owen, *The Doctrine of the Saints' Perseverance*, in *Works*, 11:353–54.

long as the Spirit of Christ dwells in any person, so long it is evident, he is Christ's, nor can he belong to the devil."[17] The Holy Spirit is "the Spirit of life": he makes those whom he indwells "free from the law of sin and death," and Christ dwells in them as their life (Rom. 8:2, 9–10).

It might be objected that the Holy Spirit can assist believers in persevering but cannot guarantee that they will do so, since this depends on the free choice of their will. However, we answer this objection by pointing out that God is able to raise spiritually dead sinners to life in Christ (Eph. 2:4–5). He does so without violating their humanity or forcing the free choice of their will, but by effectually drawing them to Christ (John 6:37, 44).[18] If God can save his enemies and slaves of sin by the regeneration and renewal of the Holy Spirit (Titus 3:5), then surely the Spirit has the power to preserve those who already love God.

The sovereign grace of God does not preserve his people automatically apart from their own wills, but the Spirit works in them so that they willingly persevere by faith in the grace of Christ. The Canons of Dort (Head 5, Arts. 6–7) say,

> God, who is rich in mercy, according to His unchangeable purpose of election, does not wholly withdraw the Holy Spirit from His own people, even in their melancholy falls; nor suffers them to proceed so far as to lose the grace of adoption, and forfeit the state of justification, or to commit the sin unto death; nor does He permit them to be totally deserted, and to plunge themselves into everlasting destruction.
>
> For in the first place, in these falls He preserves in them the incorruptible seed of regeneration from perishing or being totally lost; and again, by His Word and Spirit, certainly and effectually renews them to repentance, to a sincere and godly sorrow for their sins, that they may seek and obtain remission in the blood of the Mediator, may again experience the favor of a reconciled God, through faith adore His mercies, and henceforward more diligently work out their own salvation with fear and trembling.[19]

A crucial part of perseverance is prayer, for by prayer the saint obtains more grace to sustain his faith. A decline in prayer is the beginning of

17. Witsius, *The Economy of the Covenants*, 3.13.27 (2:70).
18. On the sovereign power of effectual calling and regeneration, see chaps. 16 and 18.
19. *The Three Forms of Unity*, 155.

backsliding; the end of prayer threatens to asphyxiate the spiritual life. However, the Holy Spirit is the divine author of the prayers of God's children. He is "the spirit of grace and of supplications," by whom God's people mourn over their sins and look to Christ crucified (Zech. 12:10). He is "the Spirit of adoption, whereby we cry, Abba, Father" (Rom. 8:15). Paul says, "The Spirit also helpeth our infirmities: for we know not what we should pray for as we ought: but the Spirit itself maketh intercession for us with groanings which cannot be uttered" (v. 26). By the Spirit's influence, those in Christ keep panting after the grace of their Lord, and thus receive what they need to persevere.

Therefore, let us persevere by "praying always . . . in the Spirit" (Eph. 6:18). Thomas Manton said, "If you fall, be not utterly discouraged." Rather, pray, "I have gone astray like a lost sheep; seek thy servant; for I do not forget thy commandments" (Ps. 119:176). And, Manton said, "when you stand, let it incite you to love and thankfulness." Say, "O give thanks unto the Lord; for he is good: for his mercy endureth for ever" (136:1).[20]

The doctrine of perseverance is a sweet comfort to those engaged in the battle to mortify sin and live unto God in obedience. However, the spiritual sluggard who refuses to make diligent use of the means of grace and the moral hypocrite who lives in unrepented sin have no right to claim these promises. John Murray wrote, "We may entertain the faith of our security in Christ only as we persevere in faith and holiness to the end."[21] The promise of preservation is pilgrim's food; none other has a right to it.

Summary: Resting on the Character of the Triune God

The Canons of Dort (Head 5, Rej. 1) say that "the perseverance of true believers . . . follows out of election, and is given the elect in virtue of the death, the resurrection and intercession of Christ."[22] The perseverance of the saints is "not in consequence of their own merits or strength, but of God's free mercy," as the Canons (Head 5, Art. 8) say, for Christians would backslide to their eternal ruin apart from grace, but "with respect to God, it is utterly impossible, since His counsel cannot be changed nor His promise fail; neither can the call according to His purpose be revoked, nor the merit, intercession, and preservation of Christ be ren-

20. Manton, *Sermons upon John 17*, in *Works*, 10:306–7.
21. Murray, *Redemption Accomplished and Applied*, 155.
22. *The Three Forms of Unity*, 159.

dered ineffectual, nor the sealing of the Holy Spirit be frustrated or obliterated."[23]

We persevere by God's grace. It would be a mistake to ground our hope of perseverance on confidence in ourselves. Instead, our confidence that we will persevere rests on our faith in the attributes of the Savior, who elected, purchased, and sanctifies his people. John Brown of Haddington raised the following questions to show that the "total or final fall" of God's saints from the state of grace "is altogether inconsistent with the perfections of God":

- How can he, who is unchangeable, hate those whom he once loved with an everlasting love?
- How can he, who is infinitely just, demand full satisfaction for their sins from Christ, and yet punish them for ever in hell?
- How can he, who is infinitely wise and powerful, begin an important work without being able and willing to finish it?
- How can he, who is infinitely faithful, engage himself by promise and oath to do that which he is either unable or unwilling to perform?[24]

Like every aspect of soteriology, the doctrine of perseverance reveals the glory of God. Therefore, it enriches our souls immensely when we meditate upon it, for through it we perceive more of the beauty of the Lord. Wilhelmus à Brakel said, "Therefore, acknowledge the certainty of your spiritual state and you will behold the sovereign grace, goodness, power, longsuffering, faithfulness, and immutability of God. . . . This will give you reason for adoration, to the praise and worship of the glorious perfections of God." Furthermore, "be encouraged in all perplexities; trust in the Lord who will also perfect that which concerneth you, will guide you with His counsel, and afterward receive you to glory." In the midst of the spiritual war, let this doctrine stir you to "be valiant in the battle, while trusting God's safekeeping."[25] As Paul says, "Therefore, my beloved brethren, be ye stedfast, unmoveable, always abounding in the work of the Lord, forasmuch as ye know that your labour is not in vain in the Lord" (1 Cor. 15:58).

23. *The Three Forms of Unity*, 155–56.
24. Brown, *Systematic Theology*, 437–38.
25. Brakel, *The Christian's Reasonable Service*, 4:300.

Running with Perseverance for the Heavenly Prize

While the Christian life is certainly one of resting our faith upon the Lord, it is not a rest of inactivity, but a rest that empowers strenuous activity "by faith," as Hebrews 11 tells us. The perseverance of the saints demands their greatest efforts. Watson said, "Christians do not arrive at perseverance when they sit still and do nothing. . . . We arrive at salvation in the use of means; as a man comes to the end of a race by running, to a victory by fighting."[26]

In the previous chapter, we looked at the teachings of the epistle to the Hebrews about apostasy. This same epistle also sets forth several principles for how the Christian must run the race so that, by the grace of Christ, he will not fall away but enter the heavenly rest.

Pay Careful Attention to God's Word

Hebrews 2:1 says, "Therefore we ought to give the more earnest heed to the things which we have heard, lest at any time we should let them slip." Literally the text says that "it is necessary" (*dei*) for us "to pay much more attention" (*prosechō*) to the Word so that "we may not drift away" (*pararreō*). The first Greek word implies strong necessity. The second and third words were both used in nautical settings for the securing of a ship near a harbor against drifting away under force of the wind, tide, or currents.[27] Later, the writer compares our hope in God's promise to "an anchor of the soul, both sure and stedfast" (6:19). The picture then is this: Christians have found refuge in the harbor of Christ's promises, but the forces of this world constantly pull them away. The greatest danger is not sudden apostasy so much as gradual drifting from Christ. We must drop anchor and cling to the Word.

One of the first signs of backsliding is a lazy and poorly focused mindset toward God's Word. Perhaps a Christian's soul is being hardened by a proud, critical, and self-sufficient spirit; growing dull by the intoxicating influence of lust; or indulging the laziness that resents the hard labor of hearing and obeying. If he would persevere in the faith, he must wake up, focus his mind, and cling to the Word. Murray said, "Perseverance means the engagement of our persons in the most intense and concentrated devo-

26. Watson, *A Body of Divinity*, 280.

27. David L. Allen, *Hebrews*, The New American Commentary 35 (Nashville: Broadman & Holman, 2010), 191–92; and Walter Riggans, *Hebrews*, Focus on the Bible Commentary (Fearn, Ross-shire, Scotland: Christian Focus, 1998), 30.

tion to those means which God has ordained for the achievement of his saving purpose."[28]

The writer to the Hebrews warns that when we hear God's voice in the Bible, we have two options: to harden our hearts against what the Holy Spirit is saying or to embrace it into our hearts by faith (Heb. 3:7–8; 4:2). The people of Israel took the path of gradual hardening, and it proved disastrous for them when they were excluded from God's rest. Hebrews 4:11 exhorts us, "Let us labour therefore to enter into that rest, lest any man fall after the same example of unbelief." Listening to the Word requires diligent labor, not least because the Word is God's sword to pierce our hearts and to expose the condition of our souls (vv. 12–13).

Rather than toying with God's Word so that we become "dull of hearing," we must seriously engage our minds with its doctrines and put it into practice so that we grow into mature Christians who "have their senses exercised to discern both good and evil" (Heb. 5:11–6:1). The Canons of Dort (Head 5, Art. 14) say, "As it has pleased God, by the preaching of the gospel, to begin this work of grace in us, so He preserves, continues, and perfects it by the hearing and reading of His Word, by meditation thereon, and by the exhortations, threatenings, and promises thereof, as well as by the use of the sacraments."[29]

One crucial means to stir up our minds to read and hear the Word is to consider who speaks to us. He is the Lord of heaven and earth, and the only Savior. Hebrews 12:25 says, "See that ye refuse not him that speaketh. For if they escaped not who refused him that spake on earth, much more shall not we escape, if we turn away from him that speaketh from heaven." The author of the Bible is the One whose voice will shake all things, leaving only his kingdom (vv. 26–27). Therefore, when we worship God, we must sit under the preaching of the Word "with reverence and godly fear: for our God is a consuming fire" (vv. 28–29). Yet he is also the God of infinite grace, and we may draw near to him reverently but without terror because of Jesus Christ the Mediator, whose blood was shed for our sins (vv. 24).

This principle of drawing near to God in the Word should shape our meditations on the Holy Scriptures every day. Jerry Bridges asked, "Do

28. Murray, *Redemption Accomplished and Applied*, 155.
29. *The Three Forms of Unity*, 158.

we spend time with God or do we just read a chapter in the Bible?" When we read the Bible, we must do so not as an end to itself, but as a means "to meet with God, to have God speak to us and to respond to him."[30] By regular communion with God in the Word we will be rooted and established in the faith.

Establish in Your Mind the Supremacy of Christ

Hebrew 3:1 says, "Wherefore, holy brethren, partakers of the heavenly calling, consider the Apostle and High Priest of our profession, Christ Jesus." Here again we find an exhortation to exercise our minds. William Gouge (1575–1653) noted that the Greek word translated as "consider" (*katanoeō*) means to examine or think thoroughly about something (10:24; cf. Luke 12:24, 27). Such consideration of truths has the benefits that "the understanding will better conceive them, the memory retain them, the heart relish them, and so a man may be brought to make the better use of them." Gouge then said, "If anything in the world is to be seriously considered, surely Christ above all, and that in his excellencies."[31]

The great topic of Hebrews is the supremacy of Jesus Christ. God's Son is the remedy to apostasy and is the life of persevering faith. Christ is supreme over Moses and the prophets (Heb. 1:1–3; 3:5–6). The Son is supreme over the angels (1:4–14). He is supreme over the old covenant priests, for his person is sinless, his offering is perfect, his intercession is heavenly, and his ministry is everlasting (4:14–10:18). Consequently, the crucial command for perseverance is to "consider . . . Christ Jesus" (3:1). All apostasy at its core consists of a rejection of Christ crucified in favor of some other way of becoming holy by false religion or happy by sin's pleasures (6:6; 10:29; 13:4–6). The soul of perseverance is esteeming Christ as supremely excellent, beautiful, and worthy, so that like Moses we count "the reproach of Christ greater riches than the treasures in Egypt" (11:26). Therefore, feed your heart with the glory and grace of God's Son.

Lean on Christ's Intercession in Your Prayers

The epistle to the Hebrews encourages believers going through trials with the knowledge that the Priest seated in heaven for us is our own flesh

30. Jerry Bridges, "Four Essentials to Finishing Well," in *Stand: A Call for the Endurance of the Saints*, ed. John Piper and Justin Taylor (Wheaton, IL: Crossway, 2008), 21.

31. William Gouge, *Commentary on Hebrews*, 2 vols. (1866; repr., Birmingham, AL: Solid Ground, 2006), 1:205–6.

and blood. Hebrews 2:17–18 says, "Therefore he had to be made like his brothers in every respect, so that he might become a merciful and faithful high priest in the service of God, to make propitiation for the sins of the people. For because he himself has suffered when tempted, he is able to help those who are being tempted" (ESV).

Christ welcomes our cries for help. Even though he is glorified in heaven, he remains a "merciful and faithful high priest." He remembers his sufferings and temptations, and can help us in our struggles to persevere. Thomas Goodwin wrote, "Christ took to heart all that befell him as deeply as might be; he slighted no cross, either from God or men, but had and felt the utmost load of it. Yea, his heart was made more tender in all sorts of affections than any of ours, even as it was in love and pity; and this made him 'a man of sorrows,' and that more than any other man was or shall be."[32]

Therefore, we can pray boldly. Hebrews 4:14–16 says, "Seeing then that we have a great high priest, that is passed into the heavens, Jesus the Son of God, let us hold fast our profession. For we have not an high priest which cannot be touched with the feeling of our infirmities; but was in all points tempted like as we are, yet without sin. Let us therefore come boldly unto the throne of grace, that we may obtain mercy, and find grace to help in time of need."

Christ is moved with sympathy for our sorrows and temptations. Goodwin argued that "infirmities" include both our troubles and temptations, for the epistle addressed people facing persecution, material losses, and the possibility of martyrdom (Heb. 10:32–34; 12:4). A high priest must be someone who "can have compassion on the ignorant, and on them that are out of the way" (5:2). Even our sins and foolish choices awaken Christ's compassion.[33]

Goodwin wrote, "Your very sins move him to pity more than to anger . . . even as the heart of a father is to a child that hath some loathsome disease, or as one is to a member of his body that hath the leprosy, he hates not the member, for it is his flesh, but the disease, and that provokes him to pity the part affected the more."[34]

32. Goodwin, *The Heart of Christ in Heaven unto Sinners on Earth*, in *Works*, 4:141. See Joel R. Beeke, "Thomas Goodwin on Christ's Beautiful Heart," in *The Beauty and Glory of Christ*, ed. Joel R. Beeke (Grand Rapids, MI: Reformation Heritage Books, 2011), 135–54.

33. Goodwin, *Heart of Christ in Heaven unto Sinners on Earth*, in *Works*, 4:111–12.

34. Goodwin, *Heart of Christ in Heaven unto Sinners on Earth*, in *Works*, 4:149.

Therefore, in your weakness and sin, cry out to the Father with an eye upon the merciful Lord seated at his right hand. Christ is full of tenderness for you, dear child of God. He does not despise your struggles, for he remembers his own. Seek grace and mercy from God in your time of need, and through this brotherly High Priest God will give you grace that is sufficient for you to glorify him in all your trials.

As you lean on Christ to make your prayers acceptable to God and find the grace that you need, constantly remind yourself of what we discussed earlier in this chapter: Christ intercedes on the basis of his perfect and effective sacrifice (1 John 2:1–2). He is not merely the merciful and sympathetic Priest, but also the Priest who has paid for your sins and purchased your complete salvation. Therefore, by his intercession God is pleased with you, eager to listen to your prayers, and zealous to give you grace and mercy in your time of need.

Stand upon the Promises of God

Hebrews 6:17–20 says, "God, willing more abundantly to shew unto the heirs of promise the immutability of his counsel, confirmed it by an oath: that by two immutable things, in which it was impossible for God to lie, we might have a strong consolation, who have fled for refuge to lay hold upon the hope set before us: which hope we have as an anchor of the soul, both sure and stedfast, and which entereth into that within the veil; whither the forerunner is for us entered, even Jesus, made an high priest for ever after the order of Melchisedec."

This text draws together the three strands of truth that we have already observed and weaves them into an unbreakable cord of hope. First, God gave us his promise to be "an anchor of the soul" so that we do not drift away from Christ. Second, God exalted Christ as the supreme and eternal High Priest of his people. Third, Christ went "within the veil" as "the forerunner"—that is, as our intercessor who entered heaven before us to guarantee that we will follow him.

The practical implication of this text is that we must grasp this threefold cord for our "strong consolation" by absolute confidence that God's promises are true. Thomas Schreiner writes, "Any doubt about being inheritors of the promise should be removed, for what God has pledged will certainly be fulfilled. . . . He wouldn't be God if he could lie."[35]

35. Thomas R. Schreiner, *Commentary on Hebrews*, Biblical Theology for Christian Proclamation (Nashville: Holman Reference, 2015), 202–3.

We stand upon the Word of God by grasping specific promises. Consider a few of God's promises that are precious to believers as they strive to persevere through trials:

- "The Lord is my shepherd; I shall not want. . . . Surely goodness and mercy shall follow me all the days of my life: and I will dwell in the house of the Lord for ever" (Ps. 23:1, 6).
- "The Lord is my light and my salvation; whom shall I fear? The Lord is the strength of my life; of whom shall I be afraid? . . . Wait on the Lord: be of good courage, and he shall strengthen thine heart: wait, I say, on the Lord" (Ps. 27:1, 14).
- "Because he hath set his love upon me, therefore will I deliver him: I will set him on high, because he hath known my name. He shall call upon me, and I will answer him: I will be with him in trouble; I will deliver him, and honour him. With long life will I satisfy him, and shew him my salvation" (Ps. 91:14–16).
- "Fear thou not; for I am with thee: be not dismayed; for I am thy God: I will strengthen thee; yea, I will help thee; yea, I will uphold thee with the right hand of my righteousness" (Isa. 41:10).
- "No weapon that is formed against thee shall prosper; and every tongue that shall rise against thee in judgment thou shalt condemn. This is the heritage of the servants of the Lord, and their righteousness is of me, saith the Lord" (Isa. 54:17).

Christians persevere in faith, and faith is the hand of the soul grasping the promises of God. Therefore, strengthen your faith by frequently laying hold and gripping tightly the precious words of God, for in them God has given you the knowledge of him, and hence, everything necessary for life and godliness (2 Pet. 1:3–4).

Share in the Worship, Love, and Accountability of the Church

Perseverance is not an individual effort, but a community project. The epistle to the Hebrews appeals to tempted believers to stand together against the forces that would draw them away from Christ. The church must exercise brotherly accountability and admonition. Hebrews 3:12–13 says, "Take heed, brethren, lest there be in any of you an evil heart of unbelief, in departing from the living God. But exhort one another daily, while it is called To day; lest any of you be hardened through the deceitfulness of sin." We must cultivate relationships with believers in which there is no offense in a loving rebuke, a friendly correction, or a brotherly exhortation.

We must have Christian friends who know us. Richard Phillips said, "If we do not know the nature of our fellow believers' struggles, and if we do not share ours with them, then we will never be able to follow through with this command. The result, in that case, will be that people among us will fall prey to sin."[36] Left to our own resources, we too often fool ourselves into rationalizing our spiritual decline and compromise with sin.

The church should also be a community of godly examples for us to imitate. This, too, is an important aspect of perseverance. Hebrews 6:11–12 says, "We desire that every one of you do shew the same diligence to the full assurance of hope unto the end: that ye be not slothful, but followers of them who through faith and patience inherit the promises." The word translated as "followers" (*mimētēs*) means imitators. Few things stir Christians to courageous endurance in the faith as well as knowing the brave spiritual exploits of their brothers and sisters, many of whom have gone ahead of us to glory. They are "a cloud of witnesses" around us as we press on in Christ (12:1). Christians must remember those who have preached the Word of God to them, imitate their faith, and consider how they conducted themselves to the end (13:7).

The center of the church's corporate life is its public worship, and such worship features largely in the call to perseverance. After climaxing doctrinally in its consideration of the finished work of Christ on the cross, the epistle exhorts its readers practically to "draw near" by faith "into the holiest," not as isolated individuals, but as "the house of God," God's living temple on earth (Heb. 10:19–22). With the gathered church, we renew our confession of faith (v. 23), consider how we may provoke one another to love and good works (v. 24), and exhort one another to press on as the day of the Lord draws ever nearer (v. 25). None of these activities is possible if we are "forsaking the assembling of ourselves together" (v. 25).

There are powerful spiritual realities present in our public worship, for Christ is among us. The church militant on earth participates in "the heavenly Jerusalem" in its worship, joining with the celestial city to adore the living God in the presence of "Jesus the mediator of the new cove-

36. Richard D. Phillips, *Hebrews*, Reformed Expository Commentary (Phillipsburg, NJ: P&R, 2006), 110.

nant" (Heb. 12:22–24). As Christians worship together, they eat from an altar far greater than that of any earthly temple, strengthening their hearts with the grace of Christ (13:9–10). Though they are rejected by this world (vv. 11–14), they have the privilege of offering up worship to God through Jesus Christ and collecting their offerings to minister to the needs of the poor, and "God is well pleased" (vv. 15–16). In the church, they also enjoy another powerful means of perseverance: the watchful guidance of the elders who shepherd their souls (v. 17).

Public worship must be complemented by a lifetime of love and mutual service. We must not forget that the pursuit of holiness cannot be done in alienation from other Christians, but we must "follow peace with all men, and holiness, without which no man shall see the Lord" (Heb. 12:14). Therefore, not only public worship, but private acts of brotherly love, hospitality, and ministering to persecuted brethren are crucial for the perseverance of God's people (13:1–3). The persevering saints draw each other forward in a beautiful web of relationships, like a phalanx of spiritual soldiers who stand and fight as one.

Run the Race with Your Eyes on Christ the Victor

Perseverance is at its core following Christ to the end. Therefore, perseverance demands looking to the Lord Jesus as disciples who aspire to become like their Master. The call to perseverance in Hebrews climaxes in this statement:

> Wherefore seeing we also are compassed about with so great a cloud of witnesses, let us lay aside every weight, and the sin which doth so easily beset us, and let us run with patience the race that is set before us, looking unto Jesus the author and finisher of our faith; who for the joy that was set before him endured the cross, despising the shame, and is set down at the right hand of the throne of God. For consider him that endured such contradiction of sinners against himself, lest ye be wearied and faint in your minds. (Heb. 12:1–3)

The Christian life is a marathon, not a sprint. It is not just making it through another day, but God "bringing many sons unto glory" (Heb. 2:10). The exhortation tells us that Christianity requires sustained effort over the long haul. A. W. Pink said, "The principal thoughts suggested by the figure of the 'race' are rigorous self-denial and discipline, vigorous exertion, persevering endurance."[37] Jesus Christ is the supreme and victorious runner. To run the race "looking unto Jesus" is to take up his heartfelt cry and make it our own: "I come to do thy will, O God" (10:9). This is the fruit of the new covenant grace mediated to us through Christ: the law is within our hearts, and we delight to do God's will (Ps. 40:8; Heb. 8:10).

All the efforts of a Christian to persevere arise from Christ, and they all return to Christ as the great goal of our perseverance. We run the race by his grace, and we run the race to meet him in glory, where he sits at God's right hand. At the finish line, we will see the King in his beauty (Isa. 33:17). We will be with him and will behold his glory (John 17:24). It is the essence of persevering faith that though we do not yet see Christ, we believe in him and love him (1 Pet. 1:7–8). Therefore, let us fill our mind's eye with his glory now, so that we will have strong motivation to endure to the end—for the end is worth it. Christ is worth it.

We conclude this call to perseverance with the benediction at the close of this great epistle: "Now the God of peace, that brought again from the dead our Lord Jesus, that great shepherd of the sheep, through the blood of the everlasting covenant, make you perfect in every good work to do his will, working in you that which is wellpleasing in his sight, through Jesus Christ; to whom be glory for ever and ever. Amen" (Heb. 13:20–21).

Sing to the Lord

Resolved to Persevere by Grace

Lord, hear the right, regard my cry,
My prayer from lips sincere;
Send Thy approval from on high,
My righteousness make clear.
Thou in the night my heart hast tried,
Nor found it turned from Thee aside.

With steadfast courage I design
No wrong to speak or do;
Thy path of life I choose for mine
And walk with purpose true.
For help, O God, I cry to Thee,
Assured that Thou wilt answer me.

37. A. W. Pink, *An Exposition of Hebrews* (Grand Rapids, MI: Baker, 1954), 894.

O Thou that ever savest those
Whose trust on Thee is stayed,
Preserving them from all their foes
By Thy almighty aid,
Let me Thy lovingkindness see,
Thy wondrous mercy, full and free.

When I in righteousness at last
Thy glorious face shall see,
When all the weary night is past,
And I awake with Thee
To view the glories that abide,
Then, then I shall be satisfied.

Psalm 17
Tune: Longfellow
The Psalter, No. 32
For an alternative version of Psalm 17 with the same tune, see *Trinity Hymnal—Baptist Edition*, No. 735

Questions for Meditation or Discussion

1. What two illustrations of the doctrine of preservation and perseverance do the authors draw from John Bunyan's *The Pilgrim's Progress*? What do they teach us?
2. How can a Christian find hope of his ultimate salvation in God the Father?
3. What does the Bible reveal about Christ's redemption that makes it a cause for confidence that the future of his people is secure?
4. How does the intercession of Christ assure believers that they will be saved to the end?
5. What cause do Christians have to trust in the Holy Spirit for their preservation in grace?
6. Why would the loss of any of God's true people dishonor the character of God?
7. Why is it crucial for believers to pay careful attention to the Word in order to avoid falling away?
8. What is a promise of God that is especially precious to you as you strive to overcome trials and temptations? Why is it so precious?

9. In what ways is it especially important to consider Christ and look to him in order to persevere?
10. What temptations are most dangerous to your soul in this season of your life? How can you use the principles of this chapter to overcome them?

Questions for Deeper Reflection

11. Someone says, "I have been a Christian for a long time, and, honestly, I've found the church to be more of a hindrance than a help in persevering in the faith." How do you respond?
12. Prepare a detailed outline of a talk that you will give on this topic: "The Importance of Prayer in the Perseverance of the Saints."
13. How would you encourage someone who is walking with God but deeply depressed and fearful that he will lose his salvation to rest his hope not in himself but in the triune God?

Section C

The Holy Spirit and the Experience of Salvation (Experientia Salutis)

32

The Indwelling, Leading, and Filling of the Holy Spirit

The Spirit of the living God comes to manifest God's presence in his people in a transformational and relational manner. Having traced the Spirit's work through the history of salvation (*historia salutis*)—from creation to Christ to new creation—and through the order of salvation (*ordo salutis*) as he applies Christ's redemption in all its facets to individual people, we now begin to look at the Holy Spirit's operations according to the experience of salvation (*experientia salutis*). John Calvin said, "We observe this distinction between the theoretical knowledge derived from the Word of God and what is called the experimental knowledge of his grace." Though God "must first be sought in his Word," he also "shows himself present in operation."[1] Of course, much of what we have already considered regarding the history and order of salvation is experiential, but in this section of our systematic theology we focus particularly on how the Spirit's work appears in Christian experience through such matters as assurance, inward godliness, and obedience.

Reformed experiential Christianity is not a mystical approach to religion that separates religious experience from biblical truth, but neither is it an approach that rests in intellectual knowledge alone. Rather, as the Holy

1. Calvin, *Commentaries*, on Ps. 27:9. On "experimental" or experiential theology, see *RST*, 1:125–27. See also Beeke, *Living for God's Glory*, 255–74; and Joel R. Beeke, *Reformed Preaching: Proclaiming God's Word from the Heart of the Preacher to the Heart of His People* (Wheaton, IL: Crossway, 2018), 23–56.

Spirit opens the eyes of faith to enable the believer to apprehend the gospel of Christ, the Spirit manifests the glory of God in the believer's heart and transforms the character and conduct of his life. This is not a prophetic vision but a very real experience of God. John says, "No man hath seen God at any time. If we love one another, God dwelleth in us, and his love is perfected in us. Hereby know we that we dwell in him, and he in us, because he hath given us of his Spirit" (1 John 4:12–13). Hence, Christian experience flows directly from the work of the Holy Spirit.

The Indwelling of the Holy Spirit

The foundation of an experiential faith is the Holy Spirit's dwelling within believers, for he manifests the glory of God in their hearts by his transformational work. The Belgic Confession (Art. 9) says, "The Holy Ghost is our Sanctifier by His dwelling in our hearts."[2] There is a profound mystery about this truth. Octavius Winslow (1808–1878) said, "The bare thought that the 'high and lofty One, inhabiting eternity, whose name is Holy' [cf. Isa. 57:15], should dwell with man, yes, *in* him . . . seems almost too illimitable and glorious for a poor finite mind to grasp."[3] Yet the Holy Scriptures reveal this incomprehensible truth for our faith, comfort, joy, and holiness.

The Promise of the Spirit's Indwelling

God told his people that the indwelling of the Holy Spirit is necessary for a life of obedience from the heart: "I will put my Spirit within you, and cause you to walk in my statutes and be careful to obey my rules" (Ezek. 36:27 ESV). This is a powerful, energetic indwelling that effectively produces life and obedience. God promised, "I will put my Spirit within you, and you shall live" (37:14 ESV). George Smeaton said that the Holy Spirit "is given to inhabit his people . . . not by a mere inactive presence, but by an efficacious inhabitation which must be regarded as animating and pervading all the faculties and powers of the human mind."[4] Those "having not the Spirit" are people who "walk after their own ungodly lusts" (Jude 18–19).

2. *The Three Forms of Unity*, 24.
3. Octavius Winslow, *The Work of the Holy Spirit: An Experimental and Practical View* (Edinburgh: Banner of Truth, 1961), 88, emphasis original.
4. Smeaton, *The Doctrine of the Holy Spirit*, 211.

Christ said that the Holy Spirit would "abide with you for ever," and "he dwelleth with you, and shall be in you" (John 14:16–17). "For ever" means that this is a permanent indwelling. It is also a Trinitarian indwelling, for where the Spirit dwells, there the Father and the Son also take up their abode (v. 23). Hence, "the Spirit is the agent of the indwelling" of God, as Robert Letham says, for "in the coming of the Spirit to indwell, the Father and the Son are indivisibly present."[5] John writes, "Hereby we know that he abideth in us, by the Spirit which he hath given us" (1 John 3:24; cf. 4:15).

The Spirit indwells every believer: "But ye are not in the flesh, but in the Spirit, if so be that the Spirit of God dwell in you. Now if any man have not the Spirit of Christ, he is none of his" (Rom. 8:9). Paul says, "That good thing which was committed unto thee keep by the Holy Ghost which dwelleth in us" (2 Tim. 1:14). Christians have "received . . . the Spirit . . . by the hearing of faith" (Gal. 3:2; cf. v. 14). This is the very act of faith in Christ crucified by which a person is justified (vv. 1, 6). Sinclair Ferguson says, "There is no other mode of receiving the Spirit, then, than by faith's reception of Christ. To have Christ is to have the Spirit."[6]

The Spirit dwells in the inner man, what the Bible calls the heart, the center of human thoughts, emotions, and choices, and the source of human activity. Paul says to God's adopted sons, "God hath sent forth the Spirit of his Son into your hearts" (Gal. 4:6). He adds, "God's love has been poured into our hearts through the Holy Spirit who has been given to us" (Rom. 5:5 ESV).

When the Bible speaks of God dwelling in a place or person, we must remember that this is anthropomorphic language. The word translated as "dwell" (*oikeō*, Rom. 8:9, 11) literally means to inhabit a "house" (*oikos*, cf. 1 Cor. 7:12–13), as if God were a man dwelling in his home (cf. John 14:23). But God transcends all dwellings in his immensity (1 Kings 8:27)—the Spirit is infinite and omnipresent (Ps. 139:7).[7] Therefore, God's dwelling refers to his special presence, his activity to reveal himself and reign in relationship to his people (Ex. 29:45–46; John 14:20–21).[8] The Spirit's indwelling is not about his physical location but a particular kind of action: the Spirit works to manifest God's special presence within his people. Hence,

5. Letham, *Systematic Theology*, 601.
6. Ferguson, *The Holy Spirit*, 92.
7. Perkins, *An Exposition of the Symbol*, in *Works*, 5:311.
8. On God's special presence versus his omnipresence, see *RST*, 1:650–51.

we cannot reduce indwelling to mere influence; the Holy Spirit is personally present in believers just as God's glory inhabited the temple in Jerusalem.[9]

Therefore, the indwelling of the Spirit means that God has given himself to his people, for the Holy Spirit is God. Athanasius said, "It is through the Spirit that we are all said to be partakers of God [citing 1 Cor. 3:16–17]. . . . If the Holy Spirit were a creature, we should have no participation of God in him."[10] Augustine said, "The Holy Spirit is the gift of God, the gift being Himself indeed equal to the Giver."[11] This divine self-giving is crucial for experiential communion with God. Wilhelmus à Brakel said that believers have a "desire which can only be satisfied with the Infinite One. . . . God Himself must be and is their portion, and they are united to God in Christ. . . . Thus the believer does not merely have the gifts of the Spirit, but he has the Spirit Himself."[12]

Where God manifests his presence, he does so as the Lord. William Perkins said, "The Holy Ghost has full disposition of the heart, as when a man comes to dwell in a house whereof he is lord he has liberty to govern it after his own will. . . . Look where the Holy Ghost dwells, there He will be Lord, governing both heart, mind, will, and affections."[13]

Richard Sibbes said, "Let us give up the government of our souls to the Spirit. It is for our safety so to do, as being wiser than ourselves who are unable to direct our own way. It is our liberty to be under a wisdom and goodness larger than our own. Let the Spirit think in us, desire in us, pray in us, live in us, do all in us; labor ever to be in such a frame as we may be fit for the Spirit to work upon." Sibbes continued, "A musical instrument, though in tune, soundeth nothing unless it be touched. Let us lay ourselves open to the Spirit's touch."[14] He also said, "He must rule. He will have the keys delivered to him; we must submit to his government. And when he is in the heart, he will subdue by little and little all high thoughts, rebellious risings, and despairing fears."[15] Our souls are the battlefield on which the Spirit marches, and he will have the final victory. To be sure, the greatest battles were won first on Calvary and then in our hearts when

9. Smeaton, *The Doctrine of the Holy Spirit*, 212–14.

10. *The Letters of Saint Athanasius concerning the Holy Spirit*, 1.24 (125–26).

11. Augustine, *The Enchiridion*, chap. 37, in *NPNF*[1], 3:250.

12. Brakel, *The Christian's Reasonable Service*, 1:181.

13. Perkins, *An Exposition of the Symbol*, in *Works*, 5:311–13. See Henry, *Commentary on the Whole Bible*, on Rom. 8:9 (2211).

14. Sibbes, *A Fountain Sealed*, in *Works*, 5:426. This paragraph is adapted from Beeke and Jones, *A Puritan Theology*, 576–77. Used with permission.

15. Sibbes, *A Fountain Sealed*, in *Works*, 5:431.

we were brought to new birth, but we must also fight daily battles in our life of sanctification. Our ever-present foes—the flesh, the world, and the Devil—will unceasingly strive to tear up the foundation on which we stand as children of the Most High.

The Spirit's presence does not nullify the presence of remaining sin in believers, but it does make it impossible for sin to reign over us. John Owen said, "He enters into no soul as his habitation, but at the same instant he dethrones sin, spoils it of its dominion, and takes the rule of the soul into the hand of his own grace."[16] For the Spirit indwells and leads as the Spirit of life in Christ.

The Spirit of Life, the Spirit of Christ

The Spirit indwells those in union with Christ as the Spirit of Christ. Paul's declaration, "If any man have not the Spirit of Christ, he is none of his" (Rom. 8:9), appears toward the end of a passage in which Paul describes how God has brought his people into a new spiritual state through the work of Christ. God sent his Son to become a man and bear the condemnation for sin (v. 3) so that "there is therefore now no condemnation to them which are in Christ Jesus" (v. 1). Consequently, "the Spirit of life in Christ Jesus" has liberated them "from the law of sin and death" (v. 2), and they "walk not after the flesh, but after the Spirit" (v. 4).[17] Though once dominated and directed by "the flesh," the sinful nature of mankind fallen in Adam, they are now dominated and directed by "the Spirit," who forms them as the new creation in union with Christ.

Paul defines the fleshly "mind" or mindset (*phronēma*) as "enmity against God," a deadly and deeply ingrained rebellion against his law (Rom. 8:6–7). The indwelling of the Spirit places believers in a radically new state: "So then they that are in the flesh cannot please God. But ye are not in the flesh, but in the Spirit, if so be that the Spirit of God dwell in you" (vv. 8–9). By implication, those indwelt by the Holy Spirit can and do please God and obey his laws because they have been given another mindset.[18]

Winslow said, "The work of holiness forms a great and glorious part of His operation as the Indweller of His people. He has come to restore, not only order, but purity to the temple. He has come to restore the reign of

16. Owen, *Pneumatologia*, in *Works*, 3:551.

17. The preposition translated as "after" in Rom. 8:4 (*kata* with an object in the accusative case) most likely means "according to" (cf. v. 27) or "because of" (cf. v. 28).

18. Pink, *The Holy Spirit*, 95–96.

holiness, to set up the law of God in the soul, to unfold its precepts, and to write them upon the heart, and, shedding abroad the love of Christ, under its gentle but powerful constraint to lead the believer to 'run the way of God's commandments.'"[19]

This transformation must be viewed according to believers' vital union with Christ: the Holy Spirit is "the Spirit of life *in* Christ Jesus" (Rom. 8:2). Thus, Paul moves seamlessly from discussing the indwelling of the Spirit (v. 9) to speaking of "Christ . . . in you" (v. 10). This shows "the mode of Christ's dwelling in us"—that is, "by the Spirit."[20] The new spiritual life that animates believers is the life of the risen Lord Jesus, and thus they will also share in his resurrection from the dead (v. 11). Caspar Olevianus said that "the office and purpose of the Holy Spirit given to us . . . [is] that through faith the Spirit might unite us to Christ as closely as possible and might achieve similar results in both members and Head, seeing as it is the same Spirit, the same life and glory."[21]

Paul says, "Your body is the temple of the Holy Ghost which is in you" (1 Cor. 6:19). Again, this is true by union with Christ (vv. 15, 17). The temple where God "dwelleth" (*oikeō*), whether viewed as each believer's body or the whole church, belongs to God and is holy (3:16–17). The temple is the dwelling place of God, and God's glory in Christ shines by the Spirit in the believer's heart (2 Cor. 3:18; 4:4–6). Therefore, those indwelt by the Holy Spirit must separate themselves from sin and pursue practical holiness (6:14–7:1). The redeemed are not their own, and so must live for the glory of God (1 Cor. 6:19–20).

The more we cultivate an awareness that the Holy Spirit dwells within us, the more we will be motivated to conduct ourselves in the fear of God and with a high sense of our privilege to have God himself condescend to make us his home. Perkins said, "If a man be to entertain but an earthly prince or some man of state, he would be sure to have his house in a readiness and all matters in order against his coming, so as everything might be pleasing unto so worthy a guest."[22] Owen exhorted believers to preach to themselves, "Hath the Lord chosen my poor heart for his habitation? Hath he said, 'I delight in it, and there will I dwell for ever'? . . . And shall I be so

19. Winslow, *The Work of the Holy Spirit*, 100. See Jer. 31:33; Rom. 5:5; 2 Cor. 5:14–15; Ps. 119:32, in that order.
20. Calvin, *Commentaries*, on Rom. 8:10.
21. Olevianus, *An Exposition of the Apostles' Creed*, 124.
22. Perkins, *An Exposition of the Symbol*, in *Works*, 5:321.

foolish, so unthankful, as willingly to defile the habitation which he hath chosen? Shall I suffer vain thoughts, foolish lusts, distempered affections, worldly aims, to put in themselves upon him there?"[23]

Furthermore, the Spirit is not a passive guest, so to speak, but the Lord who produces all holy thoughts and desires in our souls. Therefore, entertaining the Spirit involves a cooperative receptivity to his sacred work. Sibbes said, "When we have any good motion by the ministry of the word, or by conference [spiritual discussions with other believers], or by reading of good things . . . let us entertain them, let the Spirit dwell and rule in us. It is the most blessed lodger that ever we entertained in all our lives."[24]

The Leading of the Holy Spirit

The Spirit of God indwells believers to reorient their lives and move them in a new spiritual direction by his application of the Word to their hearts.

The Promise of the Spirit's Leading

Throughout redemptive history, the Holy Spirit has led God's renewed people by providing special revelation and applying that revelation to their souls so that they walk in the highway of holiness to their inheritance in God's glory (cf. Isaiah 35).[25] The Holy Spirit was the divine agent of God's leading of Israel out of Egypt and through the wilderness by the prophetic ministry of Moses and the pillar of cloud and fire (Isa. 63:11, 14; cf. Neh. 9:19–20).[26] The Spirit also appears as the internal teacher of each saint in Psalm 143:10: "Teach me to do thy will; for thou art my God: thy spirit is good; lead me into the land of uprightness."[27]

Just as the Spirit led Israel through the wilderness, so Jesus "was led [*agō*] by the Spirit into the wilderness" (Luke 4:1). The Spirit's leading of Jesus apparently involved both the special revelation that Christ should fast from eating food and the application of God's written Word, particularly the book of Deuteronomy, which Christ quoted three times, to empower him to engage in spiritual combat with Satan and to obey God under extreme temptation (vv. 2–13).

23. Owen, *The Doctrine of the Saints' Perseverance*, in *Works*, 11:361.

24. Sibbes, *A Description of Christ*, in *Works*, 1:23; cf. Joel R. Beeke, "Richard Sibbes on Entertaining the Holy Spirit," in *The Beauty and Glory of the Holy Spirit*, ed. Beeke and Pipa, 227–45.

25. Pink, *The Holy Spirit*, 115.

26. On Isa. 63:10–14, see the section on the Spirit of presence in chap. 3.

27. On Ps. 143:10, see the section on explicit statements that the Spirit sanctified old covenant saints in chap. 3.

Christ promised the Spirit's guidance to his apostles after his death and resurrection to complete the gift of special revelation to the church. The Lord Jesus said, "When he, the Spirit of truth, is come, he will guide you into all truth: for he shall not speak of himself. . . . He shall glorify me: for he shall receive of mine, and shall shew it unto you" (John 16:13–14). The verb translated as "guide" (*hodēgeō*) is the same used in the Septuagint's rendering of Psalm 143:10 and Isaiah 63:14. Just as God led Israel by his Spirit's ministry through such means as the prophetic words of Moses, so the Holy Spirit led the apostles through the revelations granted by Christ. These revelations were written down in the New Testament (cf. Eph. 3:1–6).[28] Since the completion of God's written Word, the Spirit's leading now consists not in the gift of new special revelation but in the application to men's souls of the truths already revealed in the Old and New Testaments.[29]

The leading of the Spirit is a vital aspect of every Christian's life. Paul says, "For as many as are led by the Spirit of God, they are the sons of God" (Rom. 8:14; cf. Gal. 5:18). Whoever is not led by the Spirit is not a child of God.[30] The word translated as "led" (*agō*) is the same term used of the Spirit's leading of God's Son (Luke 4:1). This, combined with the theme of adoptive sonship (Rom. 8:15–17), suggests that the Holy Spirit's work to direct and empower God's Son in his obedience under temptation overflows into the lives of God's adopted children. The present tense of the verb translated as "led" implies a continuous influence from the Holy Spirit (v. 14)—the ordinary work of the Spirit to produce obedient sons of God.

Though some Christians use the phrase "led by the Spirit" to identify their inward impulses as revelations of God's will for them,[31] there is nothing in Romans 8 about inner divine promptings to take particular actions apart from the Word of God. Rather, Paul is writing about obedience to God's law and pleasing him (vv. 8–9), denying sinful desires and putting to death sinful deeds (vv. 12–13), and suffering with Christ in order to be glorified with him (vv. 17–18). J. I. Packer said, "*Leads* is rightly taken

28. On John 16:12–14 as a promise of divine inspiration to the apostles, see *RST*, 1:325–26.

29. On the cessation of special revelation, see *RST*, 1:409–57 (chaps. 23–24).

30. Contrary to Lewis Sperry Chafer, who called this leading "a superhuman life" and said, "The leading of the Spirit is not experienced by all in whom the Spirit dwells." The believer who is not "yielded" but "self-directed" is "helpless and a failure." Chafer, *He That Is Spiritual*, 65, 106–7.

31. Walvoord, *The Holy Spirit*, 199. This is an example of continuing special revelation. Against regarding one's feelings as divine revelation, see *RST*, 1:452–55.

to mean 'guides,' but the guidance in view here is not a revealing to the mind of divine directives hitherto unknown; it is, rather, an impelling of our wills to pursue and practice and hold fast that sanctity whose terms we know already."[32]

Someone might object that the Spirit's work to lead God's children involves emotions (Gal. 5:17–18), implying subjective guidance from the Spirit through our desires.[33] In reply, we acknowledge that the Spirit's leading is an experiential reality that involves the whole inner man, including emotions. However, there is no reference in Galatians 5:16–26 to those emotions providing specific guidance regarding God's will that is not already revealed explicitly or implicitly in the Holy Scriptures. Rather, the emotions (love, joy, etc.) are part of our heartfelt obedience to God's commandments according to the new covenant promise that God inscribes his laws on the heart so that Christians delight to do God's will (Ps. 40:8; 2 Cor. 3:3). We are not to determine God's will merely by our feelings but, rather, to test our impulses and desires by the "safe and sure criterion" of "the written Word of God, and by it all must be measured," as A. W. Pink said.[34] Hence, "to be led by the Spirit" means "to have the direction of one's life as a whole determined by the Spirit,"[35] to be "ruled by his Spirit," which means "sanctification."[36]

The leading of the Spirit consists of *illuminating* and *effectually directing* believers by God's Word. Our problem by nature is both ignorance of the law of God and unwillingness to perform our duty. Happily, the leading of the Holy Spirit deals with this twofold problem. The psalmist prays for this leading when he asks for understanding: "Teach me, O Lord, the way of thy statutes; and I shall keep it unto the end. Give me understanding, and I shall keep thy law" (Ps. 119:33–34); and for the willingness to obey: "Make me to go in the path of thy commandments; for therein do I delight. Incline my heart unto thy testimonies, and not to covetousness" (vv. 35–36).

To be "led by the Spirit" involves the same combination of divine sovereignty and human activity spoken of in the ancient promise: "I will put my spirit within you, and cause you to walk in my statutes, and ye

32. Packer, *Keep in Step with the Spirit*, 118, emphasis original.
33. Thus, Grudem, *Systematic Theology*, 642–43.
34. Pink, *The Holy Spirit*, 113.
35. Moo, *The Epistle to the Romans*, 498.
36. Calvin, *Commentaries*, on Rom. 8:14. See Warfield, *The Holy Spirit*, 32–35.

shall keep my judgments, and do them" (Ezek. 36:27). God's people must "walk" in obedience, which involves the thoughts, affections, and choices of their hearts. However, their walking is caused by the leading of the Spirit. Paul writes, "Work out your own salvation. . . . For it is God which worketh in you both to will and to do of his good pleasure" (Phil. 2:12–13).[37]

The Warning against Grieving the Spirit

The Holy Spirit led the people of Israel through various prophetic and miraculous means, "but they rebelled, and vexed his holy Spirit: therefore he was turned to be their enemy, and he fought against them" (Isa. 63:10). The Hebrew verb translated as "vexed" (*'astab*) means to grieve in a way that provokes anger (Gen. 34:7; 45:5; 1 Sam. 20:34); when used of God, it communicates that sin offends him and brings his wrath (Gen. 6:6; Ps. 78:40). Israel at that time consisted mostly of unbelievers who rejected God's word and fell under the wrath of God (Ps. 95:8–11).

There is also a sense in which believers in Christ can grieve the Spirit, though they have been justified and will be saved from God's wrath (Rom. 5:9). Paul says, "Grieve not the holy Spirit of God, whereby ye are sealed unto the day of redemption" (Eph. 4:30). The Greek verb translated as "grieve" (*lypeō*) refers to emotional sorrow (2 Cor. 6:10), including taking offense at someone's actions (Rom. 14:13–15).[38] It is here used anthropomorphically of the offense of sin in God's sight, though our sins cannot hurt God or reduce his infinite joy (Job 35:6–7).[39] The context makes it clear that what grieves the Spirit is unrepented sin, such as lying, stealing, sinful anger, lack of love, or sexual impurity in speech or action (Eph. 4:25–5:6).

Sibbes said that sins of the body grieve the Spirit "as defiling his temple" and carrying away our love and delight from the things of God, but "as the Holy Ghost is a Spirit, so spiritual sins grieve him most—as pride, envy."[40] We can also grieve the Spirit, Sibbes said,

37. Smeaton, *The Doctrine of the Holy Spirit*, 217.

38. The verb *lypeō* is often associated with provoking anger. See Gen. 4:5; 45:5; Neh. 5:6; Est. 1:12; 2:21; Isa. 8:21; 57:17; Ezek. 16:43; Jonah 4:1, 4, 9 LXX.

39. On God's self-sufficiency and joy, and biblical descriptions of his grieving over sin, see *RST*, 1:645–48, 844–49, 854–55. See also Owen, *Communion with God*, in *Works*, 2:265; and *Pneumatologia*, in *Works*, 4:414.

40. Sibbes, *A Fountain Sealed*, in *Works*, 5:419. This paragraph is adapted from Beeke and Jones, *A Puritan Theology*, 584. Used by permission.

"when the mind is troubled with a multitude of business; when the soul is like a mill where one cannot hear another." We become so "drowned in the world" that we cease to give attention to Christ and "the things of heaven." Activity is not synonymous with spirituality, as popular Christian culture would have us believe. Rather, we are called to humble dependence. As Sibbes said, "This grieves the Holy Spirit also when men take the office of the Spirit from him, that is, when we will do things in our own strength and by our own light, as if we were gods to ourselves."[41]

Paul's words emphasize both the fearful majesty and faithful mercy of the Spirit, who is displeased by the sins of Christians. Majesty shines in the unprecedented title "Holy Spirit of God" (Eph. 4:30).[42] He is "the Spirit who is characterized by holiness and who is God himself at work in believers."[43] Therefore, we should regard his presence in us with holy fear and avoid offending him. Mercy pulses in the phrase "sealed unto the day of redemption." Though the Spirit will never break that seal and forsake believers, they can forfeit the sweet experiential comfort of that seal and suffer great darkness of soul.[44] Therefore, do not grieve the Holy Spirit.

Owen said, "The Holy Ghost, in his infinite love and kindness towards me, hath condescended to be my comforter; he doth it willingly, freely, powerfully. What have I received from him! In the multitude of my perplexities how hath he refreshed my soul! Can I live one day without his consolations? . . . Shall I grieve him by negligence, sin, and folly?"[45] Owen warned, "Consider who he is . . . and withal that he is a free, infinitely wise, and holy agent in all that he doth, who came freely unto you, and can withdraw from you; and grieve him not."[46]

The Duty of Walking in the Spirit

Paul says, "Walk in the Spirit, and ye shall not fulfil the lust of the flesh" (Gal. 5:16). The verb translated as "walk" (*peripateō*) refers to one's pattern of conduct, and the present imperative implies a continuous

41. Sibbes, *A Fountain Sealed*, in *Works*, 5:422.
42. While the Spirit is often called the "Holy Spirit" and the "Spirit of God," this is the only place in the Scriptures where both titles are combined as "Holy Spirit of God."
43. Lincoln, *Ephesians*, 307.
44. On the sealing and witness of the Spirit, see chap. 34.
45. Owen, *Communion with God*, in *Works*, 2:266.
46. Owen, *Pneumatologia*, in *Works*, 4:413.

or repeated duty. To "walk in the Spirit" most likely means to walk in the path of the Spirit's leading (v. 18), in this context the path of Spirit-produced love that fulfills the laws of God (vv. 5–6, 13–14, 22).[47] We might paraphrase, "Let your whole conduct be according to the external rule of God's Word and the holy motions of the indwelling Holy Spirit, who moves you to obey that Word."[48]

Walking by the Spirit requires engaging in combat: "For the flesh lusteth against the Spirit, and the Spirit against the flesh" (Gal. 5:17). Sibbes said, "Where there is no conflict, there is no Spirit of Christ at all."[49] Yet those "led of the Spirit" are not condemned for their sins or powerless to overcome them: "Ye are not under the law" (v. 18). As we saw earlier, to be led by the Spirit is to be dominated and directed by the Spirit's life-giving and sanctifying influence. Those excluded from "the kingdom of God" are characterized by "the works of the flesh," such as "adultery," "idolatry," "witchcraft," "strife," and "drunkenness" (vv. 19–21). To walk in the Spirit is to fight against those sins as the people who belong to Christ and "have crucified the flesh with the affections and lusts" by union with him in his crucifixion (v. 24).

Furthermore, to walk in the Spirit is to cultivate and practice "the fruit of the Spirit," which is "love, joy, peace, longsuffering, gentleness, goodness, faith, meekness, temperance" (Gal. 5:22–23).[50] Paul comments, "Against such things there is no law," which is "an understatement given for rhetorical effect,"[51] because people who act that way keep God's law (v. 14). By calling these qualities "the fruit of the Spirit," Paul reminds us that they are produced only by the life the Holy Spirit supplies in Christ and not by our strength.

Though walking in the Spirit requires relying on the Spirit, it also involves intentional effort to direct one's heart and life to holiness. When Paul says, "If we live in the Spirit, let us also walk in the Spirit" (Gal. 5:25), he does not repeat himself but uses a different verb for "walk" (*stoicheō*),

47. In the Greek text, *pneuma* is a simple dative modifying *peripateō*. Though the dative case may indicate means ("by the Spirit"), that verb commonly takes a dative of circumstance or manner to describe the way in which one walks. Blass, Debrunner, and Funk, *A Greek Grammar of the New Testament and Other Early Christian Literature*, 198.5 (106–7). Paul uses this same syntax to call people to "walk . . . not in orgies and drunkenness, not in sexual immorality and sensuality, not in quarreling and jealousy" (Rom. 13:13 ESV) and to say of Titus's love and pure motives, "Walked we not in the same spirit? . . . in the same steps?" (2 Cor. 12:18).

48. Adapted from Poole, *Annotations upon the Holy Bible*, on Gal. 5:16 (3:658).

49. Sibbes, *A Description of Christ*, in *Works*, 1:22.

50. We will discuss each of the fruit of the Spirit in chap. 36.

51. Longenecker, *Galatians*, 263.

which means literally to walk in ranks[52] and figuratively to follow a law or rule.[53] Packer paraphrased, "Keep in step with the Spirit."[54] One does this by fleeing the sins the Spirit condemns in the Word, such as pride and envy (v. 26), and strenuously pursuing the righteousness the Spirit commands in the Word, such as meekness (6:1).

A keen awareness that the Holy Spirit always accompanies us in our walk with God will greatly strengthen our cheerful resolve to do God's will. James Buchanan said, "The consideration of the continued presence and constant operation of the Spirit of God in the soul of every true believer is fitted at once to encourage and animate him in the path of holy obedience, and to impress him with an awful sense of reverence and godly fear."[55]

The Filling of the Holy Spirit

Though every Christian has the Holy Spirit and is led by him (Rom. 8:9, 14), there are degrees to the Spirit's work in people's lives. When Christ poured out the Holy Spirit on his disciples at Pentecost, "they were all filled with the Holy Ghost" (Acts 2:4). We have noted several indications that Pentecost was a unique step in redemptive history.[56] However, there is nothing unique about the filling of the Spirit, for it appears many times in the Holy Scriptures.

The Promise of the Spirit's Filling

The filling of the Spirit gives greater wisdom and power for service. The Lord "filled" (Hebrew *male'*, LXX Greek *empimplēmi*) his servant Bezaleel with the Spirit of God to give him wisdom and skill to construct the tabernacle (Ex. 31:3; 35:31). The same Hebrew and Greek terms are used to say that Joshua was "full" of the Spirit of wisdom to lead Israel (Deut. 34:9) and Micah was "full" of the Spirit to preach powerfully to Israel of its sin (Mic. 3:8). These words are also used when God's glory cloud "filled" the tabernacle and temple.[57] As we have already seen, the divine

52. *TDNT*, 7:666–67; cf. "walk [*stoicheō*] in the steps of that faith of our father Abraham" (Rom. 4:12).

53. Acts 21:24; Gal. 6:16; Phil. 3:16.

54. Packer, *Keep in Step with the Spirit*, 11.

55. James Buchanan, *The Office and Work of the Holy Spirit* (London: Banner of Truth, 1966), 244.

56. On the uniqueness of Pentecost, see chap. 5.

57. Ex. 40:34–35; 1 Kings 8:10–11; 2 Chron. 5:14; 7:1–2; Ezek. 10:4. In the LXX version of these texts, *male'* is rendered with *empimplēmi* in 2 Chron. 5:14; in the rest it is *pimplēmi*; cf. *plērēs* in Isa. 6:1, 3 LXX.

glory cloud is associated with the Holy Spirit.[58] The prophets looked forward to a restoration of the temple when it would again be filled with the glory of the Lord,[59] and they even spoke of a time when his glory would fill the whole earth.[60]

In the New Testament, being "filled" with the Holy Spirit is expressed through three Greek words that derive from the same root but are used with distinct nuances.[61] The verb *pimplēmi* is used several times in Luke and Acts for empowerment for a specific task.[62] A different verb (*plēroō*) is used to speak of another dimension of the Spirit's filling—namely, continuously filling people with godly character.[63] Empowerment for service and for godliness converge in the use of the adjective translated as "full" (*plērēs*) to describe Christians walking characteristically in the fullness of the Spirit's graces.[64]

Therefore, the Bible indicates that people may receive multiple, continual, or even increasing fillings by the Holy Spirit for faith, obedience, wisdom, and power. God may grant this filling to individuals or to groups.[65] Sometimes God fills people with the Spirit after they have been seeking his grace in prayer (Acts 1:14; 2:4; 4:31). Christ teaches his disciples to ask the Father for the Holy Spirit like children asking their fathers for food (Luke 11:11–13)—which suggests a regular, repeated supply, not a once-for-all endowment. Some believers, such as Stephen and Barnabas, were characteristically filled with the Spirit (Acts 6:5; 11:24). But in other instances, God fills his servants with the Spirit to meet an immediate need for power without any mention of prior seeking or preparation, as Peter and Paul

---

58. On the Spirit of presence, see chap. 3.

59. Ezek. 43:5; 44:4; Hag. 2:7.

60. Ps. 72:19; Hag. 2:7; cf. Isa. 11:9; Hab. 2:14.

61. "Fill" (*pimplēmi*, aorist *eplēs-*), "fill" (*plēroō*), and "full" (*plērēs*) share the same root (*plē-*). See *TDNT*, 6:283. On the distinct uses of the verbs in Luke-Acts, see Ferguson, *The Holy Spirit*, 89.

62. Consider the filling (*pimplēmi*) of Elizabeth, Zacharias, and John for prophetic ministry (Luke 1:15, 41, 67); the disciples to speak in tongues (Acts 2:4); Peter (v. 14; 4:8, 13); the church to speak God's word (v. 31); and Paul (9:17; 13:9). The verb is used in the aorist tense (*eplēs-*, except the future in Luke 1:15), which well suits the idea that God filled people for the particular ministries with which these texts associate the filling.

63. Consider the filling (*plēroō*) of the disciples with joy and the Holy Spirit (Acts 13:52), the church with praise (Eph. 5:18), and possibly Paul's word in Rom. 15:13: "Now the God of hope fill [*plēroō*] you with all joy and peace in believing, that ye may abound in hope, through the power of the Holy Ghost." The verb *plēroō* in Acts 13:52 and Eph. 5:18 is in the imperfect and present tenses, signifying a continuing or repeated act.

64. Consider Christ being "full" (*plērēs*) of the Holy Spirit when led by the Spirit to overcome the Devil's temptations (Luke 4:1–2); the appointing of men "full of the Holy Ghost and wisdom" (Acts 6:3); Stephen as "a man full of faith and of the Holy Ghost" (v. 5), "full of faith and power" (v. 8), and "full" of the Holy Spirit when submitting to martyrdom (7:55–60); and Barnabas, "a good man, and full of the Holy Ghost and of faith" (11:24).

65. On groups being filled with the Spirit, see Acts 2:4; 4:31; 13:52; Eph. 5:18–21.

experienced (4:8; 13:9). Those apostles had both been filled before (2:4; 9:17). This need not imply that they had lost the filling and regained it, but indicates that to be filled with the Spirit—which we must remember is a physical figure of speech for a divine person's activity—allows for different degrees and dimensions of the Spirit's work that vary over time.

There is a great need for Christian men, women, and children who are filled with the Holy Spirit. Edward Bickersteth said, "In this holy anointing is our strength both for communion with God and service among men. Was Jesus full of the Holy Ghost? We are commanded, 'Be ye filled with the Spirit.'"[66] The filling of the Spirit is essential to the church's spiritual progress. Ernest Reisinger (1919–2004) said that "without the Spirit there will be no conviction, . . . no conversions, . . . no spiritual growth. . . . The greatest need in the church today is a manifestation of the power of the Holy Spirit."[67]

The Christian's Responsibility to Be Filled by the Spirit

Paul says, "Be not drunk with wine, wherein is excess; but be filled with the Spirit" (Eph. 5:18). "Be filled" (*plērousthe*) is a present imperative passive verb, which implies the obligation of all the saints continuously or repeatedly to receive the influence of the Spirit so that he fills them.[68]

The contrast with drunkenness (cf. Acts 2:4, 13) implies receiving a mind-altering, behavior-changing influence in pursuit of happiness. Charles Hodge commented, "Men are said to be filled with wine when completely under its influence; so they are said to be filled with the Spirit when he controls all their thoughts, feelings, words, and actions."[69] Wine is associated with joy,[70] and the Spirit grants God's children supernatural joy.[71] Just as people get drunk by drinking wine, so Christians who seek spiritual refreshment are filled with the Spirit by exercising faith in Christ (John 7:37–39). However, whereas too much wine produces "excess" (*asōtia*), a wasted, self-destructive life, the power of the Holy Spirit produces a wise, careful, diligent life of doing God's will (Eph. 5:15–18). We cannot pretend to be filled with the Spirit if we violate "the unity of the

66. Bickersteth, *The Holy Spirit*, 84.

67. Ernest Reisinger, *The Church's Greatest Need* (Pensacola, FL: Chapel Library, n.d.), 4–5.

68. Compare the present passive imperative verb to "be transformed" by the renewing of the mind (Rom. 12:2) or, negatively, to not "be deceived" (1 Cor. 6:9; 15:33).

69. Hodge, *Ephesians*, 220.

70. Judg. 9:13; Ps. 104:15; Eccles. 9:7; 10:19; Song 1:2, 4; Isa. 22:13; 24:11; Zech. 10:7.

71. Ps. 51:12; Luke 10:21; Acts 13:52; Rom. 14:17; 15:13; Gal. 5:22; 1 Thess. 1:6.

Spirit" with proud, harsh, impatient, unloving conduct (4:2–3) or "grieve . . . the holy Spirit of God" by unrepented sin (v. 30).

Paul describes the Spirit-filled church with four participial clauses (Eph. 5:19–21):

- Bible-saturated worship: "speaking to yourselves [or one another][72] in psalms and hymns and spiritual songs" (cf. Col. 3:16).
- Heart-engaging worship: "singing and making melody in your heart to the Lord."
- Trinity-adoring worship: "giving thanks always for all things unto God and the Father in the name of our Lord Jesus Christ."
- Authority-honoring worship: "submitting yourselves one to another in the fear of God," which Paul proceeds to explain as honoring and obeying authorities in the home and society (Eph. 5:22; 6:1, 5).

Paul's exposition of the Spirit-filled life is notable for its focus on the church. John Stott said, "The two chief spheres in which this fullness is manifest are worship and fellowship."[73] The Spirit does not fill us to act as isolated individuals but as members of a well-ordered, worshiping community—the body of Christ.

Filling is a theme that appears repeatedly in Paul's epistle to the Ephesians, reminding us that the filling of the Spirit is Christ's "fulness" in his body (Eph. 1:23) whereby Christ lovingly dwells in his people through the Spirit so they are "filled with all the fulness of God" (3:16–21); thus, Christ may "fill all things" with God's glory and bring his people to maturity in his likeness (4:10, 13). This theme of filling ties into the typological-prophetic theme of God filling his temple and, ultimately, the whole earth with his glory.

In summary, being filled with the Spirit involves the holistic practice of godliness, including avoidance of influences that cloud and corrupt our minds, meditation on God's Word as our wisdom, exercising faith in Christ as the Mediator of God's fullness, repentance of sin and obedience to God's commands, rejoicing in God and seeking satisfaction in him, prayer for God's power and presence in our lives, adoration and thanksgiving in the presence of the triune God, participation in the assemblies of the church

72. The word translated as "yourselves" (plural *heautos*) has the sense of "one another" in 1 Cor. 6:7; Eph. 4:32; Col. 3:13, 16; Heb. 3:13; 1 Pet. 4:10, and this is the best interpretation of the term in Eph. 5:19 as well.

73. Stott, *Baptism and Fullness*, 59.

for biblical worship, and submission to God-ordained authorities in order to honor the Lord. This reminds us that the Spirit-filled life is not a different kind of life from that possessed by all people in Christ (the error of two-level Christianity), for the Spirit indwells them all. Rather, it is a different degree of the Spirit's influence.[74]

To be filled with the Spirit is not merely to receive power but to be filled with God himself in his loving self-disclosure. In other words, we must not pursue the Spirit's filling merely because we find God useful but because he is infinitely glorious (Eph. 3:19–21; 5:18–20). Being filled with the Spirit is an act of worship that enables greater worship. As Augustine said, the triune God is love, the very fountain of love and life, and the Spirit of God calls us to drink of this fountain—yes, "to drink of Himself."[75]

Praying for Revival

The need of the church to be filled with the Spirit calls Christians to pray for revival. The term *revival* originates in the biblical prayers that God would "revive" (*piel* of *khayah*) or "quicken" his people—that is, to renew their life (Pss. 80:18; 85:6; Hab. 3:2). These Old Testament prayers expressed the desire for a comprehensive renewal of Israel's national prosperity, but since that prosperity in the old covenant depended on the renewal of obedience and of true worship, they were also prayers for spiritual revival.

Revival may be defined as *a special season when God the Holy Spirit does his usual works in the church through the Word with unusual power for the glory of God*.[76] We cannot make, plan, or manipulate a revival. Charles Finney taught that "revival is the result of the right use of the appropriate means," and we may expect its attainment "with great certainty with the use of the appropriate means."[77] However, the Spirit works when and where he chooses (John 3:8; 1 Cor. 12:11). While we should ask God to send revival, we cannot cause or trigger it.[78] The Spirit of revival is the Spirit of Christ, for the Spirit comes through Christ to the glory of Christ

74. On the error of two-level Christianity (carnal versus Spirit-filled), see chap. 28.

75. Augustine, *Homilies on the Epistle of John*, 7.6, in *NPNF*[1], 7:503.

76. See Lloyd-Jones, "Revival: An Historical and Theological Survey" (1959), in *The Puritans*, 1–2.

77. Charles G. Finney, *Lectures on Revival of Religion*, 6th ed. (New York: Leavitt, Lord & Co.; Boston: Crocker & Brewster, 1835), 12, 14. On Finney's Pelagian tendencies, see chap. 16.

78. Sometimes people claim that God promises national revival if the church prays and repents of sin: "If my people, which are called by my name, shall humble themselves, and pray, and seek my face, and turn from their wicked ways; then will I hear from heaven, and will forgive their sin, and will heal their land" (2 Chron. 7:14). However, the promise to "heal their land" is a pledge to restore Israel's physical "land" from covenantal curses such as drought or locust infestation (v. 13). If people do the things mentioned here, then God has already revived them spiritually.

(John 14:16–17; 16:14). Sibbes said, "Those ages wherein the Spirit of God is most, is where Christ is most preached."[79] Unusual works such as miracles are no proof of revival by the Spirit (2 Thess. 2:9). Packer wrote, "Revival is God touching minds and hearts in an arresting, devastating, exalting way. . . . It is God accelerating, intensifying, and extending the work of grace that goes on in every Christian's life. . . . It is the near presence of God giving new power to the gospel of sin and grace."[80]

The New Testament prototype for revival is Pentecost (Acts 2). Pentecost teaches us much about the genuine marks of revival. First, authentic revival is always a sovereign work of God in Christ through the Holy Spirit (v. 33). The existence, depth, timing, and numbers of revival are all determined by God: "The Lord added to the church daily such as should be saved" (v. 47; cf. 11:18, 21–24; 13:48). Second, authentic revival is usually, though not always, preceded by a remarkable effusion of prayer (1:14). Revivals have often been prompted, under the Spirit's tutelage, by a felt need for prayer, which in turn prompted prayer meetings that were the seeds of revivals (4:31). Third, revival usually begins in the church with those who have already been born again. The small group of disciples was blessed with the Spirit's outpouring at Pentecost, and through them God converted thousands (2:1–4, 41). Fourth, in authentic revival, remarkable spiritual growth results from the Spirit joining himself to the Word of God to produce powerful and faithful preaching. The Spirit filled those already instructed by Christ and then transformed many souls when Peter preached from the Psalms and Prophets (vv. 14–36). Fifth, during revival, the Holy Spirit searches hearts with the truth to expose sin and incites repentance. Peter's sermon aimed at the conscience (v. 36), convicted sinners of sin (v. 37), and called them to repentance (v. 38). Sixth, Spirit-worked revival is always accompanied by saving faith in Jesus: "Whosoever shall call on the name of the Lord shall be saved" (v. 21). Peter's sermon was a proclamation of Christ's grace and glory from beginning to end.[81]

Ferguson says, "In some respects, Pentecost may be viewed as the inaugural revival of the New Testament epoch."[82] However, revival is not

---

79. Sibbes, *A Description of Christ*, in *Works*, 1:23.

80. J. I. Packer, "The Glory of God and the Reviving of Religion: A Study in the Mind of Jonathan Edwards," in *A God-Entranced Vision of All Things: The Legacy of Jonathan Edwards*, ed. John Piper and Justin Taylor (Wheaton, IL: Crossway, 2004), 100.

81. This paragraph is adapted from Joel R. Beeke, "The Age of the Spirit and Revival," 40–46. Used by permission.

82. Ferguson, *The Holy Spirit*, 90.

limited to the unique redemptive historical event at Pentecost. Long before Pentecost, God granted Israel seasons of corporate spiritual renewal (2 Chron. 29:36; 30:10–12; Ezra 5:1–5). After Pentecost, we find the church in Jerusalem again praying fervently together for God's assistance and being filled with the Spirit with fresh power (Acts 4:31). Therefore, we have biblical warrant for hoping that God will send revival again.

We should desire and seek revival today. If one considers Paul's prayers for the churches, it is difficult to imagine that he is praying for anything less than a remarkable revival of the churches by God's Spirit (Eph. 1:15–20; 3:14–21; Col. 1:9–12), even churches that he strongly commends (Phil. 1:9–11). Therefore, the churches of Christ should pray for revival regularly and fervently. Our prayers for the advance of Christ's kingdom should aim high, for God "is able to do exceeding abundantly above all that we ask or think, according to the power that worketh in us" (Eph. 3:20). Yet our prayers should be tempered with realism, recognizing that revival brings the difficulties of serving many new converts, standing against the world's intensified persecution, and avoiding "the false fire of fanaticism, the false zeal of errant teachers, and the false strategies of orthodox overdoers and divisive firebrands majoring in minors."[83]

If we truly long for a mighty work of the Spirit in the future, then we will faithfully cultivate the Spirit's fruit in the present. Some generations never see revival. Yet when faithful men and women serve God with perseverance in times of great darkness, they sow the seeds that God causes to grow when he does send revival. Furthermore, the greatest "revival" of the church will be shared by all believers, for it will take place when our Lord returns and raises the dead to enjoy the fullness of life, holiness, and glory in his presence. Therefore, let us pray, "Thy kingdom come" (Matt. 6:10) with an eye on revival but ultimately on Christ's coming in glory.

Sing to the Lord

Praying for the Spirit's Work

Come, O come, thou quick'ning Spirit,
God from all eternity!
May thy power never fail us;
Dwell within us constantly.

83. Packer, "The Glory of God and the Reviving of Religion," in *A God-Entranced Vision of All Things*, ed. Piper and Taylor, 104.

Then shall truth and life and light
Banish all the gloom of night.

Grant our hearts in fullest measure
Wisdom, counsel, purity,
That we ever may be seeking
Only that which pleaseth thee.
Let thy knowledge spread and grow,
Working error's overthrow.

Show us, Lord, the path of blessing;
When we trespass on our way,
Cast, O Lord, our sins behind thee
And be with us day by day.
Should we stray, O Lord, recall;
Work repentance when we fall.

Holy Spirit, strong and mighty,
Thou who makest all things new,
Make thy work within us perfect
And the evil foe subdue.
Grant us weapons for the strife
And with vict'ry crown our life.

Heinrich Held
Tune: Lux Prima
Trinity Hymnal—Baptist Edition, No. 247

Questions for Meditation or Discussion

1. How do we know that all God's saved people are indwelt by the Holy Spirit?
2. What does it mean that the Spirit "indwells" people given that he is omnipresent?
3. Show from the Scriptures that the indwelling of the Spirit is an active and sanctifying presence.
4. How was the Spirit engaged in leading ancient Israel? The apostles after Christ's resurrection?
5. Whom does the Holy Spirit personally lead today? How does he lead them?

6. What does it mean to grieve the Holy Spirit? How can believers avoid doing that?
7. A friend says, "I know that my pastor is walking in the Spirit because his life is full of miracles." How do you respond? How do you explain what it means to walk in the Spirit?
8. What does the Bible teach about being filled with the Spirit?
9. What is revival? Should we seek revival today? How?
10. Are you indwelt by the Holy Spirit? Filled by the Holy Spirit? How do you know?

Questions for Deeper Reflection

11. What is the connection between the indwelling of the Spirit and union with Christ?
12. How are both faith and obedience involved in walking in the Spirit?
13. What difference should it make in the life of Christians to know that the Holy Spirit, not just a power but the divine person, is dwelling in them wherever they go? How can Christians cultivate a continual awareness of his presence?

33

Assurance of Salvation, Part 1

A Balanced, Biblical, Reformed Approach

"Assurance is the conscious confidence that we are in a right relationship with God through Christ," writes Sinclair Ferguson. "It is the confidence that we have been justified and accepted by God in Christ, regenerated by the Spirit, and adopted into his family, and that through faith in him we will be kept for the day when our justification and adoption are consummated in the regeneration of all things."[1] Such assurance is broad in both terminology and scope. It is described in the Bible as "full assurance of understanding" and "full assurance of hope" (Col. 2:2; Heb. 6:11). There are a number of key reasons for seeking to attain to and grow in assurance, not the least of which is the fact that our thinking about assurance of faith shapes our understanding of spiritual life. We may indeed be orthodox in many areas of the Christian faith and yet be quite unsound in our understanding of this vital doctrine of the Word of God.

We live in a time when far too many people are wrongly convinced that they are Christians, and they usually base this conviction on some form of presumption or "easy believism." But they do not exhibit the marks of a true work of saving grace. How awful it will be for such men and

1. Sinclair B. Ferguson, "The Reformation and Assurance," *The Banner of Truth*, no. 643 (April 2017): 20 (full article, 20–23). Portions of this chapter are adapted from Joel R. Beeke, *Knowing and Growing in Assurance of Faith* (Fearn, Ross-shire, Scotland: Christian Focus, 2017); and Beeke, *The Quest for Full Assurance*. Used by permission.

women on judgment day when Christ denies to have ever known them (Matt. 7:21–23)! On the other hand, there are those who adhere to a type of "hard believism." There may be solid reasons for them to believe they are children of God, but they set the bar too high or look for evidences they have no right to expect. A true understanding of assurance reveals that the fruit of the new birth in a person's life is indispensable evidence of salvation, but it also demonstrates that genuine, albeit tiny, marks of grace should never be despised.

Thomas Brooks (1608–1680) entitled his key work on assurance *Heaven on Earth*[2] partly because having assurance greatly enriches the lives of God's people with peace, hope, and joy now, even while it quickens our longing for the world to come. It enriches our communion with God, stimulates our zeal in Christian service, quickens our sanctification, and emboldens us in our witness to the gospel before a dying world.

Assurance is the nerve center of doctrine put into *use*—that is, God's truth applied to our lives. It is linked to the work of the Spirit at every point in the chain of salvation, touching every facet of our Christian life and experience. Assurance is broad in scope, profound in depth, and glorious in height. To be sure, full assurance is not essential to saving faith, but it is vital for the well-being of our faith. Yes, it is possible to be saved without assurance, but it is not possible to be a healthy Christian without assurance.

In this chapter, after dealing with a few introductory matters, we shall focus on a variety of issues related to assurance of salvation by working through the most significant confessional chapter ever penned on this subject: Westminster Confession of Faith, chapter 18. This chapter well represents the codification of the historic Reformed view of assurance of salvation down to the present day, and in many ways it expresses a balanced, biblical approach.

Why Do Many Christians Lack Full Assurance?

Despite its importance, far too many professing Christians lack genuine assurance. Some claim to never wrestle with assurance even though their lives show little, if any, marks of genuine Christianity. It is horrifying to think that their presumption may very well pave the road to hell for them. Others say that they long for assurance but cannot ever seem to find it. It

2. Thomas Brooks, *Heaven on Earth*, in *The Works of Thomas Brooks*, ed. Alexander Grosart, 6 vols. (1864; repr., Edinburgh: Banner of Truth, 1980), 2:301–534.

is a painfully personal matter for them, for they have struggled desperately with assurance, sometimes for many years.

A genuine believer may struggle with assurance for various reasons, such as:

- a conscious awareness of sin, especially indwelling sin
- false conceptions of God's character and of his gospel
- lack of clarity on justification by faith
- failure in certain instances to confess Christ openly
- being disobedient and backslidden
- being ignorant of what constitutes evidence of grace
- possessing a doubting or negative disposition
- being unclear with regard to the circumstances of one's conversion
- looking for the wrong kind of experience
- lack of acknowledging what God has done savingly in one's soul
- being attacked by Satan

On the other hand, a believer may gain assurance by prayerfully meditating on the promises of God, then appropriating them by faith, and finally by examining his life in light of the marks God has given in his Word. Christians need a Word-directed, Spirit-empowered self-examination regarding whether they indeed are true Christians. A believer should never remain satisfied with mere conjecture or presumption concerning his eternal destiny.

Is Assurance of Faith Biblical and Normative?

The possibility of assurance has been a point of controversy since the Reformation. The Roman Catholic Church, while affirming that Christians can have a measure of hope that they are saved and will enjoy God's eternal blessing, nevertheless denied the certainty of assurance. The Council of Trent decreed, "Even as no pious person ought to doubt of the mercy of God, of the merit of Christ, and of the virtue and efficacy of the sacraments, even so each one, when he regards himself, and his own weakness and indisposition, may have fear and apprehension touching his own grace; seeing that *no one can know with a certainty of faith*, which cannot be subject to error, *that he has obtained the grace of God*."[3] This denial of

3. The Council of Trent, session 6, chap. 9, in *The Creeds of Christendom*, ed. Schaff, 2:99, emphasis added.

certainty to the believer's assurance and commendation of spiritual anxiety has profound practical effects.

True Christians yearn for God's affirmation that they are indeed saved by Christ. The Scriptures are filled with stories of God's servants finding assurance of his saving mercies toward them. For example, Christ said to a woman, "Thy sins are forgiven. . . . Thy faith hath saved thee; go in peace" (Luke 7:48, 50). These words must have greatly increased her assurance. Furthermore, she had a measure of assurance prior to this blessed word from the Savior, for Christ's parable about the debtors hinges on the fact that her love for him, demonstrated in her lavish devotion, sprang from knowing that her sins were forgiven (vv. 41–47). Hence, Christ both teaches and models the principle that assurance is an important ingredient in healthy Christian love and worship. If assurance were unattainable, then Christ could not command, "Rejoice, because your names are written in heaven" (Luke 10:20).[4]

There is, however, a direct proportionality between saving faith and assurance. Strong faith tends to embrace strong assurance, and weak faith tends to embrace weak assurance. All of Scripture affirms that assurance is grounded on a faith that receives God's gracious redemption in Christ and rests secure in his word of promise.[5]

In the Old Testament, faith and assurance are often bound together. At the call of God, Abraham set out "by faith" from Ur of the Chaldees in search of an unknown country (Heb. 11:8). From this point in his pilgrimage, his faith grew in both depth of conviction and breadth of vision until he became "strong in faith, giving glory to God; and being fully persuaded that, what [God] had promised, he was able also to perform" (Rom. 4:20–21). The idea of faith as resting or relying on the Lord is found throughout the entire Old Testament.[6] The Psalms, in particular, revel in assurance of faith, even amid the intense struggle for faith by the believer as he battles sin, the world, and the Devil.[7] David says, "The LORD is my light and my salvation; whom shall I fear?" and "I trusted in thee, O LORD: I said, Thou art my God" (Pss. 27:1; 31:14). The Psalms teach believers to say, "Surely

4. Perkins, *An Exposition of the Symbol*, in *Works*, 5:336.

5. Parts of this section are summarized from Robert Letham, "The Relationship between Saving Faith and Assurance of Salvation" (ThM thesis, Westminster Theological Seminary, 1976).

6. 2 Kings 18:5, 22; 1 Chron. 5:20; Pss. 86:2; 143:8; Prov. 3:5; 16:20; 28:25; Jer. 49:11; Zeph. 3:2.

7. Pss. 4:6–8; 18:1–3; 22:1–6; 35:3; 42:1–5; 73:21–28.

goodness and mercy shall follow me all the days of my life: and I will dwell in the house of the Lord for ever" (23:6).

In the New Testament, God's new utterance in the words and deeds of Christ brings fuller assurance of a present salvation (Heb. 1:1–2). Types and promises are all fulfilled through its inaugurated Christ-centered eschatology as the Spirit's work in his people intensifies (cf. Joel 2:28; Acts 2:16–21). Paul says, "Ye have received the Spirit of adoption, whereby we cry, Abba, Father. The Spirit itself beareth witness with our spirit, that *we are the children of God*" (Rom. 8:15–16). John says, "We do *know* that we know him" and "These things have I written unto you that believe on the name of the Son of God; *that ye may know that ye have eternal life*" (1 John 2:3; 5:13). Believers can know they are eternally secure in God's preserving hand (John 10:28–29; 2 Tim. 1:12; 1 Pet. 1:5). Indeed, by being assured of their calling, they can be assured of their eternal predestination by God and ultimate glorification, for "whom he did predestinate, them he also called: and whom he called, them he also justified: and whom he justified, them he also glorified" (Rom. 8:30).

Therefore, assurance of salvation is possible for the believer in Christ and is ordinarily attainable through faith and obedience to God's Word. However, not all believers possess assurance, and not all assurance is genuine.

Three Possibilities concerning Assurance

No group of theologians worked harder or were better at spelling out the biblical doctrine of assurance of faith than the seventeenth-century Puritans.[8] The Puritan doctrine of assurance was formally codified by the Westminster Confession of Faith in chapter 18, "Of the Assurance of Grace and Salvation"—in our opinion, the preeminent chapter devoted to assurance in any of the various Reformed confessions. It is biblical, experiential, and pastoral as it spells out assurance for us in four short paragraphs. Under several headings, this chapter will unpack these four paragraphs, and we shall see what we can learn about this vital subject from this theological masterpiece.

8. At least twenty-five members of the Westminster Assembly wrote books on the doctrines of faith and assurance. See Joel R. Beeke, "The Assurance Debate: Six Key Questions," in *Drawn into Controversie: Reformed Theological Diversity and Debates within Seventeenth-Century British Puritanism*, ed. Michael A. G. Haykin and Mark Jones (Göttingen: Vandenhoeck & Ruprecht, 2011), 264.

The first paragraph presents the three possibilities that pertain to assurance. It states,

> Although hypocrites and other unregenerate men may vainly deceive themselves with false hopes and carnal presumptions of being in the favour of God, and estate of salvation (Job 8:13–14; Mic. 3:11; Deut. 29:19; John 8:41) (which hope of theirs shall perish [Matt. 7:22–23]): yet such as truly believe in the Lord Jesus, and love Him in sincerity, endeavouring to walk in all good conscience before Him, may, in this life, be certainly assured that they are in the state of grace (1 John 2:3; 3:14, 18–19, 21, 24; 5:13), and may rejoice in the hope of the glory of God, which hope shall never make them ashamed (Rom. 5:2, 5).[9]

False Assurance

The confession begins its explanation of the doctrine of assurance by addressing the first possibility, that of "false hopes and carnal presumptions." False assurance, these Puritan Christians believed, is a real danger. This is one of the ways that sin deceives men and women. People are apt to deceive themselves into a false peace based on an assurance grounded only on an all-too-optimistic view of themselves.

Unrepentant sinners may delude themselves into believing that God favors them. The prophet Micah says, "The heads thereof judge for reward, and the priests thereof teach for hire, and the prophets thereof divine for money: yet will they lean upon the LORD, and say, Is not the LORD among us? None evil can come upon us" (Mic. 3:11; cf. Isa. 48:1–2). But such sinners will be sadly disappointed. Christ gives this sobering preview of judgment day: "Many will say to me in that day, Lord, Lord, have we not prophesied in thy name? And in thy name have cast out devils? And in thy name done many wonderful works? And then will I profess unto them, *I never knew you*: depart from me, ye that work iniquity" (Matt. 7:22–23).

Anthony Burgess (d. 1664), a Westminster divine and one of the best Puritan writers on the subject of assurance,[10] said, "We are possessed with

9. *Reformed Confessions*, 4:254.

10. See Anthony Burgess, *Spiritual Refining: The Anatomy of True and False Conversion; A Treatise of Grace and Assurance wherein are Handled the Doctrine of Assurance, The Use of Signs in Self-Examination, How True Graces may be Distinguished from Counterfeit, Several True Signs of Grace, and Many False Ones* (1662; repr., Ames, IA: International Outreach, 1996). Sermons 1–11 and 116–18 have been edited for the modern reader in Anthony Burgess, *Faith Seeking Assurance*, ed. Joel R. Beeke (Grand Rapids, MI: Reformation Heritage Books, 2015). For a good summary of Burgess's life and insights into his part in the Westminster Assembly, including its

self-love and carnal confidence, and upon this foundation it is impossible to build a good superstructure. All of the piercing and discovering sermons that the prophets and Christ delivered to the Jews and Pharisees could not shake their rotten foundation because of their carnal confidence and vain trust in themselves."[11] Counterfeit assurance is so deeply engrained in our fallen nature that only the Lord can open our eyes that we may see our true condition.

True Assurance

True assurance is the next possible frame of mind in which we may find ourselves. Paragraph 18.1 of the confession plainly declares that assurance is indeed possible for Christians, but it also emphasizes that assurance cannot be obtained without our Lord Jesus. Every aspect of paragraph 18.1 ties assurance to Christ in saying that we must believe in *him*, love *him*, and walk before *him*. The apostle John says, "God hath given to us eternal life, and this life is in his Son. He that hath the Son hath life; and he that hath not the Son of God hath not life" (1 John 5:11–12). The privilege of those who "have peace with God through our Lord Jesus Christ," Paul says, is to "rejoice in hope of the glory of God" (Rom. 5:1–2).

There were indeed some Puritans who felt that full assurance was quite hard to obtain, but others stressed that believers may ordinarily obtain comfortable degrees of true assurance of their salvation. William Guthrie (1620–1665) wrote, "A man's interest in Christ, or his gracious state may be known, and that with more certainty than people conjecture; yea, and the knowledge of it may be more easily attained unto than many imagine; for not only hath the Lord commanded men to know their interest in Him as a thing attainable, but many of the saints have attained unto the clear persuasion of their interest in Christ and in God as their own God."[12]

Saving Faith, Yet Little or No Conscious Assurance

Finally, paragraph 18.1 of the Westminster Confession stresses a third possible state for Christians: they may possess saving faith without the joy and full assurance that they possess it. Peter addressed the "brethren" who had

---

deliberations on assurance, see Jonathan L. Master, *A Question of Consensus: The Doctrine of Assurance after the Westminster Confession* (Minneapolis: Fortress, 2015), 63–66, 81–139.

11. Burgess, *Faith Seeking Assurance*, 24–25.

12. William Guthrie, *The Christian's Great Interest* (London: Banner of Truth, 1969), 5; cf. Jonathan Edwards, *The Religious Affections* (London: Banner of Truth, 1961), 255.

the same "precious faith" that he had and said, "Give diligence to make your calling and election sure" (2 Pet. 1:1, 10). Paul prays, "Now the God of hope fill you with all joy and peace in believing, that ye may abound in hope, through the power of the Holy Ghost" (Rom. 15:13). Thus, Burgess said that assurance is "not of absolute necessity to salvation: it's not a necessary effect of our calling and election at all times."[13]

Assurance deepens the joy of faith, but it must be emphasized that it is not essential to salvation. God justifies believers through faith *alone* in Christ *alone*. Assurance is the conscious knowledge and enjoyment of that justification. A genuine believer may feel that he or she walks in darkness (Isa. 50:10).[14] Burgess acknowledged that this is agonizing, more painful than broken bones.[15] It is hardly an ideal state. The Bible offers much practical help to those who are in this state by specifying three major sources of assurance, which are also identified in the confession.

The Foundations of Assurance

The Westminster Confession (18.2) goes to the very heart of the way to attain personal assurance of salvation when it clarifies the foundations of assurance thus:

> This certainty is not a bare conjectural and probable persuasion grounded upon a fallible hope (Heb. 6:11, 19); but an infallible assurance of faith founded upon the divine truth of the promises of salvation (Heb. 6:17–18), the inward evidence of those graces unto which these promises are made (2 Peter 1:4–5, 10–11; 1 John 2:3; 3:14; 2 Cor. 1:12), the testimony of the Spirit of adoption witnessing with our spirits that we are the children of God (Rom. 8:15–16), which Spirit is the earnest of our inheritance, whereby we are sealed to the day of redemption (Eph. 1:13–14; 4:30; 2 Cor. 1:21–22).[16]

It is vital not to confuse the grounds of *assurance* with the grounds of *salvation*.[17] As John Murray noted, "When we speak of the grounds of assurance, we are thinking of the ways in which a believer comes to entertain this assurance, not of the grounds on which his salvation rests.

13. Burgess, *Spiritual Refining*, 672.
14. Ferguson, *The Whole Christ*, 178.
15. Burgess, *Spiritual Refining*, 26.
16. *Reformed Confessions*, 4:254.
17. Paul Helm, *Calvin and the Calvinists* (Edinburgh: Banner of Truth, 1982), 28, 75.

The grounds of salvation are as secure for the person who does not have full assurance as for the person who has."[18]

In this sense, the confession presents three grounds of assurance:[19] a primary, objective ground ("the divine truth of the promises of salvation") and two secondary, subjective grounds ("the inward evidence of those graces unto which these promises are made" and "the testimony of the Spirit of adoption witnessing with our spirits"). Let us look at each of these in turn.

The Divine Promises in Christ

God's promises in Christ are the chief ground for a Christian's assurance. Assurance is the fruit that grows naturally from faith, and "faith cometh by hearing, and hearing by the word of God" (Rom. 10:17). As Brooks wrote,

> The promises of God are a Christian's *magna charta*, his chiefest evidences for heaven. Divine promises are God's deed of gift; they are the only assurance which the saints must show for their right and title to Christ, to His blood, and to all the happiness and blessedness that comes by Him. . . . The promises are not only the food of faith, but also the very life and soul of faith; they are a mine of rich treasures, a garden full of the choicest and sweetest flowers; in them are wrapped up all celestial contentments and delights.[20]

Burgess argued that it "is a more noble and excellent way" to find assurance of faith by relying on God's promises in Christ outside of us than it is to come to assurance by seeing the evidences of grace within us.[21] This stress on God's promises in Christ Jesus implies a number of things for the Christian experience of assurance.

First, we can never gain assurance by looking to ourselves or anything that we have produced without also eyeing God's promises. We must focus on God's faithfulness in Christ revealed in the various gospel promises recorded in the New Testament. Paul tells us in 2 Corinthians 1:18–20, "But as God is true, our word toward you was not yea and nay. For the Son

18. Murray, *Collected Writings*, 2:270.
19. Buchanan, *The Doctrine of Justification*, 184; cf. Louis Berkhof, *The Assurance of Faith* (Grand Rapids, MI: Eerdmans, 1939), 49–68.
20. Brooks, *A Cabinet of Jewels*, in *Works*, 3:254–55.
21. Burgess, *Faith Seeking Assurance*, 140; cf. *Spiritual Refining*, 51.

of God, Jesus Christ, who was preached among you . . . was not yea and nay, but in him was yea. For all the promises of God in him are yea, and in him Amen, unto the glory of God by us." Here Paul tells us that God does not speak out of both sides of his mouth. His glorious promises in the Lord Jesus cannot fail because God is ever true to his Word. Thus, our assurance lies in the truthful character of our God, who manifests himself supremely in the person and finished work of his Son. The very same offers of grace and gospel promises that direct us to salvation are quite sufficient to lead us to assurance.

Second, with the growth of assurance, God's promises become more and more real to the believer. The promises of God and assurance of faith serve to reinforce each other. This is because God's promises are the road on which Christ meets the soul. So Thomas Goodwin wrote, "If one promise belongs to thee, then all do; for every one conveys [the] whole Christ in whom all the promises are made and who is the matter of them."[22] William Spurstowe (c. 1605–1666) wrote, "The promises are instrumental in the coming of Christ and the soul together; they are the warrant by which faith is emboldened to come to him, and take hold of him; but the union which faith makes is not between a believer and the promise, but between a believer and Christ."[23] The promises provide a foundation for our assurance, and our assurance gives strength to our faith so that we can make further appropriation of the promises, and this, in turn, brings us into a fuller personal communion with the Lord Jesus.

Third, the Christ-centeredness of personal assurance is prominent in God's promises, for Jesus Christ himself is the "sum, foundation, seal, [and] treasury of all the promises" of God.[24] "Let thy eye and heart, first, most, and last, be fixed upon Christ, then will assurance bed and board with thee," said Brooks.[25] Burgess wisely advised his readers to beware of an obsessive and overambitious introspection when he wrote, "We should not so gaze upon ourselves to find graces in our hearts that we forget those acts of faith whereby we immediately close with Christ and rely upon Him only for our justification."[26]

22. Goodwin, *A Child of Light Walking in Darkness*, in *Works*, 3:321.
23. William Spurstowe, *The Wells of Salvation Opened: or, A Treatise Discerning the Nature, Preciousness, and Usefulness of the Gospel Promises and Rules for the Right Application of Them* (London: T. R. & E. M. for Ralph Smith, 1655), 44–45.
24. Edward Reynolds, *Three Treatises of the Vanity of the Creature. The Sinfulness of Sinne. The Life of Christ* (London: B. B. for Rob Bastocke and George Badger, 1642), 1:365.
25. Brooks, *Heaven on Earth*, in *Works*, 2:524.
26. Burgess, *Faith Seeking Assurance*, 114; cf. *Spiritual Refining*, 41.

Finally, even though subjective phenomena may sometimes *feel* more real than faith in God's promises, such experiences give less glory to God than direct embrace of the divine promises by faith. Burgess said, "Trusting in God and in Christ when we feel nothing but guilt and destruction in ourselves is the greatest honor we can give to God. Therefore, though living by signs is more comfortable to us, living by faith is a greater honor to God."[27]

When Christian was confined in Doubting Castle in John Bunyan's *Pilgrim's Progress*, Giant Despair beat him and threatened to kill him the next day. But that night Christian recalled that he had "a key . . . called promise" in one of his pockets. Using the key, he opened all the castle's locks and escaped.[28] Bunyan's message is unmistakable: the key was there all along. Therefore, we have nothing to fear, for God delights in seeing his children take up his promises and put them to good use. They are always at the ready, always in our pocket, so to speak. We need not be hesitant of embracing and believing them—that is, believing in Jesus Christ, who is the content of the promises. As we do so, we find to our amazement and delight that Giant Despair is utterly unable to keep us as his prisoner.

The objective promise embraced by faith is infallible because it is *God's* comprehensive and faithful covenant promise. Consequently, subjective evidence, though needed, must always be considered as secondary for it is often intermixed with human convictions and feelings even when it gazes on the work of God. All exercises of saving faith apprehend to some degree the primary ground of the divine promises in Christ.

The Evidences of Saving Grace: The Syllogisms

While God's promises are the primary ground of assurance, they are not the sole ground. It is true that if we examine ourselves apart from resting in the divine promises by faith, we may become proud of our achievements or be brought down to despair when we realize how much sin still abides within our frame. John Calvin said, "If you contemplate yourself, that is sure damnation. But since Christ has been so imparted to you with all his benefits that all his things are made yours, that you are made a member of him, indeed one with him, his righteousness overwhelms your sins; his

27. Burgess, *Faith Seeking Assurance*, 156; cf. *Spiritual Refining*, 57.
28. Bunyan, *The Pilgrim's Progress*, in *Works*, 3:142–43.

salvation wipes out your condemnation; with his worthiness he intercedes that your unworthiness may not come before God's sight."[29]

But there are also professing Christians who claim they possess assurance of grace because they rest in the promises of God alone for salvation, yet their lives demonstrate no real evidence to confirm or vindicate their profession. Christ said, "Ye shall know them by their fruits" (Matt. 7:16). And his apostle John identified the necessary fruits if we would have assurance that we are true believers (1 John 2:3, 5; 3:14; 5:2). Since unconverted sinners may have a kind of belief, Calvin said, "Believers are taught to examine themselves carefully and humbly, lest the confidence of the flesh creep in and replace assurance of faith."[30]

So how should self-examination be done? What are the evidences we are to look for? And how can we be sure that our conclusions are accurate? These are the kinds of questions thoughtful Christians have asked in the past and are still asking today. The Westminster Confession (18.2) addresses these very questions when it says that assurance of faith is grounded not only on the promises of God embraced by faith but also on "the inward evidence of those graces unto which these promises are made."

A note of caution: the confession does not encourage any mistaken idealism or perfectionism. As sinners saved by grace, we will find that faithful self-examination brings to light evidence that we still groan under the burden of remaining sin and infirmity. If our search for evidence of grace is a demand for "all or nothing," we shall have nothing. No one in this life ever has it all!

The logic of assurance is that evidence of the grace of God at work in Christians confirms the reality and genuineness of faith and, hence, the reality of one's election and salvation.[31] William Ames wrote, "He who rightly understands the promise of the covenant cannot be sure of his salvation, unless he perceive in himself true faith and repentance."[32] Reformed theologians helped believers to recognize the saving grace of God in themselves by means of logical arguments called *syllogisms*, which were based on what is called the *reflex act* of faith to reflect upon itself.[33] By the

29. Calvin, *Institutes*, 3.2.24.

30. Calvin, *Institutes*, 3.2.11. For Calvin's views on self-examination, see Beeke, *The Quest for Full Assurance*, 59–64.

31. Wollebius, *Compendium*, 1.4.(2).xv (53).

32. Ames, *The Marrow of Theology*, 1.30.17 (173).

33. Perkins, *An Exposition of the Symbol*, in *Works*, 5:337; and Flavel, *The Method of Grace*, in *Works*, 2:330.

reflex, or reflective, act of faith, the Holy Spirit highlights his activity in the believer, enabling him to conclude that his faith is saving faith because its exercises have a salvific character. Thus, the logic of assurance involves faith gazing upon itself in its acts in response to God and his Word. Burgess put it this way:

> First, there are the *direct acts* of the soul, whereby the soul immediately and directly responds to some object. Second, there are *reflex acts* of the soul, by which the soul considers and observes what acts it does. It's as if the eye is turned inward to see itself. The Apostle John expresses this fully, saying, "We do know that we know" (1 John 2:3). So, when we believe in God, that is a direct act of the soul; when we repent of sin, because God is dishonored, that is a direct act; but when we know that we do believe, and that we do repent of our sin, that is a reflex act.[34]

Burgess and other Reformed theologians talked about two closely related, albeit distinct, syllogisms that strengthen assurance—the practical (outward) syllogism and the mystical (inward) syllogism.[35] The practical syllogism was based on good works. It emphasized that the Christian's life of obedience provides confirmation of his experience of grace. The argument went thus:

> *Major premise*: According to the Bible, only those who possess true saving faith experience the Spirit's witness that their lives possess the fruits of sanctification in good works.
>
> *Minor premise*: I cannot deny that by the grace of God I have received the Spirit's witness that I possess the fruits of sanctification in good works.
>
> *Conclusion*: I must therefore be a partaker of saving faith.

An excellent biblical example is found in 1 John, which often uses the practical syllogism in a succinct form. For example: "Hereby we do know that we know him, if we keep his commandments" (2:3)—that is, "Those who know him keep his commandments; I keep his commandments; therefore, I know that I know him" (cf. 3:14; 5:2). In later chapters we will

34. Burgess, *Spiritual Refining*, 672.

35. Cornelis Graafland, "Van *syllogismus practicus* naar *syllogismus mysticus*," in *Wegen en Gestalten in het Gereformeerd Protestantisme*, ed. W. Balke, C. Graafland, and H. Harkema (Amsterdam: Ton Bolland, 1976), 105–22.

study obedience to God's commandments, in part to help people examine themselves for evidences of saving grace.[36]

The mystical syllogism was based on the Christian's internal virtues. It went something like this:

> *Major premise*: According to the Word of God, only those who have genuine faith will experience the Spirit's confirmation of inward grace and godliness.
>
> *Minor premise*: I cannot deny that by the grace of God I experience the Spirit's witness to inward grace and godliness.
>
> *Conclusion*: I must therefore be a partaker of saving faith.

A helpful biblical example of the mystical syllogism is found in the internal virtues laid out by Christ in the Beatitudes. Christ offers a brief description of the people who have divine warrant to count themselves blessed by God and part of his kingdom, focusing especially on the inward qualities of being poor in spirit, mourning, exhibiting meekness, hungering and thirsting for righteousness, showing mercy to others, having purity in heart, and being peacemakers (Matt. 5:3–9). Similarly, Paul lists "the fruit of the Spirit" to identify the characteristics of those who belong to Christ and are indwelt by his Spirit (Gal. 5:22–24). We will study these marks of grace in subsequent chapters.[37]

The mystical syllogism was to be based on the Holy Spirit's saving graces rather than the nonsaving operations of the Spirit, such as awakenings and stirrings of conscience, or mere external obedience and religious conformity.

How do we actually put the syllogisms and the reflex act of faith into practice? Let's assume you are spiritually distressed as you feel quite unspiritual, distant from God, and lukewarm in your faith. In fact, you can hardly pray, which makes you question if you have any faith at all. You turn to the Scriptures, but even special promises of God that were once quite precious to you in the past—such as 1 John 1:9, "If we confess our sins, he is faithful and just to forgive us our sins, and to cleanse us from all unrighteousness"—now seem hollow and unreachable. What should you do?

36. See the expositions of the Ten Commandments in chaps. 37–40.
37. See the expositions of the Beatitudes and the fruit of the Spirit in chaps. 35–36.

Turn to some of the marks of grace that are presented in Scripture. Pray to the Spirit to illuminate them for you, and then, as you think about your life, if you can say with confidence that any one of these evidences is your experience, you can be certain that you are a child of God—even if you cannot see any of the other evidences in your life. Let us assume you turn to 1 John 2:5, "But whoso keepeth his word, in him verily is the love of God perfected: hereby know we that we are in him." You would then ask yourself, praying for Spirit-illumined reflection, "Am I a keeper of Christ's Word?" Perhaps as you gaze at your life you remember how often you have broken God's Word and commandments, and you have to confess, "I'm afraid I can't see much, if anything, of that evidence of grace in me right now." But this does not mean you give up! Move on to yet another evidence of grace.

You keep reading until you get to 1 John 3:14, "We know that we have passed from death unto life, because we love the brethren." Again, you ask yourself syllogistically, knowing that only those who are the true children of God actually love the brethren, "Do I have a genuine love for the people of God?" Perhaps you can reply, "Yes, I certainly cannot deny that I do have a special love for God's people. I love to be with them, and I consider them my true brothers and sisters. I treasure seeing Christ in them. I serve them with my prayers, time, attention, abilities, and resources." You conclude, therefore, "I must truly be a child of God."

If you see one of these marks of grace in your life (such as love of fellow Christians), then you may be sure that since God does a complete work of salvation in his people, you also undoubtedly have all the other marks of grace, including that one mentioned in 1 John 2:5, even though you cannot see that in the present. An unbeliever does not have any of the marks of grace, so the presence of one indicates a real work of saving grace and, ultimately, the presence of the others. Though these evidences possess a discriminatory effect in exposing those who are counterfeit Christians, they are meant to solidify, comfort, and strengthen believers' faith and assurance, not drive them to despair.

The Testimony of the Holy Spirit

The Westminster Confession (18.2) further teaches that we obtain assurance as believers by the testimony of the Holy Spirit himself. In the words of the confession, assurance is also founded on "the testimony of the

Spirit of adoption witnessing with our spirits that we are the children of God . . . , which Spirit is the earnest of our inheritance, whereby we are sealed to the day of redemption."[38]

In the next chapter, we will study in more detail the meaning of biblical descriptions of the Holy Spirit's work in assurance.[39] However, we must remember that the internal work of the Spirit is a profound mystery (John 3:8). We should allow for the sovereign freedom of the Spirit to work as and when he wills. We must also allow freedom of conscience to those who differ about the finer details of the Spirit's witness.

Most of the members of the Westminster Assembly maintained one of two emphases. Some believed that the Holy Spirit simply bears witness with our spirits that the inward and outward evidences of grace in us are true so that we may be assured we are children of God. According to these theologians, there is then actually only one secondary ground of assurance: the Holy Spirit witnesses with our spirits concerning the evidences of grace.[40]

Other Puritan theologians argued that though the Spirit witnesses through the evidences of grace in our lives, he also can give a direct witness to the believer's heart through the Scriptures that can substantially augment his assurance and comfort, especially in times of great need.[41] For example, when the Spirit applies to the soul a special promise such as "I have loved thee with an everlasting love: therefore with lovingkindness have I drawn thee" (Jer. 31:3) with unction and palpable sweetness—such that the believer experiences what amounts to a profound depth of communion with God, is all but overwhelmed by his love, and has an acute sight of the beauty and glory of Christ—such a direct witness of the Spirit to the believer can give a large boost to his assurance. At such times, the believer is conscious that this intimately personal application of Scripture to the soul is an amazingly appropriate text for his particular need.

It needs to be underlined, however, that the assembly's divines were united in their assertion that the Spirit's witness is always tied to, and may never contradict, the Word of God. The work of the Spirit in union with

38. *Reformed Confessions*, 4:254.

39. On the Spirit's work as sealing, earnest, witness, and firstfruits, see chap. 34.

40. Burgess, *Faith Seeking Assurance*, 122; cf. *Spiritual Refining*, 44.

41. Samuel Rutherford, *A Survey of the Spirituall Antichrist* (London: by J. D. & R. I. for Andrew Crooke, 1648), 238–39; Henry Scudder, *The Christian's Daily Walk* (repr., Harrisonburg, VA: Sprinkle, 1984), 338; Brooks, *Heaven on Earth*, in *Works*, 2:518–23; Goodwin, *Of the Creatures*, in *Works*, 7:66; and *Of the Object and Acts of Justifying Faith*, in *Works*, 8:362–63, 366–67.

the Word is absolutely essential to every part of true assurance. As Burgess said, "As a man by the power of free will is not able to do any supernatural good thing, so neither by the strength of natural light can he discern the gracious privileges God bestows upon him (1 Cor. 2:12)."[42] Without the work of the Spirit, the promises of God may lead a person to self-deceit, carnal presumption, and a fruitless life. And without the inner illumination of the Spirit, self-examination invariably tends to introspection, bondage, and legalism. Seeking the witness of the Spirit apart from the promises of God and biblical inward evidence leads to an unbiblical mysticism, doctrinal antinomianism, and excessive emotionalism.

No matter which of the above two views one takes, it is critical to maintain that the Holy Spirit bears witness always with and through his Word. We must never separate the Holy Spirit's saving graces from the Word or highlight one at the expense of the other. And we must never separate the three grounds of assurance discussed above. The promises of God, the evidences of grace, and the testimony of the Holy Spirit are designed to work in tandem so as to produce a true and well-grounded assurance. A deepening realization of these truths helps us to grow in assurance.

The Cultivation of Assurance

As we noted earlier, Peter says, "Give diligence to make your calling and election sure" (2 Pet. 1:10). But just how is assurance cultivated? This is the burden of paragraph 18.3 of the Westminster Confession, which lists five practical issues dealing with assurance:

> This infallible assurance doth not so belong to the essence of faith, but that a true believer may wait long, and conflict with many difficulties, before he be partaker of it (1 John 5:13; Isa. 50:10; Mark 9:24; Ps. 88; 77:1–12): yet, being enabled by the Spirit to know the things which are freely given him of God, he may, without extraordinary revelation, in the right use of ordinary means, attain thereunto (1 Cor. 2:12; 1 John 4:13; Heb. 6:11–12; Eph. 3:17–19). And therefore it is the duty of every one to give all diligence to make his calling and election sure (2 Peter 1:10), that thereby his heart may be enlarged in peace and joy in the Holy Ghost, in love and thankfulness to God, and in strength

42. Anthony Burgess, *The True Doctrine of Justification Asserted and Vindicated, from the Errors of Papists, Arminians, Socinians, and More Especially Antinomians* (London: by Robert White, for Thomas Underhil, 1648), 272–73.

and cheerfulness in the duties of obedience (Rom. 5:1–2, 5; 14:17; 15:13; Eph. 1:3–4; Ps. 4:6–7; 119:32), the proper fruits of this assurance; so far is it from inclining men to looseness (1 John 2:1–2; Rom. 6:1–2; Titus 2:11–12, 14; 2 Cor. 7:1; Rom. 8:1, 12; 1 John 3:2–3; Ps. 130:4; 1 John 1:6–7).[43]

The Organic Relation of Faith to Assurance

First, there is a delicate balance in the Westminster divines' doctrine of assurance. They closely connect assurance to faith by calling it "an infallible assurance of faith" (18.2) but distinguish assurance from faith by saying that "this infallible assurance doth not so belong to the essence of faith" that a person with faith may lack full assurance (18.3).[44] The word *so* is important in this last statement: the divines were not making an absolute separation between assurance and faith, but a distinction.

What is the relationship of faith to assurance? Is the kernel of assurance to be found within faith? Most Reformed divines have answered yes,[45] for it is by faith in Christ that believers have "boldness" (*parrēsia*) to draw near to God (Eph. 3:12; Heb. 4:16; 10:19, 22). Paul describes how the gospel was preached to the Thessalonians not "in word only, but also in power, and in the Holy Ghost, and in much assurance" (1 Thess. 1:5). Faith contains in itself the seed of assurance, for "faith is the substance of things hoped for, the evidence of things not seen" (Heb. 11:1), which means that faith embraces invisible realities with certainty.[46]

But we must also distinguish saving faith from the assurance of faith. "It is one thing for me to believe, and another thing for me to believe that I believe," said Brooks.[47] Assurance of salvation is not identical to saving faith but is its fruit.[48] As such, assurance is certainly linked to faith, and the degree to which it is enjoyed is dependent on the health, vigor, and maturity of faith.[49] Justification, however, is by faith alone—even frail, feeble faith—and not by assurance.[50] Whether assurance is strong or weak,

43. *Reformed Confessions*, 4:254.

44. *Reformed Confessions*, 4:254.

45. Beeke, *The Quest for Full Assurance*, 147–50.

46. Turretin, *Institutes*, 15.17.14 (2:621). On Heb. 11:1, see the section on the object of saving faith in chap. 20.

47. Brooks, *Heaven on Earth*, in *Works*, 2:316.

48. Ames, *The Marrow of Theology*, 1.28.24 (167).

49. Ames, *The Marrow of Theology*, 1.27.19 (163).

50. John Downe, *A Treatise of the True Nature and Definition of Justifying Faith* (Oxford: I. Lichfield for Edward Forrest, 1635), 12–13.

Christ's righteousness appropriated by the weakest faith is nonetheless perfect and utterly sufficient to save.[51]

The Time Element in Faith's Maturation

Second, according to the Westminster Confession, "a true believer may wait long, and conflict with many difficulties, before he be partaker of" assurance (18.3), but the relationship between faith and assurance is usually strengthened over time, "growing up in many to the attainment of a full assurance" (14.3).[52] This process is implied in Peter's exhortation to "give diligence" to the pursuit of assurance (2 Pet. 1:10). Usually grace increases with age, and as faith grows, so do the other graces. Of course, age and experience do not ensure assurance, and it is not impossible for God to implant faith and full assurance simultaneously. As in conversion, God is always sovereign in the dispensing of assurance. Typically, however, as Burgess said, "He works it by degrees,"[53] so that the believer's doubts about his own salvation diminish bit by bit as he or she grows in grace (vv. 5–10).

The Means of Attaining Assurance

Third, the Westminster Confession (18.3) goes on to insist that "[the believer] may, without extraordinary revelation, *in the right use of ordinary means*, attain" to assurance.[54] Burgess noted, "It's a well-ordered assurance in the constant and diligent use of the means."[55] Four means are predominant in this regard: the Scriptures,[56] the sacraments,[57] prayer,[58] and enduring affliction (including conflicts, doubts, trials, and temptations).[59] These are the most common means God employs to increase assurance, for they are the means of spiritual growth.

51. John Rogers, *The Doctrine of Faith: Wherein Are Particularly Handled Twelve Principall Points, which Explaine The Nature and Use of It* (London: N. Newbery and H. Overton, 1629), 201.

52. *Reformed Confessions*, 4:250, 254.

53. Burgess, *The True Doctrine of Justification*, 152.

54. *Reformed Confessions*, 4:254, emphasis added.

55. Anthony Burgess, *CXLV Expository Sermons upon the Whole 17th Chapter of the Gospel according to St. John* (London: Abraham Miller for Thomas Underhill, 1656), 356.

56. Thomas Watson, *Heaven Taken by Storm* (Morgan, PA: Soli Deo Gloria, 1994), 12–15.

57. Burgess, *Faith Seeking Assurance*, 145–46; cf. *Spiritual Refining*, 53; and Robert Bruce, *The Mystery of the Lord's Supper*, trans. and ed. Thomas F. Torrance (Richmond, VA: John Knox Press, 1958), 82.

58. Burgess, *Faith Seeking Assurance*, 174–75; cf. *Spiritual Refining*, 673. See also Burgess, *The True Doctrine of Justification*, 273.

59. Burgess, *Faith Seeking Assurance*, 97; cf. *Spiritual Refining*, 35.

It is not the use of the means per se that increases assurance but the use of the means to flourish in Christlikeness. John says, "Hereby perceive we the love of God, because he laid down his life for us: and we ought to lay down our lives for the brethren. . . . My little children, let us not love in word, neither in tongue; but in deed and in truth. And hereby we know that we are of the truth, and shall assure our hearts before him" (1 John 3:16, 18–19).

The Duty of Seeking Assurance

Fourth, the Westminster Confession (18.3) says, "It is the duty of every [believer] to give all diligence to make his calling and election sure."[60] Paul says, "Examine yourselves, whether ye be in the faith; prove your own selves. Know ye not your own selves, how that Jesus Christ is in you, except ye be reprobates?" (2 Cor. 13:5).[61] In short, God commands us to pursue assurance with prayer and fervency, and promises that he will bless such a pursuit. "A good improvement of what we have of the grace of God at present, pleases God, and engages him to give us more," Bunyan wrote, going on to urge his readers, "Therefore, get more grace."[62] This stress by the Puritans on duty was reinforced by their conviction that assurance can never be considered as solely the privilege of exceptional saints, but that it is normative for every believer to at least some degree.

The Fruit of Assurance

Finally, the Westminster Confession (18.3) stresses that assurance is productive of God-glorifying, delightful fruit so that the believer's "heart may be enlarged in peace and joy in the Holy Ghost, in love and thankfulness to God, and in strength and cheerfulness in the duties of obedience . . . , the proper fruits of this assurance; so far is it from inclining men to looseness."[63] Assurance raises God-glorifying and soul-satisfying affections. It brings forth holy living particularly marked by spiritual peace, joy-filled love, humble gratitude, cheerful obedience, and a heartfelt mortification of sin. In a word, assurance enables faith to attain ever-greater

60. *Reformed Confessions*, 4:254.

61. The word translated as "reprobates" (2 Cor. 13:5) means failing to pass the test and, hence, being rejected. It is not to be connected to the doctrine of eternal reprobation, for God reveals no signs of reprobation in this life.

62. Bunyan, *A Holy Life the Beauty of Christianity*, in *Works*, 2:546.

63. *Reformed Confessions*, 4:254.

heights from which all other aspects of Christian character flow. This tonic of faith results in a fresh release of spiritual energy in every area of a person's life as a Christian.[64]

Assurance Lost and Renewed

Like the faithful pastors they were, the Puritan divines who met at Westminster concluded their historic chapter on assurance with a crisp but comprehensive paragraph (18.4) on how believers can temporarily lose their assurance of faith and, if such happens, the possibility of its renewal:

> True believers may have the assurance of their salvation divers ways shaken, diminished, and intermitted; as, by negligence in preserving of it, by falling into some special sin which woundeth the conscience and grieveth the Spirit; by some sudden or vehement temptation, by God's withdrawing the light of His countenance, and suffering even such as fear Him to walk in darkness and to have no light (Song 5:2–3, 6; Ps. 51:8, 12, 14; Eph. 4:30–31; Ps. 77:1–10; Matt. 26:69–72; Ps. 31:22; 88; Isa. 50:10): yet are they never utterly destitute of that seed of God, and life of faith, that love of Christ and the brethren, that sincerity of heart, and conscience of duty, out of which, by the operation of the Spirit, this assurance may, in due time, be revived (1 John 3:9; Luke 22:32; Job 13:15; Ps. 73:15; 51:8, 12; Isa. 50:10); and by the which, in the mean time, they are supported from utter despair (Mic. 7:7–9; Jer. 32:40; Isa. 54:7–10; Ps. 22:1; 88).[65]

The Causes of a Loss of Assurance

The reasons for a loss of assurance are often found in the believer. They include negligence in the means of grace and spiritual slothfulness, falling into sin, or yielding to a temptation. The lesson is obvious: *the Christian cannot enjoy high levels of assurance while he persists in low levels of obedience*. Burgess concluded, "It is therefore an unworthy thing to complain about the loss of God's favor and assurance if all your duties and performances are careless and withered."[66]

The Canons of Dort (Head 5, Art. 5) say that when believers commit great sins, "they very highly offend God, incur a deadly guilt, grieve the

64. Brooks, *Heaven on Earth,* in *Works*, 2:406–13.
65. *Reformed Confessions*, 4:254–55.
66. Burgess, *Faith Seeking Assurance*, 95; cf. *Spiritual Refining*, 34–35.

Holy Spirit, interrupt the exercise of faith, very grievously wound their consciences, and sometimes lose the sense of God's favor for a time, until on their returning into the right way of serious repentance, the light of God's fatherly countenance again shines upon them."[67] Therefore, the canons (Head 5, Art. 10) state that assurance springs not only from faith in God's promises and the testimony of the Holy Spirit, but also "from a serious and holy desire to preserve a good conscience and to perform good works."[68]

Another reason for a loss of assurance lies not in the believer's life as such but in God. In the mystery of his sovereign will, he may withdraw the light of his countenance or permit a believer to be tried with vehement temptations or intensified afflictions that do violence to his peace and joy. This may have the purpose of allowing the believer to "taste and see how bitter sin is." Or it may be to "keep us low and humble." Again, it may be so that the believer learns to treasure assurance more or to depend more fully on the grace of Christ, and thus seeks after a closer walk with God.[69] Both God's withdrawals and his placing of trials in the believer's path are rooted in his fatherly discipline, which teaches right walking; his fatherly sovereignty, which teaches dependence; and his fatherly wisdom, which teaches that he knows and does what is best for his own. In his wisdom, God ordains these trials for the benefit of his elect and, in the final analysis, for his glory. Hence, as William Gurnall wrote, "The Christian must trust in a withdrawing God."[70]

The Revival of Assurance

Whatever the reasons for the loss of assurance, the Westminster Confession emphasizes that in due time it can be renewed. Even in the believer's most difficult struggles, the Holy Spirit abides within him and bears him up, keeping him from "utter despair." In fact, the child of God may be losing assurance even while he or she advances in grace.[71]

The *grace* and *essence* of faith remain within the believer even if he is blind to the *acts* and *practice* of faith. This gracious preservation of faith

---

67. *The Three Forms of Unity*, 154.

68. *The Three Forms of Unity*, 156. On the inseparable link between saving faith and obedience to God, see the Belgic Confession (Art. 24); and the Heidelberg Catechism (LD 24, Q. 64), in *The Three Forms of Unity*, 41–43, 88.

69. Burgess, *Faith Seeking Assurance*, 97–101; cf. *Spiritual Refining*, 35–36. See Brooks, *Heaven on Earth*, in *Works*, 2:330–34; and Goodwin, *A Child of Light Walking in Darkness*, in *Works*, 3:292–99, for similar lists.

70. Gurnall, *The Christian in Complete Armour*, 2:145.

71. Rutherford, *The Trial and Triumph of Faith*, 139–40.

holds out genuine hope for the revival of assurance, for the flame of God's life within the soul can never be totally extinguished. The embers burn, sometimes barely, but they can be fanned into the full flame of assurance by the persevering use of God's appointed means. Assurance is revived in the same way it was obtained the very first time. Believers must review their lives. They need to confess their backsliding. They have to humbly cast themselves upon their covenant-keeping God and his gracious promises in Christ, being sure to engage continually in fresh acts of ongoing renewal through faith and repentance.[72] David recovered his lost assurance (Ps. 51:12)—why shouldn't the penitent believer? We must remember that the loss here is only for a short time, for soon we shall have perfect assurance and perfect enjoyment of God forever in the eternal Celestial City.

Conclusion

The biblical, Reformed doctrine of assurance of salvation is precisely designed to undeceive the false professor of faith, to awaken the unsaved, to mature the young in grace, and to comfort the mature in faith. This doctrine inculcates a great appreciation for the biblical doctrines of vital union and communion with Christ, not morbid introspection. Christians should examine themselves and their spiritual experience because they are eager to delineate the track record of God at work in their lives so that they might attribute glory to the Father, who elects and provides such rich grace; to the Son, who redeems and intercedes for his people; and to the Spirit, who applies salvation to the people of God and sanctifies them.

Our primary ground of assurance lies in the promises of God in Christ. Those promises need to be applied to our hearts and must bear fruit in our lives. They should enable us to experience the Spirit's corroborating witness with our spirits that we are indeed the sons and daughters of God. We are called to live fruitful lives day by day, to speak well of our great assuring God, and to serve as salt in the earth.

The practical message for the true Christian is that faith must triumph in the end since it is a gift from the triune God and is secured by his Word. Therefore, we need not despair when, for a time, we do not feel its triumph. Let us all the more embrace God's sure and steadfast promise in Christ, recognizing that our certainty, both in an objective sense and a subjective one, lies wholly in Christ, for faith is of Christ and rests in him.

72. Burgess, *Spiritual Refining*, 34–35, 673–75.

Christ shall ultimately win the day in us and for us. Let us be courageous to honor Christ, and through him, the triune God, for ultimately our assurance is not about a self-confidence but about a confidence in the Father, the Son, and the Spirit. That is what faith and assurance are all about—honoring the triune God through Jesus Christ. "For of him, and through him, and to him, are all things: to whom be glory for ever. Amen" (Rom. 11:36).

Sing to the Lord

Waiting for Assurance in Conflict

Be Thou my helper in the strife,
O Lord, my strong defender be;
Thy mighty shield protect my life,
Thy spear confront the enemy.
Amid the conflict, O my Lord,
Thy precious promise let me hear.
The faithful, reassuring word:
I am thy Saviour, do not fear.

My soul is joyful in the Lord,
In His salvation I rejoice;
To Him my heart will praise accord
And bless His Name with thankful voice.
For who, O Lord, is like to Thee,
Defender of the poor and meek?
The needy Thy salvation see
When mighty foes their ruin seek.

Psalm 35
Tune: Catherine
The Psalter, No. 92
Or Tune: Altadena
Trinity Hymnal—Baptist Edition, No. 740

Questions for Meditation or Discussion

1. How does God's Word show it is possible for believers to enjoy assurance of their salvation?
2. What three possibilities concerning assurance does the Westminster Confession describe?

3. How do God's promises provide a foundation for assurance?
4. What are the practical and mystical syllogisms? How are they rightly used?
5. What passages of Scripture provide us with evidences of genuine salvation?
6. What does the Holy Spirit do to give assurance to God's children?
7. How does a Christian cultivate assurance in his heart?
8. What benefits does Spirit-worked assurance produce in a believer's life?
9. What measure of genuine assurance do you have? What is the basis of that assurance?
10. If you are saved by grace, what can you do to grow in your assurance of salvation? If you are not saved, then how can you be saved?

Questions for Deeper Reflection

11. What is the danger of separating assurance from saving faith? What is the danger of identifying the two as the same thing?
12. Given the different approaches to the witness of the Holy Spirit, what do you think is more biblical? Why?

34

Assurance of Salvation, Part 2

The Sealing, Earnest, Witness, and Firstfruits of the Spirit

Assurance of salvation would be impossible apart from the ministry of the indwelling Holy Spirit. The Spirit is involved in every dimension of assurance, for it is he who applies God's promises to the heart by faith in Christ, produces inward godliness and outward good works that confirm one's regeneration, and draws forth childlike prayer to the Father.

It might be objected that we do not need the Holy Spirit to enjoy assurance, for we can rationally deduce our salvation by understanding God's promises and observing our faith and good works. Anthony Burgess answered this objection by noting that our assurance requires the power of the Spirit because we must overcome guilty consciences, remaining unbelief, and Satan's accusations. Furthermore, "evangelical confidence" is "wholly supernatural," just as faith in Christ and holiness are supernatural.[1] Though assurance is based on the Word and evidence in our lives, our ability to make use of these grounds of assurance comes from the Spirit. Burgess quipped, "There may be pleasant flowers in a garden, yet if we have not light, we cannot see them."[2]

---

1. Anthony Burgess, *An Expository Comment, Doctrinal, Controversial, and Practical, upon the Whole First Chapter of the Second Epistle of St Paul to the Corinthians* (London: by A. M. for Abel Roper, 1661), 636–37.
2. Burgess, *An Expository Comment*, 641.

Therefore, we need the Holy Spirit to have assurance. To supplement and deepen the doctrine of assurance presented in the last chapter, we will examine four metaphors that the apostle Paul uses to describe how God assures his people through the Spirit: sealing, earnest, witness, and firstfruits.[3] We will conclude this study with a summary statement about each metaphor.

The Sealing of the Holy Spirit

One precious picture of the Spirit's work is that God *seals* his people with the Holy Spirit. This is a doctrine revealing what the Spirit has already done for all Christians, with rich experiential and practical implications for the Christian life.

Exegetical Theology of the Spirit's Sealing

Paul teaches that "all the promises of God" are yes and amen in Jesus Christ. He adds, "Now he which stablisheth [confirms] us with you in Christ, and hath anointed us, is God; who hath also sealed us, and given the earnest of the Spirit in our hearts" (2 Cor. 1:20–22). Since the word translated as "anointed" (*chrisas*) refers to the work of the Holy Spirit in uniting people to "Christ" (*christos*) and his official work,[4] it is likely that the whole series of actions here—"anointed . . . sealed . . . given the earnest of the Spirit"—describes the activity of the Spirit toward all those who are in Christ.[5]

The verb translated as "sealed" (*sphragizō*) literally refers to stamping an object with a mark made by one's "seal" (*sphragis*), often an engraved cylinder or signet ring that was rolled or pressed on soft material such as clay, wax, or malleable metal to leave its image (also called a "seal" [*sphragis*]) as a mark of ownership (cf. 2 Tim. 2:19). The seal was engraved or shaped to impress an image that represented the owner or his god. In the ancient Greco-Roman world, every free man had the right to

3. Rom. 8:16, 23; 2 Cor. 1:22; 5:5; Eph. 1:13–14; 4:30.

4. See the use of *chriō* in 1 Kingdoms (1 Sam.) 16:12–13; Isa. 61:1 LXX; Luke 4:18; Acts 10:38. On Christ's anointed people, see *RST*, 2:978–79.

5. Some theologians have connected God's sealing of believers with the Father's sealing of Christ (John 6:27). Thus, Sibbes, *A Fountain Sealed*, in *Works*, 5:433; and Owen, *Pneumatologia*, in *Works*, 4:401–4. However, John never speaks of God sealing believers, and Paul never speaks of God sealing Christ. Furthermore, the Spirit is central to Paul's doctrine of sealing in Eph. 1:13 and 4:30, but is not mentioned in John 6:27 or its near context. Therefore, John and Paul may not use the metaphor in ways that overlap in meaning.

wear a signet ring, often made of iron, and to use its seal as his distinguishing mark.[6]

Sealing functioned as a means by which an owner marked objects for the purposes of authentication, commitment, and security.[7] The seal of a king authenticated a document as his decree with his royal authority.[8] By placing one's seal on a document, such as a covenant or a legal deed for the purchase of property, one committed oneself to abide by its terms.[9] A scroll or other object might also be sealed—that is, closed and secured so that it could not be opened except by proper authority or at an appointed time.[10]

Given that documents and other inanimate objects were sealed, it may seem strange to think of God sealing his people.[11] However, in the same epistle in which Paul says that God "sealed us" (2 Cor. 1:22), he also describes Christians as God's document: "the epistle of Christ ministered by us, written not with ink, but with the Spirit of the living God; not in tables of stone, but in fleshy tables of the heart" (3:3). Christians are living copies of God's covenant, so to speak, written by the regenerating and sanctifying work of the Spirit. Sealing is like writing, but the seal is the finishing touch to the document, confirming its authenticity as a true copy of God's covenant inscribed in the human heart.

Therefore, "God sealed us" means that he has marked us by the Holy Spirit to show that we are authentically his, he is bound to keep his promises to us, and he will keep us secure until we receive the fulfillment of all he has said he will do.[12] The sealing of the Spirit involves his work of definitive sanctification to make sinners into saints, for that is how God marks people as his—he renews his image in them by the Holy Spirit, just as a seal leaves its image.[13] But the metaphor particularly communicates how God works by the Spirit to give people a divinely authoritative basis

6. Smith, ed., *A Dictionary of Greek and Roman Antiquities*, s.v. *annulus* (95–97).

7. Hodge, *An Exposition of the Second Epistle to the Corinthians*, 24–25; and Garland, *2 Corinthians*, 106.

8. 1 Kings 21:8; Est. 3:12; 8:8, 10. Note the significance of a "ring" in Gen. 41:42; Est. 3:10; 8:2; cf. Jer. 22:24; Hag. 2:23. Paul uses "seal" in a figurative sense of ownership (2 Tim. 2:19) and authentication (Rom. 4:11; 1 Cor. 9:2).

9. Neh. 9:38; 10:1; Jer. 32:10–14, 44.

10. Job 14:15; Song 4:12; Isa. 29:11; Dan. 6:17; 12:4, 9; Matt. 27:66; Rev. 5:1; 20:3; 22:10.

11. In some instances, *sphragis* refers to a "brand of ownership" placed on the bodies of cattle, convicts, captives, or soldiers. Lampe, ed., *A Patristic Greek Lexicon*, sec. A.3.e (1355). However, this was a painful, humiliating brand of bondage, whereas Paul's doctrine of the Spirit's sealing emphasizes the inheritance of God's sons.

12. Cf. Rev. 7:1–8; 9:4, which is based on Ezekiel 9, though the picture there is not sealing but writing with ink.

13. Owen, *Communion with God*, in *Works*, 2:242. On definitive and progressive sanctification, see chap. 27.

for knowing they belong to him.[14] Matthew Poole said that "sealing us . . . signifies both the confirmation of the love of God to our souls, and also the renewing and sanctification of our natures."[15] We might say that sealing is definitive sanctification to give believers a divinely certified experiential basis for assurance of salvation—all through the Holy Spirit.

When and how does this sealing take place? Paul says, "In him [Christ] you also, when you heard the word of truth, the gospel of your salvation, and believed in him, were sealed with the promised Holy Spirit" (Eph. 1:13 ESV). Therefore, God seals his people at the time of their initial conversion, when they first trust in Christ alone for salvation.[16] The syntax that Paul uses appears to identify the Spirit as the seal or signet ring by which God seals believers.[17] Paul Baynes (c. 1573–1617) said, "We are confirmed touching salvation both by the Spirit of God, who is, as it were, the seal sealing, and by the graces of the Spirit, which is, as it were, the seal sealed and printed upon us."[18]

In Ephesians 1, Paul traces salvation from the Father's eternal election through the Son's blood-bought redemption to the Spirit's present gospel application to the elect and redeemed (Eph. 1:4, 7, 13). In God's plan, the identity of those whom he chose to save remains hidden until the decree is executed. However, by the sealing of the Spirit, God makes them "manifest," as John Chrysostom said, even "objects of wonder."[19] How do we know whom God has chosen and Christ has redeemed? They are those sealed by the Spirit.[20]

Since Paul says that believers "were sealed with the *promised* Holy Spirit" (Eph. 1:13 ESV), he likely means that the gift of the Spirit par-

14. See Goodwin, *An Exposition of the First Chapter of the Epistle to the Ephesians*, in *Works*, 1:229–31.

15. Poole, *Annotations upon the Holy Bible*, on 2 Cor. 1:22 (3:604).

16. The KJV renders Eph. 1:13 as "*after* that ye heard . . . *after* that ye believed, ye were sealed," apparently interpreting the aorist tense of "heard" and "believed" to indicate temporal precedence before "sealed." However, all three verbs are in the aorist tense, a construction that often implies no temporal sequence. Lincoln, *Ephesians*, 39. On the Greek syntax, see the reply to the fifth argument for Pentecostalism in chap. 5.

17. "Spirit" is in the simple dative case, modifying "were sealed" (Eph. 1:13). In other texts, the nouns translated as "seal" (*sphragis*) or "ring" (*daktylios*) are in the dative case, modifying the verb translated as "seal" (*sphragizō*, 3 Kingdoms 20:8 [1 Kings 21:8]; Est. 8:8, 10 LXX). Paul also writes of the Spirit "whereby" (*en* plus dative relative pronoun) people "are sealed" (Eph. 4:30), which may be compared to when a king sealed a pit "with his own signet" (*en* plus dative *daktylios*, Dan. 6:18 [17] LXX).

18. Paul Bayne(s), *An Entire Commentary upon the Whole Epistle of St Paul to the Ephesians* (1866; repr., Stoke-on-Trent, England: Tentmaker, 2007), 81.

19. Chrysostom, *Homilies on Ephesians*, homily 2, in *NPNF*[1], 13:56.

20. See *The Commentary of Dr. Zacharias Ursinus on the Heidelberg Catechism*, 296.

tially fulfills the promise of the ancient covenants.[21] The Spirit seals as the eschatological Spirit, poured out as a fruit of Christ's finished work of redemption and ascension into heaven to inaugurate the kingdom (Acts 2:33; Gal. 3:13–14). Though believers prior to Christ's resurrection had assurance of salvation by the Spirit (Pss. 32:1; 43:4–5; 51:11–12), the "Spirit of adoption" (Rom. 8:15) did not come in his experiential fullness until Christ was exalted (John 7:37–39).

What is the effect of this sealing? Paul says, "Grieve not the holy Spirit of God, whereby ye are sealed unto the day of redemption" (Eph. 4:30; cf. 1:14). The sealing of the Spirit, though already given to all believers in the past, has continuing experiential implications. It grants a basis for certainty of present and future salvation, "an infallible assurance of faith," as the Westminster Confession (18.2) says, because by the Spirit "we are sealed to the day of redemption."[22] The Holy Spirit is the source of all vital Christian hope,[23] and Christians grow or diminish in hope according to their relationship with the indwelling Lord. They must not grieve the Spirit or they may temporarily forfeit their sense of his sealing and the hope it confers.

Historical and Systematic Theology of the Spirit's Sealing

The biblical teaching on the sealing of the Spirit has been variously interpreted throughout history. Theologians in the early church identified this sealing with baptism.[24] This idea coordinated with the widespread belief at that time that God gives the Spirit through baptism. However, Paul simply has faith in view when he writes of being sealed with the Spirit but does not mention baptism (Eph. 1:13).[25]

Reformed theology recognizes the sealing of the Spirit as the common privilege of the regenerate church. The Belgic Confession (Art. 27) says, "We believe and profess one catholic or universal Church, which is a holy congregation of true Christian believers, all expecting their salvation in

21. Literally, "the Holy Spirit of the promise" (*tō pneumati tēs epangelias tō hagiō*, Eph. 1:13). Paul speaks of "the promise" revealed in the ancient covenants beginning with Abraham (2:12), which forecast the outpouring of the Spirit (Gal. 3:14). Alternatively, "Holy Spirit of the promise" could look forward to the promised inheritance.

22. *Reformed Confessions*, 4:254.

23. Rom. 5:5; 8:23–24; 15:13; Gal. 5:5; Eph. 1:17–18. On Christian hope, see chap. 42.

24. Chrysostom, *Homilies on 2 Corinthians*, 3.7, in *NPNF*[1], 12:293; cf. the references in Lampe, ed., *A Patristic Greek Lexicon*, s.v. *sphragizō*, sec. C; and *sphragis*, sec. C (1355–56).

25. Against the proposal that Christians are sealed by the Spirit in baptism, see Lincoln, *Ephesians*, 39–40.

Jesus Christ, being washed by His blood, sanctified and sealed by the Holy Ghost."[26] The sacraments are called "seals" in Reformed theology not because God seals people with the Spirit by means of the sacraments, but because God uses the sacraments as visible signs and confirming seals of God's covenant.[27]

John Calvin generally interpreted sealing to refer to the Spirit's work to firmly establish faith in the certainty of God's Word.[28] The Holy Spirit does confirm the Word with inner certainty when he gives faith (1 Cor. 2:4–5; 1 Thess. 1:5), but, contrary to Calvin, that is not what Paul means by God sealing us, for he is not sealing the Word but sealing the people who believe it (Eph. 1:13).[29] Calvin also acknowledged, however, that sealing can refer to the Spirit's life-giving work that distinguishes the godly from the wicked and gives them evidence of their adoption.[30] This latter interpretation of Calvin aligns with Paul's use of the term in the Scriptures.

In the controversy with Arminianism, the sealing of the Spirit has been an important aspect of the Reformed doctrine of preservation and perseverance. Left to themselves, believers would "totally fall . . . [and] perish finally," yet "with respect to God, it is utterly impossible," the Canons of Dort (Head 5, Art. 8) say, one reason for which is that "the sealing of the Holy Spirit . . . [cannot] be frustrated or obliterated."[31] This use of the doctrine of sealing is consistent with biblical usage of the term. The seal of a king secures something by his authority and is backed by his royal power: "The writing which is written in the king's name, and sealed with the king's ring, may no man reverse" (Est. 8:8). Once God has sealed his people, no one in all creation has the authority or power to break his seal and take them from him. God's seal demonstrates his unwavering intent to keep his promises to those whom he has sealed (2 Cor. 1:18–22). John Owen concluded, "Those who are sealed shall certainly be saved."[32]

26. *The Three Forms of Unity*, 47.

27. The Belgic Confession (Arts. 33–34); the Heidelberg Catechism (LD 25, Q. 66), in *The Three Forms of Unity*, 53, 55, 89; and the Westminster Confession of Faith (27.1; 28.1; 29.1), in *Reformed Confessions*, 4:265–67.

28. Calvin, *Commentaries*, on 2 Cor. 1:21; Eph. 1:13; and *Institutes*, 1.7.4–5; 3.2.12, 36; 3.24.1, 3.

29. Goodwin, *An Exposition*, in *Works*, 1:228. On the Spirit's witness to the gospel of Christ, see 1 John 5:6–8.

30. Calvin, *Commentaries*, on Eph. 4:30; and *Institutes*, 3.1.3.

31. *The Three Forms of Unity*, 155–56; cf. the Westminster Confession of Faith (chap. 12), in *Reformed Confessions*, 4:249. On preservation and perseverance, see chaps. 30–31.

32. Owen, *The Doctrine of the Saints' Perseverance*, in *Works*, 11:323–24.

Some Reformed theologians, such as Giovanni Diodati (1576–1649), interpreted the sealing of the Spirit to refer to the Spirit's work of "regeneration, marking us for his own."[33] Others, especially those of the English Puritan tradition, such as Richard Sibbes, Thomas Goodwin, and Burgess, spoke of the seal of the Spirit as communicating a high degree of subjective assurance, joy, and peace, meaning that not all Christians have the seal.[34] However, these Puritan theologians also recognized a foundational sealing that does not always manifest itself in powerful experiences but is constantly present in believers in their sanctification by the Spirit.[35] All believers are sealed, but not all sense their sealing.

While the distinctions that these Puritans made can be applied in a sound manner for the good of souls, it is wiser and more biblical to say that assurance, peace, and joy are the effects of sealing that arise from an experiential sense of the seal in the believer's conscience, for the apostle Paul says that all believers in Christ are sealed with the Spirit. All people in Christ have the indwelling Spirit to sanctify and comfort them, and this is the essence of sealing with the Spirit. Owen said, "God's sealing of believers with the Holy Spirit is his gracious communication of the Holy Ghost unto them, so to act his divine power in them as to enable them unto all the duties of their holy calling; evidencing them to be accepted with him both unto themselves and others, and asserting their preservation unto eternal salvation."[36]

Some Puritans distinguished between *mediate assurance*, which is derived by a Spirit-enabled perception of God's renewed image in one's soul, and *immediate assurance*, which is a supernatural light that directly convinces the soul of its salvation in Christ.[37] Though they described immediate assurance as an intimate and supernatural gift, they denied that it

33. Diodati, *Pious and Learned Annotations upon the Holy Bible*, on 2 Cor. 1:22; cf. on Eph. 1:13.

34. Sibbes, *A Commentary upon the First Chapter of the Second Epistle of St Paul to the Corinthians*, in *Works*, 3:457; Goodwin, *An Exposition*, in *Works*, 1:233, 236; and Burgess, *An Expository Comment*, 645–46. For modern examples, see Winslow, *The Work of the Holy Spirit*, 138–39; and D. Martyn Lloyd-Jones, *God's Ultimate Purpose: An Exposition of Ephesians 1:1–23* (Grand Rapids, MI: Baker, 1998), 250, 279.

35. Sibbes, *A Commentary*, in *Works*, 3:453, 457–58; Burgess, *An Expository Comment*, 648; and Flavel, *Sacramental Meditations*, in *Works*, 6:402, 406. See Beeke, *The Quest for Full Assurance*, 203–5.

36. Owen, *Pneumatologia*, in *Works*, 4:404. Owen was conscious that he partially disagreed with many of his fellow theologians, whose doctrine he had found "good and useful in the substance of it" (4:400–401).

37. Goodwin, *An Exposition*, in *Works*, 1:233, 241; and Poole, *Annotations upon the Holy Bible*, on Eph. 1:13 (3:664).

consists of direct revelation apart from God's written Word. Rather, they said, it comes through the Word as the Spirit applies the truths of the Word to the heart; thus, it must be tested by the Word.[38]

We should not consider any degree of assurance to arise from direct revelation from God to the soul apart from the Word. The deposit of special revelation is complete, being once for all given to all the saints.[39] However, believers commune with God through the Word (1 John 1:3–4). The faith of assurance apprehends invisible spiritual realities so that we know them with certainty, joy, and peace (1 Thess. 1:4–6; Heb. 11:24–27). The holiness of heart and life by which the Spirit manifests his presence is supernatural in origin and power (Ezek. 36:27). Faith and holiness not only serve as evidence to support assurance, but their very activity moves the soul to rest on the Lord and delight in him. Owen said, "Yea, in the very graces themselves of faith and uprightness of heart, there is such a seal and stamp, impressing the image of God upon the soul, as, without any reflex act or actual contemplation of those graces themselves, have an influence into the establishment of the souls of men in whom they are unto a quiet, comfortable, assured repose of themselves upon the love and faithfulness of God."[40]

Therefore, when the Spirit gives full assurance, the Christian not only acknowledges the fact of his salvation but can rightly say, "The Lord loves me and is with me. How sweet and awesome is the presence of my God! I am his, and he is mine." However, strictly speaking, we do not find warrant in the Scriptures for two kinds of assurance (immediate and mediate) but for varying degrees of assurance arising from varying degrees of the Spirit's illumination (Eph. 1:17–18). These degrees include the possibility of Word-based experiences that flood the heart with a sense of Christ's presence and love, and fill believers with the supernatural fullness of God (3:14–19). All assurance involves the Spirit applying the Word in exercises of faith and holiness.

Practical Implications of the Spirit's Sealing

Though all Christians have been sealed with the Spirit, an experiential sense of that sealing imparts a powerful stream of motivation for coura-

38. Sibbes, *A Commentary*, in *Works*, 3:456; *A Fountain Sealed*, in *Works*, 5:440–41; and Goodwin, *An Exposition*, in *Works*, 1:233, 236–37.

39. On the cessation of special revelation, see *RST*, 1:409–57 (chaps. 23–24).

40. Owen, *The Doctrine of the Saints' Perseverance*, in *Works*, 11:83.

geous Christianity that we should desire and seek. Burgess said that by a "sense" of their sealing with the Spirit, "sanctified persons" can "daily walk more and more boldly, joyfully, and thankfully, notwithstanding all discouragements to the contrary, till they be made completely happy in heaven."[41] Baynes said, "Seeing God hath thus sealed to us our salvation, we should, *ergo*, labour to be fully persuaded touching this his grace toward us. Though true believers are not always sure of their salvation in their sense and judgement, yet they should ever strive to this."[42]

People need not only saving and sanctifying grace from the Spirit but what Burgess called "the experimental feeling of it." There is a difference between what is true of all Christians and the extent to which they experience it. Burgess said, however, that "there is an order in the works of God's Spirit"—namely, that he, first, enlightens the mind; second, sanctifies the will and affections; and third, witnesses and seals to his people these gracious works. Burgess continued, "To look therefore for consolation before sanctification, is preposterous."[43]

Christians should respond to the doctrine of the Spirit's sealing with great gratitude to their Lord and Savior. God has sealed and secured them as his people. They can know they are his and rejoice as the Spirit produces his sweet fruits in them and stirs up the spiritual fragrance of holiness (cf. Song 4:12–16). As a result of the outpoured Spirit, God's people spring up with vitality, and "one shall say, I am the LORD's; and another shall call himself by the name of Jacob" (Isa. 44:3–5). What hope they can have, knowing that they are already the temple of the living God! "Hereby know we that we dwell in him, and he in us, because he hath given us of his Spirit" (1 John 4:13). Knowing they are his, they can know they will always be his.

Furthermore, Christians should cherish the Spirit's sealing and labor to grow in the consciousness of that sealing as well as to prevent anything from obscuring or diminishing their sense of it. They should flee from the sins that grieve the Spirit, for though the Spirit will not forsake them, he may withdraw their sense of his sealing and thus reduce their hope in the coming day of redemption (Eph. 4:30). By walking in the Spirit, they keep in step with the God of hope (Gal. 5:5, 16, 25).[44]

---

41. Burgess, *An Expository Comment*, 632. He later unpacked this statement (641–42).
42. Bayne(s), *An Entire Commentary upon . . . Ephesians*, 81.
43. Burgess, *An Expository Comment*, 641.
44. On grieving and walking in the Spirit, see chap. 32.

The Earnest of the Holy Spirit

Paul connects sealing with the Spirit to the *earnest* of the Spirit. He says that God "hath also sealed us, and given the earnest of the Spirit in our hearts" (2 Cor. 1:22). God made us heirs of immortality, for which we "groan," and he "also hath given unto us the earnest of the Spirit" (5:4–5).

The Greek word translated as "earnest" (*arrabōn*) or "guarantee" (ESV) refers to a pledge of future payment, "a 'deposit' which pays part of the total debt and gives a legal claim . . . 'earnest-money' ratifying a compact. . . . It always implies an act which engages to something bigger."[45] Chrysostom said, "For did He not purpose to give the whole, He would never have chosen to give 'the earnest' and to waste it without object or result."[46] This implies that the activity of the Holy Spirit in believers is a foretaste of glory, the first installment of their eternal inheritance in Christ. Colin Kruse comments, "It was by the Spirit that Christ was raised from the dead with his resurrection body. The same Spirit has been given to Christians as a guarantee that they too shall in their turn be raised up and clothed with a resurrection body."[47]

Paul says, "Ye were sealed with that holy Spirit of promise, which is the earnest of our inheritance until the redemption of the purchased possession, unto the praise of his glory" (Eph. 1:13–14). "The redemption of the purchased possession" refers to God's completion of the salvation of his people at Christ's return.[48] God gave his people the Spirit as an earnest to assure them they are truly his heirs and will receive their inheritance when he gives them full redemption from all evil. Matthew Henry said, "The earnest is part of payment, and it secures the full sum: so is the gift of the Holy Ghost; all his influences and operations, both as a sanctifier and a comforter, are heaven begun, glory in the seed and bud."[49]

The word translated as "earnest" appears in the Old Testament only in the account of Judah giving a "pledge" to a woman (Tamar) as a guaran-

---

45. *TDNT*, 1:475. See also Bayne(s), *An Entire Commentary upon . . . Ephesians*, 82.

46. Chrysostom, *Homilies on 2 Corinthians*, 3.4, on 2 Cor. 1:21–22, in *NPNF*[1], 12:290.

47. Kruse, *2 Corinthians*, 115. See Rom. 1:4; 8:11.

48. The ESV renders the phrase "until we acquire possession of it" (Eph. 1:14). But the KJV translation is more literal: "until the redemption of the purchased possession" (cf. ESV mg.). Paul elsewhere uses the word translated as "redemption" (*apolytrōsis*) for God's redeeming of his people (Rom. 3:24; 1 Cor. 1:30; Eph. 1:7; Col. 1:14), including one occasion for their future deliverance from all evil by the resurrection of the body (Rom. 8:23; cf. Luke 21:28). God does not redeem their inheritance but redeems them. The word translated as "purchased possession" (*peripoiēsis*), when not used in a verbal sense for the act of acquiring (1 Thess. 5:9; 2 Thess. 2:14; Heb. 10:39), refers to God's people as his special treasure (Mal. 3:17 LXX; 1 Pet. 2:9). See Hodge, *Ephesians*, 36; and Lincoln, *Ephesians*, 41–42.

49. Henry, *Commentary on the Whole Bible*, on Eph. 1:14 (2308).

tee of future payment, a pledge consisting of his "signet," or "seal," and other items (Gen. 38:17–20).[50] Later, she brought these objects out as legal evidence of the transaction in order to preserve her life and establish her offspring as the true sons of Judah (vv. 25–26).[51] In a similar but far more sacred way, God has given the Holy Spirit to believers as a down payment on their future inheritance and a pledge that assures them of their eternal life as his children. Burgess said, "Grace is an earnest of glory."[52]

As a financial metaphor, the earnest of the Spirit encourages Christians to reflect on the riches of glory they possess in Christ. Not many saints are rich or noble in this world (1 Cor. 1:26). Some, especially those suffering severe persecution, dwell in "poverty," but Christ says to them, "Thou art rich" (Rev. 2:9; cf. James 2:5), for God has raised them with Christ "so that in the coming ages he might show the immeasurable riches of his grace in kindness toward us in Christ Jesus" (Eph. 2:7 ESV). God mercifully gives them a pledge to confirm their true wealth: the indwelling Holy Spirit. Like a few golden coins given to a pauper to pay for his journey to the palace where he will receive a prince's crown and inheritance, the indwelling Spirit both sustains believers in their perseverance and cheers their hearts with a sure and certain hope of the glory of God. Whenever people perceive in themselves faith in Christ, repentance of sin, love for God, love for the brethren, and obedience to the commandments, they can say, "These graces are from the Holy Spirit. He dwells in me as the down payment of my future inheritance as an heir of God. I am rich!"

Therefore, let us walk in cooperation with the Spirit's sanctifying work and in communion with his comforting presence. William Shishko says, "Just as Christians live out of and enjoy the practical implications of their justification, adoption, and union with Christ in His death and resurrection, so we are meant to live out of and enjoy the down payment of the Holy Spirit as that which seals us."[53]

The peace and joy of assurance that a Christian derives from the Spirit are a great help to holy service to the Lord. John Flavel said that when God grants a powerful sense of assurance to believers, "they enjoy heaven upon

---

50. Hebrew *'erabon*, rendered into Greek in the LXX as *arrabōn*.

51. Though the relationship of Judah and Tamar is a sordid affair, in God's holy providence their union produced the line of David and Jesus Christ (Matt. 1:1–3). Hence, in some ways it foreshadows God's grace in Christ.

52. Burgess, *An Expository Comment*, 651.

53. William Shishko, "The Sealing and Witnessing Work of the Holy Spirit," in *The Beauty and Glory of the Holy Spirit*, ed. Beeke and Pipa, 178. We omit Shishko's parenthetical Scripture references.

earth, a joy beyond all the joys of this world." This assurance produces in them "inflamed love [for God] . . . renewed care and diligence . . . deep abasement and great humblings . . . increased strength . . . desires of the soul after heaven . . . [and] mortification to the world," for its beauties cannot compare to the glory now seen in God.[54]

The Witness of the Holy Spirit

Paul also uses the metaphor of judicial testimony for the Spirit's assuring work when he writes, "The Spirit itself beareth witness with our spirit, that we are the children of God" (Rom. 8:16). The Holy Spirit gives authoritative testimony that entitles believers to conclude they have been adopted by God and are his heirs in Christ (v. 17). This *witness* is the remedy for spiritual "bondage" that produces "fear" (v. 15).

The prefix of the verb translated as "bear witness with" (*symmartyreō*, Rom. 8:16) may imply a twofold witness: the Spirit witnesses "with" (*syn*) our spirit, which cries, "Abba, Father" (v. 15).[55] However, the force of the prefix on this verb often disappears, so that the word can simply mean "witness, testify, confirm."[56] Since the cry "Abba, Father" arises from the Spirit's work in the heart (v. 15; cf. Gal. 4:6), some theologians find it difficult to conceive of the Spirit and our spirit functioning as two distinct witnesses. Therefore, it is possible to interpret Romans 8:16 as referring to the singular witness of the Spirit.[57] Since both the dual and singular interpretations of this witness acknowledge the Spirit's work to give a sense of adoption in the human spirit, the two interpretations are not far apart.

How does the Holy Spirit testify to the spirits of believers that God has adopted them as his children? The Spirit causes them to know God's love revealed in the gospel and to respond to it with faith and love. The preceding context in Romans 8 does not speak of special revelations given directly to individual Christians,[58] but of the new spiritual state of those who have the indwelling Spirit, a state in which they are no longer ruled

54. Flavel, *Sacramental Meditations*, in *Works*, 6:407–8.

55. Murray, *The Epistle to the Romans*, 1:297–98; and Ferguson, *The Holy Spirit*, 184.

56. *TDNT*, 4:508–9. Paul elsewhere uses the verb where no cowitness is in view (Rom. 2:15; 9:1).

57. Leon Morris, *The Epistle to the Romans*, The Pillar New Testament Commentary (Grand Rapids, MI: Eerdmans, 1988), 316–17; and Colin G. Kruse, *The Epistle to the Romans*, The Pillar New Testament Commentary (Grand Rapids, MI: Eerdmans, 2012), 339.

58. Jonathan Edwards warned, "Many have been the mischiefs that have arisen from that false and delusive notion of the witness of the Spirit, that it is a kind of inward voice, suggestion, or declaration from God to a man, that he is beloved of him, and pardoned, elected, or the like." *Religious Affections*, in *WJE*, 2:239.

by enmity against God (Rom. 8:7–9). The Spirit gives them life (v. 10), empowers them to put sin to death (v. 13), and leads them in the way of holiness so that they relate to God as his sons (v. 14).[59] The "Spirit of adoption" gives them a sense of God's fatherly love; thus, they cry out to him in their need, "Abba, Father" (v. 15).

The great means of the Spirit's witness to God's fatherly love is the gospel of Jesus Christ. Paul says, "God's love has been poured into our hearts through the Holy Spirit who has been given to us" (Rom. 5:5 ESV). This love is objectively revealed in the gospel of Christ crucified (vv. 6–8) and subjectively applied by the Holy Spirit to the heart as we persevere in faith and obedience through many trials (vv. 1–4). Goodwin said that the Spirit's witness "is always in and with the word, and according to it."[60] "Poured into our hearts" communicates abundance. Owen said, "The Comforter gives a sweet and plentiful evidence and persuasion of the love of God to us, such as the soul is taken, delighted, satiated withal."[61] Therefore, the Spirit bears witness through a twofold illumination. He illuminates the heart to perceive the love of the Father in the gospel. He also illuminates the soul to see in itself the reality of God's saving grace as that grace is described in the Word.

To use legal language, we can say that the Holy Spirit testifies in the hearts of believers to the Father's judicial decree to adopt them as his sons and daughters. Owen pictured a courtroom setting where a man is seeking to establish his legal claim: "In the midst of the trial, a person of known and approved integrity comes into the court, and gives testimony fully and directly on the behalf of the claimer; which stops the mouths of all his adversaries, and fills the man that pleaded with joy and satisfaction."[62] Likewise, the Spirit confirms to a believer that he is God's child.

Paul's doctrine of the witness of the Spirit is similar to John's teaching about the Holy Spirit as the Advocate (*paraklētos*), a person of standing who appears in court to plead on behalf of a friend or client. Those who obey Christ are rejected and condemned by this world. However, God has not left them as "orphans," but has sent the Spirit as their Advocate (John 14:16–18 KJV mg., ESV). One aspect of the Spirit's work as an Advocate is to testify to believers that they are loved

59. On the indwelling and leading of the Spirit, see chap. 32.
60. Goodwin, *The Object and Acts of Justifying Faith*, in *Works*, 8:367.
61. Owen, *Communion with God*, in *Works*, 2:240.
62. Owen, *Communion with God*, in *Works*, 2:241.

by God so that they know they are in union with the Father through Christ (vv. 20–23).[63] The Spirit applies Christ's Word to give peace to his disciples (vv. 26–27).

A vivid illustration of the hope granted in the Spirit's sealing, earnest, and witness may be found in a prophetic action of Jeremiah. When Babylon besieged Jerusalem and its doom was sure, the Lord commanded Jeremiah to take the seemingly insane step of purchasing a field in Anathoth (Jer. 32:1–9). In a way that echoes Israel's salvation by God, the text twice states that Jeremiah had the right of "redemption" to buy the land from his cousin, as well the right of "inheritance" (vv. 7–8).[64] Jeremiah wrote out a deed of purchase, "sealed" it (v. 10, also vv. 11, 44),[65] obtained "witnesses" (v. 10, also vv. 25, 44), and paid the price. The documents were stored "in an earthen vessel, that they may continue many days" (v. 14). The immediate purpose of Jeremiah's actions was "that there might be a public and a general notice, that he himself might be able to claim that land for ever."[66] But Jeremiah's act was also a sign that God would restore his people to the land and renew them spiritually according to "an everlasting covenant with them," in which neither the Lord nor his people would turn away from each another (vv. 37–44). In the darkest times of God's people, they might rest assured that the Lord was their Redeemer (31:11; 50:34) and their future blessing in the inheritance was "sealed" according to his purchase and promise until their full redemption appeared. In a similar way, in the new covenant, God's people are sealed by God—though the treasure is hidden in jars of clay and outwardly they are perishing—so that they bear in their hearts the glorious writing of the covenant that guarantees their inheritance, by which the Spirit bears witness to them (cf. 2 Cor. 3:3; 4:6–7, 16–18).

The witness of the Spirit provides divinely authoritative testimony to our salvation so we can have certainty of being God's children. There is no greater witness and no more important case pertinent to our future happiness. Therefore, let us honor the Holy Spirit and receive his witness as God's own testimony. Octavius Winslow said, "Human testimony is feeble

63. On Christ's promise of the Paraclete, see chap. 5.

64. The word translated as "redemption" (*ge'ullah*) is used elsewhere for redeeming family property or enslaved family members (Lev. 25:24–32; 48–52; Ruth 4:6–7), and it is cognate to "redeem" (*ga'al*) and "redeemer" (*go'el*). The word translated as "inheritance" (*yerushah*), derived from the verb (*yarash*), is used of Israel's taking its inheritance in the land (Gen. 15:7; Ex. 6:8; Jer. 32:23; etc.).

65. The term *sphragizō* appears in Jer. 39(32):10, 11, 25, 44 LXX.

66. Goodwin, *An Exposition*, in *Works*, 1:231.

here. Your minister, your friend, schooled as they may be in the evidences of experimental godliness, cannot assure your spirit that you are 'born of God.' God the eternal Spirit alone can do this. He alone is competent. . . . This alone will do for a dying hour."[67]

The Firstfruits of the Holy Spirit

The last metaphor that Paul uses for the Spirit's assuring work is *firstfruits*. In a context about all creation groaning in hope of deliverance and liberty, Paul says that we "which have the firstfruits of the Spirit, even we ourselves groan within ourselves, waiting for the adoption, to wit, the redemption of our body" (Rom. 8:23). God has given his people the first beginnings of the Spirit's work in them that will overflow to them in Christ forever.[68]

The word translated as "firstfruits" (*aparchē*) literally refers to the first portion of an agricultural harvest, which the Lord required Israel to offer to him.[69] The term is used several times in the New Testament for the first part of a larger quantity to follow.[70] Paul speaks of believers groaning for their future resurrection in connection to both the earnest (2 Cor. 5:4–5) and the firstfruits (Rom. 8:23), showing how closely related the two metaphors are.

Paul is teaching that the indwelling of the Holy Spirit is the first installment of God's eschatological blessing by the Spirit that will bring believers and creation as a whole out of "bondage" into "the glorious liberty of the children of God" (Rom. 8:21). The presence and activity of the Holy Spirit remind them that God has saved them from their former bondage to sin and will one day deliver them from bondage to all misery. Consequently, the Spirit causes them to "groan" in expectation and longing for the completion of their salvation as God's adopted sons. Israel's "groaning" once rose up to the Lord, and he acted to "redeem" his "son" from bondage in Egypt (Ex. 2:24; 4:22–23; 6:5–6). God ordained that the offering of the firstfruits be the occasion of remembering their redemption

67. Winslow, *The Work of the Holy Spirit*, 173.

68. John Murray proposed that in the phrase translated as "firstfruits of the Spirit," the genitive case is partitive, as in firstfruits of the whole harvest, indicating "the pledge of the plenitude of the Spirit to be bestowed at the resurrection." *The Epistle to the Romans*, 1:306. It is also possible to interpret the genitive as epexegetical or appositional, which identifies the firstfruits with the Spirit or his work. Kruse, *The Epistle to the Romans*, 349.

69. Ex. 22:28 (29); 23:19; Lev. 2:12 (10); 23:10; Num. 15:20–21; Deut. 18:4; 26:10 LXX. By extension, *aparchē* could be used of other offerings and contributions (Lev. 22:12; Num. 5:9 LXX), such as precious materials for the tabernacle (Ex. 25:2–3; 35:5; 36:6; 39:1 [38:24] LXX).

70. Rom. 11:16; 16:5; 1 Cor. 15:20, 23; 16:15; James 1:18; Rev. 14:4, though the last text may emphasize the sense of an offering to God and not the first part of a larger group.

from Egypt and rejoicing in his goodness (Deut. 26:1–11). Today, God's children in Christ groan for their redemption from all bondage to enjoy full and eternal liberty (Rom. 8:21–23, 26).[71]

It is no coincidence that Paul also describes the resurrected Christ as the "firstfruits" (*aparchē*) of his people who will rise from the dead at Christ's return (1 Cor. 15:20, 23). The new covenant fullness of the Spirit comes to Christ's people as a consequence of his exaltation, which inaugurates the kingdom. Christians have the firstfruits of the Spirit because Christ has risen as the firstfruits of the future resurrection, for "the last Adam" rose as the "quickening spirit" (v. 45)—that is, the life giver of the new humanity by his Spirit.[72] When they rise with Christ, believers will receive the full harvest of the Spirit, and even their bodies will become "spiritual"—that is, they will be completely ruled and vivified by the Holy Spirit (v. 44). By the earnest and firstfruits of the Spirit, believers in Christ already participate in the life of the resurrection.[73]

The metaphor of firstfruits implies the tension between the "already" and the "not yet" in the eschatology of the New Testament. Israel gathered the firstfruits *after* taking possession of its inheritance in the land. However, the firstfruits of the Spirit belong to God's people while they still long for their complete redemption. Therefore, the Spirit's assuring work comes to believers as an aspect of the inaugurated kingdom of God while they still wait to enter the kingdom in its glory. This tension is profoundly experiential for believers as they taste the firstfruits of grace now but suffer, groan, and hope for what they do not see (Rom. 8:17–18, 24–25). This tension reminds us that inward struggle is not inconsistent with assurance of salvation. Assurance involves hope, hope awakens longing, and longing makes us groan.

The sense of firstfruits as an offering to God may also color Paul's use of this term. That is not to suggest that believers offer the Holy Spirit to God, but Paul's reference to the "firstfruits of the Spirit" appears in the context of the cries and groans believers lift up to God in their prayerful submission to his will and hope in his salvation (Rom. 8:15, 23, 26–27). Later in this

71. Note the use of "groan" (*stenagmos*) in Ex. 2:24; 6:5 LXX, the same word used in Rom. 8:26 and cognate to the verbs translated as "groan" in Rom. 8:22–23; "bondage" (*douleia*) in Ex. 6:6 LXX, the same word used in Rom. 8:21; and "redeem" (*lytroō*) in Ex. 6:6, cognate to "redemption" (*apolytrōsis*) in Rom. 8:23.

72. S. M. Baugh, *Ephesians*, Evangelical Exegetical Commentary (Bellingham, WA: Lexham Press, 2015), 101.

73. Vos, *The Pauline Eschatology*, 163–65.

epistle, Paul urges believers to offer themselves as "living sacrifices" in holy service to God's will (12:1–2), somewhat like the offering of the firstfruits.[74] Paul says he preaches the gospel "that the offering up of the Gentiles might be acceptable, being sanctified by the Holy Ghost" (15:16; cf. 16:5). The Spirit's sanctifying work makes us a pleasing offering to the Lord, even in our weakness and mortality as we wait for glory. Our sorrows are part of what we offer to the Lord, for we suffer in faith and obedience.

The meaning of firstfruits as an offering to the Lord reminds us that the Spirit's assuring work is not ultimately for our sake but for the glory of God. To be sure, the Spirit's gracious operations give life and happiness to his elect, but they do not stop there. The Lord said, "I give waters in the wilderness, and rivers in the desert, to give drink to my people, my chosen. This people have I formed for myself; they shall shew forth my praise" (Isa. 43:20–21). If we are drinking of the living water of the Spirit, then we must put our joy into practice by giving God the praise all our lives—indeed, to eternity—for himself, his glorious salvation, and our assurance of that salvation.

Conclusion

God has revealed the work of the Holy Spirit in giving assurance of salvation to his children through four metaphors with overlapping, mutually enriching meanings.

The *legal metaphor of a seal* communicates that God marks believers as his people with the work of the Holy Spirit to impress upon them his holy image in Christ. Those whom God has sealed by divine authority will most certainly be saved to the end. All true Christians are sealed with the Spirit, and yet the recognition of that seal and experience of its effects in peace and joy vary from believer to believer. The metaphor of a seal focuses on the Spirit's work of definitive sanctification—that is, regeneration and its immediate fruit in conversion.

74. The firstfruits were not burnt but were a "wave offering" (*tenupah*) the priests were to "wave" (*nup*) to the Lord, after which they were given to the priests to sustain their ministry (Lev. 23:17, 20). The portions of meat from the peace offerings given to the priests are also called wave offerings waved to the Lord (10:12–15). When God instructed Aaron to offer the Levites to him for his service, Aaron was to "wave them as a wave offering" to God (*nup tenupah*, Num. 8:11, 13, 15, 21). Hence, the Levites served God as living sacrifices, like the firstfruits and peace offerings. The Lord later promised in the context of the new covenant that his covenant with the Levites would continue forever and they would multiply like the sand of the sea—indications that the whole people of God would become Levites and priests (Jer. 33:18–26). See *RST*, 2:666, 1103–8.

The *financial metaphor of an earnest* teaches us that the gift of the Holy Spirit is God's down payment on the gracious inheritance that he promises in Christ. Since the Lord has already given believers the Spirit of the risen Christ to work his spiritual life in their souls, they may rest assured that he will give them the full riches of resurrection life at Christ's return. The metaphor of an earnest draws particular attention to the indwelling of the Spirit as the sanctifier and giver of life within God's children.

The *judicial metaphor of a witness* reveals the Holy Spirit's inward testimony to the believer's spirit that God has adopted him into his family. This testimony is not a private form of special revelation but the personal application of the gospel promises to the heart through the graces of saving faith and childlike love. Though Satan and this world accuse believers, the Spirit vindicates them in the court of their consciences as the rightful children of God—an anticipation of God's gracious verdict on judgment day. The metaphor of a witness emphasizes the Spirit's continuing work of illumination and progressive sanctification.

Finally, the *agricultural metaphor of firstfruits* tells us that the Holy Spirit's presence and holy operations in the believer are the beginnings of the full harvest of holiness and happiness that the Spirit will bring when Christ comes in glory. As Christians recognize the firstfruits of the Spirit in themselves, they celebrate God's goodness and offer themselves to the Lord for his glory while simultaneously hungering for the full harvest of life that will transform God's people and the world, over which they will exercise dominion as those created in God's image. The metaphor of firstfruits is closely tied to the Spirit's work to incite believers to groan in desire and expectation of glory.

Together, these four metaphors illustrate the Spirit's work to persuade God's children that they are the people of the living God: they belong to their covenant Lord, and he belongs to them. What a gift of love is the Spirit from the Father in the Son! As a result of this gift, the believer may enjoy the comfort of confessing that "I with body and soul, both in life and death, am not my own, but belong unto my faithful Savior Jesus Christ," that Christ "so preserves me that without the will of my heavenly Father, not a hair can fall from my head," and that "by His Holy Spirit, He also assures me of eternal life, and makes me sincerely willing and ready, henceforth, to live unto Him."[75]

75. The Heidelberg Catechism (LD 1, Q. 1), in *The Three Forms of Unity*, 68.

Sing to the Lord

Praying for the Spirit of Grace and Assurance

Gracious Spirit, Dove Divine,
Let thy light within me shine;
All my guilty fears remove,
Fill me full of heav'n and love.

Speak thy pard'ning grace to me,
Set the burdened sinner free;
Lead me to the Lamb of God,
Wash me in his precious blood.

Life and peace to me impart;
Seal salvation on my heart;
Breathe thyself into my breast,
Earnest of immortal rest.

Let me never from thee stray,
Keep me in the narrow way,
Fill my soul with joy divine,
Keep me, Lord, for ever thine.

John Stocker
Tune: Mercy
Trinity Hymnal—Baptist Edition, No. 245

Questions for Meditation or Discussion

1. Why do we need the work of the Holy Spirit to enjoy assurance of salvation?
2. What does the metaphor of sealing mean in Paul's teaching of being "sealed" with the Spirit?
3. Whom does God seal? When? How? Prove your answers from Scripture.
4. What is the difference between being sealed with the Spirit and having a sense of that seal? Why is that distinction important for Christian experience?
5. What is an "earnest"? How are the Spirit's indwelling and activity like an earnest?

6. What is the meaning of the legal metaphor of the Spirit's "witness" that believers are the children of God?
7. What means does the Spirit use to give this witness? How does he do this?
8. What does Paul mean when he says we have "the firstfruits of the Spirit" (Rom. 8:23)?
9. How would you describe your own experience of the Spirit's assuring work? In what ways do you desire to grow? What steps could you take to pursue this growth?

Questions for Deeper Reflection

10. How are the earnest and firstfruits of the Spirit examples of the inaugurated eschatology of the New Testament? How is this reflected in the tensions of Christian experience?
11. A friend says, "I know I am a child of God because the Holy Spirit tells me so in my heart. I hear him speak to me every day." Another responds, "God does not speak to us today. Assurance is simply a matter of comparing our faith and obedience to the Word and concluding that we are saved." How do you respond in a way that highlights the supernatural work of the Spirit in assurance but does not separate his work from God's Word?

35

The Marks of Grace in Christian Character, Part 1

The Beatitudes

Although God saves people from a vast diversity of cultures and works through a remarkable variety of circumstances, he saves one people by one Christ through one Spirit. There are distinguishing marks of saving grace, consisting of moral character and obedience to God's commandments, all by a living faith in Christ. Such godliness is definitive for distinguishing authentic Christianity and directive for growth in the Christian life.

In this chapter and the next, we will discuss how God's grace manifests itself in Christian character, first by looking at Christ's Beatitudes and then Paul's list of the fruit of the Spirit. In subsequent chapters, we will examine obedience to God's moral law summarized in the Ten Commandments, because the most practical display of authentic salvation is keeping God's commandments.

Introduction to the Beatitudes

The word *beatitude* (from Latin *beatitudo*) literally means "blessedness, happiness." It often is used for statements in the Bible beginning "Blessed is" or "Blessed are." The most recognized beatitudes are Christ's eight pithy sayings that begin the Sermon on the Mount (Matt. 5:3–10).[1]

Christ, the Prophet of God's Kingdom and Righteousness

The Lord Jesus Christ came preaching "the gospel of the kingdom" (Matt. 4:23; 9:35). The coming of the kingdom is God's conquest of evil powers and restoration of his reign over man by his word and Spirit for his glory in Christ.[2] Christ's Sermon on the Mount focuses on the righteousness required by the "kingdom."[3] Christ says, "Except your righteousness shall exceed the righteousness of the scribes and Pharisees, ye shall in no case enter into the kingdom of heaven" (5:20). The wicked persecute God's people "for righteousness' sake" (v. 10). Jesus exhorts, "Seek ye first the kingdom of God, and his righteousness" (6:33). This righteousness is a life centered on God and his will, consisting of obeying God's commandments (chap. 5) and seeking the Father's pleasure and reward instead of man's praise and earth's treasures (chap. 6).[4] In theological language, this righteousness is not merely the result of justification but especially that of sanctification; it is the fruit (good works) that grows from the tree of faith, as Martin Luther said.[5] William Perkins commented that in this sermon Christ teaches believers to lead holy lives by clarifying the meaning of the ancient law of God.[6]

Christ preached the Sermon on the Mount when large crowds began gathering to him in response to his miracles (Matt. 4:23–5:2). In it, he searches hearts with the bright light of the Word and, with the sharp edge of the truth, discriminates between two gates and two ways, one leading to life and the other to destruction (7:13–14). Christ is the risen and living Prophet of the kingdom, and he still speaks through this sermon to show the unconverted their need for a profound change of heart lest they be cast into hell (5:29–30), to assure the converted of their blessedness (v. 3), and to point the way for his people to grow into excellence in the kingdom (v. 19).

1. Matthew 5:11–12 is not a ninth beatitude but an expansion of the eighth (v. 10). Note the shift from the third person ("blessed are the") to the second ("blessed are ye").

2. On the kingdom of God as distinguished from his essential sovereignty, see *RST*, 2:1112–15.

3. See "kingdom" (*basileia*) in Matt. 5:3, 10, 19–20; 6:10, 13, 33; 7:21.

4. Hendriksen, *Exposition of the Gospel according to Matthew*, 263, 274; and France, *Matthew*, 99, 116.

5. Luther, *The Sermon on the Mount*, on Matt. 5:6, in *LW*, 21:26.

6. Perkins, *An Exposition of Christ's Sermon on the Mount*, on Matt. 5:1–2, in *Works*, 1:173–74.

God's Kingdom Blessing on Repentant Sinners

Shortly before the Beatitudes, Matthew presents a summary of Christ's preaching: "Repent: for the kingdom of heaven is at hand" (Matt. 4:17). The first and last beatitudes both take the form "Blessed are . . . for theirs is the kingdom of heaven" (5:3, 10). The fourth and eighth beatitudes explicitly mention "righteousness" (vv. 6, 10). Therefore, the Beatitudes expand on the call to repentance and the promise of the kingdom by describing the marks of people who have truly turned from sin to God in Jesus Christ to walk in righteousness.[7]

It is crucial to interpret the Beatitudes according to the contextual themes of kingdom, repentance, and righteousness. For example, "Blessed are the poor in spirit" (Matt. 5:3) is not about having a mindset that renounces earthly wealth as one's trust and treasure[8] or about humility in general,[9] but about knowing one's spiritual poverty because one lacks righteousness.[10] The saying "Blessed are they that mourn" (v. 4) is not a declaration of God's general mercy to the suffering or a promise of universal salvation ("they shall be comforted").[11] Rather, it refers to mourning over one's sins and lack of righteousness,[12] a devastating realization in light of the coming kingdom.

There is a linear structure in the Beatitudes in which each quality builds upon those that precede it—poverty producing mourning, and so on. This is not a chronological sequence, but a structure of logical relations.[13] The first four beatitudes focus on internal qualities of the heart, which lay the foundation for the focus in the next four on how God's people relate to the world around them.[14] There is also a parallel structure in the Beatitudes,[15] as shown in Table 35.1 below.

---

7. If it is objected that the beatitudes of Luke 6:20–23 do not mention righteousness but only physical suffering, we respond that Christ often used physical things as metaphors for spiritual realities (cf. vv. 37–49) and that the sermon on "the plain" (v. 17) may differ in some ways from the Sermon on the Mount.

8. Luther, *The Sermon on the Mount*, on Matt. 5:3, in *LW*, 21:13–15.

9. Augustine, Sermon 3.1 (53.1), in *NPNF*[1], 6:266; Jerome, *Commentary on Matthew*, 1.5.3, cited in *ACCS/NT*, 1a:81; John Calvin, *Sermons on the Beatitudes*, trans. Robert White (Edinburgh: Banner of Truth, 2006), 20–21; and *Commentaries*, on Matt. 5:3.

10. Perkins, *An Exposition of Christ's Sermon on the Mount*, on Matt. 5:3, in *Works*, 1:180–81.

11. Jürgen Moltmann says, "The grieving are Jesus's brothers and sisters, and fellow citizens of the kingdom of God, whether they know it or not." *The Coming of God: Christian Eschatology*, trans. Margaret Kohl (Minneapolis: Fortress, 1996), 126–27.

12. Chrysostom, *Homilies on Matthew*, 15.4, on Matt. 5:4, in *NPNF*[1], 10:93.

13. Hendriksen, *Exposition of the Gospel according to Matthew*, 267–68.

14. Luther, *The Sermon on the Mount*, on Matt. 5:10, in *LW*, 21:45.

15. On the "cumulative order" and the "parallel" structure of the Beatitudes, see Bartel Elshout, *Christ's Portrait of the Christian: An Exposition of the Beatitudes* (Grand Rapids, MI: Biblical Spirituality Press, 2019), 7, 14–18.

Internal	Relation to World	Experiential Connection
1. Poverty in Spirit	5. Mercy	A sense of need makes one merciful to the needy (James 2:12–13).
2. Mourning	6. Pure in Heart	Heartfelt repentance produces inward purity (James 4:8–9).
3. Meekness	7. Peacemaking	Humble gentleness promotes peace (James 3:13–18).
4. Hunger and Thirst for Righteousness	8. Persecuted for Righteousness	Pursuit of righteousness provokes persecution for righteousness.

Table 35.1. Parallel Structure in the Beatitudes

Christ declares the people who have these characteristics to be "blessed" (*makarios*). In biblical usage, being "blessed" might not involve immediate happiness,[16] but speaks of being destined for future felicity because of one's covenantal relationship with God through faith, a relationship exercised in fear, wisdom, and keeping his commandments.[17] The opposite of declaring someone "blessed" is the proclamation of "woe" or being under God's judgment, which Christ made against the proud and unrepentant (Matt. 11:21; 23:13–29; Luke 6:20–26). God himself is supremely and infinitely "blessed" (1 Tim. 1:11; 6:15), and he is pleased to share his joy with his people through Christ (Matt. 25:21; John 15:11).[18] The blessedness of God is his "ineffable and inconceivable good" and "indescribable beauty," as Gregory of Nyssa said, but God can share a similar blessedness with us since he made man in his image and is restoring man to that image by his saving grace.[19]

Christ is the Prophet of grace, and his message begins with indicatives of blessing from the gracious and loving God before the imperatives of the law.[20]

16. Job 5:17; Ps. 93 [94]:12 LXX; 1 Pet. 3:14; 4:14.

17. See the uses of "blessed" (*'ashrey*, translated *makarios* in the LXX) in Deut. 33:29; Pss. 1:1; 2:12; 32:1–2; 33:12; 34:8; 40:4; 84:4–5; 89:15; 112:1; 128:1; 144:15; 146:5; Prov. 3:13; 28:14; Isa. 30:18; 56:2.

18. John Piper, *The Pleasures of God* (Portland, OR: Multnomah, 1991), 23.

19. Gregory of Nyssa, *Homilies on the Beatitudes: An English Version with Commentary & Supporting Studies*, ed. Hubertus R. Drobner and Albert Viciano (Leiden: Brill, 2000), homily 1.2 (25). On God's infinite beatitude, or joy, see *RST*, 1:844–49.

20. Henry, *Commentary on the Whole Bible*, on Matt. 5:3–12 (1628); and Morris, *The Gospel according to Matthew*, 95.

The six central promises of the Beatitudes are stated in the Greek future tense, indicating that believers' full happiness waits until the kingdom comes in glory (Matt. 5:4–9). However, the first and last promises, "theirs is the kingdom of heaven" (vv. 3, 10), employ a present tense "is" (*estin*), for the kingdom already belongs to Christians in the grace of Christ. Since they are "blessed," they are justified by faith alone, for God can only bless those whom he has delivered from condemnation and curse and counted righteous in Christ (Gal. 3:8–14).[21]

The Internal Marks of the Kingdom Heirs

In the first four beatitudes, Christ reveals the way to life, and it is a way of paradoxes—the way down is the way up, to be low is to be high, to have nothing is to possess all, to bear the cross is to wear the crown, and to go backward is to go forward (Matt. 16:24; 19:30).

Poverty in Spirit

In the first beatitude, Jesus says, "Blessed are the poor in spirit: for theirs is the kingdom of heaven" (Matt. 5:3). The word translated as "poor" (*ptōchos*) does not literally refer to a laborer who lacks wealth,[22] but to a beggar who depends on charity to survive.[23] Also, the Lord does not here refer to economic poverty, though God may use hardship as a means to promote spiritual poverty, and persecution often impoverishes the godly. Jeremiah Burroughs said that many people "are outwardly poor, and yet proud, stubborn, profane, and ungodly, scorning at godliness and religion; certainly these are cursed poor."[24] Christ blessed the "poor in spirit," poor in the attitude of their inner man.[25]

In the Old Testament, "poor" (*ptōchos*) often refers to the needy and oppressed whom the Lord saves and honors.[26] The Psalms frequently identify the "poor" as those who put their trust in God and walk in his

21. Thomas Watson, *The Beatitudes: An Exposition of Matthew 5:1–12* (Edinburgh: Banner of Truth, 1971), 35.

22. Compare *penēs*, a "poor" man who is not rich and is vulnerable to oppression or may need a loan but who has a regular way of making a living as a hired worker (Ex. 23:6; Deut. 15:11; 24:14–15; 2 Kingdoms [2 Sam.] 12:1–4 LXX).

23. Ex. 23:11; Lev. 19:10; 23:22; 1 Kingdoms (1 Sam.) 2:8; Prov. 19:7; 22:9; Isa. 58:7 LXX; Matt. 11:5; 26:9; Luke 14:13, 21; 16:20, 22; 21:3; Rom. 15:26; Gal. 2:10.

24. Burroughs, *The Saints' Happiness*, 11.

25. Compare "the poor in spirit" (*hoi ptōchoi tō pneumati*) in Matt. 5:3 to "the humble in spirit" (*tous tapeinous tō pneumati*) in Ps. 33:19 (34:18) LXX. Thus, it means "those whose spirit is poor." Willoughby C. Allen, *A Critical and Exegetical Commentary on the Gospel according to St Matthew*, 3rd ed. (Edinburgh: T&T Clark, 1907), 39.

26. 1 Kingdoms (1 Sam.) 2:8; 22:28; Pss. 9:19 (18); 11:6 (12:5); 34 (35):10; 73 (74):21; 112 (113):7 LXX.

ways.[27] In Isaiah's prophecy, poverty sometimes takes on a sense of spiritual neediness: the "poor" are those dying of thirst for whom the Lord will pour out rivers in the wilderness (Isa. 41:17–18), even the Holy Spirit (32:15; 44:3) who anoints the messianic preacher of good news to the "poor" (61:1).[28] This poverty consists of humility before the Holy One, contrition over sin, and trembling at his word (57:15; 66:1–2; cf. Ezra 9:4; 10:3).

Therefore, inward poverty is God centered and gospel driven. Richard Baxter (1615–1691) said many people think of humility in terms of painful emotions and bodily self-denial, but the great exercise of seeking humility is to "strive for such a sight of your sinfulness and nothingness, as will teach you highly to esteem of Christ." Baxter added that "the most powerful means to take down pride . . . [is] to look seriously to God, and set yourselves before his eyes, . . . [for] one sight of God by a lively faith, would make you know with whom you have to do, and teach you to abhor yourselves as vile."[29]

Christ takes up this prophetic doctrine of inward poverty and weaves it into his preaching of repentance of sin; hence, "poor in spirit" refers to those who trust in the Lord for salvation because they have no righteousness of their own.[30] The sinner sees himself as a spiritual beggar, unable to live on his own good deeds, absolutely dependent on the Lord.[31] He must have Christ and his Spirit or he will perish. Thomas Watson pointed out that there is a difference between being "spiritually poor" and "poor in spirit," for "he who is without grace is spiritually poor, but he is not poor in spirit; he does not know his spiritual beggary (Rev. 3:17)."[32] Poverty in spirit is a sense of one's emptiness of righteousness before God, which disposes one to treasure and receive Christ.[33] Watson said, "If the hand be full of pebbles, it cannot receive gold."[34]

27. Pss. 13 (14):6; 21:25 (22:24); 24 (25):16; 33:7 (34:6); 36 (37):14; 71 (72):12–13 LXX.

28. The words translated as "poor" (*ptōchos*), "mourn" (*pentheō*), and "comfort" (*parakaleō*) in Matt. 5:3–4 all appear in Isa. 61:1–2 LXX. Eusebius, *The Proof of the Gospel: Being the Demonstratio Evangelica of Eusebius of Caesarea*, trans. W. J. Ferrar, 2 vols., Translations of Christian Literature, Series 1, Greek Texts (London: Society for Promoting Christian Knowledge; New York: Macmillan, 1920), 9.10 (2:172–73); and D. A. Carson, "Matthew," in *The Expositor's Bible Commentary*, ed. Gaebelein, 8:130.

29. Richard Baxter, *A Christian Directory* (1846; repr., Morgan, PA: Soli Deo Gloria, 1996), 208.

30. Poole, *Annotations upon the Holy Bible*, on Matt. 5:3 (3:20).

31. Hendriksen, *Exposition of the Gospel according to Matthew*, 269; John R. W. Stott, *The Message of the Sermon on the Mount (Matthew 5–7): Christian Counter-Culture*, The Bible Speaks Today (Downers Grove, IL: InterVarsity Press, 1985), 38–39; and Morris, *The Gospel according to Matthew*, 95.

32. Watson, *The Beatitudes*, 41.

33. Henry, *Commentary on the Whole Bible*, on Matt. 5:3 (1628); and Robert Jamieson, A. R. Fausset, and David Brown, *Commentary Critical and Explanatory on the Whole Bible*, 2 vols. (1871; repr., Oak Harbor, WA: Logos Research Systems, 1997), 2:17.

34. Watson, *The Beatitudes*, 43.

In his parable in which "two men went up into the temple to pray," Christ illustrates the difference between those who "trusted in themselves that they were righteous, and despised others" and the poor in spirit (Luke 18:9–10). Christ says that the Pharisee prayed, "God, I thank thee, that I am not as other men are, extortioners, unjust, adulterers, or even as this publican. I fast twice in the week, I give tithes of all that I possess" (vv. 11–12). Jonathan Edwards said that the false humility of "spiritual pride" makes a man "apt to think highly of his attainments in religion, as comparing himself with others."[35] Christ next says that the other man, a tax collector, said, "God be merciful to me a sinner" (v. 13). Here was a beggar—not financially but spiritually. Christ says, "This man went down to his house justified rather than the other: for every one that exalteth himself shall be abased; and he that humbleth himself shall be exalted" (v. 14). Gardiner Spring (1785–1873) said, "Humility consists in a just view of our own character, and in the disposition to abase ourselves as low as the vileness of our character requires."[36]

Poverty in spirit is the right posture of the whole life of discipleship, from beginning to end. It is not merely about becoming a Christian. It was to a *church* that Christ said, "Thou sayest, I am rich, and increased with goods, and have need of nothing; and knowest not that thou art wretched, and miserable, and poor, and blind, and naked" (Rev. 3:17).

True inward poverty must be distinguished from false humility. Regarding oneself as completely worthless is not humility but an insult to one's Maker, who created man in his image and values him much more than animals.[37] Poverty of spirit arises from knowing man's original nobility as God's image bearer, which makes our treason against him truly heinous.

The Christian's acknowledgment that he is a spiritual beggar does not mean he should deny that God's regenerating grace has produced any good in him (Ezek. 36:27; Luke 8:15; Acts 11:24).[38] Rather, inward poverty is a humbling recognition that prior to conversion no one does good in God's sight, and after conversion no one is worthy of being counted righteous according to his works (Rom. 3:10–12, 27–28). Moral evil still stains the believer's motives and obedience (7:21; Gal. 5:17). Hence, as Spring said,

35. Edwards, *Religious Affections*, in *WJE*, 2:320.
36. Gardiner Spring, *Essays on the Distinguishing Traits of Christian Character* (New York: Dodge & Sayre, 1813), 130.
37. On the sanctity of man's life as God's image bearer, see *RST*, 2:200.
38. On the power and fruitfulness of regeneration, see chap. 17.

"he will not be apt to think highly of his own virtues, nor consider himself injured if he is not highly esteemed by others."[39]

Wilhelmus à Brakel said, "They know that they are not worthy that . . . the sun shines upon them, or that they walk upon the earth, enjoying the fellowship of men, having a piece of bread to eat, and having clothing for their body. Rather, they are worthy of having been cast into hell long ago."[40] John Gill said that a Christian's humility shows itself "in ascribing all he is and has to the grace of God; confessing that he has nothing but what he has received . . . it is of the free grace of God alone, that he . . . shall be saved."[41] Thus, spiritual beggars treasure Christ as their justification and sanctification, and continually beg God for more grace.[42] Apart from Christ, they are doomed to perish in their sins; but in Christ, they are rich in eternal felicity (2 Cor. 8:9). "Blessed are the poor in spirit: for theirs is the kingdom of heaven" (Matt. 5:3).

Mourning

In the second beatitude, the Lord Jesus says, "Blessed are they that mourn: for they shall be comforted" (Matt. 5:4). The word translated as "mourn" (*pentheō*) is not used for reactions to minor disappointments, but for grieving great losses, such as the deaths of loved ones.[43] People often express mourning by weeping, an outward display of inward grief.[44] In Matthew 5:4, the grieving is over sin,[45] since Christ speaks in the context of his call to repentance and righteousness; thus, this is "godly sorrow" (2 Cor. 7:10–11).[46] Those who love God also grieve over the sins of other people (Ps. 119:53, 136, 158). Robert Harris (1581–1658) said that just as "the chief good" is God, so "the good man looks upon sin (both his own and others') as the greatest evil."[47] William Hendriksen commented, "It grieves them that God, their own God whom they love, is

39. Spring, *Essays on the Distinguishing Traits of Christian Character*, 139.

40. Brakel, *The Christian's Reasonable Service*, 4:70.

41. Gill, *Body of Divinity*, 801.

42. Burroughs, *The Saints' Happiness*, 19.

43. Gen. 23:2; 37:34–35; 50:3; 1 Kingdoms (1 Sam.) 6:19, etc. LXX.

44. Gen. 37:35; 2 Kingdoms 19:2 (2 Sam. 19:1) LXX; Mark 16:10; Luke 6:25; James 4:9; Rev. 18:11, 15, 19.

45. Chrysostom, *Homilies on Matthew*, 15.4, on Matt. 5:4, in *NPNF*[1], 10:93; Hilary of Poitiers, cited in Thomas Aquinas, *Catena Aurea: Commentary on the Four Gospels, Collected out of the Works of the Fathers*, 4 vols. in 7 (Oxford: John Henry Parker, 1841–1845), on Matt. 5:4 (1.1:150).

46. See the section on the comprehensiveness of repentance in chap. 19.

47. Robert Harris, *The Way to True Happiness, Delivered in Twenty-Four Sermons upon the Beatitudes*, ed. Don Kistler (Morgan, PA: Soli Deo Gloria, 1998), 62.

being dishonored."[48] The Stoics viewed mourning as an illogical passion to be avoided,[49] but Christ teaches that mourning over sin against God is essential to ultimate happiness in his kingdom. The present tense of "mourn" implies that this is a continuous or repeated mourning throughout the Christian life.

The poor in spirit mourn because their lack of righteousness forfeits their right to eternal life and makes them worthy of the fires of hell (Matt. 5:22, 29–30). They mourn, however, not merely because of the consequences of their sins but for the evil of sin against God, for he is "the great King" (v. 35), whose name is to be "hallowed" and whose will is to be done (6:9–10; 7:21). They have "a broken and a contrite heart" that moves them to pray, "Against thee, thee only, have I sinned, and done this evil in thy sight" (Ps. 51:4, 17).

We must beware of grief merely over sin's consequences, for that does not involve true repentance unto salvation, as seen in Ahab (1 Kings 21:27–29; 22:37–38). In contrast, Josiah mourned when he heard the threat of divine wrath against Israel, and he "turned to the Lord with all his heart" and sought to obey "all the law of Moses" (2 Kings 22:19; 23:25). Thus, blessed mourning over sin is more than conviction of sin, which precedes repentance (Ps. 32:3–4; Acts 2:37) but may not issue in repentance (Acts 24:24–26).[50] Edwards said that "evangelical humiliation" is different from "legal humiliation" because only the former involves seeing "the hateful nature of sin" in light of "the beauty of God's holiness and moral perfection."[51]

Repentance over sin breaks the heart as one turns to God with trust in his goodness (Luke 15:17–19). The Lord says, "'Return to me with all your heart, with fasting, with weeping, and with mourning; and rend your hearts and not your garments.' Return to the Lord your God, for he is gracious and merciful, slow to anger, and abounding in steadfast love; and he relents over disaster" (Joel 2:12–13 ESV). Indeed, it is the sight of God's goodness, love, grace, and mercy that breaks the heart, for it pierces us with a horrible sense that we have sinned against such a good God.[52] Watson said, "Gospel tears must drop from the eye of faith."[53]

---

48. Hendriksen, *Exposition of the Gospel according to Matthew*, 270. See also Ezra 10:6; Ezek. 9:4.
49. Epictetus, *Discourses*, 2.13.17; 4.1.52, cited in *TDNT*, 6:41.
50. On conviction of sin versus conversion, see the discussion of preparatory grace in chap. 13.
51. Edwards, *Religious Affections*, in *WJE*, 2:311.
52. Gill, *Body of Divinity*, 715, 717.
53. Watson, *The Beatitudes*, 64.

While Christ's disciples should not wallow in misery—for God commands them to rejoice in the Lord always (Phil. 4:4)—they should regularly mourn over sin in themselves, their families, their churches, and their nations. John Stott said, "Was Paul wrong to groan, 'Wretched man that I am! Who will deliver me from this body of death?', and to write to the sinful church of Corinth: 'Ought you not rather to mourn?' I think not. I fear that we evangelical Christians, by making much of grace, sometimes thereby make light of sin."[54]

Christ says, "Blessed are they that mourn: for they shall be comforted" (Matt. 5:4). Paradoxically, the way to true happiness is not to shield ourselves against all pain but to embrace God-loving, sin-hating, soul-healing pain. Those who by regenerating grace mourn over sin will receive the comfort of dwelling in a kingdom free from sin and its consequences. Already they have the comfort of hearing Christ pronounce them "blessed." This strangely comforting sorrow, as Harris said, "lightens the heart and pulls the sting out of all crosses. It is not a vexing, blubbering sorrow, but rational, quieting, and such as gives contentment."[55]

Meekness

The third beatitude of our Lord is "Blessed are the meek: for they shall inherit the earth" (Matt. 5:5). The word rendered as "meek" (*praus* or *praos*) does not refer to weakness but to an inward disposition of humility, peace, and strength that makes one slow to anger (Prov. 16:32). Brakel said that a meek person has "an even-tempered and stable disposition of heart" and is not irritable, having "as many spines as a porcupine does" or being "as prickly as a thorn bush."[56]

Christian meekness involves gracious humility and love. The world knows a shadow of meekness that is self-centered, an outward mildness essential to friendship and good statesmanship.[57] Plato recommended that people be "gentle [*praos*] to their friends and harsh to their enemies."[58] But Moses exemplified true meekness when he prayed for his sister, Miriam, after she criticized him and sought to wrest power from him (Num. 12:1–3, 13).[59] Chromatius (fl. 400) said, "The meek are those who are

54. Stott, *The Message of the Sermon on the Mount*, 41–42. He cited Rom. 7:24; 1 Cor. 5:2.
55. Harris, *The Way to True Happiness*, 65.
56. Brakel, *The Christian's Reasonable Service*, 4:84–85.
57. See the discussion of *prautēs* in *TDNT*, 6:646.
58. Plato, *The Republic*, 2.15.375c (1:169).
59. Gill, *Body of Divinity*, 802.

gentle, humble and unassuming, simple in faith and patient in the face of every affront."[60] In the New Testament, meekness is associated with humility, quietness, patience, and peace (as opposed to envying and strife).[61] Amazingly, meekness characterizes the Lord Jesus himself, even in his kingly office.[62] Therefore, it characterizes those who bear Christ's image by regeneration (Col. 3:8–12). Edwards said, "Truly gracious affections . . . are attended with the lamblike, dovelike spirit and temper of Jesus Christ, . . . such a spirit of love, meekness, quietness, forgiveness and mercy, as appeared in Christ."[63]

The words of Christ allude directly to Psalm 37:9, 11: "For evildoers shall be cut off: but those that wait upon the Lord, they shall inherit the earth. . . . The meek shall inherit the earth; and shall delight themselves in the abundance of peace."[64] The psalm calls the godly to refrain from anxiety and anger while trusting in the Lord—even if the wicked flourish and plot to destroy his people—because the Lord will punish his enemies and give the inheritance to the godly. Meekness is directed first toward the Lord in submitting to his will and second to men in forbearance.[65]

Meekness is a supernatural grace in Christ. It should not be confused with a quiet and mild personality, timidity, or a fearful compliance with God's commands out of a guilty conscience. Meekness flows from the dynamic of repentance already outlined in the previous beatitudes. The Christian who is poor in spirit realizes he has no right to demand anything, for his sin has made him a beggar before God. As Watson said, the "spiritually meek" person "does not quarrel with the instructions of the Word, but with the corruptions of his heart."[66] He receives the Word "with meekness" (James 1:21). He is willing to wait on the Lord. A humble beggar waits patiently for help, but a proud and rebellious man sighs and complains if he is not served at once.[67] Those who mourn have their proud hearts broken over their sins, which disposes them to bear patiently and gently with others who sin against them. They accept sorrow as their lot in

60. Chromatius, *Tractates on Matthew*, 17.4.1–2, cited in *ACCS/NT*, 1a:82.

61. See the use of *praus* and its cognates in Matt. 11:29; 21:5; Eph. 4:2; Col. 3:12; 2 Tim. 2:24–25; Titus 3:2; James 3:13–17; 1 Pet. 3:4.

62. Ps. 45:4; Zech. 9:9; Matt. 11:29; 21:5.

63. Edwards, *Religious Affections*, in *WJE*, 2:344–45. See also *WJE*, 2:350, quoted in *RST*, 2:1163.

64. Compare *hoi de praeis klēronomēsousin gēn* (Ps. 36 [37]:11 LXX) with *makarioi hoi praeis, hoti autoi klēronomēsousin tēn gēn* (Matt. 5:5); cf. also *klēronomēsousin tēn gēn* (Isa. 61:7 LXX).

65. Perkins, *An Exposition of Christ's Sermon on the Mount*, on Matt. 5:5, in *Works*, 1:188.

66. Watson, *The Beatitudes*, 106. See James 1:18.

67. Harris, *The Way to True Happiness*, 35.

this world but look to the coming kingdom for their full comfort. Rather than saying, "I deserve better," they acknowledge, "I deserve far worse—I am amazed that God is so good to me."

Christ's commendation of meekness raises questions about rights and authority. A meek person calmly and respectfully stands up for his legal rights as a citizen if faithfulness to God, justice, and love for people require it (Acts 16:37; 21:39; 22:25). But meekness also makes a person flexible and cooperative toward others, willing to regard the concerns of others as more important than his own (Phil. 2:3–4).[68] If God has entrusted a Christian with authority over others, then he must exercise that authority with "the meekness and gentleness of Christ" (2 Cor. 10:1). Teachers and leaders in the church should be exemplary in exercising authority with meekness (2 Tim. 2:24–25; 1 Pet. 5:3). This does not prohibit the use of power by parents to discipline children (Prov. 23:13–14); by homeowners to practice self-defense, including using deadly force (Ex. 22:2–3); or by civil officials to punish criminals (Rom. 13:4). Authority is a stewardship that cannot be abdicated. However, meekness does mean that disciplinary or punitive action must not be done in pride, rage, or bloodlust, but with humility, benevolence, and sober self-control (Gal. 6:1).

Though the meek might seem to capitulate to their adversaries and make themselves into losers, Christ said, "Blessed are the meek: for they shall inherit the earth" (Matt. 5:5). They shall receive the inheritance promised to Abraham—not just the Promised Land but the new creation to which it points.[69] Paradoxically, their meek willingness to let go of all will gain all for them in the end. The kingdom has come in their humble self-restraint and, thus, will come to them in its glory. As medieval Bible scholars said, "The meek, who have possessed themselves, shall possess hereafter the inheritance of the Father."[70]

Hunger and Thirst for Righteousness

In the fourth beatitude, Christ says, "Blessed are they which do hunger and thirst after righteousness: for they shall be filled" (Matt. 5:6). Christ

68. Brakel, *The Christian's Reasonable Service*, 4:82–83.

69. In Psalm 37, the "land" or "earth" (*'erets*, rendered *gē* in the LXX) refers immediately to the Promised Land (vv. 3, 9, 11, 22, 29, 34). To "inherit" the "land" (the promise of several of those verses) is to receive what God promised to the patriarchs (Gen. 15:7; 28:4) and later the nation of Israel (Lev. 20:24; Num. 33:53; Deut. 1:8, etc.).

70. *Glossa Ordinaria*, cited in Aquinas, *Catena Aurea*, on Matt. 5:5 (1:149).

takes up the ordinary language of satisfying physical hunger and thirst[71] and applies it to the righteousness of God's kingdom (6:33), the righteousness that distinguishes the godly from the wicked (5:10).[72] True hunger and thirst (rarely experienced by those living in affluent nations today) are all-consuming desires that, if left unmet, result in death. Thus, they aptly illustrate man's desperate need for salvation by the Lord (Ps. 107:5–9).[73] Though the citizens of God's kingdom are meek, they are not apathetic. They desire holiness. Their spiritual poverty must be remedied by a divine provision of righteousness. Their mourning over sin cannot be consoled unless sinning is replaced by being right with God and doing his will.

Those convinced of their spiritual poverty hunger for the justification that only the imputation of Christ's righteousness can supply (Phil. 3:8–9). However, as noted earlier, in the Sermon on the Mount, "righteousness" refers particularly to obedience to God's will revealed in the precepts of his law and exercised in relationships to others. God reveals his righteousness in his laws. He orders the community of his people with righteousness. God honors his righteousness in salvation through the "double grace" of justification and sanctification.[74]

The present tense of the verbs translated as "hunger" and "thirst" communicates that this desire continues through the Christian life as a longing to be practically and perfectly holy. It is a desire not merely for the benefits of righteousness but for righteousness itself, "not only because I am convinced in my conscience that I cannot go to heaven, or I must go to hell if I have it not," Burroughs said, but "I see this righteousness [as] lovely and excellent in itself."[75] It is what Edwards called "spiritual appetite": "The more a true saint loves God with a gracious love, the more he desires to love him, and the more uneasy he is at his want of love to him."[76] Gill said that "love to God manifests itself . . . [in] a desire to be like him; one that loves another, endeavors to imitate him; and such that love the Lord are followers of him, as dear children, and are obedient ones,

---

71. The word translated as "filled" (*chortazō*) means to satisfy with food (Matt. 14:20; 15:33, 37, etc.).

72. Some people interpret "hunger and thirst after righteousness" to mean that the poor long for justice when unjustly oppressed. Such a desire for justice is implied in the beatitude on persecution (Matt. 5:10; cf. Rev. 6:10). However, Christ uses "righteousness" in the Sermon on the Mount for a life of doing God's righteous will by his grace. Henry, *Commentary on the Whole Bible*, on Matt. 5:6 (1629).

73. The same verbs translated as "hunger" (*peinaō*), "thirst" (*dipsaō*), and "fill" or "satisfy" (*chortazō*) appear in both Ps. 106 (107):5, 9 LXX and Matt. 5:6.

74. See *RST*, 1:814–25.

75. Burroughs, *The Saints' Happiness*, 109.

76. Edwards, *Religious Affections*, in *WJE*, 2:376–77.

and desirous of being holy, as he is holy, in all manner of conversation [conduct]; nor can they be thoroughly satisfied and contented until they awake in his likeness."[77]

Yet as spiritual beggars, they have nothing to purchase this heavenly food and must seek it entirely by grace (Isa. 55:1). This is no hunger for self-righteousness, but a longing for God's righteousness. Sinners cannot produce good fruit until the tree is made good—that is, until God's grace changes their very nature (Matt. 7:16–20; 12:33–36). Therefore, their hunger and thirst for righteousness is "for God, for the living God" (Ps. 42:2); for Christ, the Bread of Life; and for the Holy Spirit, the river of living water (John 6:35; 7:37).

Hunger and thirst are proactive passions. To meet the crying needs of their bodies, men will labor all day (Prov. 16:26; Eccles. 6:7). Hence, spiritual hunger and thirst drive men to "seek first the kingdom of God and his righteousness" (Matt. 6:33 ESV). Burroughs said, "It is a ruling desire—that is, all desires are ordered by the desire after this righteousness."[78] This shows itself in an active pursuit of holiness. Burroughs continued, "These desires are very industrious desires. They are not idle desires. . . . If thou hast a desire to get grace, to get righteousness, if thou dost thirst for it, then this will follow: thy heart will follow hard after God in the use of all means that God is pleased to afford."[79] Like Christ, they count the doing of God's will to be their food (John 4:34; cf. Deut. 8:3; Job 23:12); that is their great priority. When such a person faces a difficult decision, the great and overriding question he asks is not "How will this affect my temporal success or happiness?" but "What must I do to obey God?"

Christ promises, "Blessed are they which do hunger and thirst after righteousness: for they shall be filled" (Matt. 5:6). When Christ comes with his kingdom, his people will see in themselves and each other a flawless image of God and likeness to his incarnate Son, Jesus Christ. Peter says, "We, according to his promise, look for new heavens and a new earth, wherein dwelleth righteousness" (2 Pet. 3:13). However, the future tense of "shall be filled" reveals that believers will never be satisfied "till all the ransomed church of God be saved, to sin no more."[80]

---

77. Gill, *Body of Divinity*, 764. He alluded to Eph. 5:1; 1 Pet. 1:14–15; and Ps. 17:15, in that order.

78. Burroughs, *The Saints' Happiness*, 110.

79. Burroughs, *The Saints' Happiness*, 111.

80. William Cowper, "There Is a Fountain Filled with Blood," in *Trinity Hymnal—Baptist Edition*, No. 188.

The Kingdom Heirs' Relation to the World

Whereas the first four beatitudes focus on negative qualities of felt spiritual need, the last four emphasize the positive qualities of the true kingdom citizens in relation to the world around them, including the world's hostile response to those qualities.

Mercy

In the fifth beatitude, Christ says, "Blessed are the merciful: for they shall obtain mercy" (Matt. 5:7). In the Gospel of Matthew, the term "merciful" (*eleēmōn*) and its cognates are used of alms for the poor, healing, deliverance from demons, and forgiving debts.[81] Perkins said, "Mercy is a holy compassion of heart, whereby a man is moved to help another in his misery."[82] Therefore, to be "merciful" is to be generously giving and graciously forgiving toward people in need.

Philosophers in Greco-Roman culture extolled the four virtues of wisdom, fortitude, temperance, and justice—but not mercy.[83] The famous "clemency" (*clementia*) of Julius Caesar (100–44 BC) to some of his conquered enemies was not mercy but merely "a new way of conquest." Those whom he spared regarded his clemency as a strategic "mistake" and murdered him.[84] Lucius Annaeus Seneca (4 BC–AD 65) told Nero (AD 37–68) that clemency is laudable leniency in executing punishment, but mercy (*misericordia*) to those in misery is a weakness.[85] The world is willing to show a counterfeit mercy, which arises from such selfish motives as kindness merely to those who love us or are like us (Matt. 5:46–47) or a hypocritical desire for man's praise (6:1–4). Paul warns, "Though I bestow all my goods to feed the poor," without love in the heart, "it profiteth me nothing" (1 Cor. 13:3). The mercy exercised by the blessed man flows from faith, love, and the fear of the Lord (Psalm 112).

Mercy is a Christian grace that grows from the roots of the graces mentioned in previous beatitudes. Mercy flows sweetly from broken

---

81. See the use of *eleēmōn*, *eleos*, *eleeō*, and *eleēmosunē* in Matt. 6:1–4; 9:27; 15:22; 17:15; 18:33; 20:30–31.

82. Perkins, *An Exposition of Christ's Sermon on the Mount*, on Matt. 5:7, in *Works*, 1:198; cf. Brakel, *The Christian's Reasonable Service*, 4:114; and *RST*, 1:785.

83. Hendriksen, *Exposition of the Gospel according to Matthew*, 276. See Plato, *The Republic*, 4.6.427e (1:347).

84. Adrian Goldsworthy, *Augustus: First Emperor of Rome* (New Haven, CT: Yale University Press, 2014), 64, 129.

85. Seneca, *On Mercy (De Clementia)*, 2.3.1–2.5.5, in *Seneca: Moral Essays*, trans. John W. Basore, 3 vols., Loeb Classical Library 214 (London: William Heinemann, 1928), 1:435–41.

hearts when sinners have tasted of God's mercy. In their meekness, they are not preoccupied with their own needs and desires, but consider the wants of others. They hunger and thirst for righteousness, and "mercy" to people in need is a central demand of God's righteous law, though often overlooked by legalistic hypocrites (Matt. 9:13; 12:7; 23:23). As noted above,[86] mercy for others in need especially flows from poverty of spirit, for the poor know they themselves need mercy from the righteous Judge (18:33). God saves them by sheer mercy (Eph. 2:4; Titus 3:5; 1 Pet. 1:3). James says, "So speak and so act as those who are to be judged under the law of liberty. For judgment is without mercy to one who has shown no mercy. Mercy triumphs over judgment" (James 2:12–13 ESV).

The practice of mercy is costly, but a merciful heart is "willing to part with much for others," Burroughs said, for it sees the good that giving will do for one's brothers and the glory that will go to God, who is the true owner of all our property.[87] Indeed, merciful people practice mercy with a sense of joy and privilege, believing "it is more blessed to give than to receive" (Acts 20:35).[88] Like Job and Tabitha, their lives are characterized by good works of compassion and justice to the poor and vulnerable (Job 29:12–17; 31:16–22; Acts 9:36, 39).[89] The love of God dwells in them, and they love their brothers with practical acts of sharing material goods (1 John 3:16–18).

By God's grace, the merciful obey the command "Be ye kind one to another, tenderhearted, forgiving one another, even as God for Christ's sake hath forgiven you" (Eph. 4:32). They are inclined to cover the sins of others if possible without injustice, and they hate malicious gossip (Prov. 10:12; 17:9). However, it is not malicious to report criminal activity to civil authorities (29:24) or to call on leaders in the church to discipline its members for unrepented sin (Matt. 18:15–17), for it is a mercy to correct sinners (Prov. 27:5–6), and their punishment and restraint is a mercy to their victims (31:8–9).

When Jesus says, "Blessed are the merciful: for they shall obtain mercy" (Matt. 5:7), he links his disciples' compassionate character with their ultimate salvation. A direct relationship exists between how a person treats

86. On the parallel structure of the Beatitudes, see Table 35.1 on p. 814.
87. Burroughs, *The Saints' Happiness*, 136.
88. Henry, *Commentary on the Whole Bible*, on Matt. 5:7 (1629).
89. Brakel, *The Christian's Reasonable Service*, 4:122.

the needy and how God treats that person.[90] Later in the same Gospel, Christ teaches that on judgment day he will welcome into the kingdom people distinguished by their works of mercy toward brethren who lacked food, drink, shelter, or clothing, or suffered sickness or imprisonment (Matt. 25:34–40). This does not mean that mercy merits eternal life, for Christ said, "They shall obtain mercy," not that they shall get what they deserve.[91] Augustine said, "You hear the voice of a beggar, but before God you are yourself a beggar."[92] Rather, the play on words between "merciful" and "obtain mercy" suggests that the merciful bear the renewed image of the merciful God and thus show themselves to be saved by his grace. Genuine works of mercy are evidences of salvation by the God of mercy.

Purity in Heart

Christ says in the sixth beatitude, "Blessed are the pure in heart: for they shall see God" (Matt. 5:8). The word translated as "pure" (*katharos*) can be used of purity, as in "pure gold" (Rev. 21:18, 21), but may also mean "clean" (Luke 11:41), the same term used in the ceremonial law regarding "clean" and "unclean" (Lev. 10:10 LXX). In ancient Israel, remaining clean was a matter of relating to the external world in a manner that avoided contamination by contact with things incompatible with God's holiness.

Given that Christ's sermon takes aim at the hypocritical righteousness of the Jewish scribes and Pharisees regarding obedience to God's law (Matt. 5:17–20), Christ has in view being "clean" inwardly versus a mere outward cleanliness according to the ceremonial law and human traditions (15:1–20). Jesus later castigates the scribes and Pharisees because they "make clean the outside of the cup and of the platter, but within they are full of extortion and excess," calling them to "cleanse first that which is within" (23:25–26). True righteousness requires repenting of malicious anger and evil lust (5:22, 29), loving one's enemies (v. 44), and seeking to please God and set one's heart on his heavenly treasure (6:4, 6, 18–21).

Therefore, "pure in heart" means being inwardly cleansed from the moral pollution of the world. Poor in spirit and meek, the pure in heart have been cleansed from the filth of self-righteousness and pride. In place

---

90. Prov. 14:31; 17:5; 19:17; 21:13; 22:9.
91. Perkins, *An Exposition of Christ's Sermon on the Mount*, on Matt. 5:7, in *Works*, 1:202.
92. Augustine, Sermon 53.5, cited in *ACCS/NT*, 1a:85; cf. *NPNF*[1], 6:267.

of such God-denying attitudes have come hunger and thirst for true, God-pleasing righteousness. God has taught them to be merciful, for "to visit the fatherless and widows in their affliction" is an essential component of "pure [*katharos*] religion" that is "undefiled before God" (James 1:27).

Purity of heart is especially related to mourning over sin, for only a broken heart turns from sin to embrace inward godliness (Matt. 5:4, 8). James says, "Draw nigh to God, and he will draw nigh to you. Cleanse your hands, ye sinners; and purify your hearts, ye double minded. Be afflicted, and mourn, and weep: let your laughter be turned to mourning, and your joy to heaviness" (James 4:8–9). Watson told those seeking purity of heart to go to "the bath of Christ's blood" and "the bath of tears," saying, "This water of contrition is healing and purifying."[93]

While a pure heart could describe moral perfection, which is impossible in this age (Prov. 20:9),[94] the Scriptures also use this language to simply describe the state of those truly converted by saving grace. Watson called it "evangelical purity."[95] It is more than sincerity, which may be mistaken (Gen. 20:3–5); it is inner godliness according to God's Word.[96] The natural state of fallen man is inward defilement that pollutes everything he thinks and does (Titus 1:15). God cleanses sinners by spiritual washing when he saves them.[97] A man with a "pure heart" is a person of authentic godliness whom the God of salvation welcomes into his holy presence and blesses (Ps. 24:3–5).[98] Peter tells all those who are "born again" to "love one another with a pure heart fervently," because "ye have purified your souls . . . unto unfeigned love of the brethren" (1 Pet. 1:22–23). Paul describes true Christians as people who "call on the Lord out of a pure heart" (2 Tim. 2:22) and says that love flows from a "pure heart" (1 Tim. 1:5). Perkins commented that when the Holy Spirit makes a person "pure in heart," he creates saving faith, mortifies inward corruption, renews God's image, and works a constant resolution not to sin in any way, but to strive to please God in all of life.[99]

The Lord Jesus promises, "Blessed are the pure in heart: for they shall see God" (Matt. 5:8). This is the "one thing" that the godly desire above

93. Watson, *The Beatitudes*, 193.

94. On the theological error of perfectionism, see chap. 28.

95. Watson, *The Beatitudes*, 171.

96. Hendriksen, *Exposition of the Gospel according to Matthew*, 276–77.

97. Acts 10:15; 11:9; 15:9; 1 Cor. 6:11; Eph. 5:26; Titus 3:5. See the section on definitive sanctification in chap. 27.

98. The LXX renders "pure of heart" (*bar-lebab*) as *katharos tē kardia* in Ps. 23 (24):4.

99. Perkins, *An Exposition of Christ's Sermon on the Mount*, on Matt. 5:8, in *Works*, 1:204.

all else: "to behold the beauty of the LORD" (Ps. 27:4). Augustine said, "To behold God is the end and purpose of all our loving activity."[100] When God grants a new heart that loves him, he also ensures that this person will enjoy whom he loves: "Delight thyself also in the LORD; and he shall give thee the desires of thine heart" (37:4). What the godly have enjoyed in communion with God is only the foretaste of what Christ promises. Christ's "blessed" (*beati* in the Latin Vulgate) will ultimately issue in the beatific vision of God's glory—their "blessed hope" (Titus 2:13).

Peacemaking

The seventh beatitude of our Lord Jesus is "Blessed are the peacemakers: for they shall be called the children of God" (Matt. 5:9). The word translated as "peacemaker" (*eirēnēpoios*) is rare,[101] but its meaning as a compound of "make" (*poieō*) and "peace" (*eirēnē*) is clear. Though "peace" can simply mean the avoidance or cessation of conflict (Josh. 9:15), in its fullest sense, drawing on the Old Testament concept of *shalom*, it means living in harmonious and just relationships with God and one another, from which comes all other blessings and prosperity.[102]

Christians might read "blessed are the peacemakers" with puzzlement or even perplexity because they are not involved in counseling estranged spouses or friends, much less arbitrating business disputes or making treaties between nations. However, the peacemaking in view here consists of the exercise of Christlike character to build a community of peace based on a mutual commitment to love and justice. Brakel said that peaceableness is an inner disposition that moves a believer to work toward "the maintaining of a relationship with his neighbor characterized by sweet unity . . . in the way of truth and godliness."[103]

True peacemaking eludes the unconverted, who are "hateful, and hating one another" (Titus 3:3). Sinners may have a sense of peace, but it is the false peace of Satan's undisturbed reign over their lives (Luke 11:20–21), the peace of a graveyard. True peace is from the Lord, but sinners are at

100. Augustine, Sermon 53.5, cited in *ACCS/NT*, 1a:86; cf. *NPNF*[1], 6:267.

101. The term *eirēnēpoios* in Matt. 5:9 appears nowhere else in the New Testament or LXX. The related verb *eirēnēpoieō* is found in Prov. 10:10 LXX (no equivalent in the Hebrew text) and Col. 1:20. See also "be at peace" or "live in peace" (*eirēneuō*) in Mark 9:50; Rom. 12:18; 2 Cor. 13:11; 1 Thess. 5:13.

102. C. L. Feinberg, "Peace," in *Evangelical Dictionary of Theology*, ed. Elwell, 833; Morris, *The Apostolic Preaching of the Cross*, 237–44; and *NIDOTTE*, 4:130–35.

103. Brakel, *The Christian's Reasonable Service*, 4:91.

war with him. "Peace, peace to him that is far off, and to him that is near, saith the Lord; and I will heal him. But the wicked are like the troubled sea, when it cannot rest, whose waters cast up mire and dirt. There is no peace, saith my God, to the wicked" (Isa. 57:19–21). True peace begins with reconciliation between God and sinners by faith in Jesus Christ (Rom. 5:1).[104] God calls the people whom he reconciled to himself (Eph. 2:16) to "walk worthy . . . with all lowliness and meekness, with longsuffering, forbearing one another in love; endeavouring to keep the unity of the Spirit in the bond of peace" (4:1–3). Watson said, "By nature we are of a fierce cruel disposition," but "grace turns the vulture into a dove."[105]

Therefore, peacemaking is the fruition of all the previous beatitudes. The poor in spirit are significantly mortified in their pride, removing a great cause of strife (Prov. 21:24; 22:10). Their mourning over sin softens their once-irreconcilable hearts and shows those whom they have wronged that they are truly repentant (Luke 17:3–4). They hunger and thirst not for their own advancement and glory, but for righteousness, which energizes them for the hard work of seeking peace. Their mercy endears them to others and draws together a community of love (Col. 3:12–15). They are not hypocrites passionate for legalism, but from their pure hearts comes sincere love for God and man. Jerome (347–420) said, "For what avails it to make peace between others, while in your own heart are wars of rebellious vices."[106] They pursue holiness, and hence, they seek and pursue peace.[107] Therefore, the blessed peacemaker loves only the peace that God loves—not a peace that compromises truth and holiness.[108]

Being a peacemaker is especially related to being meek (Matt. 5:5, 9). James says that the wisdom from above is demonstrated in "meekness," whereas earthly wisdom is accompanied by "bitter envying and strife in your hearts." He continues, "But the wisdom that is from above is first pure, then peaceable, gentle, and easy to be intreated, full of mercy and good fruits, without partiality, and without hypocrisy. And the fruit of righteousness is sown in peace of them that make peace" (James 3:13–14, 17–18). With meekness, peacemakers refuse to take revenge on those who wrong them (Rom. 12:17–21) but seek to pacify the wrath of others, bear

104. On Christ's work of reconciliation, see *RST*, 2:1001–3.
105. Watson, *The Beatitudes*, 206.
106. Jerome, cited in Aquinas, *Catena Aurea*, on Matt. 5:9 (1:154).
107. Ps. 34:14; Rom. 14:19; 2 Tim. 2:22; Heb. 12:14; 1 Pet. 3:11.
108. Burroughs, *The Saints' Happiness*, 202.

patiently with their offenses, and win them over with good deeds (Prov. 15:1, 18; 25:15).

Christ promises, "Blessed are the peacemakers: for they shall be called the children [literally sons] of God" (Matt. 5:9).[109] The future tense of the verb translated as "shall be called" points to the public manifestation of the coming kingdom (v. 19), when God the Father will publicly acknowledge believers as his own children and the brethren of his incarnate Son. They do not merit adoption by their peacemaking but receive it as a free gift through faith in Christ (John 1:12). However, their peaceable ways of loving and praying for their enemies show their likeness to their Father, who gives many good gifts to those who sin against him (Matt. 5:44–45). Already, God is at work through their peace-loving ways to build the kingdom of peace in the church that follows the Prince of Peace (Isa. 9:6–7).

Suffering Persecution

In the eighth and last beatitude, the Lord Jesus says, "Blessed are they which are persecuted for righteousness' sake: for theirs is the kingdom of heaven" (Matt. 5:10). The word translated as "persecute" (*diōkō*) means to "pursue"; here it means pursuing with malicious intent to harm (v. 44; 10:23; 23:34). The wicked hunt God's people, as if righteousness makes them dangerous or despicable vermin. Christ expands on this beatitude: "Blessed are ye, when men shall revile you, and persecute you, and shall say all manner of evil against you falsely, for my sake. Rejoice, and be exceeding glad: for great is your reward in heaven: for so persecuted they the prophets which were before you" (5:11–12).

Remarkably, the world responds to the humble, meek, merciful, pure, and peaceable character of God's children with hatred. Being "persecuted for righteousness' sake" arises particularly from hungering and thirsting "after righteousness" (Matt. 5:6, 10). Sinners hate righteousness, for they hate God and love sin (Rom. 8:7–8; 1 John 3:12).[110]

Persecution may reach the level of physical violence, but Christ notes that it begins with words: insults ("revile") and false accusations ("say all manner of evil against you falsely"). Such hard words against the righteous might be whispered in petty gossip, barked out in cruel mockery and ugly nicknames, libelously published in media, or falsely testified in courts and

109. On God's adoption of those whom he saves, see chaps. 25–26.
110. Burroughs, *The Saints' Happiness*, 212.

high councils of power. What the world regards as evil reputations are used to justify treating the saints as if they were the scum of the earth (1 Cor. 4:13).[111] As Paul says, "All that will live godly in Christ Jesus shall suffer persecution" (2 Tim. 3:12). Watson said, "Christ died to take the curse from us, yet not to take away the cross from us."[112]

Unlike qualities highlighted in the previous seven beatitudes, persecution is not a good to be desired but an evil to be endured. However, enduring persecution is a mark of grace because it shows that God's people do not belong to this world but to Christ, whom the world hates (John 15:18–20). When they are persecuted "for righteousness' sake," Christ says, they suffer "for my sake" (Matt. 5:10–11) and show themselves true disciples of the Master, who was accused of being the Devil (10:25). They are willing to confess Christ before men and are not ashamed of him (v. 32). When they persevere under persecution, they show that their repentance is not superficial and that the "root" of true conversion is in them (13:20–21). God has granted them spiritual eyes to perceive the hidden kingdom, and they will gladly give up everything to gain this great treasure (vv. 11–16, 44). Their sufferings mark them as one people with the prophets who have been persecuted and martyred through the ages (23:34–35). Hence, Watson said, "the nature of Christianity is . . . sanctity joined with suffering."[113]

Let us be careful, though, not to provoke persecution by our failure to be like Christ, for there is no reward in being arrogant and obnoxious, and civil authorities rightly punish those who commit crimes. Watson said that "the thief on the cross" was indeed saved by Christ, and "he died a saint, but not a martyr," for he suffered for his wrongdoings.[114] Peter says, "If ye be reproached for the name of Christ, happy are ye; for the spirit of glory and of God resteth upon you: on their part he is evil spoken of, but on your part he is glorified. But let none of you suffer as a murderer, or as a thief, or as an evildoer, or as a busybody in other men's matters. Yet if any man suffer as a Christian, let him not be ashamed; but let him glorify God on this behalf" (1 Pet. 4:14–16). By the Spirit "of glory," God will uphold his persecuted people with supernatural grace, for the Spirit's graces are foretastes of the glory to come.

111. Henry, *Commentary on the Whole Bible*, on Matt. 5:10–12 (1630).
112. Watson, *The Beatitudes*, 259.
113. Watson, *The Beatitudes*, 269.
114. Watson, *The Beatitudes*, 266.

Christ promises those persecuted for the sake of righteousness, "Theirs is the kingdom of heaven," and exhorts them, "Rejoice, and be exceeding glad: for great is your reward in heaven" (Matt. 5:10, 12). God will not allow them to be losers on his account: what they gain will far outweigh what they lose (19:29). They need not fear the reproach of men, for sinners will perish but salvation is forever (Isa. 51:7–8). If the wicked pursue them out of the earth, they will only drive them sooner to heaven.[115] Persecution hurts the body and may break the heart, as it did Jesus (Ps. 69:20), especially when it comes from one's own family (Matt. 10:21, 34–36). However, by God's grace renewing their inner man with eternal hope (2 Cor. 4:16–17), believers can live "as sorrowful, yet alway rejoicing; as poor, yet making many rich; as having nothing, and yet possessing all things" (6:10). The bloody opposition of sinners is their Father's loving rod to discipline them so that they will share in his holiness (Heb. 12:4–6, 10). Persecution is God's chisel and saw by which he cuts and squares the stones—that is, each one of his people—to fit his heavenly temple.[116]

Practical Conclusion to the Beatitudes

In the Beatitudes, we hear the voice of the living Christ addressing us personally and individually. By the illumination of the Spirit, allow his words to search you. Christ is mercifully uncovering the state of your soul by his revelation of the internal marks of saving grace. Walk slowly through these questions and answer each one as God gives you light. Has God shown you that you are a spiritual beggar, empty of any claim to righteousness or right to eternal life in yourself, worthy of only condemnation and hell? Do you mourn over your sins and the sins of others, not merely because of sin's consequences to you but because sin itself is hateful to the good and loving God? Has the Lord softened you so that your pride and obstinacy have to some extent been melted into meekness toward God and others? Do you hunger and thirst for the righteousness that only Christ can give you—a righteousness that shows itself practically in a life of obeying the commandments of God by a Spirit-worked love?

The Lord Jesus is also searching your life by the marks of grace according to how you relate to the world around you. How has God's mercy to you in your spiritual poverty produced a response of mercy to others in

115. Poole, *Annotations upon the Holy Bible*, on Matt. 5:10 (3:21).
116. Watson, *The Beatitudes*, 259.

need, both in your attitude and actions? Are you merely concerned with outward forms of religious purity, or has God cleansed your heart with brokenhearted repentance, a true faith in Christ, and authentic love for him, his Word, and his people? Are you a divisive person who constantly strives with others, even sincere Christians, or does your meek and gentle spirit tend to build relationships of peace and reconciliation, especially with fellow disciples of Christ? Lastly, has God worked in you a practical righteousness that provokes the world's sneers, insults, or worse forms of persecution?

It may be that you have read this chapter and found it to be like a story of a foreign land you have never visited; you have no personal experience with the qualities that Christ sets forth in the Beatitudes. If you are honest, they seem unrealistic and foolish. If that is your case, then the kingdom of heaven does not belong to you. You are a stranger to Christ and his ways. You are on the broad road to destruction. You have not yet repented of your sin. But Jesus Christ is speaking to you through his Word in his mercy. He is calling you to himself. We plead with you to call on the Lord Jesus to save you and, by his Spirit's regenerating power, to cause you to turn from your self-righteousness and sin to the Savior.

However, it may be that you read this chapter and now find Christ's words resonating with your heart and life. You sense your unworthiness, and yet, by the Spirit's enlightening grace, you are compelled to acknowledge honestly that God has planted these gracious seeds in your soul and they are bearing fruit in your life. If so, then rejoice, dear brother or sister. Do not allow your spiritual poverty to hinder you from humbly receiving Christ's infallible pronouncement about your spiritual state. God has given you saving grace. Yours is the kingdom, and therefore, you will be comforted, receive the whole earth as your inheritance, be satisfied in a world of righteousness, receive mercy from God, see his glory, and be honored as his beloved son or daughter forever. You are blessed! Therefore, give glory to God!

But if this is your state, then Christ intends for his words to deepen your sense of spiritual need and stir greater hunger and thirst. He is clearing away worldly confusion about the truly blessed person (it is not earthly prosperity) and clarifying the direction you must go. He is calling you to move ahead in the ways of the kingdom that he has revealed. His Beatitudes not only show us the doorway into the kingdom (conversion) but also the road to its glory (sanctification). Continue to follow Christ in the blessed way, and seek to grow in these qualities for the glory of his name. This is the way to full assurance. *Soli Deo gloria!*

Sing to the Lord

Rejoicing in the Blessed Life

How blest the man who fears the Lord
And greatly loves God's holy will;
His children share his great reward,
And blessings all their days shall fill.

Abounding wealth shall bless his home,
His righteousness shall still endure,
To him shall light arise in gloom,
For he is merciful and pure.

The man whose hand the weak befriends
In judgment shall his cause maintain;
A peace unmoved his life attends,
And long his mem'ry shall remain.

Of evil tidings not afraid,
His trust is in the Lord alone;
His heart is steadfast, undismayed,
For he shall see his foes o'erthrown.

With kind remembrance of the poor,
For their distress his gifts provide;
His righteousness shall thus endure,
His name in honor shall abide.

Psalm 112
Tune: Welton
The Psalter, No. 305

Questions for Meditation or Discussion

1. What important themes is Christ addressing in the context of the Beatitudes? What do those themes imply about how we should interpret the Beatitudes?

2. In what ways do the Beatitudes have a linear structure? How do they have a parallel structure?
3. What does "righteousness" mean in the Beatitudes and the rest of the Sermon on the Mount?
4. What does "blessed" mean? How does Christ's repeated affirmation that his people are blessed ground the whole Sermon on the Mount on God's saving grace? How is being blessed related to justification?
5. For each of the eight beatitudes, explain the meaning of Christ's words and discuss the character quality he highlights in light of other passages in the Holy Scriptures.
6. What should you conclude about your spiritual state based on the Beatitudes? Why?
7. If you are one of God's blessed ones, what is one area highlighted by the Beatitudes in which you especially need to grow? If you are not one of God's blessed ones, then what should you do?

Questions for Deeper Reflection

8. How would you prove that the Beatitudes are not describing a higher level of spirituality or holiness but the basic character of all those saved by God's grace in Christ?
9. Choose one beatitude and write a devotional showing how the grace that it describes is beautiful and desirable in the sight of both God and his people.

36

The Marks of Grace in Christian Character, Part 2

The Fruit of the Spirit

The Bible describes the distinctive character and activity of those saved by God's grace as their "fruit" (Mark 4:7–8). John the Baptist said, "Bring forth therefore fruits meet [suitable] for repentance. . . . Every tree which bringeth not forth good fruit is hewn down, and cast into the fire" (Matt. 3:8, 10). Using similar language, Christ says, "Every tree that bringeth not forth good fruit is hewn down, and cast into the fire. Wherefore by their fruits ye shall know them" (7:19–20; cf. 12:33). By union with Christ, those who once produced only evil in their lives become fruitful branches producing a life pleasing to God (John 15:5).[1] The Heidelberg Catechism (LD 24, Q. 64) says, "It is impossible that those, who are implanted into Christ by a true faith, should not bring forth fruits of thankfulness."[2]

The apostle Paul also sometimes uses "fruit" in this way to represent a life of godly character: "all goodness and righteousness and truth" (Eph. 5:9). He prays that the saints may be "filled with the fruits of righteousness, which are by Jesus Christ, unto the glory and praise of God" (Phil. 1:11). In this chapter, we will examine Paul's list of "the fruit of the

1. On images of union and communion with God in Christ, see chap. 9.
2. *The Three Forms of Unity*, 88.

Spirit"—namely, "love, joy, peace, longsuffering, gentleness, goodness, faith, meekness, temperance" (Gal. 5:22–23).

Introduction to the Fruit of the Spirit

Before we examine the meaning of the individual fruit, we must ask how this list functions in Paul's exhortation in Galatians 5 and why Paul gives the list its particular order.

The Significance of the Spirit's Fruit in Context

Paul exhorted the Galatians to "walk in the Spirit" by conducting themselves according to God's holy Word and the holy desires by which the Spirit was leading them to obey that Word (Gal. 5:16, 25). Believers are engaged in an inward conflict between the Spirit and the flesh (v. 17), but they can fight this battle because they are "led of the Spirit" and "not under the law" (v. 18)—that is, they are God's adopted children indwelt by the sanctifying Spirit (Rom. 8:14). By contrast, perishing sinners experience no such conflict, for they are condemned by God's law to slavery to their lusts (3:19; 6:14–17; cf. Gal. 3:10, 22–23; 4:21–31).

To clarify these two paths and two kinds of people, Paul lists "the works of the flesh" (Gal. 5:19–21) and "the fruit of the Spirit" (vv. 22–23). Of the works of the flesh, Paul says, "They which do such things shall not inherit the kingdom of God" (v. 21), but instead are on the path to destruction (6:8). When Paul says, "Now the works of the flesh are manifest" (5:19), he means they are plain to see, and hence, those who persist in unrepented sin are plainly not God's children and heirs (cf. 1 John 3:10). After listing the fruit of the Spirit, Paul says, "They that are Christ's have crucified the flesh with the affections and lusts" (Gal. 5:24), for by sharing in Christ's death and resurrection they have decisively broken from the mastery of sin to walk in the path of holiness by God's grace (Rom. 6:1–4, 21–24).[3]

Therefore, the contrasting lists of the works of the flesh and the fruit of the Spirit function to discriminate between perishing, unrepentant sinners and God's regenerated children. Furthermore, these two lists serve to direct believers in their continuing battle to put sin to death and live unto God through Jesus Christ.

3. On union with Christ in his death and resurrection, see chaps. 10 and 27. On regeneration as a participation in Christ's resurrection, see chap. 17.

The Old Testament background for Paul's phrase "fruit of the Spirit" is the promise that those who trust in the Lord and walk in his ways will be fruitful in life.[4] God promised to pour out the Holy Spirit to transform this barren world into a fruitful place filled with justice, righteousness, and peace (Isa. 32:15–17). This would take place through Christ the King (v. 1), the "branch" of David's line who "shall bear fruit,"[5] for "the Spirit of the LORD shall rest upon him" (11:1–2 ESV), producing wisdom, the fear of the Lord, justice, righteousness, faithfulness, and peace (vv. 3–9). Consequently, the Spirit-vivified Israel (44:3–5) would no longer be a vineyard producing bad fruit (5:1–7), but would "fill the face of the world with fruit" (27:6), for the Holy One gives life to the inner man of his humble people (57:15). They are part of his new creation.[6]

The phrase "fruit of the Spirit" teaches that these qualities are produced only by the Holy Spirit, though shadows of them appear in civil virtues.[7] People united to Christ derive their spiritual life and activity from the Spirit—they "live in the Spirit" (Gal. 5:25) by the resurrection life of Christ, for Paul says, "Christ liveth in me" (2:20). This does not release Christians from their responsibility to produce this fruit, but it grounds all their efforts to obey God on his grace working in them, both the willing and the doing coming through the obedient and exalted Lord Jesus (Phil. 2:5–13). They are God's "new creation" in Christ (2 Cor. 5:17; Gal. 6:15 ESV).

The fruit of the Spirit is the character of Jesus Christ, the Spirit-filled Lord. The Lord Jesus is the exemplar of divine love (Gal. 2:20; Eph. 5:2, 25). He is the joyful (John 15:11), peaceful (Isa. 9:6), patient (1 Tim. 1:16), and meek Son of God (Matt. 11:29), who "went about doing good" (Acts 10:38). The Holy Spirit who indwells God's children is "the Spirit of his Son" (Gal. 4:6). To look to the fruit of the Spirit is to look unto Jesus. Irenaeus said, "For the glory of God is a living man; and the life of man consists in beholding God."[8]

4. Pss. 1:1–3; 92:12–15; Jer. 17:7–8; Hos. 14:4–8.

5. The verb *parah*, translated as "grow" (Isa. 11:1) or "bear fruit" (ESV), is used for being fruitful in the creation account and the patriarchal promises of offspring (Gen. 1:22, 28; 9:1, 7; 17:6; 28:3; 35:11).

6. Isa. 41:17–20; 45:8; 57:19; 65:17–18. See chap. 8 and G. K. Beale, "The Old Testament Background of Paul's Reference to 'the Fruit of the Spirit' in Galatians 5:22," *Bulletin for Biblical Research* 15, no. 1 (2005): 1–38.

7. Calvin, *Commentaries*, on Gal. 5:22; and Perkins, *Commentary on Galatians*, on Gal. 5:22–23, in *Works*, 2:382–83. Similar expressions, such as "fruit of the tree," "fruit of the womb" (children), or "fruit of the mouth" (speech), show the source that produces the fruit (Gen. 3:2–3; 30:2; Ex. 10:15; Lev. 27:30; Prov. 12:14).

8. Irenaeus, *Against Heresies*, 4.20.7, in *ANF*, 1:490.

The Order of the Spirit's Fruit in Paul's List

It is difficult to discern whether Paul lists the fruit of the Spirit in a particular order. Some scholars have arranged the nine fruit in three triplets:

1. love, joy, and peace
2. longsuffering (patience), gentleness (kindness), and goodness
3. faith (faithfulness), meekness, and temperance (self-control)

It has been proposed that the first triplet pertains to the mind, the second to relationships, and the third to conduct. Alternatively, the first is oriented toward God, the second toward other people, and the third toward oneself. However, these distinctions seem artificial; for example, all the fruit begin in the mind, and love is both toward God and toward other people.[9]

Perhaps a more helpful arrangement is a chiastic pattern for the fruit following love:

<table>
<tr><td></td><td>A1. Joy</td><td></td><td></td><td></td></tr>
<tr><td></td><td></td><td>B1. Peace</td><td></td><td></td></tr>
<tr><td></td><td></td><td></td><td>C1 Longsuffering (Patience)</td><td></td></tr>
<tr><td>Christlike</td><td></td><td></td><td></td><td>D1. Gentleness (Kindness)</td></tr>
<tr><td>Love</td><td></td><td></td><td></td><td>D2. Goodness</td></tr>
<tr><td></td><td></td><td></td><td>C2. Faith (Faithfulness)</td><td></td></tr>
<tr><td></td><td></td><td>B2. Meekness</td><td></td><td></td></tr>
<tr><td></td><td>A2. Temperance (Self-Control)</td><td></td><td></td><td></td></tr>
</table>

As we will see, the words translated as "gentleness" and "goodness," appearing at the core of this chiasm (D), most likely take a nearly synonymous meaning—love's kind disposition to do good. "Longsuffering" (C1) and "faith" (or "faithfulness"; C2) directly reinforce each other as the Christian lives a consistent godly life despite his sorrows and trials. As we saw in our study of the Beatitudes, "peace" (B1) in ourselves and with others is inseparable from "meekness" (B2).[10] "Joy" in the Lord (A1) gives a Christian strength for "temperance" (or "self-control"; A2) regarding earthly joys, and the latter shows that the former is not a lawless hedonism but a wise and righteous joy. However, we present this structure

9. Timothy George, *Galatians*, The New American Commentary 30 (Nashville: Broadman & Holman, 1994), 399.

10. See chap. 35.

tentatively, knowing that there are many organic interrelations among the fruit of the Spirit. What is clear is the preeminence of love.

The Central Fruit of the Spirit: Christlike Love

"Love" (*agapē*, Gal. 5:22), sometimes translated as "charity,"[11] is the one comprehensive fruit of the Spirit.[12] Paul says that saving faith "worketh by love" (v. 6), we must "by love serve one another" (v. 13), and the duty required by God's law is summed up in "love thy neighbor as thyself" (v. 14). Martin Luther said, "It would have sufficed to list only love, for this expands into all the fruit of the Spirit."[13] Love is essential to the Christian life (1 Cor. 13:1–3). Augustine said, "When there is a question as to whether a man is good, one does not ask what he believes, or what he hopes, but what he loves."[14] Jonathan Edwards said, "All that virtue which is saving, and distinguishing of true Christians from others, is summed up in Christian or divine love."[15]

Christ's Revelation of Love

As we noted in our study of God's love under the locus of theology proper, our understanding of love is best derived not so much from lexical studies of *agapē* as from God's revelation of love in Christ.[16] In a broad sense, the whole Bible is a revelation of love. However, the preeminent revelation of love comes through Jesus Christ. We have already noted that love is revealed in the example of Jesus as he lived his life in perfect conformity to the will of the Father. Here we present several other Scripture passages in which Christ shows the glory of love.

God reveals love in the gospel of Christ (Rom. 5:6–8; 1 John 4:7–10). God's work of redemption shows us that God's love is Trinitarian (Matt. 3:16–17; John 3:34–35). The Father loves the sinners he saves and unites to himself through his Son (17:23–24). The supreme demonstration of love is the gospel: "For God so loved the world, that he gave his only begotten Son, that whosoever believeth in him should not perish, but have

11. The KJV translates *agapē* as "charity" in two dozen texts of the New Testament (cf. Latin *caritas* or *charitas*).

12. Speaking of one "fruit" is consistent with the singular number of the Greek word (*karpos*, Gal. 5:22), a term that can take the plural number (Matt. 3:8; 7:16–20; Phil. 1:11; 2 Tim. 2:6), though its singular may be used in a collective sense for multiple fruits (Matt. 13:8; 1 Cor. 9:7; James 5:18).

13. Luther, *Lectures on Galatians*, on Gal. 5:22, in *LW*, 27:93.

14. Augustine, *Enchiridion*, chap. 117, in *NPNF*[1], 3:274.

15. Edwards, *Charity and Its Fruits*, in *WJE*, 8:131.

16. See the study of God's love in *RST*, 1:788–99.

everlasting life" (3:16). Christ is our model for imitation in loving one another (Eph. 5:2, 25).

The Lord mandates love in the law of Christ, especially in the two great commandments on which the whole law hangs (Matt. 22:37–40): "Thou shalt love the Lord thy God with all thine heart, and with all thy soul, and with all thy might" (Deut. 6:5) and "Thou shalt love thy neighbour as thyself" (Lev. 19:18).

Christ instructs us about love in the Sermon on the Mount: "Love your enemies, bless them that curse you, do good to them that hate you, and pray for them which despitefully use you, and persecute you; that ye may be the children of your Father which is in heaven: for he maketh his sun to rise on the evil and on the good, and sendeth rain on the just and on the unjust. For if ye love them which love you, what reward have ye? Do not even the publicans [tax collectors] the same?" (Matt. 5:44–46) and "Whatever you wish that others would do to you, do also to them, for this is the Law and the Prophets" (7:12 ESV).

Christ illustrates love in the parable of the good Samaritan, who saw a man left half dead by robbers and "had compassion on him, and went to him, and bound up his wounds, pouring in oil and wine, and set him on his own beast, and brought him to an inn, and took care of him" (Luke 10:33–34). Christ also illustrates love in the parable of the prodigal son, in which the father saw his repentant son returning home "and had compassion, and ran, and fell on his neck, and kissed him," and ordered, "Bring forth the best robe, and put it on him; and put a ring on his hand, and shoes on his feet: and bring hither the fatted calf, and kill it; and let us eat, and be merry: for this my son was dead, and is alive again; he was lost, and is found" (15:20–24).

Christ clarifies what love is when he says, "He that hath my commandments, and keepeth them, he it is that loveth me: and he that loveth me shall be loved of my Father, and I will love him, and will manifest myself to him. . . . If a man love me, he will keep my words: and my Father will love him, and we will come unto him, and make our abode with him" (John 14:21, 23) and "Greater love hath no man than this, that a man lay down his life for his friends" (15:13).

A Systematic Description of Christlike Love

Love is difficult if not impossible to define precisely, but God's Word describes it with abundant clarity for the purposes of our knowledge, self-examination, and sanctification. Based on the Scripture passages surveyed in the previous section, we offer this description of how love acts: *Christ-like, Spirit-produced love is giving oneself to glorify God and do good to people graciously and righteously for the sake of friendship.* We will expand on this description piece by piece.

First, *love is giving oneself to glorify God.* God requires us to love him with all our heart, soul, and might (Deut. 6:5), which demands that we direct all our life, energy, and activity to serve him according to his commandments (10:12–13; 2 Kings 23:25). Love leads us to fulfill this principle: "Whether therefore ye eat, or drink, or whatsoever ye do, do all to the glory of God" (1 Cor. 10:31). To love God is to live unto the Lord as one who belongs entirely to him.[17] Such love is exemplified in God the Son incarnate, who said that he would lay down his life in obedience to God so "that the world may know that I love the Father" (John 10:17–18; 14:31). The Westminster Shorter Catechism (Q. 1) succinctly and beautifully states, "Man's chief end [main purpose] is to glorify God and to enjoy him for ever."[18]

Our love adds nothing to God but manifests his glory. God has no needs for us to meet or sorrow for us to relieve, for he is self-sufficient.[19] Rather, we glorify God as the all-sufficient Lord and Savior of his people. David says, "I will love thee, O Lord, my strength. The Lord is my rock, and my fortress, and my deliverer; my God, my strength, in whom I will trust; my buckler, and the horn of my salvation, and my high tower. I will call upon the Lord, who is worthy to be praised: so shall I be saved from mine enemies" (Ps. 18:1–3). Love for God has three major dimensions: (1) seeking the glory of his name, the advance of his kingdom, and the doing of his will (Matt. 6:9–10); (2) adoring and delighting in his beauty (Ps. 27:4); and (3) expressing thanks for his kindness and grace (116:1, 12).[20]

How are these three major dimensions worked out in practice—that is, what are some specific ways believers may lovingly glorify God? By the Spirit's grace, we glorify God by confessing our sins to him, forsaking them, and taking refuge in Christ's righteousness for forgiveness and

17. Rom. 6:11; 14:8–9; 2 Cor. 5:14–15; Gal. 2:19. On living to the Lord, see *RST*, 2:1175–79.

18. *Reformed Confessions*, 4:353.

19. On God's aseity and sufficiency, see *RST*, 1:645–49.

20. Spring, *Essays on the Distinguishing Traits of Christian Character*, 71–75; and William S. Plumer, *Vital Godliness: A Treatise on Experimental and Practical Piety* (1864; repr., Harrisonburg, VA: Sprinkle, 1993), 331–37.

salvation; by trusting God and surrendering our entire lives, including all our trials, into his loving and fatherly hands; by walking cheerfully and humbly before God and our neighbors in increasing conformity to Christ's image; and by fervently setting our minds on the things that are above and longing to be with God forever.

Strong love makes us zealous: "fervent in spirit; serving the Lord" (Rom. 12:11). Thomas Aquinas said, "Zeal . . . arises from the intensity of love."[21] Edwards said, "Christian zeal [is] . . . indeed a flame, but a sweet one: or rather it is the heat and fervor of a sweet flame. For the flame of which it is the heat, is no other than that of divine love."[22] No zeal burns hotter or more sweetly than the Father's love for his Son (Isa. 9:7). Insofar as God's love dwells in men, they too are zealous for Christ. William Plumer said, "Genuine love to Christ does not regard any service it can render, or any sacrifice it can make, as too great for the honor of Christ."[23] Zealous love moved a godly woman to pour fragrant ointment worth a year's wages on Jesus while others stood amazed at this lavish gift (Mark 14:3–9).

Spirit-worked love for God is absolute and all-consuming (Rom. 12:1). Since God is the infinite good (Ps. 36:5–9) and the giver of all finite good (James 1:17), love for the one true God rightly demands our whole being (Deut. 6:5) and the subordination of all other loves to him (Matt. 10:37). In every spark of love that is the fruit of the Spirit, there is the glad assertion, "The Lord he is God; and there is none else" (Deut. 4:35; cf. Isa. 45:22).

Second, *love is giving oneself to do good to people.* This is evident both in the gospel of God's love and in the parable of the good Samaritan. Love shows kindness (1 Cor. 13:4) and requires us to lay down our lives for one another (John 15:12–13) and to do good (Matt. 5:44).

Doing good to other people can take various forms.[24] We might give them good things that they need or that would increase their happiness, whether spiritual goods, by praying for their salvation or speaking God's truth to them, or temporal goods, such as food, drink, clothing, medicine, or money. We might give our time and labor to help them, such as by cleaning their homes, teaching or counseling them, or providing political

21. Aquinas, *Summa Theologica*, Part 2.1, Q. 28, Art. 4, Answer.
22. Edwards, *Religious Affections*, in *WJE*, 2:352. See Joel R. Beeke and James A. La Belle, *Living Zealously*, Deepen Your Christian Life (Grand Rapids, MI: Reformation Heritage Books, 2012).
23. Plumer, *Vital Godliness*, 356.
24. See Edwards, *Charity and Its Fruits*, in *WJE*, 8:207–9.

or legal advocacy. We also might reduce their suffering, such as through companionship or by asking questions and listening sympathetically.

Love is an orientation of one's whole life to live for the good of others—indeed, to die if necessary. God did not merely give salvation but gave "his only begotten Son" (John 3:16). Christ "gave himself" for his people to die for their sins.[25] He set the pattern for his people to follow: "By this we know love, that he laid down his life for us, and we ought to lay down our lives for the brothers" (1 John 3:16 ESV; cf. John 10:11, 15, 17; 15:13). Ordinarily, this does not require dying for others but living for others in daily sacrifice.

People might consider themselves to be loving because they do some good works, but Christlike love consists of an orientation of the whole life to serve others (Gal. 5:13). Rather than viewing themselves as lords to be served, believers follow Christ in making themselves servants and viewing their lives as resources to give to others (Matt. 20:26–28).

Love is an active principle: faith "worketh by love" (Gal. 5:6). John says, "If anyone has the world's goods and sees his brother in need, yet closes his heart against him, how does God's love abide in him? Little children, let us not love in word or talk but in deed and in truth" (1 John 3:17–18 ESV). Thus, an essential test of love is the good that one does to help those who lack necessities, especially brethren in Christ (Matt. 25:34–40).

Third, *love is giving oneself graciously*, for it comes not from any goodness inherent in man but from the loving and lovely nature of God. The gospel of Christ's cross displays God's love for unworthy sinners (Rom. 5:6–8). Christ commands us to love those who hate us because of who our Father is (Matt. 5:44–45). William Perkins said, "The love of God is a holy affection whereby we love God in Christ for Himself. . . . The love of our neighbor is to love him simply, in and for the Lord, and for no other by-respect."[26]

Edwards said, "Love to God is the foundation of a gracious love to men. Men are loved either because they are in some respect like God, either they have the nature or spiritual image of God; or because of their relation to God as his children, as his creatures, as those who are beloved of God, or those to whom divine mercy is offered."[27]

25. Gal. 1:4; 2:20; Eph. 5:25; 1 Tim. 2:6; Titus 2:14; cf. Eph. 5:2; Heb. 9:14.
26. Perkins, *Commentary on Galatians*, on Gal. 5:22–23, in *Works*, 2:383.
27. Edwards, *Charity and Its Fruits*, in *WJE*, 8:133–34.

God works love in human hearts by his grace. All Christian love is gracious, for it originates "of God; and every one that loveth is born of God" (1 John 4:7). "Herein is love, not that we loved God, but that he loved us. . . . We love him, because he first loved us" (vv. 10, 19).

Love motivates Christians to do good to others though they anticipate no repayment from them—as a free gift of grace. Christ says, "If ye love them which love you, what thank have ye? For sinners also love those that love them. And if ye do good to them which do good to you, what thank have ye? For sinners also do even the same. And if ye lend to them of whom ye hope to receive, what thank have ye? For sinners also lend to sinners, to receive as much again" (Luke 6:32–34). Christlike love intentionally gives to those who cannot give back to us, trusting in the God of love to reward us at the resurrection (14:12–14). The beauty of love is that it finds its reward in the beloved, as Paul says, "For what is our hope, or joy, or crown of rejoicing? Are not even ye in the presence of our Lord Jesus Christ at his coming? For ye are our glory and joy" (1 Thess. 2:19–20).

Fourth, *love is giving oneself righteously*. The same apostle who writes, "God is love," also says, "God is light"—that is, he is truth and righteousness (1 John 1:5; 4:8). His love did not deny his justice but satisfied it by sending "his Son to be the propitiation for our sins" (4:10). Love is not morally indifferent, for love "rejoiceth not in iniquity, but rejoiceth in the truth" (1 Cor. 13:6). Jesus Christ says, "He that hath my commandments, and keepeth them, he it is that loveth me" (John 14:21). Plumer said, "We may know that we love God by our cheerful, earnest obedience to his will."[28]

Therefore, we never have the right to disobey God's moral law and to justify our unrighteous behavior on the basis of love. Paul says, "Let love be genuine. Abhor what is evil; hold fast to what is good" (Rom. 12:9 ESV)—that is, cling to what is pleasing to God and according to his holy will (vv. 1–2). The word translated as "genuine" (*anypokritos*) literally means "without hypocrisy" (cf. James 3:17). By implication, any so-called love that does not move us to hate sin and cling to good is a false love that puts on a show to please people. Our love must be an image of God's love, and "the righteous Lord loveth righteousness" (Ps. 11:7); indeed, "He loveth righteousness and judgment: the earth is full of the goodness of the Lord" (33:5).

28. Plumer, *Vital Godliness*, 343.

The righteousness of love implies that the acts of love are guided by wisdom, for we are stewards of God's resources (Matt. 25:14–30) and must be faithful to our responsibilities in family, church, and so on (Gal. 6:7, 10; 1 Tim. 5:8). When God gives an increase in love, he generally accompanies it with an increase in discernment (cf. Heb. 5:14), for love is pure and holy (Phil. 1:9–10), and the wisdom from above is gentle and merciful (James 3:17).

Fifth, *love is giving oneself for the sake of friendship*. Love tends to create relationships of friendship, fellowship, and partnership if it is mutual. We might define friendship as "the personal bond of shared life."[29] God's general goodness to mankind would lead them to turn to him if it were not for their hard and unrepentant hearts (Rom. 2:4–5). God gave his Son in love to effectually reconcile sinners to himself so that believers would have eternal life, which consists of knowing him experientially (John 3:16; 17:3; Rom. 5:6–11). When by God's grace a person loves and obeys Christ, the Father and the Son respond with the love of delight in that person, reveal themselves further to him, and manifest their presence in him (John 14:21, 23). Amazingly, the Lord counts his people as his "friends" (15:13–15).[30] Therefore, as Aquinas said, Christian love is friendship.[31] Friendship begins with God. John Mason (d. 1694) said, "How can we expect to live with God in heaven, if we love not to live with him on earth?"[32]

Love, in its most realized sense, is benevolence (the will to do good) and complacency (delight in one's beloved).[33] John says he proclaimed the gospel "that ye also may have fellowship with us: and truly our fellowship is with the Father, and with his Son Jesus Christ" (1 John 1:3). Augustine said that love is a living principle that unites or seeks to unite the one who loves with his beloved.[34] Wilhelmus à Brakel said that love that is worked by God engages the heart of God's children "with desires to have harmonious fellowship with their neighbor."[35]

Mutual love unites our lives with each other. Scripture speaks of "thy friend, which is as thine own soul," though it demands that our love for

---

29. Joel R. Beeke, *Friends and Lovers: Cultivating Companionship and Intimacy in Marriage* (Adelphi, MD: Cruciform, 2012), 11.
30. See also 2 Chron. 20:7; Isa. 41:8; Luke 12:4; James 2:23.
31. "*Charitas est amicitia.*" Aquinas, *Summa Theologica*, Part 2.2, Q. 23, Art. 1; cf. Q. 27, Art. 2; Part. 2.1; Q. 28, Art. 1.
32. *Select Remains of the Rev. John Mason* (New York: G. & C. Carvill et al., 1825), 68.
33. On God's love of benevolence and love of complacency, see *RST*, 1:794–97.
34. Augustine, *On the Trinity*, 8.10.14, in *NPNF*[1], 3:124.
35. Brakel, *The Christian's Reasonable Service*, 4:53.

the Lord must be supreme (Deut. 13:6). Jonathan loved David "as his own soul," and their souls were knit together as one (1 Sam. 18:1, 3; 20:17). Augustine wrote, "Well did one say of his friend, 'Thou half of my soul,' for I felt that my soul and his soul were but one soul in two bodies."[36] Given the intensity of love that can be shared between friends, and the grief of losing a friend, Augustine prayed, "Blessed be he who loveth Thee, and his friend in Thee, and his enemy for Thy sake."[37] Only God can create "true friendship" by bonding people together with the love poured out by the Holy Spirit.[38]

Christians "are one body in Christ, and every one members one of another" (Rom. 12:5). Christian love leads us not only to do good but to build good relationships with one another in "brotherly love" (vv. 9–16), even with our enemies by overcoming evil with good insofar as it is in our power (vv. 17–21).

Friendship involves mutual loyalty, affection, unity, communication, knowledge, joy, and partnership in shared concerns (Phil. 1:3–8, 24–26; 2:19–30).[39] As brethren in God's household, believers share the highest common concern: obedience to God's will (Matt. 12:50). Their chosen companions are faithful men and women who fear the Lord (Pss. 101:6; 119:63). Jonathan Holmes notes that "biblical friendship" is not "an end in itself" but exists when people are "bound together by a common faith in Jesus Christ, [and] pursue him and his kingdom with intentionality and vulnerability."[40] Such friendship, Holmes says, requires "constancy, candor, carefulness, and counsel."[41]

We cannot overestimate the importance of brotherly love in the Christian life. The apostle John explains that love for God's children is evidence that one belongs to the same Spirit-renewed family: "We know that we have passed from death unto life, because we love the brethren. He that loveth not his brother abideth in death" (1 John 3:14; cf. 4:20–5:1).

---

36. Augustine, *Confessions*, 4.6.11, in *NPNF*[1], 1:71.
37. Augustine, *Confessions*, 4.9.14, in *NPNF*[1], 1:72.
38. Augustine, *Confessions*, 4.4.7, in *NPNF*[1], 1:70.
39. On the nature of friendship, see Ex. 33:11; Deut. 13:6; Job 2:11; 6:14; 19:21; 42:10; Prov. 17:17; 22:24–25; 27:5–6, 9–10, 17; John 15:13–15. See also Joel R. Beeke and Michael A. G. Haykin, *How Should We Cultivate Biblical Friendship?*, Cultivating Biblical Godliness (Grand Rapids, MI: Reformation Heritage Books, 2015).
40. Jonathan Holmes, *The Company We Keep: In Search of Biblical Friendship* (Adelphi, MD: Cruciform, 2014), 27.
41. Holmes, *The Company We Keep*, 47.

Diagnostic Questions about Christlike Love

The systematic description of love in the previous section provides us with questions we can use for self-examination. If you believe you might have Christlike love, you can test it by asking yourself the following questions:

- Am I actively glorifying God and serving other people for their good at some cost to myself, or is my love a mere wish or feeling that leads to little or no action?
- Am I a servant who gives away my life to others or a lord who seeks to make others serve and honor me—even to honor me for my good works?
- Do I sincerely desire in my heart to do good to others, or are my acts of love compelled by other considerations?
- Do I love and serve others despite their sins, simply because of God's grace, or do I withhold love from those I deem unworthy or who have wronged me?
- Do I love people in ways that show love for God and obedience to his holy laws, or do I view love as morally indifferent, perhaps even an excuse for sin?
- Am I loving people as persons created in God's image, with respect for their thoughts and feelings, or do I treat people as if they were things to be used?
- Insofar as it depends on me, am I building lasting friendships with the people whom I love, or am I keeping my distance and isolating myself?
- Do I have a special love for God's people and delight in spiritual fellowship with them, such that I would be willing to lay down my life for the brethren?

Christlike love that shows itself in good works is a primary mark of grace for our assurance. It is also an evidence to show the world. Christ says, "A new commandment I give unto you, That ye love one another; as I have loved you, that ye also love one another. By this shall all men know that ye are my disciples, if ye have love one to another" (John 13:34–35).

The Other Fruit of the Spirit: The Beauties of Christlike Love

Paul says, "Love is patient and kind; love does not envy or boast; it is not arrogant or rude. It does not insist on its own way; it is not irritable or resentful; it does not rejoice at wrongdoing, but rejoices with the truth. Love bears all things, believes all things, hopes all things, endures all things" (1 Cor. 13:4–7 ESV). It is evident from this statement that the other fruit of the Spirit (joy, patience, kindness, meekness, etc.) are an exposition of love.

The Spirit's Fruit of Joy

The second fruit of the Spirit that Paul names after love is joy. The word translated as "joy" (*chara*, Gal. 5:22) means happiness or gladness, and it is used in other contexts for worldly joy (James 4:9) and superficial and passing pleasures (Prov. 14:13; Joel 1:12 LXX). However, those in Christ have joy of a different source and character—joy from the Holy Spirit.[42]

Even in times of great hardship, the Lord can give his people joy that is better than earthly prosperity and feasting (Ps. 4:7). They rejoice because they know God's name and trust in him (9:2, 10; 32:10–11; 33:21). They rejoice in his Word because it is righteous (19:8; 119:14, 111, 162). Through the ordinances of public worship, they draw near to God, "unto God my exceeding joy" (43:4; cf. 16:11), and "serve the Lord with gladness" (100:2). His presence with his people is like a river that makes them glad (36:8–9; 46:4–5). They observe with joy his just and righteous works as he reigns over the world (48:11; 67:4; 97:1, 8, 11–12).

Spiritual joy does not come from earthly goods or success, but through communion with God by faith. God's people rejoice *in the Lord* (1 Sam. 2:1). Habakkuk says, "Though the fig tree should not blossom, nor fruit be on the vines, the produce of the olive fail and the fields yield no food, the flock be cut off from the fold and there be no herd in the stalls, yet I will rejoice in the Lord; I will take joy in the God of my salvation. God, the Lord, is my strength; he makes my feet like the deer's; he makes me tread on my high places" (Hab. 3:17–19 ESV).

Authentic Spirit-worked joy is distinguished by its God-centered orientation from merely natural joy (Ps. 104:15; Acts 14:17), sinful joy (Prov. 2:14; 15:21; 1 Pet. 4:3), idolatrous joy (Acts 7:41; 1 Cor. 10:7), and hypocritical joy at God's Word that manifests no true and enduring change of heart (Mark 6:20; 12:37; Luke 8:13; John 5:35). True spiritual joy is Christ's own joy, as we see when he rejoices by the Spirit in the glory of

42. Luke 10:21; Acts 13:52; Rom. 14:17; 15:13; 1 Thess. 1:6.

the Father's sovereign grace (Luke 10:20–21) and in doing the Father's will and enjoying communion with his love (John 15:10–11).

The chief distinguishing mark of spiritual joy is that it accompanies Christlike love. As Augustine said, joy is having and delighting in what one loves, and the goodness or evil of one's joy depends on what one loves.[43] The Spirit moves people to rejoice because they love God; his attributes, will, and works are their delight. Their hearts echo the cry "Rejoice in the Lord, O ye righteous: for praise is comely for the upright. . . . For the word of the Lord is right; and all his works are done in truth" (Ps. 33:1, 4). Joy in God is love for God, "the sweet motion of the heart toward God," as Brakel said, by which they "delight themselves in God, and in a joyous embrace of His will, fully surrender themselves in His service."[44]

Hence, spiritual joy is completely compatible with sorrow over our sins or those of other people, for sin is contrary to God, our great joy, and to the well-being of people created in his image. Indeed, those who grieve most over sin rejoice most over salvation.[45] We also must make allowance for Christians who, like William Cowper (1731–1800), are sometimes "covered with the ooze and mud of melancholy."[46] Even when a Christian's joy is hindered by fears about his own salvation, as John Evans (1679–1730) said, "it is the habitual and fixed judgment of his mind, that Christ and his benefits are more fit to be rejoiced in, than all worldly good."[47]

The Spirit also moves people to rejoice because they love their neighbors as themselves. They rejoice with God and the angels when they hear that a perishing sinner has repented and been saved (Luke 15:5–7, 9–10, 23–24, 32). This is the joy that causes the one who "sheweth mercy" to do so "with cheerfulness"; it stirs the members of Christ's body to "rejoice with them that do rejoice" (Rom. 12:8, 15), for when "one member be honoured, all the members rejoice with it" (1 Cor. 12:26). It is the joy of the "cheerful giver" (2 Cor. 9:7). It moves a man to say, "I will very gladly

43. Augustine, *The City of God*, 14.7, in *NPNF*[1], 2:267.

44. Brakel, *The Christian's Reasonable Service*, 3:264. This quotation is taken from Brakel's definition of love for God.

45. John W. Sanderson, *The Fruit of the Spirit: A Study Guide* (Grand Rapids, MI: Zondervan, 1972), 64–65.

46. William Cowper, Letter to William Hatley, Oct. 5, 1793, in *The Works of William Cowper: His Life, Letters, and Poems*, ed. T. S. Grimshawe, 7th ed. (London: William Tegg, 1865), 428.

47. John Evans, *Practical Discourses concerning the Christian Temper* (London: Richard Baynes, 1825), 152.

spend and be spent for you" (12:15) and "We are glad, when we are weak, and ye are strong" (13:9). It is the joy of love.[48]

Though Christlike joy is a fruit of the Holy Spirit, it is the duty of every child of God to seek this grace and "rejoice in the Lord always" (Phil. 4:4 ESV). Jerry Bridges noted that a Christian's joy can be hindered by unrepented sin and the divine discipline it incurs (Pss. 32:3–4; 51:12; Heb. 12:11), trusting in our own righteousness (Phil. 3:1–3), focusing on ministry success (Luke 10:17–20), or failing to count trials as God's means to mature us (James 1:2–4).[49] The apostle Paul writes, "Rejoice evermore. Pray without ceasing. In every thing give thanks: for this is the will of God in Christ Jesus concerning you" (1 Thess. 5:16–18). Let us therefore seek God's grace in fervent prayer that we may be "strengthened with all might, according to his glorious power, unto all patience and longsuffering with joyfulness" (Col. 1:11).

Do you consider God, Christ, and his kingdom to be your supreme joys? Do you serve the Lord with gladness, delighting in his greatness and goodness? Are you happiest when serving other people? That is the character of Jesus Christ.

The Spirit's Fruit of Peace

In the Holy Scriptures, the words translated as "peace" (Hebrew *shalom*, Greek *eirēnē*) refer to harmonious relationships that are according to justice and to the prosperity that such relationships bring to individuals and the community.[50] The Lord is called the "God of peace,"[51] for "The LORD Is Peace" (Judg. 6:24 ESV). Sinners do not know the way of peace, being alienated from God and each other (Rom. 3:10–17). They may, however, have a false spiritual peace, a deluded security while they refuse to repent of sin and ignore God's warnings of judgment.[52] But this is not genuine peace, for "there is no peace . . . for the wicked (Isa. 48:22; 57:21 ESV).

God creates an objective peace between himself and his people by the reconciliation that he accomplished through Christ.[53] Christ *is* our peace in his priestly reconciliation of us to God (Eph. 2:14–16), his prophetic

48. Perkins, *Commentary on Galatians*, on Gal. 5:22–23, in *Works*, 2:384; cf. *An Exposition of the Symbol*, in *Works*, 5:317.
49. Bridges, *The Practice of Godliness*, 109–13.
50. On peace as prosperity or well-being, see Pss. 35:27; 73:3; Jer. 29:7, 11.
51. Rom. 15:33; 16:20; Phil. 4:9; 1 Thess. 5:23; Heb. 13:20.
52. Deut. 29:19; Jer. 6:14–15; 8:11–12; Ezek. 13:10, 16; Mic. 3:5; 1 Thess. 5:3.
53. See *RST*, 2:1001–3.

announcement of the gospel of peace (Acts 10:36, 43; Rom. 10:15; Eph. 2:17), and his kingly reign (Mic. 5:2–5; Zech. 9:9–10). He merits peace, proclaims peace, works peace, and preserves peace. Christ, the Prince of Peace, came to bring his kingdom of peace (Isa. 9:6–7), which has already begun in the work of the Holy Spirit (32:15–18; Rom. 14:17). Unlike the false peace of hypocrites, this royal peace comes from the true "God of peace" who makes his people holy by the grace of Christ (1 Thess. 5:23; Heb. 13:20–21).

Christ's spiritual peace has corporate and individual dimensions. Corporately, God is creating a people of peace (Eph. 4:3; Col. 3:15) whose Spirit-formed, Christlike character promotes human relationships of peace, which we discussed in our study of the Beatitudes.[54] This peace is an outworking of their obedience in loving their neighbors as themselves.

Individually, believers enjoy subjective, inward "peace," like the internal "joy" listed before it in the fruit of the Spirit (Gal. 5:22), for they are the recipients of God's blessed peace: "Peace be on them, and mercy, and upon the Israel of God" (6:16). John Gill said, "The gospel of peace . . . speaks peace to the conscience of sinners, when Christ comes by his Spirit, and preaches peace unto them, and makes the word effectual to such a purpose."[55] There is "no condemnation" for believers in Christ (Rom. 8:1). Consequently, by the indwelling Spirit (v. 9) they have received a mindset of "life and peace," an inward state of reconciled and submissive harmony with God, in contrast to "death" and "enmity against God" (vv. 6–7).

Such inner divine peace relieves believers' minds of the fear that God's holiness will destroy them, and it strengthens them to serve him (Judg. 6:23–24; Dan. 10:19). It empowers them to fearlessly persevere though the world persecutes them (Ps. 4:8; John 14:27; 16:33). It gives them quietness and rest by trusting in the Lord (Isa. 7:4; 26:3; 30:15). It assures them of forgiveness (Luke 7:48–50), for their consciences have been cleansed by the blood of Christ (Heb. 9:14).

The believer who experientially enjoys this peace confesses, "The Lord is my shepherd; I shall not want. He maketh me to lie down in green pastures: he leadeth me beside the still waters" (Ps. 23:1–2), literally "waters of quietness" (KJV mg.). Andrew Fuller (1754–1815) said that

54. See the section on peacemakers in chap. 35.
55. Gill, *Body of Divinity*, 783.

peace consists of "that sweet tranquility of soul which arises from a well-grounded persuasion of being accepted by God," together with "that sweet satisfaction which possesses the mind from a view of God sitting at the helm of the universe, and having the management of all our concerns."[56]

God's people must work to maintain their inner peace. They must follow Paul's instructions so that "the peace of God, which passeth all understanding, shall keep [their] hearts and minds through [in] Christ Jesus": first, bringing all their requests to God with thanksgiving; second, setting their thoughts on God's perfections and whatever reflects them; and third, putting into practice holistic obedience to God's Word (Phil. 4:6–8). "Great peace have they which love thy law: and nothing shall offend them [make them stumble]" (Ps. 119:165). The essence of inner peace is the presence of the reconciled God—"the God of peace shall be with you" (Phil. 4:9).[57] Brakel said, "Peace consists in fellowship between the believing soul and God, this being characterized by oneness of heart, intimacy, friendliness, and love."[58] The enjoyment of this peaceful fellowship with God was pictured in Israel's eating the "peace offering" (Lev. 7:15, 20; Deut. 27:7) and now in the Lord's Supper (1 Cor. 10:16).[59] The peaceful believer says, "I love God and his will above all; therefore, I can be content in all circumstances, so long as I have him" (cf. Phil. 4:10–19). Peace is resting in God as one's "portion" (Ps. 73:25–26) so that in great calamities one can "quietly wait for the salvation of the LORD" (Lam. 3:24, 26).

Do you have the peace of a good conscience, knowing that your sins are forgiven and you are counted righteous by God for Christ's sake? Are you seeking peace in your relationships with other people? Do you have an experience of inner quietness because God is with you? This is the fruit of God's Spirit, poured out through Jesus Christ.

The Spirit's Fruit of Longsuffering or Patience

The word translated as "longsuffering" (*makrothymia*, Gal. 5:22) is a compound of terms meaning "long to wrath" (*makros* and *thymos*)—that is, "slow to anger." The adjective (*makrothymos*) renders God's attribute "slow to anger" in the Septuagint (Ex. 34:6; Num. 14:18, etc. LXX).[60]

56. Andrew Fuller, "The Peace of God," in *The Complete Works of the Rev. Andrew Fuller*, ed. Joseph Belcher, 3 vols. (Philadelphia: American Baptist Publication Society, 1845), 1:362–63.
57. See also Ps. 23:4; Isa. 41:10; Rom. 15:33; 2 Cor. 13:11; 2 Thess. 3:16.
58. Brakel, *The Christian's Reasonable Service*, 2:440.
59. Sanderson, *The Fruit of the Spirit*, 71.
60. On God's patience, see *RST*, 1:787–88. *Makrothymos* does not appear in the New Testament.

God often waits patiently before punishing sinners with his wrath (Rom. 9:22; 1 Tim. 1:16).

Edwards said, "A Christian spirit disposes persons meekly to bear ill which is received from others, or the injuries which others do them"—that is, to bear such wrongs "without doing anything to revenge them . . . with a continuance of love in the heart . . . without losing the quietness and repose of our minds," and with a willingness "to suffer considerably in our own interest for the sake of peace." Edwards noted that this fruit is called "*long*suffering" because it bears "a great deal of injurious treatment from others . . . [for] a great while."[61]

Longsuffering in men is frequently praised in the biblical Wisdom Literature as essential to wisdom, self-control, dignity, and good relationships.[62] Longsuffering bears kindly with people who offend, wrong, or injure a person (Matt. 18:26, 29; Eph. 4:2). Perkins noted that refraining from vengeance is wise because "we are often ignorant of the minds of men, in their actions, and of the true circumstances thereof." Since "anger is a sudden affection," this requires preparing our hearts "beforehand when we are quiet."[63] Thus, longsuffering is a form of love for other people: love "suffereth long" (*makrothymeō*)—that is, it exercises patience (1 Cor. 13:4).

Longsuffering also denotes patience under sorrow or injustice as one waits for the Lord's deliverance and reward.[64] A believer is greatly helped to grow in longsuffering when he meditates on the fact that no matter how badly he is being mistreated by another person, he has never been treated as badly as he himself has treated Christ. He never suffers nearly as much as he deserves. Furthermore, the believer can trust that God will not fail to keep his promises to his people. Bridges said, "To develop patience in the face of mistreatment by others, we must also develop a conviction about the faithfulness of God to work on our behalf."[65] The apostle Peter says, "Let them that suffer according to the will of God commit the keeping of their souls to him in well doing, as unto a faithful Creator" (1 Pet. 4:19).

Another term for "patience" (*hypomonē*) refers to perseverance under hardship. The godly are characterized by their endurance through trials

61. Edwards, *Charity and Its Fruits*, in *WJE*, 8:186, 189–92.
62. Prov. 14:29; 15:18; 16:32; 19:11; 25:15; Eccles. 7:8.
63. Perkins, *Commentary on Galatians*, on Gal. 5:22–23, in *Works*, 2:384.
64. Col. 1:11–12; Heb. 6:12, 15; James 5:7–8, 10.
65. Bridges, *The Practice of Godliness*, 169.

by trusting and obeying God's Word in hope until they attain to the promised glory.[66] Patience is essential to salvation: the one who "endureth [*hypomenō*] to the end shall be saved" (Matt. 10:22; cf. 24:13; James 1:12), just as Christ "for the joy that was set before him endured the cross, despising the shame, and is set down at the right hand of the throne of God" (Heb. 12:2).

The unconverted may exhibit a kind of patience in their courageous endurance of suffering to win glory for themselves or their nation.[67] Or they may be quietly resigned to suffering, believing their fate to be decreed by implacable gods or determined in an impersonal universe.[68]

However, Christian "patience" is motivated by hope that "the Lord is very pitiful, and of tender mercy" (James 5:11). Brakel said, "Patience is the believer's spiritual strength which he has in God whereby he, in the performance of his duty, willingly, with composure, joyfully, and steadfastly endures all the vicissitudes of life, having a hope that the outcome will be well."[69]

Christlike patience is especially driven by love, which "endureth all things" (1 Cor. 13:7). Stephen Charnock said that "the true nature of patience in regard of God . . . [is] a submission to God's sovereignty . . . acknowledging the supreme authority over him, and that he ought to be ordered by the will, and to the glory of God, more than by his own will, and for his own ease."[70] This is not fatalism but love for God, which leads the godly to say, "The Lord gave, and the Lord hath taken away; blessed be the name of the Lord" (Job 1:21). By faith that God is working all things for his glory in the good of his elect people (Rom. 8:28–29; Eph. 1:11–12), the patient Christian "endure[s] all things for the elect's sakes, that they may also obtain the salvation which is in Christ Jesus with eternal glory" (2 Tim. 2:10).

Do you restrain yourself from taking revenge on those who hurt and offend you because you love them? Are you trusting God and waiting patiently on him to deliver you from trials? Do your attitude and speech

66. Pss. 9:19 (18); 38:8 (39:7); 61:6 (62:5); 70 (71):5 LXX; Luke 8:15; Rom. 2:7; 5:3–4; 8:25; 15:4–5; 1 Thess. 1:3; Heb. 10:36; 12:1; James 1:3–4; Rev. 1:9; 2:2–3.

67. See Titus's speech to his soldiers in Josephus, *Wars of the Jews*, 6.1.5.33–44, in *Works*, 728–29; and the letter of Seneca, *Ad Lucilium Epistulae Morales*, trans. Richard M. Gummere, 3 vols., Loeb Classical Library 076 (London: William Heinemann, 1920), 67.9–10 (2:41).

68. For an example of resignation to materialistic determinism, see the quote of Bertrand Russell in *RST*, 2:1135.

69. Brakel, *The Christian's Reasonable Service*, 3:413.

70. Charnock, *The Existence and Attributes of God*, in *Works*, 2:499.

show that you love God and his will more than your own will? That is the character of Jesus Christ and those united to him by the Holy Spirit.

The Spirit's Fruit of Gentleness or Kindness

The word translated as "gentleness" (*chrēstotēs*, Gal. 5:22) or "kindness" (ESV) refers to benevolence to others, a disposition to do what is helpful or useful to them. It often translates "good" (*tob*) in the Septuagint.[71] This term is used to describe God's general goodness to mankind (Rom. 2:4). God is "kind" (*chrēstos*) to "unthankful" and "evil" people (Luke 6:35). He regenerates sinners because of his "kindness" (Titus 3:4–5) and will show "the exceeding riches of his grace in his kindness" in coming ages to those in Christ (Eph. 2:7).[72] Paul contrasts God's "goodness" (*chrēstotēs*) to believers and his "severity" in judging unbelievers (Rom. 11:22).

Human love necessarily involves kindness. Love "is kind" (*chrēsteuomai*, 1 Cor. 13:4). Man in the state of sin does not show this benevolence (Rom. 3:12), but God commands Christians to put on "kindness" (Col. 3:12) because of his love and forgiveness to them (Eph. 4:32). Kindness emphasizes the disposition of love to gladly do good to others, and since we have already given an exposition of love, we need not elaborate much more on kindness here.

However, before we leave this topic, we would point out the importance of kindness in our speech. Solomon says, "There is one whose rash words are like sword thrusts, but the tongue of the wise brings healing" (Prov. 12:18 ESV). Again, he writes, "A soft answer turneth away wrath: but grievous words stir up anger. . . . A wholesome [healing] tongue is a tree of life" (15:1, 4). Mary Beeke says, "It's like tea being infused into hot water. Will we infuse complaints, disgust, impatience, and irritation into the teapot of our home? Or will it be flavored with kindness, warmth, safety, comfort, appreciation, and love?"[73]

Are you gentle and kind toward other people? Does it please you to do good to them, even if you are not noticed and rewarded for it? Do your words communicate, both in content and tone, that other people are valuable? That is the image of Christ.

---

71. Pss. 13 (14):1, 3; 20:4 (21:3); 24 (25):7; 30:20 (31:19); 36 (37):3; 64:12 (65:11); 67:11 (68:10), etc. LXX.

72. On the goodness or kindness of God, see *RST*, 1:783–84.

73. Mary Beeke, *The Law of Kindness: Serving with Heart and Hands* (Grand Rapids, MI: Reformation Heritage Books, 2007), 187.

The Spirit's Fruit of Goodness

The word translated as "goodness" (*agathōsynē*, Gal. 5:22), not a common term in the New Testament,[74] refers to the quality of being or doing "good" (*agathos*), the opposite of "evil" or "bad" (Rom. 9:11; 12:9; 2 Cor. 5:10). Goodness has a broad meaning including moral righteousness, that which is pleasing to God, excellence, and benefit or usefulness. However, the biblical usage favors the idea of benefit. In the Greek Septuagint translation of the Old Testament, "goodness" (*agathōsynē*) refers to benefit given or enjoyed.[75] The confession that God is "good" is often coordinated with his "mercy" (*eleos*) continuing forever.[76] "Good" (*agathos*) and "kind" (*chrēstos*) can even be used interchangeably.[77]

Shortly after listing the fruit of the Spirit, Paul says, "Let us do good [*agathos*] unto all men" (Gal. 6:10). A "good" person has a loveliness in people's eyes that a "righteous" person might not (Rom. 5:7), implying that goodness, while including that which is morally pleasing to God according to his law (2:10; 7:12), especially connotes kindness to others (12:20–21; 13:4; 2 Cor. 9:8–9). This is the "goodness" that God has created in his people (Rom. 15:14; Eph. 5:9).

Therefore, we conclude that "goodness," like "gentleness" or "kindness" mentioned before it, refers to a disposition to do good to others. F. F. Bruce (1910–1990) suggested that in this context it could be rendered "generosity."[78] Jerry Bridges said, "Kindness and goodness are so closely related that they are often used interchangeably. These two traits . . . involve an active desire to recognize and meet the needs of others."[79] As we stated in our description of love, this is the very essence of Christian love. By listing these qualities among the fruit of the Spirit, indeed at the center

---

74. The term *agathōsynē* appears only in Rom. 15:14; Gal. 5:22; Eph. 5:9; 2 Thess. 1:11 in the New Testament.

75. See Judg. 8:35; 2 Chron. 24:16; Esdras B 19:25, 35; 23:31 (Neh. 9:25, 35; 13:31); Eccles. 4:8; 5:10, 17 (11, 18); 6:3, 6; 7:14; 9:18 LXX. The Greek term *agathōsynē* renders the Hebrew *tubah*, which in these texts and elsewhere refers to benefit (Gen. 44:4; 50:20; Ex. 18:9; Deut. 23:6; 28:11; 30:9, etc.).

76. 1 Chron. 16:34; 2 Chron. 5:13; 7:3; Ezra 3:11; Ps. 117 (118):1–4.

77. Compare "O give thanks unto the Lord; for he is good [*agathos*]: for his mercy endureth for ever" (Ps. 117 [118]:1 LXX) with the same statement using the other word for "good" (*chrēstos*, Ps. 135 [136]:1 LXX). See also "do good" (*chrēstotēs*, Ps. 36 [37]:3 LXX) as compared with "do good" (*agathos*, v. 27).

78. F. F. Bruce, *The Epistle to the Galatians*, The New International Greek Testament Commentary (Grand Rapids, MI: Eerdmans, 1982), 253.

79. Bridges, *The Practice of Godliness*, 189.

of the eight fruits subsequent to love, Paul emphasizes that Spirit-produced love moves a person to acts that help other people.

Are you good to other people? Do you help others at your own expense? Would a review of your actions demonstrate that you are generous with your time, abilities, money, and possessions? That is the character of a person united to Christ by the Spirit.

The Spirit's Fruit of Faith or Faithfulness

The word translated as "faith" (*pistis*, Gal. 5:22) can refer to either faith (vv. 5–6) or, less commonly in the New Testament, to faithfulness (Matt. 23:23; Rom. 3:3; Titus 2:10).[80] Though every other reference to "faith" in Galatians refers to faith, two factors make it highly likely that Paul intends "faithfulness" here. First, Paul surely would have given saving faith a place of prominence, but this quality appears near the middle of the list. Second, the other fruit of the Spirit pertain to aspects of love, but saving faith is not love. Therefore, "faith" here means "faithfulness."[81]

It is a fundamental axiom about the Lord that he is a "faithful" (*pistos*) God, which makes him the rock of his people (Deut. 7:9; 32:4 LXX). He is completely worthy of our trust, for he will most surely do what he has said and his words are entirely true (Num. 23:19; Titus 1:2). He acts with consistent righteousness and love (Ps. 111:7–8; Lam. 3:22–23).[82]

Since God is "true" (*pistos*), his servants must also be true to their word and to the God whom they represent (2 Cor. 1:18). A faithful person does not lie (Prov. 14:5). Faithfulness shows itself in both small and great matters (Luke 16:10). God's servant must prove "faithful" (1 Cor. 4:2), and it is the "faithful" servant who will receive honor and reward from the Lord when he returns (Matt. 24:45; 25:21, 23). Faithfulness is rare: "Most men will proclaim every one his own goodness: but a faithful man who can find?" (Prov. 20:6). Yet God promised to make his people a "faithful city" (Isa. 1:26). By God's grace, the believer practices faithfulness consistently across his various activities, public and private. George Bethune (1805–1862) said, "He will so govern his conduct in business, that he will not fear to open his books with his heart before the eyes of God, or to meet

80. For *pistis* as faithfulness, see also Deut. 32:20; 1 Kingdoms (1 Sam.) 26:23; 2 Chron. 34:12; Neh. 9:8; Ps. 32 (33):4; Prov. 3:3; 12:22; 14:22; Hos. 2:20 LXX.

81. The English word *faith* still occasionally carries the sense of "faithfulness," as in, "He acted in good faith."

82. On God's truth and faithfulness, see *RST*, 1:805–10.

the final appeal of both debtor and creditor to the Judge of quick and dead, who discerns the thoughts and detects the most secret sin."[83]

Therefore, faithfulness consists not merely of civil honesty, a virtue that can be found among unbelievers, but of living steadily in the fear of God. "He that walketh uprightly, and worketh righteousness, and speaketh the truth in his heart. . . . In whose eyes a vile person is contemned; but he honoureth them that fear the LORD. He that sweareth to his own hurt, and changeth not" (Ps. 15:2, 4). John Sanderson (1916–1998) said, "The faithfulness God has worked in His children is . . . an attachment to truth, a determination to persevere in it, that will not be shaken even when it is apparent that it will hurt the pocketbook, or will interfere with one's pleasure, or will mean the loss of an opportunity for personal advancement."[84] The greatest test of faithfulness is perseverance through suffering; hence, faithfulness is closely related to longsuffering and patience.[85]

Christian faithfulness is Christlike faithful love. The Christian's faithfulness is an image of God's character as "the faithful God who keeps covenant and steadfast love," and faithful people are those who "keep" God's covenant—"those who love him and keep his commandments" (Deut. 7:9, 12 ESV). Our faithfulness is the finite human reflection of God's infinite "steadfast love" (*khesed*), which is his "faithful love and affectionate loyalty."[86] This faithful love is what God desires,[87] for it is his very character and delight (Jer. 9:24; Mic. 7:18).

Are you a faithful Christian? Is there a consistent righteousness in your life, both in public and in private? Are you a person of God's Word and a person of your own word? God is faithful, Christ is faithful, and those indwelt by the Spirit are faithful as well.

The Spirit's Fruit of Meekness

The fruit of the Spirit translated as "meekness" (*praotēs*, Gal. 5:23) or "gentleness" (ESV) refers to humble self-restraint that makes one gentle to-

83. George W. Bethune, *The Fruit of the Spirit*, 4th ed. (New York: Board of Publication of the Reformed Protestant Dutch Church, 1859), 213.

84. Sanderson, *The Fruit of the Spirit*, 107.

85. See the chiastic structure proposed in the section on the order of the fruit earlier in this chapter.

86. This definition is cited from *RST*, 1:788.

87. See the use of *khesed* in Jer. 2:2; Hos. 4:1; 6:4, 6; 10:12; 12:6; Mic. 6:8, variously translated as "kindness," "mercy," and "goodness."

ward those with whom one might be harsh. We have already discussed this quality in the chapter on the Beatitudes and therefore may treat it more briefly here.[88] In that chapter, we noted that meekness qualifies a person to be a peacemaker (James 3:13–18),[89] for meekness involves inner quietness and calmness derived from knowing peace with God, which makes one humble and gentle toward God and one's neighbor.

It should be evident that meekness, too, is a form of Christlike love, for meekness toward God makes a Christian submissive to his will, and meekness toward people makes him willing to defer to their concerns before his own. It is important to include meekness at this point of our consideration of the Spirit's fruit lest we think that Christian faithfulness and temperance make a person severe with others. Love exercises its power to deal tenderly with people whenever possible for God's glory and their good.

Do you deny your pride and cultivate humility before God so that you are gentle with people? Are you curbing your sinful tendency to strive with others and growing in a quiet and meek spirit? Do you forgive those who sin against you and overlook many offenses? Such things are produced by the Holy Spirit when he joins a person to Jesus Christ.

The Spirit's Fruit of Temperance or Self-Control

The word translated as "temperance" (*enkrateia*, Gal. 5:23) or "self-control" (ESV) is a compound of words meaning "strength within" (*kratos* and *en*). The cognate verb (*enkrateuomai*) is used for the power to control one's weeping when full of emotion (Gen. 43:31 LXX), refrain from sexual activity when one desires it (1 Cor. 7:9), and discipline one's body in diet and exercise to train for athletic events (9:24–25). Therefore, "temperance" as a fruit of the Spirit is the Spirit-worked power to control oneself to conform to God's will despite inward passions and circumstances that might provoke us to sin.[90]

Self-control is an inward power, and though invisible it is more excellent than strength of body or military force. The man who can control himself has greater power than one who conquers a city (Prov. 16:32). Such self-control includes being "slow to anger," and so overlaps with longsuffering and patience. However, "he that hath no rule over his own

88. See the section on meekness in chap. 35.
89. See the section on peacemakers in chap. 35.
90. For a discussion of sober-mindedness (*sōphronismos*), sometimes translated as "self-control," see chap. 41.

spirit is like a city that is broken down, and without walls"—that is, he is easily conquered and controlled (25:28). Charles Bridges commented, "He yields himself to the first assault of his ungoverned passions."[91] A major area of life demanding self-control is one's speech (Prov. 13:3; 21:23). James says, "If any man among you seem to be religious, and bridleth not his tongue, but deceiveth his own heart, this man's religion is vain" (James 1:26). Self-control not only restrains bad behaviors but empowers us to engage in good behaviors with diligence and perseverance. "The soul of the sluggard craves and gets nothing, while the soul of the diligent is richly supplied" (Prov. 13:4 ESV).

Philosophers and moralists often praise self-control. Socrates (d. 399 BC) said, "Should not every man hold self-control to be the foundation of all virtue, and first lay this foundation firmly in his soul? For who without this can learn any good or practise it worthily? Or what man that is the slave of his pleasures is not in an evil plight body and soul alike?"[92] People can exercise self-control for many reasons, even to the point of mistreatment of the body, without any spiritual benefit (Isa. 58:3–7; Jer. 14:12; Col. 2:20–23). Bethune said, "A thief, who abstains from intoxication merely that he may more securely commit crime . . . can scarcely be called virtuous, though he may exert some self-command. It is in him one selfish principle overcoming another that is weaker."[93] Similarly, a self-righteous man might fast from food so that he can boast in his piety and impress other men—without pleasing God (Matt. 6:16; Luke 18:12).

Distinctively Christian self-control is motivated by Christlike love and directed by God's Word. The Christian is not to view his body as evil but as united to Christ and indwelt by the Holy Spirit (1 Cor. 6:15, 19). Self-control is not for the ultimate purpose of following human requirements or meeting personal goals, but for "the keeping of the commandments of God" (7:19). When Paul speaks of exercising temperance and mastering his body, he does so with regard to adapting himself to cultural norms (such as food) to be a "servant unto all" that he might win them to the gospel (9:19–27). As he applies this principle to how we should enjoy life

91. Bridges, *A Commentary on Proverbs*, 483.
92. Cited in Xenophon, *Memorabilia*, 1.5.4–5, in *Memorabilia and Oeconomicus; Symposium and Apology*, trans. E. C. Marchant and O. J. Todd, Loeb Classical Library 168 (London: William Heinemann, 1923), 67.
93. Bethune, *The Fruit of the Spirit*, 258–59.

in an idolatrous world, he makes clear that the reason for refusing certain foods is not because the body or its pleasures are evil—"for the earth is the Lord's, and the fulness thereof"—but because we must love God and serve one another: "Whether therefore ye eat, or drink, or whatsoever ye do, do all to the glory of God" (1 Cor. 10:26 [citing Ps. 24:1], 31).

Another distinctively Christlike trait of self-control is that Christians refuse to be ruled by their bodies because of their hope in the resurrection of the body (1 Cor. 6:13–14; Phil. 3:19–21). In other words, they do not restrain their bodies because the body is evil but because the body belongs to Christ and will one day fully glorify him. It is because we know that this age of darkness is passing away and the age of light is coming that Paul says, "Let us walk properly as in the daytime, not in orgies and drunkenness, not in sexual immorality and sensuality, not in quarreling and jealousy. But put on the Lord Jesus Christ, and make no provision for the flesh, to gratify its desires" (Rom. 13:13–14 ESV).

People exercise temperance or self-control based on what they love as their greatest joy. Augustine said, "Temperance is love giving itself entirely to that which is loved."[94] Christlike temperance is seeking first God, his kingdom, and his righteousness above the pleasures and comforts of this world. Therefore, by ending his list of the Spirit's fruit with temperance or self-control, Paul completes the circle by returning to where he began it: Christlike love, especially in its exercise of spiritual joy.

Do you exercise self-control over your passions because you love God and people more than your own pleasure and ease? Are you denying yourself for the sake of obedience? Do you have a hope in the kingdom of God that moves you to say no to some good things in this present age so that you may enjoy better things in the age to come? That is the character of a person united to Christ by the Holy Spirit of God.

Practical Conclusion to the Fruit of the Spirit

Paul concludes his list of the fruit of the Spirit by saying, "Against such there is no law" (Gal. 5:23). The word translated as "such" (plural *toioutos*) suggests that Paul could have listed other qualities, such as humility, hope, and so on.[95] The fruit of the Spirit encompass every dimension of keeping God's law through the indwelling activity of the Holy Spirit.

94. Augustine, *Of the Morals of the Catholic Church*, 15.25, in *NPNF*[1], 4:48.
95. Augustine, *On Continence*, chap. 9, in *ACCS/NT*, 8:90.

We do well to remember after a study of the fruit of the Spirit that, as Sanderson said, "the mere reading about them will not produce them."[96] Neither should we think that the word *fruit* implies an effortless result, for trees invest an enormous amount of energy into the production of fruit. Both before and after listing the fruit of the Spirit, Paul commands believers to "walk in the Spirit" (Gal. 5:16, 25), which requires that they make intentional, disciplined, and prolonged effort to live according to the Spirit's ways.[97]

Furthermore, we must not be satisfied to perform only occasional acts of love or to love in meager degrees, but should pray and labor for a great fullness of ripe, mature fruit in our lives. As we stated earlier in this study, the fruit of the Spirit is nothing less than the loving character and moral excellence of Jesus Christ. Christians should strive to reach that high and heavenly goal and look forward to heaven, where they shall finally attain it in perfection.

By a prayerful dependence on the grace of God and the work of his Spirit, pursue love as a holistic cluster of spiritual fruit. Love God and your fellow human beings not with a grim or resentful sorrow over what love costs you, but with joy in God, who is infinitely lovely. Seek peace in your heart and with others by your works of love and your delight in the presence of the God of peace.

Let your love be longsuffering and patient, persevering in submission to God and mercy to others in hope that God will bring you to his glory, which you love more than life itself. Show your love in works of practical kindness and goodness to others while cultivating an inner disposition that loves to do good and to see others prosper, especially in eternal life.

Exercise yourself in faithfulness so your love is consistent with God's faithful character and trustworthy Word. Follow Christ in the ways of meekness to allow your gentle humility to show the wise and winsome character of Jesus. Discipline yourself with self-control such that your attitudes, words, and actions all reflect your willing posture as an obedient servant of God and a loving servant of other people.

Cultivate the fruit of the Spirit in the garden of your life, and by God's grace your life will be increasingly full of the sweet fragrance of Jesus

96. Sanderson, *The Fruit of the Spirit*, 126.
97. On the duty of walking in the Spirit, see chap. 32.

Christ. You will discover that the Holy Spirit is sculpting and painting the image of Christ upon your soul, which is the hope of glory.

Sing to the Lord

Love, Joy, and Peace in Christ

I've found the pearl of greatest price!
My heart doth sing for joy;
And sing I must, for Christ is mine!
Christ shall my song employ.
(Repeat first verse as refrain)

Christ is my Prophet, Priest, and King;
My Prophet full of light,
My great High Priest before the Throne,
My King of heav'nly might.

For he indeed is Lord of lords,
And he the King of kings;
He is the Sun of righteousness
With healing in his wings.

Christ is my peace; he died for me,
For me he shed his blood;
And as my wondrous Sacrifice,
Offered himself to God.

Christ Jesus is my all in all,
My comfort and my love;
My life below, and he shall be
My joy and crown above.

John Mason
Tune: Jerusalem
Trinity Hymnal—Baptist Edition, No. 592

Questions for Meditation or Discussion

1. In Galatians 5, what is the significance of the fruit of the Spirit? What does that imply about how we might make application of this list?

2. What are some major ways that Christ revealed the meaning of love?
3. What description of love do the authors present? Show briefly how each part of the description is based on the Holy Scriptures.
4. How is Spirit-worked joy different from earthly joys?
5. How can a Christian cultivate inner peace?
6. What is longsuffering? How do we imitate God when we exercise it?
7. What does it mean, practically speaking, to show kindness and goodness to people?
8. Why is faithfulness essential to the Christian life?
9. How is meekness an exercise of love?
10. What is the difference between Christian self-control and that of the world?
11. Does your life exhibit the fruit of the Spirit? If not, how can you obtain it? If so, which of the fruit of the Spirit is most obviously in need of growth in your life? What practical steps will you take toward that goal?

Questions for Deeper Reflection

12. What do the authors tentatively propose regarding the order or structure of the fruit of the Spirit? What are the strengths and weaknesses of this approach?
13. Someone says, "I have to admit that I don't have much kindness or meekness, but I don't see why such things are important to keeping the law of God." How do you respond?

37

Obedience to God's Law, Part 1

Introduction and the First Two Commandments

The experience of salvation transforms our relationship to God's law. Justification delivers believers from the curse of the law and credits to them Christ's perfect obedience. Sanctification changes them so that they are able to do good works according to God's law. The Heidelberg Catechism (LD 33, Q. 90–91) says that spiritual life in Christ "is a sincere joy of heart in God, through Christ, and with love and delight to live according to the will of God in all good works," and good works are "only those which proceed from a true faith, are performed according to the law of God, and to His glory; and not such as are founded on our imaginations or the institutions of men."[1]

Therefore, believers need God's law. In the spiritual darkness of this world, the believer says of God's law, "Thy word is a lamp unto my feet, and a light unto my path" (Ps. 119:105). Paul says, "The law is holy, and the commandment holy, and just, and good" (Rom. 7:12). Christians "delight in the law of God" (v. 22). While the law can neither justify nor sanctify us, we need the revelation of righteousness God provides in the law. This is because while biblical spirituality is centered on union with Christ and empowered by the Holy Spirit, it is directed by the law of God. Augustine said, "By the

1. *The Three Forms of Unity*, 99–100.

precept He gave, God commended obedience, which is, in a sort, the mother and guardian of all the virtues in the reasonable creature."[2]

It may seem strange to encounter chapters on God's law in a systematic theology. However, classic Reformed theologies included sections expounding the Ten Commandments, for Reformed theologians insisted that theology is not merely theoretical but also practical.[3] Willem Teellinck (1579–1629) said, "The true Christian faith is knowledge that leads to godliness."[4] This requires that we "heartily wish and sincerely desire to understand as much as we can of the revealed will of God concerning us," and so we should pray with Psalm 119:33, "Teach me, O Lord, the way of thy statutes; and I shall keep it unto the end."[5]

Introduction to the Ten Commandments

God's Word reveals that the law given to Moses has three dimensions: moral, ceremonial, and judicial. Moral law refers to precepts of righteousness that obligate all mankind. As we argued in our treatment of covenant theology, the Ten Commandments summarize the moral law.[6] They themselves are summarized in the two great commandments to love God and to love our neighbors.[7] The Ten Commandments are, as Augustine said, "a harp of ten strings" on which we can make beautiful music to God (cf. Ps. 144:9).[8]

The Historical Setting and Preface of the Ten Commandments

The Lord spoke the Ten Commandments after he descended on Mount Sinai to engage the Israelites in a covenant requiring them to obey him as his holy people (Ex. 19:1–8). The voice of God proclaimed the commandments with an awesome display of his majestic holiness (vv. 9–25) to instill in Israel the fear of the Lord (20:19–20). The Lord inscribed the commandments on tablets of stone by his own power (31:18; 34:1).

The Ten Commandments are called "the words of the covenant" (Ex. 34:28) or simply "his covenant" (Deut. 4:13). They epitomized Israel's obligations to the Lord. Moses repeated them when Israel was poised to

2. Augustine, *The City of God*, 14.12, in *NPNF*[1], 2:273. The "precept" here is God's command to Adam.
3. See *RST*, 1:50–51, 60–62.
4. Willem Teellinck, *The Path of True Godliness*, trans. Annemie Godbehere, ed. Joel R. Beeke, Classics of Reformed Spirituality (Grand Rapids, MI: Reformation Heritage Books, 2003), 31.
5. Teellinck, *The Path of True Godliness*, 36–37.
6. On the moral, ceremonial, and judicial law, see *RST*, 2:683–94.
7. The Westminster Shorter Catechism (Q. 41–42), in *Reformed Confessions*, 4:359.
8. Augustine, Sermon 9.6, in *Works*, III/1:264.

enter the Promised Land (Deut. 5:1–21). Yet they were not merely for Israel, "for this is your wisdom and your understanding in the sight of the nations, which shall hear all these statutes, and say, Surely this great nation is a wise and understanding people" (4:6–8).

The Lord prefaced the Ten Commandments by saying, "I am the LORD thy God, which have brought thee out of the land of Egypt, out of the house of bondage" (Ex. 20:2). In so doing, he grounded our motivation to keep the law on three bases.[9] First, we must obey his commandments because he is the sovereign and faithful Lord over all his creation.[10] Second, he is "thy God," the God who has given himself in covenant to the seed of Abraham and has taken them to be his people (Gen. 17:7; Ex. 6:7). John Calvin said, "He holds out the promise of grace to draw them by its sweetness to a zeal for holiness."[11] Third, he saved Israel from slavery in Egypt, keeping his covenant in a massive display of sovereign grace (Ex. 2:24; 19:4–6). Similarly, Christians have been saved from slavery to sin and death by the grace of Christ.

These grounds or motives for obedience foreshadowed the great work of salvation promised in God's eternal covenant, according to which Christ gave himself to redeem a people for God and make them zealous to do what pleases him (Titus 2:14; Heb. 13:20–21). J. V. Fesko says, "We might state the prologue for today as: 'I am the LORD your God, who brought you out of slavery to Satan, sin, and death, by the life, death, and resurrection of Christ.'"[12] Thomas Boston said, "All men are obliged to keep these commandments, for God is Lord of all: but the saints especially; for besides being their Lord, he is their God and Redeemer too."[13]

We must not underestimate what an astounding thing it is for us that the holy God says to sinners, "I am the LORD thy God." The Lord's words ground all true obedience to the Ten Commandments on the sovereign grace of the triune God. Ebenezer Erskine said, "These words, 'I am the Lord thy God,' contain the leading promise of the covenant of grace; and there is more in them than heart can conceive, or tongue express; for here is an infinite God, Father, Son, and Holy Ghost, making over himself in two or three words to man upon earth. O what can he give more than himself! And what will he not

---

9. The Westminster Shorter Catechism (Q. 44), in *Reformed Confessions*, 4:359.

10. On the meaning of the divine name "the LORD" or "I AM" (Ex. 3:14), denoting his sovereign, independent lordship and faithful covenantal presence with his people, see *RST*, 1:549–65 (chap. 29).

11. Calvin, *Institutes*, 2.8.13.

12. J. V. Fesko, *The Rule of Love: Broken, Fulfilled, and Applied* (Grand Rapids, MI: Reformation Heritage Books, 2009), 12.

13. Boston, *An Illustration of the Doctrines of the Christian Religion*, in *Works*, 2:90.

give when he gives himself!"[14] This is because the words of the preface reflect the eternal purpose "in the heart of God" toward the elect, are "proclaimed to the visible church" in Israel and now also among the Gentiles, and are to be personally "applied and possessed in a way of believing" when taken up "in the hand of faith." In them, God commits himself to be "the soul's portion and inheritance forever," and in giving himself gives all life, light, love, honor, riches, and joy—for all who reside in him. "He engages that all the attributes and perfections of his glorious nature shall jointly conspire and be forthcoming for thy good," Erskine said. Whatever "the infinite and eternal God" can do for our benefit will not be lacking for those who have him as their God.[15] It is out of this overflowing fullness of grace that we obey the Ten Commandments, not out of our wisdom or willpower but out of Jesus Christ, the Mediator of the covenant of grace. It should not offend us, then, that this God would demand that we offer up all we are to him in obedience after he has given all that he is to us in his Son. The preface to the Ten Commandments shows that the covenant unfurled at Mount Sinai was not a covenant of works but an administration of the covenant of grace.[16]

The Form of the Ten Commandments

The "ten commandments" (Ex. 34:28; Deut. 4:13; 10:4) are literally the "ten words" (Greek *deka logoi*, hence, the "Decalogue"). However, God did not explicitly number the commandments, and there are more than ten verbal commands in the list.

In Judaism, what we call the preface (Ex. 20:2) is considered the first "word," and the prohibitions of other gods and graven images are counted as the second (vv. 3–6). However, the preface contains no command, whereas the "words" that follow do.

Roman Catholic and Lutheran theologians, following Augustine, count the first commandment to be the prohibitions against other gods and idols (vv. 3–6), the ninth to be the prohibition against coveting one's neighbor's house (v. 17), and the tenth to be the prohibition against coveting his wife, servants, or possessions (v. 17).[17] However, there is a distinction between whom

14. Ebenezer Erskine, *A Treasure of Gospel Grace Digged out of Mount Sinai*, in *The Whole Works of the Late Rev. Ebenezer Erskine*, 3 vols. (Edinburgh: Ogle & Murray et al., 1871), 2:22. On the Lord's promise to be their God and to take them as his people as the central promise of the covenant of grace, see *RST*, 2:658–61.

15. Erskine, *A Treasure of Gospel Grace Digged out of Mount Sinai*, in *Works*, 2:23–25.

16. On the relation of the Mosaic covenant to the covenant of works and the covenant of grace, see *RST*, 2:626–32.

17. *Catechism of the Catholic Church*, secs. 2066–67; and the Small Catechism (1.1–22), in *The Book of Concord*, 351–54; cf. Augustine, Letters, 55.11.20, in *NPNF*[1], 1:309.

we may not worship (false gods) and how we may not worship (images). Both Josephus and Origen distinguished these as two commandments.[18] Furthermore, Moses's later restatement of the Ten Commandments changed the order in listing what we may not covet, making the Augustinian enumeration impossible (Deut. 5:21). Paul treats the whole prohibition against coveting as one: "The law had said, Thou shalt not covet" (Rom. 7:7).[19]

Therefore, the Ten Commandments are best numbered as in the table below:

Commandment	Statement or Summary
First	Thou shalt have no other gods before me.
Second	Thou shalt not make unto thee any graven image.
Third	Thou shalt not take the name of the Lord thy God in vain.
Fourth	Remember the sabbath day, to keep it holy.
Fifth	Honor thy father and thy mother.
Sixth	Thou shalt not kill.
Seventh	Thou shalt not commit adultery.
Eighth	Thou shalt not steal.
Ninth	Thou shalt not bear false witness.
Tenth	Thou shalt not covet.

Table 37.1. The Ten Commandments

The comprehensiveness of these ten words asserts God's authority over every facet of human existence. The first four commandments pertain directly to our relationship to God, and the latter six to our relationships with people. This division is often referred to as the "two tables" of the law.[20] The two tables correspond to what Christ called the "great

18. Josephus, *Antiquities of the Jews*, 3.91, in *Works*, 85; and Origen, *Homilies on Exodus*, 8.2–3, in *Homilies on Genesis and Exodus*, trans. Ronald E. Heine, The Fathers of the Church 71 (Washington, DC: The Catholic University of America Press, 1982), 318–20.

19. Godefridus Udemans, *The Practice of Faith, Hope, and Love*, trans. Annemie Godbehere, ed. Joel R. Beeke, Classics of Reformed Spirituality (Grand Rapids, MI: Reformation Heritage Books, 2012), 194–95.

20. The Ten Commandments were written on two stone tablets (Ex. 31:18; 32:15; 34:1, 4, 29; Deut. 4:13; 5:22; 9:10–11, 15, 17; 10:1, 3; 1 Kings 8:9; 2 Chron. 5:10), but the Scriptures do not tell us which commandments were inscribed on which tablets or if God wrote two copies of the commandments, one copy on each tablet.

commandment," regarding our duty to God, and the "second," regarding our duty to man (Matt. 22:37–40).

The Rules of Interpretation for the Ten Commandments

To recognize the Ten Commandments as a summary of the moral law and discern the richness of their instruction, we need to interpret them according to the following rules.[21]

First, *negative prohibitions imply positive duties, and vice versa.* God revealed eight of the Ten Commandments in a negative form—"Thou shalt not," or the like. However, by revealing what he hates and forbids, God also reveals by implication what he loves and requires. For example, the prohibition against adultery shows that God values faithful love in marriage.[22]

Second, *precepts regarding external acts imply inward attitudes and affections.* Many of the commandments focus on outward acts, but the tenth commandment prohibits sinful desires, showing that God is concerned with the heart. In the second commandment, the Lord speaks of people who "hate me" and people who "love me" (Ex. 20:5–6). Therefore, the moral law addresses the heart, as Christ stated in the Sermon on the Mount (Matt. 5:8, 21–22, 27–28). This property of the commandments is called *the spirituality of the law* (Rom. 7:7–14).[23]

Third, *the Ten Commandments express God's created order* (Genesis 1). The very form of the two accounts links them, for both contain ten words from God.[24] The second and fourth commandments allude to the creation account (Ex. 20:4, 11). The prohibitions against murder and adultery (vv. 13–14) grow out God's creation of man in his image (Gen. 1:26; 9:5–6) and his institution of marriage between one man and one woman (2:18–24).[25] Therefore, the Ten Commandments reveal the ethical implications of God's *creation ordinances*, structures that God built into human life as created in his image. Creation ordinances include dominion over the earth, work, marriage, parent-

21. Similar lists of rules for interpreting the Ten Commandments appear in many Reformed writings. For example, see the Westminster Larger Catechism (Q. 99), in *Reformed Confessions*, 4:320–21; Thomas Watson, *The Ten Commandments* (Edinburgh: Banner of Truth, 1965), 45–48; and Turretin, *Institutes*, 11.6.1–8 (2:34–36).

22. Çalvin, *Institutes*, 2.8.9.

23. Cf. Calvin, *Institutes*, 2.8.6.

24. The "ten words" are introduced by "And God [*Elohim*] spake all these words, saying [*'amar*]" (Ex. 20:1), and Gen. 1:1–2:3 contains ten instances of the phrase "And God said" (*wayo'mer Elohim*, in 1:3, 6, 9, 11, 14, 20, 24, 26, 29; and *wayo'mer lahem Elohim*, in v. 28). Furthermore, Gen. 1:1 and Ex. 20:1 each contain seven Hebrew words and twenty-eight Hebrew letters, unlikely a mere coincidence.

25. On the roots of the Decalogue in Genesis 1–2, see *RST*, 2:685–86.

ing, and the holy rest of the Sabbath (Genesis 1–2).[26] The moral law of the Ten Commandments is God's revelation to Israel of the *natural law* embedded in human nature by the Creator.[27] What all men know in their consciences (Rom. 1:32; 2:14–15), though dimmed and distorted by sin (1 Tim. 4:2; Titus 1:15), God revealed with greater clarity and purity in the Decalogue and writes with effectual power on the heart in salvation (Jer. 31:33).[28]

Fourth, since the Ten Commandments express God's created order for conduct and the attitudes of the heart, *specific precepts reveal broadly applicable principles* so that we may know what pleases our Creator in all of life.[29] For example, the prohibition against bearing "false witness" specifically addresses perjury in judicial cases (Ex. 20:16), but it reveals God's love for the truth and the value of a good reputation, and hence, it instructs us regarding the evil of gossip, fraud in business dealings, and so on. Each commandment represents a whole area of righteousness and a whole family of sins, as shown in the table below.[30]

Commandment	Domain of Righteousness or Sin
First	God's unique glory
Second	God's prescribed worship
Third	God's awesome name
Fourth	God's holy day
Fifth	Proper human authority
Sixth	Sacred human life
Seventh	Faithful human sexuality
Eighth	Rightful human property
Ninth	True human testimony
Tenth	Submissive human contentment

Table 37.2. The Ten Domains of Righteousness or Sin

26. For studies of the creation ordinances, see Murray, *Principles of Conduct*, 27–106; and Greg Nichols, *Lectures in Systematic Theology*, ed. Rob Ventura, 7 vols. (Seattle: CreateSpace Independent Publishing Platform, 2017–), 2:237–391.

27. Calvin, *Institutes*, 2.8.1; cf. Irenaeus, *Against Heresies*, 4.15.1, in *ANF*, 1:479.

28. Nichols, *Lectures in Systematic Theology*, 2:369; cf. Irenaeus, *Against Heresies*, 4.16.3, in *ANF*, 1:481.

29. Calvin, *Institutes*, 2.8.8.

30. We introduced the idea of ten domains of actual sin in *RST*, 2:440–41.

Fifth, *the Ten Commandments require conduct that helps other people obey their precepts*. For example, the precept against adultery implies that we should speak or dress in a manner that helps people practice sexual purity. The command to honor one's father and mother implies the duty of parents to act in an honorable fashion toward their children.

Sixth, *the Ten Commandments are fulfilled in love*. The second commandment links obedience to love for God (Ex. 20:6). Shortly after reciting the Decalogue, Moses said, "Thou shalt love the LORD thy God" (Deut. 6:5). This summarizes the first four commandments. Moses also said, "Thou shalt love thy neighbour as thyself: I am the LORD" (Lev. 19:18). This principle summarizes the last six commandments. Thus, the whole law depends, Christ teaches us, on loving God and loving our neighbors (Matt. 22:37–40).

Seventh, *the Ten Commandments assert the supremacy of God*. God is the Lawgiver (Ex. 20:1); his lordship, covenant, and grace provide the great motivations for obedience (v. 2); and the first four commandments all pertain to him (vv. 3–11). The Hebrew text employs nearly three times as many words for the first four commandments as for the next six.[31] William Ames said that obedience is "towards God, for he is at once its standard, its object, and its end."[32] We cannot separate justice from religion. Calvin said, "It is vain to cry up righteousness without religion. . . . Not only is religion the chief part but the very soul, whereby the whole breathes and thrives."[33] As Herman Bavinck pointed out, God is the authoritative source of the law, his righteousness is the archetype of all its precepts, and his glory is the aim of all true morality.[34]

With these seven rules in hand, we are prepared to study each of the Ten Commandments. While we cannot develop a full system of ethics, we will expound each commandment, explore its relation to creation and love, and discuss some applications.

The First Commandment: God's Unique Glory

The Lord says, "Thou shalt have no other gods before me" (Ex. 20:3; Deut. 5:7). Literally the text says, "There shall not be to you other gods toward my face."

31. The number of Hebrew words in each commandment is: first (seven), second (forty-three), third (seventeen), fourth (fifty-five), fifth (fifteen), sixth (two), seventh (two), eighth (two), ninth (five), and tenth (fifteen). Thus, the first four commandments use 122 words, while the last six use just forty-one.

32. Ames, *The Marrow of Theology*, 2.1.12 (220).

33. Calvin, *Institutes*, 2.8.11.

34. Herman Bavinck, *Reformed Ethics*, ed. John Bolt et al., 3 vols. (Grand Rapids, MI: Baker Academic, 2019–), 1:66.

The Exegesis of the First Commandment

God prohibits his people from having "other gods," whether by calling on their names (Ex. 23:13), worshiping them, or serving them (Deut. 6:14; 8:19; 11:16). The language "there shall not be to you [*leka*] other gods [*elohim*]" is reminiscent of the covenantal formula "to be a God [*Elohim*] unto thee [*leka*]" (Gen. 17:7; cf. Ex. 6:7; Lev. 11:45; 26:12). This commandment admonishes Israel to keep its exclusive covenant with the Lord as his faithful spouse (Ex. 34:15–16). The preface to the Ten Commandments makes it clear that this commandment forbids the worship of any deity except the God who saved Israel from Egypt (Ex. 20:2).

The phrase translated as "before me" (*'al-panaya*) does not refer to giving other gods a higher priority than the Lord, but it means "to my face" or "in my sight" (Isa. 65:3; Jer. 6:7). Calvin said, "This is like a shameless woman who brings in an adulterer before her husband's very eyes."[35] Everything takes place before God's eyes (Prov. 15:3). However, this was especially true for God's covenant people, who dwelt near his holy presence in the tabernacle. When Israel sought "other gods," the Lord cast them "out of [his] sight" (*me'al-panay*) by banishing them into exile (Jer. 7:9, 15).[36] In Christ, the church is God's temple (1 Cor. 3:16–17). Therefore, Christians must remember that God is with them and is jealous over their worship (10:20–22).

While the first four commandments all pertain to worshiping and glorifying God, the first commandment specifies *the only God whom we must worship*. As Martin Luther said, "We are to fear, love, and trust God above all things."[37]

The First Commandment and Creation

"In the beginning God created the heaven and the earth" (Gen. 1:1) and all that they contain. Therefore, there is only one true God, and whatever people or things man elevates as other gods are either sheer fictions or part of God's creation. Moses says, "The Lord he is God in heaven above, and upon the earth beneath [note the allusion to creation]: there is none else" (Deut. 4:39).

35. Calvin, *Institutes*, 2.8.16.

36. See also 2 Kings 23:27; 2 Chron. 7:20; Jer. 15:1; 23:39; 32:31.

37. The Small Catechism (1.2), in *The Book of Concord*, 351. The catechism makes this truth central to all piety, beginning its explanation of each subsequent commandment by saying, "We are to fear and love God, so that," and so on (352–54).

The Holy Scriptures sharply distinguish "the true God" from "the gods that have not made the heavens and the earth" (Jer. 10:10–11). "For the LORD is great, and greatly to be praised: he is to be feared above all gods. For all the gods of the nations are idols: but the LORD made the heavens" (Ps. 96:4–5). The word translated as "idols" (plural *elil*) means "something worthless" (Job 13:4; Jer. 14:14; Zech. 11:17). God alone is eternal, all-powerful, and the source of all good. Therefore, we should worship no one that is not by nature God (Gal. 4:8).[38]

It might puzzle us why God would say "thou shalt have no other gods" (Ex. 20:3) when there are no other gods (Deut. 4:39; Isa. 45:22). People falsely create gods out of their own imagination. Paul says, "An idol is nothing in the world, and . . . there is none other God but one" (1 Cor. 8:4). Yet there is a reality behind the fiction. Jochem Douma (1931–2020) said, "People worship powerful forces within creation as if these were deities." For example, "Baal was the god of rain, thunder, and fertility." The creation account provides a crucial polemic against deifying the powers that God made. This polemic needs to be heard in secularized societies as well as pagan ones. Douma said, "The erotic, the desire for power, reason, nature, tradition, and conscience—each of these can be absolutized in ways both uncultured and very refined."[39] There are many people "whose God is their belly"—that is, their physical desires—"who mind earthly things" (Phil. 3:19). People become spiritual "adulterers and adulteresses" with the world by allowing their "lusts" for earthly pleasures and possessions to rule them (James 4:1–4). When people turn God's good gifts into gods, they end up worshiping demons (Deut. 32:17; 1 Cor. 10:20–21), for it was Satan who enticed man to choose the creature over the Creator, blinding people to his glory (Gen. 3:1–6; cf. 2 Cor. 4:4).

The First Commandment and Love

The prohibition against other gods implies the duty of wholehearted devotion to the Lord by faith in his Word. "Hear, O Israel: The LORD our God is one LORD: and thou shalt love the LORD thy God with all thine heart, and with all thy soul, and with all thy might" (Deut. 6:4–5). The repetition of "all" emphasizes that love for the Lord must perme-

38. On the uniqueness of the Creator, see *RST*, 2:63–65.

39. J. Douma, *The Ten Commandments: Manual for the Christian Life*, trans. Nelson D. Kloosterman (Phillipsburg, NJ: P&R, 1996), 16–17.

ate everything we are and do. Since God is unique, our hearts should not be divided (Ps. 86:11; Jer. 32:39). The call to love God grows out of faith in his revelation of his unique divine nature as "one LORD." All sins against God arise from unbelief toward his Word.[40] Though the law does not reveal the gospel, it does oblige us to believe all that God says in his Word.[41]

Augustine said that God is "the chief end after which we are told to strive with supreme affection."[42] He explained, "Following after God is the desire of happiness; to reach God is happiness itself. We follow after God by loving Him; we reach Him, not by becoming entirely what He is, but in nearness to Him, and in wonderful and immaterial contact with Him, and in being inwardly illuminated and occupied by His truth and holiness."[43] James Grier (1932–2013) said that the first commandment claims "the ultimate allegiance of life" and mandates "an unquestioned loyalty and commitment to the true and living God who has redeemed us," around whom "we organize all of our life" and without whom "our life would go to absurdity and there would be no focus and purpose."[44]

If we would love the Lord, then we must obey his commandments. Moses says, "Choose life . . . that thou mayest love the LORD thy God, and that thou mayest obey his voice, and that thou mayest cleave unto him: for he is thy life" (Deut. 30:19–20). Wilhelmus à Brakel said, "This [obedience] consists in acknowledging the Lord's majesty and His worthiness to be obeyed . . . joy in being subject to Him, in willingly offering to do whatever it pleases the Lord to command . . . as well as in the zealous and complete execution of the task."[45]

Jesus Christ exemplified the keeping of the great commandment in offering himself up completely to God, saying, "I come . . . to do thy will, O God" (Heb. 10:7). Jesus worshiped God alone (Matt. 4:10). He went resolutely to the cross "that the world may know that I love the Father" (John 14:31). Those united to Christ in his death and resurrection no longer "live unto themselves, but unto him" (2 Cor. 5:14–15).

---

40. Bavinck, *Reformed Ethics*, 1:139.
41. Boston, *An Illustration of the Doctrines of the Christian Religion*, in *Works*, 2:94.
42. Augustine, *Of the Morals of the Catholic Church*, 8.13, in *NPNF*[1], 4:44–45.
43. Augustine, *Of the Morals of the Catholic Church*, 11.18, in *NPNF*[1], 4:46.
44. James Grier, "The Ten Words: Moral Choices Begin with the Ten Commandments," Lecture 1, Grand Rapids Baptist Seminary, Grand Rapids, MI, 1991, SoundCloud, audio lecture, https://soundcloud.com/grand-rapids-theological-seminary/series-10-words-lesson-1-james-grier/s-n7Yt8, 51:50–52:36.
45. Brakel, *The Christian's Reasonable Service*, 3:101.

Some Ethical Applications of the First Commandment

The first commandment teaches that we must embrace and practice biblical monotheism—that is, belief in the one true God and adoration toward him alone. Philosophies and religions contrary to biblical monotheism, such as atheism, polytheism, pantheism, panentheism, and finite theism, offend God and destroy men's souls.[46] Furthermore, no mere creature should be the object of our worship, not even an apostle (Acts 10:25–26) or a holy angel (Col. 2:18; Rev. 19:10; 22:8–9). We should choose to die rather than to offer worship to a false god (Dan. 3:18, 28) or to forsake praying and giving thanks to the true God (6:1–10).

Roman Catholics claim that when they bow to the saints and angels, they do not offer them the "adoration" (*latria*) due to God alone, but only the "veneration" (*dulia*) that it is appropriate to give to created persons.[47] The highest kind of honor for creatures (*hyperdulia*) is given to the Virgin Mary.[48] However, the meanings of *latria* and *dulia* do not support the idea of two categories of worship, one for God and one for man.[49] Many Roman Catholics clearly worship Mary when they bow before her images and call on her as the Mother of the Church, the heavenly "Queen over all things," and "Advocate, Helper, Benefactress, and Mediatrix."[50] Furthermore, Thomas Aquinas argued that "adoration" (*latria*) should be given to images of Christ and his cross for his sake.[51]

---

46. On these false views of God, see *RST*, 1:584–605 (chap. 31).

47. On the distinction, see Aquinas, *Summa Theologica*, Part 2.2, Q. 103. See Augustine, *The City of God*, 10.1, 3; 20:21 in *NPNF*[1], 2:180–82, 262, though Augustine does not in these texts use *dulia* to justify the worship of martyrs and saints.

48. Aquinas, *Summa Theologica*, Part 2.2, Q. 104, Obj. 2 and Reply Obj. 2; Part 3, Q. 25, Art. 5.

49. Brakel, *The Christian's Reasonable Service*, 3:91–92; and Turretin, *Institutes*, 11.7.10 (2:41). These terms are Latinized versions of the Greek words *latreia* and *douleia*. The term *latreia* often refers to the worship of God (Rom. 12:1; Heb. 9:1; Rev. 7:14). The verb *latreuō* is used in prohibitions against worshiping anyone but God (Matt. 4:10; Rom. 1:25), but it is sometimes used for serving man (Deut. 28:48 LXX), as is the related noun *latreuton* (Ex. 12:16; Lev. 23:7–8, etc. LXX). The term *douleia* means a state of being the slave (*doulos*) of a master, whom one is bound to serve (*douleuō*, 1 Tim. 6:1–2). The word *douleia* is poorly suited to describe the honor that men give to the saints, unless those saints are their lords. Paul rebukes the Galatians: "When ye knew not God, ye did service [*douleuō*] unto them which by nature are no gods" (Gal. 4:8). We must be "serving [*douleuō*] the Lord" (Rom. 12:11). God's demand for exclusive worship cannot be deflected merely by claiming to give only *douleia* to men and angels, for one cannot "serve [*douleuō*] two masters" (Matt. 6:24; Luke 16:13). The deeper question is whether we honor men as fits their status as mere men or as if they were gods.

50. *Catechism of the Catholic Church*, secs. 966, 968–70, 975. Though all grace and glory is said to flow from the mediation of Christ, Mary supposedly cooperates with Christ uniquely in accomplishing and applying salvation.

51. Aquinas, *Summa Theologica*, Part 3, Q. 25, Arts. 3–4. Francis Turretin said that Aquinas's judgment on this matter was also held by Alexander of Hales, Bonaventure, Gabriel Biel, and many others. *Institutes*, 11.9.5 (2:53).

Thus, we conclude that the distinction of *latria* and *dulia* fails to guard people against idolatry. While we certainly must show honor to human beings (1 Pet. 2:17), this does not justify lifting up praise and petitions to mere men and angels in heaven. We must avoid every hint of polytheism but worship the triune God alone.

Worship is inseparable from trust. Though it is good to trust faithful people (Prov. 31:11), there is a kind of trust that belongs only to God,[52] and the Lord curses those who put such trust in mere men (Jer. 17:5). Luther said, "A 'god' is the term for that to which we are to look for all good and in which we are to find refuge in all need. Therefore, to have a god is nothing else than to trust and believe in that one with your whole heart."[53] We exercise divine trust whenever we look to someone or something as if he or it had divine attributes. For example, praying to saints assumes they always have the knowledge and power to help us wherever we are—practical omnipresence, omniscience, and omnipotence. Neither should we trust money or possessions to be our treasure, but must trust in God, who will give his servants treasure in the heavenly kingdom (Matt. 6:19–24, 33; 1 Tim. 6:15–20). Godefridus Udemans (c. 1581–1649) said, "We must remember there is only one true God who created heaven and earth (Isa. 45:20; Jer. 10:12). Everything else is merely a creature or created thing, which cannot help us without God."[54]

Another way in which people violate the first commandment is by using sorcery to obtain supernatural power or knowledge from the spirit world.[55] This is polytheism, whether it takes the form of shamanism, fortune-telling, astrology, or psychic power, or is incorporated into a religion such as Hinduism or Buddhism.[56] The Lord condemns such practices as an abomination.[57] Sorcery is a form of false prophecy, a sinful means of seeking supernatural direction for a happy life.[58] Rather than seek spirits, people should seek the Lord by faith and obedience to his Word (1 Chron.

52. The Heidelberg Catechism (LD 34, Q. 95), in *The Three Forms of Unity*, 102.
53. The Large Catechism (1.2), in *The Book of Concord*, 386.
54. Udemans, *The Practice of Faith, Hope, and Love*, 204.
55. Sorcery is to be distinguished from illusions and sleight of hand to entertain audiences.
56. On polytheism, see *RST*, 1:588–90. As we note there, some forms of practical polytheism are pantheistic or panentheistic in their belief systems.
57. Ex. 22:18; Lev. 19:26, 31; 20:6, 27; Deut. 18:9–14.
58. Douma, *The Ten Commandments*, 25. Note the contrast between "these nations . . . *hearkened* unto [listened to] observers of times, and unto diviners" and "the Lord thy God will raise up unto thee a Prophet from the midst of thee, of thy brethren, like unto me; unto him ye shall *hearken*" (Deut. 18:14–15).

10:13–14; Isa. 8:19–20). Where the name of Jesus Christ is magnified, people turn away from occult practices (Acts 19:17–20).

Positively speaking, the prohibition against other gods implies that we must give to the true God the love of our whole being. The Westminster Larger Catechism (Q. 104) says,

> The duties required in the first commandment are, the knowing and acknowledging of God to be the only true God, and our God (1 Chron. 28:9; Deut. 26:17; Isa. 43:10; Jer. 14:22); and to worship and glorify him accordingly (Ps. 95:6–7; Matt. 4:10; Ps. 29:2), by thinking (Mal. 3:16), meditating (Ps. 63:6), remembering (Eccl. 12:1), highly esteeming (Ps. 71:19), honouring (Mal. 1:6), adoring (Isa. 45:23), choosing (Josh. 24:15, 22), loving (Deut. 6:5), desiring (Ps. 73:25), fearing of him (Isa. 8:13); believing him (Ex. 14:31); trusting (Isa. 26:4), hoping (Ps. 130:7), delighting (Ps. 37:4), rejoicing in him (Ps. 32:11); being zealous for him (Rom. 12:11; Num. 25:11); calling upon him, giving all praise and thanks (Phil. 4:6), and yielding all obedience and submission to him with the whole man (Jer. 7:28; James 4:7); being careful in all things to please him (1 John 3:22), and sorrowful when in any thing he is offended (Jer. 31:18; Ps. 119:136); and walking humbly with him (Mic. 6:8).[59]

If we are to worship only the true God and live in faithful love to him, then we must know who he is and what he commands amid the many gods and religions of this world. Thomas Watson said, "We must know God in his attributes, as glorious in holiness, rich in mercy, and faithful in promises. We must know him in his Son."[60] We must give God our full attention when engaged in public worship and hearing his Word, for his Word has infinitely more importance than all the world (Isa. 40:15–17). Watson said, "Would a king take it well at our hands, if, when speaking to us, we should be playing with a feather?"[61] Udemans said that we must diligently read the Holy Scriptures, learn catechisms, listen to sermons, and "put our knowledge in the fear of the Lord into practice, for in this the Lord will further reveal His will (Ps. 25:12)."[62]

Exclusive devotion to the true God requires us to reject false doctrines that corrupt our knowledge of God. Paul speaks of his "godly jealousy"

59. *Reformed Confessions*, 4:322.
60. Watson, *The Ten Commandments*, 50.
61. Watson, *The Ten Commandments*, 54.
62. Udemans, *The Practice of Faith, Hope, and Love*, 217.

over the church as a bride betrothed to "one husband," Jesus Christ, when false teachers sought to draw church members away from simple devotion to Christ by preaching "another Jesus," imparting "another spirit," or teaching "another gospel" (2 Cor. 11:1–4; cf. Gal. 1:8–9).

Our duty regarding the first commandment includes our responsibility to promote the worship of the true God in the world by publicly declaring his glory to others (Ps. 96:3–4) and living in a manner consistent with his Word so that people "see [our] good works, and glorify [our] Father which is in heaven" (Matt. 5:16).

The Second Commandment: God's Prescribed Worship

The Lord says, "Thou shalt not make unto thee any graven image, or any likeness of any thing that is in heaven above, or that is in the earth beneath, or that is in the water under the earth: thou shalt not bow down thyself to them, nor serve them" (Ex. 20:4–5; cf. Deut. 5:8–9). He adds this motive: "For I the Lord thy God am a jealous God, visiting the iniquity of the fathers upon the children unto the third and fourth generation of them that hate me; and shewing mercy unto thousands of them that love me, and keep my commandments" (Ex. 20:5–6; cf. Deut. 5:9–10).

The Exegesis of the Second Commandment

This commandment does not forbid all visual art (which was employed in the tabernacle, Ex. 25:18; 26:1), but all visual representations of a divine being or use of such imagery for worship.[63] The word translated as "graven image" (*pesel*) always refers in the Holy Scriptures to the image of a divine being, whether shaped of stone, metal, or wood.[64] It can refer to an image that is meant to depict the true God, for Moses said that the Lord appeared on Mount Sinai as a formless fire lest the people make a "graven image" (Deut. 4:15–16). Idols were used by those claiming to worship "the Lord" (Ex. 32:5; Judg. 17:1–6). The word translated as "likeness" (*temunah*) refers to a visible appearance, often a visible manifestation of God's glory.[65] Here it is the likeness of

63. Udemans, *The Practice of Faith, Hope, and Love*, 226.

64. *NIDOTTE*, 3:645; 4:516. See Ex. 20:4; Lev. 26:1; Deut. 4:16, 23, 25; 5:8; 27:15; Judg. 17:3–4; 18:14, 17–18, 20, 30–31; 2 Kings 21:7; 2 Chron. 33:7; Ps. 97:7; Isa. 40:19–20; 42:17; 44:9–10, 15, 17; 45:20; 48:5; Jer. 10:14; 51:17; Nah. 1:14; Hab. 2:18.

65. Ex. 20:4; Num. 12:8; Deut. 4:12, 15–16, 23, 25; 5:8; Job 4:16; Ps. 17:15.

anything in "heaven," "earth," or the "water"—an allusion to God's creation of the world (Gen. 1:1–2, 20). Therefore, an idol is a man-made visual representation of a being regarded as God or a god, formed in the likeness of a creature.

Though an idol may be called by the name of a god (1 Sam. 5:2–7), the idol is distinct from the deity it represents, as is recognized by many idolaters.[66] Augustine noted that more refined idolaters say, "I worship not this visible thing, but the divinity which doth invisibly dwell therein."[67] Aaron said, "These be thy gods, O Israel, which brought thee up out of the land of Egypt," but the people had seen him make the golden calf after their departure from Egypt (Ex. 32:4); thus, the calf was not regarded as God, but as a representation of God. Multiple idols in different locations can represent the same deity (1 Kings 12:28–29). The deity is thought to be especially present in the idol,[68] and so people pray to it for the deity to save them (Isa. 44:17; 45:20).

An idol is a means of accessing the presence and controlling the power of a deity through man's rituals and offerings. Douma said that attempting to make an image of the Lord misconstrues (1) his "freedom," for he "controls man and will not allow himself to be controlled"; (2) his "majesty," for his glory cannot be captured by the work of human hands; and (3) his "covenant," for images are unneeded since God has committed himself to be with his people by his promises.[69]

The second commandment contains two prohibitions that mutually reinforce each other to fence out idolatry: "Thou shalt not make" such an image and "Thou shalt not bow down thyself to them, nor serve them."[70] The combination rules out making an image of someone regarded as divine, even if one claims not to use it for worship, and it forbids bowing before an image or praying toward it, even if one claims it is not a representation of a divine being.[71]

The words "thou shalt not make unto thee" teach us that man is prohibited from worshiping God through means that man makes for himself.

66. Hodge, *Systematic Theology*, 3:294, 301.

67. Augustine, *Expositions on the Book of Psalms*, 115.3 (5:286). See also Lactantius, *The Divine Institutes*, 2.2, in *ANF*, 7:41.

68. John I. Durham, *Exodus*, Word Biblical Commentary (Nashville: Thomas Nelson, 1987), 285.

69. Douma, *The Ten Commandments*, 38–43.

70. Prohibitions against making images of God or gods also appear in Ex. 34:17; Lev. 19:4; 26:1; Deut. 27:15.

71. Calvin, *Institutes*, 2.8.17.

How, then, does God will to be known and served? The Decalogue begins, "And God spake all these words" (Ex. 20:1). When Moses repeated the Ten Commandments, he first said, "The Lord talked with you face to face in the mount out of the midst of the fire" (Deut. 5:4). The Lord appeared in a formless fire so that Israel would not make an image of him, and he communicated with the people through words (4:15–16, 36). The implication is clear: God chooses to be worshiped through his words. Ironically, God commanded Moses to "cut" (*pasal*) the stone tablets for the Ten Commandments (Ex. 34:1), for God's alternative to a "graven image" (*pesel*) is his Word.

The second commandment pertains to *the outward means of worship*. God prohibits not only the worship of other gods but also depicting the object of worship through images, in stark contrast to the Gentile world. Instead, the commandment enjoins worship through the Word.

The Second Commandment and Creation

Like the first commandment, the second is based on God's creation of the world.[72] Paul argues, "God that made the world and all things therein, seeing that he is Lord of heaven and earth, dwelleth not in temples made with hands. . . . Forasmuch then as we are the offspring of God, we ought not to think that the Godhead is like unto gold, or silver, or stone, graven by art and man's device" (Acts 17:24, 29). As Watson said, if an artist made an image of a king in the shape of an insect, he would be very offended. Likewise, it dishonors the living God to try to represent him with a dead image, and the Creator of all things with an image created by man.[73]

Idolatry does not arise from a legitimate pursuit of God but from man's refusal to glorify God or give him thanks, plunging him into the morally degrading worship of creation instead of the Creator (Rom. 1:21–32). A man-made image does not draw people near to God but is "a teacher of lies" (Hab. 2:18). The only image of God he has authorized is the living image in righteous human beings, especially Jesus Christ (Col. 1:15; 3:10). Hence, the New Testament also condemns idolatry.[74] Whenever God has

72. On the uniqueness of the Creator and the Creator-creature distinction, see *RST*, 2:63–65.

73. Watson, *The Ten Commandments*, 59–60.

74. Acts 7:41; 15:20, 29; 21:25; Rom. 1:23; 2:22; 1 Cor. 8:1–10; 10:14, 19, 28; 12:2; 2 Cor. 6:16; Gal. 5:20; Col. 3:5; 1 Thess. 1:9; 1 Pet. 4:3; 1 John 5:21; Rev. 2:14, 20; 9:20; 13:14–15; 14:9, 11; 15:2; 16:2; 19:20; 20:4.

saved sinners by his Word and Spirit, they have "turned to God from idols to serve the living and true God; and to wait for his Son from heaven, whom he raised from the dead" (1 Thess. 1:9–10).

The Second Commandment and Church History

Since early Christianity drew many of its converts from among idol worshipers, the ancient church strongly opposed images of divine beings. Athenagoras of Athens (fl. 176) said, "Because the multitude, who cannot distinguish between matter and God, or see how great is the interval which lies between them, pray to idols made of matter, are we therefore, who do distinguish and separate the uncreated and the created . . . to come and worship images?"[75] Clement of Alexandria (c. 150–c. 215) argued that the infinite God cannot be "represented by the form of a living creature," but "we shall find the divine likeness and the holy image in the righteous soul, when it is blessed in being purified and performing blessed deeds."[76] Origen (c. 185–c. 254) wrote of Christians as "those who, being taught in the school of Jesus Christ, have rejected all images and statues."[77] The church in its earliest centuries avoided images of Jesus, although it did use religious symbols such as a fish, a shepherd, grapes, or a dove.[78]

Images did gradually make their way into Christian church buildings, but not without opposition.[79] The Synod of Elvira (canon 36) decreed at the beginning of the fourth century, "Pictures are not to be placed in churches, so that they do not become objects of worship and adoration."[80] Epiphanius (d. 403), bishop of Salamis, visited a church building and tore down a curtain that "bore an image either of Christ or of one of the saints," for it was "contrary to the teaching of the Scriptures."[81]

One justification for including images in the church is that they serve as "books for the laity," an idea attributed to Gregory the Great, though

75. Athenagoras, *A Plea for the Christians*, chap. 15, in *ANF*, 2:135.
76. Clement of Alexandria, *The Stromata*, 7.5–6, in *ANF*, 2:530–31.
77. Origen, *Against Celsus*, 7.41, in *ANF*, 4:627.
78. Schaff, *History of the Christian Church*, 3:563–71; and Ivor J. Davidson, *The Birth of the Church: From Jesus to Constantine, A.D. 30–312*, The Baker History of the Church 1 (Grand Rapids, MI: Baker, 2004), 292–93. Irenaeus notes that some Gnostic heretics had pictures of Jesus that they venerated. *Against Heresies*, 1.25.6, in *ANF*, 1:351.
79. See Turretin, *Institutes*, 11.9.14–17 (57–60).
80. Cited in John B. Carpenter, "Answering Eastern Orthodox Apologists regarding Icons," *Themelios* 43, no. 3 (2018): 428 (full article, 417–33).
81. Cited in Jerome, Letters, 51.9, in *NPNF*^{2}, 6:89.

the specific phrase appeared later in the medieval period.[82] It is true that Gregory said that pictures are like books for the illiterate to read. However, he referred to "images of saints" and depictions of "histories of the saints," not images of God or Christ, and he strongly forbade the adoration of images.[83]

Images became a central part of the devotion of the medieval church in conjunction with the rising importance of relics (the remains of martyrs and saints) in popular devotion. However, there were seasons in church history when groups of professing Christians reacted strongly against images and destroyed them (iconoclasm).[84] The Second Council of Nicaea (787) decreed in the face of this opposition that church buildings should contain icons of Jesus Christ, his mother, and the angels and saints; that these images should be honored, loved, and venerated, and that no building should be consecrated for Christian worship without containing the relics of dead saints.[85] Aquinas said, "Because in the New Testament God was made man, He can be adored in His corporeal image."[86] The Council of Trent stated, "By the images which we kiss, and before which we uncover the head, and prostrate ourselves, we adore Christ, and we venerate the saints."[87] Late medieval art includes manlike images of God the Father and the Trinity.[88]

Though theologians present elaborate defenses of this image worship (as mentioned earlier regarding *latria* and *dulia*), the counsel of Petrus van der Hagen (1641–1671) remains helpful: "Do not listen to what they are saying, but look at what they are doing."[89] When people go on holy pilgrimages to visit images and uncover their heads to salute them, bow to them, burn candles and incense before them, kiss them, and pray to them, is this anything other than the worship of idols?

Early Reformed theologians rejected such images as idols. The Second Helvetic Confession (chap. 4) says, "Although Christ took upon Him

82. The phrase "books for the laity" (*libri laicorum*) is traced to twelfth-century theologian Peter Comestor.

83. Gregory the Great, Epistles, 9.105, 11.13, in *NPNF*², 13:23, 53–54.

84. See Leslie Brubaker and John Haldon, *Byzantium in the Iconoclast Era, c. 680–850: A History* (Cambridge: Cambridge University Press, 2011).

85. Acts of the Second Council of Nicaea (AD 787), in *NPNF*², 14:550, 560, 573.

86. Aquinas, *Summa Theologica*, Part 3, Q. 25, Art. 3, Reply Obj. 1.

87. Council of Trent, session 25, "On the Invocation, Veneration, and Relics of Saints, and on Sacred Images," in *The Creeds of Christendom*, ed. Schaff, 2:202.

88. For example, consider Michelangelo's (1475–1564) depiction in the Sistine Chapel of the Father reaching out to Adam, or Andrei Rublev's (d. c. 1430) icon of the Trinity as three men.

89. Petrus van der Hagen, cited in Douma, *The Ten Commandments*, 65.

man's nature, yet He did not, therefore, take it that He might set forth a pattern for carvers and painters. He denied that He came 'to destroy the Law and the prophets' (Matt. 5:17), but images are forbidden in the Law and the prophets."[90] Reformed orthodox theologians also opposed images of Christ.[91]

The Second Commandment and Love

The Lord attaches to the second commandment a motivation directly related to love. He says that he is "a jealous God" (Ex. 20:5), his jealousy being the infinite intense energy of his holiness, expressed both in love and in wrath.[92] The Lord warns that his punishment will fall on "them that hate me" (v. 5), implying that idolatry is an act of hatred against him. William Perkins paraphrased, "You may think that your use of idols kindles in you a love of Me, but it is so far from that that all such as use them . . . hate Me."[93] When the Lord says that his judgment falls on "the third and fourth generation of them that hate me" (v. 5), he communicates not that "they must pay for the sins of their forefathers," but, as Udemans said, "punishment will fall on those who follow in the footsteps of their forefathers."[94] The Lord promises, however, that he will show "mercy unto thousands of them that love me, and keep my commandments" (v. 6), implying that the obedient avoidance of idolatry is an act of love toward him that brings multigenerational blessings for those children who walk in their parents' godly ways ("thousands" of generations "that love me," cf. Deut. 7:9; Ps. 105:8).

True worship is an act of love for God that aims to please him by following his Word. Moses told the people of Israel that when they entered the land of Canaan, they must not ask, "How did these nations serve their gods?" (Deut. 12:30). The rule for how people should worship is "Everything that I command you, you shall be careful to do. You shall not add to it or take from it" (Deut. 12:32 ESV). This rule has come to be known as the *regulative principle of worship*.[95] The regulative principle

90. *Reformed Confessions*, 2:815.

91. Watson, *The Ten Commandments*, 60–62; James Durham, *A Practical Exposition of the Ten Commandments*, ed. Christopher Coldwell (Dallas, TX: Naphtali Press, 2002), 95–96; Udemans, *The Practice of Faith, Hope, and Love*, 232; Brakel, *The Christian's Reasonable Service*, 3:109–10; Brown, *Questions and Answers on the Shorter Catechism*, 219; and Gill, *Body of Divinity*, 992.

92. On God's jealousy, see *RST*, 1:829–32.

93. Perkins, *A Golden Chain*, chap. 21, in *Works*, 6:76.

94. Udemans, *The Practice of Faith, Hope, and Love*, 229.

95. A full exposition and explanation of the regulative principle of worship will be given under the locus of ecclesiology in *RST*, vol. 4 (forthcoming).

is a rule of love, for it aims to honor God in his holiness by bringing to him only the worship that he has commanded (Lev. 10:1–3). Israel built the tabernacle and instituted the priesthood exactly "as the LORD commanded."[96] Ames said, "No instituted worship is lawful unless God is its author and ordainer. . . . For no one besides God can know what will be acceptable to him and impart that virtue to worship to make it effectual and profitable to us. Nothing can honor God unless it comes from him as the author."[97]

Obedience to the second commandment is also an act of love for our neighbors. As noted above, our partaking or rejecting of idolatry has a great impact on future generations. Furthermore, the pure worship of God tends to engender love for one's neighbors as God's image bearers, whereas idolatry corrupts the soul and, by God's just judgment, leads to uncontrolled lust for selfish pleasure by attaching one's greatest aspirations and fears to created things (Rom. 1:21–32). Guarding the purity of the church's worship is an act of compassion, for it preserves the public means of grace for the blessing of many now and in times to come.

Some Ethical Applications of the Second Commandment

The Westminster Larger Catechism (Q. 109) says that "the sins forbidden in the second commandment" include "the making any representation of God, of all or of any of the three persons, either inwardly in our mind, or outwardly in any kind of image or likeness of any creature whatsoever; all worshipping of it, or God in it or by it; the making of any representation of feigned deities, and all worship of them, or service belonging to them."[98] Even objects not originally designed to be idols should be destroyed if people begin to worship them (Num. 21:8–9; 2 Kings 18:4).[99] The second commandment presents no obstacle, however, to the use of pictures of mere men and women for the purposes of education or art.

God the Son incarnate is the supreme, living, visible image of the invisible God (2 Cor. 4:4; cf. John 1:18; 14:9). However, his incarnation does not permit man-made pictures of Jesus, for Christ is fully God, the object of our worship, and such images would become idols. The New Testament nowhere authorizes images of Jesus and never provides us with a physical

96. Ex. 39:1, 5, 7, 21, 26, 29, 31; 40:19, 21, 25, 27, 29, 32.
97. Ames, *The Marrow of Theology*, 2.13.10, 13 (279).
98. *Reformed Confessions*, 4:324.
99. Boston, *An Illustration of the Doctrines of the Christian Religion*, in *Works*, 2:151.

description of him on which to base such a portrayal.[100] The claim that images help us to think of Christ creates a moral dilemma: either people think of Christ without worshiping him (which dishonors God's Son) or they worship the Lord through an image (which is idolatry).[101] The Word of God is sufficient to reveal Christ for our faith and love, even for the instruction of children (2 Tim. 3:15–17). Rather than regard images as "books for the laity," we "must not pretend to be wiser than God, who will have His people taught, not by dumb [mute] images, but by the lively preaching of His Word," as the Heidelberg Catechism (LD 35, Q. 98) says.[102]

The second commandment also forbids directing our worship toward the image of any created person or thing. Places where the church gathers for worship should not contain artistic depictions of Mary or the saints, lest people take them as idols in their hearts. Francis Turretin said, "That ought to be distant from sacred places which does not belong to the worship of God and is joined with the danger of idolatry."[103] We must be cautious about placing material or electronic images of any kind before the worshiping congregation, for we should not underestimate the hold that idolatry has over the human heart and the temptation it presents even to believers. Israel placed idols in the holy courts of God's own temple (Ezekiel 8), and people today can do the same in their churches. Watson said, "Our nature is as prone to this sin as dry wood to take fire."[104]

Worship that pleases God is done in the simplicity of faith and obedience to his Word, not with added activities thought to enhance holiness or intimacy with God. Idolatry centers worship on the visible, but Christ teaches that "God is a Spirit: and they that worship him must worship him in spirit and in truth" (John 4:24). Worship through man-made ceremonies is closely connected to idolatry, for such ceremonies attach sacred value to material objects, whether holy garments, fluids, containers, furniture, or buildings, that God has not consecrated by his Word to be means of grace, and man has no power to make them to be such means.[105] God has authorized his chosen ordinances of worship, and we

100. The vision of Christ in Revelation 1 is not a description of his actual appearance but a collage of metaphorical images based on the Old Testament. For example, Christ does not have a sword proceeding from his mouth (Rev. 1:16).

101. John Murray, "Pictures of Christ," *Reformed Herald* 16, no. 9 (February 1961): 65–66.

102. *The Three Forms of Unity*, 103. See Perkins, *A Golden Chain*, chap. 21, in *Works*, 6:77.

103. Turretin, *Institutes*, 11.10.7 (2:64).

104. Watson, *The Ten Commandments*, 62.

105. Ames, *The Marrow of Theology*, 2.13.34–35 (281).

must use them alone. Paul said of the Lord's Supper that "I have received of the Lord that which also I delivered unto you" (1 Cor. 11:23), just as he delivered the gospel he received by divine revelation (15:3; cf. Gal. 1:12).

Philip Ryken says, "What the image always wants to do in worship is to distract us from hearing the Word. The crucifix, the icon, the drama, and the dance—these things are not aids to worship, but make true worship all but impossible. In a visual age, we need to be all the more careful not to look at the image, but to listen to the Word."[106] Grier said, "Israel was very discontent with a faceless God who only spoke." People are the same today, restless under worship that does not move their senses with visible glory. However, as Grier said, "the speech of God is intended to communicate the presence of the living God for the vital fellowship of those who are bonded to him through redemption."[107]

The prohibition against idolatry also has surprisingly broad applications that we might not consider to be religious matters. Paul says, "Mortify therefore your members which are upon the earth; fornication, uncleanness, inordinate affection, evil concupiscence, and covetousness, which is idolatry" (Col. 3:5). Whenever we set our hearts on something visible as the means of obtaining happiness or glory, we make it an idol that directly opposes the love of God (1 John 2:15–17; 5:21). Pornography puts people in bondage not only because it violates the seventh commandment but also because it bonds our adoration to images.[108] But the problem is much broader than pornography. We must guard our hearts in a world that parades before our eyes beautiful people, emblems of wealth, and symbols of military and political power.

Positively speaking, churches should search the Scriptures to see what God commands in the New Testament for his worship. Calvin said, "Above all, when it is a matter of worshiping God, we are not to give any attention whatever to our imagination. But we are to follow in all simplicity what he has ordained by his Word, without adding anything to it at all."[109] The Westminster Shorter Catechism (Q. 50) says, "The second

106. Philip Graham Ryken, *Written in Stone: The Ten Commandments and Today's Moral Crisis* (Wheaton, IL: Crossway, 2003), 81.

107. Grier, "The Ten Words," Lecture 2, SoundCloud, audio lecture, https://soundcloud.com/grand-rapids-theological-seminary/series-10-words-lesson-2-james-grier, 39:52–40:25.

108. Further discussion of pornography may be found in chap. 39 under the seventh commandment.

109. *John Calvin's Sermons on the Ten Commandments*, ed. and trans. Benjamin W. Farley (Grand Rapids, MI: Baker, 1980), 66; cf. Calvin, *Sermons on Deuteronomy*, 188.

commandment requireth the receiving, observing, and keeping pure and entire, all such religious worship and ordinances as God hath appointed in his word."[110]

We also have a responsibility to influence other people to turn from idols to serve the living God (Acts 14:15). If we are the heads of households, we should cleanse our houses from idols so that our families can worship the Lord (Gen. 35:1–7). As an act of love for God and compassion on precious human souls, we should grieve over men's idolatry and call them to repent of it and trust in the risen Lord Jesus (Acts 17:16–18).

Sing to the Lord

Praising the Lord as the Only God

Sing to the Lord, sing His praise, all ye peoples,
New be your song as new honors ye pay;
Sing of His majesty, bless Him forever,
Show His salvation from day to day.

Tell of His wondrous works, tell of His glory,
Till through the nations His name is revered;
Praise and exalt Him for He is almighty,
God over all let the Lord be feared.

Vain are the heathen gods, idols and helpless;
God made the heav'ns, and His glory they tell;
Honor and majesty shine out before Him,
Beauty and strength in His temple dwell.

Psalm 96
Tune: Wesley
The Psalter, No. 259
Trinity Hymnal—Baptist Edition, No. 65

Questions for Meditation or Discussion

1. What is the preface to the Ten Commandments? What does it teach us about motivations to obey God's commandments?
2. What rules should we follow in interpreting and applying the Ten Commandments?

110. *Reformed Confessions*, 4:360.

3. What does the first commandment say? In your own words, express what it means.
4. How is the first commandment grounded in God's creation of the world?
5. How does the first commandment call us to love God?
6. What is one specific application of the first commandment that convicts you that you need to change? How will you faithfully and diligently make use of God's grace to change?
7. What does the second commandment say? What does it mean?
8. How is the second commandment based on God's work of creation?
9. How did the church's response to the second commandment vary from the early church through the medieval period and into the Reformation era?
10. How is obedience to the second commandment an expression of love?
11. What is one way you tend to break the second commandment? How can you repent or strengthen your repentance in this area of life by the grace of God?

Questions for Deeper Reflection

12. What do Roman Catholic theologians mean by the distinction between *latria*, *dulia*, and *hyperdulia*? Critique this distinction biblically, theologically, experientially, and practically.
13. Given that idolatry is a sinful attempt to use visible images to access superhuman power, knowledge, and goodness, and to control them to do our will, what are the major idols of your culture? In your answer, be sensitive to the fact that idols may not be openly religious but may appear in secular guise.
14. Does the incarnation of God the Son justify our making pictures of Jesus? Is it right to pray or give worship to Christ while looking at such a picture? Base your answers on Scripture and sound reasoning. If you answer the first question yes and the second no, explain why.

38

Obedience to God's Law, Part 2

The Third and Fourth Commandments

Love for God entails a desire to glorify his name, especially in the public worship of his people. Psalm 92 is denoted as "A Psalm or Song for the sabbath day," and begins, "It is a good thing to give thanks unto the LORD, and to sing praises unto thy name, O most High" (v. 1). The people who love the name of the Lord also love the holy rest of his Sabbath (Isa. 56:6), for on that day they gather to God's house, which is a "house of prayer for all people" (v. 7).

Having begun our exposition of love for God in the first and second of the Ten Commandments, we now continue by examining the third and fourth commandments, in which we are instructed to love God's name and devote his special day to worshiping him.

The Third Commandment: God's Awesome Name

The Lord says, "Thou shalt not take the name of the LORD thy God in vain; for the LORD will not hold him guiltless that taketh his name in vain" (Ex. 20:7; Deut. 5:11).

The Exegesis of the Third Commandment

The Lord has revealed himself by various names, including "the LORD," "God," "Most High," "God Almighty," and so on.[1] However, the "name"

1. On the divine name "the LORD" (*YHWH*, traditionally Jehovah), see *RST*, 1:549–65 (chap. 29). On the names and titles "God" (*Elohim*), "Most High" (*'Elyon*), "God Almighty" (*El Shaddai*), "Lord" (*Adonai*), and "the LORD of hosts" (*YHWH Seb'aot*), see *RST*, 1:760–63.

of the Lord includes every aspect of his revealed glory, such as his attributes of love and justice (Ex. 33:19; 34:5–7), the majesty shining in his works (9:16; 15:3), and his manifest presence (23:21; Deut. 12:5, 11).[2]

The verb translated as "take" (*nasa'*) means to bear or lift up and can be used of lifting up one's voice loudly.[3] To take the "name" (*shem*) of a deity is to worship him by name (Ps. 16:4). Prayer, an important part of worship, is calling on "the name of the LORD."[4] Another element of worship is to swear oaths by God's "name" (Deut. 6:13; 10:20). God forbade Israel to invoke other gods or swear by them (Ex. 23:13; Josh. 23:7). He also said, "Ye shall not swear by my name falsely, neither shalt thou profane the name of thy God: I am the LORD" (Lev. 19:12).

The word translated as "vain" (*shawe*) or "vanity" means "useless" or "false" (Ex. 23:1; Ps. 127:1–2); "in vain" (*lashawe*) means "for nothing" (Jer. 2:18; 4:30; 6:29; 46:11). Occasionally, "vain" refers to false gods or idols (Ps. 31:6; Jer. 18:15; Jonah 2:8), a poke at their powerlessness to answer the prayers of their worshipers. When God's enemies take him "in vain" (*lashawe*), they "speak against thee wickedly" (Ps. 139:20).[5]

Therefore, to "take the name of the LORD thy God in vain" means to speak about God's names, attributes, works, or presence as if he were nothing, distant, powerless, or dead. God forbids this irreverence and says that he "will not hold him guiltless that taketh his name in vain" (Ex. 20:7)—that is, God will punish the one who violates this commandment (34:7).

God's name is "glorious and fearful" (Deut. 28:58), and so, as the Heidelberg Catechism (LD 36, Q. 99) says, we must "use the holy name of God no otherwise than with fear and reverence."[6] John Calvin said, "Whatever our mind conceives of God, whatever our tongue utters, should savor of his excellence, match the loftiness of his sacred name, and lastly, serve to glorify his greatness."[7] However, sinners lack the fear of God (Ps. 36:1; Rom. 3:18). Consequently, they speak lightly of him as if he were powerless, distant, or dead. They swear oaths in his name that they have no serious intention to keep.

2. On the significance of God's "name," see *RST*, 1:520–21.
3. Gen. 21:16; Judg. 9:7; Ps. 93:3; Isa. 24:14.
4. Gen. 4:26; 12:8; 13:4; 21:33; 26:25; 1 Kings 18:24; 2 Kings 5:11; Ps. 116:4, 13, 17; Joel 2:32; Zeph. 3:9.
5. In Ps. 139:20, the words "thy name" are not in the Hebrew text but are added by translators.
6. *The Three Forms of Unity*, 103.
7. Calvin, *Institutes*, 2.8.22.

The first commandment specifies the God whom we worship, the second regulates the outward means of worship, and the third mandates *reverence for the God whom we worship*. The Westminster Shorter Catechism (Q. 54–55) says, "The third commandment requireth the holy and reverent use of God's names, titles, attributes, ordinances, word, and works," and it "forbiddeth all profaning or abusing of anything whereby God maketh himself known."[8]

The Third Commandment and Creation

The creation account reveals God's sovereignty over names, for it was the Creator who authoritatively "called" the day, night, heaven, earth, and seas by their names (Gen. 1:5, 8, 10). The passage does not explicitly speak of the "name" of the Lord, but his name as "God" (*Elohim*) is pervasive in Genesis 1:1–2:3 and as "the LORD God" (*YHWH Elohim*) in 2:4–25. God's work of creation reveals his glory as the unique, eternal, personal, powerful, authoritative, wise, and good Lord.[9] The creation of the universe shows God's worthiness of all reverence.

The majesty of the Creator's works calls us to reverence his name: "For, lo, he that formeth the mountains, and createth the wind. . . . The LORD, The God of hosts, is his name" (Amos 4:13). He is the Lord who "maketh the seven stars and Orion, and turneth the shadow of death into the morning, and maketh the day dark with night: that calleth for the waters of the sea, and poureth them out upon the face of the earth: The LORD is his name" (5:8).

The Third Commandment and Love

Fear toward God goes hand in hand with love for him (Deut. 6:2, 5; 10:12), for the fear of the Lord that God blesses is not a selfish dread of his punishment but an awe-filled delight in his majesty and righteousness (Ps. 112:1; cf. Neh. 1:11 ESV). The people of God are those who love his name (Pss. 5:11; 69:36; 119:132; Isa. 56:6).

Taking up God's name in worship with love and fear is essential to glorifying him. William Ames said that this commandment requires using the means of grace in the worship of God with inward "reverence . . . [in] a due prizing of the worth of such things . . . [and] fear of too much

8. *Reformed Confessions*, 4:360.
9. On the work of creation as a unique display of God's glory, see *RST*, 2:61–73.

familiarity by which such things might be desecrated," as well as "devotion . . . [with] readiness to perform those things which belong to the worship of God . . . [and] delight in performing them."[10] Outwardly, this zeal for God's name expresses itself in worship characterized by "order and decency" so that all things are done "in a way to make for the most edification."[11]

Obedience to the third commandment also serves the purpose of loving our neighbors. If we engage in irreverent speech, it tends to corrupt those who hear us. This is an act of hatred because irreverence destroys people (Prov. 13:13; 28:14). Conversely, if we guard our speech to avoid taking God's name in vain and instead speak reverently of his greatness, we promote the fear of God in others (Mal. 3:16). If by God's grace we can influence others to fear the Lord, we give them a gift worth more than "great treasure" (Prov. 15:16).

No man exhibited more love for God's glory than Jesus Christ. He taught his disciples to pray "Hallowed be thy name" as their first request before God (Matt. 6:9). Zeal for God's house consumed him and moved him to drive people out of it when they made it a safe place for greed and hypocrisy (Mark 11:15–17; John 2:13–17). When Christ drew near to the time of his suffering under God's wrath as our Surety, he steeled himself with the resolve to complete his mission and cried out, "Father, glorify thy name" (John 12:27–28). The night he was betrayed, he prayed, "I have glorified thee on the earth: I have finished the work which thou gavest me to do" (17:4). Having died in obedience to the Father, Christ was exalted to the highest place and given the "name which is above every name" (Phil. 2:8–9). Now the church's service to the glory of God revolves around the "name" of Jesus Christ, God the Son incarnate.[12]

Some Ethical Applications of the Third Commandment

The most obvious application of the prohibition against taking God's name in vain is to avoid blaspheming or cursing God (Lev. 24:10–16). Blasphemy is speaking about God in a manner that mocks and insults him (Isa. 37:4–6, 23; cf. 36:18–20).

10. Ames, *The Marrow of Theology*, 2.14.14–17 (284).

11. Ames, *The Marrow of Theology*, 2.14.20–21 (285). He cites 1 Cor. 14:26, 40.

12. It is remarkable how the divine "name" is virtually taken over by references to the "name" of Jesus Christ in the New Testament. See Acts 2:38; 3:16; 4:10, 12 (and often in Acts); Rom. 1:5; 10:13; 1 Cor. 1:2, 10; 5:4; 6:11; Eph. 5:20; Phil. 2:10; Col. 3:17; 2 Thess. 1:12; 3:6; Heb. 1:4; James 2:7; 1 Pet. 4:14; 1 John 3:23; 5:13; Rev. 2:3, 13; 3:8.

However, the third commandment is not limited to blasphemy, for it forbids any speaking of God lightly. Such violations of the third commandment are called "profanity" because they treat what is sacred as if it were common or ordinary (Latin *profanus*). Thomas Watson said, "We take God's name in vain . . . when we use God's name in idle discourse. He is not to be spoken of but with a holy awe upon our hearts. To bring his name in at every turn, when we are not thinking of him, to say, 'O God!' or, 'O Christ!' . . . is to take God's name in vain."[13] Profanity includes cursing, calling on God to damn people to hell out of personal frustration, which is quite different than warning them about "the damnation of hell" in the fear of God (Matt. 23:33).

Frivolous oaths—the quickly rattled off "I swear to God!"—also take the Lord's name in vain. Christ forbids such oaths, even those that avoid God's name but still invoke something sacred by association with him, and he requires us to speak plainly and honestly (Matt. 5:33–37; 23:16–22; cf. James 5:12). The swearing of oaths is permitted, as we see by the examples of Christ and Paul,[14] but an oath must be taken in the fear of God by his name alone (Deut. 6:13) and with sincere resolve to do what one promises (Lev. 19:12).[15]

The positive side of the third commandment is the duty to tell God's wonders to our children (Ps. 78:4), praise and thank him among his people (35:18; 111:1), and declare his glory among the nations (96:3). Johannes Wollebius said, "The confession of God's name means the daily acknowledgement, for God's glory, freely and openly before men, of the truth known through his word."[16] Confessing Jesus as Lord is one of the most basic impulses of saving faith (Rom. 10:10; 2 Cor. 4:13). Christ says, "Whosoever therefore shall confess me before men, him will I confess also before my Father which is in heaven" (Matt. 10:32).

We honor God's name by using his Word as he intends, not for man's entertainment, intellectual curiosity, or pride. John Dod (c. 1549–1645)

13. Watson, *The Ten Commandments*, 85.

14. Matt. 26:63–64; Rom. 1:9; 2 Cor. 1:23; 11:31; Phil. 1:8; 1 Thess. 2:5. For other godly people swearing oaths, see Gen. 21:24; 26:31; 31:53–54; Ruth 3:13; 1 Kings 18:10. God himself swears oaths (Ps. 110:4; Heb. 6:13).

15. See Calvin, *Institutes*, 2.8.26; the Heidelberg Catechism (LD 37, Q. 101–2), in *The Three Forms of Unity*, 104; and the Westminster Confession of Faith (chap. 22), in *Reformed Confessions*, 4:260–61.

16. Wollebius, *Compendium*, 2.6.(3).8a (219).

said, "One must never talk of God's Word, but that he may bring some glory to God and some good edification to men."[17]

We also honor God's name by singing his praise in public worship. John Brown of Haddington said that people profane God's name by neglecting to join the church in singing, lacking sincere affections suitable for what is sung, paying more attention to the music than the heart, or quickly becoming weary of worship.[18] James Grier warned, "It is possible to violate the third commandment as you sit in the worship service and sing. . . . You will say things in praise to him that are not meant. You will indeed without fervor or commitment go through all the external motions and use the Name over and over and over again, while all the time in your life you are in disobedience to his will."[19]

Obedience to the precept regarding God-honoring speech requires a heart that fears the Lord. Christ teaches that "blasphemies" come "out of the heart" (Matt. 15:19). Therefore, talk that slights God comes from a heart that does not feel the weight of his glory (cf. v. 18). We need the Lord to do as he promised: "I will put my fear in their hearts" (Jer. 32:40). We should pray, "Thou art great, and doest wondrous things: thou art God alone. Teach me thy way, O Lord; I will walk in thy truth: unite my heart to fear thy name" (Ps. 86:10–11).

Christians must walk cautiously, lest we do anything that causes others to blaspheme God (Rom. 2:17–24). God's people are called by his name.[20] Christians must be obedient to God and submissive to the human authorities over them "that the name of God and his doctrine be not blasphemed" (1 Tim. 6:1), but instead "that they may adorn [display the beauty of] the doctrine of God our Saviour in all things" (Titus 2:10). The Lord insists, "My name shall be great among the nations" (Mal. 1:11). Let us offer ourselves as means by which God fulfills this promise.

The Fourth Commandment: God's Holy Day

The Lord says, "Remember the sabbath day, to keep it holy. Six days shalt thou labour, and do all thy work: but the seventh day is the sabbath of the Lord thy God: in it thou shalt not do any work, thou, nor thy son, nor

17. John Dod, *A Plaine and Familiar Exposition of the Ten Commandements*, 17th ed. (London: by I. D. for Thomas and Jonas Man, 1628), 92.

18. Brown, *Questions and Answers on the Shorter Catechism*, 225.

19. Grier, "The Ten Words," Lecture 3, SoundCloud, audio lecture, https://soundcloud.com/grand-rapids-theological-seminary/series-10-words-lesson-3-james-grier, 20:55–21:36.

20. Deut. 28:10; 2 Chron. 7:14; Isa. 43:7; Dan. 9:18–19; Amos 9:12.

thy daughter, thy manservant, nor thy maidservant, nor thy cattle, nor thy stranger that is within thy gates," and gives this reason: "For in six days the LORD made heaven and earth, the sea, and all that in them is, and rested the seventh day: wherefore the LORD blessed the sabbath day, and hallowed it" (Ex. 20:8–11).

Moses's repetition of this commandment differs from the original in the opening words, "Keep the sabbath day," and in the reason given: "That thy manservant and thy maidservant may rest as well as thou. And remember that thou wast a servant in the land of Egypt, and that the LORD thy God brought thee out thence through a mighty hand and by a stretched out arm: therefore the LORD thy God commanded thee to keep the sabbath day" (Deut. 5:12–15).

The Exegesis of the Fourth Commandment

The word translated as "sabbath" (*shabbat*) comes from a verb meaning to "cease" or "rest" (*shabat*, Gen. 8:22; Ex. 5:5). The rest that God commands is not a cessation of all activity but an interruption of ordinary labor, the "work" (*mela'kah*) of one's daily vocation.[21] This rest from vocational labor extends to all workers, even to servants and livestock. One purpose of the Sabbath day is that people and animals may rest regularly, find refreshment, and not be oppressed by their labor (Ex. 23:12; Deut. 5:14). Even in seasons of plowing and harvesting, the Israelites were to rest on the Sabbath day (Ex. 34:21). The Sabbath required the cessation of commercial production, traffic, and trade (Neh. 10:31; 13:15–22; Jer. 17:19–27).

The other purpose of the Sabbath is to set aside a day for worship in the assembly of God's people. God commands them to "keep it holy" or "hallowed" and to "sanctify" it (*piel* of *qadash*, Ex. 20:8, 11; Deut. 5:12). The Sabbath is a day for holy "convocation" (*miqra'*, Lev. 23:3), which means a meeting of people called together (Num. 10:2). The people are to give themselves to praise, as is illustrated in Psalm 92, "A Psalm or Song for the sabbath day," which commends public worship of God in both morning and evening with remembrance of his works and praising him (Ps. 92:1–5).[22]

21. Gen. 39:11; Prov. 18:9; 22:29; Jonah 1:8.

22. The "psaltery" and "harp" were instruments that the Levites played in the courts of the sanctuary (1 Chron. 15:16, 28; 16:5; 25:1, 6; 2 Chron. 5:12), and thus their mention in Ps. 92:3 suggests public worship.

At Mount Sinai, the Lord commanded Israel to "remember" (*zakar*) the Sabbath (Ex. 20:8), a word that denotes not merely the exercise of the memory but thoughtful activity, especially the faithful keeping of a covenant.[23] Moses later said that Israel must "keep" (*shamar*) the Sabbath (Deut. 5:12), a verb meaning to "guard," implying vigilant effort. The Lord calls the Sabbath "my holy day" (Isa. 58:13). For the sake of his honor, we must guard it from being profaned as if it were a common thing (56:2, 6), just as the Levites guarded the holy places (Num. 3:32). God says, "Ye shall keep the sabbath therefore; for it is holy unto you" (Ex. 31:14).

The fourth commandment mandates *the day* to be set apart from our ordinary work for public worship. Together with the first three commandments, the Sabbath law completes God's revelation of man's duties of worship toward God. We are to worship the holy God by the holy means he ordains with the holy reverence he deserves on the holy day he chooses. Calvin said, "We have one definite day of the week which is to be completely spent in hearing God's word, in prayers and petitions, and in meditating upon his works so that we may rejoice in him."[24]

It might be objected that the fourth commandment is a ceremonial law in the Mosaic covenant, was fulfilled in Christ, and so has passed away in its literal significance.[25]

In reply, we note that, as we have argued elsewhere, God elevated the Ten Commandments above the rest of the law by declaring it immediately by his own voice to Israel, writing it by his power on stone tablets, commanding that it be placed in the ark of the covenant, and moving Moses to declare it a second time.[26] To drop one of the Ten Commandments is to unravel the moral law. Indeed, when considered in terms of the number of words, the fourth commandment stands at the center of the Decalogue.[27] Though given with Israel's situation in view, the Decalogue summarizes the unchanging precepts of God's moral law and thus transcends the Mosaic

23. Gen. 8:1; 9:15–16; 19:29; 30:22; Ex. 2:24; 6:5; 32:13; Lev. 26:42, 45; Num. 10:9; 15:39–41; Deut. 9:27; 1 Chron. 16:15; Pss. 103:18; 105:8; 106:45; 111:5; Jer. 14:21; Ezek. 16:60; Amos 1:9.

24. John Calvin, *Sermons on Genesis, Chapters 1—11*, trans. Rob Roy McGregor (Edinburgh: Banner of Truth, 2009), 130.

25. Wayne Grudem, *Christian Ethics: An Introduction to Biblical Moral Reasoning* (Wheaton, IL: Crossway, 2018), 346–51.

26. Ex. 20:1, 19; 25:16; 31:18; Deut. 4:13–14; 5:1–21; 10:1–5. See *RST*, 2:684–86.

27. In the 163 Hebrew words of the Ten Commandments in Exodus 20, the word at the center is "to the LORD" (*laYHWH*) in the phrase literally translated as "sabbath to the LORD your God" (v. 10).

covenant. To establish this point, we will trace the Sabbath principle from creation to the church after the resurrection of Jesus Christ.

The Fourth Commandment and Creation

At Mount Sinai, the Lord explicitly linked the fourth commandment to his creation of the world: "For in six days the LORD made heaven and earth, the sea, and all that in them is, and rested the seventh day: wherefore the LORD blessed the sabbath day, and hallowed it" (Ex. 20:11).

The first creation account concludes, "Thus the heavens and the earth were finished, and all the host of them. And on the seventh day God ended his work which he had made; and he rested on the seventh day from all his work which he had made. And God blessed the seventh day, and sanctified it: because that in it he had rested from all his work which God created and made" (Gen. 2:1–3). The word translated as "rested" (*shabat*), meaning to "cease," is the verb cognate to "sabbath," sometimes used for man's Sabbath rest (Ex. 23:12; 34:21). Thus, God kept the first Sabbath himself. One passage of Scripture even says God "rested, and was refreshed" (31:17), but since God does not need rest, this was a sign for man to "be refreshed" (23:12).

Therefore, the holy rest of the Sabbath is a creation ordinance, not merely a ceremonial law instituted for Israel as a distinctive nation but part of the moral fabric of the universe. The principle that men must set apart holy days for the worship of God as he ordains is embedded in the human conscience and is evident in religions around the world.[28] The divine nature requires that men have times devoted to worship, the divine wisdom determines that man should set aside one day in seven for this purpose, and the divine will chooses the particular day.

It might be objected that God did not command Adam to keep the Sabbath, and therefore, Genesis 2:1–3 does not reveal the institution of the Sabbath for man.

In reply, we maintain that Scripture does not say that God merely rested but also "blessed" and "sanctified" the day (Gen. 2:3). For God to bless the day was to declare by his effectual word that it would be a day of blessing—not for him but for his creatures (cf. Gen. 1:22, 28), so they would rest

28. Nicholas Bownd, *Sabbathum Veteris et Novi Testamenti: or, The True Doctrine of the Sabbath*, ed. Chris Coldwell (Dallas, TX: Naphtali Press; Grand Rapids, MI: Reformation Heritage Books, 2015), 55–56.

and worship him.[29] Greg Nichols says, "God gave man the Sabbath Day as the epitome of his generosity as Creator."[30] To "hallow" or "sanctify" (*piel* of *qadash*, Gen. 2:3; Ex. 20:11) something is to dedicate it for the purpose of worship in God's holy presence, such as when God sanctified the tabernacle, the altar, and the priests (Ex. 29:44; Lev. 8:10–12). Franciscus Junius (1545–1602) said that God's sanctifying of the day implies man's duty to treat it as holy.[31] Furthermore, man was created in God's image, with a natural impulse to imitate God. God's rest, unnecessary for the deity, was presented as a model for Adam's imitation.[32] Calvin said, "God rested; then he blessed this rest, that in all ages it might be held sacred among men: or he dedicated every seventh day to rest, that his own example might be a perpetual rule . . . that they, being released from all other business, might the more readily apply their minds to the Creator of the world."[33]

It might be further objected that God did not institute the Sabbath at creation because there is no record in the Holy Scriptures of the keeping of the Sabbath until after Israel's exodus.

In reply, we note that the Holy Scriptures do not tell us of anyone in Israel keeping the Sabbath between Moses and the reign of David (1 Chron. 9:32; 23:31), though God commanded Sabbath keeping in the law of Moses (Neh. 9:14). The Scriptures pass by many events in history in silence, and we should not make an argument from silence.[34] Furthermore, the fall of man corrupted man's practice of creation ordinances, as we see in early cases of polygamy (Gen. 4:19).[35]

However, the silence of Scripture does not mean that the Sabbath was entirely neglected by the patriarchs, for the gospel and the moral law have ever been part of God's special revelation. The Lord says, "Abraham obeyed my voice, and kept my charge, my commandments, my statutes, and my laws" (Gen. 26:5). Athanasius said, "What Moses taught, that Abraham observed; and what Abraham observed, that Noah and Enoch acknowledged. . . . For Abel too in this way witnessed, knowing what he

29. Vermigli, *The Common Places*, 374.

30. Nichols, *Lectures in Systematic Theology*, 2:363.

31. Franciscus Junius, *Protoktisia, seu Creationis a Deo Factae, et in Ea Prioris Adami ex Creatione Integri & ex Lapsu Corrupti, Historia* (Amsterdam: Johannes Commelinus, 1589), 61–62. Cited in Bownd, *The True Doctrine of the Sabbath*, 41.

32. Nichols, *Lectures in Systematic Theology*, 2:363–64.

33. Calvin, *Commentaries*, on Gen. 2:3. See also Wollebius, *Compendium*, 2.7.(2) (221).

34. It may be significant that there is a reference to a seven-day "week" in the time of the patriarchs (Gen. 29:27–28).

35. Ames, *The Marrow of Theology*, 2.15.10 (289).

had learned from Adam, who himself had learned from that Lord," who spoke the same law and gospel through all the prophets.[36]

Finally, it may be objected that the creational Sabbath is a type of rest in Christ (Heb. 4:4–11), and, therefore, has been abolished by his accomplishing that rest in his death and resurrection.

In reply, we observe that the rest spoken of in Hebrews 4 is the eternal rest of God's people. The Sabbath continues to point ahead to this rest after Christ's death and resurrection, for we have not yet entered the new heaven and new earth. Marriage is a creation ordinance that typifies God's union with his people through Christ (Eph. 5:31–32), but mankind will transcend marriage only at the resurrection (Matt. 22:30). In the same way, we continue to need one day in seven for refreshment and worship until we enter into our eternal rest: "There remaineth therefore a rest [a keeping of the sabbath, KJV mg.] to the people of God" (Heb. 4:9).[37]

The Fourth Commandment and the Old Covenant

The Lord began calling Israel to practice the Sabbath before giving the Ten Commandments at Mount Sinai. God daily provided manna in the wilderness as an object lesson in trusting him and keeping the Sabbath (Ex. 16:22–31). On the sixth day, Israel found two days' supply of manna, but none appeared on the seventh day, for it was "the rest of the holy sabbath unto the LORD" (v. 23). At this point, the people of Israel were God's people simply by virtue of the covenant made with Abraham (2:24; 3:6–7; 6:4–5). Yet they kept the Sabbath.

In the Ten Commandments, the fourth commandment reiterated the Sabbath principle to Israel. However, the obligation to keep the Sabbath was not limited to Israel but included the "stranger that is within thy gates" (Ex. 20:10)—that is, people outside the covenant who dwelt in Israelite cities but were excluded from eating the Passover (12:45). Therefore, the Sabbath was not merely a ceremonial law for Israel's worship but contained a universal moral principle.[38]

However, God did add some temporary features to the Sabbath under the Mosaic covenant, including its function as a covenantal sign and ad-

36. Athanasius, *De Decretis*, 2.5, in *NPNF*², 4:153.

37. The term translated as "rest" (*sabbatismos*) in Heb. 4:9 is different from other terms rendered as "rest" in that context. It is a noun derived from the verb meaning to "rest on the sabbath" (*sabbatizō*, Ex. 16:30; Lev. 23:32; etc.).

38. Joseph A. Pipa, *The Lord's Day* (Fearn, Ross-shire, Scotland: Christian Focus, 1997), 59.

ditional restrictions and sanctions for its observance. After the revelation of the Ten Commandments, the Lord said, "Verily my sabbaths ye shall keep: for it is a sign between me and you throughout your generations; that ye may know that I am the Lord that doth sanctify you" (Ex. 31:13). Just as the rainbow and circumcision were signs of God's covenants with Noah and Abraham (Gen. 9:12–13, 17; 17:11), the Sabbath was a sign of God's national covenant with Israel by which he took them as his holy people. This covenantal significance of the Sabbath was a type foreshadowing the complete holiness that God would bring to his people in Christ (Zech. 14:20–21). The Sabbath foreshadowed the "rest" that they would enjoy in the inheritance,[39] which God would secure by his victorious kingdom through the anointed King.[40] This rest pointed beyond the acquisition of the Promised Land (Ps. 95:11) to the ultimate inheritance of believers in glory (Heb. 3:7–4:11).[41]

Although the fourth commandment is part of the summary of the moral law, not every aspect of the Sabbath reflects the unchanging moral order of God. The choice of a particular day and the specifics of how it is to be observed are determined by God as he wills. Some theologians prefer to simply call these aspects of the Sabbath *positive law*, which means a law not derived by necessity from divine nature or human nature but added by God's authoritative will.[42] Other theologians also think it appropriate to say that the Sabbath is partly moral law and partly *ceremonial law*, the latter a particular kind of positive law that consisted of divine ordinances of external worship that foreshadowed Christ.[43]

39. Deut. 3:20; 12:9–10; Josh. 21:44; 22:4; 23:1.

40. 2 Sam. 7:11; 1 Kings 5:4; 8:56; 1 Chron. 22:9, 18; 23:25.

41. Augustine, *The City of God*, 11.8, 22.30, in *NPNF*[1], 2:209, 511.

42. Bownd, *The True Doctrine of the Sabbath*, 70–81; Ames, *The Marrow of Theology*, 2.15.12–25 (291–94); Anthony Burgess, *Vindiciae Legis: or, a Vindication of the Morall Law and the Covenants, from the Errours of Papists, Arminians, Socinians, and More Especially, Antinomians*, 2nd ed. (London: by James Young, for Thomas Underhill, 1647), 148; and Daniel Cawdrey and Herbert Palmer, *Sabbatum Redivivum: or the Christian Sabbath Vindicated . . . The First Part* (London: by Robert White, for Thomas Underhill, 1645), 1–48. John Brown of Haddington said that the specification of the day "is changeable, but not properly ceremonial." *Questions and Answers on the Shorter Catechism*, 230. Wilhelmus à Brakel argued extensively that the sabbath is in no respects a ceremonial law. *The Christian's Reasonable Service*, 3:149–83.

43. Aquinas, *Summa Theologica*, Part 2.2, Q. 122, Art. 4, Reply Obj. 1; Perkins, *Commentary on Galatians*, on Gal. 4:10, in *Works*, 2:276; *A Golden Chain*, chap. 23, in *Works*, 6:100–101; Synod of Dort, in *Acta et Documenta Synodi Nationalis Dordrechtanae (1618–1619)*, vol. 1, *Acta of the Synod of Dordt (1618–1619)*, ed. Donald Sinnema, Christian Moser, and Herman J. Selderhuis (Göttingen: Vandenhoeck & Ruprecht, 2015), session 164 (166); Wollebius, *Compendium*, 2.7.(2).v (222); Durham, *A Practical Exposition of the Ten Commandments*, 207; and Turretin, *Institutes*, 11.13.19 (2:84).

The law of Moses expanded the Sabbath requirement from the simple instruction revealed at creation to a more demanding ordinance. Not even the kindling of a fire in one's home was permitted (Ex. 35:3). Each Sabbath, the priests performed extra duties of ceremonial worship (Lev. 24:8; Num. 28:9–10). God also instituted other holy Sabbath days besides the seventh day.[44] He commanded the land's yearlong Sabbath, a rest from agriculture every seven years (Lev. 25:1–7), with another yearlong Sabbath every fifty years on the Jubilee (vv. 8–13).

The judicial law penalized Sabbath breaking severely. Profaning the Sabbath by one's ordinary work was a capital offense.[45] Willfully breaking the Sabbath was a gross violation of Israel's status as God's "sacral society," as Nichols observes.[46] For Israel to reject the Sabbath was to rebel against the Lord who had sanctified the nation and, thus, to provoke him to bring about the people's national exile from the land (Ezek. 20:12–13, 20–24).

The Fourth Commandment and Christ's Teaching

Jesus Christ often taught in synagogues on the Sabbath (Luke 4:16, 31; 6:6; 13:10), and his first disciples were Sabbath-observing Jews (23:56). However, the Pharisees accused Christ and his followers of breaking the Sabbath, especially by his healing of people on that day.[47]

Christ's response to these accusations is quite instructive for us when compared to his response to accusations regarding the washing of hands. In the latter case, Christ explained that true uncleanness was not a matter of external things but of sin from the heart, thereby showing that God was declaring all things clean and abolishing the ceremonial law (Mark 7:1–5, 14–23; cf. Luke 11:37–41). Similarly, when challenged by a Samaritan about the proper place of worship, Christ taught that location no longer mattered—abolishing the old covenant temple (John 4:20–24). However, when criticized about the Sabbath, Christ did not abolish it but instead explained the true keeping of the Sabbath through works of necessity, piety, and mercy (Mark. 2:23–3:6). (We will explore his teaching when we draw out ethical implications of the fourth commandment in the last

44. Ex. 12:16; Lev. 16:29, 31; 23:7–8, 21, 24–25, 28, 30–32, 35–36; Num. 28:18, 25; 29:1, 7, 12, 35.

45. Ex. 31:14–15; 35:2; Num. 15:30–36.

46. Nichols, *Lectures in Systematic Theology*, 2:371.

47. Luke 6:7; 13:10; 14:1–3; John 5:15–16; 9:15–16.

part of this chapter.) This is the same approach Christ took to other moral laws: correcting the corruptions of human traditions and drawing out the true applications of these moral laws, which Christ did not abolish but fulfilled (Matt. 5:17–48).[48]

It might be objected that Christ gave these teachings about the Sabbath while he and his disciples were under the law of Moses, prior to his death and resurrection.

In reply, we answer that the Gospels were written after Christ's death and resurrection for the instruction of Christians under the new covenant. Christians are disciples of Jesus Christ, and therefore, they must follow his teachings and not discard them as relics of a previous age or dispensation. Christ taught his disciples to keep the Sabbath according to the law of love.

Christ says, "The sabbath was made for man, and not man for the sabbath" (Mark 2:27). He does not say that the Sabbath was made for Israel, but for "man," and alludes to God's creation of man on the sixth day and institution of the Sabbath on the seventh day (Gen. 1:26–2:3).[49] Christ's meaning is that the Sabbath serves to benefit us as human beings; mankind needs this day of rest and sacred worship. Grier said, "The sabbath was made for man's well-being. It was not made for man's restriction. It was not made to truncate and to ruin man's life. It was made to enrich man and to expand man's life."[50]

Furthermore, the Lord Jesus says, "The Son of man is Lord also of the sabbath" (Mark 2:28). The Old Testament often calls the day "the holy sabbath unto the Lord" or "the sabbath of the Lord," or it reinforces the Sabbath commandment with the assertion "I am the Lord."[51] For Christ to declare himself "Lord" of the Sabbath is to claim deity, to assert that he is the Lawgiver and to make himself the focal point of the Sabbath celebration. Truly, "one greater than the temple" has come (Matt. 12:6). Far from renouncing the Sabbath, Christ's disciples must

48. See the discussion of Christ's doctrine of the threefold law in *RST*, 2:688–91.

49. Though the verb translated as "was made" (*ginomai*) has a wide variety of uses, it well fits allusions to the work of creation (John 1:3, 10), for it appears several times in Genesis 1 for God's creative commands ("Let there be") and their effectual results (Gen. 1:3, 6, etc. LXX) as well as the first man's coming to life (2:7 LXX). Note also the parallel between Christ's words "The sabbath was made for [*dia*] man, and not man for [*dia*] the sabbath" (Mark 2:27) and Paul's words "Neither was the man created for [*dia*] the woman; but the woman for [*dia*] the man" (1 Cor. 11:9). In both cases, the argument stands on the order of creation (v. 8; cf. 1 Tim. 2:13).

50. Grier, "The Ten Words," Lecture 4, SoundCloud, audio lecture, https://soundcloud.com/grand-rapids-theological-seminary/series-10-words-lesson-4-james-grier, 44:31–48.

51. Ex. 16:23, 25; 20:10; 31:13, 15; 35:2; Lev. 19:3, 30; 23:3, 38; 25:2, 4; 26:2; Deut. 5:14 LXX. Note that in both Mark 2:28 and these citations from the LXX, "Lord" translates *Kyrios*.

keep it even more devoutly because of their love and submission to the Lord Jesus Christ, God the Son incarnate. Should we think that Christ said he was Lord of the Sabbath, told his disciples it was made for man's benefit, and taught them how to keep it rightly just so he could abolish it a short time later? Walter Chantry says that such an argument "makes nonsense of Jesus' words."[52]

The Gospel of Matthew presents Christ's conflict with the Pharisees over the Sabbath immediately after Christ's invitation "Come unto me, all ye that labour and are heavy laden, and I will give you rest. Take my yoke upon you, and learn of me; for I am meek and lowly in heart: and ye shall find rest unto your souls. For my yoke is easy, and my burden is light" (Matt. 11:28–30). The verb translated as "give rest" (*anapauō*) and the noun "rest" (*anapausis*) are used several times of Sabbath rest.[53] In contrast to man-made legalism, Christ offers himself as the giver of true Sabbath rest—not merely an outward cessation of actions but an inward peace of humbly and meekly resting in God and his will. True Sabbath keeping requires submission to Christ as our Lord and Teacher ("my yoke") and learning from him in the way of discipleship.

One more reference to the Sabbath in Christ's teaching invites our attention. In his discourse about the coming judgment, the Lord Jesus warned his disciples to flee from Judea into the mountains when they saw Gentile armies surrounding Jerusalem (Luke 21:20–21). Christ said, "Pray ye that your flight be not in the winter, neither on the sabbath day" (Matt. 24:20). Evidently, Christ anticipated that his disciples would be keeping the Sabbath when God's wrath would fall on Jerusalem—a prophecy fulfilled in AD 70, four decades after Christ rose again.[54]

It is sometimes said that the Sabbath no longer applies to Christians because the New Testament does not repeat the fourth commandment. However, the teaching of Jesus Christ in the Gospels is part of the New Testament. It is a false hermeneutic that insists that Christians need follow only the explicit commands of the New Testament Epistles.[55]

52. Walter Chantry, *Call the Sabbath a Delight* (Edinburgh: Banner of Truth, 1991), 57.

53. Ex. 16:23; 23:12; 31:15; 35:2; Lev. 16:31; 23:3; 25:2, 4; Deut. 5:14 LXX.

54. On Matt. 24:20 and the Christian sabbath, see Udemans, *The Practice of Faith, Hope, and Love*, 288–90.

55. Indeed, the New Testament does not need to repeat a teaching of the Old Testament for it to regulate our lives. The third commandment is not so repeated (Ex. 20:7). Neither is the prohibition against sexual perversion with animals (Ex. 22:19; Lev. 18:23; 20:15–16). The question is whether the teaching in view expresses a moral principle grounded in the order of creation. The fourth commandment does precisely that.

The Fourth Commandment and Apostolic Christianity

When the Lord Jesus suffered on the cross for our sins, a supernatural darkness came upon the land (Luke 23:44). Christ died on the cross as the Sabbath drew near (v. 54; John 19:31). The penalty of death imposed on creation due to man's sin had descended to its nadir in the death of the incarnate Lord. His great work of accomplishing redemption was "finished" (John 19:30). During the seventh day of the week, his body rested in the grave, and the next day he rose from the dead around the time that the sun's light dawned on the land. The fact that every Gospel says that he rose on "the first day of the week" marks the day as particularly important.[56]

The resurrection accounts allude to the first day of creation, when God created the world and brought light out of darkness (Gen. 1:1–5). Christ's resurrection was the dawning of the new creation of life and immortality (Eph. 2:5–7, 10; 2 Tim. 1:10), the pinnacle and turning point of history (Gal. 4:4). Paul says, "Christ being raised from the dead dieth no more; death hath no more dominion over him" (Rom. 6:9). "In Christ," the "new creation" has arrived, for "the old has passed away; behold, the new has come" (2 Cor. 5:17 ESV). Therefore, it is no surprise that the timing of the Sabbath, which was grounded on the order of the first creation, has been changed to commemorate the beginning of the new creation on the first day.

The Gospel of John further emphasizes the day by stating, "Then the same day at evening, being the first day of the week, when the doors were shut where the disciples were assembled for fear of the Jews, came Jesus and stood in the midst, and saith unto them, Peace be unto you" (John 20:19). John had already written that it was on "the first day of the week" when Christ rose (v. 1). By repeating the phrase, he associated the first day with enjoying fellowship with the Lord in his messianic peace through the power of the Holy Spirit and the forgiveness of sins (vv. 21–23). Christ appeared again announcing peace "after eight days" (v. 26), which in the inclusive method of counting time was again the first day of the week.[57]

Luke also provides evidence that the Lord's holy day had shifted from the seventh to the first day of the week in the book of Acts. Christ poured

56. Matt. 28:1; Mark 16:2; Luke 24:1; John 20:1. Literally, "the first day of the week" is "first of sabbaths" (*mia [tōn] sabbatōn*), where "sabbaths" functions as an idiom for a week of seven days (Luke 18:12).

57. Carson, *The Gospel according to John*, 657. Note also the references to the "eighth day" in old covenant rituals (Lev. 9:1; 12:3; 14:10, 23; 15:14, 29; 22:27; 23:36, 39; Num. 6:10; 29:35; Ezek. 43:27).

out the Holy Spirit on the church on the day of Pentecost (Acts 2), which fell on the first day of the week (Lev. 23:16). Luke records that later, "upon the first day of the week, when the disciples came together to break bread, Paul preached unto them" (Acts 20:7). Apart from references to the Jewish Sabbath, this is the only instance in Acts where Luke identifies a particular day of the week, and he uses the exact phrase that he used earlier for the day of Christ's resurrection (Luke 24:1). Here, then, is an early testimony to Christians meeting on the first day of the week to hear the preaching of God's Word and perhaps to celebrate the Lord's Supper (cf. Luke 22:19; Acts 2:42; 1 Cor. 10:16).[58]

We also find in the book of Acts that when Christ rose from the dead, he fulfilled the ancient prophecy "The stone which the builders refused is become the head stone of the corner" (Ps. 118:22; cf. Acts 4:10–11). The prophecy continues, "This is the day which the Lord hath made; we will rejoice and be glad in it" (Ps. 118:24).[59] To "make" (*'asah*) a day means to appoint a particular day for a special event, such as a feast (1 Kings 12:32–33). The psalm proceeds to describe a festival of worship at God's house (Ps. 118:26–29). Even if this psalm had an initial fulfilment in the monarchy of David's house, it points ahead to a greater fulfillment in Christ and his resurrection.[60] George Swinnock said, "The precedent verses [before Ps. 118:24] are a prophetical prediction of Christ's resurrection. . . . The Lord's day is the highest thanksgiving-day, and deserveth . . . to be a day of feasting and gladness, and a good day."[61]

Paul, too, asserted the sanctification of the first day of the week for Christian worship: "Now concerning the collection for the saints: as I directed the churches of Galatia, so you also are to do. On the first day of every week, each of you is to put something aside and store it up, as he may prosper, so that there will be no collecting when I come" (1 Cor. 16:1–2 ESV). Paul mandated that the churches take a collection weekly so that the money would be ready as soon as he arrived to take to the poor believers in Jerusalem (v. 3; cf. Rom. 15:25–28). Financial gifts are offerings (Phil. 4:18; Heb. 13:16), acts of religious "service" or worship

58. John R. W. Stott, *The Message of Acts: To the Ends of the Earth*, The Bible Speaks Today (Downers Grove, IL: InterVarsity Press, 1994), 319.

59. Boston, *An Illustration of the Doctrines of the Christian Religion*, in *Works*, 2:192.

60. Note the references to Ps. 118:22–26 in Matt. 21:9, 42; 23:39; Mark 11:9–10; 12:10–11; Luke 13:35; 20:17; John 12:13; 1 Pet. 2:7. The words translated as "save now" (*hoshi'ah n'a*, Ps. 118:25) are the basis of "hosanna."

61. Swinnock, *The Christian Man's Calling*, in *Works*, 1:239–40.

(2 Cor. 9:12). The apostolic mandate implied a general practice among the Christian churches to gather on the first day of the week; indeed, such meetings were required to keep Paul's command.

However, Paul also denied that Christians are under the strictures of the old covenant Sabbath: "Let no man therefore judge you in meat, or in drink, or in respect of an holyday [feast], or of the new moon, or of the sabbath days" (Col. 2:16). Paul declared the freedom of Christians from observing the seventh day and the burdensome Mosaic Sabbath regulations that prohibited kindling a fire at home; required extra burnt offerings, additional holy days, and Sabbath years; and punished Sabbath breakers with death. However, Paul was addressing old covenant ceremonial regulations; he did not nullify the creation ordinance of weekly holy rest.

In light of the accounts of Christ's resurrection, his appearances to the apostles, Pentecost, and the practice of the early church, it is not difficult to identify what day John meant when he said, "I was in the Spirit on the Lord's day" (Rev. 1:10). It was the first day of the week, the day of Christ's resurrection. The adjective translated as "Lord's" (*kyriakos*) means belonging to a lord (*kyrios*). It appears elsewhere in the New Testament only in reference to "the Lord's supper"—that is, the supper instituted by the Lord Jesus in remembrance of him and his death (1 Cor. 11:20, 23–25). Similarly, the "Lord's day" is the day set apart by him for his worship.[62] The early church, while insisting that Christians are not bound by the Jewish Sabbath, observed the first day of the week, "the Lord's day," as the day of Christian public worship.[63]

The biblical phrase "Lord's day" (Rev. 1:10) points to a Christian appropriation of the Sabbath principle, for Christ says that he is "the Lord" of "the sabbath" (Luke 6:5). God refers to "the sabbath" as "my holy day . . . the holy of the LORD" (Isa. 58:13). It is not likely that the disciples of Christ, rooted as they were in the Old Testament, would have set apart one

62. Ames, *The Marrow of Theology*, 2.15.2 (287).

63. Ignatius, *Epistle to the Magnesians*, chap. 9, in *ANF*, 1:62; *Didache*, 14.1–3, in Lightfoot, *The Apostolic Fathers*, 234; Justin Martyr, *First Apology*, chap. 47, in *ANF*, 1:186; Dionysius of Corinth, cited in Eusebius, *Church History*, 4.23.11, in *NPNF*², 1:201; Tertullian, *Apology*, chap. 16, in *ANF*, 3:31; *Ad Nationes*, 1:13, in *ANF*, 3:123; Athanasius, *Defence against the Arians*, sec. 11, in *NPNF*², 4:106; *Defence of His Flight*, chap. 6, in *NPNF*², 4:257; Chrysostom, *Homilies on 1 Corinthians*, 43.2, in *NPNF*¹, 12:259; Anonymous, *Constitutions of the Holy Apostles*, 7.36, in *ANF*, 7:474; Constantine, cited in Eusebius, *Life of Constantine*, 4.18–20, in *NPNF*², 1:544–45; and Augustine, Letters, 36.12.28, in *NPNF*¹, 1:268–69. Sometimes early church writers called it "the eighth day." Thus, *The Epistle of Barnabas*, chap. 15, in *ANF*, 1:147; and Tertullian, *On Idolatry*, chap. 14, in *ANF*, 3:70; cf. Justin Martyr, *Dialogue with Trypho*, chap. 138, in *ANF*, 1:268.

day in seven for holy worship without recognizing its roots in the Sabbath. However, we should also acknowledge that the identity of the "Lord" as Jesus Christ situates the "Lord's day" in a new covenant context, not the law of Moses. Thus, the Lord's Day is the *Christian* Sabbath.

It might be objected that Paul makes the observance of special days to be a matter of mere personal conviction: "One man esteemeth one day above another: another esteemeth every day alike. Let every man be fully persuaded in his own mind" (Rom. 14:5).

In reply, we observe that the objection implies that "the first day of the week . . . would not be distinguished from any other day as the memorial of Christ's resurrection and could not properly be regarded as the Lord's day"—indeed, that observing "a day commemorating our Lord's resurrection would be a feature of the person weak in faith" (cf. v. 1), as John Murray commented.[64] Was John weak in faith when observing the Lord's Day (Rev. 1:10)? Certainly not.

What, then, are we to make of Paul's teaching in Romans 14? Though it is not clear exactly what Paul was addressing in the Roman church, he spoke often of eating and drinking.[65] The issues included dietary laws (v. 14) and either old covenant feasts or special days of fasting from eating meat or drinking wine (v. 21; cf. Dan. 10:3).[66] In any case, Paul did not reduce all matters of eating and drinking to personal convictions, for then there would be no obligation to observe the Lord's Supper or avoid drunkenness.[67] In the same way, this passage does not reduce all days to matters of indifference. It does not nullify the Sabbath revealed at creation, reiterated in the fourth commandment, clarified by Christ, and appropriated by the apostles.[68]

It might also be objected that the observance of any holy days is legalism, for Paul said with alarm, "Ye observe days, and months, and times, and years" (Gal. 4:10).

In reply, we clarify that Paul was alarmed because the Galatians' observance of these days indicated their pursuit of righteousness by works (Gal.

64. Murray, *The Epistle to the Romans*, 2:257.

65. Rom. 14:2–3, 6, 14–15, 17, 20–23.

66. It is possible that the special "day" in view was appointed for people to abstain from some or all foods. Thus, Chrysostom, *Homilies on Romans*, on Rom. 14:5, in *NPNF*[1], 11:523; and Douma, *The Ten Commandments*, 134. There were special days of fasting in the Mosaic law (Lev. 16:29–31; 23:27–32; Num. 29:7) and Jewish tradition (Luke 5:33; 18:12).

67. Ames, *The Marrow of Theology*, 2.15.32 (297). Christ mandates the Lord's Supper: "this do" (1 Cor. 11:24–25).

68. Perkins, *Commentary on Galatians*, on Gal. 4:10, in *Works*, 2:276.

2:16; 5:4). Is it legalism to set aside a day of rest to celebrate God's glory in the finished work of Jesus Christ? J. V. Fesko says, "Israel worked six days, then rested on the last day of the week. . . . We, on the other hand, rest first, then work in gratitude for the completed work of Christ. Each Lord's day . . . we rest from our labors and celebrate our redemption from the bondage of Satan, sin, and death."[69]

The Fourth Commandment and Love

The Lord never intended for the Sabbath to be merely an external exercise or one focused on what people cannot do. The Sabbath is a call to love and joy. God says that if we "call the sabbath a delight . . . then shalt thou delight thyself in the LORD" (Isa. 58:13–14). In the "Song for the sabbath day," we are taught to sing, "It is a good thing to give thanks unto the LORD, and to sing praises unto thy name, O most High" and "Those that be planted in the house of the LORD shall flourish in the courts of our God" (Ps. 92:1, 13).

Ray Ortlund says, "The Sabbath is meant to structure our weekly schedules around glorifying and enjoying God together. . . . The Sabbath is God's way of saying, 'No, your highest values will not be professional and commercial. They will only end up destroying you and others through you. Your highest values will be worship and freedom and delight, enriching you and all around you.'"[70]

As an aspect of the law of love, the Sabbath must never be distorted into an occasion for malice or neglect toward the needs of people. God designed the Sabbath to give refreshment to people and animals, not to burden them (Ex. 23:12; Deut. 5:14). Christ rebuked the Pharisees for their legalistic approach to the Sabbath, saying, "If ye had known what this meaneth, I will have mercy, and not sacrifice, ye would not have condemned the guiltless" (Matt. 12:7).

Some Ethical Applications of the Fourth Commandment

The Westminster Confession of Faith (21.8) says, "This Sabbath is then kept holy unto the Lord, when men, after a due preparing of their hearts, and ordering of their common affairs before-hand, do not only observe an

69. Fesko, *The Rule of Love*, 64.
70. Raymond C. Ortlund Jr., *Isaiah: God Saves Sinners*, Preaching the Word (Wheaton, IL: Crossway, 2005), 391.

holy rest, all the day, from their own works, words, and thoughts about their worldly employments and recreations, but also are taken up, the whole time, in the public and private exercises of His worship, and in the duties of necessity and mercy."[71]

We must prepare for the Lord's Day if we are to keep it well. Watson said, "We should look upon this day as the best day in the week."[72] We must pray for ourselves, our churches, and our pastors. We must put things in order in our homes so that we are ready for a day of "holy rest," "holy services," and "holy affections," as Benjamin Beddome (1717–1795) said. The evening before the Sabbath, we should avoid activities that fill our minds with earthly thoughts, lest they follow us into the next morning. However, Beddome clarified, "should not the Sabbath then be begun and ended in the evening? No. For we read that the Sabbath ended when it 'began to dawn' towards the first day of the week (Matt. 28:1)."[73]

As we have noted, the fourth commandment requires us to rest from our ordinary vocations on the first day of the week and to allow others under our authority or whose services we employ to rest as well (Ex. 20:8–10). Heads of households have a special responsibility to direct their families to keep the Sabbath (v. 10). Godefridus Udemans said, "A father does not obey God if he observes the Sabbath but does not care what his family does."[74]

Like all God's commands, the Sabbath requires self-denial and self-control. The Lord promises his blessing on those who "turn" the "foot" in regard to the Sabbath (Isa. 58:13), a figure of speech for thoughtful self-control and disciplined obedience (Ps. 119:59; cf. v. 101). Alec Motyer said, "The Sabbath calls for careful, thoughtful living."[75] The Lord also warns against "doing thy pleasure" (Isa. 58:13) on his holy day, which means doing whatever we please (46:10; 48:14). Joseph Pipa says, "In our modern idiom we could paraphrase it 'doing your own thing.' . . . He is calling us to turn aside from lesser pleasures in order to seek the greater pleasures He has in store for us in the day."[76] Ryan McGraw writes, "Worldly recreations on the Sabbath are no more appropriate than if a

71. *Reformed Confessions*, 4:260.
72. Watson, *The Ten Commandments*, 96.
73. Benjamin Beddome, *A Scriptural Exposition of the Baptist Catechism*, biographical sketch by Michael A. G. Haykin, intro. James Renihan (Birmingham, AL: Solid Ground, 2006), 112–13.
74. Udemans, *The Practice of Faith, Hope, and Love*, 285.
75. Motyer, *The Prophecy of Isaiah*, 483.
76. Pipa, *The Lord's Day*, 18.

groom paused in the middle of his wedding ceremony to check the scores of a football game."[77]

The aim of the Sabbath is to set our hearts on God. The prohibition against worldly recreations should not be understood to forbid doing anything that we enjoy on the Sabbath. At the Synod of Dort, Dutch Reformed divines said that observing the Lord's Day requires ceasing from "all recreations that hinder the worship of God."[78] Calvin said,

> We must apply this rest to a higher purpose. We must refrain from our own business which might hinder us from the minding of God's works, and we must call upon his name and exercise ourselves in his Word. If we spend the Lord's day in . . . playing and gaming, is that a good honoring of God? Nay, is it not a mockery, yea and a very [desecrating] of his name? . . .
>
> Furthermore we must understand, that the Lord's day was not appointed all only to the hearing of sermons, but to the end that we should apply the rest of the time to the praising of God. . . . It is not to keep the ceremony so [strictly] as it was under the bondage of the law, for we have not the figure or shadow any more. But it serves to call us together . . . to dedicate that day wholly unto him.[79]

Sabbath rest does not mean inactivity. Christ teaches that keeping the Sabbath is consistent with works of necessity, mercy, and piety. The Pharisees criticized his disciples because on the Sabbath they gathered enough food from the fields for a meal (Mark 2:23; cf. Deut. 23:25). Christ used the example of David eating the holy bread to show that rules regarding sacred worship, including the Sabbath, must not be construed so as to deny men their basic necessities: "The sabbath was made for man, and not man for the sabbath" (Mark 2:25–27). Therefore, Christ authorizes us to do those tasks necessary to preserve our life and health on the Lord's Day. Francis Turretin said that the Christian Sabbath does not prohibit people "to kindle a fire, nor to cook food, nor to take up arms against an enemy, nor to prosecute [finish] a journey begun by land or sea."[80] Wollebius said,

---

77. Ryan M. McGraw, *The Day of Worship: Reassessing the Christian Life in Light of the Sabbath* (Grand Rapids, MI: Reformation Heritage Books, 2011), 52.

78. *Acta et Documenta Synodi Nationalis Dordrechtanae*, session 164 (1:166–67). English translation in Casey B. Carmichael, *A Continental View: Johannes Cocceius's Federal Theology of the Sabbath*, Reformed Historical Theology 41 (Göttingen: Vandenhoeck & Ruprecht, 2019), 82.

79. Calvin, *Sermons on Deuteronomy*, 204. "Desecrating" was originally "unhallowing," and "strictly" was "strait." Cf. Calvin, *Sermons on the Ten Commandments*, 109–10.

80. Turretin, *Institutes*, 11.14.24, 26 (2:97–98).

"Anything, which cannot, without serious loss, be postponed for another day, is excepted."[81] This, of course, does not justify putting ourselves in an emergency by poor planning and preparation; it refers to divine providences we cannot avoid. We also should be sensitive to the refreshing benefit of moderate exercise for adults, such as taking a walk, and times of play for children to facilitate alertness when we return to public worship.[82]

Christ also teaches that the Sabbath is a day for works of mercy to prevent or relieve misery (Matt. 12:11; Mark 3:4). Therefore, God is pleased with the Sabbath work of Christian doctors, nurses, caregivers, emergency responders, owners of livestock, soldiers, police officers, and those who maintain basic public services such as power, communications, and the hospitality industry.[83] However, insofar as we are able to plan and order our lives, provision must be made so that all workers can regularly rest and participate as often as possible in Lord's Day worship. Furthermore, God is pleased when his people use their free time on the Sabbath to visit the sick or to practice hospitality.

The Sabbath is especially a day for works of piety. Christ pointed out to the Pharisees that "on the sabbath days the priests in the temple profane the sabbath, and are blameless"—that is, they work on the Sabbath but do not sin in doing so (Matt. 12:5; cf. John 7:22). The labors of pastors, teachers, and those who help to facilitate worship receive God's blessing on the Lord's Day. Furthermore, God blesses people traveling to church, "though they are far distant in situation of dwelling from the common place of meeting," as Nicholas Bownd (c. 1551–1613) said.[84] At the heart of the practice of piety on the Lord's Day is meditation on God's glory as he reveals himself in the Word. The Word of God is the great means of grace, and the Lord's Day is our greatest opportunity to make use of it so that it controls our whole lives. The Sabbath is "the market-day of the soul," when we stock up on spiritual goods for the week's necessities.[85]

God blessed the Sabbath to be a blessing to us. The Lord promises that if you "call the sabbath a delight, the holy [day] of the LORD . . . then shalt thou delight thyself in the LORD; and I will cause thee to ride upon

81. Wollebius, *Compendium*, 2.7.(2).viii (222).

82. For advice about helping children honor the Lord's Day when not with the gathered church, see Pipa, *The Lord's Day*, 189–96.

83. See Udemans, *The Practice of Faith, Hope, and Love*, 284.

84. Bownd, *The True Doctrine of the Sabbath*, 215.

85. Watson, *The Ten Commandments*, 97.

the high places of the earth, and feed thee with the heritage of Jacob thy father" (Isa. 58:13–14). To "ride upon the high places of the earth" alludes to God's abundant provision for Israel in the wilderness (Deut. 32:13). The "heritage" of Jacob is not just the Promised Land, but the spiritual and eternal blessings of Christ (Isa. 54:17), for by union and communion with him, believers can already "begin in this life the eternal Sabbath."[86]

Looking ahead to eternal glory, Robert Murray M'Cheyne (1813–1843) said, "This is the reason why we love the Lord's Day. This is the reason why we 'call the Sabbath a delight.'" When a believer steps away from his desk at the office or his station in the factory, sets aside his work clothes and worldly cares, and comes to the house of God, it is like the dawn of the resurrection. When he sits under the preaching of God's Word and hears the voice of the pastor leading and feeding his soul, it reminds him of the day when "the Lamb which is in the midst of the throne shall feed them, and shall lead them unto living fountains of waters: and God shall wipe away all tears from their eyes" (Rev. 7:17). When he joins in singing psalms of praise, it reminds him that one day he will join his voice with those of myriads of angels and redeemed men to worship God and the Lamb. Thus, M'Cheyne wrote, "A well-spent Sabbath we feel to be a day of heaven upon earth."[87]

Sing to the Lord

A Song for the Sabbath

How good it is to thank the Lord,
And praise to Thee, Most High, accord,
To show Thy love with morning light,
And tell Thy faithfulness each night;
Yea, good it is Thy praise to sing,
And all our sweetest music bring.

O Lord, with joy my heart expands
Before the wonders of Thy hands;
Great works, Jehovah, Thou has wrought,

86. The Heidelberg Catechism (LD 38, Q. 103), in *The Three Forms of Unity*, 105.

87. Robert Murray M'Cheyne, "I Love the Lord's Day," in *Memoirs and Remains of Robert Murray M'Cheyne*, ed. Andrew Bonar (1892; repr., Edinburgh: Banner of Truth, 1995), 596–97. The sentences between the quotes are slightly paraphrased from M'Cheyne's own words. This paragraph is taken from Joel R. Beeke and Paul M. Smalley, "Delighting in God: A Guide to Sabbath-keeping," *Puritan Reformed Journal* 11, no. 1 (2019): 22 (full article, 5–24). Used by permission.

Exceeding deep Thy ev'ry thought;
A foolish man knows not their worth,
Nor he whose mind is of the earth.

The righteous man shall flourish well,
And in the house of God shall dwell;
He shall be like a goodly tree,
And all his life shall fruitful be;
For righteous is the Lord and just,
He is my Rock, in Him I trust.

Psalm 92
Tune: Christine
The Psalter, No. 250
Or Tune: St. Petersburg
Trinity Hymnal—Baptist Edition, No. 535

Questions for Meditation or Discussion

1. What is the third commandment? What does it mean?
2. How does the obligation of the third commandment arise naturally from who God reveals himself to be in the creation of the world?
3. How is obedience to the third commandment a form of love?
4. How has reading this material opened your eyes in a new way to your responsibility to keep the third commandment? How has it shown your responsibility toward other people?
5. What is the fourth commandment? What does it mean?
6. How is the fourth commandment grounded on God's work of creation? What does that imply about the relevance of the commandment for us today?
7. How did God expand the scope and severity of the Sabbath requirements in the law of Moses?
8. When the Pharisees challenged Jesus Christ about the Sabbath, how did he respond? How does that compare to how Christ treated the Mosaic laws regarding ceremonial cleanliness and uncleanliness?
9. What evidence is there in Acts and the New Testament Epistles that apostolic Christianity observed the first day of the week as the Lord's Day?
10. How is obedience to the fourth commandment a way to love God and man?

11. After reading this chapter, what do you believe about the Sabbath and the Lord's Day? How will you put that into practice?

Questions for Deeper Reflection

12. Does treating God's name as holy mean that Christians should never swear an oath or make a sacred vow? If so, why? If not, then what does it mean for oaths? In your answer, address the meaning of Christ's teaching in Matthew 5:33–37; 23:16–22.
13. What does Paul mean when he says, "Let no man therefore judge you in . . . the sabbath days" (Col. 2:16)? What practical application should that teaching have in our lives?
14. What practical advice would you give to a new Christian who desires to "call the sabbath a delight" (Isa. 58:13)?
15. Should our expectations for conduct on the Lord's Day be different for children than for adults? Why or why not? And if so, how?

39

Obedience to God's Law, Part 3

The Fifth through Seventh Commandments

The first four commandments direct our love for God; the last six instruct us in how to love our neighbors.[1] These two loves cannot be separated. John says, "If a man say, I love God, and hateth his brother, he is a liar, . . . [for] he who loveth God . . . [must] love his brother also" (1 John 4:20–21). William Plumer said, "No possible devotion to prescribed forms of religious worship is ever pleasing to the Almighty, or can save a people from ruin, unless they learn 'to seek judgment [justice], relieve the oppressed, judge the fatherless, plead for the widow' (Isa. 1:17)."[2] Love for men is measured by obedience to God's laws: "By this we know that we love the children of God, when we love God, and keep his commandments" (1 John 5:2).

Although the last six commandments are associated with the virtues of civil society, in context they are required as acts of obedience to the Lord. They give no basis for what J. V. Fesko calls "Godless and Christless ethics."[3] John Brown of Haddington noted that civil acts "are religious obedience" when done "from love and regard to God, chiefly for his glory, depending on his promised strength, and hoping for acceptance

1. On love and the virtues that accompany it, see chap. 36.
2. William S. Plumer, *The Law of God, as Contained in the Ten Commandments, Explained and Enforced* (1864; repr., Harrisonburg, VA: Sprinkle, 1996), 344.
3. Fesko, *The Rule of Love*, 71.

only through Christ."[4] Sins such as adultery and murder harm people but primarily wrong God (Ps. 51:4).

The precepts regarding other people are generally much shorter than those regarding God, three consisting of only two Hebrew words each. Yet the simplicity of these precepts conceals a marvelous depth of instruction, for in them the Lord asserts his lordship over every aspect of human activity: authority, life, sexuality, property, truth in communication, and desire.

The Fifth Commandment: Proper Human Authority

The Lord says, "Honour thy father and thy mother: that thy days may be long upon the land which the LORD thy God giveth thee" (Ex. 20:12). The version in Deuteronomy is somewhat longer: "Honour thy father and thy mother, as the LORD thy God hath commanded thee; that thy days may be prolonged, and that it may go well with thee, in the land which the LORD thy God giveth thee" (Deut. 5:16).

The Exegesis of the Fifth Commandment

The verb translated as "honour" (*kabad*) has the literal meaning "to be weighty" and, thus, "to treat as important, honor, glorify." It can be used of honoring God or man.[5] A synonym of "honor" is "fear"—not terror but reverence and awe.[6] God commands, "Ye shall fear every man his mother, and his father" (Lev. 19:3). The opposite of "honor" and "fear" is "despise" and "lightly esteem" (1 Sam. 2:30; Mal. 1:6). The covenant of law said, "Cursed be he that setteth light by [treats with contempt] his father or his mother" (Deut. 27:16). William Ames wrote, "Honor is an acknowledgement of the dignity or excellence of another."[7] Thomas Watson said, "Children are to show honour to their parents, by a reverential esteem of their persons," exercised "inwardly, by fear mixed with love," and "outwardly, both in word and gesture."[8]

Therefore, the fifth commandment requires us to regard our parents as important and worthy of our respect, and it prohibits us from regarding them lightly. The command is not contingent on their moral worthiness. Furthermore, it does not depend on gender; both "father" and "mother"

4. Brown, *Questions and Answers on the Shorter Catechism*, 237.
5. Ex. 14:4, 17, 18; Lev. 10:3; Num. 22:17, 37; 1 Sam. 15:30.
6. Deut. 28:58; Isa. 25:3; cf. Ps. 22:23; Mal. 1:6.
7. Ames, *The Marrow of Theology*, 2.17.9–10 (308–9).
8. Watson, *The Ten Commandments*, 128.

are included. Exodus 20:12 places "father" first (cf. 21:15, 17; Lev. 20:9), but Leviticus 19:3 reverses the order.[9] We are to honor them simply because they are our parents, because God's providence has set them over us, and because God commands us to honor them.[10]

As motivation for honoring parents, God said the Israelites would enjoy a long and good life in the land that he had promised to Abraham. The Lord attached the same pledge to Israel's obedience to the law in general.[11] Treating parents with contempt was one of the many offenses for which God sent Israel into exile (Ezek. 22:7, 15). Since God adopted Israel as his son in the covenant (Ex. 4:22),[12] the obedience of children to their parents was the training ground for obeying the Lord.

However, the fifth commandment particularly addresses individuals (note the singular words "thy father and thy mother"). Honoring one's parents is an aspect of the wisdom that tends toward a longer and happier life.[13] In ancient Israel, a person who persistently dishonored his parents could be put to death by the civil authorities (Deut. 21:18–21), and any person who commits this sin will die under God's curse (Prov. 30:17). Conversely, the person who honors his father and mother forms habits of gratitude and submission to authority that foster other virtues and protect against life-ruining vices. This is no absolute promise of health and wealth, but honoring authority from a heart obedient to the Lord does bring joy and blessing that the rebellious forfeit.

Paul applies this promise to obedient children "in the Lord," whether Jews or Gentiles, "that it may be well with thee, and thou mayest live long on the earth" (Eph. 6:3). This is another evidence that the Ten Commandments, though framed especially for Israel, present universal moral principles that continue to guide and encourage those in Christ.

The Fifth Commandment and Creation

Human beings are worthy of honor because God created them in his image (Gen. 1:26–27).[14] Bearing the divine image exalts people above the other earthly creatures and enables them to exercise the dominion that God

9. Douma, *The Ten Commandments*, 162.
10. Calvin, *Institutes*, 2.8.36.
11. Deut. 4:40; 5:29; 6:3, 18; 11:9; 22:7; 25:15; 30:18; 32:47.
12. On God's national adoption of Israel, see chap. 25.
13. Prov. 3:1–2, 16; 4:10; 9:11; 10:27.
14. On the doctrine of the image of God, see *RST*, 2:161–206 (chaps. 8–10). On the image of God in fallen man, see *RST*, 2:168–69, 196–97.

gave to them (v. 28). God gave man "glory and honour" and "dominion" over creation (Ps. 8:5–6). Though the image of God in man is defiled and distorted by sin, relics of it remain in all human beings (Gen. 9:5–6), and it is being renewed and restored in the righteousness of those united to Christ (Eph. 4:24; Col. 3:10).

A fundamental responsibility that God gave to his image bearers is procreation and parenting (Gen. 1:27–28). The family is a creation ordinance and a basic unit of human society, structuring relationships by the roles of father, mother, son, daughter, husband, and wife (2:24). Family is central to history: Genesis presents its histories under the headings of fathers and their genealogies.[15] Therefore, God has mandated that we honor our fathers and mothers.

However, this honorable status of bearing the image of God belongs not only to fathers and mothers but to all human beings. We should respect people older than we are (Lev. 19:32; Isa. 3:5; 1 Tim. 5:1–2), acknowledge those who are praiseworthy (2 Cor. 8:22–23), respect our colleagues (Phil. 2:3), and treat those under our authority as our brothers (Deut. 17:20).[16] This should affect how we treat the lowest of men, lest we dishonor their Maker (Prov. 14:31). Since the honor of bearing God's image is associated with dominion, people with special authority are worthy of special honor. In the Bible, the term "father" often refers to civil and spiritual leaders.[17] Peter says, "Honour all men. Love the brotherhood. Fear God. Honour the king" (1 Pet. 2:17). We must honor authorities, for "the powers that be are ordained of God" (Rom. 13:1, 7). John Calvin said, "Father and mothers, magistrates and all who exercise authority, are lieutenants of God and represent him."[18]

The fifth commandment is a frontal assault on our pride, for we are by nature bent to demand honor from all but give it to none, for we think of ourselves as lords.[19] Ames said, "The beginning of all honor given to our neighbor . . . is humility."[20] It is no accident that this commandment begins the second table of the law. Ames added, "Honor has first place among

15. Gen. 5:1; 6:9; 10:1; 11:10, 27; 25:12, 19; 36:1, 9; 37:2.

16. Perkins, *A Golden Chain*, chap. 24, in *Works*, 6:108–9.

17. Gen. 45:8; Judg. 17:10; 18:19; 1 Sam. 24:11; 2 Kings 2:12; 5:13; 6:21; 13:14; Job 29:16; Isa. 22:21–22; 1 Cor. 4:14–15; cf. 1 Tim. 1:2; 2 Tim. 2:1; 1 John 2:1; 3:18; 3 John 4. Deborah was "a mother in Israel" (Judg. 5:7).

18. Calvin, *Sermons on the Ten Commandments*, 138.

19. Calvin, *Sermons on the Ten Commandments*, 136.

20. Ames, *The Marrow of Theology*, 2.17.66 (313).

the duties owed to our neighbor. . . . It is the bond and foundation of all other relationships of justice to be maintained towards our neighbor."[21]

The Fifth Commandment and Love

To honor our fathers and mothers is to love them, to value and esteem them as God's gifts to us. To them we owe our very existence and our nature as those created in God's image. In most cases, we have also received from our parents provision, affection, and instruction. If our parents have lived honorable lives, they pass on to us the dignity of their name and a network of supportive relationships in their community. These are debts we can never repay, but we can give joy to our parents by honoring them and receiving whatever wisdom they offer us. Proverbs 23:22–25 says, "Hearken unto thy father that begat thee, and despise not thy mother when she is old. Buy the truth, and sell it not; also wisdom, and instruction, and understanding. The father of the righteous shall greatly rejoice: and he that begetteth a wise child shall have joy of him. Thy father and thy mother shall be glad, and she that bare thee shall rejoice."[22]

Similarly, we are to love our other leaders and do what we can to put joy into their work. Paul exhorts believers to recognize the church officers who "are over you in the Lord, and admonish you; and to esteem them very highly in love" (1 Thess. 5:12–13). Church members are commanded, "Obey them that have the rule over you, and submit yourselves: for they watch for your souls, as they that must give account, that they may do it with joy, and not with grief: for that is unprofitable for you" (Heb. 13:17).

Honor is not a stiff salute to someone we hate but an inward affection of love that moves us to give honor to one another (Rom. 12:9–10). Honor says, "I value you as someone whom God created in his image and appointed to this high position." Godefridus Udemans said, "Without love, neither authority nor submission will survive very long."[23]

The ultimate reason to honor one's father, mother, and other authorities is the Lord. Moses says, "Honour thy father and thy mother, as the Lord thy God hath commanded thee" (Deut. 5:16). Submission to people arises from the fear of the Lord (Eph. 5:21). Though we must love our parents, Christ says, "He that loveth father or mother more than me is

21. Ames, *The Marrow of Theology*, 2.17.13 (309).
22. See also Prov. 10:1; 15:20; 17:21, 25; 19:13; 23:15; 27:11; 29:3, 15.
23. Udemans, *The Practice of Faith, Hope, and Love*, 318.

not worthy of me: and he that loveth son or daughter more than me is not worthy of me" (Matt. 10:37). Christ himself honored his earthly parents (Luke 2:51) and made provision for his mother's care when his death drew near (John 19:26–27). However, Christ's great priority throughout his life was to do his Father's will (4:34; 5:30; 6:38–39), and in obedience to his Father's will he gave his all, even life itself (Matt. 26:42; Phil. 2:8).

Some Ethical Applications of the Fifth Commandment

The Heidelberg Catechism (LD 39, Q. 104) says that God requires "that I show all honor, love and fidelity, to my father and mother, and all in authority over me, and submit myself to their good instruction and correction, with due obedience; and also patiently bear with their weaknesses and infirmities, since it pleases God to govern us by their hand."[24]

Obedience to the fifth commandment obviously begins with young children. Paul says, "Children, obey your parents in the Lord: for this is right. Honour thy father and mother" (Eph. 6:1–2). Again, Paul says, "Children, obey your parents in all things: for this is well pleasing unto the Lord" (Col. 3:20). The term translated as "children" (plural *teknon*) refers to offspring that a mother "bears" (*tiktō*); it can refer to "children" of any age (1 Tim. 5:4), but it can be used specifically for minor children in the household (Deut. 3:19 LXX). Here Paul addresses minor children as distinct from adult "wives," "husbands," and "fathers" (Eph. 5:22, 25; 6:4; Col. 3:18–19, 21).[25]

As an act of love and obedience to God, children should obey the rules and directions of their parents, insofar as those rules do not hinder them from keeping the laws of God. Watson said, "A child should be the parents' echo; when the father speaks, the child should echo back obedience."[26] The duty of obedience ceases with the onset of adulthood, though a child living in his parents' home must still observe their household rules. Only when a child becomes an adult and moves out of his parents' home does he become fully independent of their governing authority (Gen. 2:24).

When children or teenagers find themselves in conflict with their parents, they must work to build trust with them and overcome barriers. James Beeke gives the following counsel: first, "be honest" with your

24. *The Three Forms of Unity*, 105.
25. Grudem, *Christian Ethics*, 368.
26. Watson, *The Ten Commandments*, 130.

parents, "even when you have done wrong." Second, "ask for their permission" to do things, for "this conveys your respect for their authority." Third, "convey your love to your parents" by thanking them and offering to help them. Fourth, "speak with, and listen to, your parents" about your life and concerns. Fifth, "try to understand your parents," even when you disagree with them, by appreciating their responsibility, authority, love for you, and concerns. Sixth, "pray for your parents," for they bear tremendous burdens.[27]

However, the requirement to honor one's parents is much broader than obedience, and the duty of rendering honor continues throughout life, a duty that extends to one's father-in-law and mother-in-law (Ex. 4:18; 18:5–8, 24; Ruth 1:14–18).

Sons and daughters should show respect to their parents through their words, postures, facial expressions, and gestures. In the ancient world, adults (even important leaders) rose to greet their parents and bowed before them.[28] How honor is shown varies from culture to culture, but children should greet their parents courteously and affectionately, addressing them with respectful titles (such as "Father" and "Mother" or, in some families, "Sir" and "Ma'am"). When their parents speak to them, they should put aside media (print or electronic) and listen quietly, attentively, and patiently. Their verbal and nonverbal communication should convey a sense that their parents have a special dignity and value to them above their peers. Cursing, striking, robbing, or threatening harm to one's parents are disgraceful and heinous sins.[29] Speaking contemptuously about one's parents and disregarding their honorable position are marks of proud, self-righteous, self-centered, untrustworthy, and unjust people who gladly oppress others.[30]

People should listen attentively to their fathers and mothers, and insofar as their instruction agrees with the Word of God, receive their wisdom.[31] Moses listened to his father-in-law's advice and consequently arranged the judicial system of Israel more wisely (Ex. 18:24). Of course, foolish and wicked counsel from parents should not be followed, but even

27. James W. Beeke, *Bible Doctrine for Teens and Young Adults*, 3 vols. (Chilliwack, BC: Timothy Christian School Publication Department, 1994), 2:474.

28. Ex. 18:7; 1 Kings 2:19; cf. Gen. 48:12; Lev. 19:32. For other examples of bowing to men, see Gen. 18:2; 19:1; 23:7, 12; 33:3, 6–7; 42:6; 43:26, 28; Ex. 11:8; Ruth 2:10; 1 Sam. 2:36; 20:41; 24:8; 25:23, 41, etc.

29. Ex. 21:15, 17; Lev. 20:9; Prov. 19:26; 20:20; 28:24; 30:17; 1 Tim. 1:9.

30. Prov. 30:11–14; Rom. 1:29–32; 2 Tim. 3:1–4.

31. Prov. 1:8; 4:1–6; 6:20; 13:1; 23:22.

unconverted parents may have helpful advice about some practical matters. People should earnestly desire and respectfully seek the counsel and blessing of their parents regarding whom they marry, though adults do not absolutely need their parents' blessing to legitimately get married.[32]

When parents grow old or become unable to provide for themselves, their children must not despise them (Prov. 23:22) but care for their needs (Gen. 45:10–11; Matt. 15:4–6). When discussing the church's care for widows, Paul says, "But if a widow has children or grandchildren, let them first learn to show godliness to their own household and to make some return to their parents, for this is pleasing in the sight of God. . . . But if anyone does not provide for his relatives, and especially for members of his household, he has denied the faith and is worse than an unbeliever" (1 Tim. 5:4, 8 ESV).

The command to honor our parents implies that they should conduct themselves in an honorable fashion. Paul says, "Fathers, provoke not your children to wrath: but bring them up in the nurture and admonition of the Lord" (Eph. 6:4). In another epistle, Paul adds this reason: "lest they be discouraged" (Col. 3:21). Therefore, parents should provide for their minor children what they need to live and flourish, and train them in the ways of God.[33]

Parental authority is given by God to serve and benefit children, not so that parents may use or control them for their own selfish ends (2 Cor. 12:14–15). Saul sinned against his son by angrily insulting and violently attacking him—and provoked him to righteous outrage (1 Sam. 20:30, 33–34). John Davenant (1572–1641) said, "It is proper to govern children with gravity and prudence: but it is not proper to exasperate them by bitterness and cruelty."[34] John Dod said that when parents must discipline their children, "it must be done in great compassion and mercy," along with prayer that God would give the parents "wise hearts" to discipline rightly and the children "soft hearts . . . [to] receive it humbly and meekly." Dod warned that no matter how much a child may deserve correction, "to fly upon him in a passion" shows much sin

32. Wollebius, *Compendium*, 2.11.(3).iv–vi (241). See Turretin, *Institutes*, 11.16.15 (2:108).

33. For more instruction on parenting and family life, see Joel R. Beeke, *Parenting by God's Promises: How to Raise Children in the Covenant of Grace* (Lake Mary, FL: Reformation Trust, 2011); and William Gouge, *Building a Godly Home*, ed. Joel R. Beeke and Scott Brown, 3 vols. (Grand Rapids, MI: Reformation Heritage Books, 2013–2014).

34. John Davenant, *An Exposition of the Epistle of St. Paul to the Colossians*, trans. Josiah Allport, Geneva Series of Commentaries, 2 vols. in 1 (1831–1832; repr., Edinburgh: Banner of Truth, 2005), 2:192.

and foolishness, and will harden the child's heart and make him bitter, stubborn, and fierce.[35] When parents physically injure children by violence, children have the right to call on civil and church authorities to intervene for their protection.

We have concentrated on the applications of the fifth commandment to parent-child relationships, for that is its explicit focus, but as we noted earlier, the commandment reveals our duty with respect to all human authorities, illustrated in the table below.

Authority from the Triune God						
Administrated by Christ, the Mediator-King						
Rightly Exercised by Spirit-Empowered Obedience to the Word						
Domestic Authority		*Civil Authority*		*Economic Authority*		*Ecclesiastical Authority*
Marriage	*Family*	*Government*	*Military*	*Education*	*Business*	*Church*
Husbands	Parents	Civil Officials & Officers	Officers (Commissioned & Noncommissioned)	Boards of Directors, Administrators, & Teachers	Owners, Boards of Directors, Officers, & Supervisors	Church Office Bearers
Wives	Children	Citizens & Aliens	Soldiers, Sailors, & Civilian Employees	Staff & Students	Employees	Members & Other Attendees

Table 39.1. Examples of Human Authority under God

Every position of authority should garner its proper respect. God commands us to give respect, obedience, and taxes to civil rulers (Rom. 13:1–7; Titus 3:1; 1 Pet. 2:13–17). Plumer said, "It is the duty of all men to treat all the officers of the government from the highest to the lowest with respect, and to give to each the honour that is his due, never using reviling or railing language to them or concerning them."[36] It is a sin

35. Dod, *A Plaine and Familiar Exposition of the Ten Commandments*, 179–80.
36. Plumer, *The Law of God*, 384.

to curse a civil ruler (Ex. 22:28), and also very foolish (Eccles. 10:20). People should seek to please those in authority over them, not argue or talk back when given instruction, and be faithful stewards of the resources those in authority entrust to their management (Titus 2:9–10). Christians should honor the pastors and elders of their churches, support them with financial gifts, imitate their faith and virtue, and give them obedience and submission insofar as they faithfully teach God's Word and direct the church in an orderly manner.[37] Believers are obligated to pray for civil leaders (1 Tim. 2:1–4) and for gospel preachers (Eph. 6:19–20; 2 Thess. 3:1–2). Conversely, leaders in civil government and the church should conduct themselves with dignity, mercy, justice, and the fear of God.[38] These manifold kinds of authority remind us, as Jochem Douma said, that human "authority is always limited authority and is bordered by other spheres of authority."[39]

The Sixth Commandment: Sacred Human Life

The Lord says, "Thou shalt not kill" (Ex. 20:13; Deut. 5:17).

The Exegesis of the Sixth Commandment

The word translated as "kill" (*ratsakh*), which appears forty-seven times in the Bible, is never used for killing an animal but only a human being.[40] In the judicial law of Moses and the account of the allocation of the Promised Land, it is used for both a "manslayer" who accidentally has killed another human being and a "murderer" who has killed his victim with a deadly weapon or hateful intent.[41] Only twice is the term used for capital punishment imposed on murderers, in phrases that may be literally translated as "he shall kill the killer" (Num. 35:27, 30). In other Old Testament books, the term is used once for a man in danger of being killed by a lion (Prov. 22:13) and several times for malicious murder or assassination of man by man.[42]

37. 1 Cor. 9:7–14; Gal. 6:6; Phil. 2:29; 1 Thess. 5:12; 1 Tim. 5:17–20; Heb. 13:7, 17; 1 Pet. 5:5.

38. Ex. 18:21; Psalm 82; 1 Tim. 3:1–13; 4:12. The respective duties of pastors and people will be explored under the locus of ecclesiology in *RST*, vol. 4 (forthcoming).

39. Douma, *The Ten Commandments*, 187.

40. On man's responsibility to care for God's other creatures, see the section on the eighth commandment and creation in chap. 40.

41. Num. 35:6, 11–12, 15–33; Deut. 4:42; 19:3–6; 22:26; Josh. 20:1–6; 21:13, 21, 27, 32, 38. Mere manslaughter did not bring the death penalty but only the necessity of fleeing to a city of refuge.

42. Judg. 20:4; 1 Kings 21:19; 2 Kings 6:32; Job 24:14; Pss. 62:3; 94:6; Isa. 1:21; Jer. 7:9; Hos. 4:2; 6:9. In Ps. 62:3, "ye shall be slain" might be better translated as "you murder" (cf. LXX).

The specificity of *ratsakh* is notable. It is not used for slaughtering animals or killing in war, and is used only rarely for the death penalty. Several other Hebrew words translated as "slay" or "kill" refer to the deaths of animals or men, whether by murder, judicial execution, warfare, divine judgment, or dangerous beasts.[43] Therefore, the translation "You shall not murder" (Ex. 20:13 ESV) is warranted,[44] as long as it is understood to include manslaughter by gross negligence (cf. 21:28–30).

The Sixth Commandment and Creation

Like the fifth commandment, the sixth is grounded on God's creation of man in his image (Gen. 1:26). The life of human beings has special value because God made them to represent him on the earth.[45] Calvin said, "If we do not wish to violate the image of God, we ought to hold our neighbor sacred."[46] Just as the triune God is personal, so each man is a person in his image, someone unique, with a rational, volitional nature, who stands in relationships to other people.[47] Viewing each human being as a person with his or her own feelings will lead us to keep the Golden Rule to do to others as we would have them do to us (Matt. 7:12).

Love is properly directed toward people, not things. The Holy Scriptures portray the love of things in a negative light.[48] If we view people as things, we will not love them but treat them as merchandise to be bought, used, sold, or destroyed (Ezek. 27:13; Joel 3:3; Rev. 18:13). But if we view them as people created in the image of God, we will regard them as the most precious of God's earthly creations, cherish their lives, and treat them with kindness and respect.

The doctrine of God's image affirms the value of human life. People have dignity far above that of animals—as beautiful and marvelous as

43. Consider some representative uses of "slay" or "kill" (*harag*, Gen. 4:8; 20:4; 34:25; Ex. 4:23; 13:15; Lev. 20:15, 16; Num. 31:7–8, 17, 19; Deut. 13:9), "slain" or "pierced" (*khalal*, Gen. 34:27; Num. 19:16; 23:24; 31:8; 2 Chron. 13:17), "smite," "kill," or "slay" (*nacah*, Gen. 4:15; 14:15; 37:21; Ex. 2:11–13; Lev. 24:17–18, 21; Num. 3:13), "slay" or "kill," literally "cause to die" (*hiphil* of *mut*, Gen. 18:25; 37:18; 38:7; Ex. 21:29; Num. 35:21), and "slay" or "kill" (*shakhat*, Gen. 22:10; 37:31; Lev. 1:5; Num. 14:16; Judg. 12:6; 1 Kings 18:40).

44. R. Alan Cole, *Exodus*, Tyndale Old Testament Commentaries 2 (Downers Grove, IL: InterVarsity Press, 1973), 167; and Douglas K. Stuart, *Exodus*, The New American Commentary 2 (Nashville: Broadman & Holman, 2006), 462.

45. On the image of God in fallen man, see *RST*, 2:168–69, 196–97.

46. Calvin, *Institutes*, 2.8.40.

47. For a description of a person in the doctrine of the Trinity, see *RST*, 1:931–33. On the image of the Creator and rational, volitional personality, see *RST*, 2:163–64, 201.

48. Gen. 27:4; Prov. 20:13; 21:17; Eccles. 5:10; Isa. 1:23; Hos. 3:1; 9:1; Matt. 6:24; 1 Tim. 6:10; 2 Tim. 4:10; 1 John 2:15–17. Love for God's Word and righteousness is love for God (Ps. 119:97; Prov. 22:11; 2 Thess. 2:10).

those creatures are.[49] However, man's value is not absolute but derived from above. Since man is created in God's image, he exists for God's glory.

The Sixth Commandment and the Death Penalty

Man's creation in the image of God results in the sanctity of human life; it is not that all men are holy, but that they all bear some resemblance to the God who is holy. Hence, we must treat people with a sacred respect above the animals. God authorized man to kill and eat animals but warned that no man may murder another man (Gen. 9:3, 5). The Lord said, "Whoso sheddeth man's blood, by man shall his blood be shed: for in the image of God made he man" (v. 6). Calvin said, "It's as if our Lord were saying, 'You wage war against me when you seek to hurt each other in this way, for I have implanted my image in you.'"[50]

Therefore, there is no contradiction in applying the death penalty to murderers. Objecting to capital punishment because God says, "Thou shalt not kill," fails to recognize the most common nuance of the word translated as "kill": "Thou shalt not *murder.*" If it is a contradiction to carry out capital punishment on a murderer, then God contradicted himself in his own law.[51] The malicious destruction of a person created in the image of God merits the most severe punishment that men can impose. For this reason, the Creator and Judge placed the "sword"—that is, the power to shed blood—in the hands of the civil magistrate (Rom. 13:4).[52]

Neither is the death penalty contrary to the command to love all men. Christ's instruction "Resist not evil: but whosoever shall smite thee on thy right cheek, turn to him the other also" (Matt. 5:39) refers to not taking personal revenge for being slapped in the face.[53] Christ often preached in brief, absolute phrases without explaining the exceptions to the rule (consider "give to him that asketh thee," v. 42). Francis Turretin said, "Christian charity [love] . . . can love the persons and punish the crimes. It would be a violation of the law of charity to leave the desperately wicked unpunished as pernicious to the republic and injurious to the good."[54] John Feinberg and Paul Feinberg (1938–2004) said, "As a private individual I may turn the other cheek when unjustly attacked. However, my

49. On the sanctity and dignity of human life as created in God's image, see *RST*, 2:200–201.
50. Calvin, *Sermons on the Ten Commandments*, 155.
51. For a list of fifteen capital crimes under the Mosaic covenant, see *RST*, 2:626n51.
52. On God's punishment of sin through civil government, see *RST*, 2:459–61.
53. Carson, "Matthew," in *The Expositor's Bible Commentary*, ed. Gaebelein, 8:156.
54. Turretin, *Institutes*, 11.17.4 (2:112).

responsibilities are quite different when I stand in the position of a guardian of a third party as a civil magistrate or parent. Because I am responsible for their lives and welfare, I must resist, even with force, unjust aggression against them."[55]

However, the value of human life means that the civil government must implement the death penalty only under the rule of law and with strong evidence of the guilt of the accused (Num. 35:30; Deut. 17:6). Otherwise, the death penalty easily becomes state-sponsored murder at the hands of a tyrant or an angry mob. Also, if a state uses corporal punishment rather than the death penalty, it must regulate that punishment so that it is not excessive or degrading (Deut. 25:1–3).

The Sixth Commandment and Love

The sixth commandment has far broader applications than merely forbidding actions that kill another person, for it exposes the evil of malice against other human beings. Christ teaches that "murders" come "out of the heart" (Matt. 15:19). In saying this, Jesus is fully in accord with the Old Testament, for a man was punished as a "murderer" if he killed another person out of "hatred" or "enmity" (Num. 35:20–21). Christ draws out the spirituality of the law, explaining that "Thou shalt not kill" condemns sinful anger and insults (Matt. 5:21–22). John says, "Whosoever hateth his brother is a murderer: and ye know that no murderer hath eternal life abiding in him" (1 John 3:15). If it is objected that "this commandment seems only to speak of murder," the Heidelberg Catechism (LD 40, Q. 106) reminds us, "In forbidding murder, God teaches us that He abhors the causes thereof, such as envy, hatred, anger, and desire of revenge; and that He accounts all these as murder."[56] Watson said, "Malice is mental murder."[57]

In opposition to such malicious hostility, God's law commands a love that reasons with sinners and forgives the repentant: "Thou shalt not hate thy brother in thine heart: thou shalt in any wise rebuke thy neighbour, and not suffer sin upon him. Thou shalt not avenge, nor bear any grudge against the children of thy people, but thou shalt love thy neighbour as thyself: I am the LORD" (Lev. 19:17–18). Likewise, Christ applies the sixth

55. John S. Feinberg and Paul D. Feinberg, *Ethics for a Brave New World*, 2nd ed. (Wheaton, IL: Crossway, 2010), 646.

56. *The Three Forms of Unity*, 106.

57. Watson, *The Ten Commandments*, 139.

commandment to our responsibility to make reconciliation when a breach has taken place in one of our relationships (Matt. 5:23–26). We must cultivate "those virtues which restrain us from any hurt of our neighbor," which are, as Ames said, "meekness, patience, long-suffering, and . . . forgiveness of wrong."[58]

The Lord Jesus Christ was so far from committing murder that he went about healing people, even a man who had come for his arrest and murder (Luke 22:51). Christ endured his own murder with meekness and love, praying for those who crucified him (23:34). Rising from the dead, he sent forth preachers to proclaim to Israel that they had murdered their own Messiah—not to condemn them, but that they might repent and be forgiven (Acts 2:36; 3:14–15; 7:52). When Christ returns to destroy his enemies and cast them into the second death, he will do so not in malice but with a clear demonstration of the justice of their punishment for the sins they committed (Matt. 16:27; Rev. 19:11; 20:11–15).

Some Ethical Applications of the Sixth Commandment

The sixth commandment prohibits murder. God hates "hands that shed innocent blood" (Prov. 6:16–17). Matthew Poole summarized the commandment this way: "Thou shalt not kill . . . any man or woman, without authority, and without just cause."[59]

Murder is murder regardless of the social status or ethnic background of the victim (Job 24:14; Ps. 94:6). The economic and national differences among people are little compared to their common participation in the image of God. John Gill said, "All mankind are our neighbours; they are all the offspring of God, and near akin to one another, being all of one man's blood."[60] Therefore, the sixth commandment condemns racism—that is, prejudice, hatred, and injustice against people because they belong to other nations or have different skin colors.[61] God's law says, "The stranger that dwelleth with you shall be unto you as one born among you, and thou shalt love him as thyself; for ye were strangers in the land of Egypt: I am the LORD your God" (Lev. 19:34).[62]

58. Ames, *The Marrow of Theology*, 2.18.15–16 (315). On these virtues, see chaps. 35–36.
59. Poole, *Annotations upon the Holy Bible*, on Ex. 20:13 (1:160).
60. Gill, *Body of Divinity*, 770; cf. Acts 17:26, 28.
61. *Racism* is a problematic term because there is only one human race. The science of the nineteenth and early twentieth centuries falsely divided mankind into different races.
62. See also the discussion of slavery in chap. 40 under the eighth commandment.

The Lord has great tenderness for children (Mark 10:13–16), and especially children who have no advocate (Ex. 22:22–24). Israel provoked God's wrath when they "had slain their children to their idols" (Ezek. 23:39). When an Egyptian pharaoh commanded infanticide for newborn Hebrew boys, the midwives bravely resisted his decree in the fear of God, as did Moses's parents by faith in God (Ex. 1:15–2:4; Heb. 11:23). It is a sin for parents to violently injure, torture, or kill their children or to abandon them, neglect their basic needs, or expose them to the elements and wild beasts.[63] Parents should discipline children (Prov. 13:24), but Paul says, "Fathers, provoke not your children to anger, lest they be discouraged" (Col. 3:21).

It is sin against God to kill unborn children in the womb (Ex. 21:22–23; Amos 1:13), unless without intervention both the mother and the child would die. God's Word reveals the human personhood of each child from conception when Job and David speak of God making them in their mothers' womb with the personal "I" and "me" (Job 10:10–11; Ps. 139:13–16).[64] The personhood of each child in the womb is scientifically established by the formation at conception of a human individual with his or her own genetic code distinct from the mother. Ultrasound imaging shows how quickly the embryo develops a heart (three weeks) and takes a recognizably human form (eight weeks).[65] Calvin said, "The fetus, though enclosed in the womb of its mother, is already a human being. . . . If it seems more horrible to kill a man in his own house than in a field, because a man's house is his place of most secure refuge, it ought surely to be deemed more atrocious to destroy a fetus in the womb."[66]

The prohibition of murder also condemns suicide, or self-murder,[67] for the wrongfulness of killing does not arise from the lack of a person's consent but from his status as a person created in God's image. This God-centered evaluation of human life contrasts sharply with that of secularism. David Hume wrote in his defense of suicide, "The life of a man is of no

63. Udemans, *The Practice of Faith, Hope, and Love*, 345.

64. See also references to unborn children as persons in Gen. 25:22–23; Ps. 51:5; Luke 1:35, 41–44.

65. For a brief discussion of arguments concerning abortion, see Joel R. Beeke and James W. Beeke, *Is Abortion Really So Bad?* (Pensacola, FL: Chapel Library, 2015), also available at https://www.chapellibrary.org/read/iars. See also Grudem, *Christian Ethics*, 566–83. A full treatment may be found in Randy Alcorn, *Prolife Answers to Prochoice Arguments*, 2nd ed. (Colorado Springs, CO: Multnomah, 2000).

66. Calvin, *Commentaries*, on Ex. 21:22.

67. Note the sad cases of Saul (1 Sam. 31:3–4), Ahithophel (2 Sam. 17:23), Zimri (1 Kings 16:18–19), and Judas (Matt. 27:3–5).

greater importance to the universe than that of an oyster."[68] However, God made man in his image, gives life to each individual, and calls everyone to a life of good works. Udemans said, "We are each placed into this life by our Creator according to our calling, much as soldiers are placed in their battle lines. Therefore, without God's consent and permission, we ought not to run away from or end what we are called to do."[69] Turretin explained that a man who commits suicide sins greatly against God, "who alone is the Lord of life"; against himself, by failing to "preserve his own flesh"; "against the state by destroying one of her citizens"; against his family, by "plunging all his relatives into disgrace, grief and mourning"; and, if he is a Christian, against his church, by bringing grief and disgrace on Christianity.[70]

People can murder themselves slowly by getting drunk with alcoholic beverages or abusing other mind-altering or body-destroying substances (Prov. 23:29–35). It is a true proverb that drunkenness kills more people than the sword.[71] Since the mid-twentieth century, scientists have understood that smoking tobacco causes serious health problems, forms an addition to a drug called nicotine (no less so when used in electronic forms such as "vaping"), and may become the gateway to the abuse of more harmful drugs. Drunkenness and drug abuse not only harm the abuser's body, but often lead to vicious, lazy, immoral, and destructive behavior that ordinarily would be restrained.[72] The use of intoxicating, addictive substances contradicts the biblical call to spiritual alertness ("Let us watch and be sober," 1 Thess. 5:6) and protecting ourselves from all that enslaves ("All things are lawful for me, but I will not be brought under the power of any," 1 Cor. 6:12).

It is murder to assist a person in committing suicide, even if the intent is to relieve the person from suffering (euthanasia). This might be done directly by a physician or by the patient using a means provided by a physician. It could involve using a chemical or procedure that destroys life or withholding food or water. In any case, it is the unlawful destruction of human life created in God's image.[73] David justly killed a man who claimed

68. David Hume, "On Suicide," in *The Philosophical Works of David Hume*, 4 vols. (Boston: Little, Brown and Co., 1854), 4:540.

69. Udemans, *The Practice of Faith, Hope, and Love*, 341. Udemans distinguished between suicidal "people who are insane" and "those who take their own lives with intentional premeditation."

70. Turretin, *Institutes*, 11.17.23 (2:116–17).

71. Latin: *plures necat crapula quam gladius*.

72. Prov. 20:1; 23:20–21; 31:4–5; Eph. 5:18; 1 Pet. 4:3.

73. On euthanasia, see Feinberg and Feinberg, *Ethics for a Brave New World*, 157–226; and Grudem, *Christian Ethics*, 587–603.

to have helped Saul kill himself (2 Sam. 1:9–10, 14–16). When Paul saw his jailer prepare to commit suicide, he shouted, "Do thyself no harm!" (Acts 16:28). We should likewise intervene when people are suicidal and call on the proper authorities to help. It is another matter, however, for a person to choose not to receive further medical treatment when it has become clear he will die. This is not suicide but acceptance of death, which for a Christian is not despair but hope (Phil. 1:21–23).

Civil authorities have the right and responsibility to use deadly force to protect law-abiding citizens and punish evildoers (Rom. 13:4), whether criminals in their nations or other nations at war with their own.[74] However, their authority does not permit them to take life without just cause, such as when a king uses his power to murder someone to seize his property (1 Kings 21:19). The people should not consent to civil officials bent on committing bloody crimes, but should oppose them (1 Sam. 14:45; 2 Kings 6:32). Even when a nation must go to war, it should do so with sobriety and sadness. Augustine noted that people say, "The wise man will wage just wars," but he replied, "As if he would not all the rather lament the necessity of just wars. . . . For it is the wrongdoing of the opposing party which compels the wise man to wage just wars."[75]

At the heart of the sixth commandment is a prohibition against malicious hatred that delights in the death or harm of other people (Prov. 24:17). "Let all bitterness, and wrath, and anger, and clamour, and evil speaking, be put away from you, with all malice" (Eph. 4:31). We are not to nurture vengeful spirits against those who wrong us but to entrust our cases to the justice and wrath of God (Rom. 12:17–21). Sin should provoke our righteous hatred and abhorrence (v. 9; cf. Pss. 97:10; 119:163; 139:21–22). However, we should love our enemies and other wicked people, and pray for their salvation (Matt. 5:43–45). Our words should not be full of a serpent's venom (Ps. 140:3) or pierce like a sword (Prov. 12:18). To "bless our Lord and Father" and "curse people who are made in the likeness of God" is a contradiction (James 3:9 ESV).

The sixth commandment requires us to love our neighbors as ourselves (Lev. 19:18), especially with regard to their life and well-being. This as-

74. The Westminster Confession of Faith (23.2), in *Reformed Confessions*, 4:261. On the principles of just war, such as that it must be conducted by public authority (not private individuals), for a just cause and by just principles, and under necessity when peaceful means have failed, see Aquinas, *Summa Theologica*, Part 2.2, Q. 40, Art. 1; Wollebius, *Compendium*, 2.8.(3).i–vii (237–38); and Grudem, *Christian Ethics*, 529–31.

75. Augustine, *The City of God*, 19.7, in *NPNF*[1], 2:405.

sumes natural self-love (Matt. 7:12; Eph. 5:29), for our lives are good gifts from God to be cherished and enjoyed with gratitude (Ps. 34:12; Eccles. 9:7–10; 1 Tim. 4:4).[76] Caring for one's own life includes regular recreation for the body and mind, including athletics, music, riddles, and amateur science.[77] When we are sick, we should take medicine likely to preserve life and restore strength (1 Tim. 5:23). We should take reasonable and lawful precautions to preserve our lives from danger, such as fleeing from violent men (Matt. 10:23; Acts 9:23–24). If a person is threatened with harm by a member of his own household, it may be necessary to leave the home, at least temporarily (Gen. 27:42–44). If flight is impossible, then it is wise to hide in a safe place until the danger passes: "A prudent man foreseeth the evil, and hideth himself: but the simple pass on, and are punished" (Prov. 22:3; 27:12). When neither flight nor hiding is possible, or if we are attacked in our own homes, then we may fight to defend ourselves or those under our care. People have the right to use force in self-defense against those who would injure or kill them (Ex. 22:2), which includes the moral right to carry weapons (Neh. 4:17–18; Luke 22:35–38). However, people should not seek to execute justice privately but rely on the civil authorities to punish evildoers, for God has appointed civil authorities to implement his just wrath (Rom. 12:19–13:7).

Every man has the responsibility to preserve and advance the life of his neighbors in a manner consistent with justice. We should share necessities with those lacking them (Ps. 112:9), even with our personal enemies (Prov. 25:21). Our first responsibility is to our own families (1 Tim. 5:8) and then the church (Gal. 6:10), and we should not support those who are able but unwilling to work to support themselves (2 Thess. 3:10).

People must take reasonable precautions to keep their property from harming others, such as corralling dangerous animals or fencing off places where people might fall, lest their negligence make them culpable in the death of others (Ex. 21:28–36; Deut. 22:8). They must speak out for those who are unjustly being taken away to death and seek to rescue them, which is especially the responsibility of kings and others in civil authority (Prov. 24:11–12; 31:1, 8–9).

Above all, the sixth commandment enjoins upon us a heartfelt concern for the spiritual state and eternal destiny of every person, including

76. See Wollebius, *Compendium*, 2.8.(2).2a (224).
77. Perkins, *A Golden Chain*, chap. 25, in *Works*, 6:122–23.

ourselves. The first and greatest "murderer" is "the devil" (John 8:44), and he seeks the everlasting ruin of sinners. False teachers come "to steal, to kill, and to destroy" people, but Christ says, "I am come that they might have life, and that they might have it more abundantly" (10:10). Therefore, we must be willing to relinquish this temporary life by obedience to Christ's commands and commission to gain eternal life (Matt. 10:39; 16:25; Acts 20:24). We must avoid anything that would contribute to the damnation of precious souls and seek to show them by word and deed the Savior.

The Seventh Commandment: Faithful Human Sexuality

The Lord says, "Thou shalt not commit adultery" (Ex. 20:14; cf. Deut. 5:18).[78]

The Exegesis of the Seventh Commandment

The word translated as "commit adultery" (*na'p*) refers to sexual immorality that violates an existing marriage covenant—that is, sex when one of the participants is married to someone else (Lev. 20:10; cf. 18:20; Deut. 22:22–24). It is a shameful sin that people generally conceal (Job 24:15), and when discovered, it provokes jealous, even violent, rage (Prov. 6:28–35), though its perpetrators may feel fully justified in satisfying their lusts (30:20).

The Seventh Commandment and Creation

The prohibition against adultery expresses a moral implication of God's creation ordinance of marriage. God created humanity in two genders, male and female, both bearing his image, and ordained the lifelong covenant of marriage between one man and one woman as the only legitimate context for sexual activity and procreation, as well as a blessed means for companionship and partnership in exercising dominion over the earth (Gen. 1:27–28; 2:18–25).[79] Calvin said, "If anything ought to be holy in all human life, it's the faith that a husband has in his wife and her faith in him," for "God presides over marriages."[80] The law of God reveals his great displeasure at

78. The words "neither shalt thou" that open the seventh, eighth, ninth, and tenth commandments in their second form (Deut. 5:18–21) reflect the addition of the Hebrew conjunction "and" (*vav*) to the first word "not" (*l'o*). The Hebrew text of the seventh and eighth commandments is otherwise identical to their first form (Ex. 20:14–15).

79. "Marriage is the individual joining of one man and woman by lawful consent for a mutual communication of their bodies and community of life together." Ames, *The Marrow of Theology*, 2.19.19 (318); cf. the Westminster Confession of Faith (24.1–2), in *Reformed Confessions*, 4:263.

80. Calvin, *Sermons on the Ten Commandments*, 169–70.

sexual activity outside of marriage, including fornication (premarital sex), adultery, incest, homosexuality, and bestiality.[81] We discussed human gender and sexuality extensively under the doctrine of creation.[82]

God designed marriage as the union of one man and one woman (Gen. 2:24; Mark 10:7–8), ruling out polygamy (marriage involving three or more people). It is true that some patriarchs and kings practiced polygamy without divine rebuke,[83] but this was an example of God's longsuffering with his people despite their sins. The Scriptures attest to the strife and misery such relationships engendered.[84] In the New Testament, being the husband of one wife or the wife of one husband is clearly the standard of moral excellence in marriage (1 Tim. 3:2, 12; 5:9).

Other serious violations of God's design for marriage include distorting sex into an act of domination and violence (rape, Deut. 22:25–27) or a perverse means of making money (prostitution, Lev. 19:29). In both cases, sexuality is cut off from the committed love of marriage between one man and one woman who treat each other with the dignity fitting for those who bear the image of God.

God made the human body good, and the enjoyment of loving sexual activity in marriage is a good gift to "be received with thanksgiving" and "sanctified by the word of God and prayer" (1 Tim. 4:3–5). Those who rebel against God's commands and give themselves to illicit sex commit sin against their own bodies (1 Cor. 6:18). They "dishonour their own bodies" by giving God's noble creation over to the ruling power of unclean lust—an ironic consequence of worshiping the creature rather than the Creator (Rom. 1:24–25).

The Seventh Commandment and Divorce

The Lord Jesus appealed to the creation ordinance of marriage when debating with the Pharisees about divorce, citing God's creation of man as male and female and the institution of marriage (Matt. 19:4–6). The law of Moses simply regulated the process of divorce (Deut. 24:1–4). Some people took advantage of this situation to divorce their wives for any cause (Matt. 19:3). However, Christ said, "Moses because of the hardness of

81. Ex. 22:16–17; Lev. 18:6–23; 20:11–12, 14–17; Deut. 22:13–21; Rom. 1:24–27; 1 Cor. 5:1; 6:9–10; Heb. 13:4, etc.

82. On man's gender and sexuality as rooted in God's creation, see *RST*, 2:207–28 (chap. 11).

83. Gen. 16:3; 29:20–30; Judg. 8:30; 2 Sam. 2:2; 3:2–5; 5:13; 1 Kings 11:1–3; 1 Chron. 3:1–9; 11:21; 13:21.

84. Gen. 16:4–6; 21:9–14; 29:31–30:24; 37:2–4; 1 Sam. 1:1–6.

your hearts suffered you to put away your wives: but from the beginning it was not so. And I say unto you, Whosoever shall put away his wife, except it be for fornication, and shall marry another, committeth adultery: and whoso marrieth her which is put away doth commit adultery" (vv. 8–9). Marriage is not merely a contract that may be dissolved at will but is a divinely sanctioned covenant that binds two people together for life. Christ says, "What therefore God hath joined together, let not man put asunder" (v. 6). Christ permits (but does not require) divorce and remarriage when the marriage covenant has been violated by sexual sin ("fornication"; cf. 5:32). Leon Morris commented, "*Fornication* strictly means sexual relations between unmarried people. But the term was used more widely than that and came to signify irregular sexual unions of all kinds."[85]

It might be objected that in Gospel parallels Christ allows no exception and simply says, "Whosoever shall put away his wife, and marry another, committeth adultery against her" (Mark 10:11; cf. Luke 16:18). Therefore, it is said that Christ does not allow for any remarriage. Some speculate that Matthew added the words "except it be for fornication" because it was the custom of his church.

In reply, we affirm that the divine inerrancy of the Holy Scriptures requires us to view the exception clause in Matthew 19:9 as a faithful testimony to Christ's teaching.[86] Its omission from the parallel statements in Mark and Luke should not trouble us, for Christ often declared general principles without detailing every exception to the rule—just as preachers do today. Craig Blomberg comments, "Probably Mark simply takes this exception for granted, since in both the Jewish and Greco-Roman cultures divorce and remarriage were universally permitted and often mandatory following adultery."[87]

It might also be objected that disallowing all remarriage after divorce is a wiser approach because it elevates the sanctity of marriage as a lifelong, unbreakable commitment.

In reply, we say that we cannot be wiser than Christ and must follow his teachings on divorce. Furthermore, our Lord's allowance for divorce and remarriage in the case of sexual sin greatly exalts the sanctity of marriage, for it highlights the heinous evil of adultery. It is as if Christ were saying, "Marriage is such a solemn and sacred bond that only a gross vio-

85. Morris, *The Gospel according to Matthew*, 483, emphasis original.
86. On the inerrancy of the Holy Scriptures, see *RST*, 1:371–94 (chaps. 20–21).
87. Blomberg, *Matthew*, 292.

lation of the marital covenant can justify its dissolution. Most sins, as evil as they are, do not qualify as such a violation. However, adultery is such a horrible transgression against God's will for marriage that God releases the innocent party from his or her obligation to remain in the relationship." Christ's teaching also allows us to show justice and compassion to the innocent party, who should not be forced to spend the rest of his or her life alone because of another's sin.

The apostle Paul likewise teaches that marriage is a lifelong commitment. He says, "For the woman which hath an husband is bound by the law to her husband so long as he liveth; but if the husband be dead, she is loosed from the law of her husband. So then if, while her husband liveth, she be married to another man, she shall be called an adulteress: but if her husband be dead, she is free from that law; so that she is no adulteress, though she be married to another man" (Rom. 7:2–3). An essential part of marriage, Paul says, is the husband and wife sharing their bodies in "due benevolence," a euphemism for sexual intimacy (1 Cor. 7:2–5).

Paul instructs a believer married to an unbeliever not to seek divorce as long as the unbeliever is "pleased to dwell with" the believing spouse (1 Cor. 7:12–14). However, he says, "If the unbelieving [spouse] depart, let him depart. A brother or a sister is not under bondage in such cases: but God hath called us to peace" (1 Cor. 7:15).[88] Hence, Paul teaches that prolonged or irreversible abandonment also constitutes grounds for divorce and remarriage.[89] It may be asked how Paul's release of an abandoned spouse from marriage is consistent with Christ's teaching that only adultery justifies divorce. Some divines would say that abandonment is essentially the same as adultery in its violation of the marital covenant. Other divines would say that someone who abandons a spouse has for all practical purposes divorced him or her, and that in divorce the innocent party is seeking legal recognition of what is already a reality.[90]

88. Note the similarity of Paul's teaching to the Mosaic statute that a man who marries a maidservant but then refuses to give her full food, clothing, or sexual rights as a wife must release her as a free woman (Ex. 21:7–11).

89. Brakel, *The Christian's Reasonable Service*, 3:206–7. It might be objected that Paul's words apply only to an unbeliever. However, if a believer deserts his or her spouse without biblical grounds, then the church should begin the process of discipline, which culminates in excommunication if the offender does not repent (Matt. 18:15–18). Consequently, the believing spouse should treat the deserting spouse as an unbeliever. The process of church discipline would be an important part of testing whether the breach in the marriage is curable. See John M. Frame, *The Doctrine of the Christian Life* (Phillipsburg, NJ: P&R, 2008), 780.

90. Udemans said, "If an unbeliever leaves his spouse because he despises her faith, the marriage is annulled.... If the deserting spouse stays away for a considerable time, the innocent party is free,

Aside from sexual immorality, few sins damage the marital relationship more than reviling speech and violent actions. When one spouse is physically violent toward the other, the innocent party should seek a safe place to reside and appeal to authorities in the civil government and the church to intervene. Even if the victim of physical or severe verbal mistreatment is the one who leaves the home, it is the offender who must be considered guilty of desertion.

The Westminster Confession of Faith (24.6) says, "Nothing but adultery, or such wilful desertion as can no way be remedied by the Church, or civil magistrate, is cause sufficient of dissolving the bond of marriage."[91] The words "as can no way be remedied" imply that abandonment justifies divorce only after sincere and persistent attempts at reconciliation by the innocent spouse have been rejected by the other party, except where the offender has sinned in such a manner as irreversibly destroys the marital relationship, such as attempting to severely injure or murder his or her spouse.[92]

The Seventh Commandment and Love

The seventh commandment, like the other precepts of the second table, instructs us in one aspect of our duty to love one another. Paul quotes the sixth through tenth commandments and says that they are summarized "in this saying, namely, Thou shalt love thy neighbour as thyself" (Rom. 13:9). Therefore, sexual purity and faithfulness to one's spouse are crucial aspects of loving one another. The world often confuses sexual lust with love (Prov. 7:18). However, Paul contrasts them by opening his list of "the works of the flesh" with "adultery, fornication, uncleanness, [and] lasciviousness," but then saying that "the fruit of the Spirit is love, joy, peace," and so on (Gal. 5:19, 22). Watson said, "Adultery sows discord. It destroys peace and love, the two best flowers that grow together in a family."[93] Adultery tears apart families, churches, societies, and nations.

Christ was tempted "in all points," including sexual temptation, but remained pure and spotless, without sin (Heb. 4:15; 1 Pet. 1:19). He took no earthly wife, for his spiritual bride consists of the whole regenerate church,

---

under the watchful eye and verdict of lawful judges, to ask for an annulment of the first marriage and permission for another." *The Practice of Faith, Hope, and Love*, 388.

91. *Reformed Confessions*, 4:263.

92. Hungarian *Confessio-Catholica*, in *Reformed Confessions*, 2:541, 617.

93. Watson, *The Ten Commandments*, 158.

whom he faithfully loved and gave himself to sanctify (Eph. 5:25–27). Christian marriages are to be pictures of the relationship between Christ and his church (vv. 31–32). When Christ returns, he will punish this unfaithful and ungodly world for the spiritual whore it has been and gather his saints to himself for the wedding feast of the Lamb (Rev. 19:1–8). As we wait for him, we are to keep ourselves as a pure virgin with eyes only for her bridegroom (2 Cor. 11:2–3). This spiritual significance of marriage is a major reason why physical fornication and adultery are such grave sins: fornicators and adulterers, though made in God's image, grossly misrepresent the Lord of faithful love.

Some Ethical Applications of the Seventh Commandment

The Westminster Shorter Catechism (Q. 71) says, "The seventh commandment requireth the preservation of our own and our neighbour's chastity, in heart, speech and behaviour."[94] People must repent of sexual sin in order to pursue eternal life with God. Paul says, "Know ye not that the unrighteous shall not inherit the kingdom of God? Be not deceived: neither fornicators, nor idolaters, nor adulterers, nor effeminate, nor abusers of themselves with mankind [both terms refer to homosexuality] . . . shall inherit the kingdom of God" (1 Cor. 6:9–10). Though the nations wallow in impurity (Eph. 4:17–19), new obedience is possible by the power of God's grace; referring to the list of sins quoted above, Paul adds, "And such were some of you: but ye are washed, but ye are sanctified, but ye are justified in the name of the Lord Jesus, and by the Spirit of our God" (1 Cor. 6:11).

Faithfulness in our sexuality stands at the heart of our calling as Christians. Paul says, "For this is the will of God, even your sanctification, that ye should abstain from fornication. . . . For God hath not called us unto uncleanness, but unto holiness. He therefore that despiseth, despiseth not man, but God, who hath also given unto us his holy Spirit" (1 Thess. 4:3, 7–8). We must have zero tolerance for lustful talk, lustful looks, lustful reading, lustful dress, and lustful touch, for lust is not love; rather, it defiles desire, contradicts our holy calling, corrupts our conversations, and damns sinners to hell.[95]

---

94. *Reformed Confessions*, 4:363.

95. Joel R. Beeke, "Zero Tolerance for Lust," sermon on Ephesians 5:3–4, The Gospel Trumpet, http://www.gospeltrumpet.net/uploads/3/1/6/5/31658911/zero_tolerance_for_lust.pdf.

Our Lord Jesus Christ says, "Ye have heard that it was said by them of old time, Thou shalt not commit adultery: but I say unto you, That whosoever looketh on a woman to lust after her hath committed adultery with her already in his heart" (Matt. 5:27–28). Samuel Willard said, "We must resist and suppress lascivious thought. We ought to withstand them at their first starting, and cast them out as soon as we discover them to have gotten into our minds.... Think that if we are consecrated temples to the Spirit of God, we ought to keep the house clean."[96] Though overcoming these lusts requires supernatural divine grace, Christ's blood-bought victory is implemented through his disciples' strenuous battles against sin. It requires nothing less than plucking out the eye and cutting off the hand that makes us stumble (vv. 29–30)—not by literal self-mutilation, which has little power to curb sins of the heart, but by amputating occasions of sexual temptation from our lives, lest they destroy us. Watson warned, "As a man may die of an inward bleeding, so he may be damned for the inward boilings of lust, if it be not mortified."[97]

Sexual purity in an unclean world requires the thoughtful and diligent use of means. The Westminster Larger Catechism (Q. 138) reminds us that "the duties required in the seventh commandment" include "watchfulness over the eyes and all the senses (Job 31:1); temperance (Acts 24:24–25), keeping of chaste company (Prov. 2:16–20), modesty in apparel (1 Tim. 2:9); marriage by those that have not the gift of continency (1 Cor. 7:2, 9), conjugal love (Prov. 5:19–20), and cohabitation (1 Peter 3:7)."[98]

The call to sexual holiness requires us to take decisive action to avoid sexually lascivious media. Pornography, especially that on the internet, has become a massive problem in the modern world because it is easily accessible from virtually any location and may be viewed privately. We must implement David's holy resolve: "I will set no wicked thing before mine eyes: I hate the work of them that turn aside; it shall not cleave to me" (Ps. 101:3).

Visual media and music that promote sin or entice us to immoral thoughts, even if they are not explicitly pornographic, should be avoided. Those who think that it is nothing to fill their eyes and ears with sinful entertainment should consider Tertullian's words about the pagan stage plays of his day: "If we ought to abominate all that is immodest, on what

96. Willard, *A Compleat Body of Divinity*, 671.
97. Watson, *The Ten Commandments*, 153.
98. *Reformed Confessions*, 4:333.

ground is it right to hear what we must not speak? . . . Why, in the same way, is it right to look on what it is disgraceful to do?"[99]

Sexual temptation often prevails through the power of words. Paul condemns coarse language and sexually titillating humor: "But fornication, and all uncleanness, or covetousness, let it not be once named among you, as becometh saints; neither filthiness, nor foolish talking, nor jesting, which are not convenient: but rather giving of thanks" (Eph. 5:3–4). Proverbs warns against being caught by the sweet and smooth words of a seductress (Prov. 5:3; 6:24; 7:5, 21; 22:14). Seductive speech need not be erotic, especially at first, but it blinds our minds by flattering our pride and entangling our affections.

One of the best means to address strong sexual desire is God's provision of sexual pleasure in godly marriage (1 Cor. 7:2, 9). Some Christians have extraordinary gifts to live celibate lives (v. 7; cf. Matt. 19:10–12). Ordinarily, unmarried Christian young adults should pursue marriage by diligent prayer to God, seeking the assistance of godly parents, pastors, and friends, and taking opportunities to befriend other unmarried Christians. Married couples should enjoy physical intimacy with each other on a regular basis, except by mutual consent for the purpose of prayer (1 Cor. 7:3–5) or as medical conditions necessitate. Let us not underestimate the power of sexual desire but use the means God gives. Calvin said, "Let no one cry out to me . . . that with God's help he can do all things. For God helps only those who walk in his ways."[100] We should not merely treat sexual activity in marriage as a necessary evil to avoid sin, but as part of our calling to love our spouses with desire and delight (Prov. 5:18–19).[101]

A question of conscience may be raised concerning touching one's own body for sexual self-stimulation (masturbation). Some people have observed that the Holy Scriptures do not explicitly forbid such behavior, and therefore, it must be permitted by God. However, it tends to draw a person into sexual fantasy, which violates Christ's prohibition against lust. Self-stimulation also turns one's sexuality inward for self-pleasing, whereas God designed sexual activity to happen in a context of giving oneself to delighting in and pleasing another person.

99. Tertullian, *De Spectaculis*, chap. 18, in *ANF*, 3:87.
100. Calvin, *Institutes*, 2.8.42.
101. On ways in which the gospel fosters healthy sexuality in marriage, see Beeke, *Friends and Lovers*, 45–86.

Satan has reduced sexuality to an impersonal technique for physical pleasure, divorced it from real relationships, and elevated it into an idol to be worshiped. R. Kent Hughes says, "The magnificent, multidimensional marital sexuality of the Bible has been shrinkwrapped into a flat-sided, single-dimensioned, materialist package. . . . Key to this reductionistic view of sex is the regarding of sex as essentially a skill. . . . Yet paradoxically, this reductionistic sex is held on the level of 'religion' in general culture."[102]

As we put off sexual lust and impurity, we must put on self-denying love. Given that marriage is a creation ordinance, it is not surprising that one key to sexual faithfulness is learning to view ourselves and other people as God's image bearers, not mere animals driven by fleshly desires or objects to be used. Attaining our greatest potential as human beings does not require sexual activity—which Jesus Christ never had—but humbly serving other people for the glory of God. This is true greatness and true joy.

If we are in a situation where our sexual desires are frustrated, rather than turn to self-pity or, worse yet, acts of immorality, let us devote ourselves to praising and rejoicing in the Lord and loving and serving the people in our families, churches, and communities. Let us seek first God's kingdom and busy ourselves in Christian service and fellowship with the saints. Whatever our marital status or degree of sexual satisfaction in marriage, we should remember that marriage and sexual activity are temporary gifts from God, and God's children will graduate to greater joys when Christ returns (Luke 20:34–36).

Sing to the Lord

Brotherly Love

Blest be the tie that binds
Our hearts in Christian love:
The fellowship of kindred minds
Is like to that above.

Before our Father's throne
We pour our ardent prayers;
Our fears, our hopes, our aims, are one,
Our comforts and our cares.

102. R. Kent Hughes, *Set Apart: Calling a Worldly Church to a Godly Life* (Wheaton, IL: Crossway, 2003), 79–80.

We share our mutual woes,
Our mutual burdens bear,
And often for each other flows
The sympathizing tear.

When we asunder part,
It gives us inward pain;
But we shall still be joined in heart,
And hope to meet again.

From sorrow, toil, and pain,
And sin, we shall be free;
And perfect love and friendship reign
Through all eternity.

John Fawcett
Tune: Boyston
Or Tune: Dennis
Trinity Hymnal—Baptist Edition, No. 285

Questions for Meditation or Discussion

1. What does the word "honour" mean in the fifth commandment?
2. How is the fifth commandment grounded on God's creation of man in his image?
3. What does the fifth commandment teach us about honoring people outside of the parent-child relationship?
4. What are some practical ways in which people must honor their parents aside from obedience?
5. What can we learn from the specific meaning of the verb translated as "kill" in the sixth commandment?
6. What does God's creation of man in his image imply about murder? About the proper civil penalty for murder?
7. How can we murder others in our hearts? What inward qualities does the sixth commandment require us to cultivate by God's grace?
8. What does God's creation of man and institution of marriage in the garden of Eden reveal about his will for human sexuality?
9. Under what circumstances is a person justified in seeking a legal divorce from his or her spouse? Apart from those circumstances, what does divorce and remarriage result in? Why?

10. How are you guarding yourself against sexual immorality in heart and body? Is there more that you need to do to protect yourself? If so, what?

Questions for Deeper Reflection

11. Under what circumstances should a minor child disobey his parents or even seek to escape from their presence? Make sure to refer to the sixth and seventh commandments.
12. Imagine that a friend tells you he is having suicidal thoughts. What reasons would you give him not to kill himself?
13. Write a detailed plan of action for someone who has engaged in a habit of viewing pornography for several years but now desires to thoroughly repent and walk in purity.

40

Obedience to God's Law, Part 4

The Eighth through Tenth Commandments and Conclusion

A significant portion of the good that people have in this world consists of material possessions, knowledge of the truth, and the enjoyment of these blessings without being disturbed by others. Love for our neighbors requires respecting their rights to their property, speaking the truth to them and about them, and rejoicing in their prosperity without envy. When we love our neighbors in these ways, we love the God who made them. Therefore, we must give our consideration to the eighth, ninth, and tenth commandments.

The Eighth Commandment: Rightful Human Property

The Lord says, "Thou shalt not steal" (Ex. 20:15; cf. Deut. 5:19).

The Exegesis of the Eighth Commandment

The verb translated as "steal" (*ganab*; cf. noun *gannab*, "thief") refers to the unlawful taking of another's property.[1] Stealing can be done by

1. Figuratively, to "steal" (*ganab*) the "heart" means to deceive (Gen. 31:20, 26; 2 Sam. 15:6). The *hithpael* of *ganab* means to move stealthily, to "steal away" (2 Sam. 19:3). The *pual* of *ganab* means "was secretly brought" (Job 4:12). Hence, sometimes "steal," in the sense of taking something stealthily, has a positive meaning, such as when the men of Jabesh-gilead "had stolen" the

various means, including by fraud and deceit: "Ye shall not steal, neither deal falsely, neither lie one to another" (Lev. 19:11). Thieves often act in secrecy (Judg. 17:2) or under cover of darkness (Job 24:14), for stealing is shameful (Jer. 2:26). It is theft to embezzle property placed under one's management by its owner (Gen. 30:33) or to take for oneself goods entrusted to one's safekeeping by a neighbor (Ex. 22:12). Theft can also be associated with the threat or use of violent force (Luke 3:14), or breaking into someone's home (Ex. 22:2; Joel 2:9). People also steal when they find lost property but do not return it even though they know its owner (Deut. 22:1), act as accomplices of thieves in helping or hiding their crimes (Prov. 29:24), or use legal or political means to unjustly take someone's possessions (Isa. 1:23).[2]

Stealing is a sin, just as murder and adultery are sins (Jer. 7:9; Hos. 4:2). Stealing to satisfy one's basic needs, such as food, should evoke sympathy, but it still is a sin worthy of punishment (Prov. 6:30–31). When the poor steal, they dishonor the name of their God (30:8–9). God's curse shall fall on the unrepentant thief (Zech. 5:3). Paul includes "thieves" among those who will not "inherit the kingdom of God" (1 Cor. 6:10).

The Eighth Commandment and Creation

The prohibition against stealing implies the right to own personal property.[3] This right is grounded on God's creation of man in his image to "have dominion . . . over all the earth" (Gen. 1:26; cf. Pss. 8:5–8; 115:16). As God's image bearer, man is not the ultimate owner of the other creatures but is the Creator's steward, responsible to rule as his representative. God is the owner of all his creation (Ex. 9:29; 19:5; Ps. 24:1; cf. Lev. 25:23).[4] Nevertheless, God commissioned man to "subdue" (*kabash*) the earth, which means to conquer and bring it under peaceful control (1 Chron. 22:18), and to "have dominion" (*radah*) over it, which means to rule it as a king or royal official (1 Kings 4:24; 9:23).[5] Therefore, man's right to use the creatures was granted to him, Samuel Willard said, "by God the Creator and great Landlord; and he was to be God's tenant."[6]

---

remains of Saul and Jonathan from the Philistines, who were desecrating them (2 Sam. 21:12), or when Jehoshabeath "stole" Joash and hid him from murderous Athaliah (2 Chron. 22:11).

2. Wollebius, *Compendium*, 2.12.(2).ii (246–47).
3. Ames, *A Sketch of the Christian's Catechism*, 187.
4. On God's authority over the world, see *RST*, 1:767–69; 2:69–70.
5. On the dominion of God's image bearers, see *RST*, 2:129–30, 165–66.
6. Willard, *A Compleat Body of Divinity*, 686.

As God's servant-kings on earth, human beings have a responsibility to care for the other creatures. Though plants and animals are not people created in God's image and may be killed for man's use or protection (Gen. 9:2–6), they still have value as the handiwork of God. The law of Moses enjoined kindness to animals, whether one's own livestock, that of other people, or wild animals.[7] Even trees were protected by the law from needless destruction (Deut. 20:19–20). Solomon identifies kindness to one's animals as a mark of righteousness: "A righteous man regardeth the life of his beast: but the tender mercies of the wicked are cruel" (Prov. 12:10). Christ assumed that people of common decency would rescue their livestock from danger, even on the Sabbath (Luke 13:15; 14:5). Therefore, "thou shalt not steal," rooted in the creation mandate, implies our responsibility not to recklessly destroy the earth and its living creatures but to care for and cultivate them, for they are the common property of mankind under God. As the Heidelberg Catechism (LD 42, Q. 110) says, the eighth commandment of God forbids, among other things, "all abuse and waste of His gifts."[8]

God not only gave mankind authority over the whole earth but gave the first man authority over a particular place in the earth: the garden of Eden,[9] which God charged Adam to serve and keep (Gen. 2:8, 15). This is the root of each man's and woman's ownership of private property and personal vocation to cultivate it for the good of mankind to the glory of God. We read that, afterward, each of Adam's sons brought an offering to the Lord: Cain brought "his offering" from the harvest of the land he farmed, and Abel "his offering" from "his flock" (4:1–5). Therefore, personal property is attested in the earliest days of the human race.

Property is one of the goods that God bestows on man. The material world is not to be viewed as worthless or evil, but as something God created and views as "good" (Gen. 1:31). Therefore, we should not despise property but receive it with thanksgiving from God's hand and use it prayerfully with faith and obedience to his Word (1 Tim. 4:4–5). Man's physical life depends on his use of material goods provided by God (Ps. 104:23, 27; Acts 14:17).

Man's creation in God's image also teaches us not to regard material goods as more important than people. Theft is a serious crime, but the law of Moses did not require the death penalty for theft; rather, the thief had

7. Ex. 23:4–5; Lev. 22:28; Deut. 22:1–4, 6–7; 25:4.
8. *The Three Forms of Unity*, 108.
9. On the garden of Eden, see *RST*, 2:136–37.

to make restitution to the owner (Ex. 22:1–6; Lev. 6:1–5). In this manner, the value of the thief's life was esteemed higher than the goods he stole, but he was required to remedy the loss he caused to others who also bore God's image.

The Eighth Commandment and Slavery

In the Bible, stealing includes kidnapping a human being and enslaving him. Though the law of Moses prescribed restitution as the penalty for stealing property, in the case of stealing people or selling those stolen,[10] it mandated the death penalty (Ex. 21:16; Deut. 24:7). Israel would have recalled the great crime that Joseph's brothers committed against him by selling him into slavery (Gen. 37:28; 40:15). Enslaving people involves a failure to honor them (a violation of the moral principle in the fifth commandment) and often leads to murder (a violation of the sixth) or sexual sin (the seventh). However, slavery especially violates the eighth commandment, for it steals a man's labor and liberty to enjoy his possessions. Augustine noted that God created man in his image to rule over the creatures, not to be ruled, and thus, the enslavement of one man by another is the consequence of sin entering the world, though it is better to be the slave of a man than the slave of sinful lust.[11] Paul includes "menstealers" (*andrapodistēs*) among the kinds of people condemned by God's law (1 Tim. 1:9–10).[12] The book of Revelation describes "Babylon," a city symbolizing the sinful world that God will destroy, as characterized in part by its human trafficking (Rev. 18:13; cf. Ezek. 27:13; Joel 3:3).

Hence, the Westminster Larger Catechism (Q. 142) includes "manstealing" among those sins forbidden in the eighth commandment.[13] Wilhelmus à Brakel said that this commandment forbids "the theft of human beings," noting that "this sin is committed in those countries where slave trade is practiced."[14] Gisbertus Voetius and Bernardus Smytegelt (1665–1739) similarly condemned the slave trade.[15] Richard Baxter said,

10. The phrase "or if he be found in his hand" (Ex. 21:16) indicates that not just the kidnapper but anyone involved in trafficking the enslaved person falls under this law's judgment. Stuart, *Exodus*, 488.

11. Augustine, *The City of God*, 19.15, in *NPNF*[1], 2:411.

12. An *andrapodon*, literally "foot-man," was a slave or captive (3 Macc. 7:5), and an *andrapodistēs* a "slave-dealer or kidnapper." Liddell and Scott, *A Greek-English Lexicon*, 128.

13. *Reformed Confessions*, 4:335. See Boston, *An Illustration of the Doctrines of the Christian Religion*, in *Works*, 2:295.

14. Brakel, *The Christian's Reasonable Service*, 3:216. He also noted the trafficking of children and youths (216–17).

15. Cited in Douma, *The Ten Commandments*, 287.

> To go as pirates and catch up poor negroes or people of another land, that never forfeited life or liberty, and to make them slaves, and sell them, is one of the worst kinds of thievery in the world; and such persons are to be taken for the common enemies of mankind; and they that buy them and use them as beasts, for their mere commodity, and betray, or destroy, or neglect their souls, are fitter to be called incarnate devils than Christians, though they be no Christians whom they so abuse.[16]

The Bible insists that human beings are to regard each other as fundamentally equal before God. All people are descended from one father and mother (Gen. 2:7; 3:20; Acts 17:26).[17] Alexander McLeod (1774–1833) said that according to the Bible, people from Europe, Asia, Africa, and America are "different members of the same great family."[18] Job says, "If I did despise the cause of my manservant or of my maidservant, when they contended with me; What then shall I do when God riseth up? And when he visiteth, what shall I answer him? Did not he that made me in the womb make him? And did not one fashion us in the womb?" (Job 31:13–15). Joseph Caryl (1602–1673) commented, "A servant's cause must not be slighted. God hath set masters over their servants, but he hath not given them a liberty to trample them under their feet; servants are under their masters' power, not under their lusts." He noted that both masters and servants are equally the objects of Christ's saving grace, equally accountable to God the Judge, and equally created by God in the womb—indeed, servants not uncommonly have stronger bodies and more intelligent minds than their masters.[19]

It is true that the Bible does not explicitly call for the abolition of slavery, and God permitted and regulated various forms of bondage in the Old and New Testaments. The Holy Scriptures allowed the Israelites to enter into arrangements of temporary servitude to pay debts or to suffer punishment for crimes, but required that they be treated as indentured servants, not slaves.[20] The law allowed for corporal punishment of disobedient servants, but it penalized inflicting injury or death on them (Ex. 21:20, 26–27). Israelites could purchase foreigners as permanent slaves (Lev.

16. Baxter, *A Christian Directory*, 462.

17. On the importance of the historical Adam for the unity of mankind, see *RST*, 2:148–50.

18. Alexander McLeod, *Negro Slavery Unjustifiable*, 11th ed. (New York: Alexander McLeod, 1863), 10. The book was originally published in 1802.

19. Joseph Caryl, *An Exposition with Practicall Observations Continued upon the Thirtieth and Thirty first Chapters of the Book of Job* (London: by M. Simmons for Elisha Wallis, 1659), 429, 440–41, 444.

20. Ex. 21:2; 22:3; Lev. 25:39–43; Deut. 15:12; 2 Kings 4:1.

25:44–46) and enslave enemies from other nations who surrendered to their armies (Deut. 20:10–11), but were forbidden to oppress foreigners; they were to treat them with the same justice as other Israelites.[21] If a slave ran away from his master and took refuge among the Israelites, they were not to return him to his master or oppress him (Deut. 23:15–16). Therefore, as Abraham Booth said, the servitude permitted by God under the law of Moses cannot be compared to the cruel enslavement of Africans in the North Atlantic slave trade.[22]

In Christ, given his accomplishment of redemption and fuller revelation of God's will, there is neither Jew nor Gentile, slave nor free (Gal. 3:28; Col. 3:11). This implies that we should treat all people at least as well as God required the Israelites to treat each other. God only permits forms of servitude that preserve human dignity, whereas chattel slavery is forbidden.[23] Paul reminds earthly "masters" that "your Master also is in heaven; neither is there respect of persons [favoritism or prejudice] with him" (Eph. 6:9). He urged Philemon to receive his formerly runaway but now repentant slave Onesimus "not now as a servant, but above a servant, a brother beloved.... Receive him as myself" (Philem. 16–17). The New Testament did not call for the abolition of slavery because such a demand would have overthrown society and caused much bloodshed (about a third of the population of the Roman Empire consisted of slaves). However, God's Word instills principles of equality and brotherly love that make it impossible for one person to treat another as mere property. Thus, the Bible contains the seeds of abolition that have borne good fruit over the course of Christian history.

The Eighth Commandment and Love

Since men, women, and children are embodied beings, a significant part of how we love them is by respecting, protecting, and seeking to advance

21. Ex. 12:49; 20:10; 22:21; 23:9; Lev. 19:33–34; 24:22; Num. 35:15; Deut. 1:16; 10:18–19; 14:29; 16:11, 14; 24:14, 17, 19–21.

22. Abraham Booth, *Commerce in the Human Species, and the Enslaving of Innocent Persons, Inimical to the Laws of Moses and the Gospel of Christ*, in *The Works of Abraham Booth*, 3 vols. (London: W. Button & Son et al., 1813), 3:190–94. Against slavery, see also Spurgeon, *The New Park Street Pulpit*, 6:155.

23. William Gouge, *Of Domestical Duties*, ed. Greg Fox (Edinburgh, IN: Puritan Reprints, 2006), 117, 485–89, 495. The laws of Puritan New England in the mid-seventeenth century gave African slaves essentially the same rights and protections of Hebrew servants under the Old Testament law. Francis Bremer, *The Puritan Experiment: New England Society from Bradford to Edwards* (Hanover, NH: University Press of New England, 1995), 205–8. Sadly, their rights were increasingly constricted until slavery was gradually abolished in Massachusetts in the late eighteenth century as inconsistent with that state's constitution.

their material wealth. Stealing, cheating, robbing, and enslaving are acts of hatred. Paul says that "thou shalt not steal," along with the other commandments, "is briefly comprehended in this saying, namely, Thou shalt love thy neighbour as thyself" (Rom. 13:9).

Applied to the motives of the heart, the eighth commandment forbids greed and avarice, the lustful intent to acquire by any means more wealth and the beautiful and glorious things it affords. The Scriptures teach us to pray, "Incline my heart unto thy testimonies, and not to covetousness" (Ps. 119:36). The word translated as "covetousness" (*betsa'*) is not related to that rendered "covet" in the tenth commandment; rather, it means "unjust gain,"[24] such as money gotten by violence (Jer. 22:17), by abuse of power and bribery (Ex. 18:21; 1 Sam. 8:3; Isa. 33:15), or by prophesying flattering lies to win the support of men (Jer. 6:13–14). This noun is used to designate a person who is "greedy for gain" (Prov. 1:19; 15:27).[25] The noun was sometimes rendered with the Greek word translated as "greediness" (*pleonexia*, Jer. 22:17; Hab. 2:9 LXX), literally "craving or grasping for more." Christ says, "Take heed, and beware of covetousness [*pleonexia*]: for a man's life consisteth not in the abundance of the things which he possesseth" (Luke 12:15; cf. Mark 7:22; Rom. 1:29). Paul warns that the "covetous" (greedy, *pleonektēs*) will not "inherit the kingdom of God" (1 Cor. 6:10).

Love for our neighbors should engender respect for their rights to own and enjoy their property. The law of Moses forbade a creditor from walking into a debtor's home to take the collateral for a loan; he had to wait outside while the owner brought it out (Deut. 24:10–11). The law also forbade keeping a poor man's cloak as collateral, lest he be exposed to the cold of the night (Ex. 22:26–27; Deut. 24:12–13). Such laws protect the dignity of all people.

The opposite of stealing is not merely avoiding theft but working and giving. Paul says, "Let him that stole steal no more: but rather let him labour, working with his hands the thing which is good, that he may have [something] to give to him that needeth" (Eph. 4:28). William Ames said, "Quietly and diligently let him follow an occupation which agrees with the will of God and the profit of men."[26] Paul exhorts Christians "that with

24. The word *betsa'* may also have the more neutral sense of "profit" (Job 22:3; Ps. 30:9; Mal. 3:14).

25. "Greedy for gain" translates the noun combined with its cognate participial verb (*botse'a batsa'*). The same phrase appears in the Hebrew text of Jer. 6:13; 8:10; Hab. 2:9.

26. Ames, *The Marrow of Theology*, 2.20.26 (322).

quietness they work, and eat their own bread" (2 Thess. 3:12). However, they must not stop at mere self-love but love their neighbors as themselves. John says, "If anyone has the world's goods and sees his brother in need, yet closes his heart against him, how does God's love abide in him?" (1 John 3:17 ESV). Loving our neighbors also calls for reasonable steps to preserve their property when it is in danger of being damaged or destroyed (Ex. 23:4–5). However, true love does not encourage people who are capable of work to live like dependent children, but calls them to share in the dignity of exercising dominion over God's world. Paul goes so far as to say, "If any would not work, neither should he eat" (2 Thess. 3:10).

Although the eighth commandment primarily focuses on love for our neighbors, it directs us ultimately to love God, the Lord of all people and property. "The rich and poor meet together: the Lord is the maker of them all" (Prov. 22:2). God's providence distributes possessions among men, and to steal another's property is "just as if we ourselves invaded the very rule of God," as Ames said.[27] Thomas Boston said, "Eye God in these matters, as he who is your witness, and will be your judge to them. Set the Lord before you in your business, and you will fear to step wrong."[28]

Greed is a great offense to God because "covetousness [*pleonexia*] . . . is idolatry" (Col. 3:5). It is a betrayal of the love we owe to God. Brian Rosner says that greed "to acquire and keep for yourself more and more money and material things is an attack on God's exclusive rights to human love and devotion, trust and confidence, and service and obedience."[29] No one exemplified the love of God more than his Son, Jesus Christ, who refused an offer to gain the whole world by bowing to Satan (Luke 4:5–8), but instead humbled himself and embraced the cross so that he might make many rich in his eternal kingdom.[30]

Some Ethical Applications of the Eighth Commandment

The Westminster Shorter Catechism (Q. 74) summarizes the requirement of the eighth commandment as "the lawful procuring and furthering the wealth and outward estate of ourselves and others."[31] George Swinnock wrote, "In all thy contracts, purchases, and sales, cast an eye upon that

---

27. Ames, *A Sketch of the Christian's Catechism*, 188.
28. Boston, *An Illustration of the Doctrines of the Christian Religion*, in *Works*, 2:310.
29. Brian S. Rosner, *Greed as Idolatry: The Origin and Meaning of a Pauline Metaphor* (Grand Rapids, MI: Eerdmans, 2007), 173.
30. Fesko, *The Rule of Love*, 107–8.
31. *Reformed Confessions*, 4:363.

golden rule, mentioned by our Saviour, 'Therefore all things whatsoever ye would that men should do to you, do ye even so to them: for this is the law and the prophets' (Matt. 7:12)."[32] The Golden Rule calls us to "commutative justice," which Ames defined as "equality between what is given and what is received,"[33] or as Johannes Wollebius said, "equity with regard to both the goods and to the price."[34]

One form of stealing is dishonesty in buying and selling. The Holy Scriptures condemn the use of false weights and measures.[35] We also must not use deceitful means of cheating people out of the goods or services that they think they are purchasing, such as falsely representing materials as precious metals or stones when they are not or intentionally and covertly mingling low-quality or defective products with the good products we advertise.[36]

It is also stealing to intentionally damage or destroy the property of a neighbor (vandalism), including defacing it or marking it with graffiti without the owner's permission. Public property, such as schools and parks, is subject to the authority of the civil government, not the whims of every individual citizen. A person is culpable for harming the property of others, in some cases even if he did not intend the damage. The law of Moses teaches us this principle of general equity when it says, "If a man shall cause a field or vineyard to be eaten, and shall put in his beast, and shall feed in another man's field; of the best of his own field, and of the best of his own vineyard, shall he make restitution. If fire break out, and catch in thorns, so that the stacks of corn, or the standing corn, or the field, be consumed therewith; he that kindled the fire shall surely make restitution" (Ex. 22:5–6).

The prohibition against stealing people's material goods implies the value of human labor to make or obtain those goods. We must not fail to promptly pay those who have rendered their labor according to a prior agreement made with us.[37] James rebukes the wicked rich: "Behold, the hire of the labourers who have reaped down your fields, which is of you kept back by fraud, crieth: and the cries of them which have reaped are

32. Swinnock, *The Christian Man's Calling*, in *Works*, 2:201.

33. Ames, *The Marrow of Theology*, 2.16.69 (307). On commutative and distributive justice in God, see *RST*, 1:814.

34. Wollebius, *Compendium*, 2.12.(2).iii.d (247).

35. Lev. 19:35; Prov. 11:1; 16:11; Amos 8:5.

36. Perkins, *A Golden Chain*, chap. 27, in *Works*, 6:134.

37. Lev. 19:13; Deut. 24:15; Prov. 3:27–28.

entered into the ears of the Lord of sabaoth [the Lord of hosts]" (James 5:4). If even an animal should be rewarded for its work, how much more is a human laborer "worthy of his reward" (Deut. 25:4; 1 Tim. 5:18). This application not only condemns someone who withholds payment to laborers (Jer. 22:13), but also rebukes a person who refuses to pay them a just and fair wage, for in effect he pays for only part of their work. God condemns as oppression all unjust treatment of workers regarding their wages (Mal. 3:5).

Theft may take place through the abuse of power by those in positions of civil authority or wealth. It is tragic when those in power oppress people who have no one to comfort them (Eccles. 4:1). Rulers are too often characterized by what they take from their nations instead of what they give (1 Sam. 8:10–18). People in positions of civil authority should aspire to complete their public service with good consciences that they have never unjustly taken anyone's property or oppressed the poor (12:3–4).

Perhaps the most valuable kind of physical property is land. The Old Testament repeatedly rebuked those who moved the "landmarks" that identified property boundaries, for to do so was to steal another family's inheritance.[38] The year of Jubilee provided for the restoration of land to its heirs to prevent any family from being cast into long-term poverty and oppression (Lev. 25:13). Although the judicial law no longer binds us, and in modern society the lives of many people do not depend on raising crops on their own land, we should still follow the general equity of these laws and protect the homes and lands of people from unjust seizure or encroachment by other individuals or the civil government.

In the Old Testament, God forbade his people from charging each other interest on loans (usury).[39] A prohibition against charging interest persisted in the Christian church into the medieval period.[40] However, John Calvin argued that the biblical prohibition against usury pertained to the economic exploitation of the poor, to whom interest-free loans were acts of mercy to help them out of desperate situations. Calvin said, "Only those unjust exactions are condemned whereby the creditor, losing sight of equity, burdens and oppresses his debtor." It certainly should not

38. Deut. 19:14; 27:17; Job 24:2; Prov. 22:28; 23:10; Hos. 5:10.

39. Ex. 22:25; Lev. 25:36–37; Deut. 23:19–20; Neh. 5:7–13; Ps. 15:5; Prov. 28:8; Jer. 15:10; Ezek. 18:8, 13, 17; 22:12. See the Heidelberg Catechism (LD 42, Q. 110), in *The Three Forms of Unity*, 108; and the Westminster Larger Catechism (Q. 142), in *Reformed Confessions*, 4:335.

40. Lombard, *The Sentences*, 3.37.5.3 (3:155); and Aquinas, *Summa Theologica*, Part 2.2, Q. 78, Art. 1.

be considered usury, he added, if a creditor should charge interest on a loan taken by a wealthy man in order to profit from some investment.[41] Furthermore, modern economies do not function in the same manner as ancient and medieval ones, so lending money with interest today can help advance the financial estate of those taking the loans if they wisely manage them. However, the sin of usury is still committed when creditors charge excessive interest rates or otherwise put conditions on loans that tend to put people in a downward spiral of debt leading to financial disaster. We must also remember that debt creates obligation and can place a person in bondage to his creditors (Prov. 22:7; cf. Deut. 28:44). Believers should be willing to offer personal loans to those in need without seeking any profit for themselves (Luke 6:35). However, it is wicked to borrow money and refuse to pay it back (Ps. 37:21).

If you have stolen from others, then you should make restitution, if possible, to those who have suffered loss, paying them back what was wrongfully taken and more. Restitution of wrongfully obtained money or goods is the requirement of justice (2 Sam. 12:6) and the evidence of genuine repentance and salvation (Ezek. 33:15; Luke 19:8–9).[42] If a large amount was stolen, it might take time to repay it, for one must still provide for one's own family (1 Tim. 5:8). However, it is far better to have a good conscience with God and man than to "stuff your pillow with thorns," as Thomas Watson put it, by living with a constant sense of guilt.[43]

The ordinary path to material prosperity for ourselves and our community, God's Word teaches us, is diligent labor in our vocations. "The hand of the diligent maketh rich" (Prov. 10:4).[44] Laziness is wastefulness, a destroyer of our time and a robber of those who employ us (18:9). Diligence is not merely working hard but giving careful attention and thought to managing one's property (27:23–27) with an eye toward future needs (6:6–11; 20:4).

Cotton Mather (1663–1728) said, "God hath made man a societal creature. We expect benefits from human society. It is but equal that human

41. Calvin, *Commentaries*, on Ex. 22:25. See John Calvin, "On Usury," in *Calvin's Ecclesiastical Advice*, trans. Mary Beaty and Benjamin W. Farley, foreword by John Haddon Leith (Louisville, KY: Westminster/John Knox, 1991), 139–43; Perkins, *A Golden Chain*, chap. 27, in *Works*, 6:135–36; Wollebius, *Compendium*, 2.12.(2).2 (249); and Turretin, *Institutes*, 11.19.7–21 (2:124–29).

42. Boston, *An Illustration of the Doctrines of the Christian Religion*, in *Works*, 2:290.

43. Watson, *The Ten Commandments*, 167.

44. See also Prov. 11:27; 12:24, 27; 13:4; 14:23; 21:5; 22:29; 23:1.

society should receive benefits from us. We are beneficial to human society by the works of that special occupation in which we are to be employed, according to the order of God."[45] Parents should provide their children with training in the character, knowledge, and skills necessary for them to flourish as adults. Workers should seek to produce high-quality goods and services that will help their customers prosper. Managers should administrate labor and resources with wisdom and honesty. Scientists should pursue technologies and medicines that benefit people's lives. Civil officials should promote peace, justice, and a reliable infrastructure so that citizens can flourish. Older people should mentor younger ones so that each generation can build on the wisdom of its predecessors. "Whatsoever ye do, do it heartily, as to the Lord, and not unto men; knowing that of the Lord ye shall receive the reward of the inheritance: for ye serve the Lord Christ" (Col. 3:23–24).

We must add to diligent service the self-restraint not to indulge ourselves in too much luxury, for pleasing our flesh will drain our resources: "He that loveth pleasure shall be a poor man: he that loveth wine and oil shall not be rich" (Prov. 21:17). God has not given riches to the wealthy so they can live like kings while neglecting the destitute (Luke 16:19–20), but to be "rich in good works" (1 Tim. 6:18).

The Ninth Commandment: True Human Testimony

The Lord says, "Thou shalt not bear false witness against thy neighbour" (Ex. 20:16; cf. Deut. 5:20).

The Exegesis of the Ninth Commandment

The word translated as "witness" (*'ed*) refers to a person, object, or discourse that demonstrates whether someone has fulfilled his legal or covenantal duty (Ex. 22:13; Deut. 17:6; 31:19). Therefore, this commandment explicitly prohibits giving false testimony regarding a legal dispute or judicial charge (perjury).

The Lord expands on this principle in the book of the covenant: "You shall not spread a false report. You shall not join hands with a wicked man to be a malicious witness. You shall not fall in with the many to do evil, nor shall you bear witness in a lawsuit, siding with the many, so as

45. Cotton Mather, *A Christian at His Calling*, cited in Leland Ryken, *Worldly Saints: The Puritans as They Really Were* (Grand Rapids, MI: Zondervan, 1986), 31.

to pervert justice, nor shall you be partial to a poor man in his lawsuit" (Ex. 23:1–3 ESV).

Though people might be fooled by false testimony or secretly smile because it favors their interests, God will most certainly punish the lying witness (Prov. 19:5, 9). In ancient Israel, if investigation proved a man to be a false witness, he was to suffer the same punishment that would have fallen on the one falsely accused (Deut. 19:16–21).

The Ninth Commandment and Creation

The Creator is the speaking God whose word has such truth that it brings things into reality (Gen. 1:3). God spoke truth to himself in the intra-Trinitarian counsel concerning man (v. 26). The Creator also spoke to man with words of blessing and command to direct his choices (vv. 28–30). And he spoke the words of his covenant (2:16–17).

The Tempter said that God's words were not trustworthy (Gen. 3:1, 4–5). Satan is the original liar (John 8:44). The very word translated as "devil" (*diabolos*) means "slanderer."[46] However, God has proven himself to be abundantly true and faithful in all he says and does (Gen. 24:27; 32:10; Ex. 34:6; Deut. 32:4).[47] God cannot lie, as his Word repeatedly affirms.[48] God's law requires that man, his image bearer, also be true and faithful.

The law forbids lying to one another (Lev. 19:11). The Lord hates "a lying tongue" (Prov. 6:17; cf. 12:22). So also, "a righteous man hateth lying" (13:5). Paul says, "Put on the new man, which after God is created in righteousness and true holiness. Wherefore putting away lying, speak every man truth with his neighbour" (Eph. 4:24–25). Lying is such an evil sin that John warns that "all liars" will "have their part in the lake which burneth with fire and brimstone: which is the second death" (Rev. 21:8).

A lie is an act of verbal communication in which something believed to be false is intentionally presented as if true.[49] To be mistaken about the facts one communicates is not to lie. Likewise, it is not a lie to hide people in danger of being unjustly killed (1 Kings 18:3–4; 2 Kings 11:1–3), to

46. On biblical terms used for Satan and the demons, see *RST*, 1:1134–36.

47. On God's truth and faithfulness, see *RST*, 1:805–10.

48. Num. 23:19; 1 Sam. 15:29; Titus 1:2; Heb. 6:18.

49. See Aquinas, *Summa Theologica*, Part 2.2, Q. 110, Art. 1; and Turretin, *Institutes*, 11.20.2 (2:129). In some cases, a gesture may be considered the equivalent of verbal communication if its significance is established by common custom, such as nodding the head for "Yes" or pointing the index finger in answer to a question such as "Who struck you?"

disguise oneself to conceal one's identity for a just cause (1 Kings 20:38, 41), to speak ambiguously to enemies (2 Kings 6:19), or to order soldiers to retreat in order to draw out one's enemies and ambush them (Josh. 8:3–8; cf. 2 Sam. 5:22–25). Furthermore, it is not a lie to tell part of the truth while remaining silent about another part, particularly if telling the whole truth would expose people to unjust harm (1 Sam. 16:1–5).

The Ninth Commandment and Love

In the ninth commandment, the words "against thy neighbour" highlight the significance of keeping this precept in order to love our neighbors as ourselves (Ex. 20:16). False testimony is extremely dangerous to the innocent: "A man that beareth false witness against his neighbour is a maul, and a sword, and a sharp arrow" (Prov. 25:18). Not only does a lying witness make an innocent party liable to civil penalties but he also creates discord (6:19).

Lying is an act of hatred (Prov. 26:28). One of the most precious gifts we can give to our neighbors is to speak the truth in love (Eph. 4:15). Whether we tell the truth or lie has massive implications for all human relationships, for people cannot live and work together in harmony unless they trust one another. Ames said, "Lying disturbs every faith [trust] in which the bond and foundation of human society exists."[50]

It might be objected that in some cases it is more loving to tell a lie than the truth. For some people, this objection suffices to justify telling all manner of lies to avoid hurting other people's feelings. However, God commands us to speak the difficult truth to our brothers and sisters regarding their sins because we love them (Lev. 19:17–18). Proverbs 27:5–6 says, "Open rebuke is better than secret love. Faithful are the wounds of a friend; but the kisses of an enemy are deceitful."

Others support lying only in more serious cases. Is it not better that we should lie so that innocent people might escape with their lives, as Rahab did to protect the Israelite spies hiding in her home in Jericho (Josh. 2:1–7)? Rahab is commended in the Bible for her actions (Heb. 11:31; James 2:25). Or what of the Hebrew midwives in Egypt, who, when Pharaoh commanded them to slay all newborn Hebrew boys, disobeyed him and excused themselves by saying, "The Hebrew women are not as

50. Ames, *A Sketch of the Christian's Catechism*, 190–91.

the Egyptian women; for they are lively, and are delivered ere [before] the midwives come in unto them" (Ex. 1:15–21)?

John Frame argues that we are obligated to not bear false witness against our neighbors only with respect to people who have the relation to us of "neighbor," but "we have no obligation to tell the truth to people who, for example, seek innocent life."[51] He supports this claim with a number of scriptural examples in which "someone misleads an enemy, without incurring any condemnation, and sometimes even being commended."[52]

In response, we argue that if we applied the same principle of interpretation to "love thy neighbour" (Lev. 19:18), it would limit the scope of our responsibility, whereas Christ taught that this command includes "love your enemies" (Matt. 5:43–44). The word translated as "neighbour" (*re'a*), while it can mean "friend," can also mean simply one's "fellow" or "another person."[53] It can be used of people who are each other's mortal enemies.[54]

How, then, should we understand the examples in the Bible of people telling lies? It may be that the midwives did not lie to Pharaoh, but that they arranged to arrive after the births of children so that the Hebrew mothers had time to hide their newborn sons (Ex. 1:19). Given that Pharaoh was murdering children, the midwives had no obligation to cooperate with him.

However, let us suppose that the midwives lied. They are commended not for their lies but for fearing God (Ex. 1:21). Rahab clearly lied, but she is commended in Scripture for her faith in the Lord and for hiding the Israelite spies.[55] God's Word never commends anyone for telling lies. Augustine said that in cases such as these, "it is not the deceit, but their good intention, that is justly praised, and sometimes even rewarded. It is quite enough that the deception should be pardoned."[56] We also recognize that such lies are not as heinous as other lies aggravated by the intent to mock, murder, steal, and so on. Augustine said, "Every lie is a sin, though

51. Frame, *The Doctrine of the Christian Life*, 839.

52. Frame, *The Doctrine of the Christian Life*, 836. For full responses, see Vern S. Poythress, "Why Lying Is Always Wrong: The Uniqueness of Verbal Deceit," *Westminster Theological Journal* 75 (2013): 83–95; and Grudem, *Christian Ethics*, 309–38.

53. See Francis Brown, Samuel Rolles Driver, and Charles Augustus Briggs, *The Enhanced Brown-Driver-Briggs Hebrew and English Lexicon* (Oxford: Clarendon, 1977), 945–46.

54. Ex. 2:13; 11:2; 21:18; 32:17; Judg. 7:22; 1 Sam. 14:20; 2 Sam. 2:16; 2 Kings 3:23; 2 Chron. 20:23; Pss. 12:2; 28:3. The word *re'a* is variously translated by the KJV in these texts.

55. Josh. 2:9–13; 6:17, 25; Heb. 11:31; James 2:25.

56. Augustine, *Enchiridion*, chap. 22, in *NPNF*[1], 3:245.

it makes a great difference with what intention. . . . For the sin of the man who tells a lie to help another is not so heinous as that of the man who tells a lie to injure another."[57]

Frame presents other examples of deception in the Bible, but these, too, do not advance the case for justified lying.[58] Some examples pertain to military maneuvers, telling part of the truth, or speaking ambiguously, none of which are lies, as we explained at the end of the previous section. There are several biblical examples of people telling lies or performing deceptive acts, but the Scriptures do not commend these acts, leaving open the question of whether they are sinful acts committed under the pressure of great danger.[59] In another case (Jer. 38:24–28), the words spoken may have been true if incomplete (37:20), or this may be an example of lying out of fear. Two other examples refer to God's sovereignty over demonic deception but do not say that God lied (1 Kings 22:19–23; 2 Thess. 2:11). As we noted above, God never lies, not even to his enemies.

It is sometimes urged that lying is necessary because it is the only way to save people's lives. However, a basic principle of God-fearing ethics is to obey God's commandments and entrust the results to him: "Trust in the Lord with all thine heart; and lean not unto thine own understanding. In all thy ways acknowledge him, and he shall direct thy paths" (Prov. 3:5–6). We do not know how God might intervene. Godefridus Udemans said, "Righteousness does not need the protection of lies, for it is protected by the shield of God Almighty."[60] We should do all that we can in good conscience to defend the innocent from oppressors and tyrants, but we must not think that we help God's cause by lying.

Paul firmly rejects the argument "Let us do evil, that good may come" (Rom. 3:8). As Augustine pointed out, arguing for the legitimacy of lying to avoid a greater evil sets a precedent to justify theft, adultery, or other sins in order to avoid tragedy.[61] Our love for our fellow man must be governed by our love for God and keeping his commandments (1 John 5:2). Love for God is love for truth, for God is truth (John 14:6; 1 John 5:6), the "God of truth" (Deut. 32:4). We follow Jesus Christ, who is "the

57. Augustine, *Enchiridion*, chap. 18, in *NPNF*[1], 3:243. On the degrees of sin, see *RST*, 2:445–47.

58. Frame, *The Doctrine of the Christian Life*, 836.

59. 1 Sam. 19:12–17; 20:6; 21:13; 27:10; 2 Sam. 15:34; 17:19–20.

60. Udemans, *The Practice of Faith, Hope, and Love*, 456.

61. Augustine, *Enchiridion*, chap. 22, in *NPNF*[1], 3:245.

faithful and true witness" (Rev. 3:14). Therefore, God's people must "love the truth" (Zech. 8:19).

Some Ethical Applications of the Ninth Commandment

The Westminster Shorter Catechism (Q. 77) says, "The ninth commandment requireth the maintaining and promoting of truth between man and man (Zech. 8:16), and of our own and our neighbour's good name (3 John 12), especially in witness-bearing (Prov. 14:5, 25)."[62] We should be people of truth, whose word is trustworthy. People often think that lying is necessary to advance and prosper, but the opposite is true: "The lip of truth shall be established for ever: but a lying tongue is but for a moment" (12:19).

Bearing false witness against one's neighbor is not limited to court but can take place in private homes and at the workplace by the lips of a gossip and slanderer (Rom. 1:29–30; 2 Cor. 12:20; 1 Tim. 5:13). The Lord says that the person who is welcome in his holy presence is "he that walketh uprightly, and worketh righteousness, and speaketh the truth in his heart. He that backbiteth not with his tongue, nor doeth evil to his neighbour, nor taketh up a reproach against his neighbour" (Ps. 15:2–3).[63] The law of Moses says, "Thou shalt not go up and down as a talebearer among thy people" (Lev. 19:16). Gossip is not merely telling lies but also spreading private information that others need not know. Solomon teaches, "A talebearer revealeth secrets: but he that is of a faithful spirit concealeth the matter" (Prov. 11:13). Gossips divide friends (16:28) and keep strife burning (26:20). Such lies might seem like a joke, but they destroy people's lives (vv. 18–19).[64] Watson rightly said that a person who speaks slander has "the devil in his tongue" and the person who listens to slander has "the devil in his ear."[65]

A good reputation has great value, better "than great riches, . . . than silver and gold" (Prov. 22:1). We should not try to lift up ourselves and our party by mocking and insulting others, but bear patiently with insults

62. *Reformed Confessions*, 4:363.

63. The verb translated as "backbiteth" (*ragal*) in Ps. 15:3 literally means to go by "foot" (*regel*) and commonly refers to spying, but on occasion means to go about slandering (2 Sam. 19:27).

64. This also might be the meaning of Prov. 18:8; 26:22, but the word translated as "wounds" (*hithpael* participle of *laham*) does not appear elsewhere in the Bible. It may be related to a similar Arabic term meaning to eagerly swallow, hence signifying delicious food quickly gobbled up that goes "down into the innermost parts of the belly." In that case, the proverb may indicate that gossip, when welcomed, deeply affects the listener.

65. Watson, *The Ten Commandments*, 169–70.

and speak kind and gentle words.[66] William Perkins said, "Such quips as sting others, though they be a pleasure for some who hear, yet are they very offensive" to those at whom they are aimed.[67] We should reserve our strongest reproaches for those who knowingly oppose God's truth and subvert righteousness (Matthew 23; Acts 13:10). Even if we know that someone has sinned, we should desire to deal with his sin as privately as possible (Prov. 10:12; 17:9; Matt. 1:19; 18:15). We must beware posting information publicly when it might prove to be a false witness. Udemans warned, "Defamatory writers are worse than thieves, for they steal people's honor, which is more costly than gold."[68]

We should guard one another's reputations insofar as honesty, wisdom, and justice allow. For this reason, Proverbs instructs us to respond prudently when we hear accusations about others:

- Be slow to judge, and listen patiently and carefully: "He that answereth a matter before he heareth it, it is folly and shame unto him" (18:13).
- Seek accurate information and godly wisdom about the matter: "The heart of the prudent getteth knowledge; and the ear of the wise seeketh knowledge" (18:15).
- Give a fair hearing to both sides of the dispute: "He that is first in his own cause seemeth just; but his neighbour cometh and searcheth him" (18:17).

God's prohibition of lying and requirement of speaking truth should make us slow to speak in general, especially in matters that stir us to passionate emotion (James 1:19). Speaking argumentative words is like spilling water—you can never take them back (Prov. 17:14). One offense can build walls that last a lifetime (18:19). Therefore, let us exercise self-control in our speech (James 1:26). "The heart of the righteous studieth to answer: but the mouth of the wicked poureth out evil things" (Prov. 15:28).

The Tenth Commandment: Submissive Human Contentment

The Lord concludes the Ten Commandments by saying, "Thou shalt not covet thy neighbour's house, thou shalt not covet thy neighbour's wife, nor

66. Prov. 9:7; 11:12; 12:16; 14:21; 15:1; 17:5; 21:24; 22:10; 1 Cor. 4:12; Titus 3:2; 1 Pet. 2:23.
67. Perkins, *A Golden Chain*, chap. 28, in *Works*, 6:144.
68. Udemans, *The Practice of Faith, Hope, and Love*, 458.

his manservant, nor his maidservant, nor his ox, nor his ass, nor any thing that is thy neighbour's" (Ex. 20:17). Moses repeated the commandment with slight variations: "Neither shalt thou desire thy neighbour's wife, neither shalt thou covet thy neighbour's house, his field, or his manservant, or his maidservant, his ox, or his ass, or any thing that is thy neighbour's" (Deut. 5:21).

The Exegesis of the Tenth Commandment

The verb translated as "covet" (*khamad*) means to desire. It can be used of evil desire, such as coveting something that does not belong to you (Ex. 34:24; Deut. 7:25). It can also be used of good desires (Ps. 19:10), even God's desires or choices (68:16). The same can be said of the parallel verb translated as "desire" (*awah*).[69] The Holy Scriptures do not condemn desire per se, and they do not call us to eliminate desire in a quest for so-called pure rationality.

What, then, is wrong with the coveting prohibited in the tenth commandment? The people and objects wrongly desired belong to another. Note the repetition: "thy neighbour's . . . thy neighbour's . . . his . . . his . . . his . . . his . . . any thing that is thy neighbor's" (Ex. 20:17). Forbidden coveting is "envy," which may be defined as "painful or resentful awareness of an advantage enjoyed by another joined with a desire to possess the same advantage."[70] Sinful coveting is not the desire for a wife, food, housing, or other legitimate blessings when one lacks them. It is proud jealousy that claims what rightfully belongs to another, leading to inward anger and hatred and outward theft and violence. Micah says, "They covet fields, and take them by violence; and houses, and take them away: so they oppress a man and his house, even a man and his heritage" (Mic. 2:2). Coveting is rebellion against the God who has forbidden us to have certain relationships or possessions, as when his providence puts them in the rightful possession of another or his law prohibits them to us.

It might be asked how the tenth commandment differs from other precepts in the second table of the law, which also imply God's prohibition of sexual lust (the seventh commandment) and greed (the eighth). We answer first by saying that one might covet one's neighbor's spouse or servant for

69. Deut. 5:21; 12:20; 14:26; Ps. 132:13. The Greek word (*epithymeō*) used in the LXX to translate these two Hebrew terms in Ex. 20:17 and Deut. 5:21 (cf. Rom. 7:7; 13:9) can also refer to either good or evil desires (Matt. 5:28; 13:17; Luke 22:15; Gal. 5:17).

70. *Merriam-Webster's Collegiate Dictionary*, s.v. "envy."

reasons other than sex, such as for that person's skill, diligence, pleasant personality, or advantageous connections in the community. However, the tenth commandment also directs our attention to a deeper problem. Sexual lust and materialistic greed are sins that involve an intentional *choice* to engage the mind in sinful thoughts.[71] The tenth commandment addresses sinful *desire* (the meaning of "covet"), which involves the inclination or disposition of the heart, but not necessarily a conscious choice.[72] God's Word does not teach that emotions are entirely neutral.[73] The desire for evil is evil and arises from an evil heart.[74] Love and fear toward God require us to "hate evil" (Ps. 97:10; Prov. 8:13; cf. Rom. 12:9).

It might be further objected that we can be tempted to sin without sinning. This is true, and we must distinguish between temptation and sin or we will be plagued by false guilt. In mere temptation, some enticement to sin is presented to a person's mind or senses (Matt. 4:1–11). However, if the person responds to that temptation with an inward delight in the idea of sinning, even without the full consent of the will, he has sinned in the heart,[75] for he has not loved the Lord his God with all his heart (Deut. 6:5).[76]

The "motions of sin," literally its "passions or affections" (plural *pathēma*), are sin (Rom. 7:5; cf. Gal. 5:24).[77] Paul said that the law com-

71. On sexual lust, Christ said that adultery in the heart is committed by "whoever looketh on a woman to lust [*pros to epithymēsai*] after her," using syntax implying intentional choice (Matt. 5:28). On greed, note the intentionality reflected in Job's words: "If I have made gold my hope, or have said to the fine gold, Thou art my confidence; if I rejoiced because my wealth was great, and because mine hand had gotten much" (Job 31:24–25).

72. Calvin's Catechism of 1545 (Q. 213–16), in *Reformed Confessions*, 1:495–96; Perkins, *A Golden Chain*, chap. 29, in *Works*, 6:149; and Turretin, *Institutes*, 11.21.11–12 (2:136–37). For an application of this principle to the sinful desire for homosexual activity (Rom. 1:26–27), see *RST*, 2:221–26.

73. We are not suggesting, for example, that sadness is always sinful (Acts 8:2) because God commands us to rejoice (Phil. 4:4). However, the complex relation of emotion to duty is evident in that believers are sometimes commanded to grieve (Rom. 12:15) but should not grieve "as others which have no hope" (1 Thess. 4:13).

74. Douma, *The Ten Commandments*, 351; and Frame, *The Doctrine of the Christian Life*, 845.

75. Perkins, *A Golden Chain*, chap. 29, in *Works*, 6:149.

76. Ames, *A Sketch of the Christian's Catechism*, 194. The Reformed position articulated here stands in contrast to the Roman Catholic doctrine: "Concupiscence [lust or covetousness viewed as an inclination to sin] stems from the disobedience of the first sin. It unsettles man's moral faculties and, *without being in itself an offense*, inclines man to commit sins." In Roman Catholic theology, concupiscence is rooted in "a certain tension" in man as "a composite being, spirit and body." Adam's sin deprived mankind of original holiness and weakened the power of the spirit to rule the body, resulting in a tendency toward sin. *Catechism of the Catholic Church*, secs. 417–18, 2515–16, emphasis added. On original righteousness as *donum superadditum* and the Roman view of original sin, see *RST*, 2:180–81, 374–75. On the debate between Reformed theologians and Roman Catholic theologians on this matter, see Udemans, *The Practice of Faith, Hope, and Love*, 475–82; and Turretin, *Institutes*, 11.21.4–14 (2:134–37).

77. The Westminster Confession of Faith (6.5), in *Reformed Confessions*, 4:242.

mands "thou shalt not covet [*epithymeō*]," but "sin, taking occasion by the commandment, wrought in me all manner of concupiscence [coveting or lust, *epithymia*]" (Rom. 7:7–8). Even as a believer who delighted in God's law, Paul still observed the "sin that dwelleth in me," for "evil is present with me" (vv. 20–22). Sadly, sin has corrupted the whole person so that the "old man," human nature fallen in Adam, "is corrupt according to the deceitful lusts" (Eph. 4:22).[78] Sin resides not merely in our outward actions and spoken words, or merely in our chosen attitudes to pursue evil, but even in the desires and inclinations of our hearts, for merely coveting someone or something that God has forbidden is a transgression of God's law, and thus, it is sin (1 John 3:4).

The Tenth Commandment and Creation

The prohibition against coveting that which belongs to one's neighbor is grounded on God's sovereignty over all he created and his goodness in making it.[79] The Lord made man, placed him in Eden, caused all manner of desirable and good trees to grow, and gave man permission to eat of the trees, but forbade him to eat of one (Gen. 2:7–9, 15–17).[80]

Satan tempted the first man and woman to distrust the goodness and justice of their Creator and disobey his prohibition (Gen. 3:1–5). The first motion of this unbelief in Eve's heart consisted of coveting: "The woman saw that the tree was good for food, and that it was pleasant to the eyes, and a tree to be desired [or coveted, *niphal* of *khamad*] to make one wise" (v. 6).[81] God had revealed that the fruit of that tree did not belong to them, but they said, in effect, "We need it. We want it. We have a right to it. We will get it." Since Adam's sin, human beings repeatedly run up against God's prohibitions that tell them that something they perceive as good does not rightfully belong to them, but they insist that God is not good to withhold it, it is rightfully theirs, and they will get it.

The Tenth Commandment and Love

Covetousness is selfishness. Paul warns, "Men shall be lovers of their own selves, covetous" (2 Tim. 3:2). Ames said, "An inordinate love of ourselves

78. On the total depravity of man, see *RST*, 2:400–405.

79. On the authority and goodness of the Creator, see *RST*, 2:69–70, 72–73.

80. The word translated as "pleasant" (*niphal* of *khamad*) in Gen. 2:9 is a form of the same word rendered as "covet," meaning that which is desirable.

81. On the temptation and first sin of man, see *RST*, 2:346–51.

is the cause of covetousness."[82] The opposite of sinful coveting is love for our neighbors. Paul says, "Love is patient and kind; love does not envy or boast; it is not arrogant or rude. It does not insist on its own way; it is not irritable or resentful" (1 Cor. 13:4–5 ESV). Covetousness makes us resent our neighbors' prosperity and pine after getting it for ourselves, but love moves us to "rejoice with them that do rejoice, and weep with them that weep" (Rom. 12:15). The Westminster Larger Catechism (Q. 147) describes this as "such a charitable frame of the whole soul toward our neighbour, as that all our inward motions and affections touching him, tend unto, and further all that good which is his."[83] This sympathy among believers is reinforced by their mutual relationships as fellow members in Christ's body: "Whether one member suffer, all the members suffer with it; or one member be honoured, all the members rejoice with it" (1 Cor. 12:26).

The covetousness forbidden in the tenth commandment takes the greatest love of our hearts and directs it to creatures rather than the Creator (Rom. 1:23, 25). John warns, "Love not the world, neither the things that are in the world. If any man love the world, the love of the Father is not in him. For all that is in the world, the lust of the flesh, and the lust of the eyes, and the pride of life, is not of the Father, but is of the world" (1 John 2:15–16). James admonishes those who quarrel and war to consider that their fighting comes from coveting what they do not have, and coveting exposes them as spiritual adulterers and adulteresses against God (James 4:1–4).

Repentance from covetousness entails learning "full contentment" with God's will for us:[84] "Let your conversation [manner of life] be without covetousness; and be content with such things as ye have: for he hath said, I will never leave thee, nor forsake thee" (Heb. 13:5). If we have the Lord as our covenant God, then we can be content with food and clothing for our bodies (1 Tim. 6:8) and his grace and strength for our souls (2 Cor. 12:9; Phil. 4:11–13). We can say to Christ, "Lord, show us the Father, and it is enough for us" (John 14:8 ESV). Therefore, in the tenth commandment we have come full circle and returned to the beginning of the Decalogue. Though formerly envious of the physical prosperity enjoyed by the wicked, we learn by grace to pray with Asaph, "Whom have I in

82. Ames, *The Marrow of Theology*, 2.22.15 (329).
83. *Reformed Confessions*, 4:337.
84. The Westminster Shorter Catechism (Q. 80), in *Reformed Confessions*, 4:364.

heaven but thee? And there is none upon earth that I desire beside thee. My flesh and my heart faileth: but God is the strength of my heart, and my portion for ever" (Ps. 73:25–26). The reason why we need not and must not covet anything belonging to our neighbors is that God says, "I am the Lord thy God. . . . Thou shalt have no other gods before me" (Ex. 20:2–3).

Some Ethical Applications of the Tenth Commandment

The tenth commandment teaches us that obedience to God's law requires right affections in the heart, not just right motions of the body. Therefore, we must heed the Word: "Keep thy heart with all diligence; for out of it are the issues of life" (Prov. 4:23). As the Heidelberg Catechism (LD 44, Q. 113) says, this commandment requires "that even the smallest inclination or thought contrary to any of God's commandments never rise in our hearts; but that at all times we hate all sin with our whole heart, and delight in all righteousness."[85]

We have a duty to protect our affections from the entrancing siren calls of this world.[86] We must guard our hearts from media that would excite covetous lusts. We must be alert to the influence of commercial advertising on our hearts.[87] We must avoid places and practices of gambling, which cultivates and rewards greed, wastes money that God gives us to use for his glory, and enslaves people to practices that lead to the destruction of marriages and families. We must place against our hearts the sharp edge of Paul's words: "They that will be rich fall into temptation and a snare, and into many foolish and hurtful lusts, which drown men in destruction and perdition. For the love of money is the root of all [kinds of] evil: which while some coveted after, they have erred from the faith, and pierced themselves through with many sorrows" (1 Tim. 6:9–10).

Let us examine ourselves for signs of covetousness. Watson said that we can recognize a covetous person by the preoccupation of his thoughts, efforts, and talk with the things of this world instead of God and his eternal

85. *The Three Forms of Unity*, 109.

86. For a practical treatment of this subject, see Owen, *The Nature, Power, Deceit, and Prevalency of the Remainders of Indwelling Sin in Believers*, in *Works*, 6:245–51.

87. This is not to condemn marketing and advertising as inherently sinful practices; they are necessary parts of commerce. Douma said, "Someone who delivers a good product should be allowed to recommend it." However, Douma also noted that modern advertising skillfully makes a "constant appeal to people's lust for consumption." In the end, both the advertiser and the consumer must examine their practices by God's Word. We cannot blame advertisers for our coveting. Douma, *The Ten Commandments*, 346–47.

kingdom. Such a person willingly forsakes spiritual goods to obtain earthly goods and is willing to sin to get this world.[88]

This commandment calls us to redirect our minds and hearts toward Christ, to "seek those things which are above, where Christ sitteth on the right hand of God" (Col. 3:1). This is possible only by exercising trust in the Word, for "this is the victory that overcometh the world, even our faith" (1 John 5:4). The prohibition against coveting is not a condemnation of strong desire but a summons to love God with all the energy of our hearts: "Delight thyself also in the LORD; and he shall give thee the desires of thine heart" (Ps. 37:4). Faith, Watson said, "not only purifies the heart, but satisfies it; it makes God our portion, and in him we have enough." Therefore, to overcome covetousness, we must "covet spiritual things more." Let us "pray for a heavenly mind" by the uplifting power of the Holy Spirit.[89]

The tenth commandment shows us that we need more than better behavior; we must be born again by the power of the Holy Spirit (John 3:3). We must have new hearts and God's indwelling Spirit (Ezek. 36:26–27). By nature, mankind is "foolish, disobedient, deceived, serving divers lusts and pleasures, living in malice and envy, hateful, and hating one another"; the only deliverance from this bitter covetousness is salvation "by the washing of regeneration, and renewing of the Holy Ghost," whom God pours out "through Jesus Christ our Saviour" (Titus 3:3–6). Only the Holy Spirit can change us from the inside out. Furthermore, the law's demands upon our hearts reveal our need for the imputation of Christ's righteousness. Ames said, "A complete and accurate fulfilling of the law is impossible even to the faithful by the grace bestowed upon them in this life."[90]

We must look to Christ crucified as the conqueror of all our sin, including its secret lusts (Gal. 5:24). Christ's death is the death of sin in believers. John Owen said,

> Consider the sorrows he underwent, the curse he bore, the blood he shed, the cries he put forth, the love that was in all this to your souls, and the mystery of the grace of God therein. Meditate on the vileness, the demerit, and the punishment of sin as represented in the cross, the blood, the death of Christ. Is Christ crucified for sin, and shall not our

88. Watson, *The Ten Commandments*, 175–76.
89. Watson, *The Ten Commandments*, 179–80.
90. Ames, *The Marrow of Theology*, 2.22.20 (330).

> hearts be crucified with him unto sin? Shall we give entertainment unto that, or hearken unto its dalliances, which wounded, which pierced, which slew our dear Lord Jesus? God forbid! Fill your affections with the cross of Christ, that there may be no room for sin.[91]

Practical Conclusion to the Ten Commandments

The Ten Commandments function in many different ways. They are designed by God to bar the way to heaven against unclean and unsanctified intruders. Their inflexibility and severity should move us to fear God. However, at the same time, the Ten Commandments lead us to grace. They cause us to understand that we need the love of God and the merits of Christ. And then the Ten Commandments define sin, a clarity of definition we desperately need in this present age when everyone does what is right in his own eyes. In all these ways, the commandments reveal the character of God, what he loves, what he hates, and who he is.

We should take up the law and employ it according to its three uses: civil, evangelical, and didactic.[92] First, we should apply the law in its *civil use* to regulate human society and restrain sinful conduct (1 Tim. 1:9–10).[93] By what standard should parents direct their children, business owners their employees in their business operations, pastors and elders the members of their churches, and civil leaders the officers and the citizens of their nations? Mere pragmatism will lead us to shortsighted expediency but long-term disaster, for no one can lead well and no people can flourish without justice and righteousness (Prov. 8:12–16; 14:34). God alone can provide us with a standard that will resonate with the consciences of all men, and that standard is his moral law. While we need wisdom to properly apply the law to the different spheres of life (for the state is not the church, the church is not the family, and none of the above is a business), our only ground for requiring our fellow human beings to submit rationally to human regulations about their conduct is the basis of such regulations in divine commandments.

Second, we should apply the law in its *evangelical use* to awaken sinners to their guilt and danger and to drive them to the gospel of Jesus Christ.[94]

91. Owen, *The Nature, Power, Deceit, and Prevalency of the Remainders of Indwelling Sin in Believers*, in *Works*, 6:250–51.

92. On the three uses of the law, see *RST*, 2:694–97.

93. Luther, *Lectures on Galatians*, in *LW*, 26:308–9; and Calvin, *Institutes*, 2.7.10.

94. Luther, *Lectures on Galatians*, in *LW*, 26:148, 150; and Calvin, *Institutes*, 2.7.6–7.

The Westminster Larger Catechism (Q. 96) says, "The moral law is of use to unregenerate men, to awaken their consciences to flee from the wrath to come, and to drive them to Christ; or, upon their continuance in the estate and way of sin, to leave them inexcusable, and under the curse thereof."[95] The civil use of the law focuses on outward actions, but the evangelical use searches the heart to reveal the evil of not only our deeds but our innermost being (Mark 7:20–23). The law is essential to evangelism, and thus, to the life of the church. Without the evangelical use of the law combined with the merciful call to repentance, the professing church ceases to cherish the gospel, dies from the inside out, and becomes puffed up with empty self-righteousness (Rev. 3:1–3, 14–19).

Third, we should apply the law in its *didactic use* to instruct believers in how to love and please their gracious and forgiving God.[96] The law puts hands and feet on love, so to speak, so that we can see how Christ-like love leads people to act toward their God and their neighbors. The law should be our constant conversational partner in life (Deut. 6:6–8) so that we can say, "O how love I thy law! It is my meditation all the day" (Ps. 119:97). While the law does not give us detailed instructions for every situation, marinating our minds in its precepts and putting it into practice will cause us by grace to mature in wisdom and discernment (Rom. 12:2; Heb. 5:13–14).

It might be thought that attention to the law would make Christians legalistic, but on the contrary, a constant consultation of the law makes them appreciate "how much they are bound to Christ for his fulfilling it, and enduring the curse thereof in their stead, and for their good."[97] The gospel-driven church is a law-directed church. Samuel Bolton (1606–1654) said, "The law sends us to the gospel for our justification, and the gospel sends us to the law to frame our conversation [conduct]; and our obedience to the law is nothing else but the expression of our thankfulness to that God, who hath so freely justified us."[98] The Heidelberg Catechism (Q. 115) says that God would have ministers to preach the Ten Commandments so that "all our lifetime we may learn more and more to know our sinful nature, and thus become the more earnest in seeking the remission

95. *Reformed Confessions*, 4:320.

96. Luther, the Small Catechism (1.1–22), in *The Book of Concord*, 351–54; and Calvin, *Institutes*, 2.7.12.

97. The Westminster Larger Catechism (Q. 97), in *Reformed Confessions*, 4:320.

98. Samuel Bolton, *The True Bounds of Christian Freedome* (London: for P.S., 1656), 100.

of sin and righteousness in Christ; likewise, that we constantly endeavor and pray to God for the grace of the Holy Spirit, that we may become more and more conformable to the image of God, till we arrive at the perfection proposed to us in a life to come."[99] Indeed, as Ames said, the law of God gives "a goal to which we may direct our gaze in all our attempts" and hope for "the perfection of the life that we will live in the future world."[100]

Sing to the Lord

Contentment in Obedience

Father, I know that all my life is portioned out for me;
The changes that are sure to come, I do not fear to see:
I ask thee for a present mind, intent on pleasing thee.

I would not have the restless will that hurries to and fro,
Seeking for some great thing to do, or secret thing to know;
I would be treated as a child, and guided where I go.

I ask thee for the daily strength, to none that ask denied,
A mind to blend with outward life, while keeping at thy side,
Content to fill a little space, if thou be glorified.

In service which thy will appoints there are no bonds for me;
My secret heart is taught the truth that makes thy children free;
A life of self-renouncing love is one of liberty.

Anna L. Waring
Tune: Morwellham
Trinity Hymnal—Baptist Edition, No. 444

Questions for Meditation or Discussion

1. How is the eighth commandment grounded in God's creation of man?
2. What do the Holy Scriptures teach about slavery?
3. Why is stealing contrary to love? What does love require of us with respect to our neighbors' property?
4. What does the ninth commandment require of us in court? In ordinary life?

---

99. *The Three Forms of Unity*, 109.
100. Ames, *A Sketch of the Christian's Catechism*, 196.

5. On what basis do some people argue that sometimes love requires us to lie? How can we answer their argument?
6. How can we avoid the sin of gossip when we hear bad things about others?
7. What does "covet" mean? What does the tenth commandment prohibit?
8. How was coveting the first motion of sinful unbelief in the human heart?
9. Someone says, "Coveting cannot be sinful, for it's no sin just to desire something." How do you respond?
10. For each of the three uses of the law, what are you responsible to do to make use of the law in your calling, position in society, and relationships with other people?

Questions for Deeper Reflection

11. A friend launches into an angry and scornful diatribe against the Bible because, he says, it is the tool of oppressors and slaveholders. Write him a gentle but instructive reply.
12. The authors say, "The gospel-driven church is a law-directed church." What do they mean? Do you agree? Why or why not? What will happen to a church that seeks to be driven by the gospel but not directed by the law of God?

41

The Fear of the Lord, Self-Denial, Sober Watchfulness, and Recovery from Backsliding

Although we have studied numerous evidences of God's saving grace, including the traits highlighted by Christ in the Beatitudes, Paul's list of the fruit of the Spirit, and the obedience to God's moral law summarized in the Ten Commandments, there is another characteristic of the godly life so essential that no treatment of practical holiness would be complete without it. That is the fear of the Lord.

Though the modern mind shies away from the idea of fearing God and tends to regard such fear as barbaric and psychologically damaging, God says in his Word that fearing him is necessary to both holiness and happiness (Psalm 112). Indeed, the fear of the Lord springs naturally from faith in his promises and engenders hope in his love. David says, "Oh how great is thy goodness, which thou hast laid up for them that fear thee; which thou hast wrought for them that trust in thee before the sons of men!" (31:19).

Therefore, in this chapter we will provide a brief exposition of the fear of the Lord and some qualities that flow from it: self-denial and taking up our cross, and spiritual sobriety and watchfulness. We will then briefly consider how to recover if we backslide from God.

The Fear of the Lord

The fear of God is a central and holistic duty of godliness. Solomon says, "Let us hear the conclusion of the whole matter: Fear God, and keep his commandments: for this is the whole duty of man. For God shall bring every work into judgment, with every secret thing, whether it be good, or whether it be evil" (Eccles. 12:13–14). The fear of the Lord is a pervasive theme in the Holy Scriptures. It frequently appears in the books of Moses.[1] It has multiple real-life examples in the historical books.[2] It fills the Psalms,[3] and it is foundational to biblical Wisdom Literature.[4] The prophets extol it and sternly rebuke those who lack it.[5] The New Testament confirms it as entirely consistent with the gospel of Jesus Christ.[6] John Murray said, "The fear of God is the soul of godliness."[7]

The Kinds of Fear toward God

The Bible speaks about different ways in which people might fear God. We see that there are distinctions within the fear of God in Moses's words to Israel after the Lord appeared in glory and declared the Ten Commandments: "Fear not: for God is come to prove you, and that his fear may be before your faces, that ye sin not" (Ex. 20:20). In other words, the Israelites were to put off one kind of fear but embrace another kind that would purify their lives. That raises a question: What kinds of fear are there?

First, there is a *formal, hypocritical fear of God* that consists of outward acts of worship toward the true God while the heart remains far from

1. Gen. 3:10; 15:12; 20:11; 22:12; 28:17; 31:42, 53; 42:18; Ex. 1:17, 21; 3:6; 9:20, 30; 14:31; 15:11, 16; 18:21; 20:20; Lev. 19:14, 30, 32; 25:17, 36, 43; 26:2; Deut. 4:10, 34; 5:5, 29; 6:2, 13, 24; 7:21; 8:6; 10:12, 17, 20–21; 13:4; 14:23; 17:13, 19; 25:18; 26:8; 28:58, 65–67; 31:12–13.

2. Josh. 4:24; 22:25; 24:14; 1 Sam. 11:7; 12:14, 18, 24; 2 Sam. 6:9; 7:23; 23:3; 1 Kings 18:3, 12; 2 Kings 4:1; 17:24–39, 41; 1 Chron. 13:12; 16:30; 2 Chron. 6:31, 33; 14:14; 17:10; 19:7; 20:29; Neh. 1:5, 11; 4:14; 5:9, 15; 7:2; 9:32.

3. Pss. 2:11; 5:7; 14:5; 15:4; 19:9; 22:23, 25; 25:12, 14; 31:19; 33:8, 18; 34:7, 9, 11; 36:1; 40:3; 45:4; 47:2; 52:6; 53:5; 55:19; 60:4; 61:5; 64:9; 65:5, 8; 66:3, 5, 16; 67:7; 68:35; 72:5; 76:7–8, 11–12; 77:16; 85:9; 86:11; 89:7; 90:11; 96:4, 9; 97:4; 99:3; 102:15; 103:11, 13, 17; 106:22; 111:5, 9–10; 112:1; 114:7; 115:11, 13; 118:4; 119:38, 63, 74, 79, 120; 128:1, 4; 130:4; 135:20; 145:6, 19; 147:11.

4. Job 1:1, 8–9; 2:3; 6:14; 13:10–11; 23:15; 25:2; 28:28; 31:23; 37:22, 24; Prov. 1:7, 29; 2:5; 3:7; 8:13; 9:10; 10:27; 13:13; 14:2, 16, 26–27; 15:16, 33; 16:6; 19:23; 22:4; 23:17; 24:21; 28:14; 31:30; Eccles. 3:14; 5:7; 7:18; 8:12–13; 12:13.

5. Isa. 2:10, 19, 21; 8:13; 11:2–3; 19:16–17; 25:3; 29:13, 23; 33:6, 14; 50:10; 59:19; 63:17; Jer. 2:19; 5:22, 24; 10:7; 26:19; 32:21, 39–40; 33:9; 44:10; Dan. 6:26; 9:4; Hos. 3:5; 10:3; Joel 2:11, 31; Amos 3:8; Jonah 1:9–10, 16; Mic. 7:17; Hab. 3:2; Zeph. 2:11; 3:7; Hag. 1:12; Mal. 1:6, 14; 2:5; 3:5, 16; 4:2, 5.

6. Matt. 10:28; Luke 1:50; 12:5; 23:40; Acts 2:43; 5:5, 11; 9:31; 10:2, 22, 35; 13:16, 26; Rom. 3:18; 8:15; 11:20; 2 Cor. 5:11; 7:1, 11; Eph. 5:21; Phil. 2:12; Col. 3:22; Heb. 4:1; 5:7; 10:27, 31; 11:7; 12:28; 1 Pet. 1:17; 2:17; 3:15; Rev. 11:18; 14:7; 15:4; 19:5.

7. Murray, *Principles of Conduct*, 229.

him (Isa. 29:13). The Scriptures say that people imported by Assyria into Samaria learned to "fear" the Lord in the sense of worshiping him as one among many gods, and yet it also says they did not "fear" him or keep his commandments (2 Kings 17:24–41).

Second, there is a *temporary, emotional fear of God* that people may experience when they see or hear of God's mighty works (Ex. 14:31; 15:14–16; Luke 5:26; 7:16). This kind of awe or dread does not accompany love for God or instill lasting faithfulness, though it may move people to change their behavior to avoid his judgment (Ex. 9:20) or to refrain from attacking God's people (2 Chron. 17:10; 20:29).

Third, there is a *conscientious, moral fear of God* that falls short of conversion but restrains people from doing acts of injustice (Gen. 20:11; 42:18; Deut. 25:18; Luke 18:4; 23:40). John Bunyan called this "a fear of God that flows even from the light of nature."[8] It can also be an effect of God's Word on the consciences of unbelievers. This may be the sense in which Gentiles feared God such that they conducted themselves justly and honored the God of Israel while still needing salvation through faith in Jesus Christ (Acts 10:2, 22, 35; 13:16, 26).

Fourth, there is a *tormenting, servile fear of God* that arises from an accusing conscience and anticipation of his wrath against violators of his law.[9] Such fear is a precursor to the terror of judgment day (Isa. 2:10, 19, 21). Servile fear does not in itself lead men to conversion or faithfulness (Acts 24:25) because it tends toward a view of God as harsh and unloving (Luke 19:21). This is the fear of which John says, "There is no fear in love; but perfect love casteth out fear: because fear hath torment. He that feareth is not made perfect in love" (1 John 4:18).

Servile fear may stir a concern for salvation in the hearts of the lost, leading them to cry out, "What must we do to be saved?" (cf. Acts 2:37; 16:30). Thus, God may use it as a preparation for conversion.[10] It would be foolish and extremely wicked "not to be afraid of God when there is reason to be afraid," as Murray said.[11] However, servile fear should not be cherished in the hearts of those already saved and adopted by God, for it arises from spiritual bondage (Rom. 8:15). Augustine said, "Fear, so to

8. Bunyan, *A Treatise on the Fear of God*, in *Works*, 1:445. On John Bunyan's doctrine of the fear of God, see Joel R. Beeke and Paul M. Smalley, *John Bunyan and the Grace of Fearing God* (Phillipsburg, NJ: P&R, 2016), 31–137.

9. Gen. 3:10; Lev. 26:17; Deut. 28:65–67; Job 13:10–11; Prov. 28:1; Isa. 33:14; Heb. 10:27, 31.

10. On conviction of sin as a preparation for conversion, see chap. 13.

11. Murray, *Principles of Conduct*, 233.

say, prepared the place for charity [love]. But when once charity has begun to inhabit, the fear which prepared the place for it is cast out." Augustine compared this fear to a needle used in sewing: unless the needle of guilty fear goes first, the thread of love does not enter the mind; however, the needle does not remain but is pulled out after the thread is sewn into the fabric.[12]

Lastly, there is a fear that pleases the Lord, the *filial, evangelical fear of God*, where "filial" means childlike in trust, love, and obedience (Deut. 10:12; Ps. 103:10–18) and "evangelical" indicates that such fear accompanies faith in the gospel of God's saving love (Pss. 31:19; 33:18).[13] Peter says that believers should live "as obedient children," being holy in all their conduct because God is holy, and since the God they call upon as "Father" is the impartial Judge, they should live as pilgrims "here in fear," knowing that they were redeemed "with the precious blood of Christ" (1 Pet. 1:14–19). Though grounded in faith (Heb. 11:7), this fear is nevertheless far more than respect; it is true fear, for God is dreadfully holy even when he comes in grace (Gen. 15:12; 28:17). At the heart of this sacred fear is a desire in believers to please their God and to avoid all that displeases him (2 Cor. 5:9–11).[14] John Brown of Edinburgh said, "The happiness of Christians is in the love of God, and the light of his countenance is the life of their life. It matters little to them that the world frowns on them, if he smiles; and it matters little to them that the world smiles, if he frowns."[15]

Therefore, unconverted people may have many kinds of fear toward God, but Paul rightly says of mankind, "There is no fear of God before their eyes," in the sense of filial fear (Rom. 3:18). John Calvin said, "The wicked fear God not because they are afraid of incurring his displeasure, if only they could do so with impunity; but because they know him to be armed with the power to take vengeance, they shake with fright on hearing of his wrath. . . . But believers . . . both fear offending God more than punishment, and are not troubled by fear of punishment, as if it hung over their necks."[16]

---

12. Augustine, *Homilies on 1 John*, 9.4, in *NPNF*[1], 7:515. Augustine used the word "bristle" to refer to a needle.

13. Gill, *Body of Divinity*, 726.

14. Wollebius, *Compendium*, 2.3.(3).6a (199); and Brakel, *The Christian's Reasonable Service*, 3:295.

15. Brown, *Expository Discourses on the First Epistle of the Apostle Peter*, 103.

16. Calvin, *Institutes*, 3.2.27.

The Grace of Fear

The filial fear of God is a gift of his sovereign grace to change sinners into his covenant people: "I will give them one heart, and one way, that they may fear me for ever, for the good of them, and of their children after them: and I will make an everlasting covenant with them, that I will not turn away from them, to do them good; but I will put my fear in their hearts, that they shall not depart from me" (Jer. 32:39–40). This grace of fear is so powerful that it effectually guards the believer from full and final apostasy so that he perseveres with Christ to the end.[17]

God gives this grace to his people in Christ by the Holy Spirit. Jesus Christ is anointed by the Spirit "of the fear of the LORD" in order to pour out that Spirit on his people (Isa. 11:2; 44:3–5). The Spirit-filled church is one that fears the Lord (Acts 9:31; Eph. 5:18, 21). Murray said, "The church walks in the fear of the Lord because the Spirit of Christ indwells, fills, directs, and rests upon the church and the Spirit of Christ is the Spirit of the fear of the Lord."[18]

As a grace of Christ, the filial fear of God has a distinct character that makes it different from anything found naturally in fallen mankind. Archibald M'Lean (1723–1812) said,

> Both believers and unbelievers have their fears; but they arise from very different sources, and have quite opposite effects. The fears of unbelievers arise from unworthy thoughts of God; a distrust of his power, faithfulness, and goodness; and also from a prevailing love of this present world and its enjoyments. . . . But that godly fear which is proper to believers, arises from a just view, reverence, and esteem of the character of God, and a supreme desire of his favour as their chief happiness; and is a fear lest they should offend him and incur his just displeasure; such a fear of him as outweighs all the allurements of sin on the one hand, and all the terrors of present sufferings for righteousness sake on the other.[19]

Whereas servile fear is a mixture of terror and hatred toward God, energized only by self-love, filial fear is fear animated by love for God.[20] Moses could say in almost the same breath, "Now these are the commandments, the

---

17. On the perseverance of the saints, see chaps. 30–31.
18. Murray, *Principles of Conduct*, 230.
19. Archibald M'Lean, *Paraphrase and Commentary on the Epistle to the Hebrews*, on Heb. 4:1, in *The Works of Mr. Archibald M'Lean*, 6 vols. in 7 (London: William Jones, 1823), 5.1:126–27.
20. Brakel, *The Christian's Reasonable Service*, 3:292–93.

statutes, and the judgments, which the LORD your God commanded to teach you . . . that thou mightest fear the LORD thy God, to keep all his statutes and his commandments" and "Thou shalt love the LORD thy God with all thine heart, and with all thy soul, and with all thy might" (Deut. 6:1–2, 5). This dual response of love and fear arises from knowing the magnificent goodness and merciful greatness of God. Bunyan said that Christ is the King with such "beauty and glory that whoso sees him must both love and fear him."[21] Michael Reeves writes, "Right fear does not stand in tension with love for God. . . . True fear of God is true love for God defined: it is the right response to God's full-orbed revelation of himself in all his grace and glory."[22]

Frederick William Faber (1814–1863) said,

They love Thee little, if at all,
Who do not fear Thee much;
If love is Thine attraction, Lord!
Fear is Thy very touch.

Our blessedness will be to bear
The sight of Thee so near;
And thus eternal love will be
But the ecstasy of fear.[23]

This gracious fear of God engages a person's whole being, including his emotions, for it is sometimes described as trembling before God (Pss. 2:11; 119:120; Phil. 2:12). However, the essence of fearing the Lord is a mindset illuminated by a believing awareness of his holy glory. People fear God when they know his name—that is, his divine nature (1 Kings 8:43). Thus, "the fear of the LORD is the beginning of wisdom: and the knowledge of the holy is understanding" (Prov. 9:10; cf. 1:7; 15:33; Ps. 111:10).[24] A God-fearing person rejoices in God's majesty (Ps. 2:11) and delights to fear the Lord (Neh. 1:11).[25] The fear of God is practical wisdom that guides a person's decisions: "The fear of the LORD, that is wisdom; and to depart from evil is understanding" (Job 28:28; cf. Prov. 3:7; 14:16).

21. Bunyan, *The Holy War*, in *Works*, 3:299.

22. Michael Reeves, *Rejoice and Tremble: The Surprising Good News of the Fear of the Lord*, Union (Wheaton, IL: Crossway, 2021), 53.

23. Frederick William Faber, *Faber's Hymns* (New York: Thomas Y. Crowell & Co., 1894), 100–101.

24. "The holy" (*qedoshim*, Prov. 9:10) is the plural of the adjective *qadosh*, perhaps plural to agree with the plural "God" (*Elohim*), as in "holy God" (*Elohim qedoshim*, Josh. 24:19).

25. Brakel, *The Christian's Reasonable Service*, 3:294, 297. In the phrase "desire to fear thy name" (Neh. 1:11), the word translated as "desire" (*khapets*) means to delight or be pleased.

Godly fear energizes a Godward life with boldness and zeal, for "in the fear of the LORD is strong confidence. . . . The fear of the LORD is a fountain of life" (Prov. 14:26–27). John Gill said, "It is a fearless fear; a man that fears the Lord has no reason to fear anything, or what any man or devil can do unto him; he may say as David did, 'The LORD is my light and my salvation, whom shall I fear?' (Ps. 27:1)."[26] Indeed, filial fear strengthens the assurance that God has forgiven the believer's sins (Ps. 103:10–12), regards him with fatherly compassion (vv. 13–14), and loves him with an eternal love (v. 17). Thomas Manton said, "The more any is given to the fear of God, the more assurance they have of God's love, and readiness to hear them at the throne of grace."[27]

The Christian Pursuit of Godly Fear

The fear of God is mandatory, indeed essential, for the Christian life. Peter commands us, "Fear God" (1 Pet. 2:17). Paul places fear at the heart of progressive sanctification, saying, "Work out your own salvation with fear and trembling" (Phil. 2:12) and "Let us cleanse ourselves from all filthiness of the flesh and spirit, perfecting holiness in the fear of God" (2 Cor. 7:1). Christ equips his servants to face persecution with the words "Fear not them which kill the body, but are not able to kill the soul: but rather fear him which is able to destroy both soul and body in hell" (Matt. 10:28). Fear is essential for worship (Ps. 5:7), for we "serve God acceptably with reverence and godly fear" (Heb. 12:28).[28]

Let us never rest complacently in the degree of our fear toward God: "God is *greatly* to be feared" (Ps. 89:7). We must fear him supremely, for he is the Supreme Being: "The LORD is great, and greatly to be praised: he is to be feared above all gods" (Ps. 96:4). George Swinnock said, "If God be so great a God, how greatly is he to be reverenced! Canst thou do too much service for him, or give too much glory to him? Can thy love to him be too great, or can thy fear of him be too great, or can thy labour for him be too great, when this God is so great?"[29]

---

26. Gill, *Body of Divinity*, 726.

27. Manton, *Several Sermons on the CXIX Psalm*, in *Works*, 6:407.

28. On the fear of God in worship, according to the Holy Scriptures and as expounded by the Puritans, see Arnold L. Frank, *The Fear of God: A Forgotten Doctrine* (Ventura, CA: Nordskog, 2007), 152–70.

29. Swinnock, *Heaven and Hell Epitomized*, in *Works*, 3:329–30. See J. Stephen Yuille, *Puritan Spirituality: The Fear of God in the Affective Theology of George Swinnock*, Studies in Christian History and Thought (Eugene, OR: Wipf and Stock, 2007), 71–78.

How can we grow in this precious grace of the fear of God? Since God plants fear in the heart (Jer. 32:40), let us go to God and petition him for more of that grace. Let us say, "Teach me thy way, O Lord; I will walk in thy truth: unite my heart to fear thy name" (Ps. 86:11). Jerry Bridges added, "After prayer, the next ingredient for growth in fearing God is regular, consistent exposure of our minds and hearts to His Word. This exposure should involve reading it for ourselves, hearing it taught, and studying it for ourselves."[30]

What we learn about God from the Word must be spiritually digested by meditation. Think often of the greatness of God and praise him: "There is none like unto thee, O Lord; thou art great, and thy name is great in might. Who would not fear thee, O King of nations?" (Jer. 10:6–7). Murray said, "The controlling sense of the majesty and holiness of God and the profound reverence which this apprehension elicits constitute the essence of the fear of God."[31]

Though it may seem strange, we cultivate evangelical fear by meditating on God's grace in the gospel: "There is forgiveness with thee, that thou mayest be feared" (Ps. 130:4). Bunyan said, "There is nothing in heaven or earth that can so *awe* the heart as the grace of God."[32] God promised that his people would "fear the Lord and his goodness" after he saved them from their spiritual adultery (Hos. 3:5). Nothing stirs reverence in the heart as much as meditating on Christ dying for wicked sinners and rising again in triumph over all the powers of evil. Look to Christ by faith, fellowship with him through the Word and sacraments, and imitate him. Jesus Christ is anointed by the Spirit of the fear of the Lord, so seek for his Spirit to fill you with that fear (Eph. 5:18, 21).

As you meditate on this God of holiness and grace, remind yourself constantly that you live each moment before his eyes (Prov. 15:3). Albert Martin notes that a crucial ingredient in the fear of God is "a pervasive sense of His presence." Martin says, "There is no place or circumstance in which we find ourselves, but . . . we are conscious that God is here with us. He is here in all His majesty, holiness, fatherly love and compassion, and immensity."[33]

---

30. Jerry Bridges, *The Joy of Fearing God* (Colorado Springs, CO: Waterbrook, 1997), 121.
31. Murray, *Principles of Conduct*, 237.
32. Bunyan, *The Water of Life*, in *Works*, 3:546, emphasis original.
33. Albert N. Martin, *The Forgotten Fear: Where Have All the God-Fearers Gone?* (Grand Rapids, MI: Reformation Heritage Books, 2015), 62.

Stay alert to sins especially contrary to the fear of God, such as pride (Rom. 11:20), failing to take to heart God's judgment on sinners (Jer. 3:8), grasping after unjust gain (Ex. 18:21), abusing power to exploit others (Neh. 5:15), refusing to show compassion to those in need (Job 31:16–23), and disrespect for one's elders and irreverence toward God's worship (Lev. 19:30, 32). Put those sins to death, lest like weeds they choke the fear of God out of your soul. Beware of a hardened heart, the great enemy of godly fear (Isa. 63:17).

Beware, too, of sinful fears. A legalistic "spirit of bondage" may masquerade as the fear of God, but it is quite opposite to a childlike trust and love toward the Lord (Rom. 8:15). Johannes Wollebius said, "Filial fear proceeds from the love of God, servile fear from fear and even hatred of God. . . . Filial fear attracts man to God, but servile fear pulls man away from God."[34] Another sinful fear is the fear of man: "The fear of man bringeth a snare: but whoso putteth his trust in the LORD shall be safe" (Prov. 29:25). We do owe a kind of fear toward men—that is, a deep respect for their positions of authority—but we should fear men as men and fear God as God.[35] If you are tempted to cowardice before men that hinders your obedience to God, remember that "God hath not given us the spirit of fear; but of power, and of love, and of a sound mind" (2 Tim. 1:7).[36] John Flavel said that inordinate fear "magnifies and exalts the creature, and puts it, as it were, into the room and place of God."[37] Thus, God says, "I, even I, am he that comforteth you: who art thou, that thou shouldest be afraid of a man that shall die, and of the son of man which shall be made as grass; and forgettest the LORD thy maker, that hath stretched forth the heavens, and laid the foundations of the earth" (Isa. 51:12–13). The Christian's goal is not to become more fearful in general but to increase and abound in the fear of the Lord.

Self-Denial

The fear of the Lord moves us to deny ourselves of anything contrary to God's glory or will. This principle is powerfully illustrated in the Lord's

34. Wollebius, *Compendium*, 2.3.(3).6b (199).

35. Gill, *Body of Divinity*, 722–23. See Lev. 19:3; 1 Sam. 12:18; Prov. 24:21; Rom. 13:7; Eph. 5:33; 6:5; Heb. 12:9.

36. The word translated as "fear" (*deilia*) in 2 Tim. 1:7 and its cognates are used of unbelieving fear or sinful cowardice (Matt. 8:26; Mark 4:40; John 14:27; Rev. 21:8), not the godly fear of the Lord.

37. Flavel, *A Practical Treatise of Fear*, in *Works*, 3:250.

testing of Abraham by commanding him to sacrifice his only son, whom he loved, as a burnt offering (Gen. 22:1–2). After Abraham laid Isaac on the altar and raised the knife to kill him, the Lord intervened and said, "Lay not thine hand upon the lad, neither do thou any thing unto him: for now I know that thou fearest God, seeing thou hast not withheld thy son, thine only son from me" (v. 12). It is remarkable that when God commended his servant for this remarkable act of obedience, he chose not to highlight his faith or love but his *fear* of God. Matthew Henry commented, "The best evidence of our fearing God is our being willing to serve and honour him with that which is dearest to us, and to part with all to him or for him."[38] Therefore, the fear of the Lord is the vital principle of godly self-denial by which we willingly offer up to God all we are for his glory (Rom. 12:1).

There is no Christianity without self-denial. The Lord Jesus Christ said, "If any man will come after me, let him deny himself, and take up his cross daily, and follow me" (Luke 9:23). Calvin said that "the denial of ourselves" is the "first step" of the Christian life and "the sum of the Christian life."[39] The words "if any man" show the universal scope of Christ's teaching: no one can be a disciple of Christ without doing this. To "deny" (*aparneomai*, or in some other texts *arneomai*) is "to say no" and, hence, to negate, reject, or refuse to acknowledge.[40] Denying oneself entails more than just saying no to certain desires; as is clear from "take up his cross daily, and follow me," it is a radical self-negation for the purpose of learning from, obeying, and imitating Christ.

Christ's requirement that each disciple take up his own cross is a call to voluntarily engage in a difficult, laborious, and even painful endeavor.[41] People should "count the cost" of following Christ (Luke 14:28–33). The apostolic exhortation to new Christians is "to continue in the faith, and . . . we must through much tribulation enter into the kingdom of God" (Acts 14:22). Believers must sacrifice to serve and must suffer persecution for their confession of Christ. Thomas Hooker said, "You must not think to go to heaven on the feather-bed: if you will be Christ's disciples, you must take up his cross, and it will make you sweat."[42] Thomas Watson

38. Henry, *Commentary on the Whole Bible*, on Gen. 22:11–14 (53).
39. Calvin, *Institutes*, 3.7, title and sec. 1.
40. *TDNT*, 1:468–71.
41. The expression to "take up" (aorist *airō*) a "cross" (*stauros*), which Christ used to describe discipleship (Matt. 16:24; Mark 8:34; 10:21; Luke 9:23), is the same used of Simon of Cyrene's bearing Christ's cross to Calvary after Jesus could carry it no farther (Matt. 27:32; Mark 15:21).
42. Thomas Hooker, *The Christian's Two Chief Lessons: Self-Denial and Self-Trial* (Ames, IA: International Outreach, 1997), 57.

said, "A Christian must deny his ease," for lazy people are unwilling to till up their hearts, pull out the weeds of sin, and sow the seed of righteousness—and thus never "reap a harvest of glory" (cf. Gal. 6:7–9).[43] Neither is this the acute pain of a quickly passing crisis, but the chronic suffering of continual self-denial: "Let him deny himself, and take up his cross *daily*" (Luke 9:23).

The cross was an instrument of death (Phil. 2:8). We must put away all that is incompatible with Christ and his demands on our lives. This includes both those things that are inherently sinful and those things that are good in themselves but must be renounced to keep Christ's Word. In a parallel text, the Lord Jesus says that taking up the cross requires that we "hate" our dearest family members and our own lives (Luke 14:25–27)—that is, that our love for Christ as our Lord far exceeds our love for them, and we willingly accept their persecution for Christ's sake rather than renounce him (Matt. 10:33–38; cf. 19:29). Campegius Vitringa (1659–1722) said, "Self-denial is when a Christian willingly renounces all his sins and vices. . . . But not only this, self-denial is the virtue by which the believer is willing to lay aside even the helps and comforts of this life, any good thing whatsoever, if it is in the interests of the glory of God."[44]

To take up the cross means to renounce our self-righteousness, for only a condemned lawbreaker died on a cross, a sign of God's curse (Deut. 21:22–23). The cross is what we deserve and what Christ took for us (Gal. 3:10, 13). Thus, self-denial arises from knowing the doctrines of sin and grace. Walter Chantry says, "Nothing leads to self-repudiation so much as spiritual meditation on the corruption and wickedness of your heart. . . . The truth that I am a foul rebel and that God is the author of amazing grace leads to the devotional act of self-denial, which in turn must demonstrate itself in daily living."[45]

Carrying the cross means forsaking our pride and lust for honor among men. The cross was not a heroic, admirable way to die (1 Cor. 1:23), for it was an instrument of humiliation and shame (Heb. 12:2) and a display of weakness (2 Cor. 13:4). Thus, the "self" we especially must deny to follow

43. Thomas Watson, *The Duty of Self-Denial (and Ten Other Sermons)* (Morgan, PA: Soli Deo Gloria, 1996), 16.

44. Campegius Vitringa, *The Spiritual Life*, trans. and ed. Charles K. Tefler, foreword by Richard A. Muller (Grand Rapids, MI: Reformation Heritage Books, 2018), 44.

45. Walter J. Chantry, *The Shadow of the Cross: Studies in Self-Denial* (Edinburgh: Banner of Truth, 1981), 9–10.

Christ is our self-righteous, self-sufficient pride.[46] Manton said, "That self which we must hate or deny is that self which stands in opposition to God or competition with him, and so jostleth [contends] with him for the throne . . . it is the great idol of the world, ever since the fall, when men took the boldness to depose and lay aside God, as it were, self succeeded in the throne."[47] It is our pride that insists that we grasp what we desire or think we have a right to have, rather than forsaking it for Christ. It is our pride that insists on people honoring us, but as Jeremiah Burroughs said, "We must deny ourselves by being willing to suffer the most disgraceful thing that can be put upon us for the cause of Christ."[48]

Christ concludes his call to self-denial by saying simply, "Follow me" (Luke 9:23). No one denied himself more than Christ, God the Son incarnate (Phil. 2:6–8). Manton said, "We should not murmur, we cannot be worse used than Christ was. . . . Christ was a pattern of suffering from the cradle to the cross."[49] No one received higher glory and honor than Christ did from God the Father (vv. 9–11). Thus, Christ attracts us to the path of self-denial by the promise of joining him: "He that loveth his life shall lose it; and he that hateth his life in this world shall keep it unto life eternal. If any man serve me, let him follow me; and where I am, there shall also my servant be: if any man serve me, him will my Father honour" (John 12:25–26).

What we gain is worth the pain. After issuing the call to self-denial, Christ proceeds to say, "For whosoever will save his life shall lose it: but whosoever will lose his life for my sake, the same shall save it. For what is a man advantaged, if he gain the whole world, and lose himself, or be cast away?" (Luke 9:24–25). In the paradox of Christ's words lies a principle of hope: Christ's disciples renounce themselves and this world to gain life in the age to come. The context is Christ's coming in the glory of God to judge the world and establish his kingdom (v. 26). Hence, self-denial is not really self-hatred but self-love illuminated by God's wisdom and directed by love for God. We do not seek to harm ourselves but to avoid the greatest loss and gain the supreme and only lasting good—the Lord and his kingdom. Indeed, while we take up the burden of the cross, we lay down

46. Hooker, *The Christian's Two Chief Lessons*, 32–38.

47. Manton, *A Treatise of Self-Denial*, in *Works*, 15:182.

48. Jeremiah Burroughs, *Moses' Self-Denial*, ed. Don Kistler (Grand Rapids, MI: Soli Deo Gloria, 2010), 19.

49. Manton, *A Treatise of Self-Denial*, in *Works*, 15:188.

the far heavier burdens of our pride and sins, and so find that Christ's yoke is far easier and his burden far lighter than that of the world (Matt. 11:28–30). Samuel Rutherford said, "His cross is the sweetest burden that ever I bare; it is such a burden as wings are to a bird, or sails are to a ship, to carry me forward to my harbour."[50]

Similarly, Paul says that God's grace trains us "that, denying ungodliness and worldly lusts, we should live soberly, righteously, and godly, in this present world; looking for that blessed hope, and the glorious appearing of the great God and our Saviour Jesus Christ; who gave himself for us, that he might redeem us from all iniquity, and purify unto himself a peculiar people, zealous of good works" (Titus 2:12–14). Though such lusts once ruled us (3:3), we now deny these evil desires because God's grace has planted in us a new desire to serve him and a new hope to see his glory. This is self-denial, for these lusts have been so woven into the fabric of our souls that we must "deny whatever our reason and will dictate" insofar as it is necessary to obey God's commandments, as Calvin said.[51] However, by denying ourselves, we gain the eternal enjoyment of God's glory in Christ. Therefore, Watson said, "for the attaining of self-denial, . . . be convinced of the incomparable excellency of Christ."[52]

Just as Christ teaches his disciples to take up their crosses, so Paul teaches the saints in Christ to view themselves as having already been crucified with Christ (Gal. 2:20; 5:24; 6:14). Like a condemned criminal carrying his cross to the place of his execution, a Christian should regard himself as a dead man—dead to sin and this world. Indeed, Christians are truly dead to sin by virtue of their union with Christ (Rom. 6:11). They are dead to self, for "he died for all, that they which live should not henceforth live unto themselves, but unto him which died for them, and rose again" (2 Cor. 5:15). This, then, is the antithesis: the people of this world live for themselves, but the people of Christ live for him. Such a wholehearted giving of self to God is an act of worship that is possible only by the power of the fear of the Lord. Paul puts it succinctly: "Know ye not that . . . ye are not your own? For ye are bought with a price: therefore glorify God" (1 Cor. 6:19–20).

---

50. *Letters of Samuel Rutherford*, ed. Andrew A. Bonar (Edinburgh: Oliphant Anderson & Ferrier, 1891), 262.

51. Calvin, *Institutes*, 3.7.3.

52. Watson, *The Duty of Self-Denial*, 35.

We can love one another only by denying ourselves.[53] By nature, our pride swells to divine proportions, and we insist that others serve us. Love, however, "does not envy or boast; it is not arrogant or rude. It does not insist on its own way; it is not irritable or resentful" (1 Cor. 13:4–5 ESV). Paul says, "Let nothing be done through strife or vainglory; but in lowliness of mind let each esteem other better than themselves. Look not every man on his own things, but every man also on the things of others" (Phil. 2:3–4). Our love has become bent inward upon ourselves; by Christ's grace, we must bend it outward to love our neighbors as ourselves (Lev. 19:18).

Understanding the purpose of Christian self-denial helps us to guard against distorting it into unbiblical asceticism.[54] Christ's disciples do not view God's creatures as evil but as good and to be enjoyed with thanksgiving (1 Tim. 4:4). Their rule for what they must deny themselves is the Word of God, not man's traditions or philosophies (v. 5). They do not regard pain or the neglect of physical needs and desires as inherently spiritual. Rather, they deny only that which opposes their intent to walk in the path of obedience by faith in Jesus Christ. The question that they ask is neither "Is this permissible?" (maximal earthly pleasure) nor "Is this absolutely necessary?" (minimal earthly pleasure), but "How will this help me to love God and love my neighbor?" (purposeful self-denial). They are like a man who has found a treasure hidden in a field or a pearl of great price, who gladly sells all that he has to acquire it—not because possessions are evil but to gain a greater treasure (Matt. 13:44–46).

Sober Watchfulness

As we noted earlier in this chapter, the fear of the Lord is wisdom, a mindset controlled by the awareness of God, leading to affections and actions according to what God loves and hates. Paul exhorts believers to cultivate a constant awareness of God's gracious love for them (Eph. 5:1–2) and his righteous wrath upon the disobedient (v. 6) so that they discern what is pleasing to God (v. 10) and live wisely in a wicked age by doing his will (vv. 15–17). In this context, Paul uses the metaphor of being illuminated and transformed by Christ's "light," resulting in clear thinking and righteous separation from the shameful corruption of the world (vv. 7–14). This

53. Calvin, *Institutes*, 3.7.5.
54. On asceticism as a false path to holiness, see chap. 28.

Spirit-filled mentality and lifestyle is the opposite of drunkenness and dissipation (v. 18). We have seen in our study of self-denial that Paul teaches that "denying ungodliness and worldly lusts, we should live soberly, righteously, and godly, in this present world" (Titus 2:12). Therefore, the fear of the Lord and the self-denial of Christian discipleship entail spiritual sobriety.

The word translated as "soberly" (*sōphronōs*, Titus 2:12) is one term in a group of words referring to a sound, rational mind that enables discretion and self-restraint.[55] This quality is the polar opposite of the twisted thinking and bizarre behavior that flows from either demon possession or insanity.[56] However, spiritual sobriety is not mere mental health in a secular sense, for all sin is demonic insanity, being rebellion against the all-good and all-powerful God. Rather, true sobriety is a gift of divine grace by the Holy Spirit: "God hath . . . given us the spirit of . . . a sound mind [*sōphronismos*]" (2 Tim. 1:7). This spiritual renewal of the mind enables a person to make a realistic assessment of himself instead of being puffed up with pride (Rom. 12:2–3). It gives discretion in even such mundane matters as dressing with modesty (1 Tim. 2:9). Paul says that young women and young men should be taught to be sober-minded (Titus 2:4–6), commends it in motherhood (1 Tim. 2:15), and requires it as a character quality in church elders (3:2; Titus 1:8). All Christians must seek to develop clear and sane thinking in the fear of God instilled by the Spirit through his Word.

Peter ties spiritual sobriety to the closely related virtue of watchfulness[57] when he says, "But the end of all things is at hand: be ye therefore sober, and *watch* unto prayer" (1 Pet. 4:7). The word translated as "watch" (*nēphō*), also rendered in other texts as "be sober," can be used of vigilance against danger (5:8) while waiting for deliverance (1:13). Paul uses the term to contrast the spiritual alertness of believers as they wait for Christ's return to the spiritual sleepiness and drunkenness of the wicked (1 Thess. 5:6–8). In the same context (v. 6), Paul also employs another Greek term for "watch" (*grēgoreō*) that is often used in the New Testament, especially for spiritual alertness.[58] Another term of wakefulness (*agrypneō*) appears in a few Scripture passages.[59] The same idea is communicated by

---

55. *TDNT*, 7:1097–98. The word group includes *sōphrōn*, *sōphronizō*, *sōphroneō*, *sōphronōs*, *sōphrosynē*, and *sōphronismos*. The canonical LXX avoids these terms.

56. See the use of *sōphroneō* in Mark 5:15; Luke 8:35; 2 Cor. 5:13; and *sōphrosynē* in Acts 26:25.

57. We briefly introduced the topic of watchfulness in *RST*, 2:473–74.

58. Matt. 24:42–43; 25:13; 26:38, 40–41; Mark 13:34–35, 37; 14:34, 37–38; Luke 12:37, 39; Acts 20:31; 1 Cor. 16:13; Col. 4:2; 1 Thess. 5:10; 1 Pet. 5:8; Rev. 3:2–3; 16:15.

59. Mark 13:33; Luke 21:36; Eph. 6:18; Heb. 13:17.

the verb to "look" or "see" (*blepō*), as in to look at ourselves (2 John 8), our conduct (Eph. 5:15), and our brethren in Christ (Heb. 3:12). Spiritual alertness also appears in several uses of the verb translated as "take heed" or "beware" (*prosechō*).[60]

John Owen offered the following definition of watchfulness: "A universal carefulness and diligence, exercising itself in and by all ways and means prescribed by God, over our hearts and ways, the baits and methods of Satan, the occasions and advantages of sin in the world, that we be not entangled."[61] Brian Hedges says that spiritual watchfulness has four ingredients: wakefulness (versus spiritual slumber), attentiveness (to Christ, ourselves, and each other), vigilance (against sin and Satan), and expectancy (for the coming of the Lord).[62]

Bunyan reminded us that watchfulness flows from the fear of God:

> It [godly fear] makes them watch their hearts, and take heed to keep them with all diligence, lest they should, by one or another of its flights, lead them to do that which in itself is wicked (Prov. 4:23; Heb. 12:15). It makes them watch, lest some temptation from hell should enter into their heart to the destroying of them (1 Pet. 5:8). It makes them watch their mouths, and keep them also, at sometimes, as with a bit and bridle, that they offend not with their tongue, knowing that the tongue is apt, being an evil member, soon to catch the fire of hell, to the defiling of the whole body (James 3:2–7). It makes them watch over their ways, look well to their goings, and to make straight steps for their feet (Ps. 39:1; Heb. 12:13). Thus this godly fear puts the soul upon its watch, lest from the heart within, or from the devil without, or from the world, or some other temptation, something should surprise and overtake the child of God to defile him, or to cause him to defile the ways of God, and so offend the saints, open the mouths of men, and cause the enemy to speak reproachfully of religion.[63]

Christians must keep watch against temptation and sin. The Lord Jesus Christ told his disciples, as the great temptation of his passion was about to fall upon them all, "Watch and pray, that ye enter not into temptation:

60. Matt. 6:1; 7:15; 10:17; 16:6, 11–12; Luke 12:1; 17:3; 20:46; 21:34; Acts 20:28; 1 Tim. 4:13; Heb. 2:1; 2 Pet. 1:19.

61. Owen, *Of Temptation*, in *Works*, 6:100–101.

62. Brian G. Hedges, *Watchfulness: Recovering a Lost Spiritual Discipline* (Grand Rapids, MI: Reformation Heritage Books, 2018), 18–34.

63. Bunyan, *A Treatise on the Fear of God*, in *Works*, 1:462–63.

the spirit indeed is willing, but the flesh is weak" (Matt. 26:41). In this case, watchfulness had a physical component: the disciples were tired, but they needed to stay awake and pray with Christ for divine deliverance from Satan's assault (vv. 38, 40). Spiritual alertness often requires physical self-control so that our bodies' desires for sleep or other kinds of refreshment do not make us dull to urgent spiritual dangers or opportunities.

However, watchfulness is primarily alertness and alacrity toward spiritual things. It keeps us attentive to hearing and keeping God's Word (Prov. 8:34). We must pay attention not only to the Word but also to how we are paying attention to the Word: "Take heed therefore how ye hear" (Luke 8:18). Therefore, Christians must be alert to the Word and to themselves as they seek to obey the Word in this world. In this regard, "watchfulness is a careful observing of our hearts and diligent looking to our ways, that they may be pleasing and acceptable unto God," as Richard Rogers (1551–1618) said.[64]

Believers must also watch for the coming of Christ, maintaining a posture of constant readiness to meet their Lord: "Of that day and that hour knoweth no man, no, not the angels which are in heaven, neither the Son, but the Father. Take ye heed, watch and pray: for ye know not when the time is" (Mark 13:32–33). Christians should watch for their Lord like servants who wait expectantly for their master to return, ready to greet him, even if he does not come until the middle of the night (Luke 12:35–40). Contrary to such watchfulness is the spiritual sleep of this world, which pretends that the Lord will never come to judge it (1 Thess. 5:2–8). Watching for Christ's return motivates watching against sin, for Christ comes to glorify his people in his holy likeness (1 John 3:2–3) and to judge all men for their deeds (Matt. 25:1–30). Christ says, "Behold, I come as a thief. Blessed is he that watcheth, and keepeth his garments, lest he walk naked, and they see his shame" (Rev. 16:15).

Paul combines the duty of watchfulness with the call to continual prayer (Col. 4:2). He concludes his teaching on spiritual warfare by saying, "Praying always with all prayer and supplication in the Spirit, and watching thereunto with all perseverance and supplication for all saints" (Eph. 6:18). Watchfulness in prayer is the attitude and alertness of a soldier in battle, ready to face his enemy with the strength of the Lord (v. 10),

64. Richard Rogers, *Holy Helps for a Godly Life*, ed. Brian G. Hedges, Puritan Treasures for Today (Grand Rapids, MI: Reformation Heritage Books, 2018), 38.

both to defend against satanic attacks (vv. 11–13, 16) and to send forth the Word with divine power (vv. 17, 19–20). "Watch and pray" expresses a wartime mentality, a sense that God's people are threatened by imminent danger from their enemies (cf. Neh. 4:9). The watchful Christian is a good soldier of Christ, prepared to manfully stand for truth and righteousness (1 Cor. 16:13).

Sober watchfulness should not be confused with anxiety. The spiritual warrior keeps watch in the confidence of Christ's complete victory and supreme power (Eph. 1:19–23; 6:10–13). Watchfulness is not the hyperalertness of someone who mistakenly thinks he must control everything to be safe. God our Father is in control, and we need never fear that he will neglect to provide for his children or fail to bring them to his kingdom (Luke 12:30–32). However, God's warrior-child longs to please his Father and to do good to other people, while he is painfully conscious that his remaining sin, Satan's subtle tricks, and the world's temptations and persecutions continually strive to make him fall into painful and shameful transgressions. Watchfulness is of the very essence of the perseverance of the saints to the end.

Watchfulness is both an individual duty and a corporate responsibility. Watching in prayer can be an intensely lonely experience, especially when suffering isolates us (Ps. 102:7). However, God's people are called to watch over each other. The elders of the church "watch for your souls, as they that must give account" (Heb. 13:17). They know that false teachers will arise in the churches, even from among the elders, and therefore must stay alert as shepherds guarding the sheep from wolves (Acts 20:28–31). This duty of mutual watchfulness, though, is not limited to the shepherds of the church. All believers have this responsibility: "Take heed, brethren, lest there be in any of you an evil heart of unbelief, in departing from the living God. But exhort one another daily, while it is called To day; lest any of you be hardened through the deceitfulness of sin" (Heb. 3:12–13). Mutual watchfulness is not a climate of suspicion and ill will but an atmosphere of brotherly love. Watching over each other to provoke one another to good works is one of the primary reasons why we assemble as a church (10:24–25).

Proud people feel no need to keep watch, for they are sure they are safe. However, the Bible teaches us that we must *constantly* keep watch: "Watch thou in all things" (2 Tim. 4:5). Hedges says, "The watchful believer never takes a day off."[65] We are not to watch only when we sense danger but when we feel strong: "Let him that thinketh he standeth take heed lest he fall" (1 Cor. 10:12). Furthermore, we must watch "with all perseverance" (Eph. 6:18), lest we begin well but lapse into dullness and lethargy. Victory over temptation and growth in godliness do not happen automatically, and many a Christian has sadly fallen because of careless walking.

Recovery from Backsliding

The Christian life is a race that we run "looking unto Jesus" until by grace we join him in glory (Heb. 12:1–2).[66] However, on the road to heaven, Christians may experience backsliding, a season of weakened faith and obedience, and increasing sin. Wilhelmus à Brakel described backsliding as "spiritual winter" in one's life, "the very opposite of growth."[67] Andrew Fuller wrote that backsliding among professing Christians is "their having sinned, and not repented of their deeds."[68] Signs of backsliding are coldness in prayer, indifference under the Word, growing inner corruptions, increasing love of the world, declining love for believers, and man-centered hopes.

What should a professing Christian do if he discovers he has backslidden? He should take his condition very seriously, for backsliding, if left unchecked, will stop at nothing short of apostasy. William Plumer said, "He who is determined to see how far he may decline in religion and yet be restored, will lose his soul."[69] It is crucial for the backslidden Christian to exercise himself in the fear of God, for it is by the fear of God that the Lord keeps people from departing from him (Jer. 32:40). It is true that a child of God cannot fully and finally fall away,[70] but a backslider's repentance demonstrates that his faith is real. This is no time to slumber spiritually but to shake oneself awake, begin to keep watch, and take every necessary step to deny oneself, take up one's cross, and follow Jesus Christ. Thus, a proper response to backsliding engages each of the virtues we have highlighted in this chapter.

65. Hedges, *Watchfulness*, 13.

66. This section is a greatly abridged adaption of Beeke, *Getting Back in the Race*, 16, 22, 41–102. Used by permission.

67. Brakel, *The Christian's Reasonable Service*, 4:159–60.

68. Andrew Fuller, *The Backslider: His Nature, Symptoms, and Recovery* (1801; repr., Birmingham, AL: Solid Ground, 2005), 48.

69. Plumer, *Vital Godliness*, 148.

70. On the preservation and perseverance of the saints, see chaps. 30–31.

We find gracious guidance for the restoring of backsliders in the Lord's words to Israel in Hosea 14. There we see that backsliders must return to the Lord, receive his grace, and recover their spiritual vitality.

First, backsliders must *return to the Lord*. Returning requires repentance. Hosea 14:1 says, "O Israel, return unto the LORD thy God; for thou hast fallen by thine iniquity." This is not merely breaking off a bad habit but recognizing that you have forsaken God to pursue idols, which can never satisfy, and you must return to him, the fountain of living waters (Jer. 2:13). Richard Sibbes said that a person who is seeking happiness and hope from mere creatures "is restless still until he come unto Jehovah, who is the all-sufficient, universal good, who fills and fills the soul abundantly."[71] To that end, remember how you formerly obeyed the Lord, and acknowledge how bad is your present spiritual condition (Rev. 2:4–5; 3:17). Look deep into the motives of your heart, and grieve over the evil of your sins (2 Cor. 7:10), confessing them with sorrow to the Lord (Ps. 32:5). Flee from sin, pursue righteousness, and seek the Lord.[72]

God has provided you with a pathway home, a pathway paved with the means of grace. Hosea 14:2 says, "Take with you words, and turn to the LORD: say unto him, Take away all iniquity, and receive us graciously: so will we render the calves of our lips." God gives you "words," his Word, to guide you back to him. Humble yourself like a newborn babe, and crave once again the Word as your necessary milk (1 Pet. 2:2). God's Word even teaches you how to pray. William Gurnall wrote, "Prayer is nothing but the promise reversed, or God's Word formed into an argument, and retorted by faith upon God again."[73] Pray for the Holy Spirit like a hungry child asks his Father for food (Luke 11:11–13). And do not neglect public worship ("the calves of our lips," a picture of praise taken from the sacrifices), for Christ is specially present in the public meetings of his people as they gather for worship and training in discipleship (Matt. 18:20; 28:18–20).

We travel the pathway of the means of grace by exercising faith. Hosea 14:3 expresses the confident reliance of trusting in the Lord alone: "Asshur shall not save us; we will not ride upon horses: neither will we say any more to the work of our hands, Ye are our gods: for in thee the fatherless findeth mercy." In other words, do not trust in mere men

71. Sibbes, *The Returning Backslider*, in *Works*, 2:253.

72. On repentance, see chap. 19.

73. Gurnall, *The Christian in Complete Armour*, 2:88.

("Asshur"), in your own power or resources ("horses"), or in the idols you have made. Seek "life, in all its richness and fullness" from the Lord, and trust that he alone is sufficient for all things.[74] This faith must receive and rest in Jesus Christ, for he is the only Mediator between God and man.[75]

Second, backsliders must *receive the grace of God.* Hosea 14:4 highlights three graces in Christ that are especially precious to those who have wandered from the Lord. The first two are prefaced by the Lord's "I will," sealing the promise as a gift of sovereign grace. These are promises that all backsliders who repent and believe in Christ can claim as their own:

- There is the grace of sanctification: "I will heal their backsliding." This is a promise that God himself will purify them of their bent to depart from him and instill in his repentant ones a contrary bent to cling to him (Jer. 3:22). Backslider, are you afraid that your fickle heart will never stay with God? Trust in his sanctifying power to hold you in his hand and in his faithfulness to never let you go (John 10:28).
- There is the grace of adoption: "I will love them freely." God's love for his people is the love of an adoptive father for his dear, chosen children (Hos. 11:1–4). Do you fear that your sins against light and grace have made it impossible for God to love you and rejoice over you? Grasp hold of that word "freely." Sibbes wrote, "Doth not a father and mother love their child freely? What doth the child deserve of the father and mother a great while? Nothing. But the mother hath many a weary night and foul hand with it. Hath God planted an affection in us to love our children freely; and shall not God much more, who gives this love and plants it in us, be admitted to love freely?"[76]
- There is the grace of justification: "For mine anger is turned away from him." Here God promises complete propitiation of his wrath and reconciliation of sinners to himself. Does guilt overwhelm your soul? Or do you feel that you are not nearly sorry enough for your sins? Remind yourself that God's forgiveness has never rested on

74. Raymond C. Ortlund Jr., *Whoredom: God's Unfaithful Wife in Biblical Theology* (Grand Rapids, MI: Eerdmans, 1996), 49.

75. On faith in Jesus Christ and its exercises, see chaps. 20–21.

76. Sibbes, *The Returning Backslider*, in *Works*, 2:317.

> your works, your repentance, or your faith, but is based on Christ alone. John says, "If we confess our sins, he is faithful and just to forgive us our sins, and to cleanse us from all unrighteousness." And how? Because "we have an advocate with the Father, Jesus Christ the righteous: and he is the propitiation for our sins" (1 John 1:9; 2:1–2).

Although sanctification, adoption, and justification are granted to all believers upon conversion and these graces never fail, backslidden Christians need to receive a renewed sense of the reality and power of these graces in their lives. They need to draw living water from these wells of salvation for the strengthening of assurance and the increase of the Spirit's operations in their souls.

Third, backsliders must *recover spiritual vitality*. This is done by communion with God through union with the Lord Jesus Christ. God says in Hosea 14:5–7, "I will be as the dew unto Israel: he shall grow as the lily, and cast forth his roots as Lebanon. His branches shall spread, and his beauty shall be as the olive tree, and his smell as Lebanon. They that dwell under his shadow shall return; they shall revive as the corn, and grow as the vine: the scent thereof shall be as the wine of Lebanon." Sibbes wrote, "God's love is a fruitful love. Wheresoever he loves, he makes things lovely."[77]

Perhaps, backsliding Christian, you have come to think that your sins have made it impossible for you ever to flourish spiritually again. Dear believer, you underestimate the magnitude of God's grace in Christ. Edward Reynolds wrote that God gave us this beautiful image of a prospering and fruitful plant "to encourage us in prayer to beg for an answer, not according to the defect and narrowness of our own low conceptions, but according to the fullness of God's own abundant mercies." He said, "God delights to have his people beg great things of him, to implore the performance of 'exceeding great and precious promises' (2 Pet. 1:4); to pray for a share in 'the unsearchable riches of Christ,' to know things which pass knowledge, and to 'be filled with all the fulness of God' (Eph. 3:8, 18, 19)."[78]

Yet the Lord notes in Hosea 14:8, "Ephraim shall say, What have I to do any more with idols? I have heard him, and observed him: I am like a green fir tree. From me is thy fruit found." Mark those words: "From

77. Sibbes, *The Returning Backslider*, in *Works,* 2:330.

78. Edward Reynolds, "Israel's Prayer in Time of Trouble, with God's Gracious Answer Thereunto: An Explication of the Fourteenth Chapter of Hosea," in Jeremiah Burroughs et al., *An Exposition of the Prophecy of Hosea* (1865; repr., Beaver Falls, PA: Soli Deo Gloria, 1989), 658.

me is thy fruit found." Do not think you can live a fruitful life apart from God. None of the idols to which you have devoted yourself can offer it. Christ says, "I am the vine, ye are the branches: He that abideth in me, and I in him, the same bringeth forth much fruit: for without me ye can do nothing" (John 15:5). Herein is both a promise and a warning: "Who is wise, and he shall understand these things? Prudent, and he shall know them? For the ways of the LORD are right, and the just shall walk in them: but the transgressors shall fall therein" (Hos. 14:9). This is a word to us all, whether we are unrepentant and perishing in our sins, newly converted believers, believers who have backslidden, or flourishing Christians who need to continue to walk in the fear of God.

God offers us so much in Hosea 14! Plumer wrote, "Here are promised rich supplies of free grace, securing pardon of sin, the indwelling of the Holy Spirit, deep-rooted vigor, increase of grace and of fruitfulness, usefulness to those under his influence, a sweet savor of piety at all times, together with an utter renunciation of idols and self-dependence."[79] Will you receive what he offers? Let us look to Jesus Christ as our life, our only life, and our abundant life.

Sing to the Lord

The Blessedness of Fearing God

Praise ye the Lord. The man is blessed
Who fears the Lord aright.
The man who finds in His commands
His pleasure and delight,
His children shall be mighty men
Upon the earth renowned;
The generation of the just
In blessing shall abound.

That man is good who graciously
And freely gives and lends,
Who justly governs his affairs,
Who truth and right extends.
There surely is not anything
That ever shall him move;

79. Plumer, *Vital Godliness*, 171.

The righteous man's memorial
Shall everlasting prove.

When he shall evil tiding hear
He shall not be afraid;
His heart is fixed; his confidence
Upon the Lord is stayed.
Established firmly is his heart;
He shall not fearful be,
Until upon his enemies
He his desire shall see.

Psalm 112
Tune: Topanga Canyon
Trinity Hymnal—Baptist Edition, No. 768

Questions for Meditation or Discussion

1. What five kinds of fear toward God do the Holy Scriptures reveal? Provide a short description and Scripture proof for each.
2. What is the source of godly, filial fear?
3. What is the difference between servile fear and filial fear?
4. How should a Christian seek to grow in the fear of God?
5. What did Christ mean when he said, "If any man will come after me, let him deny himself, and take up his cross daily, and follow me" (Luke 9:23)?
6. What does the Bible mean when it charges us to be "sober" or of "sound mind"?
7. What is the Christian's duty with respect to being watchful?
8. What is backsliding in the Christian life? What are its signs?
9. Outline how Hosea 14 shows us that backsliders can be restored.
10. What is one way that reading this chapter has convicted you of sin? What is one way it has comforted you? How can you put each of these into practical application?

Questions for Deeper Reflection

11. Write a brief article explaining how the fear of God is not a contradiction of the gospel of Jesus Christ but instead fosters healthy godliness. Include an explanation of 1 John 4:18.

12. An old friend contacts you, confessing that she has backslidden far from the Lord and committed such grave sins over the last year that she is afraid there is no hope for her restoration. How do you respond?

42

Prayer and the Hope of Glorification

Nothing is more characteristic of the child of God than that he prays to God. Prayer is as natural to the regenerate soul as breathing is to a living body. J. C. Ryle said, "A habit of prayer is one of the surest marks of a true Christian."[1] When the Lord told Ananias that Saul of Tarsus had been converted, he said, "Behold, he prayeth" (Acts 9:11). No doubt, Saul had prayed many prayers in his life as a self-righteous Pharisee. However, Saul, now Paul the apostle, later identifies prayer as a characteristic effect of becoming a child of God: "Ye have received the Spirit of adoption, whereby we cry, Abba, Father" (Rom. 8:15).

In prayer, the Christian lifts up to God the holy desires stirred within him by the Spirit-empowered exercises of faith and love. Prayer is often the first outward expression of saving faith when a person calls on the name of the Lord Jesus to save him (Acts 2:21; Rom. 10:13). Calling on the name of the Lord characterizes the saints of God (1 Cor. 1:2; 2 Tim. 2:22). Christ described the prayer life of God's children as one of repeatedly asking and receiving, seeking and finding, knocking and having doors opened for them (Matt. 7:7–11).

We will not attempt in this chapter to give anything close to a full theology of prayer. All systematic theology, rightly applied, is a theology of prayer. We have sprinkled our systematic theology with regular appli-

1. J. C. Ryle, *Home Truths*, 4th ed. (Ipswich, England: William Hunt, 1859), 2:106.

cations of doctrine to prayer.[2] Here we simply aim to conclude our treatment of the doctrines of the Holy Spirit and salvation with a description of prayer, a practical exhortation to prayer, and a discussion of hope in our future in glory—for hope is the soul's expectant longing for the great object of our desires and prayers.

A Description of Christian Prayer

While people of many religions offer prayer to their gods, here we deal with that prayer that the only true God produces by his grace in those who believe in his gospel so that they call on his name.[3] Prayer is a "necessary" part of the Christian life, as the Heidelberg Catechism (LD 45, Q. 116) reminds us, "because it is the chief part of thankfulness which God requires of us; and also, because God will give His grace and Holy Spirit to those only, who with sincere desires continually ask them of Him, and are thankful for them."[4] The psalmist says, "What shall I render unto the Lord for all his benefits toward me? I will take the cup of salvation, and call upon the name of the Lord" (Ps. 116:12–13). A "cup" symbolizes one's portion from the Lord, whether blessing or wrath.[5] Therefore, a truly grateful response to God's grace involves receiving by faith the grace he has given and calling on him for more grace.

2. See the discussions of prayer in relation to illumination in the study and preaching of the Word (*RST*, 1:17, 148–49, 368; 2:733, 974); a right response to God's Word (1:191); scientific studies (1:226); evangelism and missions (1:470–71; 2:414, 877, 983); God's sovereign power (1:778); communion with the Trinity (1:945–51); God's eternal decree (1:976); providence (1:1077); guardian angels (1:1127–28); spiritual warfare against Satan (1:1155); man's creation as a priest (2:311); human sin (2:404, 439); confession of sin (2:469); grace to overcome sin (2:472–73); suffering in union with Christ (2:493); the new covenant promises (2:652–53); faith in the covenant God (2:708–10); the names of Christ (2:750); calling upon and worshiping Christ (2:772–73); family worship (2:983); Christ in Gethsemane (2:1049–50); Christ's intercession (2:1088–1103); and the believer's priestly ministry to God (2:1103–7). In this volume, consider the discussions of prayer in relation to the church's worship (in chap. 3); speaking in tongues (chaps. 5–7); pastoral prayer for healing (chap. 7); practical applications of the doctrines of preparatory conviction (chap. 13) and regeneration (chap. 18); the spiritual exercise of repentance (chap. 19); kinds of faith that do not save (chap. 20); disciplines to cultivate holiness (chap. 29); the transformation of one's relationship to God by adoption (chap. 26); persevering by God's preserving grace (chap. 31); and praying for revival by the Holy Spirit (chap. 32).

3. Our intent in focusing on Christian prayer is not to discourage unbelievers from crying out to the true God when they sense their need for his mercy. Prayer to the Creator is the duty of all mankind. Though the prayers of the wicked are an abomination to God (Prov. 28:9), the Lord is merciful and may hear their cries (1 Kings 21:27–29; Jonah 1:14–15). An unrepentant sinner may begin praying for salvation from God's wrath while under conviction of sin, but at some point may find that he has been regenerated and is praying in faith and repentance. Far worse is the case of those who refuse to pray at all, for their prayerlessness provokes God's wrath (Ps. 79:6; Jer. 10:25).

4. *The Three Forms of Unity*, 110.

5. Pss. 11:6; 16:5; 23:5; 75:8. Some interpreters have seen a reference to the drink offering here (cf. Num. 15:5, 7, 10), but the expression "cup of salvation" suggests a gift from the Lord, not an offering to him. Derek Kidner, *Psalms 73–150: An Introduction and Commentary*, Tyndale

What is Christian prayer? The Baptist Catechism (Q. 105) synthesizes answers from the Westminster Shorter Catechism (Q. 98) and Larger Catechism (Q. 178) to say, "Prayer is an offering up of our desires to God (Ps. 62:8), by the assistance of the Holy Spirit (Rom. 8:26) for things agreeable to His will (1 John 5:14), in the name of Christ (John 16:23), believing (Matt. 21:22; James 1:6); with confession of our sins (Ps. 32:5–6; Dan. 9:4) and thankful acknowledgment of His mercies (Phil. 4:6)."[6] This description has the following components:

First, *Christian prayer is presenting our desires to God.* The cited proof text says, "Trust in him at all times; ye people, pour out your heart before him: God is a refuge for us" (Ps. 62:8). When men seek to destroy us with slanderous lies (vv. 3–4) and acts of oppression and robbery (vv. 9–10), God is our rock, salvation, and glory (vv. 1–2, 5–7). Therefore, we can pour out the concerns of our souls into his fatherly lap,[7] so to speak, knowing that he will be our eternal refuge and carry us in his everlasting arms (Deut. 33:27). Thus, childless Hannah was able to take her cries to the Lord, and though the priest mistook her silent but passionate petitions for drunkenness, she could say, "No, my lord, I am a woman of a sorrowful spirit: I have drunk neither wine nor strong drink, but have poured out my soul before the LORD" (1 Sam. 1:15). Though prayer is typically framed in spoken words, John Calvin said that "the essentials of prayer are set in the mind and heart, or rather that prayer itself is properly an emotion [*affectus*] of the heart within, which is poured out and laid open before God, the searcher of hearts."[8] John Bunyan said, "When thou prayest, rather let thy heart be without words, than thy words without a heart."[9]

Second, *Christian prayer is offered only to God.* The Heidelberg Catechism (LD 45, Q. 117) says that we must "pray to the one true God only, who hath manifested Himself in His Word."[10] The Westminster Larger Catechism (Q. 179) gives us the biblical reasons why we are to pray to God alone: "God only being able to search the hearts, hear the requests, pardon the sins, and fulfil the desires of all; and only to be believed in, and

Old Testament Commentaries 16 (Downers Grove, IL: InterVarsity Press, 1975), 445. The word translated as "cup" (*kos*) is not used of the drink offering.

6. *Reformed Confessions*, 4:587; cf. 347, 367.

7. Calvin, *Commentaries*, on Ps. 89:38.

8. Calvin, *Institutes*, 3.20.29. On Calvin's doctrine of prayer, see Joel R. Beeke, "The Communion of Men with God," in *John Calvin: A Heart for Devotion, Doctrine, and Doxology*, ed. Burk Parsons (Lake Mary, FL: Reformation Trust, 2008), 231–46.

9. Bunyan, "Dying Sayings," in *Works*, 1:65.

10. *The Three Forms of Unity*, 110.

worshipped with religious worship; prayer, which is a special part thereof, is to be made by all to him alone, and to none other."[11] To pray to saints or angels is to practically ascribe to them attributes belonging only to God.[12]

Third, *Christian prayer is possible only by the power of the Holy Spirit.* In relation to his work in prayer, he is "the spirit of grace and of supplications" (Zech. 12:10). Paul says to the redeemed and adopted children of God, "Because ye are sons, God hath sent forth the Spirit of his Son into your hearts, crying, Abba, Father" (Gal. 4:6). We argued in an earlier chapter that the indwelling of God's Spirit is necessary for all holy works (Ezek. 36:27).[13] Certainly his work is necessary for people to call on the name of the Lord, for Paul says, "No man can say that Jesus is the Lord, but by the Holy Ghost" (1 Cor. 12:3). Thus, Paul also says, "the Spirit also helpeth our infirmities: for we know not what we should pray for as we ought" (Rom. 8:26). The apostle commends praying "in the Spirit" (Eph. 6:18; cf. Jude 20), which most likely means with or by the influences of the Holy Spirit.[14] The Westminster Larger Catechism (Q. 182) explains that "the Spirit helpeth our infirmities, by enabling us to understand both for whom, and what, and how prayer is to be made; and by working and quickening in our hearts (although not in all persons, nor at all times, in the same measure) those apprehensions, affections, and graces which are requisite for the right performance of that duty."[15]

Fourth, *Christian prayer is performed by faith in Jesus Christ.* The Westminster Larger Catechism (Q. 181) explains, "The sinfulness of man, and his distance from God by reason thereof, being so great, as that we can have no access into his presence without a mediator (John 14:6; Isa. 59:2; Eph. 3:12); and there being none in heaven or earth appointed to, or fit for, that glorious work but Christ alone (John 6:27; Heb. 7:25–27; 1 Tim. 2:5), we are to pray in no other name but his only (Col. 3:17; Heb. 13:15)."[16] All God's people through the ages have drawn near to him by faith in the promised Mediator.[17] The incarnate Christ taught his disciples to pray explicitly in his name (John 14:13–14; 16:24), which means, as the

11. *Reformed Confessions*, 4:347.
12. See the section on some ethical applications of the first commandment in chap. 37.
13. See the section on the necessity of the indwelling of the Spirit for obedience in chap. 3.
14. Compare the use of the same phrase (*en pneumati*) in Eph. 2:22; 3:5; 5:18 (cf. Rom. 2:29; 8:9; 14:17; 1 Cor. 12:3; 1 Thess. 1:5; 1 Pet. 1:12) or *en tō pneumati* in Eph. 2:18.
15. *Reformed Confessions*, 4:347–48. See Owen, *A Discourse of the Work of the Holy Spirit in Prayer*, in *Works*, 235–350.
16. *Reformed Confessions*, 4:347.
17. On the continuity of the gospel through the ages, see *RST*, 2:565–83 (chap. 29).

Larger Catechism (Q. 180) says, "to ask mercy for his sake; not by bare mentioning of his name, but by drawing our encouragement to pray, and our boldness, strength, and hope of acceptance in prayer, from Christ and his mediation."[18] Praying in Christ's name goes hand in hand with praying in the Spirit, for we pray in the Spirit by approaching the Father through the Son (Eph. 2:18).

George Downame (1563–1634) said that we must ask "how it cometh to pass that man being stained and polluted with sin, and by reason thereof an enemy of God, should have any access to God, or be admitted to any speech with him, who is most just and terrible, a consuming fire, and hating all iniquity with perfect hatred." Downame answered, "Therefore of necessity a mediator was to come between God and man, who reconciling us unto God, and covering our imperfections, might make both our persons and our prayers acceptable unto God."[19]

Fifth, *Christian prayer is according to God's preceptive will.*[20] John says, "This is the confidence that we have in him, that, if we ask any thing according to his will, he heareth us" (1 John 5:14). The Westminster Larger Catechism (Q. 184) says, "We are to pray for all things tending to the glory of God, the welfare of the church, our own or others' good; but not for any thing that is unlawful."[21] The prayers of the wicked are an abomination to God (Prov. 15:8; 28:9). Likewise, petitions for good things displease God when asked out of evil motives (Ps. 66:18; James 4:3).

In the Lord's Prayer, Christ gives us a brief directory for praying according to God's will (Matt. 6:9–13).[22] Jesus teaches us to pray with faith in God's mercy and majesty ("our Father which art in heaven"). Then he presents six model petitions, three concerning God's glory and three con-

---

18. *Reformed Confessions*, 4:347. See Calvin, *Institutes*, 3.20.17.

19. George Downame, *A Godly and Learned Treatise of Prayer* (Cambridge: by Roger Daniel for Nicolas Bourn, 1640), 68.

20. On God's preceptive will as distinguished from his decretive will, see *RST*, 1:764–67.

21. *Reformed Confessions*, 4:348.

22. Two of the most helpful expositions for guidance in prayer remain those on the Lord's Prayer found in the Heidelberg Catechism (LD 45–52, Q. 116–29) and the Westminster Shorter Catechism (Q. 99–107). Many longer expositions of the Lord's Prayer have been written, some of which are nearly systematic theologies unto themselves. For examples from Reformed orthodoxy, see Perkins, *An Exposition of the Lord's Prayer in the Way of Catechizing, Serving for Ignorant People*, in *Works*, 5:415–79; Manton, *A Practical Exposition of the Lord's Prayer*, in *Works*, 1:1–254; and Herman Witsius, *Sacred Dissertations on the Lord's Prayer*, trans. William Pringle (Grand Rapids, MI: Reformation Heritage Books, 2010). See also other expositions of the portions of either of the catechisms mentioned above, such as Theodorus VanderGroe, *The Christian's Only Comfort in Life and Death: An Exposition of the Heidelberg Catechism*, trans. Bartel Elshout, ed. Joel R. Beeke, 2 vols. (Grand Rapids, MI: Reformation Heritage Books, 2016), 2:419–532; and Thomas Watson, *The Lord's Prayer* (Edinburgh: Banner of Truth, 1960).

cerning our needs. "Hallowed be thy name" is not a praise but a petition that people would know that God is holy and honor him for who he is (Isa. 29:23; Ezek. 36:23).[23] "Thy kingdom come" asks God to establish his reign among men, presently in Christ's work by the Spirit and ultimately by Christ's return in glory (Luke 17:20–24). "Thy will be done in earth, as it is in heaven" seeks grace for people to obey God's preceptive will and submit to his decretive will (Matt. 26:42). "Give us this day our daily bread" looks to the Father to provide for all our material needs so we can have life and strength to serve him (6:25–26, 31–33). We pray, "Forgive us our debts, as we forgive our debtors" because even as justified and adopted children of God, we still incur his fatherly displeasure against our sins and need his forgiveness. In the last petition, "Lead us not into temptation, but deliver us from evil," we acknowledge our spiritual vulnerability to Satan (26:41) and call on God to rescue us from all sin and misery. The conclusion to the Lord's Prayer, "For thine is the kingdom, and the power, and the glory, for ever," echoes David's praise of God's sovereign self-sufficiency (1 Chron. 29:11), for our confidence in prayer arises from God alone. We end with "Amen" to affirm that we sincerely desire these petitions and trust that God has heard them and will answer according to his love and wisdom (Neh. 5:13; 8:6). This is how God wants his people to pray.

Sixth, *Christian prayer is made with confession of sin.* "If we confess our sins, he is faithful and just to forgive us our sins, and to cleanse us from all unrighteousness" (1 John 1:9). The Heidelberg Catechism (LD 45, Q. 117) says that one prerequisite for God-pleasing prayer is "that we rightly and thoroughly know our need and misery, that so we may deeply humble ourselves in the presence of His divine majesty."[24] Thus, Abraham referred to himself as "dust and ashes" in his prayer (Gen. 18:27), and Jacob confessed, "I am not worthy of the least of all the mercies, and of all the truth, which thou hast shewed unto thy servant" (32:10). We saw in the Lord's Prayer that Christ teaches his disciples to ask the Father for forgiveness of their sins as often as they pray for their physical needs—daily (Matt. 6:11–12).

Seventh, *Christian prayer is accompanied by thanksgiving and adoration.* David says, "I will bless the Lord at all times: his praise shall continually be in my mouth" (Ps. 34:1; cf. James 5:13). Paul says, "Rejoice

23. See Joel R. Beeke, "Hallowing God's Name," in *Let Us Pray*, ed. Don Kistler (Orlando, FL: The Northampton Press, 2011), 37–56.
24. *The Three Forms of Unity*, 110.

in the Lord always; again I will say, rejoice. . . . Do not be anxious about anything, but in everything by prayer and supplication with thanksgiving let your requests be made known to God" (Phil. 4:4, 6 ESV). He adds, "Rejoice evermore. Pray without ceasing. In every thing give thanks: for this is the will of God in Christ Jesus concerning you" (1 Thess. 5:16–18).

Praise and thanksgiving are our duty in prayer and the means to stir our faith into active exercise so that we can pray well. When reading the prayers of the Old Testament saints, one is deeply impressed with their fearful sense of God's greatness, their humility before him as unworthy sinners, and their confident reliance on his mercy and faithfulness.[25] Likewise, the epistles of Paul sparkle with continual thanksgiving for God's saving grace and feature many petitions that God would strengthen those whom he has saved according to the riches of his glory in Christ Jesus, with the result that Paul's petitions often sound like praises.[26] The more we fill our minds and mouths with the glory of God in Jesus Christ, the more richly and prayerfully we will pray.

A Practical Exhortation to Prayerful Praying

James, when commending Elijah as a model for effectual prayer, says that he "prayed earnestly" (James 5:17)—literally he "prayed in his prayer" (KJV mg.).[27] Alexander Ross (1888–1954) commented that that idiom communicates intensity: "A man may pray with his lips and yet not pray with an intense desire of the soul."[28] We might call it *prayerful praying*. Our prayers are often more prayerless than prayerful. They are exercises in mere words rather than communion with the living God. Yet how precious is prayer in his presence! Thomas Brooks said, "Ah! How often, Christians, hath God kissed you at the beginning of prayer, and spoke peace to you in the midst of prayer, and filled you with joy and assurance, upon the close of prayer!"[29]

25. Gen. 18:23–32; 32:9–12; Ex. 32:11–13; 33:12–18; Num. 14:13–19; 1 Kings 18:36–37; 1 Chron. 17:16–27; 29:10–19; 2 Chron. 6:12–42; Neh. 1:4–11; 9:4–38; Isa. 37:14–20; Jer. 32:16–25; Dan. 9:1–19.

26. Rom. 1:8–12; 1 Cor. 1:4–9; Eph. 1:15–23; 3:14–21; Phil. 1:3–6, 9–11; Col. 1:3–14; 1 Thess. 1:3–5; 3:9–13; 2 Thess. 1:3, 11–12; 2:13.

27. Greek *proseuchē proseuxato*. This section is adapted from Joel R. Beeke, "Prayerful Praying Today," in *Taking Hold of God: Reformed and Puritan Perspectives on Prayer*, ed. Joel R. Beeke and Brian G. Najapfour (Grand Rapids, MI: Reformation Heritage Books, 2011), 223–40. Used by permission.

28. Alexander Ross, *The Epistles of James and John*, The New International Commentary on the New Testament (Grand Rapids, MI: Eerdmans, 1954), 102.

29. Brooks, *Heaven on Earth*, in *Works*, 2:369.

The giants of church history dwarf us in true prayer. Martin Luther spent two hours of every day alone with God.[30] Yet such prayer took tremendous effort and self-discipline. Luther said, "Prayer is a difficult matter and hard work. It is far more difficult than preaching the Word or performing other official duties in the church. . . . This is the reason why it is so rare."[31] The wife of Joseph Alleine (1634–1668) said of her husband,

> All the time of his health, he did rise constantly at or before four of the clock, and on the Sabbath sooner, if he did wake. He would be much troubled if he heard any smiths, or shoemakers, or such tradesmen, at work at their trades, before he was in his duties with God; saying to me often, "O how this noise shames me! Doth not my Master deserve more than theirs?" From four till eight he spent in prayer, holy contemplations, and singing of psalms, which he much delighted in, and did daily practice alone, as well as in his family.[32]

In more recent history, we also remember the fervent prayers of the church in Korea, where hundreds of people meet daily for prayer before the sun rises, a tradition that goes back a hundred years.[33] So we are surrounded by a cloud of witnesses of faithful men and women whose prayers rebuke our prayerless praying.

The Problem of Prayerless Praying

Let each of us begin with ourselves. Does our personal use of the weapon of prayer bring us shame rather than glory? Is it a missile that shatters satanic powers, or is it like a harmless toy that Satan sleeps beside? We are usually more concerned about what our listeners think of our words than our communication with God. Where is our prayerful passion for the presence of God? We must go beyond complaining about our weak prayers and repent of our coldness.

What is the condition of your prayer life? Perhaps you have never experienced a powerful prayer life. You may repeat words of prayer in a

---

30. Andrew Kosten, translator's introduction to Martin Luther, *Devotions and Prayers of Martin Luther* (Grand Rapids, MI: Baker, 1965), 5.

31. Martin Luther, *What Luther Says: A Practical In-Home Anthology for the Active Christian*, comp. Ewald M. Plass (St. Louis, MO: Concordia, 1959), 1088 (3476, 3478).

32. Richard Baxter, Theodosia Alleine, et al., *Life and Death of the Rev. Joseph Alleine . . . to which Are Added, His Christian Letters* (New York: Robert Carter, 1840), 106.

33. Myung Hyuk Kim, "Lessons from the Prayer Habits of the Church in Korea," in *Teach Us to Pray: Prayer in the Bible and the World*, ed. D. A. Carson (Grand Rapids, MI: Baker, 1990), 235–38.

religious meeting or over a meal. You may cry out to God for some pressing need but never possess the Spirit of prayer. Does your soul ever pant after God in Christ? If not, you are still dead in your sins. You must cry out to God, begging him to make you alive in Christ. You must look to the Lord Jesus for salvation.

Perhaps you once prayed in your prayers, but your prayers became more a matter of words than heart-to-heart communion with God. Thomas Adam (1701–1784) confessed, "I pray faintly, and with reserve, merely to quiet conscience. . . . Prayer and other spiritual exercises are often a weariness to me. . . . Whenever I attempt to pray for others, I am soon made sensible that I do it in a cold, heartless manner; a plain indication that love is not at the bottom.[34] David Clarkson said, "We should be sensible who it is with whom we have to do," and warned that if "we pray with sleepy, drowsy, listless hearts," we make light of the great God, our needs, our best interest, and our spiritual duty toward him—and hence, we offend God.[35]

We must confront our prayerless praying, confess it to God, and plead for the renewal of our souls. Prayer is the thermometer of our spiritual condition. Prayerless praying is a symptom of our entanglement with the love of this world and trust in its wealth, for prayer is our sighing after the world to come. Augustine said, "In the darkness, then, of this world, in which we are pilgrims absent from the Lord as long as 'we walk by faith and not by sight' [2 Cor. 5:6–7] the Christian soul ought to feel itself desolate, and continue in prayer, and learn to fix the eye of faith on the word of the divine sacred Scriptures, as 'on a light shining in a dark place, until the day dawn, and the day-star arise in our hearts' [2 Pet. 1:19]."[36]

Practical Steps toward Prayerful Praying

Prayerful praying does not happen automatically. It requires the exercise of self-control. We must preach to ourselves, as David did: "Why art thou cast down, O my soul? And why art thou disquieted in me? Hope thou in God: for I shall yet praise him for the help of his countenance" (Ps. 42:5) and "Bless the Lord, O my soul, and forget not all his benefits" (103:2).

34. Thomas Adam, *Private Thoughts on Religion* (Glasgow: Chalmers and Collins, 1824), 68, 73, 76.

35. Clarkson, "Pray for Everything," in *Works*, 2:177.

36. Augustine, Letters, 130.2.5, in *NPNF*[1], 1:461. With the word "desolate," Augustine reminded his reader, a rich widow, that none of her temporal prosperity was real riches, which yet awaited her in Christ's kingdom.

First, *remember the value of prayer.* Daniel preferred to die rather than give up prayer (Dan. 6:6–10). Appreciate the value of unanswered as well as answered prayer. William Carey (1761–1834) labored as a missionary for eight years before baptizing the first convert to Christ under his ministry, but he said, "I feel that it is good to commit my soul, my body, and my all, into the hands of God. Then the world appears little, the promises great, and God an all-sufficient portion."[37] And if unanswered prayer is sweet, how much sweeter are answers to prayers! Thomas Watson said, "The angel fetched Peter out of prison, but it was prayer that fetched the angel."[38] We may not have much money or property to bequeath to future generations, but we can pass on a heritage far more valuable than silver or gold: a treasury of prayers that we lifted up for their good.

Second, *maintain the priority of prayer*. Our Lord said in John 15:5, "Without me ye can do nothing." Struggle to avoid prayerless praying whether in private devotions or public prayers. If you cannot put your feelings into words, at least groan before the Lord and trust that the Holy Spirit is groaning with you (Rom. 8:23, 26–27). Put prayer first. Remember this wise counsel: "You can do *more* than pray, *after* you have prayed. But you can *not* do more than pray *until* you have prayed."[39] Even if your prayers seem lifeless, do not stop praying. Dullness may be beyond your immediate ability to overcome, but refusing to pray at all is the fruit of presumption, self-sufficiency, and slothfulness. When even the outward form of prayer is gone, all is gone. It is easy to pray when you are like a sailboat gliding forward in a favoring wind. But you must also pray when you are like an icebreaker smashing your way through an arctic sea. Watch and pray "with all perseverance" (Eph. 6:18).

Third, *keep a blood-washed conscience for boldness in prayer*. Nothing keeps us from the holy presence of God like a guilty, accusing conscience. It is one thing to affirm the doctrine of Christ's mediation, but it is yet another to bring specific transgressions into the light of God so that "the blood of Jesus Christ his Son cleanseth us from all sin" (1 John 1:7). In the Old Testament, unclean people had to purify themselves with water

---

37. Cited in Timothy George, *Faithful Witness: The Life and Mission of William Carey* (Birmingham, AL: New Hope, 1991), 104, 131.

38. Thomas Watson, *A Divine Cordial* (1663; repr., Wilmington, DE: Sovereign Grace, 1972), 18.

39. S. D. Gordon, *Quiet Talks on Prayer* (New York: Fleming H. Revell, 1904), 16, emphasis original. Attributed to John Bunyan in I. D. E. Thomas, comp., *The Golden Treasury of Puritan Quotations* (Chicago: Moody, 1975), 210.

mixed with the ashes of a sacrificed heifer (Numbers 19). The writer to the Hebrews says that if that sufficed for ceremonial purification, "how much more shall the blood of Christ, who through the eternal Spirit offered himself without spot to God, purge your conscience from dead works to serve the living God?" (Heb. 9:14). Go quickly to Jesus Christ as soon as your conscience smites you and find cleansing, forgiveness, and liberty in his blood so that you draw near to God (10:19; Eph. 3:12).

Fourth, *speak with sincerity in prayer*. To pray with your mouth what is not truly in your heart is hypocrisy (Isa. 29:13)—unless you are confessing the coldness of your heart and crying out for heartwarming grace. Sometimes a sincere prayer, such as Psalm 119, is long and carefully crafted. Other times, a sincere prayer is quite simple: "God be merciful to me a sinner" (Luke 18:13). Either way, settle for nothing less than sincerity in your prayer. Brooks said, "God looks not at the elegancy of your prayers, to see how neat they are; nor yet at the geometry of your prayers, to see how long they are; nor yet at the arithmetic of your prayers, to see how many they are; nor yet at the music of your prayers, nor yet at the sweetness of your voice, nor yet at the logic of your prayers; but at the sincerity of your prayers, how hearty they are."[40]

Fifth, *cultivate a spirit of continual prayer*. Paul says, "Pray without ceasing" (1 Thess. 5:17). In addition to set times of prayer (cf. Acts 3:1) and private devotions (Matt. 6:6), develop a habit of regularly shooting short prayers up to heaven (Neh. 2:4). Whenever you feel the least impulse to pray, do so. If you come across an emergency, pray for those involved. If you are talking to someone who mentions a need, ask if you can pray for him and do so immediately. Nurture in yourself a constant awareness of living in God's presence, and consciously walk with him through the day (Gen. 5:22, 24; 6:9). Alleine said, "I am never quiet till I am in my old way of communion with God; like the needle in the compass, that is restless till it be turned towards the pole."[41] Though we cannot constantly be speaking prayers, we can live continually in a spirit of prayer—a heart desiring communion with God, begun here and completed hereafter. Augustine said, "What else is intended by the words of the apostle: 'Pray without ceasing,' than, 'Desire without intermission, from him alone who can give it, a happy life, which no life can be but that which is eternal'?"[42] In prayer

40. Brooks, *The Privy Key of Heaven*, in *Works*, 2:256.
41. Joseph Alleine, Letter to his Wife, in Baxter and Alleine, *Life and Death*, 248.
42. Augustine, Letters, 130.9.18, in *NPNF*[1], 1:465.

we seek happiness, and "happy is that people, whose God is the Lord" (Ps. 144:15).[43] To live unto God is to pray continually.

Sixth, *exercise a broad and organized ministry of intercession.* Godly prayer cannot be constricted to the needs of our little circle of family members and friends, but includes intercession in love for many people.[44] In the Lord's Prayer, Christ taught his disciples to pray to *our* Father for *our* physical and spiritual needs (Matt. 6:9–13). The apostle Paul calls for "supplication for all saints" (Eph. 6:18), which, while it cannot refer to every Christian in the world, certainly summons us to a broad ministry of intercession. Paul prayed constantly for believers and churches in many places, though he was a remarkably busy person whose life was full of conflicts and trials. We can follow his example by keeping prayer lists and, with God's help, using them to help organize our prayers. You might have various lists of people for whom you pray daily, weekly, or monthly. Pray through your church directory, dividing the list to cover a reasonable number of people each day. Use other prayer directories to pray through a list of missionaries supported by your church or denomination. Attend reports by visiting missionaries, read their newsletters, and pray for them whenever you get news—before you forget. Do not allow yourself to slack off in intercession; it is likely the most important ministry you will ever perform.

Seventh, *read the Bible for prayer and pray the Bible to God.* We must listen to God if we would learn how to speak to him. Christ says, "If ye abide in me, and my words abide in you, ye shall ask what ye will, and it shall be done unto you" (John 15:7). In the persecuted house churches in China, many Christians had no Bibles, but their prayers were full of Scripture, based on passages they had memorized.[45] Therefore, read and memorize the Bible with the intent of responding to God's Word with prayer. Lift up his attributes in adoration, turn his commandments into confession of sin, remember his mighty works of salvation and provision with thanksgiving, and grasp his promises and make them into supplications

43. Augustine, Letters, 130.13.24, in *NPNF*[1], 1:466–67. It might be objected that prayer expresses more than just desire for eternal life and communion with God but also our daily, physical needs. True enough, but why do we desire for our physical needs to be met? Such desire cannot end in the things themselves but in the way they are useful for us to enjoy God. See Augustine, *On Christian Doctrine*, 1.3–5, 22, in *NPNF*[1], 2:523–24, 527–28.

44. James W. Beeke and Joel R. Beeke, *Developing a Healthy Prayer Life: 31 Meditations on Communing with God* (Grand Rapids, MI: Reformation Heritage Books, 2010), 24–28.

45. David Wang, "Lessons from the Prayer Habits of the Church in China," in *Teach Us to Pray*, ed. Carson, 251.

that God would do what he has said. Thomas Manton said, "One good way to get comfort is to plead the promise of God in prayer. . . . Show him his handwriting; God is tender of his word."[46] Take up biblical prayers to guide your prayers, such as the prayers of Paul.[47] Learn, pray, and sing the Psalms. Athanasius said that the Psalms are a picture of all the motions of the soul, a spiritual mirror in which we both see ourselves and discern a pattern for drawing near to God with all our hearts.[48]

Eighth, *use biblical variety and balance in prayer*. Paul teaches us to be praying "with all prayer and supplication" (Eph. 6:18). The Scriptures present various kinds of prayer: praise of God's glories, confession of our sins, lamentation over our miseries, petition for our needs (spiritual and physical), thanksgiving for God's mercies, intercession for others (our family members, friends, churches, nations, and the world), and our affirmation of God's willingness and ability to answer. The Bible also presents different contexts for prayer: private prayer, family prayer, prayer with friends, prayer meetings, and prayer in public worship. We tend to favor some forms of prayer to the neglect of others. Periodically examine your prayers to see if they are out of balance, and give more time and energy to aspects of prayer that you are neglecting.

Ninth, *believe that God answers the prayers of his children*. Faith in God is essential to answered prayer (Mark 11:22–24; James 1:5–6). It can be discouraging, even heart sickening, to pray and not receive (Prov. 13:12). We may be inclined to cry, "How long wilt thou forget me, O LORD? For ever? How long wilt thou hide thy face from me?" (Ps. 13:1). But we must also say, "I have trusted in thy mercy" (v. 5). The Lord Jesus teaches us that our confidence in prayer is confidence in the Father's goodness to his children (Matt. 7:9–11). The Lord teaches us to address him as "thou that hearest prayer" (Ps. 65:2). Thomas Goodwin said that God cherishes the prayers of his people: "They are all before him, and he sets them in his view, as we do letters of friends, which we stick in our windows, that we remember to answer them, or lay them not out of our bosoms, that we might be sure not to forget them."[49] Therefore, it is

---

46. Manton, *Several Sermons upon the CXIX Psalm*, in *Works*, 6:242.

47. See D. A. Carson, *A Call to Spiritual Reformation: Priorities from Paul and His Prayers* (Grand Rapids, MI: Baker, 1992). A second edition was issued as *Praying with Paul* (Grand Rapids, MI: Baker Academic, 2014).

48. Athanasius, *Letter to Marcellinus*, secs. 10–12, in *The Life of Anthony and the Letter to Marcellinus*, trans. Robert C. Gregg, pref. William A. Clebsch, The Classics of Western Spirituality (New York: Paulist Press, 1980), 108–11.

49. Goodwin, *The Return of Prayers*, in *Works*, 3:361.

essential that we fight against doubt: "Lord, I believe; help thou mine unbelief" (Mark 9:24). Do not think that God hears other believers' prayers but not yours, which is to accuse him of favoritism. Allow the fiery trial of unanswered prayer to refine your faith so that you may learn a deeper trust and fuller submission to your faithful God. When God's ways seem to contradict his Word, then, as Calvin said, we are "permitted to pour into His bosom the difficulties which torment us, in order that He may loosen the knots which we cannot untie."[50]

Tenth, *take hold of the triune God in prayer*. It is impossible to solve prayerless praying by our own strength. Yet God does not call us to passively wait for him to give us some experience before we pray, but to work out our salvation because he is working in us (Phil. 2:12–13). Prayer demands an energetic exercise of faith. David says, "Unto thee, O Lord, do I lift up my soul" (Ps. 25:1). God dwells in our prayers most when our minds most dwell on God (cf. 22:3). Calvin said that "communion of men with God" is the rich and heavenly benefit of prayer. The Reformer wrote, "Words fail to explain how necessary prayer is, and in how many ways the exercise of prayer is profitable. . . . In short, it is by prayer that we call him to reveal himself as wholly present to us."[51] Wrestle with God until he blesses you (Gen. 32:24–30).

Therefore, when you pray, meditate on the gospel of God. Consider how the Father, the Son, and the Holy Spirit draw sinners to God. Paul says, "For through him [Christ Jesus] we both have access by one Spirit unto the Father" (Eph. 2:18). Lean heavily on the Spirit to lead you into fellowship with God, trust in Christ to make your prayers effectual by his grace, and rest in the love of the Father who sent both Son and Spirit (2 Cor. 13:14). Do not use God merely to gain something you want, but seek him so you may glorify and enjoy him (1 Chron. 16:10–11). If prayer is the hand of faith grasping after the object of love's desire, then use your prayers to grasp God himself—and you will discover to your delight that he is grasping you.

May no one who reads this book ultimately fall under the verdict of Isaiah 64:7: "There is none that calleth upon thy name, that stirreth up himself to take hold of thee." Instead, may God give us all grace to take hold of him by praying in our prayers.

---

50. Calvin, *Commentaries*, on Gen. 18:25.
51. Calvin, *Institutes*, 3.20.2.

The Hope of Glorification

As a Godward expression of desire, prayer is closely allied with hope, the anticipation that God will satisfy our desires through Christ. Godefridus Udemans said, "Hope is also active in prayer. Prayer is a means to strengthen hope and to receive the things hoped for, for hope gives birth to desire, and desire produces prayer."[52] Augustine said that the hope of believers is summarized in petitions of the Lord's Prayer for eternal and temporal blessings.[53] The great object of Christ's prayer is "that they also, whom thou hast given me, be with me where I am; that they may behold my glory" (John 17:24). So, too, the highest petition of God's child is "Come, Lord Jesus" (Rev. 22:20).

Therefore, the conclusion of our treatment of the Holy Spirit and the experience of salvation coincides with the last element in the *ordo salutis*—namely, glorification. The doctrine of glorification includes the entrance of the believing soul into Christ's presence and a state of perfect holiness at death, the resurrection from the dead, the rewards of grace given at judgment day, and the eternal rest and bliss of the saints in the new heaven and new earth. The doctrine of glorification is a point at which soteriology overlaps with eschatology, so we will reserve our treatment of it for the last volume of our systematic theology.[54] However, we will end our study of salvation with a meditation on the grace of hope and how it shapes the Christian life.

The Grace of Christian Hope

In general, hope is a human expectation of some future good.[55] William Plumer said, "Hope consists of desire and expectation."[56] The Holy Scriptures employ various terms for hope. The three major Hebrew word groups for hope (from the verbs *qavah*, *yakhal*, and *shabar*) all refer to waiting with expectation for something desirable.[57] Their sense is well represented

52. Udemans, *The Practice of Faith, Hope, and Love*, 119.
53. Augustine, *Enchiridion*, chaps. 114–15, in *NPNF*[1], 3:274.
54. See the locus of eschatology in *RST*, vol. 4 (forthcoming).
55. See Jer. 8:15; 14:19; Acts 24:26; 27:20; 1 Cor. 9:10.
56. Plumer, *Vital Godliness*, 307.
57. The first verb (*qavah*, Ps. 130:5) appears forty-seven times in the Old Testament. See its cognate nouns *tiqvah* (Pss. 9:18; 62:5; 71:5; Jer. 29:11) and *miqveh* (Jer. 14:8; 17:13; 50:7). The second verb (*yakhal*, Ps. 130:5, 7) appears forty-one times. See its cognate noun *tokhelet* (Ps. 39:7; Prov. 10:28; 11:1; 13:12) and the related word *yakhil* (Lam. 3:26). The third verb (*shabar*), used eight times, means to look (*qal*, Neh. 2:13, 15) and, hence (in the *piel*), to wait with hope and expectation (Pss. 104:27; 119:166; 145:15; Isa. 38:18). See its cognate noun *sheber* (Pss. 119:116; 146:5).

in Psalm 130:5–7: "I wait [*qavah*] for the LORD, my soul doth wait [*qavah*], and in his word do I hope [*yakhal*]. My soul waiteth for the Lord more than they that watch for the morning: I say, more than they that watch for the morning. Let Israel hope [*yakhal*] in the LORD: for with the LORD there is mercy, and with him is plenteous redemption"; and in Psalm 145:15: "The eyes of all wait [*shabar*] upon thee; and thou givest them their meat in due season." In the New Testament, "hope" consistently translates one Greek verb (*elpizō*, thirty-one times) and the related noun (*elpis*, fifty-four times). This verb is also rendered "trust" in the King James Version, perhaps influenced by the Septuagint.[58] The noun "hope" (*elpis*) can refer to objective hope ("the hope which is laid up for you in heaven," Col. 1:5) or subjective hope in the heart ("that your faith and hope might be in God," 1 Pet. 1:21).

Christian hope is a saving grace (2 Thess. 2:16) produced by the new birth by the power of the risen Christ (1 Pet. 1:3, 21). People outside of God's covenantal promise have "no hope" (Eph. 2:12), but all believers in Christ share "one hope" (4:4). Waiting on the Lord is a defining mark of the people whom God is saving and will bring to the inheritance (Pss. 25:3, 5, 21; 37:9, 34). Isaac Ambrose said, "If we long for his coming, then will he come to satisfy our longings."[59]

The Scriptures command, "Hope in God" (Ps. 43:5). The Lord is called "the hope of Israel" (Jer. 14:8). John Gill said, "It is the abundance of his mercy, grace, and goodness, which lays a solid foundation for hope in him, and encourages to it" (cf. Ps. 130:7).[60] Though believers may hope to receive many good things from God, the ultimate object of Christian hope is the living God himself (1 Tim. 4:10; 5:5; 6:17) and eternal life with him (Titus 1:2; 3:7). Though most people would say they want to go to heaven, Calvin noted, "If you examine the plans, the efforts, the deeds, of anyone, there you will find nothing else but earth."[61] Hence, the world lives for vanity and vapor (Eccles. 1:2; James 4:14), the quickly passing-away objects of its lusts (1 John 2:16–17). By contrast, the "blessed hope" of the church is "the appearing of the glory of our great God and Savior Jesus Christ" (Titus 2:13 ESV). Such hope reflects the sanctification of the

58. The LXX ordinarily used *elpizō* to translate "trust" (*batakh*, forty-seven times). It also used the same Greek word group to translate many instances of the Hebrew words for hope, as well as for "seek refuge" (*khasah*). *TDNT*, 2:521–22.

59. Ambrose, *Looking unto Jesus*, 670–71. In that context, he cited Rom. 8:22–23; 1 Cor. 1:7; Phil. 3:20; 2 Tim. 4:8; Heb. 9:28; 2 Pet. 3:12.

60. Gill, *Body of Divinity*, 754.

61. Calvin, *Institutes*, 3.9.1.

heart's deepest motives to desire God supremely (Isa. 26:8). "The LORD is my portion, saith my soul; therefore will I hope in him" (Lam. 3:24).

Hope, subjectively considered, is a complex of saving graces, for it has an organic and symbiotic relation to faith and love.[62] In the exercise of hope, we act with both future-oriented faith in God and love for God, desiring to glorify and enjoy him completely and eternally. Such hope issues in peace and joy that mingle with present sorrows and strengthen the believer.

Hope is inseparable from faith: "Faith is the substance of things hoped for, the evidence of things not seen" (Heb. 11:1). Calvin said, "Faith believes God to be truthful; hope waits for him to show his truth at the right occasion. Faith believes God to be our Father; hope waits for him ever to act as such toward us. Faith believes eternal life has been given us; hope waits for it sometime to be revealed."[63] Paul says that, having received justification and grace by faith in Christ, we "rejoice in hope of the glory of God" (Rom. 5:1–2). This hope in God increases as we pass through various trials and grow in character (vv. 3–4). Hope in the Lord cannot end in shame, for God has already proven his love in Christ and poured it out by his Spirit (vv. 5–8), and he will most certainly give full salvation to those whom he has already reconciled to himself by Christ's blood (vv. 9–11).

By hope, we reach in faith for what we do not yet fully possess: "Now hope that is seen is not hope. For who hopes for what he sees? But if we hope for what we do not see, we wait for it with patience" (Rom. 8:24–25 ESV). Thus, our hope is full of holy groaning (vv. 22–23). As Augustine said, God uses the stress of waiting to stretch out our desires and give us a greater capacity to enjoy him while emptying us of desires for this world so that he may fill us to the utmost with himself.[64] The Holy Spirit leads us in this painful preparation for glory by igniting hopeful desires that flame forth in prayer. Believers have received "the Spirit of adoption, whereby we cry, Abba, Father" (v. 15). God's children are bound by the Spirit to Christ so "that we suffer with him" and will "be also glorified together" with him (v. 17). All creation waits for "the glorious liberty of the children of God" (v. 21). Our cries to the Father express how we "groan within ourselves, waiting for the adoption, . . . the redemption of our body" (v. 23). Thus,

62. Note the mention of faith, hope, and love together in 1 Cor. 13:13; Gal. 5:5–6; Eph. 1:15–18; 4:2–6; Col. 1:4–5; 1 Thess. 1:3; 5:8; Heb. 6:10–12; 1 Pet. 1:21–22.

63. Calvin's Catechism of 1537 and 1538 (Art. 21), in *Reformed Confessions*, 1:430.

64. Augustine, *Homilies on 1 John*, 4.6, in *NPNF*[1], 7:485.

the Spirit who intercedes within us with unutterable groanings (v. 27) is the Spirit of resurrection (v. 11), projecting into our prayerful longings the hope of our glorification with Christ. We desire the grace and the glory that this world cannot supply because we have "the firstfruits of the Spirit" (v. 23).[65]

However, hope already brings into the present an anticipation of the joys promised for the future so that we are "rejoicing in hope; patient in tribulation; continuing instant in prayer" (Rom. 12:12). Paul says, "Now the God of hope fill you with all joy and peace in believing, that ye may abound in hope, through the power of the Holy Ghost" (15:13). Through hope, the Holy Spirit brings the joy and peace of God's kingdom into our hearts here and now (14:17). William Ames went so far as to say that hope is the beginning of *glorification*: the "sense of the love of God shining forth in Christ . . . [and] undoubting hope and expectation of the enjoyment of all those good things which God has prepared for his own," resulting in "consolation, peace, and unspeakable joy . . . the first fruits of glory."[66]

The potent joy of hope arises from faith working through love, for it is love that delights in God's glory, kingdom, and righteousness so much that it waits patiently to obtain them. Paul says that love "beareth all things, believeth all things, hopeth all things, endureth all things" (1 Cor. 13:7). Ambrose said, "Hope is of good things to come; hope is an act of the will extending itself towards that which it loves as future."[67] Therefore, Christian hope is only as strong as a Christian's love for God, for how can we hope for that which we do not desire?

The Experiential Exercise of Christian Hope

God's means of producing hope is his Word: "For whatsoever things were written aforetime were written for our learning, that we through patience and comfort of the scriptures might have hope" (Rom. 15:4). The believer can confess, "I hope in thy Word" (cf. Ps. 119:49, 74, 81, 114, 147). The Bible is the book of hope. Hope rests in God's revelation of his faithful love (*khesed*) and his "holy name," instilling confidence that he will save those who fear him (Pss. 33:18–22; 147:11).[68] In particular, God creates hope by the gospel of Christ, for "in him will the Gentiles hope" (Rom.

65. On the firstfruits of the Spirit, see chap. 34.
66. Ames, *The Marrow of Theology*, 1.30.8, 10, 21 (172–73).
67. Ambrose, *Looking unto Jesus*, 669.
68. On God's faithful love (*khesed*), sometimes translated as "mercy," see *RST*, 1:788.

15:12 ESV). Hope depends on the confidence that the God who made these promises cannot lie (Titus 1:2; Heb. 6:18). Whereas people commonly say, "I hope so" as a mere wish, biblical hope in God is a solid "expectation" with "great certainty" obtained "by faith" in God's true Word, as Ames said.[69] Plumer wrote, "True religious hope is . . . no vain persuasion, no idle dream, but a sure expectation. It rests upon an immovable foundation, God's unchanging word and oath and covenant."[70] Therefore, seek to grow in your hope by reading the Holy Scriptures and receiving its revelations of unseen, eternal realities as absolute truth. Learn to live by what you cannot see simply because God tells you it is so and he is faithful.

We nourish hope by meditating on the heavenly glory of Christ. Paul says, "If ye then be risen with Christ, seek those things which are above, where Christ sitteth on the right hand of God. Set your affection on things above, not on things on the earth" (Col. 3:1–2). John Owen said, "The especial object of hope is eternal glory (Col. 1:27; Rom. 5:2). The peculiar use of it is to support, comfort, and refresh the soul, in all trials, under all weariness and despondencies, with a firm expectation of a speedy entrance into that glory, with an earnest desire after it. Wherefore, unless we acquaint ourselves, by continual meditation, with the reality and nature of this glory, it is impossible it should be the object of a vigorous, active hope." He added that Christians are like people who have begun a long sea voyage to a land where they have been promised "a place of rest and an inheritance"; when "their voyage proves long and wearisome, their difficulties many, and their dangers great, . . . they have nothing to relieve and encourage themselves with but the hope and expectation of the country whither they are going."[71]

God creates hope in Christ by the power of the Holy Spirit (Rom. 15:13). Hope is not merely a doctrine we affirm about the future. Hope flows from vital union with Christ by the indwelling Spirit, who transforms us into Christ's image: "Christ in you, the hope of glory" (Col. 1:27). The Christ who dwells in us by his Spirit, sharing his resurrection life with us now, is the Christ who sits at God's right hand, securing our place in the kingdom of glory, and who one day will appear and raise us up by the same Spirit (Rom. 8:9–11; Col. 3:1–4).

69. Ames, *The Marrow of Theology*, 2.6.8–9 (247).
70. Plumer, *Vital Godliness*, 310.
71. Owen, *Phronēma tou Pneumatos, or, the Grace and Duty of Being Spiritually Minded*, in *Works*, 7:322.

Hope in Christ has many sanctifying effects on the believer's life. It equips the Christian to submit to proper authority while enduring injustice (1 Pet. 3:5 ESV) so that in the imitation of Christ the believer entrusts himself to the God "who judges justly" (2:23 ESV). "Say not thou, I will recompense evil; but wait on the LORD, and he shall save thee" (Prov. 20:22). Hope adds a winsome beauty to Christian character, making opportunities for us to tell others why we have this holy optimism (1 Pet. 3:15).

Springing from faith and wedded to love, Christian hope embraces our brothers and sisters with the confidence that God will keep his promises to them (2 Cor. 1:7, 13; 1 Thess. 2:19). Learning to view other Christians as "heirs together [with us] of the grace of life" motivates us to treat them with honor and affection (1 Pet. 3:7). Hope gives boldness for witness and ministry (3:12), for our covenant God has promised to give life-giving, soul-transforming power to his Word by the Holy Spirit (vv. 6, 17–18).

Hope drives us to prayer, especially prayer for God's kingdom to come. The more our prayers are formed by an awareness that this world is passing away and our inheritance lies with Christ in glory, the more our prayers will focus on his kingdom. We see this in the life of Calvin, who found himself unable to complete his lectures on the prophecy of Ezekiel because of his failing health and concluded his commentary with this prayer:

> Grant, Almighty God, since we have already entered in hope upon the threshold of our eternal inheritance, and know that there is a certain mansion for us in heaven after Christ has been received there, who is our head, and the first-fruits of our salvation: Grant, I say, that we may proceed more and more in the course of thy holy calling until at length we reach the goal, and so enjoy that eternal glory of which thou affordest us a taste in this world, by the same Christ our Lord. Amen.[72]

Hope has a universal purifying influence, for it anticipates with joy the coming of the Pure One: "When he shall appear, we shall be like him; for we shall see him as he is. And every man that hath this hope in him purifieth himself, even as he is pure" (1 John 3:2–3). Wilhelmus à Brakel said, "The result of hope is holy industry. Hope neither causes us to be inactive nor will it tolerate occupation with other things. . . . The end in view causes us to be active and to take the means in hand."[73] Desiring to be like Christ and

72. Calvin, *Commentaries*, on Ezek. 20:44.
73. Brakel, *The Christian's Reasonable Service*, 3:324.

believing that God will bring them to this goal in perfection, believers "exercise" themselves "unto godliness" (1 Tim. 4:7). They "by patient continuance in well doing seek for glory and honour and immortality" (Rom. 2:7).

Hope empowers martyrs to persevere courageously unto death for the glory of Christ (Phil. 1:20). Christian hope does not make us immune from grief, but it transforms how we grieve (1 Thess. 4:13). Waiting on God may reduce us over time to great weariness (Ps. 69:3). By the fortitude of hope, the saints wage war against inner despondency and overcome despair (42:5, 11; 43:5). Together with faith and love, hope is an indispensable part of the spiritual armor that believers must wear to overcome this world and live as those prepared for the day of the Lord (1 Thess. 5:8).

In all circumstances, hope walks hand in hand with "patience" (*hypomonē*) or the exercise of endurance (*hypomenō*).[74] Hope brings a quiet, humble contentment in God, so that the believer is like a weaned child resting in his mother's arms (Psalm 131). This is because hope teaches us to quietly submit to God's will while we wait on him: "Be still before the Lord and wait patiently for him" (37:7 ESV); "For God alone my soul waits in silence; from him comes my salvation" (62:1 ESV).[75] Ames said, "One fruit of this patience is the silence in which we rest on the will of God and repress all carnal thoughts that stir us up to lose patience or struggle against it."[76]

The saints must persevere in hope to the end so that they will stand without reproach before God (Col. 1:22–23; Heb. 3:6; 6:11). Peter exhorts, "Wherefore gird up the loins of your mind [a figure of speech for being prepared for action], be sober, and hope to the end for the grace that is to be brought unto you at the revelation of Jesus Christ" (1 Pet. 1:13). However, believers not only wait on the Lord for complete salvation but also for present strength to endure to the end (Isa. 40:31): "Wait on the Lord: be of good courage, and he shall strengthen thine heart: wait, I say, on the Lord" (Ps. 27:14).

What amazing blessings come to us through the grace of hope! Owen said, "Hope is a glorious grace. . . . By it we are purified, sanctified, saved."[77] Plumer said, "Genuine Christian hope . . . makes us patient in tribulation, . . . gives courage in facing danger, and fortitude in enduring

---

74. Rom. 5:4; 8:25; 12:12; 15:4; 1 Cor. 13:7; 1 Thess. 1:3. On patience or longsuffering, see chap. 36.

75. The words *damam* (Ps. 37:7) and *dumiyah* (62:1) refer to quietness (4:4; 22:2; 30:12; 31:17; 39:2; 62:5; 131:2). Note the marginal readings in Pss. 37:7; 62:1 KJV.

76. Ames, *The Marrow of Theology*, 2.6.18 (248).

77. Owen, *Phronēma tou Pneumatos*, in *Works*, 7:321.

pain, . . . [is] the great animating principle in labor, . . . is the great nourisher of Christian joy," and by it believers through the ages have "disarmed death of all his terrors."[78]

Therefore, we conclude our study of the Holy Spirit and salvation with hope. Few graces exemplify the power and presence of the Holy Spirit in our lives as much as an indomitable hope, undaunted by the hatred of the wicked and nourished and sweetened by love for God and our neighbors. Hope energizes the Christian life and motivates Christian ministry. Yet hope also humbles us, reminding us God may not give us today what we need for tomorrow but make us wait each day for his supply. Hope weans us from this world and sharpens our appetite for the glory of God. Hope is the realistic optimism of faith, resting on Christ's finished work and looking to him as our all in all now and forever. "Therefore, my beloved brethren, be ye stedfast, unmoveable, always abounding in the work of the Lord, forasmuch as ye know that your labour is not in vain in the Lord" (1 Cor. 15:58).

Thank God for the Holy Spirit's work to produce such saving, persevering, and certain hope within us. *Soli Deo gloria*!

Sing to the Lord

Calling on the Lord, Waiting on the Lord

From out the depths I cry, O Lord, to Thee;
Lord, hear my call;
I love Thee, Lord, for Thou dost heed my plea,
Forgiving all;
If Thou shouldst mark our sins, who then could stand?
But grace and mercy dwell at Thy right hand.

I wait for God, the Lord, and on His word
My hope relies;
My soul still waits and looks unto the Lord
Till light arise;
I look for Him to drive away my night,
Yea, more than watchmen look for morning light.

Hope in the Lord, ye waiting saints, and He
Will well provide,
For mercy and redemption full and free

78. Plumer, *Vital Godliness*, 316–20.

With Him abide;
From sin and evil, mighty though they seem,
His arm almighty will His saints redeem.

Psalm 130
Tune: Sandon
The Psalter, No. 362
Trinity Hymnal—Baptist Edition, No. 463

Questions for Meditation or Discussion

1. What are the seven elements in the authors' description of Christian prayer? Provide a Scripture reference to support each of them.
2. What do the authors mean by "prayerless praying"? What are some signs of it?
3. What is the value of prayer when we do not receive a speedy and favorable answer?
4. Why is it crucial to confess our sins and keep a fresh sense of being washed by the blood of Christ in order to have a vibrant prayer life?
5. How can a Christian "pray without ceasing" (1 Thess. 5:17)?
6. Describe in specifics how you are regularly interceding in prayer for other people. What are some ways you could pray for more people or groups, and pray better?
7. What does it mean to "read the Bible for prayer and pray the Bible to God"?
8. How can a believer "take hold" of God and commune with him in prayer?
9. What is the grace of hope? How does it relate to faith and love?
10. How would you describe the influence of hope on your life? What difference would it make if your hope were to increase tenfold? How might you seek to grow in hope?

Questions for Deeper Reflection

11. What is a specific way that a Christian might become imbalanced and fail to use biblical variety in prayer? How would that imbalance affect his whole spiritual life?
12. Write a fifteen-minute devotional on the topic "The Power of Christian Hope: Its Source and Effects."

Bibliography

Works Cited in This Volume

For abbreviations such as *ANF*, *LW*, etc.,
see the list in the front matter.

* Denotes a frequently consulted work or series.

Creeds and Confessions

Acta et Documenta Synodi Nationalis Dordrechtanae (1618–1619). Vol. 1, *Acta of the Synod of Dordt (1618–1619)*. Edited by Donald Sinnema, Christian Moser, and Herman J. Selderhuis. Göttingen: Vandenhoeck & Ruprecht, 2015.

The Arminian Confession of 1621. Translated and edited by Mark A. Ellis. Princeton Theological Monograph Series. Eugene, OR: Pickwick, 2005.

The Book of Concord: The Confessions of the Evangelical Lutheran Church. Edited by Robert Kolb and Timothy J. Wengert. Translated by Charles Arand, Eric Gritch, Robert Kolb, William Russell, James Schaaf, Jane Strohl, and Timothy J. Wengert. Minneapolis: Fortress, 2000.

Catechism of the Catholic Church. New York: Doubleday, 1994.

The Creeds of Christendom. Edited by Philip Schaff. Revised by David S. Schaff. 3 vols. Grand Rapids, MI: Baker, 1983.

A Declaration of Some of the Fundamental Principles of Christian Truth, as Held by the Religious Society of Friends; Adopted by Friends' Conference Held in Richmond, Indiana, U.S.A. Richmond, IN: Nicholson & Bro., 1887.

The Heidelberg Catechism, in German, Latin, and English: With an Historical Introduction. Edited by E. V. Gerhart, John W. Nevin, Henry Harbaugh, John S. Kessler, Daniel Zacharias, William Heyser, Rudolph K. Kelker, and Lewis H. Steiner. New York: Charles Scribner, 1863.

* *Reformed Confessions of the 16th and 17th Centuries in English Translation: 1523–1693*. Compiled by James T. Dennison Jr. 4 vols. Grand Rapids, MI: Reformation Heritage Books, 2008–2014.

* *The Three Forms of Unity*. Edited and introduced by Joel R. Beeke. Birmingham, AL: Solid Ground, 2010.

Psalms and Hymns

Latin Hymns, with English Notes. Edited by F. A. March. New York: Harper & Brothers, 1896.

* *The Psalter, with Doctrinal Standards, Liturgy, Church Order, and Added Chorale Section*. Preface by Joel R. Beeke and Ray B. Lanning. 1965. Reprint, Grand Rapids, MI: Eerdmans for Reformation Heritage Books, 2003.

A Selection of Hymns for Public Worship. Compiled by William Gadsby. Harpenden, England: Gospel Standard Strict Baptist Trust, 1978.

* *Trinity Hymnal—Baptist Edition*. Revised by David Merck. Suwanee, GA: Great Commission Publications, 1995.

The United Methodist Hymnal. Nashville: The United Methodist Publishing House, 1989.

Annotated Sacred and Apocryphal Writings

Apocrypha and Pseudepigrapha of the Old Testament in English. Edited by R. H. Charles. 2 vols. Oxford: Clarendon, 1913.

The Apocryphal New Testament: Being the Apocryphal Gospels, Acts, Epistles, and Apocalypses. Edited by Montague R. James. Rev. ed. Oxford: Oxford University Press, 1953.

(Douay-Rheims New Testament) *The New Testament of Jesus Christ, Translated Faithfully into English out of the Authentical Latin . . . in the English College of Rhemes*. Rhemes (Rheims or Reims), France: John Fogney, 1582.

The Dutch Annotations upon the Whole Bible. Translated by Theodore Haak. London: by Henry Hills, for John Rothwell, Joshua Kirton, and Richard Tomlins, 1657.

The Orthodox Study Bible: New Testament and Psalms. Edited by Joseph Allen, Michel Najim, Jack Norman Sparks, and Theodore Stylianopoulos. Nashville: Thomas Nelson, 1993.

The Reformation Heritage KJV Study Bible. Edited by Joel R. Beeke, Michael P. V. Barrett, Gerald M. Bilkes, and Paul M. Smalley. Grand Rapids, MI: Reformation Heritage Books, 2014.

Language Resources

Blass, F., and A. Debrunner. *A Greek Grammar of the New Testament and Other Early Christian Literature*. Translated and edited by Robert W. Funk. Chicago: The University of Chicago Press, 1961.

Bretzke, James T. *Consecrated Phrases: A Latin Theological Dictionary; Latin Expressions Commonly Found in Theological Writings*. 3rd ed. Collegeville, MN: Liturgical Press, 2013.

Brown, Francis, Samuel Rolles Driver, and Charles Augustus Briggs. *The Enhanced Brown-Driver-Briggs Hebrew and English Lexicon*. Oxford: Clarendon, 1977.

Kittel, Gerhard, Geoffrey W. Bromiley, and Gerhard Friedrich, eds. *Theological Dictionary of the New Testament*. 10 vols. Grand Rapids, MI: Eerdmans, 1964.

Lampe, G. W. H., ed. *A Patristic Greek Lexicon*. Oxford: Oxford University Press, 1961.

Lewis, Charlton T., and Charles Short, eds. *A New Latin Dictionary*. New York: Harper & Brothers; Oxford: Clarendon, 1879.

Liddell, Henry George, and Robert Scott. *A Greek-English Lexicon*. Revised by Henry Stuart Jones and Roderick McKenzie. Oxford: Oxford University Press, 1996.

Merriam-Webster's Collegiate Dictionary. 11th ed. Springfield, MA: Merriam-Webster, 2003.

Muller, Richard A. *Dictionary of Latin and Greek Theological Terms: Drawn Principally from Protestant Scholastic Theology*. 2nd ed. Grand Rapids, MI: Baker Academic, 2017.

Silva, Moisés, ed. *The New International Dictionary of New Testament Theology and Exegesis*. 5 vols. Grand Rapids, MI: Zondervan, 2014.

VanGemeren, Willem A., ed. *The New International Dictionary of Old Testament Theology and Exegesis*. 5 vols. Grand Rapids, MI: Zondervan, 1997.

Wallace, Daniel B. *Greek Grammar beyond the Basics: An Exegetical Syntax of the New Testament*. Grand Rapids, MI: Zondervan, 1996.

Theological, Historical, Philosophical, and General Works

Adam, Thomas. *Private Thoughts on Religion*. Glasgow: Chalmers and Collins, 1824.

Akin, Daniel L. *1, 2, 3 John*. The New American Commentary 38. Nashville: Broadman & Holman, 2001.

Alcorn, Randy. *Prolife Answers to Prochoice Arguments*. 2nd ed. Colorado Springs, CO: Multnomah, 2000.

Alexander, Archibald. *Thoughts on Religious Experience*. Reprint, Edinburgh: Banner of Truth, 1967.

Alexander, Donald L., ed. *Christian Spirituality: Five Views of Sanctification*. Downers Grove, IL: InterVarsity Press, 1988.

Allen, David L. *Hebrews*. The New American Commentary 35. Nashville: Broadman & Holman, 2010.

Allen, David L., and Steve W. Lemke, eds. *Whosoever Will: A Biblical-Theological Critique of Five-Point Calvinism*. Nashville: Broadman & Holman, 2010.

Allen, John L., Jr. *Pope Benedict XVI: A Biography of Joseph Ratzinger*. London: Continuum, 2000.

Allen, Leslie C. *Psalms 101–50, Revised*. Word Biblical Commentary. Nashville: Thomas Nelson, 2002.

Allen, Willoughby C. *A Critical and Exegetical Commentary on the Gospel according to St Matthew*. 3rd ed. Edinburgh: T&T Clark, 1907.

Ambrose, Isaac. *Looking unto Jesus: A View of the Everlasting Gospel; or, The Soul's Eyeing of Jesus, as Carrying on the Great Work of Man's Salvation, from First to Last*. Philadelphia: J. B. Lippinscott & Co., 1856.

* Ames, William. *The Marrow of Theology*. Translated by John D. Eusden. Grand Rapids, MI: Baker, 1968.

———. *A Sketch of the Christian's Catechism*. Translated by Todd M. Rester. Classic Reformed Theology 1. Grand Rapids, MI: Reformation Heritage Books, 2008.

Amos, N. Scott. *Bucer, Ephesians and Biblical Humanism: The Exegete as Theologian*. Studies in Early Modern Religious Tradition, Culture and Society. New York: Springer, 2015.

Anonymous [Dutch Reformed Divines]. *The Dutch Annotations upon the Whole Bible*. Translated by Theodore Haak. London: by Henry Hills, for John Rothwell, Joshua Kirton, and Richard Tomlins, 1657.

Anonymous [Westminster Divines]. *Annotations upon All the Books of the Old and New Testament*. London: Evan Tyler, 1657.

Anselm. *The Prayers and Meditations of St. Anselm*. Translated by Benedicta Ward. Harmondsworth, England: Penguin, 1973.

Aquinas, Thomas. *Catena Aurea: Commentary on the Four Gospels, Collected out of the Works of the Fathers*. 4 vols. in 7. Oxford: John Henry Parker, 1841–1845.

———. *Commentary on the Letter of Saint Paul to the Hebrews*. Edited by John Mortensen and Enrique Alarcón. Translated by Fabian R. Larcher.

Lander, WY: The Aquinas Institute for the Study of Sacred Doctrine, 2012.

* ———. *Summa Theologica*. Translated by the Fathers of the English Dominican Province. 22 vols. London: R. & T. Washbourne, 1914.

Arminius, Jacob. *The Works of James Arminius*. Translated by James Nichols and William Nichols. 3 vols. Grand Rapids, MI: Baker, 1991.

Ascol, Thomas K., and Nathan A. Finn, eds. *Ministry by His Grace and for His Glory: Essays in Honor of Thomas J. Nettles*. Cape Coral, FL: Founders, 2011.

Athanasius. *The Letters of Saint Athanasius concerning the Holy Spirit*. Translated and edited by C. R. B. Shapland. London: Epworth, 1951.

———. *The Life of Anthony and the Letter to Marcellinus*. Translated by Robert C. Gregg. Preface by William A. Clebsch. The Classics of Western Spirituality. New York: Paulist Press, 1980.

Auber, Harriet. *The Spirit of the Psalms, or, a Compressed Version of Select Portions of the Psalms of David, Adapted to Christian Worship*. London: for T. Cadell and C. & J. Rivington, 1829.

Augustine. *The Enchiridion on Faith, Hope, and Love*. Washington, DC: Regnery, 1996.

———. *Expositions on the Book of Psalms*. 6 vols. Oxford: John Henry Parker; London: F. and J. Rivington, 1847.

———. *The Works of Saint Augustine: A Translation for the 21st Century*. 42 vols. Hyde Park, NY: New City, 1995–2015.

Balke, W., C. Graafland, and H. Harkema, eds. *Wegen en Gestalten in het Gereformeerd Protestantisme*. Amsterdam: Ton Bolland, 1976.

Ballor, Jordan J., David S. Sytsma, and Jason Zuidema, eds. *Church and School in Early Modern Protestantism: Studies in Honor of Richard A. Muller on the Maturation of a Theological Tradition*. Studies in the History of Christian Traditions. Leiden: Brill, 2013.

Barabas, Steven. *So Great Salvation: The History and Message of the Keswick Conference*. Chicago: Fleming H. Revell, 1952.

Barker, Kenneth L. *Micah, Nahum, Habakkuk, Zephaniah*. The New American Commentary 20. Nashville: Broadman & Holman, 1999.

Barrett, Matthew, ed. *The Doctrine on Which the Church Stands or Falls: Justification in Biblical, Theological, Historical, and Pastoral Perspectives*. Wheaton, IL: Crossway, 2019.

———, ed. *Reformation Theology: A Systematic Summary*. Wheaton, IL: Crossway, 2017.

———. *Salvation by Grace: The Case for Effectual Calling and Regeneration.* Phillipsburg, NJ: P&R, 2013.

Barrett, Michael P. V. *Complete in Him: A Guide to Understanding and Enjoying the Gospel.* 2nd ed. Grand Rapids, MI: Reformation Heritage Books, 2017.

Barth, Karl. *Christ and Adam: Man and Humanity in Romans 5.* Translated by T. A. Smail. Eugene, OR: Wipf and Stock, 1956.

———. *Church Dogmatics.* Edited by G. W. Bromiley and T. F. Torrance. 4 vols. in 14. London: T&T Clark, 1936–1977.

———. *Dogmatics in Outline.* Translated by G. T. Thomson. New York: Harper and Row, 1959.

Baugh, S. M. *Ephesians.* Evangelical Exegetical Commentary. Bellingham, WA: Lexham Press, 2015.

* Bavinck, Herman. *Reformed Dogmatics.* Edited by John Bolt. Translated by John Vriend. 4 vols. Grand Rapids, MI: Baker Academic, 2003–2008.

———. *Reformed Ethics.* Edited by John Bolt with Jessica Joustra, Nelson D. Kloosterman, Antoine Theron, and Dirk van Keulen. 3 vols. Grand Rapids, MI: Baker Academic, 2019–.

———. *Saved by Grace: The Holy Spirit's Work in Calling and Regeneration.* Translated by Nelson D. Kloosterman. Edited by J. Mark Beach. Grand Rapids, MI: Reformation Heritage Books, 2008.

———. *The Wonderful Works of God.* Translated by Henry Zylstra. Glenside, PA: Westminster Seminary Press, 2019. Previously released as *Our Reasonable Faith.*

Baxter, Richard. *A Christian Directory.* 1846. Reprint, Morgan, PA: Soli Deo Gloria, 1996.

Baxter, Richard, Theodosia Alleine, et al. *Life and Death of the Rev Joseph Alleine . . . to which Are Added, His Christian Letters.* New York: Robert Carter, 1840.

Bayne(s), Paul. *An Entire Commentary upon the Whole Epistle of St Paul to the Ephesians.* 1866. Reprint, Stoke-on-Trent, England: Tentmaker, 2007.

Beale, G. K. "The Old Testament Background of Paul's Reference to 'the Fruit of the Spirit' in Galatians 5:22." *Bulletin for Biblical Research* 15, no. 1 (2005): 1–38.

Beardslee, John W., III, ed. and trans. *Reformed Dogmatics: Seventeenth-Century Reformed Theology through the Writings of Wollebius, Voetius, and Turretin.* Grand Rapids, MI: Baker, 1965.

Beddome, Benjamin. *A Scriptural Exposition of the Baptist Catechism.* Biographical sketch by Michael A. G. Haykin. Introduced by James Renihan. Birmingham, AL: Solid Ground, 2006.

Beeke, James W. *Bible Doctrine for Teens and Young Adults.* 3 vols. Chilliwack, BC: Timothy Christian School Publication Department, 1994.

Beeke, James W., and Joel R. Beeke. *Developing a Healthy Prayer Life: 31 Meditations on Communing with God.* Grand Rapids, MI: Reformation Heritage Books, 2010.

Beeke, Joel R. "The Age of the Spirit and Revival." *Puritan Reformed Journal* 2, no. 2 (July 2010): 32–51.

———, ed. *The Beauty and Glory of Christ.* Grand Rapids, MI: Reformation Heritage Books, 2011.

———, ed. *The Beauty and Glory of the Father.* Grand Rapids, MI: Reformation Heritage Books, 2013.

———. "Cultivating Holiness." *Reformation and Revival Journal* 4, no. 2 (Spring 1995): 81–112.

———. *The Epistles of John.* Darlington, England: Evangelical Press, 2006.

———. *A Faithful Church Member.* Darlington, England: Evangelical Press, 2011.

———. *Friends and Lovers: Cultivating Companionship and Intimacy in Marriage.* Adelphi, MD: Cruciform, 2012.

———. *Getting Back in the Race: The Cure for Backsliding.* Adelphi, MD: Cruciform, 2011.

———. *Heirs with Christ: The Puritans on Adoption.* Grand Rapids, MI: Reformation Heritage Books, 2008.

———. *Knowing and Growing in Assurance of Faith.* Fearn, Ross-shire, Scotland: Christian Focus, 2017.

———. *Living for God's Glory: An Introduction to Calvinism.* Lake Mary, FL: Reformation Trust, 2008.

———. *Parenting by God's Promises: How to Raise Children in the Covenant of Grace.* Lake Mary, FL: Reformation Trust, 2011.

———. *Puritan Reformed Spirituality: Historical, Experiential, and Practical Studies for the Whole of Life.* Darlington, England: Evangelical Press, 2020.

———. *The Quest for Full Assurance: The Legacy of Calvin and His Successors.* Edinburgh: Banner of Truth, 1999.

———. *Reformed Preaching: Proclaiming God's Word from the Heart of the Preacher to the Heart of His People.* Wheaton, IL: Crossway, 2018.

Beeke, Joel R., and Michael P. V. Barrett. *A Radical, Comprehensive Call to Holiness.* Fearn, Ross-shire, Scotland: Christian Focus, 2020.

Beeke, Joel R., and James W. Beeke. *Is Abortion Really So Bad?* Pensacola, FL: Chapel Library, 2015.

Beeke, Joel R., and Michael A. G. Haykin. *How Should We Cultivate Biblical Friendship?* Cultivating Biblical Godliness. Grand Rapids, MI: Reformation Heritage Books, 2015.

Beeke, Joel R., and Mark Jones. *A Puritan Theology: Doctrine for Life*. Grand Rapids, MI: Reformation Heritage Books, 2012.

Beeke, Joel R., and James A. La Belle. *Living Zealously*. Deepen Your Christian Life. Grand Rapids, MI: Reformation Heritage Books, 2012.

Beeke, Joel R., and Steven J. Lawson. *Root and Fruit: Harmonizing Paul and James on Justification*. Conway, AR: Free Grace Press, 2020.

Beeke, Joel R., and Brian G. Najapfour, eds. *Taking Hold of God: Reformed and Puritan Perspectives on Prayer*. Grand Rapids, MI: Reformation Heritage Books, 2011.

Beeke, Joel R., and Joseph A. Pipa, eds. *The Beauty and Glory of the Holy Spirit*. Grand Rapids, MI: Reformation Heritage Books, 2012.

Beeke, Joel R., and Paul M. Smalley. "Delighting in God: A Guide to Sabbath-keeping." *Puritan Reformed Journal* 11, no. 1 (2019): 5–24.

———. "Images of Union and Communion with Christ." *Puritan Reformed Journal* 8, no. 2 (2016): 125–36.

———. *John Bunyan and the Grace of Fearing God*. Phillipsburg, NJ: P&R, 2016.

———. *Prepared by Grace, for Grace: The Puritans on God's Ordinary Way of Leading Sinners to Christ*. Grand Rapids, MI: Reformation Heritage Books, 2013.

* ———. *Reformed Systematic Theology*. 4 vols. Wheaton, IL: Crossway, 2019–.

Beeke, Mary. *The Law of Kindness: Serving with Heart and Hands*. Grand Rapids, MI: Reformation Heritage Books, 2007.

Beilby, James K., Paul Rhodes Eddy, and Steven E. Enderlein, eds. *Justification: Five Views*. Downers Grove, IL: InterVarsity Press, 2011.

Beisner, E. Calvin. *The Auburn Avenue Theology, Pros and Cons: Debating the Federal Vision*. Fort Lauderdale, FL: Knox Theological Seminary, 2004.

Belleville, Linda. "'Born of Water and Spirit': John 3:5." *Trinity Journal* 1NS (1980): 125–41.

Benner, David G., and Peter C. Hill. *Baker Encyclopedia of Psychology and Counseling*. 2nd ed. Grand Rapids, MI: Baker, 1999.

Berkhof, Louis. *The Assurance of Faith*. Grand Rapids, MI: Eerdmans, 1939.

* ———. *Systematic Theology*. Edinburgh: Banner of Truth, 1958.

Berkouwer, G. C. *Faith and Justification*. Studies in Dogmatics. Grand Rapids, MI: Eerdmans, 1954.

Bernard of Clairvaux. *Concerning Grace and Free Will*. Translated and edited by Watkin W. Williams. London: Society for Promoting Christian Knowledge, 1920.

———. *The Life and Works of Saint Bernard, Abbot of Clairvaux*. Edited by John Mabillon. Translated by Samuel J. Eales. 4 vols. London: John Hodges, 1896.

———. *The Love of God*. Translated by Marianne Caroline and Coventry Patmore. 2nd ed. London: Burns and Oates, 1884.

Bethune, George W. *The Fruit of the Spirit*. 4th ed. New York: Board of Publication of the Reformed Protestant Dutch Church, 1859.

Bickersteth, Edward Henry. *The Holy Spirit: His Person and Work*. Reprint, Grand Rapids, MI: Kregel, 1959.

Bilkes, Gerald M. *Mercy Revealed: A Cross-Centered Look at Christ's Miracles*. Grand Rapids, MI: Reformation Heritage Books, 2015.

Billings, J. Todd. *Union with Christ: Framing Theology and Ministry for the Church*. Grand Rapids, MI: Baker Academic, 2011.

Blomberg, Craig L. *Interpreting the Parables*. 2nd ed. Downers Grove, IL: IVP Academic, 2012.

———. *Matthew*. The New American Commentary 22. Nashville: Broadman & Holman, 1992.

Boardman, W. E. *The Higher Christian Life*. Boston: Henry Hoyt, 1858.

Bock, Darrell L. *Acts*. Baker Exegetical Commentary on the New Testament. Grand Rapids, MI: Baker Academic, 2007.

Boda, Mark J. *'Return to Me': A Biblical Theology of Repentance*. New Studies in Biblical Theology. Downers Grove, IL: InterVarsity Press, 2015.

Boersma, Karla, and Herman J. Selderhuis, eds. *More than Luther: The Reformation and the Rise of Pluralism in Europe*. Refo500 Academic Studies 55. Göttingen: Vandenhoeck & Ruprecht, 2019.

Bolt, John. "Common Grace and the Christian Reformed Synod of Kalamazoo (1924): A Seventy-Fifth Anniversary Retrospective." *Calvin Theological Journal* 35, no. 1 (April 2000): 7–36.

Bolton, Samuel. *The True Bounds of Christian Freedom*. London: for P. S., 1656.

Bonar, Horatius. *God's Way of Holiness*. Reprint, Pensacola, FL: Mt. Zion Publications, 1994.

Booth, Abraham. *The Reign of Grace, from Its Rise to Its Consummation*. 1st American ed. New York: T. Allen, 1793.

———. *The Works of Abraham Booth*. 3 vols. London: W. Button & Son et al., 1813.

Borchert, Gerald L. *John 1–11*. The New American Commentary 25A. Nashville: Broadman & Holman, 1996.

Boston, Thomas. *Human Nature in Its Fourfold State*. Edinburgh: Banner of Truth, 1964.

———. *The Whole Works of the Late Rev. Thomas Boston*. Edited by Samuel M'Millan. Introduced by Joel R. Beeke and Randall J. Pederson. 12 vols. Reprint, Stoke-on-Trent, England: Tentmaker, 2002.

Bowler, Kate. *Blessed: A History of the American Prosperity Gospel*. Oxford: Oxford University Press, 2013.

Bownd, Nicholas. *Sabbathum Veteris et Novi Testamenti: or, The True Doctrine of the Sabbath*. Edited by Chris Coldwell. Dallas, TX: Naphtali Press; Grand Rapids, MI: Reformation Heritage Books, 2015.

Boyce, James P. *Abstract of Systematic Theology*. 1887. Reprint, Cape Coral, FL: Founders, 2006.

* Brakel, Wilhelmus à. *The Christian's Reasonable Service*. Translated by Bartel Elshout. Edited by Joel R. Beeke. 4 vols. Grand Rapids, MI: Reformation Heritage Books, 1992–1995.

Brand, Chad Owen, ed. *Perspectives on Spirit Baptism: Five Views*. Nashville: B&H Academic, 2004.

Bremer, Francis. *The Puritan Experiment: New England Society from Bradford to Edwards*. Hanover, NH: University Press of New England, 1995.

Bretschneider, Carolus Gottlieb et al., eds. *Corpus Reformatorum*. 101 vols. Halis Saxonum: Apud C. A. Schwetschke et Filium, 1834–1959.

Bridge, William. *The Works of the Rev. William Bridge*. 5 vols. London: Thomas Tegg, 1845.

Bridges, Charles. *A Commentary on Proverbs*. Edinburgh: Banner of Truth, 1968.

Bridges, Jerry. *The Joy of Fearing God*. Colorado Spring, CO: Waterbrook, 1997.

———. *The Practice of Godliness*. Colorado Springs, CO: NavPress, 1996.

Bright, Bill. *Have You Made the Wonderful Discovery of the Spirit-Filled Life?* Peachtree City, GA: Cru, 2018.

Bromiley, Geoffrey W., ed. *The International Standard Bible Encyclopedia*. Rev. ed. 4 vols. Grand Rapids, MI: Eerdmans, 1979–1988.

Brooks, James A. *Mark*. The New American Commentary 23. Nashville: Broadman & Holman, 1991.

Brooks, Thomas. *The Works of Thomas Brooks*. Edited by Alexander Grosart. 6 vols. 1864. Reprint, Edinburgh: Banner of Truth, 1980.

Brown, Colin. *Miracles and the Critical Mind*. Exeter, England: Paternoster; Grand Rapids, MI: Eerdmans, 1984.

Brown, John, of Edinburgh. *Expository Discourses on the First Epistle of the Apostle Peter*. New York: Robert Carter and Brothers, 1855.

Brown, John, of Haddington. *Questions and Answers on the Shorter Catechism*. Grand Rapids, MI: Reformation Heritage Books, 2006.

———. *Systematic Theology: A Compendious View of Natural and Revealed Religion*. Grand Rapids, MI: Reformation Heritage Books, 2015.

Brown, John, of Wamphray. *The Life of Justification Opened*. N.p.: 1695.

Brown, Raymond E., Joseph A. Fitzmyer, and Roland E. Murphy, eds. *The New Jerome Biblical Commentary*. Englewood Cliffs, NJ: Prentice Hall, 1990.

Brubaker, Leslie, and John Haldon. *Byzantium in the Iconoclast Era, c. 680–850: A History*. Cambridge: Cambridge University Press, 2011.

Bruce, Alexander B. *The Miraculous Element in the Gospels*. New York: A. C. Armstrong and Son, 1902.

Bruce, F. F. *The Epistle to the Galatians*. The New International Greek Testament Commentary. Grand Rapids, MI: Eerdmans, 1982.

———. *The Epistle to the Hebrews*. The New International Commentary on the New Testament. Grand Rapids, MI: Eerdmans, 1964.

Bruce, Robert. *The Mystery of the Lord's Supper*. Translated and edited by Thomas F. Torrance. Richmond, VA: John Knox Press, 1958.

Brunner, Emil. *Dogmatics*. Vol. 1, *The Christian Doctrine of God*. Translated by Olive Wyon. Philadelphia: The Westminster Press, 1950.

Bucer, Martin. *Praelectiones Doctiss. in Epistolam D. P. ad Ephesios . . . Anno MD.L. & LI.* Basileae: Apud Petrum Pernam, 1562.

Buchanan, James. *The Doctrine of Justification*. 1867. Reprint, Grand Rapids, MI: Baker, 1955.

———. *The Office and Work of the Holy Spirit*. London: Banner of Truth, 1966.

Budgen, Victor. *The Charismatics and the Word of God: A Biblical and Historical Perspective on the Charismatic Movement*. 2nd ed. Darlington, England: Evangelical Press, 1989.

Bullinger, Heinrich. *The Decades of Henry Bullinger*. Translated by H. I. Edited by Thomas Harding. 5 decades in 4 vols. Cambridge: Cambridge University Press, 1849–1852.

Bunyan, John. *The Works of John Bunyan*. Edited by George Offor. 3 vols. 1854. Reprint, Edinburgh: Banner of Truth, 1991.

Burgess, Anthony. *CXLV Expository Sermons upon the Whole 17th Chapter of the Gospel according to St. John*. London: Abraham Miller for Thomas Underhill, 1656.

———. *An Expository Comment, Doctrinal, Controversial, and Practical, upon the Whole First Chapter of the Second Epistle of St Paul to the Corinthians*. London: by A. M. for Abel Roper, 1661.

———. *Faith Seeking Assurance*. Edited by Joel R. Beeke. Grand Rapids, MI: Reformation Heritage Books, 2015.

———. *Spiritual Refining: The Anatomy of True and False Conversion; A Treatise of Grace and Assurance wherein are Handled the Doctrine of Assurance, The Use of Signs in Self-Examination, How True Graces may be Distinguished from Counterfeit, Several True Signs of Grace, and Many False Ones*. 1662. Reprint, Ames, IA: International Outreach, 1996.

———. *The True Doctrine of Justification Asserted and Vindicated, from the Errors of Papists, Arminians, Socinians, and More Especially Antinomians*. London: by Robert White, for Thomas Underhil, 1648.

———. *Vindiciae Legis: or, a Vindication of the Morall Law and the Covenants, from the Errours of Papists, Arminians, Socinians, and More Especially, Antinomians*. 2nd ed. London: by James Young, for Thomas Underhill, 1647.

Burgess, Stanley M. *The Holy Spirit: Eastern Christian Traditions*. Peabody, MA: Hendrickson, 1989.

———. *The Holy Spirit: Medieval Roman Catholic and Reformation Traditions (Sixth–Sixteenth Centuries)*. Peabody, MA: Hendrickson, 1997.

Burgess, Stanley M., and Eduard M. Van der Maas, eds. *The New International Dictionary of Pentecostal and Charismatic Movements*. Rev. and exp. ed. Grand Rapids, MI: Zondervan, 2002.

Burke, Trevor J. *Adopted into God's Family: Exploring a Pauline Metaphor*. New Studies in Biblical Theology. Downers Grove, IL: InterVarsity Press, 2006.

Burroughs, Jeremiah. *Moses' Self-Denial*. Edited by Don Kistler. Grand Rapids, MI: Soli Deo Gloria, 2010.

———. *The Saints' Happiness, Together with the Several Steps Leading Thereunto: Delivered in Divers Lectures on the Beatitudes*. 1867. Reprint, Ligonier, PA: Soli Deo Gloria, 1992.

Burroughs, Jeremiah, Thomas Hall, and Edward Reynolds. *An Exposition of the Prophecy of Hosea*. Edited by James Sherman. 1865. Reprint, Beaver Falls, PA: Soli Deo Gloria, 1989.

Calvin, John. *Calvin's Ecclesiastical Advice*. Translated by Mary Beaty and Benjamin W. Farley. Foreword by John Haddon Leith. Louisville, KY: Westminster/John Knox, 1991.

* ———. *Commentaries*. 22 vols. Grand Rapids, MI: Baker, 2003.

———. *Golden Booklet of the True Christian Life*. Translated by Henry J. Van Andel. Grand Rapids, MI: Baker, 1952.

* ———. *Institutes of the Christian Religion*. Edited by John T. McNeill. Translated by Ford Lewis Battles. 2 vols. Library of Christian Classics. Philadelphia: Westminster Press, 1960. Cited as *Institutes*.

———. *John Calvin's Sermons on the Ten Commandments*. Edited and translated by Benjamin W. Farley. Grand Rapids, MI: Baker, 1980.

———. *Sermons on the Acts of the Apostles: Chapters 1–7*. Translated by Rob Roy McGregor. Edinburgh: Banner of Truth, 2008.

———. *Sermons on the Beatitudes*. Translated by Robert White. Edinburgh: Banner of Truth, 2006.

———. *Sermons on Deuteronomy*. 1583. Facsimile reprint, Edinburgh: Banner of Truth, 1987.

———. *Sermons on Genesis, Chapters 1–11*. Translated by Rob Roy McGregor. Edinburgh: Banner of Truth, 2009.

———. *Tracts Relating to the Reformation*. Translated by Henry Beveridge. 3 vols. Edinburgh: Calvin Translation Society, 1844.

Cameron, Nigel M. de S., and Sinclair B. Ferguson, eds. *Pulpit & People: Essays in Honour of William Still on His 75th Birthday*. Edinburgh: Rutherford House, 1986.

Campbell, Constantine R. *Paul and Union with Christ: An Exegetical and Theological Study*. Grand Rapids, MI: Zondervan, 2012.

Carmichael, Casey B. *A Continental View: Johannes Cocceius's Federal Theology of the Sabbath*. Reformed Historical Theology 41. Göttingen: Vandenhoeck & Ruprecht, 2019.

Carpenter, John B. "Answering Eastern Orthodox Apologists Regarding Icons." *Themelios* 43, no. 3 (2018): 417–33.

Carson, D. A. *A Call to Spiritual Reformation: Priorities from Paul and His Prayers*. Grand Rapids, MI: Baker, 1992. A second edition was issued as *Praying with Paul*. Grand Rapids, MI: Baker Academic, 2014.

———. *The Gospel according to John*. The Pillar New Testament Commentary. Grand Rapids, MI: Eerdmans, 1991.

———. *Showing the Spirit: A Theological Exposition of 1 Corinthians 12–14*. Grand Rapids, MI: Baker, 1987.

———, ed. *Teach Us to Pray: Prayer in the Bible and the World*. Grand Rapids, MI: Baker, 1990.

Carson, D. A., Peter T. O'Brien, and Mark A. Seifrid, eds. *Justification and Variegated Nomism: A Fresh Appraisal of Paul and Second Temple Judaism*. 2 vols. Grand Rapids, MI: Baker Academic, 2001, 2004.

Cartledge, Mark J., ed. *Speaking in Tongues: Multi-Disciplinary Perspectives*. Studies in Pentecostal and Charismatic Issues. Eugene, OR: Wipf and Stock, 2006.

Caryl, Joseph. *An Exposition with Practicall Observations Continued upon the Thirtieth and Thirty first Chapters of the Book of Job*. London: by M. Simmons for Elisha Wallis, 1659.

Cawdrey, Daniel, and Herbert Palmer. *Sabbatum Redivivum: or the Christian Sabbath Vindicated . . . The First Part*. London: by Robert White, for Thomas Underhill, 1645.

Chadwick, Owen, trans. and ed. *Western Asceticism*. Library of Christian Classics. Philadelphia: Westminster, 1958.

Chafer, Lewis Sperry. *He That Is Spiritual*. Rev. ed. Philadelphia: Sunday School Times Co., 1919.

———. *Systematic Theology*. 8 vols. Dallas, TX: Dallas Seminary Press, 1948.

Chalmers, Thomas. *The Expulsive Power of a New Affection*. London: Hatchard and Co., 1861.

Chantry, Walter J. *Call the Sabbath a Delight*. Edinburgh: Banner of Truth, 1991.

———. *The Shadow of the Cross: Studies in Self-Denial*. Edinburgh: Banner of Truth, 1981.

———. *Signs of the Apostles: Observations on Pentecostalism Old and New*. 2nd ed. Edinburgh: Banner of Truth, 1976.

Charnock, Stephen. *The Complete Works of Stephen Charnock*. 5 vols. Edinburgh: James Nichol, 1864.

Chemnitz, Martin. *Chemnitz's Works*. 9 vols. St. Louis, MO: Concordia, 2008.

———. *Justification: The Chief Article of Christian Faith as Expounded in Loci Theologici*. Translated by J. A. O. Preus. Edited by Delpha H. Preus. St. Louis, MO: Concordia, 1985.

Chesterton, G. K. *Orthodoxy*. New York: John Lane, 1908.

Christian Reformed Church. *1924 Acts of Synod*. Translated by Henry De Mots. Grand Rapids, MI: Archives of the Christian Reformed Church, 2000.

Ciampa, Roy E., and Brian S. Rosner. *The First Letter to the Corinthians*. The Pillar New Testament Commentary. Grand Rapids, MI: Eerdmans; Nottingham, England: Apollos, 2010.

Clark, R. Scott. *Caspar Olevian and the Substance of the Covenant*. Edinburgh: Rutherford House, 2005.

———, ed. *Covenant, Justification, and Pastoral Ministry*. Phillipsburg, NJ: P&R, 2007.

———. "*Iustitia Imputata Christi*: Alien or Proper to Luther's Doctrine of Justification?" *Concordia Theological Quarterly* 70 (2006): 269–310.

Clarkson, David. *The Works of David Clarkson*. 3 vols. 1864. Reprint, Edinburgh: Banner of Truth, 1988.

Clowney, Edmund P. *The Message of 1 Peter: The Way of the Cross*. The Bible Speaks Today. Downers Grove, IL: InterVarsity Press, 1988.

Cole, Graham A. *He Who Gives Life: The Doctrine of the Holy Spirit*. Foundations of Evangelical Theology. Wheaton, IL: Crossway, 2007.

Cole, R. Alan. *Exodus*. Tyndale Old Testament Commentaries 2. Downers Grove, IL: InterVarsity Press, 1973.

Cole, Thomas. *A Discourse of Regeneration, Faith and Repentance*. London: Thomas Cockerill, 1689.

Coles, Elisha. *A Practical Discourse of God's Sovereignty*. London: Nath. Hiller, 1699.

Colliander, Tito. *Way of the Ascetics: The Ancient Tradition of Discipline and Inner Growth*. Translated by Katherine Ferré. Introduced by Kenneth Leech. Crestwood, NY: St. Vladimir's Seminary Press, 1985.

Collier, Jay T. *Debating Perseverance: The Augustinian Heritage in Post-Reformation England*. Oxford Studies in Historical Theology. Oxford: Oxford University Press, 2018.

Colquhoun, John. *Repentance*. London: Banner of Truth, 1965.

———. *Sermons, Chiefly on Doctrinal Subjects*. Edinburgh: J. & D. Collie, 1836.

Combs, William W. "Romans 12:1–2 and the Doctrine of Sanctification." *Detroit Baptist Seminary Journal* 11 (2006): 3–24.

Contarini, Gasparo. *Gasparis Contareni Cardinalis Opera*. Paris: Apud Sebastinanum Nivellium, 1571.

Cotton, John. *The Correspondence of John Cotton*. Edited by Sargent Bush Jr. Chapel Hill: University of North Carolina Press, 2001.

———. *A Practical Commentary, or an Exposition with Observations, Reasons, and Uses upon the First Epistle Generall of John*. London: by R. I. and E. C. for Thomas Parkhurst, 1656.

———. *The Way of Life, Or, Gods Way and Course, in Bringing the Soule into, and Keeping It in, and Carrying It on, in the Ways of Life and Peace*. London: by M. F. for L. Fawne and S. Gellibrand, 1641.

Cowper, William. *The Works of William Cowper: His Life, Letters, and Poems*. Edited by T. S. Grimshawe. 7th ed. London: William Tegg, 1865.

Culver, Robert Duncan. *Systematic Theology: Biblical and Historical*. Fearn, Ross-shire, Scotland: Christian Focus, 2005.

Currid, John D. *A Study Commentary on Genesis: Genesis 1:1–25:18*. EP Study Commentary. Darlington, England: Evangelical Press, 2003.

Dagg, John. *Manual of Theology*. 2 parts. Charleston, SC: Southern Baptist Publication Society, 1859.

Dallimore, Arnold. *George Whitefield: The Life and Times of the Great Evangelist of the 18th Century Revival*. 2 vols. Edinburgh: Banner of Truth, 1970, 1980.

Davenant, John. *An Exposition of the Epistle of St. Paul to the Colossians*. Translated by Josiah Allport. Geneva Series of Commentaries. 2 vols. in 1. 1831–1832. Reprint, Edinburgh: Banner of Truth, 2005.

Davidson, Ivor J. *The Birth of the Church: From Jesus to Constantine, A.D. 30–312*. The Baker History of the Church 1. Grand Rapids, MI: Baker, 2004.

Davies, Samuel. *Sermons by the Rev. Samuel Davies*. 3 vols. Philadelphia: Presbyterian Board of Publication, 1864.

Davis, John Jefferson. "The Perseverance of the Saints: A History of the Doctrine." *Journal of the Evangelical Theological Society* 34, no. 2 (June 1991): 213–28.

Dayton, Donald W. *Theological Roots of Pentecostalism*. Grand Rapids, MI: Zondervan, 1987.

* Demarest, Bruce. *The Cross and Salvation: The Doctrine of Salvation*. Foundations of Evangelical Theology. Wheaton, IL: Crossway, 1997.

Demaus, R. *Hugh Latimer: A Biography*. Rev. ed. London: Religious Tract Society, 1881.

Denlinger, Aaron Clay, ed. *Reformed Orthodoxy in Scotland: Essays on Scottish Theology, 1560–1775*. London: Bloomsbury T&T Clark, 2015.

Dickson, David. *Therapeutica Sacra, Shewing Briefly the Method of Healing the Diseases of the Conscience, concerning Regeneration*. Edinburgh: Evan Tyler, 1664.

Dieter, Melvin E., Anthony A. Hoekema, Stanley M. Horton, J. Robertson McQuilkin, and John F. Walvoord. *Five Views on Sanctification*. Counterpoints. Grand Rapids, MI: Zondervan, 1987.

Diodati, John (Giovanni). *Pious and Learned Annotations upon the Holy Bible*. 3rd ed. London: by James Flesher, for Nicholas Fussell, 1651.

Dod, John. *A Plaine and Familiar Exposition of the Ten Commandements*. 17th ed. London: by I. D. for Thomas and Jonas Man, 1628.

Douma, J. *The Ten Commandments: Manual for the Christian Life*. Translated by Nelson D. Kloosterman. Phillipsburg, NJ: P&R, 1996.

Downame, George. *A Godly and Learned Treatise of Prayer*. Cambridge: by Roger Daniel for Nicolas Bourn, 1640.

Downe, John. *A Treatise of the True Nature and Definition of Justifying Faith.* Oxford: I. Lichfield for Edward Forrest, 1635.

Dunn, James D. G. *Jesus and the Spirit: A Study of the Religious and Charismatic Experience of Jesus and the First Christians as Reflected in the New Testament.* Grand Rapids, MI: Eerdmans, 1975.

Durham, James. *A Practical Exposition of the Ten Commandments.* Edited by Christopher Coldwell. Dallas, TX: Naphtali Press, 2002.

Durham, John I. *Exodus.* Word Biblical Commentary. Nashville: Thomas Nelson, 1987.

Dutton, Anne. *Selected Spiritual Writings of Anne Dutton: Eighteenth-Century, British-Baptist, Woman Theologian.* Edited by JoAnn Ford Watson. 7 vols. Macon, GA: Mercer University Press, 2003–2015.

Eck, John. *Enchiridion of Commonplaces: Against Luther and Other Enemies of the Church.* Translated by Ford Lewis Battles. Grand Rapids, MI: Baker, 1979.

Edwards, James R. *The Gospel according to Mark.* The Pillar New Testament Commentary. Grand Rapids, MI: Eerdmans, 2002.

Edwards, Jonathan. *The Religious Affections.* London: Banner of Truth, 1961.

* ———. *The Works of Jonathan Edwards.* 26 vols. New Haven, CT: Yale University Press, 1957–2008.

Elshout, Bartel. *Christ's Portrait of the Christian: An Exposition of the Beatitudes.* Grand Rapids, MI: Biblical Spirituality Press, 2019.

Elwell, Walter A., ed. *The Evangelical Dictionary of Theology.* Grand Rapids, MI: Baker, 1984.

Emmrich, Martin. "'Amtscharisma': Through the Eternal Spirit (Hebrews 9:14)." *Bulletin for Biblical Research* 12, no. 1 (2002): 17–32.

Engelsma, David J. *Common Grace Revisited: A Response to Richard J. Mouw's* He Shines in All That's Fair. Grandville, MI: Reformed Free Publishing, 2003.

Erickson, Millard J. *Christian Theology.* 3rd ed. Grand Rapids, MI: Baker Academic, 2013.

Erskine, Ebenezer. *The Whole Works of the Late Rev. Ebenezer Erskine.* 3 vols. Edinburgh: Ogle & Murray et al., 1871.

Eusebius. *The Proof of the Gospel: Being the Demonstratio Evangelica of Eusebius of Caesarea.* Translated by W. J. Ferrar. 2 vols. Translations of Christian Literature, Series 1, Greek Texts. London: Society for Promoting Christian Knowledge; New York: Macmillan, 1920.

Evans, John. *Practical Discourses Concerning the Christian Temper.* London: Richard Baynes, 1825.

Evans, Robert F. *Pelagius: Inquiries and Reappraisals*. New York: Seabury, 1968.

Evans, William B. "Déjà Vu All over Again? The Contemporary Reformed Soteriological Controversy in Historical Perspective." *Westminster Theological Journal* 72, no. 1 (Spring 2010): 135–51.

———. *Imputation and Impartation: Union with Christ in American Reformed Theology*. Studies in Christian History and Thought. Milton Keynes, UK: Paternoster, 2008.

———. "Three Current Reformed Models of Union with Christ." *Presbyterion* 41, nos. 1–2 (Fall 2015): 12–30.

Faber, Frederick William. *Faber's Hymns*. New York: Thomas Y. Crowell & Co., 1894.

Fairweather, Eugene R., ed. *A Scholastic Miscellany: Anselm to Ockham*. Library of Christian Classics. Philadelphia: Westminster, 1956.

Fee, Gordon D. *God's Empowering Presence: The Holy Spirit in the Letters of Paul*. Peabody, MA: Hendrickson, 1994.

Feinberg, John S., and Paul D. Feinberg. *Ethics for a Brave New World*. 2nd ed. Wheaton, IL: Crossway, 2010.

Ferguson, Sinclair B. *Children of the Living God*. Colorado Springs, CO: NavPress, 1987.

———. *The Christian Life: A Doctrinal Introduction*. Edinburgh: Banner of Truth, 1989.

———. *The Grace of Repentance*. Wheaton, IL: Crossway, 2010.

* ———. *The Holy Spirit*. Contours in Christian Theology. Downers Grove, IL: InterVarsity Press, 1996.

———. "The Reformation and Assurance." *The Banner of Truth*, no. 643 (April 2017): 20–23.

———. *The Whole Christ: Legalism, Antinomianism, and Gospel Assurance—Why the Marrow Controversy Still Matters*. Wheaton, IL: Crossway, 2016.

Fesko, J. V. *Beyond Calvin: Union with Christ and Justification in Early Modern Reformed Theology (1517–1700)*. Reformed Historical Theology 20. Göttingen: Vandenhoek and Ruprecht, 2012.

———. *Justification: Understanding the Classic Reformed Doctrine*. Phillipsburg, NJ: P&R, 2008.

———. "Methodology, Myths, and Misperceptions: A Response to William B. Evans." *Westminster Theological Journal* 72, no. 2 (Fall 2010): 391–402.

———. "Romans 8.29–30 and the Question of the *Ordo Salutis*." *Journal of Reformed Theology* 8 (2014): 35–60.

———. *The Rule of Love: Broken, Fulfilled, and Applied*. Grand Rapids, MI: Reformation Heritage Books, 2009.

Finney, Charles G. *An Autobiography*. 1876. Reprint, Westwood, NJ: Fleming H. Revell, 1908.

———. "Lecture XIV: The Holy Spirit of Promise." *The Oberlin Evangelist* 1, no. 18 (August 14, 1839): 137–38.

———. "Lecture XV: The Covenants." *The Oberlin Evangelist* 1, no. 19 (August 28, 1839): 145–47.

———. *Lectures on Revival of Religion*. 6th ed. New York: Leavitt, Lord & Co.; Boston: Crocker & Brewster, 1835.

———. *Lectures on Systematic Theology: Embracing Ability, (Natural, Moral, and Gracious,) Repentance, Impenitence, Faith and Unbelief, Justification, Sanctification, Election, Reprobation, Divine Purposes, Divine Sovereignty, and Perseverance*. Oberlin, OH: James M. Fitch, 1847.

———. *Lectures on Systematic Theology: Embracing Lectures on Moral Government, Together with Atonement, Moral and Physical Depravity, Regeneration, Philosophical Theories, and Evidences of Regeneration*. Oberlin, OH: James M. Fitch, 1846.

Fiorenza, Francis Schüssler, and John P. Galvin, eds. *Systematic Theology: Roman Catholic Perspectives*. 2 vols. Minneapolis: Fortress, 1991.

Fisher, Edward. *The Marrow of Modern Divinity*. 1645. Reprint, Fearn, Ross-shire, Scotland: Christian Focus, 2009.

Fisher, James, Ebenezer Erskine, and Ralph Erskine. *The Assembly's Shorter Catechism Explained*. Lewes, East Sussex, UK: Berith, 1998.

* Flavel, John. *The Works of John Flavel*. 6 vols. 1820. Reprint, Edinburgh: Banner of Truth, 1968.

Foster, George B. "Kaftan's Dogmatik." *The American Journal of Theology* 2, no. 4 (October 1898): 802–27.

Fox, Matthew. *The Coming of the Cosmic Christ*. New York: HarperCollins, 1988.

Frame, John M. *The Doctrine of the Christian Life*. Phillipsburg, NJ: P&R, 2008.

France, R. T. *Matthew*. Tyndale New Testament Commentaries 1. Downers Grove, IL: InterVarsity Press, 1985.

Frank, Arnold L. *The Fear of God: A Forgotten Doctrine*. Ventura, CA: Nordskog, 2007.

Frankfort, Henri. *Kingship and the Gods: A Study of Ancient Near Eastern Religion as the Integration of Society & Nature*. Chicago: University of Chicago Press, 1948.

Fraser, James. *A Treatise on Sanctification: An Explication of Romans Chapters 6, 7, and 8:1–4*. Rev. ed. 1897. Reprint, Audubon, NJ: Old Paths, 1992.

Fuller, Andrew. *The Backslider: His Nature, Symptoms, and Recovery*. 1801. Reprint, Birmingham, AL: Solid Ground, 2005.

———. *The Complete Works of the Rev. Andrew Fuller*. Edited by Joseph Belcher. 3 vols. Philadelphia: American Baptist Publication Society, 1845.

Gaebelein, Frank E., ed. *The Expositor's Bible Commentary*. 12 vols. Grand Rapids, MI: Zondervan, 1976.

Gaffin, Richard B. *Perspectives on Pentecost: New Testament Teaching on the Gifts of the Holy Spirit*. Phillipsburg, NJ: Presbyterian and Reformed, 1979.

———. *Resurrection and Redemption: A Study in Paul's Soteriology*. 2nd ed. Phillipsburg, NJ: Presbyterian and Reformed, 1987.

Garland, David E. *2 Corinthians*. The New American Commentary 29. Nashville: Broadman & Holman, 1999.

Garner, David B. *Sons in the Son: The Riches and Reach of Adoption in Christ*. Phillipsburg, NJ: P&R, 2016.

Geisler, Norman L. *Miracles and the Modern Mind: A Defense of Biblical Miracles*. Grand Rapids, MI: Baker, 1992.

Geisler, Norman L., and Abdul Saleeb. *Answering Islam: The Crescent in the Light of the Cross*. Grand Rapids, MI: Baker, 1993.

George, Timothy. *Faithful Witness: The Life and Mission of William Carey*. Birmingham, AL: New Hope, 1991.

———. *Galatians*. The New American Commentary 30. Nashville: Broadman & Holman, 1994.

Gilbertson, Richard. *The Baptism of the Holy Spirit: The Views of A. B. Simpson and His Contemporaries*. Camp Hill, PA: Christian Publications, 1993.

Gill, John. *The Cause of God and Truth*. 1855. Reprint, Paris, AK: The Baptist Standard Bearer, 1992.

* ———. *A Complete Body of Doctrinal and Practical Divinity*. 1839. Reprint, Paris, AR: The Baptist Standard Bearer, 1995. Cited as Gill, *Body of Divinity*.

———. *The Glory of God's Grace Displayed, In Its Abounding over the Aboundings of Sin*. London: Aaron Ward, 1724.

———. *Sermons and Tracts*. 1815. Reprint, Streamwood, IL: Primitive Baptist Library, 1981.

Gillham, Bill. *What God Wishes Christians Knew about Christianity*. Eugene, OR: Harvest House, 1998.

Glover, Peter, ed. *The Signs and Wonders Movement—Exposed*. Epsom, Surrey, UK: Day One, 1997.

Goldsworthy, Adrian. *Augustus: First Emperor of Rome*. New Haven, CT: Yale University Press, 2014.

Gomarus, Franciscus. *Opera Theologica Omnia*. 2 vols. Amsterdam: Joannis Janssonii, 1644.

* Goodwin, Thomas. *The Works of Thomas Goodwin*. 12 vols. 1861–1866. Reprint, Grand Rapids, MI: Reformation Heritage Books, 2006.

Gordon, A. J. *In Christ; Or, The Believer's Union with His Lord*. Boston: Gould and Lincoln, 1872.

Gordon, S. D. *Quiet Talks on Prayer*. New York: Fleming H. Revell, 1904.

Gouge, William. *Building a Godly Home*. Edited by Joel R. Beeke and Scott Brown. 3 vols. Grand Rapids, MI: Reformation Heritage Books, 2013–2014.

———. *Commentary on Hebrews*. 2 vols. 1866. Reprint, Birmingham, AL: Solid Ground, 2006.

———. *Of Domestical Duties*. Edited by Greg Fox. Edinburgh, IN: Puritan Reprints, 2006.

Greendyk, J. "The Danger of Resisting the Holy Spirit (1)." *The Banner of Sovereign Grace Truth* 5, no. 5 (May/June 1997): 115–16.

Gregory the Great. *Morals on the Book of Job*. 3 vols. Oxford: John Henry Parker, 1844.

Gregory of Nyssa. *Homilies on the Beatitudes: An English Version with Commentary & Supporting Studies*. Edited by Hubertus R. Drobner and Albert Viciano. Leiden: Brill, 2000.

Grier, James. "The Ten Words: Moral Choices Begin with the Ten Commandments." Unpublished audio lectures. Grand Rapids, MI: Grand Rapids Baptist Seminary, 1991.

Gross, Edward N. *Miracles, Demons, and Spiritual Warfare: An Urgent Call for Discernment*. Grand Rapids, MI: Baker, 1990.

Grudem, Wayne, ed. *Are Miraculous Gifts for Today?* Counterpoints. Grand Rapids, MI: Zondervan, 1996.

———. *Christian Ethics: An Introduction to Biblical Moral Reasoning*. Wheaton, IL: Crossway, 2018.

*———. *Systematic Theology: An Introduction to Biblical Doctrine*. Grand Rapids, MI: Zondervan, 1994.

Gundry, Robert H. *Commentary on the New Testament: Verse-by-Verse Explanations with a Literal Translation*. Peabody, MA: Hendrickson, 2010.

———. "'Ecstatic Utterance' (N.E.B.)?" *The Journal of Theological Studies*, New Series, 17, no. 2 (October 1966): 299–307.

———. "Why I Didn't Endorse 'The Gospel of Jesus Christ: An Evangelical Celebration.'" *Books and Culture* 7, no. 1 (January/February 2001): 6–9.

Gurnall, William. *The Christian in Complete Armour*. 2 vols. in 1. 1864. Reprint, Edinburgh: Banner of Truth, 2002.

Guthrie, William. *The Christian's Great Interest*. London: Banner of Truth, 1969.

Hagin, Kenneth E. *What Faith Is*. 5th ed. Tulsa, OK: Hagin Evangelistic Association, 1972.

Hamilton, James M., Jr. *God's Indwelling Presence: The Holy Spirit in the Old and New Testaments*. NAC Studies in Bible and Theology. Nashville: B&H Academic, 2006.

Harris, Robert. *The Way to True Happiness, Delivered in Twenty-Four Sermons upon the Beatitudes*. Edited by Don Kistler. Morgan, PA: Soli Deo Gloria, 1998.

Hawthorne, Gerald F. *The Presence and the Power: The Significance of the Holy Spirit in the Life and Ministry of Jesus*. Dallas, TX: Word, 1991.

Hawthorne, Gerald F., Ralph P. Martin, and Daniel G. Reid, eds. *Dictionary of Paul and His Letters*. Downers Grove, IL: InterVarsity Press, 1993.

Haykin, Michael A. G., ed. *The Life and Thought of John Gill (1697–1771): A Tercentennial Appreciation*. Leiden: Brill, 1997.

Haykin, Michael A. G., and Mark Jones, eds. *Drawn into Controversie: Reformed Theological Diversity and Debates within Seventeenth-Century British Puritanism*. Göttingen: Vandenhoeck & Ruprecht, 2011.

Hedges, Brian G. *Watchfulness: Recovering a Lost Spiritual Discipline*. Grand Rapids, MI: Reformation Heritage Books, 2018.

Heidegger, Johann. *The Concise Marrow of Christian Theology*. Translated by Casey Carmichael. Introduced by Ryan Glomsrud. Classic Reformed Theology 4. Grand Rapids, MI: Reformation Heritage Books, 2019.

Heinz, Johann. *Justification and Merit: Luther vs. Catholicism*. Berrien Springs, MI: Andrews University Press, 1981.

Helm, Paul. *Calvin and the Calvinists*. Edinburgh: Banner of Truth, 1982.

Hendriksen, William. *Exposition of the Gospel according to John*. New Testament Commentary. Grand Rapids, MI: Baker, 1953.

———. *Exposition of the Gospel according to Matthew*. New Testament Commentary. Grand Rapids, MI: Baker, 1979.

———. *Exposition of Paul's Epistle to the Romans*. Vol. 1, *Chapters 1–8*. New Testament Commentary. Grand Rapids, MI: Baker, 1980.

Hengstenberg, E. W. *Commentary on the Psalms*. Translated by P. Fairbairn and J. Thomson. 3 vols. Edinburgh: Thomas Clark, 1845.

Henry, Matthew. *Matthew Henry's Commentary on the Whole Bible: Complete and Unabridged in One Volume*. Peabody, MA: Hendrickson, 1994.

Hesselink, I. John. "Calvin, Theologian of Sweetness." *Calvin Theological Journal* 37 (2002): 318–32.

Hewitt, Thomas. *The Epistle to the Hebrews*. Tyndale New Testament Commentary. Grand Rapids, MI: Eerdmans, 1960.

Hicks, John Mark. "The Righteousness of Saving Faith: Arminian versus Remonstrant Grace." *Evangelical Journal* 9 (Spring 1991): 27–39.

———. "The Theology of Grace in the Thought of Jacobus Arminius and Philip van Limborch: A Study in the Development of Seventeenth-Century Dutch Arminianism." PhD diss., Westminster Theological Seminary, 1985.

Hodge, Archibald A. *Outlines of Theology*. Rev. ed. New York: Robert Carter and Brothers, 1879.

Hodge, Charles. *Commentary on the Epistle to the Romans*. Rev. ed. Philadelphia: Alfred Martien, 1873.

———. *Ephesians*. 1856. Reprint, Edinburgh: Banner of Truth, 1991.

———. *An Exposition of the Second Epistle to the Corinthians*. New York: A. C. Armstrong & Son, 1891.

———. *Systematic Theology*. 3 vols. Reprint, Peabody, MA: Hendrickson, 1999.

Hodges, Zane C. *Absolutely Free! A Biblical Reply to Lordship Salvation*. Grand Rapids, MI: Zondervan, 1989.

Hoekema, Anthony A. *Holy Spirit Baptism*. Grand Rapids, MI: Eerdmans, 1972.

———. *Saved by Grace*. Grand Rapids, MI: Eerdmans, 1989.

Hoeksema, Herman. *Reformed Dogmatics*. 2nd ed. Grandville, MI: Reformed Free Publishing, 2004–2005.

———. *A Triple Breach in the Foundation of the Reformed Truth*. Grand Rapids, MI: C. J. Doorn, 1925.

Hoglund, Jonathan. *Called by Triune Grace: Divine Rhetoric and the Effectual Call*. Studies in Christian Doctrine and Scripture. Downers Grove, IL: IVP Academic, 2016.

Holmes, Jonathan. *The Company We Keep: In Search of Biblical Friendship*. Adelphi, MD: Cruciform, 2014.

Hooker, Thomas. *The Application of Redemption, by the Effectual Work of the Word, and Spirit of Christ, for the Bringing Home of Lost Sinners to God. The First Eight Books*. London: Peter Cole, 1656.

———. *The Christian's Two Chief Lessons: Self-Denial and Self-Trial*. Ames, IA: International Outreach, 1997.

———. *The Soules Vocation or Effectual Calling to Christ*. London: by John Haviland, for Andrew Crooke, 1638.

Hopkins, Ezekiel. *The Works of Ezekiel Hopkins*. Edited by Charles W. Quick. 3 vols. Philadelphia: Leighton Publications, 1874.

Horton, Michael S., ed. *Christ the Lord: The Reformation and Lordship Salvation*. Eugene, OR: Wipf and Stock, 1992.

———. *The Christian Faith: A Systematic Theology for Pilgrims on the Way*. Grand Rapids, MI: Zondervan, 2011.

———. *Justification*. 2 vols. New Studies in Dogmatics. Grand Rapids, MI: Zondervan, 2018.

———. *Rediscovering the Holy Spirit: God's Perfecting Presence in Creation, Redemption, and Everyday Life*. Grand Rapids, MI: Zondervan, 2017.

Houston, Thomas. *The Adoption of Sons, Its Nature, Spirit, Privileges, and Effects: A Practical and Experimental Treatise*. Paisley: Alex. Garner et al., 1872.

Huber, Karen C. "The Pelagian Heresy: Observations on Its Social Context." PhD diss., Oklahoma State University, 1979.

Huey, F. B., Jr. *Jeremiah, Lamentations*. The New American Commentary 16. Nashville: Broadman & Holman, 1993.

Hughes, R. Kent. *Set Apart: Calling a Worldly Church to a Godly Life*. Wheaton, IL: Crossway, 2003.

Hume, David. *Essays and Treatises on Several Subjects*. Vol. II. New ed. London: A. Millar et al., 1768.

———. *The Philosophical Works of David Hume*. 4 vols. Boston: Little, Brown and Co., 1854.

Husbands, Mark, and Daniel J. Treier, eds. *Justification: What's at Stake in the Current Debates*. Downers Grove, IL: InterVarsity Press, 2004.

Innocent IV. *Super Libros Quinque Decretalium*. Frankfurt, 1570.

Irons, Charles Lee. *The Righteousness of God: A Lexical Examination of the Covenant-Faithfulness Interpretation*. Wissenschaftliche Untersuchungen Zum Neuen Testament, 2/386. Tübingen: Mohr Siebeck, 2015.

Jackson, Samuel Macauley, ed. *The New Schaff-Herzog Encyclopedia of Religious Knowledge*. 13 vols. New York; London: Funk & Wagnalls, 1908–1914.

James, John Angell. *Pastoral Addresses, Chiefly on the Subject of Christian Duty*. New York: Robert Carter and Brothers, 1852.

Jamieson, Robert, A. R. Fausset, and David Brown. *Commentary Critical and Explanatory on the Whole Bible*. 2 vols. 1871. Reprint, Oak Harbor, WA: Logos Research Systems, 1997.

Jang, Sung Joon, and Aaron B. Franzen. "Is Being 'Spiritual' Enough without Being Religious? A Study of Violent and Property Crimes among Emerging Adults." *Criminology* 51, no. 3 (August 2013): 595–627.

Jedin, Hubert. *A History of the Council of Trent*. Translated by Dom Ernest Graf. 2 vols. Edinburgh: Thomas Nelson, 1957.

Jewel, John. *The Works of John Jewel*. Edited by Richard William Jelf. 8 vols. Oxford: Oxford University Press, 1848.

Johnson, Gary L. W., and Guy P. Waters, eds. *By Faith Alone: Answering the Challenges to the Doctrine of Justification*. Wheaton, IL: Crossway, 2006.

Johnson, Marcus Peter. *One with Christ: An Evangelical Theology of Salvation*. Wheaton, IL: Crossway, 2013.

Johnston, Mark. *Child of a King*. Focus on Faith. Fearn, Ross-shire, Scotland: Christian Focus, 1997.

Jones, Mark. *Antinomianism: Reformed Theology's Unwelcome Guest?* Phillipsburg, NJ: P&R, 2013.

Josephus, Flavius. *The Works of Josephus: Complete and Unabridged*. Translated by William Whiston. New ed. Peabody, MA: Hendrickson, 1987.

Junius, Franciscus. *Protoktisia, seu Creationis a Deo Factae, et in Ea Prioris Adami ex Creatione Integri & ex Lapsu Corrupti, Historia*. Amsterdam: Johannes Commelinus, 1589.

Kaftan, Julius. *Dogmatik*. Tübingen: J. C. B. Mohr, 1920.

Keener, Craig S. *Acts: An Exegetical Commentary*. Vol. 1, *Introduction and 1:1–2:47*. Grand Rapids, MI: Baker Academic, 2012.

Kelly, Douglas F. *Systematic Theology: Grounded in Holy Scripture and Understood in the Light of the Church*. 2 vols. to date. Fearn, Ross-shire, Scotland: Christian Focus, 2008, 2014.

Kelly, J. N. D. *Early Christian Creeds*. 3rd ed. London: Continuum, 1972.

Kendall, R. T. *Once Saved, Always Saved*. Carlisle, Cumbria, England: Paternoster, 1997.

Kent, Homer. *The Epistle to the Hebrews*. Grand Rapids, MI: Baker, 1972.

Kenyon, E. W. *The Two Kinds of Faith: Faith's Secret Revealed*. Lynnwood, WA: Kenyon's Gospel Publishing, 1998.

Kersten, G. H. *Reformed Dogmatics: A Systematic Treatment of Reformed Doctrine Explained for the Congregations*. Translated by Joel R. Beeke and J. C. Weststrate. 2 vols. Grand Rapids, MI: Netherlands Reformed Book and Publishing Committee, 1980.

Kidner, Derek. *Genesis: An Introduction and Commentary*. Tyndale Old Testament Commentaries. Downers Grove, IL: InterVarsity Press, 1967.

———. *Psalms 1–72: An Introduction and Commentary on Books I and II of the Psalms*. Tyndale Old Testament Commentaries. Downers Grove, IL: InterVarsity Press, 1973.

———. *Psalms 73–150: An Introduction and Commentary*. Tyndale Old Testament Commentaries. Downers Grove, IL: InterVarsity Press, 1975.

Kistler, Don, ed. *Justification by Faith Alone: Affirming the Doctrine by Which the Church and the Individual Stands or Falls*. Morgan, PA: Soli Deo Gloria, 1995.

———. *Let Us Pray*. Orlando, FL: The Northampton Press, 2011.

Kitchen, John A. *Proverbs*. A Mentor Commentary. Fearn, Ross-shire, Scotland: Christian Focus, 2006.

Klein, George L. *Zechariah*. The New American Commentary 21B. Nashville: Broadman & Holman, 2008.

Klooster, Fred H. "Aspects of the Soteriology of Karl Barth." *Journal of the Evangelical Theological Society* 2, no. 2 (Spring 1959): 6–14.

Knapp, Henry. "Augustine and Owen on Perseverance." *Westminster Theological Journal* 62, no. 1 (Spring 2000): 65–87.

Knight, George W., III. *The Pastoral Epistles: A Commentary on the Greek Text*. The New International Greek Testament Commentary. Grand Rapids, MI: Eerdmans; Carlisle, Cumbria, England: Paternoster, 1992.

Kolakowski, Leszek. *God Owes Us Nothing: A Brief Remark on Pascal's Religion and the Spirit of Jansenism*. Chicago: University of Chicago Press, 1995.

Kolb, Robert. *Bound Choice, Election, and the Wittenberg Theological Method: From Martin Luther to the Formula of Concord*. Minneapolis: Fortress, 2017.

Kolb, Robert, and Charles P. Arand. *The Genius of Luther's Theology: A Wittenberg Way of Thinking for the Contemporary Church*. Grand Rapids, MI: Baker Academic, 2008.

Köstenberger, Andreas J. *A Theology of John's Gospel and Letters*. Grand Rapids, MI: Zondervan, 2009.

Köstenberger, Andreas J., and Robert W. Yarbrough, eds. *Understanding the Times: New Testament Studies in the Twenty-First Century; Essays in Honor of D. A. Carson*. Wheaton, IL: Crossway, 2011.

Kruse, Colin G. *2 Corinthians: An Introduction and Commentary*. Tyndale New Testament Commentaries 8. Downers Grove, IL: InterVarsity Press, 1987.

———. *The Epistle to the Romans*. The Pillar New Testament Commentary. Grand Rapids, MI: Eerdmans, 2012.

Kuiper, Herman. *By Grace Alone: A Study in Soteriology*. Grand Rapids, MI: Eerdmans, 1955.

———. *Calvin on Common Grace*. Grand Rapids, MI: Smitter, 1928.

Kuyper, Abraham. *Common Grace*. Translated by Nelson D. Kloosterman and Ed M. van der Maas. Edited by Jordan J. Ballor and Stephen J. Grabill. Introduced by Richard J. Mouw. 2 vols. to date. Abraham Kuyper Collected Works in Public Theology. Bellingham, WA: Lexham Press; Grand Rapids, MI: Acton Institute, 2015, 2019.

———. *The Work of the Holy Spirit*. Translated by Henri de Vries. Introduced by B. B. Warfield. Grand Rapids, MI: Eerdmans, 1946.

Lane, Anthony N. S. *Bernard of Clairvaux: Theologian of the Cross*. Cistercian Studies Series 248. Collegeville, MN: Liturgical Press, 2013.

———. *Justification by Faith in Catholic-Protestant Dialogue: An Evangelical Assessment*. London: T&T Clark, 2002.

Lea, Thomas D., and Hayne P. Griffin. *1, 2 Timothy, Titus*. The New American Commentary 34. Nashville: Broadman & Holman, 1992.

Letham, Robert. "The Relationship between Saving Faith and Assurance of Salvation." ThM thesis, Westminster Theological Seminary, 1976.

———. *Systematic Theology*. Wheaton, IL: Crossway, 2019.

———. *Union with Christ: In Scripture, History, and Theology*. Phillipsburg, NJ: P&R, 2011.

Lightfoot, J. B. *The Apostolic Fathers*. Edited by J. R. Harmer. London: Macmillan and Co., 1912.

Lincoln, Andrew T. *Ephesians*. Word Biblical Commentary 42. Dallas, TX: Word, 1990.

———. *Truth on Trial: The Lawsuit Motif in the Fourth Gospel*. Peabody, MA: Hendrickson, 2000.

Lloyd-Jones, D. Martyn. *The Baptism and Gifts of the Spirit*. Edited by Christopher Catherwood. Grand Rapids, MI: Baker, 1994.

———. *God's Ultimate Purpose: An Exposition of Ephesians 1:1–23*. Grand Rapids, MI: Baker, 1998.

———. *Great Doctrines of the Bible*. Vol. 2, *God the Holy Spirit*. Wheaton, IL: Crossway, 1997.

———. *The Puritans: Their Origins and Successors*. Edinburgh: Banner of Truth, 1987.

———. *Triumphant Christianity*. Studies in the Book of Acts 5. Wheaton, IL: Crossway, 2006.

Locke, John. *An Essay concerning Human Understanding*. 4th ed. London: Awnsham and John Churchil; and Samuel Manship, 1700.

———. *The Works of John Locke*. 9 vols. 12th ed. London: For C. and J. Rivington et al., 1824.

Lombard, Peter. *The Sentences*. Translated by Giulio Silano. 4 vols. Toronto: Pontifical Institute of Mediaeval Studies, 2007–2010.

Longenecker, Richard N. *Galatians*. Word Biblical Commentary 41. Nashville: Thomas Nelson, 1990.

Lossky, Vladimir. *The Mystical Theology of the Eastern Church*. Crestwood, NY: St. Vladimir's Seminary Press, 1976.

Luther, Martin. *Devotions and Prayers of Martin Luther*. Translated by Andrew Kosten. Grand Rapids, MI: Baker, 1965.

———. *Lectures on Romans*. Edited and translated by Wilhelm Pauck. Library of Christian Classics. Louisville: Westminster John Knox, 1961.

* ———. *Luther's Works*. Edited by Jaroslav Pelikan, Helmut T. Lehmann, Christopher Boyd Brown, and Benjamin T. G. Mayes. 80 vols. St. Louis, MO: Concordia, 1958–2020.

———. *What Luther Says: A Practical In-Home Anthology for the Active Christian*. Compiled by Ewald M. Plass. St. Louis, MO: Concordia, 1959.

MacArthur, John, Jr. *The Gospel according to Jesus: What Is Authentic Faith?* Rev. ed. Grand Rapids, MI: Zondervan, 2008.

MacArthur, John, and Richard Mayhue, eds. *Biblical Doctrine: A Systematic Summary of Bible Truth*. Wheaton, IL: Crossway, 2017.

Macaskill, Grant. *Union with Christ in the New Testament*. Oxford: Oxford University Press, 2013.

Machen, J. Gresham. *Christianity and Liberalism*. 1923. Reprint, Grand Rapids, MI: Eerdmans, 1992.

Macleod, Donald. *A Faith to Live By: Understanding Christian Doctrine*. Rev. ed. Fearn, Ross-shire, Scotland: Christian Focus, 2002.

Mannermaa, Tuomo. *Christ Present in Faith: Luther's View of Justification*. Minneapolis: Fortress, 2005.

Manton, Thomas. *The Works of Thomas Manton*. 22 vols. London: James Nisbet, 1873.

Marquart, Kurt E. "Luther and Theosis." *Concordia Theological Quarterly* 64, no. 3 (July 2000): 182–205.

Marshall, I. Howard. *Kept by the Power of God: A Study of Perseverance and Falling Away*. Minneapolis: Bethany Fellowship, 1969.

Marshall, Stephen. *The Works of Mr Stephen Marshall . . . The First Part*. London: Peter Cole and Edward Cole, 1661.

Marshall, Walter. *The Gospel Mystery of Sanctification*. Grand Rapids, MI: Reformation Heritage Books, 1999.

Martin, Albert N. *The Forgotten Fear: Where Have All the God-Fearers Gone?* Grand Rapids, MI: Reformation Heritage Books, 2015.

———. *Union with Christ*. Toronto: Toronto Baptist Seminary, 1978.

Mason, John. *Select Remains of the Rev. John Mason*. New York: G. & C. Carvill et al., 1825.

Master, Jonathan L. *A Question of Consensus: The Doctrine of Assurance after the Westminster Confession*. Minneapolis: Fortress, 2015.

Mawhinney, Allen. "*Yiothesia* in the Pauline Epistles: Its Background, Use and Implications." PhD diss., Baylor University, 1982.

McCormack, Bruce L., ed. *Justification in Perspective: Historical Developments and Contemporary Challenges*. Grand Rapids, MI: Baker Academic, 2006.

McGrath, Alister E. *Iustitia Dei: A History of the Christian Doctrine of Justification*. 2 vols. Cambridge: Cambridge University Press, 1986.

———. *The Sunnier Side of Doubt*. Grand Rapids, MI: Zondervan, 1990.

McGraw, Ryan M. *The Day of Worship: Reassessing the Christian Life in Light of the Sabbath*. Grand Rapids, MI: Reformation Heritage Books, 2011.

M'Cheyne, Robert Murray. *Memoirs and Remains of Robert Murray M'Cheyne*. Edited by Andrew Bonar. 1892. Reprint, Edinburgh: Banner of Truth, 1995.

McLeod, Alexander. *Negro Slavery Unjustifiable*. 11th ed. New York: Alexander McLeod, 1863.

Melanchthon, Philip. *The Chief Theological Topics: Loci Praecipui Theologici 1559*. Translated by J. A. O. Preus. 2nd ed. St. Louis, MO: Concordia, 2011.

———. *Commonplaces: Loci Communes 1521*. Translated by Christian Preus. St. Louis, MO: Concordia, 2014.

Melick, Richard R. *Philippians, Colossians, Philemon*. The New American Commentary 32. Nashville: Broadman & Holman, 1991.

Meyendorff, John. *Byzantine Theology: Historical Trends and Doctrinal Themes*. 2nd ed. New York: Fordham University Press, 1979.

Migne, J. P., ed. *Patrologia Latina*. 221 vols. Paris: J. P. Migne, 1841–1865.

Miley, John. *Systematic Theology*. 2 vols. New York: Eaton and Mains, 1892, 1894.

M'Lean, Archibald. *The Works of Mr. Archibald M'Lean*. 6 vols. in 7. London: William Jones, 1823.

Moltmann, Jürgen. *The Coming of God: Christian Eschatology*. Translated by Margaret Kohl. Minneapolis: Fortress, 1996.

Moo, Douglas J. "Divine Healing in the Health and Wealth Gospel." *Trinity Journal* 9, no. 2 (Fall 1988): 191–209.

———. *The Epistle to the Romans*. The New International Commentary on the New Testament. Grand Rapids, MI: Eerdmans, 1996.

———. *The Letter of James*. The Pillar New Testament Commentary. Grand Rapids, MI: Eerdmans, 2000.

Morris, Leon. *The Apostolic Preaching of the Cross*. 3rd ed. Grand Rapids, MI: Eerdmans, 1965.

———. *The Epistle to the Romans*. The Pillar New Testament Commentary. Grand Rapids, MI: Eerdmans, 1988.

———. *The Gospel according to John*. The New International Commentary on the New Testament. Grand Rapids, MI: Eerdmans, 1995.

———. *The Gospel according to Matthew*. The Pillar New Testament Commentary. Grand Rapids, MI: Eerdmans; Leicester, England: Apollos, 1992.

Motyer, J. A. *The Message of James: The Tests of Faith*. Downers Grove, IL: InterVarsity Press, 1985.

———. *The Prophecy of Isaiah: An Introduction and Commentary*. Downers Grove, IL: InterVarsity Press, 1993.

Mouw, Richard J. *He Shines in All That's Fair: Culture and Common Grace*. Grand Rapids, MI: Eerdmans, 2001.

Muller, Richard A. *Calvin and the Reformed Tradition: On the Work of Christ and the Order of Salvation*. Grand Rapids, MI: Baker Academic, 2012.

Murray, Iain H. *The Invitation System*. Edinburgh: Banner of Truth, 1967.

———. *Spurgeon and Hyper-Calvinism: The Battle for Gospel Preaching*. Edinburgh: Banner of Truth, 1995.

* Murray, John. *Collected Writings of John Murray*. 4 vols. Edinburgh: Banner of Truth, 1982.

———. *The Epistle to the Romans*. The New International Commentary on the New Testament. 2 vols. Grand Rapids, MI: Eerdmans, 1968.

———. "Pictures of Christ." *Reformed Herald* 16, no. 9 (February 1961): 65–66.

———. *Principles of Conduct: Aspects of Biblical Ethics*. Grand Rapids, MI: Eerdmans, 1957.

* ———. *Redemption Accomplished and Applied*. Grand Rapids, MI: Eerdmans, 1955.

Musculus, Wolfgang. *Commonplaces of Christian Religion*. London: n.p., 1578.

Naselli, Andrew David. "Keswick Theology: A Survey and Analysis of the Doctrine of Sanctification in the Early Keswick Movement." *Detroit Baptist Seminary Journal* 13 (2008): 17–67.

———. *Let Go and Let God? A Survey and Analysis of Keswick Theology*. Bellingham, WA: Lexham Press, 2010.

Nathan, Rich, and Ken Wilson. *Empowered Evangelicals: Bringing Together the Best of the Evangelical and Charismatic Worlds*. Rev. ed. Boise, ID: Ampelon, 2009.

Naylor, Peter. *A Study Commentary on 2 Corinthians*. EP Study Commentary. Darlington, England: Evangelical Press, 2002.

Newman, John. *The Popish Doctrine of Merit and Justification Considered*. 3rd ed. London: R. Ford and R. Hett, 1735.

Newton, John. *Wise Counsel: John Newton's Letters to John Ryland, Jr.* Edited by Grant Gordon. Edinburgh: Banner of Truth, 2009.

Newton, John, and William Cowper. *Olney Hymns*. London: W. Oliver, J. Buckland, and J. Johnson, 1779.

Nichols, Greg. *Lectures in Systematic Theology*. Edited by Rob Ventura. 7 vols. Seattle: CreateSpace Independent Publishing Platform, 2017–.

Nichols, James, ed. *Puritan Sermons, 1659–1689*. 6 vols. Reprint, Wheaton, IL: Richard Owen Roberts, 1981.

Oberman, Heiko. *The Dawn of the Reformation: Essays in Late Medieval and Early Reformation Thought*. Edinburgh: T&T Clark, 1986.

———. *The Harvest of Medieval Theology: Gabriel Biel and Late Medieval Nominalism*. Durham, NC: Labyrinth, 1963.

O'Brien, Peter T. *The Epistle to the Philippians*. The New International Greek Testament Commentary. Grand Rapids, MI: Eerdmans, 1991.

Oden, Thomas, ed. *Ancient Christian Commentary on Scripture: New Testament*. 12 vols. Downers Grove, IL: InterVarsity Press, 2005–2006.

———, ed. *Ancient Christian Commentary on Scripture: Old Testament*. 15 vols. Downers Grove, IL: InterVarsity Press, 2001–2005.

———. *John Wesley's Scriptural Christianity: A Plain Exposition of His Teaching on Christian Doctrine*. Grand Rapids, MI: Zondervan, 1994.

———. *The Justification Reader*. Grand Rapids, MI: Eerdmans, 2002.

———. *Systematic Theology*. 3 vols. Peabody, MA: Prince, 1992.

Olevianus, Caspar. *An Exposition of the Apostles' Creed*. Translated by Lyle D. Bierma. Grand Rapids, MI: Reformation Heritage Books, 2009.

Olson, Roger E. *Against Calvinism*. Grand Rapids, MI: Zondervan, 2011.

———. *Arminian Theology: Myths and Realities*. Downers Grove, IL: InterVarsity Press, 2006.

Origen. *Homilies on Genesis and Exodus*. Translated by Ronald E. Heine. The Fathers of the Church 71. Washington, DC: The Catholic University of America Press, 1982.

Ortlund, Raymond C., Jr. *Isaiah: God Saves Sinners*. Preaching the Word. Wheaton, IL: Crossway, 2005.

———. *Whoredom: God's Unfaithful Wife in Biblical Theology*. Grand Rapids, MI: Eerdmans, 1996.

Ott, Ludwig. *Fundamentals of Catholic Dogma*. Edited by James C. Bastible. Translated by Patrick Lynch. Cork: Mercier, 1962.

Owen, John. *An Exposition of the Epistle to the Hebrews*. 7 vols. Reprint, Edinburgh: Banner of Truth, 1991.

* ———. *The Works of John Owen*. Edited by William H. Goold. 16 vols. 1850–1853. Reprint, Edinburgh: Banner of Truth, 1965.

Ozment, Steven E. *The Age of Reform (1250–1550): An Intellectual and Religious History of Late Medieval and Reformation Europe*. New Haven, CT: Yale University Press, 1980.

Packer, J. I. *Evangelism and the Sovereignty of God*. Downers Grove, IL: InterVarsity Press, 1976.

———. *Faithfulness and Holiness: The Witness of J. C. Ryle*. Wheaton, IL: Crossway, 2002. Contains *Holiness* by J. C. Ryle.

———. *Keep in Step with the Spirit*. Old Tappan, NJ: Fleming H. Revell, 1984.

Palamas, Gregory. *The Triads*. Edited by John Meyendorff. Translated by Nicholas Gendle. The Classics of Western Spirituality. New York: Paulist, 1983.

Palmer, Phoebe. *The Way of Holiness*. New York: Piercy and Reed, 1843.

Pao, David W. *Acts and the Isaianic New Exodus*. Eugene, OR: Wipf and Stock, 2016.

Parsons, Burk, ed. *John Calvin: A Heart for Devotion, Doctrine, and Doxology*. Lake Mary, FL: Reformation Trust, 2008.

Pattison, E. Mansell. "Behavioral Science Research on the Nature of Glossolalia." *Journal of the American Scientific Affiliation* 20 (September 1968): 73–86.

Pearse, Edward. *The Best Match: The Soul's Espousal to Christ*. Edited by Don Kistler. Grand Rapids, MI: Soli Deo Gloria, 1994.

Peck, George. *The Scripture Doctrine of Christian Perfection Stated and Defended: With a Critical and Historical Examination of the Controversy, Ancient and Modern*. 3rd ed. New York: Lane & Scott, 1848.

Pelagius. "The Christian Life and Other Essays." Translated by Ford Lewis Battles. Pittsburgh: s.n., 1972.

Pelikan, Jaroslav. *The Christian Tradition: A History of the Development of Doctrine*. 5 vols. Chicago: University of Chicago Press, 1975–1991.

Pemble, William. *The Workes of the Late Learned Minister of God's Holy Word, Mr William Pemble*. 4th ed. Oxford: by Henry Hall for John Adams, 1659.

* Perkins, William. *The Works of William Perkins*. Series edited by Joel R. Beeke and Derek W. H. Thomas. 10 vols. Grand Rapids, MI: Reformation Heritage Books, 2014–2020.

Perrin, Nicholas, and Richard B. Hays, eds. *Jesus, Paul, and the People of God: A Theological Dialogue with N. T. Wright*. Downers Grove, IL: InterVarsity Press, 2011.

Peterson, David G. *The Acts of the Apostles*. The Pillar New Testament Commentary. Grand Rapids, MI: Eerdmans; Nottingham, England: Apollos, 2009.

Peterson, Robert A. *Adopted by God: From Wayward Sinners to Cherished Children*. Phillipsburg, NJ: P&R, 2001.

———. *Salvation Applied by the Spirit: Union with Christ*. Wheaton, IL: Crossway, 2015.

Petry, Ray C., ed. *Late Medieval Mysticism*. Library of Christian Classics. Philadelphia: Westminster, 1957.

Phillips, Richard D. *Hebrews*. Reformed Expository Commentary. Phillipsburg, NJ: P&R, 2006.

Philo of Alexandria. *The Works of Philo: Complete and Unabridged*. Translated by C. D. Yonge. New ed. Peabody, MA: Hendrickson, 1995.

Pighius, Albertus. *Hierarchiae Ecclesiasticae*. Coloniae Agrippinae (Cologne or Köln), Germany: Arnoldi Birckmanni, 1572.

Pink, Arthur W. *The Doctrine of Sanctification*. Swengel, PA: Reiner, 1975.

———. *An Exposition of Hebrews*. Grand Rapids, MI: Baker, 1954.

———. *The Holy Spirit*. Grand Rapids, MI: Baker, 1970.

———. *Practical Christianity*. Grand Rapids, MI: Guardian Press, 1974.

———. *Studies on Saving Faith*. Swengel, PA: Reiner, 1974.

Pinnock, Clark H., ed. *The Grace of God and the Will of Man*. Minneapolis: Bethany House, 1989.

———. *Grace Unlimited*. Minneapolis: Bethany House, 1975.

Pinson, J. Matthew, ed. *Four Views on Eternal Security*. Counterpoints. Grand Rapids, MI: Zondervan, 2002.

Pipa, Joseph A. *The Lord's Day*. Fearn, Ross-shire, Scotland: Christian Focus, 1997.

Piper, John. *Counted Righteous in Christ: Should We Abandon the Imputation of Christ's Righteousness?* Wheaton, IL: Crossway, 2002.

———. *Finally Alive: What Happens When We Are Born Again*. Fearn, Ross-shire, Scotland: Christian Focus, 2009.

———. *The Future of Justification: A Response to N. T. Wright*. Wheaton, IL: Crossway, 2007.

———. *The Pleasures of God*. Portland, OR: Multnomah, 1991.

Piper, John, and Justin Taylor, eds. *A God-Entranced Vision of All Things: The Legacy of Jonathan Edwards*. Wheaton, IL: Crossway, 2004.

———, eds. *Stand: A Call for the Endurance of the Saints*. Wheaton, IL: Crossway, 2008.

Piper, Noël. *Faithful Women and Their Extraordinary God*. Wheaton, IL: Crossway, 2005.

Plato. *The Republic*. Vol. 1, *Books 1–5*. Translated by Paul Shorey. Rev. ed. Loeb Classical Library 237. Cambridge, MA: Harvard University Press, 1937.

Plumer, William S. *The Law of God, as Contained in the Ten Commandments, Explained and Enforced*. 1864. Reprint, Harrisonburg, VA: Sprinkle, 1996.

———. *Studies in the Book of Psalms*. Philadelphia: J. B. Lippincott and Co., 1867.

———. *Vital Godliness: A Treatise on Experimental and Practical Piety*. 1864. Reprint, Harrisonburg, VA: Sprinkle, 1993.

Pollock, John C., and Ian Randall. *The Keswick Story: The Authorized Version of the Keswick Convention*. New ed. Fort Washington, PA: CLC Publications, 2006.

* Polyander, Johannes, Antonius Walaeus, Antonius Thysius, and Andreas Rivetus. *Synopsis Purioris Theologiae, Synopsis of a Purer Theology: Latin Text and English Translation*. Translated by Riemer A. Faber. Edited by Dolf te Velde, Rein Ferwerda, Willem J. van Asselt, William den Boer, Riemer A. Faber, Henk van den Belt, and Harm Goris. 3 vols. Studies in Medieval and Reformation Traditions: Texts and Sources. Leiden: Brill, 2014, 2016, 2020.

Poole, Matthew. *Annotations upon the Holy Bible*. 3 vols. New York: Robert Carter and Brothers, 1853.

Pope, William. *A Compendium of Christian Theology*. 3 vols. London: Wesleyan Conference Office, 1877.

Poythress, Vern S. "Why Lying Is Always Wrong: The Uniqueness of Verbal Deceit." *Westminster Theological Journal* 75 (2013): 83–95.

Preston, John. *The Breast-plate of Faith and Love*. 1634. Facsimile reprint, Edinburgh: Banner of Truth, 1979.

———. *Remaines of that Reverend and Learned Divine, John Preston*. London: for Andrew Crooke, 1634.

Prior, Kenneth. *The Way of Holiness: A Study in Christian Growth*. Downers Grove, IL: InterVarsity Press, 1982.

Purnell, Robert. *The Way Step by Step to Sound and Saving Conversion, With a Clear Discovery of the Two States, Viz: Nature, and Grace*. London: by T. Childe, and L. Parry, for Edw. Thomas, 1659.

Rainbow, Paul A. *Johannine Theology: The Gospel, the Epistles, and the Apocalypse*. Downers Grove, IL: IVP Academic, 2014.

Reeves, Michael. *Rejoice and Tremble: The Surprising Good News of the Fear of the Lord*. Union. Wheaton, IL: Crossway, 2021.

Reisinger, Ernest. *The Church's Greatest Need*. Pensacola, FL: Chapel Library, n.d.

Reymond, Robert L. *A New Systematic Theology of the Christian Faith*. Nashville: Thomas Nelson, 1998.

———. *What about Continuing Revelations and Miracles in the Presbyterian Church Today?* Nutley, NJ: Presbyterian and Reformed, 1977.

Reynolds, Edward. *Three Treatises of the Vanity of the Creature. The Sinfulness of Sinne. The Life of Christ*. London: B. B. for Rob Bastocke and George Badger, 1642.

———. *The Works of the Right Rev. Edward Reynolds*. 6 vols. 1826. Reprint, Morgan, PA: Soli Deo Gloria, 1998.

Richardson, Alan, and John Bowden, eds. *The Westminster Dictionary of Theology*. Philadelphia: Westminster Press, 1983.

Ridderbos, Herman. *Paul: An Outline of His Theology*. Translated by John Richard de Witt. Grand Rapids, MI: Eerdmans, 1975.

Riddlebarger, Kim. *First Corinthians*. The Lectio Continua Expository Commentary on the New Testament. Powder Springs, GA: Tolle Lege, 2013.

Riggans, Walter. *Hebrews*. Focus on the Bible Commentary. Fearn, Ross-shire, Scotland: Christian Focus, 1998.

* Roberts, Alexander, and James Donaldson. Revised by A. Cleveland Coxe. *The Ante-Nicene Fathers*. 9 vols. New York: Charles Scribner's Sons, 1918. Includes cited works written by Athenagoras, Clement, Clement of Alexandria, Cyprian, Ignatius, Irenaeus, Justin Martyr, Lactantius, Novatian, Origen, and Tertullian.

Robertson, O. Palmer. "Genesis 15:6: New Covenant Expositions of an Old Covenant Text." *Westminster Theological Journal* 42, no. 2 (Spring 1980): 259–90.

———. "Tongues: Sign of Covenantal Curse and Blessing." *Westminster Theological Journal* 38, no. 1 (January 1975): 43–53.

Rogers, John. *The Doctrine of Faith: Wherein Are Particularly Handled Twelve Principall Points, which Explaine The Nature and Use of It*. London: N. Newbery and H. Overton, 1629.

Rogers, Richard. *Holy Helps for a Godly Life*. Edited by Brian G. Hedges. Puritan Treasures for Today. Grand Rapids, MI: Reformation Heritage Books, 2018.

Rollock, Robert. *In Epistolam Pauli Apostoli ad Ephesios*. Edinburgh: Robertus Waldegrave, 1590.

———. *In Epistolam S. Pauli Apostoli ad Romanos*. Rev. ed. Genevae: Apud Franc. le Preux, 1595.

Rosner, Brian S. *Greed as Idolatry: The Origin and Meaning of a Pauline Metaphor*. Grand Rapids, MI: Eerdmans, 2007.

Ross, Alexander. *The Epistles of James and John*. The New International Commentary on the New Testament. Grand Rapids, MI: Eerdmans, 1954.

Rutherford, Samuel. *Christ Dying and Drawing Sinners to Himselfe*. London: by J. D. for Andrew Crooke, 1647.

———. *Letters of Samuel Rutherford*. Edited by Andrew A. Bonar. Edinburgh: Oliphant Anderson & Ferrier, 1891.

———. *A Survey of the Spirituall Antichrist*. London: by J. D. & R. I. for Andrew Crooke, 1648.

———. *The Trial and Triumph of Faith*. Edinburgh: The Assembly's Committee, 1845.

Ruthven, Jon Mark. *On the Cessation of the Charismata: The Protestant Polemic on Post-Biblical Miracles*. Word and Spirit Monograph Series 1. Rev. ed. Tulsa, OK: Word & Spirit, 2011.

———. *What's Wrong with Protestant Theology?* Tulsa, OK: Word & Spirit, 2013.

Ryken, Leland. *Worldly Saints: The Puritans as They Really Were*. Grand Rapids, MI: Zondervan, 1986.

Ryken, Philip Graham. *Written in Stone: The Ten Commandments and Today's Moral Crisis*. Wheaton, IL: Crossway, 2003.

Ryle, J. C. *Expository Thoughts on John*. 2 vols. New York: Robert Carter & Brothers, 1879.

———. *Holiness: Its Nature, Hindrances, Difficulties, and Roots*. Foreword by D. Martyn Lloyd-Jones. Cambridge: James Clarke & Co., 1956.

———. *Home Truths*. 4th ed. Ipswich, England: William Hunt, 1859.

———. *Old Paths*. 2nd ed. London: William Hunt and Co., 1878.

Ryrie, Charles C. *Basic Theology: A Popular Systematic Guide to Understanding Biblical Truth*. Wheaton, IL: Victor, 1986.

———. *So Great Salvation: What It Means to Believe in Jesus Christ*. Wheaton, IL: Victor, 1989.

Samarin, William J. *Tongues of Men and Angels: The Religious Language of Pentecostalism*. New York: Macmillan; London: Collier-Macmillan, 1972.

Sanders, E. P. *Paul and Palestinian Judaism: A Comparison of Patterns of Religion*. Philadelphia: Fortress, 1977.

Sanderson, John W. *The Fruit of the Spirit: A Study Guide*. Grand Rapids, MI: Zondervan, 1972.

Schaff, Philip. *History of the Christian Church*. 8 vols. 3rd ed. New York: Charles Scribner's Sons, 1891.

* ———, ed. *A Select Library of Nicene and Post-Nicene Fathers of the Christian Church, First Series*. 14 vols. New York: Christian Literature Co., 1888. Includes cited works written by Aurelius Augustine and John Chrysostom.

* Schaff, Philip, and Henry Wace, eds. *A Select Library of Nicene and Post-Nicene Fathers of the Christian Church, Second Series*. 14 vols. New York: Christian Literature Co., 1894. Includes cited works written by Ambrose, Athanasius, Basil, John Cassian, Cyril of Jerusalem, Eusebius, Gregory the Great, Gregory of Nazianzus, Gregory of Nyssa, and Jerome.

Schaver, J. L. *The Polity of the Churches*. 3rd ed. 2 vols. Chicago: Church Polity Press, 1947.

Schleiermacher, Friedrich. *The Christian Faith*. Edited by H. R. Mackintosh and J. S. Stewart. 2 vols. New York: Harper and Row, 1963.

Schmid, Heinrich. *The Doctrinal Theology of the Evangelical Lutheran Church, Verified from the Original Sources*. Revised by Charles A. Hay and Henry E. Jacobs. Philadelphia: Lutheran Publication Society, 1889.

Schortinghuis, Wilhelmus. *Essential Truths in the Heart of a Christian*. Translated by Harry Boonstra and Gerrit W. Sheeres. Edited by James A. De Jong. Classics of Reformed Spirituality. Grand Rapids, MI: Reformation Heritage Books, 2009.

Schreiner, Thomas R. *1, 2 Peter, Jude*. The New American Commentary 37. Nashville: Broadman & Holman, 2003.

———. *Commentary on Hebrews*. Biblical Theology for Christian Proclamation. Nashville: Holman Reference, 2015.

———. *Faith Alone: The Doctrine of Justification*. Grand Rapids, MI: Zondervan, 2015.

Schreiner, Thomas R., and Bruce A. Ware, eds. *The Grace of God, the Bondage of the Will: Biblical and Practical Perspectives on Calvinism*. Grand Rapids, MI: Baker, 1995.

Scudder, Henry. *The Christian's Daily Walk*. Reprint, Harrisonburg, VA: Sprinkle, 1984.

Seeberg, Reinhold. *Text-Book of the History of Doctrines*. Translated by Charles E. Hay. 2 vols. Rev. ed. Philadelphia: Lutheran Publication Society, 1905.

Seifrid, Mark A. *Christ, Our Righteousness: Paul's Theology of Justification*. New Studies in Biblical Theology. Downers Grove, IL: InterVarsity Press, 2000.

Seneca. *Ad Lucilium Epistulae Morales*. Translated by Richard M. Gummere. 3 vols. Loeb Classical Library 076. London: William Heinemann, 1920.

———. *Seneca: Moral Essays*. Translated by John W. Basore. 3 vols. Loeb Classical Library 214. London: William Heinemann, 1928.

Shank, Robert. *Life in the Son: A Study of the Doctrine of Perseverance*. Minneapolis: Bethany House, 1989.

Shaw, Robert. *An Exposition of the Confession of Faith of the Westminster Assembly of Divines*. 8th ed. Glasgow: Blackie and Son, 1857.

Shedd, William G. T. *Dogmatic Theology*. 2 vols. New York: Charles Scribner's Sons, 1888.

Shelfer, Lochlan. "The Legal Precision of the Term '*parakletos*.'" *Journal for the Study of the New Testament* 32, no. 2 (2009): 131–50.

* Sibbes, Richard. *The Works of Richard Sibbes*. Edited by Alexander B. Grosart. 7 vols. 1862–1864. Reprint, Edinburgh: Banner of Truth, 1973.

Smeaton, George. *The Doctrine of the Holy Spirit*. Foreword by W. J. Grier. Edinburgh: Banner of Truth, 2016.

Smedes, Lewis. *All Things Made New: A Theology of Man's Union with Christ*. Grand Rapids, MI: Eerdmans, 1970.

Smith, Hannah Whitall. *The Christian's Secret to a Happy Life*. Rev. ed. Chicago: F. H. Revell, 1883.

Smith, Robert Pearsall. *Holiness through Faith*. Rev. ed. New York: Anson D. F. Randolph & Co., 1870.

Smith, William, ed. *Dictionary of Greek and Roman Antiquities*. 2nd ed. London: Walton and Maberly, 1859.

Sommers, Charles G., William R. Williams, and Levi L. Hill, eds. *The Baptist Library: A Republication of Standard Baptist Works*. 3 vols. Prattsville, NY: Robert H. Hill, 1843.

Spring, Gardiner. *Essays on the Distinguishing Traits of Christian Character*. New York: Dodge & Sayre, 1813.

Sproul, R. C. *The Gospel of God: An Exposition of Romans*. Fearn, Ross-shire, Scotland: Christian Focus, 1994.

———. *The Mystery of the Holy Spirit*. Wheaton, IL: Tyndale House, 1990.

Spurgeon, C. H. *The Metropolitan Tabernacle Pulpit*. 57 vols. Edinburgh: Banner of Truth, 1969.

———. *The New Park Street Pulpit*. 6 vols. in 3. Pasadena, TX: Pilgrim, 1975.

Spurstowe, William. *The Wells of Salvation Opened: or, A Treatise Discerning the Nature, Preciousness, and Usefulness of the Gospel Promises and Rules for the Right Application of Them*. London: T. R. & E. M. for Ralph Smith, 1655.

Stanglin, Keith D. *Arminius on the Assurance of Salvation: The Context, Roots, and Shape of the Leiden Debate, 1603–1609*. Brill's Series in Church History 27. Leiden: Brill, 2007.

Stanglin, Keith D., and Thomas H. McCall. *Jacob Arminius: Theologian of Grace*. Oxford: Oxford University Press, 2012.

Stedman, Rowland. *The Mystical Union of Believers with Christ*. London: by W. R. for Thomas Parkhurst, 1668.

Stott, John R. W. *Baptism and Fullness: The Work of the Holy Spirit Today*. Downers Grove, IL: InterVarsity Press, 1975.

———. *The Letters of John: An Introduction and Commentary*. Tyndale New Testament Commentaries 19. Downers Grove, IL: InterVarsity Press, 1988.

———. *Men Made New: An Exposition of Romans 5–8*. Downers Grove, IL: InterVarsity Press, 1966.

———. *The Message of Acts: To the Ends of the Earth*. The Bible Speaks Today. Downers Grove, IL: InterVarsity Press, 1994.

———. *The Message of the Sermon on the Mount (Matthew 5–7): Christian Counter-Culture*. The Bible Speaks Today. Downers Grove, IL: InterVarsity Press, 1985.

Strong, Augustus H. *Systematic Theology*. 3 vols. Philadelphia: Griffith and Rowland, 1909.

Stuart, Douglas K. *Exodus*. The New American Commentary 2. Nashville: Broadman & Holman, 2006.

Summers, Thomas. *Systematic Theology: A Complete Body of Wesleyan Arminian Divinity*. Edited by John J. Tigert. 2 vols. Nashville: Publishing House of the Methodist Episcopal Church, South, 1888.

Swinnock, George. *The Works of George Swinnock*. 5 vols. 1868. Reprint, Edinburgh: Banner of Truth, 1992.

Synan, Vinson. *The Holiness-Pentecostal Tradition: Charismatic Movements in the Twentieth Century*. 2nd ed. Grand Rapids, MI: Eerdmans, 1997.

Tchividjian, Tullian. *Jesus + Nothing = Everything*. Wheaton, IL: Crossway, 2011.

Teellinck, Willem. *The Path of True Godliness*. Translated by Annemie Godbehere. Edited by Joel R. Beeke. Classics of Reformed Spirituality. Grand Rapids, MI: Reformation Heritage Books, 2003.

Thiselton, Anthony C. *1 Corinthians: A Shorter and Pastoral Commentary*. Grand Rapids, MI: Eerdmans, 2006.

———. *The First Epistle to the Corinthians*. The New International Greek Testament Commentary. Grand Rapids, MI: Eerdmans; Carlisle, Cumbria, England: Paternoster, 2000.

Thomas, Geoffrey. *The Holy Spirit*. Grand Rapids, MI: Reformation Heritage Books, 2011.

Thomas, I. D. E., comp. *The Golden Treasury of Puritan Quotations*. Chicago: Moody, 1975.

Toplady, Augustus. *Hymns and Sacred Poems, on a Variety of Divine Subjects, Comprising the Poetical Remains of the Rev. Augustus M. Toplady*. London: Daniel Sedgwick, 1860.

Torrey, R. A. *The Baptism with the Holy Spirit*. Chicago: The Bible Institute Colportage Association, 1895.

Traill, Robert. *The Works of Robert Traill*. 4 vols. in 2. 1810. Reprint, Edinburgh: Banner of Truth, 1975.

Trumper, Tim J. R. "An Historical Study of the Doctrine of Adoption in the Calvinistic Tradition." PhD diss., University of Edinburgh, 2001.

* Turretin, Francis. *Institutes of Elenctic Theology*. Translated by George Musgrave Giger. Edited by James T. Dennison Jr. 3 vols. Phillipsburg, NJ: P&R, 1992–1997.

Udemans, Godefridus. *The Practice of Faith, Hope, and Love*. Translated by Annemie Godbehere. Edited by Joel R. Beeke. Classics of Reformed Spirituality. Grand Rapids, MI: Reformation Heritage Books, 2012.

Ursinus, Zacharias. *The Commentary of Dr. Zacharias Ursinus on the Heidelberg Catechism*. Translated by G. W. Williard. 2nd American ed. Columbus: Scott & Bascom, 1852.

Ussher, James. *A Body of Divinity*. Edited by Michael Nevarr. Birmingham, AL: Solid Ground, 2007.

VanderGroe, Theodorus. *The Christian's Only Comfort in Life and Death: An Exposition of the Heidelberg Catechism*. Translated by Bartel Elshout. Edited by Joel R. Beeke. 2 vols. Grand Rapids, MI: Reformation Heritage Books, 2016.

VanDrunen, David, ed. *The Pattern of Sound Doctrine: Systematic Theology at the Westminster Seminarie; Essays in Honor of Robert B. Strimple*. Phillipsburg, NJ: P&R, 2004.

van Genderen, J., and W. H. Velema. *Concise Reformed Dogmatics*. Translated by Gerrit Bilkes and Ed M. van der Maas. Phillipsburg, NJ: P&R, 2008.

van Mastricht, Petrus. *Theoretical-Practical Theology*. Vol. 2. Translated by Todd M. Rester. Edited by Joel R. Beeke. Grand Rapids, MI: Reformation Heritage Books, 2019.

———. *Theoretico-Practica Theologia*. New ed. 2 vols. Trajecti ad Rhenum: Thomae Appels, 1699.

———. *A Treatise on Regeneration*. New Haven, CT: Thomas and Samuel Green, 1770.

Van Til, Cornelius. *Common Grace and the Gospel*. Phillipsburg, NJ: Presbyterian and Reformed, 1972.

Venema, Cornelis P. *The Gospel of Free Acceptance in Christ: An Assessment of the Reformation and New Perspective on Paul*. Edinburgh: Banner of Truth, 2006.

Vermigli, Peter Martyr. *The Common Places*. Translated by Anthonie Marten. N.p., 1583.

Vitringa, Campegius. *The Spiritual Life*. Translated and edited by Charles K. Tefler. Foreword by Richard A. Muller. Grand Rapids, MI: Reformation Heritage Books, 2018.

Voltaire (Francois-Marie Arouet). *The Works of Voltaire*. Edited by Tobias Smollett. Revised and translated by William F. Fleming. Introduced by Oliver H. G. Leigh. 22 vols. Paris: E. R. DuMont, 1901.

Vos, Geerhardus. *The Pauline Eschatology*. Princeton, NJ: Geerhardus Vos, 1930.

* ———. *Reformed Dogmatics*. Translated and edited by Richard B. Gaffin et al. 5 vols. Bellingham, WA: Lexham Press, 2012–2016.

Wagner, C. Peter. *The Third Wave of the Holy Spirit: Encountering the Power of Signs and Wonders Today*. Ann Arbor, MI: Servant, 1988.

Waldron, Samuel E. *The Crux of the Free Offer of the Gospel*. Greenbrier, AR: Free Grace Press, 2019.

———. *To Be Continued? Are the Miraculous Gifts for Today?* Merrick, NY: Calvary Press, 2005.

Wallace, Daniel B. "The Semantic Range of the Article-Noun-*Kai*-Noun Plural Construction in the New Testament." *Grace Theological Journal* 4, no. 1 (1983): 59–84.

Wallace, Robert. *A Plain Statement and Scriptural Defence of the Leading Doctrines of Unitarianism*. Chesterfield, England: for the author, by T. Woodhead et al., 1819.

Walther, C. F. W. *Walther's Works: All Glory to God*. St. Louis, MO: Concordia, 2016.

Walvoord, John F. *The Holy Spirit: A Comprehensive Study of the Person and Work of the Holy Spirit*. Grand Rapids, MI: Zondervan, 1991.

Ware, Timothy. *The Orthodox Church*. New ed. London: Penguin, 1997.

Warfield, B. B. *Biblical and Theological Studies*. Edited by Samuel G. Craig. Philadelphia: Presbyterian and Reformed, 1968.

———. *Counterfeit Miracles*. 1918. Reprint, Edinburgh: Banner of Truth, 1972.

———. *Faith and Life: 'Conferences' in the Oratory of Princeton Seminary*. New York and London: Longmans, Green, and Co., 1916.

———. *Perfectionism*. 2 vols. New York: Oxford University Press, 1931.

———. *The Person and Work of the Holy Spirit*. Introduced by Sinclair B. Ferguson. Birmingham, AL: Solid Ground, 2010.

———. *The Saviour of the World: Sermons Preached in the Chapel of Princeton Theological Seminary*. New York and London: Hodder and Stoughton, 1913.

———. *The Works of Benjamin B. Warfield*. 10 vols. Bellingham, WA: Logos Research Systems, 2008.

Waters, Guy. *A Christian's Pocket Guide to Being Made Right with God: Understanding Justification*. Fearn, Ross-shire, Scotland: Christian Focus, 2012.

———. *Justification and the New Perspectives on Paul: A Review and Response*. Phillipsburg, NJ: P&R, 2004.

Watson, Richard. *Theological Institutes*. 2 vols. New York: Lane and Scott, 1851.

Watson, Thomas. *The Beatitudes: An Exposition of Matthew 5:1–12*. Edinburgh: Banner of Truth, 1971.

* ———. *A Body of Divinity*. Edinburgh: Banner of Truth, 1965.

———. *A Body of Practical Divinity . . . with a Supplement of Some Sermons*. London: Thomas Parkhurst, 1692.

———. *A Divine Cordial*. 1663. Reprint, Wilmington, DE: Sovereign Grace, 1972.

———. *The Doctrine of Repentance*. Puritan Paperbacks. Edinburgh: Banner of Truth, 1987.

———. *The Duty of Self-Denial (and Ten Other Sermons)*. Morgan, PA: Soli Deo Gloria, 1996.

———. *Heaven Taken by Storm*. Morgan, PA: Soli Deo Gloria, 1994.

———. *The Lord's Prayer*. Edinburgh: Banner of Truth, 1960.

———. *The Ten Commandments*. Edinburgh: Banner of Truth, 1965.

Wengert, Timothy J. *Law and Gospel: Philip Melanchthon's Debate with John Agricola of Eisleben over* Poenitentia. Texts and Studies in Reformation and Post-Reformation Thought. Grand Rapids, MI: Baker, 1997.

Wesley, John. *Explanatory Notes upon the New Testament*. 2nd ed. London, 1757.

———. *Free Grace, A Sermon Preach'd at Bristol*. Bristol: S. & F. Farley, 1739.

———. *John Wesley's Sermons: An Anthology*. Edited by Albert C. Outler and Richard P. Heitzenrater. Nashville: Abingdon, 1991.

———. *The Works of John Wesley*. 10 vols. 3rd ed. 1872. Reprint, Grand Rapids, MI: Baker, 1979.

Whately, William. *The New Birth*. London: Joane Man and Benjamin Fisher, 1635.

Whitaker, William. *An Answere to the Ten Reasons of Edmund Campian . . . [and] the Sum of the Defence of Those Reasons by John Duraeus*. Translated by Richard Stocke. London: by Felix Kyngston, for Cuthbert Burby and Edmund Weaver, 1606.

———. *Responsionis ad Decem Illas Rationes, Quibus Fretus Edmundus Campianus . . . Defensio contra Confutationem Ioannis Duraei*. London: Excudebat Henricus Midletonus impensis Thomae Chardi, 1584.

White, James R. *The God Who Justifies*. Minneapolis: Bethany House, 2001.

Whitefield, George. *Sermons of George Whitefield*. Edited by Lee Gatiss. 2 vols. Wheaton, IL: Crossway, 2012.

Wiggers, G. F. *An Historical Presentation of Augustinism and Pelagianism from the Original Sources*. Translated and edited by Ralph Emerson. Andover, MA: Gould, Newman, and Saxton, 1840.

Willard, Samuel. *The Child's Portion: or the Unseen Glory of the Children of God, Asserted, and Proved: Together with Several Other Sermons*. Boston: Samuel Green, 1684.

* ———. *A Compleat Body of Divinity*. 1726. Facsimile reprint, New York: Johnson Reprint, 1969.

Williams, J. Rodman. *Renewal Theology*. 3 vols. Grand Rapids, MI: Zondervan, 1990.

Winslow, Octavius. *The Work of the Holy Spirit: An Experimental and Practical View*. Edinburgh: Banner of Truth, 1961.

Wisse, G. *Godly Sorrow*. St. Thomas, ON: Free Reformed, 1998.

Wisse, Maarten, Marcel Sarot, and Willemien Otten, eds. *Scholasticism Reformed: Essays in Honour of Willem J. van Asselt*. Leiden: Brill, 2010.

Witherington, Ben, III. *The Problem with Evangelical Theology: Testing the Exegetical Foundations of Calvinism, Dispensationalism and Wesleyanism*. Waco, TX: Baylor University Press, 2005.

Witsius, Herman. *The Economy of the Covenants between God and Man.* 2 vols. 1822. Reprint, Grand Rapids, MI: Reformation Heritage Books, 2010.

———. "The Efficacy and Utility of Baptism." Translated by William Marshall and J. Mark Beach. Edited by J. Mark Beach. *Mid-America Journal of Theology* 17 (2006): 121–90.

———. *Sacred Dissertations on the Apostles' Creed.* 2 vols. 1823. Reprint, Grand Rapids, MI: Reformation Heritage Books, 2010.

———. *Sacred Dissertations on the Lord's Prayer.* Translated by William Pringle. Grand Rapids, MI: Reformation Heritage Books, 2010.

Wolever, Terry. *The Life of John Gano, 1727–1804: Pastor-Evangelist of the Philadelphia Association.* Philadelphia Association Series. Springfield, MO: Particular Baptist Press, 2012.

* Wollebius, Johannes. *Compendium Theologiae Christianae.* In *Reformed Dogmatics: Seventeenth-Century Reformed Theology through the Writings of Wollebius, Voetius, and Turretin.* Edited and translated by John W. Beardslee III. Grand Rapids, MI: Baker, 1965.

Wood, Leon J. *The Holy Spirit in the Old Testament.* Grand Rapids, MI: Zondervan, 1976.

Wright, N. T. *Justification: God's Plan and Paul's Vision.* New ed. Downers Grove, IL: InterVarsity Press, 2016.

———. *What Saint Paul Really Said: Was Paul of Tarsus the Real Founder of Christianity?* Grand Rapids, MI: Eerdmans, 1997.

Xenophon. *Memorabilia and Oeconomicus; Symposium and Apology.* Translated by E. C. Marchant and O. J. Todd. Loeb Classical Library 168. London: William Heinemann, 1923.

Young, Edward J. *The Book of Isaiah.* 3 vols. Grand Rapids, MI: Eerdmans, 1969.

Young, William. "Historic Calvinism and Neo-Calvinism (Part 1)." *Westminster Theological Journal* 36, no. 1 (Fall 1973): 48–64; "Part 2." Issue 36, no. 2 (Winter 1974): 156–73.

Yuille, J. Stephen. *Puritan Spirituality: The Fear of God in the Affective Theology of George Swinnock.* Studies in Christian History and Thought. Eugene, OR: Wipf and Stock, 2007.

Zanchi, Girolamo. *De Religione Christiana Fides—Confession of Christian Religion.* Vol. 1. Edited by Luca Baschera and Christian Moser. Studies in the History of Christian Traditions. Leiden: Brill, 2007.

Zwingli, Ulrich. *On Providence and Other Essays.* Edited by William John Hinke. 1922. Reprint, Durham, NC: Labyrinth, 1983.

General Index

Scripture Index

Luke

2 Corinthians

1 Thessalonians